K. LINK
421-0890 (W)
845-2197 (H)

Summer '94

W9-CHC-240

University Casebook Series

October, 1993

ACCOUNTING AND THE LAW, Fourth Edition (1978), with Problems Pamphlet (Successor to Dohr, Phillips, Thompson & Warren)

George C. Thompson, Professor, Columbia University Graduate School of Business.
Robert Whitman, Professor of Law, University of Connecticut.
Ellis L. Phillips, Jr., Member of the New York Bar.
William C. Warren, Professor of Law Emeritus, Columbia University.

ACCOUNTING FOR LAWYERS, MATERIALS ON (1980)

David R. Herwitz, Professor of Law, Harvard University.

ADMINISTRATIVE LAW, Eighth Edition (1987), with 1993 Case Supplement and 1983 Problems Supplement (Supplement edited in association with Paul R. Verkuil, Dean and Professor of Law, Tulane University)

Walter Gellhorn, University Professor Emeritus, Columbia University.
Clark Byse, Professor of Law, Harvard University.
Peter L. Strauss, Professor of Law, Columbia University.
Todd D. Rakoff, Professor of Law, Harvard University.
Roy A. Schotland, Professor of Law, Georgetown University.

ADMIRALTY, Third Edition (1987), with 1991 Statute and Rule Supplement

Jo Desha Lucas, Professor of Law, University of Chicago.

ADVOCACY, see also Lawyering Process

AGENCY, see also Enterprise Organization

AGENCY—PARTNERSHIPS, Fourth Edition (1987)

Abridgement from Conard, Knauss & Siegel's Enterprise Organization, Fourth Edition.

AGENCY AND PARTNERSHIPS (1987)

Melvin A. Eisenberg, Professor of Law, University of California, Berkeley.

ANTITRUST: FREE ENTERPRISE AND ECONOMIC ORGANIZATION, Sixth Edition (1983), with 1983 Problems in Antitrust Supplement and 1993 Case Supplement

Louis B. Schwartz, Professor of Law, University of Pennsylvania.
John J. Flynn, Professor of Law, University of Utah.
Harry First, Professor of Law, New York University.

BANKRUPTCY, Third Edition (1993)

Robert L. Jordan, Professor of Law, University of California, Los Angeles.
William D. Warren, Professor of Law, University of California, Los Angeles.

BANKRUPTCY AND DEBTOR–CREDITOR LAW, Second Edition (1988)

Theodore Eisenberg, Professor of Law, Cornell University.

UNIVERSITY CASEBOOK SERIES—Continued

BUSINESS ASSOCIATIONS, AGENCY, PARTNERSHIPS, AND CORPORATIONS (1991), with 1993 Supplement

William A. Klein, Professor of Law, University of California, Los Angeles.
Mark Ramseyer, Professor of Law, University of California, Los Angeles.

BUSINESS CRIME (1990), with 1993–94 Case Supplement

Harry First, Professor of Law, New York University.

BUSINESS ORGANIZATION, see also Enterprise Organization

BUSINESS PLANNING (1991)

Franklin Gevurtz, Professor of Law, McGeorge School of Law.

BUSINESS PLANNING, Temporary Second Edition (1984)

David R. Herwitz, Professor of Law, Harvard University.

BUSINESS TORTS (1972)

Milton Handler, Professor of Law Emeritus, Columbia University.

CHILDREN IN THE LEGAL SYSTEM (1983), with 1990 Supplement (Supplement edited in association with Elizabeth S. Scott, Professor of Law, University of Virginia)

Walter Wadlington, Professor of Law, University of Virginia.
Charles H. Whitebread, Professor of Law, University of Southern California.
Samuel Davis, Professor of Law, University of Georgia.

CIVIL PROCEDURE, see Procedure

CIVIL RIGHTS ACTIONS (1988), with 1993 Supplement

Peter W. Low, Professor of Law, University of Virginia.
John C. Jeffries, Jr., Professor of Law, University of Virginia.

CLINIC, see also Lawyering Process

COMMERCIAL AND DEBTOR–CREDITOR LAW: SELECTED STATUTES, 1993 EDITION

COMMERCIAL LAW, Third Edition (1992)

Robert L. Jordan, Professor of Law, University of California, Los Angeles.
William D. Warren, Professor of Law, University of California, Los Angeles.

COMMERCIAL LAW, Fifth Edition (1993)

E. Allan Farnsworth, Professor of Law, Columbia University.
John O. Honnold, Professor of Law Emeritus, University of Pennsylvania.
Curtis R. Reitz, Professor of Law, University of Pennsylvania.
Steven L. Harris, Professor of Law, University of Illinois.
Charles Mooney, Jr., Professor of Law, University of Pennsylvania.

COMMERCIAL PAPER, see also Negotiable Instruments

COMMERCIAL PAPER AND BANK DEPOSITS AND COLLECTIONS (1967), with Statutory Supplement

William D. Hawkland, Professor of Law, University of Illinois.

UNIVERSITY CASEBOOK SERIES—Continued

COMMERCIAL TRANSACTIONS—Principles and Policies, Second Edition (1991)

Alan Schwartz, Professor of Law, Yale University.
Robert E. Scott, Professor of Law, University of Virginia.

COMPARATIVE LAW, Fifth Edition (1988)

Rudolf B. Schlesinger, Professor of Law, Hastings College of the Law.
Hans W. Baade, Professor of Law, University of Texas.
Mirjan P. Damaska, Professor of Law, Yale Law School.
Peter E. Herzog, Professor of Law, Syracuse University.

COMPETITIVE PROCESS, LEGAL REGULATION OF THE, Revised Fourth Edition (1991), with 1993 Selected Statutes Supplement

Edmund W. Kitch, Professor of Law, University of Virginia.
Harvey S. Perlman, Dean of the Law School, University of Nebraska.

CONFLICT OF LAWS, Ninth Edition (1990), with Revised 1993 Supplement

Willis L. M. Reese, Professor of Law, Columbia University.
Maurice Rosenberg, Professor of Law, Columbia University.
Peter Hay, Professor of Law, University of Illinois.

CONSTITUTIONAL LAW, CIVIL LIBERTY AND INDIVIDUAL RIGHTS, Second Edition (1982), with 1992 Supplement

William Cohen, Professor of Law, Stanford University.
John Kaplan, Professor of Law, Stanford University.

CONSTITUTIONAL LAW, Ninth Edition (1993), with 1993 Supplement

William Cohen, Professor of Law, Stanford University.
Jonathan D. Varat, Professor of Law, University of California, Los Angeles.

CONSTITUTIONAL LAW, Twelfth Edition (1991), with 1993 Supplement (Supplement edited in association with Frederick F. Schauer, Professor, Harvard University)

Gerald Gunther, Professor of Law, Stanford University.

CONSTITUTIONAL LAW, INDIVIDUAL RIGHTS IN, Fifth Edition (1992) (Reprinted from CONSTITUTIONAL LAW, Twelfth Edition), with 1993 Supplement (Supplement edited in association with Frederick F. Schauer, Professor, Harvard University)

Gerald Gunther, Professor of Law, Stanford University.

CONSUMER TRANSACTIONS, Second Edition (1991), with Selected Statutes and Regulations Supplement

Michael M. Greenfield, Professor of Law, Washington University.

CONTRACT LAW AND ITS APPLICATION, Fourth Edition (1988)

Arthur Rosett, Professor of Law, University of California, Los Angeles.

CONTRACT LAW, STUDIES IN, Fourth Edition (1991)

Edward J. Murphy, Professor of Law, University of Notre Dame.
Richard E. Speidel, Professor of Law, Northwestern University.

UNIVERSITY CASEBOOK SERIES—Continued

CONTRACTS, Sixth Edition (1993)

John P. Dawson, late Professor of Law, Harvard University.
William Burnett Harvey, Professor of Law and Political Science, Boston University.
Stanley D. Henderson, Professor of Law, University of Virginia.

CONTRACTS, Fourth Edition (1988)

E. Allan Farnsworth, Professor of Law, Columbia University.
William F. Young, Professor of Law, Columbia University.

CONTRACTS, Selections on (statutory materials) (1992)

CONTRACTS, Second Edition (1978), with Statutory and Administrative Law Supplement (1978)

Ian R. Macneil, Professor of Law, Cornell University.

COPYRIGHT, PATENTS AND TRADEMARKS, see also Competitive Process; see also Selected Statutes and International Agreements

COPYRIGHT, PATENT, TRADEMARK AND RELATED STATE DOCTRINES, Revised Third Edition (1993), with 1993 Selected Statutes Supplement and 1981 Problem Supplement

Paul Goldstein, Professor of Law, Stanford University.

COPYRIGHT, Unfair Competition, and Other Topics Bearing on the Protection of Literary, Musical, and Artistic Works, Fifth Edition (1990), with 1993 Statutory and Case Supplement

Ralph S. Brown, Jr., Professor of Law, Yale University.
Robert C. Denicola, Professor of Law, University of Nebraska.

CORPORATE ACQUISITIONS, The Law and Finance of (1986), with 1993 Supplement

Ronald J. Gilson, Professor of Law, Stanford University.

CORPORATE FINANCE, Brudney and Chirelstein's Fourth Edition (1993)

Victor Brudney, Professor of Law, Harvard University.
William W. Bratton, Jr., Professor of Law, Rutgers University, Newark.

CORPORATION LAW, BASIC, Third Edition (1989), with Documentary Supplement

Detlev F. Vagts, Professor of Law, Harvard University.

CORPORATIONS, see also Enterprise Organization and Business Organization

CORPORATIONS, Sixth Edition—Concise (1988), with 1993 Case Supplement and 1993 Statutory Supplement

William L. Cary, late Professor of Law, Columbia University.
Melvin Aron Eisenberg, Professor of Law, University of California, Berkeley.

CORPORATIONS, Sixth Edition—Unabridged (1988), with 1993 Case Supplement and 1993 Statutory Supplement

William L. Cary, late Professor of Law, Columbia University.
Melvin Aron Eisenberg, Professor of Law, University of California, Berkeley.

CORPORATIONS AND BUSINESS ASSOCIATIONS—STATUTES, RULES, AND FORMS, 1993 Edition

UNIVERSITY CASEBOOK SERIES—Continued

ETHICS AND PROFESSIONAL RESPONSIBILITY (1981) (Reprinted from THE LAWYERING PROCESS)

Gary Bellow, Professor of Law, Harvard University.
Bea Moulton, Legal Services Corporation.

EVIDENCE, Seventh Edition (1992)

John Kaplan, late Professor of Law, Stanford University.
Jon R. Waltz, Professor of Law, Northwestern University.
Roger C. Park, Professor of Law, University of Minnesota.

EVIDENCE, Eighth Edition (1988), with Rules, Statute and Case Supplement (1993)

Jack B. Weinstein, Chief Judge, United States District Court.
John H. Mansfield, Professor of Law, Harvard University.
Norman Abrams, Professor of Law, University of California, Los Angeles.
Margaret Berger, Professor of Law, Brooklyn Law School.

FAMILY LAW, see also Domestic Relations

FAMILY LAW, Third Edition (1992)

Judith C. Areen, Professor of Law, Georgetown University.

FAMILY LAW AND CHILDREN IN THE LEGAL SYSTEM, STATUTORY MATERI- ALS (1981)

Walter Wadlington, Professor of Law, University of Virginia.

FAMILY PROPERTY LAW, Cases and Materials on Wills, Trusts and Future Interests, Star Edition (1991)

Lawrence W. Waggoner, Professor of Law, University of Michigan.
Richard V. Wellman, Professor of Law, University of Georgia.
Gregory Alexander, Professor of Law, Cornell Law School.
Mary L. Fellows, Professor of Law, University of Minnesota.

FEDERAL COURTS, Ninth Edition (1992)

Charles T. McCormick, late Professor of Law, University of Texas.
James H. Chadbourn, late Professor of Law, Harvard University.
Charles Alan Wright, Professor of Law, University of Texas, Austin.

FEDERAL COURTS AND THE FEDERAL SYSTEM, Hart and Wechsler's Third Edition (1988), with 1993 Case Supplement, and the Judicial Code and Rules of Procedure in the Federal Courts (1993)

Paul M. Bator, Professor of Law, University of Chicago.
Daniel J. Meltzer, Professor of Law, Harvard University.
Paul J. Mishkin, Professor of Law, University of California, Berkeley.
David L. Shapiro, Professor of Law, Harvard University.

FEDERAL COURTS AND THE LAW OF FEDERAL–STATE RELATIONS, Second Edition (1989), with 1993 Supplement

Peter W. Low, Professor of Law, University of Virginia.
John C. Jeffries, Jr., Professor of Law, University of Virginia.

FEDERAL PUBLIC LAND AND RESOURCES LAW, Third Edition (1993), with 1990 Statutory Supplement

George C. Coggins, Professor of Law, University of Kansas.
Charles F. Wilkinson, Professor of Law, University of Oregon.
John D. Leshy, Professor of Law, Arizona State University.

UNIVERSITY CASEBOOK SERIES—Continued

FEDERAL RULES OF CIVIL PROCEDURE and Selected Other Procedural Provisions, 1993 Edition

FEDERAL TAXATION, see Taxation

FIRST AMENDMENT (1991), with 1993 Supplement

William W. Van Alstyne, Professor of Law, Duke University.

FOOD AND DRUG LAW, Second Edition (1991), with Statutory Supplement

Peter Barton Hutt, Esq.
Richard A. Merrill, Professor of Law, University of Virginia.

FUTURE INTERESTS (1970)

Howard R. Williams, Professor of Law, Stanford University.

FUTURE INTERESTS AND ESTATE PLANNING (1961), with 1962 Supplement

W. Barton Leach, late Professor of Law, Harvard University.
James K. Logan, formerly Dean of the Law School, University of Kansas.

GENDER DISCRIMINATION, see Women and the Law

GOVERNMENT CONTRACTS, FEDERAL, Successor Edition (1985), with 1989 Supplement

John W. Whelan, Professor of Law, Hastings College of the Law.

GOVERNMENT REGULATION: FREE ENTERPRISE AND ECONOMIC ORGANIZATION, Sixth Edition (1985)

Louis B. Schwartz, Professor of Law, Hastings College of the Law.
John J. Flynn, Professor of Law, University of Utah.
Harry First, Professor of Law, New York University.

HEALTH CARE LAW AND POLICY (1988), with 1992 Supplement

Clark C. Havighurst, Professor of Law, Duke University.

HINCKLEY, JOHN W., JR., TRIAL OF: A Case Study of the Insanity Defense (1986)

Peter W. Low, Professor of Law, University of Virginia.
John C. Jeffries, Jr., Professor of Law, University of Virginia.
Richard C. Bonnie, Professor of Law, University of Virginia.

IMMIGRATION LAW AND POLICY (1992)

Stephen H. Legomsky, Professor of Law, Washington University.

INJUNCTIONS, Second Edition (1984)

Owen M. Fiss, Professor of Law, Yale University.
Doug Rendleman, Professor of Law, College of William and Mary.

INSTITUTIONAL INVESTORS (1978)

David L. Ratner, Professor of Law, Cornell University.

INSURANCE, Second Edition (1985)

William F. Young, Professor of Law, Columbia University.
Eric M. Holmes, Professor of Law, University of Georgia.

INSURANCE LAW AND REGULATION (1990)

Kenneth S. Abraham, University of Virginia.

UNIVERSITY CASEBOOK SERIES—Continued

INTERNATIONAL LAW, see also Transnational Legal Problems, Transnational Business Problems, and United Nations Law

INTERNATIONAL LAW IN CONTEMPORARY PERSPECTIVE (1981), with Essay Supplement

Myres S. McDougal, Professor of Law, Yale University.
W. Michael Reisman, Professor of Law, Yale University.

INTERNATIONAL LEGAL SYSTEM, Third Edition (1988), with Documentary Supplement

Joseph Modeste Sweeney, Professor of Law, University of California, Hastings.
Covey T. Oliver, Professor of Law, University of Pennsylvania.
Noyes E. Leech, Professor of Law Emeritus, University of Pennsylvania.

INTRODUCTION TO LAW, see also Legal Method, On Law in Courts, and Dynamics of American Law

INTRODUCTION TO THE STUDY OF LAW (1970)

E. Wayne Thode, late Professor of Law, University of Utah.
Leon Lebowitz, Professor of Law, University of Texas.
Lester J. Mazor, Professor of Law, University of Utah.

JUDICIAL CODE and Rules of Procedure in the Federal Courts, Students' Edition, 1993 Revision

Daniel J. Meltzer, Professor of Law, Harvard University.
David L. Shapiro, Professor of Law, Harvard University.

JURISPRUDENCE (Temporary Edition Hardbound) (1949)

Lon L. Fuller, late Professor of Law, Harvard University.

JUVENILE, see also Children

JUVENILE JUSTICE PROCESS, Third Edition (1985)

Frank W. Miller, Professor of Law, Washington University.
Robert O. Dawson, Professor of Law, University of Texas.
George E. Dix, Professor of Law, University of Texas.
Raymond I. Parnas, Professor of Law, University of California, Davis.

LABOR LAW, Eleventh Edition (1991), with 1993 Statutory Supplement and 1992 Case Supplement

Archibald Cox, Professor of Law, Harvard University.
Derek C. Bok, President, Harvard University.
Robert A. Gorman, Professor of Law, University of Pennsylvania.
Matthew W. Finkin, Professor of Law, University of Illinois.

LABOR LAW, Second Edition (1982), with Statutory Supplement

Clyde W. Summers, Professor of Law, University of Pennsylvania.
Harry H. Wellington, Dean of the Law School, Yale University.
Alan Hyde, Professor of Law, Rutgers University.

LAND FINANCING, Third Edition (1985)

Norman Penney, late Professor of Law, Cornell University.
Richard F. Broude, Member of the California Bar.
Roger Cunningham, Professor of Law, University of Michigan.

LAW AND MEDICINE (1980)

Walter Wadlington, Professor of Law and Professor of Legal Medicine, University of Virginia.

Jon R. Waltz, Professor of Law, Northwestern University.

Roger B. Dworkin, Professor of Law, Indiana University, and Professor of Biomedical History, University of Washington.

LAW, LANGUAGE AND ETHICS (1972)

William R. Bishin, Professor of Law, University of Southern California.

Christopher D. Stone, Professor of Law, University of Southern California.

LAW, SCIENCE AND MEDICINE (1984), with 1989 Supplement

Judith C. Areen, Professor of Law, Georgetown University.

Patricia A. King, Professor of Law, Georgetown University.

Steven P. Goldberg, Professor of Law, Georgetown University.

Alexander M. Capron, Professor of Law, University of Southern California.

LAWYERING PROCESS (1978), with Civil Problem Supplement and Criminal Problem Supplement

Gary Bellow, Professor of Law, Harvard University.

Bea Moulton, Professor of Law, Arizona State University.

LEGAL ETHICS (1992)

Deborah Rhode, Professor of Law, Stanford University.

David Luban, Professor of Law, University of Maryland.

LEGAL METHOD (1980)

Harry W. Jones, Professor of Law Emeritus, Columbia University.

John M. Kernochan, Professor of Law, Columbia University.

Arthur W. Murphy, Professor of Law, Columbia University.

LEGAL METHODS (1969)

Robert N. Covington, Professor of Law, Vanderbilt University.

E. Blythe Stason, late Professor of Law, Vanderbilt University.

John W. Wade, Professor of Law, Vanderbilt University.

Elliott E. Cheatham, late Professor of Law, Vanderbilt University.

Theodore A. Smedley, Professor of Law, Vanderbilt University.

LEGAL PROFESSION, THE, Responsibility and Regulation, Second Edition (1988)

Geoffrey C. Hazard, Jr., Professor of Law, Yale University.

Deborah L. Rhode, Professor of Law, Stanford University.

LEGISLATION (1993)

William D. Popkin, Professor of Law, Indiana University at Bloomington.

LEGISLATION, Fourth Edition (1982) (by Fordham)

Horace E. Read, late Vice President, Dalhousie University.

John W. MacDonald, Professor of Law Emeritus, Cornell Law School.

Jefferson B. Fordham, Professor of Law, University of Utah.

William J. Pierce, Professor of Law, University of Michigan.

LEGISLATIVE AND ADMINISTRATIVE PROCESSES, Second Edition (1981)

Hans A. Linde, Judge, Supreme Court of Oregon.
George Bunn, Professor of Law, University of Wisconsin.
Fredericka Paff, Professor of Law, University of Wisconsin.
W. Lawrence Church, Professor of Law, University of Wisconsin.

LOCAL GOVERNMENT LAW, Second Revised Edition (1986)

Jefferson B. Fordham, Professor of Law, University of Utah.

MASS MEDIA LAW, Fourth Edition (1990), with 1993 Supplement

Marc A. Franklin, Professor of Law, Stanford University.
David A. Anderson, Professor of Law, University of Texas.

MUNICIPAL CORPORATIONS, see Local Government Law

NEGOTIABLE INSTRUMENTS, see Commercial Paper

NEGOTIABLE INSTRUMENTS, Fourth Edition (1993)

E. Allan Farnsworth, Professor of Law, Columbia University.

NEGOTIABLE INSTRUMENTS AND LETTERS OF CREDIT (1992) (Reprinted from Commercial Law), Third Edition (1992)

Robert L. Jordan, Professor of Law, University of California, Los Angeles.
William D. Warren, Professor of Law, University of California, Los Angeles.

NEGOTIATION (1981) (Reprinted from THE LAWYERING PROCESS)

Gary Bellow, Professor of Law, Harvard Law School.
Bea Moulton, Legal Services Corporation.

NEW YORK PRACTICE, Fourth Edition (1978)

Herbert Peterfreund, Professor of Law, New York University.
Joseph M. McLaughlin, Dean of the Law School, Fordham University.

OIL AND GAS, Sixth Edition (1992)

Richard C. Maxwell, Professor of Law, Duke University.
Stephen F. Williams, Judge of the United States Court of Appeals.
Patrick Henry Martin, Professor of Law, Louisiana State University.
Bruce M. Kramer, Professor of Law, Texas Tech University.

ON LAW IN COURTS (1965)

Paul J. Mishkin, Professor of Law, University of California, Berkeley.
Clarence Morris, Professor of Law Emeritus, University of Pennsylvania.

PENSION AND EMPLOYEE BENEFIT LAW (1990), with 1993 Supplement

John H. Langbein, Professor of Law, University of Chicago.
Bruce A. Wolk, Professor of Law, University of California, Davis.

PLEADING AND PROCEDURE, see Procedure, Civil

POLICE FUNCTION, Fifth Edition (1991), with 1993 Supplement

Reprint of Chapters 1–10 of Miller, Dawson, Dix and Parnas's CRIMINAL JUSTICE ADMINISTRATION, Fourth Edition.

PREPARING AND PRESENTING THE CASE (1981) (Reprinted from THE LAWYERING PROCESS)

Gary Bellow, Professor of Law, Harvard Law School.
Bea Moulton, Legal Services Corporation.

PROCEDURE (1988), with Procedure Supplement (1991)

Robert M. Cover, late Professor of Law, Yale Law School.
Owen M. Fiss, Professor of Law, Yale Law School.
Judith Resnik, Professor of Law, University of Southern California Law Center.

PROCEDURE—CIVIL PROCEDURE, Sixth Edition (1990), with 1993 Supplement

Richard H. Field, late Professor of Law, Harvard University.
Benjamin Kaplan, Professor of Law Emeritus, Harvard University.
Kevin M. Clermont, Professor of Law, Cornell University.

PROCEDURE—CIVIL PROCEDURE, Successor Edition (1992)

A. Leo Levin, Professor of Law Emeritus, University of Pennsylvania.
Philip Shuchman, Professor of Law, Rutgers University.
Charles M. Yablon, Professor of Law, Yeshiva University.

PROCEDURE—CIVIL PROCEDURE, Fifth Edition (1990), with 1993 Supplement

Maurice Rosenberg, Professor of Law, Columbia University.
Hans Smit, Professor of Law, Columbia University.
Rochelle C. Dreyfuss, Professor of Law, New York University.

PROCEDURE—PLEADING AND PROCEDURE: State and Federal, Sixth Edition (1989), with 1993 Case Supplement

David W. Louisell, late Professor of Law, University of California, Berkeley.
Geoffrey C. Hazard, Jr., Professor of Law, Yale University.
Colin C. Tait, Professor of Law, University of Connecticut.

PROCEDURE—FEDERAL RULES OF CIVIL PROCEDURE, 1993 Edition

PRODUCTS LIABILITY AND SAFETY, Second Edition (1989), with 1993 Case and Statutory Supplement

W. Page Keeton, Professor of Law, University of Texas.
David G. Owen, Professor of Law, University of South Carolina.
John E. Montgomery, Professor of Law, University of South Carolina.
Michael D. Green, Professor of Law, University of Iowa.

PROFESSIONAL RESPONSIBILITY, Fifth Edition (1991), with 1993 Selected Standards on Professional Responsibility Supplement

Thomas D. Morgan, Professor of Law, George Washington University.
Ronald D. Rotunda, Professor of Law, University of Illinois.

PROPERTY, Sixth Edition (1990)

John E. Cribbet, Professor of Law, University of Illinois.
Corwin W. Johnson, Professor of Law, University of Texas.
Roger W. Findley, Professor of Law, University of Illinois.
Ernest E. Smith, Professor of Law, University of Texas.

PROPERTY—PERSONAL (1953)

S. Kenneth Skolfield, late Professor of Law Emeritus, Boston University.

PROPERTY—PERSONAL, Third Edition (1954)

Everett Fraser, late Dean of the Law School Emeritus, University of Minnesota.
Third Edition by Charles W. Taintor, late Professor of Law, University of Pittsburgh.

UNIVERSITY CASEBOOK SERIES—Continued

PROPERTY—INTRODUCTION, TO REAL PROPERTY, Third Edition (1954)

Everett Fraser, late Dean of the Law School Emeritus, University of Minnesota.

PROPERTY—FUNDAMENTALS OF MODERN REAL PROPERTY, Third Edition (1992)

Edward H. Rabin, Professor of Law, University of California, Davis.
Roberta Rosenthal Kwall, Professor of Law, DePaul University.

PROPERTY, REAL (1984), with 1988 Supplement

Paul Goldstein, Professor of Law, Stanford University.

PROSECUTION AND ADJUDICATION, Fourth Edition (1991), with 1993 Supplement

Reprint of Chapters 11–26 of Miller, Dawson, Dix and Parnas's CRIMINAL JUSTICE ADMINISTRATION, Fourth Edition.

PSYCHIATRY AND LAW, see Mental Health, see also Hinckley, Trial of

PUBLIC UTILITY LAW, see Free Enterprise, also Regulated Industries

REAL ESTATE PLANNING, Third Edition (1989), with Revised Problem and Statutory Supplement (1991)

Norton L. Steuben, Professor of Law, University of Colorado.

REAL ESTATE TRANSACTIONS, Third Edition (1993), with Statute, Form and Problem Supplement (1993)

Paul Goldstein, Professor of Law, Stanford University.
Gerald Korngold, Professor of Law, Case Western Reserve University.

RECEIVERSHIP AND CORPORATE REORGANIZATION, see Creditors' Rights

REGULATED INDUSTRIES, Second Edition (1976)

William K. Jones, Professor of Law, Columbia University.

REMEDIES, Third Edition (1992)

Edward D. Re, Professor of Law, St. John's University.
Stanton D. Krauss, Professor of Law, University of Bridgeport.

REMEDIES (1989)

Elaine W. Shoben, Professor of Law, University of Illinois.
Wm. Murray Tabb, Professor of Law, Baylor University.

SALES, Third Edition (1992)

Marion W. Benfield, Jr., Professor of Law, Wake Forest University.
William D. Hawkland, Professor of Law, Louisiana State Law Center.

SALES (1992) (Reprinted from Commercial Law) Third Edition (1992)

Robert L. Jordan, Professor of Law, University of California, Los Angeles.
William D. Warren, Professor of Law, University of California, Los Angeles.

SALES AND SECURED FINANCING, Sixth Edition (1993)

John Honnold, Professor of Law Emeritus, University of Pennsylvania.
Steven L. Harris, Professor of Law, University of Illinois.
Charles Mooney, Jr., Professor of Law, University of Pennsylvania.
Curtis R. Reitz, Professor of Law, University of Pennsylvania.

UNIVERSITY CASEBOOK SERIES—Continued

SALES LAW AND THE CONTRACTING PROCESS, Second Edition (1991) (Reprinted from Commercial Transactions) Second Edition (1991)

Alan Schwartz, Professor of Law, Yale University.
Robert E. Scott, Professor of Law, University of Virginia.

SALES TRANSACTIONS: DOMESTIC AND INTERNATIONAL LAW (1992)

John Honnold, Professor of Law Emeritus, University of Pennsylvania.
Curtis R. Reitz, Professor of Law, University of Pennsylvania.

SECURED TRANSACTIONS IN PERSONAL PROPERTY, Third Edition (1992) (Reprinted from COMMERCIAL LAW, Third Edition (1992))

Robert L. Jordan, Professor of Law, University of California, Los Angeles.
William D. Warren, Professor of Law, University of California, Los Angeles.

SECURITIES REGULATION, Seventh Edition (1992), with 1993 Selected Statutes, Rules and Forms Supplement, and 1993 Cases and Releases Supplement

Richard W. Jennings, Professor of Law, University of California, Berkeley.
Harold Marsh, Jr., Member of California Bar.
John C. Coffee, Jr., Professor of Law, Columbia University.

SECURITIES REGULATION, Second Edition (1988), with Statute, Rule and Form Supplement (1991)

Larry D. Soderquist, Professor of Law, Vanderbilt University.

SECURITY INTERESTS IN PERSONAL PROPERTY, Second Edition (1987)

Douglas G. Baird, Professor of Law, University of Chicago.
Thomas H. Jackson, Dean of the Law School, University of Virginia.

SECURITY INTERESTS IN PERSONAL PROPERTY, Second Edition (1992)

John Honnold, Professor of Law Emeritus, University of Pennsylvania.
Steven L. Harris, Professor of Law, University of Illinois.
Charles W. Mooney, Jr., Professor of Law, University of Pennsylvania.

SELECTED STANDARDS ON PROFESSIONAL RESPONSIBILITY, 1993 Edition

SELECTED STATUTES AND INTERNATIONAL AGREEMENTS ON UNFAIR COMPETITION, TRADEMARK, COPYRIGHT AND PATENT, 1993 Edition

SELECTED STATUTES ON TRUSTS AND ESTATES, 1992 Edition

SOCIAL RESPONSIBILITIES OF LAWYERS, Case Studies (1988)

Philip B. Heymann, Professor of Law, Harvard University.
Lance Liebman, Professor of Law, Harvard University.

SOCIAL SCIENCE IN LAW, Second Edition (1990)

John Monahan, Professor of Law, University of Virginia.
Laurens Walker, Professor of Law, University of Virginia.

TAXATION, FEDERAL INCOME (1989)

Stephen B. Cohen, Professor of Law, Georgetown University.

TAXATION, FEDERAL INCOME, Second Edition (1988), with 1993 Supplement (Supplement edited in association with Deborah H. Schenk, Professor of Law, New York University)

Michael J. Graetz, Professor of Law, Yale University.

TAXATION, FEDERAL INCOME, Seventh Edition (1991)

James J. Freeland, Professor of Law, University of Florida.

Stephen A. Lind, Professor of Law, University of Florida and University of California, Hastings.

Richard B. Stephens, late Professor of Law Emeritus, University of Florida.

TAXATION, FEDERAL INCOME, Successor Edition (1986), with 1993 Supplement

Stanley S. Surrey, late Professor of Law, Harvard University.

Paul R. McDaniel, Professor of Law, Boston College.

Hugh J. Ault, Professor of Law, Boston College.

Stanley A. Koppelman, Professor of Law, Boston University.

TAXATION, FEDERAL INCOME, OF BUSINESS ORGANIZATIONS (1991), with 1993 Supplement

Paul R. McDaniel, Professor of Law, Boston College.

Hugh J. Ault, Professor of Law, Boston College.

Martin J. McMahon, Jr., Professor of Law, University of Kentucky.

Daniel L. Simmons, Professor of Law, University of California, Davis.

TAXATION, FEDERAL INCOME, OF PARTNERSHIPS AND S CORPORATIONS (1991), with 1993 Supplement

Paul R. McDaniel, Professor of Law, Boston College.

Hugh J. Ault, Professor of Law, Boston College.

Martin J. McMahon, Jr., Professor of Law, University of Kentucky.

Daniel L. Simmons, Professor of Law, University of California, Davis.

TAXATION, FEDERAL INCOME, OIL AND GAS, NATURAL RESOURCES TRANSACTIONS (1990)

Peter C. Maxfield, Professor of Law, University of Wyoming.

James L. Houghton, CPA, Partner, Ernst and Young.

James R. Gaar, CPA, Partner, Ernst and Young.

TAXATION, FEDERAL WEALTH TRANSFER, Successor Edition (1987)

Stanley S. Surrey, late Professor of Law, Harvard University.

Paul R. McDaniel, Professor of Law, Boston College.

Harry L. Gutman, Professor of Law, University of Pennsylvania.

TAXATION, FUNDAMENTALS OF CORPORATE, Third Edition (1991), with 1993 Supplement

Stephen A. Lind, Professor of Law, University of Florida and University of California, Hastings.

Stephen Schwarz, Professor of Law, University of California, Hastings.

Daniel J. Lathrope, Professor of Law, University of California, Hastings.

Joshua Rosenberg, Professor of Law, University of San Francisco.

TAXATION, FUNDAMENTALS OF PARTNERSHIP, Third Edition (1992), with 1993 Supplement

Stephen A. Lind, Professor of Law, University of Florida and University of California, Hastings.

Stephen Schwarz, Professor of Law, University of California, Hastings.

Daniel J. Lathrope, Professor of Law, University of California, Hastings.

Joshua Rosenberg, Professor of Law, University of San Francisco.

UNIVERSITY CASEBOOK SERIES—Continued

TAXATION OF CORPORATIONS AND THEIR SHAREHOLDERS (1991), with 1993 Supplement

David J. Shakow, Professor of Law, University of Pennsylvania.

TAXATION, PROBLEMS IN THE FEDERAL INCOME TAXATION OF PARTNER-SHIPS AND CORPORATIONS, Second Edition (1986)

Norton L. Steuben, Professor of Law, University of Colorado.
William J. Turnier, Professor of Law, University of North Carolina.

TAXATION, PROBLEMS IN THE FUNDAMENTALS OF FEDERAL INCOME, Second Edition (1985)

Norton L. Steuben, Professor of Law, University of Colorado.
William J. Turnier, Professor of Law, University of North Carolina.

TORT LAW AND ALTERNATIVES, Fifth Edition (1992)

Marc A. Franklin, Professor of Law, Stanford University.
Robert L. Rabin, Professor of Law, Stanford University.

TORTS, Eighth Edition (1988)

William L. Prosser, late Professor of Law, University of California, Hastings.
John W. Wade, Professor of Law, Vanderbilt University.
Victor E. Schwartz, Adjunct Professor of Law, Georgetown University.

TORTS, Third Edition (1976)

Harry Shulman, late Dean of the Law School, Yale University.
Fleming James, Jr., Professor of Law Emeritus, Yale University.
Oscar S. Gray, Professor of Law, University of Maryland.

TRADE REGULATION, Third Edition (1990), with 1993 Supplement

Milton Handler, Professor of Law Emeritus, Columbia University.
Harlan M. Blake, Professor of Law, Columbia University.
Robert Pitofsky, Professor of Law, Georgetown University.
Harvey J. Goldschmid, Professor of Law, Columbia University.

TRADE REGULATION, see Antitrust

TRANSNATIONAL BUSINESS PROBLEMS (1986)

Detlev F. Vagts, Professor of Law, Harvard University.

TRANSNATIONAL LEGAL PROBLEMS, Third Edition (1986), with 1991 Revised Edition of Documentary Supplement

Henry J. Steiner, Professor of Law, Harvard University.
Detlev F. Vagts, Professor of Law, Harvard University.

TRIAL, see also Evidence, Making the Record, Lawyering Process and Preparing and Presenting the Case

TRUSTS, Sixth Edition (1991)

George G. Bogert, late Professor of Law Emeritus, University of Chicago.
Dallin H. Oaks, President, Brigham Young University.
H. Reese Hansen, Dean and Professor of Law, Brigham Young University.
Claralyn Martin Hill, J.D., Brigham Young University.

TRUSTS AND ESTATES, SELECTED STATUTES ON, 1992 Edition

TRUSTS AND WILLS, see also Decedents' Estates and Trusts, and Family Property Law

UNIVERSITY CASEBOOK SERIES—Continued

UNFAIR COMPETITION, see Competitive Process and Business Torts

WATER RESOURCE MANAGEMENT, Fourth Edition (1993)

A. Dan Tarlock, Professor of Law, IIT Chicago–Kent College of Law.

James N. Corbridge, Jr., Chancellor, University of Colorado at Boulder, and Professor of Law, University of Colorado.

David H. Getches, Professor of Law, University of Colorado.

WOMEN AND THE LAW (1992)

Mary Joe Frug, late Professor of Law, New England School of Law.

WILLS AND ADMINISTRATION, Fifth Edition (1961)

Philip Mechem, late Professor of Law, University of Pennsylvania.

Thomas E. Atkinson, late Professor of Law, New York University.

WRITING AND ANALYSIS IN THE LAW, Second Edition (1991)

Helene S. Shapo, Professor of Law, Northwestern University.

Marilyn R. Walter, Professor of Law, Brooklyn Law School.

Elizabeth Fajans, Writing Specialist, Brooklyn Law School.

University Casebook Series

EDITORIAL BOARD

DAVID L. SHAPIRO
DIRECTING EDITOR
Professor of Law, Harvard University

EDWARD L. BARRETT, Jr.
Professor of Law Emeritus, University of California, Davis

ROBERT C. CLARK
Dean of the School of Law, Harvard University

OWEN M. FISS
Professor of Law, Yale Law School

GERALD GUNTHER
Professor of Law, Stanford University

THOMAS H. JACKSON
Provost University of Virginia

HERMA HILL KAY
Dean of the School of Law, University of California, Berkeley

PAGE KEETON
Professor of Law, University of Texas

ROBERT L. RABIN
Professor of Law, Stanford University

CAROL M. ROSE
Professor of Law, Yale University

CASS R. SUNSTEIN
Professor of Law, University of Chicago

SAMUEL D. THURMAN
Professor of Law Emeritus, University of Utah

THE LAW AND ETHICS OF LAWYERING

SECOND EDITION

By

GEOFFREY C. HAZARD, JR.
Sterling Professor of Law, Yale Law School

SUSAN P. KONIAK
Professor of Law
Boston University School of Law

ROGER C. CRAMTON
Robert S. Stevens Professor of Law
Cornell Law School

Westbury, New York
THE FOUNDATION PRESS, INC.
1994

COPYRIGHT © 1990 THE FOUNDATION PRESS, INC.
COPYRIGHT © 1994 By THE FOUNDATION PRESS, INC.
    615 Merrick Ave.
    Westbury, N.Y. 11590–6607
    (516) 832–6950

All rights reserved
Printed in the United States of America

Library of Congress Cataloging-in-Publication Data
Hazard, Geoffrey C.
 The law and ethics of lawyering / by Geoffrey C. Hazard, Jr.,
Susan P. Koniak, and Roger C. Cramton. — 2nd ed.
  p. cm. — (University casebook series)
 Includes index.
 ISBN 1–56662–120–8
 1. Legal ethics—United States—Cases. 2. Lawyers—United States
—Discipline—Cases. I. Koniak, Susan P. II. Cramton, Roger C.
III. Title. IV. Series.
KF306.A4H39 1994
174'.3'0973—dc20   93–36968

H., K. & C. Law & Ethics of Lawyering 2nd Ed. UCS

TEXT IS PRINTED ON 10% POST CONSUMER RECYCLED PAPER

To Beth and Harriet

To Morris, Esther and Jay

To the memory of Robert M. Cover

*

PREFACE

This book seeks to fulfill its title. Thus, first of all it contains cases. Cases are at the same time sources of legal doctrine in the law governing law practice, a mirror of the minds of judges in interpreting what lawyers do, and "war stories" of difficult situations that lawyers confront. This book also contains statutes and rules of professional conduct. Statutes reflect public sentiment about right and wrong in transactions in which lawyers are involved, such as managing a service enterprise, buying and selling property, administering criminal justice and paying taxes. The rules of professional conduct are formulated primarily through the authorship of lawyers. Hence, those rules are a mirror of the minds of lawyers in interpreting their own work. All of these legal sources project visions of the practice of law, but the visions are not the same. Therein lies an important part of the tale.

The book also contains source materials on ethics and morals, from Plato and since. The practice of law is not fully intelligible without reference to these great philosophical issues in ethics and to ethical standards of the community at large. Community ethical standards inform the minds of clients and opposite parties with whom a lawyer deals, the minds of officials and other lawyers with whom lawyers must work, and the minds of jurors, judges and disciplinary committees before whom a lawyer may be called to account. Neither is the practice of law fully intelligible without reference to the inner mind of each of us who engages in law practice. Every act a lawyer does, or fails to do, appears somehow in her own mind's eye. The accumulation of these impressions is not only professional experience but personal identity as well. Every lawyer should continually ask herself: What kind of memories will this leave with me? Contemplating the morality of practicing law does not come too soon in law school. Indeed if not started then it may come too late, or never.

The materials in the book also reflect the variousness of lawyers' situations in practice. Some of the cases and rules involve big firm corporate practice. Others involve small firm lawyers and sole practitioners and such transactions as drafting a will, handling a divorce or defending a criminal accused. Situation in practice makes a difference in the kind of matters a lawyer handles and therefore the kind of ethical problems she encounters. Situation in practice also makes a difference in the kinds of political, economic and moral resources a lawyer has for dealing with ethical problems. In these respects, lawyers are very different from each other. Yet they are alike in being governed by a common body of law and professional lore and being obliged, in the end, to resolve ethical dilemmas alone on the basis of personal judgment.

The book covers a wide range not only in the foregoing respects but in fields of legal subject matter. We include distillates of agency law, criminal law and procedure, civil procedure, evidence law, tort law, contract law, securities law and corporation law, and make reference to tax law and the law of wills, estate planning and marital dissolution. This cannot be avoided if the problems of legal ethics are to be adequately comprehended. The stuff of law practice includes all legal subjects, and law practice performed competently and ethically requires dealing with unfamiliar areas of law. In the "pervasive method" of teaching legal ethics, ethical problems are implanted in the context of a body of some other law in some other course. This book represents the "pervasive method" in reverse.

G.C.H., JR.
S.P.K.
R.C.C.

October 1993

NOTE ON EDITORIAL PRACTICES

The editorial practices followed in the book require brief explanation. In general we have reprinted cases rather fully in a desire to provide class material that retains the detail and texture of the originals. We have not carried this approach so far as to preserve passages that are repetitious or irrelevant. Authorities cited in principal cases have been pruned out, leaving only those citations that build an understanding of the course as a whole or that a curious student might want to examine. Our notes contain some citations to cases and secondary sources, but in this edition these are placed in footnotes so as not to interrupt the flow of the text. We have discussed and cited all of the materials that we think a careful instructor or diligent student might want to examine for class purposes. See the Table of Cases and Table of Books and Articles.

Omissions from principal cases or quoted materials are indicated in all instances, with the exceptions noted below. Periods (. . .) signal the omission of words, sentences or citations from within a paragraph (although in some instances citations are omitted without indication). A centered ellipsis (. . .) indicates the omission of a paragraph or more. Most of the footnotes in principal cases and quoted materials have been discarded. Those footnotes which have been included retain their original number. Notation of the elimination of dissenting opinions is provided. In a few instances we have corrected obvious typographical errors in the original, or changed italic to roman typeface.

*

ACKNOWLEDGEMENTS

We thank the hundreds of students and lawyers in our professional experience who have helped us to try and understand this subject. Special thanks go to Professor Charles W. Wolfram of Cornell Law School, whose detailed comments on a tentative version of the second edition were extremely helpful. Very special thanks also go to Susan Evans, J.D. 1992, Cornell University, whose careful editorial eye, good judgment and perseverance greatly improved the text of the book. Research assistants who contributed to the second edition include Julia Lee, Richard McCaffrey and Lenore Neerbasch, students at the Cornell Law School, and Christine Biancheria at the University of Pittsburgh School of Law. Jack Glezen at Cornell provided exceptional assistance in the preparation of the manuscript.

We owe continued thanks to many who contributed to the first edition: LuAnn Driscoll, Ruth Jencks, Karen Knochel, Darleen Mocello, Carolyn Rohan, Barbara Salopek and Hillary Sonet, who typed various portions of the manuscript. We thank Kathleen C. Cleary, Andrew B. Klaber, Kristen A. Lee, Daniel Lee and Lauren Schlecker, research assistants at the University of Pittsburgh School of Law, who worked so earnestly on the first edition. Especially, we thank Margaret M. Egler, J.D. 1988, University of Pittsburgh, for her tireless efforts, critical eye, good spirit and sincere dedication to this project.

We thank each other for a lovely law partnership.

G.C.H., Jr.
S.P.K.
R.C.C.

We thank the authors and holders of copyrights for permission to publish excerpts, as follows:

American Bar Association, Formal Opinion 342 (November 24, 1975). Copyright © by the American Bar Association and reprinted with its permission.

American Bar Association, Formal Opinion 352 (July 7, 1985). Copyright © by the American Bar Association and reprinted with its permission.

Julie Amparano, A Lawyer Flourishes by Suing Corporations and Their Shareholders, Wall Street Journal (April 28, 1987). Copyright © 1987 The Wall Street Journal.

Association of the Bar of the City of New York, Committee on Professional and Judicial Ethics, Inquiry Reference 80–23. Reprinted with permission.

ACKNOWLEDGEMENTS

Derrick A. Bell, Jr., Serving Two Masters: Integration Ideals and Client Interests in School Desegregation Litigation, 85 Yale L.J. 470 (1976). Reprinted with permission of the Yale Law Journal Company and Fred B. Rothman & Company.

Sissela Bok, Lying: Moral Choice in Public and Private Life (1978). Copyright © 1978 by Sissela Bok and reprinted with her permission and the permission of Pantheon Books.

Sissela Bok, Secrets (1982). Copyright © 1983 by Sissela Bok and reprinted with her permission and the permission of Pantheon Books.

Louis D. Brandeis, The Opportunity in the Law (1905), in Brandeis, Business: A Profession (1914).

Steven Brill, The Stench of Room 202. Reprinted with permission from the April 1987 issue of The American Lawyer. Copyright © 1987 The American Lawyer.

John C. Coffee, Jr., Understanding the Plaintiff's Attorney: The Implications of Economic Theory for Private Enforcement of Law Through Class and Derivative Actions, 86 Colum.L.Rev. 669 (1986). Reprinted with permission.

Robert M. Cover, Violence and the Word, 95 Yale L.J. 1601 (1986). Reprinted with permission of the Yale Law Journal Company and Fred B. Rothman & Company.

Roger C. Cramton, The Lawyer as Whistleblower: Confidentiality and the Government Lawyer, 5 Geo.J.Legal Ethics 292 (1991). Reprinted with the permission of the publisher, copyright © 1991 Georgetown Journal of Legal Ethics and Georgetown University.

Barbara A. Curran, Two Nationwide Surveys: 1989 Pilot Assessments of the Unmet Legal Needs of the Poor and of the Public Generally. Reprinted with permission of Barbara A. Curran, the American Bar Association and the American Bar Foundation. Copyright © 1990 American Bar Association.

District of Columbia Office of Bar Counsel, Have a Complaint About an Attorney? (1993). Reprinted with permission.

Norman Dorsen and Leon Friedman, Disorder in the Courtroom (1973). Copyright © 1973 by Association of the Bar of the City of New York. Reprinted with permission.

Federal Bar Association, Professional Ethics Committee, Opinion 73–1: The Government Client and Confidentiality, 32 Fed.B.J. 71 (1973). Reprinted with permission of the Federal Bar Association and the Federal Bar Journal.

Monroe H. Freedman, Perjury: The Lawyer's Trilemma, 1 Litigation 26 (No. 1 Winter, 1975). Reprinted with permission of the Section of

Litigation, American Bar Association.

James J. Fuld, Lawyers' Standards and Responsibilities in Rendering Opinions, 33 Bus.Law. 1295 (1978). Copyright © 1978 by the American Bar Association and reprinted with its permission and the permission of its Section of Business Law. All rights reserved.

William J. Genego, The Future of Effective Assistance of Counsel: Performance Standards and Competent Representation, 22 American Crim.L.Rev. 181 (1984). Copyright © 1984 jointly by American Criminal Law Review and the author and reprinted with the permission of both.

Carol Gilligan, In a Different Voice (1982). Copyright © 1980 by Carol Gilligan. Reprinted with permission of the publisher, Harvard University Press.

Erving Goffman, Asylums: Essays on the Social Situation of Mental Patients and Other Inmates (1961). Copyright © 1961 by Erving Goffman. Reprinted with permission.

Robert W. Gordon, The Ideal and the Actual in the Law, in Gawalt, ed., the New High Priests: Lawyers in Post–Civil War America (1984). Reprinted with permission.

Geoffrey C. Hazard, Jr., Disciplinary Process Needs Major Reform, National Law Journal, August 1, 1988, p. 13. Reprinted with permission.

Geoffrey C. Hazard, Jr., Ethics in the Practice of Law (1978). Reprinted with permission of Yale University Press.

Geoffrey C. Hazard, Jr., How Far May a Lawyer Go in Assisting a Client in Legally Wrongful Conduct?, 35 U.Miami L.Rev. 669 (1981). Reprinted with the permission of the University of Miami Law Review.

Geoffrey C. Hazard, Jr., Permissive Affirmative Action on Behalf of Blacks, 1987 U.Ill.L.Rev. 379. Copyright © 1987 University of Illinois Law Review, Board of Trustees of the University of Illinois. Reprinted with permission.

Geoffrey C. Hazard, Jr., Rectification of Client Fraud: Death and Revival of a Professional Norm, 33 Emory L.J. 271 (1984). Reprinted with permission of the Emory Law Journal.

Geoffrey C. Hazard, Jr., Securing Courtroom Decorum, 80 Yale L.J. 433 (1970). Reprinted with permission of the Yale Law Journal Company and Fred B. Rothman & Company.

Geoffrey C. Hazard, Jr., Triangular Lawyer Relationships: An Exploratory Analysis, 1 Geo.J. of Leg. Ethics 15 (1987). Reprinted with permission of the Georgetown Journal of Legal Ethics.

Kenney F. Hegland, Moral Dilemmas in Teaching Trial Advocacy, 32 J.Legal Educ. 69 (1982). Reprinted with permission of the author and the Journal of Legal Education.

Ronald L. Hirsch, Are You on Target?, The Barrister Magazine, Vol. 12, No. 1, p. 17. Reprinted with permission.

Oliver W. Holmes, Jr., The Path of Law in Collected Legal Papers (1920), also appears 10 Harv.L.Rev. 457 (1897).

David Hoffman, A Course in Legal Study (1836).

Robert Keeton, Trial Tactics and Methods (2d ed. 1973). Copyright © 1973 by Little, Brown and Company and reprinted with its permission.

Duncan Kennedy, Legal Education and the Reproduction of Hierarchy (1983). Reprinted with permission of the author.

Susan P. Koniak, The Law Between the Bar and the State, 70 N.C.L.Rev. 1389 (1992). Reprinted with permission of North Carolina Law Review.

Steven C. Krane, The Attorney Unshackled: SEC Rule 2(e) Violates Clients' Sixth Amendment Right to Counsel, 57 Notre Dame Lawyer 50 (1981). Copyright © 1981 by Notre Dame Law Review, University of Notre Dame. Reprinted with permission.

Charles R. Lawrence III, The Id, the Ego and Equal Protection: Reckoning with Unconscious Racism, 39 Stan.L.Rev. 317 (1987). Copyright © 1987 by the Board of Trustees of the Leland Stanford Junior University. Reprinted with permission.

David Luban, Lawyers and Justice: An Ethical Study xiv–xv, 297–98 (1988). Copyright © 1988 Princeton University Press.

David Luban, Paternalism and the Legal Profession, 1981 Wis.L.Rev. 454. Reprinted with the permission of the Wisconsin Law Review.

Stewart Macaulay, Law Schools and the World Outside Their Doors II: Some Notes on Two Recent Studies of the Chicago Bar, 32 J.Legal Educ. 506 (1982). Reprinted with permission of the author and the Association of American Law Schools.

Jonathan R. Macey and Geoffrey P. Miller, The Plaintiffs' Attorney's Role in Class Action and Derivative Litigation: Economic Analysis and Recommendations for Reform, 58 U.Chi.L.Rev. 1 (1991). Reprinted with permission of the University of Chicago Law Review.

Morton Mintz, At Any Cost: Corporate Greed, Women, and the Dalkon Shield. Copyright © 1985 by Morton Mintz. Reprinted with permission of Pantheon Books, a division of Random House, Inc.

Plato, Gorgias in the Dialogues of Plato, translated by Benjamin Jowett (1898). Copyright © 1898 by D. Appleton and Company.

Deborah L. Rhode, Class Conflicts in Class Actions, 34 Stan.L.Rev. 1183 (1982). Copyright © 1982 by the Board of Trustees of the Leland Stanford Junior University. Reprinted with permission.

Deborah L. Rhode, Perspectives on Professional Women, 40 Stan.L.Rev. 1163 (1988). Copyright © 1988 by the Board of Trustees of the Leland Stanford Junior University. Reprinted with permission.

Simon H. Rifkind, The Lawyer's Role and Responsibility in Modern Society, 30 The Record of the Association of the Bar of the City of New York 534 (1975). Reprinted with permission of the author and the Association. Copyright © 1975 Association of the Bar of the City of New York.

Douglas E. Rosenthal, Lawyer and Client, Who's in Charge? Copyright © 1974 by the Russell Sage Foundation and reprinted with its permission.

Eric Schnapper, Legal Ethics and the Government Lawyer, 32 The Record 649 (1979).

Geraldine Segal, Blacks in the Law (University of Pennsylvania Press 1985). Reprinted with permission.

William H. Simon, The Ideology of Advocacy, 1978 Wisconsin Law Review 30. Copyright © 1978 Wisconsin Law Review. Reprinted with the permission of the Wisconsin Law Review.

Harlan Fiske Stone, The Public Influence of the Bar, 48 Harv.L.Rev. 1 (1934). Reprinted with permission of the Harvard Law Review.

Stuart Taylor, Jr., Ethics and the Law: A Case History, New York Times Magazine (January 9, 1983). Reprinted with permission. Copyright © 1983 by the New York Times Company.

Richard Wasserstrom, Lawyers and Revolution, 30 U.Pitt.L.Rev. 125 (1968). Reprinted with permission of University of Pittsburgh Law Review.

Richard Wasserstrom, Lawyers as Professionals: Some Moral Issues, 5 Human Rights 1 (1975). Reprinted with permission.

Stephen Wexler, Practicing Law for Poor People (1970). Reprinted with permission of the Yale Law Journal Company and Fred B. Rothman & Company from The Yale Law Journal, Vol. 79, pp. 1049–1067.

Charles W. Wolfram, Modern Legal Ethics 33–38 (1986). Reprinted with permission of the author and West Publishing Company. Copyright © 1986 West Publishing Company.

*

NOTES ON BIBLIOGRAPHY
AND RESEARCH

Research on legal and ethical problems arising in the practice of law
is a daunting business because of the number and variegated nature of
relevant materials. There is much more to the subject than ethics codes
and opinions; the law of lawyering is influenced by practice context,
which then leads to the institutional arrangements and procedural and
substantive law of particular fields of practice (e.g., a matrimonial lawyer
faced with a tax counseling problem, a white collar criminal defense
lawyer whose client is charged with RICO violations, a law firm whose
corporate client is fighting a hostile takeover). Given the scope of the
subject, the goal here is not to be encyclopedic but to point the way to a
few of the most salient sources.

I. BASIC STUDY AND RESEARCH

For the student seeking a quick overview of a topic or an introduction to relevant legal sources, several useful books and treatises are
available:

Charles W. Wolfram, *Modern Legal Ethics* (West, 1986) (an excellent
treatise, providing a comprehensive review of the subject; a second
edition is in preparation).

Geoffrey C. Hazard, Jr. and W. William Hodes, *The Law of
Lawyering* (Prentice-Hall, 2d ed. 1990) (a useful treatise, supple-
mented annually, that deals mainly with the Model Rules of
Professional Conduct and brings in case authority only occasionally).

Richard H. Underwood and William H. Fortune, *Trial Ethics* (1988)
(a sound treatise, supplemented annually, with coverage somewhat
broader than its title).

Ronald E. Mallen and Jeffrey M. Smith, *Legal Malpractice* (West, 3d
ed. 1989) (this multi-volume treatise, with annual pocket parts, is
the standard reference work on its subject).

Monroe H. Freedman, *Understanding Lawyers' Ethics* (Matthew
Bender, 1990) (a provocative and interesting student handbook that
provides a vigorous defense of adversary ethics).

For research purposes, the *ABA/BNA Lawyers' Manual on
Professional Conduct*, a multi-volume looseleaf service that is updated
biweekly, is an extremely valuable resource. Its "Manual" volume contains a treatise-like treatment of most relevant issues; its "Ethics
Opinions" volume is the best available collection of synopses of state and
local bar association ethics committee opinions; and the "Current
Reports" volume contains biweekly digests of recent developments.

In 1985 the American Law Institute began work on a *Restatement of the Law Governing Lawyers* under the guidance of its director, Geoffrey C. Hazard, Jr., one of the coauthors of this book. Professor Charles W. Wolfram of the Cornell Law School serves as Chief Reporter. Tentative drafts on a number of topics have been considered at ALI annual meetings and are available at many law libraries. The Tentative Drafts currently available deal with the following subjects: (1) T.D. No. 1 (April 11, 1988), T.D. No. 2 (April 7, 1989), and T.D. No. 3 (April 10, 1990)--all dealing with attorney-client privilege and confidentiality; (2) T.D. No. 4 (April 10, 1991)--dealing with conflicts of interest and the financial and property relationship between client and lawyer; and (3) T. D. No. 5 (March 16, 1992)--the work-product doctrine and the basic elements of the client-lawyer relationship. Future drafts will deal with advocacy, advising and counseling, lawyer liability, delivery of legal services and regulation of the legal profession. The Restatement should be completed by about 1996.

II. EDIFICATION AND AMUSEMENT

Legal journalism: The *New York Times* (particularly on Fridays) and the *Wall Street Journal* (daily in section B) feature stories and columns dealing with lawyers and legal ethics. Every issue of the weekly *National Law Journal* contains several articles or stories relating to professional responsibility. The monthly *American Lawyer* also focuses on lawyer behavior and legal ethics. Topical material from these and other journalistic sources can suggest facts and issues that enrich understanding of legal ethics or the course on the subject.

Novels, movies, and TV shows: *L.A. Law*, especially in its first two years, dealt with a variety of legal ethics problems. A number of excellent (and many mediocre) movies portray lawyers and their ethical problems. For an annotated guide as of 1987, see Roger C. Cramton, *Audiovisual Materials on Professional Responsibility* (ABA, 1987). Many novels feature lawyer heroes or villains: Some noteworthy examples include James Gould Cozzens, *By Love Possessed* (1957) and *The Just and the Unjust* (1942); Charles Dickens, *Bleak House* (1853); William Faulkner, *Intruder in the Dust* (1948); George V. Higgins, *Kennedy for the Defense* (1980) and *Penance for Kennedy* (1985); Harper Lee, *To Kill a Mockingbird* (1960); Anthony Trollope, *Orley Farm* (1862); and Scott Turow, *Presumed Innocent* (1987) and *Burden of Proof* (1990).

Biography. Biographies and autobiographies of famous lawyers (e.g., John Adams, Abraham Lincoln, Clarence Darrow, John W. Davis, O. W. Holmes, Jr., Samuel Williston) are illuminating and sometimes inspiring. Falling into the inspiring category are Richard Kluger, *Simple Justice* (1977), a treatment of the role of lawyers in the fight against school segregation, and Anthony Lewis, *Gideon's Trumpet* (1964), a prize-winning account of Abe Fortas' pro bono work for the prevailing defendant in Gideon v. Wainwright (see p. 193 below).

III. AMERICAN BAR ASSOCIATION PROFESSIONAL CODES AND STANDARDS OF CONDUCT

1. *Model Rules of Professional Conduct* (adopted initially in 1983; amended from time to time). Reprinted in ABA/BNA Lawyers' Manual on Professional Conduct 01:101 and in the various standards supplements published annually by law book publishers. The Model Rules serve as the basis for state lawyer codes in 38 states as of September 1993. The ABA/BNA Lawyers' Manual on Professional Conduct 01:3 provides a state-by-state list of the states that have revised their ethics rules since 1983 and, for those states, the major ways in which a state's rules depart from the Model Rules.

> *Legislative history:* ABA Center for Professional Responsibility, Legislative History of the Model Rules of Professional Conduct: Their Development in the ABA House of Delegates (1987) (chronological summary of work of Kutak Commission and of discussion of Model Rules in six meetings of the House of Delegates). See also, Ted Schneyer, Professionalism as Bar Politics: The Making of the Model Rules of Professional Conduct, 1989 Law & Soc.Inquiry 677 (summarizing and interpreting the legislative history).

> *Annotations.* See ABA Center for Professional Responsibility, Annotated Model Rules of Professional Conduct (2d ed. 1992) (a comprehensive discussion of the case law, ethics opinions and other authorities relating to each provision of the Model Rules).

2. *Model Code of Professional Responsibility* (1969; amended through 1981 but no longer updated or recommended by the ABA). The Model Code continues to provide the framework for the lawyer codes in more than a dozen states, although a number of these states have revised their versions of the Code to incorporate provisions of the Model Rules (e.g., New York, Oregon and Virginia). The Model Code is reprinted in ABA/BNA Lawyers' Manual on Professional Conduct 01.301 and in the various standards supplements. An annotated version covers developments to 1977: Oliver Maru (ed.), Annotated Model Code of Professional Responsibility (American Bar Foundation, 1979).

3. *Standards for Criminal Justice* (4 vols.) (2d ed. 1980). The standards are guidelines for the criminal justice system in Restatement form (black-letter statements followed by explanatory comments). The chapters dealing with The Prosecution Function and The Defense Function contain standards of conduct applicable, respectively, to prosecutors and defense counsel. The standards are frequently cited.

4. *Miscellaneous ABA standards.* The ABA House of Delegates has adopted standards on a number of matters relevant to the law and ethics of lawyering. The most important are listed below (the page reference is to the ABA/BNA Lawyers' Manual on Professional Conduct, where the standards are reprinted):

Model Rules for Lawyer Disciplinary Enforcement (1989) (01:601).

Model Rules for Lawyers' Funds for Client Protection (1989) (01:5001).

Standards for Imposing Lawyer Sanctions (1986) (01:801).

Lawyers' Creed of Professionalism and Lawyers' Pledge of Professionalism (1988) (01:401).

5. *Ethics opinions.* The Standing Committee on Ethics and Professional Responsibility is charged with interpreting the ABA's professional standards and recommending amendments. Since 1983 the Formal and Informal Opinions have primarily referred to the Model Rules, although the opinions also discuss Model Code provisions and other standards. From 1970-1983 the opinions interpreted the Model Code; prior to 1970 they interpreted the Canons of Professional Ethics. The opinions have been published in various forms.

Much of the material discussed here is also available on the computerized legal research services, LEXIS and WESTLAW.

LEXIS *Library*: ABA; *Files*: FOPIN (Formal Opinions), INFOP (Informal Opinions) and Codes.

WESTLAW *Databases*: ABA; *Files*: LS-ABAEO (ABA Opinions); AMBAR (abstracts of ABA documents), and JDDD (judicial discipline and disability digest).

IV. FEDERAL AND STATE STATUTES AND COURT RULES

The codes, standards and ethic opinions produced by the American Bar Association, a voluntary association of lawyers, carry weight because of the prestige of the Association and the care with which this work is done. But the recommendations and views of the ABA are not formal law except and to the extent that federal and state law makers embody the ABA's views in legislation, court rules, judicial decisions, state-adopted ethics codes and administrative regulations and decisions. This formal law is found in the same way that other law is found—by legal research into the law of the United States or that of a particular state. The paragraphs that follow contain some illustrative examples relevant to the law of lawyering; many others could be cited.

1. *Federal.* Procedural rules applicable to the federal courts impose duties on lawyers who have entered an appearance in a proceeding in a federal court. E.g., Federal Rules of Civil Procedure, Rule 11, 16(f), 26(g), and 37. See text at pp. 151-154. Local rules of federal district courts also impose important (and varying) duties. Similarly, a number of federal statutes deal with the responsibilities of lawyers currently or formerly employed by the federal government. See, e.g., Federal Conflict of Interest Act, 18 U.S.C. §§ 201-219 (discussed at p. 725 below). Federal departments and agencies usually have adopted one of the ABA codes as

a "guideline" to govern the conduct of the agency's lawyers. Agency regulations often govern admission to practice and discipline before an agency. See text at p. 779 below.

2. *State.* Each state regulates the legal profession and the practice of law in a somewhat different manner. Judicial decisions, statutes and procedural rules deal with many matters of importance to lawyers (e.g., attorney-client privilege, attorney liens, bar admission, conflicts of interest). In all states, a set of court-adopted rules provides professional standards applicable to lawyers in disciplinary proceedings. Today, the ABA Model Rules on Professional Conduct provides the basic framework in most states (with much local variation). State and local bar associations issue ethics opinions interpreting a lawyer's ethical responsibilities. The following paragraphs deal briefly with California and New York, important states with approximately one-fourth of the nation's lawyers, but states that are somewhat atypical in their pattern of regulation of lawyers.

California. The California Business and Professions Code contains extensive provisions governing, for example, bar admission, disciplinary authority of the courts, unlawful practice of law, contingency fee agreements, unlawful solicitation, arbitration of attorney's fees, funds for provision of legal services to indigent persons and other matters. The California Supreme Court adopted the California Rules of Professional Conduct (1988, effective 1989), codified in Cal.Bus. & Prof.Code § 6076 et seq. The California ethics rules are unique in that they follow neither the ABA Model Rules nor ABA Model Code. Some major subjects, such as confidentiality, are left to statute and case law. California statutes, ethics code and ethics opinions are collected in a publication of the State Bar: California State Bar Compendium on Professional Responsibility (a looseleaf set with annual updates).

New York. New York's ethics rules were revised in 1990. In New York, unlike other states, the intermediate appellate courts, not the state's high court, issue court rules. The four Appellate Divisions adopted uniform rules governing professional conduct in 1990. The Appellate Divisions are also responsible for professional discipline. The current rules maintain the structure of the Model Code but include many changes incorporating provisions from the Model Rules. Ethics opinions are issued by state and local bar associations (all private associations) and published in their publications, the New York Law Journal and in other legal newspapers.

V. OTHER SOURCES

The vast literature bearing on lawyers and their work is too expansive to list here. A start is made in the Table of Books and Articles, which lists the books and articles cited in this book and used extensively in its preparation. Excellent bibliographies containing many other materials are found in a number of recent books:

Richard L. Abel, *American Lawyers* (Oxford, 1990) (this bibliography is especially comprehensive in its inclusion of sociological and other materials relating to theories of the profession).

John Flood, *The Legal Profession in the United States* (American Bar Foundation, 3d ed., 1989) (an annotated, selective bibliography that emphasizes theoretical and empirical studies of the American legal profession).

Charles W. Wolfram, *Modern Legal Ethics* (West, 1986) (in addition to copious citations to cases, rules, ethics opinions and statutes, the footnotes include a wide array of other relevant literature).

SUMMARY OF CONTENTS

TABLE OF CONTENTS

TABLE OF CONTENTS

TABLE OF CONTENTS

TABLE OF CONTENTS

TABLE OF CONTENTS

TABLE OF BOOKS AND ARTICLES

This table lists the books, monographs and articles used in the preparation of this book and cited therein. For further bibliographic help, see the Note on Bibliography and Research, p. xv above.

Books are listed first under the author's name in chronological order. Articles by the same author follow, also in chronological order. Anonymous student work is listed under the name of the law review in which it appeared.

Abel, Richard L.
American Lawyers (1989)
Delegalization, reprinted in G. Hazard and D. Rhode, The Legal Profession: Responsibility and Regulation 388 (2d ed. 1988)
Lawyers, in Leon Lipson and Stanton Wheeler, eds., Law and the Social Sciences (1988)
Legal Services (1981), reprinted in G. Hazard and D. Rhode, The Legal Profession: Responsibility and Regulation 417 (2d ed. 1988)

Akerlof, George A.
The Market for Lemons: Quality Uncertainty and the Market Mechanism, 84 Q.J.Econ. 488 (1970)

American Bar Association
Center for Professional Responsibility, The Legislative History of the Model Rules of Professional Conduct (1987)
——, 1990 Survey on Lawyer Discipline Systems (1992)
Commission on Professionalism, "... In the Spirit of Public Service:" A Blueprint for the Rekindling of Lawyer Professionalism [report of the Stanley Commission, reprinted in 112 F.R.D. 243 (1986)]
Lawyer Regulation for a New Century: Report of the Commission on Evaluation of Disciplinary Enforcement (1992) [McKay Commission Report]
Opinions of the Committee on Professional Ethics (1967)
Report of ABA Task Force on Minorities in the Legal Profession (Jan. 10, 1986)

American Bar Association—Cont'd
Section of Corporation, Banking, and Business Law, Report of the Ad Hoc Civil RICO Task Force (1985)
——, Special Report by the TriBar Opinion Committee, The Remedies Opinion, 46 Bus.Law. 959 (1991)
——, Third-Party Legal Opinion Report, 47 Bus.Law. (Nov.1991)
Section of Legal Education and Admissions to the Bar, A Review of Legal Education in the United States, Law Schools and Bar Admissions Requirements [an annual publication]
——, Task Force Report on Law Schools and the Profession, Legal Location and Professional Development—An Educational Continuum (1992) [the McCrate Report]
——, and National Conference of Bar Examiners (NCBE), Comprehensive Guide to Bar Admission Requirements 1993-1994 [an annual publication]
Standards for Lawyer Discipline and Disability Proceedings (1979)
Standing Committee on Ethics and Professional Responsibility, Rules of Procedure
Standing Committee on Professional Discipline, Statistical Report: Sanctions Imposed in Public Discipline of Lawyers 1986-1990 (1991)
Statement of Policy Adopted by the American Bar Association Regarding Responsibilities and Liabilities of Lawyers in Advising with Respect to the Compliance by Clients with Laws Administered by the Securities and Exchange Commission, 61 A.B.A.J. 1085 (1975)

Wade, John W.
On Frivolous Litigation: A Study of Tort Liability and Procedural Sanctions, 14 Hofstra L.Rev. 433 (1986)

Waid, Brian J.
Ethical Problems of the Class Action Practitioner: Continued Neglect by the Drafters of the Proposed Model Rules of Professional Conduct, 27 Loy.L.Rev. 1047 (1981)

Warren, Charles
A History of the American Bar (2d ed. 1966)

Washington University Law Quarterly
Note, Model Rule 2.2 and Divorce Mediation: Ethics Guideline or Ethics Gap?, 65 Wash.U.L.Q. 223 (1987)

Wasserstrom, Richard
Lawyers and Revolution, 30 U.Pitt.L.Rev. 125 (1968)
Lawyers as Professionals: Some Moral Issues, 5 Human Rights 1 (1975)
Legal Education and the Good Lawyer, 34 J.Legal Educ. 155 (1984)
Roles and Morality, in David Luban (ed.), The Good Lawyer (1984)

Watson, Andrew S.
Some Psychological Aspects of Teaching Professional Responsibility, 16 J.Legal Educ. 1 (1963)

Weckstein, Donald T.
Maintaining the Integrity and Competence of the Legal Profession, 48 Tex. L.Rev. 267 (1970)

Weiler, Paul C. et al.
Reporters' Study, Enterprise Responsibility for Personal Injury (American Law Institute, Apr. 15, 1991)

Weinstein, Jack B.
Some Ethical and Political Problems of a Government Lawyer, 18 Me.L.Rev. 155 (1966)

Wexler, Stephen
Practicing Law for Poor People, 79 Yale L.J. 1049 (1970)

White, James Boyd
The Ethics of Argument: Plato's Gorgias and the Modern Lawyer, in White, Heracles' Bow, c. 10 (1985)

White, James J.
Machiavelli and the Bar: Ethical Limitations on Lying in Negotiation, 1980 Am.Bar Found.Research J. 926

White, James P.
Legal Education in the Era of Change: Law School Autonomy, 1987 Duke L.J. 292

Whitman, Alfred D.
A Proposed Solution to the Problem of Perjury in Our Courts, 39 Dickinson L.Rev. 127 (1955)

Wigmore, John H.
Evidence (McNaughton ed., 1961)

Wilkins, David B.
Who Should Regulate Lawyers?, 105 Harv. L.Rev. 799 (1991)

Williston, Samuel B.
Life and Law (1940)

Windt, Allan D.
Insurance Claims and Disputes: Representation of Insurance Companies and Insureds (1982)

Winslow, Gerald R.
Triage and Justice (1982)

Wizner, Stephen and Berkman, Miriam
Being a Lawyer for a Child Too Young to be a Client: A Clinical Study, 68 Neb.L.Rev. 330 (1989)

Wolfman, Bernard and Holden, James P.
Ethical Problems in Modern Tax Practice (2d ed. 1985)

Wolfman, Bernard, Holden, James P. and Harris, Kenneth L.
Standards of Tax Practice: Professional Responsibility and Ethics (CCH, 1991)

Wolfram, Charles W.
Modern Legal Ethics (1986)
Client Perjury, 50 S.Cal.L.Rev. 809 (1977)
The Code of Professional Responsibility as a Measure of Attorney Liability in Civil Litigation, 30 S.C.L.Rev. 281 (1979)
The Second Set of Players: Lawyers, Fee Shifting, and the Limits of Professional Discipline, 47 Law & Contemp.Probs. 293 (1984)
Hide and Secrets: The Boundaries of Privilege, Legal Times, Apr. 3, 1989
Lawyer Turf and Lawyer Regulation—The Role of the Inherent—Powers Doctrine, 12 U.Ark.Little Rock L.J. 1 (1989–90)

Word, James C.
Risk and Knowledge in Interspousal Conflicts of Interest, 7 Whittier L.Rev. 943 (1985)

TABLE OF CASES

Principal cases are in italic type. Non-principal cases are in roman type. References are to Pages.

TABLE OF OTHER AUTHORITIES

TABLE OF OTHER AUTHORITIES

lxxxiii

TABLE OF OTHER AUTHORITIES

THE LAW AND ETHICS
OF LAWYERING

*

Chapter 1

RELATIONSHIP OF LAW, LAWYERS AND ETHICS

A. INTRODUCTION

This book is about the law and ethics of lawyering.[1] Each of these terms has depth, complexity and multiple shades of meaning. Law and ethics, which are related yet distinct concepts, are part of a general subject that includes all aspects of the concept of obligation. As used here, *ethics* refers to imperatives regarding the welfare of others that are recognized as binding upon a person's conduct in some more immediate and binding sense than *law* and in some more general and impersonal sense than *morals*. While acknowledging the place in the philosophical universe of ethical theories that deny the existence of an imperative regarding the welfare of others, such as ethical egoism, our concern here is with the relationship between rules that are believed to exist and the conduct to which they are thought to refer.

Ethical rules are not merely moral sentiments that have attained a certain publicity and formality nor are they merely a subspecies of legislation—rules that differ from law only in that their enforcement is relatively informal. Ethics rules emerge from a process of subjective deliberation leading to a decision about what one ought to do and from interpersonal exchanges establishing what a group believes one should have done. In the real world of acting, judging and being judged, ethics is best regarded as all of these—deliberation about how one should act given the existence of rules established by a consensus that one shares substantially if not unreservedly.

This book, however, is not about ethics generally but about the law and ethics of lawyering, a variegated set of activities that cannot be reduced to the two paradigms of the advocate in litigation and the counselor or advisor in the law office. Common elements of a lawyer's role and function, however, suggest two general problems. First, a lawyer's training and activity as a legal technician demythologizes the law. The lawyer, more than the lay person, is conscious of the ambiguities of the law's commands, the frequently specious or conflicting character of its policy and the frailties of its interpreters. The lawyer's professional function consists largely of providing counsel for clients about how, on the one hand, to escape or mitigate the incidence

---

1. Some of the material in this introduction is drawn, with permission of the publisher, Yale University Press, from Geoffrey C. Hazard, Jr., Ethics in the Practice of Law 1–3, 11–14, and 19–21 (1978).

of the law's obligations, or, on the other, to enlarge or detail its enforcement. The essence of these activities is the manipulation of governmental authority and the language and social processes through which that authority is exercised. The lawyer as counselor gives at least lip service to the idea that the law's obligations are real, but she is bound to advise on the extent to which they are mere formalities or even less. What view should she take of rules that address her own conduct? Are they legal regulations whose burdens the lawyer may minimize or obviate by technical advice delivered professionally to herself, or are they strictures of conscience whose only meaning is in their observation?

A second problem of legal ethics arises from the fact that a client is in the picture. Ethics, seriously discussed as in Western philosophy, usually speak in terms that require treating all other persons on an equal footing. That is, ethical norms are cast as universals in which in principle every "other" is entitled to equal respect and consideration in the calculation of the actor's alternatives and course of action. On the other hand, professional ethics give priority to an "other" who is a client and in general require subordination of everyone else's interests to that of the client. Indeed, the central problem in professional ethics can be described as the tension between the client's preferred position resulting from the professional connection and the position of equality that everyone else is accorded by general principles of morality and legality.

Although many modern moral philosophers frame rules of behavior in universal (Kantian) terms, only in a rigorous system taken seriously is there an expectation that they will be applied without regard to special circumstances. In other religious and philosophic traditions, as well as in folk ethics, it is accepted that a person owes one kind of duty to a member of her family (or village or working group) and another to those with whom a relationship is more remote. The possibility of such discrimination opens up a range of questions: How does one rank the various "others" (spouse, child, cousin, next-door neighbor, fellow worker, compatriot, etc.) and how does one rank different kinds of obligations (to refrain from killing, to refrain from stealing, to forbear, to counsel forbearance by others, to come to another's aid, to sacrifice one's self for another, etc.). These questions pose great philosophic difficulties for all universalistic ethical conceptions, a fact that may explain why these conceptions are usually expressed in wholly abstract terms. They pose similar difficulties in practical application, so that folk ethics is a mishmash of homilies, legalistic formulations of various duty relationships and resignation to subjective ethical choice.

We lead our daily lives by making ethical discriminations in these terms, but we are left defenseless against charges of inconsistency, casuistry and discrimination. The burden of these charges can be lifted by attributing responsibility to the force of circumstances. Thus we say that no one volunteers to have to distinguish between her spouse and child, employer and customer, or neighbor and the building inspector.

When events conscript us into doing so, we make ethical distinctions because we must in order to continue to function. At the level of principle, therefore, many modern conceptions of ethics posit a system of universals, while in day-by-day application ethics involves a more complicated scheme of distinctions and excuses based on role, relationships and practical necessity.

The rules governing a lawyer's office are neither a system of universal rules nor a set of injunctions to be virtuous in responding to situational exigencies. Rules of legal ethics are <u>not universal</u> because they give a preferred position to clients; the office of lawyer begins with having to make distinctions among persons. At least in an immediate sense, the rules are not based on practical necessity, for no one is compelled to become a lawyer and, ordinarily at least, no lawyer is compelled to take a particular case. While in some situations a lawyer is supposed to act with perfect neutrality among others, a lawyer usually intervenes in relationships between others with a pre-disposition to treat the one who is her client with greater solicitude than she treats the other, regardless of the merits of their respective positions.

According to any "nonlegal" ethics, intervention on these terms is difficult to justify. It violates the principle of equal treatment inherent in all forms of universalist ethics. It lacks the involuntarism that is present in the ethical dilemmas of everyday life. For the lawyer does not merely encounter choices between the conflicting interests of others but makes a business out of such encounters, and takes partisan positions for money. Thus, her vocation violates the concepts of ethics held both by philosophers and in folklore.

If the profession were uniformly an elite, it would be unlikely to have adopted a formal code and so the problem of disobeying that code would not arise. Shared norms would be enforced by informal means such as peer pressure. Our relatively heterogeneous legal profession, however, seems to require positive legislation to resolve questions of conduct about which a consensus is lacking. But positive legislation is inevitably simplistic to some degree, and thus an incomplete guide in delicate situations. A truly conscientious and self-confident practition-er would not feel bound to follow the letter of the law when her personal judgment dictated a different course. Hence, the concept of a principled violation of the rules of ethics introduces what is in fact a triple standard—conscience for some, code for others and lip-service for still others. This state of affairs, whether desirable or not, necessarily results from the admission that conduct can be at the same time unlawful and right.

The profession's codes of legal ethics govern a number of matters that are very important to the public interest but either trivially obvious or largely irrelevant to ethics as such. These include:

• Rules requiring that a lawyer be truthful and honest.

- Rules regulating competition among lawyers (advertising, solicitation, etc.), which are subsumed under the rubric of assisting "the legal profession in fulfilling its duty to make legal counsel available."

- Rules regulating competition from outside the profession. The substance of these rules is that lawyers should prevent nonlawyers from doing anything that is the "practice of law," whatever that may include.

Putting these aside, the ethics codes—and the bulk of this book—deal with essentially four problems:

- Prohibited assistance: What kinds of things is a lawyer prohibited from doing for a client?

- Competence: What measures will assure competent lawyering?

- Confidentiality: What information learned by a lawyer should she treat as secret, and from whom, and under what conditions may the secrecy be lifted?

- Conflicts of interest: When and to what extent is a lawyer prohibited from acting because there is a conflict of interest between her clients or between herself and a client?

These are all tough problems, and not only for lawyers. What is perhaps not fully appreciated, by lawyers and lay people alike, is that similar problems arise in everyday life. If this fact were appreciated by lawyers, they might be able to perceive and to discuss the problems free of the introverted assumption that lawyers alone can appreciate their complex and stressful nature. If lay people recognized the similarity, they might regard the lawyers' ethical dilemmas with greater comprehension and perhaps even greater sympathy.

Many illustrations might be suggested from other walks of life, at work and at home, of problems involving prohibited assistance, confidentiality and conflict of interest. A few will suffice to make the point. Thus, regarding prohibited assistance: Do you help a friend by lying to the police? Omit adverse information when asked to evaluate a former student or employee? Help sell stock that may be overvalued? Maintain the "character of a neighborhood" by not renting to an African American? Regarding confidentiality: What should a parent do who knows that a child has stolen something from a store? A pediatrician who discovers physical abuse of a child by its parents? A teacher who finds out that a student has been using drugs? An accountant who knows that a client is understating income for tax purposes? Regarding conflicts of interest: Does a parent send a healthy child to college rather than send a sick one to the Mayo Clinic? A plant manager trim on safety systems to keep her company financially afloat? A doctor order hospitalization because medical insurance will not otherwise cover the patient? A supervisor commend a subordinate who may become a rival?

If there is any peculiarity about these problems as they are confronted by lawyers, it is that a lawyer confronts them every day and is supposed to resolve them in a fashion that is compatible with a conception of her professional role. The ethics codes and the law of lawyering undertake to tell her how she should do so.

B. WHO AMONG US?

1. Adversary Ethics

Disclosure of Adverse Evidence

[handwritten: driver of car π was in]

SPAULDING v. ZIMMERMAN

Supreme Court of Minnesota, 1962.
263 Minn. 346, 116 N.W.2d 704.

GALLAGHER, JUSTICE.

Appeal from an order of the District Court of Douglas County vacating and setting aside a prior order of such court dated May 8, *[handwritten: procedure]* 1957, approving a settlement made on behalf of David Spaulding on March 5, 1957, at which time he was a minor of the age of 20 years; and in connection therewith, vacating and setting aside releases executed by him and his parents, a stipulation of dismissal, an order for dismissal with prejudice, and a judgment entered pursuant thereto.

The prior action was brought against defendants by Theodore Spaulding, as father and natural guardian of David Spaulding, for injuries sustained by David in an automobile accident, arising out of a *[handwritten: Facts]* collision which occurred August 24, 1956, between an automobile driven by John Zimmerman, in which David was a passenger, and one owned by John Ledermann and driven by Florian Ledermann.

On appeal defendants contend that the court was without jurisdiction *[handwritten: Appeal]* to vacate the settlement solely because their counsel then possessed information, unknown to plaintiff herein, that at the time he was suffering from an aorta aneurysm which may have resulted from the accident, because (1) no mutual mistake of fact was involved; (2) no duty rested upon them to disclose information to plaintiff which they could assume had been disclosed to him by his own physicians; (3) insurance limitations as well as physical injuries formed the basis for the settlement; and (4) plaintiff's motion to vacate the order for settlement and to set aside the releases was barred by the limitations provided in Rule 60.02 of Rules of Civil Procedure.[2]

After the accident, David's injuries were diagnosed by his family physician, Dr. James H. Cain, as a severe crushing injury of the chest with multiple rib fractures; a severe cerebral concussion, probably with petechial hemorrhages of the brain; and bilateral fractures of the

---

2. [Editors' note:] Minnesota Rule 60.02 is substantially identical to Rule 60(b) of the Federal Rules of Civil Procedure.

[handwritten: D's atty knew of aorta aneurysm when entered settlement.]

clavicles. At Dr. Cain's suggestion, on January 3, 1957, David was examined by Dr. John F. Pohl, an orthopedic specialist, who made X-ray studies of his chest. Dr. Pohl's detailed report of this examination included the following:

> " ... The lung fields are clear. The heart and aorta are normal."

Nothing in such report indicated the aorta aneurysm with which David was then suffering. On March 1, 1957, at the suggestion of Dr. Pohl, David was examined from a neurological viewpoint by Dr. Paul S. Blake, and in the report of this examination there was no finding of the aorta aneurysm.

In the meantime, on February 22, 1957, at defendants' request, David was examined by Dr. Hewitt Hannah, a neurologist. On February 26, 1957, the latter reported to Messrs. Field, Arvesen, & Donoho, attorneys for defendant John Zimmerman, as follows:

> "The one feature of the case which bothers me more than any other part of the case is the fact that this boy of 20 years of age has an aneurysm, which means a dilatation of the aorta and the arch of the aorta. Whether this came out of this accident I cannot say with any degree of certainty and I have discussed it with the Roentgenologist and a couple of Internists.... Of course an aneurysm or dilatation of the aorta in a boy of this age is a serious matter as far as his life. This aneurysm may dilate further and it might rupture with further dilatation and this would cause his death.
>
> "It would be interesting also to know whether the X-ray of his lungs, taken immediately following the accident, shows this dilatation or not. If it was not present immediately following the accident and is now present, then we could be sure that it came out of the accident."

Prior to the negotiations for settlement, the contents of the above report were made known to counsel for defendants Florian and John Ledermann.

The case was called for trial on March 4, 1957, at which time the respective parties and their counsel possessed such information as to David's physical condition as was revealed to them by their respective medical examiners as above described. It is thus apparent that neither David nor his father, the nominal plaintiff in the prior action, was then aware that David was suffering the aorta aneurysm but on the contrary believed that he was recovering from the injuries sustained in the accident.

On the following day an agreement for settlement was reached wherein, in consideration of the payment of $6,500, David and his father agreed to settle in full for all claims arising out of the accident.

Richard S. Roberts, counsel for David, thereafter presented to the court a petition for approval of the settlement, wherein David's injuries were described as:

> " ... severe crushing of the chest, with multiple rib fractures, severe cerebral concussion, with petechial hemorrhages of the brain, bilateral fractures of the clavicles."

Attached to the petition were affidavits of David's physicians, Drs. James H. Cain and Paul S. Blake, wherein they set forth the same diagnoses they had made upon completion of their respective examinations of David as above described. At no time was there information disclosed to the court that David was then suffering from an aorta aneurysm which may have been the result of the accident. Based upon the petition for settlement and such affidavits of Drs. Cain and Blake, the court on May 8, 1957, made its order approving the settlement.

Early in 1959, David was required by the army reserve, of which he was a member, to have a physical checkup. For this, he again engaged the services of Dr. Cain. In this checkup, the latter discovered the aorta aneurysm. He then reexamined the X-rays which had been taken shortly after the accident and at this time discovered that they disclosed the beginning of the process which produced the aneurysm. He promptly sent David to Dr. Jerome Grismer for an examination and opinion. The latter confirmed the finding of the aorta aneurysm and recommended immediate surgery therefor. This was performed by him at Mount Sinai Hospital in Minneapolis on March 10, 1959.

Shortly thereafter, David, having attained his majority, instituted the present action for additional damages due to the more serious injuries including the aorta aneurysm which he alleges proximately resulted from the accident. As indicated above, the prior order for settlement was vacated. In a memorandum made a part of the order vacating the settlement, the court stated:

> "The facts material to a determination of the motion are without substantial dispute. The only disputed facts appear to be whether ... Mr. Roberts, former counsel for plaintiff, discussed plaintiff's injuries with Mr. Arvesen, counsel for defendant Zimmerman, immediately before the settlement agreement, and, further, whether or not there is a causal relationship between the accident and the aneurysm.
>
> "Contrary to the ... suggestion in the affidavit of Mr. Roberts that he discussed the minor's injuries with Mr. Arvesen, the Court finds that no such discussion of the specific injuries claimed occurred prior to the settlement agreement on March 5, 1957.
>
> " ... the Court finds that although the aneurysm now existing is causally related to the accident, such finding is for the purpose of the motions only and is based solely upon the opinion expressed by Dr. Cain (Exhibit 'F'), which, so far as the Court can find from the

numerous affidavits and statements of fact by counsel, stands without dispute.

. . .

Findings

"The mistake concerning the existence of the aneurysm was not mutual. For reasons which do not appear, plaintiff's doctor failed to ascertain its existence. By reason of the failure of plaintiff's counsel to use available rules of discovery, plaintiff's doctor and all his representatives did not learn that defendants and their agents knew of its existence and possible serious consequences. Except for the character of the concealment in the light of plaintiff's minority, the Court would, I believe, be justified in denying plaintiff's motion to vacate, leaving him to whatever questionable remedy he may have against his doctor and against his lawyer.

Adverse vs Non-Adverse Relationships

"That defendants' counsel concealed the knowledge they had is not disputed. The essence of the application of the above rule is the character of the concealment. Was it done under circumstances that defendants must be charged with knowledge that plaintiff did not know of the injury? If so, an enriching advantage was gained for defendants at plaintiff's expense. There is no doubt of the good faith of both defendants' counsel. There is no doubt that during the course of the negotiations, when the parties were in an adversary relationship, no rule required or duty rested upon defendants or their representatives to disclose this knowledge. However, once the agreement to settle was reached, it is difficult to characterize the parties' relationship as adverse. At this point all parties were interested in securing Court approval. . . .

"When the adversary nature of the negotiations concluded in a settlement, the procedure took on the posture of a joint application to the Court, at least so far as the facts upon which the Court could and must approve settlement is concerned. It is here that the true nature of the concealment appears, and defendants' failure to act affirmatively, after having been given a copy of the application for approval, can only be defendants' decision to take a calculated risk that the settlement would be final. . . ."

ROL

1. The principles applicable to the court's authority to vacate settlements made on behalf of minors and approved by it appear well established. With reference thereto, we have held that the court in its discretion may vacate such a settlement, even though it is not induced by fraud or bad faith, where it is shown that in the accident the minor sustained separate and distinct injuries which were not known or considered by the court at the time settlement was approved. . . .

Holding

2. From the foregoing it is clear that in the instant case the court did not abuse its discretion in setting aside the settlement which it had approved on plaintiff's behalf while he was still a minor. It is undisputed that neither he nor his counsel nor his medical attendants were aware that at the time settlement was made he was suffering from an

aorta aneurysm which may have resulted from the accident. The seriousness of this disability is indicated by Dr. Hannah's report indicating the imminent danger of death therefrom. This was known by counsel for both defendants but was not disclosed to the court at the time it was petitioned to approve the settlement. While no canon of ethics or legal obligation may have required them to inform plaintiff or his counsel with respect thereto, or to advise the court therein, it did become obvious to them at the time, that the settlement then made did not contemplate or take into consideration the disability described. This fact opened the way for the court to later exercise its discretion in vacating the settlement and under the circumstances described we cannot say that there was any abuse of discretion on the part of the court in so doing under Rule 60.02(6) of Rules of Civil Procedure [which permits the court to set aside a judgment on motion made more than a year after entry for "any other reason justifying relief from the operation of the judgment"]. . . .

ROGOSHESKE, J., [who served as the trial judge in the case and was subsequently elevated to the Supreme Court,] took no part in the consideration or decision of this case.

Disclosure of Adverse Evidence

What was Zimmerman's duty to Spaulding? What responsibility did the defense-paid doctor have to Spaulding? What were Zimmerman's lawyers' responsibilities to Zimmerman? To the doctor they hired? To Spaulding?

Fed.R.Civ.P. 35(a) provides that upon motion showing good cause a court may order a party to submit to a physical or mental examination. Rule 35(b) provides that the medical report from any such examination (or any examination agreed to by the parties without court order) shall be supplied to the party examined upon that party's request. In general, the turnover obligation exists whether the examination is ordered by the court or agreed to by the parties. Similar rules apply in state courts.

Spaulding's lawyers could have obtained a copy of the defense expert's report if they had asked the right questions or made the right motions. Does the negligence of Spaulding's lawyers (or of one or more of his doctors) excuse or mitigate the silence of Zimmerman's lawyers (or the doctor they hired)?

The result in *Spaulding* turns on the special responsibilities of a court toward a minor and the special responsibilities of lawyers to the court. If Spaulding had attained the age of majority, the court would have left Spaulding to seek redress against his doctor and his lawyer. Does this game-like framework, in which clients are bound by the actions of their lawyers, lose sight of David Spaulding? Why doesn't the court base its ruling on the seriousness of the undisclosed facts rather than on Spaulding's minority?

Absent special circumstances, such as mutual mistake, fraud on the court or concealment from the court, courts will not set aside a judgment because a lawyer has concealed adverse evidence from the opposing party. In Brown v. County of Genesee,[3] an employment discrimination case, plaintiff Brown through her lawyer made it clear to defense counsel during settlement negotiations that Brown "would not settle unless [she] were paid at a rate of pay she would have received had she been hired on June 16, 1982." Both Brown and her lawyer believed the highest rate of pay to which this would entitle her was Step C pay; and they therefore settled for Step C pay. In fact, she would have been eligible for Step D pay, a higher rate. At the time of settlement, defense counsel "did not know, but he believed it probable that Brown and her counsel" mistakenly believed that Step C was the ceiling for employees hired on June 16, 1982. Defense counsel said nothing to correct Brown and her lawyer's mistaken belief. The district court vacated the settlement, but the Sixth Circuit reversed, holding that, "absent some misrepresentation or fraudulent conduct, [the defendant] had no duty to advise [Brown or her counsel] of any such factual error...." The court pointed out that Brown's counsel could have discovered the correct information about the pay scales by either examining public documents or asking the right questions in discovery: "The failure of Brown's counsel ... cannot be imputed to the [defendant] as unethical or fraudulent."[4]

Apparently only one case, Virzi v. Grand Trunk Warehouse & Cold Storage Co.,[5] states that a lawyer has a duty to reveal adverse information to an opposing party in civil litigation. In Virzi the court set aside a $35,000 settlement in a personal injury action because the plaintiff's lawyer had concealed the fact that the plaintiff, viewed by both parties as an excellent witness, had died of causes unrelated to the lawsuit. The court said:

> Candor and honesty necessarily require disclosure of such a significant fact as the death of one's client. Opposing counsel does not have to deal with his adversary as he would deal in the marketplace. Standards of ethics require greater honesty, greater candor, and greater disclosure, even though it might not be in the interest of the client or his estate.[6]

As in Spaulding, however, the specific holding in Virzi rests on a concealment from the court, rather than on a failure to disclose to an adverse party: Because the plaintiff's lawyer did not move for a substitution of parties under Rule 25 of the Federal Rules of Civil Procedure, the court "enter[ed] an order of settlement for a non-

---

3. 872 F.2d 169 (6th Cir.1989).

4. 872 F.2d at 175.

5. 571 F.Supp. 507 (E.D.Mich.1983).

6. 571 F.Supp. at 512.

existent party." Causing the court to do this constituted concealment and justified setting aside the settlement.

In civil litigation, is a lawyer who knows of evidence that would establish the claim or defense of the opposing party (a) required to remain silent, (b) required to disclose the adverse evidence, or (c) permitted to take either path? Suppose a lawyer represents an apartment house landlord. A tenant has sued on behalf of his child, who sustained serious injury from falling either through a negligently created gap in a porch railing or down the porch stairs. The landlord's lawyer has discovered an eyewitness, unknown to the tenant, who will support the claim that the infant fell through the gap. Without this witness the case will be dismissed for failure of proof. An ethics opinion on these facts concluded that "the conduct of the defendant's attorney [in moving to dismiss the plaintiff's case without disclosing] is not professionally improper. The fact of infancy does not call for a different reply." [7]

porch
CAfC
witnesses

Consider a further hypothetical, also based on a well-known ethics opinion.[8] At a sentencing hearing, a judge asks the prosecutor whether the convicted defendant has a prior criminal record. The prosecutor replies that he does not. Defense counsel, who knows that her client has been convicted of two armed robberies in another jurisdiction, remains silent. The trial judge, "because this is a first offense," gives the defendant a suspended sentence. Did defense counsel act properly? Should she have volunteered information about the prior conviction? What if she had argued for a suspended sentence on the basis of the defendant's "clean record?" [9]

Procedural rules impose duties on litigating parties that alter the responsibilities of their lawyers.[10] Fed.R.Civ.P. 26(e), for example,

---

7. New York County Lawyer's Ass'n Comm. on Prof. Ethics, Op. 309 (1933). Why the double negative in the Committee's formulation? In his autobiography, Samuel Williston recounts a situation in which he, as a young lawyer, sat silently (and uncomfortably) as an opposing witness was unable to supply a crucial fact established by a document in Williston's possession. Samuel B. Williston, Life and Law 271 (1940), discussed in Charles P. Curtis, It's Your Law 17 (1954). Curtis argues that the situation of the lawyer for the party with the burden of proof is different than that of the lawyer whose client is in a defensive posture, but this position appears to be a relic of a bygone procedural era in which a defendant by making a general denial could require the plaintiff to prove all the elements of a prima facie case.

8. ABA Formal Op. 287 (June 27, 1953).

9. The majority of the ethics committee, relying on Canon 37 of the Canons of Professional Ethics, concluded that, if the lawyer's information came from her client, she should remain silent. A concurring member stated that the same position should be taken even if the lawyer's information came from her own work rather than from the client. Two dissenting members stated that Canons 15, 22, 29 and 41, taken together, "require the lawyer to see that his client gives to the court the truth about [the client's] criminal record or the lawyer must do so himself." Does Model Rule 1.6, extending the duty of confidentiality to all "information relating to the representation of a client," resolve the clash between Canon 37 and the other canons cited?

10. A proposed amendment to Fed.R.Civ.P. 26, which will go into effect on December 1, 1993 unless postponed or rejected by Congress, illustrates the effect of procedural rules on the disclosure obligations of lawyers. The controversial amendment requires mutual disclosure of "discoverable information relevant to disputed facts alleged with particulari-

FRCP 26(e) *Supplementa* *of Info*

provides that a party is not required to supplement a response made in discovery to include information later acquired as long as the response was complete when made. The rule then lists several exceptions to this general statement. Consider some of these exceptions:

- A party owes a duty to supplement seasonably any response concerning the substance of expert testimony expected to be offered at trial. Rule 26(e)(1)(B).

- A party owes a duty to amend seasonably any response if the party learns the response was based on information that the party now knows was incorrect when the statement was made. Rule 26(e)(2)(A).

- A party owes a duty to amend seasonably any response if the party "knows that the response though correct when made is no longer true and the circumstances are such that a failure to amend the response is in substance a knowing concealment." Rule 26(e)(2)(B).

The Advisory Committee Notes explain that the latter two exceptions cover situations in which a "lawyer obtains actual knowledge that a prior response is incorrect" but that the exceptions do not impose a continuing obligation to check prior answers. All answers must, however, be supplemented if a court so orders or if an opposing party makes a new discovery request for supplemental answers. Rule 26(e)(3). Moreover, under Rule 26(g), a lawyer must sign all discovery requests and responses. This signature constitutes a warranty that *"after a reasonable inquiry,"* the lawyer believes the request or response complies with the discovery rules. (Emphasis added.) False answers, whether knowingly or negligently made, violate the discovery rules.

Such rules, however, provide no help to the Spauldings or Browns of this world, whose lawyers fail to ask the right questions. Normally, the legal system does not protect a party in civil litigation from the laziness, incompetence or failure of the party's lawyer. In Link v. Wabash R. Co.,[11] upholding an involuntary dismissal of an injured railroad worker's federal tort claim for failure of his lawyer to attend a pretrial conference, Justice Harlan stated:

> There is certainly no merit to the contention that dismissal of petitioner's claim because of his counsel's unexcused conduct imposes an unjust penalty on the client. Petitioner voluntarily chose this attorney as his representative in the action, and he cannot now avoid the consequences of the acts or omissions of this freely selected agent. Any other notion would be wholly inconsistent with our system of representative litigation, in which each party is

ty in the pleadings." The amendment would require parties to disclose, without a prior discovery request, such core information as the names of potential witnesses, including experts, documentary evidence and data regarding damages and insurance. Under the amended rule, would Zimmerman's lawyers have been required to disclose their information concerning the extent of Spaulding's injury to him?

11. 370 U.S. 626 (1962).

deemed bound by the acts of his lawyer-agent and is considered to have "notice of all facts, notice of which can be charged upon the attorney." [12]

2. Introduction to Ethical Codes

Three times in its history the American Bar Association (ABA) has issued a model code for regulation of the conduct of lawyers. As a voluntary organization of lawyers, the ABA's actions do not have the force of law. However, the ABA has long been recognized as the leading national organization of lawyers, and it has succeeded in convincing state courts, state legislatures, federal courts and federal agencies to adopt some form of its model codes, giving the codes, as so adopted, the effect of law.

[margin handwriting: No force of Law, but adopted mostly + have effect of Law.]

Canons of Professional Ethics

In the 19th century the states left regulation of the profession to common law precedent and occasional statutory pronouncements. Alabama adopted the first formal code of ethics in 1887, codifying a series of published lectures on ethics by David Hoffman of Baltimore and George Sharswood of Philadelphia. A number of other states followed Alabama's lead in the ensuing two decades.

The ABA in 1908 adopted the Canons of Professional Ethics, alluded to in *Spaulding*. As with most state ethics codes of the era, the Canons owed a great debt to the Hoffman and Sharswood antecedents. The Canons originally numbered 32, but expanded to 47 by the end of the 1930s. Even at 47, the Canons were brief, written in broad language with a high moral tone. Criticism of the Canons centered on the need for more specificity. Despite their ambiguities, bar associations and state courts gave the Canons wide recognition. They remained in force in the states until the early 1970s.

[margin handwriting: Canons of prof. Ethics]

Model Code of Professional Responsibility

In 1964 Lewis F. Powell, Jr., then president of the ABA, appointed a committee to examine the Canons and suggest revisions. This committee proposed the Model Code of Professional Responsibility, which the ABA adopted in 1969. Almost every state thereafter adopted some form of the Model Code. The Model Code also became operative in federal courts because most federal district courts adopted the Model

---

12. 370 U.S. at 633–34. Justice Black, dissenting, complained that visiting "the sins or faults or delinquencies of a lawyer ... upon his client ... is to ignore the practicalities and realities of the lawyer-client relationship." 370 U.S. at 646. The injured worker, having lost his damage claim due to his lawyer's failure, is left with the possibility of a malpractice remedy against the lawyer. Some courts, however, are willing to give the client a second chance in some circumstances. See, e.g., Carroll v. Abbott Laboratories, Inc., 32 Cal.3d 892, 187 Cal.Rptr. 592, 654 P.2d 775, (1982) (client may obtain relief from an involuntary dismissal based on his lawyer's "positive misconduct" or "excusable neglect," but not for "inexcusable neglect" as in the failure in this case to respond to discovery requests).

Code by local court rule.[13]

The 1969 Model Code has a much more complicated format than the 1909 Canons. The Model Code contains nine Canons, which function as chapter headings. Each Canon contains both Ethical Considerations [ECs] and Disciplinary Rules [DRs]. The Preamble and Preliminary Statement of the Model Code explains its structure as follows:

> The Canons are statements of axiomatic norms, expressing in general terms the standards of professional conduct expected of lawyers in their relationships with the public, with the legal system, and with the legal profession. They embody the general concepts from which the Ethical Considerations and the Disciplinary Rules are derived.

> The Ethical Considerations are aspirational in character and represent the objectives toward which every member of the profession should strive. They constitute a body of principles upon which the lawyer can rely for guidance in many specific situations.

> The Disciplinary Rules, unlike the Ethical Considerations, are mandatory in character. The Disciplinary Rules state the minimum level of conduct below which no lawyer can fall without being subject to disciplinary action.... An enforcing agency, in applying the Disciplinary Rules, may find interpretive guidance in the basic principles embodied in the Canons and in the objectives, reflected in the Ethical Considerations.

This statement suggests greater clarity to the Model Code's structure than in fact exists. For example, although the Ethical Considerations (ECs) supposedly are aspirational statements, some sound like commands, e.g., EC 5–15: "A lawyer should never...." Other ECs elaborate on the Disciplinary Rules (DRs) by providing concrete examples of what the latter mean, e.g., EC 3–8 and EC 5–24. Not surprisingly, courts and bar disciplinary bodies have sometimes applied Ethical Considerations as though they were Disciplinary Rules.

Aside from problems of structure, the Model Code has been criticized for embodying outdated assumptions about what lawyers do and how they do it. The Model Code primarily reflects a vision of lawyers in a courtroom, as equal advocates competing under the watchful eye of a judge, who stands ready to correct overzealousness by either party. This vision provides little practical guidance to a lawyer negotiating a transaction, drafting documents, or counseling clients, or even one engaged in pretrial matters. The Model Code also envisions lawyers operating alone in practice or with a few partners, equal in status and responsibility. Of course, lawyers today practice in large organiza-

13. Some district courts adopted the Model Code as promulgated by the ABA but most adopted the Code as amended by the state in which the federal court sits. Federal courts are not required to abide by the ethics rules adopted in the state in which they sit. Under Fed.R.Civ.P. 83, federal district courts may establish their own rules for lawyers practicing in the district. See, e.g., United States v. Walsh, 699 F.Supp. 469, 472 (D.N.J.1988) (Model Rule 1.11 applies in district court, not Rule 1.11 as amended in New Jersey's version of the Rules).

tions—large law firms, government offices, corporations—with hierarchical structures in which lawyers at various levels have different degrees of responsibility and control over their work. Finally, the Model Code imagines a client as an individual, not a collection of individuals nor an inanimate legal entity such as a corporation or a government agency. Thus, the Model Code leaves a lawyer representing a corporation or a class with little enlightenment on such basic issues as the identity of the client.

Model Rules of Professional Conduct 1983

ABA President William Spann in 1977 appointed a Commission on the Evaluation of Professional Responsibility, popularly known as the Kutak Commission after its Chairman Robert J. Kutak, to recommend changes to the Model Code of Professional Responsibility. The Kutak Commission concluded that the ethics rules needed a new formulation with a cleaner structure and a basis in a modern conception of the lawyer's role. The Kutak Commission, unlike the committee that drafted the Model Code, worked largely in the open: The Commission held public hearings and circulated its working drafts to the bar and public alike for comment. The resulting debate over the professional responsibility of lawyers was unprecedented in scope and intensity. In 1983, the ABA House of Delegates, after amending several key provisions of the Kutak final draft, adopted the Model Rules of Professional Conduct, with a recommendation to states and to federal courts and agencies that the Model Rules replace their respective versions of the Model Code.[14]

The format of the Model Rules follows that used by the Restatements of Law produced by the American Law Institute: black-letter rules followed by explanatory comments. The Rules also reflect a more modern concept of a lawyer's role. For example, M.R. 1.13 addresses the lawyer who represents an entity as distinct from an individual; M.R. 2.1 addresses the lawyer as advisor; M.R. 2.2, the lawyer as intermediary; M.R. 2.3, the lawyer as evaluator of a matter for the use of third parties; M.R. 5.1 describes the responsibilities of a partner or supervisory lawyer; M.R. 5.2 is the counterpart rule for the lawyer who is a subordinate.

As of August 1993, 36 states and the District of Columbia had adopted some version of the Model Rules. Some states—for example, New York, North Carolina, Oregon and Virginia—have decided to retain their version of the Model Code although often with numerous adjustments based on provisions in the Model Rules. California's code has elements of both the Model Rules and the Model Code, but omits significant material found in both. The federal courts, including the

14. The legislative history of the Model Rules is discussed by Ted Schneyer, Professionalism as Bar Politics: The Making of the Model Rules of Professional Conduct, 1989 Law & Soc. Inquiry 677. For a more detailed history, see ABA Center for Professional Responsibility, The Legislative History of the Model Rules of Professional Conduct (1987).

Supreme Court, cite both the Model Rules and the Model Code as authority in decisions concerning a lawyer's professional conduct.

Other Sources of Ethical Guidance

The ABA has generated two other important sets of rules governing the conduct of lawyers: the ABA Standards Relating to the Administration of Criminal Justice and the Model Code of Judicial Conduct. The Standards, which have not been embodied in formal rules of courts or agencies, do not have the same force of law as the adopted versions of the Model Code or Model Rules. However, state and federal courts frequently rely on the Standards as authority for proper conduct by prosecutors and defense counsel. The Model Code of Judicial Conduct, originally adopted by the ABA in 1972, applies to judges and has been adopted in most states and the federal courts. A thorough revision in 1990 resulted in a new Model Code of Judicial Conduct, now under consideration by state and federal courts. The regulation of judges in these codes imposes controls on relationships between judges and lawyers.

Ethics opinions are another source of guidance. The ABA Standing Committee on Ethics and Professional Responsibility issues formal and informal opinions on ethical questions. These opinions do not have the force of law, but they are sometimes cited by courts. In theory a formal opinion responds to a question of general interest, whereas an informal opinion is a response to a question "comparatively narrow in scope." [15] Some ethics opinions limit themselves to "ethics" and refuse to take a position on matters of "law."

State and local bars also issue ethics opinions. Some states publish editions of the state ethical code with annotations that include state and local ethics opinions. State and local bar ethics opinions may provide guidance and usually offer a good defense to a disciplinary charge, but they do not have the status of law. Court decisions provide the only truly authoritative interpretation of ethics rules. When court precedent conflicts with a bar opinion, the court's opinion governs.

Other voluntary associations of lawyers promulgate ethical codes applicable to their members. The Federal Bar Association, composed primarily of lawyers engaged in the practice of federal law, adopted the Model Rules of Professional Conduct for Federal Lawyers in 1990. The Association of American Trial Lawyers, composed primarily of claimants' lawyers, became dissatisfied with the process and emerging content of the ABA's Model Rules; it published a competing ethics code in 1982, the American Lawyer's Code of Conduct (ALCC). Organizations of specialized practitioners often publish special rules for their mem-

---

15. ABA, Opinions of the Committee on Professional Ethics 6 (1967); ABA Standing Committee on Ethics and Professional Responsibility, Rules of Procedure 3. See Wolfram, Modern Legal Ethics 65–67 (1986) for a general discussion of ethics committees and opinions. The ethics opinions of the ABA are reviewed and criticized in Ted Finman and Ted Schneyer, The Role of Bar Association Ethics Opinions in Regulating Lawyer Conduct, 29 UCLA L. Rev. 67 (1981) (analyzing 21 opinions issued under 1969 Model Code).

bers (e.g., matrimonial lawyers). Several major law book publishers issue annual volumes compiling most of the ethics codes we have mentioned.[16]

Ethics Rules and *Spaulding*

The Canons of Professional Ethics were in effect in Minnesota when the *Spaulding* case was decided. The court stated that "no canon of ethics or legal obligation may have required [defense counsel] to inform plaintiff [of the aneurysm]." Is that a correct statement? Read the following provisions of the Canons of Professional Ethics in your standards supplement: Canon 15 (How Far a Lawyer May Go in Supporting a Client's Cause), Canon 22 (Candor and Fairness), Canon 31 (Responsibility for Litigation), Canon 37 (Confidences of a Client), Canon 41 (Discovery of Imposition and Deception) and Canon 44 (Withdrawal From Employment as Attorney or Counsel).

Minnesota adopted a version of the Model Rules of Professional Conduct in 1985. How would the *Spaulding* case have been decided if the Model Rules had been in effect at the time? See especially Model Rules 1.3, 1.6, 1.16, 3.3 and 4.1.

C. PERSPECTIVES ON MORALITY OF THE LAWYER'S ROLE

1. Lawyer as Friend?

In examining the question, "Can a lawyer be a good person?", Professor Charles Fried has sought to justify the lawyer's disregard for the interests of others by drawing an analogy to friendship: [17]

> [M]y analogy shall be to friendship, where the freedom to choose and to be chosen expresses our freedom to hold something of ourselves in reserve, in reserve even from the universalizing claims of morality. These personal ties and the claims they engender may be all-consuming, as with a close friend or family member, or they may be limited, special-purpose claims, as in the case of the client or patient. The special-purpose claim is one in which the beneficiary, the client, is entitled to all the special consideration within the limits of the relationship which we accord to a friend or a loved one. It is not that the claims of the client are less intense or demanding: they are only more limited in their scope. After all, the ordinary concept of friendship provides only an analogy....

. . .

16. Thomas D. Morgan and Ronald D. Rotunda, 1993 Selected Standards of Professional Responsibility (Foundation Press); Stephen Gillers and Roy D. Simon, Jr., 1993 Regulation of Lawyers: Statutes and Standards (Little, Brown & Co.); John S. Dzienkowski, Selected Statutes, Rules and Standards on the Legal Profession (West Publishing Co.1993).

17. Charles Fried, The Lawyer as Friend: The Moral Foundations of the Lawyer-Client Relation, 85 Yale L.J. 1060 (1976).

If[, however,] personal integrity lies at the foundation of the lawyer's right to treat his client as a friend, then surely consideration for personal integrity—his own and others'—must limit what he can do in friendship. Consideration for personal integrity forbids me to lie, cheat, or humiliate, whether in my own interests or those of a friend, so surely they prohibit such conduct on behalf of a client, one's legal friend.... [18]

Lawyers, of course, may easily be distinguished from "real" friends. For example, unlike friends, lawyers are paid and are granted a special franchise by the state to give legal advice, and friendship is an "open" contract that the parties are continuously free to redefine or revoke.[19] Do such distinctions suggest different moral responsibilities for lawyers? Professor William Simon describes Fried's portrayal of the lawyer-client relationship as more like prostitution than friendship.[20]

What would a good friend of Zimmerman's have advised him to do?

2. Lawyer's Partisan and Amoral Role

RICHARD WASSERSTROM
"LAWYERS AS PROFESSIONALS: SOME MORAL ISSUES"

5 Human Rights 1 (1975).[21]

In this paper I examine two moral criticisms of lawyers which, if well-founded, are fundamental....

The first criticism centers around the lawyer's stance toward the world at large. The accusation is that the lawyer-client relationship renders the lawyer at best systematically amoral and at worst more than occasionally immoral in his or her dealings with the rest of mankind.

The second criticism focuses upon the relationship between the lawyer and the client. Here the charge is that it is the lawyer-client relationship which is morally objectionable because it is a relationship in which the lawyer dominates and in which the lawyer typically, and perhaps inevitably, treats the client in both an impersonal and a paternalistic fashion.

. . .

Although I am undecided about the ultimate merits of either criticism, I am convinced that each is deserving of careful articulation and assessment, and that each contains insights that deserve more

---

18. Id. at 1071, 1083.

19. For a critique of Fried's analogy to friendship, see Edward A. Dauer and Arthur A. Leff, Correspondence, 86 Yale L.J. 573 (1977).

20. William H. Simon, The Ideology of Advocacy, 1978 Wis.L.Rev. 29, 108.

21. Copyright © 1975 by the American Bar Association, Section of Individual Rights and Responsibilities, and Southern Methodist University.

acknowledgment than they often receive. My ambition is, therefore, more to exhibit the relevant considerations and to stimulate additional reflection, than it is to provide any very definite conclusions.

I.

... [T]he first issue I propose to examine concerns the ways the professional-client relationship affects the professional's stance toward the world at large. The primary question that is presented is whether there is adequate justification for the kind of moral universe that comes to be inhabited by the lawyer as he or she goes through professional life. For at best the lawyer's world is a simplified moral world; often it is an amoral one; and more than occasionally, perhaps, an overtly immoral one.

. . .

... [O]ne central feature of the professions in general and of law in particular is that there is a special, complicated relationship between the professional, and the client or patient. For each of the parties in this relationship, but especially for the professional, the behavior that is involved is to a very significant degree, what I call, role-differentiated behavior....

. . .

... [W]here the attorney-client relationship exists, it is often appropriate and many times even obligatory for the attorney to do things that, all other things being equal, an ordinary person need not, and should not do. What is characteristic of this role of a lawyer is the lawyer's required indifference to a wide variety of ends and consequences that in other contexts would be of undeniable moral significance. Once a lawyer represents a client, the lawyer has a duty to make his or her expertise fully available in the realization of the end sought by the client, irrespective, for the most part, of the moral worth to which the end will be put or the character of the client who seeks to utilize it. Provided that the end sought is not illegal, the lawyer is, in essence, an amoral technician whose peculiar skills and knowledge in respect to the law are available to those with whom the relationship of client is established. The question, as I have indicated, is whether this particular and pervasive feature of professionalism is itself justifiable. At a minimum, I do not think any of the typical, simple answers will suffice.

One such answer focuses upon and generalizes from the criminal defense lawyer.... The received view within the profession (and to a lesser degree within the society at large) is that having once agreed to represent the client, the lawyer is under an obligation to do his or her best to defend that person at trial, irrespective, for instance, even of the lawyer's belief in the client's innocence....

But ... the irrelevance of the guilt or innocence of an accused client by no means exhausts the altered perspective of the lawyer's conscience, even in criminal cases. For in the course of defending an accused, an attorney may have, as a part of his or her duty of representation, the obligation to invoke procedures and practices which are themselves morally objectionable and of which the lawyer in other contexts might thoroughly disapprove. And these situations, I think, are somewhat less comfortable to confront. For example, in California, the case law permits a defendant in a rape case to secure in some circumstances an order from the court requiring the complaining witness, that is the rape victim, to submit to a psychiatric examination before trial.[2] For no other crime is such a pretrial remedy available. In no other case can the victim of a crime be required to undergo psychiatric examination at the request of the defendant on the ground that the results of the examination may help the defendant prove that the offense did not take place. I think such a rule is wrong and is reflective of the sexist bias of the law in respect to rape.... Nonetheless, it appears to be part of the role-differentiated obligation of a lawyer for a defendant charged with rape to seek to take advantage of this particular rule of law—irrespective of the independent moral view he or she may have of the rightness or wrongness of such a rule.

Nor, it is important to point out, is this peculiar, strikingly amoral behavior limited to the lawyer involved with the workings of the criminal law. Most clients come to lawyers to get the lawyers to help them do things that they could not easily do without the assistance provided by the lawyer's special competence....

And in each case, the role-differentiated character of the lawyer's way of being tends to render irrelevant what would otherwise be morally relevant considerations. Suppose that a client desires to make a will disinheriting her children because they opposed the war in Vietnam. Should the lawyer refuse to draft the will because the lawyer thinks this a bad reason to disinherit one's children? Suppose a client can avoid the payment of taxes through a loophole only available to a few wealthy taxpayers. Should the lawyer refuse to tell the client of a loophole because the lawyer thinks it an unfair advantage for the rich? Suppose a client wants to start a corporation that will manufacture, distribute and promote a harmful but not illegal substance, e.g., cigarettes. Should the lawyer refuse to prepare the articles of incorporation for the corporation? In each case, the accepted view within the profession is that these matters are just of no concern to the lawyer *qua* lawyer. The lawyer need not of course agree to represent the client (and that is equally true for the unpopular client accused of a heinous crime), but there is nothing wrong with representing a client whose aims and purposes are quite immoral. And having agreed to do so, the lawyer is required to provide the best possible assistance, without regard to his or her disapproval of the objective that is sought.

2. Ballard v. Superior Court, 64 Cal.2d 159, 410 P.2d 838, 49 Cal.Rptr. 302 (1966). [Editors' note:] Cal. Pen. Code § 1112, effective Jan. 1, 1981, prohibited a trial court from ordering any witness or victim in any sexual assault prosecution to submit to a psychiatric or psychological examination for the purpose of assessing credibility. The constitutionality of the statute was upheld in People v. Armbruster, 163 Cal.App.3d 660, 210 Cal.Rptr. 11 (3d Dist.1985).

The lesson, on this view, is clear. The job of the lawyer, so the argument typically concludes, is not to approve or disapprove of the character of his or her client, the cause for which the client seeks the lawyer's assistance, or the avenues provided by the law to achieve that which the client wants to accomplish.... And the difficulty I have with all of this is that the arguments for such a way of life seem to be not quite so convincing to me as they do to many lawyers. I am, that is, at best uncertain that it is a good thing for lawyers to be so professional—for them to embrace so completely this role-differentiated way of approaching matters.

. . .

... [F]or most lawyers, most of the time, pursuing the interests of one's clients is an attractive and satisfying way to live in part just because the moral world of the lawyer is a simpler, less complicated, and less ambiguous world than the moral world of ordinary life....

But there is, of course, also an argument which seeks to demonstrate that it is good and not merely comfortable for lawyers to behave this way.

It is good, so the argument goes, that the lawyer's behavior and concomitant point of view are role-differentiated because the lawyer *qua* lawyer participates in a complex institution which functions well only if the individuals adhere to their institutional roles.

For example, when there is a conflict between individuals, or between the state and an individual, there is a well-established institutional mechanism by which to get that dispute resolved. That mechanism is the trial in which each side is represented by a lawyer whose job it is both to present his or her client's case in the most attractive, forceful light and to seek to expose the weaknesses and defects in the case of the opponent.

When an individual is charged with having committed a crime, the trial is the mechanism by which we determine in our society whether or not the person is in fact guilty. Just imagine what would happen if lawyers were to refuse, for instance, to represent persons whom they thought to be guilty.... The private judgment of individual lawyers would in effect be substituted for the public, institutional judgment of the judge and jury. The amorality of lawyers helps to guarantee that every criminal defendant will have his or her day in court.

. . .

Nor is the amorality of the institutional role of the lawyer restricted to the defense of those accused of crimes.... The attorney may think it wrong to disinherit one's children because of their views about the Vietnam war, but here the attorney's complaint is really with the laws of inheritance and not with his or her client. The attorney may think the tax provision an unfair, unjustifiable loophole, but once more the complaint is really with the Internal Revenue Code and not with the client who seeks to take advantage of it.... If lawyers were to substitute their own private views of what ought to be legally permissible and impermissible for those of the legislature, this would constitute a surreptitious and undesirable shift from a democracy to an oligarchy of lawyers. For given the fact that lawyers are needed to effectuate the wishes of clients, the lawyer ought to make his or her skills available to those who seek them without regard for the particular objectives of the client.

. . .

As I indicated earlier, I do believe that the amoral behavior of the *criminal* defense lawyer is justifiable. But I think that [justification] depends at least as much upon the special needs of an accused as upon any more general defense of a lawyer's role-differentiated behavior. As a matter of fact I think it likely that many persons such as myself have been misled by the special features of the criminal case. Because a deprivation of liberty is so serious, because the prosecutorial resources of the state are so vast, and because, perhaps, of a serious skepticism about the rightness of punishment even where wrongdoing has occurred, it is easy to accept the view that it makes sense to charge the defense counsel with the job of making the best possible case for the accused—without regard, so to speak, for the merits. This coupled with the fact that it is an adversarial proceeding succeeds, I think, in justifying the amorality of the criminal defense counsel. But this does not, however, justify a comparable perspective on the part of lawyers generally. Once we leave the peculiar situation of the criminal defense lawyer, I think it quite likely that the role-differentiated amorality of the lawyer is almost certainly excessive and at times inappropriate. . . .

Moreover, even if I am wrong about all this, four things do seem to me to be true and important.

First, all of the arguments that support the role-differentiated amorality of the lawyer on institutional grounds can succeed only if the enormous degree of trust and confidence in the institutions themselves is itself justified. . . . To the degree to which the institutional rules and practices are unjust, unwise or undesirable, to that same degree is the case for the role-differentiated behavior of the lawyer weakened if not destroyed.

Second, it is clear that there are definite character traits that the professional such as the lawyer must take on if the system is to work. What is less clear is that they are admirable ones. Even if the role-differentiated amorality of the professional lawyer is justified by the virtues of the adversary system, this also means that the lawyer *qua* lawyer will be encouraged to be competitive rather than cooperative; aggressive rather than accommodating; ruthless rather than compassionate; and pragmatic rather than principled. . . . It is surely neither accidental nor unimportant that these are the same character traits that are emphasized and valued by the capitalist ethic—and on precisely analogous grounds. Because the ideals of professionalism and capitalism are the dominant ones within our culture, it is harder than most of us suspect even to take seriously the suggestion that radically different styles of living, kinds of occupational outlooks, and types of social institutions might be possible, let alone preferable.

Third, there is a special feature of the role-differentiated behavior of the lawyer that distinguishes it from the comparable behavior of other professionals. What I have in mind can be brought out through the following question: Why is it that it seems far less plausible to talk critically about the amorality of the doctor, for instance, who treats all patients irrespective of their moral character than it does to talk critically about the comparable amorality of the lawyer? ...

... The lawyer lives with and within a dilemma that is not shared by other professionals. If the lawyer actually believes everything that he or she asserts on behalf of the client, then it appears to be proper to regard the lawyer as in fact embracing and endorsing the points of view that he or she articulates. If the lawyer does not in fact believe what is urged by way of argument, if the lawyer is only playing a role, then it appears to be proper to tax the lawyer with hypocrisy and insincerity. To be sure, actors in a play take on roles and say things that the characters, not the actors, believe. But we know it is a play and that they are actors. The law courts are not, however, theaters, and the lawyers both talk about justice and they genuinely seek to persuade. The fact that the lawyer's words, thoughts, and convictions are, apparently, for sale and at the service of the client helps us, I think, to understand the peculiar hostility which is more than occasionally uniquely directed by lay persons toward lawyers....

Fourth, ... we do pay a social price for that way of thought and action. For to become and to be a professional, such as a lawyer, is to incorporate within oneself ways of behaving and ways of thinking that shape the whole person. It is especially hard, if not impossible, because of the nature of the professions, for one's professional way of thinking not to dominate one's entire adult life.... In important respects, one's professional role becomes and is one's dominant role, so that for many persons at least they become their professional being. This is at a minimum a heavy price to pay for the professions as we know them in our culture, and especially so for lawyers. Whether it is an inevitable price is, I think, an open question, largely because the problem has not begun to be fully perceived as such by the professionals in general, the legal profession in particular, or by the educational institutions that train professionals.

II.

The role-differentiated behavior of the professional also lies at the heart of the second of the two moral issues I want to discuss, namely, the character of the interpersonal relationship that exists between the lawyer and the client.* As I indicated at the outset, the charge that I want to examine here is that the relationship between the lawyer and the client is typically, if not inevitably, a morally defective one in which the client is not treated with the respect and dignity that he or she deserves.

. . .

A+y/π
In eQuality

... [O]ne pervasive, and I think necessary, feature of the relationship between any professional and the client or patient is that it is in some sense a relationship of inequality. This relationship of inequality is intrinsic to the existence of professionalism. For the professional is, in some respects at least, always in a position of dominance vis-á-vis the client, and the client in a position of dependence vis-á-vis the professional. . . .

To begin with, there is the fact that one characteristic of professions is that the professional is the possessor of expert knowledge of a sort not readily or easily attainable by members of the community at large. Hence, in the most straightforward of all senses the client,

"dependency typically, is dependent upon the professional's skill or knowledge because the client does not possess the same knowledge.

Moreover, virtually every profession has its own technical language, a private terminology which can only be fully understood by the members of the profession. The presence of such a language plays the dual role of creating and affirming the membership of the professionals within the profession and of preventing the client from fully discussing or understanding his or her concerns in the language of the profession.

. . .

In addition, because the matters for which professional assistance is sought usually involve things of great personal concern to the client, it is the received wisdom within the professions that the client lacks the perspective necessary to pursue in a satisfactory way his or her own best interests, and that the client requires a detached, disinterested representative to look after his or her interests. . . .

Finally, as I have indicated, to be a professional is to have been acculturated in a certain way. It is to have satisfactorily passed through a lengthy and allegedly difficult period of study and training. It is to have done something hard. Something that not everyone can do. Almost all professions encourage this way of viewing oneself; as having joined an elect group by virtue of hard work and mastery of the mysteries of the profession. In addition, the society at large treats members of a profession as members of an elite by paying them more than most people for the work they do with their heads rather than their hands, and by according them a substantial amount of social prestige and power by virtue of their membership in a profession. It is

---

* [Editors' note:] The moral aspects of the lawyer-client relationship are considered below in Chapter 6. See p. 474 below for further discussion of Professor Wasserstrom's views.

hard, I think, if not impossible, for a person to emerge from professional training and participate in a profession without the belief that he or she is a special kind of person, both different from and somewhat better than those nonprofessional members of the social order. It is equally hard for the other members of society not to hold an analogous view of the professionals. And these beliefs surely contribute, too, to the dominant role played by a professional in any professional-client relationship.

. . .

... It is, I believe, indicative of the state of legal education and of the profession that there has been to date extremely little self-conscious concern even with the possibility that these dimensions of the attorney-client relationship are worth examining—to say nothing of being capable of alteration. That awareness is, surely, the prerequisite to any serious assessment of the moral character of the attorney-client relationship as a relationship among adult human beings.

Notes on Role Morality

How would Wasserstrom have a lawyer deal with Zimmerman to accord Zimmerman the "respect and dignity that he ... deserves"?

Wasserstrom accepts the role-based morality of the criminal defense lawyer while rejecting such morality for lawyers in other situations. Are his arguments distinguishing the criminal lawyer persuasive? Are not his arguments against the role-morality of other lawyers equally applicable to the criminal defense lawyer? For example, are trust and confidence in the criminal justice system more warranted than trust and confidence in the civil system? Should we be less concerned with the character traits nourished by role-morality in criminal defense lawyers than with the traits fostered in civil litigators?

Suppose Zimmerman was a criminal defendant who possessed knowledge that, if disclosed, would save another's life but would also result in Zimmerman's imprisonment. Would the morality of his lawyer's action in keeping the information secret differ from that lawyer's morality in doing the same in the civil case?

In Nebraska v. Harper,[22] Harper, who had been convicted of poisoning several people, claimed that his trial counsel had provided ineffective representation because the lawyer had "permitted" Harper to tell the court the kind of poison he had administered to victims who were still alive. This disclosure allowed the victims to get appropriate medical treatment. The trial court allowed the disclosure but excluded

[handwritten margin notes: Nebraska v. Harper poison]

22. 214 Neb. 911, 336 N.W.2d 597 (1983).

from evidence the fact that Harper had provided the information. In rejecting the claim of ineffective assistance of counsel, the court said:

> [R]efusal ... to disclose would have only served as an aggravating circumstance. To now suggest that [the lawyer] should not have permitted Harper to disclose ... is totally without basis. The lives of three individuals hung in the balance. Effective assistance of counsel does not require such callous behavior as [now] suggested by Harper.[23]

Wasserstrom describes a lawyer's moral universe as defined by client interests and restricted only by the dictates of law. He says that conduct permissible under law includes immoral behavior that should not be condoned. His argument assumes that the boundary between lawful and unlawful conduct is discernible, discerned and respected by most lawyers. The problem, according to Wasserstrom and most other commentators on this subject, is not that lawyers are lawless but that compliance with law does not ensure "moral" behavior. Yet Wasserstrom acknowledges, in a part of his article not reprinted here, that the Watergate scandal, which involved many lawyers, prompted renewed concern about legal ethics. The lawyers involved in Watergate, however, committed acts that were illegal as well as immoral. Does the amorality of role-differentiated lawyer behavior lead to lawlessness?

In 1984 Wasserstrom revisited the issues discussed in his 1975 article, reprinted above, and advanced some arguments in support of lawyers' role-differentiated morality.[24] First, he suggested, a better range of moral outcomes may result overall if lawyers simply play their assigned adversarial roles in the legal system without bothering about other considerations. Second, the legitimate expectations of clients, who retain lawyers with the traditional role in mind, may justify the lawyers' conforming to the morality of the expected adversarial role. These and other arguments in support of the "standard conception" of the lawyer's role often appear in the literature.[25] Wasserstrom, however, expressed doubt as to whether such arguments, characterized as "weak," support the lawyer's amoral role other than in the special case of criminal defense.

---

23. 336 N.W.2d at 600.

24. Richard Wasserstrom, Roles and Morality, in David Luban (ed.), The Good Lawyer 25 (1984).

25. See, e.g., Monroe H. Freedman, Understanding Lawyers' Ethics (1990) (defending adversarial ethics as essential to the vindication of individual autonomy and individual rights); Stephen L. Pepper, The Lawyer's Amoral Ethical Role: A Defense, A Problem, and Some Possibilities, 1986 Am.Bar Found.Research J. 613 (lawyer's adversarial role is essential to provide people with meaningful access to law in all its forms).

3. Perspective of the Bad Man *an atty's "Ends"*

OLIVER WENDELL HOLMES, JR.
"THE PATH OF THE LAW," COLLECTED LEGAL PAPERS

Pp. 167–169, 171–175 (1920).
Appears also in 10 Harv.L.Rev. 457–462 (1897).

When we study law we are not studying a mystery but a well-known profession. We are studying what we shall want in order to appear before judges, or to advise people in such a way as to keep them out of court. The reason why it is a profession, why people will pay lawyers to argue for them or to advise them, is that in societies like ours the command of the public force is intrusted to the judges in certain cases, and the whole power of the state will be put forth, if necessary, to carry out their judgments and decrees. People want to know under what circumstances and how far they will run the risk of coming against what is so much stronger than themselves, and hence it becomes a business to find out when this danger is to be feared. The object of our study, then, is prediction, the prediction of the incidence of the public force through the instrumentality of the courts.

... If you want to know the law and nothing else, you must look at it as a bad man, who cares only for the material consequences which such knowledge enables him to predict, not as a good one, who finds his reasons for conduct, whether inside the law or outside of it, in the vaguer sanctions of conscience. The theoretical importance of the distinction is no less, if you would reason on your subject aright. The law is full of phraseology drawn from morals, and by the mere force of language continually invites us to pass from one domain to the other without perceiving it, as we are sure to do unless we have the boundary constantly before our minds....

The confusion with which I am dealing besets confessedly legal conceptions. Take the fundamental question. What constitutes the law? You will find some text writers telling you that it is something different from what is decided by the courts of Massachusetts or England, that it is a system of reason, that it is a deduction from principles of ethics or admitted axioms or what not, which may or may not coincide with the decisions. But if we take the view of our friend the bad man we shall find that he does not care two straws for the axioms or deductions, but that he does want to know what the Massachusetts or English courts are likely to do in fact. I am much of his mind. The prophecies of what the court will do in fact, and nothing more pretentious, are what I mean by the law.

Take again a notion which as popularly understood is the widest conception which the law contains—the notion of legal duty, to which already I have referred. We fill the word with all the content which we draw from morals. But what does it mean to a bad man? Mainly, and in the first place, a prophecy that if he does certain things he will be subjected to disagreeable consequences by way of imprisonment or compulsory payment of money. But from his point of view, what is the difference between being fined and being taxed a certain sum for doing, a certain thing?...

———

Lawyer as Bad Man

Holmes says the bad man's perspective is necessary "if you want to know the law and *nothing else* ...." What are the consequences for the lawyer of adopting this perspective? Is it possible to keep the bad man's perspective in one's office and not have it intrude on the rest of one's life? [26] What are the consequences of this view for the client?

How would Holmes have advised Zimmerman's lawyers to counsel Zimmerman?

Holmes' "bad man" presumably would be interested not only in what the courts of Massachusetts would say but also in the likelihood that a prosecutor or private person would bring his actions before a court. If the courts would hold the client liable, but the local prosecutor is unlikely to discover the violation, should the lawyer so inform the client? How should the likelihood of prosecution affect the advice the lawyer gives the client? If Holmes' lawyer found out that the judge could be bought, should she tell her client this too? [27]

Critique of the Bad Man's Perspective

Professor William Simon's restatement and critique of the "lawyer as bad man" is cast in terms of the acceptance by many lawyers of a positivist world view.[28] Simon's critique of the positivist lawyer is based on the observation that such a lawyer's notion of the advocate's role is inconsistent with that lawyer's idea of the relation between the law and personal ends. The positivist sees the lawyer as enhancing a client's autonomy by enabling the client to make the fullest use of his freedom to pursue his own ends. The lawyer does so ostensibly by using "[her] objective knowledge of the precise, regular, mechanical operation of the legal system to predict the consequences of alternative courses of action" (p. 52). The client, however, cannot give a satisfacto-

---

26. See Thomas L. Shaffer, Faith and the Professions 71–110 (1987) (discussing whether it is possible or desirable to separate professional morality from personal morality). See also Shaffer, The Theology of the Two Kingdoms, 17 Valparaiso L.Rev. 17 (1983).

27. Other materials on the morality of the lawyer's role and relationship with clients include: Douglas E. Rosenthal, Lawyer & Client: Who's In Charge? (1974); Alan H. Goldman, The Moral Foundations of Professional Ethics, ch. 3 (1980); Andrew L. Kaufman, Book Review, 94 Harv.L.Rev. 1504 (1981) (reviewing Goldman); David Luban (ed.), The Good Lawyer: The Lawyers' Roles and Lawyers' Ethics (1984) (collection of articles on the morality of the lawyer's role); Ted Schneyer, Moral Philosophy's Standard Misconception of Legal Ethics, 1984 Wis.L.Rev. 1529; Stephen L. Pepper, The Lawyer's Amoral Ethical Role: A Defense, A Problem and Some Possibilities, 1986 Am.Bar Found.Research J. 613; Thomas L. Shaffer, Legal Ethics and the Good Client, 36 Cath.U.L.Rev. 319 (1987); William F. Simon, Ethical Discretion in Lawyering, 101 Harv.L.Rev. 1083 (1988).

28. William H. Simon, The Ideology of Advocacy, 1978 Wisconsin L. Rev. 30, 52 ff.

ry account of his situation without the lawyer's knowledge of legal relevance. The lawyer for her part has no way of divining the client's goals, or ends, by herself, since they are subjective and peculiar to the individual. Any speculation by the lawyer would reveal merely the interference of the lawyer's own biases or ends. The positivist lawyer's dilemma is that she cannot advise her client without referring to ends, yet she cannot refer to ends without jeopardizing her client's own autonomy via the lawyer's biases.

The lawyer's strategy for dealing with this dilemma is to impute *Imputing* certain basic ends to the client, and then to work to advance these ends, *Ends to* even though this weakens the premise of the absolute individuality of *the π.* the client's ends. Thus, the personal injury claimant is presumed to be interested only in the largest award, and the criminal defendant is presumed to be interested only in being relieved of all responsibility for his conduct. Imputed ends are invariably extremely selfish ones, primarily involving "maximization of freedom of movement and the accumulation of wealth" (p. 54).

This procedure offers one way to avoid potentially "dangerous" (and time-consuming) inquiries into a client's ends from the beginning, and, if the ends selected are shared, the lawyer does advance the client's actual needs to some degree while advancing the ends that the lawyer imputes to him.

... The client of whom Positivism is most solicitous is the naive person, face to face with the alien force of the state, threatened with a massive disruption of his life. Confronted with the need to act in this strange situation, the client must make sense of it as best he can. The lawyer puts himself forth quite plausibly as the client's best hope of mastering his predicament. If [the client] is to avoid being overwhelmed by chaos, he must acquiesce in his lawyer's definition of the situation. He must think in a manner which gives coherence to the advice he is given. He may begin to do this quite unconsciously. If he is at all aware of the change, he is likely to see it as a defensive posture forced on him by the hostile intentions of opposing parties.... His only strategy of survival requires that he see himself as the lawyers and the officials see him, as an abstraction, a hypothetical person with only a few crude, discrete ends. He must assume that his subtler ends, his long-range plans, and his social relationships are irrelevant to the situation at hand. This is the profound and unintended meaning of Holmes's remark:

"If you want to know the law and nothing else, you must look at it as a bad man, who cares only for the material consequences which such knowledge enables him to predict, not as a good one, who finds his reasons for conduct, whether inside the law or outside of it, in the vaguer sanctions of conscience."

The role of the bad man, conceived as an analytical device for the lawyer, becomes, under pressure of circumstances, a psychological reality for the client.

. . .

Despite its complete irrationality, this Positivist strategy [of imposing ends on the client] has become so widely accepted that many lawyers have come to equate the manipulation of the client ... with neutral advice to the client on his rights. For instance, lawyers constantly express astonishment at the willingness of intelligent laymen, aware of their rights, to make inculpatory statements to the authorities. They can think of no other explanation for this phenomenon besides confusion or pressure from the interrogators, and they thus conclude that no one can be expected to make an "informed decision" on such matters without the assistance of counsel. But the lawyer's assistance does not take the form of neutral information or the alleviation of pressure. Along with his knowledge of the law, the lawyer brings [her] own prejudices and [her] own psychological pressures. These derive from the conception of the roles of lawyer and client which is implicit in Positivism generally and in the strategy of imputed ends. As Justice Jackson put it, "[A]ny lawyer worth his salt will tell the suspect in no uncertain terms to make no statement to the police under any circumstances." [66] The Positivist lawyer is not an advisor, but a lobbyist for a peculiar theory of human nature.

The Legal Realism Problem

Positivist v. Naturalist

The positivist interpretation of law in part reacted against a natural law interpretation, which held that law expresses inevitable and therefore "natural" justice. Does the legal system deliver natural justice? Or, at best, moderately effective controls on "bad men"? If the latter, shouldn't a lawyer advise her client on that basis? Every sensitive person wishes for more caring conduct toward others than the "bad man" delivers. But how can legal process deliver or compel such conduct? [29] How do you feel about pursuing a vocation that, unlike medicine or teaching, is not generally considered a "caring profession"?

Holmes is celebrated as a precursor of "legal realism," today a widely held jurisprudential position. Legal realism places great emphasis on the indeterminacy and manipulability of law. If only law—not morality—limits a lawyer's conduct, moral input or constraint in the lawyer-client relationship is reduced or eliminated. [30] For example,

---

66. Watts v. Indiana, 338 U.S. 49, 59 (1949); cf. Justice Jackson's remark on his experience of civil practice in Jamestown, N.Y., " ... a lawyer there, if he was consulted on a matter, usually dominated the matter, no matter who the businessman was." E. Gerhart, America's Advocate: Robert M. Jackson 63 (1958).

29. For a sophisticated modern presentation of a positivist perspective, see Joseph Raz, The Authority of Law: Essays on Morality and Law 250–61 (1979) (defending the view that a positivist lawyer would have a qualified respect for law that would lead her to obey most laws of a reasonably just and good society).

30. See Pepper, supra, at 625 et seq.

a lawyer's emphasis on "law" may influence a business concern assessing and planning conduct that poses risk of personal injury or death to third persons in perceiving the problem as involving only legal risks and economic costs and not moral issues (such as the conduct being "bad" or "wrong" or "unfair"). An amoral, realist lawyer thus may encourage an industrial client to engage in as much pollution as the lawyer believes the client can get away with, viewing the "law" solely as a prediction of the risks and benefits of what officials are likely to do, including the likelihood of being caught and of stiff sanctions being applied.

One response to the legal realism problem is to encourage lawyers to engage in moral dialogue with clients, who retain responsibility for determining the objectives of representation. A second response is to ask lawyers to reject the premise that assisting a client by unjust means or toward an unjust goal is morally permissible. Professor David Luban argues that it is wrong to assume that everything legally right is also morally right.[31] A good society wants people not only to make their own choices, but to make *good* choices. Increasing individual autonomy is good only if the consequences are good or neutral, but not when the act chosen is bad, such as telling a lie or humiliating a truthful witness.

> When getting the client whatever he or she wants is conceived of as the lawyer's preponderant professional obligation, it is psychologically natural to reduce the dissonance between that obligation and legality by understanding the law as *whatever I can get officials to give my client.* .... If you think winning is the most important thing, you will eventually think winning is the only thing. Take the normative content out of the lawyer's role and the lawyer will feel impelled to take the normative content out of law as well and define it ... as victor's spoils pure and simple.[32]

4. Relational Feminism

CAROL GILLIGAN
IN A DIFFERENT VOICE

Pp. 25–29 (1982).[33]

The dilemma that these eleven-year-olds were asked to resolve was one in the series devised by [Lawrence] Kohlberg to measure moral development in adolescence by presenting a conflict between moral norms and exploring the logic of its resolution. In this particular

---

31. David Luban, The Lysistratian Prerogative: A Response to Stephen Pepper, 1986 Am.Bar Found. Research J. 637.

32. Id. at 648.

33. Copyright © 1982 by Carol G. Gilligan. Published by Harvard University Press. Reprinted by Permission.

dilemma, a man named Heinz considers whether or not to steal a drug which he cannot afford to buy in order to save the life of his wife. In the standard format of Kohlberg's interviewing procedure, the description of the dilemma itself—Heinz's predicament, the wife's disease, the druggist's refusal to lower his price—is followed by the question, "Should Heinz steal the drug?" The reasons for and against stealing are then explored through a series of questions that vary the parameters of the dilemma in a way designed to reveal the underlying structure of moral thought.

Jake, at eleven, is clear from the outset that Heinz should steal the drug. Constructing the dilemma, as Kohlberg did, as a conflict between the values of property and life, he discerns the logical priority of life and uses that logic to justify his choice.

> For one thing, a human life is worth more than money, and if the druggist only makes $1,000, he is still going to live, but if Heinz doesn't steal the drug, his wife is going to die. (*Why is life worth more than money?*) Because the druggist can get a thousand dollars later from rich people with cancer, but Heinz can't get his wife again. (*Why not?*) Because people are all different and so you couldn't get Heinz's wife again.

Asked whether Heinz should steal the drug if he does not love his wife, Jake replies that he should, saying that not only is there "a difference between hating and killing," but also, if Heinz were caught, "the judge would probably think it was the right thing to do." Asked about the fact that, in stealing, Heinz would be breaking the law, he says that "the laws have mistakes and you can't go writing up a law for everything that you can imagine."

. . .

[In contrast to Jake's answers are Amy's.] Asked if Heinz should steal the drug, she replies. . . .

> Well, I don't think so. I think there might be other ways besides stealing it, like if he could borrow the money or make a loan or something, but he really shouldn't steal the drug—but his wife shouldn't die either.

Asked why he should not steal the drug, she considers neither property nor law but rather the effect that theft could have on the relationship between Heinz and his wife:

> If he stole the drug, he might save his wife then, but if he did, he might have to go to jail, and then his wife might get sicker again, and he couldn't get more of the drug, and it might not be good. So, they should really just talk it out and find some other way to make the money.

Seeing in the dilemma not a math problem with humans but a narrative of relationships that extends over time, Amy envisions the wife's continuing need for her husband and the husband's continuing concern for his wife and seeks to respond to the druggist's need in a way that would sustain rather than sever connection. . . . Since Amy's moral judgment is grounded in the belief that "if somebody has something that would keep somebody alive, then it's not right not to give it to them," she considers the problem in the dilemma to arise not from the druggist's assertion of rights but from his failure of response.

. . . Failing to see the dilemma as a self-contained problem in moral logic, she does not discern the internal structure of its resolution; . . . she constructs the problem differently. . . .

Instead, seeing a world comprised of relationships rather than people standing alone, a world that coheres through human connection rather than through systems of rules, she finds the puzzle in the dilemma to lie in the failure of the druggist to respond to the wife. Saying that "it is not right for someone to die when their life could be saved," she assumes that if the druggist were to see the consequences of his refusal to lower his price, he would realize that "he should just give it to the wife and then have the husband pay back the money later." Thus she considers the solution to the dilemma to lie in making the wife's condition more salient to the druggist or, that failing, in appealing to others who are in a position to help.

Just as Jake is confident the judge would agree that stealing is the right thing for Heinz to do, so Amy is confident that, "if Heinz and the druggist had talked it out long enough, they could reach something besides stealing." . . .

Putting People First

How would Jake analyze the moral predicament of the lawyers in *Spaulding*? How would Amy? Can you improve on their analyses?

A prominent psychologist, Mihaly Csikszentmihalyi, has reflected on Gilligan's alternative vision of moral development and selfhood: [34]

> Mr. Kohlberg's moral hierarchy was reasonably convincing and widely accepted, but it led to some disturbing results. When girls were asked to justify their moral choices, they often failed to arrive at the "highest" form of moral reasoning. Instead of using abstract rules of justice to decide whether an action was right or wrong, they kept wondering who would suffer by the action. They would then rate as best the choice that led to the least harm. If Mr. Kohlberg's argument was correct, it seemed that women's moral reasoning was underdeveloped. This was a conclusion that many famous psychologists, including Freud and Piaget, had held to be true all along.
>
> Ms. Gilligan did not reject Mr. Kohlberg's findings, but simply reinterpreted them. Basically, she asked: why should we believe

34. Mihaly Csikszentmihalyi, More Ways Than One to Be Good, Book Review, N.Y.Times Book Review 6 (May 28, 1989).

that the sequence of moral stages through which boys pass constitutes moral development *tout court*? What comes later does not necessarily represent a higher order of morality. Perhaps the girls' abiding concern for human relatedness and personal responsibility is not a lower form of reasoning, but an equally sophisticated and vital perspective, complementing the more masculine concern for rights and justice.

In retrospect, this hardly seems like a revolutionary concept. Of course, it is often the case with new ideas that after they have been stated, people will say: "Why didn't I think of it? It was so obvious." But Ms. Gilligan, either because she focused on a very concrete and clear issue (the hierarchy of moral arguments), or because she delved into it with great zest and eloquence, or because she happened to be writing at the right historical moment, was able to make her ideas the common currency of the academic world.

In the long run, however, the most important aspect of her work may not be her reinterpretation of morality, but her insistence that our entire conception of the self must be revised in the light of what we can learn from women's experiences. The ideal self has commonly been understood as hard, independent, detached, autonomous, capable of distancing itself from other people and from its own emotions. Indeed, if one looks back on the theories of selfhood developed by American social scientists over the past century or so, from those of Charles Horton Cooley to George Herbert Mead, Erving Goffman and the "symbolic interactionist" school of sociology, one gets the impression that the self is something like a ferret hiding in its hole, ready to pounce on any moving thing it can kill and drag into its lair. Motivated by nothing except a fierce individualistic need to survive and prevail, it neither asks for nor gives quarter. Any signs of grace or sympathy are only to deceive the unwary. By contrast, Ms. Gilligan suggests that care and responsibility for the well-being of others represent qualities at least as desirable as the ones associated with the traditional image of the self. This picture of a self that is responsive and dependent on others is a definite improvement.

... [Instead of emphasizing] the detached act of looking ... Ms. Gilligan instead resorts continuously to the metaphor of the voice. It is not by looking that the self develops, but by talking and listening. Through communication with others, sharing their concerns and desires, we understand ourselves and our responsibilities in the world. The self gains strength in becoming part of a web of relationships, not in accumulating power.

. . .

One disturbing finding that seems to emerge [in the later book by Gilligan and others] is that as girls become involved in the institutional roles of the world as men—the more they advance in school, or in the professions—their "voices" change into masculine baritones. The concern with care and personal involvement is never totally expunged, but increasingly it gets displaced by recourse to impersonal justice. In the old days, psychologists would have interpreted this to mean that women learn higher forms of moral reasoning as they move into the complexity of the "real" world. Now, thanks to Ms. Gilligan's insights, we cannot be so sure.[35]

D. PITFALLS FOR THE UNWARY

1. Shaping and Using Law and Facts

Both legal education and legal practice attune lawyers to the ambiguity of law and facts. The first-year law student who reads the proverbial statute prohibiting vehicles in the park [36] might think she knows what the statute means, but the law professor quickly demonstrates how slippery words can be. Does the statute include motorcycles? Bicycles? Baby carriages? An army truck used as a war memorial? A similar process occurs in law firms when new associates find out the many ways to characterize their client's behavior. Facts that seem clearly to show negligence reemerge under a partner's skillful hands as facts demonstrating great care and caution. Taking advantage of ambiguity that exists and creating ambiguity where none appeared before are skills that every lawyer cultivates. Beyond some line, however, exercise of these skills may lead to trouble.

In <u>Matter of Krueger</u> [37] the client, while living in Illinois, retained Krueger, a Wisconsin lawyer, to represent him in a divorce proceeding. Krueger counseled the client to rent a room in Wisconsin to satisfy the residency requirement for a divorce action under Wisconsin law. The client did so for two weeks. Krueger thereafter filed for the client a divorce petition alleging that the client had been a resident of Wisconsin for more than six months and of the county in question for more than 30 days. The court-appointed referee in a disciplinary proceeding found that the client initially gave Krueger some reason to believe that he could meet Wisconsin's residency requirements; the referee also found "that diverse opinions could exist concerning the client's residency at the time the action was commenced." Krueger did not tell his client to testify falsely but did tell him how to "manifest an intention to continue his Wisconsin residency, despite the presence of facts indicat-

---

35. See also Mary F. Belenky et al., Women's Ways of Knowing: The Development of Self, Voice and Mind (1986). Gilligan's thesis and methodology have been criticized by other feminists: See, e.g., Cynthia F. Epstein, Deceptive Distinctions: Sex, Gender, and the Social Order 76–94 (1988).

36. Herbert L.A. Hart, The Concept of Law 121 (1961).

37. 103 Wis.2d 192, 307 N.W.2d 184 (1981).

ing a specific intention to abandon a Wisconsin domicile...." Krueger was publicly reprimanded for unprofessional conduct.

What did Krueger do wrong? Should Krueger have refused to tell the client what the courts would consider as evidence of an intention to stay in Wisconsin once Krueger had reason to believe the client would not stay? Is it proper to keep such information from a client? What did Krueger do that went beyond giving realistic advice about Wisconsin domicile law?

Legal philosophy today generally interprets law as uncertain and malleable to a greater degree than the positivist approach. Most forms of legal positivism asserted that law in its various forms—statutory, common and natural—was discoverable, i.e., had an inherent meaning apart from the will of its reader or interpreter. Judges could be right or wrong about what the law was. Legal realism, which understood law as "what courts do", supplanted positivism as the dominant jurisprudential perspective. Law was what judges said it was; the lawyer's job was to predict what that might be. See the Holmes' excerpt printed above at p. 27. What judges did and would do—in other words, what the law was and would be—could be understood as a function of the societal values held by judges, who as products of their environment would act in a manner consistent with historical and cultural norms. Understanding those norms, the values of the society that produced judges, was the key to understanding law. More recently, Critical Legal Studies takes the realist critique of positivism one step further. Law is to be understood as the product of neither rational thought nor shared societal values. Law is power exercised by judges as state officials. Their will—their commitment to their own values and the use of power—determines the content of law.

If law is the exercise of power or a prediction of what courts will do, why was Krueger wrong to help his client act in a way that would produce a more favorable ruling by the courts? How does a lawyer interpret the requirement of Canon 7 of the Model Code that representation of a client remain "within the bounds of the law" when many modern concepts of law reject the notion that law has bounds? Where is the line between presenting evidence in the light most favorable to one's client, permitted under EC 7–6, and making false statements about the facts, prohibited by M.R. 3.3 and DR 7–102(A)(5)?

2. Are Lawyers Immune From Law's Prohibitions?

Introductory Note

When lawyers act not as advocates but as counselors, advisors, negotiators, etc., the law treats them very much as it treats lay persons performing similar roles. Hence, the same law that applies to all people regardless of profession governs lawyers most of the time. The law makes an exception, however, for advocates, who act not in the real world but in a staged world with its own set of rules—the theater of a court—where the lawyer is governed by the special rules governing the legal theater. The suspension of the general law (and the substitution of special rules) for the advocate arises not from membership in the profession but from the courtroom theater and the lawyer's part in it.

The fact that an advocate operates under special rules in a courtroom operates as a source of confusion for many lawyers and as an excuse for misconduct by others.[38] The extent to which laws of general application apply to lawyers outside the courtroom will be considered in depth in the next chapter. The special rules that govern the advocate in court are considered in Chapter 5. The following case examines the line between the paradigms of in-court behavior and office conduct.

COMMONWEALTH v. STENHACH

Superior Court of Pennsylvania, 1986.

356 Pa.Super. 5, 514 A.2d 114, appeal denied, 517 Pa. 589, 534 A.2d 769 (1987).

HESTER, JUDGE:

Two criminal defense attorneys have appealed from convictions for hindering prosecution and tampering with evidence arising from their conduct while representing a defendant in a murder trial. Appellants George and Walter Stenhach were young public defenders appointed to represent Richard Buchanan, a man charged with first degree murder. Following Buchanan's directions, appellants recovered a rifle stock used in the homicide. Allegedly believing that disclosure of the rifle stock would be legally and ethically prohibited, appellants did not deliver it to the prosecutor until ordered to do so by the court during the prosecution's case. After Buchanan's conviction of third degree murder, appellants were charged with hindering prosecution, 18 Pa.C.S. § 5105(a)(3), tampering with physical evidence, § 4910(1), criminal conspiracy, § 903, and criminal solicitation, § 902. A jury found both appellants guilty of hindering prosecution, a third degree felony, and tampering, a second degree misdemeanor. In addition, George was convicted of solicitation, and Walter of conspiracy. Each was sentenced to twelve months probation and a fine of $750.

Their appeal raises questions relating to the interplay of the fifth and sixth amendments to the United States Constitution, the statutory attorney-client privilege, and the Pennsylvania Code of Professional Responsibility, in which appellants challenge their duty to deliver evidence to the prosecution. Appellants also raise a due process challenge to the criminal statutes which prohibit hindering prosecution and tampering with evidence when these statutes are applied to criminal

---

38. "One of the least supportable excesses of M. Freedman, Lawyer's Ethics in an Adversary System (1975), is the extension of arguments for client-oriented lawyer action from the area of advocacy to the entirely different field of client counseling. As a glaring example, arguments for a lawyer's exclusive focus on the interests of his or her client that Professor Freedman develops, in the context of the criminal defense function, he then applies without qualification to lawyers who advise clients about non-criminal law matters when issuing securities, id. at 20–24." Wolfram, Modern Legal Ethics 697 n. 45 (1986).

defense attorneys, claiming the statutes are unconstitutionally over-broad; the statutory defense of justification; and allegations of numer-ous trial errors in evidentiary and other rulings. Amicus curiae briefs by the Pennsylvania Trial Lawyers Association, the National Associa-tion of Criminal Defense Lawyers and the Public Defender Association of Pennsylvania all support reversal of the judgments of sentence.

Holding

We reject appellants' argument that their retention of physical evidence was proper under existing law. We hold, however, that the statutes under which they were convicted are unconstitutionally over-broad as applied to criminal defense attorneys. Accordingly, we do not address appellants' claims of trial error, but order appellants dis-charged.

Background

In March, 1982, Theodore Young was killed in Potter County. The following day Richard Buchanan and an accomplice were arrested and charged with first degree murder. Appellant George Stenhach, part-time Public Defender of Potter County, undertook Buchanan's defense immediately. He petitioned for appointment of an investigator to assist in Buchanan's defense, and former police officer Daniel Weidner was appointed as Buchanan's investigator. During a confidential con-ference among Stenhach, Weidner and Buchanan, Buchanan described the death of Theodore Young. He said that Young had attacked him

Facts

with two knives and that during the attack, Young had died after he was shot, hit by Buchanan's car, then struck by Buchanan's rifle, causing the stock of the rifle to break off. Buchanan and his accom-plice had then disposed of the weapons and other items relating to Young's death. During the conference, Weidner and Buchanan pre-pared a map identifying the location of some of these items.

Appellant Walter Stenhach, George's younger brother, was practic-ing law in partnership with George, and assisted in Buchanan's defense. Appellants George and Walter Stenhach had graduated from law school in 1978 and 1980, respectively, and had been admitted to practice in Pennsylvania in 1979 and 1981. They discussed the information re-ceived from Buchanan, and decided to pursue the theory of self-defense and to attempt to gather evidence supporting that theory. Accordingly, they ordered Weidner to search for the items Buchanan had described, and to retrieve as many as he could find.

On the same day, Weidner found the broken rifle stock and brought it back to appellants' office. He did not find the barrel, which was eventually discovered by the prosecutor and introduced into evi-dence at Buchanan's trial. Weidner was unable to locate the knives allegedly used by the victim, and no knives were ever found. When Weidner delivered the rifle stock to appellants, they stored it inside a paper bag in a desk drawer in their office.

Weidner had been a police officer for twenty years and was per-forming his first defense investigation in the Buchanan case. He expressed his concern as many as twenty times during the five months before Buchanan's trial that appellants were violating the law by withholding the rifle stock. Based on their research of case law, the Constitution, Pennsylvania statutes and the Pennsylvania Code of Professional Responsibility, appellants repeatedly told Weidner that the weapon was protected by the attorney-client privilege and that Weidner and appellants had a legal duty to preserve Buchanan's confidential communications which led to discovery of the weapon.

On the fourth day of Buchanan's murder trial, during an in-camera hearing, the prosecutor questioned Weidner about the rifle stock. Appellants objected on the ground that an answer would violate the attorney-client privilege. The trial judge overruled the objection, holding the privilege inapplicable to physical evidence, and ordered Weidner to answer. After Weidner testified how he had located and retrieved the rifle stock, the judge ordered its production, and appellants brought it from their office. The stock was not entered into evidence during Buchanan's trial by the prosecution or by the defense.

After Buchanan's conviction, the prosecutor, District Attorney Leber, charged appellants with hindering prosecution and tampering with evidence for withholding the rifle stock. Due to Leber's role as a prospective witness against appellants, a prosecutor was appointed by the state attorney general's office.

At appellants' trial, the primary witnesses for the Commonwealth were Buchanan, Leber and Weidner. Due to Buchanan's invocation of his fifth amendment privilege while his conviction was on direct appeal, the trial court allowed the transcript of Buchanan's testimony in his murder trial to be read into evidence against appellants to establish the evidentiary nature of the rifle stock in question. Leber testified concerning its concealment, its production, and the effect on the prosecution of Buchanan. Weidner testified about discovery and seizure of the evidence as well as appellants' acts and statements regarding continuing retention of the weapon after its discovery.

Appellants in turn testified about the various authorities which allegedly justified their belief that they were obligated to retain the rifle stock to protect their client. They attempted to offer the expert testimony of law professor John Burkoff to establish a justification defense based on the ethical standards applicable to attorney conduct. The trial judge did not permit Burkoff to testify, nor did he instruct the jury on the defense of justification.

Following conviction and sentencing, this appeal was filed. Appellants argue four issues. First, they challenge the trial court's interpretation of the statutes as requiring production of the physical evidence without a court order. Second, they argue they were denied due process of law in that the hindering prosecution and evidence tampering statutes are unconstitutionally vague or overbroad as applied to defense attorneys when literal compliance would require them to violate their statutory, ethical and constitutional duties to their clients.

Third, they claim the trial court erred in refusing to permit presentation of a justification defense. Fourth, they argue that the trial court committed reversible error [in failing to sustain a number of appellants' objections]. . . .

① **Duty to Deliver** — *See top pg 44 for RoL*

Appellants' first argument is that they had no duty to turn over the rifle stock to the prosecutor until ordered to do so by the court. We reject this argument. Although we have no Pennsylvania cases on point, the decisions in other jurisdictions appear to be virtually unanimous in requiring a criminal defense attorney to deliver physical evidence in his possession to the prosecution without court order. It is true that most of the cases arose in the context of appeals from criminal convictions challenging the effectiveness of counsel who had turned over physical evidence, or in the context of litigation of discovery orders or in the context of contempt proceedings against attorneys who failed to produce evidence. The sole case in which an attorney was charged with a criminal offense resulted in the only holding that the concealed evidence was protected by the attorney-client privilege. We join the overwhelming majority of states which hold that physical evidence of crime in the possession of a criminal defense attorney is not *RoL* subject to a privilege but must be delivered to the prosecution.

precedent — most cases deal w/ π appeal for poor Representation.

Analysis Turning to the law in other jurisdictions, we note the much-quoted case of State v. Olwell, 64 Wash.2d 828, 394 P.2d 681 (1964). A criminal defense attorney had been held in contempt of court following his refusal to answer questions or produce weapons at a coroner's inquest, in defiance of a subpoena duces tecum. [The subpoena sought production of the defendant's weapon, a knife.] The appellate court reversed the finding of contempt, holding that the subpoena was defective on its face for invading the confidential relationship between attorney and client so that refusal to testify against the client was not contemptuous. Id. at 833, 394 P.2d 681. The court went on to state that the attorney was required to produce the weapon on his own motion, and that the jury was not to learn the source of the evidence.

ORDER to produce violate Confidentiality. But atty must do so on his own motion

We do not, however, by so holding, mean to imply that evidence can be permanently withheld by the attorney under the claim of the attorney-client privilege. Here, we must consider the balancing process between the attorney-client privilege and the public interest in criminal investigation. We are in agreement *balance* that the attorney-client privilege is applicable to the knife held by appellant, but do not agree that the privilege warrants the attorney, as an officer of the court, from withholding it after being properly requested to produce the same. The attorney should not be a depository for criminal evidence (such as a knife, other weapons, stolen property, etc.), which in itself has little, if any, material value for the purposes of aiding counsel in the preparation of the defense of his client's case. Such evidence given the attorney during legal consultation for information purposes and used by the attorney in preparing the defense of his client's case whether or not the case ever goes to trial, could clearly be withheld for a reasonable period of time. It follows that the attorney, after a reasonable period, should, as an officer of the court, on his own motion turn the same over to the prosecution.

Could ≠ hold for reasonable time.

We think the attorney-client privilege should and can be preserved even though the attorney surrenders the evidence he has in his possession. The prosecution, upon receipt of such evidence from an attorney, where charge against the attorney's client is contemplated (presently or in the future), should be well aware of the existence of the attorney-client privilege. Therefore, the state when attempting to introduce such evidence at the trial, should take extreme precautions to make certain that the source of the evidence is not disclosed in the presence of the jury and prejudicial error is not committed. By thus allowing the prosecution to recover such evidence, the public interest is served, and by refusing the prosecution an opportunity to disclose the source of the evidence, the client's privilege is preserved and a balance is reached between these conflicting interests.

Because of atty/π, priv., can't disclose source to Jury or = prejudicial Error. —

Balance

Id. at 833–34, 394 P.2d 681. We have quoted at length from *Olwell* because most of the cases which follow cite or quote it and raise the same issues addressed in the above passage.

People v. Meredith, 29 Cal.3d 682, 175 Cal.Rptr. 612, 631 P.2d 46 (1981), reached similar conclusions. A murder defendant told his attorney where he had abandoned physical evidence of the crime [the wallet of the murder victim, which the defendant had taken from the victim, attempted to burn, and left in a burn barrel behind his residence]. The attorney's investigator retrieved the evidence, the attorney examined it and then turned it over to the police, and the evidence was admitted at trial along with testimony of the investigator describing the location of the evidence. On appeal from his conviction, the defendant conceded the admissibility of the physical evidence, but challenged the admissibility of the testimony regarding its location. The court held that the testimony did not violate the attorney-client privilege. "When defense counsel alters or removes physical evidence, he necessarily deprives the prosecution of the opportunity to observe that evidence in its original condition or location.... To extend the attorney-client privilege to a case in which the defense removed evidence might encourage defense counsel to race the police to seize critical evidence." Id. 175 Cal.Rptr. at 612, 631 P.2d at 46.

testimony Re: location ↓ No Atty/π priv. violation.

In People v. Lee, 83 Cal.Rptr. 715, 3 Cal.App.3d 514 (1970), the court also concluded that physical evidence in the possession of an attorney was not privileged [shoes stained with the victim's blood delivered to the defense lawyer by the client's wife]....

Morrell v. State, 575 P.2d 1200 (Alaska Supreme Ct.1978), is another direct appeal from a criminal conviction raising the issue of ineffectiveness of trial counsel following his delivery of incriminating physical evidence to the police [a kidnapping plan prepared by the defendant in advance of the crime]. A third party had discovered the evidence and brought it to the attorney. Unsure of his duties, he sought guidance from the ethics committee of the state bar association. The committee advised him to return the evidence to the finder, explaining the laws pertaining to concealment of evidence. Counsel did so, and assisted the third party in delivering the evidence to the police. The court held that counsel was not ineffective, stating:

> As [appellant] notes, authority in this area is surprisingly sparse. The existing authority seems to indicate, however, that a criminal defense attorney has an obligation to turn over to the prosecution physical evidence which comes into his possession, especially where the evidence comes into the attorney's possession through acts of a third party who is neither a client of the attorney nor an agent of a client. After turning over such evidence, an attorney may have either a right or a duty to remain silent as to the circumstances under which he obtained such evidence. . . .

Id. at 1207. After reviewing cases involving duties of attorneys in possession of incriminating physical evidence, the court summarized their holdings

> From the foregoing cases emerges the rule that a criminal defense attorney must turn over to the prosecution real evidence that the attorney obtains from his client. Further, if the evidence is obtained from a non-client third party who is not acting for the client, then the privilege to refuse to testify concerning the manner in which the evidence was obtained is inapplicable.

Id. at 1210.

Another case in which defense counsel, who had received physical evidence incriminating his client from a third party, sought the advice of the state bar association ethics committee is Hitch v. Pima County Superior Court, 146 Ariz. 588, 708 P.2d 72 (Supreme Ct.1985). The committee's opinion advised him he had a legal obligation to deliver the evidence to the prosecution. He informed the court of the evidence and the ethics committee opinion, whereupon the court ordered him to turn over the evidence and to withdraw from the case. His client, prior to trial, appealed that order.

The Arizona Supreme Court, referring to "Ethical Standard to Guide [A Lawyer] Who Receives Physical Evidence Implicating His Client in Criminal Conduct," proposed by the Ethics Committee of the Criminal Justice Section of the American Bar Association, 29 Crim. L.Rptr. 2465–66 (August 26, 1981), held that the attorney might return the evidence to its source if he could do so without destroying the evidence, or he must turn it over to the prosecution. Counsel's reasonable belief that the third-party source, a friend of the client, might cause destruction or concealment of the evidence necessitated its delivery to the prosecution. The court also rejected the procedure utilized in the District of Columbia whereby such evidence is given to the local bar association for subsequent delivery to the prosecutor. The court believed that such anonymous transmittal would frequently destroy the evidentiary significance of the physical item, which often depends upon where and under what circumstances it was found. Citing People v. Nash, 110 Mich.App. 428, 447, 313 N.W.2d 307, 314 (1981), the court stated that "it is simpler and more direct for defendant's attorney to turn the matter over to the state as long as it is understood that the prosecutor may not mention in front of the jury the fact that the evidence came from the defendant or his attorney." *Hitch,* supra, 708 P.2d at 79. Finding no dereliction in the attorney's representation of his client, the court held that he need not withdraw unless "the client [believes] his attorney no longer has his best interest in mind." Id.

Cannot Anonymously Deliver.

The only case we have found involving criminal prosecution of an attorney for failure to deliver physical evidence is People v. Belge, 83 Misc.2d 186, 372 N.Y.S.2d 798 (1975). Representing a murder defendant and relying on an insanity defense, counsel investigated his client's claim that he had committed other murders and discovered one of the bodies hidden in a cemetery. He left the body *in situ* and did not reveal his discovery until his client's trial. After the murder trial, counsel was indicted for the offenses of failure to assure that a decent burial be accorded the dead and failure to report to authorities the death of a person without medical attendance. Not surprisingly,

On-point prosecution of an atty

> Public indignation reached the fever pitch.... A hue and cry went up from the press and other news media.... However, the [Constitution] attempts to preserve the dignity of the individual and to do that guarantees him the services of an attorney who will bring to the bar and to the bench every conceivable protection from the inroads of the state against such rights as are vested in the [C]onstitution for one accused of crime. Among those substantial constitutional rights is that a defendant does not have to incriminate himself. His attorneys were bound to uphold that concept and [to] maintain what has been called a sacred trust of confidentiality.

dismissed

372 N.Y.S.2d at 801–02. The court held that counsel had "conducted himself as an officer of this Court with all the zeal at his command to protect the constitutional rights of his client," id. at 803, and dismissed the indictment.

The court did state, however, that the attorney's conduct in balancing his client's rights against the public interest in the administration of justice was, "in a sense, obstruction of justice." The court believed the grand jury was "grasping at straws," and that if instead of charging the attorney with violation of a "pseudo-criminal statute," it had charged him with obstruction of justice under a proper statute, the court would have been faced with a much more difficult decision. Id.

may have convicted under obstruction of justice

With the exception of *Belge,* id., the foregoing cases provide a consistent body of law, which we adopt. To summarize, a criminal

RoL defense attorney in possession of physical evidence incriminating his client may, after a reasonable time for examination, return it to its source if he can do so without hindering the apprehension, prosecution, conviction or punishment of another and without altering, destroying or concealing it or impairing its verity or availability in any pending or imminent investigation or proceeding. Otherwise, he must deliver it to the prosecution on his own motion. In the latter event, the prosecution is entitled to use the physical evidence as well as information pertaining to its condition, location and discovery but may not disclose to a fact-finder the source of the evidence. We thus reject appellants' contention that their conduct was proper and that they had no duty to deliver the rifle stock to the prosecution until they were ordered to do so.

(2) **Due Process: Overbreadth** *pitting atty Duties to π's against Statutory Constraints*

Appellants' second argument is that the statutes against hindering prosecution and tampering with evidence are unconstitutionally vague or overbroad as applied to attorneys engaged in the representation of criminal defendants, and hence their enforcement against appellants was a denial of due process. We agree. Our discussion of appellants' first argument, while holding that defense attorneys have an affirmative duty to deliver physical evidence to the prosecution, clearly demonstrates that there are conflicting concerns facing defense attorneys in possession of incriminating physical evidence. Moreover, we are not aware of *any* case in *any* state in which an attorney was convicted of a crime for conduct similar to that of appellants....

denial of Due process ① Both overbroad and vague statutes deny due process in two ways: they do not give fair notice to people of ordinary intelligence that their contemplated activity may be unlawful, and ② they do not set reasonably clear guidelines for law enforcement officials and courts, thus inviting arbitrary and discriminatory enforcement....

Analysis We hold that the statutes at issue in this case are overbroad when applied to attorneys representing criminal defendants. The literal language of each section is relatively clear. Section 5105(a)(3) states that a person is guilty of hindering prosecution "if, with intent to hinder the ... conviction ... of another for crime, he ... conceals ... evidence of the crime ... regardless of its admissibility in evidence...." Section 4910 provides that a person is guilty of tampering with physical evidence "if, believing that an official proceeding ... is pending ..., he ... conceals or removes any record, document or thing with intent to impair its verity or availability in such proceeding...." The clarity of the language is delusive, for it prohibits conduct which cannot constitutionally be prohibited along with conduct which clearly can. In certain circumstances, an attorney might conceal evidence with the intent of impairing its availability in his client's criminal trial and with the intent of hindering his client's conviction.

An example of such circumstances might involve an attorney whose client gives him a handwritten account of involvement in the crime he is charged with committing. If the attorney were to destroy the statement or retain it in his file, he would be guilty of violating the literal terms of the statutes against hindering prosecution and tampering with evidence. Yet no one would suggest the attorney should give the document to the prosecutor; indeed, to do so would be an egregious violation of the attorney's duties to his client.

The functions of the attorney counseling a criminal defendant have a constitutional dimension. In opposing unreasonable searches and seizures, in preventing self-incrimination and in rendering effective assistance of counsel, the defense attorney is charged with the protection of fourth, fifth and sixth amendment rights. In performing these functions, the defense attorney might run afoul of the statutes against hindering prosecution and tampering with evidence; thus he may not have adequate notice of what conduct might be a crime, and he is subject to the threat of arbitrary and discriminatory prosecution.

Beyond the obvious example stated above, there is little or no guidance for an attorney to know when he has crossed the invisible line into an area of criminal behavior. There are no prior cases in this jurisdiction in which a criminal defense attorney has been convicted of violating these statutes. We have discussed many of the similar cases from other jurisdictions, none of which addresses the precise issues facing us in this case. Although we focused on the uniformity we found in those cases as to disposition of physical evidence, they express a great deal of doubt and reflect great diversity as to the grayer areas of ethical usage of evidence of all sorts. Attorneys face a distressing paucity of dispositive precedent to guide them in balancing their duty of zealous representation against their duty as officers of the court. Volumes are filled with other potential sources of guidance, such as ethical codes and comments thereto, both proposed and adopted, advisory opinions by ethics committees and myriad articles in legal periodicals. The plethora of writings exemplifies the profession's concern with the problem, and although they may help to clarify some of the issues, they fail to answer many of the difficult questions in this area of legal practice.

In the cases discussed in the preceding section, we find many statements which belie the seeming consistency in their approach to the problem. *People v. Belge*, supra, of course, dismissing the indictment against an attorney who had withheld evidence, focused on the rights of a criminal defendant rather than the society's interest in criminal law enforcement:

> A trial is in part a search for truth, but it is only partly a search for truth. The mantle of innocence is flung over the defendant to such an extent that he is safeguarded by rules of evidence which frequently keep out absolute truth, much to the chagrin of juries. Nevertheless, this has been a part of our system since our laws were taken from the laws of England and over these

many years has been found to best protect a balance between the rights of the individual and the rights of society.

Belge, supra, 372 N.Y.S.2d at 801. Another example is *In re Gartley,* supra, wherein this court stated:

> Not only is effective assistance of counsel a constitutional mandate, it is also necessary to an adversary system of justice. Assuredly, counsel's assistance can be made safely and readily available only when the client is free from the apprehension of disclosure.

> . . .

Finally, *Hitch v. Pima County Superior Court,* supra, although holding that an attorney has a duty to deliver incriminating evidence to the prosecutor, added:

> We note also that the lawyer's role as a zealous advocate is an important one, not only for the client but for the administration of justice. We have chosen an adversary system of justice in which, in theory, the state and the defendant meet as equals—"strength against strength, resource against resource, argument against argument." United States v. Bagley, [473 U.S. 667, 694] n. 2 (1985) (Marshall, J., dissenting). In order to close the gap between theory and practice and thereby ensure that the system is working properly, a defendant must have an attorney who will fight against the powerful resources of the state. It is only when this occurs that we can be assured that the system is functioning properly and only the guilty are convicted.

Hitch, supra, 708 P.2d at 76.

Two cases cited in the previous section involved attorneys who had sought advisory opinions from ethics committees when confronted with problems related to disposition of physical evidence. Their action was salutary, but underscores the dilemma facing criminal defense attorneys in similar situations. Not only is the resort to guidance from an ethics committee a time-consuming process,[2] it is a process totally inconsistent with the precision which must attend a valid criminal statute to inform its subjects of what specific behavior is proscribed.

Another symbol of the dilemma is its extensive treatment in legal periodicals. Of the many articles which have been cited by the parties in this case, we have found several to be helpful and noteworthy.[3]

2. The court in *Hitch,* supra, explained the result of seeking advice in that case:

We note that the prosecution in this matter has been delayed for over a year while this issue is being resolved. We believe that the recourse to the State Bar Ethics Committee, while proper and commendable, resulted in an excessive delay. We hope that in the future the State Bar Ethics Committee will be more prompt in responding to requests for opinions when, as here, a criminal prosecution is held in abeyance awaiting the opinion of the Committee.

Id. 708 P.2d at 79 n. 3.

3. See Comment, Ethics, Law and Loyalty: The Attorney's Duty to Turn Over Incriminating Physical Evidence, 32 Stan.L.Rev. 977 (1980); Comment, The Right of a Criminal Defense Attorney to Withhold Physical Evidence Received from His Client, 38

Nonetheless, the writings exemplify a variety of approaches and suggestions, and indicate that an evidentiary problem related to incriminating evidence might arise in divers contexts in the representation of criminal defendants. It is not incumbent upon attorneys to digest the legal periodicals in order to conform their conduct to a criminal statute. The statutes involved in this case embrace conduct which is constitutionally protected as well as conduct which may validly be prohibited, and there is no line between the two which can be ascertained with any assurance whatsoever.

Even if it were possible, it is not the function of this court to provide an advisory opinion as to various examples of attorney conduct not involved in this case which might or might not violate the statutes we are reviewing. We note that other jurisdictions have enacted criminal statutes which address the unique role of defense attorneys in the administration of criminal justice and do not subject them to rules identical with those applicable to the public. *See* Clark v. State, 159 Tex.Cr.R. 187, 261 S.W.2d 339 (1953) (statute specifically excluded from liability one who aids an offender in preparing his defense). We note, also, as the Pennsylvania Supreme Court iterated in *Estate of Pedrick*, that the courts have the power, outside the context of criminal sanctions, to regulate the conduct of attorneys practicing before them, and that the Pennsylvania Supreme Court has established a Disciplinary Board together with comprehensive rules for dealing with apparent attorney misconduct. 505 Pa. [530,] 542, 482 A.2d [215,] 221.

For these reasons, we hold that the statutes which prohibit hindering prosecution and tampering with physical evidence are unconstitutionally overbroad when applied to attorneys representing criminal defendants.

Accordingly, the judgments of sentence are vacated and appellants discharged.

Did the Lawyers in *Stenhach* Commit a Crime?

The court in *Stenhach* rejects the argument that the lawyers had no duty to turn over the evidence. The court not only "adopts" the rule of other jurisdictions that a lawyer has a responsibility under the ethics rules to turn over incriminating physical evidence, but speaks as though this duty were in force when the lawyers in this case acted. Why is the court confident that lawyers can observe the line between ethical and unethical conduct but not between criminal and legal conduct? Why isn't the court concerned about the potential "chilling effect" of the disciplinary rules?

The lawyers claimed that they had conducted exhaustive research and concluded they were "obligated" to retain the rifle stock. Howev-

U.Chi.L.Rev. 211 (1970); Comment, Disclosure of Incriminating Physical Evidence: The Defense Attorney's Dilemma, 52 U.Colo.L.Rev. 419 (1981).

er, as the court's review of the case law shows, all the decided cases, with the exception of *Belge*,[39] had held that there was a duty to turn over such evidence. Does *Belge* support the Stenhachs' claim of immunity? Despite the consistency of court decisions in this area, lawyers have long been confused about their duties as to incriminating physical evidence. A Virginia lawyer was disciplined by a federal court in In re Ryder,[40] a seminal case, for removing from his client's safe deposit box a sawed-off shot gun and the proceeds of a bank robbery and placing those items in a safe deposit box under the lawyer's own name. Ryder had consulted with several other lawyers, including a former judge, as to what he should do with the evidence. All those consulted were uncertain, but none recommended the "correct" course of conduct, i.e., turning the evidence over to law enforcement officials. Neither did any suggest that Ryder might be criminally liable as an accomplice for retaining and concealing money stolen from the bank. The confusion might be attributed to the fact that *Ryder* was one of the first opinions decided on this question, but this fact does not explain why no one considered the stolen-property statute as even potentially applicable.

This failure to consider general criminal statutes may be due to the assumption that lawyers are immune from laws of general applicability, but even so *Ryder* does not explain the continuing confusion of lawyers like the Stenhach brothers. In 1980 a commentator wrote:

> The attorney [in possession of incriminating physical evidence] has little guidance on how to resolve [her conflicting responsibilities as an officer of the court and as an advocate of the client]. Neither the attorney-client privilege nor ethical rules nor statutes nor constitutional doctrines give a clear signal to the attorney seeking both to maintain loyalty to her client and to be properly candid with the court. The attorney in possession of incriminating physical evidence confronts a series of rules most of which indicate the importance of the value of loyalty to the client but none of which quite provides the loyal attorney with a *safe harbor* from discipline or criminal penalties.[41]

Recent articles continue to bemoan the confusion in this area.[42] The confusion may have less to do with conflicting legal standards, however, than with a perceived conflict between what the law actually requires and what lawyers believe to be their duty, i.e., not to harm or betray their clients.

Spaulding v. Zimmerman, supra, assumes that a lawyer has no duty to disclose adverse evidence to the opposing party in the absence of

39. See the discussion of the *Dead Bodies Case*, p. 53 below.

40. 263 F.Supp. 360 (E.D.Va.1967), aff'd, 381 F.2d 713 (4th Cir.1967).

41. Note, Ethics, Law, and Loyalty: The Attorney's Duty to Turn Over Incriminating Physical Evidence, 32 Stan.L.Rev. 977, 980 (1980) (emphasis added).

42. See, e.g., Norman Lefstein, Incriminating Physical Evidence, The Defense Attorney's Dilemma, and the Need for Rules, 64 N.C.L.Rev. 897 (1986).

a proper request.   Why is a different approach applied to physical evidence of crime?

3. Lawyers and Incriminating Evidence

Ethics Rules   *Rule BK., pg. 420*

DR 7–102(A)(3) of the Model Code provides that "a lawyer shall not conceal or knowingly fail to disclose that which he is required by law to reveal"; and DR 7–109(A) states, "A lawyer shall not suppress any evidence that he or his client has a legal obligation to reveal or produce."   Finally, DR 7–102(A)(8) directs that "a lawyer shall not knowingly engage in other illegal conduct or conduct contrary to a Disciplinary Rule."   Thus, the Model Code takes the clear position that on this issue, as on all others under DR 7–102(A)(8), other law trumps the general duty of loyalty to the client.

Can't act unlawfully

The Model Rules follow the Model Code with respect to incriminating evidence.   M.R. 3.4(a) states, "A lawyer shall not *unlawfully* obstruct another party's access to evidence, or *unlawfully* alter, destroy or conceal a document or other material having potential evidentiary value.   A lawyer shall not counsel or assist another person to do any such act."   (Emphasis added.)   M.R. 1.2(d) and M.R. 8.4(a) and (b), which prohibit lawyer conduct that is "criminal or fraudulent," also subject lawyers to general criminal law.

The question then is: What does law require?

First, criminal laws in all jurisdictions make the concealment or destruction of evidence criminal although the circumstances that trigger the statutes vary from one state to another.   Some states prohibit destruction only when a person "knows" a legal proceeding is ongoing or about to be instituted; other states prohibit destruction when a person "believes" a proceeding is pending or about to be instituted; and still other states prohibit destruction with intent to prevent the production of the evidence.[43]   Few of these statutes make exception for lawyers.   But see Clark v. State,[44] holding that the Texas concealment statute contains an implied exclusion for lawyers, and the approval of this approach in *Stenhach*.

when is an act by an atty un-lawful?

Contraband statutes, which make the possession of certain items illegal, exist in all jurisdictions and make no exceptions for criminal defense lawyers.[45]   Prohibited items generally include instrumentalities

Contraband Statutes = unlawful

43. See, e.g., Model Penal Code § 242.3 (1962); 18 U.S.C. § 1000; West's Ann.Cal.Pen. Code § 135; Minn.Stat.Ann. § 609.63(1), (7); N.Y.—McKinney's Penal Law § 205.50.

44. 159 Tex.Crim. 187, 261 S.W.2d 339 (1953).

45. At least one commentator has suggested that the contraband statutes be amended to provide an exception for lawyers. Note, Ethics, Law, and Loyalty: The Attorney's Duty to Turn Over Incriminating Physical Evidence, 32 Stan.L.Rev. 977, 995 (1980). This commentator also suggests an exception for lawyers under the concealment and destruction of evidence statutes, arguing that a lawyer's duty of loyalty to a client should preclude having to provide the prosecution with physical evidence.

of crime (such as a murder weapon), illegal weapons and drugs and other controlled substances.[46]

Judicial decisions, as pointed out in *Stenhach*, are unanimous in holding that the ethics rules, read in conjunction with the concealment and contraband laws, require a lawyer to deliver physical evidence when those laws would be violated by retaining the evidence. There is some question, as *Stenhach* demonstrates, whether courts will uphold the use of criminal sanctions against criminal defense lawyers whose conduct violates these laws, but none that lawyers may be disciplined for such conduct under the ethics rules. But see *Stenhach II*, discussed below.

Case Law on a Lawyer's Obligations as to Incriminating Evidence [47]

Generally, a lawyer must not act or assist in the destruction or unlawful concealment of evidence.[48] This means that a lawyer must not take affirmative steps to conceal evidence, such as those taken by the lawyers in *Stenhach*.[49] If a lawyer leaves evidence where she finds it, she cannot be compelled to reveal information gained from a privileged communication. However, once physical evidence [50] is taken from its original resting place, the lawyer must not do anything that would conceal or destroy either the evidence itself or evidence of its location or condition.

Once a lawyer possesses physical evidence, she must not return that evidence to its source (whether the client or a third person) if she has reason to believe that the evidence will be destroyed or unlawfully concealed or that the chain of evidence will be broken. In light of the risk of subsequent destruction or concealment, the majority of jurisdictions require the lawyer to hand over to the proper authorities *all* physical evidence.[51]

---

46. See, e.g., Model Pen.Code § 5.06–.07 (1962) (possession of criminal instruments and weapons); West's Ann.Cal.Pen.Code § 12020 (Supp.1980) (possession of illegal weapons); West's Ann.Cal.Health & Safety Code § 11377 (Supp.1980) (possession of drugs and controlled substances); Uniform Controlled Substances Act § 401(c).

47. The lawyer's responsibilities as to evidence in civil cases are discussed in Chapter 5 below at pp. 381–84 (false evidence) and 455 (improper means).

48. The word "unlawful" distinguishes what might be called "lawful concealment", i.e., the legal steps an attorney may take to suppress evidence inadmissible under evidence rules or obtained through a violation of the client's constitutional rights or the legal steps a lawyer may take to prevent the opposing party in a civil case from gaining access to privileged material.

49. See, e.g., Hitch v. Pima County Court, 146 Ariz. 588, 708 P.2d 72 (1985); People v. Meredith, 29 Cal.3d 682, 175 Cal.Rptr. 612, 631 P.2d 46 (1981).

50. Throughout this discussion we are speaking of *physical* evidence. A bright line exists between the lawyer's possession of physical evidence and her knowledge of testimonial evidence. The lawyer has a duty to keep the testimonial evidence of past criminal activity confidential.

51. See, e.g., State ex rel. Sowers v. Olwell, 64 Wash.2d 828, 394 P.2d 681 (1964); People v. Lee, 3 Cal.App.3d 514, 83 Cal.Rptr. 715 (1970); Morrell v. State, 575 P.2d 1200 (Alaska 1978).

[handwritten margin notes: 2 Caveats, to handing over physical evidence. 1 = Lawful Concealment]

Two caveats limit this rule. The first concerns evidence created as part of a defense, such as a statement by a defendant prepared for his lawyer on what the defendant knew about the bank's security system. Such evidence falls under the protective umbrella of the attorney-client privilege and thus need not be turned over to authorities as physical evidence. The fact that certain communications between client and lawyer are in physical form does not change their privileged status. If the client prepared a written statement for some purpose other than assisting in the defense, e.g., the client kept a journal of her criminal activities as they took place, the document qualifies as physical evidence and is not protected by the attorney-client privilege. In Morrell v. State,[52] where a third party gave the defense lawyer kidnap plans written out by the defendant, the court held that the lawyer acted properly in returning the plans to the third party and advising him to turn them over to the police.[53]

The second caveat involves evidence that the state could not compel a defendant to produce against his will. If a personal diary, for example, is constitutionally protected against compulsory production by an accused, the protection continues once possession is transferred to the accused's lawyer.[54] Some earlier cases, including *Ryder*, extended protection to "merely evidentiary articles" that are not contraband or the fruits or instrumentalities of crime. The Supreme Court's later repudiation of the "mere evidence" rule narrowed sharply the category of protected physical evidence, whether retained by the client or given to the client's lawyer.[55]

Even if a lawyer must eventually turn over all physical evidence, courts allow the lawyer to retain the evidence for a "reasonable" period of time for investigatory purposes. As long as the defense then stipulates to the "chain of possession, location or condition of the evidence," the prosecution may not disclose to the jury from whom or in what manner the evidence was obtained.[56] Requiring the defense to stipulate to the evidence's original location and source prevents the defendant from "destroying" the evidence by negating its probative value. On the other hand, restricting the prosecution's disclosure of the source of the evidence protects a privileged communication—the client's statement to the lawyer of the source or location of the evidence. The physical evidence itself is not privileged. As the court in People v. Meredith said:

[handwritten margin notes: Reasonable period; source = privileged]

> To bar admission of testimony concerning the original condition and location of the evidence ... permits the defense to "destroy"

52. 575 P.2d 1200 (Alaska 1978).

53. Accord: State v. Carlin, 7 Kan.App.2d 219, 640 P.2d 324 (1982) (lawyer ordered to surrender an incriminating tape recording made by the client).

54. See, e.g., State v. Superior Court, 128 Ariz. 253, 625 P.2d 316 (1981).

55. Warden v. Hayden, 387 U.S. 294, 306–307 (1967), repudiated the "mere evidence" rule. See the discussion of fourth amendment protection of diaries or letters in Chapter 4 below at p. 254.

56. People v. Meredith, supra, 631 P.2d at 54; see also *Olwell*, supra.

critical information; it is as if . . . the wallet in this case bore a tag bearing the words "located in the trash can by Scott's residence," and the defense by taking the wallet, destroyed this tag.[57]

The District of Columbia version of the Model Rules provides that a lawyer shall not counsel or assist concealment or destruction of evidence "if the lawyer reasonably should know that the evidence is or may be the subject of discovery or subpoena in any pending or imminent proceeding."[58] The comments to the D.C. rules, which include a detailed summary of federal and D.C. criminal provisions relating to physical evidence, rely on a D.C. ethics opinion stating that the "test is whether destruction of [a] document is directed at concrete litigation that is either pending or almost certain to be filed":

> Because of the duty of confidentiality under Rule 1.6, the lawyer is generally forbidden to volunteer information about physical evidence received from a client without the client's consent after consultation.[59]

The D.C. Rules also contain a unique procedure:

> In some cases, the Office of Bar Counsel will accept physical evidence from a lawyer and then turn it over to the appropriate persons; in those cases this procedure is usually the best means of delivering evidence to the proper authorities without disclosing the client's confidences.[60]

Other courts have rejected this procedure because it may result in erasing the chain of evidence so completely as to render the evidence meaningless: [61]

> Not all items have evidentiary significance in and of themselves. In this case, for instance, the watch is not inculpatory per se; rather, it is the fact that the [victim's] watch was found in defendant's jacket that makes the watch material evidence. By returning the watch anonymously to the police, this significance is lost. Assuming investigating officials are even able to determine to what case the evidence belongs, they may never be able to reconstruct where it was originally discovered or under what circumstances.[62]

Do the rules change when a lawyer obtains the evidence from a third person rather than from a client? When the source is the client or the client's agent, the attorney-client privilege usually prevents the prosecution from compelling the lawyer to testify as to the origin of the

57. 631 P.2d at 53.

58. D.C. Rules of Professional Conduct, Rule 3.4(a) (adopted March 1, 1990 by the D.C. Court of Appeals). The rules are reprinted in Thomas D. Morgan and Ronald D. Rotunda, 1994 Selected Standards on Professional Responsibility.

59. D.C. Rules of Professional Conduct, Comment [5] to Rule 34.

60. Id.

61. Hitch v. Pima County, 146 Ariz. 588, 708 P.2d 72 (1985).

62. 708 P.2d at 78–79.

evidence as long as the defense makes an appropriate stipulation as to the evidence's original location and condition. When the source is a third person, however, the courts hold that the privilege no longer applies. See, e.g., *Olwell*, supra.

Given the case law, how could the lawyers in *Stenhach* have conducted extensive research, as they testified they did, and still have reached the conclusion they did? Apparently they approached their research with the goal of building a legal argument to justify retention of the rifle stock. What question might they have asked instead?

The *Dead Bodies* Case [63]

This case has gained a special place in the annals of legal ethics. A murder defendant, Robert Garrow, confessed to his lawyers, Belge and Armani, that he had committed the crime charged, as well as three other murders. The police had not yet discovered the bodies of two of those victims. Following Garrow's directions, the two lawyers found the bodies of Alicia Hauk, a 16–year–old high school student, and Susan Petz, a 21–year–old Boston University journalism student. Petz had disappeared after going camping in the Adirondacks with Dan Porter, a third murder victim whose body the police had already discovered. Hauk had disappeared a month before Petz and Porter. The lawyers photographed the two women's bodies but told no one of their discovery.

Petz's parents, knowing that police suspected Garrow of the murder of their daughter's camping partner, feared that she too was dead. They pleaded with Garrow's lawyers, Belge and Armani, for knowledge about their daughter, but the lawyers remained silent. Six months later, Garrow testified at his trial about the Hauk and Petz murders as part of an ultimately unsuccessful insanity defense. At a press conference Belge and Armani acknowledged they had known the location of the two women's bodies for many months but had remained silent. The lawyers, however, had offered to help the police solve the Petz and Hauk cases in exchange for a plea bargain promise that Garrow would be committed to a mental hospital, an offer the prosecutor had rejected.

Community outrage over the case resulted in criminal charges against one of the lawyers, Belge, for violating a New York law that requires a decent burial for the dead and the reporting of any death that occurs without medical attention. The trial court granted a motion to dismiss based on attorney-client privilege. The appeals' court affirmed, holding that the privilege "effectively shielded the defendant attorney from his actions which would otherwise have violated the Public Health Law." The court, however, expressed its "serious concern" with the argument that the privilege is absolute: "We believe that an attorney must protect his client's interests, but also must observe basic human standards of decency, having due regard to the

---

63. People v. Belge, 50 A.D.2d 1088, 376 N.Y.S.2d 771 (4th Dept.1975), aff'd, 41 N.Y.2d 60, 390 N.Y.S.2d 867, 359 N.E.2d 377 (1976). The facts stated in the text are drawn from the reported opinions and from Tom Alibrandi with Frank H. Armani, Privileged Information (1984).

need that the legal system accord justice to the interests of society and its individual members." [64]   After the appellate court's decision, the Committee on Professional Ethics of the New York State Bar Association issued an opinion stating that the ethical rules required the lawyers' silence. [65]

The court in *Stenhach* notes that *Belge* dismissed a criminal prosecution against a lawyer who had failed to take affirmative steps to disclose physical evidence to law enforcement officials.   *Belge*, however, is distinguishable on other grounds.   The lawyers in that case never had possession of the evidence nor did they conceal or alter the evidence: They looked at the bodies in their original resting places and left them there.

Did the lawyers in *Belge* act immorally?   Would an anonymous tip of the location of the bodies have satisfied professional, legal and moral duties?   Would disclosure have been proper if the uncertainty concerning her daughter had constituted a grave threat to Mrs. Petz's life?

Why Lawyers Are Not Prosecuted for Concealing Evidence

Prosecutors have shown little interest in prosecuting lawyers for violating the evidence or contraband statutes.   Although there may be many reasons for this, including collegial sympathy, the primary reasons include the following: (1) Most of the evidence statutes require proof of "specific" or "willful" intent, e.g., intent to hinder the prosecution, and prosecutors appreciate that defense lawyers will claim to have concealed with intent only to fulfill their professional responsibility; (2) prosecutors tend to exercise their discretion against bringing charges against one who acted without malicious intent or bad faith, even if the statute does not require evil purpose; and (3) prosecutors may share the assumption that lawyers are somehow immune from liability.

Stenhach II

In Office of Disciplinary Counsel v. Stenhach, [66] the Pennsylvania disciplinary board unanimously refused to discipline the Stenhach brothers for their conduct.   The board found that the Stenhachs, who "resolved in favor of their client doubts as to the bounds of law," acted in good faith and were guilty only of "zealous advocacy."   The board's opinion, however, provides little comfort to Pennsylvania lawyers who receive and retain physical evidence of a crime.   At the time the Stenhachs acted, the board emphasized, no Pennsylvania decision had held that physical evidence must be turned over to authorities; but the turnover rule first announced in *Stenhach I* changed the law of Pennsylvania prospectively.   Further, the board observed, the prosecutor, who knew or should have known that the Stenhachs had acquired physical evidence, did not seek to compel its production.   The Sten-

64.   376 N.Y.S.2d 771, 772.

65.   N.Y. State Bar Ass'n Comm. on Prof. Ethics Op. 479 (1978).

66.   No. 479, slip op. at 25–27 (Pa.Supr.Ct.Disciplinary Board Aug. 8, 1989) (*Stenhach II*).

hachs' action did not impair the integrity of the criminal process because the prosecution neither needed nor used the rifle stock as evidence in the case.

Is the rule in Pennsylvania after *Stenhach II* that a lawyer may retain incriminating evidence so long as it is not vital to the prosecution? Since the time that the Stenhach brothers acted, Pennsylvania has adopted a version of the Model Rules that includes a provision substantially similar to M.R. 3.4(a). Does this clarify the rule in Pennsylvania? Does a lawyer in Pennsylvania who retains the murder weapon or any other material evidence that incriminates the client run a serious risk of being disciplined for such conduct? If so, what explains *Stenhach II*?

Should Nixon Have Burned the Tapes?

The Watergate burglary took place on June 17, 1972. Shortly thereafter, criminal investigators discovered evidence indicating that some persons connected with the Nixon administration were implicated. Over a year later, during the course of an investigation conducted by a Senate committee, an aide to President Richard Nixon revealed that tapes existed of all conversations in the president's office. The committee sought to compel production of relevant tapes, but the courts ultimately held the committee's subpoena to be unauthorized by statute.[67] A criminal investigation of Watergate, however, began soon after the Watergate burglary. In April 1974, a special prosecutor, who had taken over the criminal investigation, issued a second subpoena seeking production of the tapes. The Supreme Court upheld the validity of the second subpoena in July 1974 against plausible claims of executive privilege.[68]

Nixon later claimed that he should have destroyed the tapes: "I had bad advice from well-intentioned lawyers who had sort of the cockeyed notion that I would be destroying evidence."[69] Was Nixon given sound advice? At what point, if at all, would destruction of the tapes have violated the federal obstruction of justice statute, infra, p. 69, or the D.C. ethics rule, supra, p. 52? What moral or practical reasons support advice not to destroy the tapes?

Document Retention and Destruction

Lawyers who handle civil matters for white-collar clients are unlikely to encounter dead bodies, sawed-off shotguns or paper bags of $100 bills. They nevertheless encounter serious questions concerning concealment or destruction of physical evidence. For example, a company official might seek advice as to what documents may be "harmful" in a rumored antitrust investigation. A pharmaceutical company might ask whether it may destroy test results that reveal harmful side

---

67. Senate Select Committee v. Nixon, 366 F.Supp. 51 (D.D.C.1973).

68. United States v. Nixon, 418 U.S. 683 (1974). President Nixon resigned on Aug. 9, 1974, only four days after transcripts of the subpoenaed conversations were released.

69. John Herbers, Former Aide Interviews Nixon, N.Y. Times, Apr. 9, 1984, at p. 8.

effects of a drug that the company has marketed. Even if destruction of documents is not a crime, there are practical questions that must be considered. Documents may offer protection against false accusations (e.g., President Nixon might have wanted to retain the tapes because they would protect him against accusations that others implicated in the Watergate coverup might make against him). Destruction has other consequences:

1) 2° Evidence

> The destruction of a document to prevent its use at trial precludes that party from later introducing secondary evidence to prove the document's contents, but does not bar the opposing party from doing so. Moreover, the intentional destruction of a document to prevent its use at trial, even when not illegal, creates an adverse inference that a party's whole case is weak. Finally, any questions asked of a client under oath concerning the destruction must be answered honestly to avoid outright perjury. It is possible that the answers will be as damaging as the actual contents of the destroyed documents.[70]

2) Adverse Inference

3) testimony as to + perjury

70. Note, Legal Ethics and the Destruction of Evidence, 88 Yale L.J. 1665, 1675 (1979). See also John M. Fedders and Lauryn H. Guttenplan, Document Retention and Destruction: Practical, Legal and Ethical Considerations, 56 Notre Dame L. 5 (1980).

Chapter 2

CONFORMITY TO THE LAW

I have been asked many times as regard to particular practices or agreements as to whether they were legal or illegal under the Sherman [antitrust] law. One gentleman said to me: "We do not know where we can go." To which I replied, "I think your lawyers ... can tell you where a fairly safe course lies. If you are walking along a precipice no human being can tell you how near you can go to that precipice without falling over, because you may stumble on a loose stone, you may slip and go over; but anybody can tell you where you can walk perfectly safe within convenient distance of that precipice." The difficulty which men have felt ... has been rather that they wanted to go to the limit rather than that they have wanted to go safely.[1]

Louis D. Brandeis

A. CRIMINAL LAW

1. Fraud and Criminal Complicity

UNITED STATES v. BENJAMIN

United States Court of Appeals, Second Circuit, 1964.
328 F.2d 854.

Before MOORE, FRIENDLY and KAUFMAN, CIRCUIT JUDGES.

FRIENDLY, CIRCUIT JUDGE.

This appeal concerns another of those sickening financial frauds which so sadly memorialize the rapacity of the perpetrators and the gullibility, and perhaps also the cupidity, of the victims. It is unusual in that the vehicle, American Equities Corporation, owned nothing at all—and, in a happier sense, in that the SEC was able to nip the fraud quite early in the bud. The appellants are Milton Mende, the principal promoter, Martin Benjamin, his lawyer, and Bernard Howard, a certified public accountant. After trial in the District Court for the Southern District of New York before Judge Palmieri without a jury, all three were convicted of conspiring willfully by use of interstate commerce to sell unregistered securities and to defraud in the sale of securities, in violation of the Securities Act of 1933, §§ 5(a) and (c), and 17(a), 15 U.S.C. §§ 77e(a) and (c), and 77q(a), sections which are imple-

---

1. Louis D. Brandeis, Hearings before Sen.Comm. on Interstate Commerce, S.Res.No. 98, 62nd Cong., 1st Sess. 1161 (1911), quoted in Harry First, Business Crimes 27 (1990).

mented criminally by § 24 of the Act, 15 U.S.C. § 77x. Mende and Benjamin were convicted also on three substantive counts for using the mails in furtherance of the fraudulent schemes in violation of 18 U.S.C. § 1341. As their sentences on the latter counts were the same as those on the conspiracy count and run concurrently with them, and as we are satisfied that their conspiracy conviction was proper, we need not concern ourselves with the mail fraud counts. Lawn v. United States, 355 U.S. 339, 362 (1958).

Since the principal claim of Howard and Benjamin relates to the sufficiency of the evidence against them, it is necessary to give some description of what went on. The scheme began in December, 1960, when Mende, then in Nevada, arranged to be put in touch with a Reno attorney, McDonald, who was reported to have some "old corporations prior to 1933" for sale. Mende's interest in corporations of such vintage was due to § 3(a)(1) of the Securities Act of 1933, 15 U.S.C. § 77c(a)(1), which confers an exemption from the need for registration on

"Any security which, prior to or within sixty days after May 27, 1933, has been sold or disposed of by the issuer or bona fide offered to the public, but this exemption shall not apply to any new offering of any such security by an issuer or underwriter subsequent to such sixty days."

He was especially attracted by a 1919 shell, then bearing the rather appropriate name of Star Midas Mining Co., Inc. Authorized to issue 1,500,000 shares with a par value of 10¢ per share, Star Midas had approximately 964,000 shares outstanding, nearly all owned by a so-called "Mahoney group." It had no assets. After arranging to purchase the Mahoney holdings for $5,000 plus a $1,500 fee, Mende instructed McDonald to change the corporate name to American Equities Corporation and to increase the authorized capital to $1,500,000 by raising the par value to $1 per share. Before closing the purchase, the funds for which were not yet available, Mende, with McDonald's cooperation, bought stock certificates and a seal reflecting these changes. The purchase was not completed until February 23, 1961, when McDonald, having previously caused appropriate resolutions to be adopted and new officers and directors of Mende's selection to be named, turned over to Reiss and Kovaleski, as Mende's representatives, the books and records of the corporation and stock certificates for the 890,000 shares owned by the selling group. At this time the name of the corporation was changed.

Mende had not waited to acquire the American Equities shares before starting to sell them. In mid-January, 1961, he ordered an additional supply of stock certificates from a Los Angeles printer. By entering a bid to buy shares he arranged for American Equities to appear in the pink and white sheets of the National Quotation Service at a price of something over $5 per share. Robert Drattell, president of Lawrence Securities, Inc., which was inactive because of financial

*Sold + used
As collateral
for loans*

difficulties, testified that Benjamin then sought to interest him in selling shares of a corporation whose alleged assets corresponded with those later shown in statements of American Equities. Benjamin indicated that if Drattell would cooperate, he might be in a position to find some way to make capital available to Lawrence Securities. Later in January, Benjamin had Drattell come to a New York hotel to meet Mende, who told Drattell and Reiter, another broker, in Benjamin's presence, that American Equities "was a holding corporation that had property, various types of property all over the United States, assets of about six and a half million dollars, liabilities of about three million dollars." Mende whetted Drattell's appetite, as Benjamin had already done, by indicating he would help to get Lawrence Securities back on its feet. Drattell said he "would need letters of opinion" and "certified financial statements," and also would need to see the transfer records which, Mende told him, were kept by "a certified public accountant out on the Coast."

Benjamin speedily filled one of Drattell's demands by handing him a signed opinion, dated January 28, 1961, headed "To Whom It May Concern: American Equities Corporation." It recited that the corporation was organized in May, 1919, "and there was at that time issued to the public, 963,067 Shares." It went on to say that in Benjamin's opinion "the aforesaid shares are presently free and tradeable pursuant to" § 3(a)(1) of the Securities Act which it quoted, and reiterated:

> "In view of the foregoing section, and further in view of the fact that the original issuance of the 963,067 Shares in May of 1919, falls directly within Section 3(1) of the Securities Act of 1933, and is therefore, in my opinion, free and tradeable." [sic]

On January 28, Benjamin with Reiter and another broker, Parks, went to Los Angeles. Mende gave 4,000 shares of American Equities to Parks and 20,000 shares to Reiter, and also handed Reiter 5,000 shares to be given to Drattell. The latter used these to obtain from the Empire Trust Company a $12,500 loan, $3,500 of which went to bolstering Lawrence Securities' depleted capital account and the balance to Reiter, Mende and Mende's wife; Drattell sent a confirmation, dated January 31, 1961, of the "purchase" of these 5,000 shares for $9,000 to "Martin Benjamin Trustee." Later, after Drattell had gone to California to view some of the supposed assets of American Equities, he and Benjamin visited the office of Reiss, the transfer agent, where Benjamin prepared two letters. One, signed by Reiss, advised as to the 5,000 shares given to Drattell "that said certificates is free stock and is not investment stock";[1] the second, dated back to January 31, and signed by "Martin Benjamin Trustee," purported to evidence the "sale" of the 5,000 shares for $9,000 and directed the distribution to Reiter and Mrs. Mende that had already been made.

used as loan collateral

---

1. By what Drattell assumed to have been a Freudian slip, the word "not" was originally typed "hot."

Reiter and Parks had also brought from California copies of a paper with a printed cover entitled "American Equities Corporation." This contained an unidentified "Pro Forma Balance Sheet" as of November 30, 1960, in fact prepared by Reiss,[2] and a sheet of descriptive material, a draft of which the judge could reasonably have found to have been written out by Benjamin. The first numbered paragraph of this recited that American Equities was "a diversified investment company formed in the State of Nevada in 1919" and that its holdings consisted of "8 Apartment Houses, 2 Hotels, 2 Office Buildings (all located in Detroit area, Michigan)" with a "gross income from the properties" of $1,061,406.51 and net income of $200,000. This was completely false; the company owned no real estate in Detroit or elsewhere. Three subsequent paragraphs gave facts and figures as to the Outpost Inn, in Arizona, Biesmeyer Boat & Plastic Co., also of Arizona, and Stanford Trailer and Marine Supply Co., of California; the description did not say just what was American Equities' interest in these companies and the only elucidation in the balance sheet was in a note indicating that the price of the Outpost Inn would be $71,000 in cash and a $79,000 note, the former being separately shown as a liability. In fact, no arrangements of any kind had been made as to the Outpost Inn, and the owner of Biesmeyer testified that in December, 1960, he had agreed to give Mende an option for a down payment of $10,000 which was never made; we are not informed as to Stanford Trailer and Marine. Finally the description stated that American Equities "has acquired a working interest of 68% of the California Molded Products," whose 1961 sales were estimated at $2,000,000 with a gross profit margin "in excess of 30.1% with a potential of 32% by April, 1961," and that American Equities was negotiating to acquire still other companies, one "doing in excess of $20,000,000.00 annually." In fact, and to Benjamin's knowledge, American Equities had not acquired any interest in California Molded Products; all it had was a month's option, dated January 16, 1961, to acquire 68% of the stock for $145,000.

In mid-January, Benjamin invited Howard, a certified public accountant who had served Benjamin and his clients, to do some work for American Equities. Howard testified he received the November 30, 1960, "Pro Forma Balance Sheet," a yellow handwritten sheet of paper listing certain real estate holdings in Detroit, and balance sheets of corporations which Mende and Benjamin claimed were "owned or controlled" by American Equities. From these materials and without any examination of books and records, he prepared a paper dated February 10, 1961, and on the following day gave copies of this to Mende who handed one to Reiter. The latter testified that this was in Howard's presence.

The paper has a cover, on the stationery of Howard as a Certified Public Accountant, which bears the legend:

2. Reiss was also convicted of conspiracy but has not prosecuted an appeal.

American Equities Corporation

December 31, 1960.

Auditors Report.

This is followed by a two-page letter in which Howard advises the company that "After an examination of the books and records of the diversified holdings of your corporation for the period ended December 31, 1960," he is submitting a report of the company as at that date, consisting of "Exhibit 'A'—Pro-forma Balance Sheet as at December 31, 1960." Next comes a section entitled "COMMENTS" informing the company that it is "a diversified investment corporation with the following holdings." These were substantially the same as in the description accompanying the November 30 statement, with the Outpost Inn, Biesmeyer, Stanford and also California Molded Products now clearly listed among them. The comment on California Molded Products anticipates 1961 sales of $2,000,000 with gross profit margin in excess of 30% and a net of better than 4%, but omits to limit the company's interest in these riches to 68%, the most that was claimed by the November 30 balance sheet. The comments say that "The statement which is pro-forma includes the disposition of $500,000 which a group of stockholders propose to advance to the corporation as a long term loan"; that $150,000 of this was to be advanced to subsidiaries for working capital and $71,000 "to repay an officer for the purchase of the assets of the Outpost Inn, Inc."; that "The assets are shown at actual cost and are calculated at the most conservative value," although "A recent appraisal of the real estate in Detroit shows an increase of approximately $2,500,000.00 over book value, which has not been reflected in the statement"; that "The accounts receivable, loans receivable, loans payable, and mortgages payable were not verified by direct communication" and inventories were taken as submitted by the management; and, finally, that "The statement reflects an accurate and true picture of the corporation's net worth after taking into consideration the proposed loan by the officers." The "Pro–Forma Balance Sheet as at December 31, 1960" showed total assets of $7,769,657.11 and a net worth of $3,681,049.70—this including $963,067.00 in the capital stock account. Howard received $200 for his two days of service in preparing the report.

. . .

American Equities stock continued to be sold until March 22, 1961, *[stopped Trading.]* when, as a result of the SEC's action, trading stopped.

Howard's principal claim is that the evidence against him was *[Howard's claim]* insufficient to show the state of mind required for a criminal conviction. He says he was performing an accountant's duties innocently if inefficiently—and for a negligible compensation, that he sheltered himself with the label "pro forma," and that he did not know his reports were to help in stock peddling but thought they were to be used solely for management purposes. His own testimony belies the last claim; he admitted knowing that the promoters intended to use the stock as collateral for loans or as part of or collateral for the purchase price in various acquisitions and that his statements were shown to prospective lenders or sellers. Since his reports were little more than a regurgitation of material handed him by the "management" and related to properties that, as he had reason to know, were not owned, the judge could properly have regarded his claim that he thought them needed for "management" purposes as incredible in the last degree. But the evidence we have summarized shows directly that he knew his reports were being used with brokers who were selling the stock. Drattell, whom he knew to be a broker interested in American Equities, telephoned him in regard to his reports, and, on Reiter's testimony, he saw Mende hand a copy of his first report to Reiter whom he knew to be similarly interested.

The argument that reports which depicted American Equities as owner of properties and companies it neither owned nor had any firm arrangements to acquire were not false because they were stated to be "pro forma" involves a complete misconception of the duties of an accountant in issuing a report thus entitled. Although pro forma statements "purport to give effect to transactions actually consummated or expected to be consummated at a date subsequent to that of the date of the statements," "auditors consider it proper to submit their report and opinion on such statements only when the nature of the transactions effected is clearly described in the statements, and when satisfactory evidence of their bona fides is available, such as actual subsequent consummation or signed firm contracts." Montgomery, Auditing Theory and Practice (6th ed. 1940), 62–63; see also Prentice-Hall Encyclopedic Dictionary of Business Finance (1960), 485. It would be insulting an honorable profession to suppose that a certified public accountant may take the representations of a corporation official as to companies it proposes to acquire, combine their balance sheets without any investigation as to the arrangements for their acquisition or suitable provision reflecting payment of the purchase price, and justify the meaningless result simply by an appliqué of two Latin words.

It is true that the Government had not merely to show that the statements were false but to present evidence from which the judge could be convinced beyond reasonable doubt of Howard's culpable state of mind. But, as Judge Hough said for this court years ago, "when that state of mind is a knowledge of false statements, while there is no allowable inference of knowledge from the mere fact of falsity, there are many cases where from the actor's special situation and continuity of conduct an inference that he *did* know the untruth of what he said or wrote may legitimately be drawn." Bentel v. United States, 13 F.2d 327, 329 (2 Cir.1926). Any accountant must know that his obligations in certifying "pro forma" statements are not satisfied by any such arithmetical exercise as Howard performed. But, as our description of the reports has indicated, there were further false assertions, some of them clearly known to Howard to be such; these constituted a basis for holding him that was independent of the falsity of the total report, as well as for discrediting his assertions of ignorance as to what was required of him. The Michigan real estate was represented to Howard not as properties to be acquired but as already owned; he claimed to have seen deeds for these properties but admitted that American Equities was not named as grantee. The statements that certain assets had not been "verified by direct communication" implied that with this qualification all assets had been verified by suitable means; they had not been. Howard made no examination of American Equities' books, which, indeed, were not available when he rendered his first report; even a most cursory inspection would have revealed that nothing had been paid when the capital stock account was written up ten-fold. His statement purported to reflect "an accurate and true picture of the corporation's net worth after taking into consideration the proposed loan by the officers"; at best it would have been accurate only if the corporation had had at least some contractual basis for the assertion of ownership, and even then only if proper provision had been made for the cost. The inclusion as an asset of over $700,000 of "Unrecovered Development Costs" of a dormant mining company known to have been through insolvency proceedings was wholly indefensible. Perhaps most damning of all was the making of a profit and loss statement including a positive assertion that the six companies were "acquired within the last few months," when Howard knew that at least some of them had not been acquired at all.

... Judge Learned Hand said in a similar context, " ... the cumulation of instances, each explicable only by extreme credulity or professional inexpertness, may have a probative force immensely greater than any one of them alone." United States v. White, 124 F.2d 181, 185 (2 Cir.1941).

In fact, however, the Government was not required to go that far. "Willful," the Supreme Court has told us, "is a word of many meanings, its construction often being influenced by its context." Spies v. United States, 317 U.S. 492, 497 (1943), citing United States v. Murdock, 290 U.S. 389, 394–396 (1933). We think that in the context of § 24 of the Securities Act as applied to § 17(a), the Government can meet its burden by proving that a defendant deliberately closed his eyes to facts he had a duty to see, compare Spurr v. United States, 174 U.S. 728 (1899) and American Law Institute, Model Penal Code, § 2.02(7), commentary in Tent.Draft No. 4, pages 129–30 (1955), or recklessly stated as facts things of which he was ignorant. Judge Hough so ruled in Bentel v. United States, supra; although that case and the similar ruling in Slakoff v. United States, 8 F.2d 9 (3 Cir.1925), were under the mail fraud statute, § 215 of the then Criminal Code, 35 Stat. 1130 (1909), the ancestor of 18 U.S.C. § 1341, which does not use the term "willfully," the Congress that passed the Securities Act scarcely meant to make life easier for defrauders. Other circuits have gone further and have held the willfulness requirement of the Securities Act to be satisfied in fraud cases by proof of representations which due diligence would have shown to be untrue. Stone v. United States, 113 F.2d 70, 75 (6 Cir.1940); United States v. Schaefer, 299 F.2d 625, 629, 632 (7 Cir.1962). In our complex society the accountant's certificate and the lawyer's opinion can be instruments for inflicting pecuniary loss more potent than the chisel or the crowbar. Of course, Congress did not mean that any mistake of law or misstatement of fact should subject an attorney or an accountant to criminal liability simply because more skillful practitioners would not have made them. But Congress equally could not have intended that men holding themselves out as members of these ancient professions should be able to escape criminal liability on a plea of ignorance when they have shut their eyes to what was plainly to be seen or have represented a knowledge they knew they did not possess. . . .

Much of what we have said as to Howard is relevant also to Benjamin's claim of insufficiency of the evidence as to his culpable state of mind. Benjamin brought Howard into the scheme; he had written out the list of assets which Howard later used in his first report; as Howard testified, Benjamin had told him to take the statements of the various companies "and just put them into a consolidated form"; and his work in connection with several of the proposed "acquisitions" gave him actual knowledge of the falsity both of the November 30 statement and of Howard's reports. But there was much more than this. His opinion letter made a positive statement that he believed all the shares of American Equities were exempt from registration, although he must have known that control of the corporation, not yet even named "American Equities Corporation," was being acquired by Mende and that the statute explicitly denied exemption to any new offerings by persons in control, a limitation of which his testimony before the SEC showed he was well aware. Yet there is abundant evidence that Benjamin knew Mende was putting American Equities shares on the market. Among the instances was the transaction outlined above with Drattell in late January wherein Benjamin received a confirmation of a purchase of 5,000 shares from "Martin Benjamin Trustee" for $9,000—at a time when the pink sheets were quoting the stock at $5 per share or more—and the distribution of part of the proceeds to Mende and his wife; yet Benjamin prepared a letter whereby the transfer agent certified these shares to be "free stock and . . . not investment stock." In another transaction, not previously mentioned, wherein Mende had a nominee, Mrs. Tanner, sell American Equities shares to relatives and friends of Paul Reicher, her father, on a basis whereby she retained $2 per share for her pains, she received a letter signed by "Martin Benjamin Trustee" acknowledging the sale of 11,000 shares to her and the receipt of $4.75 per share. Benjamin's role was far more than that of an attorney. He told Drattell he was acting as a "trustee" for some of the principals and, when Drattell sought elucidation, explained that "as a trustee and as an attorney . . . licensed in the State of New York, . . . he was not obligated to reveal any of the sources and it is enough for anyone to accept a legal document from a trustee who was an attorney and the trustee was not required to reveal the source of the legal document or who the principals were behind the legal document"—surely a novel contribution to the law of trusts. His proffer of financial aid if Drattell would undertake some distribution of American Equities afforded further basis for inferring knowledge of the intended fraud, as did his efforts falsely to minimize Mende's role when he and others were examined by the SEC. This and other evidence made a case at least as strong as that held sufficient with respect to another lawyer in United States v. Crosby, 294 F.2d 928, 938 (2 Cir.1961).

Howard and Benjamin make the complaint, standard in appeals of this sort and buttressed by the inevitable citation of Kotteakos v. United States, 328 U.S. 750 (1946), that although the indictment alleged a single conspiracy, the proof showed separate ones to sell unregistered securities and to defraud. The argument could not avail Benjamin in any event since the evidence clearly implicated him in both aspects of the scheme. See United States v. Agueci, 310 F.2d 817, 827–828 (2 Cir.1962). But the point is wholly without merit. The fraudulent acts and the unlawful failure to register information which would uncover them were essential steps in a single scheme to dupe; the limited scope of Kotteakos was explained in Blumenthal v. United States, 332 U.S. 539, 558–559 (1947) and its inapplicability to an integrated financial fraud like this was affirmed by us in United States v. Crosby, supra, 294 F.2d at 944–945. It is thus immaterial that the evidence may not have shown awareness by Howard of the part of the scheme that involved the sale of unregistered shares, United States v. Agueci, supra, and cases there cited.

Mende, as the central figure in the scheme, has not challenged the sufficiency of the evidence introduced against him. He raises several points on appeal; all seem so patently without substance as not to require discussion. We here mention only his claim that McDonald's testimony should have been excluded under the attorney-client privilege, and we do that solely to state its complete lack of merit. The relation between Mende and McDonald was not that of client and attorney but of buyer and seller; what Mende was seeking from McDonald was not legal advice but a pre–1933 corporate shell.

Affirmed.

[handwritten marginal note: atty/π privilege]

Notes on *Benjamin*

The court holds Benjamin criminally liable for activities, such as drafting an opinion letter for his client, Mende, and trying to minimize his client's role in the affair. What made those acts—routinely undertaken by lawyers—criminal on Benjamin's part?

Criminal law operates on a basic premise that bad acts alone are not enough to establish criminal liability; an actor must also have had

Benjamin's state of mind —

a culpable state of mind, the mens rea. Various states of mind satisfy the mens rea requirement, however, depending on the crime. For example, some crimes require a specific intent to do harm; others provide that negligence satisfies the mens rea component.[2] In *Benjamin* what state of mind did the government have to prove to establish the requisite mens rea?

What distinguishes mere incompetence or misplaced confidence in a client's story from the conduct of Howard and Benjamin?

What a Lawyer "Knows"—Mens Rea

Roe

In *Benjamin* the lawyer through his actions clearly facilitated the criminal scheme. The question is whether the lawyer did so with a culpable state of mind. Most jurisdictions hold that mere knowledge of another's criminal purpose does not suffice to make a person guilty of aiding and abetting the other's criminal conduct. One must associate oneself with the venture, participate in it as something one desires to bring about and seek by one's acts to make the venture succeed.[3] The court, however, may infer an intent to facilitate commission of the crime from an actor's knowledge that a principal would use the aid to commit a crime. What a lawyer knows about her client's criminal purpose is therefore critical.

Aside from criminal law sanctions, both the Model Code and the Model Rules make it unethical for a lawyer to facilitate a client's criminal or fraudulent purpose. Model Rule 1.2(d) states that a lawyer may not "counsel a client to engage, or assist a client, in conduct that the lawyer knows is criminal or fraudulent." DR 7–102(A)(7) of the Model Code bans a lawyer from actions that "counsel or assist his client in conduct that the lawyer knows to be illegal or fraudulent." Does the reach of these formulations differ? When will a lawyer be held to have known that her client is engaged in or contemplating criminal activity?

Benjamin reflects a general belief by courts that lawyers and accountants have a greater responsibility to know their client's actions and goals than do nonprofessionals in similar situations. The courts base this greater responsibility on an assumption that lawyers and other similarly situated professionals are more familiar with applicable legal limits and thus are more sensitive to facts that suggest transgression of those limits. Note that this assumption runs counter to that suggested by the paradigm of the criminal defense lawyer, who is permitted and even expected to act in court as though a client were innocent no matter what reasons the lawyer may have to believe or know otherwise. Relying on the criminal defense paradigm, lawyers

---

2. Strict liability offenses provide an exception to the basic criminal law requirement of a culpable mental state. The crimes charged against Howard and Benjamin were not strict liability crimes and so required a showing of mens rea.

3. See United States v. Peoni, 100 F.2d 401 (2d Cir.1938). For a general discussion of the various mental states required for accomplice liability, see Wayne R. LaFave and Austin Scott, Jr., Criminal Law § 6.7(b) at 579 (2d ed.1986). Some jurisdictions hold that knowledge or reason to know of another's intent to commit a crime establishes the mens rea. See, e.g., Mowery v. State, 132 Tex.Cr. 408, 105 S.W.2d 239 (1937).

often say that their job is not to judge the client but to believe in her. However, as *Benjamin* makes clear, lawyers who, while acting as counselors or advisors, "shut their eyes to what was plainly to be seen" or represent that they know something that they do not know, not only act improperly but risk criminal sanctions.[4] Thus a Colorado lawyer who received a car from his client in payment of a legal fee was found guilty of receiving stolen property.[5]

What a Lawyer Does—Actus Reus

The criminal law contains a corollary to the principle that bad acts alone are insufficient for criminal liability: Bad thoughts without an act are also insufficient. For criminal liability to attach, an act (actus reus) must be performed with the required culpable state of mind. Aiding and abetting a client's unlawful activity may result in professional discipline in addition to criminal liability.[6]

As *Benjamin* shows, an act routine in law practice—including the act of giving advice—may constitute the requisite actus reus, resulting in criminal liability if combined with the required culpable state of mind (which may be mere knowledge that a client intends to use the advice to further a criminal purpose). In United States v. Feaster,[7] for example, the court upheld a charge of aiding preparation of a false tax return in a case in which a lawyer advised an undercover agent, posing as a client, on how to avoid paying taxes. In another case a lawyer's advice to a client to destroy documents if a proceeding was instituted resulted in conviction of conspiracy to obstruct a future judicial proceeding.[8] Drafting documents with unlawful terms may also constitute assisting in illegal conduct.[9]

Professor Sanford Kadish discusses the assistance element of criminal complicity:

> Various terms are used to capture the central notions of assistance and influence. Assistance is sometimes expressed as helping, aiding, or abetting. Liability never turns, however, on the choice among these terms. All embrace ways in which one person

4. See Comment, Model Penal Code Section 2.02(7) and Wilful Blindness, 102 Yale L.J. 2231 (1993). What a lawyer as advocate "knows" about the truthfulness of a client's assertions is discussed below in Chapter 5.

5. People v. Zelinger, 179 Colo. 379, 504 P.2d 668 (1972) (lawyer failed to make appropriate further inquiry after receiving, under suspicious circumstances, a car in payment of a legal fee).

6. See People v. Kenelly, 648 P.2d 1065 (Colo.1982) (lawyer fashioned an agreement whereby client would receive money in return for being unavailable to testify at criminal trial); In re La Duca, 62 N.J. 133, 299 A.2d 405 (1973) (lawyer aided client in extorting ransom for return of stolen property).

7. 843 F.2d 1392 (6th Cir.1988) (unreported opinion, text available on WESTLAW).

8. United States v. Perlstein, 126 F.2d 789 (3d Cir.1942).

9. See, e.g., In re Giordano, 49 N.J. 210, 229 A.2d 524 (1967) (discipline for usurious loan contract); Leardi v. Brown, 394 Mass. 151, 474 N.E.2d 1094 (1985) (lawyer violates consumer protection law by including unconscionable provision in residential lease). The problem of inclusion of illegal or unenforceable provisions in documents drafted for one party to a consumer transaction is considered below in Chapter 11 at p. 1072.

may help another commit a crime, including furnishing means, whether material or informational, providing opportunities, and lending a helping hand in preparation or execution. Influence is expressed in a greater variety of terms, sometimes with over-lapping meanings, sometimes with different connotations. *Advise*, like counsel, imports offering one's opinion in favor of some action. *Persuade* is stronger, suggesting a greater effort to prevail on a person, or counseling strongly. *Command* is even stronger, imply-ing an order or direction, commonly by one with some authority over the other. *Encourage* suggests giving support to a course of action to which another is already inclined. *Induce* means to persuade, but may suggest influence beyond persuasion. *Procure* seems to go further, suggesting bringing something about in the sense of producing a result. *Instigate* as well as *incite* suggest stirring up and stimulating, spurring another to a course of action. *Provoke* is roughly equivalent to incite, with the added sense of producing a response by exploiting a person's sensitivities. *Solicit* is generally equivalent to incite in legal usage, although in common usage it suggests simply asking or proposing.

These differences in emphasis and connotation rarely have legal significance. All of these terms describe ways of influencing a person to choose to act in a particular way and therefore constitute a ground of complicity. Occasionally, however, the pre-cise form of influence affects the legal conclusion, most often where statutes employ one or more of these terms restrictively.[10]

Prepaid Legal Services for Those Engaged in Crime

In 1989 a Florida attorney was convicted of both conspiracy to import marijuana and to defraud the Internal Revenue Service by concealing the proceeds of narcotics law violations.[11] According to the government's case the lawyer collected a $10,000 fee from each person on board a boat before it left on a drug-smuggling trip. If no one was caught, the lawyer kept the money; if anyone was arrested, the lawyer would represent that person without further charge.

In In re Disbarment Proceedings,[12] several lawyers were disbarred for making advance agreements with the operators of an illegal num-bers racket to represent subordinates who were arrested. The court said:

> An attorney who agrees in advance to defend persons if and when arrested for criminal offenses whose future commission is a planned certainty, or from whose conduct such an agreement may be inferred, forfeits all right to practice law.... An attorney may defend persons accused of participating in the numbers racket as

10. Sanford H. Kadish, Complicity, Cause and Blame: A Study in the Interpretation of Doctrine, 73 Calif.L.Rev. 323, 343 (1985).

11. Wall St.J., July 20, 1989, at p. B5.

12. 321 Pa. 81, 184 A. 59 (1936).

writers, pick-up men, or bankers, and their clients need not be limited. It is not the number of persons defended that counts, but it is the regularity, character, and purpose of employment. When the purpose is to guide and aid a combination of persons engaged in crime, an attorney becomes part of the criminal system. Where a large number of cases of the same kind of crime are regularly defended by the same lawyer, where the defendants do not know and never have seen the lawyer prior to the moment of representation, and where the attorney's fees are paid by men known to be the leaders of a criminal system, a court may not only infer knowledge on his part of the criminal combination, but, from the frequency of his performance and knowledge, conclude that he becomes an actual participant therein.... [13]

2. Other Crimes

Aside from liability for aiding and abetting, lawyers who know or suspect that their clients are engaged in criminal activity may also suffer sanctions under a variety of criminal statutes. The following notes describe some of the crimes to which lawyers risk exposure.[14]

Obstruction of Justice

Obstruction of justice is a crime of large importance to lawyers.[15] The federal obstruction of justice statute, 18 U.S.C. § 1503, provides: "Whoever corruptly ... endeavors to influence, intimidate, or impede any ... officer ... of any court of the United States ... in the discharge of his duty ... or corruptly ... influences, obstructs or impedes, or endeavors to influence, obstruct, or impede, the due administration of justice, shall be fined ... or imprisoned ... or both." Conduct commonly treated as obstruction of justice includes: attempting to alter or prevent the testimony of a witness,[16] interfering with a grand jury investigation[17] and destroying evidence sought by a court or grand jury.[18]

13. 184 A. at 66.

14. In addition to the crimes discussed in the text, the Foreign Corrupt Practices Act (FCPA), 15 U.S.C. § 78m(b)(2)-(3), should be mentioned. The "books and records" provisions of the FCPA requires that every company with publicly traded securities maintain books and records that "accurately and fairly reflect" the company's transactions. SEC regulations pursuant to the FCPA carry criminal penalties and contain no scienter requirement. See SEC v. World–Wide Coin Invest., Ltd., 567 F.Supp. 724, 745–46 (N.D.Ga.1983). Lawyers who represent publicly held corporations may be guilty of aiding and abetting violations if they know of unreported transactions and have assisted the client in the failure to report.

15. Obstruction of justice served as the central charge against the Watergate defendants, many of whom were lawyers. See United States v. Haldeman, 559 F.2d 31 nn. 2–3 (D.C.Cir.1976).

16. United States v. Tedesco, 635 F.2d 902, 907 (1st Cir.1980).

17. United States v. Walasek, 527 F.2d 676 (3d Cir.1975); and United States v. Teitler, 802 F.2d 606 (2d Cir.1986).

18. United States v. Faudman, 640 F.2d 20 (6th Cir.1981).

Even if the means used to obstruct justice are not in themselves unlawful, obstruction may be found. The crime of obstruction of justice "reaches all corrupt conduct capable of producing an effect that prevents justice from being duly administered, regardless of the means employed." [19] For example, in United States v. Cintolo [20] a lawyer was convicted of obstructing justice by his advice to his client although giving advice is not in itself unlawful. The lawyer advised his client to refuse to testify before the grand jury even though the client had a valid grant of immunity. The prosecution introduced tape-recorded conversations between the lawyer and others that revealed the lawyer's purpose was to keep the grand jury from finding out about the criminal activities of others, some of whom the lawyer-defendant apparently represented. In fact, the lawyer regularly reported on his client's inclination to testify and was aware of plans to kill the client should the client decide to testify. The court stated:

> [M]eans, though lawful in themselves, can cross the line of illegality if (i) employed with a corrupt motive, (ii) to hinder the due administration of justice, so long as (iii) the means have the capacity to obstruct.

> The appellant and amici [Massachusetts Association of Criminal Defense Lawyers and National Network for the Right to Counsel] pay lip service to this principle, but maintain that different considerations come into play where criminal defense lawyers are concerned. In those [situations], they assert, a corrupt motive may not be found in conduct which is, itself, not independently illegal....

> [T]he conversion of innocent acts to guilty ones by the addition of improper intent—is what this case is all about.... Nothing in the caselaw ... suggests that lawyers should be plucked gently from the madding crowd and sheltered from the rigors of 18 U.S.C. § 1503.... [21]

Mail Fraud

The mail and wire fraud statutes, 18 U.S.C. §§ 1341, 1343, prohibit the use of the mail or of electronic transmissions to execute "any scheme or artifice to defraud, or for the purpose of obtaining money or property by false or fraudulent pretenses...." The material mailed need not itself be false; liability attaches regardless of the truth or falsity of the material if the communication of that material aids the execution of a fraud.[22] Mailings occurring after receipt of the proceeds obtained by fraud are covered if the mailings "were designed to lull the victims into a false sense of security, postpone their ultimate complaint

---

19. United States v. Silverman, 745 F.2d 1386, 1393 (11th Cir.1984); see also State v. Cogdell, 273 S.C. 563, 257 S.E.2d 748 (1979).

20. 818 F.2d 980 (1st Cir.1987).

21. 818 F.2d at 992–93, 995–96.

22. United States v. Talbott, 590 F.2d 192 (6th Cir.1978); United States v. Reid, 533 F.2d 1255 (D.C.Cir.1976).

to the authorities, and therefore make the apprehension of the defendants less likely than if no mailings had taken place." [23]

The federal courts, apart from a short hiatus after the *McNally* case,[24] have interpreted the mail fraud statutes as reaching fraudulent schemes to deprive people of intangible civic rights in addition to money and goods. For example, the courts frequently use the mail fraud statute to convict corrupt state and federal government officials (many of them lawyers) of defrauding citizens of their right to the honest service of governmental officials.[25] Typically, those cases involve a government official who has used public office for personal gain. The government also successfully prosecutes cases against private persons for schemes involving the corruption of public servants.[26] Moreover, the courts interpret the "intangible rights" theory to protect the public's right to an honest election process [27] and to allow prosecution of employees and union officials who accepted kickbacks or used confidential information for personal gain.[28]

In Carpenter v. United States,[29] decided shortly after *McNally* and before it was overturned by statute, the Wall Street Journal's "Heard on the Street" columnist, one Winans, was charged with giving two securities brokers advance notice of his column. The brokers and their clients bought and sold securities based on the probable impact of the column on the market. The lower court convicted Winans and his codefendants of violating the federal securities laws and the mail and wire fraud statutes. The Supreme Court divided 4–4 on the securities laws convictions, but unanimously affirmed the fraud convictions. The Court rejected the defendants' argument that their scheme did not deprive the Wall Street Journal of property:

> Petitioners argue that the Journal's interest in prepublication confidentiality for the "Heard" columns is no more than an intangible consideration outside the reach of § 1341; nor does that law, it is urged, protect against mere injury to reputation. This is not a case like *McNally*, however.... Here, the object of the scheme was to take the Journal's confidential business information—the

23. United States v. Maze, 414 U.S. 395, 403 (1974).

24. In McNally v. United States, 483 U.S. 350 (1987), the Supreme Court rejected the entire intangible rights line of cases, holding that the mail and wire fraud statutes only covered schemes defrauding people of property interests. Congress responded by amending the fraud statutes to overturn *McNally*. See 18 U.S.C. § 1346 (1988) ("the term 'scheme or artifice to defraud' includes a scheme or artifice to deprive another of the intangible right of honest services").

25. United States v. Holzer, 816 F.2d 304 (7th Cir.1987) (county judge); United States v. Diggs, 613 F.2d 988 (D.C. Cir.1979) (Congressman); United States v. Mandel, 591 F.2d 1347 (4th Cir.1979) (governor); United States v. Classic, 35 F.Supp. 457 (E.D.La.1940) (election commissioner).

26. See, e.g., United States v. Rauhoff, 525 F.2d 1170 (7th Cir.1975) (bribing state secretary of state).

27. See, e.g., United States v. Girdner, 754 F.2d 877 (10th Cir.1985); and United States v. Clapps, 732 F.2d 1148 (3d Cir.1984) (convictions for using the mails to falsify votes).

28. See, e.g., United States v. Bryza, 522 F.2d 414 (7th Cir.1975).

29. 484 U.S. 19 (1987).

publication schedule and contents of the "Heard" column—and its intangible nature does not make it any less 'property' protected by the mail and wire fraud statutes. *McNally* did not limit the scope of § 1341 to tangible as distinguished from intangible property rights.[30]

Lawyers always possess confidential information belonging to their clients and to third parties. Unauthorized use of such information for personal gain violates federal fraud statutes whenever the mail, a telephone or any other electronic transmission is used in the scheme.[31] Moreover, lawyers often represent clients who themselves possess confidential information. If a lawyer knows a client is using such information for personal gain, and mail or some form of electronic transmission is employed, the lawyer risks prosecution as an aider and abettor whenever the lawyer provides substantial assistance to the client's plan.[32]

Conspiracy

Conspiracy—an *agreement* to do something unlawful (or something lawful through unlawful means)—often goes hand in hand with an unlawful act and forms a separate criminal offense. Thus, in addition to substantive offenses, Benjamin was convicted of conspiracy to commit the substantive offenses. The agreement that forms the core of any conspiracy charge need not be proved through direct evidence, nor must the agreement be explicit: A tacit understanding to do something illegal in concert with others will suffice, and a tacit agreement may be proved by showing that two or more people acted in a way that permits the inference they had some form of agreement.[33] Successful withdrawal from a conspiracy requires an "affirmative act bringing home the fact of [one's] withdrawal to [one's] confederates."[34] Disclosing the conspiracy to authorities is obviously the most effective affirmative act.

Conspiracy may also constitute a tort. For example, one court held a lawyer liable for civil conspiracy when the lawyer: (1) prepared materially misleading documents to secure a bank loan for a partnership in which the lawyer was a member, (2) knew that the misleading information was being used to secure new loans and (3) benefitted from the money fraudulently obtained, which was used to pay a debt of the partnership.[35]

30. Id. at 25.

31. See, e.g., United States v. Grossman, 843 F.2d 78 (2d Cir.1988).

32. See also United States v. Bronston, 658 F.2d 920 (2d Cir.1981) (lawyer deprived his firm's client of honest services by representing another client whose interests directly conflicted).

33. Direct Sales Co. v. United States, 319 U.S. 703 (1943). On conspiracy see generally LaFave and Scott, supra, at §§ 6.4–6.5.

34. Loser v. Superior Court, 78 Cal.App.2d 30, 177 P.2d 320 (1947).

35. Hartford Accident and Indemnity Co. v. Sullivan, 846 F.2d 377 (7th Cir.1988).

RICO

The Racketeer Influenced and Corrupt Organizations Act (RICO) [36] defines "racketeering" acts to include not only murder and kidnapping but mail, wire and securities fraud. The inclusion of these latter "white-collar" crimes gives the statute a reach far beyond its original target, the "mob," and makes lawyers vulnerable to RICO charges. [37] The wide reach of RICO has engendered much criticism by many groups, including lawyers, [38] but efforts to persuade Congress to limit RICO's reach have thus far failed. [39] A 1993 decision, however, provides protection for outside lawyers who merely advise an organization subject to a racketeering claim. [40]

RICO prohibits, in any enterprise affecting interstate commerce, the following: (1) investing income derived from a pattern of racketeering, (2) acquiring or maintaining an interest through a pattern of racketeering, (3) participating in the enterprise's affairs through a pattern of racketeering and (4) conspiring to engage in any of these activities. Two acts of racketeering and the threat of continuing racketeering activity suffice to establish a "pattern" of racketeering. Thus, given the definition of racketeering acts, two instances of mail or wire fraud would satisfy the "two-act" requirement.

RICO authorizes civil remedies as well as criminal sanctions. Moreover, the Supreme Court has refused to interpret RICO as requiring a criminal conviction to support civil RICO liability: [41] " 'Proof of two acts ... without more does not establish a pattern.... [C]ontinuity plus relationship [are what] produce a pattern.' " [42] A private party

36. 18 U.S.C. §§ 1961–68 (1982 & Supp. III 1985).

37. "Only 9% of all civil RICO cases have involved allegations of criminal activity normally associated with professional criminals. The central purpose that Congress sought to promote through civil RICO is now a mere footnote." Sedima, S.P.R.L. v. Imrex Co., 473 U.S. 479, 506 (1985) (Marshall, J., dissenting).

38. "In practice, [civil RICO] frequently has been invoked against legitimate businesses in ordinary commercial settings.... [T]he ABA Task Force that studied civil RICO found that 40% of the reported cases involved securities fraud, 37% involved common-law fraud in a commercial or business setting. Many a prudent defendant, facing ruinous exposure, will decide to settle even a case with no merit. It is thus not surprising that civil RICO has been used for extortive purposes, giving rise to the very evils that it was designed to combat." Report of the Ad Hoc Civil RICO Task Force of the ABA Section of Corporation, Banking and Business Law 69 (1985).

39. The ABA House of Delegates in August 1986 passed resolutions urging Congress to change the definition of racketeering activity and to require a criminal RICO conviction as a condition precedent to civil RICO liability. For criticism of RICO liability, see Dennis O. Lynch, RICO: The Crime of Being a Criminal, Parts I & II, 87 Colum.L.Rev. 661; Parts III & IV, 87 Colum.L.Rev. 920 (1987); Note, Civil RICO is a Misnomer ..., 100 Harv.L.Rev. 1288 (1987). But see Michael Goldsmith, Civil RICO Reform: The Basis for a Compromise, 71 Minn.L.Rev. 827 (1987) (describing the criticism of RICO as overstated and proposing a moderate revision).

40. Reves v. Ernst & Young, 113 S.Ct. 1163 (1993) (an outside accounting firm to an organization experiencing financial difficulty did not "participate" in the "conduct" of the organization by failing to inform its board of directors that if a major asset was given a market rather than book value the organization would probably be insolvent).

41. Sedima, S.P.R.L. v. Imrex Co., 473 U.S. 479 (1985).

42. 473 U.S. at 496 n. 14.

who prevails on the merits in a RICO action is entitled to treble damages and litigation expenses, including attorneys' fees.

In United States v. Teitler[43] the Second Circuit affirmed the conviction of two lawyers for engaging in mail fraud, conspiring to conduct the affairs of an enterprise through a pattern of racketeering and conducting the affairs of an enterprise through racketeering. The enterprise in question was their law firm:

> [T]he method of operation employed by the enterprise included the creation of false documents and the encouragement of perjury by the firm's clients in order to inflate their injuries and expenses so as to obtain better settlements in negligence lawsuits brought by the firm.... [T]he fraud took several forms: creation of false medical bills; submission of false affidavits to document housekeeping services that were never rendered and lost wages that were never earned; referral of clients to doctors who provided backdated bills and exaggerated medical reports; and procurement of false testimony at trials and examinations before trial.... Further, when a grand jury investigation was underway, defendants Norman Teitler, head of the firm, and Maureen Murphy, an employee, allegedly tried to induce false testimony before the grand jury.[44]

3. Paying Lawyers With Proceeds of Crime

In the 1980s a series of legislative enactments aimed at organized crime and drug trafficking, coupled with more vigorous law enforcement, led to extensive litigation in which prosecutors sought to obtain information from lawyers concerning amount of fees paid, form of payment and identity of the payor. Federal racketeering and drug laws require forfeiture of assets acquired directly or indirectly through specified criminal activity. The Internal Revenue Code requires every person who receives more than $10,000 in cash in connection with a trade or business to report information concerning the transaction with the Internal Revenue Service.

If the lawyer knows that the amounts paid to her are the proceeds of ongoing criminal activity, the lawyer's action in accepting the payment is illegal because the money is either contraband or stolen property. In the typical case, however, the government does not claim that the lawyer has the requisite knowledge or mental state to establish the lawyer's criminal liability. Thus, the primary issue presented by prosecutorial efforts to discover fee arrangements and client identity and to forfeit fees is one of confidentiality: Whether the lawyer is

---

43. 802 F.2d 606 (2d Cir.1986).

44. 808 F.2d at 609. Criminal and civil RICO cases against personal injury lawyers are becoming quite common. A prominent New York City personal injury lawyer, Morris J. Eisen, and a partner, along with five nonlawyer staff, were convicted in March 1991 on charges of hiring false witnesses, manufacturing evidence and suborning perjury in a substantial number of personal injury cases. A large scandal erupted in California in 1990 involving 20 or more lawyers who are alleged to have defrauded liability insurers of more than $200 million. See Marcia Chambers, Untangling an Unholy Alliance, Nat'l L.J., Apr. 30, 1990, at p. 13.

required to divulge information concerning fee arrangements and client identity. The issues raised by these provisions are discussed below in the Koniak excerpt at p. 127 and in Chapter 4 at pp. 256–71.

B. TORT LAW

1. Negligent Misrepresentation

GREYCAS, INC. v. PROUD

United States Court of Appeals, Seventh Circuit, 1987.
826 F.2d 1560.

Before BAUER, CHIEF JUDGE, and CUMMINGS and POSNER, CIRCUIT JUDGES.

POSNER, CIRCUIT JUDGE.

Theodore S. Proud, Jr., a member of the Illinois bar who practices law in a suburb of Chicago, appeals from a judgment against him for $833,760, entered after a bench trial. The tale of malpractice and misrepresentation that led to the judgment begins with Proud's brother-in-law, Wayne Crawford, like Proud a lawyer but one who devoted most of his attention to a large farm that he owned in downstate Illinois. The farm fell on hard times and by 1981 Crawford was in dire financial straits. He had pledged most of his farm machinery to lenders, yet now desperately needed more money. He approached Greycas, Inc., the plaintiff in this case, a large financial company headquartered in Arizona, seeking a large loan that he offered to secure with the farm machinery. He did not tell Greycas about his financial difficulties or that he had pledged the machinery to other lenders, but he did make clear that he needed the loan in a hurry. Greycas obtained several appraisals of Crawford's farm machinery but did not investigate Crawford's financial position or discover that he had pledged the collateral to other lenders, who had perfected their liens in the collateral. Greycas agreed to lend Crawford $1,367,966.50, which was less than the appraised value of the machinery.

The loan was subject, however, to an important condition, which is at the heart of this case: Crawford was required to submit a letter to Greycas, from counsel whom he would retain, assuring Greycas that there were no prior liens on the machinery that was to secure the loan. Crawford asked Proud to prepare the letter, and he did so, and mailed it to Greycas, and within 20 days of the first contact between Crawford and Greycas the loan closed and the money was disbursed. A year later Crawford defaulted on the loan; shortly afterward he committed suicide. Greycas then learned that most of the farm machinery that Crawford had pledged to it had previously been pledged to other lenders.

The machinery was sold at auction. The Illinois state court that determined the creditors' priorities in the proceeds of the sale held that Greycas did not have a first priority on most of the machinery that secured its loan; as a result Greycas has been able to recover only a small part of the loan. The judgment it obtained in the present suit is the district judge's estimate of the value that it would have realized on its collateral had there been no prior liens, as Proud represented in his letter.

That letter is the centerpiece of the litigation. Typed on the stationery of Proud's firm and addressed to Greycas, it identifies Proud as Crawford's lawyer and states that, "in such capacity, I have been asked to render my opinion in connection with" the proposed loan to Crawford. It also states that "this opinion is being delivered in accordance with the requirements of the Loan Agreement" and that

> I have conducted a U.C.C., tax, and judgment search with respect to the Company [i.e., Crawford's farm] as of March 19, 1981, and except as hereinafter noted all units listed on the attached Exhibit A ("Equipment") are free and clear of all liens or encumbrances other than Lender's perfected security interest therein which was recorded March 19, 1981 at the Office of the Recorder of Deeds of Fayette County, Illinois.

The reference to the lender's security interest is to Greycas's interest; Crawford, pursuant to the loan agreement, had filed a notice of that interest with the recorder. The excepted units to which the letter refers are four vehicles. Exhibit A is a long list of farm machinery— the collateral that Greycas thought it was getting to secure the loan, free of any other liens. . . .

Proud never conducted a search for prior liens on the machinery listed in Exhibit A. His brother-in-law gave him the list and told him there were no liens other than the one that Crawford had just filed for Greycas. Proud made no effort to verify Crawford's statement. The theory of the complaint is that Proud was negligent in representing that there were no prior liens, merely on his brother-in-law's say-so. No doubt Proud *was* negligent in failing to conduct a search, but we are not clear why the *misrepresentation* is alleged to be negligent rather than deliberate and hence fraudulent, in which event Greycas's alleged contributory negligence would not be an issue (as it is, we shall see), since there is no defense of contributory or comparative negligence to a deliberate tort, such as fraud. Proud did not merely say, "There are no liens"; he said, "I have conducted a U.C.C., tax, and judgment search"; and not only is this statement, too, a false one, but its falsehood cannot have been inadvertent, for Proud knew he had not conducted such a search. The concealment of his relationship with Crawford might also support a charge of fraud. But Greycas decided, for whatever reason, to argue negligent misrepresentation rather than fraud. It may have feared that Proud's insurance policy for professional malpractice excluded deliberate wrongdoing from its coverage, or may not have wanted to bear the higher burden of proving fraud, or may have feared that an accusation of fraud would make it harder to settle the case—for most cases, of course, are settled, though this one has not been. In any event, Proud does not argue that either he is liable for fraud or he is liable for nothing.

He also does not, and could not, deny or justify the misrepresentation; but he argues that it is not actionable under the tort law of Illinois, because he had no duty of care to Greycas. (This is a diversity case and the parties agree that Illinois tort law governs the substantive issues.) He argues that Greycas had an adversarial relationship with Proud's client, Crawford, and that a lawyer has no duty of straight dealing to an adversary, at least none enforceable by a tort suit. In so arguing, Proud is characterizing Greycas's suit as one for professional malpractice rather than negligent misrepresentation, yet elsewhere in his briefs he insists that the suit was solely for negligent misrepresentation—while Greycas insists that its suit charges both torts. Legal malpractice based on a false representation, and negligent misrepresentation by a lawyer, are such similar legal concepts, however, that we have great difficulty both in holding them apart in our minds and in understanding why the parties are quarreling over the exact characterization; no one suggests, for example, that the statute of limitations might have run on one but not the other tort. So we shall discuss both.

Proud is undoubtedly correct in arguing that a lawyer has no general duty of care toward his adversary's client; it would be a considerable and, as it seems to us, an undesirable novelty to hold that every bit of sharp dealing by a lawyer gives rise to prima facie tort liability to the opposing party in the lawsuit or negotiation. The tort of malpractice normally refers to a lawyer's careless or otherwise wrongful conduct toward his own client. Proud argues that Crawford rather than Greycas was his client, and although this is not so clear as Proud supposes—another characterization of the transaction is that Crawford undertook to obtain a lawyer for Greycas in the loan transaction—we shall assume for purposes of discussion that Greycas was not Proud's client.

Therefore if malpractice just meant carelessness or other misconduct toward one's own client, Proud would not be liable for malpractice to Greycas. But in Pelham v. Griesheimer, 92 Ill.2d 13, 64 Ill.Dec. 544, 440 N.E.2d 96 (1982), the Supreme Court of Illinois discarded the old common law requirement of privity of contract for professional malpractice; so now it is possible for someone who is not the lawyer's (or other professional's) client to sue him for malpractice. The court in *Pelham* was worried, though, about the possibility of a lawyer's being held liable "to an unlimited and unknown number of potential plaintiffs," ... so it added that "for a nonclient to succeed in a negligence action against an attorney, he must prove that the primary purpose and intent of the attorney-client relationship itself was to benefit or influence the third party,".... That, however, describes this case exactly. Crawford hired Proud not only for the primary purpose, but for the sole purpose, of influencing Greycas to make Crawford a loan. The case is much like Brumley v. Touche, Ross & Co., 139 Ill.App.3d 831, 836, 93 Ill.Dec. 816, 819–20, 487 N.E.2d 641, 644–45 (1985), where a complaint that an accounting firm had negligently prepared an audit report that the firm knew would be shown to an investor in the audited corporation and relied on by that investor was held to state a claim for professional malpractice. In Conroy v. Andeck Resources '81 Year–End Ltd., 137 Ill.App.3d 375, 389–91, 92 Ill.Dec. 10, 21–22, 484 N.E.2d 525, 536–37 (1985), in contrast, a law firm that represented an offeror of securities was held not to have any duty of care to investors. The representation was not intended for the benefit of investors. Their reliance on the law firm's using due care in the services it provided in connection with the offer was not invited. Cf. Barker v. Henderson, Franklin, Starnes & Holt, 797 F.2d 490, 497 (7th Cir.1986).

All this assumes that *Pelham* governs this case, but arguably it does not, for Greycas, as we noted, may have decided to bring this as a suit for negligent misrepresentation rather than professional malpractice. We know of no obstacle to such an election; nothing is more common in American jurisprudence than overlapping torts.

The claim of negligent misrepresentation might seem utterly straightforward. It might seem that by addressing a letter to Greycas intended (as Proud's counsel admitted at argument) to induce reliance on the statements in it, Proud made himself prima facie liable for any material misrepresentations, careless or deliberate, in the letter, whether or not Proud was Crawford's lawyer or for that matter anyone's lawyer. Knowing that Greycas was relying on him to determine whether the collateral for the loan was encumbered and to advise Greycas of the results of his determination, Proud negligently misrepresented the situation, to Greycas's detriment. But merely labeling a suit as one for negligent misrepresentation rather than professional malpractice will not make the problem of indefinite and perhaps excessive liability, which induced the court in *Pelham* to place limitations on the duty of care, go away. So one is not surprised to find that courts have placed similar limitations on suits for negligent misrepresentation—so similar that we are led to question whether ... these really are different torts, at least when both grow out of negligent misrepresentations by lawyers. For example, the *Brumley* case, which we cited earlier, is a professional-malpractice case, yet it has essentially the same facts as Ultramares Corp. v. Touche, Niven & Co., 255 N.Y. 170, 174 N.E. 441 (1931), where the New York Court of Appeals, in a famous opinion by Judge Cardozo, held that an accountant's negligent misrepresentation was not actionable at the suit of a lender who had relied on the accountant's certified audit of the borrower.

The absence of a contract between the lender and the accountant defeated the suit in *Ultramares*—yet why should privity of contract have been required for liability just because the negligence lay in disseminating information rather than in designing or manufacturing a product? The privity limitation in products cases had been rejected, in another famous Cardozo opinion, years earlier. See MacPherson v. Buick Motor Co., 217 N.Y. 382, 111 N.E. 1050 (1916). Professor Bishop suggests that courts were worried that imposing heavy liabilities on producers of information might cause socially valuable information to be underproduced. See Negligent Misrepresentation Through Economists' Eyes, 96 L.Q.Rev. 360 (1980). Many producers of information have difficulty appropriating its benefits to society. The property-rights system in information is incomplete; someone who comes up with a new idea that the law of intellectual property does not protect cannot prevent others from using the idea without reimbursing his costs of invention or discovery. So the law must be careful not to weigh these producers down too heavily with tort liabilities. For example, information produced by securities analysts, the news media, academicians, and so forth is socially valuable, but as its producers can't capture the full value of the information in their fees and other remuneration the information may be underproduced. Maybe it is right, therefore—or at least efficient—that none of these producers should have to bear the full costs.... At least that was once the view; and while *Ultramares* has now been rejected, in Illinois as elsewhere— maybe because providers of information are deemed more robust today than they once were or maybe because it is now believed that auditors, surveyors, and other providers of professional services were always able to capture the social value of even the information component of those services in the fees they charged their clients—a residuum of concern remains. So when in Rozny v. Marnul, 43 Ill.2d 54, 250 N.E.2d 656 (1969), the Supreme Court of Illinois, joining the march away from *Ultramares*, held for the first time that negligent misrepresentation was actionable despite the absence of a contract, and thus cast aside the same "privity of contract" limitation later overruled with regard to professional malpractice in *Pelham*, the court was careful to emphasize facts in the particular case before it that limited the scope of its holding—facts such as that the defendant, a surveyor, had placed his "absolute guarantee for accuracy" on the plat and that only a few persons would receive and rely on it, thus limiting the potential scope of liability....

[handwritten margin note: No privity required for neg. misrep.]

Later Illinois cases, however, influenced by section 552 of the Second Restatement of Torts (1977), state the limitation on liability for negligent misrepresentation in more compact terms—as well as in narrower scope—than *Rozny*. These are cases in the intermediate appellate court, but, as we have no reason to think the Supreme Court of Illinois would reject them, we are bound to follow them.... They hold that "one who in the course of his business or profession supplies information for the guidance of others in their business transactions" is liable for negligent misrepresentations that induce detrimental reliance.... Whether there is a practical as distinct from a merely semantic difference between this formulation of the duty limitation and that of *Pelham* may be doubted but cannot change the outcome of this case. Proud, in the practice of his profession, supplied information (or rather misinformation) to Greycas that was intended to guide Greycas in commercial dealings with Crawford. Proud therefore had a duty to use due care to see that the information was correct. He used no care.

Proud must lose on the issue of liability even if the narrower, *ad hoc* approach of *Rozny* is used instead of the approach of section 552 of the Restatement. Information about the existence of previous liens on particular items of property is of limited social as distinct from private value, by which we mean simply that the information is not likely to be disseminated widely. There is consequently no reason to give it special encouragement by overlooking carelessness in its collection and expression. Where as in this case the defendant makes the negligent misrepresentation directly to the plaintiff in the course of the defendant's business or profession, the courts have little difficulty in finding a duty of care. Prosser and Keeton on the Law of Torts ... § 107, at p. 747.

There is no serious doubt about the existence of a causal relationship between the misrepresentation and the loan. Greycas would not have made the loan without Proud's letter. Nor would it have made the loan had Proud advised it that the collateral was so heavily encumbered that the loan was as if unsecured, for then Greycas would have known that the probability of repayment was slight. Merely to charge a higher interest rate would not have been an attractive alternative to security; it would have made default virtually inevitable by saddling Crawford with a huge fixed debt. To understand the astronomical interest rate that is required to make an unsecured loan a paying proposition to the lender when the risk of default is high, notice that even if the riskless interest rate is only 3 percent, the rate of inflation zero, the cost of administering the loan zero, and the lender risk-neutral, he still must charge an annual interest rate of 106 percent if he thinks there is only a 50 percent chance that he will get his principal back.

Proud argues, however, that his damages should be reduced in recognition of Greycas's own contributory negligence, which, though no longer a complete defense in Illinois, is a partial defense, renamed "comparative negligence." ... It is as much a defense to negligent misrepresentation as to any other tort of negligence.... On the issue of comparative negligence the district court said only that "defendant may have proved negligence upon the part of plaintiff but that negligence, if any, had no causal relationship to the malpractice of the defendant or the damages to the plaintiff." This comment is not easy to fathom. If Greycas was careless in deciding whether to make the loan, this implies that a reasonable investigation by Greycas would have shown that the collateral for the loan was already heavily encumbered; knowing this, Greycas would not have made the loan and therefore would not have suffered any damages.

But we think it too clear to require a remand for further proceedings that Proud failed to prove a want of due care by Greycas. Due care is the care that is optimal given that the other party is exercising due care.... It is not the higher level of care that would be optimal if potential tort victims were required to assume that the rest of the world was negligent. A pedestrian is not required to exercise a level of care (e.g., wearing a helmet or a shin guard) that would be optimal if there were no sanctions against reckless driving. Otherwise drivers would be encouraged to drive recklessly, and knowing this pedestrians would be encouraged to wear helmets and shin guards. The result would be a shift from a superior method of accident avoidance (not driving recklessly) to an inferior one (pedestrian armor).

So we must ask whether Greycas would have been careless not to conduct its own UCC search had Proud done what he had said he did— conduct his own UCC search. The answer is no. The law normally does not require duplicative precautions unless one is likely to fail or the consequences of failure (slight though the likelihood may be) would be catastrophic. One UCC search is enough to disclose prior liens, and Greycas acted reasonably in relying on Proud to conduct it. Although Greycas had much warning that Crawford was in financial trouble and that the loan might not be repaid, that was a reason for charging a hefty interest rate and insisting that the loan be secured; it was not a reason for duplicating Proud's work. It is not hard to conduct a UCC lien search; it just requires checking the records in the recorder's office for the county where the debtor lives. See Ill.Rev.Stat. ch. 26, ¶ 9–401. So the only reason to backstop Proud was if Greycas should have assumed he was careless or dishonest; and we have just said that the duty of care does not require such an assumption. Had Proud disclosed that he was Crawford's brother-in-law this might have been a warning signal that Greycas could ignore only at its peril. To go forward in the face of a known danger is to assume the risk.... But Proud did not disclose his relationship to Crawford.

The last issue concerns the amount of damages awarded Greycas....

. . .

... [T]he judge was, if anything, unduly generous to Proud, in giving Greycas only the value of the collateral on the date of default, rather than the unpaid principal of the loan. But for Proud's misrepresentations, Greycas would not have made the loan, so its damages are not just the collateral but the entire uncollectable portion of the loan together with the interest that the money would have earned in an alternative use ... We therefore conclude that the realizable value of Greycas's collateral on the date of Crawford's default was a real loss.

A final point. The record of this case reveals serious misconduct by an Illinois attorney. We are therefore sending a copy of this opinion to the Attorney Registration and Disciplinary Commission of the Supreme Court of Illinois for such disciplinary action as may be deemed appropriate in the circumstances.[45]

Affirmed.

BAUER, CHIEF JUDGE, concurring.

I am in agreement with the majority opinion. I believe that Proud would be liable without reference to legal malpractice or negligent misrepresentation. The evidence in this case indicates that he is guilty of fraud or intentional misrepresentation. He was lying when he represented that he had made U.C.C., tax and judgment searches on his brother-in-law's farm. He intended the misrepresentation to induce Greycas to make a loan to his brother-in-law; Greycas justifiably relied upon the misrepresentation in making the loan and was injured as a result. Under these facts, Proud's misrepresentation was indefensible.

―――――――

Liability to Non-Clients

Why did Greycas sue lawyer Proud for negligence rather than for intentional tort? How does the court justify holding a lawyer liable in negligence to a non-client?

In discussing comparative negligence the court points out that "[a] pedestrian is not required to exercise a level of care (e.g., wearing a helmet) that would be optimal if there were no sanctions against reckless driving." Yet later the court suggests that if Proud had disclosed to Greycas that he was Crawford's brother-in-law, "this might have been a warning signal that Greycas could ignore only at its peril. To go forward in the face of a known danger is to assume the risk." Making false statements is unethical whether or not they are made on behalf of one's brother-in-law. If made with intent to defraud, they are fraudulent regardless of the relationship between the maker and the party he is "helping." Why then should a third party be required to see the relationship as a warning signal?

Negligent Misrepresentation Cases

In Greyhound Leasing & Financial Corp. v. Norwest Bank of Jamestown,[46] as in *Greycas*, a lender, Greyhound, required a lawyer's opinion letter stating that farm equipment securing a proposed loan was unencumbered. Greyhound wanted a lawyer from the farmer's locality to write the letter because a local lawyer would be more likely to be familiar with the farmer's business activities. The farmer told the lawyer that all the equipment was brand new and not yet "owned or possessed by him." Greyhound, although it knew that some of the equipment was used, sent the lawyer documents asserting that the equipment was new, making the transaction eligible for federal credits.

45. [Editors' note:] After a disciplinary hearing in 1990, Proud was suspended for one year in Illinois.

46. 854 F.2d 1122 (8th Cir.1988).

Relying on the word of his client and the documents sent by Greyhound, the lawyer did not conduct a lien search because in North Dakota one cannot create a valid lien on farm equipment until it is "owned or possessed." The lawyer wrote a letter stating that he was "not aware of any liens or encumbrances ... created or suffered by the lessee nor have they [sic] granted or conveyed any liens or encumbrances of any nature with respect thereto." In fact, the equipment was not new and almost all was encumbered by at least one lien. Shortly after Greyhound disbursed the loan money, the farmer filed bankruptcy. Finding itself with virtually no collateral and a bankrupt debtor, Greyhound filed suit against the lawyer.

for Atty

The Eighth Circuit upheld a judgment for the lawyer. Assuming arguendo that the letter was a negligent misrepresentation, the court of appeals held that Greyhound was barred under North Dakota's doctrine of contributory negligence because its negligence exceeded the lawyer's. First, knowing the equipment was not new, Greyhound negligently prepared documents that stated otherwise in order to gain a tax benefit. Second, Greyhound negligently failed to make its own independent investigation of the lien situation.

cont. N eg.

> Greyhound claims to have paid out $1 million in reliance on the opinion of a lawyer whom it never contacted or instructed and to whom it arranged the transmittal of seriously inaccurate documents. It devised for the lawyer to sign a most equivocal form of opinion letter which does not clearly set forth the representation which Greyhound now says it thought it was getting from the lawyer, and relied upon it. It seems to us eminently reasonable to hold, as the trial judge did, that under the circumstances, Greyhound had an independent obligation to investigate the existence of liens.[47]

Is *Greyhound*'s analysis consistent with the reasoning in *Greycas*?

In Roberts v. Ball, Hunt, Hart, Brown & Baerwitz,[48] a law firm's client needed a loan and asked the firm to prepare an opinion letter that the client, a partnership, could show to its potential creditor. Knowing the intended use, the firm prepared a letter stating that the fourteen partners of the client-partnership were all general partners. The creditor, Roberts, considered this assurance critical because general partners are liable for the debts of the partnership in the event of default. The client gave the letter to Roberts, who, relying on the letter, made the loan. When the partnership defaulted and Roberts sought to collect from the partners, thirteen of the fourteen partners defended by claiming to be only limited partners. Roberts then sued the law firm for fraud and negligent misrepresentation, claiming that at the time the firm drafted the letter it knew that most of the partners believed they were limited and not general partners and were asserting

General partners vs. limited ptnrs.

47. Id. at 1125.
48. 57 Cal.App.3d 104, 128 Cal.Rptr. 901 (1976).

that position in partnership meetings. According to Roberts, the firm had a duty to disclose these material facts in the opinion letter.

defense

The firm defended by saying it had no intent to deceive and thus was not liable for fraud. The court agreed that the complaint failed to state a cause of action for fraud because there was no allegation of intent to deceive, but held that the firm might be liable for negligent misrepresentation. California, the court stated, rejects the "traditional view ... that an attorney may not ... be held liable to third persons [for negligence] because he is not in privity with them, and owes them no duty to act with care." According to the *Roberts* court, determination of a lawyer's liability to a non-client involves the balancing of various factors, including the following:

> the extent to which the transaction was intended to affect the plaintiff, the foreseeability of harm to him, the degree of certainty that the plaintiff suffered injury, the closeness of the connection between the defendant's conduct and the injury suffered, and the policy of preventing future harm.[49]

Some cases in which a lawyer assists an offeror in the sale of securities require that the lawyer exercise due diligence in checking the client's factual representations.[50] In other cases, however, adversarial negotiations with a purchaser or small group of purchasers lead to a different result: A seller's lawyer engaged in adversarial contract negotiations in connection with a sale of stock is not liable to purchasers who rely on the lawyer's negligent misrepresentations if "the duties involved, including negotiations and drafting of contractual agreements ... [are] clearly adversarial in nature" and were not intended to benefit the purchasers directly."[51]

Relaxation of Privity Requirement[52]

Traditionally, a lawyer is liable for negligence only to those in

49. 57 Cal.App.3d at 110, 128 Cal.Rptr. at 905, citing Lucas v. Hamm, 56 Cal.2d 583, 15 Cal.Rptr. 821, 364 P.2d 685, 687 (1961) (reprinted in Chapter 3 below).

50. See, e.g., Felts v. National Account Systems Association, 469 F.Supp. 54, 68 (N.D.Miss.1978) (offeror's lawyer liable to purchasers of unregistered securities for negligent failure to verify or investigate underlying material facts: "law and public policy require that the attorney exercise his position of trust and superior knowledge responsibly so as not to adversely affect persons whose rights and interests are certain and foreseeable"). See also Bradford Securities Processing Services, Inc. v. Plaza Bank & Trust, 653 P.2d 188 (Okla.1982) (bond counsel who negligently misrepresented the value and nature of bonds held liable to all foreseeable plaintiffs).

51. Astor Chauffeured Limousine Co. v. Runnfeldt Investment Corp., 1988 WL 101267 (N.D.Ill.), vacated and remanded for recomputation of damages, 910 F.2d 1540 (7th Cir.1990) (applying Illinois law). See the discussion of "adversarial" relationships in *Greycas.*

52. The lawyer's liability to third parties for professional malpractice is discussed in Chapter 3 along with liability to clients for malpractice. For discussion of policy issues concerning the liability of professionals to non-clients who rely on their work, see John A. Siliciano, Negligent Accounting and the Limits of Instrumental Tort Reform, 86 Mich. L.Rev. 1929 (1988), and Victor P. Goldberg, Accountable Accountants: Is Third–Party Liability Necessary?, 17 J.Legal Stud. 295 (1988). See also Bily v. Arthur Young and Co., 3 Cal.4th 370, 11 Cal.Rptr.2d 51, 834 P.2d 745 (Cal.1992), reviewing authorities and

privity of contract with the lawyer (typically clients).[53] Many jurisdictions still purport to adhere to this traditional rule. New York, for example, generally upholds the privity requirement.[54] Thus, in Grassi v. Tatavito Homes, Inc.,[55] the court found a seller's attorney not liable to a buyer for the lawyer's negligent misrepresentation that the seller owned the property and had title insurance. "Absent privity," the court stated, an attorney "is not liable for simple negligence."[56] Despite such pronouncements, New York courts hold a lawyer liable to non-clients for negligent misrepresentation when a legal opinion is intended to induce third parties' reliance on the lawyer's statements. In Crossland Savings FSB v. Rockwood Insurance Co.,[57] the court reconciled the two lines of cases as follows: "When a lawyer at the direction of her client prepares an opinion letter, which is addressed to the third party or which expressly invites the third party's reliance, she engages in a form of limited representation [of that third party]."[58] Compare this to the statement in *Greycas* that the lender might be considered to have been Proud's client.

Jurisdictions that, rejecting privity, hold that a lawyer may owe a duty of care to non-clients take a number of approaches. Some, following California, apply a balancing-of-factors approach giving substantial weight to whether the situation is one in which it is reasonably foreseeable that a lawyer's absence of due care will directly harm a third person.[59] The duty of care is generally limited to transactional contexts in which the lawyer is dealing directly with the injured third

holding that an auditor owes no general duty of care regarding the conduct of an audit to persons other than the client; however, an auditor is liable for negligent misrepresentation when an audit report is made to influence a transaction with a nonclient who relied on a negligent misrepresentation.

53. An English case, Robertson v. Fleming, 4 Macq.H. of L.Cas. 167 (House of Lords, Scottish Appeals, 1861), first enunciated the privity rule; Fish v. Kelly, 17 C.B. (N.S.) 194 (Common Bench 1864), restated the rule. In the United States, the most authoritative early pronouncement came in 1880 on facts strikingly similar to those in *Greycas*. National Savings Bank v. Ward, 100 U.S. 195 (1880), involved a lawyer who negligently conducted a title search, failing to find a prior conveyance; a bank loaned money to the lawyer's client relying on the lawyer's opinion letter, which asserted a clear title. The Supreme Court refused to find the lawyer liable to the bank because the bank was not in privity with the lawyer.

54. For a case with facts similar to those in *Greycas*, see Council Commerce Corp. v. Schwartz, Sachs & Kamhi, P.C., 144 A.D.2d 422, 534 N.Y.S.2d 1 (2d Dept.1988), appeal denied, 74 N.Y.2d 606, 544 N.Y.S.2d 820, 543 N.E.2d 85 (1989) (applying traditional rule, court found lawyers not liable to lender).

55. 90 A.D.2d 479, 454 N.Y.S.2d 471 (2d Dept.1982), aff'd, 58 N.Y.2d 1038, 462 N.Y.S.2d 445, 448 N.E.2d 1356 (1983).

56. 454 N.Y.S.2d at 472.

57. 700 F.Supp. 1274 (S.D.N.Y.1988) (collecting New York cases holding lawyers liable to non-clients when the lawyer's services involve a legal opinion designed to influence those persons).

58. Id. at 1282, quoting 1 Hazard and Hodes, Law of Lawyering 320 (1987).

59. See Biakanja v. Irving, 49 Cal.2d 647, 320 P.2d 16 (1958) (listing factors); Roberts v. Ball, Hunt, Hart, Brown & Baerwitz, 57 Cal.App.3d 104, 128 Cal.Rptr. 901 (1976), discussed in the prior note.

person;[60] few if any decisions hold that a lawyer in adversarial litigation has a duty of care to opposing parties.[61] Other jurisdictions, rejecting the balancing-of-factors approach as well as the privity doctrine, limit the duty of care for negligent lawyer conduct to situations in which the lawyer's services are intended to influence or benefit specific third persons. The Illinois law discussed in *Greycas* falls into this category.

2. Intentional Torts

As both the majority and concurrence in *Greycas* point out, Greycas could have sued Proud for fraud instead of negligent misrepresentation and malpractice. Proud said he conducted a U.C.C., tax and judgment search when he had not, and he lied with the intent of separating Greycas from its money. Doesn't this constitute the intentional tort of fraud?[62]

Generally, the law grants a lawyer no privilege to commit intentional torts against third parties in the course of representing a client or to assist a client in committing intentional torts against third parties. The most notable exception to this rule is the lawyer's virtually absolute privilege to make defamatory statements orally or in writing in court or which are reasonably related to a pending or contemplated litigation.[63] In addition, as with all fiduciaries, a lawyer has a qualified privilege to make statements intended to protect the interests of others.[64]

To prove the intentional torts of fraud and misrepresentation, the plaintiff must show that a lawyer intended to deceive and that the plaintiff belonged to a class of people that the lawyer might reasonably have foreseen being deceived. No special duty or relationship is necessary. If the lawyer honestly believed that the communication was

60. See Home Budget Loans, Inc. v. Jacoby & Meyers Law Offices, 207 Cal.App.3d 1277, 255 Cal.Rptr. 483 (1989) (mortgage broker insisted that debtor retain a lawyer to review mortgage documents and verify to broker that he had done so liable to broker for negligence).

61. See, e.g., Garcia v. Rodey, Dickason, Sloan, Akin & Robb, 106 N.M. 757, 750 P.2d 118 (1988) (plaintiff could not recover for constructive fraud against defendant's lawyers, who had stated before trial that they would not raise a defense and then successfully did so on appeal). Cases involving a litigation context often turn on failure to prove justifiable reliance: a litigant cannot reasonably rely on a statement by an opposing party's lawyer.

62. The basic elements of the intentional tort of misrepresentation (fraud) are: (1) a material false statement, (2) made with an intent to deceive, (3) which is reasonably relied on by a person to whom it is made (4) to that person's detriment.

63. The absolute privilege for judicial proceedings is not limited to lawyers but applies to judges, parties, witnesses and other participants. The purpose of the privilege is to ensure that adjudication is not hampered by fears of tort liability. Statements preliminary to a proceeding or given to a newspaper are only conditionally protected, if protected at all. See W. Prosser and P. Keeton, Prosser on Torts § 114 (5th ed.1984).

64. See, e.g., Pelagatti v. Cohen, 370 Pa.Super. 422, 536 A.2d 1337 (1987) (discussing both the absolute and qualified privilege); and Dano v. Royal Globe Ins. Co., 59 N.Y.2d 827, 464 N.Y.S.2d 741, 451 N.E.2d 488 (1983). See Chapter 5 below, in which the lawyer's tort liability for conduct connected to litigation is discussed along with other legal limits on the advocate's conduct of litigation or an appeal.

truthful, she lacked the intent necessary for fraud unless her belief was reckless.

Fraudulent intent may be shown by a reckless disregard for the truth or falsity of the proposition asserted. For example, in In re Flight Transportation Corporation Securities Litigation,[65] the court held that the purchasers of securities stated a cause of action for common law fraud against the law firm that had represented the securities' underwriters by alleging (1) that the firm, knowingly or in reckless disregard of the facts, either had made or had aided others in making untrue statements of material facts and had omitted to state other material facts necessary in order to make the statements made not misleading; (2) that the purchasers had relied on the untrue statements; and (3) that the firm by preparing the allegedly fraudulent prospectuses had assumed a duty to prospective purchasers.

May a lawyer ever safely rely on her client's assertions without some independent verification of the facts?

atty's
reliance
on TI's
statements

> It is claimed that a lawyer is entitled to rely on the statements of his client and that to require him to verify their accuracy would set an unreasonably high standard. This is too broad a generalization. It is all a matter of degree. To require an audit would obviously be unreasonable. On the other hand, to require a check of matters easily verifiable is not unreasonable. Even honest clients can make mistakes.[66]

In Newburger, Loeb & Co., Inc. v. Gross,[67] the Finley, Kumble law firm, through its partner Robert Persky, represented several general partners of a failing brokerage firm. Those general partners wanted to transfer the brokerage firm's assets to a newly formed corporation. New York law, however, requires that all partners consent to such a transfer unless the partnership agreement expressly provides otherwise, and some of the brokerage firm's other partners opposed the transfer. Persky reasoned that provisions in the partnership agreement granting the general partners the power to terminate the partnership included the power to transfer assets. He thus issued an opinion letter—necessary for the transfer—stating that the brokerage partnership had authority to make the transfer. Another law firm had declined to issue such an opinion.

Finding "simply no language in the partnership agreement" that could legitimately be construed as Persky concluded, the appellate court held the transfer to be a conversion and the Finley Kumble lawyers liable for assisting their clients in intentionally tortious con-

---

65. 593 F.Supp. 612 (D.Minn.1984).

66. Seidel v. Public Service Co. of New Hampshire, 616 F.Supp. 1342, 1362 (D.N.H. 1985), quoting Escott v. BarChris Constr. Corp., 283 F.Supp. 643, 690 (S.D.N.Y.1968). See also Stokes v. Lokken, 644 F.2d 779 (8th Cir.1981) (lawyer who recklessly relies on information provided by client may be liable for fraud); and Ames Bank v. Hahn, 205 Neb. 353, 287 N.W.2d 687 (1980) (lawyer may be liable for misrepresentation for making statement without any knowledge as to whether it is true).

67. 563 F.2d 1057 (2d Cir.1977).

duct. Finley Kumble claimed that because it had acted in its professional capacity, it was immune from suit by third parties for having given its clients bad advice. The court rejected this defense:

> Under New York law an attorney generally cannot be held liable to third parties for actions taken in furtherance of his role unless it is shown that he 'did something either tortious in character [in the sense of committing an intentional tort] or beyond the scope of his honorable employment.' Dallas v. Fassnacht, 42 N.Y.S.2d 415, 418 (Sup.Ct.N.Y. County 1943). Thus, while an attorney is privileged to give honest advice, even if erroneous, and generally is not responsible for the motives of his clients, admission to the bar does not create a license to act maliciously, fraudulently, or knowingly to tread upon the legal rights of others.

> . . .

> The issue here is simply whether [the trial judge] was warranted in finding that Persky had violated that standard.

> . . .

> [The trial judge] found that "[w]ithout question, Persky was at the heart of this entire matter, guiding the entire plan, carrying threats to the dissidents and knowingly counseling, advising and instituting baseless and fraudulent lawsuits to achieve the [clients'] goal." ... [I]nter alia, Persky was responsible for: (1) manipulating the settlement and assertion of [baseless claims]; (2) threatening the [other partners] with [litigation] in bad faith; (3) [making allegations about one of the other partners in a complaint] in disregard for the truth, thereby needlessly vilifying [him]; (4) issuing a false opinion letter ... thereby furthering the transfer in violation of the rights [of the other partners]; and (5) inducing and participating in the partners' breach of fiduciary obligation to [the other partners]. We find that the record supports the conclusion that Persky went "beyond the scope of his honorable employment" and the district court's finding of liability.[68]

If, however, a lawyer does not know and has no reason to know that her client is using her advice to engage in activity constituting an intentional tort, the courts hold that the lawyer is not liable. A lawyer is not liable merely for giving good faith advice.[69]

Nor is a lawyer liable merely for being near the scene of a client's tortious conduct. In Worldwide Marine Trading Corp. v. Marine Transport Service Inc.,[70] the court held that a lawyer's activities did not amount to culpable participation either in his client's tortious interference with contract or in violation of the antitrust laws. The court said

---

68.   563 F.2d at 1080.

69.   See Yoggerst v. Stewart, 623 F.2d 35 (7th Cir.1980), distinguishing *Newburger* and holding that "an attorney, offering advice in good faith is not liable for the torts of a client."

70.   527 F.Supp. 581 (E.D.Pa.1981).

that, unless the lawyer was a "stakeholder" in the alleged conspiracy, the lawyer "must [have done] more than be present at the scene, and indeed must [have done] more than merely advise":

> There is an important societal interest in protecting the lawyer from third-party lawsuits, and thus in requiring a showing of a knowingly fraudulent or tortious action by the lawyer before permitting third-party recovery from the lawyer.... A lawyer must be able to act decisively on behalf of his client, without fearing that he will provide "the deep pocket" in subsequent litigation. If his advice and activity are wrong or negligent, he is already exposed by virtue of his duty to his client. In the context of this case, for example, if plaintiffs prevail, [the lawyer] may have some cause to fear that certain defendants [his former clients] will proceed against him.[71]

Lawyers are also held liable for assisting in the intentional breach of fiduciary duties.[72] The special responsibilities of lawyers who represent fiduciaries are addressed in Chapter 8 below.

3. Assisting a Client in Tortious or Unlawful Conduct

GEOFFREY C. HAZARD, JR.
"HOW FAR MAY A LAWYER GO IN ASSISTING A CLIENT IN UNLAWFUL CONDUCT?"

35 U. of Miami L.Rev. 669 (1981).[73]

. . .

The general question to be considered is: How far may a lawyer lawfully go in providing assistance to a client that might enable the client to carry out an act that is to some degree illegal?

. . .

The services that a lawyer can provide cover a wide spectrum, regardless of the client purposes that may be involved. At one end of the spectrum is simply advice as to what the law "is," without specific aid or encouragement to the client. It is not easy to provide advice that is neutral with respect to the purposes implicit in the request for advice. Nevertheless, it is possible to give unsuggestive advice, and doing so is the least instrumental form of assistance that a lawyer can provide a client. At the other end of the spectrum of lawyer assistance is pure instrumentalism—lawyer's physical execution of a purpose that the client would like to realize but cannot or will not actually execute

71. Id. at 586.

72. See Whitfield v. Lindemann, 853 F.2d 1298 (5th Cir.1988) (liability of lawyer is not limited to amount of personal gain).

73. Copyright © 1981 by the University of Miami Law Review. Reprinted with permission.

himself. One example would be a lawyer who serves as "bagman" in an illegal payoff for a client who wishes to remain behind the scenes.

Sanction vs. prohibition

At the least instrumental end of the spectrum, the lawyer merely provides the client with an expert definition of the limits of the law, leaving it to the client to consider whether those limits should be transgressed. At the other end of the spectrum, the lawyer personally provides the means without which the client could not achieve the illicit purpose. The law clearly sanctions providing assistance at the least instrumental end of this spectrum. The law clearly prohibits conduct at the other end. But what about forms of conduct that fall within these extremes? Obviously, the farther we move away from simple, unsuggestive advice, and the closer we move toward active assistance, the farther we get from what the law encourages and permits and the closer we get to what the law abhors and proscribes. The questions raised by conduct falling in the middle of the spectrum, however, are difficult, and the answers are usually qualified. What advice should the lawyer give about the limits of the law of fraud or breach of fiduciary duty to a client who has fiduciary obligations but shows signs of being self-interested? What about a client who requests his attorney to prepare documents for a transaction whose factual particulars the client refuses to disclose but the lawyer has reason to suspect? What about a client who asks his lawyer to make frequent, but unscheduled, deposits of very large sums of cash in bank accounts bearing fictitious names? In the latter case, what if the city is Miami in 1981, and the client is twenty-four years of age?

. . .

It is rare that the lawyer fully knows a client's purposes or fully anticipates the ways in which the client might make use of the lawyer's services. Indeed, the client himself often does not fully realize his purposes until the moment of choice has come and gone. Furthermore, a lawyer does not learn of a client's purposes in a continuous narrative. Rather, revelation comes in fragments, often beginning in the historical middle rather than at the historical beginning. As the matter unfolds, it may appear to the lawyer that the portents of abuse are strong or weak, clear or ambiguous, firm or wavering. When are these portents sufficiently certain so that the lawyer "knows" that the client intends an illegal objective and is bent on its accomplishment?

It is sometimes suggested that the dilemma is false, because surely a lawyer cannot "know" what a client intends. This suggestion is either disingenuous or absurd. Of course, speaking in terms of radical epistemology, it is true that a lawyer cannot "know" what a client—or anyone else—intends. In these terms it is impossible for a lawyer to "know" anything. Yet the practice of law is based on practical knowledge, that is, practical assessments leading to empirical conclusions which form the basis for irrevocable action. Lawyers certainly possess such practical knowledge. If a lawyer can have practical knowledge of how the purposes of others may affect his client, he can have the same knowledge of how his client's purposes may affect others. It is in that sense that the lawyer can "know" when a client's purpose is illegal. . . .

The general category embraced by the term "illegality" also includes, beyond the criminal law, various torts. Certain kinds of torts are readily subsumed under the rubric of "illegality." These torts include the civil counterparts of criminal offenses that are *mala in se*: wrongful death by willful unexcused act, physically harmful battery, knowing conversion, and some forms of abuse of process. Other intentional torts, such as piracy of trade secrets or invasion of privacy, can also be included.

On the other hand, it is less apparent why negligence should be regarded as "illegal" conduct even if it results in tort liability. Yet negligence is a violation of the legal standard of reasonable care and is in this sense a violation of law. Suppose, for example, a client asks his lawyer whether compliance with old safety regulations is sufficient, and the lawyer indicates that such compliance would be sufficient because a tenuous argument can be made that new and stricter safety regulations are constitutionally invalid. If someone is injured as a result of the client's noncompliance with the new regulations, is the lawyer chargeable with having materially assisted the client in "illegal conduct"? How would the outcome be affected if that violation also entails criminal sanctions?

. . . We may feel confident about including [torts that are counterparts of serious criminal offenses], but as we move away from this core meaning, the boundaries become increasingly doubtful.

We can also approach the question from a different direction. There is a wide range of client conduct that gives rise to civil liability, but which we would not readily call "illegal" in the present context. Consider, for example, the deliberate default in performance of a contract obligation, the deliberate exercise of dominion and control over property of which another person claims ownership, or the deliberate decision to make a search and seizure of doubtful legality. Should any of these forms of conduct be categorized as "illegal" for the purpose of limiting the client endeavors that a lawyer may further?

The term "illegality" in ordinary legal parlance does not embrace breach of contract or invasion of a property interest [unless tortious conduct is involved]. Yet there are breaches of contract and invasions of personal and property interests that are more flagrant and more harmful than many torts, and indeed more harmful than many regulatory offenses.

. . .

The law of legal ethics, for example, specially presupposes the law of torts and of agency. A lawyer in the service of a client is typically an agent. But legal representation is a special kind of agency, involving legally conferred special powers that provide the lawyer with some autonomy from the client in carrying out the agency. . . .

In general, the law of agency imposes limits on what an agent may, with legal impunity, do for a principal. Section 343 of the Restatement (Second) of Agency states: "An agent who does an act otherwise a tort is not relieved from liability by the fact that he acted . . . on account of the principal, except where he is exercising . . . a privilege held by him for the protection of the principal's interests. . . ."[15] As explained in Comment b to this section, an agent's act is privileged if "a reasonable belief in the existence of facts causes an act to be privileged, and a command by the principal gives the agent reason to believe in the existence of such facts." Thus, if a client directs his lawyer to commence criminal proceedings against another, and if the lawyer "has reasonable grounds for believing the other guilty of the crime, the [lawyer] is not guilty of malicious prosecution."

Section 348 of the Restatement is also pertinent to the kinds of transactions in which lawyers can be involved. That section provides that "[a]n agent who fraudulently makes representations, uses duress, or knowingly assists in the commission of tortious fraud or duress by his principal or by others is subject to liability in tort to the injured person. . . ." The comments following section 348 make it clear that if a lawyer acts for a client in a transaction that the lawyer knows is founded on misrepresentations, the lawyer acts tortiously.[19]

. . .

The vital circumstance under the law of agency is therefore not the fact that the actor is an agent, but the existence of facts that render his actions privileged. Applying the law of agency to lawyers, the vital question is what the lawyer knows about the client's endeavor. Using defamation and false arrest as illustrations, Comment b to section 343 of the Restatement (Second) of Agency observes that if "a reasonable belief in the existence of facts causes an act to be privileged," and if what the agent (lawyer) is told by the principal (client) "gives the agent reason to believe in the existence of such facts," then the agent (lawyer) has the privilege that is conferred on innocent actors.

But what if the client's endeavor is *not* one that a "reasonable belief in the existence of facts" will cause to be privileged? For example, in the tort of conversion it is not a defense that the agent reasonably believes that the property was his principal's. This problem is explicitly addressed in section 349 of the Restatement (Second) of

---

15. Restatement (Second) of Agency § 343 (1957).

19. Comment a, for example, states: "[A]n agent who enters into transactions with a buyer knowing that the buyer is relying upon the previous misrepresentations by the principal or other agent is liable to the same extent as if he had made the previous misrepresentations." Id. Comment a. Comment c adds:

 [I]f an agent who has been given misinformation by a principal, on the strength of which he makes statements to a third person, later discovers the untruth and refrains from taking steps to inform the other party, the agent is subject to liability if subsequently the other party completes the transaction with the principal or another agent, relying in part upon the statements of the first agent.

Id. at Comment c.

Agency: An agent whose acts "would otherwise constitute trespass to or conversion of a chattel is not relieved from liability by the fact that he acts on account of his principal and reasonably, although mistakenly, believes that the principal is entitled to possession of the chattels." Under this rule, what is the situation of a lawyer who advises a client to seize property in possession of a debtor? [24]

The lawyer's knowledge is again the vital question in cases involving misrepresentations in a contract transaction. Under section 348 of the Restatement (Second) of Agency, for example, a lawyer faces liability if he "knowingly assists in the commission of tortious fraud" by his client. If the lawyer proceeds "knowing that the buyer is relying upon the previous misrepresentations by the [client]," then the lawyer is "liable to the same extent as if he had made the previous misrepresentations." [Comment a.] Moreover, if the lawyer "has been given misinformation by a [client], on the strength of which he makes statements to a third person, [and] later discovers the untruth and refrains from taking steps to inform the other party, the [lawyer] is subject to liability if subsequently the other party completes the transaction ... relying in part upon the statements of the [lawyer]." [Comment c.] Under these rules, then, a lawyer would be liable if he discovered on the eve of a closing that the other party had relied on statements by the client that the lawyer knew were false or fraudulently misleading.[28] Such conduct also would seem to be "illegal" within the meaning of DR 7–102(A)(7).

The rules of tort law are similar to the rules of agency, but are cast in terms of "persons acting in concert." That agents and principals act "in concert" is clear as a matter of ordinary usage. Section 343, Comment d of the Restatement (Second) of Agency expressly refers to section 876 of the Restatement (Second) of Torts, which is entitled "Persons Acting in Concert." Section 876 provides:

> For harm resulting to a third person from the tortious conduct of another, one is subject to liability if he
>
> > (a) does a tortious act in concert with the other or pursuant to a common design with him, or
> >
> > (b) knows that the other's conduct constitutes a breach of duty and gives substantial assistance or encouragement to the other so to conduct himself.... [30]

24. Flagg Bros., Inc. v. Brooks, 436 U.S. 149 (1978) addresses the situation of a lawyer who advises a client about seizing property in the possession of a debtor. It would seem that if the lawyer "assists" the client, and if the seizure turns out not to be legally privileged, then the lawyer, as well as the client, is prima facie legally responsible. Restatement (Second) of Agency § 343, Comment d, says that "[T]he act of the agent may play too small a part to render him legally responsible for the result, or the agent's innocence and purpose may create a privilege for him to act." It is hard to see how the lawyer's role in such a situation is "too small" to count. The comment does not indicate the scope of the privilege that could result in immunity.

28. ... [See] SEC v. National Student Marketing Corp., 457 F.Supp. 682 (D.D.C.1978) [reprinted below at p. 99]....

30. Restatement (Second) of Torts § 876 (1977).

Advice to a tortfeasor is equivalent to active participation in the tort if the advisor knows that the contemplated act is tortious, and if the advice is a "substantial factor in causing the resulting tort."

. . .

Complicity

Finally, one can look to the principles of complicity expressed in the criminal law for guidance. Section 2.06(1) of the Model Penal Code provides that "[a] person is guilty of an offense if it is committed by his own conduct or by the conduct of another person for which he is legally accountable...." [36] Section 2.06(2)(c) of the Code provides that a person is legally accountable for the conduct of another person if he is an "accomplice of such other person." And section 2.06(3)(a)(ii) provides that an accomplice is one who "aids ... in planning or committing" the offense "with the purpose of promoting or facilitating the commission of the offense." Restating these provisions, a lawyer is guilty of an offense if he aids a client in facilitating conduct that is an offense. [39]

The case law on the question is sparse.... In most of the cases, the lawyer has overtly assisted his client in accomplishing manifestly illegal purposes. Thus, courts have held that it is improper for a lawyer to give advice as to how to commit a crime or fraud [41] or how to conceal criminal or fraudulent acts. [42] These cases beget law that is not hard to formulate. There is less guidance when the conduct is less blatant, but there is enough to point the way. One case, for example, states the test ... as whether "the lawyer conveyed to the client the idea that by adopting a particular course of action [the client] may successfully [accomplish the illegal purpose]?" [43] As to the mode of assistance, courts have held that it is unlawful for a lawyer to negotiate for his client in pursuance of an illegal purpose [44] or to prepare documents to effectuate it. [45] As to the extent of knowledge that will result in complicity, the cases say not only that liability results from actual knowledge of the client's illegal purpose, but also that it results

---

36. Model Penal Code § 2.06(1) (Proposed Official Draft, 1962).

39. There is very little authority on the degree of lawyer involvement in a client's criminal endeavor that would constitute "aiding." See Johnson v. Youden, [1950] 1 K.B. 544, involving a criminal prosecution against a solicitor who effected the conveyance of real property at a price in excess of that permitted by applicable price control regulations. The action was dismissed because there was no showing that the solicitor knew about the calculation of the price such that, given his assumed knowledge of the law, he knew that the price violated the law.

41. E.g., In re Feltman, 51 N.J. 27, 237 A.2d 473 (1968).

42. E.g., Townsend v. State Bar, 32 Cal.2d 592, 197 P.2d 326 (1948); In re Giordano, 49 N.J. 210, 229 A.2d 524 (1967).

43. In re Bullowa, 223 A.D. 593, 602, 229 N.Y.S. 145, 154 (1928). See also Attorney Grievance Comm'n v. Kerpelman, 288 Md. 341, 420 A.2d 940 (1980).

44. E.g., In re La Duca, 62 N.J. 133, 299 A.2d 405 (1973).

45. E.g., Galbraith v. State Bar, 218 Cal. 329, 23 P.2d 291 (1933).

from knowledge of facts that reasonably should excite suspicion.[46]

This analysis indicates the dimensions of the lawyer's duty under criminal and civil law to refrain from "assisting" a client in conduct that is "illegal." A lawyer violates that duty if:

(1) The client is engaged in a course of conduct that violates the criminal law or is an intentional violation of a civil obligation, other than failure to perform a contract or failure to sustain a good faith claim to property;

(2) The lawyer has knowledge of the facts sufficient to reasonably discern that the client's course of conduct is such a violation; and

(3) The lawyer facilitates the client's course of conduct either by giving advice that encourages the client to pursue the conduct or indicates how to reduce the risks of detection, or by performing an act that substantially furthers the course of conduct.

Some Questions

Is a lawyer who advises a client that breaching a contract may be less costly than carrying it out liable for damages to the non-client party if the client follows the lawyer's advice? Will your answer be different if the lawyer assists a client in persuading a non-client to break a contract with a third person? When does legal advice given in connection with a client's property dispute with a third person become the intentional tort of conversion? May a lawyer advise (and defend in further litigation that may arise) a product manufacturer who is continuing to distribute a product that some juries, but not the manufacturer, believe is so unsafe as to be a "defective product?"[73] What if the product violates current state or federal safety regulations? Finally, is the lawyer liable to a non-client who is injured by improper "hardball" tactics in the courtroom that include malicious and false statements about the claimant?

Does a lawyer commit a federal civil rights violation by invoking summary procedures that have now been declared unconstitutional?

---

46. E.g., In re Wines, 370 S.W.2d 328 (Mo.1963); State ex rel. Nebraska State Bar Ass'n v. Holscher, 193 Neb. 729, 230 N.W.2d 75 (1975); In re Blatt, 65 N.J. 539, 324 A.2d 15 (1974).

73. Ford sought to justify its placement of the gas tank in Pinto cars on the ground that "the $11 increased cost on 12.5 million cars and light trucks would be almost three times greater than the estimated injury costs" (180 deaths and a similar number of serious burn injuries). This decision was revisited in a criminal trial against Ford for reckless homicide in Indiana and a California damage award of $125 million (later reduced to $6.6 million by a judge). See David Luban, Lawyers and Justice 206–34 (1989) (discussing the Pinto case). Dow Corning decided to take a more conciliatory approach in the 1992 breast implant controversy.

In Wyatt v. Cole,[74] the lawyer for one partner in a soured business venture brought a replevin proceeding in Mississippi to obtain summary possession of property his client claimed. The other partner brought a federal civil rights action under 42 U.S.C. § 1983 against the first partner and his lawyer for employing an unconstitutional summary remedy to seize property. The Court held that private individuals who use unconstitutional state procedures do not have the qualified tort immunity available to public officials.

C. SECURITIES AND REGULATORY LAW

1. Lawyer's Opinion Function

Parties to business transactions often seek legal reassurance on certain issues from opposing parties' counsel. This reassurance, known as a third-party legal opinion (or comfort letter), may be either written or oral but typically takes the form of a formal letter, the contents of which counsel haggle over as much as any other transactional point. Opinions often deal with such matters as legal authority to act, valid incorporation and compliance with particular laws, such as applicable federal and state securities laws. Some of the professional concerns connected with the opinion function are ably summarized in a well-known article by James J. Fuld.[75]

Conscientious lawyers, Fuld reports, are concerned at the risks created for lawyers by increasing requests for legal opinions of broad scope that are relied on by persons with whom the client is dealing. Lawyers who have two sets of draft opinions for each transaction, depending upon which party they represent, stimulate haggling about opinion terms and sometimes impose their will in situations in which their client has a superior bargaining position. Lawyers should be reluctant, Fuld argues, to request or provide opinions that purport to certify matters on which no lawyer can feel fully confident, such as an opinion that a corporate client is complying with all applicable federal, state and local laws. Opinions that contain factual detail about the client also imperil the client's attorney-client privilege. Nor is it responsible for a lawyer to give an opinion involving the law of another jurisdiction without involving local counsel.

To whom does the opining lawyer owe duties? Fuld states:

> ... It is clear that he has an obligation to his client, and if the lawyer addresses his opinion to a third party, he has duties to the third party. I believe, however, that the duties may not be exactly the same. To his client the lawyer owes a duty to deliver an opinion which is appropriate for the client and which the client can

---

74. 112 S.Ct. 1827 (1992). The Court left open the question whether an affirmative defense of good faith or probable cause to invoke the state procedure is available to private defendants.

75. James J. Fuld, Lawyers' Standards and Responsibilities in Rendering in Rendering Opinions, 33 Bus.Lawyer 1295 (1978).

understand and act upon; there is no one else who can help the client to understand the opinion and if necessary obtain a different opinion. But a third-party recipient is usually represented by his own lawyer, who is uniquely familiar with the third-party's particular legal and tax problems, and the opining lawyer's duties are therefore merely to give his careful opinion on the matters requested.

. . .

Whatever the law may ultimately be held to be, I would recommend that a lawyer assume that his opinion, or a summary of, or reference to, it, will be seen by persons other than the original recipient, and that the lawyer may be charged with legal responsibility for their reliance. Such an opinion should, therefore, not only attempt to limit the class of persons who may rely on the opinion, but perhaps more importantly, include all qualifications, conditions, assumptions and references to other documents in order to alert subsequent users of the opinion regarding any uncertainties involved. Anyone other than the intended recipient should be told to consult his own advisor. And, if this is understood in advance with the client, the opinion should further state that no summary of, or reference to, the opinion is to be made without the lawyer's written consent. Even all these steps may not be sufficient.... [76]

Third–Party Legal Opinions

Increasing concern over a lawyer's civil liability for third-party legal opinions has prompted bar associations across the United States to draft opinion guidelines and standards.[77] Widespread acceptance of such standards not only mitigates the risk of misunderstanding of opinion language, but also provides support to a lawyer unwilling to give a risky opinion desired by an opposing party. Agreement on standards also provides a common starting point for negotiations, perhaps reducing the "two files of opinions" phenomenon discussed by Fuld.[78]

---

76. Id. at 1309–10.

77. In addition to the ABA report described in the text, other major standardization efforts include the following: Special Report by the TriBar Opinion Committee, The Remedies Opinion, 46 Bus.Law. 959 (1991) (a joint effort of three major New York bar associations); Report of Standards for Opinions of Florida Counsel of the Special Committee on Opinion Standards of the Florida Bar Business Law Section, 46 Bus.Law. 1407 (1991); and Report of the Committee on Corporations of the Business Law Section of the State Bar of California Regarding Legal Opinions in Business Transactions, 14 Pac.L.J. 1001 (1983).

78. Other articles on rendering opinions for third parties include: Norman Redlich, Lawyers' Standards and Responsibilities in Rendering Opinions, 33 Bus.Law. 1317 (1978); and Note, Attorney Liability to Third Parties for Corporate Opinion Letters, 64 B.U.L.Rev. 415 (1984). See also ABA Statement of Policy Regarding Auditors' Requests for Information, 31 Bus.Law. 1709 (1976). For a bibliography, see Joint Committee of the Real Property Sections of the State Bar of California and the Los Angeles County Bar Assn., Report: Legal Opinions in California Real Estate Transactions, 42 Bus.Law. 1139, 1203–05 (1987).

The most significant, and potentially most far-reaching in effect, of the various third-party opinion standards efforts is the Third–Party Legal Opinion Report of the ABA's Section on Business Law.[79]   The avowed purpose of the project was to serve as "the first step toward the establishment of a national consensus as to the purpose, format and coverage of a third-party legal opinion, the precise meaning of its language and the recognition of certain guidelines for its negotiation." Do such bar association efforts present any antitrust concerns?

Opinion Letters and M.R. 2.3

The Model Code did not address evaluations of the client's affairs for use by third parties.   Model Rule 2.3, however, provides that a lawyer may undertake such an evaluation as long as (1) it is reasonable to believe that making the evaluation is compatible with the lawyer's other duties to the client, and (2) the client consents after consultation. As to the confidentiality of information learned in the course of making the evaluation, M.R. 2.3(b) states:

> Except as disclosure is required in connection with a report of an evaluation, information relating to the evaluation is otherwise protected by Rule 1.6 [the rule on confidentiality].

The Comment to 2.3 states:

> The quality of an evaluation depends on the freedom and extent of the investigation upon which it is based.   Ordinarily a lawyer should have whatever latitude of investigation seems necessary as a matter of professional judgment.   Under some circumstances, however, the terms of the evaluation may be limited.   For example, certain issues or sources may be categorically excluded, or the scope of search may be limited by the time constraints of the noncooperation of persons having relevant information.   Any such limitations which are material to the evaluation should be described in the report.   If after a lawyer has commenced an evaluation, the client refuses to comply with the terms upon which it was understood the evaluation was to have been made, the lawyer's obligations are determined by law, having reference to the terms of the client's agreement and the surrounding circumstances.

Notice that the Comment refers to law outside the Rules in determining whether disclosure of adverse information may be necessary. Whether the lawyer may withdraw and whether disclosure is necessary to avoid assisting a fraud also are answered by reference to criminal, tort and relevant statutory law.

Read Model Rule 4.1.   How is it related to M.R. 2.3?   M.R. 4.1 uses the word "knowingly."   Read the definition of "knowingly" in the

---

79. ABA Section on Business Law, Third–Party Legal Opinion Report, 47 Bus.Law. (Nov. 1991).   The report originated in a 1989 conference at which 71 practitioners presented papers.   In its final form it reflects the comments of more than 24 bar groups. The resulting "Accord," as it is referred to, contains many pages of densely written fine print and includes guidelines for negotiating a legal opinion.

Terminology section of the Model Rules. Should a different word or phrase have been substituted for "knowingly" in M.R. 4.1? What would M.R. 2.3 and 4.1 have required of the lawyer doing the lien search in *Greycas*? M.R. 4.1 is considered further in connection with the disclosure of client fraud in Chapter 4 at p. 294.

2. Aiding and Abetting a Securities Law Violation

SEC v. NATIONAL STUDENT MARKETING CORP.

United States District Court for the District of Columbia, 1978.
457 F.Supp. 682.

Before BARRINGTON PARKER, DISTRICT JUDGE.

[National Student Marketing Corporation (NSMC), which marketed products for high school and college students, was a prosperous company in 1969, or so the financial community thought. In that year NSMC expressed an interest in acquiring Interstate National Corporation, an insurance holding company.

[On June 10, 1969, NSMC's president and one of its senior vice-presidents made a presentation to the Interstate directors concerning the proposed merger. They provided the Interstate directors with NSMC's 1968 annual report, its financial report for the first half of 1969, and financial projections of earnings for the fiscal year ending on August 31, 1969. They sweetened their initial offer (1) from one share of NSMC common stock for every two shares of Interstate to two shares of NSMC stock for every three shares of Interstate; and (2) by promising the Interstate directors that they would be permitted to sell up to 25% of the NSMC shares they would acquire in a registered public offering planned for the fall of 1969.

[This resulted in an agreement in principle for the merger. NSMC and Interstate issued press releases, which included information about NSMC's earnings for the first half of fiscal year 1969.

[On August 12, 1969, the Interstate directors met to review the final version of the merger agreement. The agreement provided: (1) that both corporations warranted that the information in their Proxy statements would "be accurate and correct and [would] not omit to state a material fact necessary to make such information not misleading"; and (2) that the financial statements included "are true and correct and have been prepared in accordance with generally accepted accounting principles". It also included NSMC's specific assurance that its 1968 year-end and May 31, 1969, nine-month financial statements:

> fairly present the results of the operation of NSMC ... for the periods indicated, subject in the case of the nine-month statements to year-end audit adjustments.

[The agreement also provided that the merger was conditioned on the prior receipt by each corporation of (1) an opinion letter from the other corporation's lawyers that all transactions in connection with the merger had been taken in full compliance with applicable law; and (2) a satisfactory "comfort letter" from the other corporation's independent public accountants. Each comfort letter was to state that the accountants had no reason to believe that any material adjustments in the interim financials were required in order fairly to present the results of the operations of the company. The agreement could be terminated by mutual consent of the two corporations' boards of directors at any time prior to completion of the merger. It also gave each party the right to waive any of the conditions to that party's obligations. Finally, the agreement specified that the merger be consummated on or before November 28, 1969.

[Both corporations used proxy statements and notices of special stockholder meetings to secure stockholder approval of the proposed merger. The material sent by Interstate to its shareholders included a copy of the merger agreement, NSMC's proxy statement and NSMC's financial statement for August 31, 1968 and the nine-month interim financial statement, ending on May 31, 1969. The nine-month interim statement showed an NSMC profit of approximately $700,000. The shareholders of both companies seemed enthusiastic about the merger, approving it by large majorities.

[In mid-October Peat Marwick—the independent accountant as it happened for both Interstate and NSMC—began working on the comfort letter on NSMC's financial condition. It soon determined that NSMC's nine-month interim financials had to be adjusted so that, instead of showing a $700,000 profit for these nine months, NSMC would show a loss of almost $200,000. Peat Marwick discussed the proposed adjustments with representatives of NSMC, but neither the accountants nor NSMC told Interstate of the proposed change. Peat Marwick completed a draft of the comfort letter on the morning of the closing.

[The closing was scheduled for 2:00 p.m. on Friday, October 31, at the New York offices of the law firm of White & Case. White & Case represented NSMC, with Epley as the partner in charge of the firm's representation. Epley and several White & Case associates were at the meeting in behalf of NSMC, along with NSMC's president, Randell, and general counsel, Davies. The law firm of Lord Bissell & Brook, through its partners Meyer and Schauer, represented Interstate. Meyer was also a director and shareholder of Interstate. Interstate's president, Brown, and three other members of the Interstate board of directors and executive committee were also at the meeting in Interstate's behalf.]

. . .

Although Schauer had had an opportunity to review most of the merger documents at White & Case on the previous day, the comfort letter had not been delivered. When he arrived at White & Case on the morning of the merger, the letter was still not available, but he was informed by a representative of the firm that it was expected to arrive at any moment.

The meeting proceeded. When the letter had not arrived by approximately 2:15 p.m., Epley telephoned Peat Marwick's Washington office to inquire about it. Anthony M. Natelli, the partner in charge, thereupon dictated to Epley's secretary a letter which provided in part:

Comfort letter

> [N]othing has come to our attention which caused us to believe that:
>
> 1. The National Student Marketing Corporation's unaudited consolidated financial statements as of and for the nine months ended May 31, 1969:
>
> > a. Were not prepared in accordance with accounting principles ... followed in the preparation [of previous financial statements];
> >
> > b. Would require any material adjustments for a fair and reasonable presentation of the information shown except with respect to [NSMC's nine month interim financial statement covering the period ending on] ... May 31, 1969 ... our examination ... disclosed the following significant adjustments which in our opinion should be reflected retroactive to May 31, 1969:
> >
> > > 1. In adjusting the amortization of deferred costs at May 31, 1969 ... an adjustment of $500,000 was required....
> > >
> > > 2. In August 1969 management wrote off receivables in amounts of $300,000. It appears that the uncollectibility of these receivables could have been determined at May 31, 1969 and such charge off should have been reflected as of that date
> > >
> > > 3. Acquisition costs in the amount of $84,000 for proposed acquisitions which the Company decided not to pursue were transferred from additional paid-in capital to general and administrative expenses. In our opinion, these should have been so transferred as of May 31, 1969

· · ·

Epley delivered one copy of the typed letter to the conference room where the closing was taking place. Epley then returned to his office.

Schauer was the first to read the unsigned letter. He then handed it to Cameron Brown, advising him to read it.... [Meyer also read it.] They asked Randell and Joy a number of questions relating to the nature and effect of the adjustments. The NSMC officers gave assurances that the adjustments would have no significant effect on the predicted year-end earnings of NSMC and that a substantial portion of the $500,000 adjustments to deferred costs would be recovered. Moreover, they indicated that NSMC's year-end audit for fiscal 1969 had been completed by Peat Marwick, would be published in a couple of weeks, and would demonstrate that NSMC itself had made each of the adjustments for its fourth quarter. The comfort letter, they explained, simply determined that those adjustments should be reflected in the third quarter ended May 31, 1969, rather than the final quarter of NSMC's fiscal year. Randell and Joy indicated that while NSMC disagreed with what they felt was a tightening up of its accounting practices, everything requested by Peat Marwick to "clean up" its books had been undertaken.

At the conclusion of this discussion, certain of the Interstate representatives, including at least Brown, Schauer and Meyer, conferred privately to consider their alternatives in light of the apparent nonconformity of the comfort letter with the requirements of the Merger Agreement. Although they considered the letter a serious matter and the adjustments as significant and important, they were nonetheless under some pressure to determine a course of action promptly since there was a 4 p.m. filing deadline if the closing were to be consummated as scheduled on October 31.[20] Among the alternatives considered were: (1) delaying or postponing the closing, either to secure more information or to resolicit the shareholders with corrected financials; (2) closing the merger; or (3) calling it off completely.

The consensus of the directors was that there was no need to delay the closing. The comfort letter contained all relevant information and in light of the explanations given by Randell and Joy, they already had sufficient information upon which to make a decision. Any delay for the purpose of resoliciting the shareholders was considered impractical because it would require the use of year-end figures instead of the stale nine-month interim financials. Such a requirement would make it impossible to resolicit shareholder approval before the merger upset date of November 28, 1969, and would cause either the complete abandonment of the merger or its renegotiation on terms possibly far less favorable to Interstate. The directors also recognized that delay or abandonment of the merger would result in a decline in the stock of both companies, thereby harming the shareholders and possibly subjecting the directors to lawsuits based on their failure to close the merger. The Interstate representatives decided to proceed with the closing. They did, however, solicit and receive further assurances from the NSMC representatives that the stated adjustments were the only ones to be made to the company's financial statements and that 1969 earnings would be as predicted. When asked by Brown whether the closing could proceed on the basis of an unsigned comfort letter, Meyer responded that if a White & Case partner assured them that this was in fact the comfort letter and that a signed copy would be forthcoming from Peat Marwick, they could close. Epley gave this assurance. Meyer then announced that Interstate was prepared to proceed, the closing was consummated, and a previously arranged telephone call

20. The pressure to close on October 31 derived from a public announcement to that effect; it was therefore likely that any delay would have had an adverse impact on the stock of both companies. The 4 p.m. deadline was the closing time of the District of Columbia office where the merger documents were to be filed.

was made which resulted in the filing of the Articles of Merger at the Office of the Recorder of Deeds of the District of Columbia. Large packets of merger documents, including the required counsel opinion letters, were exchanged.[22] The closing was solemnized with a toast of warm champagne.

Unknown to the Interstate group, several telephone conversations relating to the substance of the comfort letter occurred on the afternoon of the closing between Peat Marwick representatives and Epley.... Epley was told that an additional paragraph would be added in order to characterize the adjustments. The paragraph recited that with the noted adjustments properly made, NSMC's unaudited consolidated statement for the nine-month period would not reflect a profit as had been indicated but rather a net loss, and the consolidated operations of NSMC as they existed on May 31, 1969, would show a break-even as to net earnings for the year ended August 31, 1969. Epley had the additional paragraph typed out, but failed to inform or disclose this change to Interstate. In a second conversation, after the closing was completed and the Interstate representatives had departed, Epley was informed of still another proposed addition, namely, a paragraph urging resolicitation of both companies' shareholders and disclosure of NSMC's corrected nine-month financials prior to closing. To this, he responded that the deal was closed and the letter was not needed. Peat Marwick nonetheless advised Epley that the letter would be delivered and that its counsel was considering whether further action should be taken by the firm.

The final written draft of the comfort letter arrived at White & Case late that afternoon. Peat Marwick believed that Interstate had been informed and was aware of the conversations between its representatives and Epley and of its concern about the adjustments. Because of this belief and especially since the merger had been closed

---

22. The LBB opinion letter, delivered to NSMC at the closing, reads in pertinent part:

Gentlemen:

We have acted as counsel to Interstate in connection with the merger of Interstate into NSMC pursuant to the Plan. In such capacity, we have examined the Plan together with Exhibits A, B and C thereto; the charters, by-laws and minutes of Interstate and its Subsidiaries (as defined in the Plan), corporate records, certificates of public officials and of officers and representatives of Interstate and such other documents deemed necessary to enable us to give the opinion hereinafter expressed.

Based on the foregoing and having due regard to legal considerations we deem relevant, we are of the opinion that:

. . .

7. The Plan has been duly executed and delivered by Interstate and is a valid and binding obligation in accordance with its terms and any corporate action by Interstate required in order to authorize the transactions therein contemplated has been taken.

8. To our knowledge, neither Interstate nor any Subsidiary is engaged in or threatened with any legal action or other proceeding, or has incurred or been charged with any presently pending violation of any Federal, state or local law or administrative regulation, which would materially adversely affect or impair the financial condition, business, operations, prospects, properties or assets of Interstate.

. . .

without benefit of the completed letter, Peat Marwick's counsel perceived no obligation to do anything further about the merger. Nonetheless, a signed copy of the final letter was sent to each board member of the two companies, presumably in an effort to underline the accountants' concern about consummation of the merger without shareholder resolicitation.

The signed comfort letter was delivered to the Interstate offices on Monday, November 3. It was first seen and read by Donald Jeffers, Interstate's chief financial officer. He had not been present at the October 31 closing or informed of the adjustments to the interim financials. Concerned, he contacted Brown immediately and read the letter to him. Since a meeting with other Interstate principals was scheduled for the next morning the letter was added to the other matters to be discussed.

The signed letter was virtually identical to the unsigned version delivered at the closing, except for the addition of the following two paragraphs:

> Your attention is called, however, to the fact that if the aforementioned adjustments had been made at May 31, 1969 the unaudited consolidated statement of earnings of National Student Marketing Corporation would have shown a net loss of approximately $80,000. It is presently estimated that the consolidated operations of the company as it existed at May 31, 1969 will be approximately a break-even as to net earnings for the year ended August 31, 1969.

> In view of the above mentioned facts, we believe the companies should consider submitting corrected interim unaudited financial information to the shareholders prior to proceeding with the closing.

The only other change was the reduction in the write-off to receivables from $300,000 to $200,000, making total negative adjustments to NSMC's nine-month financials in the amount of $784,000.

At the meeting the following day, the matter was fully discussed by the former Interstate principals. Of particular concern were the additional "break-even" and "resolicitation" paragraphs.[25] Brown explained what had occurred at the closing and the reasons for the decision to consummate the merger. He called Meyer at LBB, who by that time was also aware of the letter. After some discussion, it was decided that more information was needed. Brown and Jeffers agreed to contact Peat Marwick and Meyer agreed that his firm would contact Epley at White & Case.

---

25. A significant cause of their concern was a statement contained in a copy of a letter from Peat Marwick to Epley which accompanied the signed comfort letter; that letter suggested that Epley was aware of the additional paragraphs on the day of the closing. SEC Exhibit 57, Letter dated October 31, 1969, from Peat Marwick to Mr. Eplee (sic). Jeffers, however, was concerned with the adjustments in general, stating that it was very unusual for them to be included in a comfort letter, that he was surprised the Interstate representatives had closed without a signed comfort letter, and that the deferred cost adjustment of $500,000 was "a hell of a big adjustment,".

On that afternoon, Schauer contacted Epley by telephone. Epley stated that he had not known of the additional paragraphs until after the closing. He added that in any case the additions did not expand upon the contents of the earlier unsigned letter; the "break-even" paragraph simply reflected the results of an arithmetic computation of the effects of the adjustments, and the "resolicitation" paragraph was gratuitous and a matter for lawyers, not accountants. While Schauer disagreed, Epley again responded that the additional paragraphs made no difference and that NSMC regarded the deal as closed.

... Meanwhile, the market value of NSMC stock continued to increase, and the directors noted that any action on their part to undo the merger would most likely adversely affect its price. By the end of the week, the decision was made to abstain from any action. Thereafter, Brown issued a memorandum to all Interstate employees announcing completion of the merger. No effort was ever made by any of the defendants to disclose the contents of the comfort letter to the former shareholders of Interstate, the SEC or to the public in general.

D. The Stock Sales

Early in the negotiations the principal Interstate shareholders understood that they would be able to sell a portion of the NSMC stock received in the merger through a public offering planned for the fall of 1969. Various shareholders, including Brown, Tate, Allison, Bach and Meyer, intended to profit by this opportunity and sell up to 25 percent of their newly acquired stock....

White Weld [the brokerage firm handling the sales] began processing the sales on the afternoon of October 31. It subsequently sold a total of 59,500 shares of NSMC stock. The gross received was slightly less than $3 million. Brown received approximately $500,000 for his shares and Meyer received approximately $86,000 for the shares he held.... White Weld was never informed of the comfort letter adjustments before it undertook the sale as agents for the Interstate principals.

. . .

E. Subsequent Events

Following the acquisition of Interstate and several other companies NSMC stock rose steadily in price, reaching a peak in mid-December. However, in early 1970, after several newspaper and magazine articles appeared questioning NSMC's financial health, the value of the stock decreased drastically. Several private lawsuits were filed and the SEC initiated a wide-ranging investigation which led to the filing of this action.

II. THE PRESENT ACTION

[This was a civil proceeding brought by the Securities and Exchange Commission, seeking injunctive sanctions against NSMC, the NSMC representatives and the Interstate representatives for their participation in alleged securities law violations in the merger of the two companies. While the suit was in the discovery stage, NSMC and its representatives, including Peat Marwick, the Peat Marwick partner who dictated the "comfort letter" and Epley, consented to the entry of judgments of permanent injunctions against them. Epley was suspended from securities practice for 180 days. White & Case, also a defendant, entered into a settlement with the SEC. The firm agreed to follow specified procedures in handling future securities matters. Thus, the only defendants that remained before the court in this case were those who had represented Interstate: the law firm of Lord, Bissell & Brook and its two partners, Meyer and Schauer, and Brown, the former president of Interstate.] *

     ... [T]he Commission alleges that the defendants, both as principals and as aiders and abettors, violated § 10(b) of the 1934 Act,[37] Rule 10b–5 promulgated thereunder,[38] and § 17(a) of the 1933 Act,[39] through their participation in the Interstate/NSMC merger and subsequent stock sales by Interstate principals, in each instance without disclosing the material information revealed by the Peat Marwick comfort letter.

---

   * [Editors' note:] Before reading on think about what, if anything, the lawyers for Interstate did wrong. What, if anything, should they have done differently before the closing meeting? At the closing meeting? After the closing meeting?

37.   Section 10(b), 15 U.S.C. § 78j(b), reads as follows:

   It shall be unlawful for any person, directly or indirectly, by the use of any means or instrumentality of interstate commerce or of the mails, or of any facility of any national securities exchange—

* * *

   (b) To use or employ, in connection with the purchase or sale of any security registered on a national securities exchange or any security not so registered, any manipulative or deceptive device or contrivance in contravention of such rules and regulations as the Commission may prescribe as necessary or appropriate in the public interest or for the protection of investors.

38.   Rule 10b–5, 17 C.F.R. § 240.10b–5, provides:

   It shall be unlawful for any person, directly or indirectly, by the use of any means or instrumentality of interstate commerce, or of the mails or of any facility of any national securities exchange,

   (a) To employ any device, scheme, or artifice to defraud,

   (b) To make any untrue statement of a material fact or to omit to state a material fact necessary in order to make the statements made, in the light of the circumstances under which they were made, not misleading, or

   (c) To engage in any act, practice, or course of business which operates or would operate as a fraud or deceit upon any person, in connection with the purchase or sale of any security.

39.   Section 17(a), 15 U.S.C. § 77q(a), provides:

   It shall be unlawful for any person in the offer or sale of any securities by the use of any means or instruments of transportation or communication in interstate commerce or by the use of the mails, directly or indirectly—

   (1) to employ any device, scheme, or artifice to defraud, or

   (2) to obtain money or property by means of any untrue statement of a material fact or any omission to state a material fact necessary in order to make the statements made, in the light of the circumstances under which they were made, not misleading, or

   (3) to engage in any transaction, practice, or course of business which operates or would operate as a fraud or deceit upon the purchaser.

Numerous charges, all of which appear to allege secondary liability, are leveled against the attorney defendants. Schauer is charged with "participating in the merger between Interstate and NSMC," apparently referring to his failure to interfere with the closing of the merger after receipt of the comfort letter. Such inaction, when alleged to facilitate a transaction, falls under the rubric of aiding and abetting. See Kerbs v. Fall River Industries, Inc., 502 F.2d 731, 739–40 (10th Cir.1974). Both Schauer and Meyer are charged with issuing false opinions in connection with the merger and stock sales, thereby facilitating each transaction, and with acquiescence in the merger after learning the contents of the signed comfort letter. The Commission contends that the attorneys should have refused to issue the opinions in view of the adjustments revealed by the unsigned comfort letter, and after receipt of the signed version, they should have withdrawn their opinion with regard to the merger and demanded resolicitation of the Interstate shareholders. If the Interstate directors refused, the attorneys should have withdrawn from the representation and informed the shareholders or the Commission. . . .

Since any liability of the alleged aiders and abettors depends on a finding of a primary violation of the antifraud provisions, the Court will first address the issues relating to the Commission's charges against the principals. . . .

A.   Nexus With a Sale

For the SEC to prove a violation of the antifraud provisions, it must demonstrate that the alleged misconduct was "in the offer or sale" of a security under § 17(a) or "in connection with the purchase or sale" of a security under § 10(b) and Rule 10b–5. The Commission has made the requisite showing for each of the provisions with respect to the defendants' activities leading to the closing of the merger. . . .

B.   Materiality

Also essential to an alleged violation of the antifraud provisions is that the omission or misstatement be material. . . .

Initially, the sheer magnitude of the adjustments supports a finding that they were material. The interim financials issued by NSMC reflected a profit of $702,270 for the nine-month period end[ing] May 31, 1969. . . . The aggregate adjustments amounted to $884,000, thereby reducing the reported profit by 125 percent and resulting in a net loss for the nine-month period of approximately $180,000. Viewing these figures alone, it is difficult to imagine how the adjustments could not be material.

. . .

C.   Scienter

Finally, there must be proof that Brown and Meyer acted with the requisite degree of culpability. Unfortunately, the level of culpability required in an SEC injunctive action is far from certain. . . .

Though these are important issues, the resolution of which would be welcome to the securities bar, the Court concludes that they need not be decided at this time, because the conduct of Brown and Meyer in this case meets the prevailing standard for scienter.

After receiving the unsigned comfort letter at the closing, the Interstate representatives immediately expressed concern over the new information; they caucused privately and sought and received various oral assurances from the NSMC representatives. Moreover, the new information included adjustments which were far from insubstantial; they reduced the reported profit of NSMC by several hundreds of thousands of dollars and converted what had been a sizable profit into a net loss. Despite the obvious materiality of this information, especially as demonstrated by their conduct, they made a conscious decision not to disclose it. Such conduct has been found sufficient to meet the scienter requirement. McLean v. Alexander, 420 F.Supp. 1057, 1080–82 (D.Del. 1976); see Nassar & Co., Inc. v. SEC, 185 U.S.App.D.C. 125, 130 n. 3, 566 F.2d 790, 795 n. 3 (1977) (Leventhal, J., concurring); Lanza v. Drexel & Co., 479 F.2d 1277, 1305 (2d Cir.1973).

. . .

. . . Brown and Meyer expected to profit handsomely from the merger and the subsequent stock sales. They were in no haste to disseminate the comfort letter information, and in fact they never revealed the adjustments, even after NSMC's year-end audit had been released. . . .

In any event, to the extent an inference of *actual* intent to deceive, manipulate, or defraud may be inappropriate, the defendants' actions here clearly constitute "the kind of recklessness that is equivalent to wilful fraud," SEC v. Texas Gulf Sulphur Co., 401 F.2d at 868 (concurring opinion), and which also satisfies the scienter requirement. . . .

IV. AIDING AND ABETTING

The Court must now turn to the Commission's charges that the defendants aided and abetted these two violations of the antifraud provisions. The violations themselves establish the first element of aiding and abetting liability, namely that another person has committed a securities law violation. . . . The remaining elements, though not set forth with any uniformity, are essentially that the alleged aider and abettor had a "general awareness that his role was part of an overall activity that is improper, and [that he] knowingly and substantially assisted the violation." SEC v. Coffey [493 F.2d 1304, 1316 (6th Cir. 1974) cert. denied, 420 U.S. 908 (1975)].

The Commission's allegations of aiding and abetting by the defendants, seem to fall into four basic categories: (1) the failure of the attorney defendants to take any action to interfere in the consummation of the merger; (2) the issuance by the attorneys of an opinion with respect to the merger; (3) the attorneys' subsequent failure to withdraw that opinion and inform the Interstate shareholders or the SEC of the inaccuracy of the nine-month financials; and (4) the issuance by the attorneys and Brown of an opinion and letter, respectively, concerning the validity of the stock sales under Rule 133.** The SEC's position is that the defendants acted or failed to act with an awareness of the fraudulent conduct by the principals, and thereby substantially assisted the two violations. The Court concurs with regard to the attorneys' failure to interfere with the closing, but must conclude that the remaining actions or inaction alleged to constitute aiding and abetting did not substantially facilitate either the merger or the stock sales.

As noted, the first element of aiding and abetting liability has been *Analysis* established by the finding that Brown and Meyer committed primary violations of the securities laws. Support for the second element, that the defendants were generally aware of the fraudulent activity, is provided by the previous discussion concerning scienter.... Despite the obvious materiality of the information, see section III–B supra, each knew that it had not been disclosed prior to the merger and stock sale transactions. Thus, this is not a situation where the aider and abettor merely failed to discover the fraud, see Rolf v. Blyth, Eastman Dillon & Co., 570 F.2d at 52 (Mansfield, J., dissenting), or reasonably believed that the victims were already aware of the withheld information, Hirsch v. du Pont, 553 F.2d 750, 759 (2d Cir.1977)....

The final requirement for aiding and abetting liability is that the conduct provide knowing, substantial assistance to the violation. In addressing this issue, the Court will consider each of the SEC's allegations separately. The major problem arising with regard to the Commission's contention that the attorneys failed to interfere in the closing of the merger is whether inaction or silence constitutes substantial assistance. While there is no definitive answer to this question, courts have been willing to consider inaction as a form of substantial assistance when the accused aider and abettor had a duty to disclose....

Upon receipt of the unsigned comfort letter, it became clear that the merger had been approved by the Interstate shareholders on the basis of materially misleading information. In view of the obvious materiality of the information, especially to attorneys learned in securities law, the attorneys' responsibilities to their corporate client required them to take steps to ensure that the information would be disclosed to the shareholders. However, it is unnecessary to determine the precise extent of their obligations here, since it is undisputed that they took no steps whatsoever to delay the closing pending disclosure to and resolicitation of the Interstate shareholders. But, at the very least, they were required to speak out at the closing concerning the obvious materiality of the information and the concomitant requirement that the merger not be closed until the adjustments were disclosed and approval of the merger was again obtained from the Interstate shareholders. Their silence was not only a breach of this duty to speak, but in addition lent

** [Editors' note:] This refers to the legality under SEC Rule 133 of sales of stock by the Interstate principals as "insiders," following the merger.

the appearance of legitimacy to the closing,.... Contrary to the attorney defendants' contention, imposition of such a duty will not require lawyers to go beyond their accepted role in securities transactions, nor will it compel them to "err on the side of conservatism, ... thereby inhibiting clients' business judgments and candid attorney-client communications." Courts will not lightly overrule an attorney's determination of materiality and the need for disclosure. However, where, as here, the significance of the information clearly removes any doubt concerning the materiality of the information, attorneys cannot rest on asserted "business judgments" as justification for their failure to make a legal decision pursuant to their fiduciary responsibilities to client shareholders.

The Commission also asserts that the attorneys substantially assisted the merger violation through the issuance of an opinion that was false and misleading due to its omission of the receipt of the comfort letter and of the completion of the merger on the basis of the false and misleading nine-month financials. The defendants contend that a technical reading of the opinion demonstrates that it is not false and misleading, and that it provides accurate opinions as to Interstate's compliance with certain corporate formalities. Of concern to the Court, however, is not the truth or falsity of the opinion, but whether it substantially assisted the violation. Upon consideration of all the circumstances ..., the Court concludes that it did not.

Contrary to the implication made by the SEC, the opinion issued by the attorneys at the closing did not play a large part in the consummation of the merger. Instead, it was simply one of many conditions to the obligation of NSMC to complete the merger. It addressed a number of corporate formalities required of Interstate by the Merger Agreement, only a few of which could possibly involve compliance with the antifraud provisions of the securities laws. Moreover, the opinion was explicitly for the benefit of NSMC, which was already well aware of the adjustments contained in the comfort letter. Thus, this is not a case where an opinion of counsel addresses a specific issue and is undeniably relied on in completing the transaction. Compare SEC v. Coven, 581 F.2d 1020, at 1028; SEC v. Spectrum, Ltd., 489 F.2d 535 (2d Cir.1973). Under these circumstances, it is unreasonable to suggest that the opinion provided substantial assistance to the merger.

The SEC's contention with regard to counsel's alleged acquiescence in the merger transaction raises significant questions concerning the responsibility of counsel. The basis for the charge appears to be counsel's failure, after the merger, to withdraw their opinion, to demand resolicitation of the shareholders, to advise their clients concerning rights of rescission of the merger, and ultimately, to inform the Interstate shareholders or the SEC of the completion of the merger based on materially false and misleading financial statements. The defendants counter with the argument that their actions following the merger are not subject to the coverage of the securities laws.

The filing of the complaint in this proceeding generated significant interest and an almost overwhelming amount of comment within the legal profession on the scope of a securities lawyer's obligations to his client and to the investing public. The very initiation of this action, therefore, has provided a necessary and worthwhile impetus for the profession's recognition and assessment of its responsibilities in this area. The Court's examination, however, must be more limited. Although the complaint alleges varying instances of misconduct on the part of several attorneys and firms, the Court must narrow its focus to the present defendants and the charges against them.

Meyer, Schauer and Lord, Bissell & Brook are, in essence, here charged with failing to take any action to "undo" the merger. The Court has already concluded that counsel had a duty to the Interstate shareholders to delay the closing of the merger pending disclosure and resolicitation with corrected financials, and that the breach of that duty constituted a violation of the antifraud provisions through aiding and abetting the merger transaction. The Commission's charge, however, concerns the period following that transaction. Even if the attorneys' fiduciary responsibilities to the Interstate shareholders continued beyond the merger, the breach of such a duty would not have the requisite relationship to a securities transaction, since the merger had already been completed. It is equally obvious that such subsequent action or inaction by the attorneys could not substantially assist the merger.

The final contention of the SEC concerns the issuance by the attorneys and Brown of the Rule 133 opinion and letter, respectively. [These documents asserted that the Interstate directors could sell their shares without violating Rule 133.] Little discussion is necessary with respect to this charge, for the Commission has clearly failed to show that these documents substantially assisted the stock sales. Neither of the documents were required by the Merger Agreement, but were requested by NSMC at the closing of the merger. The documents were not intended for the investing public, but for the sole use of NSMC and its counsel in preparing a formal, independent opinion concerning the validity of the sales under Rule 133. Further, the documents were limited to primarily factual issues relevant to the requirements of the Rule, and in no way indicated that they could be relied upon with regard to compliance with the antifraud provisions. Under the circumstances, the Court concludes that the Rule 133 documents issued by the attorneys and Brown did not substantially assist the stock sales by Interstate principals, specifically Brown and Meyer.

Thus, the Court finds that the attorney defendants aided and abetted the violation of § 10(b), Rule 10b–5, and § 17(a) through their participation in the closing of the merger.

V. APPROPRIATENESS OF INJUNCTIVE RELIEF

Although the Commission has proved past violations by the defendants, that does not end the Court's inquiry. Proof of a past violation is not a prerequisite to the grant of injunctive relief ... but it may, in combination with other factors, warrant an inference of future misconduct by the charged party, SEC v. Manor Nursing Centers, Inc., 458 F.2d 1082, 1100 (2d Cir.1972). The crucial question, though, remains not whether a violation has occurred, but whether there exists a reasonable likelihood of future illegal conduct by the defendant....

. . .

The Commission has not demonstrated that the defendants engaged in the type of repeated and persistent misconduct which usually justifies the issuance of injunctive relief ... Instead, it has shown violations which principally occurred within a period of a few hours at the closing of the merger in 1969. The Commission has not charged, or even suggested, that the defendants were involved in similar misconduct either before or after the events involved in this proceeding. Thus, the violations proved by the SEC appear to be part of an isolated incident, unlikely to recur and insufficient to warrant an injunction....

Finally, the Commission asserts that an injunction is necessary because the professional occupations of the defendants provide significant opportunities for further involvement in securities transactions. It notes that ... Meyer, Schauer and LBB continue to be involved in various corporate activities, including securities transactions, as part of their legal practice.... [T]hat fact is countered somewhat by their professional responsibilities as attorneys and officers of the court to conform their conduct to the dictates of the law. The Court is confident that they will take appropriate steps to ensure that their professional conduct in the future comports with the law.[80]

. . .

Notes on *National Student Marketing*

National Student Marketing Corp. (NSMC), a conglomerate established to sell to college students everything from coffee mugs to computer-matched dates, was one of a number of short-lived glamour stocks in the late 1960s.[81] NSMC stock went from $1 per share in 1968 to a high of $69 per share shortly after the merger. In December 1969 *Barron's* published a negative article on NSMC, and the company reported it would post a major loss in the first quarter of 1970. Those developments exposed a mess of inflated assets, misleading statements and hidden losses. NSMC's stock plummeted, and estimates of investors' losses reached as high as $100 million. Some NSMC principals and a

---

80. [Editors' note:] The SEC appealed the district court's denial of sanctions against Lord, Bissell and Brook and its two partners and they appealed from the court's holding of substantive violations. The appeal was dismissed when the district court approved a $1.3 million settlement of related private suits against the lawyers. See Stan Crock, SEC Agrees to Settle a Landmark Case Involving National Student Marketing, Wall St.J., Jan. 2, 1982, p. 8.

81. See Burt Schorr, White & Case on Trial, 7 Juris Dr. 15 (March 1977). See also Wall St.J., Dec. 6, 1976, at p. 1.

Peat Marwick accountant were convicted of securities law violations and served prison sentences. The SEC's effort to reach the lawyers involved in the merger transaction created a tremendous stir in the corporate and securities bar.[82] The long, drawn-out litigation took nearly ten years: White & Case and Epley entered consent decrees that obligated them to follow set procedures if they suspected any foul play in securities cases; and the remaining defendants (mostly Interstate officers and their lawyers) defended on the merits, resulting in the reprinted decision.

Meanwhile, private securities fraud actions had been brought against the same parties. In 1982 nearly all of these suits were settled. The settlement provided $30 million for NSMC investors. White & Case contributed $1.95 million to the fund, and Lord, Bissell & Brook $1.3 million.[83]

The court in *National Student Marketing* sets forth three elements necessary to establish aiding and abetting a violation of § 10(b), Rule 10b–5 and § 17(a): (1) a violation of the securities law by the principal (client); (2) knowledge by the defendant that her role was part of an illegal activity; and (3) substantial assistance by the defendant in the violation.

Did Interstate's officers violate the securities laws? Did Interstate's lawyers assist in the violation? What, if anything, should the lawyers for NSMC and Interstate have done differently during the merger negotiations? Before the closing meeting? At the meeting?

The opinion letters exchanged by the lawyers were held not to be a basis of their liability. Why not?

Read Model Rule 1.13(b) and the Comment thereto. If it had been in effect when *National Student Marketing* was decided, would it have helped the lawyers avoid liability?

Liability of Lawyers as Principals

As *Benjamin* indicates, lawyers who take an active role as entrepreneur investors, directors, officers or signatories of prospectuses may be liable as principals under the securities laws provisions that impose liability without proof of wrongful intent.[84] Lawyers and accountants

---

82. Then–SEC Commissioner Sommer stated in 1974 that "in securities matters (other than those where advocacy is clearly proper) the attorney will have to function in a manner more akin to that of the auditor than to that of the advocate." Sommer, Emerging Responsibilities of the Securities Lawyer, [1973–74 Transfer Binder] Fed. Sec. L. Rep. (CCH) ¶ 79,631 (Jan. 1974). One of the reactions of the bar was to amend DR 7–102(B)(1) of the Model Code to eliminate, as a practical matter, the lawyer's duty to reveal a client's fraud in which the lawyer's services had been used. See, e.g., Junius Hoffman, On Learning of a Corporate Client's Crime of Fraud, 33 Bus.Law. 1389, 1405–07 (1978) (the amendment was one of a series of attempts by bar groups to resolve the "conflict" raised between the SEC position and the bar's conception of its primary loyalty to clients).

83. See David Lauter, Two Law Firms Pay $3M To Settle Stock Scandal, Nat'l L. J., Sept. 20, 1982, at pp. 4, 25.

84. See, e.g., *Benjamin*, supra; S.E.C. v. Manor Nursing Centers, Inc., 458 F.2d 1082 (2d Cir.1972); S.E.C. v. Coven, 581 F.2d 1020 (2d Cir.1978).

who merely advise an offeror, however, are generally not subject to liability as principals under section 12(1) of the 1933 Act.[85] Thus if a lawyer does not sign a prospectus, but provides substantial assistance in preparing or reviewing the offering materials, the lawyer generally will be held liable only as an accessory, requiring proof of wrongful intent.[86]

3. Culpable Intent

IN RE AMERICAN CONTINENTAL CORP./LINCOLN SAVINGS AND LOAN SECURITIES LITIGATION

United States District Court, District of Arizona, 1992.
794 F.Supp. 1424.

Before BILBY, D.J.:

This Opinion describes the basis of this court's rulings by order of February 14, 1992, on notions for summary judgment filed by parties to these consolidated actions.

I. PROCEDURAL HISTORY

Five separate actions are consolidated before this court [including a class action by purchasers of securities of American Continental Corp. ("ACC") and an action by Resolution Trust Co., as receiver for Lincoln Savings & Loan Association ("Lincoln"). The actions charged professionals who provided services to ACC and/or Lincoln with civil liability for violations of federal securities laws, RICO and its Arizona counterpart and also sought damages under various state law claims of fraud, negligent misrepresentation and breach of fiduciary duty.]

These actions originate from the business dealings of Charles H. Keating, Jr. ("Keating"), former chairman of ACC. The claims at issue here were brought principally against professionals who provided services to ACC and/or Lincoln Savings. These include [a long list of accounting firms, law firms, consulting firms and others. One of the law firm defendants is Jones, Day, Reavis & Pogue ("Jones Day"), a Cleveland-based law firm and two of its individual partners.]

On February 14, 1992, following lengthy discovery, extensive briefing and oral argument, and after a review of voluminous pleadings, depositions, exhibits, and other papers, this court ruled on numerous motions for summary judgment.... At that time, the court stated that it would in due course issue this Memorandum Opinion, setting forth its analysis supporting the decision to grant or deny, in whole or in part, the various motions for summary judgment.

. . .

---

85. See Pinter v. Dahl, 486 U.S. 622, 647 (1988) (section 12(1) contemplates a contractual relationship akin to that of seller and buyer of securities, but does not extend to those "whose motivation [in soliciting the sale is] solely to benefit the buyer."

86. See, e.g., Westlake v. Abrams, 565 F.Supp. 1330, 1350 (N.D.Ga.1983): "[a lawyer] cannot be held to be a controlling person merely because he renders advice in pursuing litigation on behalf of his client."

II. LAW OF GENERAL APPLICATION

(V) Section 10(b) of the [Securities and] Exchange Act

. . .

... In Hollinger v. Titin Capital Corp., 914 F.2d 1564 (9th Cir.1990), the Ninth Circuit adopted a standard for the minimal culpable mindset, referred to hereinafter by this court as "reckless scienter." The Ninth Circuit held:

> Reckless conduct may be defined as the highly unreasonable omission, involving not merely simple, or even inexcusable negligence, but an extreme departure from the standards of ordinary care, which presents a danger of misleading buyers or sellers that is either known to the defendant or so obvious that the actor must have been aware of it.

Id. at 1569. The *Hollinger* court observed that "the danger of misleading buyers must be actually known or so obvious that any reasonable [person] would be legally bound as knowing, and the omission must derive from something more egregious than even 'white heart/empty head' good faith." Id. at 1569–70. Thus, the court concluded, "recklessness is a lesser form of intent rather than a greater degree of negligence."

. . .

(2) Aiding and abetting securities fraud—or secondary liability—requires proof of the following elements: (1) the existence of an independent primary wrong; (2) knowledge by the alleged aider and abetter of the wrong and of his or her role in furthering it; and (3) substantial assistance in the wrong. Levine [v. Diamanthuset, Inc.], 950 F.2d at 1483; Roberts v. Peat, Marwick, Mitchell & Co., 857 F.2d 646, 652 (9th Cir.1988). As with a primary violation, a defendant must know of the fraud, or recklessly disregard it. Levine, 950 F.2d at 1483.

Proof of substantial assistance requires a showing that the defendant's assistance was a substantial factor in causing the plaintiff's harm. Mendelsohn v. Capital Underwriters, Inc., 490 F.Supp. 1069, 1084 (N.D. Cal.1979). "Substantial assistance means more than a little aid." Barker v. Henderson, Franklin, Starnes & Holt, 797 F.2d 490, 496 (7th Cir.1986). Where substantial assistance is premised on actual misrepresentations, the *Hollinger* standard applies. Levine,, 950 F.2d at 1484.

. . .

... If aiding and abetting liability is to be premised exclusively on silence or inaction, it may be necessary for the court to consider whether a defendant operates under a duty of disclosure.... "When it is impossible to find any duty of disclosure, an alleged aider-abettor should be found liable only if scienter of the high 'conscious intent' variety can be proved. Where some special duty of disclosure exists, then liability should be possible with a lesser degree of scienter."

. . .

Racketeering Influenced and Corrupt Organizations Act

. . .

To establish a RICO claim, plaintiffs must prove defendants intended to devise and did devise a scheme to defraud. United States v. Bohonus, 628 F.2d 1167 (9th Cir.1980). "The scheme must be reasonably calculated to deceive persons of ordinary prudence and comprehension." Id. at 1172. "Thus, the fraud must be active, not merely constructive." Id. Intent may be shown by examining the scheme itself. Id. "The fraudulent scheme need not be one which includes an affirmative misrepresentation of fact, since it is only necessary [to prove] that the scheme was calculated to deceive persons of ordinary prudence." Id. at 1172, "[D]eceitful concealment of material facts is not constructive fraud but actual fraud." Id. (citing Cacy v. United States, 298 F.2d 227, 229 (9th Cir.1961)).

The standard for aiding and abetting a RICO violation parallels that under Section 10(b).... A defendant must have knowledge or act with reckless scienter. See discussion of Section 10(b) standards, supra. This court has previously applied the reckless scienter standard to a RICO aiding and abetting action. In re ACC/Lincoln Savings Securities Litigation, MDL 834 (D.Ariz.Dec. 12, 1991)....

. . .

Common Law Fraud and Negligent Misrepresentation

Under California common law, an action for fraud and deceit requires proof of: (1) a false representation; (2) knowledge of the falsity; (3) an intent to induce reliance; (4) actual and reasonable reliance; and (5) resulting damage to the plaintiff. Secondary liability, or aiding and abetting, is defined in Restatement (Second) of Torts, 876b. It requires proof of knowledge of the primary violation, which may be inferred from the circumstances, and substantial assistance, which may be in the form of encouragement or advice. Pasadena Unified School Dist. v. Pasadena Federation of Teachers, 72 Cal.App.3d 100, 140 Cal.Rptr. 41 (1977). The aider and abetter's conduct must be a substantial factor in causing the plaintiff's harm. Rest.2d of Torts § 876 and comments.

A negligent misrepresentation claim involves the following elements: (1) a misrepresentation of past or existing material facts; (2) a lack of reasonable grounds for believing in the truth of the representation; (3) an intent to induce reliance; (4) actual and justifiable reliance; and (5) resulting damage.

[After discussing the standard for summary judgment under Fed. R.Civ.Pro. 56(c), the court granted defendants' motions for summary judgment on claims under § 18 of the Securities and Exchange Act, the

California Corporation Code and for aiding and abetting ACC/Lincoln in negligently misrepresenting the financial condition of the two companies. The opinion then considers the remaining claims against each defendant. The portion of the opinion discussing the liability of Jones, Day and two of its lawyers is reproduced here.]

V. RULINGS PERTINENT TO INDIVIDUAL DEFENDANTS

. . .

D. Jones, Day, Reavis & Pogue

Jones Day, a defendant in [four of the actions] focuses its summary judgment motion on an individual opinion letter given in connection with a 1986 registration statement. Jones Day claims this opinion letter was neither false, nor was it written in an expert capacity. Jones Day generally claims that it has not engaged in conduct for which it could be held liable because lawyers are obligated to keep their clients' confidence and to act in ways that do not discourage their clients from undergoing regulatory compliance reviews.

1. The Record

The record reveals the following facts concerning Jones Day's involvement with ACC and Keating.

Prior to joining Jones Day, defendant William Schilling was director of the FHLBB Office of Examinations and Supervision. In that capacity, he was directly involved in the supervision of Lincoln Savings. During the summer of 1985, he wrote at least one memorandum and concurred in another, expressing serious regulatory concerns about numerous aspects of Lincoln's operations. For example, he wrote:

> Under new management, Lincoln has engaged in several serious regulatory violations. Some of these violations, such as the overvaluation of real estate and failure to comply with Memorandum R–41(b), are the same type of violations that have lead to some of the worst failures in FSLIC's history.

Later in 1985, Schilling was hired by Jones Day to augment its expertise in thrift representation. On January 31, 1986, Schilling and Jones Day's Ron Kneipper flew to Phoenix to solicit ACC's business. ACC retained Jones Day to perform "a major internal audit of Lincoln's FHLBB compliance and a major project to help Lincoln deal with the FHLBB's direct investment regulations."

During the regulatory compliance audit, which Jones Day understood to be a pre-FHLBB examination compliance review, the law firm found multiple regulatory violations. There is evidence that Jones Day knew that Lincoln had backdated files, destroyed appraisals, removed appraisals from files, told appraisers not to issue written reports when their oral valuations were too low, and violated affiliated transaction regulations. Jones Day found that Lincoln did no loan underwriting and no post-closure loan followup to ensure that Lincoln's interests were being protected. Jones Day learned Lincoln had multiple "loans" which were, in fact, joint ventures which violated FHLBB regulations, made real estate loans in violation of regulations, and backdated corporate resolutions which were not signed by corporate officers and did not reflect actual meetings. There is evidence that Jones Day may have tacitly consented to removal of harmful documents from Lincoln files. For example, one handwritten notation on a memorandum memorializing Jones Day's advice not to remove documents from files reads, "If something is devastating, consider it individually." (Emphasis in original).

There is evidence that Jones Day instructed ACC in how to rectify deficiencies so that they would not be apparent to FHLBB examiners. Jones Day attorneys, including Schilling, testified that they told ACC/Lincoln personnel to provide the Jones Day-generated "to do" lists only to the attorneys responsible for rectifying the deficiencies, and to destroy the lists so that FHLB–SF would not find them in the files. For the same reason, Jones Day's regulatory compliance reports to ACC/Lincoln were oral. Jones Day paralegals testified that responsibilities for carrying out the "to do" lists were divided among Jones Day and ACC staff. Jones Day continued this work into the summer of 1986.

The evidence indicates that Jones Day may have been aware that ACC/Lincoln did not follow its compliance advice with respect to ongoing activities. There are material questions of fact concerning the procedures Jones Day used—if any—to ascertain whether their compliance advice was being heeded. The testimony suggests that Jones Day partners knew ACC/Lincoln personnel were preparing loan underwriting summaries contemporaneously with Jones Day's regulatory compliance review, even though the loan transactions had already been closed. Moreover, the evidence reveals that Jones Day attorneys participated in creating corporate resolutions to ratify forged and backdated corporate records.

On April 23, 1986, Jones Day partner Fohrman wrote:

I received Neal Millard's memo on ACC. In looking at the long list of people involved, it occurred to me that there will be times when individuals may be called upon to render legal services that might require the issuance of opinion letters from Jones, Day. As we all know, we now possess information that could affect the way we write our opinion letters and our actual ability to give a particular opinion may be severely restricted. However, this large list of individuals may not be aware of knowledge that is held by Messrs. Fein and Schilling. I would suggest that a follow up memo be issued by Ron Fein indicating that any work involving ACC which requires the issuance of opinions, must be cleared by Ron....

Also in April 1986, ACC's Jim Grogan wrote to Jones Day's Kneipper, soliciting a strategy to "sunset" the FHLBB direct investment regulation. Jones Day subsequently made multiple Freedom of

Information Act requests to FHLBB in furtherance of a direct investment rule strategy, for which Lincoln was billed. In a September 12,
1986 telephone conversation, Grogan allegedly told Kneipper: "[C]om-
ment letters were great success—FHLBB picked it up 'hook, line and
sinker' Charlie wants to do again...."

The record indicates that the concept of selling ACC debentures in
Lincoln Savings branches may have originated at an April 9, 1986 real
estate syndicate seminar given by Jones Day Defendant Ron Fein.
There is evidence that Fein may have contributed to the detailed bond
sales program outline, attending to details such as explaining how the
sales would work, and insuring that the marketing table was far
enough from the teller windows to distinguish between ACC and
Lincoln Savings employees. The evidence indicates that Jones Day
reviewed the debenture registration statement and prospectus, which is
corroborated by Jones Day's billing records. As a result, in January
1987, ACC was able to assure the California Department of Savings
Loan that:

> The process of structuring the bond sales program was reviewed by
> Kaye, Scholer and Jones Day to assure compliance not only with
> securities laws and regulations, but also with banking and FSLIC
> laws and regulations.

Moreover, there is evidence which suggests that political contributions were made on behalf of ACC, in exchange for ACC's consent that
Jones Day could "bill liberally." On June 23, 19861 Kneipper memori-
alized a phone conversation:

> (1) 1:15 p.m. Ron Kessler—in past, firm has given $amt. to PAC,
> has premium billed, & PAC contri. to candidate; concern that
> we're an out of state law firm and that a $ # in excess of $5,000.00
> would look like an unusual move; Barnett and Kessler have done
> before; question re whether and how we can get some busi. from
> GOV. for this.

> (2) 3:40 p.m. Jim Grogan Ten tickets at $1,000.00 equals $10,000.00
> Barr wants limits of $5,000.00/contribution

> Agreed that we could bill liberally in future in recognition of this.

At deposition, Kneipper testified that his note—"agreed could bill
liberally in recognition for this,"—"is what it appears to be." Jones
Day set up an Arizona Political Action Committee ("PAC") specifically
for the purpose of making a contribution to an Arizona gubernatorial
candidate. The PAC was opened on September 4, 1986 and closed in
December, 1986, after the contribution was made.

In June 1986, Jones Day solicited additional work from ACC. Jones
Day attorney Caulkins wrote, in part:

> Rick Kneipper reports that ACC is very explicit that it does not
> care how much its legal services cost, as long as it gets the best.
> He states that Keating gave him an unsolicited $250,000 retainer
> to start the thrift work, and sent another similar check also

unsolicited in two weeks. On the down side, he reports that he has never encountered a more demanding and difficult client, ...

It appears to Rick and to me that American Continental is made for us and we for them.

On October 28, 1986, Jones Day provided an opinion letter, required by Item 601(b) of SEC regulation S–K for inclusion in an ACC bond registration statement. Jones Day's opinion letter stated that the indenture was a valid and binding obligation under California law.

2. Section 10(b), RICO, and Common Law Fraud

Jones Day seeks summary judgment on Plaintiffs' claims under Section 10(b), RICO and common law fraud.

Jones Day contends that it may not be held liable for counseling its client. The line between maintaining a client's confidence and violating the securities law is brighter than Jones Day suggests, however. Attorneys must inform a client in a clear and direct manner when its conduct violates the law. If the client continues the objectionable activity, the lawyer must withdraw "if the representation will result in violation of the rules of professional conduct or other law." Ethical Rule 1.16 ("ER"). Under such circumstances, an attorney's ethical responsibilities do not conflict with the securities laws. An attorney may not continue to provide services to corporate clients when the attorney knows the client is engaged in a course of conduct designed to deceive others, and where it is obvious that the attorney's compliant legal services may be a substantial factor in permitting the deceit to continue. See Rudolph v. Arthur Andersen, supra.

The record raises material questions about whether Jones Day knew of ACC/Lincoln's fraud, but nevertheless provided hands-on assistance in hiding loan file deficiencies from the regulators, offered detailed advice about setting up the bond sales program, carried out a lobbying strategy with respect to the direct investment rule, made political contributions on ACC's behalf, reviewed SEC registration statements and prospectuses, and lent its name to a misleading legal opinion. This evidence raises material questions concerning section 10(b), RICO, AZRAC, common law fraud and deceit, and violations of Cal. Corp. Code §§ 25401 and 25504.1.

3. Section 11 Liability

Section 11 imposes liability for misleading statements made in connection with registration statements. Jones Day offers two arguments. [The court first rejected arguments that these claims were barred by statute of limitations.]

· · ·

Jones Day further contends that it cannot be held liable under Section 11 because it did not issue an "expert" opinion. Section 11 applies to misleading statements made by one "whose profession gives authority to statements made by him." 13 U.S.C. § 771. Jones Day concedes that its October 28, 1986 opinion letter was required by SEC Regulation S–K, which provides in part:

> (5) Opinion Re Legality—(i) An opinion of counsel as to the legality of the securities being registered, indicating whether they will, when sold, be legally issued, fully paid and non-assessable, and, if debt securities, whether they will be binding obligations of the registrant.

SEC Regulation S–K, Item 601( )(5).

The court holds that an attorney who provides a legal opinion used in connection with an SEC registration statement is an expert within the meaning of Section ii. See Schneider v. Traweek, 1990 U.S. Dist. LEXIS 15,563 (C.D. Cal. Sept. 5, 1990).

4. Breach of Fiduciary Duty to Lincoln

a. Statute of Limitations

Jones Day contends that claims for breach of fiduciary duty, brought by the RTC, are time-barred. RTC contends that its claims were preserved until the conservatorship was imposed.

Under the theory of adverse domination, the limitations period on a corporation's cause of action is tolled while wrongdoers control the corporation. Bornstein v. Poulos, 793 F.2d 444 (1st Cir.1986) (doctrine extends to attorney with fiduciary duty to corporation)i Fed. Sav. and Loan Ins. Corp. v. Williams, 599 F.Supp. 1184 (D. Md.1984) (limitations statute tolled while corporation is dominated by wrongdoers). In this instance, ACC/Lincoln management would not have brought claims on behalf of ACC/Lincoln, for it would have brought their own misconduct to light. Furthermore, the court finds material questions as to whether Jones Day knowingly assisted in ACC's alleged fraud. Accordingly, it is equitable to toll the statute Of limitations on Lincoln's behalf.

b. Validity of Claims

An attorney who represents a corporation has a duty to act in the corporation's best interest when confronted by adverse interests of directors, officers, or corporate affiliates. It is not a defense that corporate representation often involves the distinct interests of affiliated entities. Attorneys are bound to act when those interests conflict. There are genuine questions as to whether Jones Day should have sought independent representation for Lincoln. See Section IV(F)(5), infra.

Moreover, where a law firm believes the management of a corporate client is committing serious regulatory violations, the firm has an obligation to actively discuss the violative conduct, urge cessation of the activity, and withdraw from representation where the firm's legal services may contribute to the continuation of such conduct. Jones Day contends that it would have been futile to act on these fiduciary obligations because those controlling ACC/Lincoln would not have responded. Client wrongdoing, however, cannot negate an attorney's fiduciary duty. Moreover, the evidence reveals that attorney advice influenced ACC/Lincoln's conduct in a variety of ways. Accordingly, summary judgment as to this claim is denied.

5. Professional Negligence Claims

Jones Day issued an opinion letter that was included with ACC'S 1986 shelf registration statement. California authority provides that independent public accountants have a duty to those who are foreseeably injured from representations made in connection with publicly held corporations. While this duty does not extend to confidential advice which an attorney gives to its clients, it would apply where an attorney issues an SEC opinion letter to the public. Roberts v. Ball, Hunt., Hart, Brown & Baerwitz, 57 Cal.App.3d 104, 128 Cal.Rptr. 901 (1976); see also Int'l Mortgage Co. v. Butler Accountancy Corp., 177 Cal.App.3d 806, 223 Cal.Rptr. 218 (4th Dist.1986).

Accordingly, a question of fact remains as to whether the Yahr Plaintiffs, who purchased bonds issued pursuant to the November, 1986 shelf registration and amendments, were injured by the Jones Day opinion letter.

6. Section 12 Liability

Section 12 imposes liability only on those who offer and sell securities. 15 U.S.C. § 771. The court concludes that Jones Day's contributions to the bond sales program were those of an expert consultant rather than those of an offeror or seller. Accordingly, Jones Day's participation is insufficient to impose Section 12 liability within the meaning of the Securities Act.

. . .

Accordingly, this Memorandum Opinion affirms the court's Order of February 14, 1992 granting and denying summary judgment.[1]

Notes on *ACC/Lincoln Savings and Loan*

ACC/Lincoln is one of a large number of cases involving liability of professionals of failed thrifts. What are the acts with which Jones, Day

1. In March 1992 Jones, Day settled the claims of ACC bondholders and stockholders for $24 million. Wall St.J., Mar. 3, 1992, p. A2. The government claims against Jones, Day went to trial in April 1993 before Judge Bilby. After opening arguments, Jones, Day agreed to pay $51 million to the government in settlement of this and other cases against it. The settlement also obligated Jones, Day to follow specified procedures in any future thrift regulation and prohibited William Schilling, who worked on the Lincoln matter for Jones, Day after leaving the government, from holding any position in the banking industry or representing clients before the Office of Thrift Supervision, the agency that now regulates the savings and loan industry. See John H. Cushman, Jr., Law Firm Settles S. & L. Case, N.Y.Times, Apr. 20, 1993, p. D1. Press reports have stated that as much as $20 million of the settlement with the government will be borne by partners in the firm, with the remainder paid by the firm's malpractice insurer.

was charged? What intent is required to be shown to establish liability? *ACC/Lincoln* and *National Student Marketing* both employ the same three-part test for aiding and abetting violations and both hold that intent to deceive must be established but that recklessness meets that standard. In *National Student Marketing*, how did the court establish the wrongful intent of the lawyers for Interstate? In *ACC/Lincoln* what facts must the trier of fact accept to establish wrongful intent on the part of Jones, Day?

Does *ACC/Lincoln* permit a plaintiff to make out a case of wrongful intent even though no direct evidence shows that a lawyer knows that transaction documents are false or misleading? Compare *Benjamin*, printed earlier in this chapter, and *ACC/Lincoln* on the question of inferring wrongful intent. Are they consistent?

In Barker v. Henderson,[2] referred to in *ACC/Lincoln*, a claim that a lawyer unlawfully assisted a fraudulent securities transaction was dismissed on summary judgment because the lawyer's participation was too insubstantial. A general practitioner had assisted an organization in corporate and property matters involved in creating the project in which interests were later sold to private investors. Although the lawyer received the selling materials, he did not review or approve them and his name was not on them. The client, pursuant to the lawyer's advice, engaged a large Detroit firm to handle securities law matters; that firm settled the case against it for assisting client fraud for $612,500.

Judge Easterbrook, speaking for the court in *Barker*, used language that has been relied on by professional firms defending aiding and abetting claims:

> ... A plaintiff's case against an aider, abetter, or conspirator may not rest on a bare inference that the defendant "must have had" knowledge of the facts. The plaintiff must support the inference with some reason to conclude that the defendant has thrown in his lot with the primary violators.
>
> Law firms and accountants may act or remain silent for good reasons as well as bad ones, and allowing scienter or conspiracy to defraud to be inferred from the silence of a professional firm may expand the scope of liability far beyond that authorized in [controlling Supreme Court decisions]. If the plaintiff does not have direct evidence of scienter, the court should ask whether the fraud (or cover-up) was in the interest of the defendants. Did they gain by bilking the buyers of the securities? Cf. *Dirks*, 463 U.S. at 662–64. In this case the Firms did not gain [an accounting firm was also involved]. They received none of the proceeds from the sales. They did not receive fees for rendering advice in connection with the sales to the plaintiffs. Both Firms billed so little time to the Foundation between 1974 and 1976 (and none after October 1976)

---

2. 797 F.2d 490 (7th Cir.1986).

that it is inconceivable that they joined a venture to feather their nests by defrauding investors. They had nothing to gain and everything to lose. There is no sound basis, therefore, on which a jury could infer that the Firms joined common cause with other offenders or aided and abetted a scheme with the necessary state of mind.[3]

Is the problem in *Barker* absence of both direct evidence of wrongful intent and positive activity to facilitate the fraud? Would the result be the same if the lawyer in *Barker* had handled the securities aspect of the transaction?[4]

The court in *Barker* also stated that "an award of damages under the securities laws is not the way to blaze the trail toward improved ethical standards in the legal ... profession.... The securities law ... must lag behind changes in ethical and fiduciary standards."[5] Should ethical rules dictate who is liable under the securities laws or other regulatory law?

In DiLeo v. Ernst & Young,[6] Judge Easterbrook revisited the duty and scienter elements of aiding and abetting a securities law violation. Shareholders of a large, financially distressed Chicago bank charged its accounting firm with aiding and abetting the bank's fraud in misrepresenting its financial position. Upholding the dismissal of the complaint, Easterbrook stated:

> [A]iding and abetting [should not be treated] as an open-ended invitation to create liability without fault.... [T]here can be no liability on an aiding-and-abetting theory unless (1) someone committed a primary violation, (2) positive law obliges the abettor to disclose the truth, and (3) the abettor fails to do this, *with the same degree of scienter necessary for the primary violation.*
>
> ... The securities laws do not impose general duties to speak, Basic, Inc. v. Levinson, 485 U.S. 224, 239 & n. 17 (1988); therefore, as *Barker* held, these must usually be located in state law, if they exist at all.... [Under Illinois law] accountants must exercise care in giving opinions on the accuracy and adequacy of firms' financial statements, [but] they owe no broader duty to search and sing.... Such a duty would prevent the client from reposing in the accountant the trust that is essential to an accurate audit.... [Because companies would conceal relevant information and liability costs would burden accounting firms,] the price [of accounting services] would go up as the amount of oversight went down.[7]

---

3. 797 F.2d at 497.

4. See Roberts v. Peat, Marwick, Mitchell & Co., 857 F.2d 646 (9th Cir.1988), distinguishing *Barker* on the ground that the lawyers in *Barker*, unlike the accountants in *Roberts*, had not reviewed the selling documents before their distribution and had not put their names on the prospectus.

5. 797 F.2d at 497.

6. 901 F.2d 624 (7th Cir.1990).

7. 901 F.2d at 628–29 (emphasis added).

Judge Easterbrook also emphasized in *DiLeo*, as he had in *Barker*, that the defendant had nothing to gain from joining its client in fraud: "An [accounting firm's] greatest asset is its reputation for honesty, followed closely by its reputation for careful work. Fees for two years' audits could not approach the losses [the accounting firm] would suffer from a perception that it would muffle a client's fraud." [8] Is it correct to say that the continuing business of a major Chicago bank is not a temptation? Is this focus on economic reward too reductionist? Do professionals have other reasons for unwillingness to disrupt the ongoing transactions and business of a corporate client?

Is Silence a Safe Course?

National Student Marketing, ACC/Lincoln and the cases they rely upon hold that a lawyer must take some preventive action when the lawyer issues legal opinions and facilitates a sale of securities knowing that the client has made knowingly false representations in the selling materials. The case law is more confused when the lawyer, without issuing a legal opinion relied on by third persons, assists a client in closing a transaction knowing that the client has made material misrepresentations to those with whom the client is dealing.

At one extreme is Schatz v. Rosenberg,[9] which upheld dismissal of fraud and securities law claims against a law firm that knew its client, Rosenberg, had materially misrepresented his net worth in a transaction handled by the law firm, although not in any document prepared by the firm. Plaintiffs had agreed to sell their business to Rosenberg on terms involving $1.5 million in promissory notes personally guaranteed by Rosenberg, who provided a balance sheet showing a net worth exceeding $7 million. The law firm, which had represented Rosenberg during a period in which his financial empire was crumbling, knew that the financial statement contained material false representations. Nevertheless, it documented the transaction for Rosenberg and transmitted to plaintiffs at the closing a letter from Rosenberg stating that no material changes had occurred in his financial condition.

Dismissal of a complaint stating these facts was upheld by the Fourth Circuit: (1) No cause of action existed under federal securities laws because the law firm, which remained silent while the client made false representations, had no duty of disclosure absent a confidential or fiduciary relationship with the plaintiffs or provision of a legal opinion constituting an affirmative misrepresentation by the law firm. No affirmative misrepresentations by the law firm were involved because it merely transmitted its client's misrepresentations to the plaintiffs: "lawyers do not vouch for the probity of their clients when they draft documents reflecting their clients' promises, statements or warranties." [10] (2) No claim for relief under Maryland law existed because a

8.   901 F.2d at 629.

9.   943 F.2d 485 (4th Cir.1991).

10.   943 F.2d at 495.

lawyer is not liable in Maryland for negligent misrepresentation in the absence of privity and because a Maryland ethics requirement that the law firm under the circumstances either withdraw from representation or disclose the misrepresentations to the third person did not create a legal duty to disclose.

Another major case is Federal Deposit Ins. Corp. v. O'Melveny & Meyers,[11] in which a law firm assisted a subsidiary of a regulated bank in the sale of interests in real estate to private investors. After the bank became insolvent, the government as successor to the client bank charged the firm with professional negligence. The court of appeals reversed dismissal of the complaint, holding that the failure of the law firm to investigate whether the bank's representations were false or misleading was a breach of a duty of care "not only to the investors, but also to its client."

Are Schatz and O'Melveny distinguishable? If not, which is correct? Note that Schatz deals with liability to a non-client; O'Melveny, on the other hand, involves malpractice liability to a client.

If a lawyer makes a material and affirmative misrepresentation to a third person knowing that a third person will rely on the statement, the lawyer may have violated federal regulatory law as well as state tort law. If the lawyer's role, however, is limited to providing legal advice and documenting transactions, liability for aiding and abetting a principal's violation involves a more complicated and uncertain inquiry. Some federal courts, including the Ninth Circuit, follow a "reckless disregard" standard when the agent, knowing that the principal is making false representations, provides further assistance in closing a transaction. The Seventh Circuit cases and Schatz, on the other hand, require a non-client plaintiff to demonstrate existence of a duty of disclosure on the lawyer's part when the lawyer, in documenting a transaction, has merely remained silent. That duty, if not found in substantive regulatory law, may be found in state tort law or state ethics rules. Schatz is apparently the first case to hold that violation of a duty to take action under state ethics rules (e.g., remonstration, withdrawal or disclosure to the third person) does not result in tort liability.

The lawyers in ACC/Lincoln and Schatz represented entities whose managing agents were lying about the entities' financial status, thereby exposing the entities to liability. The entity-as-client aspect of cases like ACC/Lincoln and Schatz is addressed in Chapter 8 beginning at p. 789.

The "S & L Mess"

The insolvency of Lincoln Savings and Loan had many ramifications. Losses to the federal government in making good Lincoln's guaranteed deposits came to more than $2 billion, the largest bailout in what is commonly referred to as "the S & L mess." Keating, ACC's chairman, was convicted of state and federal fraud charges and sen-

11. 969 F.2d 744, 749 (9th Cir.1992).

tenced to lengthy prison terms. Combined settlements against various participants and their professional advisers total several hundred million dollars.[12]

The most noted case arising out of Lincoln's failure involved Kaye, Scholer, a New York City law firm that, along with Jones, Day, represented ACC/Lincoln in dealing with thrift regulators.[13] The Office of Thrift Supervision (OTS) instituted an administrative proceeding against Kaye, Scholer and three of its lawyers, seeking "restitution" of $275 million. The proceeding was accompanied by an asset preservation ("freeze") order that had the effect of threatening the financial solvency of the firm. Kaye, Scholer then quickly settled with OTS for $41 million without testing the freeze order or challenging in court the OTS actions and allegations. The firm continues to assert that the OTS actions and allegations violated its constitutional rights, were unwarranted by federal law and were inconsistent with a lawyer's professional obligations.

The *Kaye, Scholer* case has given rise to enormous discussion within the legal profession.[14] Issues relating to it will be discussed in connection with the lawyer's dilemma when she discovers in the midst of a transaction that a client is engaged in an ongoing fraud (see the client fraud section of chapter 4, p. 294 and the further complexities when the client is an organization (see chapter 8 at p. 776.

4. Conflicting Visions of the Law Governing Lawyers

SUSAN P. KONIAK
"THE LAW BETWEEN THE BAR AND THE STATE"

70 North Carolina Law Review 1389 (1992).[1]

The state and the profession have different understandings of the law governing lawyers—they have in effect different "law." [2] The law of lawyering is not inherently more amorphous, contradictory or obtuse

12. See Amy Stevens, Ernst & Young and Jones Day Law Firm to Pay $87 Million in Lincoln S & L Case, Wall St.J., Mar.31, 1992, at p. A3.

13. For discussion of *Kaye, Scholer*, see p. 792 below. The factual basis of charges against Kaye, Scholer is summarized in Susan Beck and Michael Orey, They Got What They Deserved, The American Lawyer, May 1992, at p. 68.

14. A major ABA inquiry has resulted in a comprehensive and useful report: ABA Working Group on Lawyers' Representation of Regulated Clients, Laborers in Different Vineyards? The Banking Regulators and the Legal Profession (Discussion Draft, Jan. 1993).

1. Copyright © University of North Carolina Law Review. Reprinted with permission. [Editors' note:] The footnotes in this condensation of the article have been renumbered. Some other changes in the original text, primarily updating, have been made. Changes and omissions from the original are not indicated.

2. This article uses Robert Cover's rich and original vision of law, which he articulated most fully in Robert M. Cover, The Supreme Court, 1982 Term—Foreword, Nomos and Narrative, 97 Harv.L.Rev. 4 (1983) [hereinafter Cover, Nomos].

than other law. It is not radically uncertain; it is essentially contested. There is a continuing struggle between the profession and the state over whether the profession's vision of law or the state's will reign.

II. The Inadequacy of the Traditional Understanding of the Relationship Between Law and Professional Ethics

As traditionally conceived, the domain of professional ethics begins where the law of the state leaves off.[3] By this I mean that ethics is generally understood to be about obligations above and beyond the requirements of law.[4]

Professional ethics thus conceived does not compete with state law, nor could it possibly conflict with it. Professional ethics merely supplements state law, supplying norms to govern conduct that the society at large lacks the necessary expertise to regulate[5] or for which the state's standards are insufficiently exacting. But the traditional understanding of the relationship between professional ethics and law—at least among professionals themselves—goes further than the mere statement that ethics begins where law leaves off; it also includes the notion that it is appropriate for the state to leave substantial areas of conduct in which the profession's own norms govern, i.e., that state law should "leave off" sooner rather than later. The rhetoric of the professions is filled with talk of the "right" of self-regulation, of the "encroachments" by the state into areas of professional control, and of the need to ward off increased state regulation by toughening internal controls.

In so far as the traditional understanding of the relationship between law and ethics includes an ongoing debate over the extent and nature of the "right" of self-regulation, it exposes the competition

---

3. See, e.g., William J. Goode, Community within a Community: The Professions, 22 Am.Soc.Rev. 194, 195 (1957) ("Although the occupational behavior of members is regulated by law, the professional community exacts a higher standard of behavior than does the law.").

4. The view that ethics should be about something other than and more than law is exemplified by Professor Stephen Gillers in What We Talked About When We Talked About Ethics: A Critical View of the Model Rules, 46 Ohio St.L.J. 243, 247–48 (1985), an article criticizing the Model Rules of Professional Conduct because, among other things, much of it merely repeats the injunctions of civil and criminal law. "The more [the document traces the commands of civil or criminal law] . . ., the less it can be considered a code of ethics." Id. at 246. "It is [the] extralegal realm that defines ethics." Id. at 248.

5. The classic sociological understanding of the professions is that society and individual consumers are too lacking in expertise to control or monitor adequately the performance of professionals. At the same time the larger society and individual consumers are intensely interested in controlling the conduct of professionals because of the high stakes involved in the tasks committed to professionals—high stakes both for the individual client and for the larger society because professional work implicates central social values like justice and the physical well-being of societal members. The professions and society thus "strike a bargain:" in exchange for high status, high remuneration, protection from lay competition and a significant degree of autonomy from state control, the professions adopt norms designed to protect individual consumers and the public at large, seek to educate members so they will internalize these norms and monitor compliance with and sanction deviations from such norms. See Dietrich Rueschemeyer, Lawyers and their Society 13–14 (1973) for a statement of this classic sociological explanation of professional ethics. For a similar explanation of professional ethics from an economist, see Kenneth Arrow, The Limits of Organization 36–37 (1974).

between state and group over normative space. But the nature and force of that competition is masked because the traditional understanding asserts that the domain of professional ethics does leave off where state law begins. The traditional understanding thus suggests that a consensus exists on the authoritative position of state law where state law exists. It suggests that, if the professions and the state agree on when the state has spoken and on what the state has said, the effect of the state pronouncement is to invalidate as a basis of action group norms that are in conflict with state law. These assumptions, however, are based on a naive positivism about state law; they minimize the richness and power of the group's normative vision; and they conceal the dynamic interplay between state and group norms.

Consider the following example:

By 1985, the number of criminal defense lawyers being subpoenaed before grand juries had risen dramatically,[6] and opposition to this practice by individual lawyers and the organized bar was increasing apace.[7] The state was largely unresponsive to the bar's opposition. The courts that had considered the question had rejected the lawyers' claims that client and fee identity were generally privileged from disclosure and that special procedures, such as prior judicial approval, should be required before the government is allowed to subpoena a criminal defense lawyer.[8] And while the Justice Department issued guidelines on this subject in 1985, these guidelines provided that such subpoenas could be issued upon a rather modest showing of need by the U.S. Attorney's office involved, and more important, they provided that the showing of need be made to the Department of Justice itself, not to a court.[9]

The Massachusetts bar then proposed an ethics rule making it unethical for a prosecutor to call a lawyer before a grand jury to testify about a client without prior judicial approval. The Supreme Judicial

6. This increase was in large part due to the broad forfeiture provisions of the Racketeer Influenced and Corrupt Organizations Act (RICO), 18 U.S.C. §§ 1961–68 (1982 & Supp. III, 1985) (see particularly § 1963(c)); and the Continuing Criminal Enterprise Statute (CCE), 21 U.S.C. § 853(c), which prosecutors interpreted as applying to attorney's fees. See the note above on p. 73.

7. See, e.g., Merkle & Moscarino, At Issue: Are Prosecutors Invading the Attorney–Client Relationship?, 71 A.B.A.J. 38 (1985); Pierce & Colamarino, Defense Counsel as a Witness for the Prosecution: Curbing the Practice of Issuing Grand Jury Subpoenas to Counsel for Targets of Investigations, 36 Hastings L.J. 821 (1985); and Zwerling, Federal Grand Juries v. Attorney Independence and the Attorney–Client Privilege, 27 Hastings L.J. 1263 (1976). In In re Grand Jury Subpoena (Slotnick), 781 F.2d 238 (2d Cir.1986) (en banc), amicus briefs opposing the government's use of such subpoenas and arguing for special procedures to limit the practice were filed by Association of The Bar of the City of New York, New York County Lawyers Association, New York Criminal Bar Association, National Association of Criminal Defense Lawyers and New Jersey Association of Criminal Defense Lawyers.

8. See, e.g., In re Grand Jury Proceedings (Freeman), 708 F.2d 1571, 1575 (11th Cir.1983); In re Grand Jury Proceeding (Schofield), 721 F.2d 1221, 1222–23 (9th Cir.1983); In re Klein, 776 F.2d 628, 632–33 (7th Cir.1985); In re Grand Jury Subpoena (Slotnick), 781 F.2d 238, 247–50 (2d Cir.1968) (en banc).

9. The text of the guidelines is reprinted in In re Grand Jury Subpoena to Attorney (Under Seal), 679 F.Supp. 1403, 1408 n.15 (N.D.W.Va.1988).

Court of Massachusetts adopted the rule in 1986, and the United States District Court for the District of Massachusetts refused to enjoin its operation.[10] The federal government challenged the district court decision arguing, among other things, that ethics rules should not be used to change grand jury procedures, an area governed by the Federal Rules of Criminal Procedure.[11] In United States v. Klubock,[12] the United States Court of Appeals for the First Circuit split four-four, leaving in place the district court opinion upholding the rule. In the meantime, courts have continued to hold that special procedures are neither required nor advisable under the Constitution or other law,[13] while state bars, following Massachusetts' lead, have proposed ethics rules that would require such procedures.[14]

In 1988, the American Bar Association passed its second resolution on this issue, and it called for even tighter limitations on the government's power to subpoena lawyers to testify before grand juries than those the ABA had originally proposed.[15] The courts, prosecutors and legislatures have remained largely unresponsive to the bar's position.[16] In 1990, the ABA amended the Model Rules of Professional Conduct to require prosecutors to obtain prior judicial approval before seeking to subpoena a lawyer about her client's affairs and making it unethical for

10. United States v. Klubock, 639 F.Supp. 117 (D.Mass.1986). The district court declined, however, to rule on whether the rule had been incorporated into the federal court rules for the district by virtue of the state court adoption. Id. at 121.

11. United States v. Klubock, 832 F.2d 664, 665 (1st Cir.1987) (en banc). The government made three arguments: (1) the rule was invalid under the Supremacy Clause of the Constitution because it was an attempt by state authorities to control federal prosecutors; (2) the district court lacked the power to promulgate the rule because it effected a substantial change in grand jury procedures, which should be made by amending the Federal Rules of Criminal Procedure or by separate congressional enactment; and (3) the court of appeals should exercise its supervisory powers to invalidate the law because the rule was so unwise.

12. 832 F.2d 664 (1st Cir.1987) (en banc).

13. See, e.g., United States v. Perry, 857 F.2d 1346, 1348 (9th Cir.1988); In re Nackson, 114 N.J. 527, 537, 555 A.2d 1101, 1107 (1989).

14. As of 1993, apparently six state supreme courts have adopted subpoena rules proposed by bar associations: Massachusetts, New Hampshire, Pennsylvania, Rhode Island, Tennessee and Virginia. The high courts of at least four jurisdictions have rejected a proposed subpoena rule: District of Columbia, Florida, New Jersey and New York.

15. The February 1988 resolution calls for an adversarial hearing as a prerequisite to judicial approval, whereas the 1986 resolution called for an ex parte proceeding. It also would require the prosecutor to show that the information sought is "essential" to an ongoing investigation, whereas the 1986 resolution required only a showing of "relevance."

16. For example, despite strong lobbying efforts on the part of the ABA and the National Association of Criminal Defense Lawyers (NACDL) among other bar groups, Congress has not enacted any legislative restrictions on the use of attorney subpoenas, although bills to accomplish this have been introduced. Courts have similarly rejected pleas for special procedures and pleas to expand the protection for client identity or fee information under the attorney-client privilege. See, e.g., In re Grand Jury Subpoenas ex rel. United States v. Anderson, 906 F.2d 1485, 1499 (10th Cir.1990). Moreover, while several state supreme courts have adopted bar-proposed ethics rules requiring special procedures, other state courts have rejected such proposals and no federal court has officially adopted the rule.

a prosecutor to seek judicial approval unless the information sought is not privileged, it is essential to the investigation and there is no feasible alternative means of obtaining it.[17]

In Baylson v. Disciplinary Board of Supreme Court of Pennsylvania,[18] however, the Third Circuit held that the Pennsylvania subpoena rule, which had become a local rule of federal district courts by automatic incorporation, could not be enforced against federal prosecutors because its adoption as federal law falls outside the rule-making authority of the district courts and its enforcement as state law violates the Supremacy Clause of the Constitution.[19]

This example suggests a far more active competition between state and group norms than the traditional understanding suggests, and it is far from an isolated example of this struggle over law.

III. The Profession's Ethos as Law

Law is more than a collection of rules. Rules demand explanation to have meaning. Stories must be told to create even the semblance of a shared understanding of what the rules require. Stories, in turn, demand explanation in the form of a rule—the "point" of the story. But law is not just rules and stories. Rules and stories alone (literature, history), while essential to normative discourse, are to be distinguished from law because they do not license transformations of reality through the use of force.[20] Law does. Law is rules and stories and a commitment of human will to change the world that is into the world that our rules and stories tell us ought to be. This commitment to realize the "ought" distinguishes law from utopian vision, literature and history.

Law understood as rules, the stories told about the rules and the commitment to act in accordance with those rules and stories requires no state.[21] A community and the state may share an understanding of

17. Model Rule 3.8(f) (as amended February 1990).

18. 975 F.2d 102 (3d Cir.1992).

19. The court said, 975 F.2d at 112,

... Pennsylvania does have an important interest in regulating the conduct of attorneys licensed to practice in the state. But " 'the law of the state, though enacted in the exercise of powers not controverted, must yield' when incompatible with federal legislation." Sperry, 373 U.S. at 384, quoting Gibbons v. Ogden, 9 Wheat. 1, 211 (1824). Rule 3.10, as written, is simply incompatible with federal grand jury law....

For discussion of the subpoena controversy, see Roger C. Cramton and Lisa K. Udell, State Ethics Rules and Federal Prosecutors: The Controversies Over the Anti-Contact and Subpoena Rules, 53 U.Pitt.L.Rev. 291, 359–85 (1992).

20. Cover, Nomos, supra at 9. "The creation of legal meaning cannot take place in silence. But neither can it take place without the committed action that distinguishes law from literature." Id. at 49.

21. Cover, Nomos, supra at 11 and n. 30. Professor Cover explains:

The state becomes central in the process not because it is well suited to jurisgenesis [the creation of legal meaning] nor because the cultural processes of giving meaning to normative activity cease in the presence of the state. The state becomes central only because ... an act of commitment is a central aspect of legal meaning. And violence

what constitutes the operative rule, but if they have radically different understandings of what that rule means (different stories) and each is committed to action based on its understanding, we have two distinct laws.

Why insist on calling each "law?" There are two reasons. First, by calling the bar's understanding of its responsibilities and obligations "law" I am taking a normative position. The word "law" has a rich history. It has long been used to describe normative systems other than those officially endorsed by the state: natural law, religious law, the law of the marketplace, etc. The continuing triumph of positivism can best be gauged by how the word "law" has come to be restricted in its meaning: "Law" is only that which the state speaks. Today those who dare dignify non-official norms with the name of "law" must defend their choice, while any state pronouncement is automatically dignified and implicitly legitimated with the word "law." I reject this triumph of positivism.

The second reason is practical. By reserving the label "law" for official state pronouncements and relegating the normative visions of communities to the status of "non-law" or, at best, advocacy about law, we may miss the force and effect that committed communities with their own vision of law have on state law. State law inevitably changes in the face of action taken in the name of alternative normative visions. In other words, the state must decide whether and to what extent the state and the group will be reshaped in the struggle.

Let's take an example from legal ethics. The Tax Reform Act of 1984 [22] requires people to report cash payments of $10,000 or more received in their trade or business. The person who received the money must fill in a reporting form, IRS Form 8300, which asks for the paying party's name, address, social security number, and occupation and, when applicable, for the name of the person on whose behalf the transaction was conducted. In October 1989, the IRS sent letters to 956 lawyers demanding that they fully complete these forms.[23] The lawyers had submitted incomplete forms, claiming much of the information could not be provided because it was protected by the attorney-client privilege.[24] The vast majority of lawyers receiving the IRS demand

[as to which the state has an imperfect but important monopoly] is one extremely powerful measure and test of commitment.

22. Tax Reform Act of 1984, 26 U.S.C. § 6050I.

23. Fred Strasser, Lawyers Must Name Names, Nat'l L.J., June 24, 1991, p. 18.

24. Id. This claim of privilege was asserted despite the fact that courts unanimously have held, in other contexts, that client identity and fee information are generally not protected by the privilege. See, e.g., United States v. Hodge and Zweig, 548 F.2d 1347, 1355 (9th Cir. 977) [reprinted below at p. 256]. The circumstances under which client identity and fee information might be privileged are uniformly described by the courts as quite rare. See, e.g., In re Grand Jury Subpoenas (Hirsch), 803 F.2d 493, 497 (9th Cir.1986).

letter refused to comply.[25] The IRS then issued ninety summonses to non-complying lawyers who had reported unusually large cash payments or who had declared multiple instances of cash payments over $10,000. Many, if not most, of the ninety lawyers refused to comply. The government brought a test case in the Southern District of New York to force compliance. The district court ordered the lawyers to comply, holding that nothing in the case justified departing from the general rule that client identity and fee information are not privileged.[26] After the district court ruling and with organized bar support,[27] many of the other ninety lawyers who had received summonses and the other 771 lawyers who did not respond to the IRS demand letter continued to resist.[28]

These lawyers and bar groups claimed that complying with state law (as manifested by the federal statute, the IRS regulations, the IRS activities in applying these rules to lawyers, the long-line of court precedents suggesting there is no valid claim of privilege as to client identity and fee, and the district court opinion) would violate the ethical responsibilities of the lawyers involved. For example, the president of the Criminal Trial Lawyers Association of Northern California, urging other lawyers to resist, stated: "There are ethical responsibilities we have as lawyers that foreclose giving information which may put our clients in jeopardy." [29] On appeal, the Second Circuit upheld the district court, dismissing as "without merit" the contention that the reporting requirement conflicts with the attorney-client privilege.[30] After this decision, when asked what advice he would give to

25. Alexander Stille, A Strategic Retreat for the IRS on Disclosure of Attorney Fees, Nat'l L. J., May 14, 1990, p. 3 ("Only 95 lawyers answered the letters by providing client information, according to Elle Murphy, director of public information at the IRS").

26. United States v. Fischetti Pomerantz & Russo, No. N–18–304 (VLB), slip op. at 53–4 (S.D.N.Y. Mar. 13, 1990).

27. The organized bar demonstrated its support of these lawyers in various ways. The Association of the Bar of the City of New York, the National Association of Criminal Defense Lawyers and the New York Council of Defense Lawyers filed amicus briefs on behalf of the lawyers in *Fischetti*. The American Bar Association communicated to the Justice Department that wholesale enforcement of the federal law would have a devastating impact on the attorney-client relationship. Perhaps most important for my purposes, several bars have issued ethics opinions stating or strongly suggesting that compliance with the IRS or similar state revenue agency demands is unethical, at least in the absence of a court order, and that even when a court orders exists, the lawyer may ethically choose not to comply. See, e.g., State Bar of Georgia, Advisory Op. 41 (Sept. 21, 1984); Florida Bar Staff Op. TEO88203 (1988); Nat'l Ass'n Crim. Defense Lawyers Ethical Advisory Comm. Op. 89–1 (Nov. 22, 1989); Chicago Bar Ass'n Op. 86–2 (May 11, 1988); and New Mexico Bar Op. 1989–2 (1989).

28. Steve Albert, Courting a Showdown: More Lawyers Defy IRS Demands for Client Data, Legal Times, Apr. 30, 1990, p. 2.

29. William Carlson, Drug War's Fallout on Defense Lawyers, S.F. Chron., Jan. 15, 1990, at A1. Consider also the argument of counsel in *Fischetti* : "[W]e are here because we have no choice but to be here. We are not here as willing gladiators, we are here because the government began this proceeding. We are ethically counseled, in a number of opinions that we have cited, not to disclose client identity without testing the enforceability of the statute in a court." *Fischetti*, slip. op. at 26.

30. United States v. Goldberger & Dubin, 935 F.2d 501, 504 (2d Cir.1991) (*Fischetti* on appeal). The court held that the lawyers had to await government enforcement before

lawyers in the circuit, the head of the National Association of Criminal Defense Lawyers' "8300 Task Force" commented: "I would say many people subscribe to the notion that you don't violate a confidence until you are ordered to do so by a court." [31] From the context, it is obvious he means personally ordered.

IV. Two Laws Masquerading as One

A. What We Might Expect to Find

The legal profession is, by definition, inextricably connected to the state and its laws. The state has the last say over such central matters of group definition as who may be admitted to group membership and who may be excluded. Moreover, the central privilege of membership in the profession is the right to speak to the state on behalf of another in the state's courts. Thus, the profession is dependent on the state for boundary and functional definition, central matters in the normative vision of any community. But the state's *nomos* is similarly dependent on the profession. To be a lawyer is to have a right to participate in the creation and maintenance of the state's *nomos* that is denied to other persons in the society.

As an expression of the real interdependence of the two normative worlds, we would expect to find significant areas in which the two normative worlds coincide. Further, the intensity and particular nature of the interdependence of bar and state increases the need of all involved to maintain the myth of a unitary normative system. The idea that the ministers of the state law are somehow less than faithful to that law is simply too powerful a suggestion to be incorporated easily into either the state's or the bar's normative system. Thus, we would expect to find that each normative world has developed means of masking the existence of the profession's conflicting norms.

B. The Hierarchy of Norms

For the most part, the bar and the state agree on the precepts that are relevant to the law governing lawyers: precepts contained in the Constitution of the United States; the ethics rules as embodied in various codes promulgated by the bar; the common law of lawyering, particularly the attorney-client privilege and precepts embodied in "other law," including the law of torts, criminal law, securities law and the law of procedure. I say "for the most part" for two reasons. First, the state treats ethics rules as "law" only to the extent that they are (and in the form in which they are) adopted by the state. On the other hand, the bar may treat as law ethics rules adopted by the ABA or a state bar organization but not adopted by the state. Second, the extent to which the bar accepts that precepts of "other law" govern the

challenging the summonses. "[T]he [privilege] protects only those disclosures that are necessary to obtain informed legal advice and that would not be made without the privilege." See also United States v. Leventhal, 961 F.2d 936 (11th Cir.1992) (following *Goldberger & Dubin*).

31. Strasser, supra (quoting Gerald B. Lefcourt, head of the "8300 Task Force").

conduct of lawyers is not clear. Sometimes lawyers and bar groups speak as if lawyers enjoy some form of immunity from the precepts of other law. But, even if we put aside for the moment these two areas of potential disagreement on precepts and assume that the bar and the state are in total agreement on the relevant precepts, the existence of shared precepts indicates a unitary normative system only if the precepts are ordered and interpreted by each group (the bar and the state) in the same way. They are not. In the bar's *nomos* ethics rules [32] are presumed to control when they conflict with other law, while in the state's *nomos* other law is presumed to control when it conflicts with the ethics rules.

In the state's hierarchy of norms—as it exists in theory—ethics rules occupy a relatively lowly status. Ethics rules are generally court rules not legislation, and they are more often state law, not federal law. Those two facts relegate ethics rules to a lowly status in the state's hierarchy of precepts.[33] Moreover, federal and state courts often state that the only instances in which they are bound to treat the ethics rules as binding precepts are in disciplinary proceedings against lawyers.[34] Thus, even when the ethics rules purport to speak directly on a matter and are the only existing source of precept on the question, they may be ignored with relative ease so long as the case is not a disciplinary proceeding.

The strongest evidence that the bar's hierarchy of norms differs from the state's is found in the bar narratives that explicate the rules— ethics opinions. Just as court opinions provide a body of narratives and precepts that are intended to be realized in action, ethics opinions perform a similar function in the bar's *nomos*. Ethics opinions are also a particular strong source of evidence on the content of the bar's *nomos* because they are generally not subject to prior state control. They therefore express law to which the bar, but not necessarily the state, is committed.

32. This is not to say that in the bar's *nomos* each precept in the ethics rules carries equal power to trump other law. The bar is so weakly committed to some rules that they may be said to have taken on the status of "non-law" for the bar, and thus they lack the power to trump other law.

33. First, Constitutional requirements, including those on procedure, trump all other law. Second, federal law trumps state law. Third, on matters of substantive law, legislation trumps rules adopted by courts. Fourth, on matters of procedure, federal legislation trumps rules adopted by federal courts, and federal rules of procedure adopted pursuant to congressional authorization, such as the Federal Rules of Civil Procedure, trump rules adopted by federal courts, which include ethics rules. And while in many states rules of procedure adopted by a court pursuant to the court's inherent powers, which is how ethics rules are adopted, trump conflicting state legislative pronouncements on procedure, this may be truer in theory than in practice.

34. See, e.g., W.T. Grant Co. v. Haines, 531 F.2d 671, 676–77 (2d Cir.1976) (holding that lawyer's violation of ethics rule against advising unrepresented party is insufficient basis upon which to dismiss client's lawsuit or disqualify the law firm). Courts typically consult the ethics rules in non-disciplinary cases involving a lawyer's conduct, but they treat the rules as a source of guidance rather than as binding precept. See the note on the role of ethics rules in determining a lawyer's duty of care in legal malpractice, infra at 190.

What do the ethics opinions tell us about the bar's ordering of norms? Some ethics opinions actively and openly encourage disobedience of other law.[35] They provide the strongest evidence that the bar's hierarchy of norms places ethics rules above other state precepts. Such opinions are, however, relatively rare.[36] What is surprising is that they exist at all.

Much more common are ethics opinions stating that the ethics rules permit, but do not require, compliance with other law.[37] While less dramatic, these opinions also provide evidence that the bar's hierarchy of norms presumes that ethics rules trump other norms. How else can one understand the question: Do the ethics rules permit compliance with other law? Or the answer, that compliance is permitted?

The bar's understanding that ethics rules trump other law (or qualify it or render it ambiguous) is also evident in its efforts to pass ethics rules or interpret existing rules to stop state action that the courts have held is permitted under other law. Ethics rules that would require prosecutors to get prior judicial approval and demonstrate extreme need before subpoenaing lawyers to testify before grand juries about their clients' affairs are just one example of this. Other examples include ethics rules and ethics opinions prohibiting the disclosure of client fraud in connection with the sale or purchase of securities to the Securities and Exchange Commission, purchasers, or stockholders; [38]

---

35. State Bar of New Mexico Advisory Op. 1989–2 states:

[T]he intent of the New Mexico Rules of Professional Conduct is that attorney should not reveal exactly what the federal [requirement that a lawyer report the source of a cash payment of $10,000 or more] requires [an] attorney to reveal. Thus, there is a conflict between [the two]. Our Committee does not resolve the conflict, but we [recommend that a lawyer] consistent with the highest ideals of the profession ... may, with the client's consent, agree to "make a good faith effort to determine the validity, scope, meaning or application" of the law at issue [citing a state-court-adopted ethics rule requiring confidentiality]....

36. Other examples of openly defiant ethics opinions include: State Bar Wis. Formal Op. 3–90–3 (Apr. 2, 1990) (lawyer should not make disclosure when faced with an IRS summons unless and until a court, preferably an appellate court, considers the validity of the summons and any judicial enforcement orders in this area and that court's ruling requires such disclosure."); Nat'l Ass'n Crim. Defense Lawyers Ethical Advisory Comm. Op. 89–1 (Nov. 22, 1989) (same); Chicago Bar Ass'n Op. 86–2 (May 11, 1988) (lawyer would not be condemned for filing a completed IRS form; "however, the better course ... is to file an IRS form that asserts the attorney-client privilege and gives notice ... that information has been withheld ..."); State Bar of Georgia, Advisory Op. No, 41 (Sept. 21, 1984) (a lawyer should pursue all reasonable avenues of appeal before complying with requests from state agency). Openly defiant ethics opinions are much more likely to involve certain precepts, like the rule on confidentiality, than others.

37. See, e.g., Ass'n of the Bar of New York Op. 1990–2 (Feb. 27, 1990) (lawyer may comply with Fed.R.Civ.Pro. 26(e)); Chicago Bar Ass'n. Op. 86–4 (undated) (lawyer is permitted but not required to disclose to IRS its overpayment to client if he is under a legal obligation pursuant to statute or regulation to disclose such information); ABA Comm. on Ethics and Prof. Resp., Informal Op. 1349 (1975) ("[W]e do not decide whether local criminal law makes it unlawful for S to fail to reveal the information.... If disclosure is required by such law, S may, but is not required under DR 4–101(C)(2), to make disclosure.").

38. In 1974 the ABA adopted an amendment to DR 7–102(B)(1) of the 1969 Model Code which all but eliminated the lawyer's duty to reveal a client's fraud in which the lawyer's

prohibiting the simultaneous negotiation of attorneys' fees in civil rights cases; [39] and prohibiting disclosure of information to the Legal Services Corporation. [40]

V. The Centrality of Confidentiality in the Bar's Nomos

Introduction

The bar texts discussed above show that it is confidentiality, and particularly the duty to keep client confidences from the state, more often than any other norm, which triggers the obligation to resist competing state norms, and which justifies the passage of ethics rules to "undo" state pronouncements. That the bar deems individual acts of resistance and group efforts to repeal state pronouncements as appropriate responses to state efforts to secure client confidences reveals the bar's interpretation of the norm, i.e., that it is absolute or nearly-so.

Confidentiality is a constitutional norm in the bar's *nomos*. By constitutional norm, I mean a norm so central to group definition (to that which constitutes a group) that perceived threats to the norm are understood by the group as threats against the group itself—against the group's very existence; that proposals to change the norm are seen by the group as proposals to change the essence/character/function of the group itself; and consequently that extreme action is thought to be justified in defense of the norm.

The special importance of the norm of confidentiality in the bar's *nomos* is not apparent on the face of the ethics codes as adopted by the states, nor is it readily apparent on the face of the ethics rules as drafted by the ABA. Confidentiality is not the first norm stated in the professional codes. Moreover, the language describing confidentiality in all three documents is relatively dry and straightforward, and each document contains exceptions to the duty to keep client confidences.

---

services had been used. This amendment was a response to a several court decisions that had alarmed the securities bar, including *National Student Marketing*. See, e.g., Hoffman, On Learning of a Corporate Client's Crime or Fraud, 33 Bus.Law. 1389, 1405–07 (1978) (explaining that the amendment was one of a series of attempts by bar groups to resolve the "conflict" raised between the state's position and the securities lawyers' ethical obligations). In the 1980s, this struggle over the law governing securities lawyers was played out in the ABA's adoption in 1983 of Model Rules 1.13 and 1.6. Rule 1.13, as adopted, eliminated the lawyer's discretion to disclose criminal or fraudulent corporate activity to stockholders, government agencies or those defrauded by the corporation's activities—discretion that had been included in the draft presented to the House of Delegates. Rule 1.6 eliminated the lawyer's discretion to reveal client fraud—discretion that had been included in the Kutak draft.

39. See Evans v. Jeff D., 475 U.S. 717 (1986), reprinted below at p. 548 (upholding fee waivers despite ethics opinions concluding that simultaneous negotiation of a fee award and an award on the merits is unethical). In his dissent in *Evans*, Justice Brennan invited the bar to use ethics opinions to try and outlaw simultaneous negotiations. 475 U.S. at 765 (1986). This invitation for the bar to continue its own normative understanding is consistent with Brennan's general approach of inviting alternate normative understandings to counteract Court decisions with which he disagrees.

40. See, e.g., N.H. Bar Ass'n Formal Op. No. 1988–9/13 (Feb. 9, 1989); ABA Comm. on Ethics and Prof.Resp. Informal Op. 1394 (1977); ABA Comm. on Ethics and Prof.Resp. Informal Op. 1287 (1974).

The ethics codes may mask the power of the norm of confidentiality, but the ethics opinions interpreting the codes make it plain. A pattern emerges in these opinions: rules affirming a duty or the discretion to disclose are either narrowed to the point of near-irrelevance or held to be overridden by rules requiring silence.[41]

VII. Commitment

Because the *nomos* is but the process of human action stretched between vision and reality, a legal interpretation cannot be valid if no one is prepared to live by it.[42]

We call the state's normative vision "law" because we know that the state means it. It is committed to its interpretation. It is prepared to act, using all the resources of violence at its disposal, if necessary, to enforce its interpretations. Earlier, to justify my use of the word "law" to describe the profession's normative vision, I argued that the profession means it too, that it too is committed to its interpretations. If, however, the profession's law diverges from that of the state, how can the profession maintain its commitment given the state's imperfect monopoly over violence?[43] The answer lies in understanding that commitment is not an all or nothing proposition for either the state or the community.[44] As we shall see, judges are particularly unlikely to assert their interpretive power or back their interpretations with violence in cases in which their understanding of law diverges from the bar's. The state's commitment is weak. On the other hand, the bar's commitment is relatively strong.

A. The Weakness of the State's Commitment

In cases involving the law governing lawyers, the courts show a weak commitment to state law—to the maintenance of a state *nomos*—in two basic ways. First, [the courts] are reluctant to create legal meaning and as a consequence create little. Second, they show little inclination to back with violence the legal meaning they do create. Consider the court's decision in SEC v. National Student Marketing.[45]

----

41. See discussion in Chapter 4 below, p. 295.

42. Cover, Nomos, supra at 44.

43. To appreciate the importance of the question posed in the text, consider the following quote:

> Certain efforts to [maintain a separate *nomos*] have an almost doomed character. The state's claims over legal meaning are at bottom, so closely tied to the state's imperfect monopoly over the domain of violence that the claim of a community to an autonomous meaning must be linked to the community's willingness to live out its meaning in defiance. Outright defiance, guerrilla warfare, and terrorism are, of course, the most direct responses. They are responses, however, that may—as in the United States—be unjustifiable and doomed to failure.

Cover, Nomos, supra at 52.

44. "Some interpretations are writ in blood and run with a warranty of blood as part of their validating force. Other interpretations carry more conventional limits to what will be hazarded on their behalf." Id. at 46.

45. 457 F.Supp. 682 (D.D.C.1978), reprinted above at p. 99.

In *National Student Marketing* the SEC sought to enjoin several lawyers and their law firms, claiming that they had closed a merger deal knowing that shareholder approval had been obtained on the basis of materially misleading documents. The SEC had a complete vision of law—norm, narrative and commitment—and one at odds with the bar's *nomos*. The court's decision showed commitment neither to the law it articulated nor to the court's role as interpreter of law.

The court agreed with the SEC that the lawyers had violated the securities laws by knowingly and substantially assisting their clients to commit fraud. Having articulated precepts that it is wrong to remain silent and do nothing while assisting clients in a fraudulent securities transaction, however, the court failed to connect them to the lawyers' actions in this case:

> [I]t is unnecessary to determine the precise extent of their obligations here, since ... they took no steps whatsoever to delay the closing.... But, at the very least, they were required to speak out [to their clients] at the closing.... [46]

In failing to provide a narrative, in failing to connect norms to the actions of the past, the court showed a weak commitment to its role as creator of legal meaning. The court refused to explain what parts of the world as it exists (represented in this case by the actions of the lawyers) are to be changed by its norms. It thus created little law to project into the future. Was it wrong under state law that the lawyers failed to resign? That they failed to inform officers of the corporate client not present at the meeting? That they failed to inform shareholders or the SEC? Does the law demand that lawyers in the future do any of these things? With the words "at the very least," the court admits that the narrative is incomplete, that state law has more meaning, but it does not assert its power to control that meaning. Instead, it invites the bar to provide that meaning:

> The very initiation of this action ... has provided a necessary and worthwhile impetus for the profession's recognition and assessment of its responsibilities in this area.[47]

By telling a community that it should reconsider its behavior and beliefs in light of state power whether or not the use of that power is legitimate, a court abandons its commitment to a state built on the meaning of shared principles and helps constitute a state built instead on obedience to authority.

The court explained its failure to create law by stating that further explication would be "unnecessary [to resolve the case before it]" and that it "must narrow its focus to the present defendants and the charges against them." These statements are allusions to the rule against rendering advisory opinions. The case was before the court to

46. 475 F.Supp. at 713.

47. 457 F.Supp. at 715.

determine whether an injunction was warranted against the defendants. What exactly the lawyers did wrong and the degree to which it was wrong were issues thus directly before the court. The court had to reach for the advisory opinion rule to avoid discussing these issues. This stretch demonstrates the court's weak commitment. The court uses the advisory opinion rule in a case where it does not naturally apply as an excuse not to make law. Moreover, the advisory opinion rule assumes "an ironic cast" [48] in this case: the court's refusal to grant any relief against the defendants, a matter to which we turn next, renders the entire opinion no more than advice.

The court refused to enjoin the lawyers from further violations of the securities laws; it granted the SEC no relief against the defendants. By denying relief, the court showed a weak commitment to the little law it did create and to whatever more the securities laws might mean as applied to lawyers whose clients are engaged in fraud. It refused to back its interpretation with force, and more striking, it explained that force was unnecessary, in part, because the defendants were lawyers. The court expressed its confidence that the defendants' "professional responsibilities as attorneys and officers of the court" will lead them to honor the court's interpretation without force.[49] In other words, state law will depend on the bar's *nomos* for vindication. The court thus speaks as if the bar's law were somehow stronger and more binding on group members than state law. The power of the bar's law does not trouble the court because in the court's vision the paramount precept for lawyers must be (and therefore for the court is) the obligation to comply with state law. This understanding of the hierarchy of norms contained in the ethics rules is, however, a state understanding. In the bar's *nomos* the duty to comply with other law does not, as we have seen, trump all other norms.

The evidence of weak commitment found in *National Student Marketing* is common in cases involving the law governing lawyers.

---

48. Professor Cover used this phrase to describe the thickness of legal meaning. In his example, it was the Due Process Clause's reference to "life" that had taken on an ironic cast both for opponents of the death penalty and opponents of abortion. Cover, Nomos, supra at 7. When a precept takes on an ironic cast for a community or for the society at large, those who perceive the irony will view any invocation of the precept by the state with suspicion.

49. Subsequent events suggest that weak commitment to law by a court helps the bar maintain its divergent understanding of law:

According to the allegations contained in two lawsuits that Lord, Bissell [and Brook] recently settled for twenty four million dollars, shortly after the decision in *National Student Marketing*, the firm began aggressively representing National Mortgage Equity Corporation, a controversial venture designed to capitalize on the newly emerging market in second mortgages. . . . [A]ccording to the deposition testimony of the firm's managing partner, the firm changed virtually none of its practices as a result of the SEC's prosecutions in *National Student Marketing*.

David B. Wilkins, Who Should Regulate Lawyers?, 105 Harv. L. Rev. 799, 870–871 (1992) (citing Tim O'Brien, Some Firms Never Learn: Lord Bissell's Second Escape from Fraud Charges Cost $24 Million—And It Could Happen Again, Am. Law., Oct. 1989, at 63, 64). . . .

The *Stenhach* case reprinted in Chapter 1 provides another example. Moreover, there are numerous other examples of the courts' weak commitment in cases involving the law governing lawyers: cases in which the court refuses to use force to back its interpretation; [50] cases in which the court refuses to create legal meaning; [51] cases using temporary or inherently weak boundary rules; [52] and cases in which the court suggests that the bar's understanding of law controls the court's interpretation.[53] There are, of course, counter examples.[54]

Detecting trends in something as complex as the degree of state commitment is a difficult business. There are, however, many indications that the commitment is increasing.[55] On the other hand, given how pervasive and longstanding the practice of low commitment has been and how sympathetic to the bar's vision many judges are, I would not predict a complete about face in the immediate future.

50. See, e.g., In re Thompson, 416 F.Supp. 991, 996 (S.D.Tex.1976) (refusing to hold lawyer in contempt of court's order of discharge in bankruptcy, although his threats against discharged bankrupt on behalf of unsecured creditor were "inexcusable and in obvious disregard of the purposes" of the bankruptcy act"); In re Corboy, 124 Ill.2d 29, 45, 528 N.E.2d 694, 701 (1988) (imposing no sanction because the lawyers "acted without guidance of precedent or settled opinion, and there was, apparently, considerable belief among members of the bar that they had acted properly"); Mozzochi v. Beck, 204 Conn. 490, 497, 529 A.2d 171, 174 (1987) (holding lawyers who breach their duty "to their clients and to the judicial system" by filing suit after learning that the allegations are wholly without merit are not liable for abuse of process because "[a]ny other rule would ineluctably interfere with the attorney's primary duty of robust representation."). See also In re Carter and Johnson, reprinted at p. 779 below.

51. See Barker v. Henderson, 797 F.2d 490, 497 (7th Cir.1986) (refusing to discuss "the extent to which lawyers ... should reveal their clients' wrongdoing—and to whom they should reveal," noting that "[t]he professions and the regulatory agencies will debate questions raised by cases such as this one for years to come").

52. See, e.g., Financial General Bankshares, Inc. v. Metzger, 680 F.2d 768, 775 (D.C.Cir.1982) ("the unsettled nature of District of Columbia law regarding the fiduciary duties of an attorney to a client" rendered it an abuse of discretion by the district court to decide that pendent jurisdiction claim).

53. See, e.g., United States v. Klubock, 832 F.2d 649, 654 (1st Cir.1987) (en banc) (bar's understanding of when and how lawyers are to be called before grand juries governs because the "fundamental underlying problem ... is an ethical one"); Barker v. Henderson, 797 F.2d 490, 497 (7th Cir.1986) ("[A]n award of damages under the securities laws is not the way to blaze the trail toward improved ethical standards in the legal and accounting professions.... The securities law ... must lag behind changes in ethical and fiduciary standards").

54. See, e.g., United States v. Cintolo, 818 F.2d 980 (1st Cir.1987), discussed above at p. 70; In re Grand Jury Subpoenas, ex rel. United States v. Anderson, 906 F.2d 1485, 1499 (10th Cir.1990) (upholding district court order jailing lawyers for contempt for refusing to reveal the source of their fees to the grand jury and rejecting lawyers argument that their refusal was justified by their ethical obligations); In re Solerwitz, 848 F.2d 1573 (Fed. Cir.1988) (suspending a lawyer for filing and maintaining frivolous appeals even though three ethics experts testified the lawyer's conduct was proper).

55. Goldfarb v. Virginia State Bar, 421 U.S. 773, 793 (1975), holding that activities of a mandatory bar association are not exempt from the antitrust laws, is an early and significant sign of an increased commitment to the role of state law vis a vis the profession. Another important sign is the significant erosion in the traditional rule that a lack of privity prevents third parties from suing lawyers for negligence. See, Greycas v. Proud, 826 F.2d 1560 (1st Cir.1987). The amendment of Fed.R.Civ.P. Rule 11 in 1983 (holding lawyers to a greater level of candor in pleadings and other court papers) and the adoption of similar rules in the states may be another sign of the courts' increased commitment to its vision of lawyering. Rule 11 is discussed at p. 414 below.

The Bar's Commitment: Texts of Resistance

> Whenever a community resists ... some ... law of the state, it necessarily enters into a secondary hermeneutic—the interpretation of the texts of resistance.[56]

As we have seen, the bar's sacred stories predict a crisis between a lawyer's obligations to her client and the demands of state law put forth by prosecutors, judges and other state actors.[57]

It is in the bar's texts of resistance that we find the bar's understanding of its obligation to the state and its law. The texts do not deny the obligation; they interpret it.

In the bar's texts of resistance, after deciding that something the state calls "law" conflicts with bar law the question becomes: Is that troublesome thing, which the state calls law, law for purposes of the lawyer's obligation to obey? The first interpretive move is that legislation and regulation that conflict with bar law are not "law" for purposes of this norm. The comment to Rule 1.6 itself suggests this move by omitting reference to legislation and regulation. It reads: "The lawyer must comply with the final orders of a court or other tribunal of competent jurisdiction requiring the lawyer to give information about the client." It may be that the bar treats judicial decisions as a higher form of law, in part, because it regards judges as semi-brothers and hence mediators between the state and the bar. The point here is that what counts as law is limited by this first interpretive move.

While neither legislation nor regulation are law that require obedience, bar texts emphasize that their non-law status is strictly limited to the extent that they conflict with bar law and no further. For example, while client confidentiality, according to the bar, precludes a lawyer from complying with tax law and regulations that require the lawyer to provide the client's name and other identifying information, "confidentiality ... do[es] not relieve the lawyer of the statutory duty to file the required form." [58] It "must still be filed, but the lawyer should insert ... in place of the client's name ... a statement that the lawyer and the client are asserting client confidentiality, the attorney-client privilege and, if applicable, the Fifth and Sixth Amendment privileges." [59] Resistance is to be tailored to contest the "invalid"

---

56. Cover, Nomos, supra, at 49.

57. Consider William Kunstler's response when sanctioned under Rule 11 for his conduct in suing state prosecutors for harassing Native American activists. In re Kunstler (Robinson Defense Comm. v. Britt), 914 F.2d 505, 525 (4th Cir.1990). Kunstler said: "I'll tell you this: I'm not going to pay any fine. I'm going to rot in jail if that's what I have to do to dramatize this thing. I think I could do no better thing for my country." Don J. DeBenedictis, Rule 11 Snags Lawyers, 77 A.B.A.J. 16, 17 (1991).

58. Ethics Advisory Comm. of Nat'l Ass'n of Crim. Defense Lawyers, Formal Op. 89–1 (Nov. 22, 1989); see also, State Bar Wis. Formal Op. E–90–3 (Apr. 2, 1990) (approving and incorporating NACDL Op. 89–1).

59. Id.

portion of the legislation or regulation and should not otherwise show disrespect to the state's legislation or regulation.

Moreover, while for the bar neither legislation nor regulation are "law" for purposes of the duty to obey (when they conflict with bar law), bar texts typically distinguish between the two: the obligation to resist regulation is generally greater than the obligation to resist legislation. For example, the Statement of Policy adopted by the ABA House of Delegates on the duties of lawyers to comply with the securities laws states:

> [A]ny principle of law which, except as permitted or required by the [Code of Professional Responsibility], permits or obliges a lawyer to disclose to the S.E.C. otherwise confidential information should be established *only by statute* after full and careful consideration of the public interests involved and should be resisted unless clearly mandated by law.[60]

Implicitly, this suggests greater resistance is owed SEC regulations inconsistent with bar law than legislation, which must be resisted too, but not if "clearly mandated by law." How one decides whether legislation is "clearly mandated by law" is not fully described by this ABA Statement, although a reference to "a questionable lower court decision" carries the inference that an interpretation of legislation that conflicts with the bar's law and that is supported by only a lower court decision is not "clearly mandated by law."

This brings us to the bar's next interpretive problem, whether court orders and decisions are law that must be obeyed. It is at this point that we may gauge the true nature of the bar's commitment. For at this point the state's use of force may be imminent. The comment to Rule 1.6 states that lawyers "must comply with the final orders of a court or other tribunal of competent jurisdiction." The qualifications in this sentence—"final orders" and "competent jurisdiction"—are, however, important indicators of the bar's understanding. Generally, bar texts of resistance allow a lawyer to comply with court orders, but do not require that she do so.[61] For example, the ABA has explained its understanding of the ethics rules as follows:

> If the motion to quash is denied, the lawyer must either testify or run the risk of being held in contempt.... The lawyer has an ethical duty to preserve client confidences and to test any interference with that duty in court.... If a contempt citation is upheld on appeal, however, the lawyer has little choice but to testify or go to jail. Both the Model Rules and the Model Code recognize that a

---

60. See ABA's Section of Corporation, Banking, and Business Law, Statement of Policy Adopted by the American Bar Association Regarding Responsibilities and Liabilities of Lawyers in Advising with Respect to the Compliance by Clients with Laws Administered by the Securities and Exchange Commission, 61 A.B.A. J. 1085 (1975) (emphasis added).

61. See, e.g., Ala. Formal Op. 88–76 (Sept. 1, 1988) ("If ordered to testify by the court, the lawyer may either do so or may seek appellate relief"); and Va. Bar Formal Op. 787 (Apr. 4, 1986) (similar).

lawyer's ethical duty to preserve client confidences gives way to final court orders.[62]

While this quote carefully avoids explicitly requiring resistance, the message is clear that a lawyer should resist a lower court order: ethical duty "gives way" according to the text only after a final court order, and "final court orders" are, according to the quote, orders of an appellate court. Even more telling of the bar's commitment to its law than the strong encouragement to resist lower court orders is the suggestion that bar law "gives way" to appellate orders not because they are legitimate and authoritative interpretations but because the state at this point is extremely likely to use force: "the lawyer may have little choice but to testify or go to jail." It is accommodation pure and simple that is being expressed not concession to the appellate court's role as authoritative interpreter of its law.

The view that it is the state's force and not its interpretation or its right to interpret that relieves a lawyer of the obligation to resist appellate orders is also expressed by the bar's understanding of the reach of such orders. Bar texts do not contain any suggestion of an obligation to check controlling precedent in the relevant jurisdiction before deciding whether to comply. Moreover, given the weight of authority on such issues as whether a client's identity or fees paid an attorney are privileged, it is clearly the message of these bar texts that court decisions contrary to bar law are to be understood as having decided the question before them and no more. As the NACDL put it in testifying before Congress: "Our members will litigate these issues at every turn...." [63]

This posture "is an attempt to separate completely the projection of understanding from the decree that is the direct exercise of court power. Such separation allows one to 'acquiesce' by refraining from resistance while simultaneously refusing to extend the social range of the Court's hermeneutic." [64] The efficacy of this move is dependent on the level of the courts' commitment. Courts, after all, have the means to insist that their interpretations are projected into the future: injunctions. But the likelihood of the courts using such a tool against lawyers

---

62. 83 ABA/BNA Lawyers' Man.Prof.Conduct 5, 11 (1989) (emphasis added) (citations omitted)....

63. Statement of Alan Ellis, President–Elect, and Scott Wallace, Legislative Director, on Behalf of the Nat'l Ass'n Crim. Defense Lawyers Before the Subcommittee on Government Information, Justice and Agriculture, House Committee on Government Operations, May 10, 1990 at 12 (on file with author).

64. Cover, Nomos, supra, at 54 n.146. Professor Cover is discussing Lincoln's famous remarks on the *Dred Scott* decision, Scott v. Sanford, 60 U.S. (19 How.) 393 (1857):

I do not resist [*Dred Scott*]. If I wanted to take Dred Scott from his master, I would be interfering with property.... But I am doing no such thing as that, but all that I am doing is refusing to obey it as a political rule. If I were in Congress, and a vote should come up on a question whether slavery should be prohibited in a new territory, in spite of that Dred Scott decision. I would vote that it should.

Id. (quoting Speech by Abraham Lincoln at Chicago, Illinois, July 10, 1858). Professor Cover explains that what Lincoln is saying is that "[o]ur future actions are to be governed by our own understanding, not the Court's." Id. at 54.

is remote, given how weakly committed they are to their role when they find themselves at odds with the bar. The bar's commitment, on the other hand, is, as we have just seen, strong. It is the interaction of these two levels of commitment that allows the divergence in normative understanding to continue.

Questions

Do you agree with the Cover–Koniak view that private groups, such as the ABA or a state bar association, contribute to the creation and explanation of "law"? That the organized bar's conception of the legal obligations of lawyers is at odds at some critical points with that of official lawmakers (legislatures and courts)?

Consider the persistent refusal of criminal defense lawyers to comply with IRS requests for client identity, requests that are founded in statutory requirements the courts have repeatedly upheld. Does that story indicate the importance of commitment in shaping the law? The centrality of the principle of confidentiality in the profession's normative priorities?

D. TAX LAW

Introductory Note

Lawyers representing taxpayers must decide whether legal advice or assistance constitutes prohibited assistance. Consider the following hypothetical:

> After a successful sex discrimination suit under Title VII of the Civil Rights Act of 1964, a client receives damages equal to the back wages she would have received but for the discrimination. She does not want to report the damages as taxable income. Wages, of course, are reportable income but a tort recovery for personal injuries is not. Her lawyer determines that taxability in this case depends upon whether the damages may be characterized as a substitute for back wages or analogized to a tort recovery for personal injuries (Internal Revenue Code § 104(a)(2) excludes from taxable income damages derived from "personal injuries or sickness"). The Internal Revenue Service originally characterized back-pay awards under Title VII as wages reportable as income, and the courts accepted this view.[1] The rulings and decisions were consistent until 1986 when the Tax Court accepted the tort analogy in one case. By the end of 1991, the Third and Sixth Circuits had

---

1. See, e.g., Rev.Rul. 72–341, 1972–2 C.B. 32; and Hodge v. Commissioner, 64 T.C. 616 (1975).

also found Title VII damages excludable from income.[2]   Other
federal courts continued to treat such damages as taxable income.[3]
In 1992 the U.S. Supreme Court resolved the conflict of circuits by
holding that back-pay awards in settlement of Title VII claims are
not excludable from a taxpayer's gross income.[4]

How should a lawyer advising this client in 1979 have counseled
her to treat the damages?   Would it have mattered if the lawyer
believed the tort analogy to be the best characterization despite the
contrary case law?   What about in 1986 after the Tax Court broke with
the accepted view and found Title VII damages excludable?   In early
1992 when a clear conflict between circuits existed and the Supreme
Court was considering the issue?   Even if the lawyer decided that the
damages were excludable, should the amount nonetheless be reported
to flag the IRS as to the existence of the damages and the possible
question of income?   How would these questions be answered if ABA
Formal Opinion 85–352, reprinted below, had been in effect?

ABA FORMAL OPINION 85–352

American Bar Association Standing Committee on Professional Ethics.
July 7, 1985.

The Committee has been requested by the Section of Taxation of
the American Bar Association to reconsider the "reasonable basis"
standard in the Committee's Formal Opinion 314 governing the position
a lawyer may advise a client to take on a tax return.

Opinion 314 (April 27, 1965) was issued in response to a number of
specific inquiries regarding the ethical relationship between the Internal Revenue Service and lawyers practicing before it.   The opinion
formulated general principles governing this relationship, including the
following: "[A] lawyer who is asked to advise his client in the course of
the preparation of the client's tax returns may freely urge the statement of positions most favorable to the client just as long as there is a
reasonable basis for this position."

The Committee is informed that the standard of "reasonable basis"
has been construed by many lawyers to support the use of any colorable
claim on a tax return to justify exploitation of the lottery of the tax
return audit selection process. . . .

. . . [A]s a result of serious controversy over this standard and its
persistent criticism by distinguished members of the tax bar, IRS

2.   See Threlkeld v. Commissioner, 87 T.C. 1294 (1986), aff'd, 848 F.2d 81 (6th Cir.1988);
and Metzger v. Commissioner, 88 T.C. 834 (1987), aff'd without published opinion, 845
F.2d 1013 (3d Cir.1988).

3.   See Thompson v. Commissioner, 866 F.2d 709 (4th Cir.1989); Johnston v. Harris
County Flood Control Dist., 869 F.2d 1565 (5th Cir.1989), cert. denied, 493 U.S. 1019
(1990); Watkins v. United States, 223 Ct.Cl. 731 (1980); and Sparrow v. Commissioner,
949 F.2d 434 (D.C. Cir.1991).

4.   United States v. Burke, 112 S.Ct. 1867 (1992), reversing 929 F.2d 1119 (6th Cir.).

officials and members of Congress, sufficient doubt has been created regarding the validity of the standard so as to erode its effectiveness as an ethical guideline. For this reason, the Committee has concluded that it should be restated. Another reason for restating the standard is that since publication of Opinion 314, the ABA has adopted in succession the Model Code of Professional Responsibility (1969; revised 1980) and the Model Rules of Professional Conduct (1983). Both the Model Code and the Model Rules directly address the duty of a lawyer in presenting or arguing positions for a client in language that does not refer to "reasonable basis." It is therefore appropriate to conform the standard of Opinion 314 to the language of the new rules.

This opinion reconsiders and revises only that part of Opinion 314 that relates to the lawyer's duty in advising a client of positions that can be taken on a tax return. It does not deal with a lawyer's opinion on tax shelter investment offering, which is specifically addressed by this Committee's Formal Opinion 346 (Revised), and which involves very different considerations, including third party reliance.

The ethical standards governing the conduct of a lawyer in advising a client on positions that can be taken in a tax return are no different from those governing a lawyer's conduct in advising or taking positions for a client in other civil matters. Although the Model Rules distinguish between the roles of advisor and advocate (see, for example, Model Rules 2.1 and 3.1), both roles are involved here, and the ethical standards applicable to them provide relevant guidance. In many cases a lawyer must realistically anticipate that the filing of the tax return may be the first step in a process that may result in an adversary relationship between the client and the IRS. This normally occurs in situations when a lawyer advises an aggressive position on a tax return, not when the position taken is a safe or conservative one that is unlikely to be challenged by the IRS.

[The opinion then quoted Model Rules 3.1 and 1.2(d).]

On the basis of these rules and analogous provisions of the Model Code, a lawyer, in representing a client in the course of the preparation of the client's tax return, may advise the statement of positions most favorable to the client if the lawyer has a good faith belief that those positions are warranted in existing law or can be supported by a good faith argument for an extension, modification or reversal of existing law. A lawyer can have a good faith belief in this context even if the lawyer believes the client's position probably will not prevail. (Comment to Rule 3.1; see also Model Code EC 7–4.) However, good faith requires that there be some realistic possibility of success if the matter is litigated.

This formulation of the lawyer's duty in the situation addressed by this opinion is consistent with the basic duty of the lawyer to a client, recognized in ethical standards since the ABA Canons of Professional Ethics, and in the opinions of this Committee: zealously and loyally to represent the interests of the client within the bounds of the law.

Thus, where a lawyer has a good faith belief in the validity of a position in accordance with the standard stated above that a particular transaction does not result in taxable income or that certain expenditures are properly deductible as expenses, the lawyer has no duty to require as a condition of his or her continued representation that riders be attached to the client's tax return explaining the circumstances surrounding the transaction or the expenditures.

In the role of advisor, the lawyer should counsel the client as to whether the position is likely to be sustained by a court if challenged by the IRS, as well as of the potential penalty consequences to the client if the position is taken on the tax return without disclosure. Section 6661 of the Internal Revenue Code imposes a penalty for substantial understatement of tax liability which can be avoided if the facts are adequately disclosed or if there is or was substantial authority for the position taken by the taxpayer. Competent representation of the client would require the lawyer to advise the client fully as to whether there is or was substantial authority for the position taken in the tax return. If the lawyer is unable to conclude that the position is supported by substantial authority, the lawyer should advise the client of the penalty the client may suffer and of the opportunity to avoid such penalty by adequately disclosing the facts in the return or in a statement attached to the return. If after receiving such advice the client decides to risk the penalty by making no disclosure and to take the position initially advised by the lawyer in accordance with the standard stated above, the lawyer has met his or her ethical responsibility with respect to the advice.

In all cases, however, with regard both to the preparation of returns and negotiating administrative settlements, the lawyer is under a duty not to mislead the Internal Revenue Service deliberately, either by misstatements or by silence or by permitting the client to mislead. Rules 4.1 and 8.4(c); DRs 1–102(A)(4), 7–102(A)(3) and (5).

In summary, a lawyer may advise reporting a position on a return even where the lawyer believes the position probably will not prevail, there is no "substantial authority" in support of the position, and there will be no disclosure of the position in the return. However, the position to be asserted must be one which the lawyer in good faith believes is warranted in existing law or can be supported by a good faith argument for an extension, modification or reversal of existing law. This requires that there is some realistic possibility of success if the matter is litigated. In addition, in his role as advisor, the lawyer should refer to potential penalties and other legal consequences should the client take the position advised.

———

Tax Law and Prohibited Assistance [5]

The lawyer providing tax advice or preparing a client's tax return must balance client desires against the often murky requirements of the tax code. Determining the appropriate balance is simple only in the extreme cases. For example, the lawyer may not aid a client in tax evasion, such as by failing to report clearly taxable income or by claiming deductions based on fictitious events or transactions. To assist a client in such behavior constitutes the crime of aiding and abetting tax evasion.[6] Such assistance also violates the ethical rule that a lawyer may not assist a client in crime or fraud. See M.R. 1.2(d) and DR 7–102(A)(7). On the other hand, any taxpayer may claim every "legitimate" exemption or deduction even if a plausible legal argument might be made against the claim. A lawyer violates no laws or ethical duties by aiding a client in determining what counts as "legitimate."

Between the two extremes lies a spectrum of possible balancing points, and debate over the appropriate balance has continued for at least 40 years.[7] At a minimum, for a lawyer to recommend a position, that position must not be frivolous.[8] Requiring a reasonable basis for success, as did ABA Formal Opinion 314, discussed above, demands only slightly more than the non-frivolous standard. Even the current ethical standard expressed in ABA Opinion 85–352 mandates only a realistic possibility of success, which some IRS sources have treated as about a 33 percent likelihood of success for the taxpayer should the position be litigated.[9]

Aside from meeting ethical requirements in advocating a position, a lawyer actually preparing a tax return faces a practical dilemma in determining whether to indicate on the return that claims for exemptions of income from tax, or for deductions from otherwise taxable income, are legally debatable. Such an indication may "flag" the return for special attention of the Internal Revenue Service, and that special attention in turn may result in a disallowance that otherwise would not have been imposed and consequently higher tax for the client. Given that the IRS does not audit all returns but only a small fraction of them, to the extent that the lawyer or other professional assisting the taxpayer does "flag" a client's return, the client may be worse off than if he had had no professional assistance.

5. Ethical issues in tax practice are discussed in Bernard Wolfman and James P. Holden, Ethical Problems in Modern Tax Practice (2d ed. 1985). See also Bernard Wolfman, James P. Holden, and Kenneth L. Harris, Standards of Tax Practice: Professional Responsibility and Ethics (CCH 1991); George Cooper, The Avoidance Dynamic: A Tale of Tax Planning, Tax Ethics, and Tax Reform, 80 Colum.L.Rev. 1553 (1980).

6. See, e.g., United States v. Feaster, 843 F.2d 1392 (6th Cir.1988) (unreported opinion, text available on WESTLAW).

7. See Randolph Paul, The Responsibilities of the Tax Adviser, 63 Harv.L.Rev. 377 (1950).

8. See M.R. 3.1: "A lawyer shall not ... assert or controvert an issue ... unless there is a basis for doing so that is not frivolous, which includes a good faith argument for an extension, modification or reversal of existing law...." See also DR 7–102(A)(1).

9. See Wolfman, Holden & Harris, supra, at 69.

Further complicating the situation is the fact that taxpayers have reporting responsibilities of their own under the Internal Revenue Code, with penalties for understatement of tax liabilities; and these duties do not parallel the ethical duties imposed on lawyers. In general, taxpayers can avoid an understatement penalty if either they disclose the debatable point on their tax return or there is substantial authority for their position.[10] The Catch–22 raised by disclosure has already been noted, and the substantial authority standard is not precisely defined relative to the lawyers' realistic possibility of success guideline. The lawyer thus must reconcile the two sets of standards.

Professor Michael Durst shows the anomaly in trying to require the lawyer to advise the taxpayer to adhere to a higher standard of reporting than is required by the penalty provisions of the tax law.[11] Put differently, the way to induce tax lawyers to give advice conforming to a certain standard is to impose that standard directly on the taxpayer.

One approach to resolving the ethical questions peculiar to tax practice involves analogizing the process of filing a tax return to some other legal transaction. ABA Formal Opinion 85–352 analogizes the tax return process to a pleading in litigation, wherein assertions short of frivolousness may be predicated on interpretation of law and fact most favorable to the proponent. Critics point out that pleadings are filed between parties with a ripened legal dispute, whereas a tax return is a submission of information that, in principle, is not in dispute. Another analogy might be to a securities disclosure document, such as was involved in *National Student Marketing*. Such a comparison would suggest that a tax return should disclose any fact or circumstance that a reasonable tax collector would think material in determining the amount of tax due under the return. Needless to say, the bar has not encouraged this analogy, but its very advancement does reflect the breadth of disagreement that exists as to the appropriate standard to govern a lawyer advising a client in preparing a return.

Did the ABA opinion take adequate account of the standards of candor and disclosure that govern pleadings and representations to a court? See Model Rules 3.1 and 3.3; DR 7–102(A)(2), (3) and (6). Does Model Rule 3.3(d), dealing with ex parte submissions to a tribunal, have any application? M.R. 3.3(d) provides: "In an ex parte proceeding, a lawyer shall inform the tribunal of all material facts known to the lawyer which will enable the tribunal to make an informed decision, whether or not the facts are adverse."

---

10. Current tax law does not require that a tax return conform to the standards of disclosure that apply under the securities laws. However, § 6661(b)(2)(B) of the Internal Revenue Code, 26 U.S.C. § 6661(b)(2)(B), provides for a ten percent addition to the amount of an underpaid tax if the amount of understatement exceeds ten percent of the tax due or $5,000, but the amount of understatement is reduced if "there was substantial support of [the tax treatment of an item]" or the "facts affecting the item's tax treatment are adequately disclosed in the return or in a statement attached to the return."

11. Michael Durst, The Tax Lawyer's Professional Responsibility, 39 U.Fla.L.Rev. 1027 (1987).

E. PROCEDURAL LAW

Of the bodies of law external to the rules of professional conduct that are important for lawyers, none is more significant than the law of procedure. For the lawyer, the law of procedure is a set of legal empowerments accompanied by limitations and obligations. The very term "attorney" denotes one who is an agent in legal matters, particularly litigation. Agency is itself a relationship involving powers, limitations and obligations.[12] Agency law governs lawyers in many contexts in which the rules of professional conduct are silent or incomplete. Moreover, legal regulation allows only lawyers to undertake agent relationships that involve "practice of law." [13] The term "practice of law" is indeterminate at the margin of meaning but certainly includes advocacy in criminal and civil litigation. Hence, the law of procedure has special significance for lawyers because only they may be employed as advocates.

The function of advocacy is governed by and takes its form from the law of criminal and civil procedure. The rules of procedure, although they generally address the "parties," contemplate that litigation ordinarily will be conducted by lawyers.

1. Empowerments in Procedural Law

The law of procedure is largely a set of legal empowerments. For example, Rule 4(a) of the Federal Rules of Civil Procedure begins as follows:

> Upon the filing of the complaint the clerk shall forthwith issue a summons to the plaintiff or the plaintiff's attorney....

Rule 4(a) does not say so, but rather presupposes that the attorney for the plaintiff will have drafted the complaint in conformity with the pleading rules stated in Fed.R.Civ.P. 8–12 and other provisions of the Federal Rules. Rule 4(a) similarly presupposes that the plaintiff's attorney will also have prepared the summons itself, in contemplation that the clerk will simply stamp the document, record that fact and then hand the summons back to the lawyer, who will arrange service on the defendant. Similarly, Fed.R.Civ.P. 26(a) provides that "parties may obtain discovery ... upon oral examination or written questions ...," but contemplates that attorneys will conduct discovery on behalf of parties.

Criminal procedure involves similar presuppositions. For example 18 U.S.C. § 3041 provides:

> For any offense against the United States, the offender may, by any ... judge of the United States, ... be arrested and imprisoned or released as provided in chapter 207 of this title....

12. See generally Restatement (Second) of Agency.

13. See, e.g., Florida Bar v. Brumbaugh, 355 So.2d 1186 (Fla.1978), reprinted in Chapter 10 at p. 938.

Section 3041 does not say so, but it presupposes that ordinarily a judge will order such arrest only on application of the U.S. district attorney, a lawyer for the Department of Justice or some other lawyer for the government.

Such rules and presuppositions reflect the fact that commencing criminal or civil litigation, with potentially momentous effect on the lives of the parties involved, for most practical purposes lies exclusively within the authority of people who are lawyers. The same holds for all subsequent stages of litigation. Litigation is an exercise of the power of the state over which lawyers have important control.

2. Limitations in Procedural Law

The powers that lawyers exercise in conducting litigation are subject to all kinds of limitations. These limits are the focus of Chapter 5 below. For example, Fed.R.Civ.P. 11, as amended in 1983, provides:

The signature of an attorney ... constitutes a certificate by the signer that the signer has read the pleading, motion, or other paper; that to the best of the signer's knowledge, information, and belief formed after reasonable inquiry it is well grounded in fact and is warranted by existing law or a good faith argument for the extension, modification, or reversal of existing law, and that it is not interposed for any improper purpose, such as to harass or to cause unnecessary delay or needless increase in the cost of litigation.

Another set of explicit limits appears in Fed.R.Civ.P. 37, governing discovery.

The sanction of contempt of court cuts across all activities directly involving the courts. The contempt power is founded both in common law and in statute, e.g., 18 U.S.C. § 401, which provides as regards criminal contempt:

A court of the United States shall have power to punish by fine or imprisonment ... such contempt of its authority ... as ... misbehavior of any person in its presence or so near thereto as to obstruct the administration of justice. ...

Another set of limits, pervasive in the law of procedure, involves the requirement that procedural options be exercised in timely fashion or otherwise be forfeited. Statutes of limitations, governing the time within which litigation must be commenced following the occurrence of a legal grievance, are an obvious example.[14] But virtually every procedural empowerment carries with it a limitation on the time within which it may be invoked.[15]

---

14. The failure of a lawyer to bring suit within the limitations period is the most obvious form of legal malpractice. See Ronald E. Mallen & Jeffrey M. Smith, Legal Malpractice, § 24.13 (3d ed. 1989).

15. See, e.g., Fed.R.Civ.P. 6, "Time"; Rule 60(b) (time limitations on a motion to set aside a judgment on the ground of its procurement by mistake or fraud).

Yet another restriction on lawyer powers appears in requirements of court permission for procedural steps to be taken. For example, Fed.R.Civ.P. 23, which permits an action to proceed as a class action only upon the court's authorization, provides in part:

> As soon as practicable after the commencement of an action brought as a class action, the *court* shall determine by order *whether* it is to be so maintained.[16] (Emphasis supplied.)

Similarly, Fed.R.Civ.P. 26(c) confers broad power upon the court to regulate discovery, including power to direct that "discovery not be had." [17] More generally, the courts have broad "inherent power," often expressed in capacious terms:

> A court set up by the Constitution has within it the power of self-preservation, indeed, the power to remove all obstructions to its successful and convenient operation.[18]

3. Obligations in Procedural Law

A power conferred on a lawyer by the law of procedure also carries obligations concerning how the power is exercised. Broadly speaking, a lawyer has an obligation to a client to employ litigation powers to maximize the client's interest. Model Rules 1.1 and 1.2(a). At the same time, the lawyer has an obligation not to employ those powers in a way that is illegal, fraudulent or merely for harassment. See Fed. R.Civ.P. 11, quoted above; Rule 16 (governing pretrial conferences and giving the court authority to "discourag[e] wasteful pretrial activities"); and Rule 37, referred to above. Moreover, the concept that a lawyer is an "officer of the court" implies a general obligation to conduct litigation within the limits of accepted conventions. As stated in Cohen v. Hurley:

> It is no less true than trite that lawyers must operate in a three-fold capacity, as self-employed businessmen as it were, as trusted agents of their clients, and as assistants to the court in search of a just solution of disputes.[19]

A lawyer's obligations to the court and to opposing parties in connection with litigation are codified in M.R. 3.1 through 3.8. See also M.R. 3.9, dealing with obligations in non-adjudicative proceedings. Those Rules refer to the law of procedure both expressly and impliedly. For example, a key formula in M.R. 3.1 corresponds to that in Fed. R.Civ.P. 11, quoted above. M.R. 3.1 provides:

> A lawyer shall not bring or defend a proceeding, or assert or controvert an issue therein, unless there is a basis for doing so that is not frivolous, which includes a good faith argument for an extension, modification or reversal of existing law. . . .

16. Fed.R.Civ.P. Rule 23(c)(1).
17. Fed.R.Civ.P. 26(c)(1).
18. Millholen v. Riley, 211 Cal. 29, 33, 293 P. 69, 71 (1930).
19. 366 U.S. 117, 122 (1961).

Another example of an ethical rule's reference to the law of procedure is M.R. 3.4(a), which provides:

A lawyer shall not *unlawfully* obstruct another party's access to evidence or *unlawfully* alter, destroy or conceal a document or other material having potential evidentiary value.... (Emphasis supplied.)

More generally, M.R. 3.4(c) provides:

A lawyer shall not knowingly disobey an obligation under the *rules of a tribunal* except for an open refusal based on an assertion that no valid obligation exists.... (Emphasis supplied.)

A question of proper professional conduct in litigation therefore usually depends, wholly or in part, on the law of procedure. The law of procedure, however, is itself a distillate of professional practice. After all, the modern codified version of procedural law originated in common law, which in turn reflects the historic practice of law.[20] Moreover, the law of procedure embodies the understandings of the community of practicing lawyers; procedure is understood in terms of the bar's concepts, norms and expectations about appropriate behavior in conducting litigation. Because the community of practicing lawyers differs in experience, interest, political position and ethical concepts, controversies inevitably arise over what the law of procedure permits and requires of lawyers. See generally Chapter 1 above.

This takes us back to *Commonwealth v. Stenhach*, see p. 37 above, doesn't it?

F. PROFESSIONAL DISCIPLINE

1. The Disciplinary Process

Introduction

Nearly 5,000 of the nation's 770,871 lawyers (0.6 percent) were disciplined in 1990.[21] Public sanctions were imposed on 2,323 lawyers and 2,607 others received private reprimands. These sanctions were the residue of 105,602 contacts with state disciplinary authorities concerning lawyers, which resulted in 66,745 investigated complaints, which in turn produced the public and non-public sanctions. About 20 percent of the public sanctions imposed were disbarment (including disbarment on consent, reciprocal disbarment and resignation), 30 percent were suspensions and the remainder involved less serious sanctions (public reprimand, probation, fines and restitution or re-

---

20. See generally, e.g., F. James and G. Hazard, Civil Procedure, § 1.3 et seq. (3d ed. 1984).

21. Most of the data in this paragraph is drawn from ABA Center for Professional Responsibility, 1990 Survey on Lawyer Discipline Systems (1992). The figures given are all for 1990 and, because of the time lag in handling individual cases, should not be viewed as a exact case-flow description.

quired to take a professional responsibility examination).[22]

Neglect (e.g., failing to appear in court, failure to communicate with clients) is the leading category of misconduct (28 percent of the 3,489 disciplinary offenses). Improper relationships with clients or the court, ranging from improper settlements and refusal to release documents to contempt of court, ranks second (16 percent). Improper personal behavior, including mental disability and substance abuse, is the third-ranking category (14 percent). Theft and trust account violations constitute about 12 percent of disciplinary offenses. The remaining categories are misrepresentation (8 percent), criminal activity (7 percent), fee violations (5 percent), and conflict of interest violations (2 percent).[23]

The disciplinary effort varies enormously in staffing, resources and structure from state to state.[24] California, at one end of the spectrum, spent $307 per California lawyer in 1990 investigating 6,793 complaints and disciplining 442 lawyers with a fulltime staff of 411 lawyers, investigators and others. Ohio, on the other hand, which has less than one-third as many lawyers as California, spent $24 per Ohio lawyer in the same year investigating 3,296 complaints (a substantially higher complaint rate than California) and disciplining 92 lawyers (a substantially lower disciplinary rate) with a fulltime staff of only 12. Ohio's system, like that in a number of states, relies heavily on the volunteer services of members of the bar.

Disciplinary procedure is considered further in Chapter 9 below at p. 884. At this point, however, some familiarity with disciplinary process is desirable. The disciplinary structure and procedure in the District of Columbia are fairly typical of American jurisdictions. The description below is taken from a brochure made available by Bar Counsel to those who ask about making a complaint against a lawyer.

HAVE A COMPLAINT ABOUT AN ATTORNEY?
Office of Bar Counsel, Board of Professional Responsibility.
District of Columbia Court of Appeals, 1992.

Every attorney admitted to the practice of law in the District of Columbia is obligated to observe high standards of ethical conduct and professional behavior. The Rules of Professional Conduct set forth the specific rules that govern an attorney's actions. The Office of Bar Counsel has been given jurisdiction by the District of Columbia Court of

---

22. American Bar Association Standing Committee on Professional Discipline, Statistical Report: Sanctions Imposed in Public Discipline of Lawyers 1986–1990 (1991). Because more than one sanction may be applied to a single lawyer, the total number of lawyers disciplined in 1990 is smaller than the total of reported offenses, probably about 2,500 lawyers nationwide.

23. Id. Discipline for conflict of interest violations usually involves business transactions with clients.

24. The data in this paragraph is drawn from ABA Center for Professional Responsibility, 1990 Survey on Lawyer Discipline Systems (1992).

Appeals to investigate and prosecute allegations of ethical misconduct on the part of attorneys who are members of the District of Columbia Bar.

The following are examples of behavior by an attorney that the Office of Bar Counsel may investigate:

- persistent delay or failure to answer your calls and letters
- not accounting to you for money or property held on your behalf or on behalf of third parties, or failure to return such money or property
- not keeping confidences and secrets
- acting in the same matter for you and other persons where your interests are in conflict with theirs
- taking advantage of your age or inexperience
- dishonesty or deceit
- failing to act to protect your rights
- neglecting to pursue your case
- behaving in an improper manner before a court

The jurisdiction of the Office of Bar Counsel is limited and, therefore, there are things that the Office is unable to do. Some conduct on the part of attorneys falls outside the parameters of the Rules, and Bar Counsel is unable to investigate those activities. The following are some examples of services that Bar Counsel cannot provide:

- give you legal advice
- compel an attorney to act for you
- recommend an attorney or firm by name
- tell your attorney how to proceed with your case
- represent you in an attorney malpractice matter
- collect private debts
- investigate complaints about judges, lay persons, or attorneys who are not members of the District of Columbia Bar

How to File a Complaint

Your complaint should be filed in writing either by filling out a complaint form that is available from the Office of Bar Counsel or by writing your own statement. Your statement should include your name and address, your attorney's name and address and an explanation of the circumstances and details of your complaint. Supporting documents, such as copies of a retainer agreement, proof of payment, correspondence between you and the attorney and, if a specific case is involved, the case name and number, the name of the court where the case is filed, and copies of papers filed in connection with the case may be of assistance to our investigation.

What Happens to Your Complaint

When your complaint is received, it will be reviewed to determine whether the Office of Bar Counsel has jurisdiction to investigate your allegations. Is the attorney a member of the D.C. Bar? Does the complaint allege conduct on the part of an attorney which, if true, would violate the Rules? If the answers to these questions are "yes," then your complaint will be docketed and assigned a number. A copy of your complaint will be sent to the attorney, and the attorney will be required to respond to your statements. Upon receipt of the attorney's response, we will forward a copy of the response to you for your comments.

The case is then reviewed to determine if there is enough information to make a decision regarding the case. If additional information if needed, a staff attorney investigating the case may request answers to specific questions, review the court file, interview potential witnesses, undertake legal research or subpoena additional materials.

Upon completion of the investigation, Bar Counsel will determine whether there is evidence of a violation of the Rules. If there is not clear and convincing evidence of ethical misconduct, the case must be dismissed. If there is evidence of misconduct, Bar Counsel may decide to issue an informal admonition or to petition the Board on Professional Responsibility for a hearing on the case. An informal admonition is a private form of discipline, and it functions as a warning to the attorney. The attorney is advised that Bar Counsel has determined that a violation of the Rules has occurred but that it is not necessary to institute formal disciplinary proceedings.

Petitioned cases are scheduled for a hearing before a three-member Hearing Committee consisting of two attorneys and one non-attorney. This is an adversarial hearing in which Bar Counsel acts as prosecutor. Bar Counsel does not represent individual complainants in this hearing, and you may not participate as a party. However, as the complainant, you may be called as a witness in support of Bar Counsel's case. Following the hearing, the Hearing Committee will issue a report either recommending dismissal of the charges or appropriate discipline. The recommended discipline may be for the issuance of a reprimand, a public censure, a suspension or a disbarment.

The Hearing Committee's report and recommendation are reviewed by the Board on Professional Responsibility. The Board has nine members—seven attorneys and two non-attorneys. The Board may dismiss the case, ratify an informal admonition, issue a reprimand or make a recommendation for censure, suspension or disbarment by the District of Columbia Court of Appeals. The Court of Appeals must review the record and has final authority to order the appropriate sanction.

You will be informed by a letter from our Office of the final disposition of your case following this process.

A Final Note

Filing a complaint against an attorney is a serious matter. We hope that you will make your decision only after careful consideration and after all efforts to work out the problem with your attorney have failed. The disciplinary system is designed to provide an orderly and just way to deal with complaints against attorneys. We hope that the problem that gave rise to your complaint will be resolved to your satisfaction.

---

2. Obligation to Report Professional Misconduct of Other Lawyers

One of the innovations of the Model Code was the inclusion in DR 1–103(A) of a broad mandatory obligation on the part of lawyers to report unprivileged knowledge of professional misconduct to disciplinary authorities.[25] The Model Rules narrow the scope of the obligation to report misconduct from that in the Code in two respects: (1) M.R. 8.3(a) requires a lawyer to report only those violations that raise "a substantial question as to the lawyer's honesty, trustworthiness or fitness as a lawyer in other respects"; and (2) the Rules do not require a lawyer to report if knowledge of the violation is based on client confidences, M.R. 8.3(c). In contrast, the Code requires a lawyer to report all violations, with an exception only for information based on "privileged" communications. Use of the term "privileged" suggests the exception is limited to information protected by the attorney-client privilege and not, for example, information learned from a third party in the course of representing a client.[26]

It is no secret that the duty to report professional misconduct is widely ignored. Although lawyers and judges are in the best position to learn of the wrongdoing of other lawyers, only a small proportion of disciplinary complaints are filed by them.[27] Prior to the *Himmel* case,

---

25. The Canons of Professional Ethics contained much narrower reporting obligations: Canon 28 imposed a duty to report lawyers engaged in ambulance chasing, paying runners to drum up cases and related forms of stirring up litigation. Canon 29 imposed a duty but did not require lawyers to report perjury in litigation and "dishonest and corrupt conduct." Lofty language admonished lawyers to "uphold the honor of the profession" by striving for its improvement by keeping out or removing "unfit persons."

26. ABA Comm. on Ethics and Prof. Responsibility, Formal Op. 341 (1975) interprets "privileged" as used in another provision of the Model Code, DR 7–102(B)(1), as including professional secrets as well as confidences protected by the attorney-client privilege. The reasoning of the opinion is also applicable to DR 1–103(A). Cf. the views of the Illinois court in the *Himmel* case, reprinted below. See Chapter 4 below on the difference between confidential information and privileged communications. Formal Op. 341 is discussed below at p. 296.

27. ABA Commission on Professionalism, In the Spirit of Public Service, A Blueprint for the Rekindling of Lawyer Professionalism 37 (1986): "reporting of serious misconduct of both lawyers and judges is essential [but] hardly any such reporting occurs." See generally F. Raymond Marks and Darlene Cathcart, Discipline Within the Legal Profession: Is It Self–Regulation?, 1974 Ill.L.Forum 193; Eric H. Steele and Raymond T.

reproduced below, lawyers had been disciplined for failure to report only in connection with other violations.[28] Should lawyers be disciplined for failing to report the misconduct of other lawyers?

IN RE HIMMEL

Supreme Court of Illinois, 1988.
125 Ill.2d 531, 127 Ill.Dec. 708, 533 N.E.2d 790.

JUSTICE STAMOS delivered the opinion of the court:

This is a disciplinary proceeding against respondent, James H. Himmel....

We will briefly review the facts, which essentially involve three individuals: respondent, James H. Himmel, licensed to practice law in Illinois on November 6, 1975; his client, Tammy Forsberg ...; and her former attorney, John R. Casey.

[Forsberg retained Casey in 1980 to handle a personal injury claim arising out of a motorcycle accident. Casey settled the case for $35,000, but converted the portion of the settlement check ($23,233) belonging to Forsberg. Forsberg, after complaining about Casey's conduct to the Illinois disciplinary agency, retained Himmel in 1983 to collect her money and agreed to pay him one-third of any funds recovered above $23,233. Himmel negotiated an agreement with Casey in which Casey agreed to pay Forsberg $75,000 in settlement of any claim she might have against Casey and Forsberg agreed not to initiate any criminal, civil or attorney discipline action against Casey. When Casey failed to pay the agreed amount, Himmel brought suit against him for breaching the agreement, resulting in a $100,000 judgment against Casey. Forsberg eventually received a total of $15,400 from Casey of which $10,400 was the result of Himmel's efforts. Himmel received no fee for his work.

[In 1985 Casey was disbarred by consent because of misconduct unrelated to Forsberg. In 1986 the Administrator of the Attorney Registration and Disciplinary Commission (the Commission) filed a disciplinary complaint against Himmel for failing to report Casey's misconduct in his representation of Forsberg. The Hearing Board determined that Himmel violated Rule 1–103(a) (the Illinois counterpart of DR 1–103(A)) and recommended a private reprimand. The Review Board recommended that the complaint be dismissed. The Administrator sought and obtained review in the Supreme Court.]

The Administrator now raises three issues for review: (1) whether the Review Board erred in concluding that respondent's client had

Nimmer, Lawyers, Clients, and Professional Regulation, 1976 Am.Bar Found. Research J. 917.

28. See, e.g., Attorney Grievance Comm'n v. Kahn, 290 Md. 654, 431 A.2d 1336 (1981) (lawyer disbarred for aiding unethical conduct of his law firm and failing to report); Matter of Bonafield, 75 N.J. 490, 383 A.2d 1143 (1978) (lawyer disciplined for assisting another lawyer's misconduct and for failing to report).

informed the Commission of misconduct by her former attorney; (2) whether the Review Board erred in concluding that respondent had not violated Rule 1–103(a); and (3) whether the proven misconduct warrants at least a censure.

[The court first held that a client's complaint of attorney misconduct to the disciplinary commission is not a defense to an attorney's failure to report the same misconduct.]

... We have held that the canons of ethics in the Code constitute a safe guide for professional conduct, and attorneys may be disciplined for not observing them.... The question is, then, whether or not respondent violated the Code, not whether Forsberg informed the Commission of Casey's misconduct.

As to respondent's argument that he did not report Casey's misconduct because his client directed him not to do so, we again note respondent's failure to suggest any legal support for such a defense. A lawyer, as an officer of the court, is duty-bound to uphold the rules in the Code. The title of Canon 1 [of the Code] reflects this obligation: "A lawyer should assist in maintaining the integrity and competence of the legal profession." A lawyer may not choose to circumvent the rules by simply asserting that his client asked him to do so.

As to the second issue, the Administrator argues that the Review Board erred in concluding that respondent did not violate Rule 1–103(a)....

. . .

Our analysis of this issue begins with a reading of the applicable disciplinary rules. Rule 1–103(a) of the Code states: "(a) A lawyer possessing unprivileged knowledge of a violation of Rule 1–102(a)(3) or (4) shall report such knowledge to a tribunal or other authority empowered to investigate or act upon such violation."

Rule 1–102 of the Code states: "(a) A lawyer shall not (1) violate a disciplinary rule; (2) circumvent a disciplinary rule through actions of another; (3) engage in illegal conduct involving moral turpitude; (4) engage in conduct involving dishonesty, fraud, deceit, or misrepresentation; or (5) engage in conduct that is prejudicial to the administration of justice."

These rules essentially track the language of the American Bar Association Model Code of Professional Responsibility, upon which the Illinois Code was modeled.* Therefore, we find instructive the opinion of the American Bar Association's Committee on Ethics and Professional Responsibility that discusses the Model Code's Disciplinary Rule 1–103. Informal Opinion 1210 [1972] states that under DR 1–103(a) it is the duty of a lawyer to report to the proper tribunal or authority any

---

* [Editors' note:] The Illinois version of DR 1–103(A) narrows the duty to inform to "illegal conduct involving moral turpitude" or "conduct involving dishonesty, fraud, deceit, or misrepresentation." The Model Code also requires a lawyer to report all disciplinary violations of another lawyer.

unprivileged knowledge of a lawyer's perpetration of any misconduct listed in Disciplinary Rule 1–102. The opinion states that "the Code of Professional Responsibility through its Disciplinary Rules necessarily deals directly with reporting of lawyer misconduct or misconduct of others directly observed in the legal practice or the administration of justice."

This court has also emphasized the importance of a lawyer's duty to report misconduct. In the case In re Anglin (1988), 122 Ill.2d 531, 539, 524 N.E.2d 550, because of the petitioner's refusal to answer questions regarding his knowledge of other persons' misconduct, we denied a petition for reinstatement to the roll of attorneys licensed to practice in Illinois. We stated, "Under Disciplinary Rule 1–103 a lawyer has the duty to report the misconduct of other lawyers. Petitioner's belief in a code of silence indicates to us that he is not at present fully rehabilitated or fit to practice law." Thus, if the present respondent's conduct did violate the rule on reporting misconduct, imposition of discipline for such a breach of duty is mandated.

The question whether the information that respondent possessed was protected by the attorney-client privilege, and thus exempt from the reporting rule, requires application of this court's definition of the privilege. [The court then quoted Wigmore's definition of the attorney-client privilege.] ... The record does not suggest that this information was communicated by Forsberg to the respondent in confidence. We have held that information voluntarily disclosed by a client to an attorney, in the presence of third parties who are not agents of the client or attorney, is not privileged information. (People v. Williams (1983), 97 Ill.2d 252, 295, 454 N.E.2d 220.) In this case, Forsberg discussed the matter with respondent at various times while her mother and her fiance were present. Consequently, unless the mother and fiance were agents of respondent's client, the information communicated was not privileged....

Though respondent repeatedly asserts that his failure to report was motivated not by financial gain but by the request of his client, we do not deem such an argument relevant in this case. This court has stated that discipline may be appropriate even if no dishonest motive for the misconduct exists.... In addition, we have held that client approval of an attorney's action does not immunize an attorney from disciplinary action.... We have already dealt with, and dismissed, respondent's assertion that his conduct is acceptable because he was acting pursuant to his client's directions.

Respondent does not argue that Casey's conversion of Forsberg's funds was not illegal conduct involving moral turpitude under Rule 1–102(a)(3) or conduct involving dishonesty, fraud, deceit, or misrepresentation under Rule 1– 102(a)(4). It is clear that conversion of client funds is, indeed, conduct involving moral turpitude.... We conclude, then, that respondent possessed unprivileged knowledge of Casey's conversion of client funds, which is illegal conduct involving moral turpitude, and that respondent failed in his duty to report such misconduct to the Commission. Because no defense exists, we agree with the Hearing Board's finding that respondent has violated Rule 1– 103(a) and must be disciplined.

The third issue concerns the appropriate quantum of discipline to be imposed in this case....

In evaluating the proper quantum of discipline to impose, we note that it is this court's responsibility to determine appropriate sanctions in attorney disciplinary cases.... We have stated that while recommendations of the Boards are to be considered, this court ultimately bears responsibility for deciding an appropriate sanction.... We reiterate our statement that "[w]hen determining the nature and extent of discipline to be imposed, the respondent's actions must be viewed in relationship 'to the underlying purposes of our disciplinary process, which purposes are to maintain the integrity of the legal profession, to protect the administration of justice from reproach, and to safeguard the public.' "

Bearing these principles in mind, we agree with the Administrator that public discipline is necessary in this case to carry out the purposes of attorney discipline.... [T]he evidence proved that respondent possessed unprivileged knowledge of Casey's conversion of client funds, yet respondent did not report Casey's misconduct.

This failure to report resulted in interference with the Commission's investigation of Casey, and thus with the administration of justice. Perhaps some members of the public would have been spared from Casey's misconduct had respondent reported the information as soon as he knew of Casey's conversions of client funds. We are particularly disturbed by the fact that respondent chose to draft a settlement agreement with Casey rather than report his misconduct. As the Administrator has stated, by this conduct, both respondent and his client ran afoul of the Criminal Code's prohibition against compounding a crime, which states in section 32–1: "(a) A person compounds a crime when he receives or offers to another any consideration for a promise not to prosecute or aid in the prosecution of an offender. (b) Sentence. Compounding a crime is a petty offense." (Ill.Rev.Stat. 1987, ch. 38, par. 32–1.) Both respondent and his client stood to gain financially by agreeing not to prosecute or report Casey for conversion. According to the settlement agreement, respondent would have received $17,000 or more as his fee. If Casey had satisfied the judgment entered against him for failure to honor the settlement agreement, respondent would have collected approximately $25,588.

We have held that fairness dictates consideration of mitigating factors in disciplinary cases.... Therefore, we do consider the fact that Forsberg recovered $10,400 through respondent's services, that respondent has practiced law for 11 years with no record of complaints, and that he requested no fee for minimum collection of Forsberg's funds. However, these considerations do not outweigh the serious nature of respondent's failure to report Casey, the resulting interference with the Commission's investigation of Casey, and respondent's ill-advised choice to settle with Casey rather than report his misconduct.

Accordingly, it is ordered that respondent be suspended from the practice of law for one year.

A Mandatory Duty to Inform?

The *Himmel* case sent shock waves through the bar in Illinois and nationwide.[30] It was apparently the first case in which a lawyer had been disciplined *solely* for failing to report the misconduct of another lawyer. Bar associations and individual lawyers denounced the decision, arguing the following:[31] Himmel received confidential information from his client; he used that information to pursue the client's goal of monetary recompense for Casey's wrongdoing; reporting a disciplinary violation or bringing criminal charges might have interfered with the client's objective of monetary recompense; therefore, Himmel had a duty to follow his client's instructions and not to report Casey's misconduct.[32] Does the *Himmel* opinion respond satisfactorily to this argument? Why does the duty to inform trump the explicit instructions of the client?

The distinction between information protected by the attorney-client privilege and that falling within the professional duty of confidentiality is considered in detail in chapter 4. For present purposes, it is enough to note that the term "privileged" has sometimes been interpreted to include both categories of information. Is *Himmel* also too restrictive in holding that Forsberg waived the attorney-client privilege because her mother and fiance accompanied her in meeting with Himmel?

The broad question is whether lawyers should have a mandatory, rather than discretionary, duty to inform on other lawyers. The ABA's Commission on Professionalism, reporting in 1986, argued that increased reporting by lawyers and judges of professional misconduct was "essential" to protect the public from abuses that otherwise would not be detected or deterred. To put teeth into the report obligation, the Commission stated that "an improved attitude by lawyers with respect to reporting" would result if "proceedings [were] brought in appropriate

30. See Ronald D. Rotunda, The Lawyer's Duty to Report Another Lawyer's Unethical Violations in the Wake of *Himmel*, 1988 U.Ill.L.Rev. 977.

31. Three bar associations, including the Illinois Bar Association, unsuccessfully sought rehearing of the *Himmel* case. See Paul Marcotte, The Duty to Inform, ABA J., May 1989, pp. 17–18.

32. See Maryland State Bar Ass'n, Committee on Ethics, Op. 89–46 (1989) (lawyer suing client's former lawyer for breach of fiduciary duty is not required to report where client has asked lawyer not to file a complaint against the former lawyer).

cases against lawyers who fail to do so."[33]   Perhaps the Illinois court heard this recommendation and took it seriously.

Professor Gerard Lynch is among those commentators who doubt the efficacy and desirability of a mandatory report obligation.[34]   The pejorative aspect of words like "tattle," "squeal" and "inform" reflects an inevitable and in part justifiable attitude arising from relational concerns:

> The impulse to protect one's friends and associates from harm, even from deserved punishment, is a moral and socially useful impulse precisely because it reaches beyond individual self-interest; it assimilates another's well-being to that of oneself.[35]

Lynch argues that relationships based on trust satisfy human needs of affiliation and identity; they also protect otherwise isolated individuals from the formal rigor of state power.   A rigid legalism that requires a lawyer to report all professional misconduct of other lawyers, Lynch argues, is misconceived:

> Although it would sometimes be morally correct to report wrongdoing that comes to one's attention, such action would be morally incorrect in a great number of situations.   The considerations relevant to sorting out these cases are highly complex.   The preference for laws that are narrowly drawn and easy to apply would thus counsel that the law leave individuals free to follow their consciences in deciding whether or not to inform, except in a few carefully defined situations.   Moreover, given the likelihood that people would disregard an unfocused and unpopular obligation to report the misconduct of others, little social benefit can be expected from a general rule even in those instances in which the moral obligation to inform is clearest....   [T]he law has generally declined—correctly I believe—to impose a duty to provide unsolicited information, except in situations in which the information is especially vital and a definable category of persons is particularly likely to obtain it.   The possibility of harm is too great, and the rewards too slim, to justify a general duty to inform....   The ethical codes applicable to lawyers ought to reflect the same approach that has proved acceptable to society as a whole.[36]

Which approach is better, that of the ABA Commission on Professionalism or that of Lynch?   Two jurisdictions do not have a report requirement, California and Massachusetts.[37]

Extortion as Prohibited Assistance

Although the disciplinary action in *Himmel* was grounded on the lawyer's failure to report, the Illinois court was troubled by another

---

33. Report of ABA Commission on Professionalism, supra, at 38.

34. Gerard E. Lynch, The Lawyer as Informer, 1986 Duke L.J. 491.

35. Id. at 531.

36. Id. at 535.

37. ABA/BNA Law. Manual Prof. Conduct 101:201 (1989).

aspect of the case: Both Himmel and his client "ran afoul" of the criminal code's prohibition against compounding a crime, which prohibits receiving consideration in exchange for agreeing not to prosecute or report a crime, here the original theft of the client's money.

DR 7–105(A) of the Model Code provides:

A lawyer shall not present, participate in presenting, or threaten to present criminal charges solely to obtain an advantage in a civil matter.[38]

The Model Rules do not contain a similar provision, perhaps because the criminal prohibitions against threats constituting extortion, fraud or criminal abuse are included under M.R. 8.4(b), which provides for discipline of a lawyer for "commit[ting] a criminal act that reflects adversely on the lawyer's honesty, trustworthiness or fitness as a lawyer in other respects." [39]

Does the criminal prohibition of extortion and the Model Code prohibition of threatening criminal charges prevent a lawyer from mentioning the possibility of criminal charges in civil negotiations? A 1992 ethics opinion and judicial holding give a negative response.[40]

3. Conduct Prejudicial to the Administration of Justice

Model Rule 8.4(d) replicates the requirement of DR 7–102(A)(5) that a lawyer shall not "engage in conduct that is prejudicial to the administration of justice." What conduct is proscribed by this language?

In re Masters [41]

Masters, an experienced lawyer with extensive experience as a state prosecutor before entering private practice, was consulted by a construction company that was faced with an extortion demand made by Arambasich, a business agent for the Iron Workers' Union. Arambasich had visited the foreman at one of the client's construction jobs, placed a gun on the desk and told the foreman that "he was going to shut down the job" if he wasn't paid $1,000 every six months. Because of his service as a prosecutor, Masters had personal knowledge of Arambasich's reputation for violence; he feared for the safety of the

38. The California rule is even broader. It prohibits threats to present administrative and disciplinary charges as well as criminal charges. Calif. Rules of Professional Conduct, Rule 5–100.

39. See 1 Hazard and Hodes, The Law of Lawyering § 4.4:103 (1990) (stating that the prohibition found in DR 7–105(A) was deliberately omitted from Model Rule 4.4. as redundant and also because its broad language appeared to prohibit "legitimate pressure tactics and negotiation strategies").

40. ABA Standing Comm. on Ethics and Prof. Responsibility, Formal Op. 92–363 (lawyer negotiating a civil claim is not barred from any mention of possible related criminal charges); Committee on Legal Ethics v. Printz, 187 W.Va. 182, 416 S.E.2d 720, 727 n. 4 (1992) (distinguishing between extortion and legitimate negotiations: "Receiving repayment of money taken from a victim is not extortion; however, asking a higher price (i.e., 'Give my money back and $20,000 or I'll call the cops!'") in return for the victim's silence is extortion").

41. 91 Ill.2d 413, 63 Ill.Dec. 449, 438 N.E.2d 187 (1982).

foreman, himself, and his son, who had a summer job as an ironworker in the area. Masters advised the client to pay the extortion money; and he personally delivered a series of $1,000 payments to Arambasich over a five-year period. Masters then advised the client to end the payments and to report the extortion to law enforcement officials. A federal investigation resulted in indictment and conviction of Arambasich for extortion. Masters cooperated fully in the investigation and testified against Arambasich at the trial after receiving immunity from prosecution.

Masters was charged by the Illinois disciplinary body with violating the Illinois counterparts to DR 7–102(A)(7), counseling or assisting one's client in illegal activity; and DR 1–103(A)(5), engaging in conduct prejudicial to the administration of justice. The court agreed with Masters that he was not guilty of assisting a client's criminal conduct: the client in paying extortion money was a victim of crime, not a criminal. Yet the court rejected Masters' claim that good faith advice to cooperate with the extortion under the threat of serious injury should not be grounds for discipline under DR 1–103(A)(5):

> As an attorney [and as] former State's Attorney ... [Masters] was certainly aware of the fact that the proper course of conduct was to report the extortion demand to the appropriate authorities. For a lawyer of respondent's demonstrated ability and standing at the bar to serve as the conduit through which funds were passed from the alleged victim to the extortionist was unprofessional and unseemly and served to bring the legal profession into disrepute.[42]

Masters received a one-year suspension. A dissenting judge, argued that Masters had done "nothing illegal, immoral or unethical": "The record shows that Frank Masters did nothing worse than protect his client, an innocent victim of a criminal extortion, in the only way he believed was realistically available." The dissenting opinion argued that the rule prohibiting "conduct prejudicial to the administration of justice," which had previously been applied only to misconduct in a pending or contemplated legal proceeding, was unclear and that lawyers were given no guidance concerning its scope.

A Duty to Report Crimes?

Did Masters commit a crime? Did he assist his client in the commission of a crime? If not, why was he disciplined? Would the court have disciplined him if he had known his client was paying extortion to Arambasich but had not been personally involved in the payments?

Does *Masters* obligate a lawyer to report a crime that the lawyer learns about because her client is its victim? Should lawyers have a general duty to report crimes (even though lay people ordinarily do not)? One ABA ethics opinion replies in the affirmative, providing the

42. 438 N.E.2d at 193.

lawyer's knowledge is based on unprivileged sources.[43]   But the limitation to "unprivileged sources" would radically limit the report obligation announced in *Masters*.

What Conduct Prejudices the Administration of Justice?

The courts have generally invoked the prohibition on engaging in conduct prejudicial to the administration of justice in situations similar to those chargeable as obstruction to justice: advising clients to testify falsely,[44] paying a witness, to be unavailable to testify,[45] threatening criminal prosecution and altering documents.[46]   But the courts have also used the prohibition in other contexts, such as a lawyer's false statements about a judicial officer,[47] a lawyer's false statements to bar admissions authorities [48] and a lawyer's failure to appear at a contempt hearing for his failure to make child support payments.[49]   Although some commentators have criticized the provision as overbroad and vague,[50] the courts have nevertheless sustained applications of the prohibition.[51]   Is it broader or vaguer than the federal obstruction of justice statute?

Another Illinois case, In re Corboy,[52] reflects much greater judicial tolerance of lawyer misconduct than was evidenced in *Himmel* and *Masters*.   *Corboy* involved a substantial loan by several prominent Chicago lawyers to a Cook County circuit judge, ostensibly to pay a hospital bill of the judge's mother.   In fact, unbeknownst to the lawyers providing the check, the judge used the money for other purposes.   The Illinois ethics rule corresponding to DR 7–110(A) provided that a lawyer may not "give or lend anything of value" to a judge.   The Illinois court held that the rule is a "per se" prohibition that does not require a corrupt purpose although, when read with Code of Judicial Conduct Rule 5(C)(4), the rule does not prohibit gifts implicit in "ordinary social hospitality."   Even though the loan to the judge violated several ethics rules, including M.R. 8.4(d), the court imposed no sanction on the lawyers because they "acted without the guidance of precedent or

43.   See ABA Informal Op. 1210 (1972) (discussing the duty of lawyers to report crimes when knowledge is based on unprivileged sources).

44.   See, e.g., Florida Bar v. Simons, 391 So.2d 684 (Fla.1980).

45.   People v. Kenelly, 648 P.2d 1065 (Colo.1982).

46.   In re Barrett, 88 N.J. 450, 443 A.2d 678 (1982).

47.   State v. Nelson, 210 Kan. 637, 504 P.2d 211 (1972).

48.   In re Howe, 257 N.W.2d 420 (N.D.1977).

49.   People v. Kane, 638 P.2d 253 (Colo.1981).

50.   See Donald T. Weckstein, Maintaining the Integrity and Competence of the Legal Profession, 48 Tex.L.Rev. 267, 275–76 (1970); and Comment, ABA Code of Professional Responsibility: Void for Vagueness?, 57 N.C.L.Rev. 671, 685 (1971).

51.   Howell v. State Bar of Texas, 843 F.2d 205 (5th Cir.1988); In re Keiler, 380 A.2d 119, 126 n. 7 (D.C.App.1977); Office of Disciplinary Counsel v. Campbell, 463 Pa. 472, 482, 345 A.2d 616, 621–22 (1975) (DR 1–102(A)(5) arguably vague but clear as applied to case at bar).

52.   124 Ill.2d 29, 124 Ill.Dec. 6, 528 N.E.2d 694 (1988).

settled opinion, and there was, apparently, considerable belief among members of the bar that they had acted properly." [53]

53.   528 N.E.2d at 701.

Chapter 3

COMPETENCE

I find no pleasure in saying to you that the majority of lawyers who appear in court are so poorly trained that they are not properly performing their job....

From more than twenty years of active practice ... and from more than ten years on the bench, I think I have gained a fairly reasonable ... view of what goes on in courtrooms.... [M]y appraisal of courtroom performance was so low that I began to check it with lawyers and judges in various parts of the country to see whether I misjudged....

On the most favorable view expressed, seventy-five percent of the lawyers appearing in the courtroom were deficient by reason of poor preparation, lack of ability to conduct a proper cross-examination, lack of ability to present expert testimony, ... lack of ability to frame objections ..., [and] lack of basic analytic ability in the framing of issues.... [1]

Warren E. Burger

How Widespread Is Incompetence?

Warren Burger, as an appellate judge and as Chief Justice of the United States, focused the attention of the legal profession and the public on lawyer competency with his provocative assertion in 1967 that a majority of trial lawyers were incompetent. In subsequent speeches, Burger continued to assert his belief that 75 percent might be an accurate figure, but accepted as a "working hypothesis" a lower number: "that from one-third to one-half of the lawyers who appear in serious cases are not really qualified to render fully adequate representation." [2] The resulting controversy generated much heat, some proposals for reform—usually the imposition of further educational or apprenticeship requirements on new lawyers—and a modest collection of empirical studies of lawyer behavior and attitudes.

Documenting the level of competence in the practice of law is virtually impossible. Surveys that ask lawyers or judges to estimate the frequency of incompetence are notoriously unreliable, and varying

1. Warren E. Burger, A Sick Profession?, 5 Tulsa L.J. 1 (1968) (remarks at the Winter Convention of the American College of Trial Lawyers, April 11, 1967).

2. Warren E. Burger, The Special Skills of Advocacy: Are Specialized Training and Certification of Advocates Essential to Our System of Justice?, 42 Fordham L.Rev. 227, 234 (1978).

results are reported.[3] The most careful study, by the Federal Judicial Center, revealed that when asked to rate actual levels of trial "performance" rather than to give a general impression of the frequency of incompetence, federal judges reported 8.6 percent of trial lawyer performances as incompetent and another 16.8 percent as barely adequate.[4] Surveys asking judges what proportion of trial lawyers are incompetent tend to yield somewhat larger percentages.[5] What is one to make of such figures, given the absence of reliable measures and agreement on standards of competence? Some prominent commentators have asserted that lawyers are less competent today than in the past and have attributed the decline in part to the large number of new lawyers entering the profession. What evidence would be sufficient to support or refute this assertion?

Defining "competence" is a difficult matter. The word connotes performance rather than capacity. Model Rule 1.1 defines competence with a list: "legal knowledge, skill, thoroughness and preparation reasonably necessary for the representation." Presumably the standard, like that in malpractice, is one of prudent norms of professional performance, not of client expectations. Studies of the quality of professional care suggest that, given a certain level of intelligence, education and experience, the delivery of quality professional care depends more on intangible aspirations than anything else: caring about law, caring about clients and caring about one's image of oneself as a good professional who keeps up to date and takes pride in providing quality professional services.[6]

The lawyer competency controversy triggered consideration of numerous proposals to change legal education or impose apprenticeship requirements on new entrants. The growth of clinical legal education during the 1970s and 1980s was furthered by this debate, but the apprenticeship proposals encountered academic and professional opposition. Many commentators urged caution in considering proposals to amend law school curricula as a means of reducing incompetent trial

3. See Roger C. Cramton and Erik M. Jensen, The State of Trial Advocacy and Legal Education: Three New Studies, 30 J.Leg.Ed. 253 (1979) (reviewing the literature and criticizing Burger's figures as unscientific, anecdotal and overstated).

4. Id. at 257, citing and discussing the Federal Judicial Center study reported by Anthony Partridge and Gordon Bermant, The Quality of Advocacy in the Federal Courts (1978).

5. See Eleanor Maddi, Trial Advocacy Competence: The Judicial Perspective, 1978 Am.Bar Found.Research J. 105 (reporting a survey of 40 judges in the Second Circuit, which revealed that these judges considered 10 to 12 percent of the lawyers they observed in civil and criminal cases to be incompetent; and a national survey of more than one thousand federal and state trial judges, who estimated that 20 percent of trial lawyers were incompetent, but that dropped to 13 percent when they were asked about the lawyers in the last five trials over which they had presided). See also LawPoll, 64 A.B.A.J. 832 (1978) (nationwide survey of lawyers showing that 41 percent of those responding, and 72 percent of the litigators, agreed with Burger's "working hypothesis" of one-third to one-half incompetent).

6. See Roger C. Cramton, Lawyer Competence and the Law Schools, 4 U.Ark.Little Rock L.J. 1 (1981); see also Douglas E. Rosenthal, Evaluating the Competence of Lawyers, 11 Law & Soc'y Rev. 257 (1976).

performance given how sketchy our understanding is of the relationship between competence and law school study.[7]

A. CHECKS ON INCOMPETENCE

preventive

Preventive measures designed to ensure that clients receive competent legal services begin with bar admission requirements. In general, *Bar Admission* seven years of higher education, including graduation from one of the 176 law schools approved by the ABA, are required in order to qualify for admission to the bar in American states. In addition, the bar admission process seeks to exclude those who are deficient in character or fitness. Bar examinations are designed to test legal ability and knowledge. Admission standards for law school and requirements for admission to the bar are discussed in Chapter 9 below at p. 859.

reactive

Reactive measures, which are also intended to have a deterrent effect, include professional discipline, civil liability for negligence (legal malpractice) and sanctions administered by a tribunal in which a lawyer is litigating. May ordinary Americans safely rely on this array of measures as assuring competent legal assistance at a reasonable cost?

1. Ethics Rules on Competence

The Canons of Ethics did not contain a provision on competence. Canon 6 of the Model Code recognized the importance of competence: "A Lawyer Should Represent a Client Competently." Despite grandiloquent language in the Canon's ethical considerations, the disciplinary *Discipl. Rule 6-101* rule on competence is not stringent. DR 6–101(A)(1) states that a lawyer shall not "handle a legal matter which he knows or should know that he is not competent to handle, without associating with ... a lawyer who is competent to handle it." EC 6–3 explains that this does not prevent a novice in an area of law from accepting employment in that area "if in good faith he expects to become qualified through study and investigation, as long as such preparation would not result in unreasonable delay or expense to the client." Once the representation has been accepted, DR 6–102(A)(2) provides that a lawyer shall not "handle a matter without preparation adequate in the circumstances," and DR 6–102(A)(3) prohibits the lawyer from "neglect[ing] a legal matter entrusted to him."

Model Rule 1.1 provides:

A lawyer shall provide competent representation to a client. Competent representation requires the legal knowledge, skill, thoroughness and preparation reasonably necessary for the representation.

7. See, e.g., Cramton and Jensen, supra; Christen R. Blair, Trial Lawyer Incompetence: What the Studies Suggest About the Problem, the Causes and the Cure, 11 Cap.U.L.Rev. 419 (1982); and H. Russell Cort and Jack L. Sammons, The Search for "Good Lawyering": A Concept and Model of Lawyering Competencies, 29 Clev.St.L.Rev. 397 (1980); Marvin E. Frankel, Curing Lawyers' Incompetence: Primum non Nocere, 10 Creighton L.Rev. 613 (1977).

The Comment to M.R. 1.1 states that while "[i]n many instances, the required proficiency is that of the general practitioner," nonetheless "[e]xpertise in a particular field of law may be required in some circumstances." However, the Comment also contains language similar to EC 6–5 to the effect that a novice can provide adequate representation if she engages in necessary study or associates with someone of established competence in the field.

M.R. 1.3 requires that a lawyer act with reasonable diligence, and M.R. 1.4(a) requires that a lawyer "keep a client reasonably informed of the status of the representation and promptly comply with reasonable requests for information."

Discipline for incompetence has been relatively rare.[8] Most cases have involved either egregious, repeated instances of incompetence or incompetence combined with other misconduct.[9] Court decisions and ethics opinions often state that it is inappropriate to impose discipline for conduct that amounts "only" to negligent malpractice.[10] Is this position justified?

Some states have adopted a standard of competence different from that in the Code or Rules. For example, California Rule of Prof. Conduct 3–110(A) provides that a lawyer "shall not intentionally, or with reckless disregard, or repeatedly fail to perform legal services competently." Rule 3–110(B) defines acting competently as "diligently to apply the learning and skill necessary to perform ... duties arising from employment or representation." Is this an improvement over M.R. 1.1?

2. Continuing Legal Education [11]

Voluntary continuing legal education (CLE) is a major part of a modern lawyer's professional life. CLE is a large and highly competitive industry. Virtually all bar associations, national, state and local,

8. See Susan R. Martyn, Lawyer Competence and Lawyer Discipline: Beyond the Bar? 71 Geo.L.J. 705 (1981).

9. See, e.g., Attorney Grievance Com'n v. Werner, 315 Md. 172, 553 A.2d 722 (1989) (gross neglect, multiple misrepresentations and failure to cooperate with bar authorities); Office of Disciplinary Counsel v. Henry, 664 S.W.2d 62 (Tenn.1983) (gross incompetence in four cases); In re Albert, 390 Mich. 234, 212 N.W.2d 17 (1973) (neglect of the claims of a number of clients and failure to keep clients informed of the status of their cases); In re Kennedy, 254 S.C. 463, 176 S.E.2d 125 (1970) (repeated instances of incompetence).

10. See, e.g., Florida Bar v. Neale, 384 So.2d 1264, 1265 (Fla.1980) (professional discipline for neglect should not be used "as a substitute for what is essentially a malpractice action"); Committee on Legal Ethics v. Mullins, 159 W.Va. 647, 226 S.E.2d 427 (1976). Also see ABA Informal Op. 1273 (1973) (neglect "involves more than a single act or omission"); ABA Comm. on Ethics and Prof. Resp. Formal Op. 335 n.1 (1974) (discipline for "neglect" under the Model Code requires "indifference and a consistent failure to carry out the obligations [the lawyer had] assumed to his client or a conscious disregard for the responsibility owed to his client").

11. For discussion of continuing legal education, see ALI–ABA Committee on Continuing Legal Education, CLE and the Lawyer's Responsibilities in an Evolving Profession (Arden House, 1988); Study of the Quality of Continuing Legal Education (1980); and A Model for Continuing Legal Education: Structure, Methods, and Curriculum (1980).

provide a variety of CLE programs: lectures, panels, video and audio tapes, pamphlets, checklists, books and articles. Many private publishers and other entrepreneurs also provide offerings. Some lawyers take a heavy load of courses; others never or rarely attend. It is the latter group that is suspected of needing such training most. Because of fear that those who need it most take it least, CLE has been made mandatory in most states.[12] How much CLE training is sufficient? How does a lawyer gauge whether her level of knowledge of a subject is at least average other than by going to courses to hear what other lawyers know on the subject? Is conveying such awareness a sufficient justification for mandatory CLE?

Lawyers have challenged "mandatory CLE," as it is called, on free speech, due process and other constitutional grounds, but such challenges have failed.[13]

3. Peer Review

For more than a decade the American Bar Association and the American Law Institute have experimented with "peer review" through their joint CLE enterprise, ALI–ABA. The theory behind peer review is that lawyers may maintain and improve their competence by submitting their practice methods to the scrutiny of knowledgeable colleagues for comment and constructive criticism.[14] ALI–ABA has supported experimental peer review programs in several states. However, peer review has had difficulty gaining general acceptance. Peer review procedures are invoked if a lawyer's practice is found substandard, for example, in connection with a grievance inquiry. For obvious reasons, lawyers do not wish their practice to be so designated. Also, the psychology of education suggests that it is not easy to teach someone after having called her incompetent. On the other hand, making peer review compulsory for all would be an expensive form of mandatory CLE.

Informal peer review, of course, goes on all the time. Weren't Chief Justice Burger's remarks about the competence of trial lawyers, quoted at the beginning of this chapter, essentially peer review? Isn't peer review involved in evaluating an associate in a law firm for

12. Thirty-nine states had mandatory CLE requirements as of June 1992. Nat'l L.J., June 8, 1992, p. 31 (listing states). The California requirement of 36 hours every three years requires that at least four hours be on the subject of legal ethics and that one hour each be devoted to substance abuse and the elimination of bias. Katherine Bishop, California Lawyers Must Take Refresher Courses, N.Y. Times, Aug. 9, 1991, at p. B7.

13. See, e.g., Verner v. Colorado, 716 F.2d 1352 (10th Cir.1983) (mandatory CLE does not violate lawyers' constitutional rights to due process, free speech or assembly, equal protection of the law, the 8th Amendment's prohibition against cruel and unusual punishment, or the 13th Amendment's prohibition against involuntary servitude; the state may require lawyers to take CLE courses as a condition of maintaining their licenses); see also Brown v. McGarr, 774 F.2d 777 (7th Cir.1985) (practice requirements for federal "trial bar" do not deprive lawyers of property without due process of law).

14. See ALI–ABA Committee on Continuing Professional Education, A Model Peer Review System (1980); ALI–ABA Committee on Continuing Professional Education, Law Practice Quality Evaluation: An Appraisal of Peer Review and Other Measures To Enhance Professional Performance (1987).

partnership or in establishing the shares of partners in the profits of a firm's practice? One reason law firms experience lower rates of malpractice claims than sole practitioners is that the members of a firm undergo continuous peer review in the ordinary course of the firm's practice.

4. Reputation and the Market

Traditionally, a lawyer's reputation reflected his proficiency. Reputation is established partly through the opinion of clients, but at least equally through the opinion of other lawyers. To this extent, a lawyer's reputation is the distillate of peer review. Today, reputation remains important within the circle of a lawyer's professional acquaintance. A nonspecialist practitioner located in a metropolitan area rather than a small face-to-face community, however, has a largely disconnected circle of acquaintance. Apart from well-developed legal specializations, the impersonal nature of modern law practice in urban areas means that the informal peer review expressed in professional reputation is relatively weak. Are mandatory CLE and peer review adequate to replace reputational controls in protecting against incompetence?

Why not trust the market to differentiate between competent and incompetent lawyers? The market probably operates comparatively well as a competence filter with regard to specialized types of legal services provided to sophisticated clients such as business corporations.[15] However, available evidence indicates that most individuals use a lawyer's services on only two or three occasions in a lifetime.[16] Such limited experience as a client does not provide much basis for making market comparisons. Should current and prospective clients be able to pool their experience by joining together to purchase legal services? That is what prepaid and legal services plans involve. See Chapter 10 below, discussing group legal services beginning at p. 979.

B. MALPRACTICE

Introductory Note

In 1978 the American Bar Association established the National Legal Malpractice Data Center to compile information, based on data submitted by participating insurance companies, on malpractice claims against lawyers. The Center's figures do not include claims against uninsured lawyers, about whom no statistics are available.

The Center's compilation of data reported during 1983–1985 showed that almost 50 percent of all reported malpractice claims arise

---

15. Consider, for example, the search made for the lawyer in Brobeck, Phleger & Harrison v. Telex Corp., 602 F.2d 866 (9th Cir.1979), printed at p. 515 below.

16. See Barbara A. Curran, The Legal Needs of the Public: The Final Report of a National Survey (1977).

out of real estate and personal injury matters.[17] Forty-four percent of claims involved allegations that the lawyer's knowledge of the law was faulty or inadequate; 26 percent involved poor office administration; 16 percent involved errors in client relations (e.g., conflicts of interest); 12 percent involved intentional error; and the remaining 2 percent involved miscellaneous causes.

Almost 80 percent of the claims targeted sole practitioners and lawyers from firms of two to five lawyers. Sixty-seven percent of all lawyers in private practice in 1985 practiced alone or in firms of five or fewer lawyers. About 20 percent of the claims involved lawyers in firms with six to thirty lawyers, a percentage about equal to the number of lawyers in firms of this size. About 2 percent of the claims involved lawyers in practice with more than 30 lawyers; 11.2 percent of all private-practice lawyers belonged to firms of 51 or more lawyers.[18]

The low percentage of claims against lawyers in large firms may be misleading. Large firms often have malpractice liability insurance policies with sizeable deductibles and thus may not report small claims. On the other hand, many sole and small firm practitioners may be uninsured and malpractice claims against them are not included in the statistics.

1. Overview of Tort of Malpractice

The elements of a legal malpractice claim are:

1. *Duty*. A duty of care arising from an attorney-client relationship [19] or, in those jurisdictions that have rejected privity, some other showing that there was a duty to the plaintiff, e.g., that a substantial purpose of the attorney-client relationship was to influence or benefit the plaintiff.

2. *Breach of duty*. A failure by the lawyer to exercise the care, skill or diligence that reasonably competent lawyers exercise under similar circumstances.

3. *Causation*. Cause-in-fact and proximate cause must be shown, i.e., evidence that the lawyer's failure was the actual and proximate cause of the plaintiff's injury.

4. *Harm*. Legally cognizable harm must have been caused by the lawyer's act or omission. Legal malpractice usually seeks a recovery for purely economic harm: e.g., a showing that the plaintiff would have achieved a different and more advantageous result in the transaction or litigation but for the lawyer's conduct. The

17. William H. Gates and Sheree L. Swetin, Characteristics of Legal Malpractice: Report of the National Legal Malpractice Data Center (1989).

18. See also Ronald E. Mallen, Malpractice at a Glance, 5 Calif. Lawyer 34 (July 1985).

19. See Togstad v. Vesely, Otto, Miller & Keefe, 291 N.W.2d 686 (Minn.1980), printed in Chapter 6 below at p. 481, and the notes following it for a discussion of when, for purposes of a legal malpractice claim, an attorney-client relationship will be found to exist.

availability of damages for emotional or psychic harm is a topic of current controversy and disagreement.[20]

The law of legal malpractice is a subject in itself. In the notes that follow, we touch on only a few of the many questions in this area.[21] There is a substantial literature on subsidiary problems such as use of expert testimony,[22] accrual of the cause of action and tolling of the statute of limitations through continuation of the lawyer-client relationship[23] and liability for particular types of mistakes.[24]

LUCAS v. HAMM

Supreme Court of California, 1961.
56 Cal.2d 583, 15 Cal.Rptr. 821, 364 P.2d 685.

GIBSON, CHIEF JUSTICE.

[Attorney Hamm was retained to draft a will. The testator's instructions called for creation of a trust of the residue for the benefit of the plaintiffs. Hamm prepared and the client executed a will providing that this trust of the residue would terminate "at 12 o'clock noon on a day five years after" termination of the testator's estate. After the testator's death, Hamm, as the lawyer for the testator's estate, advised plaintiffs that the trust provision was invalid under the California rule against perpetuities, which prohibits any restraint on alienation "for a period longer than 21 years after some life in being at the creation of the interest...." As a result, plaintiffs entered into a settlement with intestate heirs, receiving $75,000 less than they would have received if the instructions given by the testator had been effectuated. The plaintiffs sued Hamm, alleging that he was negligent in drafting the will. They sought money damages. The trial court dismissed the complaint for failing to state a cause of action. The plaintiffs appealed.]

... We are of the view that the extension of [a lawyer's] liability to beneficiaries injured by a negligently drawn will does not place an

---

20. See Note, An Attorney's Liability for the Negligent Infliction of Emotional Distress, 58 Fordham L.Rev.1309 (1990) (damages for emotional distress generally are limited to cases in which the client suffered a physical injury or the attorney acted egregiously, but some recent cases permit such damages without regard to the degree of lawyer negligence). See, e.g., Pinkham v. Burgess, 933 F.2d 1066 (1st Cir.1991) (affirming an award of $186,500 for emotional distress caused to a client by lawyer's negligent representation in a civil rights case).

21. For more elaborate treatment of this subject, see Ronald E. Mallen and Jeffrey M. Smith, Legal Malpractice (3d ed.1989); Wolfram, Modern Legal Ethics § 5.6 et seq. (1986); William L. Prosser and W. Page Keeton, Prosser and Keeton on Torts 185 et seq. (5th ed.1984).

22. See, e.g., Charles M. Liebson, Legal Malpractice Cases: Special Problems in Identifying Issues of Law and Fact and in the Use of Expert Testimony, 75 Ky.L.J. 1 (1986–87).

23. Joseph H. Koffler, Legal Malpractice Statutes of Limitations: A Critical Analysis of a Burgeoning Crisis, 20 Akron L.Rev. 209 (1986).

24. See, e.g., Note, Liability of Attorneys for Legal Opinions Under the Federal Securities Laws, 27 B.C.L.Rev. 325 (1986).

undue burden on the profession, particularly when we take into consideration that a contrary conclusion would cause the innocent beneficiary to bear the loss. [The court applied a balancing-of-factors approach in holding that it was reasonably foreseeable to Hamm, when he drafted the will, that absence of due care would result in harm to the intended will beneficiaries.]

It follows that the lack of privity between plaintiffs and defendant does not preclude plaintiffs from maintaining an action in tort against defendant.

. . .

The general rule with respect to the liability of an attorney for failure to properly perform his duties to his client is that the attorney, by accepting employment to give legal advice or to render other legal services, impliedly agrees to use such skill, prudence, and diligence as lawyers of ordinary skill and capacity commonly possess and exercise in the performance of the tasks which they undertake.... The attorney is not liable for every mistake he may make in his practice; he is not, in the absence of an express agreement, an insurer of the soundness of his opinions or of the validity of an instrument that he is engaged to draft; and he is not liable for being in error as to a question of law on which reasonable doubt may be entertained by well-informed lawyers....

The complaint, as we have seen, alleges that defendant drafted the will in such a manner that the trust was invalid because it violated the rules relating to perpetuities and restraints on alienation. These closely akin subjects have long perplexed the courts and the bar. Professor Gray, a leading authority in the field, stated: "There is something in the subject which seems to facilitate error. Perhaps it is because the mode of reasoning is unlike that with which lawyers are most familiar.... A long list might be formed of the demonstrable blunders with regard to its questions made by eminent men, blunders which they themselves have been sometimes the first to acknowledge; and there are few lawyers of any practice in drawing wills and settlements who have not at some time either fallen into the net which the Rule spreads for the unwary, or at least shuddered to think how narrowly they have escaped it." Gray, The Rule Against Perpetuities (4th ed. 1942) p. xi; see also Leach, Perpetuities Legislation (1954) 67 Harv.L.Rev. 1349 (describing the rule as a "technicality-ridden legal nightmare" and a "dangerous instrumentality in the hands of most members of the bar"). Of the California law on perpetuities and restraints it has been said that few, if any, areas of the law have been fraught with more confusion or concealed more traps for the unwary draftsman; that members of the bar, probate courts, and title insurance companies make errors in these matters; that the code provisions adopted in 1872 created a situation worse than if the matter had been left to the common law; and that the legislation adopted in 1951 (under which the will involved here was drawn), despite the best of intentions, added further complexities. (See 38 Cal.Jur.2d 443; Coil, Perpetuities and Restraints; A Needed Reform (1955) 30 State Bar J. 87, 88–90.)

Holding

In view of the state of the law relating to perpetuities and restraints on alienation and the nature of the error, if any, assertedly made by defendant in preparing the instrument, it would not be proper to hold that defendant failed to use such skill, prudence, and diligence as lawyers of ordinary skill and capacity commonly exercise. The provision of the will quoted in the complaint, namely, that the trust was to terminate five years after the order of the probate court distributing the property to the trustee, could cause the trust to be invalid only because of the remote possibility that the order of distribution would be delayed for a period longer than a life in being at the creation of the interest plus 16 years (the 21–year statutory period less the five years specified in the will). Although it has been held that a possibility of this type could result in invalidity of a bequest (Estate of Johnston, 47 Cal.2d 265, 269–270, 303 P.2d 1; Estate of Campbell, 28 Cal.App.2d 102, 103 et seq., 82 P.2d 22), the possible occurrence of such a delay was so remote and unlikely that an attorney of ordinary skill acting under the same circumstances might well have "fallen into the net which the Rule spreads for the unwary" and failed to recognize the danger....

[The court then considered and rejected a count of the complaint that alleged negligence by Hamm as lawyer for the estate in negotiating the settlement with the intestate heirs.]

Notes on *Lucas*

The decision in *Lucas* suggests that judges as well as lawyers have trouble understanding the rule against perpetuities. If a reasonably competent lawyer may not be expected to understand the rule against perpetuities, is it equitable that courts apply the rule to disinherit people? What about complicated tax and securities problems? Complicated issues of constitutional criminal procedure?

Is the following a fair statement of the position taken by the California Supreme Court in *Lucas?*: "California law is so confused and uncertain that citizens have to rely on lawyers; but, because the law is uncertain, lawyers cannot be held responsible for giving incompetent advice."[25] Who is in the best position to reform or simplify the California rule against perpetuities?

25. An English commentator, R. E. Megarry, criticized the *Lucas* decision as "a slur on the profession which, like the mule, will display neither pride of ancestry nor hope of posterity." Megarry, 81 L.Q.Rev. 478, 481 (1965). "The standard of competence in California thus seems to be that it is not negligent for lawyers to draft wills knowing little or nothing of the rule against perpetuities, and without consulting anyone skilled in the rule...." See also Gerald P. Johnston, Legal Malpractice in Estate Planning—Perilous Times Ahead for the Practitioner, 67 Iowa L. Rev. 629 (1982).

Would the result in *Lucas* be the same if lawyer Hamm had held himself out as limiting his practice to trusts and estates law? [26]

Malpractice Liability to Non–Clients

The traditional rule is that absent fraud, collusion, or privity of contract, an attorney is not liable to a non-client third person for professional malpractice.[27]   But a growing number of jurisdictions have abandoned the requirement of privity of contract, either by using a balancing-of-factors approach or by employing a third-party beneficiary theory.[28]

Intended Beneficiaries of a Will

A number of state courts follow the holding in Lucas v. Hamm, allowing a claim for malpractice by the intended beneficiaries of a will.[29]   In Lorraine v. Grover,[30] the Florida court reaffirmed the traditional rule that privity is required but recognized an exception for the beneficiaries of a will to whom lawyers have a "direct duty." [31]   Pennsylvania reached the same result but refused to do so under tort law.[32] Rejecting California's balancing-of-factors approach as unworkable, the Pennsylvania court settled instead on liability to the intended beneficiary under a third-party beneficiary approach.[33]

New York, however, has rejected negligence claims brought against lawyers by the intended beneficiaries of wills,[34] as well as most negligence claims by other third parties: " ... New York has not retreated from the requirement of privity in legal malpractice cases." [35]

26. See Horne v. Peckham, 97 Cal.App.3d 404, 158 Cal.Rptr. 714 (1979) (inexperienced practitioner drafting a "Clifford trust" without consulting a tax or estate planning specialist), discussed later in this section.

27. National Savings Bank v. Ward, 100 U.S. 195 (1880).

28. See the *Greycas* case and the notes that follow it in Chapter 2 above at p. 75. California's balancing-of-factors approach lists seven factors relevant to the question whether an actor has a duty of care to a third person in the absence of privity of contract. This approach, which originated in Biakanja v. Irving, 49 Cal.2d 647, 650, 320 P.2d 16 (1958) (notary public liable to intended beneficiary of a will that was denied probate because it lacked proper attestation), was extended to lawyers in *Lucas*.

29. See, e.g., Schreiner v. Scoville, 410 N.W.2d 679 (Iowa 1987); and Auric v. Continental Cas. Co., 111 Wis.2d 507, 331 N.W.2d 325 (1983).

30. 467 So.2d 315 (Fla.App.1985).

31. For a similar approach see Needham v. Hamilton, 459 A.2d 1060 (D.C.App.1983).

32. Guy v. Liederbach, 501 Pa. 47, 459 A.2d 744 (1983).

33. Restatement (Second) Contracts § 302(1) (1981) (intended beneficiaries of a contract may recover on the contract when necessary to effectuate the intention of the parties to the contract).   See also Hale v. Groce, 304 Or. 281, 744 P.2d 1289 (1987) (intended beneficiary's tort action barred by statute of limitations but may proceed under contract theory); and Stowe v. Smith, 184 Conn. 194, 441 A.2d 81 (1981) (contract approach).

34. See, e.g., Victor v. Goldman, 74 Misc.2d 685, 344 N.Y.S.2d 672 (1973), aff'd, 43 A.D.2d 1021, 351 N.Y.S.2d 956 (2d Dept.1974).

35. Calamari v. Grace, 98 A.D.2d 74, 469 N.Y.S.2d 942 (1983).   But cases applying New York law carve out an exception for legal opinions designed to influence a third person with whom a client is dealing.   See Crossland Saving FSB v. Rockwood Insurance Co., 700 F.Supp. 1274 (S.D.N.Y.1988) (holding that New York recognizes a lawyer's liability to

In Metzker v. Slocum,[36] a couple hired a lawyer to carry out an adoption, but the adoption was never perfected as a result of the lawyer's negligence. The parents subsequently divorced, and the minor child was left without support. The child sued the lawyer for negligence. The Oregon court held that the lawyer was not liable to the child, a third party to the original transaction. The court said that even applying the liberal California balancing-of-factors test for third-party liability there would be no liability because the relationship between the negligence and the harm was too tenuous and the foreseeability of harm to the child was minimal. Aren't both propositions dubious, at best?

2. Causation and Standard of Care

SMITH v. LEWIS

Supreme Court of California, 1975.
13 Cal.3d 349, 118 Cal.Rptr. 621, 530 P.2d 589.

MOSK, JUSTICE.

Defendant Jerome R. Lewis, an attorney, appeals from a judgment entered upon a jury verdict for plaintiff Rosemary E. Smith in an action for legal malpractice. The action arises as a result of legal services rendered by defendant to plaintiff in a prior divorce proceeding. The gist of plaintiff's complaint is that defendant negligently failed in the divorce action to assert her community interest in the retirement benefits of her husband.

Defendant principally contends, inter alia, that the law with regard to the characterization of retirement benefits was so unclear at the time he represented plaintiff as to insulate him from liability for failing to assert a claim therefor on behalf of his client. We conclude defendant's appeal is without merit, and therefore affirm the judgment.

In 1943 plaintiff married General Clarence D. Smith. Between 1945 and his retirement in 1966 General Smith was employed by the California National Guard. As plaintiff testified, she informed defendant her husband "was paid by the state ... it was a job just like anyone else goes to." For the first 16 years of that period the husband belonged to the State Employees' Retirement System, a contributory plan. Between 1961 and the date of his retirement he belonged to the California National Guard retirement program, a noncontributory plan. In addition, by attending National Guard reserve drills he qualified for separate retirement benefits from the federal government, also through a noncontributory plan. The state and federal retirement programs each provide lifetime monthly benefits which terminate upon the death

third parties for negligent misrepresentation in some circumstances). *Crossland* is discussed in the notes following *Greycas* in Chapter 2 above.

36. 272 Or. 313, 537 P.2d 74 (1975).

of the retiree. The programs make no allowance for the retiree's widow.

On January 1, 1967, the State of California began to pay General Smith gross retirement benefits of $796.26 per month. Payments under the federal program, however, will not begin until 1983, i.e., 17 years after his actual retirement, when General Smith reaches the age of 60. All benefits which General Smith is entitled to receive were earned during the time he was married to plaintiff.

On February 17, 1967, plaintiff retained defendant to represent her in a divorce action against General Smith. According to plaintiff's testimony, defendant advised her that her husband's retirement benefits were not community property. Three days later defendant filed plaintiff's complaint for divorce. General Smith's retirement benefits were not pleaded as items of community property, and therefore were not considered in the litigation or apportioned by the trial court. The divorce was uncontested and the interlocutory decree divided the minimal described community property and awarded Mrs. Smith $400 per month in alimony and child support. The final decree was entered on February 17, 1968.

Retirement Benefits

On July 17, 1968, pursuant to a request by plaintiff, defendant filed on her behalf a motion to amend the decree, alleging under oath that because of his mistake, inadvertence, and excusable neglect (Code Civ. Proc., § 473) the retirement benefits of General Smith had been omitted from the list of community assets owned by the parties, and that such benefits were in fact community property. The motion was denied on the ground of untimeliness. Plaintiff consulted other counsel, and shortly thereafter filed this malpractice action against defendant.

motion to Amend decree

Defendant admits in his testimony that he assumed General Smith's retirement benefits were separate property when he assessed plaintiff's community property rights. It is his position that as a matter of law an attorney is not liable for mistaken advice when well informed lawyers in the community entertain reasonable doubt as to the proper resolution of the particular legal question involved. Because, he asserts, the law defining the character of retirement benefits was uncertain at the time of his legal services to plaintiff, defendant contends the trial court committed error in refusing to grant his motions for nonsuit and judgment notwithstanding the verdict and in submitting the issue of negligence to the jury under appropriate instructions.[3]

---

3. The jury was instructed as follows:

"In performing legal services for a client in a divorce action an attorney has the duty to have that degree of learning and skill ordinarily possessed by attorneys of good standing, practicing in the same or similar locality and under similar circumstances.

"[An attorney is also required] to use reasonable diligence and his best judgment in the exercise of his skill and the accomplishment of his learning, in an effort to accomplish the best possible result for his client."

"An attorney is not liable for every mistake he may make in his practice; he is not in the absence of an express agreement, an insurer of the soundness of his opinions."

Analysis

The law is now settled in California that "retirement benefits which flow from the employment relationship, to the extent they have vested, are community property subject to equal division between the spouses in the event the marriage is dissolved." [Six California cases were cited.] Because such benefits are part of the consideration earned by the employee, they are accorded community treatment regardless of whether they derive from a state, federal, or private source, or from a contributory or noncontributory plan. In light of these principles, it becomes apparent that General Smith's retirement pay must properly be characterized as community property.

We cannot, however, evaluate the quality of defendant's professional services on the basis of the law as it appears today. In determining whether defendant exhibited the requisite degree of competence in his handling of plaintiff's divorce action, the crucial inquiry is whether his advice was so legally deficient when it was given that he may be found to have failed to use "such skill, prudence, and diligence as lawyers of ordinary skill and capacity commonly possess and exercise in the performance of the tasks which they undertake." (Lucas v. Hamm (1961) 56 Cal.2d 583, 591, 15 Cal.Rptr. 821, 825, 364 P.2d 685, 689.) We must, therefore examine the indicia of the law which were readily available to defendant at the time he performed the legal services in question.

Law in 1965 = Community property

The major authoritative reference works which attorneys routinely consult for a brief and reliable exposition of the law relevant to a specific problem uniformly indicated in 1967 that vested retirement benefits earned during marriage were generally subject to community treatment.[5] (See, e.g., Note, Pensions, and Reserve or Retired Pay, as Community Property, 134 A.L.R. 368; 15 Am.Jur.2d Community Property, § 46, p. 859; 38 Cal.Jur.2d, Pensions, § 12, p. 325; 10 Cal.Jur.2d, Community Property, § 25, p. 692; 1 Cal.Family Lawyer (Cont.Ed.Bar 1962) p. 111; 4 Witkin, Summary of Cal.Law (1960) pp. 2723–2724; cf. 41 C.J.S. Husband and Wife § 475, p. 1010 & fn. 69 and 1967 Supp. p. 1011.) A typical statement appeared in the California Family Lawyer, a work with which defendant admitted general familiarity: "Of increasing importance is the fact that pension or retirement benefits are community property, even though they are not paid or payable until after termination of the marriage by death or divorce." (1 Cal.Family Lawyer, supra, at p. 111.)

Although it is true this court had not foreclosed all conflicts on some aspects of the issue at that time, the community character of retirement benefits had been reported in a number of appellate opinions often cited in the literature and readily accessible to defendant. In Benson v. City of Los Angeles (1963), 60 Cal.2d 355, 33 Cal.Rptr. 257, 384 P.2d 649 decided four years before defendant was retained herein, we stated directly that "pension rights which are earned during the

---

5. In evaluating the competence of an attorney's services, we may justifiably consider his failure to consult familiar encyclopedias of the law. People v. Ibarra (1963) 60 Cal.2d 450, 405, 34 Cal.Rptr. 803, 386 P.2d 487.

course of a marriage are the community property of the employee and his wife." ... In *French*, decided two decades earlier, we indicated that "retire[ment] pay is community property because it is compensation for services rendered in the past." (17 Cal.2d at p. 778, 112 P.2d at p. 236.) The other cases contain equally unequivocal dicta.

We are aware, moreover, of no significant authority existing in 1967 which proposed a result contrary to that suggested by the cases and the literature, or which purported to rebut the general statutory presumption, as it applies to retirement benefits, that all property acquired by either spouse during marriage belongs to the community....

On the other hand, substantial uncertainty may have existed in 1967 with regard to the community character of General Smith's federal pension. The above-discussed treaties reveal a debate which lingered among members of the legal community at that time concerning the point at which retirement benefits actually vest. [Citations to law review literature omitted.] Because the federal payments were contingent upon General Smith's survival to age 60, 17 years subsequent to the divorce, it could have been argued with some force that plaintiff and General Smith shared a mere expectancy interest in the future benefits. Alternatively, a reasonable contention could have been advanced in 1967 that federal retirement benefits were the personal entitlement of the employee spouse and were not subject to community division upon divorce in the absence of express congressional approval.... Although we [subsequently rejected this analysis in a 1974 case], the issue was clearly an arguable one upon which reasonable lawyers could differ....

Of course, the fact that in 1967 a reasonable argument could have been offered to support the characterization of General Smith's federal benefits as separate property does not indicate the trial court erred in submitting the issue of defendant's malpractice to the jury. The state benefits, the large majority of the payments at issue, were unquestionably community property according to all available authority and should have been claimed as such. As for the federal benefits, the record documents defendant's failure to conduct any reasonable research into their proper characterization under community property law.[7] Instead, he dogmatically asserted his theory, which he was unable to support with authority and later recanted, that all noncontributory military retirement benefits, whether state or federal, were

---

7. At trial defendant testified that prior to the division of property in the divorce action, he had assumed the retirement benefits were not subject to community treatment, despite the fact General Smith had already begun to receive payments from the state: that he did not at that time undertake any research on the point nor did he discuss the matter with plaintiff; that subsequent to the divorce plaintiff asked defendant to research the question whereupon defendant discovered the *French* case which contained dictum in support of plaintiff's position; that the *French* decision caused him to change his opinion and conclude "that the Supreme Court, when it was confronted with this [the language in *French*] may hold that it [vested military retirement pay] in community property."...

immune from community treatment upon divorce. The jury could well have found defendant's refusal to educate himself to the applicable principles of law constituted negligence which prevented him from exercising informed discretion with regard to his client's rights.

As the jury was correctly instructed, an attorney does not ordinarily guarantee the soundness of his opinions and, accordingly, is not liable for every mistake he may make in his practice. He is expected, however, to possess knowledge of those plain and elementary principles of law which are commonly known by well informed attorneys, and to discover those additional rules of law which, although not commonly known, may readily be found by standard research techniques.... If the law on a particular subject is doubtful or debatable, an attorney will not be held responsible for failing to anticipate the manner in which the uncertainty will be resolved.... But even with respect to an unsettled area of the law, we believe an attorney assumes an obligation to his client to undertake reasonable research in an effort to ascertain relevant legal principles and to make an informed decision as to a course of conduct based upon an intelligent assessment of the problem. In the instant case, ample evidence was introduced to support a jury finding that defendant failed to perform such adequate research into the question of the community character of retirement benefits and thus was unable to exercise the informed judgment to which his client was entitled. (See fn. 7, ante.)

We recognize, of course, that an attorney engaging in litigation may have occasion to choose among various alternative strategies available to his client, one of which may be to refrain from pressing a debatable point because potential benefit may not equal detriment in terms of expenditure at time and resources or because of calculated tactics to the advantage of his client. But, as the Ninth Circuit put it somewhat brutally in Pineda v. Craven (9th Cir.1970) 424 F.2d 369, 372: "There is nothing strategic or tactical about ignorance...." In the case before us it is difficult to conceive of tactical advantage which could have been served by neglecting to advance a claim so clearly in plaintiff's best interest, nor does defendant suggest any. The decision to forego litigation on the issue of plaintiff's community property right to a share of General Smith's retirement benefits was apparently the product of a culpable misconception of the relevant principles of law, and the jury could have so found.

Furthermore, no lawyer would suggest the property characterization of General Smith's retirement benefits to be so esoteric an issue that defendant could not reasonably have been expected to be aware of it or its probable resolution. (Lucas v. Hamm (1961) supra, 56 Cal.2d 583, 15 Cal.Rptr. 821, 364 P.2d 685.) In *Lucas* we held that the rule against perpetuities poses such complex and difficult problems for the draftsman that even careful and competent attorneys occasionally fall prey to its traps. The situation before us is not analogous. Certainly one of the central issues in any divorce proceeding is the extent and division of the community property. In this case the question reached monumental proportions, since General Smith's retirement benefits constituted the only significant asset available to the community.[8] In undertaking professional representation of plaintiff, defendant assumed the duty to familiarize himself with the law defining the character of retirement benefits; instead, he rendered erroneous advice contrary to the best interests of his client without the guidance through research of readily available authority.

. . .

... Even as to doubtful matters, an attorney is expected to perform sufficient research to enable him to make an informed and intelligent judgment on behalf of his client.[9]

[The court rejected defendant's further argument that the $100,000 verdict was excessive. Plaintiff's expert had testified that the combined value of the two pensions was $322,032.]

The judgment is affirmed.

CLARK, JUSTICE (dissenting). ——

[The dissent argued at length that the law confronting the defendant in 1967 was not nearly as clear as the majority contended; that the legal complexity of military pensions as community property fell within the protection afforded by the *Lucas* case; and that, as a tactical matter, the defendant better served his client by securing alimony than by litigating the community property point. The dissent concluded:]

Given the uncertain status of the law, the circumstances of the parties, and the close relationship between property division and alimony payment, an ethical, diligent and careful lawyer would have avoided litigation over pension rights and instead would have sought a compensating alimony award for any inequity.... So far as appears, defendant secured such compensating award.

Accordingly, even assuming that defendant was negligent in failing to research the pension questions, the record does not furnish a balance of probabilities that his negligence—rather than the uncertain status of the law and the availability of uncontested alimony—caused plaintiff to lose a $100,000 pension award.

. . .

8. It is undisputed that the only assets the parties had to show as community property after 24 years of marriage, aside from General Smith's retirement benefits, were an equity of $1,800 in a house, some furniture, shares of stock worth $2,300, and two automobiles on which money was owing.

9. The principal thrust of the dissent is its conclusion that "even assuming that defendant was negligent in failing to research the pension questions, the record does not furnish a balance of probabilities that his negligence—rather than the uncertain status of the law and the availability of uncontested alimony—caused plaintiff to lose a $100,000 pension award." Whether defendant's negligence was a cause in fact of plaintiff's damage—an element of proximate cause—is a factual question for the jury to resolve.... Here the jury was correctly instructed that plaintiff had the burden of proving, inter alia, that defendant's negligence was a proximate cause of the damage suffered, and proximate cause was defined as "a cause which, natural and continuous sequence, produces the damage, and without which the damage would not have occurred."...

Causation of Harm

The dissent in Smith v. Lewis rests primarily on a causation argument: Was the harm caused by the failure of lawyer Lewis to conduct research or by the uncertainty of state and federal law dealing with community property interests in retirement pensions? Note that the majority treats this proximate-cause question as a question of fact for the jury (see the court's footnote 9), while the dissent would have resolved it as a matter of law. Does the decision require a lawyer to communicate legal uncertainty to her client so that the client can make decisions accordingly? [37]

Causation issues in malpractice cases are frequent and often difficult. If a lawyer's breach of duty to a client occurs in the handling of litigation and the harm suffered is the loss of a recoverable claim, the client will usually be required to prove that the underlying case would have succeeded if it had been properly brought or litigated. A failure, for example, to file a client's medical malpractice case before the limitations period expired requires proof by the client that a recovery of a specified amount would have been obtained but for the failure. This trial of a "case within a case" puts the lawyer charged with malpractice in the awkward position of defending the physician charged with malpractice (the opposing party in the case in which the lawyer's negligence occurred).

Suppose a lawyer fails to communicate a settlement offer to his client, believing that a larger recovery will be obtained at trial. The trial is lost. Does the client have a malpractice claim against the lawyer? What are the damages?

Suppose a lawyer is negligent in a number of respects in handling the defense of a client accused of crime. The client is convicted and later brings a malpractice action against her lawyer. Should the client, in order to establish that the conviction resulted from the lawyer's negligence, have to prove that she was innocent of the crime charged? [38] Or only that she would have been acquitted? [39]

Standard of Care

As set forth in *Smith,* the duty to conduct a reasonable investigation of applicable law holds lawyers to a higher standard than suggest-

37. In Procanik v. Cillo, 226 N.J.Super. 132, 543 A.2d 985 (1988), a New Jersey lawyer declined to undertake a woman's claim that her attending physician had failed to inform her that the fetus had a birth defect in time for her to obtain an abortion. At the time New Jersey tort law was unclear as to whether a cause of action for "wrongful life" would be recognized. The court held that a legal malpractice claim was not stated against the lawyer because he failed to state the law's uncertainty in his letter declining to take the case; his failure to inform the client that New Jersey law was in the process of change was not malpractice.

38. See, e.g., Carmel v. Lunney, 70 N.Y.2d 169, 518 N.Y.S.2d 605, 511 N.E.2d 1126 (1987) (failure to allege innocence of the underlying offense defeats a malpractice claim against the defense lawyer as a matter of law).

39. See, e.g., Hines v. Davidson, 489 So.2d 572 (Ala.1986).

ed by *Lucas*. What is left of *Lucas* after *Smith?*[40] *Smith* has been cited and followed in other states; *Lucas*, insofar as it creates a lower standard of care for perpetuities matters, is not followed outside California.

Should attorney Lewis have been disciplined in California? Would he be? Would the result have been different if Lewis had taken the case as a favor at no fee or a minimal fee? If his client had agreed in advance to a limited representation?

Custom

Professional Custom Sets the Standard

Professional malpractice differs from ordinary negligence in that the standard of care is determined by the skill, knowledge and diligence brought to bear on similar matters by a lawyer of ordinary competence. In ordinary negligence cases, evidence of the custom of a trade or industry is relevant and admissible either to show departure from or compliance with customary care, but custom is not dispositive. As Judge Learned Hand wrote:

> [I]n most cases reasonable prudence is in fact common prudence; but strictly it is never its measure; a whole calling may have unduly lagged in the adoption of new and available devices. It never may set its own tests, however persuasive be its usages. Courts must in the end say what is required; there are precautions so imperative that even their universal disregard will not excuse their omission.[41]

With respect to professions, standards of practice (customary care) are given greater, usually exclusive, deference. The legal standard is stated in terms of the care provided by the ordinary practitioner, and expert testimony of practice standards is ordinarily required as part of the plaintiff's prima facie case.[42] Yet a scattering of decisions have relied on Hand's dictum in holding that what expert witnesses stated as the general practice of physicians was negligent.[43] In Gleason v. Title Guarantee Co.,[44] a lawyer, instead of checking titles, relied on telephone conversations with the title company, which was the customary prac-

---

40. Wright v. Williams, 47 Cal.App.3d 802, 809 n.2, 121 Cal.Rptr. 194, 199 n.2 (1975), expressed doubts whether *Lucas v. Hamm* was still good law in California. But see Aloy v. Mash, 38 Cal.3d 413, 212 Cal.Rptr. 162, 696 P.2d 656 (1985) (employing the reasonable investigation standard of *Smith* and repeating in dicta the distinction between less difficult areas of law and the rule against perpetuities).

41. The T.J. Hooper, 60 F.2d 737, 740 (2d Cir.1932). In *The T.J. Hooper* the court found the defendant negligent for not having a working radio set aboard its tug boat. It is interesting to note that, contrary to what Hand's language suggests, most tugs did have radios at the time. See The T.J. Hooper, 53 F.2d 107, 111 (S.D.N.Y.1931).

42. For discussion of the standard of care in legal malpractice, see Wolfram, Modern Legal Ethics § 5.6 (1986).

43. The leading case is Helling v. Carey, 83 Wash.2d 514, 519 P.2d 981 (1974) (failure of ophthalmologist routinely to administer glaucoma test to patient under 40 years of age). See also Truhitte v. French Hospital, 128 Cal.App.3d 332, 180 Cal.Rptr. 152 (1982) (surgical practice of delegating to a nurse the job of keeping track of the sponges during an operation found to be negligent).

44. 300 F.2d 813 (5th Cir.1962).

tice of lawyers in that area of Florida. The court, citing *The T.J. Hooper*, said that <u>custom provides no defense if the custom is itself negligent</u>. Following this logic, even if most lawyers misunderstand the rule against perpetuities, should it be negligent for a lawyer to draft a will with future interest provisions if she does not understand the rule?

Expert Testimony

The plaintiff in a malpractice action generally must produce expert testimony to establish both the level of care owed by the attorney under the circumstances and the failure to conform to that level of care.[45] In Waldman v. Levine,[46] for example, the lawyers, without consulting a medical expert in obstetrical matters, advised the client to settle a medical malpractice claim for little more than $2,000; the client's claim was that her daughter's death after childbirth was due to obstetric malpractice. The expert in the malpractice case against the lawyers testified that failing to consult an obstetrical expert in such a case was "conduct ... below the minimum standard of care for attorneys in medical malpractice cases."[47] The court affirmed the jury's verdict against the lawyers and the award of $600,000 in damages.

Expert testimony is generally unnecessary "when the attorney's lack of care and skill is so obvious that the trier of fact can find negligence as a matter of common knowledge."[48] In Wagenmann v. Adams,[49] the lawyer, representing a client who had been arrested for disturbing the peace, told the client that his only alternatives were to leave town immediately or commit himself to a mental hospital; the lawyer took no action to secure the client's release when the client was involuntarily committed. On those facts, the court held expert testimony unnecessary to establish that the lawyer committed malpractice. Examples of other cases where courts held expert testimony to be unnecessary include: failure to take any action with regard to estate matters;[50] failure to obey client's instructions;[51] and failure to sue before expiration of limitations period.[52]

Not long ago it was extremely difficult to get one lawyer to testify against another in a malpractice action. Today, it is much easier

45. See Wagenmann v. Adams, 829 F.2d 196, 218 (1st Cir.1987); Progressive Sales v. Williams, Willeford, Boger, Grady & Davis, 86 N.C.App. 51, 356 S.E.2d 372 (1987).

46. 544 A.2d 683 (D.C.App.1988).

47. 544 A.2d at 687.

48. O'Neil v. Bergan, 452 A.2d 337, 341 (D.C.App.1982).

49. 829 F.2d 196, 220 (1st Cir.1987) (affirming a judgment against the lawyer of $50,000).

50. Sorenson v. Fio Rito, 90 Ill.App.3d 368, 373, 45 Ill.Dec. 714, 720, 413 N.E.2d 47, 53 (1980).

51. Olfe v. Gordon, 93 Wis.2d 173, 286 N.W.2d 573, 578 (1980) (client insisted that his divorce be kept out of the newspapers; lawyer promised to do so, but the law required that the divorce be published and lawyer arranged for publication without notifying client).

52. George v. Caton, 93 N.M. 370, 600 P.2d 822, 829 (1979).

although difficulty persists in some areas, especially in communities with relatively few lawyers. In Patterson v. Atlanta Bar Ass'n,[53] the plaintiffs claimed, inter alia, that individual members of the bar and various bar associations were engaged in a conspiracy to prevent lawyers from testifying as expert witnesses in malpractice cases. The court found that the plaintiffs had presented no evidence of conspiracy. Nevertheless, the filing of such a suit lends some support to the proposition that finding a lawyer to testify against another lawyer remains problematic.

National or Local Standard

Should the performance of the lawyer charged with malpractice be compared with that of the profession at large, only with that of lawyers practicing in the same jurisdiction,[54] or, most narrowly, only with that of lawyers practicing in the same or a similar locality? A national standard forces the upgrading of local performance and makes it easier for a plaintiff to obtain expert witnesses. On the other hand, the predicament of lawyers who practice more informally (and more cheaply) in small communities should not be entirely ignored.[55]

A related issue concerns whether a lawyer venturing into a field replete with specialists is or should be judged by the standards of specialized practice. For example, if a general practitioner undertakes a trademark search, will she be liable for professional negligence under the standards of trademark specialists?[56] Should the lawyer be liable for accepting the representation? Should liability depend on what the lawyer communicates to the client concerning experience and ability and what the client agrees to?[57]

In Horne v. Peckham,[58] the lawyer, after consulting "the client's *Specialist* accountant ..., a two volume set of American Jurisprudence" and a tax "expert" who, unknown to the lawyer, had been admitted to the bar only one year earlier, drew up a trust to shelter the client's money from federal taxes. Not surprisingly, the lawyer botched it, and the trust failed to accomplish its purpose. The lawyer testified that he told the client he had "no expertise in tax matters." The court affirmed the jury verdict against the lawyer for malpractice and approved a jury instruction that it "is the duty of an attorney who is a general

---

53. 373 S.E.2d 514 (Ga.1988).

54. Kellos v. Sawilowsky, 172 Ga.App. 263, 322 S.E.2d 897 (1984), held that the standard to be applied was that of lawyers practicing in the state of Georgia but noted that in practice it would make little difference whether one applied a national or local standard.

55. See Wolfram, Modern Legal Ethics 213 (1986).

56. See, e.g., Mayo v. Engel, 733 F.2d 807 (11th Cir.1984) (lawyer held not liable for professional negligence in a trademark search where the firm never held itself out to be expert in trademark work).

57. See, e.g., Walker v. Bangs, 92 Wash.2d 854, 601 P.2d 1279 (1979) (if a lawyer holds himself out as specializing in a particular field, he "will be held to the standard of performance of those who hold themselves out as specialists in the area").

58. 97 Cal.App.3d 404, 158 Cal.Rptr. 714 (1979).

practitioner to refer his client to a specialist or recommend the assistance of a specialist if under the circumstances a reasonably careful and skillful practitioner would do so."[59] If the lawyer fails to consult an expert, the courts will hold the lawyer to the standard of a specialist in the field.

3. Other Issues

Violation of Ethical Rules as a Basis for Malpractice

Generally, courts treat the violation of a relevant statute or regulation setting a standard of performance as negligence per se in tort cases based on negligence. Should violation of an ethics rule imposed on lawyers be similarly treated when the violation causes a client harm?[60]

The Preliminary Statement to the Model Code of Professional Responsibility states that the Code "does not undertake to define standards for civil liability of lawyers for professional conduct." The Scope Section of the Model Rules states: "Violation of a Rule should not give rise to a cause of action nor should it create any presumption that a legal duty has been breached."

Why not? Does this mean that reasonably careful lawyers breach the Rules on occasion? Should the ABA's attempt to confine the Rules to professional discipline be viewed as special pleading or wishful thinking?

The profession's effort to prevent plaintiffs from predicating civil liability on a violation of ethics rules has been only partially successful. Courts generally state that the violation of an ethics rule does not create a civil cause of action or constitute negligence per se.[61] On the other hand, most courts view ethics rules as relevant and admissible evidence and occasionally as creating a rebuttable presumption of negligence.[62] Expert witnesses in malpractice actions rely on the ethics

---

59. 158 Cal.Rptr. at 720.

60. For discussion of this question, see David Luban, Ethics and Malpractice, 12 Miss.Coll.L.Rev. 151 (1991) (arguing that ethical codes should be used as standards for civil liability whenever the alleged misconduct would warrant professional discipline); Charles W. Wolfram, The Code of Professional Responsibility as a Measure of Attorney Liability in Civil Litigation, 30 S.C.L. Rev. 281 (1979) (ethical code "should serve as a measure both of professional discipline and of civil liability sanctions"); and Robert Dalhquist, The Code of Professional Responsibility, 9 Ohio.No.U.L.Rev. 1 (1982) (responding to Wolfram).

61. Miami International Realty Co. v. Paynter, 841 F.2d 348, 352 (10th Cir.1988) ("Colorado courts have not decided how its Code of Professional Responsibility is to be treated as an element of proof in a malpractice case" although it appears clear that under Colorado case law the Code does not create a private cause of action).

62. See Lipton v. Boesky, 110 Mich.App. 589, 313 N.W.2d 163, 166–67 (1981): "The Code of Professional Responsibility is a standard of practice for attorneys which expresses in general terms the standards of professional conduct expected of lawyers in their relationships with the public, the legal system and the profession. Holding a specific client unable to rely on the same standards in his professional relations with his own attorney would be patently unfair. We hold that, as with statutes, a violation of the Code is rebuttable evidence of malpractice."

rules and courts cite them in malpractice decisions.[63]

Limiting Malpractice Liability by Agreement

DR 6–102 of the Model Code prohibits a lawyer from contracting with the client to limit the lawyer's malpractice liability. Model Rule 1.8(h) relaxes the absolute ban by providing that a lawyer may prospectively limit her malpractice liability to the client, but only if permitted under applicable state law *and* the client is independently represented on the limitation. Further, M.R. 1.8(h) prohibits a lawyer from settling a malpractice claim with a client or former client who is not represented by independent counsel unless the lawyer first advises the client in writing that independent representation would be appropriate. There is no similar provision in the Code.

In In re Tallon,[64] the court disciplined a lawyer for having his client sign a general release of all malpractice claims against him without first notifying the client of the nature of her potential claims, withdrawing from the representation and advising her of her right to retain independent representation in the matter.[65] Does *Tallon* mean that it is malpractice for a lawyer not to inform a client of the lawyer's prior malpractice in handling the client's matter?

Malpractice Insurance

The cost of maintaining legal malpractice insurance has risen dramatically in the last ten years. In the late 1970s, the cost of malpractice insurance per lawyer for a million-dollar limit was less than $1,000 per year; by 1990 rates in high-risk states, such as California and New York, were as high as $12,000 per lawyer for the same coverage.[66] More lawyers and firms now forego insurance altogether—"go bare." Informed observers estimate that "20 to 45 percent

---

63. See Charles W. Wolfram, The Code of Professional Responsibility as a Measure of Attorney Liability in Civil Litigation, 30 S.C.L.Rev. 281 (1979); and Wolfram, Modern Legal Ethics § 2.6.1 (1986). Washington bans specific mention of the ethics rules in expert testimony or jury instructions, although the rules may provide the substantive content of both expert testimony and jury instructions. Hizey v. Carpenter, 119 Wash.2d 251, 830 P.2d 646 (1992) (expert opinion may be based on a lawyer's failure to conform to an ethics rule but testimony must address the breach of legal duty and not a supposed breach of the ethics rules).

64. 86 A.D.2d 897, 447 N.Y.S.2d 50 (1982).

65. See also In re Weiblen, 439 N.W.2d 7 (Minn.1989) (lawyer attempted to obtain complete release from liability for any malpractice); Committee on Legal Ethics v. Hazlett, 179 W.Va. 303, 367 S.E.2d 772 (1988) (request for malpractice release as a condition of turning over client's files). Generally see Leonard E. Gross, Contractual Limitations on Attorney Malpractice Liability: An Economic Approach, 75 Kentucky L.J. 793 (1986–87).

66. Debra Moss, Going Bare: Practicing Without Malpractice Insurance, 73 A.B.A.J. 82, 83 (Dec. 1, 1987) ($10,000 per lawyer in some California cities in 1987); Rita H. Jensen, Turmoil in Malpractice, Nat'l L.J., Oct. 15, 1991, p. 3 (1990 premiums ranging from $7,000–$12,000 per lawyer in New York City). In 1990, Attorneys Liability Assurance Society (ALAS), a self-insurance group composed of preferred-risk large law firms, was charging about $3,500 per lawyer for a $10 million per occurrence, $20 million per year policy with a $250,000 deductible per claim. Jensen, supra.

of the lawyers in a given jurisdiction in private practice are without insurance." [67]

Should lawyers be required to carry malpractice insurance as a condition of practice? [68] Oregon, which requires all Oregon-based lawyers to purchase primary malpractice insurance from the state bar, is apparently the only state requiring lawyers to have insurance. [69]

Malpractice insurance comes in two major forms: (1) *Occurrence insurance* covers the lawyer for acts or omissions during the policy term, regardless of when the claim is asserted; and (2) *claims made insurance* covers only claims made during the policy term, regardless of when the act or omission took place. Because occurrence coverage is more expensive, claims made coverage is more common. But cheaper may not be better: If a lawyer retires or becomes a judge and a claims made policy expires, no coverage exists for a later claim involving acts or omissions that occurred during the policy year.

Policies for legal malpractice insurance typically exclude from coverage: (1) claims arising out of criminal acts of the lawyer; (2) claims arising out of "any dishonest, fraudulent or malicious act, error or omission" of the lawyer; and (3) "punitive or exemplary damages, fines, sanctions or penalties." In Perl v. St. Paul Fire & Marine Insurance Co.,[70] the lawyers had failed to disclose to the client that the insurance adjuster with whom the firm negotiated on the client's behalf worked for the law firm as an investigator. The court awarded the client as damages a full refund of the fees she had paid the lawyers. The lawyer's insurance company refused to pay, claiming that the policy's terms excluded such damages and that, if the damages were not excluded, the policy was void as against public policy. The court held that the policy did cover the damages: (1) The exclusion for fraudulent acts did not exclude breach of a fiduciary duty, which is "constructive" not "actual" fraud; and (2) reimbursement of attorney's fees was not the equivalent of "exemplary or punitive damages," which the policy excluded from coverage. However, the court held that a policy that insures lawyers against loss of attorney's fees upon breach of their fiduciary duties is void as against public policy. Despite the latter holding, the court's final decision stated that the policy was not void to the extent that it insured the firm as opposed to the individual lawyer

---

67. Id. (quoting Duke Nordlinger Stern of the ABA Standing Committee on Lawyer's Professional Liability). A 1987 report of the California State Bar concluded that almost one-half of California lawyers are uninsured, either because they cannot get coverage or cannot afford it. Id.

68. See Theodore J. Schneyer, Mandatory Malpractice Insurance for Lawyers in Wisconsin and Elsewhere, 1979 Wis.L.Rev. 1019 (a study on the need for mandatory insurance); and Wolfram, Modern Legal Ethics § 5.6.8 (1986) (arguing that mandatory insurance may not be efficient).

69. See Or.Rev.Stat. § 9.080; and Hass v. Oregon State Bar, 883 F.2d 1453 (9th Cir.1989) (upholding the insurance requirement against antitrust and Commerce Clause challenges).

70. 345 N.W.2d 209 (Minn.1984).

who committed the breach. Which of the court's conflicting messages is the right one?

C. EFFECTIVE ASSISTANCE OF COUNSEL UNDER THE SIXTH AMENDMENT

Introductory Note

The Sixth Amendment to the United States Constitution provides that "[i]n all criminal prosecutions, the accused shall enjoy the right ... to have the Assistance of Counsel for his defense." This provision was a clear departure from 18th century English criminal law, which did not permit a felony defendant to be represented by counsel. Until 1932, however, the Sixth Amendment provided a right to be represented only if the defendant could afford a retained lawyer or the court chose to appoint one. In Powell v. Alabama[1] the Supreme Court required Alabama to appoint counsel for the Scottsboro Boys, who had been sentenced to death in a highly controversial interracial rape case. This holding evolved first into a constitutional requirement that state courts appoint counsel if fundamental unfairness would otherwise result.[2] In 1963 Gideon v. Wainright[3] extended the right to appointed counsel to every felony case in which the defendant could not afford representation. The current rule is that counsel must be appointed in every criminal case, including misdemeanors, in which a prison sentence is imposed,[4] unless the defendant exercises the right of self-representation.[5]

A complicated body of law deals with the stage at which an individual under investigation becomes an "accused" in a "criminal prosecution" who has a right to appointed counsel. In demarcating the critical stages of a criminal prosecution at which there is a right to appointed counsel, the Court has sought to avoid impairing the investigatory activity essential for effective law enforcement. Thus, a defendant has a right to appointed counsel at a preliminary hearing at which probable cause to proceed is determined,[6] at a post-arrest lineup,[7] at

1. 287 U.S. 45, 60 (1932) (failure to appoint defense counsel for the Scottsboro Boys, who were charged and convicted of raping a white woman, was fundamentally unfair and a violation of due process). See Dan T. Carter, Scottsboro: A Tragedy of the American South (1979).

2. Betts v. Brady, 316 U.S. 455, 466 (1942). Johnson v. Zerbst, 304 U.S. 458 (1938), required the appointment of defense counsel in federal felony trials. Many states gradually adopted the same position.

3. 372 U.S. 335 (1963). See Anthony Lewis, Gideon's Trumpet (1964) for a detailed history of the case.

4. Scott v. Illinois, 440 U.S. 367 (1979) (appointed counsel not required in a misdemeanor case in which imprisonment might have been, but was not, imposed). See Lawrence Herman and Charles A. Thompson, Scott v. Illinois and the Right to Counsel: A Decision in Search of a Doctrine?, 17 Am.Crim.L.Rev. 71 (1979–80).

5. Faretta v. California, 422 U.S. 806 (1975).

6. Coleman v. Alabama, 399 U.S. 1 (1970).

7. United States v. Wade, 388 U.S. 218 (1967).

trial and sentencing, and through a first appeal;[8] but the right does not extend to discretionary appeals, habeas corpus proceedings, or other post-conviction remedies.[9] Some showing of indigency must be made for a defendant to qualify for appointed counsel. Some jurisdictions use a court-appointment system in which the court appoints a defense lawyer from a roster of eligible lawyers. Others employ a public defender system.

When a Sixth Amendment right to counsel attaches, what level of competence is required? In McMann v. Richardson,[10] the Court required that defense counsel's assistance fall "within the range of competence demanded of attorneys in criminal cases."[11] Older cases requiring a showing that defense counsel's failings constituted a "farce and mockery of justice" were gradually replaced by various tests turning on whether the lawyer's conduct was reasonable under the circumstances.[12] In the *Strickland* case, reproduced below, the Court addressed for the first time the specifics of ineffective assistance under the Sixth Amendment.[13]

1. Ineffective Assistance: The Constitutional Standard

[handwritten: Duty to Investigate]

STRICKLAND v. WASHINGTON

[handwritten: Criminal Case]

Supreme Court of the United States, 1984.
466 U.S. 668, 104 S.Ct. 2052, 80 L.Ed.2d 674.

JUSTICE O'CONNOR delivered the opinion of the Court.

[handwritten: Issue] This case requires us to consider the proper standards for judging a criminal defendant's contention that the Constitution requires a conviction or death sentence to be set aside because counsel's assistance at the trial or sentencing was ineffective.

8. Evitts v. Lucey, 469 U.S. 387 (1985).

9. Pennsylvania v. Finley, 481 U.S. 551 (1987) (state post-conviction remedy); Ross v. Moffitt, 417 U.S. 600 (1974) (discretionary further appeal); Williams v. Missouri, 640 F.2d 140, 144 (8th Cir.1981) (federal habeas corpus); United States v. Degand, 614 F.2d 176, 179 (8th Cir.1980) (federal post-conviction attack). But see Anti–Drug Abuse Act of 1988, Pub.L. 100–690, 102 Stat. 4181 (providing for appointed counsel in federal habeas corpus actions involving challenges to the death penalty); many states have similar laws for death penalty challenges, but not all. See Murray v. Giarratano, 492 U.S. 1 (1989) (describing and upholding as constitutional Virginia's system in which death row inmates seeking habeas review are provided law books not lawyers).

10. 397 U.S. 759 (1970) (defendant who had pleaded guilty after giving an allegedly coerced confession could not attack his conviction unless his lawyer's advice concerning the confession constituted ineffective assistance of counsel).

11. 397 U.S. at 770–71.

12. See Trapnell v. United States, 725 F.2d 149, 151–155 (2d Cir.1983) (abandoning the "farce and mockery" rule and summarizing the developments in other federal circuits). For an example of a pre-*Strickland* effort to develop objective standards, see Judge David Bazelon's article, The Realities of *Gideon* and *Argersinger*, 64 Geo.L.J. 811, 837–838 (1976).

13. See Vivian O. Berger, The Supreme Court and Defense Counsel: Old Roads, New Paths—A Dead End?, 86 Colum.L.Rev. 9 (1986), for a thoughtful and thorough review of the Supreme Court cases on ineffective assistance of counsel.

rejected
Counsel's advice
3 times

I

A

During a 10–day period in September 1976, respondent [David Washington] planned and committed three groups of crimes, which included three brutal stabbing murders, torture, kidnaping, severe *Crimes* assaults, attempted murders, attempted extortion, and theft. After his two accomplices were arrested, respondent surrendered to police and voluntarily gave a lengthy statement confessing to the third of the *Confessed to 3rd murder* criminal episodes. The State of Florida indicted respondent for kidnaping and murder and appointed an experienced criminal lawyer [William R. Tunkey of Miami] to represent him.

Counsel actively pursued pretrial motions and discovery. He cut his efforts short, however, and he experienced a sense of hopelessness about the case, when he learned that, against his specific advice, *Later confessed to other 2* respondent had also confessed to the first two murders. By the date set for trial, respondent was subject to indictment for three counts of first-degree murder and multiple counts of robbery, kidnaping for ransom, breaking and entering and assault, attempted murder, and conspiracy to commit robbery. Respondent waived his right to a jury trial, again acting against counsel's advice, and pleaded guilty to all charges, including the three capital murder charges.

In the plea colloquy, respondent told the trial judge that, although he had committed a string of burglaries, he had no significant prior criminal record and that at the time of his criminal spree he was under extreme stress caused by his inability to support his family.... He also stated, however, that he accepted responsibility for the crimes.... The trial judge told respondent that he had "a great deal of respect for people who are willing to step forward and admit their responsibility" but that he was making no statement at all about his likely sentencing decision.

Counsel advised respondent to invoke his right under Florida law to an advisory jury at his capital sentencing hearing. Respondent rejected the advice and waived the right. He chose instead to be sentenced by the trial judge without a jury recommendation.

In preparing for the sentencing hearing, counsel spoke with respondent about his background. He also spoke on the telephone with respondent's wife and mother, though he did not follow up on the one *Counsel Did not* unsuccessful effort to meet with them. He did not otherwise seek out *① meet c FAm* character witnesses for respondent.... Nor did he request a psychiatric examination, since his conversations with his client gave no indication that respondent had psychological problems.... *② seek character witnesses ③ Ask for psych X Am.*

Counsel decided not to present and hence not to look further for evidence concerning respondent's character and emotional state. That decision reflected trial counsel's sense of hopelessness about overcoming the evidentiary effect of respondent's confessions to the gruesome crimes. It also reflected the judgment that it was advisable to rely on the plea colloquy for evidence about respondent's background and about his claim of emotional stress: the plea colloquy communicated sufficient information about these subjects, and by forgoing the opportunity to present new evidence on these subjects, counsel prevented the State from cross-examining respondent on his claim and from putting on psychiatric evidence of its own. . . .

Counsel also excluded from the sentencing hearing other evidence he thought was potentially damaging. He successfully moved to exclude respondent's "rap sheet." . . . Because he judged that a presentence report might prove more detrimental than helpful, as it would have included respondent's criminal history and thereby would have undermined the claim of no significant history of criminal activity, he did not request that one be prepared. . . .

At the sentencing hearing, counsel's strategy was based primarily on the trial judge's remarks at the plea colloquy as well as on his reputation as a sentencing judge who thought it important for a convicted defendant to own up to his crime. Counsel argued that respondent's remorse and acceptance of responsibility justified sparing him from the death penalty. . . . Counsel also argued that respondent had no history of criminal activity and that respondent committed the crimes under extreme mental or emotional disturbance, thus coming within the statutory list of mitigating circumstances. He further argued that respondent should be spared death because he had surrendered, confessed, and offered to testify against a codefendant and because respondent was fundamentally a good person who had briefly gone badly wrong in extremely stressful circumstances. The State put on evidence and witnesses largely for the purpose of describing the details of the crimes. Counsel did not cross-examine the medical experts who testified about the manner of death of respondent's victims.

The trial judge found several aggravating circumstances with respect to each of the three murders. He found that all three murders were especially heinous, atrocious, and cruel, all involving repeated stabbings. All three murders were committed in the course of at least one other dangerous and violent felony, and since all involved robbery, the murders were for pecuniary gain. All three murders were committed to avoid arrest for the accompanying crimes and to hinder law enforcement. In the course of one of the murders, respondent knowingly subjected numerous persons to a grave risk of death by deliberately stabbing and shooting the murder victim's sisters-in-law, who sustained severe—in one case, ultimately fatal—injuries.

With respect to mitigating circumstances, the trial judge made the same findings for all three capital murders. First, although there was no admitted evidence of prior convictions, respondent had stated that he had engaged in a course of stealing. In any case, even if respondent had no significant history of criminal activity, the aggravating circumstances "would still clearly far outweigh" that mitigating factor. Second, the judge found that, during all three crimes, respondent was not suffering from extreme mental or emotional disturbance and could appreciate the criminality of his acts. Third, none of the victims was a participant in, or consented to, respondent's conduct. Fourth, respondent's participation in the crimes was neither minor nor the result of duress or domination by an accomplice. Finally, respondent's age (26) could not be considered a factor in mitigation, especially when viewed in light of respondent's planning of the crimes and disposition of the proceeds of the various accompanying thefts.

In short, the trial judge found numerous aggravating circumstances and no (or a single comparatively insignificant) mitigating circumstance. With respect to each of the three convictions for capital murder, the trial judge concluded: "A careful consideration of all matters presented to the court impels the conclusion that there are insufficient mitigating circumstances ... to outweigh the aggravating circumstances." See Washington v. State, 362 So.2d 658, 663–664 (Fla.1978), (quoting trial court findings), cert. denied, 441 U.S. 937 (1979). He therefore sentenced respondent to death on each of the three counts of murder and to prison terms for the other crimes. The Florida Supreme Court upheld the convictions and sentences on direct appeal.   *Holding* [margin note]

B   *1st Appeal* [margin note]

Respondent subsequently sought collateral relief in state court on numerous grounds, among them that counsel had rendered ineffective assistance at the sentencing proceeding. Respondent challenged counsel's assistance in six respects. He asserted that counsel was ineffective because he failed to move for a continuance to prepare for sentencing, to request a psychiatric report, to investigate and present character witnesses, to seek a presentence investigation report, to present meaningful arguments to the sentencing judge, and to investigate the medical examiner's reports or cross-examine the medical experts. In support of the claim, respondent submitted 14 affidavits from friends, neighbors, and relatives stating that they would have testified if asked to do so. He also submitted one psychiatric report and one psychological report stating that respondent, though not under the influence of extreme mental or emotional disturbance, was "chronically frustrated and depressed because of his economic dilemma" at the time of his crimes....

The trial court denied relief without an evidentiary hearing, finding that the record evidence conclusively showed that the ineffectiveness claim was meritless.... Four of the assertedly prejudicial errors required little discussion. [The trial court dealt with two of the asserted errors at greater length: the failure to investigate and present character witnesses. As to both of these grounds, the court concluded under] the standard for ineffectiveness claims articulated by the Florida Supreme Court in Knight v. State, 394 So.2d 997 (1981), that   *Denied* [margin note] respondent had not shown that counsel's assistance reflected any substantial and serious deficiency measurably below that of competent counsel that was likely to have affected the outcome of the sentencing proceeding. The court specifically found: "[A]s a matter of law, the record affirmatively demonstrates beyond any doubt that even if [counsel] had done each of the ... things [that respondent alleged counsel had failed to do] at the time of sentencing, there is not even the remotest chance that the outcome would have been any different. The plain fact is that the aggravating circumstances proved in this case were completely *overwhelming ....*"

. . .

C

Habeas Corpus

Respondent next filed a petition for a writ of habeas corpus in the United States District Court for the Southern District of Florida....

Dist. Ct.

... On the legal issue of ineffectiveness, the District Court concluded that, although trial counsel made errors in judgment in failing to investigate nonstatutory mitigating evidence further than he did, no prejudice to respondent's sentence resulted from any such error in judgment....

Ct. App

On appeal, a panel of the United States Court of Appeals for the Fifth Circuit affirmed in part, vacated in part, and remanded with instructions to apply to the particular facts the framework for analyzing ineffectiveness claims that it developed in its opinion.... The panel decision was itself vacated when ... the Eleventh Circuit ... decided to rehear the case en banc. The full Court of Appeals developed its own framework for analyzing ineffective assistance claims and reversed the judgment of the District Court and remanded the case for new factfinding under the newly announced standards.

. . .

Ct. of Appeals Framework For Analysis of Ineffective Assistance of Asms.

Turning to the merits, the Court of Appeals stated that the Sixth Amendment right to assistance of counsel accorded criminal defendants a right to "counsel reasonably likely to render and rendering reasonably effective assistance given the totality of the circumstances." The court remarked in passing that no special standard applies in capital cases such as the one before it: the punishment that a defendant faces is merely one of the circumstances to be considered in determining whether counsel was reasonably effective....

Totality of the Circumstances

[W]e granted certiorari to consider the standards by which to judge a contention that the Constitution requires that a criminal judgment be overturned because of the actual ineffective assistance of counsel.

II

S. Ct.

In a long line of cases ... this Court has recognized that the Sixth Amendment right to counsel exists, and is needed, in order to protect the fundamental right to a fair trial....

. . .

For that reason, the Court has recognized that "the right to counsel is the right to the effective assistance of counsel." ...

The Court has not elaborated on the meaning of the constitutional requirement of effective assistance in cases—presenting claims of "actual ineffectiveness." In giving meaning to the requirement, however, we must take its purpose—to ensure a fair trial—as the guide. The benchmark for judging any claim of ineffectiveness must be whether counsel's conduct so undermined the proper functioning of the adversarial process that the trial cannot be relied on as having produced a just result.

The same principle applies to a capital sentencing proceeding such as that provided by Florida law....

III

A convicted defendant's claim that counsel's assistance was so defective as to require reversal of a conviction or death sentence has two components. First, the defendant must show that counsel's performance was deficient. This requires showing that counsel made errors so serious that counsel was not functioning as the "counsel" guaranteed the defendant by the Sixth Amendment. Second, the defendant must show that the deficient performance prejudiced the defense. This requires showing that counsel's errors were so serious as to deprive the defendant of a fair trial, a trial whose result is reliable. Unless a defendant makes both showings, it cannot be said that the conviction or death sentence resulted from a breakdown in the adversary process that renders the result unreliable.

A

As all the Federal Courts of Appeals have now held, the proper standard for attorney performance is that of reasonably effective assistance.... The Court indirectly recognized as much when it stated in McMann v. Richardson, 397 U.S. [759], 770, 771, that a guilty plea cannot be attacked as based on inadequate legal advice unless counsel was not "a reasonably competent attorney" and the advice was not "within the range of competence demanded of attorneys in criminal cases." See also Cuyler v. Sullivan, 446 U.S. [335], 344. When a convicted defendant complains of the ineffectiveness of counsel's assistance, the defendant must show that counsel's representation fell below an objective standard of reasonableness.

More specific guidelines are not appropriate. The Sixth Amendment refers simply to "counsel," not specifying particular requirements of effective assistance. It relies instead on the legal profession's maintenance of standards sufficient to justify the law's presumption that counsel will fulfill the role in the adversary process that the Amendment envisions.... The proper measure of attorney performance remains simply reasonableness under prevailing professional norms.

Duties in representation of criminal D

Representation of a criminal defendant entails certain basic duties. Counsel's function is to assist the defendant, and hence counsel owes the client a duty of loyalty, a duty to avoid conflicts of interest.... From counsel's function as assistant to the defendant derives the overarching duty to advocate the defendant's cause and the more particular duties to consult with the defendant on important decisions and to keep the defendant informed of important developments in the course of the prosecution. Counsel also has a duty to bring to bear such skill and knowledge as will render the trial a reliable adversarial testing process....

These basic duties neither exhaustively define the obligations of counsel nor form a checklist for judicial evaluation of attorney performance. In any case presenting an ineffectiveness claim, the performance inquiry must be whether counsel's assistance was reasonable considering all the circumstances. Prevailing norms of practice as reflected in American Bar Association standards and the like ... are guides to determining what is reasonable, but they are only guides. No particular set of detailed rules for counsel's conduct can satisfactorily take account of the variety of circumstances faced by defense counsel or the range of legitimate decisions regarding how best to represent a criminal defendant. Any such set of rules would interfere with the constitutionally protected independence of counsel and restrict the wide latitude counsel must have in making tactical decisions.... Indeed, the existence of detailed guidelines for representation could distract counsel from the overriding mission of vigorous advocacy of the defendant's cause. Moreover, the purpose of the effective assistance guarantee of the Sixth Amendment is not to improve the quality of legal representation, although that is a goal of considerable importance to the legal system. The purpose is simply to ensure that criminal defendants receive a fair trial.

Judicial scrutiny of counsel's performance must be highly deferential. It is all too tempting for a defendant to second-guess counsel's assistance after conviction or adverse sentence, and it is all too easy for a court, examining counsel's defense after it has proved unsuccessful, to conclude that a particular act or omission of counsel was unreasonable.... A fair assessment of attorney performance requires that every effort be made to eliminate the distorting effects of hindsight, to reconstruct the circumstances of counsel's challenged conduct, and to evaluate the conduct from counsel's perspective at the time. Because of the difficulties inherent in making the evaluation, a court must indulge a strong presumption that counsel's conduct falls within the wide range of reasonable professional assistance; that is, the defendant must overcome the presumption that, under the circumstances, the challenged action "might be considered sound trial strategy." See Michel v. Louisiana, 350 U.S. [91], 101. There are countless ways to provide effective assistance in any given case. Even the best criminal defense attorneys would not defend a particular client in the same way....

The availability of intrusive post-trial inquiry into attorney performance or of detailed guidelines for its evaluation would encourage the proliferation of ineffectiveness challenges. Criminal trials resolved unfavorably to the defendant would increasingly come to be followed by a second trial, this one of counsel's unsuccessful defense. Counsel's performance and even willingness to serve could be adversely affected. Intensive scrutiny of counsel and rigid requirements for acceptable assistance could dampen the ardor and impair the independence of defense counsel, discourage the acceptance of assigned cases, and undermine the trust between attorney and client.

Thus, a court deciding an actual ineffectiveness claim must judge the reasonableness of counsel's challenged conduct on the facts of the particular case, viewed as of the time of counsel's conduct. A convicted defendant making a claim of ineffective assistance must identify the acts or omissions of counsel that are alleged not to have been the result of reasonable professional judgment. The court must then determine whether, in light of all the circumstances, the identified acts or omissions were outside the wide range of professionally competent assistance. In making that determination, the court should keep in mind that counsel's function, as elaborated in prevailing professional norms, is to make the adversarial testing process work in the particular case. At the same time, the court should recognize that counsel is strongly presumed to have rendered adequate assistance and made all significant decisions in the exercise of reasonable professional judgment.

These standards require no special amplification in order to define counsel's duty to investigate, the duty at issue in this case. As the Court of Appeals concluded, strategic choices made after thorough investigation of law and facts relevant to plausible options are virtually unchallengeable; and strategic choices made after less than complete investigation are reasonable precisely to the extent that reasonable professional judgments support the limitations on investigation. In other words, counsel has a duty to make reasonable investigations or to make a reasonable decision that makes particular investigations unnecessary. In any ineffectiveness case, a particular decision not to investigate must be directly assessed for reasonableness in all the circumstances, applying a heavy measure of deference to counsel's judgments.

The reasonableness of counsel's actions may be determined or substantially influenced by the defendant's own statements or actions. Counsel's actions are usually based, quite properly, on informed strategic choices made by the defendant and on information supplied by the defendant. In particular, what investigation decisions are reasonable depends critically on such information. For example, when the facts that support a certain potential line of defense are generally known to counsel because of what the defendant has said, the need for further investigation may be considerably diminished or eliminated altogether. And when a defendant has given counsel reason to believe that pursuing certain investigations would be fruitless or even harmful, counsel's failure to pursue those investigations may not later be challenged as unreasonable. In short, inquiry into counsel's conversations with the defendant may be critical to a proper assessment of counsel's investigation decisions, just as it may be critical to a proper assessment of counsel's other litigation decisions....

B

Atty Error must have effect on Judgment

An error by counsel, even if professionally unreasonable, does not warrant setting aside the judgment of a criminal proceeding if the error had no effect on the judgment.... The purpose of the Sixth Amendment guarantee of counsel is to ensure that a defendant has the assistance necessary to justify reliance on the outcome of the proceeding. Accordingly, any deficiencies in counsel's performance must be prejudicial to the defense in order to constitute ineffective assistance under the Constitution.

e.g. 3 prejudice

In certain Sixth Amendment contexts, prejudice is presumed. Actual or constructive denial of the assistance of counsel altogether is legally presumed to result in prejudice. So are various kinds of state interference with counsel's assistance.... Prejudice in these circumstances is so likely that case-by-case inquiry into prejudice is not worth the cost.... Moreover, such circumstances involve impairments of the Sixth Amendment right that are easy to identify and, for that reason and because the prosecution is directly responsible, easy for the government to prevent.

One type of actual ineffectiveness claim warrants a similar, though more limited, presumption of prejudice. In Cuyler v. Sullivan, 446 U.S., at 345–350, the Court held that prejudice is presumed when counsel is burdened by an actual conflict of interest. In those circumstances, counsel breaches the duty of loyalty, perhaps the most basic of counsel's duties. Moreover, it is difficult to measure the precise effect on the defense of representation corrupted by conflicting interests. Given the obligation of counsel to avoid conflicts of interest and the ability of trial courts to make early inquiry in certain situations likely to give rise to conflicts, see, e.g., Fed.Rule Crim.Proc. 44(c), it is reasonable for the criminal justice system to maintain a fairly rigid rule of presumed prejudice for conflicts of interest. Even so, the rule is not quite the *per se* rule of prejudice that exists for the Sixth Amendment claims mentioned above. Prejudice is presumed only if the defendant demonstrates that counsel "actively represented conflicting interests" and that "an actual conflict of interest adversely affected his lawyer's performance." Cuyler v. Sullivan, *supra*, 446 U.S., at 350, 348.

Conflict of interest claims aside, actual ineffectiveness claims alleging a deficiency in attorney performance are subject to a general requirement that the defendant affirmatively prove prejudice. The government is not responsible for, and hence not able to prevent, attorney errors that will result in reversal of a conviction or sentence. Attorney errors come in an infinite variety and are as likely to be utterly harmless in a particular case as they are to be prejudicial. They cannot be classified according to likelihood of causing prejudice.

Nor can they be defined with sufficient precision to inform defense attorneys correctly just what conduct to avoid. Representation is an art, and an act or omission that is unprofessional in one case may be sound or even brilliant in another. Even if a defendant shows that particular errors of counsel were unreasonable, therefore, the defendant must show that they actually had an adverse effect on the defense.

It is not enough for the defendant to show that the errors had some conceivable effect on the outcome of the proceeding. Virtually every act or omission of counsel would meet that test, ... and not every error that conceivably could have influenced the outcome undermines the reliability of the result of the proceeding. Respondent suggests requiring a showing that the errors "impaired the presentation of the defense." That standard, however, provides no workable principle. Since any error, if it is indeed an error, "impairs" the presentation of the defense, the proposed standard is inadequate because it provides no way of deciding what impairments are sufficiently serious to warrant setting aside the outcome of the proceeding.

On the other hand, we believe that a defendant need not show that counsel's deficient conduct more likely than not altered the outcome in the case. This outcome-determinative standard has several strengths. It defines the relevant inquiry in a way familiar to courts, though the inquiry, as is inevitable, is anything but precise. The standard also reflects the profound importance of finality in criminal proceedings. Moreover, it comports with the widely used standard for assessing motions for new trial based on newly discovered evidence.... Nevertheless, the standard is not quite appropriate.

... The high standard for newly discovered evidence claims presupposes that all the essential elements of a presumptively accurate and fair proceeding were present in the proceeding whose result is challenged.... An ineffective assistance claim asserts the absence of one of the crucial assurances that the result of the proceeding is reliable, so finality concerns are somewhat weaker and the appropriate standard of prejudice should be somewhat lower. The result of a proceeding can be rendered unreliable, and hence the proceeding itself unfair, even if the errors of counsel cannot be shown by a preponderance of the evidence to have determined the outcome.

Accordingly, the appropriate test for prejudice finds its roots in the test for materiality of exculpatory information not disclosed to the defense by the prosecution, ... and in the test for materiality of testimony made unavailable to the defense by Government deportation of a witness.... The defendant must show that there is a reasonable probability that, but for counsel's unprofessional errors, the result of the proceeding would have been different. A reasonable probability is a probability sufficient to undermine confidence in the outcome. *test for prejudice*

In making the determination whether the specified errors resulted in the required prejudice, a court should presume, absent challenge to the judgment on grounds of evidentiary insufficiency, that the judge or jury acted according to law. An assessment of the likelihood of a result more favorable to the defendant must exclude the possibility of arbitrariness, whimsy, caprice, "nullification," and the like. A defendant has no entitlement to the luck of a lawless decisionmaker, even if a lawless decision cannot be reviewed. The assessment of prejudice should proceed on the assumption that the decisionmaker is reasonably, conscientiously, and impartially applying the standards that govern the decision. It should not depend on the idiosyncracies of the particular decisionmaker, such as unusual propensities toward harshness or leniency. Although these factors may actually have entered into counsel's selection of strategies and, to that limited extent, may thus affect the performance inquiry, they are irrelevant to the prejudice inquiry. Thus, evidence about the actual process of decision, if not part of the record of the proceeding under review, and evidence about, for example, a particular judge's sentencing practices, should not be considered in the prejudice determination.

The governing legal standard plays a critical role in defining the question to be asked in assessing the prejudice from counsel's errors. When a defendant challenges a conviction, the question is whether there is a reasonable probability that, absent the errors, the factfinder would have had a reasonable doubt respecting guilt. When a defendant challenges a death sentence such as the one at issue in this case, the question is whether there is a reasonable probability that, absent the errors, the sentencer—including an appellate court, to the extent it independently reweighs the evidence—would have concluded that the balance of aggravating and mitigating circumstances did not warrant death.

In making this determination, a court hearing an ineffectiveness claim must consider the totality of the evidence before the judge or jury. Some of the factual findings will have been unaffected by the errors, and factual findings that were affected will have been affected in different ways. Some errors will have had a pervasive effect on the inferences to be drawn from the evidence, altering the entire evidentiary picture, and some will have had an isolated, trivial effect. Moreover, a verdict or conclusion only weakly supported by the record is more likely to have been affected by errors than one with overwhelming record support. Taking the unaffected findings as a given, and taking due account of the effect of the errors on the remaining findings, a court making the prejudice inquiry must ask if the defendant has met the burden of showing that the decision reached would reasonably likely have been different absent the errors.

IV

A number of practical considerations are important for the application of the standards we have outlined. Most important, in adjudicating a claim of actual ineffectiveness of counsel, a court should keep in mind that the principles we have stated do not establish mechanical rules. Although those principles should guide the process of decision, the ultimate focus of inquiry must be on the fundamental fairness of the proceeding whose result is being challenged. In every case the court should be concerned with whether, despite the strong presumption of reliability, the result of the particular proceeding is unreliable because of a breakdown in the adversarial process that our system counts on to produce just results.

To the extent that this has already been the guiding inquiry in the lower courts, the standards articulated today do not require reconsideration of ineffectiveness claims rejected under different standards.... In particular, the minor differences in the lower courts' precise formulations of the performance standard are insignificant: the different formulations are mere variations of the overarching reasonableness standard. With regard to the prejudice inquiry, only the strict outcome-determinative test, among the standards articulated in the lower courts, imposes a heavier burden on defendants than the tests laid down today. The difference, however, should alter the merit of an ineffectiveness claim only in the rarest case.

Although we have discussed the performance component of an ineffectiveness claim prior to the prejudice component, there is no reason for a court deciding an ineffective assistance claim to approach the inquiry in the same order or even to address both components of the inquiry if the defendant makes an insufficient showing on one. In particular, a court need not determine whether counsel's performance was deficient before examining the prejudice suffered by the defendant as a result of the alleged deficiencies. The object of an ineffectiveness claim is not to grade counsel's performance. If it is easier to dispose of an ineffectiveness claim on the ground of lack of sufficient prejudice, which we expect will often be so, that course should be followed. Courts should strive to ensure that ineffectiveness claims not become so burdensome to defense counsel that the entire criminal justice system suffers as a result.

The principles governing ineffectiveness claims should apply in federal collateral proceedings as they do on direct appeal or in motions for a new trial.... Since fundamental fairness is the central concern of the writ of habeas corpus, ... no special standards ought to apply to ineffectiveness claims made in habeas proceedings.

Finally, in a federal habeas challenge to a state criminal judgment, a state court conclusion that counsel rendered effective assistance is not a finding of fact binding on the federal court to the extent stated by 28 U.S.C. § 2254(d).... Although state court findings of fact made in the course of deciding an ineffectiveness claim are subject to the deference requirement of § 2254(d), and although district court findings are subject to the clearly erroneous standard of Federal Rule of Civil Procedure 52(a), both the performance and prejudice components of the ineffectiveness inquiry are mixed questions of law and fact.

V

Analysis

Having articulated general standards for judging ineffectiveness claims, we think it useful to apply those standards to the facts of this case in order to illustrate the meaning of the general principles. The record makes it possible to do so. There are no conflicts between the state and federal courts over findings of fact, and the principles we have articulated are sufficiently close to the principles applied both in the Florida courts and in the District Court that it is clear that the factfinding was not affected by erroneous legal principles. . . .

Application of the governing principles is not difficult in this case. The facts as described above, make clear that the conduct of respondent's counsel at and before respondent's sentencing proceeding cannot be found unreasonable. They also make clear that, even assuming the challenged conduct of counsel was unreasonable, respondent suffered insufficient prejudice to warrant setting aside his death sentence.

(1) Performance

With respect to the performance component, the record shows that respondent's counsel made a strategic choice to argue for the extreme emotional distress mitigating circumstance and to rely as fully as possible on respondent's acceptance of responsibility for his crimes. Although counsel understandably felt hopeless about respondent's prospects, nothing in the record indicates, as one possible reading of the District Court's opinion suggests, that counsel's sense of hopelessness distorted his professional judgment. Counsel's strategy choice was well within the range of professionally reasonable judgments, and the decision not to seek more character or psychological evidence than was already in hand was likewise reasonable.

The trial judge's views on the importance of owning up to one's crimes were well known to counsel. The aggravating circumstances were utterly overwhelming. Trial counsel could reasonably surmise from his conversations with respondent that character and psychological evidence would be of little help. Respondent had already been able to mention at the plea colloquy the substance of what there was to know about his financial and emotional troubles. Restricting testimony on respondent's character to what had come in at the plea colloquy ensured that contrary character and psychological evidence and respondent's criminal history, which counsel had successfully moved to exclude, would not come in. On these facts, there can be little question, even without application of the presumption of adequate performance, that trial counsel's defense, though unsuccessful, was the result of reasonable professional judgment.

(2) Prejudice

With respect to the prejudice component, the lack of merit of respondent's claim is even more stark. The evidence that respondent says his trial counsel should have offered at the sentencing hearing would barely have altered the sentencing profile presented to the sentencing judge. As the state courts and District Court found, at most this evidence shows that numerous people who knew respondent thought he was generally a good person and that a psychiatrist and a psychologist believed he was under considerable emotional stress that did not rise to the level of extreme disturbance. Given the overwhelm- *Holding* ing aggravating factors, there is no reasonable probability that the omitted evidence would have changed the conclusion that the aggravating circumstances outweighed the mitigating circumstances and, hence, the sentence imposed. Indeed, admission of the evidence respondent now offers might even have been harmful to his case: his "rap sheet" would probably have been admitted into evidence, and the psychological reports would have directly contradicted respondent's claim that the mitigating circumstance of extreme emotional disturbance applied to his case.

Our conclusions on both the prejudice and performance components of the ineffectiveness inquiry do not depend on the trial judge's testimony at the District Court hearing. We therefore need not consider the general admissibility of that testimony, although, that testimony is irrelevant to the prejudice inquiry. Moreover, the prejudice question is resolvable, and hence the ineffectiveness claim can be rejected, without regard to the evidence presented at the District Court hearing. The state courts properly concluded that the ineffectiveness claim was meritless without holding an evidentiary hearing.

Failure to make the required showing of either deficient performance or sufficient prejudice defeats the ineffectiveness claim. Here there is a double failure. More generally, respondent has made no showing that the justice of his sentence was rendered unreliable by a breakdown in the adversary process caused by deficiencies in counsel's assistance. Respondent's sentencing proceeding was not fundamentally unfair.

We conclude, therefore, that the District Court properly declined to issue a writ of habeas corpus. The judgment of the Court of Appeals is accordingly

Reversed.[14]

[Justice Brennan joined in the Court's opinion, but dissented from the judgment on the ground that capital punishment was violative of the Eighth Amendment. *Cruel + unusual*

[Justice Marshall, dissenting, first attacked the refusal of the Court to adopt more specific standards to govern the performance of defense counsel. He argued that to tell the lower courts that counsel in a criminal case must act like " 'a reasonably competent attorney' is to tell them nothing" and that the Court should not have disapproved of the admirable job that lower courts had been doing in creating workable objective standards of reasonableness. Second, he expressed strong disagreement with the "prejudice" standard adopted by the Court. He argued that prejudice could not be determined after the fact and should be presumed if incompetence of defense counsel had been established. A more fundamental problem with the prejudice standard, he argued,

14. [Editors' note:] David Washington was executed in Florida on July 13, 1984.

was that it treated the Sixth Amendment's guarantee of effective assistance of counsel as if its only purpose was to ensure that the innocent were not convicted:]

> ... In my view, the guarantee also functions to ensure that convictions are obtained only through fundamentally fair procedures. The majority contends that the Sixth Amendment is not violated when a manifestly guilty defendant is convicted after a trial in which he was represented by a manifestly ineffective attorney. I cannot agree. Every defendant is entitled to a trial in which his interests are vigorously and conscientiously advocated by an able lawyer. A proceeding in which the defendant does not receive meaningful assistance in meeting the forces of the State does not, in my opinion, constitute due process. [466 U.S. at 711.]

[Justice Marshall also criticized the majority's repeated emphasis on the heavy presumption in favor of competence that the lower courts were admonished to apply. Finally, he argued that a separate and higher standard for effective assistance of counsel should be applied in capital cases. Applying these considerations to the facts of the case, Justice Marshall concluded:]

> If counsel had investigated the availability of mitigating evidence, he might well have decided to present some such material at the hearing. If he had done so, there is a significant chance that respondent would have been given a life sentence. In my view, those possibilities, conjoined with the unreasonableness of counsel's failure to investigate, are more than sufficient to establish a violation of the Sixth Amendment and to entitle respondent to a new sentencing proceeding. [466 U.S. at 719.]

Deficient Professional Performance

What did Washington's defense lawyer do or not do that was said to constitute ineffective assistance? Would his conduct have subjected him to professional discipline under the Model Rules or the Model Code? What is the relevance of ABA Standards Relating to the Administration of Criminal Justice, especially Standard 4–4.1 dealing with the duty to investigate, to professional discipline or the constitutional claim of ineffective assistance of counsel? [15] Would Washington's lawyer have been liable to Washington for malpractice?

Professor William Genego argues that Washington's lawyer could not have made a "tactical" or "strategic" decision not to use psychiatric evidence or character evidence when he had made no inquiry as to

---

15. The Standards, first approved in 1968 and revised in 1979 and 1991, are reproduced in Thomas D. Morgan and Ronald D. Rotunda, 1993 Selected Standards on Professional Responsibility (1993).

what such evidence might show.[16]   A lawyer cannot know whether evidence will be helpful until the lawyer obtains it; if the evidence is unfavorable or its introduction will permit the prosecutor to pursue harmful paths otherwise unavailable, a tactical decision not to offer the evidence can then be made.   Pursuing any available evidence, Genego argues, should be required, especially when someone's life is at stake, as in Washington's sentencing hearing.   Should the courts hold counsel to a higher standard in death penalty cases? [17]   The ABA has proposed special standards for capital cases.[18]

The Court's deference to professional standards, combined with the repeated assertion of a strong presumption of competency, suggests that the Court believes substandard performance by defense counsel is extremely rare.   Is this confidence misplaced?   Professor Vivian Berger argues that it flies in the face of evidence that "counsel inadequacy poses a very severe, if difficult to measure, problem." [19]   She cites a number of factors that suggest a "grave" problem: (1) the observations of informed observers (recall the statements of former Chief Justice Burger on p. 169 supra); (2) studies of the prevalent conditions under which defense services are made available that report "the crushing caseloads of public defenders and the cut-rate fees for appointed counsel," circumstances that "stamp a 'stigma of inferiority' on the in forma pauperis bar" and "promote lackluster performance by discouraging careful investigation"; [20] and (3) the modern revolution in constitutional criminal procedure that has made criminal defense a much more complex and demanding field of practice.   Perhaps a familiarity with these conditions has led the courts' grappling with ineffective assistance issues to take the approach of "legitimating 'necessary evils' ".[21]

16. William J. Genego, The Future of Effective Assistance of Counsel: Performance Standards and Competent Representation, 22 Amer.Crim.L.Rev. 181, 196–97 (1984) (arguing that a psychiatric examination of Washington and exploration of character evidence might have supported mitigating factors under the Florida death penalty statute or, at a minimum, permitted Washington's claim of mental stress to be "presented in a more favorable light").

17. See State v. Davis, 116 N.J. 341, 561 A.2d 1082, 1089 (1989) (refusing to interpret the state constitution as requiring a more stringent test of competency in death penalty cases than the test in *Strickland*). Arguments for a higher standard are developed by Margaret J. Radin, Cruel Punishment and Respect for Persons: Super Due Process for Death, 53 S.Cal.L.Rev. 1143 (1980); and Charles L. Black, Capital Punishment: The Inevitability of Caprice and Mistake (2d ed. 1981).

18. ABA, Toward a More Just and Effective System of Review in State Death Penalty Cases (Ira P. Robbins, Reporter, August 1990).

19. Vivian O. Berger, The Supreme Court and Defense Counsel: Old Roads, New Paths—A Dead End?, 86 Colum.L.Rev. 9, 64 (1986).

20. Id. at 60–61. The institutional arrangements for the selection and compensation of appointed counsel also result in many defendants being represented either by young and inexperienced defense counsel, who are learning by trial and error, or by senior counsel who are burned out and cynical. Id. at 62.

21. See Genego, supra note 16, at 201:

Inadequate representation is a major institutional problem. By all accounts there are far too many defendants who are represented by inadequate counsel; the courts cannot, in the limited context of granting postconviction relief, adequately respond to the problem. When confronted with such fundamental issues in the criminal justice

If so, why isn't the Court more candid and honest about current conditions?

Is the Sixth Amendment violated when the appointed defense counsel in a complex federal mail fraud case is a real estate lawyer who has never tried a jury case? In United States v. Cronic,[22] decided the same day as *Strickland*, the Court held that it is not enough to show that the lawyer was not an experienced criminal lawyer; the defendant must show specific errors.[23] May a lawyer under such circumstances decline to serve? United States v. Wendy [24] held it improper to hold appointed counsel in contempt of court for refusing to proceed to trial because he was a tax lawyer who had never tried a case before.[25]

Required Showing of Prejudice

Except in certain limited circumstances, discussed below, the convicted defendant must show a "reasonable probability" that, but for counsel's unprofessional errors, the result would have been different. Doesn't the Court's test collapse two questions into one? (Was a right violated? What remedy, if any, should be accorded?) Is this tort-like standard, requiring proof of harm in order to establish the invasion of a right, appropriate? Contrast Justice Marshall's view that automatic reversal should flow from a demonstration that counsel's performance was seriously inadequate. Does the Court's statement that lower courts need not consider counsel's performance "[i]f it is *easier* to dispose of an ineffectiveness claim on the ground of lack of sufficient prejudice, *which we expect will often be so*," invite lower courts "to avoid refining more detailed criteria for lawyer conduct" and suggest "that virtually all challenges to counsel can be readily rejected"? [26]

Effect of *Strickland*

A 1988 law review survey of the case law, reporting nearly five years' experience under *Strickland*, discovered 702 federal appellate

system, courts have tended to respond by legitimating "necessary evils," such as when the Supreme Court upheld the constitutionality of plea bargaining.

G.K. Chesterton once suggested that abuses in the legal system arose not because police or judges were "wicked" or "stupid" but simply because they had "gotten used to it." G. K. Chesterton, The Twelve Men, in Tremendous Trifles 57–58 (1955).

22. 466 U.S. 648 (1984).

23. See also People v. Perez, 24 Cal.3d 133, 155 Cal.Rptr. 176, 594 P.2d 1 (1979) (en banc) (upholding the representation of indigent defendants with their consent by "certified" law students supervised by an attorney).

24. 575 F.2d 1025 (2d Cir.1978).

25. See also State v. Gasen, 48 Ohio App.2d 191, 356 N.E.2d 505 (1976) (reversing a contempt citation of a public defender who refused to proceed with a preliminary hearing because the court had not given him time to read the file on the case or consult with the defendants); and Easley v. State, 334 So.2d 630 (Fla.App.1976) (lawyer not in contempt because he had an obligation to tell defendant that he lacked competence to proceed).

26. Berger, supra note 19, at 86–87 (emphasis added). The Court refers to ineffectiveness claims as entailing an "intrusive post-trial inquiry," the availability of which needs to be restricted so as not to "encourage the proliferation of ineffectiveness challenges."

cases involving ineffective assistance claims.[27] The ineffectiveness claim was sustained in only 30 cases or 4.27 percent. In six of the twelve circuits, accounting for 165 of the 702 cases, no defendant had prevailed in a claim of ineffective assistance of counsel. In the other six circuits, four to six percent of the defendants were successful in making the claim. The exception was the Seventh Circuit, in which nearly 10 percent of the defendants succeeded. Do these figures, which are lower than the estimates of trial lawyer incompetence reported by knowledgeable observers and available survey research,[28] indicate that perhaps only the Seventh Circuit is ensuring that criminal defendants receive competent representation? Or are the other circuits following the dictates of *Strickland* more faithfully? Of course, some substandard defense lawyering is corrected at the trial court level without further appeal or in the state courts on direct review or by an earlier collateral attack.

The 1988 survey contains a troubling statistic: Of the 672 cases rejecting the defendant's claim, 291 (43.3 percent) did so on the ground that prejudice had not been shown. In other words, in almost half of the cases, the defendant's allegations of bungling by the lawyer were "relegated to [the] 'guilty anyway' category." [29] In the 291 "no prejudice" cases, the courts rarely addressed the performance of counsel. Nevertheless, in 37 "no prejudice" cases (5.27 percent) the court indicated that counsel's performance was less than adequate. In 227 cases the courts found that counsel's performance was adequate, and in 154 cases the courts found neither inadequate performance nor prejudice. The data suggest that, although *Strickland* said it was *not* adopting an outcome-determinative test, lowers courts are applying *Strickland* as if it had.

Examples of "Competent" Representation After *Strickland*

In Mitchell v. Kemp,[30] Mitchell pleaded guilty to killing a 14–year-old boy and seriously wounding the boy's mother during an armed robbery of a convenience store. Mitchell made two confessions shortly after being taken into custody. Mitchell's defense lawyer interviewed some of the police officers involved in taking the confessions, but did not interview the one who had signed the Miranda form because he did not like that officer and believed the others had spoken truthfully. He made no attempt to interview any witnesses to obtain mitigating character evidence because Mitchell's father had been uncooperative in two phone calls and Mitchell had said he did not want his family

[handwritten margin note: Killed 14 y/o Boy + Wounded mother]

---

27. Note, How To Thread the Needle: Toward a Checklist–Based Standard for Evaluating Ineffective Assistance of Counsel Claims, 77 Geo.L.J. 413, 458–461 (1988).

28. Former Chief Justice Burger's "working hypothesis" that at least one-third to one-half of trial lawyers are incompetent, see p. 169 above, may be an overstatement. But the more modest estimates provided by the judges in the Maddi or Partridge and Bermant studies (see p. 170 above) suggest that 9–12 percent of trial lawyer performances are inadequate.

29. Note, supra, at 433.

30. 762 F.2d 886 (11th Cir.1985), cert. denied, 483 U.S. 1026 (1987).

involved. The court of appeals affirmed the district court's rejection of the claims of ineffective assistance of counsel. The failure to investigate the voluntariness of the confessions by talking with each police officer was not prejudicial because of the guilty plea and the state's proof of the crimes. The failure to produce character evidence raised a "difficult question," but was affirmed on the ground that it was the result of strategic choices.

Justice Marshall, joined by Justices Brennan and Blackmun, dissented from the denial of certiorari. Justice Marshall concluded that permitting these failures interpreted the Sixth Amendment guarantee to require "no more than that 'a person who happens to be a lawyer is present at trial alongside the accused.'"

> Counsel's failure to investigate mitigating circumstances left him ignorant of the abundant information that was available to an attorney exercising minimal diligence in fighting for Billy Mitchell's life. The affidavits of individuals who would have testified on petitioner's behalf fill 170 pages of the record in the District Court....

> Had defense counsel tapped these resources, he would have been able to present the sentencing judge with a picture of a youth who, despite growing up in "the most poverty-stricken and crime-ridden section of Jacksonville, Florida," had impressed his community as a person of exceptional character. He had been captain of the football team; leader of the prayer before each game; an above-average student; an active member of the student council, school choir, church choir, glee club, math club, and track team; a boy scout; captain of the patrol boys; and an attendant to the junior high school queen.

> . . .

> An account of what happened to this well-adjusted young person was also readily available to anyone who took the time to ask. When petitioner was 16 years old, his parents were divorced, and soon thereafter petitioner ... and two friends were arrested for attempted robbery. Petitioner professed his innocence, but was persuaded by his father to plead guilty, because "things would go easier for him." The charges against the two friends were dropped. Petitioner was sentenced to six months in prison, where he was subjected to repeated violent homosexual attacks, experienced severe depression, and lost 30 pounds. When he was released, he continued to be highly depressed, and eventually committed the crime for which he received a sentence of death.

> Counsel's explanation for his total lack of preparation for the sentencing hearing is that he carried an "ace in the hole." His sole strategy for representing his client's interests rested on his belief that, under Georgia law, the State would not be permitted to introduce any evidence of aggravating circumstances of which the defense had not been notified in writing. Prior to sentencing, the

State had provided petitioner's counsel with oral notice of the aggravating circumstances upon which it would rely, but had not furnished written notice. Although the state statute upon which counsel's theory relied did not mention written notice, and no court decision had ever required that such notice be in writing, counsel was content to rest his entire defense, and the fate of his client, on an untried legal theory. At sentencing, counsel took the first opportunity to object to the admission of aggravating evidence of which he had not received prior written notice; the court promptly overruled his objection, and the "ace in the hole" was gone....

... [P]etitioner's attorney also claimed that he had not wished to present any mitigating character evidence because that would have opened the door to the State's introduction of petitioner's prior conviction.... In this case, [such a decision] was patently unreasonable.'.... Moreover, under state law, the prior conviction would have been admissible even though the defense put on no evidence. If counsel in this case made any decisions at all, they were barren of even minimal supporting information or knowledge.

· · ·

As a result of counsel's nonfeasance, no one argued to the sentencing judge that petitioner should not die. The judge heard only a technical argument regarding the admissibility of aggravating circumstances without prior written notice, which he consistently rejected, in addition to a reference to petitioner's youth.... Prejudice to the defendant's case is obvious when not even a suggestion that petitioner's life had some value, that his crime was aberrational, or that he was suffering from severe depression reached the ears and the conscience of the sentencing judge.... The judge heard not even a plea for mercy.[31]

Can a failure to investigate ever suffice to establish ineffective assistance of counsel? In Kimmelman v. Morrison,[32] the Supreme Court held counsel ineffective when his failure to conduct pretrial discovery resulted in a failure to raise an objection under the Fourth Amendment to illegally seized evidence.[33] Nonetheless, in the vast majority of cases even a complete failure to investigate does not lead to reversal.[34]

31. 483 U.S. at 1027–31. Billy Mitchell was executed on September 1, 1987.

32. 477 U.S. 365, 366 (1986).

33. See also Sullivan v. Fairman, 819 F.2d 1382, 1391–3 (7th Cir.1987) (failure to contact witnesses whose testimony contradicted that of government's witnesses was ineffective and prejudicial); Grooms v. Solem, 923 F.2d 88 (8th Cir.1991) (ineffective assistance where lawyer failed to investigate defendant's potential alibi); and Capps v. Sullivan, 921 F.2d 260 (10th Cir.1990) (ineffective assistance where lawyer failed to investigate witnesses who could have provided defendant with an entrapment defense).

34. See, e.g., Burger v. Kemp, 483 U.S. 776 (1987) (no investigation of mitigating evidence for presentation at defendant's capital sentencing hearing held not unreasonable); Ballou v. Booker, 777 F.2d 910, 914 (4th Cir.1985) (failure to interview rape victim or examining physicians not unreasonable when counsel already "knew" what happened); Aldrich v. Wainwright, 777 F.2d 630, 633 (11th Cir.1985) (failure to interview state's

The *Strickland* standard may seem to guarantee precious little protection for a criminal defendant at trial, but one should keep in mind that not even this standard protects a convicted defendant from the consequences of her attorney's incompetence in a habeas proceeding. Because there is no right to counsel in habeas proceedings, the Court has held that *Strickland* does not apply.[35] The severity of this holding is apparent once one understands that in almost all instances a lawyer's procedural mistake in a habeas proceeding results in forfeiture of the client's claim to a new trial.[36]

Constitutional Role of Defense Counsel

According to *Strickland*, the purpose of the Sixth Amendment guarantee of effective assistance of counsel is "to ensure that the adversarial testing process works to produce a *just* result," "a fair trial whose result is *reliable*." Assuming this standard vision of counsel's role is appropriate, does the *Strickland* standard as applied guarantee this? Consider *Mitchell v. Kemp,* supra. Was the sentencing result there reliable? What does it mean to say a sentencing result was reliable?

The next question to consider is whether the Court's version of counsel's role is appropriate. Professors Berger and Genego argue that *Strickland's* hindsight evaluation of fairness in terms of effects neglects process concerns relating to counsel's role in the adversary system: [37]

> The role of an attorney for a defendant facing criminal prosecution is not, however, to see that his or her client received a fair trial and that a just outcome resulted. The attorney's role is to do everything ethically proper to see that the client receives the most favorable outcome possible—whether or not it produces an outcome which society considers just.[152] Society relies on the adversary system to produce just results from partisan advocacy. The guiding principle in determining whether an attorney has provided effective representation must then be whether he or she discharged the role of partisan advocate faithfully and zealously, not whether the performance yielded what a court views as a just result.[38]

witnesses or otherwise investigate, along with counsel's admission that he was "totally unprepared," demonstrated unreasonable performance, but not prejudicial); Hoots v. Allsbrook, 785 F.2d 1214, 1221 (4th Cir.1986) (failure to investigate unreasonable but not prejudicial).

35. Coleman v. Thompson, 111 S.Ct. 2546 (1991).

36. Id. (applying the habeas procedural default rule of Wainright v. Sykes, 433 U.S. 72 (1977), and holding that incompetence of counsel does not fulfill the "cause and prejudice" exception to the default rule).

37. See Berger, supra note 19, at 93–96, and Genego, supra note 16, at 198–202.

152. [Footnote from Genego article:] Model Code of Professional Responsibility Canon 7 (1979). Ethical Consideration 7–1 states: "The duty of a lawyer, both to his client and the legal system, is to represent his client zealously within the bounds of the law...." Id. at EC 7–1. For an in depth discussion of the lawyer's role within the adversary system, see M.H. Freedman, Lawyers Ethics In An Adversary System 9–26 (1975).

38. Genego, supra note 16, at 200.

Does the Constitution require a state to require its defense lawyers to conform to a "total commitment to client" model of lawyering? Does it provide a federal remedy for every departure from that model? What weight should be given to the three "f-words" impliedly emphasized by the Court: federalism (respect for state court adjudications of fact and law); efficiency (the social cost of reversing every conviction that might have been affected by deficient professional performance); and finality (reducing incentives for endless and repeated federal challenges to criminal convictions that have survived at least two prior reviews)? Isn't there a great danger that the Court's approach, as Justice Marshall argued, limits the success of ineffectiveness claims to defendants who can prove they were innocent?

Under Professor Genego's approach, does defense counsel have an incentive to seed error into a criminal case that is a clear loser by failing to do a competent job? [39] Like all rules, the ineffectiveness rule itself may be put to tactical use by counsel more concerned with "winning for client" than with either just results or the integrity of the adjudicatory process. How likely is such behavior? What controls would minimize the risk?

Professor Berger contrasts the Court's many decisions that enhance the dependence of client on defense counsel by binding the client by counsel's actions,[40] with *Strickland*, which provides very limited protection against incompetent lawyering to the ignorant and vulnerable client. The Court, in simultaneously maximizing the defendant's need for competent representation and minimizing the Constitution's competence safeguard, has made the lawyer—with her broad power to decide matters contrary to the client's wishes—not simply another "indignity" the indigent defendant must bear, but also potentially the client's greatest enemy.[41]

When Prejudice Is Presumed

In *Strickland* the Court stated that prejudice will be presumed in certain limited circumstances: when there has been an "actual or constructive denial of the assistance of counsel altogether," or when the government interferes with counsel's assistance in such a way that "prejudice ... is so likely that case-by-case inquiry into prejudice is not worth the cost." The Court also made it clear that a defendant need

---

39. This issue was raised by Justice Rehnquist in Wainwright v. Sykes, 433 U.S. 72, 89 (1977), and responded to in that case by Justices Brennan and Marshall, dissenting, 433 U.S. at 102 and note 4.

40. Numerous decisions dealing with collateral attack on guilty pleas and availability of the federal habeas remedy bind a convicted defendant by her lawyer's advertent or inadvertent actions in raising or not raising particular issues. See Berger at 17–25 (discussing habeas and guilty plea decisions). Other decisions permit defense counsel to decide important matters either without consulting the defendant or against the defendant's expressed desires. See, e.g., Jones v. Barnes, 463 U.S. 745 (1983) (lawyer, not client, decides what arguments are presented in an appellate brief), considered below at 505. These constitutional decisions make the criminal defendant very dependent on the competence of defense counsel.

41. Berger, supra note 19, at 11.

not show prejudice when his trial was conducted without counsel despite her desire for representation or when counsel in a criminal case was under an actual conflict of interest.[42]

Since *Strickland*, the Court has affirmed that prejudice also is not required in the following two situations. The (first) is failure to file an *Anders* brief. Anders v. California [43] requires appellate counsel in criminal cases who seek leave to withdraw based on their judgment that an appeal is meritless to file a brief referring to anything in the record that might arguably support the appeal. Such a brief is called an *Anders* brief. Failure to file an *Anders* brief requires reversal; no showing of prejudice is required, nor may such conduct be labeled harmless error.[44] The (second) situation is when the defendant is prevented from conferring with her counsel for any significant period of time.[45]

Apart from these situations, the courts have dispensed with the requirement of demonstrating prejudice in relatively few instances. The category of "actual or constructive denial" of the assistance of counsel is interpreted quite narrowly, not reaching cases in which defense counsel had mental problems during the trial [46] or suffered from drug addiction.[47] Where a denial has been found, the courts have sometimes used the doctrine of harmless error to avoid reversal.[48]

Government interference with the right to counsel must be egregious before prejudice will be presumed. "Not all government interference triggers the per se [prejudice] rule. The common thread in cases where the government's conduct was found to be 'egregious' is conduct which jeopardizes the integrity of the legal process." [49]

Are there specific blunders by counsel that are so blatantly incompetent that no separate showing of prejudice should be required? What

42. See Cuyler v. Sullivan, reprinted in Chapter 7 below at p. 661.

43. 386 U.S. 738 (1967).

44. Penson v. Ohio, 488 U.S. 75 (1988).

45. See Geders v. United States, 425 U.S. 80 (1976) (defendant not allowed to confer with counsel during overnight trial recess). In Perry v. Leeke, 488 U.S. 272 (1989), the Court reaffirmed that a violation of *Geders* was not subject to the requirement that prejudice be shown, but held that *Geders* was not violated when the defendant was prevented from conferring with counsel during a 15–minute trial recess, that prejudice therefore had to be shown and that it was not.

46. In Smith v. Ylst, 826 F.2d 872 (9th Cir.1987), psychiatric reports showed that the defendant's lawyer suffered "paranoid psychotic reactions" during the trial, but the court upheld the conviction because the defendant failed to show prejudice.

47. See Berry v. King, 765 F.2d 451, 454 (5th Cir.1985) (no presumption of prejudice on showing that defense counsel was addicted to drugs, and prejudice not shown by counsel's stipulation to virtually all elements of the crime when state could easily have proved the elements).

48. See, e.g., Thomas v. Kemp, 796 F.2d 1322, 1326–27 (11th Cir.1986) (defendant, facing capital charge, was denied presence of a lawyer at preliminary hearing; no reversal because harmless error); Siverson v. O'Leary, 764 F.2d 1208 (7th Cir.1985) (defense counsel's absence during jury deliberations and when jury returned verdict presumed prejudicial, but error harmless).

49. United States v. Perry, 857 F.2d 1346, 1349 (9th Cir.1988) (giving examples).

about failing to remove for cause an obviously biased juror? [50]

Effective Assistance of Counsel Under State Constitutions

The state courts—the laboratories of our federal judicial system—are free to develop more rigorous standards for judging effective assistance of counsel under state constitutional provisions. However, almost all follow *Strickland*.[51] Some states employ somewhat different verbal formulation but it is not clear that the differences result in different outcomes.[52]

[handwritten margin note: State cts = Free to Impose more rigorous standard?]

Perhaps the most serious problem in day-to-day administration is the inadequate compensation provided for court-appointed lawyers who represent indigent defendants in serious criminal cases.[53] In most states compensation provisions for court-appointed counsel are substantially less than the prevailing rates for privately retained lawyers.[54] Rates of compensation are as low as $10 an hour. Statutory provisions generally limit compensation to a maximum allowance ranging from $100 to $5,000, with most states imposing a limitation on felony cases between $500 and $1,000. Would the issues presented by *Strickland* be so troublesome if state courts did it right the first time by providing defendants with competent lawyers receiving adequate compensation and supported with adequate investigative resources?

A Preventive Approach?

Professional discipline, civil malpractice liability and after-the-fact review of ineffective assistance claims share the common characteristic that they come along after the damage, if any, is done. Would preventive measures be more effective? Judge Bazelon sought unsuccessfully to commit the Court of Appeals for the District of Columbia to

50. Compare Presley v. State, 750 S.W.2d 602 (Mo.App.1988) (holding that prejudice is presumed in this situation), with Wicker v. McCotter, 783 F.2d 487 (5th Cir.1986) (holding such conduct was a strategic choice).

51. See, e.g., State v. Nash, 143 Ariz. 392, 694 P.2d 222 (1985); People v. Ledesma, 43 Cal.3d 171, 233 Cal.Rptr. 404, 729 P.2d 839 (1987); People v. Albanese, 104 Ill.2d 504, 85 Ill.Dec. 441, 473 N.E.2d 1246 (1984); State v. Davis, 116 N.J. 341, 561 A.2d 1082 (1989). South Carolina has adopted a somewhat different prejudice test. See Frett v. State, 298 S.C. 54, 378 S.E.2d 249 (1988) (prejudice established if defendant shows that conduct of trial, not necessarily its outcome, would have altered his position in a beneficial way).

52. See, e.g., Commonwealth v. Buehl, 510 Pa. 363, 508 A.2d 1167 (1986), holding that the Pennsylvania Constitution requires the same showing of prejudice as in *Strickland* but a different inquiry as to counsel's performance: The court asks whether the course the defendant suggests counsel should have pursued is frivolous; if not, then the court asks whether the course counsel chose "had some reasonable basis designed to serve the interests of [the] client." 508 A.2d at 1174.

53. The Federal Criminal Justice Act, 18 U.S.C. § 3006A(d), provides for compensation at hourly rates of $60 per hour in court and $40 per hour for office and investigative work, unless the Judicial Conference determines that a higher rate not to exceed $75 per hour is justified for a circuit or a particular district; the maximum amount for handling a felony case is $3,500 for each attorney; and larger payments may be made "for extended or complex representation" with judicial approval.

54. See Note, The Breath of the Unfee'd Lawyer: Statutory Fee Limitations and Ineffective Assistance of Counsel in Capital Litigation, 90 Mich.L.Rev. 626, 627 (1991) (arguing that fee limitations deprive indigent defendants of their right to effective assistance of counsel).

a prophylactic approach involving a more active role on the part of the trial judge.[55] For example, the trial judge would require the defense lawyer to submit a checklist and report indicating that "a complete investigation" has been performed and "reviewing the steps he has taken in pretrial preparation, including what records were obtained, which witnesses were interviewed, when the defendant was consulted, and what motions were filed." [56] Justice O'Connor's opinion in *Strickland* rejected this approach, arguing that a "set of rules" for defense counsel "would interfere with the constitutionally protected independence of counsel and restrict the wide latitude counsel must have in making tactical decisions." How would requiring defense counsel, for example, to take certain investigatory steps interfere with the defendant's rights?

If monitoring by trial judges "poses risks of violating defendants' rights by the very process designed to protect them," [57] what alternatives are desirable? Some possible types of systemic reform are continuing legal education, professional certification or specialization requirements for practice in certain courts or subjects, more clinically oriented law school training, higher pay and greater auxiliary resources for assigned counsel and structural changes in the delivery of defense services. How likely are these changes? How effective would they be? Professor Berger urges the Court to play an educative role in defining ineffective assistance, but concludes that constitutionalizing lawyer behavior (except at the extremes) is neither appropriate nor wise: "[O]ther institutions [will] have to carry the lion's share of the remedial burden." [58]

2. Malpractice Claims Against Criminal Defense Lawyers

In Ferri v. Ackerman [59] the Supreme Court held that counsel appointed in federal criminal cases under the Criminal Justice Act of 1964 enjoy no inherent immunity from malpractice claims. Yet a successful malpractice claim against either a retained or appointed defense lawyer must circumvent a number of hurdles. In some states a defendant must establish his innocence of the crime involved to establish that his lawyer's conduct resulted in harm.[60] Several courts have held that when a criminal defendant's ineffective assistance of counsel claim has been fully heard and denied, the doctrine of collateral

---

55. United States v. Decoster, 624 F.2d 196, 215 (D.C. Cir.1976) (en banc, Bazelon and Wright, dissenting).

56. 624 F.2d at 297.

57. Berger, supra note 19, at 114, note 528.

58. Id. at 115.

59. 444 U.S. 193 (1979).

60. See, e.g., Carmel v. Lunney, 70 N.Y.2d 169, 518 N.Y.S.2d 605, 511 N.E.2d 1126 (1987) ("the undisturbed determination of the client's guilt in the subsequent criminal prosecution precludes him, as a matter of law, from recovering for civil damages flowing from the allegedly negligent representation"); compare Hines v. Davidson, 489 So.2d 572 (Ala.1986) (criminal defendant required to show that he would have been acquitted but for the lawyer's negligence).

estoppel bars a subsequent civil malpractice suit against the lawyer.[61] In Zeidwig v. Ward [62] the court reasoned:

> If we were to allow a claim in this instance, we would be approving a policy that would approve the imprisonment of a defendant for a criminal offense . . . but which would allow the same defendant to collect from his counsel damages . . . because he was improperly imprisoned.[63]

Does this result in criminal defense lawyers being held to a lesser standard in malpractice cases than civil lawyers? [64]

In Polk County v. Dodson,[65] the Supreme Court held that a public defender "when performing a lawyer's traditional functions as counsel to a defendant in a criminal proceeding" does not act "under color of state law" within the meaning of 42 U.S.C. § 1983. The plaintiff had sued under § 1983, claiming that his rights to counsel and to due process were violated when his counsel moved to withdraw on the ground that he thought plaintiff's appeal was frivolous. In Tower v. Glover,[66] the Court held that § 1983 applies when a plaintiff alleges that the public defender conspired with state officials to ensure the plaintiff's conviction.

61. See, e.g., Knoblauch v. Kenyon, 163 Mich.App. 712, 415 N.W.2d 286 (1987); Johnson v. Raban, 702 S.W.2d 134 (Mo.App.1985).

62. 548 So.2d 209 (Fla.1989).

63. 548 So.2d at 214.

64. For a case awarding malpractice damages after the defendant's criminal conviction had been overturned, see Holliday v. Jones, 215 Cal.App.3d 102, 264 Cal.Rptr. 448 (1989).

65. 454 U.S. 312, 325 (1981). State prosecutors are absolutely immune from liability under § 1983 for conduct in initiating and trying criminal cases, but not for giving legal advice to police prior to an application for a search warrant. Burns v. Reed, 111 S.Ct. 1934 (1991).

66. 467 U.S. 914 (1984).

Chapter 4

CONFIDENTIALITY

Introductory Note

The law governing client confidences has two sources: agency law and the law of evidence. Lawyers, like all agents, have a duty to treat information from and about their principals as confidential to the extent that the principal so intends and a duty not to use information about the principal against the principal or for the personal gain of the agent.[1] These duties continue after the agency ends. The professional duty of confidentiality in the ethics codes, discussed later in this chapter, expands the agency duty. The professional duty governs the lawyer in all activities and at all times: in the law office, in public settings, in private social gatherings. Breach of confidentiality may lead to one or more of a number of remedies.[2]

The professional duty of confidentiality is also broader than the attorney-client privilege of evidence law: The professional duty protects information about the client that the lawyer learns from third parties; the privilege extends only to information transmitted directly between client and lawyer. Neither the professional duty of confidentiality nor its agency counterpart, however, allow the lawyer-agent to refuse to testify or produce evidence about confidential matters in court or before other government bodies that have the power to compel testimony, such as administrative agencies or legislative committees. This is where the attorney-client privilege comes into play.

The law of evidence excludes some evidence as presumptively unreliable, e.g., evidence that violates the hearsay rule. It excludes other evidence to protect an interest or relationship, e.g., the marital relationship, deemed of sufficient importance that the law tolerates the loss of reliable evidence to protect that interest. Exclusionary rules of the latter type are known as privileges. Because recognizing a privilege impairs a tribunal's pursuit of truth, courts interpret privileges narrowly and place the burden on the proponent of privilege to prove that its elements have been met.

---

1. Agency law requires an agent "not to use or to communicate information confidentially given him by the principal or acquired by him during the course of or on account of his agency," subject to a power of the agent to reveal information when necessary to protect the superior interest of a third person. Restatement (Second) of Agency § 395, and comment f (1958).

2. A lawyer's breach of confidentiality may lead to professional discipline or malpractice liability or both. In addition, agency law provides the basis for other remedies, such as tort or contract damages and injunctive relief.

Because the attorney-client privilege prevents testimonial disclosure of a client's communications, commentators over the years have attacked the privilege as a device by which lawyers assist wrongdoers in concealing their wrongs "in the face of a specific demand for its disclosure by the very person suffering the wrong." [3] In the early 1800s Jeremy Bentham put this objection forcefully, urging the elimination of the privilege: "What, then, would be the consequence? That a guilty person will not in general be able to derive so much assistance from his law advisor, in the way of concerting a false defense, as he may do at present." [4] Bentham's single-minded devotion to the truth-seeking aspect of adjudication has not prevailed in the courts, which have accorded greater weight to a client's interest in freedom of consultation with a legal advisor. What reasons support the privilege? Are these reasons inconsistent with a modification of the privilege so as to make it inapplicable if a strong need for the privileged matter arises in a trial? [5]

The modern rationale for the attorney-client privilege is that the privilege encourages open communication between clients and their lawyers, serving both the interests of clients who need effective legal representation and society's interests in having clients advised about the legality of proposed actions and effectively represented in the adversary process.

The attorney-client privilege is recognized in every jurisdiction either by statute or common law. In federal courts the contours of the privilege are determined by federal law on issues of federal law and by state law on state law matters. [6]

English common law recognized the privilege as early as the 16th century, although English courts did not fully accept the privilege until after 1800. [7] The privilege has developed in the United States through common law decisions and statutory enactments and not as a matter of constitutional right. Federal and state constitutions, however, recognize rights supported by the attorney-client privilege, namely the privilege against self-incrimination and the right to counsel. The relationship between the Fifth Amendment privilege against self-incrimination and the attorney-client privilege is considered in the *Fisher* case below.

3. See Geoffrey C. Hazard, Jr., An Historical Perspective on the Attorney–Client Privilege, 66 Calif.L.Rev. 1061, 1062 (1978) (discussing attacks on the privilege).

4. Jeremy Bentham, Rationale of Judicial Evidence (1827), quoted in John H. Wigmore, 7 Evidence 569 (McNaughton ed., 1961).

5. See Note, The Attorney–Client Privilege: Fixed Rules, Balancing, and Constitutional Entitlement, 91 Harv.L.Rev. 464 (1977).

6. As adopted in 1975, Fed.Evid.Rule 501 requires federal courts to follow state privilege law in all cases in which "state law supplies the rule of decision." In cases in which federal substantive law applies, Rule 501 provides that privilege claims are to be decided by "the common law, interpreted in the light of reason and experience."

7. Geoffrey C. Hazard, Jr., An Historical Perspective on the Attorney–Client Privilege, 66 Calif.L.Rev. 1061, 1070 (1978) (discussing the history of the privilege). See also Max Radin, The Privilege of Confidential Communication Between Lawyer and Client, 16 Calif.L.Rev. 487 (1928).

The relationship between the Sixth Amendment's right to counsel and the attorney-client privilege has uncertain contours.[8] The federal court decisions agree that *government use* of information protected by the attorney-client privilege may infringe the defendant's Sixth Amendment right to counsel, though they differ on what is material infringement.[9] These decisions assume the existence of a state privilege and implicitly acknowledge its importance to the Sixth Amendment's right to counsel in criminal trials. They strongly suggest that, should a state legislature abolish the attorney-client privilege, the courts would hold the statute unconstitutional. This point remains a theoretical one because no state is likely to abolish the privilege. The more important and more difficult question is whether the courts would hold that a narrowing of the privilege violates a criminal defendant's right to counsel. Thus far the courts have shown no inclination to require any particular scope for the privilege under the Sixth Amendment. On the other hand, no state has sought to restrict the privilege significantly.

A. ATTORNEY-CLIENT PRIVILEGE

The scope of the attorney-client privilege is a complicated subject. The materials that follow provide only an overview.[10]

The precise formulation of the attorney-client privilege varies from jurisdiction to jurisdiction.[11] The most concise and best-known statement of the attorney-client privilege is Wigmore's classic formulation, which sets out eight elements:

[1] Where legal advice of any kind is sought

[2] from a professional legal adviser in his capacity as such,

[3] the communications relating to that purpose,

[4] made in confidence

[5] by the client,

---

8. See Marano v. Holland, 179 W.Va. 156, 366 S.E.2d 117 (1988) (citing cases suggesting but not holding that the Sixth Amendment right to counsel includes some form of attorney-client privilege). On the connection between the Sixth Amendment and the privilege, see David E. Seidelson, The Attorney–Client Privilege and Clients' Constitutional Rights, 6 Hofstra L.Rev. 693 (1978).

9. See United States v. Mastroianni, 749 F.2d 900 (1st Cir.1984) (describing the differences among the circuit courts).

10. Generally see John W. Strong et al., McCormick on Evidence c. 10 (4th ed. 1992); Wolfram, Modern Legal Ethics § 6.3 et seq. (1986); 8 John H. Wigmore, Evidence § 2291 (J. McNaughton rev. ed. 1961); and Developments in the Law—Privileged Communications, 98 Harv.L.Rev. 1450, 1501 et seq. (1985). Proposed Federal Rule of Evidence 503 (1972), although not adopted by Congress, is viewed by courts and commentators as an authoritative summary of the common law of the attorney-client privilege.

11. See Wolfram, Modern Legal Ethics 250–68 (1986), for a modern discussion of the privilege. The American Law Institute is now engaged in preparing a Restatement of the Law Governing Lawyers. Sections 118–34 deal with the attorney-client privilege. See Restatement of the Law Governing Lawyers, Tent. Draft No. 2 (adopted at May meeting, 1989).

[6]   are at his instance permanently protected

[7]   from disclosure by himself or by the legal adviser,

[8]   except the protection be waived.[12]

1. Aspects of the Privilege

A "Client" Seeking "Legal Advice" From a "Lawyer"

The attorney-client privilege does not protect privacy per se; the rule protects privacy only in the context and for the purpose of encouraging full disclosure to a legal advisor by one seeking legal services. A "client" is a person who consults with a lawyer to obtain legal advice including, of course, a lawyer who seeks legal advice from another lawyer. A "lawyer" is a person whom the client reasonably believes is a lawyer; "legal advice" turns on the intent of the client in making the communication.[13] For example, the privilege does not cover a person who seeks business advice or who speaks to a lawyer merely as a friend. Payment of a fee, however, is not required; and preliminary conversations for the purpose of obtaining representation are privileged even if the lawyer subsequently declines the representation. Termination of the attorney-client relationship does not end the privilege; protection continues indefinitely.[14]

Privileged Communications

Client communications to a lawyer—whether oral, written, or non-verbal (e.g., rolling up a sleeve to reveal a tattoo)—are privileged if relevant to the legal subject matter on which the client seeks legal assistance. Observations or things that are evidence of events and occurrences are not privileged, except in the form in which a client communicates them to a lawyer. Thus a client may be compelled to testify about events involving the client if no other privilege, such as the Fifth Amendment privilege against self-incrimination, prevents disclosure. And the client's lawyer may be compelled to testify to facts about the client's appearance (e.g., a cut or bruise the lawyer observes on the client's face); the lawyer's observations are not client communications.

The privilege protects documents if prepared for the purpose of seeking a lawyer's advice but not preexisting documents or those prepared for another purpose (e.g., tax working papers) even if turned over to a lawyer.[15] Physical evidence of a crime also falls outside of the

---

12. 8 Wigmore on Evidence § 2292 (McNaughton ed.1961).

13. Proposed Fed.R.Evid. 503 contains definitions of these terms. The privilege protects a client who has a good-faith but mistaken belief that the person from whom legal advice is sought is a licensed lawyer.

14. See Matter of Doe (Stuart), 408 Mass. 480, 562 N.E.2d 69 (1990) (murder suspect's conversations with his lawyer continued to be privileged after the suspect's death by suicide; a balancing-of-interests test held inappropriate).

15. See Fisher v. United States, 425 U.S. 391 (1976), reprinted below at p. 243.

privilege.[16] The client's name, the fact that the client has retained the lawyer, details of the retainer or fee and who paid it and the client's whereabouts are generally not privileged.[17] A major exception to the privilege, known as the crime-fraud exception, is considered separately later in this chapter.

It is worth repeating that underlying facts or evidence are not protected by the privilege but only a client's communications to a lawyer made for the purpose of obtaining legal advice.[18] Thus a lawyer's client may be required to testify concerning any fact unless the information is protected by some other privilege, such as the Fifth Amendment privilege against self-incrimination. The attorney-client privilege, which applies only to what the client has told the lawyer and vice versa, "is not intended to enable a client to keep secret all information that might prove to be damaging," but only to insure "that clients do not suffer as a result of consulting lawyers and confiding in them." The privilege "is not intended to give the client exclusive property rights in all information discovered by counsel while acting on the client's behalf." [19]

A "Communication" "Made in Confidence"

Because the purpose of the privilege is to facilitate effective legal assistance, the privilege is lost if the communication is not made in secrecy. The presence of third persons (other than agents of the lawyer or client who are necessary to protect the interests of the client) destroys the privilege.[20] Lawyers cannot provide legal advice without the assistance of secretaries, investigators and paralegals; their presence does not affect the privilege. Communications made for public consumption or intended for a non-lawyer are not privileged (e.g., a

---

16. See Commonwealth v. Stenhach, 356 Pa.Super. 5, 514 A.2d 114 (1986), reprinted supra at p. 37.

17. See the extensive discussion of these issues below at p. 256.

18. An example may clarify the point. Suppose C, a client, who has been involved in an accident, goes to a lawyer, L, for legal advice concerning her potential rights and liabilities. She speaks fully and frankly about the incident to L, who assures her that everything she says is confidential and will not be disclosed. Her communications include the information that T, a third person, was a witness to the incident. L's later investigation discovers that W also has relevant evidence. Will the privilege prevent the opposing party from offering the evidence of T, C or W? Clearly not. Although C or L cannot be required to testify without C's consent as to any information that C has communicated to L, the privilege does not deny the opposing party access to T's testimony or even to C's knowledge of T's existence as a witness. Under modern procedural systems, C may be compelled by proper discovery to disclose T's existence and T may be deposed or called as a witness. Nor does the privilege extend to what T or W or other third persons communicate to L (although this will be protected information under the professional codes and will receive limited protection under the work-product immunity doctrine).

19. Stephen A. Saltzburg, Communications Falling Within the Attorney–Client Privilege, 66 Iowa L.Rev. 811, 816 (1981).

20. See, e.g., In re Himmel, 125 Ill.2d 531, 127 Ill.Dec. 708, 533 N.E.2d 790 (1988) (communication in front of mother and fiancé not privileged); Bolyea v. First Presbyterian Church of Wilton, 196 N.W.2d 149 (N.D.1972) (communication in front of others not privileged because not necessary to the preparation of a deed). See also United States v. Pipkins, 528 F.2d 559 (5th Cir.1976).

suicide note addressed to a relative but turned over to a lawyer). Also, a client waives the privilege if, after communicating privileged information to a lawyer, she disseminates the information to third persons.

Communications From Lawyer to Client

The classic formulation of the privilege by Wigmore limits it to communications made by a client to a lawyer. What about the lawyer's advice to the client? Some courts hold that all communications from lawyer to client are privileged, even when initiated by the lawyer. This approach relies in part on the lawyer's duty to keep the client informed and assumes that any statement by the lawyer would reveal a confidence previously entrusted to her by the client.[21] The other approach extends the privilege to lawyer statements only when the court finds that the statements in fact reveal the substance of a client confidence.[22]

Joint Clients and Cooperating Parties

If two or more persons jointly retain a lawyer to represent them in a matter, communications made by any of the clients to the lawyer on the subject of the joint representation are not privileged against use by one joint client against another.[23] This rule, referred to as the "co-client rule," is an exception to the general rule that disclosure to third persons waives the privilege. The issue arises most often when one co-client feels her interests have been inadequately represented and sues another co-client or the lawyer.[24] The theory behind abrogation of the privilege in such cases is that the joint clients intend their communications to be secret from the rest of the world but not from one another.[25] Courts generally do not allow one joint client to waive the privilege for use against (or by) a third party except that a joint client may waive the privilege as to her own statements.[26]

A lawyer should consider and discuss with clients the limited scope of the privilege in joint client relationships before entering into a representation of multiple clients. See M.R. 2.2(a)(1) (lawyer who acts as an intermediary between clients must consult with each client on,

21. See, e.g., In re LTV Securities Litigation, 89 F.R.D. 595, 602 (N.D.Tex.1981); Hercules, Inc. v. Exxon Corp., 434 F.Supp. 136, 144–45 (D.Del.1977); Jack Winter, Inc. v. Koratron Company, Inc., 54 F.R.D. 44, 46 (N.D.Cal.1971).

22. See, e.g., American Standard Inc. v. Pfizer, Inc., 828 F.2d 734 (Fed.Cir.1987); United States v. Amerada Hess Corp., 619 F.2d 980, 986 (3d Cir.1980).

23. See Proposed Fed.R.Evid. 503(d)(5). For discussion of the co-client rule see Wolfram, Modern Legal Ethics § 6.4.8 (1986).

24. See, e.g., Brennan's, Inc. v. Brennan's Restaurants, Inc., 590 F.2d 168 (5th Cir.1979), reprinted at p. 696 below.

25. But see Ogden v. Groves, 241 So.2d 756 (Fla.App.1970) (attorney could testify only to statements by joint clients made in one another's presence, not to private statements by any of the joint clients to the lawyer).

26. See, e.g., American Mut. Liab. Ins. Co. v. Superior Court, 38 Cal.App.3d 579, 113 Cal.Rptr. 561, 573 (1974); Western Fuels Ass'n v. Burlington No. R.R., 102 F.R.D. 201, 203 (D.Wyo.1984). But see Tunick v. Day, Berry & Howard, 40 Conn.Supp. 216, 486 A.2d 1147, 1149 (1984) (in suit against shared lawyer for malpractice, one of the joint clients could waive the privilege of other joint clients who were not parties to the suit).

inter alia, "the effect on the attorney-client privilege"). The conflict of interest ramifications of a lawyer simultaneously representing more than one person engaged in a joint endeavor in which there are both common and differing interests are considered in Chapter 7 below at p. 671.

The "pooled information" or joint defense doctrine is another exception to the general rule that disclosure to third parties waives the attorney-client privilege. The pooled information exception applies to certain communications between parties who share a common interest in defending against or attacking a common litigational opponent but who are represented by separate lawyers.[27] This exception, which facilitates cooperation in litigation, protects communications only if and so long as a community of interest on one or more issues exists between the parties and only with respect to communications that serve the purpose of advancing the common interests. As with co-clients, a falling out between cooperating co-parties leads to loss of privilege.

2. Corporations and the Attorney–Client Privilege

UPJOHN v. UNITED STATES

Supreme Court of the United States, 1981.
449 U.S. 383, 101 S.Ct. 677, 66 L.Ed.2d 584.

JUSTICE REHNQUIST delivered the opinion of the Court.

We granted certiorari in this case to address important questions concerning the scope of the attorney-client privilege in the corporate context and the applicability of the work-product doctrine in proceedings to enforce tax summonses. . . .

I

Petitioner Upjohn Co. manufactures and sells pharmaceuticals here and abroad. In January 1976 independent accountants conducting an audit of one of Upjohn's foreign subsidiaries discovered that the subsidiary made payments to or for the benefit of foreign government officials in order to secure government business. The accountants so informed petitioner, Mr. Gerard Thomas, Upjohn's Vice President, Secretary, and General Counsel. Thomas is a member of the Michigan and New York Bars, and has been Upjohn's General Counsel for 20 years. He consulted with outside counsel and R.T. Parfet, Jr., Upjohn's Chairman of the Board. It was decided that the company would conduct an internal investigation of what were termed "questionable

---

27. See Proposed Fed.R.Evid. 503(b)(3), providing that the privilege extends to communications between a client "or his lawyer to a lawyer representing another in a matter of common interest." See, e.g., United States v. McPartlin, 595 F.2d 1321 (7th Cir.1979); Eisenberg v. Gagnon, 766 F.2d 770 (3d Cir.1985). But see Government of the Virgin Islands v. Joseph, 685 F.2d 857 (3d Cir.1982) (defendant gave statement to co-defendant's lawyer implicating defendant but exonerating a co-defendant; court held that privilege did not apply because statement was not given as part of common strategy).

payments." As part of this investigation the attorneys prepared a letter containing a questionnaire which was sent to "All Foreign General and Area Managers" over the Chairman's signature. The letter began by noting recent disclosures that several American companies made "possibly illegal" payments to foreign government officials and emphasized that the management needed full information concerning any such payments made by Upjohn. The letter indicated that the Chairman had asked Thomas, identified as "the company's General Counsel," "to conduct an investigation for the purpose of determining the nature and magnitude of any payments made by the Upjohn Company or any of its subsidiaries to any employee or official of a foreign government." The questionnaire sought detailed information concerning such payments. Managers were instructed to treat the investigation as "highly confidential" and not to discuss it with anyone other than Upjohn employees who might be helpful in providing the requested information. Responses were to be sent directly to Thomas. Thomas and outside counsel also interviewed the recipients of the questionnaire and some 33 other Upjohn officers or employees as part of the investigation.

On March 26, 1976, the company voluntarily submitted a preliminary report to the Securities and Exchange Commission on Form 8–K disclosing certain questionable payments. A copy of the report was simultaneously submitted to the Internal Revenue Service, which immediately began an investigation to determine the tax consequences of the payments. Special agents conducting the investigation were given lists by Upjohn of all those interviewed and all who had responded to the questionnaire. On November 23, 1976, the Service issued a summons pursuant to 26 U.S.C. § 7602 demanding production of:

> "All files relative to the investigation conducted under the supervision of Gerard Thomas to identify payments to employees of foreign governments and any political contributions made by the Upjohn Company or any of its affiliates since January 1, 1971 and to determine whether any funds of the Upjohn Company had been improperly accounted for on the corporate books during the same period.

> "The records should include but not be limited to written questionnaires sent to managers of the Upjohn Company's foreign affiliates, and memorandums or notes of the interviews conducted in the United States and abroad with officers and employees of the Upjohn Company and its subsidiaries."

The company declined to produce the documents specified in the second paragraph on the grounds that they were protected from disclosure by the attorney-client privilege and constituted the work product of attorneys prepared in anticipation of litigation. On August 31, 1977, the United States filed a petition seeking enforcement of the summons under 26 U.S.C. §§ 7402(b) and 7604(a) in the United States District Court for the Western District of Michigan. . . .

II

Federal Rule of Evidence 501 provides that "the privilege of a witness ... shall be governed by the principles of the common law as they may be interpreted by the courts of the United States in light of reason and experience." The attorney-client privilege is the oldest of the privileges for confidential communications known to the common law. 8 J. Wigmore, Evidence § 2290 (McNaughton rev. 1961). Its purpose is to encourage full and frank communication between attorneys and their clients and thereby promote broader public interests in the observance of law and administration of justice. The privilege recognizes that sound legal advice or advocacy serves public ends and that such advice or advocacy depends upon the lawyer's being fully informed by the client. As we stated last Term in Trammel v. United States, 445 U.S. 40, 51 (1980): "The lawyer-client privilege rests on the need for the advocate and counselor to know all that relates to the client's reasons for seeking representation if the professional mission is to be carried out." And in Fisher v. United States, 425 U.S. 391, 403 (1976), we recognized the purpose of the privilege to be "to encourage clients to make full disclosure to their attorneys." This rationale for the privilege has long been recognized by the Court, see Hunt v. Blackburn, 128 U.S. 464, 470 (1888).... Admittedly complications in the application of the privilege arise when the client is a corporation, which in theory is an artificial creature of the law, and not an individual; but this Court has assumed that the privilege applies when the client is a corporation, United States v. Louisville & Nashville R. Co., 236 U.S. 318, 336 (1915), and the Government does not contest the general proposition.

The Court of Appeals, however, considered the application of the privilege in the corporate context to present a "different problem," since the client was an inanimate entity and "only the senior management, guiding and integrating the several operations, ... can be said to possess an identity analogous to the corporation as a whole." The first case to articulate the so-called "control group test" adopted by the court below, Philadelphia v. Westinghouse Electric Corp., 210 F.Supp. 483, 485 (ED Pa.), petition for mandamus and prohibition denied sub nom. General Electric Co. v. Kirkpatrick, 312 F.2d 742 (CA3 1962), reflected a similar conceptual approach:

> "Keeping in mind that the question is, Is it the corporation which is seeking the lawyer's advice when the asserted privileged communication is made?, the most satisfactory solution, I think, is that if the employee making the communication, of whatever rank he may be, is in a position to control or even to take a substantial part in a decision about any action which the corporation may take upon the advice of the attorney, ... then, in effect, *he is (or personifies) the corporation* when he makes his disclosure to the lawyer and the privilege would apply." (Emphasis supplied.)

Such a view, we think, overlooks the fact that the privilege exists to protect not only the giving of professional advice to those who can act on it but also the giving of information to the lawyer to enable him to give sound and informed advice.... The first step in the resolution of any legal problem is ascertaining the factual background and sifting through the facts with an eye to the legally relevant. See ABA Code of Professional Responsibility, Ethical Consideration 4–1:

> "A lawyer should be fully informed of all the facts of the matter he is handling in order for his client to obtain the full advantage of our legal system. It is for the lawyer in the exercise of his independent professional judgment to separate the relevant and important from the irrelevant and unimportant. The observance of the ethical obligation of a lawyer to hold inviolate the confidences and secrets of his client not only facilitates the full development of facts essential to proper representation of the client but also encourages laymen to seek early legal assistance."

See also Hickman v. Taylor, 329 U.S. 495, 511 (1947).

In the case of the individual client the provider of information and the person who acts on the lawyer's advice are one and the same. In the corporate context, however, it will frequently be employees beyond the control group as defined by the court below—"officers and agents ... responsible for directing [the company's] actions in response to legal advice"—who will possess the information needed by the corporation's lawyers. Middle-level—and indeed lower-level—employees can, by actions within the scope of their employment, embroil the corporation in serious legal difficulties, and it is only natural that these employees would have the relevant information needed by corporate counsel if he is adequately to advise the client with respect to such actual or potential difficulties. This fact was noted in Diversified Industries, Inc. v. Meredith, 572 F.2d 596 (CA8 1978) (en banc):

> "In a corporation, it may be necessary to glean information relevant to a legal problem from middle management or non-management personnel as well as from top executives. The attorney dealing with a complex legal problem 'is thus faced with a "Hobson's choice". If he interviews employees not having "the very highest authority", their communications to him will not be privileged. If, on the other hand, he interviews *only* those employees with the "very highest authority", he may find it extremely difficult, if not impossible, to determine what happened."' Id., at 608–609 (quoting Weinschel, Corporate Employee Interviews and the Attorney–Client Privilege, 12 B.C.Ind. & Com.L.Rev. 873, 876 (1971)).

The control group test adopted by the court below thus frustrates the very purpose of the privilege by discouraging the communication of relevant information by employees of the client to attorneys seeking to render legal advice to the client corporation. The attorney's advice will also frequently be more significant to noncontrol group members than to those who officially sanction the advice, and the control group test makes it more difficult to convey full and frank legal advice to the employees who will put into effect the client corporation's policy. See, e.g., Duplan Corp. v. Deering Milliken, Inc., 397 F.Supp. 1146, 1164 (DSC 1974) ("After the lawyer forms his or her opinion, it is of no immediate benefit to the Chairman of the Board or the President. It must be given to the corporate personnel who will apply it").

The narrow scope given the attorney-client privilege by the court below not only makes it difficult for corporate attorneys to formulate sound advice when their client is faced with a specific legal problem but also threatens to limit the valuable efforts of corporate counsel to ensure their client's compliance with the law. In light of the vast and complicated array of regulatory legislation confronting the modern corporation, corporations, unlike most individuals, "constantly go to lawyers to find out how to obey the law," Burnham, The Attorney–Client Privilege in the Corporate Arena, 24 Bus.Law. 901, 913 (1969), particularly since compliance with the law in this area is hardly an instinctive matter, see, e.g., United States v. United States Gypsum Co., 438 U.S. 422, 440–441 (1978) ("the behavior proscribed by the [Sherman] Act is often difficult to distinguish from the gray zone of socially acceptable and economically justifiable business conduct"). The test adopted by the court below is difficult to apply in practice, though no abstractly formulated and unvarying "test" will necessarily enable courts to decide questions such as this with mathematical precision. But if the purpose of the attorney-client privilege is to be served, the attorney and client must be able to predict with some degree of certainty whether particular discussions will be protected. An uncertain privilege, or one which purports to be certain but results in widely varying applications by the courts, is little better than no privilege at all. The very terms of the test adopted by the court below suggest the unpredictability of its application. The test restricts the availability of the privilege to those officers who play a "substantial role" in deciding and directing a corporation's legal response. Disparate decisions in cases applying this test illustrate its unpredictability. Compare, e.g., Hogan v. Zletz, 43 F.R.D. 308, 315–316 (ND Okl.1967), aff'd in part sub nom. Natta v. Hogan, 392 F.2d 686 (CA10 1968) (control group includes managers and assistant managers of patent division and research and development department), with Congoleum Industries, Inc. v. GAF Corp., 49 F.R.D. 82, 83–85 (ED Pa.1969), aff'd, 478 F.2d 1398 (CA3 1973) (control group includes only division and corporate vice presidents, and not two directors of research and vice president for production and research).

The communications at issue were made by Upjohn employees to counsel for Upjohn acting as such, at the direction of corporate superiors in order to secure legal advice from counsel. As the Magistrate found, "Mr. Thomas consulted with the Chairman of the Board and outside counsel and thereafter conducted a factual investigation to determine the nature and extent of the questionable payments *and to be in a position to give legal advice to the company with respect to the payments.*" (Emphasis supplied.) Information, not available from upper-echelon management, was needed to supply a basis for legal advice concerning compliance with securities and tax laws, foreign laws, currency regulations, duties to shareholders, and potential litigation in each of these areas. The communications concerned matters within the scope of the employees' corporate duties, and the employees themselves were sufficiently aware that they were being questioned in order that the corporation could obtain legal advice. The questionnaire identified Thomas as "the company's General Counsel" and referred in its opening sentence to the possible illegality of payments such as the ones on which information was sought. App. 40a. A statement of policy accompanying the questionnaire clearly indicated the legal implications of the investigation. The policy statement was issued "in order that there be no uncertainty in the future as to the policy with respect to the practices which are the subject of this investigation." It began "Upjohn will comply with all laws and regulations," and stated that commissions or payments "will not be used as a subterfuge for bribes or illegal payments" and that all payments must be "proper and legal." Any future agreements with foreign distributors or agents were to be approved "by a company attorney" and any questions concerning the policy were to be referred "to the company's General Counsel." This statement was issued to Upjohn employees worldwide, so that even those interviewees not receiving a questionnaire were aware of the legal implications of the interviews. Pursuant to explicit instructions from the Chairman of the Board, the communications were considered "highly confidential" when made, and have been kept confidential by the company. Consistent with the underlying purposes of the attorney-client privilege, these communications must be protected against compelled disclosure.

The Court of Appeals declined to extend the attorney-client privilege beyond the limits of the control group test for fear that doing so would entail severe burdens on discovery and create a broad "zone of silence" over corporate affairs. Application of the attorney-client privilege to communications such as those involved here, however, puts the adversary in no worse position than if the communications had never taken place. The privilege only protects disclosure of communications; it does not protect disclosure of the underlying facts by those who communicated with the attorney:

> "[T]he protection of the privilege extends only to *communications* and not to facts. A fact is one thing and a communication concerning that fact is an entirely different thing. The client cannot be compelled to answer the question, 'What did you say or write to the attorney?' but may not refuse to disclose any relevant fact within his knowledge merely because he incorporated a statement of such fact into his communication to his attorney." Philadelphia v. Westinghouse Electric Corp., 205 F.Supp. 830, 831 (ED Pa.1962).

See also Diversified Industries, 572 F.2d, at 611; State ex rel. Dudek v. Circuit Court, 34 Wis.2d 559, 580, 150 N.W.2d 387, 399 (1967) ("the courts have noted that a party cannot conceal a fact merely by revealing it to his lawyer"). Here the Government was free to question the employees who communicated with Thomas and outside counsel. Upjohn has provided the IRS with a list of such employees, and the IRS has already interviewed some 25 of them. While it would probably be more convenient for the Government to secure the results of petitioner's internal investigation by simply subpoenaing the questionnaires and notes taken by petitioner's attorneys, such considerations of convenience do not overcome the policies served by the attorney-client privilege. As Justice Jackson noted in his concurring opinion in Hickman v. Taylor, 329 U.S., at 516: "Discovery was hardly intended to enable a learned profession to perform its functions ... on wits borrowed from the adversary."

Needless to say, we decide only the case before us, and do not undertake to draft a set of rules which should govern challenges to investigatory subpoenas. Any such approach would violate the spirit of Federal Rule of Evidence 501.... While such a "case-by-case" basis may to some slight extent undermine desirable certainty in the boundaries of the attorney-client privilege, it obeys the spirit of the Rules. At the same time we conclude that the narrow "control group test" sanctioned by the Court of Appeals in this case cannot, consistent with "the principles of the common law as ... interpreted ... in the light of reason and experience," Fed.Rule Evid. 501, govern the development of the law in this area.

III

Our decision that the communications by Upjohn employees to counsel are covered by the attorney-client privilege disposes of the case so far as the responses to the questionnaires and any notes reflecting responses to interview questions are concerned. The summons reaches further, however, and Thomas has testified that his notes and memoranda of interviews go beyond recording responses to his questions. To the extent that the material subject to the summons is not protected by the attorney-client privilege as disclosing communications between an employee and counsel, we must reach the ruling by the Court of Appeals that the work-product doctrine does not apply to summonses issued under 26 U.S.C. § 7602.[6]

The Government concedes, wisely, that the Court of Appeals erred and that the work-product doctrine does apply to IRS summonses....

As we stated last Term, the obligation imposed by a tax summons remains "subject to the traditional privileges and limitations." United States v. Euge, 444 U.S. 707, 714 (1980). Nothing in the language of the IRS summons provisions or their legislative history suggests an

---

6. The following discussion will also be relevant to counsel's notes and memoranda of interviews with the seven former employees should it be determined that the attorney-client privilege does not apply to them.

intent on the part of Congress to preclude application of the work-product doctrine. Rule 26(b)(3) codifies the work-product doctrine, and the Federal Rules of Civil Procedure are made applicable to summons enforcement proceedings by Rule 81(a)(3).... While conceding the applicability of the work-product doctrine, the Government asserts that it has made a sufficient showing of necessity to overcome its protections. The Magistrate apparently so found. The Government relies on the following language in *Hickman* :

> "We do not mean to say that all written materials obtained or prepared by an adversary's counsel with an eye toward litigation are necessarily free from discovery in all cases. Where relevant and nonprivileged facts remain hidden in an attorney's file and where production of those facts is essential to the preparation of one's case, discovery may properly be had.... And production might be justified where the witnesses are no longer available or can be reached only with difficulty." 329 U.S., at 511.

The Government stresses that interviewees are scattered across the globe and that Upjohn has forbidden its employees to answer questions it considers irrelevant. The above-quoted language from *Hickman*, however, did not apply to "oral statements made by witnesses ... whether presently in the form of [the attorney's] mental impressions or memoranda." Id., at 512, 67 S.Ct., at 394. As to such material the Court did "not believe that any showing of necessity can be made under the circumstances of this case so as to justify production.... If there should be a rare situation justifying production of these matters petitioner's case is not of that type." Id., at 512–513, 67 S.Ct., at 394–395.... Forcing an attorney to disclose notes and memoranda of witnesses' oral statements is particularly disfavored because it tends to reveal the attorney's mental processes, 329 U.S., at 513 ("what he saw fit to write down regarding witnesses' remarks"); id., at 516–517 ("the statement would be his [the attorney's] language, permeated with his inferences") (Jackson, J., concurring).[8]

Rule 26 accords special protection to work product revealing the attorney's mental processes. The Rule permits disclosure of documents and tangible things constituting attorney work product upon a showing of substantial need and inability to obtain the equivalent without undue hardship. This was the standard applied by the Magistrate. Rule 26 goes on, however, to state that "[i]n ordering discovery of such materials when the required showing has been made, the court shall protect against disclosure of the mental impressions, conclusions, opinions or legal theories of an attorney or other representative of a party concerning the litigation." Although this language does not specifically refer to memoranda based on oral statements of witnesses, the

---

8. Thomas described his notes of the interviews as containing "what I considered to be the important questions, the substance of the responses to them, my beliefs as to the importance of these, my beliefs as to how they related to the inquiry, my thoughts as to how they related to other questions. In some instances they might even suggest other questions that I would have to ask or things that I needed to find elsewhere."

Hickman court stressed the danger that compelled disclosure of such memoranda would reveal the attorney's mental processes. It is clear that this is the sort of material the draftsmen of the Rule had in mind as deserving special protection. See Notes of Advisory Committee on 1970 Amendment to Rules, 28 U.S.C.App., p. 442.

Based on the foregoing, some courts have concluded that *no* showing of necessity can overcome protection of work product which is based on oral statements from witnesses. See, e.g., In re Grand Jury Proceedings, 473 F.2d 840, 848 (CA8 1973) (personal recollections, notes, and memoranda pertaining to conversation with witnesses); In re Grand Jury Investigation, 412 F.Supp. 943, 949 (ED Pa.1976) (notes of conversation with witness "are so much a product of the lawyer's thinking and so little probative of the witness's actual words that they are absolutely protected from disclosure"). Those courts declining to adopt an absolute rule have nonetheless recognized that such material is entitled to special protection. See, e.g., In re Grand Jury Investigation, 599 F.2d 1224, 1231 (CA3 1979) ("special considerations ... must shape any ruling on the discoverability of interview memoranda ...; such documents will be discoverable only in a 'rare situation' "); Cf. In re Grand Jury Subpoena, 599 F.2d 504, 511–512 (CA2 1979).

We do not decide the issue at this time. It is clear that the Magistrate applied the wrong standard when he concluded that the Government had made a sufficient showing of necessity to overcome the protections of the work-product doctrine. The Magistrate applied the "substantial need" and "without undue hardship" standard articulated in the first part of Rule 26(b)(3). The notes and memoranda sought by the Government here, however, are work product based on oral statements. If they reveal communications, they are, in this case, protected by the attorney-client privilege. To the extent they do not reveal communications, they reveal the attorneys' mental processes in evaluating the communications. As Rule 26 and *Hickman* make clear, such work product cannot be disclosed simply on a showing of substantial need and inability to obtain the equivalent without undue hardship.

While we are not prepared at this juncture to say that such material is always protected by the work-product rule, we think a far stronger showing of necessity and unavailability by other means than was made by the Government or applied by the Magistrate in this case would be necessary to compel disclosure....

CHIEF JUSTICE BURGER, concurring in part and concurring in the judgment.

... I agree fully with the Court's rejection of the so-called "control group" test, its reasons for doing so, and its ultimate holding that the communications at issue are privileged. As the Court states, however, "if the purpose of the attorney-client privilege is to be served, the attorney and client must be able to predict with some degree of certainty whether particular discussions will be protected." For this very reason, I believe that we should articulate a standard that will govern similar cases and afford guidance to corporations, counsel advising them, and federal courts.

... [T]he Court should make clear now that, as a general rule, a communication is privileged at least when, as here, an employee or former employee speaks at the direction of the management with an attorney regarding conduct or proposed conduct within the scope of employment. The attorney must be one authorized by the management to inquire into the subject and must be seeking information to assist counsel in performing any of the following functions: (a) evaluating whether the employee's conduct has bound or would bind the corporation; (b) assessing the legal consequences, if any, of that conduct; or (c) formulating appropriate legal responses to actions that have been or may be taken by others with regard to that conduct....

Scope of the Corporate Privilege

What test does *Upjohn* provide for determining the scope of the corporate privilege? Does it make privileged every communication between a corporation's lawyers and any of its employees?

The strongest argument for the "control group" test is that the test prevents too broad a "zone of silence" over corporate affairs. After *Upjohn* might a corporation route all corporate documents through its general counsel's office ostensibly to keep its lawyer informed but actually to set up a later claim of privilege? Would such a plan work?

Under *Upjohn* may the IRS use compulsory process to obtain the following: (1) The accounting report prepared by the outside accounting firm that first raised the subject of "questionable payments?" (2) A memorandum, prepared by the manager of Upjohn's Turkish operations on his own initiative, detailing illegal payments to Turkish officials and reports of similar payments made by other Upjohn employees in Greece and Italy? Does it make a difference whether the report or memorandum is addressed to Upjohn's chairman, Parfet, or to its general counsel, Thomas? Is the privilege inapplicable to either document because it was not made "at the direction of corporate superiors in order to secure legal advice from counsel"?[28] Is the privilege inapplicable because the document comes from a non-employee or the information it contains does not relate to the employee's duties for the corporation? Does Chief Justice Burger's formulation of the privilege answer these hypothetical situations?[29]

Suppose Upjohn executives decide to offer government agencies an airtight case against the Turkish manager on condition that claims

28. See John E. Sexton, A Post–Upjohn Consideration of the Corporate Attorney–Client Privilege, 57 N.Y.U.L.Rev. 443, 508–10 (1982).

29. See Robert Stern, Attorney–Client Privilege: Supreme Court Repudiates the Control Group Test, 67 A.B.A.J. 1142, 1146 (1981).

involving other "questionable payments" are dropped. Can the manager prevent Upjohn from delivering his questionnaire and interview responses to the government? [30]

Why a Corporate Privilege?

The *Upjohn* case appears to have quieted concerns emanating from lower court decisions about the application of the attorney-client privilege to corporations. In its extreme form, the question was whether an artificial entity such as a corporation qualifies as a "client" for purposes of the privilege. Considerations of individual dignity and autonomy that undergird the Fifth Amendment privilege against self-incrimination and the Sixth Amendment right to counsel are limited to natural persons. If the attorney-client privilege rests on similar considerations, should artificial legal entities be confined to the work-product immunity? [31]

A federal district judge startled the corporate bar in 1962 by holding that only natural persons, not corporations, were "clients." [32] Although subsequent decisions rejected this position, the Third Circuit evolved the "control group test" as a limitation on the corporate privilege.[33] Does *Upjohn* settle the question of the applicability of the attorney-client privilege to corporations? Note that state courts are not bound by federal evidence law; even in federal courts, state law governs testimonial privileges insofar as state-created claims and defenses are involved.[34] Federal and state decisions also apply the privilege to other artificial entities, such as partnerships, unincorporated associations and governmental bodies.

Who May Claim the Privilege on Behalf of a Corporation?

The current management of a corporation controls the privilege on behalf of the corporation. When management is replaced, the successor controls the privilege. This may result in decisions to waive the

---

30. See Sexton, supra, 57 N.Y.U.L.Rev. 443 (1982); Note, The Attorney–Client Privilege and the Corporate Client: Where Do We Go After Upjohn?, 81 Mich.L.Rev. 665 (1983).

31. Note that an individual's attorney-client privilege extends only to information supplied by that person to a lawyer. Communications relating to the client from third persons, however closely related to the individual client, are not privileged. Yet *Upjohn* extends the corporate attorney-client privilege to information from anyone related to the corporation. Does this make the corporate attorney-client privilege broader than that available to individuals?

32. Radiant Burners, Inc. v. American Gas Ass'n, 207 F.Supp. 771, 209 F.Supp. 321 (N.D.Ill.1962), rev'd, 320 F.2d 314 (7th Cir.1963).

33. City of Philadelphia v. Westinghouse Elec. Corp., 210 F.Supp. 483 (E.D.Pa.1962), left standing on appeal, 312 F.2d 742 (3d Cir.1962).

34. *Upjohn* is not controlling in state courts or in federal diversity cases. See, e.g., Consolidated Coal Co. v. Bucyrus–Erie Co., 89 Ill.2d 103, 59 Ill.Dec. 666, 432 N.E.2d 250 (1982) (*Upjohn* rejected; control group test applied). However, most states reach the same result as *Upjohn*. See, e.g., Leer v. Chicago, Milwaukee, S.P. & Pac. Ry., 308 N.W.2d 305 (Minn.1981); and Marriott Corp. v. American Academy of Psychotherapists, Inc., 157 Ga.App. 497, 277 S.E.2d 785 (1981). Also see Rossi v. Blue Cross and Blue Shield, 73 N.Y.2d 588, 542 N.Y.S.2d 508, 540 N.E.2d 703 (1989) (discussing limits of the privilege when house counsel are involved).

privilege that may be embarrassing to members of the prior management.[35] Moreover, shareholders in a derivative suit may successfully
challenge management's decision to invoke the privilege and thereby
gain access to otherwise confidential corporate communications.[36]

Speaking With Corporate Employees or Advising Them Not to Speak With Opposing Counsel

The Court in *Upjohn* states that the IRS may question the employees from whom Upjohn's general counsel obtained information. Would
such questioning violate professional constraints against direct contact
with another lawyer's clients? See Model Rule 4.2 and DR 7–104(A)(1).
If the employees refuse to cooperate informally, will a subpoena be
effective? What if an employee refuses to respond on grounds that his
answers may incriminate him? Whether an opposing party may contact employees of an organization directly without notifying the organization's lawyer is considered in Chapter 6 below at p. 574.

In *Upjohn* corporate employees were "forbidden ... to answer
questions" that were posed by government lawyers which the company
considered irrelevant. Could Upjohn also insist that one of its lawyers
be present when the IRS interviews an employee? Model Rule 3.4(f)
provides:

> A lawyer shall not ... request a person other than a client to
> refrain from voluntarily giving relevant information to another
> party unless: (1) the person is a relative or an employee or other
> agent of a client; and (2) the lawyer reasonably believes that the
> person's interests will not be adversely affected by refraining from
> giving such information.

Recall that urging some one not to give evidence may sometimes
constitute the crime of "obstruction of justice." Is there a clear line
between protecting a client by urging employees not to cooperate with
an adversary and obstructing another party's access to evidence?

Governmental Clients and Attorney–Client Privilege

The scope of the attorney-client privilege as applied to governmental clients has been less well explored than the scope of the privilege in
general. Professor Wolfram argues that the privilege should be given a
narrow reading in this context because of the countervailing policies of
open government. Freedom of information statutes contain specified
exceptions and the lawyer work-product doctrine provides more limited
but essential protection in litigation contexts.[37]

---

35. See Commodity Futures Trading Commission v. Weintraub, 471 U.S. 343 (1985)
(court-appointed successor may waive the corporation's privilege).

36. See Garner v. Wolfinbarger, 430 F.2d 1093 (5th Cir.1970) (setting out factors to be
considered in whether to grant shareholders access to otherwise privileged information).
This case and its progeny are discussed in Chapter 8 below at p. 774.

37. See Wolfram, Modern Legal Ethics § 6.5.6 (1986); see also Roger C. Cramton, The
Lawyer as Whistleblower: Confidentiality and the Government Lawyer, 5 Geo.J.Legal
Ethics 291 (1991).

3. Work–Product Doctrine

The work-product doctrine is connected to, but different from, the attorney-client privilege.[38] As *Upjohn* demonstrates, the work-product rule governs documents prepared by lawyers in anticipation of litigation that do not include communications protected by the privilege.

The leading case on the work-product doctrine is Hickman v. Taylor.[39] In *Hickman* the Court recognized a qualified immunity for the work product of lawyers, holding that such material was discoverable only upon a substantial showing of "necessity or justification." *Hickman* has been codified in Federal Rule of Civil Procedure 26(b)(3), which provides in part:

> [A] party may obtain discovery of [material] . . . otherwise discoverable under . . . this rule and prepared in anticipation of litigation . . . only upon showing that the party seeking discovery has substantial need of the materials in the preparation of his case and that he is unable without undue hardship to obtain the substantial equivalent of the materials by other means. In ordering discovery of such materials when the required showing has been made, the court shall protect against disclosure of the mental impressions, conclusions, opinions, or legal theories of an attorney . . . concerning the litigation.

Material other than a lawyer's mental impressions, theories and opinions is called "fact work product." Fact work product has been held discoverable for impeachment purposes,[40] because a witness is unavailable or hostile,[41] because of the delay or expense that would be incurred if the opposing party were not given access to the material[42] and where the passage of time makes the material otherwise inaccessible.[43] Does *Upjohn* raise the level of hardship required to obtain fact work product?

Lawyer's Mental Impressions and Theories

The language in Fed.R.Civ.Proc. Rule 26(b)(3) and in corresponding state formulations of the work-product doctrine accords the mental impressions, opinions and theories of the lawyer special protection. *Upjohn* left open the issue of whether mental impressions and the like are absolutely protected from discovery. What showing of need did the

---

38. On the work-product doctrine see generally Special Project: The Work Product Doctrine, 68 Cornell L.Rev. 760 (1983). See also Proposed Restatement of the Law Governing Lawyers §§ 136–43 (Tent. Draft No. 5, Mar. 16, 1992).

39. 329 U.S. 495 (1947).

40. Brennan v. Engineered Products, 506 F.2d 299 (8th Cir.1974); Dingler v. Halcyon, 50 F.R.D. 211 (E.D.Pa.1970).

41. Xerox v. IBM, 64 F.R.D. 367 (S.D.N.Y.1974) (witness lost memory); Fidelity & Deposit Co. v. S. Stefan Strauss, Inc., 52 F.R.D. 536 (E.D.Pa.1971) (witness employee of adversary); Almaguer v. Chicago, R.I. & P.R., 55 F.R.D. 147 (E.D.Neb.1972) (witness hostile).

42. Arney v. Geo. A. Hormel & Co., 53 F.R.D. 179 (D.Minn.1971).

43. Hamilton v. Canal Barge Co., 395 F.Supp. 975 (D.La.1974).

IRS make in *Upjohn*?   After *Upjohn*, what showing is required to overcome work-product protection?

Most state courts follow the lead of *Upjohn*, holding that absent some extreme necessity the mental impressions of lawyers are not discoverable.[44]   Others hold that under no circumstances are mental impressions discoverable.[45]

Material Prepared in Anticipation of Litigation

As formulated in *Hickman* and codified in Rule 26(b)(3), the work-product rule protects only material prepared in "anticipation of litigation."   *Upjohn* demonstrates that this may include reports prepared prior to the filing of a complaint.   On the other hand, "the work product rule does not come into play merely because there is a remote prospect of future litigation."[46]   The scope of the phrase "prepared in anticipation of litigation" thus is uncertain:

> Courts have attempted to explain exactly what anticipation of litigation means, but such efforts have not helped to resolve the issue.   For example, some courts indicate that a party ... anticipates litigation where there is a "substantial probability" of "imminent" litigation or when there is a "prospect" of litigation.   Another requirement is that there be "some possibility" of litigation; however, a "mere possibility" of litigation is not enough.   Other courts have stated that there must be an "eye" towards litigation or that litigation need only be a reasonable "contingency."   These methods for redefining the word anticipation do little more than say that litigation is anticipated when litigation is anticipated.[47]

Whether material was prepared in anticipation of litigation is an important question for insurance companies.   Are all claims investigations "in anticipation of litigation"?   Two positions have emerged. Most courts say that litigation is not "anticipated" until an attorney has become involved and has either prepared the documents herself or requested their preparation.[48]   Under this rule, unless the insurer's

---

44.   See, e.g., Klaiber v. Orzel, 148 Ariz. 320, 714 P.2d 813 (1986); Consolidation Coal Co. v. Bucyrus–Erie Co., 89 Ill.2d 103, 59 Ill.Dec. 666, 432 N.E.2d 250 (1982); and Parks v. United States, 451 A.2d 591 (D.C.App.1982).

45.   See, e.g., Broussard v. State Farm Mutual, 519 So.2d 136 (La.1988); Dennie v. Metropolitan Medical Center, 387 N.W.2d 401 (Minn.1986).

46.   Diversified Industries, Inc. v. Meredith, 572 F.2d 596, 604 (8th Cir.1977).   See also Sims v. Knollwood Park Hospital, 511 So.2d 154 (Ala.1987) (fact that litigation eventually ensues is not, by itself, enough to designate materials prepared by a lawyer as work product prepared in anticipation of litigation).

47.   Note, Work Product Discovery: A Multifactor Approach to the Anticipation of Litigation Requirement in Federal Rule of Civil Procedure 26(b)(3), 66 Iowa L.Rev. 1277, 1277–78 (1981) (footnotes omitted).

48.   See McDougall v. Dunn, 468 F.2d 468, 474–75 (4th Cir.1972); State Farm Fire & Casualty v. Perrigan, 102 F.R.D. 235, 237–38 (W.D.Va.1984); American Banker's Insurance v. Colorado Flying Academy, 97 F.R.D. 515, 517–18 (D.Colo.1983).   See generally Brian L. Woodward, Insurance Companies and Work Product Immunity Under Indiana Trial Rule 26(b)(3): Indiana Adopts a Fact–Sensitive Approach, 19 Ind.L.Rev. 139, 141–42 (1986).

investigation has been performed at the request or under the direction of an attorney, the materials resulting from the investigation are "conclusively presumed to have been made in the ordinary course of business and not in anticipation of litigation." [49]   One court has given the following rationale for this approach:

> Because a substantial part of an insurance company's business is to investigate claims made by an insured against the company or by some other party against an insured, it must be presumed that such investigations are part of the normal business activity of the company and that reports and witness' statements compiled by or on behalf of the insurer in the course of such investigations are ordinary business records as distinguished from trial preparation materials.[50]

The alternative position treats virtually all insurance investigations as made in anticipation of litigation.[51]   Liability insurers who investigate claims do anticipate litigation, but should work-product protection be provided for the work of claims investigators who are nominally supervised by a lawyer?   What degree of attorney involvement in a claims investigation should be required to satisfy the "anticipation of litigation" requirement? [52]

The work-product rule does not cover material prepared as part of a future or ongoing crime or fraud, whether or not in anticipation of litigation.[53]

Who May Invoke Attorney–Client and Work–Product Protection?

The client, not the lawyer, "owns" the attorney-client privilege, which means that a lawyer cannot successfully invoke the privilege if the client has waived it.[54]   As to work-product protection, courts disagree as to whether the protection is the client's, the lawyer's or belongs to both.   The proposed Restatement of the Law Governing Lawyers states the majority rule that "work product immunity may be

49.   Henry Enterprises v. Smith, 225 Kan. 615, 592 P.2d 915, 920 (1979).

50.   Hawkins v. District Court, 638 P.2d 1372, 1378 (Colo.1982) (en banc, quoting Thomas Organ Co. v. Jodranska Slobodna Plovida, 54 F.R.D. 367, 373 (N.D.Ill.1972)).

51.   See Ashmead v. Harris, 336 N.W.2d 197, 201 (Iowa 1983);   Firemen's Fund Insurance v. McAlpine, 120 R.I. 744, 391 A.2d 84, 89–90 (1978).

52.   See National Farmers Union Property and Casualty Co. v. District Court, 718 P.2d 1044 (Colo.1986) (memoranda prepared by lawyers for insurance company not protected by work product rule because lawyers were performing same function as claims adjuster and the resulting report is an ordinary business record of the company, which is discoverable);   Longs Drug Store v. Howe, 134 Ariz. 424, 657 P.2d 412 (1983).   Compare Shelton v. American Motors Corp., 805 F.2d 1323, 1329 (8th Cir.1986) ("selection and compilation of documents [by lawyer] ... reflects legal theories and thought processes which are protected as work product").

53.   See, e.g., In re Doe, 662 F.2d 1073, 1079–80 (4th Cir.1981);   In re Antitrust Grand Jury, 805 F.2d 155 (6th Cir.1986).   See also the discussion below at p. 265 of the crime-fraud exception to the attorney-client privilege.

54.   See the discussion of waiver below at p. 271.

invoked by or for the client on whose behalf it was prepared." [55] Some courts hold that the lawyer as well as the client must consent to disclosure.[56] A few decisions hold that a lawyer in some situations may resist disclosure of work product in the face of a client's request for it.[57]

Unlike the attorney-client privilege, which clearly continues after the lawyer-client relationship is terminated, work-product protection may terminate at the end of the litigation for which the material was prepared or may continue thereafter. The courts are split on the issue.[58] What, if anything, in the rationale for the work-product rule suggests that its duration be limited?

Accountants Versus Lawyers

Federal securities laws require publicly held corporations to file financial statements that include an independent audit. The accountant must determine whether a corporation has sufficient reserve funds to handle any additional taxes that might arise. Typically, the outside auditor prepares work sheets reviewing the company's own evaluation of its tax liability and outlining the corporation's other possible areas of tax vulnerability. Arthur Young & Co. performed this function for one of its clients, Amerada Hess Corp. The IRS, during an investigation of Amerada's taxes, asked for the work sheets for particular tax years; when Amerada instructed Arthur Young not to produce them, the IRS sought court enforcement of its summons. The Court unanimously held that "tax accrual workpapers prepared by a corporation's independent certified public accountant in the course of regular financial audits are [subject to] disclosure in response to an Internal Revenue Service summons." [59]

The decision reflected the broad statutory authority of the IRS to compel production of taxpayer records and the desirability, in a tax system that relies on voluntary reporting, of assuring government access. But the contrasting treatment given to IRS summonses in *Upjohn* and *Arthur Young* did not go unnoticed. Reliable audits depend upon candor and full disclosure in the provision of information. Accounting firms asserted that failure to protect an auditor's working papers would reduce the flow of information from corporate clients,

---

55. Restatement of Law Governing Lawyers § 139 (Tent.Draft No. 5, Mar. 16, 1992) (discussing cases in the Reporter's Note).

56. See, e.g., In re Special September 1978 Grand Jury, 640 F.2d 49 (7th Cir.1980).

57. In Lasky, Haas, Cohler & Munter v. Superior Court, 172 Cal.App.3d 264, 218 Cal.Rptr. 205 (1985), the court so held but the conclusion in that case may have been affected by the fact that the client's request apparently was under legal coercion from a third party. The court observed that its holding would not preclude a client from obtaining material relevant to a legal malpractice case.

58. See United States v. IBM Corp., 66 F.R.D. 154, 178 (S.D.N.Y.1974) (terminates with the end of litigation); In re Murphy, 560 F.2d 326, 334 (8th Cir.1977) (protection extends to all future litigation).

59. United States v. Arthur Young & Co., 465 U.S. 805 (1984).

reducing the reliability of independent audits.[60]

Chief Justice Burger, writing for the Court in *Arthur Young*, rejected the argument that "a work-product immunity for accountants' tax accrual workpapers is a fitting analogue to the attorney work-product doctrine established in Hickman v. Taylor."

> ... The *Hickman* work-product doctrine was founded upon the private attorney's role as the client's confidential advisor and advocate, a loyal representative whose duty it is to present the client's case in the most favorable possible light. An independent certified public accountant performs a different role. By certifying the public reports that collectively depict a corporation's financial status, the independent auditor assumes a *public* responsibility transcending any employment relationship with the client. The independent public accountant performing this special function owes ultimate allegiance to the corporation's creditors and stockholders, as well as to [the] investing public. This "public watchdog" function demands that the accountant maintain total independence from the client at all times and requires complete fidelity to the public trust. To insulate from disclosure a certified public accountant's interpretations of the client's financial statements would be to ignore the significance of the accountant's role as a disinterested analyst charged with public obligation.

> We cannot accept the view that [without the protection of confidentiality] a corporation might be tempted to withhold from its auditor certain information relevant and material to a proper evaluation of its financial statements.... [T]he independent certified public accountant cannot be content with the corporation's representations that its tax accrual reserves are adequate; the auditor is ethically and professionally obligated to ascertain for himself as far as possible whether the corporation's contingent tax liabilities have been accurately stated. If the auditor were convinced that the scope of the examination had been limited by management's reluctance to disclose matters relating to the tax accrual reserves, the auditor would be unable to issue an unqualified opinion as to the accuracy of the corporation's financial statements. Instead, the auditor would be required to issue a qualified opinion, an adverse opinion, or a disclaimer of opinion, thereby notifying the investing public of possible potential problems inherent in the corporation's financial reports. Responsible corporate management would not risk a qualified evaluation of a corporate taxpayer's financial posture to afford cover for questionable positions reflected in a prior tax return. Thus, the independent auditor's obligation to serve the public interest assures that the integrity of the securities markets will be preserved, without the need for

60. See Stephen Wermiel, Justices Allow Review by IRS of Audit Papers, Wall St.J., Mar. 22, 1984, p. 2.

a work-product immunity for accountants' tax accrual workpapers.[61]

Are you satisfied that the arguments for lawyer confidentiality are better than those for accountant confidentiality? Are lawyers always acting as "advocates" and accountants always as "auditors?" In a world in which different service professions compete for business, *Upjohn* and *Arthur Young* give lawyers something to sell that accountants and others do not—a large but uncertain degree of protection against compelled disclosure. Does the attorney-client privilege, as applied in *Upjohn*, provide an artificial stimulus for large organizations to hire lawyers whenever trouble is afoot in an effort to shield dirty linen from public scrutiny and response?

4. Documents, Attorney–Client Privilege and the Bill of Rights

FISHER v. UNITED STATES

Supreme Court of the United States, 1976.
425 U.S. 391, 96 S.Ct. 1569, 48 L.Ed.2d 39.

MR. JUSTICE WHITE delivered the opinion of the Court.

In these two cases we are called upon to decide whether a summons directing an attorney to produce documents delivered to him by his client in connection with the attorney-client relationship is enforceable over claims that the documents were constitutionally immune from summons in the hands of the client and retained that immunity in the hands of the attorney.

... In our view the documents were not privileged either in the hands of the lawyers or of their clients....

[In one of the two cases, United States v. Kasmir, 499 F.2d 444 (5th Cir.1974), two special agents of the Internal Revenue Service visited Dr. E.J. Mason's medical office, informed him that his tax returns for 1969, 1970, and 1971 were under investigation, and gave him Miranda warnings. When the agents asked to see Mason's books and records, Mason called his accountant, Candy, who advised him to say nothing and not to produce his records. Candy then called Kasmir, a lawyer, whom Mason retained as his attorney later the same day. Early the next morning, at Mason's direction, Candy delivered various records and documents to Mason, who then turned them over to Kasmir as his attorney. The next day the IRS served a summons on Kasmir directing him to produce "the following records of Tannebaum Bindler & Lewis [the accounting firm].

"1. Accountant's workpapers pertaining to Dr. E.J. Mason's books and records of 1969, 1970 and 1971.

"2. Retained copies of E.J. Mason's income tax returns for 1969, 1970 and 1971.

---

61. 465 U.S. at 817–19.

"3. Retained copies of reports and other correspondence between Tannenbaum Bindler & Lewis and Dr. E.J. Mason during 1969, 1970 and 1971."

[When Kasmir refused to comply with the summons, the government sought enforcement. The district court granted enforcement, but the court of appeals reversed. United States v. Kasmir, 499 F.2d 444 (5th Cir.1974). The second case, United States v. Fisher, 500 F.2d 683 (3d Cir.1974), reached a result contrary to *Kasmir*. In *Fisher* the IRS sought analyses by the taxpayers' accountant of income and expenses, which had been prepared from canceled checks and deposit receipts of the taxpayers' businesses, and later turned over to their lawyer. In *Fisher* as in *Kasmir*, the attorney claimed that enforcement would involve compulsory self-incrimination of the taxpayers in violation of their Fifth Amendment privilege, would involve a seizure of the papers without necessary compliance with the Fourth Amendment and would violate the taxpayers' right to communicate in confidence with their attorneys.]

II

All of the parties in these cases and the Court of Appeals for the Fifth Circuit have concurred in the proposition that if the Fifth Amendment would have excused a *taxpayer* from turning over the accountant's papers had he possessed them, the *attorney* to whom they are delivered for the purpose of obtaining legal advice should also be immune from subpoena. Although we agree with this proposition for the reasons set forth in Part III, infra, we are convinced that, under our decision in Couch v. United States, 409 U.S. 322 (1973), it is not the taxpayer's Fifth Amendment privilege that would excuse the *attorney* from production.

The relevant part of that Amendment provides:

"No person ... shall be *compelled* in any criminal case to be a *witness against himself.*" (Emphasis added.)

The taxpayer's privilege under this Amendment is not violated by enforcement of the summonses involved in these cases because enforcement against a taxpayer's lawyer would not "compel" the taxpayer to do anything—and certainly would not compel him to be a "witness" against himself. The Court has held repeatedly that the Fifth Amendment is limited to prohibiting the use of "physical or moral compulsion" exerted on the person asserting the privilege.... In Couch v. United States, supra, we recently ruled that the Fifth Amendment rights of a taxpayer were not violated by the enforcement of a documentary summons directed to her accountant and requiring production of the taxpayer's own records in the possession of the accountant. We did so on the ground that in such a case "the ingredient of personal compulsion against an accused is lacking." 409 U.S., at 329....

Here, the taxpayers are compelled to do no more than was the taxpayer in *Couch*. The taxpayers' Fifth Amendment privilege is therefore not violated by enforcement of the summonses directed toward their attorneys. This is true whether or not the Amendment would have barred a subpoena directing the taxpayer to produce the documents while they were in his hands.

The fact that the attorneys are agents of the taxpayers does not change this result. *Couch* held as much, since the accountant there was also the taxpayer's agent, and in this respect reflected a longstanding view. In Hale v. Henkel, 201 U.S. 43, 69–70 (1906), the Court said that the privilege "was never intended to permit [a person] to plead the fact that some third person might be incriminated by his testimony, even though he were the agent of such person.... [T]he Amendment is limited to a person who shall be compelled in any criminal case to be a witness against *himself*." (Emphasis in original.) "It is extortion of information from the accused himself that offends our sense of justice." Couch v. United States, supra, 409 U.S., at 328.... Agent or no, the lawyer is not the taxpayer. The taxpayer is the "accused," and nothing is being extorted from him.

Nor is this one of those situations, which *Couch* suggested might exist, where constructive possession is so clear or relinquishment of possession so temporary and insignificant as to leave the personal compulsion upon the taxpayer substantially intact. 409 U.S., at 333.... In this respect we see no difference between the delivery to the attorneys in these cases and delivery to the accountant in the *Couch* case. As was true in *Couch*, the documents sought were obtainable without personal compulsion on the accused.

... Here, the taxpayers retained any privilege they ever had not to be compelled to testify against themselves and not to be compelled themselves to produce private papers in their possession. *This* personal privilege was in no way decreased by the transfer. It is simply that by reason of the transfer of the documents to the attorneys, those papers may be subpoenaed without compulsion on the taxpayer. The protection of the Fifth Amendment is therefore not available. "A party is privileged from producing evidence but not from its production." Johnson v. United States, 228 U.S., at 458....

The Court of Appeals for the Fifth Circuit suggested that because legally and ethically the attorney was required to respect the confidences of his client, the latter had a reasonable expectation of privacy for the records in the hands of the attorney and therefore did not forfeit his Fifth Amendment privilege with respect to the records by transferring them in order to obtain legal advice. It is true that the Court has often stated that one of the several purposes served by the constitutional privilege against compelled testimonial self-incrimination is that of protecting personal privacy. But the Court has never suggested that every invasion of privacy violates the privilege. Within the limits imposed by the language of the Fifth Amendment, which we necessarily observe, the privilege truly serves privacy interests; but the Court has never on any ground, personal privacy included, applied the Fifth

Amendment to prevent the otherwise proper acquisition or use of evidence which, in the Court's view, did not involve compelled testimonial self-incrimination of some sort.[5]

The proposition that the Fifth Amendment protects private information obtained without compelling self-incriminating testimony is contrary to the clear statements of this Court that under appropriate safeguards private incriminating statements of an accused may be overheard and used in evidence, if they are not compelled at the time they were uttered, Katz v. United States, 389 U.S. 347, 354 (1967); Osborn v. United States, 385 U.S. 323, 329–330 (1966); and Berger v. New York, 388 U.S. 41, 57 (1967); cf. Hoffa v. United States, 385 U.S. 293, 304 (1966); and that disclosure of private information may be compelled if immunity removes the risk of incrimination. Kastigar v. United States, 406 U.S. 441 (1972). If the Fifth Amendment protected generally against the obtaining of private information from a man's mouth or pen or house, its protections would presumably not be lifted by probable cause and a warrant or by immunity. The privacy invasion is not mitigated by immunity; and the Fifth Amendment's strictures, unlike the Fourth's, are not removed by showing reasonableness. The Framers addressed the subject of personal privacy directly in the Fourth Amendment. They struck a balance so that when the State's reason to believe incriminating evidence will be found becomes sufficiently great, the invasion of privacy becomes justified and a warrant to search and seize will issue. They did not seek in still another Amendment—the Fifth—to achieve a general protection of privacy but to deal with the more specific issue of compelled self-incrimination.

We cannot cut the Fifth Amendment completely loose from the moorings of its language, and make it serve as a general protector of privacy—a word not mentioned in its text and a concept directly addressed in the Fourth Amendment. We adhere to the view that the Fifth Amendment protects against "compelled self-incrimination, not [the disclosure of] private information." United States v. Nobles, 422 U.S. 225, 233 n. 7 (1975).

Insofar as private information not obtained through compelled self-incriminating testimony is legally protected, its protection stems from other sources[6]—the Fourth Amendment's protection against seizures

---

5. There is a line of cases in which the Court stated that the Fifth Amendment was offended by the use in evidence of documents or property seized in violation of the Fourth Amendment. Gouled v. United States, 255 U.S. 298, 306 (1921); Agnello v. United States, 269 U.S. 20, 33–34 (1925); United States v. Lefkowitz, 285 U.S. 452, 466–467 (1932); Mapp v. Ohio, 367 U.S. 643, 661 (1961) (Black, J., concurring). But the Court purported to find elements of compulsion in such situations. "In either case he is the unwilling source of the evidence, and the Fifth Amendment forbids that he shall be compelled to be a witness against himself in a criminal case." Gouled v. United States, supra, 255 U.S., at 306. . . . In any event the predicate for those cases, lacking here, was a violation of the Fourth Amendment. Cf. Burdeau v. McDowell, supra, 256 U.S. 465, 475–476 (1921).

6. In Couch v. United States, 409 U.S. 322 (1973), on which taxpayers rely for their claim that the Fifth Amendment protects their "legitimate expectation of privacy," the Court differentiated between the things protected by the Fourth and Fifth Amendments. "We hold today that no Fourth or Fifth Amendment claim can prevail where, as in this

without warrant or probable cause and against subpoenas which suffer from "too much indefiniteness or breadth in the things required to be 'particularly described,"' Oklahoma Press Pub. Co. v. Walling, 327 U.S. 186, 208 (1946); In re Horowitz, 482 F.2d 72, 75–80 (CA2 1973) (Friendly, J.); the First Amendment, see NAACP v. Alabama, 357 U.S. 449, 462 (1958); or evidentiary privileges such as the attorney-client privilege.[7]

III

... The taxpayers in these cases, however, have from the outset consistently urged that they should not be forced to expose otherwise protected documents to summons simply because they have sought legal advice and turned the papers over to their attorneys. . . .

Confidential disclosures by a client to an attorney made in order to obtain legal assistance are privileged. 8 J. Wigmore, Evidence, § 2292 (McNaughton rev. 1961) (hereinafter Wigmore); McCormick § 87, p. 175. The purpose of the privilege is to encourage clients to make full disclosure to their attorneys. 8 Wigmore § 2291, and § 2306, p. 590; McCormick § 87, p. 175, § 92, p. 192. . . . As a practical matter, if the client knows that damaging information could more readily be obtained from the attorney following disclosure than from himself in the absence of disclosure, the client would be reluctant to confide in his lawyer and it would be difficult to obtain fully informed legal advice. However, since the privilege has the effect of withholding relevant information from the factfinder, it applies only where necessary to achieve its purpose. Accordingly it protects only those disclosures—necessary to obtain informed legal advice—which might not have been made absent the privilege. In re Horowitz, supra, 482 F.2d 72, at 81 (Friendly, J.); United States v. Goldfarb, supra, 328 F.2d 280; 8 Wigmore, § 2291, p. 554; McCormick, § 89, p. 185. This Court and the lower courts have thus uniformly held that pre-existing documents which could have been obtained by court process from the client when he was in possession may also be obtained from the attorney by similar process following transfer by the client in order to obtain more informed legal advice. Grant v. United States, 227 U.S. 74, 79–80 (1913); 8 Wigmore § 2307 and cases there cited; McCormick § 90, p. 185. . . . State ex rel. Sowers v. Olwell, 64 Wash.2d 828, 394 P.2d 681 (1964). The purpose of the privilege requires no broader rule. Pre-existing documents obtainable from the client are not appreciably easier to obtain from the attorney after transfer to him. Thus, even absent the attorney-client privilege,

case, there exists no legitimate expectation of privacy and no semblance of governmental compulsion against the person of the accused." Id., 409 U.S., at 336. . . .

7. The taxpayers and their attorneys have not raised arguments of a Fourth Amendment nature before this Court and could not be successful if they had. The summonses are narrowly drawn and seek only documents of unquestionable relevance to the tax investigation. Special problems of privacy which might be presented by subpoena of a personal diary, United States v. Bennett, 409 F.2d 888, 897 (CA2 1969) (Friendly, J.), are not involved here.

First Amendment values are also plainly not implicated in these cases.

clients will not be discouraged from disclosing the documents to the attorney, and their ability to obtain informed legal advice will remain unfettered. It is otherwise if the documents are not obtainable by subpoena duces tecum or summons while in the exclusive possession of the client, for the client will then be reluctant to transfer possession to the lawyer unless the documents are also privileged in the latter's hands. . . . We accordingly proceed to the question whether the documents could have been obtained by summons addressed to the taxpayer while the documents were in his possession. The only bar to enforcement of such summons asserted by the parties or the courts below is the Fifth Amendment's privilege against self-incrimination. . . .

IV

The proposition that the Fifth Amendment prevents compelled production of documents over objection that such production might incriminate stems from Boyd v. United States, 116 U.S. 616 (1886). *Boyd* involved a civil forfeiture proceeding brought by the Government against two partners for fraudulently attempting to import 35 cases of glass without paying the prescribed duty. The partnership had contracted with the Government to furnish the glass needed in the construction of a Government building. The glass specified was foreign glass, it being understood that if part or all of the glass was furnished from the partnership's existing duty-paid inventory, it could be replaced by duty-free imports. Pursuant to this arrangement, 29 cases of glass were imported by the partnership duty free. The partners then represented that they were entitled to duty-free entry of an additional 35 cases which were soon to arrive. The forfeiture action concerned these 35 cases. The Government's position was that the partnership had replaced all of the glass used in construction of the Government building when it imported the 29 cases. At trial, the Government obtained a court order directing the partners to produce an invoice the partnership had received from the shipper covering the previous 29–case shipment. The invoice was disclosed, offered in evidence, and used, over the Fifth Amendment objection of the partners, to establish that the partners were fraudulently claiming a greater exemption from duty than they were entitled to under the contract. This Court held that the invoice was inadmissible and reversed the judgment in favor of the Government. The Court ruled that the Fourth Amendment applied to court orders in the nature of subpoenas duces tecum in the same manner in which it applies to search warrants, id., at 622, . . . and that the Government may not, consistent with the Fourth Amendment, seize a person's documents or other property as evidence unless it can claim a proprietary interest in the property superior to that of the person from whom the property is obtained. Id., at 623–624. . . . The invoice in question was thus held to have been obtained in violation of the Fourth Amendment. The Court went on to hold that the accused in a criminal case or the defendant in a forfeiture action could not be forced to produce evidentiary items without violating the Fifth Amendment as well as the Fourth. More specifically, the Court declared, "a compulsory production of the private books and papers of the owner of goods sought to be forfeited ... is compelling him to be a witness against himself, within the meaning of the Fifth Amendment to the Constitution." Id., at 634–635.... Admitting the partnership invoice into evidence had violated both the Fifth and Fourth Amendments.

Among its several pronouncements, *Boyd* was understood to declare that the seizure, under warrant or otherwise, of any purely evidentiary materials violated the Fourth Amendment and that the Fifth Amendment rendered these seized materials inadmissible. Gouled v. United States, 255 U.S. 298 (1921).... That rule applied to documents as well as to other evidentiary items—"[t]here is no special sanctity in papers, as distinguished from other forms of property, to render them immune from search and seizure, if only they fall within the scope of the principles of the cases in which other property may be seized...." Gouled v. United States, supra, 255 U.S., at 309.... Private papers taken from the taxpayer, like other "mere evidence," could not be used against the accused over his Fourth and Fifth Amendment objections.

Several of *Boyd's* express or implicit declarations have not stood the test of time....

[T]he Fifth Amendment does not independently proscribe the compelled production of every sort of incriminating evidence but applies only when the accused is compelled to make a *testimonial* communication that is incriminating. We have, accordingly, declined to extend the protection of the privilege to the giving of blood samples, Schmerber v. California, 384 U.S. 757, 763–764, (1966); to the giving of handwriting exemplars, Gilbert v. California, 388 U.S. 263, 265–267 (1967); voice exemplars, United States v. Wade, 388 U.S. 218, 222–223 (1967); or the donning of a blouse worn by the perpetrator, Holt v. United States, 218 U.S. 245 (1910). Furthermore, despite *Boyd*, neither a partnership nor the individual partners are shielded from compelled production of partnership records on self-incrimination grounds. Bellis v. United States, 417 U.S. 85 (1974). It would appear that under that case the precise claim sustained in *Boyd* would now be rejected for reasons not there considered.

· · ·

A subpoena served on a taxpayer requiring him to produce an accountant's workpapers in his possession without doubt involves substantial compulsion. But it does not compel oral testimony; nor would it ordinarily compel the taxpayer to restate, repeat, or affirm the truth of the contents of the documents sought. Therefore, the Fifth Amendment would not be violated by the fact alone that the papers on their face might incriminate the taxpayer, for the privilege protects a person only against being incriminated by his own compelled testimonial communications. Schmerber v. California, supra; United States v. Wade, supra, and Gilbert v. California, supra. The accountant's workpapers are not the taxpayer's. They were not prepared by the taxpayer, and they contain no testimonial declarations by him. Furthermore, as far as this record demonstrates, the preparation of all of the papers sought in these cases was wholly voluntary, and they cannot be said to contain compelled testimonial evidence, either of the taxpayers or of anyone else.[11] The taxpayer cannot avoid compliance with the subpoena merely by asserting that the item of evidence which he is required to produce contains incriminating writing, whether his own or that of someone else.

The act of producing evidence in response to a subpoena nevertheless has communicative aspects of its own, wholly aside from the contents of the papers produced. Compliance with the subpoena tacitly concedes the existence of the papers demanded and their possession or control by the taxpayer. It also would indicate the taxpayer's belief that the papers are those described in the subpoena. Curcio v. United States, 354 U.S. 118, 125 (1957). The elements of compulsion are clearly present, but the more difficult issues are whether the tacit averments of the taxpayer are both "testimonial" and "incriminating" for purposes of applying the Fifth Amendment. These questions perhaps do not lend themselves to categorical answers; their resolution may instead depend on the facts and circumstances of particular cases or classes thereof. In light of the records now before us, we are confident that however incriminating the contents of the accountant's workpapers might be, the act of producing them—the only thing which the taxpayer is compelled to do—would not itself involve testimonial self-incrimination.

It is doubtful that implicitly admitting the existence and possession of the papers rises to the level of testimony within the protection of the Fifth Amendment. The papers belong to the accountant, were prepared by him, and are the kind usually prepared by an accountant working on the tax returns of his client. Surely the Government is in no way relying on the "truth-telling" of the taxpayer to prove the existence of or his access to the documents. 8 Wigmore § 2264, p. 380. The existence and location of the papers are a foregone conclusion and the taxpayer adds little or nothing to the sum total of the Government's information by conceding that he in fact has the papers. Under these circumstances by enforcement of the summons "no constitutional rights

---

11. The fact that the documents may have been written by the person asserting the privilege is insufficient to trigger the privilege, Wilson v. United States, 221 U.S. 361, 378 (1911). And, unless the Government has compelled the subpoenaed person to write the document, cf. Marchetti v. United States, 390 U.S. 39 (1968); Grosso v. United States, 390 U.S. 62 (1968), the fact that it was written by him is not controlling with respect to the Fifth Amendment issue. Conversations may be seized and introduced in evidence under proper safeguards, Katz v. United States, 389 U.S. 347 (1967); Osborn v. United States, 385 U.S. 323 (1976); Berger v. New York, 388 U.S. 41 (1967); United States v. Bennett, 409 F.2d, at 897 n. 9, if not compelled. In the case of a documentary subpoena the only thing compelled is the act of producing the document and the compelled act is the same as the one performed when a chattel or document not authored by the producer is demanded. McCormick § 128, p. 261.

are touched. The question is not of testimony but of surrender." In re Harris, 221 U.S. 274, 279 (1911).

When an accused is required to submit a handwriting exemplar he admits his ability to write and impliedly asserts that the exemplar is his writing. But in common experience, the first would be a near truism and the latter self-evident. In any event, although the exemplar may be incriminating to the accused and although he is compelled to furnish it, his Fifth Amendment privilege is not violated because nothing he has said or done is deemed to be sufficiently testimonial for purposes of the privilege. This Court has also time and again allowed subpoenas against the custodian of corporate documents or those belonging to other collective entities such as unions and partnerships and those of bankrupt businesses over claims that the documents will incriminate the custodian despite the fact that producing the documents tacitly admits their existence and their location in the hands of their possessor. E.g., Wilson v. United States, 221 U.S. 361 (1911); Dreier v. United States, 221 U.S. 394 (1911); United States v. White, 322 U.S. 694 (1944); Bellis v. United States, 417 U.S. 85 (1974); *In re Harris*, supra. The existence and possession or control of the subpoenaed documents being no more in issue here than in the above cases, the summons is equally enforceable.

Moreover, assuming that these aspects of producing the accountant's papers have some minimal testimonial significance, surely it is not illegal to seek accounting help in connection with one's tax returns or for the accountant to prepare workpapers and deliver them to the taxpayer. At this juncture, we are quite unprepared to hold that either the fact of existence of the papers or of their possession by the taxpayer poses any realistic threat of incrimination to the taxpayer.

As for the possibility that responding to the subpoena would authenticate [12] the workpapers, production would express nothing more than the taxpayer's belief that the papers are those described in the subpoena. The taxpayer would be no more competent to authenticate

---

12. The "implicit authentication" rationale appears to be the prevailing justification for the Fifth Amendment's application to documentary subpoenas. Schmerber v. California, 384 U.S., at 763–764 ... ("the privilege reaches ... the compulsion of responses which are also communications, for example, compliance with a subpoena to produce one's papers. Boyd v. United States, 116 U.S. 616"); Couch v. United States, 409 U.S., at 344, 346 ... (Marshall, J., dissenting) (the person complying with the subpoena "implicitly testifies that the evidence he brings forth is in fact the evidence demanded"); United States v. Beattie, 522 F.2d 267, 270 (CA2 1975) (Friendly, J.) ("[a] subpoena demanding that an accused produce his own records is ... the equivalent of requiring him to take the stand and admit their genuineness"), cert. pending, Nos. 75–407, 75–700; 8 Wigmore § 2264, p. 380 (the testimonial component involved in compliance with an order for production of documents or chattels "is the witness' assurance, compelled as an incident of the process, that the articles produced are the ones demanded"); McCormick § 126, p. 268 ("[t]his rule [applying the Fifth Amendment privilege to documentary subpoenas] is defended on the theory that one who produces documents (or other matter) described in the subpoena duces tecum represents, by his production, that the documents produced are in fact the documents described in the subpoena"); People v. Defore, 242 N.Y. 13, 27, 150 N.E. 585, 590 (1926) (Cardozo, J.) ("A defendant is 'protected from producing his documents in response to a subpoena duces tecum, for his production of them in court would be his voucher of their genuineness.' There would then be 'testimonial compulsion'").

the accountant's workpapers or reports [13] by producing them than he would be to authenticate them if testifying orally. The taxpayer did not prepare the papers and could not vouch for their accuracy. The documents would not be admissible in evidence against the taxpayer without authenticating testimony. Without more, responding to the subpoena in the circumstances before us would not appear to represent a substantial threat of self-incrimination. Moreover, in Wilson v. United States, supra; Dreier v. United States, supra; United States v. White, supra; Bellis v. United States, supra; and *In re Harris*, supra, the custodian of corporate, union, or partnership books or those of a bankrupt business was ordered to respond to a subpoena for the business' books even though doing so involved a "representation that the documents produced are those demanded by the subpoena," Curcio v. United States, 354 U.S., at 125.... [14]

Whether the Fifth Amendment would shield the taxpayer from producing his own tax records in his possession is a question not involved here; for the papers demanded here are not his "private papers," see Boyd v. United States, supra, 116 U.S., at 634–635.... We do hold that compliance with a summons directing the taxpayer to produce the accountant's documents involved in these cases would involve no incriminating testimony within the protection of the Fifth Amendment.

· · ·

MR. JUSTICE STEVENS took no part in the consideration or disposition of these cases.

MR. JUSTICE BRENNAN, concurring in the judgment.

I concur in the judgment. Given the prior access by accountants retained by the taxpayers to the papers involved in these cases and the wholly business rather than personal nature of the papers, I agree that the privilege against compelled self-incrimination did not in either of these cases protect the papers from production in response to the summonses. See Couch v. United States, 409 U.S. 322, 335–336 (1973); id., at 337 (Brennan, J., concurring). I do not join the Court's opinion, however, because of the portent of much of what is said of a serious crippling of the protection secured by the privilege against compelled production of one's private books and papers....

---

13. In seeking the accountant's "retained copies" of correspondence with the taxpayer in No. 74–611, we assume that the summons sought only "copies" of original letters sent from the accountant to the taxpayer—the truth of the contents of which could be testified to only by the accountant.

14. In these cases compliance with the subpoena is required even though the books have been kept by the person subpoenaed and his producing them would itself be sufficient authentication to permit their introduction against him.

Documents Given to a Lawyer by a Client [62]

If the client had created the subpoenaed documents solely to assist the lawyer in preparing a defense, would the result in *Fisher* have been different? What if the lawyer had prepared the documents in anticipation of the IRS's bringing suit against the lawyer's client?

The *Fisher* Court held that under the attorney-client privilege pre-existing documents in the hands of the lawyer are exempt from subpoena only if under the Fifth Amendment the documents would be exempt from subpoena in the hands of the client. The question then became whether the Fifth Amendment would protect the client from having to produce the documents. On this question the Court held that compelled production does not violate the Fifth Amendment unless the compulsion is both "testimonial" and "incriminating." The documents here apparently were incriminating. Why were they not considered testimonial?

The Court went to considerable pains to differentiate a lawyer's direct reliance on the client's Fifth Amendment rights and the derivative use of the attorney-client privilege by the lawyer to raise the Fifth Amendment question. In doing so, did not the Court expand the normal contours of the attorney-client privilege? What is the "confidential communication made for purposes of obtaining legal advice" when the client delivers his accountant's files concerning him to his lawyer?

Extending the attorney-client privilege to include material that would have been privileged on other grounds, such as the Fifth Amendment, had the material remained in the client's hands makes a great deal of sense because such an extension avoids putting a client in a worse position than he would have been in if he had not consulted a lawyer. On the other hand, requiring that the material be otherwise privileged prevents a client from obtaining a better position in terms of non-production of evidentiary material just because he has delivered it to a lawyer. If delivery to a lawyer alone rendered material immune from production, lawyers would be engaged in the warehouse business; and a race to discover and transmit papers would accompany suspicion of an impending government investigation.

Would the result in *Fisher* have differed if the papers involved had been the books and records of Dr. Mason's medical practice rather than those of his accountant? In United States v. Doe [*Doe I*],[63] the government subpoenaed business records from the sole proprietor of a restaurant. The Court held that the documents were not themselves privileged under the Fifth Amendment, clearing up any doubt remaining

---

62. On the issues raised by *Fisher* and *Doe I*, see Robert H. Heidt, The Fifth Amendment Privilege and Documents—Cutting Fisher's Tangled Line, 49 Mo.L.Rev. 439 (1984); Robert P. Mosteller, Simplifying Subpoena Law: Taking the Fifth Amendment Seriously, 73 Va.L.Rev. 1 (1987); and Note, Fifth Amendment Privilege for Producing Corporate Documents, 84 Mich.L.Rev. 1544 (1986).

63. 465 U.S. 605 (1984).

after *Fisher* as to whether an individual's business records enjoyed some special Fifth Amendment privilege not accorded to the records of a partnership or corporation. The Court held, however, that the act of producing the documents was sufficiently "testimonial" to give the defendant a Fifth Amendment right to refuse absent a grant of use immunity.

In a subsequent unrelated case with the same title, *Doe II,*[64] the Court upheld a lower court order obtained by the government requiring a suspect to sign a form stating that he consented to the surrender by a foreign bank to prosecutors of the records of any accounts that he might have. Justice Blackmun's opinion for the majority of five said the compelled signature was "not testimonial in nature" because the government-drafted form was worded hypothetically and did not require the suspect to admit whether or not he in fact had a foreign bank account. The opinion relied on decisions requiring a suspect to provide blood, handwriting and voice samples.

Whither *Boyd*?

The argument, rejected in *Doe I*, that some special protection under the Fifth Amendment should be accorded an individual's business records comes from Boyd v. United States,[65] one of the earliest Fourth and Fifth Amendment cases to be decided by the Supreme Court. In sweeping language, *Boyd* suggested that the Fifth and Fourth Amendments protected the private papers of an individual, "his dearest property." [66] Subsequent cases replaced *Boyd* 's "property-oriented" view of the Fifth Amendment with an analysis concerned only with whether the act of producing the documents was itself testimonial and incriminatory.[67] After *Doe I*, special protection for papers may exist only for non-business papers of an individual.[68]

Other doctrinal developments have continued to narrow the application of any vestiges of the *Boyd* doctrine.[69] One line of cases has

64. Doe v. United States [*Doe II*], 487 U.S. 201 (1988).

65. 116 U.S. 616 (1886).

66. 116 U.S. at 628.

67. See Wayne R. LaFave and Jerold H. Israel, Criminal Procedure 398–407 (1985) for discussion of the case law dealing with self-incrimination and the production of documents.

68. Compare In re Three Grand Jury Subpoenas, dated January 5, 1988, 847 F.2d 1024 (2d Cir.1988) (issue of personal papers undecided by *Doe*), with Butcher v. Bailey, 753 F.2d 465 (6th Cir.1985) (there may be protection for personal private papers); and In re Grand Jury Proceedings on February 4, 1982, 759 F.2d 1418 (9th Cir.1985) (no protection for personal papers).

69. In *Doe I*, Justice O'Connor's concurring opinion asserted

that the Fifth Amendment provides absolutely no protection for the contents of private papers of any kind. The notion that the Fifth Amendment protects the privacy of papers originated in *Boyd v. United States,* but our decision in *Fisher v. United States* sounded the death-knell for *Boyd.* ... Today's decision puts a long-overdue end to that fruitless search.

465 U.S. at 618. Justices Brennan and Marshall, dissenting in *Doe,* took issue with Justice O'Connor's burial of *Boyd*, an obituary not explicitly endorsed by the majority opinion.

developed the "entity exception": The self-incrimination privilege is not available to a corporation, union, partnership, or other structured organization operating as a joint entity.[70] Moreover, the custodian of entity records may not rely on a personal privilege to refuse to produce the records even though the records are highly incriminating to the custodian.[71] Finally, the "required records" doctrine holds that requiring a person to keep records of certain business activities and to make those records available for government inspection does not violate the self-incrimination clause.[72] Consider the application of the required records doctrine to a state rule requiring lawyers to keep records of client trust accounts and to make them available for random audits by state bar auditors.

Searches of Law Offices

Fisher dealt with a subpoena and not a search warrant. Even where a defendant has a Fifth Amendment right to refuse to *produce* documents in compliance with a subpoena, she has no Fifth Amendment right to refuse to allow the police to conduct a search pursuant to a valid search warrant or a search otherwise constitutional under the Fourth Amendment. Therefore, if the government seeks to search a lawyer's office for incriminating documents, the lawyer's objections must be grounded in the Fourth Amendment or the attorney-client privilege. If the search is not unreasonable under the Fourth Amendment and the documents are not covered by the attorney-client privilege (because, for example, they were not created to communicate with the lawyer), the courts will uphold the validity of the search.[73] A federal statute, however, requires prosecutorial guidelines for searches

Boyd is an example of an interesting jurisprudential phenomenon. From a very early point, the Court both identified *Boyd* as the seminal case on constitutional criminal procedure and began to move away from it. The history of constitutional criminal procedure can best (and perhaps only) be understood as a long struggle with *Boyd*. In an important sense, Justice O'Connor is probably right: The Court is unlikely to use *Boyd* to protect an individual's privacy interest in material objects. But it is apparently difficult for the Court to dismiss as "wrong" a case it has found worthy of struggling with for so long.

70. See, e.g., Hale v. Henkel, 201 U.S. 43 (1906) (corporation); United States v. White, 322 U.S. 694 (1944) (union); Bellis v. United States, 417 U.S. 85 (1974) (law partnership consisting of three partners and six employees); In re Grand Jury Proceedings (Shiffman), 576 F.2d 703 (6th Cir.1978) (tenants in common engaged in financial transaction of real property under an assumed name).

71. Braswell v. United States, 487 U.S. 99 (1988) (individual custodian of records of his closely held corporation compelled to produce those records even if the very act of handing them over would incriminate him); Curcio v. United States, 354 U.S. 118 (1957).

72. Shapiro v. United States, 335 U.S. 1 (1948) (sales records required to be kept by Emergency Price Control Act); California v. Byers, 402 U.S. 424 (1971) (upholding against Fifth Amendment objections "hit and run" statute requiring a driver involved in a motor vehicle accident to stop and report the accident); cf. Grosso v. United States, 390 U.S. 62 (1968) (privilege against self-incrimination is a defense to criminal prosecutions for violation of registration and taxing provisions of the federal wagering statutes).

73. See, e.g., Andresen v. Maryland, 427 U.S. 463 (1976) (a warrant-authorized search and seizure of business records constitutes a taking by the government, not testimonial compulsion protected by the Fifth Amendment).

of offices of lawyers and others.[74]

Cases dealing with law office searches generally involve lawyers who themselves are the target of the search. In *Impounded I*,[75] the affidavit supporting the search warrant asserted probable cause to believe that the law firm and some of its lawyers were engaged in tax evasion and mail fraud. The alleged scheme involved the firm's failure to report accurately its share of personal injury awards. The government seized approximately 420 complete files from the office and documents from other closed personal injury files. The district court held the search unconstitutional because the warrant was overbroad in that it allowed the search and seizure of client files without particular allegations of underreporting of settlements in those particular cases. The court of appeals upheld the search. It noted that searches of law offices were not per se unreasonable under the Fourth Amendment and that the proper role of the court was "to 'scrutinize carefully the particularity and breadth of the warrant authorizing the search, the nature and scope of the search, and any resulting seizure.' "[76] The breadth of the alleged scheme—a broad and ongoing effort by the firm and many of its lawyers to defraud the government—kept the search from being overbroad. Privileged information, the court held, could be protected by requiring the government to obtain leave of the court before examining any of the seized items.[77]

5. Fee Arrangements, Client Identity and the Crime–Fraud Exception

UNITED STATES v. HODGE AND ZWEIG

United States Court of Appeals, Ninth Circuit, 1977.
548 F.2d 1347.

Before BROWNING, CHIEF JUDGE, and SMITH and KENNEDY, CIRCUIT JUDGES.

KENNEDY, CIRCUIT JUDGE:

The principal issues on this appeal are whether information demanded by an Internal Revenue Service subpoena is protected by the

74. See also 42 U.S.C. §§ 2000aa–11, which requires the Attorney General to issue guidelines for searches of lawyer's offices and the offices of other professionals whose relationships with their clients are protected by privileges, e.g., doctors and clergy. The resulting guidelines for searches of lawyer's offices appear at 37 Crim.L.Rep. (BNA) 2479.

75. In re Impounded Case (Law Firm) [Impounded I], 840 F.2d 196 (3d Cir.1988). For discussion of subpoenas to lawyers seeking information relating to clients, see Koniak excerpt, supra p. 129, and the note on this topic at p. 268 below.

76. 840 F.2d at 200, quoting Klitzman, Klitzman & Gallagher v. Krut, 744 F.2d 955, 959 (3d Cir.1984). In *Klitzman* the appellate court held the search overbroad because the warrant authorized a wholesale search and seizure of the firm's business records although only one lawyer was the target of the grand jury's suspicion.

77. A later stage of the same case turned on the client-fraud exception to the attorney-client privilege. In re Impounded Case (Law Firm) [Impounded II], 879 F.2d 1211 (3d Cir.1989).

attorney-client privilege, by the fifth amendment privilege against self-incrimination, or by the rule which prohibits issuance of an IRS summons for an improper purpose.

Messrs. Richard A. Hodge and Robert M. Zweig, appellants here, are both members of the State Bar of California and are partners in the practice of law. From all indications in the record, they acted ethically and professionally throughout this matter. This decision may provide further guidance for the proper discharge of their professional responsibilities.

In November 1973, Special Agent Christopher of the IRS issued a summons pursuant to 26 U.S.C. § 7602 directed to appellants, individually and as a law partnership. The summons directed the attorneys to produce various business records pertaining to a client, one Joseph Ernest Sandino, Jr., for the calendar years 1970, 1971, and 1972. The requested information pertains to: (1) payments received by the attorneys from Sandino for legal services rendered to him; (2) payments received from Sandino for services rendered to Rena Sandino Joseph, Cindy Purdy, and Stephen Purdy; (3) payments received from Sandino on behalf of any other person; (4) payments received from any other person on behalf of Sandino. The attorneys refused to comply with the summons. The United States thereupon petitioned the district court for enforcement. The court directed compliance, and the attorneys appeal.[1]

About the same time as the IRS inquiry into Sandino's financial affairs, a protracted grand jury investigation centering around alleged drug activities of Sandino and some of his confederates was in progress. In order that we may properly consider appellants' claims in this case, it is useful to summarize the chronology of these two investigations.

In 1971, a federal grand jury in Nevada began an inquiry into an alleged conspiracy to import drugs by a group that government prosecutors sometimes called "the Sandino Gang." Hodge and Zweig represented several witnesses and suspects called before the grand jury, including Joe Sandino, Rena Joseph, Cindy Purdy, Bernard See, and Robert Gordon. The record before us does not indicate whether Stephen Purdy was a target of the drug investigation. In January 1972, Hodge was called before the grand jury and was asked to disclose information pertaining to fee arrangements and retainer agreements with clients who were being investigated by the grand jury. Zweig was subpoenaed by the grand jury in April 1972 and was asked similar questions. On each occasion, the attorneys refused to answer, invoking both the attorney-client privilege and the fifth amendment privilege against self-incrimination on behalf of themselves and their clients. See and Gordon were subsequently tried for various drug related offenses, including conspiracy to import marijuana, and were found

1. The California Attorneys for Criminal Justice and the American Civil Liberties Union jointly filed a brief as amici curiae.

guilty. We affirmed their convictions on appeal. United States v. See, 505 F.2d 845 (9th Cir.1974).

In March 1974, Sandino and several of his associates were charged with conspiracy to import marijuana. In the indictment, the Government alleged that as part of the conspiracy, the conspirators had agreed to provide bail and legal services for participants who were apprehended by law enforcement officials in the course of the criminal activities. Sandino, Rena Joseph, Cindy Purdy, and others eventually pleaded guilty to conspiracy charges and were sentenced.[2]

While the above criminal prosecution was pending, the IRS was continuing its tax investigation. Appellants failed to comply with the IRS summons of November 1973, and in August 1974, the district court ordered that the summons be enforced. This appeal followed. In light of this background, we turn to the contentions of the parties.

Appellants raise three grounds for reversing the district court's order enforcing the IRS summons. They first argue that the summons was issued solely to gather information in aid of the pending criminal prosecution, and as such was issued for an improper purpose. Second, appellants assert that the fifth amendment bars enforcement of the summons, since compelled disclosure of the requested information would violate their own privilege against self-incrimination and that of their clients. Finally, they claim that the requested information is protected by the attorney-client privilege. We consider these contentions in order.

[On the first issue the court holds that the summons was properly issued.]

Self–Incrimination

Appellants, asserting their own rights and the rights of Sandino, argue that disclosure of the requested records would violate the fifth amendment privilege against self-incrimination.[7] They contend that disclosure would subject them and Sandino to prosecution for various drug violations that were being investigated at the time the summons was issued.

As to appellants' assertion of the privilege on their own behalf, the trial court, citing Zicarelli v. New Jersey State Commission of Investigation, 406 U.S. 472, 478 (1972), concluded that appellants had "not demonstrated such a real danger of prosecution as would justify quashing the summons on the ground of fifth amendment protection." We

---

2. These persons pleaded guilty to a superseding information that charged that the conspiracy began on or about June 1, 1971 and continued until November 21, 1974. It also charged that as part of the conspiracy, defendants would provide money to be used for bail and legal services for the members of the conspiracy apprehended in the course of the unlawful activity. In addition, Sandino alone pleaded guilty to a second count in the information, charging him with interstate travel to aid an unlawful enterprise, in violation of 18 U.S.C. §§ 1952, 2.

7. Whether disclosure of these records would violate the fifth amendment rights of appellants' unnamed clients was neither considered by the trial court nor pressed on appeal. We do not reach that issue here.

cannot say that the court's determination is clearly erroneous. See United States v. Hart, 546 F.2d at 801–02.

Neither is disclosure of the information at issue precluded by assertion of the fifth amendment on behalf of Sandino. Sandino entered a plea of guilty to the first count of the drug-related criminal conspiracy charge and has been sentenced. It does not appear that any further charge is pending against Sandino at this time, nor do appellants contend that additional charges are anticipated. We conclude that Sandino is no longer in danger of incriminating himself and thus may not raise the fifth amendment as a bar to compelled testimony. It follows that appellants may not raise the fifth amendment on Sandino's behalf.[8]

Attorney–Client Privilege

Appellants next contend that the attorney-client privilege precludes enforcement of the IRS summons. They assert the privilege on behalf of Sandino and other named clients, and on behalf of unnamed clients whose identity would necessarily be disclosed if the summons were enforced.

Before the effective date of the Federal Rules of Evidence, this circuit applied the law of the state in which the attorney-client relationship arose to determine whether or not a communication was privileged. Baird v. Koerner, 279 F.2d 623, 632 (9th Cir.1960). . . . We . . . hold that [now] the Federal Rules of Evidence govern our determination.

Fed.R.Evid. 501 provides in relevant part [that "the privilege of a witness . . . shall be governed by the principles of the common law as they may be interpreted by the courts of the United States in the light of reason and experience."] Accordingly, we turn to an examination of federal common law in order to rule on appellants' claim that the information requested in the IRS summons is protected by the attorney-client privilege.

As a general rule, where a party demonstrates that there is a legitimate need for a court to require disclosure of such matters, the identity of an attorney's clients and the nature of his fee arrangements with his clients are not confidential communications protected by the attorney-client privilege. In re Michaelson, 511 F.2d 882, 889 (9th Cir.1975); Baird v. Koerner, 279 F.2d at 630; accord, United States v. Jeffers, 532 F.2d 1101, 1115 (7th Cir.1976); 8 J. Wigmore, Evidence § 2313 (McNaughton rev. 1961). The IRS has demonstrated that the information at issue is sought for a legitimate purpose—the collection of tax revenues. As a threshold matter, therefore, the information is not privileged.

---

8. We do not understand appellants to argue that disclosure is barred because it would incriminate Sandino in income tax violations, nor do we think that appellants could successfully make such an argument. See Couch v. United States, 409 U.S. 322 (1973); United States v. Cromer, 483 F.2d 99 (9th Cir.1973).

The general rule, however, is qualified by an important exception: A client's identity and the nature of that client's fee arrangements may be privileged where the person invoking the privilege can show that a strong probability exists that disclosure of such information would implicate that client in the very criminal activity for which legal advice was sought. Baird v. Koerner, 279 F.2d at 630. While in Baird we enunciated this rule as a matter of California law, the rule also reflects federal law. See In re Grand Jury Proceedings, 517 F.2d 666, 671 (5th Cir.1975); Tillotson v. Boughner, 350 F.2d 663, 666 (7th Cir.1965). Appellants contend that the Baird exception applies to this case.

The Baird exception is entirely consonant with the principal policy behind the attorney-client privilege. "In order to promote freedom of consultation of legal advisors by clients, the apprehension of compelled disclosure from the legal advisors must be removed; hence the law must prohibit such disclosure except on the client's consent." 8 J. Wigmore, supra, § 2291, at 545. In furtherance of this policy, the client's identity and the nature of his fee arrangements are, in exceptional cases, protected as confidential communications.

As noted at the outset, the summons directs appellants to supply information pertaining to four types of transactions. The summons first requests information pertaining to legal fees paid by Sandino on his own behalf. There is no doubt that Sandino played an active role in the drug conspiracy; indeed, he pleaded guilty to that offense. Disclosure of this first category of information could in no way further implicate Sandino in criminal activity connected to the drug conspiracy, nor could it identify a suspect heretofore unknown to the Government. We do not understand appellants to argue otherwise. The Baird rule therefore does not apply to this request. The trial court did not err in ordering appellants to disclose information pertaining to legal fees paid by Sandino on his own behalf.

The second demand in the summons seeks information concerning payments made by Sandino to the attorneys on behalf of Rena Joseph and Cindy Purdy. The Baird rule is similarly inapplicable to that information. Those two persons, along with Sandino, pleaded guilty to the drug conspiracy; there is no indication that further charges are anticipated. Disclosure of this information would therefore not implicate these persons in the very criminal activity for which they sought legal advice. The trial court was correct in ordering disclosure of this information.

The summons also seeks information concerning payments made by Sandino on behalf of Stephen Purdy and unnamed clients, and by unnamed clients on behalf of Sandino. The record gives no indication whether Stephen Purdy was under investigation as a participant in the drug conspiracy; nor is there any evidence before us that he has been indicted or convicted of offenses arising out of the drug investigation. Likewise, we cannot know of the extent of involvement, if any, of possible unnamed clients. The question whether this information is protected by lawyer-client privilege is therefore considerably more troublesome.

Once a party seeking disclosure has met the initial burden of showing that it has a legitimate interest in the information requested, the individual asserting the privilege must demonstrate that the conditions of the *Baird* rule are satisfied. Appellants in this case have met that initial burden as to Stephen Purdy and the unnamed clients. The conspiracy indictment charged that the conspirators agreed to furnish bail and legal fees for those individuals apprehended in the course of the criminal enterprise. If appellants are required to divulge information that would show that the principal conspirator paid Stephen Purdy's legal fees, Stephen Purdy would no doubt be linked to the criminal enterprise by that disclosure. Similarly, disclosure of information pertaining to payments made by or on behalf of unnamed clients could implicate these unnamed clients in the drug conspiracy. Consequently, as a threshold matter, the information appears to be covered by the attorney-client privilege under the *Baird* rationale.[10]

Our inquiry is not at an end, however. Because the attorney-client privilege is not to be used as a cloak for illegal or fraudulent behavior, it is well established that the privilege does not apply where legal representation was secured in furtherance of intended, or present, continuing illegality. United States v. Friedman, 445 F.2d 1076, 1086 (9th Cir.1971); see Clark v. United States, 289 U.S. 1, 15 (1933).... The crime or fraud exception applies even where the attorney is completely unaware that his advice is sought in furtherance of such an improper purpose. United States v. Friedman, 445 F.2d at 1086; see Clark v. United States, 289 U.S. at 15.

To invoke the exception successfully, the party seeking disclosure (here the Government) must make out a prima facie case that the attorney was retained in order to promote intended or continuing criminal or fraudulent activity. United States v. Friedman, 445 F.2d at 1086; see Clark v. United States, 289 U.S. at 15; O'Rourke v. Darbishire, [1920] A.C. at 604. The record on appeal and the supplemental briefs and documents establish such a prima facie case. The information sought by the IRS concerns transactions with the appellants during 1970, 1971, and 1972. The superseding information to which Joe Sandino, Rena Joseph, and Cindy Purdy pleaded guilty charged that the conspiracy began at least as early as June 1971 and ended on November 21, 1974. In fact, there is strong evidence that the conspiracy began earlier, in 1970. The guilty pleas further demonstrate that as an integral part of the conspiracy the participants agreed to furnish bail and legal expenses for conspirators who might be apprehended by law enforcement officials. Presumably, such an agreement was designed to hinder any criminal drug prosecution arising out of the

---

10. Our analysis assumes, of course, that appellants could show that Stephen Purdy and the various unnamed individuals whose identity they seek to protect are clients. If not, the attorney-client privilege is inapplicable in any event.

conspiracy; as such, the agreement constituted part of the consideration for engaging in the conspiratorial activity.[11]

In light of the above, we conclude that a prima facie case exists that payments to appellants, if any, made during the years 1970, 1971, and 1972 by and on behalf of Sandino were made pursuant to the conspiratorial agreement and thus in furtherance of the continuing drug conspiracy. We therefore hold that disclosure of the information requested in the IRS summons is required.

The IRS summons in this case was issued to accomplish a legitimate governmental purpose, viz. the collection of revenues. As noted in our consideration of Donaldson v. United States, [400 U.S. 517 (1971),] the summons was not intended to gather information in aid of the drug investigation. The allegation in the conspiracy indictment charging that the conspirators agreed to furnish each others' legal fees was not a device to circumvent the attorney-client privilege, and the pleas of guilty to the drug offenses by various conspirators establish the existence of such an agreement.

In our legal system the client should make full disclosure to the attorney so that the advice given is sound, so that the attorney can give all appropriate protection to the client's interest, and so that proper defenses are raised if litigation results. The attorney-client privilege promotes such disclosure by promising that communications revealed for these legitimate purposes will be held in strict confidence. The privilege encourages persons to seek advice as to future conduct. But so important is full disclosure that the law recognizes the privilege even if the advice is sought by one who has already committed a bad act. Thus, the attorney-client privilege is central to the legal system and the adversary process. For these reasons, the privilege may deserve unique protection in the courts.

But a *quid pro quo* is exacted for the attorney-client confidence: the client must not abuse the confidential relation by using it to further a fraudulent or criminal scheme, and as a condition to continued representation, the lawyer is required to advise the client to cease any unlawful activities that the lawyer perceives are occurring. Law and society consent to the attorney-client privilege on these preconditions. By insisting on their observance, we safeguard the privilege itself and protect the integrity of the professional relation.

Because neither the client's identity nor the nature of his fee arrangements are generally privileged, the intrusive effect of our ruling in this case is minimal. And to the extent that appellants' clients had an expectation of confidentiality, that expectation was ill-founded; it has been sufficiently shown that the attorneys were retained in furtherance of a continuing conspiracy. There was a failure of one of the essential preconditions of the privilege. While this is a difficult case, we are convinced that disclosure is required.

11. This is manifestly not a case where the attorneys were retained in order that the clients could ascertain whether or not some future course of action was lawful.

Affirmed.

_____

Fee Arrangements and Client Identity

Courts generally hold that fee arrangements and client identity are not privileged.[1] Why is this the general rule?

In *Baird*[2] the client had substantially underreported his income to the IRS and feared the imposition of penalties. His lawyer sent a check to the IRS, withholding the client's name and explaining why. The Ninth Circuit upheld the lawyer's refusal to reveal his client's name, stating that "it may well be the link that could form a chain of testimony necessary to convict an individual of a federal crime."[3]

While courts frequently cite *Baird* as an exception to the general rule, they rarely apply the exception.[4] In In re Grand Jury Subpoenas (Hirsch),[5] the Ninth Circuit explicitly disapproved the oft-cited description of *Baird* in *Hodge and Zweig*, stating that "it is not the law that the requisites of the attorney-client privilege are met whenever evidence regarding the fees paid the attorney would implicate the client in a criminal offense regarding which the client sought legal advice." According to the *Hirsch* court, *Baird* involved "a unique factual situation": "[U]nder the facts of that case, the client's identity was in substance [itself] a confidential communication."[6] In other words, the court read *Baird* as protecting fee and identity information that would implicate the client in criminal activity only when the client communicated that information to the lawyer as part of seeking legal advice and not merely as a necessary corollary to advice-getting. Is this a sensible distinction? When the court calls *Baird*'s facts unique, might it be referring to the fact that the lawyer and client were acting to rectify

1. See United States v. Haddad, 527 F.2d 537 (6th Cir.1975); Colton v. United States, 306 F.2d 633 (2d Cir.1962); McCormick on Evidence § 9 (4th ed. 1992). See also In re Michaelson, 511 F.2d 882 (9th Cir.1975) (general rule that fees not privileged also applies to identity of person who paid the client's fees); In re Grand Jury Subpoena (Wine), 841 F.2d 230 (8th Cir.1988) (same). But see United States v. Sims, 845 F.2d 1564 (11th Cir.1988) (fee information privileged when it would give the identity of a previously undisclosed client/suspect). Also see Corry v. Meggs, 498 So.2d 508 (Fla.App.1986) (state statutory privilege includes fees and identity).

2. Baird v. Koerner, 279 F.2d 623, 632 (9th Cir.1960).

3. 279 F.2d at 633.

4. See, e.g., In re Slaughter, 694 F.2d 1258 (11th Cir.1982), and In re Grand Jury Proceedings, 680 F.2d 1026 (5th Cir.1982) (en banc) (both holding the exception is limited and narrow). See also In re Grand Jury Subpoena (Wine), 841 F.2d 230 (8th Cir.1988) (finding *Baird* inapplicable and noting the Ninth Circuit's limitation of *Baird* to its facts).

5. 803 F.2d 493 (9th Cir.1986).

6. Id. at 497. See also In re Grand Jury Matter (French), 969 F.2d 995 (11th Cir.1992) (lawyer must identify clients who may have paid him with counterfeit money; *Baird*'s "last link" exception does not protect testimony which may incriminate client but only communications made for purposes of legal advice).

the client's prior fraud? [7]

Other Client Identity Issues

Client's Physical Characteristics

The attorney-client privilege protects only "communications" that are intended to be "confidential." Thus, the physical characteristics of a client, such as complexion, demeanor and dress, are not generally considered privileged because they are neither "communications" nor matters which in the usual case a client considers confidential.[8] Should a lawyer be permitted to testify over a client's objection on observations of the client's demeanor that speak to the client's competence? [9]

The Hit–and–Run Driver

The *Baltes* case in 1988 attracted substantial media attention.[10] The client showed up at lawyer Krischer's office, stated his name and said that he had been involved in a hit-and-run auto accident in which a man in the road had been run over. He asked Krischer to negotiate a resolution of the matter with the authorities but not to reveal his identity. Without identifying the client, Krischer asked another lawyer to negotiate with the state's attorney. Baltes, the plaintiff in this civil suit against the nameless client, sought to compel Krischer to divulge the client's identity. The court held that the Florida statutory attorney-client privilege protected identity. Leaving the scene of an accident, without providing statutorily required information to the police or others involved in the accident, was not an ongoing crime. The court also held that neither the lawyer nor the client could be compelled to allow the plaintiff to examine the client's car or photographs of it as this might reveal his identity. How does the *Baltes* decision square with the holding in *Fisher*?

Client Whereabouts

Communications about a client's whereabouts generally are not privileged.[11] For a discussion of whether the confidentiality rules

7. May a lawyer assist a client in returning stolen property without revealing the client's identity? The cases go both ways. See Dean v. Dean, 607 So.2d 494 (Fla.App. 4th Dist.1992) (client's identity is privileged; dissent discusses cases holding that acting as a conduit for return of stolen property is not "legal advice").

8. United States v. Kendrick, 331 F.2d 110 (4th Cir.1964).

9. See *Kendrick* (yes); Gunther v. United States, 230 F.2d 222 (D.C.Cir.1956) (no).

10. Baltes v. Doe (Fla.Cir.Ct.1988) is not reported. The case is summarized in Dean v. Dean, 607 So.2d 494, 495–96 (Fla.App. 4th Dist.1992). For discussion of *Baltes,* see Charles W. Wolfram, Hide and Secrets: The Boundaries of Privilege, Legal Times, Apr. 3, 1989, p. 23.

11. See, e.g., In re Walsh, 623 F.2d 489 (7th Cir.1980); Burden v. Church of Scientology, 526 F.Supp. 44 (M.D.Fla.1981) (information on whereabouts needed to serve complaint); Commonwealth v. Maguigan, 511 Pa. 112, 511 A.2d 1327 (1986) (whereabouts of fugitive client not privileged). Compare In re Grand Jury Subpoena (Field), 408 F.Supp. 1169 (S.D.N.Y.1976) (client's new address privileged, despite general rule, because it was communicated to lawyer as part of obtaining legal advice about moving). But see In the

permit a lawyer to disclose voluntarily a client's whereabouts, see the notes preceding the *Hawkins* case below at p. 336.

Lawyer Resistance to Reporting Cash Receipts

Case law on fee arrangements and client identity notwithstanding, many lawyers continue to act on the belief and assert the position that fees and identity are generally privileged.[12] One illuminating example is the controversy between the bar and the federal government over reporting cash receipts. The Tax Reform Act of 1984[13] and regulations implementing it require anyone who receives a cash payment of more than $10,000 in a trade or business to report to the IRS the paying party's name, address, social security number, occupation and, when applicable, the name of the person on whose behalf the transaction was conducted.[14]

The organized resistance of lawyers and bar associations to this reporting requirement is discussed in the Koniak article reprinted in chapter 2, beginning at p. 132. Although lawyers have not succeeded in efforts to exempt themselves by statute, regulation, interpretation or constitutional challenge,[15] the refusal of many criminal defense lawyers to identify clients has stymied the IRS, requiring it to bring enforcement proceedings to obtain a court order requiring a particular lawyer to provide the identity of the payor. Is lawyer resistance to this statutory and judicial law justified?

Crime–Fraud Exception

As Justice Cardozo said:

> The privilege takes flight if the relation is abused. A client who consults an attorney for advice that will serve him in the commission of a fraud will have no help from the law.[1]

Matter of Nackson, 221 N.J.Super. 187, 534 A.2d 65 (1987) (where other means available for obtaining information on fugitive client lawyer could not be compelled to disclose).

12. See also the material below on subpoenaing lawyers before grand juries.

13. Tax Reform Act of 1984, Pub. L. No. 98–369, 98 Stat. 494 (1984) (codified as amended in 26 U.S.C.).

14. 26 U.S.C. § 6050I (1991). See generally the note on p. 269 below on paying lawyers with the proceeds of crime.

15. In the test case challenging the report requirement, the Second Circuit dismissed as "without merit" the contention that the reporting requirement conflicts with the attorney-client privilege: "[T]he identification in Form 8300 of respondents' clients who make substantial cash fee payments is not a disclosure of privileged information ... even though it might incriminate the client." United States v. Goldberger & Dubin, 935 F.2d 501, 504 (2d Cir.1991): "[T]he [privilege] protects only those disclosures that are necessary to obtain informed legal advice and that would not be made without the privilege." See also United States v. Leventhal, 961 F.2d 936 (11th Cir.1992) (following *Goldberger & Dubin*).

1. Clark v. United States, 289 U.S. 1, 15 (1933). On the crime/fraud exception and its relation to confidentiality, see Geoffrey C. Hazard, Jr., An Historical Perspective on the Attorney–Client Privilege, 66 Calif.L.Rev. 1061 (1978), with which compare David Fried, Too High a Price for the Truth: The Exception to the Attorney–Client Privilege for Contemplated Crimes and Frauds, 64 N.C.L.Rev. 443 (1986) (arguing that the exception is interpreted too broadly and criticizing *Hodge & Zweig*), and Earl Silbert, The Crime

The crime-fraud exception is a corollary to the prohibition against assisting a client to commit a fraud or crime, as noted in the next to the last paragraph in *Hodge and Zweig*. The crime-fraud exception applies to ongoing criminal activity as well as to future criminal activity, but does not apply to past crimes about which the law encourages the seeking of legal counsel. The distinction between past crimes and ongoing ones is clear in principle. However, many a lawyer has fallen into difficulty by treating an ongoing fraud as a past crime. See the *O.P.M.* case below at p. 300. An undiscovered, unrectified fraud may be considered as ongoing, not past, so long as the consequences of the fraud continue.

The court in *Hodge and Zweig* notes that the "exception applies even where the attorney is completely unaware that his advice is sought in furtherance of ... an illegal purpose." Why? The inquiry into the client's state of mind involves drawing fine distinctions between legitimate advice on matters of uncertain legality, on the one hand, and counseling a criminal course of conduct, on the other. In *Ohio–Sealy*,[2] a lawyer was engaged in an effort to restructure a restrictive trade agreement violative of antitrust law to achieve the same effect without running afoul of Supreme Court precedent. Despite documents revealing the clients' belief that their activities would ultimately be found illegal, the court declined to find the lack of good faith on the clients' part that triggers the crime-fraud exception. The clients' belief was read as an evaluation of the weakness of their position, not as an awareness of wrongdoing.[3] But another factfinder might have reached the opposite conclusion on the same record.

Should the crime-fraud exception apply when the client is unaware that the intended purpose is illegal? In In re Impounded Case (Law Firm) [*Impounded II*],[4] the law firm, asserting the privilege on behalf of its innocent clients, claimed that the crime-fraud exception did not apply when the alleged criminality was solely that of the law firm. The court rejected this argument, holding that the privilege would have to yield to the societal interest of bringing to justice lawyers engaged in criminal activities.[5]

May a judge examine material claimed to be privileged to determine whether the privilege applies? Once the judge has examined the evidence, how is she to determine whether the exception applies? In United States v. Zolin,[6] the Court held that a federal district court, at the request of the party seeking access to allegedly privileged material,

---

Fraud Exception to the Attorney–Client Privilege and Work–Product Doctrine, 23 Am. Crim.L.Rev. 351 (1986).

2. Ohio–Sealey Mattress Mfg. Co. v. Kaplan, 90 F.R.D. 21 (N.D.Ill.1980).

3. *Ohio–Sealey* also holds that the crime-fraud rule obliges the lawyer to advise the client to stop any unlawful activity in which the lawyer discovers the client is engaged.

4. 879 F.2d 1211 (3d Cir.1989).

5. But see State v. Green, 493 So.2d 1178, 1182 (La.1986) (lawyer's criminal intent of which client was unaware will not trigger crime-fraud exception).

6. 491 U.S. 554 (1989).

may review the material in camera to determine whether the crime-fraud exception applies. The in camera inspection may be made upon " 'a showing of a factual basis adequate to support a good faith belief by a reasonable person,' ... that in camera review ... may reveal evidence to establish the claim that the crime-fraud exception applies." [7] The Court also held that the content of the communication revealed in the in camera inspection could be used in determining whether a crime or fraud was involved.[8] What opportunity should be afforded the asserter of the privilege to rebut the evidence that the exception applies? [9]

While most civil frauds are criminal as well, the exception applies whether or not the fraud involves criminal liability.[10] Should the crime-fraud exception extend to the client's intent to commit any intentional tort? Professor Wolfram suggests that "fraud" is and should be read as a catchall phrase to include any intentional wrong "involving a client acting with bad faith...." [11] The relationship between antitrust law, the First Amendment and the attorney-client privilege is considered in a number of cases.[12]

Procedures for Invoking the Privilege

To assert the privilege, most courts hold that the witness must appear, testify and invoke the privilege in response to a particular question.[13] The burden is then on the witness to prove that all the elements of the privilege are present.[14] In determining whether the lawyer has asserted a valid claim of privilege, the district court may use an *in camera* proceeding to prevent the release of information which the assertion of privilege is designed to prevent. See United States v. Zolin, supra, on the review of allegedly privileged material in camera.

7. Id. at 572, quoting Caldwell v. District Court, 644 P.2d 26, 33 (Colo.1982).

8. State law may differ from *Zolin*. For example, under Cal.Evid.Code § 915(a) the content of the communication may not be used to determine whether an exception to the privilege applies.

9. See Company X v. United States, 857 F.2d 710 (10th Cir.1988) (determination that exception applies may be made upon ex parte showing and judge need not first examine all documents in camera).

10. See In re Burlington Northern, Inc., 822 F.2d 518 (5th Cir.1987) (civil violation of the antitrust laws is a "fraud" sufficient to trigger the exception to the attorney-client privilege); Natta v. Zletz, 418 F.2d 633 (7th Cir.1969) (fraud upon the Patent and Trademark Office triggers the exception).

11. Wolfram, Modern Legal Ethics § 6.4.10 (1986).

12. See, e.g., In re Burlington Northern, Inc., 822 F.2d 518 (5th Cir.1987), dealing with the *Noerr–Pennington* doctrine: petitioning of the government, which includes suing and in some cases defending a suit, is exempt from the antitrust laws unless the petitioning is a mere sham to cover violation of the antitrust laws. Eastern Railroad Presidents Conference v. Noerr Motor Freight, Inc., 365 U.S. 127 (1961); United Mine Workers v. Pennington, 381 U.S. 657 (1965). *In re Burlington Northern* involved a claim of sham litigation. The plaintiffs sought access to conversations between the defendants and their lawyers to prove their claim of a sham defense.

13. In re Certain Complaints Under Investigation, 783 F.2d 1488, 1518 (11th Cir.1986) (collecting cases).

14. In re Grand Jury Empanelled February 14, 1978 (Markowitz), 603 F.2d 469 (3d Cir.1979).

The lawyer generally has a duty to invoke the privilege when called to testify about privileged matters; the client need not specially request that the lawyer do so.[15] If the court finds that the matter is not privileged, the lawyer is not obliged to continue to refuse to testify in order to appeal the ruling. A lawyer's refusal to comply with a court ruling that the privilege is inapplicable involves some risk because a contempt citation may result in immediate imprisonment and continuing sanctions.[16]

Attorney–Client Privilege and the "War on Crime"

Federal and state efforts to crack down on drug conspiracies and organized crime activities have led in recent decades to a number of measures that have deeply concerned criminal defense lawyers, bar associations and a number of scholars and judges. In the eyes of some, these measures are an assault on the lawyer's "sacred trust" to maintain client confidences; the assault, many lawyers believe, simultaneously undermines the attorney-client privilege and threatens a criminal defendant's Sixth Amendment right to counsel. Government intrusion into the attorney-client relation is said to create conflicts of interest between lawyer and client and damage a lawyer's ability to provide effective representation.

Subpoenas to Lawyers

One concern involves an increasing use by prosecutors of subpoenas requesting lawyers to testify before grand juries on matters relating to client identity, fee arrangements or client affairs.[17] *Hodge and Zweig*, in which two lawyers were summoned before a grand jury and asked questions about fee arrangements and client identity, provides an example. The controversy growing out of subpoenas to lawyers is reported in the Koniak excerpt, reprinted in chapter 2 at p. 127. Efforts by defense lawyers and bar associations to shape grand jury law to provide for a court hearing prior to issuance of subpoenas to lawyers were rejected by the courts. Bar associations counterattacked by seeking to amend ethics codes to make it unethical for a prosecutor to subpoena a lawyer without a prior judicial determination made after a showing of need in an adversary hearing. The high courts of several states adopted such rules, which were in turn attacked by federal

15. EC 4–4; Comment to Model Rule 1.6. See also United States v. Hodgson, 492 F.2d 1175, 1177 (10th Cir.1974).

16. See Maness v. Meyers, 419 U.S. 449, 458–459 (1975). For an extreme case see Dike v. Dike, 75 Wash.2d 1, 448 P.2d 490 (1968) (trial judge had lawyer booked and held in jail until bail was paid; the court upheld the trial court's ruling on the privilege, but vacated its contempt order).

17. For discussion of law and controversy bearing on increased use of lawyer subpoenas, see Susan P. Koniak, The Law Between the Bar and the State, 70 N.C.L.Rev. 1389 (1992), above at p. 129; Roger C. Cramton and Lisa K. Udell, State Ethics Rules and Federal Prosecutors: The Controversies Over the Anti–Contact and Subpoena Rules, 53 U.Pitt.L.Rev. 291, 359–85 (1992); and Fred C. Zacharias, A Critical Look at Rules Governing Grand Jury Subpoenas of Attorneys, 76 Minn.L.Rev. 917 (1992).

prosecutors as violative of federal grand jury law.[18] Federal prosecutors are prevailing in the courts but a subpoena rule, now incorporated in Model Rule 3.8(f) by a 1990 amendment, has been adopted in at least six states.

The controversy over the subpoena rule demonstrates the bar's use of the ethics rules as a competing source of norms to the courts' interpretation of the law. Having failed in efforts to persuade Congress or the courts to adopt its interpretation of the Sixth Amendment, the attorney-client privilege and grand jury law, the bar sought to achieve its objectives by shifting the focus to a lawmaking arena—ethics rules— in which the bar has a more influential role.[19] Is that appropriate?

Forfeiture of Crime Proceeds

Fee forfeiture statutes are the second measure giving rise to concern. Their existence is a major reason prosecutors seek information from lawyers by subpoena. Under a battery of federal statutes— RICO, CCE and the Comprehensive Crime Control Act of 1984 [20]—fees paid to a lawyer for a criminal defense are subject to forfeiture if the money was realized from illegal activity. Moreover, the government may seek forfeiture not only at the inception of the representation but after the criminal proceeding that results in conviction. Thus a private criminal defense lawyer is taking substantial financial risks when she takes a case where the fee money may be subject to forfeiture, as it may be in any narcotics case and many RICO cases.[21]

In 1989, the Supreme Court in two 5–4 decisions held that the forfeiture provisions did not exempt assets used to pay an attorney. The defendant's assets may be frozen before conviction based on a finding of probable cause to believe that the assets are forfeitable; [22] and forfeiture of attorney's fees does not violate the defendant's Sixth Amendment right to counsel or Fifth Amendment right to due process.[23] The Court rejected "the drug merchant['s] claims that his possession of huge sums of money ... entitles him to something more

---

18. See Baylson v. Disciplinary Board of Supreme Court of Pennsylvania, 975 F.2d 102 (3d Cir.1992) (Pennsylvania subpoena rule cannot be applied to federal prosecutors because its adoption as federal law falls outside the rule-making authority of a federal district court and its enforcement as state law violates the Supremacy Clause); cf. United States v. Klubock, 832 F.2d 664 (1st Cir.1987) (en banc affirmance of Massachusetts subpoena rule, also adopted as a rule of the federal court, by an equally divided court).

19. See Roger C. Cramton and Lisa K. Udell, State Ethics Rules and Federal Prosecutors: The Controversies Over the Anti–Contact and Subpoena Rules, 53 U.Pitt.L.Rev. 291, 359–85 (1992).

20. The Racketeer Influenced and Corrupt Organizations Act (RICO), 18 U.S.C. §§ 1961–68) and Continuing Criminal Enterprise Statute (CCE), 21 U.S.C. § 848, are supplemented by the Comprehensive Crime Control Act of 1984, 18 U.S.C. § 1963(c) and 21 U.S.C. § 853(c). See the discussion of these statutes in chapter 2 at p. 73 above.

21. See generally Ass'n Bar City of New York Committee on Criminal Advocacy, The Forfeiture of Attorney Fees in Criminal Cases: A Call for Immediate Remedial Action, 41 The Record 469 (1986); A. Morgan Cloud, Forfeiting Defense Attorneys' Fees, 1987 Wis.L.Rev. 1.

22. United States v. Monsanto, 491 U.S. 600 (1989).

23. Caplin & Drysdale v. United States, 491 U.S. 617 (1989).

[than appointed counsel]." There is no "constitutional right to use the proceeds of crime to finance an expensive defense":

> Whatever the full extent of the Sixth Amendment's protection of one's right to retain counsel of his choosing, that protection does not go beyond "the individual's right to spend his own money to obtain the advice and assistance of ... counsel." ... A defendant has no Sixth Amendment right to spend another person's money for services rendered by an attorney, even if those funds are the only way that that defendant will be able to retain the attorney of his choice. A robbery suspect, for example, has no Sixth Amendment right to use funds he has stolen from a bank to retain an attorney to defend him if he is apprehended. The money, though in his possession, is not rightfully his; the government does not violate the Sixth Amendment if it seizes the robbery proceeds, and refuses to permit the defendant to use them to pay for his defense. "[N]o lawyer, in any case, ... has the right to accept stolen property, or ... ransom money, in payment of a fee.... The privilege to practice law is not a license to steal." [24]

Justice Blackmun's dissent in *Caplin & Drysdale* argued that

> [t]he right to retain private counsel serves to foster the trust between attorney and client that is necessary for the attorney to be a truly effective advocate.... When the Government insists upon the right to choose the defendant's counsel for him, that relationship of trust is undermined: counsel is too readily perceived as the Government's agent rather than his own....
>
> The right to retain private counsel also serves to assure some modicum of equality between the Government and those it chooses to prosecute. The Government can be expected to "spend vast sums of money ... to try defendants accused of crime," ... and of course will devote greater resources to complex cases in which the punitive stakes are high.... But when the Government provides for appointed counsel, there is no guarantee that levels of compensation and staffing will be even average. Where cases are complex, trials long, and stakes high, that problem is exacerbated.... Over the long haul, the result of lowered compensation levels will be that talented attorneys will "decline to enter criminal practice." ... Without the defendant's right to retain private counsel, the Government too readily could defeat its adversaries simply by outspending them. [25]

Underlying *Caplin & Drysdale* is the fact that the wealthy are more likely to receive better representation than the poor and that one's liberty, property or other important interests may depend on how good a lawyer one has. Does the majority grapple with this truth?

---

24. Id. at 626.

25. Id. at 646–47.

Does the dissent grapple with the problem any more honestly than the majority? [26]

Reporting of Cash Receipts

The third measure giving rise to concern is the reporting requirement of section 6050I of the Internal Revenue Code. This provision requires any person who receives more than $10,000 in cash in connection with a trade or business to file a report with the IRS. The implementing regulations leave no doubt that lawyers are engaged in a trade or business for purposes of the reporting requirement. The IRS provision is reinforced by the federal money laundering statute, which makes it a crime knowingly to engage in a monetary transaction with a financial institution if the amount of the transaction exceeds $10,000 and the funds are derived from specified criminal activity. If a lawyer knows that a client's fee comes from illegal activity, she cannot deposit a fee of more than $10,000 without committing a crime.[27]

6. Waiver of Attorney–Client Privilege [28]

Once a privileged communication has been made, the privilege continues indefinitely unless action or inaction of the client terminates the confidential status of the communication. The fact that the privilege survives the termination of the lawyer-client relationship and even the death of the client presents interesting questions concerning the availability to future generations of historical materials reposing in lawyer files. If, for example, John Wilkes Booth had consulted a Virginia lawyer after shooting President Lincoln, may the successor firm make those records available, or is the consent of Booth's descendants required? [29]

A client loses the privilege with respect to a particular communication either by consent or by conduct inconsistent with maintaining the

---

26. The dissent alludes to the low pay rates and meager resources of public defender and appointed counsel programs. Is this "problem" significant only in "complex" cases of the sort brought under RICO? Many non-forfeiture cases involve higher stakes—the life of the defendant, for example. Perhaps so many of those cases appear "simple" because appointed counsel does not have the resources to explore (or create) complexities. By appearing to concede that the generally inadequate resources of appointed counsel programs are only of constitutional significance in forfeiture cases, does the dissent, like the majority, perpetuate a myth that as a general matter poor defendants are accorded equal justice?

27. See Kathleen F. Brickey, Tainted Assets and the Right to Counsel—The Money Laundering Conundrum, 66 Wash.U.L.Q. 47, 47–49 (1988) (discussing the federal fee forfeiture and money laundering statutes).

28. See generally George A. Davidson and William H. Voth, Waiver of the Attorney-Client Privilege, 64 Or.L.Rev. 637 (1986); Richard L. Marcus, The Perils of Privilege: Waiver and the Litigator, 84 Mich.L.Rev. 1605 (1986).

29. There is very little law on the subject. The proposed Restatement of the Law Governing Lawyers § 112, comment d (Tent. Draft No. 2, Apr. 7, 1989), states that a lawyer may cooperate "with efforts to obtain information about clients and law practice for public purposes, such as historical research" providing "sufficient time has passed and the nature of the information is such that disclosure poses no reasonable likelihood of risk to the material interests of the client." See David A. Kaplan, Does Attorney–Client Privilege Outweigh Demands of History?, Nat'l L. J., July 4, 1988, p. 36.

privilege. Consent usually takes the form of disclosure of a privileged communication in an unprivileged setting; conduct inconsistent with maintaining the privilege includes a failure to object to an attempt by another to obtain or provide evidence of a privileged communication. Only the client may waive the privilege; but, because lawyers have implied authority to waive a client's confidentiality rights in the course of representation, waiver may flow from a lawyer's action even though the client was not consulted.[30] Whether a lawyer's disclosure constitutes an exercise of that implied authority is a question of agency law, which looks to whether the disclosure was within the course of representation and not to whether the disclosure was prudent.

Waiver by Putting–In–Issue

STATE v. VON BULOW
Supreme Court of Rhode Island, 1984.
475 A.2d 995.

MURRAY, JUSTICE.

This is an appeal by the defendant, Claus von Bulow, from a Superior Court conviction on two counts of attempting to murder his wife, Martha von Bulow....

... The defendant now appeals from the judgment of conviction entered below.

After a trial spanning six weeks, the record of which includes more than 5200 pages of transcript embodied in twenty-six volumes, Claus von Bulow was found guilty of twice attempting to murder his wife by injecting her with doses of insulin. There were no eyewitnesses to these alleged crimes. Rather, the jury found defendant guilty on the basis of circumstantial evidence.

On December 21, 1980, Martha von Bulow was found in a comatose state on her bathroom floor in the family's Newport home—Clarendon Court. She remains in that condition at a New York hospital. Approximately one year earlier, she suffered a similar episode of unconsciousness from which she quickly recovered. The occurrence of the second coma triggered the events leading up to defendant's indictment, trial, and conviction. Suspecting that defendant may have poisoned his wife, Martha von Bulow's son, Alex; her daughter Ala; and her mother, Mrs. Aitken, hired former Manhattan District Attorney Richard Kuh to investigate the cause of Mrs. von Bulow's condition.

. . .

---

30. See, e.g., United States v. Martin, 773 F.2d 579, 583–84 (4th Cir.1985) (client impliedly authorized lawyer to disclose privileged communications by authorizing lawyer to negotiate with tax agency in effort to settle a tax liability matter); Drimmer v. Appleton, 628 F.Supp. 1249, 1251 (S.D.N.Y.1986) (client, who was present in courtroom when lawyer testified to content of a privileged communication, waived privilege by remaining silent).

Kuh = Investigator/atty
For son, daughter + mother

The state continued the investigation, expanding upon the work of Kuh and the others involved in the family's investigation. Their efforts resulted in the indictment, trial, and ultimate conviction of defendant.

The defendant raises several issues on appeal to this court. We find two of them to be dispositive. These are: (1) Whether the trial justice erred in denying defendant access to certain materials in Kuh's possession and (2) whether the trial justice erred by failing to exclude the results of tests performed by state officials upon the contents of the black bag without first obtaining a search warrant. [The court's discussion of the second issue is not reproduced.]

② *Issues*

ct. only looks @ Issue #1.

. . .

[At a preliminary hearing] defendant called Kuh as a pretrial witness, serving upon him a subpoena duces tecum, which required Kuh to produce certain documents (hereinafter the Kuh documents). In particular, the subpoena directed Kuh to produce (1) telephone records, (2) time records, (3) records relating to work done by investigative agencies, and (4) records relating to interviews of witnesses. Through oral motions and requests and by the questioning of Kuh and Alex, defendant also sought disclosure of other materials, including notes of witness interviews and a summary of incriminating events turned over to the State Police.

materials In Kuh's possession

The trial justice denied the oral motions and requests of defendant and sustained objections to questions through which defendant was attempting to elicit information relative to the scope of Kuh's investigation. With regard to the materials requested in the subpoena duces tecum, the trial justice ruled that all the documents withheld by Kuh were protected by the attorney-client privilege or the work-product doctrine.

ct. Ruling

. . .

We address ourselves initially to defendant's claim that the Kuh documents were not shielded from disclosure by the attorney-client privilege. . . .

. . .

. . . An essential element that must be proved in establishing the existence of the privilege is that it has not been waived. Absent such a waiver, the communications to which Kuh and Alex referred would be protected from disclosure since the privilege normally protects a client from having to disclose even the subject matter of confidential communications with his attorney. United States v. Aronoff, 466 F.Supp. 855, 861 (S.D.N.Y.1979). The privilege may be waived, however, when there has been disclosure of a confidential communication to a third party. Id. at 862; see also Status Time Corp. v. Sharp Electronics Corp., 95 F.R.D. at 34; Haymes v. Smith, 73 F.R.D. at 576; Edmund J. Flynn Co. v. LaVay, 431 A.2d 543, 551 (D.C. 1981); State v. Driscoll, 116 R.I. 749, 757, 360 A.2d 857, 861 (1976).

RoL
① waiver

In considering whether there was a waiver of the privilege in this case, we are mindful that the attorney-client privilege operates as a narrow exception to the general rule that every person must offer testimony on all facts relevant to a judicial proceeding. Edmund J. Flynn Co. v. LaVay, 431 A.2d at 551 (citing 8 Wigmore, § 2285). Because the attorney-client privilege limits the full disclosure of the truth, it must be narrowly construed. We shall recognize the privilege, therefore, only if it has not been waived. Haymes v. Smith, 73 F.R.D. at 576.

. . .

In the present case, Alex and the other family members instructed Kuh to contact the authorities. Kuh contacted the Attorney General's office by telephone and first met with the Rhode Island State Police on February 25, 1981. At that first meeting, Kuh turned over a typewritten summary prepared by him detailing incidents that had led him and the family to conclude that defendant had attempted to kill his wife. He also turned over photocopies of medical records and information concerning defendant's trip to the Bahamas "with someone other than his wife" and generally informed the State Police of information he had obtained from his clients and from Dr. Stock. Kuh also testified that the summary contained a narration of what he had learned from his interviews of potential witnesses. On March 13, 1981, Kuh accompanied Alex to State Police headquarters, at which time all of the items found in the January 23, 1981 search were turned over, with the few exceptions noted above.

. . .

Assuming arguendo that actual confidential communications were not disclosed, the extent to which disclosures relating to the subject matter of the attorney-client relationship were made was sufficient to waive the privilege. As the court stated in United States v. Aronoff, 466 F.Supp. at 862, this principle has been referred to as "waiver by implication" and it is based on considerations of fairness.

"[W]hen [the client's] conduct touches a certain point of disclosure, fairness requires that his privilege shall cease whether he intended that result or not. He cannot be allowed, after disclosing as much as he pleases, to withhold the remainder. He may elect to withhold or to disclose, but after a certain point his election must remain final. 8 Wigmore, supra § 2327, at 636. See also McCormick on Evidence § 93, at 194 (2d ed. 1972)." Id.

Consistent with these principles of fairness, it has been held that the attorney-client privilege properly serves as a shield and not as an offensive tool of litigation. Edmund J. Flynn Co. v. LaVay, 431 A.2d at 551; see also International Telephone & Telegraph Corp. v. United Telephone Co. of Florida, 60 F.R.D. at 185. The court in *Aronoff* recognized that "[w]here a privilege-holder has made assertions about privileged communications, but has attempted to bar other evidence of those communications, there is a serious danger that his assertions are false or misleading." United States v. Aronoff, 466 F.Supp. at 862. "A party may not, therefore, insist upon protection of the privilege for damaging communications while disclosing those which it considers to be favorable to its position." Edmund J. Flynn Co. v. LaVay, 431 A.2d at 551; see also International Telephone & Telegraph Corp. v. United Telephone Co. of Florida, 60 F.R.D. at 185.

The facts of the present case are a classic example of the impermissible selective use of privileged information. While maintaining that communications were intended to be confidential, Alex and his attorney, at Alex's direction, disclosed information sufficient to trigger an investigation by the state and an indictment. These same parties later refused to disclose other evidence of the same communications. The inequity of allowing the privilege holder in this case to disclose as much as he pleased while withholding the remainder is heightened by the fact that defendant was on trial for attempted murder. The effect of excluding such evidence was therefore to deny defendant access to information that he was entitled to examine in the preparation of his defense.

[The court also held that the work-product immunity, applicable to documents not protected by the attorney-client privilege, was also waived by the same conduct. von Bulow's conviction was reversed and the case remanded for a new trial.]

Fairness Doctrine

Was the Rhode Island court in *von Bulow I* justified in penetrating the confidentiality interests of the von Bulow children in information communicated to their lawyer? Is it relevant that some of the information gathered by attorney Kuh came from third persons and included physical evidence of crime? Did the court overlook the pooled-information rule in holding that disclosures to a prosecutor by an opposing interest (children of the victim) waived the privilege? [31]

Generally, client disclosure of privileged information to third parties (or lawyer disclosure authorized by the client) destroys the privilege. [32] Even partial disclosure may destroy the privilege in some cases: When a client during litigation puts in issue a privileged communication, the client impliedly waives the privilege. The extent of the waiver may exceed the dimensions of the initial disclosure.

31. See the discussion of the pooled information or common defense exception to the attorney-client privilege above at p. 226.

32. See, e.g., Clady v. County of Los Angeles, 770 F.2d 1421 (9th Cir.1985) (general rule); United States ex rel. Edney v. Smith, 425 F.Supp. 1038 (E.D.N.Y.1976), aff'd, 556 F.2d 556 (2d Cir.1977) (implied waiver by own testimony); Weil v. Investment/Indicators, Research & Management, Inc., 647 F.2d 18, 23–25 (9th Cir.1981) (out-of-court waiver); and United States v. American Tel. & Tel. Co., 642 F.2d 1285, 1299 (D.C.Cir.1980) (same).

Underlying the implied waiver that results from a client's putting privileged information in issue is the "fairness doctrine," a forensic rule derived from the principle of evidence law that opening one part of a topic opens the whole topic. A familiar application of this principle is that a criminal defendant who takes the stand waives the privilege against self-incrimination, and hence must respond to cross-examination on all relevant matters, not merely those covered in the defendant's direct testimony.[33] The rationale of the fairness doctrine has been summarized as follows:

> "[T]he fairness doctrine" aim[s] to prevent prejudice to a party and distortion of the judicial process that may be caused by the privilege-holder's selective disclosure during litigation of otherwise privileged information. Under the doctrine the client alone controls the privilege and may or may not choose to divulge his own secrets. But it has been established law for a hundred years that when the client waives the privilege by testifying about what transpired between her and her attorney, she cannot thereafter insist that the mouth of the attorney be shut. Hunt v. Blackburn, 128 U.S. 464, 470–71 (1888). From that has grown the rule that testimony as to part of a privileged communication, in fairness, requires production of the remainder. McCormick On Evidence § 93, at 194–95 (2d ed. 1972).[34]

When the client attacks the lawyer's conduct, whether in a malpractice suit, a disciplinary charge or other setting, fairness requires that the lawyer be able to use client communications in defense.[35] By challenging a conviction based on ineffective assistance of counsel, for example, a petitioner waives the privilege to the extent necessary to resolve the claim.[36]

Waiver may also result from assertion of a claim of good faith in reliance on a lawyer's advice. In United States v. Bilzerian,[37] the defendant failed to testify that he thought his conduct was legal because the trial court had ruled that he could not do so without waiving the attorney-client privilege. The Second Circuit affirmed the subsequent conviction, holding that "the privilege may be implicitly

---

33. See United States ex rel. Edney v. Smith, supra.

34. In re von Bulow, 828 F.2d 94, 101–02 (2d Cir.1987).

35. It makes little difference whether lawyer self-defense is viewed as waiver under the fairness doctrine or as an exception to the privilege. The attorney-client privilege, it is said, does not apply "as to a communication relevant to an issue of breach of duty by the lawyer to his client or by the client to his lawyer." See Proposed Fed.R.Evid. 503(d)(3).

36. See, e.g., United States v. Woodall, 438 F.2d 1317 (5th Cir.1970) (en banc); Evans v. Raines, 800 F.2d 884 (9th Cir.1986). Also see Smith v. Estelle, 527 F.2d 430, 434 n. 9 (5th Cir.1976) (defendant's claim that he would have testified but for admission of unconstitutionally obtained confession waived the privilege as to communications relevant to determine the question).

37. 926 F.2d 1285 (2d Cir.1991). See also United States v. Miller, 600 F.2d 498, 501–02 (5th Cir.1979) (defendant waived privilege by raising defense of good faith reliance on attorney's advice).

waived when defendant asserts a claim that in fairness requires examination of protected communications": [38]

> ... Bilzerian's testimony that he thought his actions were legal would have put his knowledge of the law and the basis for his understanding of what the law required in issue. His conversations with counsel regarding the legality of his schemes would have been directly relevant in determining the extent of his knowledge and, as a result, his intent.[39]

For a discussion of the "self-defense" exception to the attorney-client privilege, which allows lawyers to reveal privileged information when their actions are at issue, see *Meyerhofer* and the notes following it, p. 286 below.

Some courts have held that disclosures made in a voluntary effort to cooperate with the government waive the privilege only as to the government—a form of limited waiver; the goal of such rulings is to encourage voluntary cooperation with the government.[40] Most courts, however, hold that disclosure to any potential adversary, including the government, constitutes a waiver as to all others.[41] A substantial case law also deals with the work-product doctrine as applied to documents voluntarily disclosed to the government.[42]

Waiver by Subsequent Disclosure: *von Bulow II*

In In re von Bulow [*von Bulow II*],[43] two children of Martha "Sunny" von Bulow brought a civil damage action in federal court against their foster father, Claus von Bulow, for attempting to kill their mother. In a Rhode Island state court, von Bulow had been acquitted of criminal charges alleging the same conduct after an initial conviction, appellate court reversal and retrial. After von Bulow's acquittal on retrial, Alan Dershowitz, who had handled the appeal from the initial conviction, published *Reversal of Fortune*, a book detailing his successful exploits on von Bulow's behalf. The book, subsequently made into a movie, partially disclosed the content of a number of communications between von Bulow and his lawyer, Dershowitz. The plaintiffs in *von Bulow II*, viewing the partial disclosures in *Reversal of*

---

38. Id. at 1292.

39. Id.

40. See, e.g., Diversified Industries, Inc. v. Meredith, 572 F.2d 596, 611 (8th Cir.1977) (en banc); Byrnes v. IDS Realty Trust, 85 F.R.D. 679, 685 (S.D.N.Y.1980).

41. In In re Subpoenas Duces Tecum, 738 F.2d 1367 (D.C.Cir.1984), Tesoro Petroleum provided the Securities and Exchange Commission with information on illegal foreign bribes in exchange for more lenient treatment from the SEC. Shareholders brought a derivative suit against the corporation and in discovery sought the documents Tesoro had provided to the SEC. The court held that the privilege was waived as to these documents, rejecting the argument that the waiver doctrine should yield to the public policy in favor of encouraging voluntary cooperation with the government. See also In re Martin Marietta, 856 F.2d 619 (4th Cir.1988).

42. See Chubb Integrated Systems v. National Bank of Washington, 103 F.R.D. 52, 67 (D.D.C.1984).

43. 828 F.2d 94 (2d Cir.1987).

Fortune as a waiver of von Bulow's attorney-client privilege, sought disclosure of the remainder of the conversations. The district court ruled broadly in favor of waiver, but von Bulow sought and obtained relief by mandamus from the Second Circuit.

The Second Circuit, after holding that the situation warranted the exercise of mandamus jurisdiction, held that von Bulow, by encouraging the publication of the book and actively promoting its sale, waived the privilege by consent with respect to information actually disclosed in the book. More importantly, however, the court held that the extrajudicial dissemination to the general public of certain privileged information did not waive the privilege as to any portions of conversations not revealed. The court distinguished the forensic rule, discussed above, which allows an opposing party to inquire into the remainder of a privileged communication after the party offers evidence of a portion of a privileged communication:

> [W]here, as here, disclosures of privileged information are made extrajudicially and without prejudice to the opposing party, there exists no reason in logic or equity to broaden the waiver beyond those matters actually revealed. Matters actually disclosed in public lose their privileged status because they obviously are no longer confidential. The cat is let out of the bag, so to speak. But related matters not so disclosed remain confidential. Although it is true that disclosures in the public arena may be "one-sided" or "misleading", so long as such disclosures are and remain extrajudicial, there is no *legal* prejudice that warrants a broad court-imposed subject matter waiver. The reason is that disclosures made in public rather than in court—even if selective—create no risk of *legal* prejudice until put at issue in the litigation by the privilege-holder. Therefore, insofar as the district court broadened petitioner's waiver to include related conversations on the same subject it was in error.[44]

Is *von Bulow II* correct in distinguishing so sharply between the forensic rule of implied waiver by putting a matter in issue and that of waiver by subsequent extrajudicial disclosure?[45] Should von Bulow's disclosure of some secret information result in forfeiture of other secret information? Should the purpose of the extrajudicial disclosures affect the extent of waiver? For example, should disclosures in a book intended to establish the innocence of a defendant, whether or not intended to mislead or prejudice, trigger a broader forfeiture than disclosures made to a government agency for purposes of assisting an

44. Id. at 102–03. The civil suit was later settled by an agreement by which von Bulow gave up all claim to his wife's estate, agreed to divorce her and relinquished all rights to write books or earn money by publicizing the case. In return, von Bulow's daughter was restored to a one-third share in her grandmother's estate and the plaintiffs agreed to drop their lawsuit. N.Y. Times, Dec. 24, 1987, at p. B1.

45. See generally Note, Fairness and the Doctrine of Subject Matter Waiver of the Attorney–Client Privilege in Extrajudicial Disclosure Situations, 1988 U.Ill.L.Rev. 999.

ongoing investigation? [46]   Should the party alleging waiver have to show that the disclosure was actually misleading, or should it be enough that the disclosure was intended to prejudice the proceedings?

Privileged Subsequent Disclosure

If a disclosure is itself privileged, as with disclosure to other lawyers who are assisting with a case,[47] it does not waive the privilege. Similarly, statements made in the course of settlement negotiations or plea bargaining are inadmissible to prove liability in subsequent litigation between the negotiating parties.[48] Supplementing the protections provided by those rules, many cautious lawyers preface any damaging disclosure in negotiations or plea bargaining by stating that the statement is made "without prejudice" or make the admission in hypothetical conditional form.

Inadvertent Disclosure

The traditional rule has been that inadvertent disclosure waives the privilege as effectively as intentional disclosure, apparently on the theory that inadvertent disclosure is inconsistent with an intention to preserve confidentiality.[49]   The reality of modern discovery, however, has made the inadvertent disclosure of privileged documents an increasing problem and the case law on this subject is changing.[50]   Some courts have rejected the traditional rule entirely,[51] others adhere to it,[52] and a growing number take a middle-ground approach, preserving the privilege unless, in effect, the disclosure resulted from the palpable negligence of either the client or her lawyer.[53]

46. In a footnote the court in *von Bulow II* left open the possibility that plaintiffs could demonstrate that "von Bulow's assertion of his attorney-client privilege is misleading or otherwise prejudicial": "assertions before trial may mislead or prejudice an adversary at trial and thereby impede the proper functioning of the judicial system." 828 F.2d at 102 n. 1.

47. See, e.g., Transmirra Prods. Corp. v. Monsanto Chemical Co., 26 F.R.D. 572, 576–77 (S.D.N.Y.1960); and the note above on the privilege between joint clients and cooperating parties. Generally see Proposed Fed.Evid.R. 501 and Revised Uniform Rule of Evidence 510.

48. See, e.g., Fed.R.Evid. 408 (statements in settlement negotiations); and Fed.R.Evid. 410(4) (statements in plea bargaining).

49. See 8 Wigmore, Evidence § 2325 at 633 (McNaughton rev. 1961).

50. See Transamerica Computer Co. v. IBM Corp., 573 F.2d 646 (9th Cir.1978).

51. Some courts seem to have abandoned the traditional rule, holding that an inadvertent disclosure does not result in waiver. See Mendenhall v. Barber–Greene Co., 531 F.Supp. 951, 954–55 (N.D.Ill.1982). Also see Kansas–Nebraska Natural Gas v. Marathon Oil Co., 109 F.R.D. 12, 21 (D.Neb.1983).

52. Recent cases adhering to the traditional rule include International Digital Systems Corp. v. Digital Equipment Corp., 120 F.R.D. 445, 450 (D.Mass.1988) (stating that the strict rule "would probably do more than anything else to instill in attorneys the need for effective precautions against such disclosure").

53. See, e.g., Lois Sportswear, U.S.A., Inc. v. Levi Strauss & Co., 104 F.R.D. 103 (S.D.N.Y.1985) (listing several factors in deciding whether the inadvertent disclosure waived the privilege: "(1) the reasonableness of the precautions to prevent inadvertent disclosure; (2) the time taken to rectify the error; (3) the scope of the discovery; (4) the extent of the disclosure; and (5) the 'overriding issue of fairness' ").

The proposed Restatement of the Law Governing Lawyers adopts the middle-ground approach:

> The question is whether the client, lawyer, or other agent was inattentive to the need to maintain confidentiality of the communication and turns on whether reasonable precautionary measures were taken to protect against disclosure or, if an inadvertent disclosure has already occurred, to recover the communication. What is reasonable depends on all the relevant circumstances...." [54]

B. PROFESSIONAL DUTY OF CONFIDENTIALITY

Introductory Note

Agency law provides that "an agent [has] a duty to the principal not to use or to communicate information confidentially given him by the principal or acquired by him during the course of or on account of his agency." [1] "Client confidential information" is a broad category including all information about the client that the lawyer has a duty to keep secret. It includes information about the client learned from other sources.

In addition to evidence and agency law, every state ethical code prescribes a duty of confidentiality, usually based on the provisions in the ABA Model Code or Model Rules. These provisions, while reflecting evidence and agency law, do not fully correspond in breadth and limits to the rules of confidentiality under that law. They might better be described as codifications of the profession's lore of confidentiality. The breadth of the exceptions to confidentiality acknowledged by the law of agency conflicts with the profession's understanding of its duty to preserve confidences. Under agency law, for example, the agent's duty of confidentiality is qualified by the agent's power to reveal confidences when necessary to protect a third party with a superior interest to the principal's interest in confidentiality. [2] Contrast the narrower exceptions in Model Rule 1.6(b).

We first consider the scope of confidentiality under the Model Code of Professional Responsibility and the Model Rules of Professional Conduct. [3] Next, we examine the exceptions.

---

54. ALI, Restatement of Law Governing Lawyers § 129, comment i (Tent. Draft No. 1, Apr. 7, 1989).

1. See Restatement (Second) of Agency §§ 395–96 (1958) § 395. See also 2 Floyd R. Mechem, Treatise on the Law of Agency § 2150 (2d ed.1914).

2. See § 395, comment (f); 2 Mechem, Treatise on the Law of Agency § 2404 (2d ed.1914).

3. See Fred C. Zacharias, Rethinking Confidentiality, 74 Iowa L.Rev. 351 (1989) for a review of the law of confidentiality and an empirical study of client and lawyer impressions of the confidentiality rule. Also see Nancy J. Moore, Limits to Attorney–Client Confidentiality: A "Philosophically Informed" and Comparative Approach to Legal

In examining the exceptions to confidentiality, two pervasive themes emerge:

(1) What relationship do the confidentiality rules envision between a lawyer and a client who is engaged in criminal or fraudulent conduct? Do the rules allow sufficient room for a lawyer to protect herself from civil and criminal liability for the client's illegal conduct? Do they adequately reinforce the prohibition against assisting a client in illegal conduct?

(2) Do the confidentiality rules properly balance the interests of clients and other societal and individual interests, such as protecting innocent third parties from harm?

The justification for the principle of client confidentiality is encouragement of clients to communicate fully with the lawyer and to seek early legal assistance even about embarrassing matters. See the Comment to M.R. 1.6 and EC 4–1. Is the exception in the law of agency, allowing disclosure to protect a "superior interest" of a third party, inadequate to serve the purposes of lawyer-client confidentiality?

Interests of Confidentiality

Another interest served by confidentiality is more closely aligned with the law of agency. To encourage people to rely on others, they must be able to trust those in whose hands they place their affairs. The duty of confidentiality is a corollary of the more general duty of loyalty. This suggests a greater duty of loyalty, and a correspondingly greater duty of confidentiality, from those in whom a greater degree of trust is placed than in ordinary agents. Lawyers are not ordinary agents. Lawyers, however, are not the only professionals who are entrusted with matters of great importance. Yet they receive greater protection for client confidences than that afforded other professionals, for example, physicians.[4] In any case, why should this duty of loyalty extend to confidences about contemplated and ongoing illegal activity?

1. Scope of Duty of Confidentiality

Model Code of Professional Responsibility

DR 4–101 of the Model Code of Professional Responsibility is the Code's principal confidentiality provision. DR 4–101(A) defines the information to be protected. DR 4–101(B) defines the scope of the duty. DR 4–101(C) sets out exceptions. The question of client fraud is treated in a separate provision, DR 7–102(B)(1). DR 4–101(D) deals with disclosure and use of confidential information by the lawyer's agents.

DR4–101

DR 4–101(A) defines two types of confidential information, "confidences" and "secrets." All subsequent provisions of the Code apply to both categories. "Confidences" refers to information protected by the attorney-client privilege under applicable law, and "secrets" refers to

Confidences & Secrets

and Medical Ethics 36 Case W.Res.L.Rev. 177 (1986); and Richardson W. Nahstoll, The Lawyer's Allegiance: Priorities Regarding Confidentiality, 41 Wash. & Lee L.Rev. 421, 433 (1984).

4. Compare the *Hawkins* case printed below at p. 337 with *Tarasoff*, which is discussed at p. 341.

other information gained in the professional relationship that the client has requested be held inviolate or the disclosure of which would be embarrassing or likely to be detrimental to the client.

The definition of "confidences" thus is a source external to the Code; it is defined by the law of evidence. The definition of "secrets" covers non-privileged information gained in the relationship, but does not cover information gained before or after the relationship. Should it? The attorney-client privilege is limited to information received from the client *during* the representation, but the agent's duty is broader, covering information "acquired . . . on account of [the] agency." Recall that the law of agency applies to lawyers. Is the agency definition better than that in the Code provision? Is the agency definition broad enough?

"Secrets" does not cover all information gained in the course of the representation, only that which the client requests be secret or which would harm or embarrass the client if disclosed. Should the lawyer be left to decide whether information would harm or embarrass the client when the client has not requested secrecy?

The distinction between "confidences" and "secrets" became a source of controversy in interpreting an ABA amendment to DR 7–102(B)(1).[5] The distinction, however, has never assumed practical importance in determining whether there is a duty of confidentiality and was abandoned in the Model Rules, see M.R. 1.6.

DR 4–101(B) provides:

Except when permitted under DR 4–101(C), a lawyer shall not knowingly:

(1) Reveal a confidence or secret of his client.

(2) Use a confidence or secret of his client to the disadvantage of the client.

(3) Use a confidence or secret of his client for the advantage of himself or of a third person, unless the client consents after full disclosure.

The Model Code specifies that "knowing" use or disclosure is a violation, apparently excluding inadvertent non-negligent disclosure. However DR 4–101(D) requires exercise of reasonable care in supervising agents who possess confidential client information, suggesting that negligent disclosure by the lawyer would violate DR 4–101(B).

Model Rules of Professional Conduct

Model Rule 1.6 is the key provision on confidentiality. It was the most hotly debated of the rules during the drafting process of the

5. See the discussion below at p. 296, describing the controversy and the ABA's resolution of it in Formal Op. 341.

Kutak Commission and on the floor of the ABA House of Delegates.[6] In the process of being adopted by the states, M.R. 1.6 has also been more significantly redrafted than any of the other model rules. The heart of the controversy involves the scope of the exceptions, discussed below.

M.R. 1.6(a) is broader than DR 4–101. First, it protects all information "relating to the representation" whether the lawyer learned the information before, during or after the representation. Second, the rule applies whether or not disclosure would harm or embarrass the client. It also eliminates the word "knowingly" from its prohibition, stating flatly "a lawyer shall not."

Using as Opposed to Revealing Client Information

Use of confidential information is governed by the rules on conflict of interest. M.R. 1.8(b) prohibits using confidential information concerning a present client to the disadvantage of that client without the client's consent given after consultation, except as M.R. 1.6 or 3.3 permit; and M.R. 1.9(c)(1) prohibits using confidential information of a former client to that client's disadvantage except as M.R. 1.6 and 3.3 permit *or* until the information has become generally known.[7] Neither M.R. 1.6, 1.8(b) nor 1.9(c)(1) prohibit the use of confidential information to benefit the lawyer when the client will not be harmed by the use. Should a lawyer be prohibited from benefiting from a client confidence in a way that does not harm the client?

Such self-dealing is prohibited by the law of agency.[8] Under some circumstances it may also constitute mail fraud.[9] Use of confidential information to benefit the lawyer may also violate federal or state laws prohibiting insider trading.

6. The Kutak Commission was the ABA body that drafted the Model Rules for consideration by the ABA House of Delegates. For a good summary of the controversy, see Ted Schneyer, Professionalism as Bar Politics: The Making of the Model Rules of Professional Conduct, 1989 J. Law & Soc. Inquiry 677.

7. Discipline is a more likely prospect when a breach of confidentiality benefits a lawyer and hurts her client. In *In re Pool*, Supreme Judicial Court, Suffolk County, Mass. (No. 83–37 BD, Jan. 17, 1984), a young lawyer, Pool, was defending a client charged with serious federal crimes. The FBI had obtained the only keys to the client's safe deposit boxes but did not know their location. Pool, who needed funds for the defense and for his unpaid fees, arranged with the federal prosecutor for access to the safe deposit boxes to remove cash in return for providing the prosecutor with information the client had given Pool concerning the location of the boxes. After Pool had removed the cash, the government seized the contents of the boxes, including a handgun and false identifications, on the basis of a search warrant that did not reveal the source of the government's information. The client later learned of Pool's conduct and filed disciplinary grievances against him. Pool was disbarred but was reinstated four years later. In re Pool, 401 Mass. 460, 517 N.E.2d 444 (1988).

8. See Restatement (Second) of Agency § 395 (1958) and the comment to § 388.

9. In Carpenter v. United States, 484 U.S. 19 (1987), discussed above at p. 71, the Court affirmed the conviction of a Wall Street Journal reporter who had traded in securities that he contemporaneously mentioned in his market gossip column. Information collected for the column was confidential information belonging to the Journal until published: "Confidential business information has long been recognized as property.... The confidential information was generated from the business and the business had a right to decide how to use it prior to disclosing it to the public." Id. at 26.

Publicly Available Information as Confidential Information

Under the Model Rules as under the Model Code, the lawyer's obligation not to *reveal* confidential information applies whether or not the information is publicly known. See M.R. 1.9(c)(2). However, M.R. 1.9(c)(1), unlike the Code, allows the *use* of generally known information against a *former* client.[10]

What interests are sacrificed by allowing a lawyer to use generally known information to the detriment of a former client? Why does Model Rule 1.8(b) not have an exception for generally known information similar to the one in M.R. 1.9(c)(1)? The law of agency allows agents to use confidential information to the disadvantage of a former principal when that information is available from public sources.[11] M.R. 1.9(c)(1)'s exception seems narrower than that of agency law in that the information must be "generally known."

Client Consent and Implied Authority to Reveal

Model Rule 1.6(a) and DR 4–101(C)(1) allow for disclosure of any client confidence if the client consents after consultation with the lawyer as to the consequences of such a decision. See also M.R. 1.8(b).

Lawyers, however, would be unable to do their job, which is to represent people, if they had to have express consent before speaking about anything that involves a confidence. The Comment to M.R. 1.6 explains:

> A lawyer is impliedly authorized to make disclosures about a client when appropriate in carrying out the representation, except to the extent that the client's instructions or special circumstances limit that authority. In litigation, for example, a lawyer may disclose information by admitting a fact that cannot properly be disputed, or in negotiation by making a disclosure that facilitates a satisfactory conclusion.

The Model Code has no similar provision on implied authority. However, the Code's definition of "secrets" as information that would embarrass or harm the client if revealed yields a similar result.

2. Self–Defense Exception

Exceptions to the professional duty of confidentiality may be classified into three broad areas: (1) protection of lawyers threatened by a claim or charge brought by the client or a third person (the self-defense exception); (2) protection of innocent third parties who are being or may be victimized by the client; and (3) prevention or rectification of fraud on the tribunal. The first two of these areas, self-defense and the

---

10. For cases on whether public information is confidential, see, e.g., City of Wichita v. Chapman, 214 Kan. 575, 521 P.2d 589, 596 (1974) (public information not a confidence); NCK Org. Ltd. v. Bregman, 542 F.2d 128, 133 (2d Cir.1976) (public information a confidence).

11. See Restatement (Second) of Agency § 395 (1958).

defense of third parties, are discussed in this chapter. The third category, fraud on the court, is considered in Chapter 5.

The self-defense exception arises primarily in three types of cases: (1) when a client charges a lawyer with wrongdoing in the course of representation; (2) when a lawyer sues the client to enforce some duty owed the lawyer, such as payment of a fee; and (3) when a third person accuses a lawyer of wrongdoing in the course of representing a client, perhaps in complicity with the client.

*_ Meyer-hofer_*

The first situation, in which the client attacks the lawyer by filing a malpractice action, a disciplinary complaint or other formal charge, raises the fewest problems. The client has waived the attorney-client privilege by putting the lawyer's representation in issue. Fairness, even due process, requires that the lawyer be permitted to use confidential information to respond to what may be false charges. The self-defense exception to the professional duty of confidentiality is an obvious corollary of this principle.

The second situation, in which the lawyer seeks to enforce a duty owed to her by her client, appears more problematic, but has strong support in agency law. It is unfair for the beneficiary of a fiduciary's services to receive those services and not perform duties owed to the fiduciary. When the lawyer sues a client to collect a fee, moreover, the claim itself involves very limited or no disclosure of client confidences, since fee arrangements are not ordinarily privileged. Confidential information will come out only if the client defends the fee action by attacking the amount charged or the lawyer's representation. Thus the client has some control of the scope of the waiver. On the other hand, the cost of maintaining confidentiality may be paying what the lawyer claims is owed, whether it is or not.

The third situation, involved in *Meyerhofer* below, is the most troublesome, since the client has no control of loss of confidentiality when disclosure flows from a third person's claim against the client's lawyer. On the other hand, when the third party's claim against the lawyer is based on wrongful conduct in which the client participated, the client may be said to bear some responsibility for the loss of the privilege.

Almost without objection the bar has agreed that the principle of confidentiality must yield to a self-defense exception for lawyers.[12] Even ATLA's competing professional code, which was in large part a response to the perceived attack on confidentiality embodied in the Kutak Commission draft of the Model Rules,[13] contains a fairly broad

---

12. For a general discussion and critique of the self-defense exception, see Henry D. Levine, Self–Interest or Self–Defense: Lawyer Disregard of the Attorney–Client Privilege for Profit and Protection, 5 Hofstra L.Rev. 783 (1977).

13. See the Preface to the American Lawyers Code of Conduct (ALCC), reprinted in T. Morgan & R. Rotunda, 1993 Selected Standards on Professional Responsibility at 238: "This code is quite frankly presented as an alternative ... to the new Rules of Professional Conduct that the ABA is apparently about to hawk as the latest thing in legal ethics." Published in 1982, the ALCC was a product of a special commission under

self-defense exception to confidentiality.[14]

The Model Code of Professional Responsibility makes no distinction between accusations against the lawyer made by a third party and those made by the client. DR 4–101(C)(4) permits the lawyer to disclose "[c]onfidences or secrets necessary to establish or collect his fee or to defend himself or his employees, or associates against an accusation of wrongful conduct."

Model Rule 1.6(b)(2) provides:

A lawyer may reveal [confidential] information to the extent the lawyer reasonably believes necessary ... to establish a claim or defense on behalf of the lawyer in a controversy between the lawyer and the client, to establish a defense to a criminal charge or civil claim against the lawyer based upon conduct in which the client was involved, or to respond to allegations in any proceeding concerning the lawyer's representation of the client.

The Comment to M.R. 1.6 emphasizes a broad reading of this exception:

The lawyer's right to respond arises when an assertion of such complicity has been made. Paragraph (b)(2) does not require the lawyer to await the commencement of an action or proceeding that charges such complicity, so that a defense may be established by responding directly to a third party who has made such an assertion.

Several bar ethics opinions take the position that the lawyer may be forthcoming with the prosecutor when she learns that she has been accused by someone, even though the prosecutor has not yet threatened prosecution.[15]

MEYERHOFER v. EMPIRE FIRE AND MARINE INS. CO.

United States Court of Appeals, Second Circuit, 1974.
497 F.2d 1190.

Before MOORE, FRIENDLY and ANDERSON, CIRCUIT JUDGES.

MOORE, CIRCUIT JUDGE:

. . .

The full import of the problems and issues presented on this appeal cannot be appreciated and analyzed without an initial statement of the facts out of which they arise.

Empire Fire and Marine Insurance Company on May 31, 1972, made a public offering of 500,000 shares of its stock, pursuant to a

the auspices of the research arm of the American Trial Lawyers Association (ATLA), composed primarily of plaintiffs' trial lawyers.

14. ALCC Rule 1.5 permits disclosure of client confidences in the lawyer's self-defense.

15. See Ass'n Bar City of New York Op. 1986–7; Mich.Op. CI–900 (1983); Maine Op. 55 (1985).

registration statement filed with the Securities and Exchange Commission (SEC) on March 28, 1972. The stock was offered at $16 a share. Empire's attorney on the issue was the firm of Sitomer, Sitomer & Porges. Stuart Charles Goldberg was an attorney in the firm and had done some work on the issue.

Plaintiff Meyerhofer, on or about January 11, 1973, purchased 100 shares of Empire stock at $17 a share. He alleges that as of June 5, 1973, the market price of his stock was only $7 a share—hence, he has sustained an unrealized loss of $1,000.... Plaintiff Federman, on or about May 31, 1972, purchased 200 shares at $16 a share, 100 of which he sold for $1,363, sustaining a loss of some $237 on the stock sold and an unrealized loss of $900 on the stock retained.

On May 2, 1973, plaintiffs, represented by the firm of Bernson, Hoeniger, Freitag & Abbey (the Bernson firm), on behalf of themselves and all other purchasers of Empire common stock, brought this action alleging that the registration statement and the prospectus under which the Empire stock had been issued were materially false and misleading. Thereafter, an amended complaint, dated June 5, 1973, was served. The legal theories in both were identical, namely, violations of various sections of the Securities Exchange Act of 1933, the Securities Exchange Act of 1934, Rule 10b–5, and common law negligence, fraud and deceit. Damages for all members of the class or rescission were alternatively sought.

The lawsuit was apparently inspired by a Form 10–K which Empire filed with the SEC on or about April 12, 1973. This Form revealed that "The Registration Statement under the Securities Act of 1933 with respect to the public offering of the 500,000 shares of Common Stock did not disclose the proposed $200,000 payment to the law firm as well as certain other features of the compensation arrangements between the Company [Empire] and such law firm [defendant Sitomer, Sitomer and Porges]." Later that month Empire disseminated to its shareholders a proxy statement and annual report making similar disclosures.

The defendants named were Empire, officers and directors of Empire, the Sitomer firm and its three partners, A.L. Sitomer, S.J. Sitomer and R.E. Porges, Faulkner, Dawkins & Sullivan Securities Corp., the managing underwriter, Stuart Charles Goldberg, originally alleged to have been a partner of the Sitomer firm, and certain selling stockholders of Empire shares.

On May 2, 1973, the complaint was served on the Sitomer defendants and Faulkner. No service was made on Goldberg who was then no longer associated with the Sitomer firm. However, he was advised by telephone that he had been made a defendant. Goldberg inquired of the Bernson firm as to the nature of the charges against him and was informed generally as to the substance of the complaint and in particular the lack of disclosure of the finder's fee arrangement. Thus informed, Goldberg requested an opportunity to prove his non-involvement in any such arrangement and his lack of knowledge thereof. At this stage there was unfolded the series of events which ultimately resulted in the motion and order thereon now before us on appeal.

Goldberg, after his graduation from [Cornell] Law School in 1966, had rather specialized experience in the securities field and had published various books and treatises on related subjects. He became associated with the Sitomer firm in November 1971. While there Goldberg worked on phases of various registration statements including Empire, although another associate was responsible for the Empire registration statement and prospectus. However, Goldberg expressed concern over what he regarded as excessive fees, the nondisclosure or inadequate disclosure thereof, and the extent to which they might include a "finder's fee," both as to Empire and other issues.

The Empire registration became effective on May 31, 1972. The excessive fee question had not been put to rest in Goldberg's mind because in middle January 1973 it arose in connection with another registration (referred to as "Glacier"). Goldberg had worked on Glacier. Little purpose will be served by detailing the events during the critical period January 18 to 22, 1973, in which Goldberg and the Sitomer partners were debating the fee disclosure problem. In summary Goldberg insisted on a full and complete disclosure of fees in the Empire and Glacier offerings. The Sitomer partners apparently disagreed and Goldberg resigned from the firm on January 22, 1973.

On January 22, 1973, Goldberg appeared before the SEC and placed before it information subsequently embodied in his affidavit dated January 26, 1973, which becomes crucial to the issues now to be considered.

Some three months later, upon being informed that he was to be included as a defendant in the impending action, Goldberg asked the Bernson firm for an opportunity to demonstrate that he had been unaware of the finder's fee arrangement which, he said, Empire and the Sitomer firm had concealed from him all along. Goldberg met with members of the Bernson firm on at least two occasions. After consulting his own attorney, as well as William P. Sullivan, Special Counsel with the Securities and Exchange Commission, Division of Enforcement, Goldberg gave plaintiffs' counsel a copy of the January 26th affidavit which he had authored more than three months earlier. He hoped that it would verify his nonparticipation in the finder's fee omission and convince the Bernson firm that he should not be a defendant. The Bernson firm was satisfied with Goldberg's explanations and, upon their motion, granted by the court, he was dropped as a defendant. After receiving Goldberg's affidavit, the Bernson firm amended plaintiff's complaint. The amendments added more specific facts but did not change the theory or substance of the original complaint.

By motion dated June 7, 1973, the remaining defendants moved "_____nt to Canons 4 and 9 of the Code of Professional Responsibility, ciplinary Rules and Ethical Considerations applicable thereto, and the supervisory power of this Court" for the order of disqualification now on appeal.

By memorandum decision and order, the District Court ordered that the Bernson firm and Goldberg be barred from acting as counsel or participating with counsel for plaintiffs in this or any future action against Empire involving the transactions placed in issue in this lawsuit and from disclosing confidential information to others.

The complaint was dismissed without prejudice. The basis for the Court's decision is the premise that Goldberg had obtained confidential information from his client Empire which, in breach of relevant ethical canons, he revealed to plaintiffs' attorneys in their suit against Empire. The Court said its decision was compelled by "the broader obligations of Canons 4 and 9." [In a footnote the court quoted ECs 4–1 and 4–4 through 4–6, DR 4–101, and ECs 9–1 and 9–6.]

There is no proof—not even a suggestion—that Goldberg had revealed any information, confidential or otherwise, that might have caused the instigation of the suit. To the contrary, it was not until after the suit was commenced that Goldberg learned that he was in jeopardy. The District Court recognized that the complaint had been based on Empire's—not Goldberg's—disclosures, but concluded because of this that Goldberg was under no further obligation "to reveal the information or to discuss the matter with plaintiffs' counsel."

Despite the breadth of paragraphs EC 4–4 and DR 4–101(B), DR 4–101(C) recognizes that a lawyer may reveal confidences or secrets necessary to defend himself against "an accusation of wrongful conduct." This is exactly what Goldberg had to face when, in their original complaint, plaintiffs named him as a defendant who wilfully violated the securities laws.

The charge, of knowing participation in the filing of a false and misleading registration statement, was a serious one. The complaint alleged violation of criminal statutes and civil liability computable at over four million dollars. The cost in money of simply defending such an action might be very substantial. The damage to his professional reputation which might be occasioned by the mere pendency of such a charge was an even greater cause for concern.

Under these circumstances Goldberg had the right to make an appropriate disclosure with respect to his role in the public offering. Concomitantly, he had the right to support his version of the facts with suitable evidence.

The problem arises from the fact that the method Goldberg used to accomplish this was to deliver to Mr. Abbey, a member of the Bernson firm, the thirty page affidavit, accompanied by sixteen exhibits, which he had submitted to the SEC. This document not only went into extensive detail concerning Goldberg's efforts to cause the Sitomer firm to rectify the nondisclosure with respect to Empire but even more extensive detail concerning how these efforts had been precipitated by counsel for the underwriters having come upon evidence showing that a similar nondisclosure was contemplated with respect to Glacier and their insistence that full corrective measures should be taken. Although Goldberg's description reflected seriously on his employer, the Sitomer firm and, also, in at least some degree, on Glacier, he was clearly in a situation of some urgency. Moreover, before he turned over the affidavit, he consulted both his own attorney and a distinguished practitioner of securities law, and he and Abbey made a joint telephone call to Mr. Sullivan of the SEC. Moreover, it is not clear that, in the context of this case, Canon 4 applies to anything except information gained from Empire. Finally, because of Goldberg's apparent intimacy with the offering, the most effective way for him to substantiate his story was for him to disclose the SEC affidavit. It was the fact that he had written such an affidavit at an earlier date which demonstrated that his story was not simply fabricated in response to plaintiff's complaint.

The District Court held: "All that need be shown ... is that during the attorney-client relationship Goldberg had access to his client's information relevant to the issues here." See Emle Industries, Inc. v. Patentex, Inc., 478 F.2d 562 (2d Cir.1973). However, the irrebuttable presumption of *Emle Industries* has no application to the instant circumstances because Goldberg never sought to "prosecute litigation," either as a party, compare Richardson v. Hamilton International Corp., 62 F.R.D. 413 (E.D.Pa.1974), or as counsel for a plaintiff party. Compare T.C. Theatre Corporation v. Warner Brothers Pictures, 113 F.Supp. 265 (S.D.N.Y.1953). At most the record discloses that Goldberg might be called as a witness for the plaintiffs but that role does not invest him with the intimacy with the prosecution of the litigation which must exist for the *Emle* presumption to attach.

In addition to finding that Goldberg had violated Canon 4, the District Court found that the relationship between Goldberg and the Bernson firm violated Canon 9 of the Code of Professional Responsibility which provides that:

> EC 9-6 Every lawyer [must] strive to avoid not only professional impropriety but also the appearance of impropriety.

The District Court reasoned that even though there was no evidence of bad faith on the part of either Goldberg or the Bernson firm, a shallow reading of the facts might lead a casual observer to conclude that there was an aura of complicity about their relationship. However, this provision should not be read so broadly as to eviscerate the right of self-defense conferred by DR 4–101(C)(4).

Nevertheless, Emle Industries, Inc. v. Patentex, Inc., supra, requires that a strict prophylactic rule be applied in these cases to ensure that a lawyer avoids representation of a party in a suit against a former here there may be the appearance of a possible violation of ce. To the extent that the District Court's order prohibits from *representing* the interests of these or any other plaintiffs in this or similar actions, we affirm that order. We also affirm so much of the District Court's order as enjoins Goldberg from disclosing material information except on discovery or at trial.

The burden of the District Court's order did not fall most harshly on Goldberg; rather its greatest impact has been felt by Bernson, Hoeniger, Freitag & Abbey, plaintiffs' counsel, which was disqualified from participation in the case. The District Court based its holding, not on the fact that the Bernson firm showed bad faith when it received Goldberg's affidavit, but rather on the fact that it was involved in a tainted association with Goldberg because his disclosures to them inadvertently violated Canons 4 and 9 of the Code of Professional Responsibility. Because there are no violations of either of these Canons in this case, we can find no basis to hold that the relationship between Goldberg and the Bernson firm was tainted. The District Court was apparently unpersuaded by appellees' salvo of innuendo to the effect that Goldberg "struck a deal" with the Bernson firm or tried to do more than prove his innocence to them. Since its relationship with Goldberg was not tainted by violations of the Code of Professional Responsibility, there appears to be no warrant for its disqualification from participation in either this or similar actions. *A fortiori* there was no sound basis for disqualifying plaintiffs or dismissing the complaint.

Order dismissing action without prejudice and enjoining Bernson, Hoeniger, Freitag & Abbey from acting as counsel for plaintiffs herein reversed.... To the extent that the orders appealed from prohibit Goldberg from acting as a party or as an attorney for a party in any action arising out of the facts herein alleged, or from disclosing material information except on discovery or at trial, they are affirmed.

Third–Party Charges Against a Lawyer

Is *Meyerhofer* a "confidentiality" or a "privilege" case? Why?

Was Goldberg justified in making his disclosure to the plaintiffs who were suing his former client? Why should the client's confidences be at the mercy of the actions of non-clients? [16]

Is it possible that Empire did not know of the obligation to disclose the fee arrangement in the prospectus? Could the fraud, if such it was, have been the firm's and not the client's? If so, does that suggest that Goldberg's initial disclosure should have been to the client rather than to the SEC?

---

16. The Model Code and Model Rules reject a distinction between an accusation made by a client and one made by a third person, see DR 4–101(C)(4) and M.R. 1.6(b)(2). ALCC Rule 1.5, on the other hand, distinguishes between the two situations: When the charge is made by a third party, disclosure of client confidences is permitted only *after charges are formally instituted;* when the charge is made by the client, disclosure may be made prior to formal proceedings. Does an exception for charges made by third parties encourage third parties to sue lawyers in an attempt to gain access to confidential information?

Model Rule 1.13 speaks of a lawyer's duties to an organizational client. It prescribes a course of conduct to be followed when a lawyer knows that an agent of the organizational client is violating a legal obligation to the client or violating the law in a manner that might be imputed to the organization [17] Under M.R. 1.13, should Goldberg have discussed the matter directly with Empire officers before going to the SEC? Would he have a duty to do so before disclosing in self-defense? The Comment to Model Rule 1.6(b)(2), the self-defense exception to confidentiality, states: "Where practicable and not prejudicial to the lawyer's ability to establish the defense, the lawyer should advise the client of the third party's assertions and request that the client respond appropriately." [18]

If the Bernson firm had had access to and had used Goldberg's affidavit to file suit against Empire, what result? In Beiny v. Wynyard [19] a prominent Wall Street firm procured attorney-client privileged documents through deception. It was held that the evidence so procured should be suppressed and the firm disqualified. A number of cases disqualify a law firm that has gained improper access to the opposing party's evidence.[20] Lawyers may also be disciplined for abuse of the self-defense exception.[21]

Although the court's opinion concentrates on Goldberg's disclosure to the plaintiffs, the earlier disclosure to the SEC raises serious questions. Goldberg, relying on cases such as *National Student Marketing*, may have believed he had an affirmative duty under federal law to prevent a securities law violation. If Goldberg did have such a duty, and if the client refused to make the required disclosure, DR 4–101(C)(3) would permit a New York lawyer to reveal the client's intention to commit a crime or fraud. But what if the fraud is that of Goldberg's firm, which has not communicated the legal problem to its client?

Does the self-defense exception of M.R. 1.6(b)(2) or DR 4–101(C)(4) permit a lawyer to disclose prior to an "accusation" when the lawyer believes one may be forthcoming? Is this what Goldberg did when he went to the SEC? Assuming Goldberg had gone to Empire and it had refused to disclose the fee arrangements in the prospectus, would

---

17. See the discussion of M.R. 1.13 in Chapter 8 below at p. 777.

18. See also Canon 41 and DR 7–102(B), provisions dealing with client fraud, which require the lawyer to ask the client to rectify before the lawyer discloses the fraud.

19. 129 A.D.2d 126, 517 N.Y.S.2d 474 (1987).

20. See, e.g., MMR/Wallace Power & Ind., Inc. v. Thames Associates, 764 F.Supp. 712 (D.Conn.1991) (disqualification of lawyer for obtaining privileged information from former employee of opposing party who was a member of that party's litigation team); American Protection Ins. Co. v. MGM Grand Hotel–Las Vegas, Inc., (D.Nev.1984 unreported), app. dismissed, 765 F.2d 925 (9th Cir.1985) (disqualification of lawyer for ex parte interrogation of other party's primary expert witness).

21. For a case where a lawyer was disciplined for using client confidences ostensibly in self-defense, see Dixon v. California State Bar, 32 Cal.3d 728, 187 Cal.Rptr. 30, 653 P.2d 321 (1982) (discipline imposed for using confidences in a suit brought by client to enjoin ~~~er from harassing client). See also Florida Bar v. Ball, 406 So.2d 459 (Fla.1981) ~~~uspended for disclosing to adoption agency that clients did not pay the lawyer's ~~~herefore might be a financial risk).

Goldberg then have been justified in going to the SEC prior to an "accusation" of wrongdoing? Even if so, was what he did "self-defense" given the proactive nature of his conduct? The more natural classification is disclosure to stop ongoing fraud rather than disclosure in self-defense, but the Model Rules treatment of client fraud disclosures makes resort to the self-defense exception necessary. See Model Rule 1.6(b)(1) (making no provision for disclosure of ongoing client fraud). This issue will be more fully explored when we take up client fraud below.

The disclosures permitted by M.R. 1.6(b)(2) are limited by the requirement that the lawyer reasonably believe they are necessary. The Comment adds: "disclosure should be no greater than the lawyer reasonably believes is necessary to vindicate innocence, the disclosure should be made in a manner which limits access to the information to the tribunal or other persons having a need to know it, and appropriate protective orders or other arrangements should be made by the lawyer to the fullest extent practicable." [22] How do Goldberg's actions match up against these standards?

Should judicial approval be required before the lawyer reveals confidences? [23] In the *First Federal* case,[24] the court read *Meyerhofer* as implicitly accepting the proposition that, in cases where the lawyer is accused of wrongdoing by a third party, "the attorney's interest in disclosure—at least to the extent necessary to defend himself—will usually outweigh the more general interest of the client in preserving confidences." [25] But procedural safeguards were adopted to protect confidentiality interests. The court ordered the lawyer to submit all proposed disclosures to the court for review in camera along with an affidavit explaining the necessity for each proposed disclosure. The client was then given the opportunity to respond to the lawyer's showing. In deciding what disclosures to allow, the court used the "reasonable necessity" standard of M.R. 1.6.

Self–Defense Exception to Attorney–Client Privilege

In an action to collect a fee, a lawyer may disclose otherwise privileged communications to establish the claim.[26] The privilege also yields to the lawyer's need to defend herself in a malpractice suit brought against her by the client.[27] If the client attacks the lawyer's work in a proceeding to which the lawyer is not a party, the privilege

22. See also the Comment's statement that the lawyer should, where practicable, inform the client and request that the client itself respond to the charges.

23. See Henry D. Levine, Self–Interest or Self–Defense: Lawyer Disregard of the Attorney–Client Privilege for Profit and Protection, 5 Hofstra L.Rev. 783, 825–26 (1977) (prior judicial approval should be required).

24. First Federal Savings & Loan Ass'n of Pittsburgh v. Oppenheim, Appel, Dixon & Co., 110 F.R.D. 557 (S.D.N.Y.1986).

25. Id. at 565.

26. See, e.g., Cannon v. U.S. Acoustics Corp., 532 F.2d 1118 (7th Cir.1976).

27. See, e.g., Nave v. Baird, 12 Ind. 318, 319 (1859).

also yields.[28]   A common example is a habeas corpus proceeding brought by a convicted person in which the claim is ineffective assistance of counsel.[29]

Statutory definitions of the attorney-client privilege include a self-defense exception.   Proposed Federal Rule of Evidence 503(d)(3), for example, allows disclosure of "communication[s] relevant to an issue of breach of duty by the lawyer to his client or by the client to his lawyer." [30]   This formulation, however, arguably provides no exception where the lawyer is accused of wrongdoing in complicity with the client, such as charged against Goldberg in the *Meyerhofer* case.

Although the court in *Meyerhofer* deals only with confidentiality and not the attorney-client privilege, that case has been read as supporting an exception to the *privilege* where lawyers are accused of wrongdoing in complicity with a client.[31]

C. CLIENT FRAUD

Introductory Note

Perhaps no other subject in professional ethics has generated more heated debate than that of a lawyer's proper course of action upon discovery of client fraud.   An historical review of the rules and ethics opinions on the subject reveals a longstanding morass of conflicting precepts: Rules imposing a duty to disclose are followed by ethics opinions interpreting those rules as requiring non-disclosure.[32]   A later rule appearing to require non-disclosure, M.R. 1.6, has a commentary that allows disclosure as long as it is done through signals instead of words.   In general, rules adopted by state courts provide for disclosure of client fraud while bar interpretations call for non-disclosure.[33]

[handwritten margin note: MR 1.6 appears to Require non-disclosure]

---

28.   See, e.g., Flood v. Commissioner, 468 F.2d 904, 905 (9th Cir.1972) (lawyer could testify to establish that settlement of former client's case was within lawyer's authority).

29.   See the cases cited above in the note on p. 276.

30.   West's Ann.Cal.Evid.Code § 958 (1966) ("no privilege ... as to a communication relevant to an issue of breach, by the lawyer or by the client, of a duty arising out of the lawyer-client relationship").

31.   See In re National Mortgage Equity Corp., 120 F.R.D. 687 (C.D.Cal.) (a law firm, which had unknowingly assisted a client in a fraudulent private-placement securities issue, could disclose otherwise privileged information to show that it was not a party to the client's fraudulent conduct), appeal dismissed, 857 F.2d 1238 (9th Cir.1988).   The case recognizes a self-defense exception to the attorney-client privilege, essentially parallel to *Meyerhofer*.

32.   Compare Canon 41 with ABA Formal Op. 287, and DR 7–102(B)(1) with ABA Formal Op. 341.

33.   Most states adopting the Model Rules have amended M.R. 1.6 to allow (and in a few instances to require) disclosure of client fraud.   See the chart of state rules on disclosure of client fraud printed below at p. 321.

1. Ethics Codes and Client Fraud

Canons of Professional Ethics

Canon 37 imposed a duty to keep confidences but, in addition to a self-defense exception, provided: "The announced intention of a client to commit a crime is not included within the confidences which [the lawyer] is bound to respect." Canon 41, which dealt directly with a lawyer's obligations upon discovery of a fraud perpetrated by a client, stated that, if the client refused to rectify the fraud, the client "should promptly inform the injured person or his counsel, so that they may take appropriate steps."[34]

Ethics opinions interpreting Canons 37 and 41 confounded the apparent clarity of the two canons. For example, ABA Formal Opinion 268 (1945) stated that a lawyer, who withdrew from representation upon learning that his client intended to commit perjury had no discretion to reveal the intended perjury to successor counsel employed to present it. Whither Canon 37? Similarly, ABA Formal Opinion 287 (1953) barred a lawyer who discovered his client had committed perjury in a civil case from disclosing the perjury because that would violate the duty to keep confidences. Whither Canon 41?

Model Code of Professional Responsibility

As initially promulgated in 1969 and as adopted in the vast majority of states, the Model Code appeared to reaffirm the explicit provisions of the Canons and overturn the contrary interpretations of the ethics opinions. DR 4–101(C)(3) thus provided: "A lawyer may reveal ... [t]he intention of his client to commit a crime and the information necessary to prevent the crime." Like Canon 37, DR 4–101(C)(3) applied to all future crimes and was discretionary.

Again like the Canons, the Model Code dealt with the discovery of past fraud in a separate provision. DR 7–102(B)(1) as originally adopted provided:

> A lawyer who receives information clearly establishing that: (1) His client has, in the course of the representation, perpetrated a fraud upon a person or tribunal shall promptly call upon his client to rectify the same, and if his client refuses or is unable to do so, he shall reveal the fraud to the affected person or tribunal.[35]

DR 7–102(B)(1) as originally promulgated did not expressly indicate that the duty to disclose fraud was an exception to the confidentiality rule, but logic suggests an exception was intended. How else could a lawyer "reveal fraud to the affected person," as required by DR 7–

---

34. Canon 41 imposed a mandatory duty to disclose both past and ongoing fraud, whether or not the lawyer's services had been used to perpetrate the fraud. For example, disclosure was required of a lawyer drawing a will who discovered that the client fraudulently had been collecting disability compensation while working full-time.

35. Unlike the Canons, however, DR 7–102(B)(1) was ambiguous as to whether the lawyer's services must have been employed in the fraud for disclosure to be mandatory. The better interpretation is that the provision does include such a requirement because the phrase "in the course of the representation" modifies "perpetrated a fraud" rather than "receives information."

102(B)(1), while at the same time obeying the injunction of DR 4–101(B) that "a lawyer shall not reveal a confidence or secret of his client"? [36] Also, a footnote to DR 7–102(B)(1) refers to DR 4–101(C)(2), which allows disclosure "when permitted under Disciplinary Rules. . . ."

In most Model Code states today, DR 7–102(B)(1) stands in its original form as stated above.

The realization that a literal reading of DR 7–102(B)(1) might require a lawyer to disclose a client's ongoing or past fraud led to an amendment of the rule in 1974 and an ethics opinion interpreting that amendment in 1975. These ABA actions left the disclosure obligation in the text of the rule but added an exception that had the effect of virtually eliminating the obligation. The 1974 ABA amendment added the following italicized "except" clause to DR 7–102(B)(1) so that it read as follows:

> [to rectify a fraud upon a person or tribunal when the client has refused to do so, a lawyer] shall reveal the fraud to the affected person or tribunal, *except when the information is protected as a privileged communication.*

The ABA may have intended the amendment to cancel the duty to reveal fraud when doing so would require revealing information prejudicial to the client. But a natural reading of the term "privileged communications" suggests a narrower meaning: Client fraud must be disclosed only if a lawyer's knowledge of the fraud came from information not protected as a "confidence" by the attorney-client privilege. The narrower reading also gains support from the argument that otherwise the amendment effectively repeals DR 7–101(B)(1). If "secrets" as well as "confidences" qualify as privileged communications, the amendment would cancel a lawyer's duty under DR 7–102(B)(1) to rectify client fraud in virtually all circumstances in which the duty could arise: In what situation could a lawyer reveal a client's fraud, the client having refused to do so, without revealing a client "secret" as that term is defined in the Code? To effectively repeal the duty to disclose fraud, while nominally preserving it, is surely disingenuous.

Despite the arguments in favor of the narrow reading, the ABA Committee on Ethics and Professional Responsibility in 1975 issued Formal Opinion 341, which officially interpreted the amendment as referring to both "confidences" and "secrets." Opinion 341 states:

> Such an interpretation does not wipe out DR 7–102(B)(1), because DR 7–102(B)(1) applies to information received from any source, and it is not limited to information gained in the professional relationship as is DR 4–101. Under the suggested interpretation, the duty imposed by DR 7–102(B) would remain in force if the information clearly establishing a fraud on a person or tribunal

---

36. "Secret" is defined in DR 4–101(A) as "information gained in the professional relationship . . . the disclosure of which would be embarrassing or would be likely to be detrimental to the client." Thus the term includes all significant information acquired during the course of representation.

and committed by a client in the course of representation were obtained by the lawyer from a third party (but not in connection with [the lawyer's] professional relationship with the client), because it would not be a confidence or secret of a client entitled to confidentiality.

In other words, a lawyer has a duty to disclose client fraud when fortuitously informed by a person, who is unaware that the lawyer is representing the client implicated, that the client committed fraud in the course of the representation. How likely is this scenario?

Only 14 states accepted the 1974 amendment to DR 7–102(B)(1) and only a few of those took a formal position on the question dealt with in Opinion 341. New York, for example, adopted the amendment in a form that included both confidences and secrets. With or without the amendment, however, the Code position on client fraud remains almost totally incoherent.

Model Rules of Professional Conduct   *must not Disclose*

The ABA special commission that drafted the Model Rules, known as the Kutak Commission, was well aware of the difficulties with the Code's approach to client fraud.[37] The commission's proposed final draft attempted to reconcile the profession's hostility to policing and "betraying" clients with the substantive law dealing both with a lawyer's liability for aiding client fraud and the crime-fraud exception to *MR 1.6(b)* the attorney-client privilege. The Kutak Commission proposal concerning client fraud, proposed Rule 1.6(b), read as follows:

> A lawyer may reveal [confidential] information to the extent the lawyer reasonably believes necessary:
>
> (1) to prevent the client from committing a criminal or fraudulent act that the lawyer reasonably believes is likely to result in ... substantial injury to the financial interests or property of another; [or] (2) to rectify the consequences of a client's criminal or fraudulent act in the furtherance of which the lawyer's services had been used....[38]

Amended (over)

Proposed Rule 1.6(b) covered prevention of a fraud, whether or not the lawyer's services had been involved, and rectification of a fraud where the lawyer's services had been used, both courses of action being discretionary and neither requiring a warning to the client.

Although the Kutak Commission viewed its proposal as a fair restatement of existing law, critics from within the profession bitterly

---

37. For an account and evaluation of the six-year process by which the ABA developed the Model Rules, see Ted Schneyer, Professionalism as Bar Politics: The Making of the Model Rules of Professional Conduct, 1989 Law & Soc.Inquiry 677 (evaluating the rule-making process as a species of de facto lawmaking by a private group and identifying common themes in the way lawyers think about legal ethics as "professionalism-in-fact").

38. Model Rules of Professional Conduct Rule 1.6(b) (Proposed Final Draft 1981).

attacked the proposed rule.[39] Those attackers repeatedly charged that permitting disclosure of client fraud in some situations constituted a "radical" change from existing law, a change that would undermine confidentiality by making clients less candid and by reducing lawyers' opportunities to channel client behavior along legal lines. Critics also argued that permitting disclosure would serve as a basis for expanded civil liability for lawyers who failed to disclose. After heated debate, the ABA House of Delegates in 1983, by a vote of 207–129, amended proposed Rule 1.6 to prohibit any disclosure of client fraud.[40] Model Rule 1.6(b) as adopted is a comprehensive and unqualified prohibition of disclosure of any client information, subject only to the homicide/bodily injury exception, the "self-defense" exception and the uncontroversial exception regarding disclosures "impliedly authorized" to carry out the representation.[41]

What does a lawyer do to protect herself in a situation where she has unwittingly been made the instrument of client fraud but cannot yet invoke the self-defense exception because no accusation has been made? The proponents of non-disclosure argue that the lawyer should resign, an action that would signal the lawyer's innocence and provide warning to other participants in a transaction that has not yet been consummated. Resignation will not provide a warning signal, however, if the fraudulent transaction has already been closed or if unsophisticated participants do not comprehend the significance of the lawyer's withdrawal. The morally conscientious lawyer, as well as the lawyer interested only in self-protection, would remain at risk in those situations.

The ABA House of Delegates in February 1983 adopted the black-letter text of amended Model Rule 1.6(b), with consideration of the Comment deferred to the August 1983 meeting. During the interim, negotiations between the opposing factions resulted in agreement on the addition of the following sentence to the Comment:

> Neither this Rule nor Rule 1.8(b) nor Rule 1.16(d) prevents the lawyer from giving notice of the fact of withdrawal, and the lawyer may also withdraw or disaffirm any opinion, document, affirmation, or the like.

39. See, e.g., Monroe H. Freedman, Lawyer–Client Confidence: The Model Rules' Radical Assault on the Traditional Role of the Lawyer, 68 A.B.A.J. 428 (1982). The attack on the confidentiality provisions of the proposed Model Rules was led by two organizations of trial lawyers: the American College of Trial Lawyers [ACTL] (primarily litigators for large corporations) and the American Trial Lawyers Association [ATLA] (primarily plaintiffs' trial lawyers).

40. See "Lawyers Vote Against Disclosure of Fraudulent Activity by Clients," N.Y. Times, Feb. 8, 1983, p. 1.

41. Note that while the Canons and Model Code dealt with client fraud on the tribunal in the same manner in which they dealt with client fraud on private parties, the Model Rules take a sharply different approach to the two problems. Although the Model Rules as adopted make no provision for disclosure of client fraud on third parties, they *mandate* disclosure of client fraud on the court. See M.R. 3.3. The question of fraud on the tribunal is considered in Chapter 5 below.

The proponents of the amended rule took the position that waving a red flag at the time of withdrawal did not involve a disclosure of confidential client information because the permitted actions, such as withdrawing a legal opinion, do not reveal a lawyer's knowledge of the details of the client's fraud. This view reconciles the "noisy withdrawal" permitted by the Comment with the black-letter text of the rule. A number of academic commentators have disagreed with this view, however, arguing that the intended warning is, in effect, the revelation of a confidence.[42] Is the "noisy withdrawal" permitted by the Comment consistent with the authoritative black-letter text? [43]

At one level the revised Comment can be understood as allowing what M.R. 1.6 itself appears to forbid: disclosure of unrectified client fraud in which the lawyer's services were used. Performance of a ritual that is intended as a signal is likely to be understood as a signal, thus revealing the information that the signal denotes. Although an effective signal may be equivalent to outright disclosure from the client's perspective, it may be materially different from the lawyer's perspective. Communicating in such an unnatural manner—avoiding direct communication—allows the bar to reaffirm the power of the norm of confidentiality even as it provides escapes from it. Moreover, banishing the "exception" to the Comment casts doubt on its existence and suggests that it should be relied on as the basis of action in only the most urgent cases. Comments, after all, are "intended as guides to interpretation, but the test of each Rule is authoritative." [44]

[handwritten margin note: noisy withdrawal as Disclosure]

The 1983 debate on client fraud was replayed at the 1991 meeting of the ABA House of Delegates.[45] The ABA's Committee on Ethics and Professional Responsibility recommended that language very similar to that deleted in 1983 be added to M.R. 1.6(b). The committee had found the 1983 version of the rule "unworkable" in the absence of a provision allowing disclosure of "the consequences of a client's criminal or fraudulent act in the commission of which the lawyer's services had been used." The committee's report stated:

> [W]e have had called to our attention situations with respect to which a literal application of the existing provisions ... dictates results which we believe to be unjust and inconsistent and which

---

42. Geoffrey C. Hazard, Jr., Rectification of Client Fraud: Death and Revival of a Professional Norm, 33 Emory L.J. 271, 305–06 (1984), stating that "the ABA wanted a statutory rule of confidentiality 'up front,' but also some kind of common law ... exception for cases of fraud or other urgent necessity.... The trouble with the solution ... adopted is that some fools may not understand that Rule 1.6 does not mean what it seems to mean." See also Ronald D. Rotunda, The Notice of Withdrawal and the New Model Rules of Professional Conduct: Blowing the Whistle and Waving the Red Flag, 63 Ore.L.Rev. 455 (1984).

43. The Preamble to the Model Rules states that "the text of each rule is authoritative" and that "[t]he Comments are intended as guides to interpretation."

44. Scope note to Model Rules.

45. 7 Law.Man.Prof.Conduct 256, 258 (Aug. 28, 1991).

threaten to unfairly subject lawyers to potential civil liability and criminal prosecution.[46]

The House of Delegates rejected the committee's proposal, 251–158.[47]

The internal professional debate over disclosure to prevent or rectify client fraud was echoed in a 1992 ABA ethics opinion.[48] The majority concluded that a lawyer, whose services had been used to obtain a bank loan on client representations that turned out to be fraudulent, must withdraw from further representation involving client transactions with the same bank; in making this mandatory withdrawal, the lawyer might withdraw "noisily" by notifying the bank that she no longer stands behind the opinion letter given at the time the loan was made. The majority relied on the Comment to Rule 1.6. Three dissenters argued that, because the lawyer's work on the loan was over, the lawyer was not required to withdraw from future loan transactions, even with the same lender, and, if the lawyer chose to withdraw, could not breach confidentiality by waving a red flag while doing so. The dissenters pointed out that the ABA House of Delegates had twice rejected proposals to amend Rule 1.6(b) to permit disclosure to prevent or rectify client fraud. A new exception to the Rule, they reasoned, must come from action by the House of Delegates.

Each state that has either adopted a version of the Model Rules or revised its ethics rules since 1983 in light of the Model Rules has given extensive consideration to the client fraud issue. Only a handful of the 37 states that have adopted some version of the Model Rules have followed M.R. 1.6 in its entirety. Most states permit a lawyer to disclose a future crime involving financial and property injury, and a majority permit or require a lawyer to act to prevent or rectify client fraud. A chart summarizing the ethics provisions of all states concerning prevention or rectification of client fraud is reproduced below at p. 321.[49]

[handwritten margin note: How states have adopted model Rule 1.6]

2. O.P.M.: A Case Study

In the following case study, a client was engaged in ongoing fraud and used the lawyers' services to perpetrate the fraud. At some point

---

46. Id. at 173 (June 19, 1991).

47. Id. at 258 (Aug. 28, 1991). John Elam, representing the American College of Trial Lawyers, argued that discretionary rectification "will become a mandate" if lawyers have "the discretion to blow the whistle" on clients. Other opponents argued that the rectification rule would subject lawyers to liability if they failed to disclose something that they had discretion to disclose. A trial lawyer posed the issue as: "Is the lawyer the policeman of the client's conduct or the repository of the client's confidences?" Id. at 258–59.

48. ABA Comm. on Ethics and Prof.Resp. Formal Op. 92–366, 8 Law.Man.Prof.Conduct 394 (Dec. 16, 1992).

49. The proposed Restatement of the Law Governing Lawyers § 117B (Tentative Draft No. 2, Apr. 17, 1989) abandons the approach of M.R. 1.6 in favor of discretionary disclosure to prevent substantial financial loss threatened by a client's criminal or fraudulent act. The ALI proposal, which has not yet been adopted, deals only with prevention, not rectification. A lawyer who discovers after a loss has occurred that her client used the lawyer's services to perpetrate a fraud must look to the self-defense exception in § 116 for the scope of the lawyer's right to disclose.

Case study

in the representation, based on the confidences of the client's managers and other knowledge gained in the course of representation, the lawyers became aware of the problem. The lawyers faced a choice between revealing the fraud, which would have constituted disclosure of client information, and withdrawing from the representation without disclosure, which the lawyers realized might leave the firm open to civil and criminal charges.

Drew but did not disclose

The O.P.M. lawyers eventually withdrew, but following the advice of their ethics consultants they refrained from disclosing the fraud to the victims or to the successor law firm that unwittingly continued the fraud. The trustee in bankruptcy later wrote:

> One thing seems clear; the firm could have followed other courses, consistent with their ethical responsibilities, that would have stopped the fraud. Instead, after receiving notice that it was dealing with a crook, it acted in a way that helped [O.P.M.] continue the fraud for eight additional months during which financial institutions were bilked out of more than $85 million. After [the first law firm] resigned, O.P.M.'s in-house legal staff and [successor counsel] closed fraudulent ... lease financings totaling approximately $15 million.[50]

In reading the O.P.M. story, consider at each stage what the lawyers should have done differently. Keep in mind that scams similar to O.P.M. have occurred repeatedly in other contexts, including the savings and loan scandals of the 1980s, the Southwest oil industry investments in the 1970s, and shaky smaller businesses every day. You may have such a business for a client.

Consider whether lawyers for O.P.M. could have been charged with aiding and abetting the fraud. What about their "ethics experts"?

other people's $

STUART TAYLOR, JR.
"ETHICS AND THE LAW: A CASE HISTORY"
New York Times Magazine, January 9, 1983, p. 31 et seq.[51].

[In December 1982 Myron S. Goodman, Mordecai Weissman and five other employees of O.P.M. Leasing Services, Inc. appeared in federal court before Judge Haight for sentencing in one of the most massive corporate frauds in American history.] Goodman and Weissman had pleaded guilty to defrauding banks and other lenders of more than $210 million before their company went bankrupt in 1981. Along the way, they had hoodwinked some of the nation's largest and most prestigious companies, including Rockwell International, American Express, Chase Manhattan Bank and Lehman Brothers Kuhn Loeb. [Goodman received a 12–year sentence and Weissman a 10–year term. Before sentencing, Goodman promised the judge that the "wrongs I have done are behind me."]

---

50. Report of the Trustee, In re O.P.M. (S.D.N.Y.1983).

51. Copyright © New York Times Magazine. Reprinted by permission.

Over his years as O.P.M.'s executive vice president, Goodman had made the same promise again and again, sometimes in tears, to the group of men who served as the company's attorneys. And over the years, they had believed him—or, at least, they had acted as though they believed him—while they carried out his directions. As a result, their firm, Singer Hutner Levine and Seeman, has been accused by some lenders of complicity in the leasing company's fraud.

. . .

Singer Hutner's experience with the O.P.M. fraud represents a dramatic illustration of the conflicts and moral ambiguities that have troubled thoughtful lawyers for many years and have now become a focus of heated public debate.

. . .

Weissman started [O.P.M.] in 1970 in a small office on Church Avenue in Brooklyn, and Goodman joined him a few months later. Weissman handled the marketing end, Goodman was the inside man, in charge of finances; they each owned half of the business. O.P.M. was Weissman's name for the company—short for "other people's money."

The company would borrow money to purchase computers and other business equipment and then lease the equipment to corporate customers. In theory, the lease payments to O.P.M. would be large enough to allow the company to service its loans with enough left over to provide a handsome profit.

The formula seemed to work magically. By the late 1970's, O.P.M. had become one of the nation's five largest computer-leasing companies, with 250 employees in 11 offices across the country, including plush headquarters on Broadway in Manhattan. It was buying multimillion-dollar computers from the likes of I.B.M. and leasing them to such corporations as American Telephone and Telegraph, Revlon and Polaroid. Prestigious banks, insurance companies and other financial institutions were glad to lend O.P.M. money, secured as it was by the obligations of the lessees to make lease payments and by the value of the computers themselves. Many of these lenders were recruited by Lehman Brothers, the company's investment banker. O.P.M. also raised cash by selling legal title to the computers to individual investors seeking tax shelters.

The two owners of O.P.M. lived well. Goodman purchased the baronial Wardwell Estate (currently valued at up to $750,000) in Lawrence, L.I., where he lived with his wife and two daughters. He decorated it lavishly, adding a disco and a small movie theater. He pledged $10 million to Yeshiva University and became the youngest trustee in its history.

In 1978, Goodman and Weissman bought a bank in Louisiana, savoring this traditional emblem of corporate success. Goodman soon found a special use for the bank, however—a kind of illegal interest-free borrowing called check-kiting. He was detected by bank officials within six months, and in March 1980 O.P.M. pleaded guilty to 22 felony counts and paid a $110,000 fine. A tearful Goodman promised his attorneys that he would never stray again.

It was the first public indication of serious legal trouble at the company, but the case attracted little notice. Not until a year later would O.P.M. go bankrupt and the story of the Goodman–Weissman machinations begin to emerge.

Almost from the start, the company was basically insolvent and survived by means of fraud and bribery. A single computer would be used as collateral for two or three loans with different banks; the value of a given piece of equipment would be inflated to obtain larger loans. (Judge Haight, at the time of sentencing, told how "Mr. Goodman would crouch under a glass table with a flashlight and Mr. Weissman would trace the forged signatures.")

To win a place in the competitive computer-leasing market, Weissman bribed employees of potential customers, and the company offered lease rates far below those of its competitors. Moreover, the company offered lessors a risky bonus. In return for granting O.P.M. a long lease of, say, seven years, customers were promised that they could cancel the contract in the event a technological breakthrough made the computers obsolete.

Goodman was pushing the company toward ever bigger loans, building the shaky pyramid ever higher, when I.B.M. announced in 1977 a forthcoming new line of computers that would revolutionize the business. O.P.M. customers soon started lining up to cancel their leases. To avoid bankruptcy, Goodman resorted to fraud on a much grander scale than ever before, as Weissman's role in the illegal actions diminished. He relied almost totally on leases supposedly entered into by Rockwell International, the huge California aerospace company. He used forged signatures, documents falsified to overstate the value of leases and computers, and loans obtained upon equipment that did not exist. Between 1978 and 1981, O.P.M. obtained from 19 banks, pension funds and other lenders more than $196 million in loans secured by phony Rockwell leases. These new loans went to meet payments on old loans until the company finally came crashing down in March 1981. Within the next year, Goodman, Weissman and five O.P.M. vice presidents would plead guilty to charges of fraud.

Andrew B. Reinhard was 26 years old, an honors graduate of Harvard Law School, when he joined a small New York law firm in 1969. When the newly created O.P.M. Leasing Services Inc. started casting about for a law firm, Myron Goodman remembered Reinhard, older brother of a boyhood friend. That was the start of the long, tumultuous relationship between the company and Singer Hutner.

All through the decade of fraud at O.P.M., Singer Hutner handled the company's legal work. That included closing loans and supplying the legal opinions that lenders relied on as to O.P.M.'s title to computers and as to the legality of O.P.M. leases. The firm also handled the personal legal affairs of "Myron and Mordy," as the owners of O.P.M. were known to Singer Hutner lawyers.

As the computer-leasing company grew, so did Singer Hutner. By 1980, it employed 29 lawyers, with offices in New York and New Orleans; in that year, it collected more than $3.2 million in fees and expenses from O.P.M.—about 60 percent of its total income. Reinhard was the third O.P.M. director, along with Weissman and Goodman, and several other Singer Hutner lawyers were company officers.

Today, looking back on that time, Singer Hutner lawyers who have testified insist that up until June 1980, they had no inkling that their chief client was engaged in large-scale fraud; they thought O.P.M. a booming, legitimate business. (According to Goodman, however, there was one partner who was a knowing, although reluctant, participant in the Rockwell fraud—Andrew Reinhard, whom Goodman described in his deposition as his closest friend aside from Weissman. Reinhard was a major target of a Federal grand jury investigation last year but was not indicted. He invoked the Fifth Amendment to avoid testifying in the sweeping bankruptcy investigation, but through his attorney, he has denied any involvement in the fraud.)

[But the trustee's subsequent report stated that:

... By early 1979 Singer Hutner had received indications that Goodman and Weissman were capable of serious illegality. Some lawyers were also aware that Weissman and Goodman had engaged in lease fraud and commercial bribery, and the firm knew that Goodman had recently perpetrated a $5 million check kiting scheme. Singer Hutner also had knowledge of facts showing that OPM was suffering severe cash shortages that provided a motive for further fraud.

In the sixteen months between the first financing of phantom Rockwell leases in February 1979 and Goodman's first confession to Singer Hutner of serious wrongdoing in June 1980, numerous facts came to Singer Hutner's attention that should have raised suspicions about the bona fides of OPM–Rockwell leases. The closings of Rockwell transactions in 1979 and 1980 differed from other closings in several significant respects. Among other things, Goodman and his accomplices directed Singer Hutner to send Rockwell's copies of financing documents to OPM after the closings and instructed the lawyers not to contact Rockwell without Goodman's prior permission. No equity participations were sold in the expensive equipment shown on numerous Rockwell leases. IBM mass storage units began to appear on purported leases to Rockwell in numbers far greater than Rockwell could possibly need. Insurance for Rockwell equipment came from OPM's insurer, despite Rockwell's contractual obligation to maintain the insurance. A number of inconsistencies and peculiarities appeared in title documents presented by the fraud team for Rockwell closings. Singer Hutner was also aware that, on certain leases, OPM made rental payments to financing institutions in the lessee's place. With all these red flags, Singer Hutner should have exercised extreme caution in closing OPM–Rockwell lease financings. Instead, until June 1980 the firm closed these transactions on a business as usual basis.]

The relationship between Singer Hutner and O.P.M. took a dramatic turn on June 12, 1980, when Joseph L. Hutner, a senior partner in the law firm, received an extraordinary visit from Myron Goodman. The O.P.M. executive indicated that he was troubled, that he might have done something wrong in his stewardship of the company—something he could not set right because it involved millions of dollars more than he could raise. But during the meeting with Hutner, which lasted for several hours as Reinhard and others shuttled in and out of the room, Goodman indicated he had no intention of telling Hutner any details unless he could be sure the attorney would not tell them to anyone else. Hutner could not give him such an assurance since the law firm also represented O.P.M. itself and thus might have to inform Weissman.

[handwritten margin notes: Goodman gues to atty & FrAuD. Secrets]

One of the matters troubling Goodman was a letter that John A. Clifton, O.P.M.'s chief in-house accountant, had told Goodman he was preparing to send to Reinhard. Clifton had discovered evidence of the Rockwell lease fraud. After consulting his own lawyer, William J. Davis, Clifton decided to turn the information over to Singer Hutner and then resign. He hoped thereby to avoid criminal prosecution while putting the onus on Singer Hutner to decide whether to blow the whistle on O.P.M. While Goodman was in Hutner's office, the letter was delivered to Reinhard's room down the hall.

During a break in the meeting in Hutner's office, Goodman and Reinhard strolled off, Goodman heading for the bathroom. Some time later they returned; Goodman had the letter. Accounts of how he obtained it differ. The lawyers say that Goodman snatched the letter unopened from Reinhard's hand or seized it from the top of his desk. Goodman says this was a "cover story" agreed upon between him and Reinhard—that in fact he found Reinhard reading the letter as he passed his office. By all accounts, Goodman took the Clifton letter with him when he left Singer Hutner that afternoon, still refusing to reveal what he had done wrong but insisting that it was all in the past.

Goodman was worried that Clifton might go to the authorities. He said he promised Clifton $50,000 to $100,000 in severance pay that, Goodman testified, was "meant to induce him to keep his mouth shut." Goodman also urged Hutner to talk with Clifton's attorney, William J. Davis of Schulman Berlin & Davis.

In his description of their meetings, Davis said that Hutner seemed to be trying to persuade him that Clifton should keep silent and should take back his letter. Davis said the conversations were "a kind of macabre dance around the issue," so elliptical and hypothetical that "nothing was fact, everything was possible." He said Hutner seemed to know more than he let on, but seemed anxious to preserve a "smoke screen" of deniability. Davis recalled: "I had visions of him clamping his hands over his ears and running out of the office."

Davis also said he had been prepared to give Hutner a copy of Clifton's letter and would have told him "as much as he wanted to know," but that Hutner told him "he didn't want it, he didn't want to know what was in it."

Hutner gave a very different account of these meetings. He insisted he did not seek to have Clifton withdraw the letter, nor did he shrink from hearing about Clifton's evidence.

Yet Davis did give Hutner and Eli R. Mattioli, a younger Singer Hutner lawyer who attended one of the meetings, some crucial information. According to a memorandum prepared by Singer Hutner at the time, Davis said Clifton had evidence that O.P.M. had perpetrated a multimillion-dollar fraud and that the opinion letters Singer Hutner had drawn up to obtain loans for O.P.M. had been based upon false documents. And Davis also passed along, Mattioli recalled, an ominous opinion from Clifton—that O.P.M., "in order to survive, would probably have to continue the same type of wrongful activity."

(accountant)
Clifton's
atty

Thus it was that in the middle of June 1980 Singer Hutner received what was tantamount to a stark warning that the law firm was deeply involved in a huge, ongoing fraud. Today, Davis recalls that he felt at the time that a turning point for Singer Hutner had arrived. "Once you come into that kind of knowledge," he says, "a whole new set of rules drops on you." Certain that Singer Hutner would have to resign and that O.P.M.'s fraud would soon be exposed, Davis says he "just sat here waiting for the shoes to drop."

It was a long wait.

The seriousness of the situation was not lost on Singer Hutner, which decided it needed some outside legal advice of its own. On June 18, the firm made an appointment with Joseph M. McLaughlin, who was dean of Fordham Law School at the time and is now a Federal District judge in New York [subsequently, McLaughlin was elevated to the United States Court of Appeals for the Second Circuit]. McLaughlin, one of Mattioli's professors at Fordham, was a leading authority on the attorney-client privilege, under which lawyers are generally prohibited from revealing secrets confided to them by their clients.

According to McLaughlin's deposition, Hutner, Mattioli and Carl J. Rubino, another Singer Hutner lawyer, arrived at his office on June 19 "in a distressed state." He said Hutner made it clear "that he wanted to act in a way that would preserve the attorney-client confidence."

But it soon became clear to McLaughlin that, given the apparent scope of the fraud and the law firm's close relationship with O.P.M., the central problem was one of "ethics, professional responsibility." He accepted a $5,000 check from Hutner as a retainer and proceeded to bring into the case a legal-ethics expert, Henry Putzel 3d, a former

Federal prosecutor who had taught the subject at Fordham and who was practicing law in New York.

The next day, at a two-and-a-half-hour meeting in Hutner's office, Hutner, Mattioli and Rubino gave McLaughlin and Putzel a detailed report on what they had learned from Goodman and Davis. The Singer Hutner lawyers stressed two major points, McLaughlin recalled in his deposition: they wanted to do the ethical thing, and they wanted to continue representing O.P.M. unless they were ethically and legally obliged to quit.

In conversations on June 25 and over the next few days, McLaughlin and Putzel gave Hutner and other members of the law firm the advice they wanted to hear. (The advice is described in detail in documents Putzel prepared at the time and in Putzel's and McLaughlin's depositions in the bankruptcy investigation.) Singer Hutner could ethically continue to represent O.P.M., giving the benefit of the doubt to Goodman's assurances that there was no ongoing fraud. The firm could continue to close new loans for O.P.M. pending efforts to find out the details of Goodman's past wrongdoing; such information would help them guard against any continuing fraud. Singer Hutner was bound to keep everything it had already learned secret, except from Weissman.

[margin note: Advice to singer-Hutner]

It was not necessary, Putzel advised, for Singer Hutner to check the authenticity of the computer-lease documents with third parties such as Rockwell before closing the new loans. As to the possibly false opinion letters and documents the firm had unwittingly provided to banks to obtain loans for O.P.M., Putzel offered another welcome opinion: Singer Hutner had no legal duty to withdraw them. He reasoned that leaving the victims of a past fraud in the dark was not an ongoing fraud.

McLaughlin and Putzel did recommend some steps aimed at stopping any efforts to commit new fraud. They said, for example, that O.P.M. should be required to certify in writing the legitimacy of each new transaction. Goodman was unfazed; he simply signed certifications he knew to be false. And he found ways to put off giving the law firm the kind of detailed description of his crimes that would have made the attorneys better able to judge the dangers of their position.

[margin note: Future steps]

While McLaughlin and Putzel advised the law firm to press Goodman to confess to them and to his partner Weissman the details of his wrongdoing, they did not initially suggest that he be pressed too hard. One reason, as Putzel explained in a deposition, was his concern that the law firm's obligations to O.P.M. might be inconsistent with giving Goodman's secrets the fullest protection. Thus, a lawyer was found to represent Goodman's personal best interests, while Singer Hutner theoretically concentrated on representing the best interests of the corporation—this though the corporation was virtually Goodman's personal fiefdom.

Goodman's new lawyer was Andrew M. Lawler, an old law-school friend of McLaughlin and, like Putzel, a former Federal prosecutor. In their depositions, McLaughlin and Putzel testified that they had placed great confidence in Lawler, and that Lawler had told Putzel that he knew of no ongoing fraud. This should, perhaps, not have been much of a surprise. Lawler's information came from Goodman, and according to Goodman's testimony, Hutner had given the executive a brief lesson in the attorney-client privilege, telling him that his disclosures to Lawler would be protected only so long as they did not indicate any ongoing fraud.

Meanwhile, as Goodman continued to stall, Lawler and Singer Hutner were dickering over the best way for Goodman to come clean about his past crimes. The object: to get at the truth but to do it in a way that would wrap it in the legal code of silence that is the attorney-client privilege.

The advice offered by Putzel and McLaughlin in June and thereafter was predicated on Singer Hutner's position that it did not "know" of any ongoing fraud by O.P.M. McLaughlin testified in his deposition that "it was basic black-letter law that they could not continue to represent O.P.M. if they were aware of an ongoing fraud, and that if they became aware, they would certainly have to resign."

Thus a little too much knowledge can be a dangerous thing for a lawyer. Some criminal-defense lawyers, for example, privately acknowledge that they are careful not to ask defendants who come to them: "Did you do it? Tell me everything." One reason: The client might answer by confessing his guilt and then go on to insist upon giving a false alibi at the trial, and the lawyer could be deemed a knowing accessory to perjury for helping him give such testimony.

Whether or not Singer Hutner purposely shielded itself from knowledge of O.P.M.'s ongoing fraud is in dispute. In a "memorandum to the file" after his meetings with Hutner in June, William Davis expressed concern about Hutner's "apparent willingness to stick his head in the sand and ignore these problems."

Singer Hutner and Putzel discounted Clifton's suspicions that the company would have to continue engaging in fraud to stay in business. As Putzel wrote in a later letter to Hutner, "Your firm was in the possession of no fact which in any way indicated the commission of an ongoing fraud." And he and Singer Hutner also accepted O.P.M.'s explanations of some strange happenings—bills of sale for computers that O.P.M. apparently did not have the money to buy; a signature on a document that looked to Mattioli like a forgery; the sudden resignation of an outside accounting firm because of its suspicion that Goodman and Weissman had been looting their corporation at a time when it was insolvent.

On July 15, for example, Alan S. Jacobs, a Singer Hutner partner who handled O.P.M.'s bank financings, discovered that O.P.M. had given the law firm two bills of sale, supposedly for different leases and different bank loans, that contained identical equipment descriptions and serial numbers. Jacobs consulted with Putzel and then checked with O.P.M., which told him there had been a typographical error. He accepted the explanation and a "corrected" document. Both the original and the corrected version proved to be phony.

Meanwhile, the lawyers were becoming increasingly upset at Goodman's continuing refusal to disclose the details of his wrongdoing. Late on the afternoon of July 22, in the middle of what Putzel recalled as "the worst lightning and thunderstorm I have ever seen in New York over the East River," Hutner telephoned Goodman and set a deadline for him to tell Weissman what he had done. Goodman responded with threats to hurl himself out the window of his huge, luxuriously appointed office.

Out the window!

"It was right out of a Grade C movie," recalled Putzel, who was in the room with Hutner. "There was wild lightning, claps of thunder, Hutner pleading with Goodman to be rational."

All through this summer of nondisclosure, Singer Hutner continued closing loans for O.P.M. without checking the legitimacy of underlying Rockwell leases. Some were legitimate, but leases securing loans of $22 million in June, $17 million in July and $22 million in August proved to be fraudulent.

Goodman tells Hunter of past fraud

In the first week of September, Goodman finally told Hutner some of the details of the fraud he had first hinted at in June, and Hutner explained it all to Putzel over lunch at the Yale Club in New York. In his deposition, Hutner recalled the meeting. "I wanted to get the hell out" of the connection with O.P.M., he said. "I was just disgusted, and I wanted [Putzel's] acquiescence." The two men tentatively agreed that the law firm should quit as O.P.M.'s counsel—though Putzel advised that the firm was not ethically obliged to do so because, he still assumed, the fraud had ended before June.

"What struck me as so, frankly, evil about this," Putzel said in his deposition, "was that the lawyers had been manipulated in this fashion." It was now apparent, he said, that "the attorneys were the instruments, the unwitting instruments, of the fraud by Goodman."

Over a period of two weeks, the members of the law firm discussed the question of quitting O.P.M. in a series of heated and emotional meetings. Meanwhile, Singer Hutner closed two more loans that proved to be fraudulent. For the first time, the law firm tried to check with Rockwell the legitimacy of the leases by mailing a verification form to a Rockwell executive in California. Goodman later recalled that when he heard the form was on its way, "I just went totally bananas." Goodman's O.P.M. henchmen intercepted the document at Rockwell and forged the executive's signature.

Singer Hutner voted formally to resign as O.P.M.'s general counsel on Sept. 23 in a daylong series of meetings punctuated by expressions of concern about the effect of a possible O.P.M. bankruptcy on the law firm's fees. Goodman was in the firm's offices that day and bitterly accused the lawyers of disloyalty, seemingly unabashed by their knowledge that he had used them to swindle banks out of tens of millions of dollars. He also described McLaughlin and Putzel as "white-shoed and ultra-Fascist attorneys" and warned the Singer Hutner lawyers to "keep their mouths shut." Later that night, according to Mattioli, Goodman stood at the head of the law firm's staircase, shaking with anger, and shouted, "If you do this and bring down the company, I will bring down this firm." Weissman was also in the law firm's offices that night, incongruously assuring those who would listen that O.P.M.'s business was better than ever and that its prospects were excellent.

Singer Hutner quit O.P.M. gradually, completing the process in December 1980. The lawyers assumed that an abrupt withdrawal would cause O.P.M. to collapse; they would handle legal business until Goodman, who had vowed that he would eventually pay back the victims of the fraud, could find new counsel. Singer Hutner's decision was in accord with Putzel's advice that the law firm could not drop its client "like a sack of potatoes." The withdrawal, he said, "had to be accomplished in a manner least likely to cause injury to the client." Still, Singer Hutner had cause to worry about its own potential liability during the withdrawal period, and the firm took steps to prevent new fraud. Its lawyers refused to proceed with new loans unless Goodman authorized them to check out the collateral with third parties such as Rockwell. They also demanded that O.P.M. cease new "tax-shelter" financings entirely, because they would almost certainly involve violations of the Federal securities laws.

Singer Hutner also moved to guard its income during the withdrawal period. Fearful that Goodman would refuse to pay its fees, and that they might be uncollectible if O.P.M. went bankrupt, the law firm announced in late September that it would do no more work for O.P.M. unless it received "an advance retainer against our customary time charges." It demanded and received $250,000 for the withdrawal period, along with $250,000 for services already performed.

Once the decision to quit O.P.M. was made, Singer Hutner had to determine what to do with its knowledge that it had been part of a giant fraud. On Putzel's advice, the law firm kept the facts to itself, telling nothing to the corporations and bankers who had been defrauded. Based on Goodman's increasingly implausible assurances that the days of fraud were over, Putzel said that the executive's secrets were still protected by the attorney-client privilege. Singer Hutner accepted that view, even after Goodman acknowledged on Sept. 29 and 30 that the outstanding fraudulent loans totaled $80 million to $90 million, about three times the amount he had confessed earlier in the month. And the law firm held fast even after receiving the worst news of all, that Goodman had been using Singer Hutner to close fraudulent loans from June through September.

The law firm responded to inquiries from lenders and other interested parties by saying that Singer Hutner and O.P.M. had "agreed" to part ways. ("Was that not a lie?" Hutner was asked, during the taking of his deposition. "It was inaccurate," he replied at first, later amending that to "more accurate than not, if not totally accurate.")

This stance played right into the hands of Goodman. He was able to continue obtaining fraudulent loans while spreading the suggestion that he had dismissed Singer Hutner and assuring business contacts that there was nothing wrong with the loans.

The close-mouthed stance was also called for by Putzel as the appropriate way of dealing with the lawyers who would fill Singer Hutner's shoes—in spite of the considerable risk that Goodman would simply lie to the new attorneys. Thus he advised Singer Hutner that it must honor Goodman's demand that Gary R. Simon, the O.P.M. in-house lawyer who was preparing to handle new loan closings, be kept in the dark.

Fearing that Goodman would use Simon, who was inexperienced in closing loans, to commit new frauds, Singer Hutner in October prepared for Simon a memorandum specifying "due diligence" verification procedures that should be used in all O.P.M. financings. But before the memorandum was delivered, it was shown to Goodman for editing; the final memo had nothing in it to make Simon suspect something was wrong with the Rockwell leases.

It soon became apparent that Simon was unlikely to discover the fraud. At one point, he told Mattioli that "if something is wrong with those deals, then I want to know it today." Mattioli did not respond.

A similar series of events was played out with Kaye, Scholer, Fierman, Hays & Handler, one of New York's largest law firms, which Goodman invited to step into Singer Hutner's place and close new loans for O.P.M. Hutner wanted to warn Peter M. Fishbein, a Kaye Scholer partner and an old friend, to stay away from O.P.M. In his deposition, Hutner quoted Putzel's response to the notion: "Oh my God, that is exactly what you can't do."

Fishbein phoned Hutner in October 1980 asking "if there was anything he should be aware of" in considering Goodman's invitation. Hutner told him only that "the decision to terminate was mutual and that there was mutual agreement that the circumstances of termination would not be discussed." Two years later, Hutner testified that "this specific thing caused me more personal pain than anything I can recall during the course of the entire O.P.M. thing, including learning that Myron was a thief."

The end result of Singer Hutner's close-mouthed policy: Goodman was able to use the unwitting Gary Simon and Kaye Scholer to close more than $15 million in loans for O.P.M. in December 1980 and early 1981 that were secured by fraudulent Rockwell leases.

The use of outside counsel like McLaughlin and Putzel has increased significantly during the post-Watergate decade as law firms have been exposed to increased public and Government scrutiny. Attorneys are more and more finding themselves in the unaccustomed role of defendants charged with complicity in their clients' illegal activities, or as targets of Government investigations of securities frauds.

Aside from the old saw that a lawyer who represents himself has a fool for a client, lawyers who find themselves in potential compromising circumstances are often willing to pay for the expertise of a specialist. That is particularly true in cases involving the fine points of legal ethics, about which many lawyers are quite ignorant. But lawyers, like other people, also hire specialists as a precautionary move, seeking advance legal clearance before taking action that might later become the focus of a lawsuit or a criminal investigation. And the more prestigious the specialist, the better.

Joseph McLaughlin, for example, given his considerable stature in the New York legal fraternity, seemed an ideal man for Singer Hutner to have in its corner. That was reflected in his fee, a healthy $12,500 for 25 hours work; that averages out to $500 an hour, a rate more than double what senior corporate lawyers in New York's big firms ordinarily charge their clients. It was about four times the rate charged by Putzel.

In his deposition, McLaughlin testified that he professed no expertise in legal ethics (except to the extent that it overlaps with the attorney-client privilege) and that he hardly knew anything about "the mechanics" of Singer Hutner's work for O.P.M. He minimized his role, calling himself a "sort of avuncular ... senior adviser" with no time "to get down to the nitty-gritty of this thing." In part, he said, that was because he was busy that summer of 1980 "running for office, in effect"—that is, jockeying for a judicial appointment. He was eventually named to a Federal District Court judgeship. Last month, he was among four men being considered for appointment to the New York Court of Appeals, the state's highest court.

After O.P.M. came tumbling down, Singer Hutner, and four co-defendants including Rockwell and Lehman Brothers, became the targets of a spate of multimillion-dollar lawsuits. The suits, brought by lenders, accused the law firm of being an accomplice in the O.P.M. crimes, on the ground that the attorneys knew or should have known they were part of an ongoing fraud. A tentative settlement of the lawsuits has been reached whereby the five defendants would pay $65 million; Singer Hutner's share would be about $10 million. But the law firm still maintains that it acted in conformity with the ethics code, as interpreted by Putzel and McLaughlin. And Putzel said in a recent interview, "I am in my own conscience absolutely convinced that the advice we gave was correct advice based on what we knew at the time."

Even the lawyers' lawyers have lawyers in the O.P.M. case, and those representing Putzel offered a written brief that summarized their client's attitude toward legal ethics. Under the adversary system of justice, they wrote: "A lawyer's primary obligation, loyalty and responsibility must be to his client, rich or poor, likeable or despicable, honest or crooked. Lawyers are not ordinary people: they sometimes are duty bound to stand up for and protect liars and thieves."

Whether or not Singer Hutner violated the ethical code, a basic question remains: Is there not something wrong with a code that can plausibly be used to justify the extreme lengths to which Singer Hutner went to protect its criminal client? Indeed, there is growing concern both inside and outside the legal profession that the current rules make it too easy for lawyers to condone or even actively assist their clients' ongoing crimes, frauds and cover-up conspiracies.

"Where Were the Lawyers?"

"Where were the lawyers [or other professionals]?" is a standard refrain after every major fraud. James P. Hassett, the court-appointed bankruptcy trustee of O.P.M., stated in his 600–page report to the bankruptcy court that the "accountants, lawyers, investment bankers, lessee representatives, bankers and other businessmen" deserved "substantial criticism" for their dealings with O.P.M. Some of the trustee's conclusions follow:

Accountants. O.P.M. had discharged its first accounting firm, Rashba & Pokart, because the firm did not "bend under Goodman's pressure" to report a positive net worth. Fox & Company, a large accounting firm based in Denver, was more compliant: Fox "departed from generally accepted accounting principles" and yielded to pressure to certify "materially false and misleading" O.P.M. financial statements for 1976, 1977 and 1978.

Investment Bankers. The trustee criticized Lehman Brothers, which arranged hundreds of millions of dollars in loans for O.P.M., for failing "to give proper weight to early warning signs" of fraud and for failing to pass on its knowledge of O.P.M.'s financial problems to the recruited lenders.[52]

---

52. The trustee said of the investment bankers:

Lehman did not discover that Goodman, Weissman, and their accomplices were forging and altering lease documents because [it] did not contact lessees or verify basic transaction facts.... Lehman's private placement memoranda expressly stated that the information they contained came from OPM and that Lehman did not vouch for its accuracy. Lehman made this disclaimer with good reason. Among other things, it did not know enough about computers to recognize as fraudulent OPM's purported leases to Rockwell of over twenty percent of the world's supply of IBM mass storage units on transactions for which Lehman arranged financing.

Lehman did know, however, that O.P.M. had repeatedly kited checks, was likely to experience a $76 million shortfall over the next five years and had a chaotic accounting

Lawyers. According to the trustee, "[l]awyers played a critical role in the massive Rockwell lease fraud." Singer Hutner had acted with "wilful blindness" to O.P.M.'s crimes or "reckless participation in them" when it helped O.P.M. obtain multimillion dollar loans with collateral that proved to be phony. The trustee concluded that Reinhard may have been "a knowing participant" in the fraud. The trustee also had some harsh words concerning the "ethics experts:"

> Singer Hutner, of course, relies on the advice it received from McLaughlin and Putzel to justify its conduct during the summer and fall of 1980. While the Trustee does not attempt to resolve the question whether that advice was consistent with the legal profession's code of ethics, it is clear that McLaughlin and Putzel could have advised other courses, consistent with Singer Hutner's ethical responsibilities, that would have stopped the fraud. Although McLaughlin and Putzel in good faith considered their advice appropriate in the circumstances, the Trustee believes it was in fact the worst possible advice from the point of view of O.P.M., the third parties with whom it dealt, Singer Hutner's successor counsel, and Singer Hutner itself. Accordingly, McLaughlin and Putzel must shoulder significant responsibility for their client's conduct.

> But Singer Hutner cannot properly shift all blame for its actions after Goodman's first confession of wrongdoing to McLaughlin and Putzel. While Singer Hutner relied on McLaughlin and Putzel for advice on its ethical obligations, McLaughlin and Putzel relied on the firm for the central factual predicate for their advice—whether the fraud was continuing. On issues like the significance of irregularities in title documents and the weight to be accorded Clifton's prediction that O.P.M. could not continue in business without further fraud, Singer Hutner was the expert.

> Viewed as a whole, the Trustee finds Singer Hutner's conduct nothing short of shocking, given the warnings it received before June 1980 and the remarkable events of the summer and early fall. Although Singer Hutner cites its ethical obligation not to injure its client unnecessarily, the most questionable aspects of Singer Hutner's conduct raise issues beyond professional ethics. Even after learning that Goodman had engaged in major wrongdoing, Singer Hutner continued to close O.P.M. debt financings without obtaining prior disclosure of the nature of the wrongdoing and without independently verifying transaction facts. No rule of professional ethics can or should exempt lawyers from the general legal proscriptions against willful blindness to their clients' crimes or reck-

system. It also knew that O.P.M.'s managers had withdrawn $1.5 million for personal purposes at a time when O.P.M. was probably insolvent. "But," reported the trustee, "Lehman continued to serve OPM until 1980 and did not disclose any of these problems to the institutions from which it solicited permanent financing for OPM."

less participation in them.[53]

Disclosure of Client Fraud?

The public reports of the O.P.M. fraud are based on an investigation by O.P.M.'s trustee in bankruptcy that delved into the files and recollections of O.P.M.'s lawyers, accountants, bankers, etc.[54] Why did the attorney-client privilege not protect this information?[55] Who was the client in the O.P.M. case?

Examine the conduct of the Singer Hutner lawyers in light of two bodies of law: the law of prohibited assistance presented in Chapter 2 and the law of professional ethics embodied in lawyer codes and ethics opinions. (Put Reinhard aside—if he was an active participant in the fraud, he concealed his knowledge from other lawyers in the firm.) Did any warning signals prior to June 1980 indicate or require further inquiry? If warning signals did exist, what explains Putzel's assertion that "no fact [in the possession of Singer Hutner] in any way indicated the commission of an ongoing fraud"?

Did the firm respond appropriately in June 1980 after the incident involving the Clifton letter and Goodman's initial confession? Why was the law firm so eager to continue its representation of O.P.M. if "ethically" possible?

What does a lawyer "know?" When, for example, does a lawyer receive information "clearly establishing that ... [h]is client has, in the course of the representation, perpetrated a fraud upon a person or tribunal ... ?" DR 7–102(B)(1). Is a lawyer entitled to believe a client's promise that no fraud continues? How much independent checking should a lawyer do if she doubts the word of a client's manager? Does a lawyer have an obligation to notify lenders, who are owed money on existing fraudulent leases or who are being asked to lend money now, that the legal opinions relating to existing leases are invalid? Does a lawyer faced with client fraud have an obligation to resign? When? What can or should the law firm tell a successor law firm?

Was the trustee's report correct in its harsh criticism of the advice Singer Hutner received from McLaughlin and Putzel? Where did the "ethics experts" look for guidance? Did they give, as the trustee said, the "worst advice possible?" What better advice was possible under

53. Report of the Trustee, In re O.P.M. (S.D.N.Y.1983). Joseph Hutner, senior partner in the Singer, Hutner firm, stated that the report was unfair to his firm, adversarial in its approach and was "the work of an ideologue." N.Y.Times, Apr. 27, 1983, p. D1.

54. The trustee was represented in the investigation by lawyers from Wilmer, Cutler & Pickering, which took formal depositions from 73 witnesses and compiled a transcript of more than 60,000 pages. The firm's fees totaled about $2.5 million. N.Y.Times, Apr. 27, 1983, pp. D1, D4.

55. See Commodity Futures Trading Comm'n v. Weintraub, 471 U.S. 343 (1985) (trustee of corporation in bankruptcy may waive corporation's attorney-client privilege with respect to pre-bankruptcy confidential communications, despite present objections of corporation's former officers and directors).

New York's law of professional responsibility [56] and the "other law" of prohibited assistance? [57]   What result if the Model Rules had been in effect in New York in 1980?   Were the ethics experts correct in concluding at each stage that, because Goodman promised to avoid any new fraudulent transactions, the prior representation involved only "past fraud?"

To the extent that professional rules and other applicable law allow discretion, how should a lawyer exercise choice in a situation such as O.P.M?   If the professional rules prohibit disclosure, should a moral lawyer engage in civil disobedience by violating the professional rule? Is the judiciary likely to support or punish a lawyer who discloses in an O.P.M.-type situation?   Consider *Meyerhofer.*   If *Benjamin* and *Meyerhofer* suggest that a lawyer should or may disclose but the ethics rules suggest a lawyer should not disclose, what might explain the existence of such contradictory normative messages?   What moral principles appear to have governed the lawyers' behavior in O.P.M?   What moral principles should the lawyers have followed?

Consider the consequences to the law firm involved in the O.P.M. case: Singer Hutner dissolved as a result of the O.P.M. case;   the reputations and careers of lawyers in the firm were adversely affected; prosecutors, grand juries and disciplinary authorities scrutinized the conduct of individual lawyers (apparently none of the lawyers was prosecuted or disciplined);   and the law, accounting and investment banking firms involved in handling O.P.M. transactions settled malpractice claims brought by victims of the fraud for $65 million (the law firm's share in this settlement was $10 million, the maximum coverage of its malpractice insurance).   Do the rules of professional conduct *require* a lawyer to act in a manner that involves such dire consequences?

What lessons does the O.P.M. story have for the future?   How can future O.P.M.s be avoided?   How can you ensure that you do not become ensnared in some similar disaster?

Representing Organizations

Much lawyering today occurs within the institutional framework of a law firm and involves continuing relationships with other organizations, private or public.   Clients are often large entities with a complex

---

56. As stated earlier, New York, the jurisdiction in which O.P.M. transactions were centered, adopted the 1974 amendment to DR 7–102(B)(1) in a form that prohibited rectification of client fraud when the lawyer's "information is protected as a confidence or secret."   But New York also adopted DR 4–101(C)(3) in its Model Code form, permitting disclosure of a client's "intention ... to commit a crime."   Note that practicing law across state lines raises important choice-of-law questions.   Many of O.P.M.'s lease transactions involved a lender, a lessee and equipment located outside of New York.   If those three contacts were in New Jersey and that state balances confidentiality and protection of third persons differently from New York, might the New Jersey standard have been applied to the New York lawyers?

57. Both *Meyerhofer,* p. 286 above, and *Benjamin,* p. 57 above, were decided by the Second Circuit, which includes New York, years before O.P.M. became Singer Hutner's client.   Are they not valid sources for determining a lawyer's responsibilities?

structure composed of constituents with somewhat differing interests. The context in which lawyers conduct their practice effects (some would say controls) how lawyers behave. Robert Gandossy has explored how Goodman and Weissman could carry on such large-scale fraudulent activities over a nine-year period without someone—a lawyer, accountant, investment banker, lender, employee or customer—blowing the whistle. Why did those people, many of them professionals with fiduciary responsibilities, fail to act on the many indications of ongoing improprieties, if not crimes? Gandossy concludes:

> Three factors were prominent in the O.P.M. debacle. First, people trusted Goodman and Weissman, and they believed that illicit activity would have been discovered by one of the many associates and employees of the firm. But many of these people worked in virtual isolation from each other, rarely communicating or sharing information and knowledge about O.P.M.'s affairs. Second, Goodman and Weissman created an image of respectability and upright citizenship for themselves and for their company, which affected what people saw. In a sense, the image they created served as a weapon that disarmed the company's victims. Third, a number of individuals who worked for and with O.P.M. were loyal to and dependent on the leasing company, which influenced their perceptions and their ability to control Goodman and Weissman.... [C]ertain social norms made it difficult to disclose information about the wrongdoing. From a very early age in our society, we are discouraged from "squealing" or "tattling" or "butting into other people's business." It is especially difficult to blow the whistle on those we are loyal and indebted to.

> [T]he O.P.M. trustee, James P. Hassett, claimed that the O.P.M. fraud was possible because of "other people's mistakes." A "variety of simple measures" by those associated with O.P.M. "could have or should have detected fraud or prevented its continuation," [Hassett's] report concluded. "Instead, in an 'after you, Alphonse' routine, all stood by in the mistaken belief that others were checking to verify that things were really as they seemed or proceeded on the unfounded assumption that others who knew about the fraud would act to stop it."

. . .

> Companies that come together for a particular project, transaction, or series of transactions, as we have seen in the O.P.M. case, generally have specific—often narrow—concerns. Within each organization, the aspects of the deal that occupy an individual's time are further differentiated. This narrow focus can make it difficult for anyone to discover illicit activity by making it possible for evidence to slip ... through the cracks.... And, because there are multiple actors, each is quick to assume that others are responsible

for certain aspects of the deal; when trouble appears, it is relatively easy to shift responsibility for acting to someone else.[58]

Aspects of the Client Fraud Problem [59]

The client fraud problem arises when a lawyer undertakes representation in a transaction that she assumes is legitimate but then, having done substantial professional work to carry out the transaction, discovers that the transaction involves fraud against a party to the transaction or some third person. Because the lawyer did not know of the fraudulent element initially, the lawyer is not personally culpable unless or until she proceeds to implement a transaction known by her to be fraudulent.[60] The representation ceases to be innocent, however, once the lawyer, with the required mental state of knowledge of the client's fraud, provides substantial assistance to the fraud, such as by preparing documents or participating in a closing. If the lawyer immediately terminates representation, she should not be charged or held guilty as an accessory, although a risk always exists that a trier of fact, looking at the transaction at some future time, will not accept the lawyer's version of the facts.

When does a lawyer "know" that her client has a fraudulent aim or purpose? Some trial lawyers profess that they cannot "know" anything, that facts exist only when a jury has found them in a verdict. This incapacity to know is a form of epistemological skepticism useful and legitimate for trial advocates, particularly those who represent criminal defendants. A lawyer's representation of a criminal defendant involves less cognitive dissonance if the lawyer does not "know" the accused is guilty. The same cognitive incapacity can help sustain the civil advocate.

The special encapsulation of knowledge that is permitted when the lawyer is acting as an advocate in litigation, however, is not ordinarily permitted when a lawyer is engaged in a non-litigation function such as representation of a client in connection with a business transaction. Thus an office lawyer may not pretend lack of knowledge when circumstances have given warning of fraud.[61] An office lawyer (or a trial advocate engaged in a counseling function such as a negotiated settlement) must gauge the significance of a fact, or set of facts, in light of what an alert lawyer familiar with the type of transaction involved

---

58. Robert P. Gandossy, Bad Business: The OPM Scandal and the Seduction of the Establishment 5–8, 206–08, 227–28 (1985).

59. This note draws, with permission, on material in Geoffrey C. Hazard, Jr., Rectification of Client Fraud: Death and Revival of a Professional Norm, 33 Emory L. J. 271 (1984).

60. A lawyer who gives substantial assistance to a fraudulent scheme is a joint tortfeasor in the client's fraud, may be guilty as an accessory to the crime of fraud, and is subject to professional discipline for rendering prohibited assistance. Ignorance based on reckless disregard of facts that should have been apparent to a reasonable lawyer may suffice to impute to the lawyer "knowledge" of fraud when she implemented the transaction. Chapter 2 above considers such issues.

61. *Benjamin* and other cases, see p. 66 above, say that a lawyer cannot "close his eyes" to facts that are readily apparent.

would know upon looking with a professional eye at the totality of circumstances there to be seen.[62]

Lawyers are unlikely to be trigger-happy in disclosing apparent client fraud because of the grave consequences involved: acrimony and possibly litigation with the client, damage to the lawyer's reputation for trustworthiness, risk of discipline for betraying a client's confidences and peer disapproval. If professional rules add further legal deterrents, the lawyer's discretion to act to prevent or rectify fraud may be reduced to the vanishing point.

At the very least, before acting, a lawyer should have a reasonable basis for concluding that fraud is involved. If the lawyer decides to act, the lawyer should proceed so as to damage the client as little as reasonably possible. Prevention is therefore better than after-the-fact rectification, since the intended fraud may simply be an ugly secret between client and lawyer. Interception after the fraud is under way, on the other hand, is likely to result in the client suffering sanctions on the basis of the lawyer's evidence. There is an unavoidable tension, however, between the proposition that the lawyer should act early, to prevent the fraud, and the requirement that the lawyer should act only on the basis of solid information.

Upon discovering clear client fraud, a lawyer has the difficult, delicate task of warning the client about the lawyer's responsibilities if the fraudulent course is pursued. Silent withdrawal is the only alternative to warning the client that, if the client goes forward, the lawyer will have to withdraw and, in addition, may wind up being an adverse witness against the client. And silent withdrawal may be inadequate in some cases to deflect the client from his purpose. When third parties have already acted in reliance, the lawyer has no good alternatives. The excruciating difficulty of the midpoint discovery situations is that anything the lawyer does at that stage will hurt the client. At some point in every transaction, a "silent" withdrawal is no longer possible, if the lawyer is to avoid liability.

Even if participation in fraud is morally intelligible in some circumstances,[63] the law cannot license some of its subjects, least of all lawyers, to assist in the commission or concealment of serious legal wrongs, such as fraud. With that possibility foreclosed, the choice becomes one of what interests are worth protecting. The self-defense exception, itself necessary and justifiable, protects the reputational and economic interests of lawyers by sacrificing confidentiality. The open questions are whether protection of third-party victims should have equivalent priority and, if so, the scope of the exception to confidentiality that should be incorporated into the lawyer codes.

62. See, e.g., *National Student Marketing*, supra p. 99.

63. James Gould Cozzens, By Love Possessed (1957), creates a fictional situation in which a lawyer's concealment of an ongoing fraud by another lawyer becomes morally intelligible.

Ethics rules abrogating client confidentiality in the interest of protecting third persons must address, first, whether lawyer disclosure should be limited to situations in which the lawyer's services in some way facilitated fraud on a third person. Contrast the situation in which representation involves a fraudulent transaction with the situation in which a lawyer, perhaps in defending tax deductions a client has taken, discovers that the client is receiving income from fraud practiced on a third party, such as embezzlement from an employer. The former situation, unlike the latter, may lead to charges against the lawyer. Moreover, the lawyer's more direct involvement in the client's wrongdoing heightens moral responsibility.

A second issue is whether a lawyer's authority to take action should cover prevention or rectification or both. The distinction between past and future crimes drawn by DR 4–101(C)(3) is difficult to apply in fraud cases. Even if the fraudulent transaction has been consummated, the fraud may be considered ongoing if the consequences are still unfolding. In a realistic sense the fraud continues until it is rectified.

Yet a third issue is whether authority to take action should be discretionary or mandatory. The Scope section of the Model Rules states that "[v]iolation of a Rule should not give rise to a cause of action nor should it create any presumption that a legal duty has been breached." The Model Code contained a similar statement.[64] Those statements, however, are given only limited effect: A number of courts have held that the standards in lawyer codes are relevant and admissible to evaluate lawyer behavior in tort actions and other legal contexts where a lawyer's conduct is in issue.[65] Given that the courts take this approach when the ethics rules take only a discretionary approach, many bar groups favor continuing a discretionary rule or having no rule at all out of fear that a mandatory rule will increase the lawyer's exposure to civil suit. For example, in those cases in which a lawyer made timely withdrawal so as to avoid any act that might substantially assist the fraud, a mandatory disclosure rule might impose civil liability for failing to disclose. A rule that allows or requires disclosure only when a lawyer reasonably believes that silent withdrawal would leave her exposed to liability as a participant minimizes this civil liability risk.[66]

64. See the Preliminary Statement to the Model Code.

65. See, e.g., Woodruff v. Tomlin, 616 F.2d 924, 936 (6th Cir.1980) (Model Code's rules are evidence of standard in legal malpractice case involving impermissible conflict of interest); Lipton v. Boesky, 110 Mich.App. 589, 313 N.W.2d 163 (1981) (evidence of Code violation creates rebuttable presumption of malpractice); and United States v. DeLucca, 630 F.2d 294, 301 (5th Cir.1980) (appropriate to consider Code provisions in determining lawyer's criminal liability for participation in conspiracy with client). But cf. Sanders v. Townsend, 582 N.E.2d 355 (Ind.1991) (lawyer's violation of ethics rule in coercing a client to settle did not state a claim for civil liability for constructive fraud but was a matter for the disciplinary commission).

66. See Rotunda, supra, 63 Ore.L.Rev. 455, 482 (1984).

The client fraud provisions of the various states, summarized in the chart below, reflect virtually every alternative suggested by the above variables.

State Ethics Rules on Client Fraud

The following chart summarizes the provisions of state legal ethics codes regarding a lawyer's privilege or obligation to disclose confidential client information to prevent or rectify a client crime or fraud other than fraud on a tribunal (perjury).[67] The issues addressed are whether a lawyer "may" or "must" or "must not" reveal confidential client information for the stated purpose. Remember that ethics codes are merely one source of the relevant law governing disclosure of client confidences. Tort law and criminal law in every jurisdiction may require a lawyer to take steps to avoid assisting unlawful conduct and federal law may sometimes be a source of obligations that preempt state law.

	Prevent a Client's Criminal Fraud	Prevent a Client's Non–Criminal Fraud	Rectify a Client's Crime or Fraud in Which Lawyer's Services Were Used
ABA Model Rules	Must Not	Must Not	Must Not
ABA Model Code	May	Must Not	Must Not
Alabama	Must Not	Must Not	Must Not
Alaska	May	Must Not	May
Arizona	May	Must Not	Must Not
Arkansas	May	Must Not	Must Not
California	Must Not	Must Not	Must Not
Colorado	May	Must Not	Must Not
Connecticut	May	Must Not	May
Delaware	Must Not	Must Not	Must Not
District of Columbia	Must Not	Must Not	Must Not
Florida	Must	Must Not	Must Not
Georgia	May	Must Not	Must
Hawaii	May	Must Not	Must
Idaho	May	Must Not	Must Not
Illinois	May	Must Not	Must Not
Indiana	May	Must Not	Must Not
Iowa	May	Must Not	Must Not
Kansas	May	Must Not	Must Not
Kentucky	Must Not	Must Not	Must Not
Louisiana	Must Not	Must Not	Must Not
Maine	May	Must Not	Must Not
Maryland	May	May	May
Massachusetts	May	Must Not	Must Not
Michigan	May	Must Not	May

67. The chart was prepared in September 1993 by lawyers of the Attorneys' Liability Assurance Society, Inc., a major legal malpractice insurer, and is reprinted with permission. For a more comprehensive state-by-state analysis of ethics rules and client confidences, see T. Morgan and R. Rotunda, 1993 Selected Standards on Professional Responsibility 126 et seq.

	Prevent a Client's Criminal Fraud	Prevent a Client's Non–Criminal Fraud	Rectify a Client's Crime or Fraud in Which Lawyer's Services Were Used
Minnesota	May	Must Not	May
Mississippi	May	Must Not	Must Not
Missouri	Must Not	Must Not	Must Not
Montana	Must Not	Must Not	Must Not
Nebraska	May	Must Not	Must Not
Nevada	May	May	May
New Hampshire	May	Must Not	Must Not
New Jersey	Must	Must	May
New Mexico	May	Must Not	Must Not
New York	May	Must Not	Must Not
North Carolina	May	Must Not	Must Not
North Dakota	May	May	May
Ohio	May	Must Not	Must
Oklahoma	May	Must Not	Must Not
Oregon	May	Must Not	Must Not
Pennsylvania	May	May	May
Rhode Island	Must Not	Must Not	Must Not
South Carolina	May	Must Not	Must Not
South Dakota	Must Not	Must Not	May
Tennessee	May	Must Not	Must Not
Texas	May	May	May
Utah	May	May	May
Vermont	May	Must Not	Must Not
Virginia	Must	Must Not	May
Washington	May	Must Not	Must Not
West Virginia	May	Must Not	Must Not
Wisconsin	Must	Must	May
Wyoming	May	Must Not	Must Not

Overall Summary

- Prevention of criminal fraud: 37 states permit, and 4 (Florida, New Jersey, Virginia and Wisconsin) require, the lawyer to disclose.

- Prevention of non-criminal fraud: 7 states permit, and 2 (New Jersey and Wisconsin) require, the lawyer to disclose.

- Rectification of crime or fraud: 14 states permit, and 3 (Georgia, Hawaii and Ohio) require, the lawyer to disclose.

3. Making False Statements to Others: M.R. 4.1

Model Rule 4.1, Truthfulness in Statements to Others, provides:

In the course of representing a client a lawyer shall not knowingly:

(a) make a false statement of material fact or law to a third person; or

(b) fail to disclose a material fact to a third person when disclosure is necessary to avoid assisting a criminal or fraudulent act by a client, unless disclosure is prohibited by Rule 1.6.

Read the definition of "knowingly" in the Terminology section of the Model Rules. Should M.R. 4.1 say "knowingly or recklessly"?

The proviso to M.R. 4.1(b), by permitting disclosure only when not prohibited by M.R. 1.6, invites lawyers to keep silent about a client's material omissions even when disclosure "is necessary to avoid assisting a criminal or fraudulent act by the client." Lawyers who read M.R. 4.1(b) this way must believe either that the ethics rules require them to risk imprisonment and civil penalties when the only alternative is to "turn in" their fraud-doing clients or that the Rules provide some sort of defense to conduct that would otherwise be criminal or civil fraud.

One possible reconciliation of M.R. 4.1(b) and the law of fraud relies on an expansive reading of the self-defense exception of M.R. 1.6(b)(2) to permit disclosure of client fraud when non-disclosure would expose a lawyer to potential civil or criminal liability. Since disclosure then would be permitted under M.R. 1.6, it would be required under M.R. 4.1(b) if "necessary to avoid assisting a criminal or fraudulent act by a client." Another possible reconciliation rests on an assumption that lawyers will understand that civil and criminal law dealing with fraud "trumps" the ethics rule, which deals only with professional discipline. Perhaps the ABA decided against discipline for lawyers who tacitly assist fraud by omitting material facts, returning the problem to the civil and criminal law. But there is no hint of these subtleties in the text of or Comment to M.R. 4.1. Will lawyers who resort to the Rule for guidance understand these subtleties?

D. CONFIDENTIALITY WHEN BODILY HARM OR DEATH MAY RESULT

Introductory Note

The ultimate test of one's commitment to principle comes in those situations when life is threatened. Are we willing to go to war to protect a principle? Are we willing to kill or be killed? To sacrifice others? Should the press be enjoined from printing troop movements if publication would threaten soldiers' lives? In the area of client confidentiality, decisions where life hangs in the balance are extremely rare—in contrast to the frequency in which substantial economic harm is threatened by client fraud. Nevertheless, examining confidentiality in those extreme situations in which life is threatened illuminates the principle at stake, our commitment to it and our compassion for the suffering of others.

Professor Robert Cover's study of the response of judges, particularly antislavery judges, to cases involving enforcement of the slave laws supplies a helpful perspective on the dramatic situations in this section.[68] In discussing the few cases that directly raised the question of the right of slaves to revolt, Cover says:

68. Robert M. Cover, Justice Accused 108 (1975).

Moralists have often sought to strip ethical issues of the complicating layers of fact and competing interests that seem to always characterize choice in society. Indeed the common association of natural right with a preexisting state of nature is itself an example of such an attempt. The tendency remains strong today as it was thousands of years ago. We have the relatively recent attempt of Professor Fuller to plumb the depths of the scope of responsibility for the taking of human life, the famous case of the speluncean explorers,[69] which itself is but an elaboration of the hypothetical of Rabbi Akiva, now two millennia old, of two men lost in the desert with enough water for one.[70] What is of interest to us is not only that philosophers should create such hypotheticals, but that where life imitated art, where events have occurred that seem in part to mirror the choices presented by these hypotheticals, jurists have seized on the cases as presenting fundamental problems about the nature of law. Thus, cases like United States v. Holmes and Regina v. Dudley and Stephens have received extended attention from jurists. [Regina v. Dudley and Stephens, 14 Q.B.D. 273 (1884) involved the killing of a boy by shipwrecked sailors in the good-faith belief that without cannibalism all would die. The boy was not consulted. In United States v. Holmes, 26 F.Cas. 360 (No. 15, 383) (C.C.D.Pa.1842), a mate directed seamen to throw passengers overboard from a lifeboat after a shipwreck. The mate reasonably believed that if all had stayed aboard, the lifeboat would have gone down.]

The same inclination to seize on dramatic and rare instances of stark moral choice and to analyze them stripped of context can be discerned in the field of legal ethics. Law teachers often illustrate the conflict between confidentiality and protection of life with the example of a client who confesses to her lawyer that she has committed a crime for which another is scheduled to be executed on the morrow. Professor Andrew Kaufman provides a real occurrence of the "execution" problem from the infamous Leo Frank case: "After the conviction of Frank had been affirmed, a client told [Judge Arthur] Powell, then a practicing attorney, that he, not Frank, had committed the murder. Powell reports that his decision not to reveal the confidential communication was eased by the commutation of Frank's sentence to life imprisonment. Shortly thereafter, Frank was lynched by a mob."[71]

The danger of such extreme examples is that, by focusing our attention on the rare and exceptional, they may train us to see moral choice only when it is presented in stark terms, allowing us to ignore

69. L. Fuller, The Case of the Speluncean Explorers, 62 Harv.L.Rev. 616 (1949).

70. Babylonian Talmud, Tractate Baba Mezia, 62a.

71. See, e.g., Andrew L. Kaufman, Problems in Professional Responsibility 212–14, 216–218 (2d ed.1984), citing Arthur Powell, I Can Go Home Again 287–292 (1943) and Powell, Privilege of Counsel and Confidential Communications, 6 Ga.Bar J. 333 (1944). Kaufman also points out that such examples are rare in practice and "are designed to test the limits of our belief in the principle of confidentiality." See Frank v. Mangum, 237 U.S. 309 (1915).

the important lesson that in searching for an "ethical" or "moral" course of action in more mundane situations the choices are apparent only after a deeper examination of context. See the Gilligan excerpt reprinted in Chapter 1 at p. 31. The hard ethical questions in life arise not only in those rare instances that mirror the moralist's stark hypotheticals, but also in the vaguer, infinitely more complex arena of ordinary life.

1. Professional Rules

As explained above, both the Canons of Professional Ethics and the Model Code of Professional Responsibility permitted disclosure of any crime, no matter how trivial, that a client intends to commit. See Canon 37 and DR 4–101(C)(3). The Model Rules restrict this permission. M.R. 1.6(b)(1) provides: "A lawyer *may* reveal [confidential] information to the extent the lawyer *reasonably believes* necessary: (1) to prevent the client from committing a *criminal* act that the lawyer *believes* is likely to result in *imminent death or serious bodily injury.*" (Emphasis added.)

M.R. 1.6(b)(1) makes disclosure permissive rather than mandatory and judges scope of disclosure by an objective standard of reasonable belief. But a lawyer's honest, even if unreasonable, belief that imminent death or serious bodily injury will result protects a lawyer who has reasonably concluded that disclosure is necessary to prevent a client's life-threatening criminal act. The ABA House of Delegates added the word "imminent" to the Rule during discussion on the floor. Why? Does "imminent" also modify "bodily injury"? And why the word "serious"? Should not any bodily injury suffice to trigger permissive disclosure?

Consider the effect of the restrictions in M.R. 1.6(b)(1) on the execution hypothetical described above. If client perjury had secured the conviction of an innocent person who was about to be executed, the lawyer might view the unrectified fraud as ongoing, future criminal conduct. If so, disclosure would be permitted. But what if the client had not participated in fraud to secure the conviction?

Recall Spaulding v. Zimmerman, printed in Chapter 1 at p. 5. Would Model Rule 1.6 have permitted disclosure to David Spaulding that he had an aneurysm? Compare proposed ALCC Rule 1.6: "A lawyer may reveal a client's confidence when and to the extent that the lawyer reasonably believes that divulgence is necessary to prevent imminent danger to human life. The lawyer shall use all reasonable means to protect the client's interests that are consistent with preventing loss of life." The ATLA commission, which put forth the ALCC, did not approve the proposed rule. The ALCC as adopted included no exception to the duty of confidentiality for disclosure either of client fraud on third parties or of the threat of death or bodily harm.

Suppose a client had engaged in fraud to secure the conviction of an innocent person for a crime committed by the client, the punishment for which was a two-year prison term. Could the lawyer disclose under M.R. 1.6? Does imprisonment amount to serious bodily harm? Does M.R. 3.3 help? Earlier drafts of the Model Rules imposed a mandatory duty to disclose information necessary "to prevent the client from committing an act that would seriously endanger the life or safety of a person, result in wrongful detention or incarceration of a person...." [72] Putting aside for the moment the change from mandatory to permissive disclosure, what is to be made of the elimination of: (1) any explicit mention of wrongful imprisonment as a ground for disclosure and (2) the right to disclose noncriminal acts of a client that would result in death or wrongful imprisonment? Do you think the bar's position reflects the fact that most lawyers would not disclose to prevent wrongful imprisonment or execution? [73]

2. Limits of Confidentiality

PEOPLE v. FENTRESS

Dutchess County Court, 1980.
103 Misc.2d 179, 425 N.Y.S.2d 485.

ALBERT M. ROSENBLATT, JUDGE.

. . .

The defendant stands indicted for intentional murder [Penal Law 125.25[1]]. While the facts adduced before the grand jury are sufficient to establish the crime, the defendant avers that the indictment must be dismissed because it is the product of tainted and inadmissible evidence, presented in violation of the attorney-client privilege, as codified in CPLR 4503....

[New York CPLR 4503 provides that "evidence of a confidential communication made between the attorney or his employee and the client in the course of professional employment ... and *evidence resulting therefrom*, shall not be disclosed (by any governmental agency in any proceeding)." (Emphasis added.) A preliminary hearing was held to determine whether the statute had been violated; the prosecution agreed that testimony concerning possible confidences at this preliminary hearing would not be viewed as a waiver of privilege in any subsequent trial.]

. . .

Albert Fentress was a schoolteacher in the City of Poughkeepsie School System.

---

72. Unofficial Drafts of Aug. 20, 1979 and Sept. 21, 1979, Rule 1.5(b)(1).

73. Consider also State v. Macumber, 112 Ariz. 569, 544 P.2d 1084 (1976): The defendant was on trial for several murders; two attorneys were prepared to testify that their client, since deceased, had confessed to them that he had committed those murders. Should the court permit the testimony over the objection of the prosecutor? In *Macumber* the court refused to hear the testimony.

Among his colleagues there for more than a decade was Enid Schwartz, a fellow teacher and personal friend, whom Fentress visited at her home once or twice yearly. Her friendship with Fentress was substantial, and was based on his having taught two of her children, as well as on the independent basis of their relationships as colleagues over the years.

One of these sons, Wallace, had been taught by Fentress in the ninth grade, and through the years had developed an independent personal friendship with him. After graduating, Wallace Schwartz and Fentress visited at each others' homes and had engaged in sports together.

After Wallace graduated from law school, and joined a civil firm in New York City, he gave Fentress his card and told him that he could call him at any time. On August 20, 1979, the Court finds the following to have occurred:

2:12 a.m. Fentress, from his home at 216 Grand Avenue in Pough-keepsie, called Wallace Schwartz at the latter's home in Hartsdale, Westchester County. The first thing that Fentress said was that he was about to kill himself. Fentress spoke in a low monotone, and was distraught, but coherent. He told Schwartz that he had just killed someone, that a terrible thing had happened, which he could not square with God, and that he was going to kill himself.

Incredulous, Wallace Schwartz said it must have been an accident, but was told it was not, and that there had been a sexual mutilation as well.

In continuing attempts to dissuade his valued friend from suicide, Wallace Schwartz told Fentress that suicide would not square anything with God, and that whatever had happened, Fentress could get help. Wallace Schwartz invited Fentress to his house, and offered to go to Fentress' house, but Fentress refused.

Wallace Schwartz then suggested various persons who might be able to call and stay with Fentress, all of whom were rejected. However, later in the conversation Fentress said he would like the local rabbi, Rabbi Zimet, to come to his house and asked Wallace Schwartz to call the rabbi for him, which Wallace Schwartz agreed to do immediately. Fentress said he would leave the door open, and wait for the rabbi. It was also agreed that the police be summoned....

Schwartz testified that it was his "legal" advice to Fentress that the police be called.

Fentress agreed, and stated that he would like to have both *Wallace Schwartz and the rabbi* present when the police arrived....

At this point, of course, Schwartz did not have firsthand knowledge of the facts, but, recognizing the urgent need for immediate action (he could not fully conclude that any victim was actually dead) and because he was some fifty miles away, he immediately attempted to arrange to contact the rabbi.[1]

2:40 a.m. Wallace Schwartz called his mother, Enid Schwartz, who lived in Poughkeepsie, to enlist her aid in calling the rabbi and arranging for him to go to Fentress' house.

Wallace Schwartz told Enid of the call he had just received, and of his extreme anxiety about Fentress having said that there had been a killing, or that he had killed someone, and that he was going to kill himself, and wanted Rabbi Zimet to come to see him. Enid, herself a close friend of Fentress, agreed to call the rabbi but said she was going to call Albert Fentress first to verify that there was a real problem there.

2:45 a.m. As soon as Enid hung up, she called and asked Fentress *what had happened.* He told her either that he had killed someone, or that there had been a killing.

Notably, she never told Fentress that Wallace Schwartz had revealed to her any of the substance of the conversation between Fentress and Wallace Schwartz.

When Enid telephoned Fentress she did not state or imply, nor could she have concluded, that Fentress had committed a crime. She knew, from Wallace, that Fentress may have killed *someone*, but she could not have concluded whether it was self-defense or the justifiable killing of an intruder, or willful murder. Her overriding concern was for the preservation of the life of her friend, Albert Fentress. When she began the conversation by asking Fentress what happened, Fentress stated that there had been a killing.

During the 2:45 a.m. conversation, Enid told Fentress that the police must be called, saying either "You must call the police" or "I am going to call the police." Fentress' response was that he would like Rabbi Zimet there waiting until the police came. She got the understanding that Albert Fentress acknowledged that it was proper for the police to come....

Notably, Fentress did not state that he wanted his attorney there, only the rabbi. This is important, in that Fentress recognized that the presence of an attorney in the case would not (or should not) stem the arrival of the police. The Court thus finds that Fentress agreed that the police be called, and further, that he did not attempt to place any condition, as to the presence of an attorney, on their being called. His wish for a rabbi, while understandable for purposes of spiritual comfort, has no legal implications whatever.

1. It should be noted, at this point, that Fentress was not and is not Jewish. While there was some peripheral discussion at the hearing about the possible clergyman-penitent relationship, the court finds it lacking. Rabbi Zimet, as it turned out, could not be reached, and through no one's fault never appeared at defendant's house or spoke to the defendant. The only connection between the defendant and the rabbi is that they both were at Wallace Schwartz' wedding where, one may speculate, they may have met.

2:50 a.m. After Enid spoke to Fentress, she immediately called Rabbi Zimet but there was no answer.

While Fentress had asked her to let him know if she reached the rabbi, she was fearful that if she informed him of her failure, he might carry out his suicide threat.

It was because she could not reach the rabbi that she decided to call the police, to protect Fentress from harming himself.

2:59 a.m. Enid Schwartz called her son Wallace, to tell him of her unsuccessful attempts to reach the rabbi, and her intention to call the police. The Court finds that the decision to call the police was made by Enid alone, although Wallace Schwartz concurred in it, principally because they both wished to prevent the defendant's suicide. Because of Wallace Schwartz' concern for Fentress' (legal) position, he cautioned his mother to be discreet in what she told the police, and to limit her remarks to the effect that there may have been a shooting at Fentress's house, and that there was fear that Fentress might commit suicide.

3:05 a.m. Enid called the police and told Officer Thomas Ghee that it was reported to her by her son, and then by Fentress, that there had been a shooting or killing at his home. She warned the police that because of Fentress' alleged suicidal intentions, it would be unwise to approach with sirens.

3:15 a.m. The police, dispatched by Sgt. Krauer, arrived at defendant's house. The lights were on and the door open. Fentress was seated next to an open window, and beckoned: "Officer, please come in and take the gun."

3:19 a.m. The defendant was given his *Miranda* warnings, according- *miRanda*
ing to Officer Perkins. The defendant declined to speak, stating that he was "waiting for his attorney," whom "he had already contacted," and whom he was expecting shortly. The police desisted questioning.

3:30 a.m. Fentress was driven to the police station, and told the police that his attorney was Wallace Schwartz. After arriving at the police station, Fentress, on three or four occasions, asked for "his attorney, Wallace Schwartz."

5:09 a.m. Wallace Schwartz arrived in Poughkeepsie, and advised the police that he was not a criminal lawyer and would not be able to properly represent the defendant. By that time Wallace Schwartz had decided to recommend Peter L. Maroulis to the defendant.

Peter L. Maroulis telephoned the police, and instructed them not to question the defendant. They had not; they did not.

. . .

The primary issues to be decided are, therefore, whether the requisites for confidentiality were established, and if so, whether they were waived by Fentress.

Wigmore, as usual, is an apt starting place, and provides the most orderly formulation of the rule. [The court quoted Wigmore's statement of the attorney-client privilege, reprinted above at p. 222.]

If Wallace Schwartz was not being consulted in a professional capacity for legal advice, the inquiry is at an end.... The district attorney argues that Wallace Schwartz was predominantly a friend, who never handled a criminal case, and was neither retained nor gave any appreciable amount of legal advice to the defendant. To be sure, he "withdrew" in favor of Mr. Maroulis at the earliest time, and made no secret of his discomfort in the unfamiliar surroundings of the criminal law.

It is well settled, however, that the professional relationship may exist in a financial vacuum, and that the absence of a fee or retainer does not alone destroy it (People v. Arroyave, 49 N.Y.2d 264, 425 N.Y.S.2d 282, 401 N.E.2d 393, January 10, 1980; Bacon v. Frisbie, 80 N.Y. 394; Gage v. Gage, 13 App.Div. 565, 43 N.Y.S. 810).

Under any view, the defendant and Wallace Schwartz were friends. And while there would be no privilege if Wallace Schwartz was acting solely as a friend, abjuring professional involvement (Kitz v. Buckmaster, 45 App.Div. 283, 61 N.Y.S. 64, mot. for lv. to app. den. 47 App.Div. 633, 62 N.Y.S. 1140), it may be inferred that the defendant communicated with Wallace Schwartz because he was not only a friend but an attorney, from whom he was seeking support, advice, and guidance. That Wallace Schwartz was in effect called upon to serve as psychologist, therapist, counselor, and friend, does not derogate from his role as lawyer (Privileged Communications, 71 Yale L.J. 1226 at 1252).

Fentress told the police on several occasions that he had an attorney, Wallace Schwartz, and was eagerly awaiting his arrival. It is indicative of his own subjective and articulated belief that he contacted his friend, Wallace Schwartz, *qua attorney* (Nichols v. Village Voice, Inc., 99 Misc.2d 822, 417 N.Y.S.2d 415), but did not, and could not, have concluded that their conversation was to be kept confidential in all respects.

Fentress urges, as he must to fit within Section 4503, that his call was for "legal advice." Ironically, the only "legal advice" which he can identify—and the Court adopts it as such—is the advice that the police must be called, the very advice which Fentress is now trying to disown. He cannot have it both ways.

Wallace Schwartz's advice was not the least bit unprofessional. Even the most seasoned criminal lawyers often "legally advise" their clients to turn themselves in for reasons which are strategic, if not moral. An experienced criminal practitioner might, of course, refrain from making that suggestion and still be on arguably stable grounds (both legally and ethically, despite the existence of an undetected body),[3] but he would have to weigh the risk of its ultimate discovery, and the disdain of a jury for any defense interposed by someone who had the cunning to suppress the corpus delicti. Duplicity is not tactically sound "legal advice." What other "legal advice" could Wallace Schwartz have given?

Had Schwartz affirmatively advised Fentress to conceal or dispose of the body, he would have been counselling the commission of a crime (Penal Law 215.40(2), impeding the discovery of evidence; People v. DeFelice, 282 App.Div. 514, 125 N.Y.S.2d 80) which involves professional actions beyond those found endurable in *Belge*. They are violative of Code of Professional Responsibility DR 1–102A(4)(5), and may thus demolish the attorney-client privilege itself.[4] According to the Code of Professional Responsibility EC 7–5, "A lawyer should never encourage or aid his client to commit criminal acts or counsel his client on how to violate the law and avoid punishment therefor."

Not every communication made to a lawyer in his professional capacity is confidential or intended to be so. As a general rule the question of privileged confidentiality depends on the circumstances.... Fentress' intentions and his reasonable expectations of confidentiality or disclosure, as expressed and inferred from his conversations are of critical importance. (See 24 Ohio State L.J., supra, at 26) Fentress, when he spoke to Wallace Schwartz at 2:12 a.m., imparted the killing, and his suicidal intentions. Wallace Schwartz told him, and he agreed, that the police would have to be called. According to testimony of Wallace Schwartz:

> "Al (Fentress) indicated that he would leave the door open for the rabbi, that the rabbi can come over, and that he would wait for the rabbi, and that at that time I, meaning me, could call the police.... *I wanted to make sure that Al understood what I intended to do.*"

> "Towards the end of the conversation the police were (again) mentioned in relation to his waiting for me with the rabbi. I believe at that time it was Al that mentioned that I could call the police at that time."

The conclusion is inescapable, and the Court has found as a fact, that Fentress did not intend to keep the corpus of the crime from the police. His renunciation of confidentiality (as to the fact of the homicide) appeared again when Enid suggested that the police be called, and

---

3. People v. Belge, 83 Misc.2d 186, 372 N.Y.S.2d 798, aff'd 50 A.D.2d 1088, 376 N.Y.S.2d 771, aff'd 41 N.Y.2d 60, 390 N.Y.S.2d 867, 359 N.E.2d 377; N.Y.State Bar Op. 479 (1978). [Editors' note: See the discussion of *Belge* (*Dead Bodies Case*) in Chapter 1 at p. 53.]

4. The privilege may not be asserted when the communication relates to the commission of a future crime, or to advise the client to suppress or destroy evidence ... or to conceal wrong doing.... The same result would follow, of course, if the attorney were to aid in impeding discovery of evidence.... Lastly, there is the actual entrustment of evidence to the lawyer. See, The Right of a Criminal Defense Attorney to Withhold Physical Evidence Received From His Client, 38 U.Chi.L.Rev. 211, 213.

Fentress again specifically disavowed any expectation of keeping the fact of the homicide from the police. Enid's testimony confirms it, and the Court has adopted as a fact, the defendant's expectations of non-confidentiality regarding the corpus:

Q: He expected the police to come?

A: I don't know what he expected. That's what he *said to me* ....

When Fentress concurred in the decision to call the police, he waived confidentiality of the *corpus*. Both to Wallace Schwartz and Enid Schwartz, he knew that disclosure to the police was inevitable both from his viewpoint and from the advice he received from his attorney, and later, from his friend, Enid Schwartz. His express eschewal of confidentiality is controlling (Rosseau v. Bleau, 131 N.Y. 177, 183, 30 N.E. 52, 53). "If the communication is made to an attorney with the knowledge and intent that it be disclosed to a third person it is fairly clear that it was not meant to be kept confidential and it is therefore not privileged." ...

After the 2:12 a.m. conversation between Fentress and Wallace Schwartz, and the 2:40 a.m. conversation between Wallace Schwartz and Enid, Fentress received a telephone call from Enid at 2:45 a.m. She did not tell Fentress that Wallace Schwartz had related to her any admissions that Fentress made to Wallace Schwartz. She began immediately by asking Fentress what happened, and he then told her that there had been a killing. They both then agreed that the police would have to be summoned ... with Fentress stating that he wanted her to call Rabbi Zimet.

At this point, for reasons which are expanded upon below, the Court finds that the conversation between Fentress and Enid, in which he divulged the killing, was a communication made independently freely by Fentress to Enid, a friend and teaching colleague whom he had known for ten years. He did not make the disclosure on the belief or expectation that Enid was an extension of Wallace Schwartz, qua attorney, or under the impression that she was Wallace Schwartz' agent for *purposes of any attorney-client* confidentiality.

The Court has found as a fact that Fentress's disclosure to her was not prompted on *constraint* of any previous disclosure that he made to Wallace Schwartz, but was independent of it, causally disconnected, and in response to a question by a friend who did not intimate to him that she was privy to any actual facts regarding his actions (United States v. Bayer, 331 U.S. 532, 540; People v. Tanner, 30 N.Y.2d 102, 106, 331 N.Y.S.2d 1, 4, 282 N.E.2d 98, 99; People v. Jennings, 33 N.Y.2d 880, 352 N.Y.S.2d 444, 307 N.E.2d 561). The little that Enid knew—of a highly ambiguous nature—she did not disclose to Fentress and he could not have reasonably believed that she was privy to any *incriminating* facts merely from her inquiry, apprehensive though it was, as to "what happened." When Fentress replied, and told her that he killed someone, no confidentiality existed or was intended by him, and any previous attorney-client privilege which may have been created by the (2:12

Waiver

a.m.) call between Fentress and Wallace Schwartz had been broken and attenuated. Thus, the evidence before the grand jury was not the "result" of any breach of attorney-client confidentiality within the meaning of CPLR 4503 even if, arguendo, complete confidentiality between Fentress and Wallace Schwartz was intended. This conclusion is confirmed by Fentress's repeated recognition and statements to Enid that the police were to be summoned. Hence, Enid was under no legal or ethical duty to refrain from calling the police. She had not only the defendant's express approval to do so, but her own unilateral and unfettered choice in the matter, just as any person is free to call the police when a friend has confided that he has killed someone and is about to kill himself.

. . .

The advice later given by Wallace Schwartz to his mother, Enid, at 2:59 a.m., that she should be discreet in what she tells the police because there "may" be an attorney-client privilege, did not and does not alter the relationship between Fentress and Enid. To the extent that there was an attorney-client relationship between Fentress and Wallace Schwartz, Enid was no part of it, nor was she in any manner acting as her son's agent, qua attorney. After her conversation with Fentress at 2:40 a.m., she was entirely free to call the police on her own for the reasons given. It is hard to conceive of anyone doing otherwise.

The defendant recognizes that the *presence* of an unnecessary third party will destroy confidentiality.... The waiver doctrine, however, is applied not only when a third non-indispensable person is present, but when such a person is let in on the secret before (Workman v. Boylan Buick, Inc., 36 A.D.2d 978, 321 N.Y.S.2d 983), during or after the attorney-client consultation. Thus, when the client, *after consultation*, reveals the contents of the consultation to someone else a waiver is effectuated (People v. Hitchman, 70 A.D.2d 695, 416 N.Y.S.2d 374). This is not new, and represents the unswerving application of the waiver doctrine on the basis of voluntary disclosures made by clients to third persons after the initial consultation....

Enid was not a person whose participation was necessary for furtherance of the professional relationship. Had she been present during the 2:12 a.m. conversation, her role as a friend could not be transmuted into that of an attorney's agent [7] or be perceived as essential to or in furtherance of the attorney-client conference (Baumann v. Steingester, 213 N.Y. 328, 332, 107 N.E. 578, 579).

. . .

The defendant's announced suicidal intentions pervade the case. Wallace Schwartz was burdened with a trilemma. He had just been told of a frightful homicide and an undiscovered victim. Secondly, Fentress said he was about to take a second life, his own. Given the

---

7. Naturally, the mere fact that Enid and Wallace Schwartz were related does not itself create agency ..., and the Court finds no other evidence to justify any finding of agency.

desperation of the call, it would not have been possible for Wallace Schwartz, or anyone else, to determine whether the victim was still alive or beyond all hope. Fentress had mentioned drinking and a sexual mutilation as well. Schwartz could not possibly travel quickly enough to save anyone's life, but he knew that lives were in serious jeopardy at the very least. The implication of Fentress' motion is that Wallace Schwartz somehow broke a confidence by telephoning his parents, who lived moments away from Fentress, who was their friend as well, for the express purpose of complying with Fentress' request that Rabbi Zimet be summoned to the scene, and to avert a suicide.

The ethical oath of secrecy must be measured by common sense....

To exalt the oath of silence, in the face of imminent death, would, under these circumstances, be not only morally reprehensible, but ethically unsound. As Professor Monroe Freedman reminds us, "At one extreme, it seems clear that the lawyer should reveal information necessary to save a life." (10 Crim.L.Bull., No. 10, p. 987). If the ethical duty exists primarily to protect the client's interests, what interest can there be superior to the client's life itself?

The issue was addressed in N.Y.State Bar op. 486 (1978) (New York State Bar Journal, August 1978). Posing the question "May a lawyer disclose his client's expressed intention to commit suicide?" the New York State Bar Association, in interpreting EC 4–2 and DR 4–101(C)(3) answered in the affirmative, despite the repeal of suicide as a crime (See, L.1919, ch. 414; Former Penal Law Sec. 2301; Meacham v. NYSMBA, 120 N.Y. 237, 242, 24 N.E. 283, 284).

Thus, even if the defendant flatly forbade Wallace Schwartz from calling the police, the ethical duty of silence would be of dubious operability. We need not decide the legal consequences of such an interdiction, having rejected the defendant's contention that he did not acquiesce in the call to the police, and having found waiver by repetition to Enid Schwartz.

. . .

Disclosures to Save Life

Does the New York statute cover only material protected by the attorney-client privilege or does it also cover material protected by the duty of client confidentiality? Is *Fentress* an attorney-client privilege case or one involving the professional duty of confidentiality?

When does talking to a friend, who happens to be a lawyer, become a privileged communication? Do you agree with the court's characterization of Wallace Schwartz's advice as legal advice?

The court says that Fentress waived confidentiality as to the homicide. Do you agree? Why did the court find that Enid Schwartz was not acting as the lawyer's agent? Is the court's reasoning persuasive?

Was the discussion of suicide necessary to this opinion? The court asks, "what interest can there be superior to the client's life itself?" and relies on the N.Y. State Bar Association opinion approving disclosure to prevent a client's suicide. Does this reliance suggest that, had Fentress not threatened suicide, the court might not have upheld the lawyer's disclosure? Would this court have approved disclosure in Spaulding v. Zimmerman, printed above at p. 5?

Would the Model Rules permit disclosure in a case like *Fentress*? A 1983 ABA ethics opinion decided that under both the Model Code and the Model Rules a lawyer could disclose his client's intent to commit suicide in a jurisdiction where suicide was no longer a crime.[74] The ethics committee cited with approval several state ethics opinions [75] and relied on EC 7–12 and Model Rule 1.14, which provide that a lawyer has special responsibilities when a client suffers from a disability. Does this imply that suicidal thoughts qualify as a disability?

A New Jersey ethics opinion [76] concluded "that where an attorney for a parent has facts that demonstrate a propensity of that parent to engage in child abuse and hence the continuing unfitness of that parent to raise its [sic] child, ... the information *must* be provided to the [state] Children's Bureau." (Emphasis added.) The ethics committee emphasized that the state's interest in child welfare makes this crime *sui generis*, thus justifying the obligation to report a "propensity" to commit it. Is this opinion wise? Recall that the prosecutor in the *Dead Bodies Case*, discussed above at p. 53, invoked a New York public health statute requiring the reporting of information concerning certain deaths.

Would the lawyers in the *Dead Bodies Case* have been subject to professional discipline if they had revealed the location of the bodies without their client's consent? Would the ethics rules have permitted the lawyers to phone in an anonymous tip providing the authorities with the location of the bodies?

Why are the moral intuitions of many lay people so much at odds with those of lawyers in situations like that involved in the *Dead Bodies Case?* The anguish of parents who do not know whether a child is alive or dead is easy to understand. Moreover, the decent treatment of the dead is a powerful moral theme in all civilizations. In the Western tradition, one need mention only *Antigone*. Lawyers, who share these cultural values, nevertheless generally believe that the values underlying confidentiality and the partisan representation of clients in the adversary system outweigh considerations of "ordinary morality." As a number of writers put it, the differentiated role

---

74. ABA Informal Op. 83–1500 (1983).

75. The cited opinions were the N.Y.S.Bar Ass'n opinion cited in *Fentress* and a similar opinion in Massachusetts, Mass.Bar Ass'n Op. 79–61 (1979).

76. N.J. Op. 280, 97 N.J.L.J. 361 (1974).

morality associated with being a lawyer displaces the more general moral principles that otherwise would prevail. See the discussion of moral perspectives on lawyering in Chapter 1 above.

The tension between ordinary morality and professional morality has a further element: In situations like that in the *Dead Bodies Case*, the concern of lay people is not just the lawyer's passive role in keeping secrets. Lawyers, such as those who represented the killer in the *Dead Bodies Case*, do more than merely remain silent: They provide active assistance in helping clients (in this situation, a guilty and repulsive person) avoid disclosure and accountability. An effective lawyer, even if aware of a client's guilt, will try to reshape reality to make the client appear innocent or, at least, not guilty beyond a reasonable doubt. This active participation in suppressing or distorting truth, burdens lawyers in the public eye with a kind of moral complicity in a client's antisocial ends. Do you agree?

Fugitive Clients

Courts usually hold that the whereabouts of a client is not privileged.[77] But is the information confidential? In other words, may a lawyer disclose absent a court order? After his conviction Garrow, the client in the *Dead Bodies Case,* escaped from the state institution in which he was confined. One of his former lawyers (who no longer represented him) provided the authorities information about Garrow's possible whereabouts based on the lawyer's interviews with, and knowledge of, Garrow. Was this disclosure proper?

A number of ethics opinions have dealt inconsistently with the dilemma confronted by a lawyer who, after a client disappears during a criminal investigation or jumps bail, learns where the client is hiding.[78] If the flight and continuing absence constitute a crime, may or must the lawyer disclose the client's whereabouts, or do the rules prohibit such disclosure? If the client refuses to accept the lawyer's advice to surrender, must the lawyer withdraw from representation? The opinions agree that the lawyer must not assist the client in remaining a fugitive, but go every which way on the other questions.[79] Is a clear rule either requiring or prohibiting disclosure desirable? Or should a lawyer have broad discretion to consider various factors such as the

77. See cases cited in the note on p. 264 above.

78. ABA Informal Op. 1141 (1970) involves a lawyer contacted by a deserter from the military. The opinion turns on the deserter's purpose in consulting the lawyer: If the deserter contacts the lawyer to discuss his rights, the lawyer should treat the client's whereabouts as privileged. If the deserter wants advice on how best to evade capture, the lawyer must advise him to turn himself in, refuse to represent him if he declines to do so, and advise him that the lawyer will reveal his whereabouts if the client, continuing in his intention to evade capture, contacts the lawyer a second time. (Is the client likely to call back?) The opinion also tries to reconcile the ABA's previous opinions on what a lawyer with a fugitive client should do.

79. Compare ABA Informal Op. 1141 (1970), reviewing some prior inconsistent opinions and concluding that the lawyer should not disclose but must withdraw, with Ass'n Bar City of N.Y. Op. 81–13, 50 U.S.L.W. 2400 (1982), concluding that the lawyer may disclose and need not withdraw.

characteristics of the client, the nature of crime, the source of the information, etc.?

3. A Duty to Warn?

HAWKINS v. KING COUNTY

Court of Appeals of Washington, Division 1, 1979.
24 Wn.App. 338, 602 P.2d 361.

[handwritten: minor]

[handwritten: Failure to disclose mental dangerous propensity]

SWANSON, ACTING CHIEF JUDGE.

Michael Hawkins, acting through his guardian ad litem, and his mother Frances M. Hawkins, appeal from a summary judgment dismissing attorney Richard Sanders from an action sounding in tort. Appellants contend Sanders, court-appointed defense attorney for Michael Hawkins, was negligent and committed malpractice by failing to divulge information regarding his client's mental state at a bail hearing. We find no error and affirm.

On July 1, 1975, Michael Hawkins was booked for possession of marijuana. Following his court appointment as Hawkins' defense counsel on July 3, 1975, Richard Sanders conferred with Hawkins for about 45 minutes, at which time Hawkins expressed the desire to be released from jail.

Also on July 3, 1975, Sanders talked with Palmer Smith, an attorney employed by Hawkins' mother Frances Hawkins, to assist in having Hawkins either hospitalized or civilly committed. Smith told Sanders then, and reiterated by letter, that Hawkins was mentally ill and dangerous. On July 8, 1975, Dr. Elwood Jones, a psychiatrist, telephoned and wrote Sanders and averred Hawkins was mentally ill and of danger to himself and others and should not be released from custody. Sanders represented that he intended to comply with his client's request for freedom. *[handwritten: π = mentally ill + dangerous.]*

On July 9, 1975, a district judge released Hawkins on a personal surety bond. At the bail hearing, Sanders did not volunteer any information regarding Hawkins' alleged illness or dangerousness, nor were any questions in that vein directed to him either by the judge or the prosecutor. Smith, Jones, and Mrs. Hawkins were informed of Hawkins' release, and all parties later met on two occasions in a counseling environment.

On July 17, 1975, about 8 days after his release, Michael Hawkins assaulted his mother and attempted suicide by jumping off a bridge, causing injuries resulting in the amputation of both legs. The Hawkinses commenced an action for damages against King County, the State of Washington, Community Psychiatric Clinic, Inc., and one of its employees on August 16, 1976, and amended the suit on November 30, 1977, to name Sanders a party defendant. Sanders filed a motion to dismiss for failure to state a claim. . . .

On appeal, the Hawkinses essentially present two arguments: First, that by his failure at the bail hearing to disclose the information he possessed regarding Michael Hawkins' mental state, defense counsel Sanders subjected himself to liability for malpractice, as court rules and the Code of Professional Responsibility mandate such disclosure on ethical and legal grounds. Second, that by the same omission Sanders negligently violated a common law duty to warn foreseeable victims of an individual he knew to be potentially dangerous to himself and others. See Tarasoff v. Regents of University of California, 17 Cal.3d 425, 131 Cal.Rptr. 14, 551 P.2d 334 (1976).

Sanders asserts the Hawkinses have failed to demonstrate that he breached any duty owed to them and, as an attorney appointed by the court to represent an indigent defendant, that he was a quasi-judicial officer, immune from civil liability.

We defined the elements of a legal malpractice action in Hansen v. Wightman, 14 Wash.App. 78, 88, 538 P.2d 1238, 1246 (1975), as

> the existence of an attorney-client relationship, *the existence of a duty on the part of a lawyer*, failure to perform the duty, and the negligence of the lawyer must have been a proximate cause of damage to the client.

[Footnote and citations omitted. Emphasis added.] The Court, in Cook, Flanagan & Berst v. Clausing, 73 Wash.2d 393, 395, 438 P.2d 865, 867 (1968) defined the standard care for Washington lawyers:

> [T]he correct standard to which the plaintiff is held in the performance of his professional services is that degree of care, skill, diligence and knowledge commonly possessed and exercised by a reasonable, careful and prudent lawyer in the practice of law in this jurisdiction.

We further note that the Code of Professional Responsibility sets standards of ethics for all members of the Bar of this state.

In considering appellants' argument that Hawkins' defense counsel breached an ethical and legal duty to disclose information to the court, we observe that a lawyer is ethically bound to advocate zealously his client's interests to the fullest extent permitted by law and the disciplinary rules. CPR 7, DR 7–101(A)(1).

Appellants argue that the information Sanders received was particularly relevant to the issues the bail-hearing judge is required to resolve on pretrial release pursuant to CrR 3.[2] In support of this contention, appellants cite DR 7–102(A)(3), which states:

---

2. The pretrial release hearing was conducted in justice court; therefore, JCrR 2.09 governs; however the provisions of JCrR 2.09 and CrR 3.2 are identical. Both rules identify the relevant factors as follows:

the length and character of the defendant's residence in the community; his employment status and history and financial condition; his family ties and relationships; his reputation, character and mental condition; his history of response to legal process; his prior criminal record; the willingness of responsible members of the community to

(A) In his representation of a client, a lawyer shall not: ... (3) Conceal or knowingly fail to disclose that which he is required by law to reveal.

Assuming without deciding that the information received by Sanders from Dr. Jones and Mrs. Hawkins' attorney did not constitute a "confidence or secret" which a lawyer generally may not reveal, neither CrR 3.2 nor JCrR 2.09 specifies who has the duty to provide facts for the court's consideration. The quoted rules state only that "the court shall, on the available information, consider the relevant facts ..." JCrR 2.09(b); CrR 3.2(b).[3] Further, the Hawkinses ignore an ethical standard of paramount importance: that an attorney must advocate zealously his client's interests to the fullest extent permissible by law and the disciplinary rules. CPR 7 DR 7–101(A)(1).

While it can be argued that the draftsmen of JCrR 2.09 assumed defense counsel would participate in furnishing information for the court, there is no indication as to the length to which defense counsel should go in revealing information damaging to his client's stated interests. Manifestly, defense counsel has an ethical duty to disclose that which he is required by law to reveal. Appellants, however, have not cited any clear provision of the law which *requires* defense counsel to volunteer information damaging to his client's expressed desire to be released from custody.

We believe that the duty of counsel to be loyal to his client and to represent zealously his client's interest overrides the nebulous and unsupported theory that our rules and ethical code mandate disclosure of information which counsel considers detrimental to his client's stated interest. Because disclosure is not "required by law," appellants' theory of liability on the basis of ethical or court rule violations fails for lack of substance.

Turning then to the Hawkinses' theory of a common law duty to warn or disclose, we note common law support for the precept that attorneys must, upon learning that a client plans an assault or other violent crime, warn foreseeable victims. See Tarasoff v. Regents, supra; State ex rel. Sowers v. Olwell, 64 Wash.2d 828, 394 P.2d 681 (1964); Dike v. Dike, 75 Wash.2d 1, 448 P.2d 490 (1968). *Olwell* and

---

vouch for the defendant's reliability and assist him in appearing in court; the nature of the charge; and any other factors indicating the defendant's ties to the community.

3. The American Bar Association's standards relating to pretrial release include this commentary: "The basic criticism of the administration of bail has been that magistrates were required to make decisions without having sufficient facts.... No agency charged with the specific duty of ascertaining facts relevant to release other than the defendant's criminal record and the nature of the present charge ordinarily exists. Unfortunately counsel, who is present in only a limited number of cases at this stage, seldom makes a special effort to supply the judicial officer with background facts.... Where public defender and other assigned lawyers provide representation on an institutional basis, they are frequently too pressed for time to make a special point of such an inquiry and, most important, to verify the information they may receive in an interview.

"The ideal system would involve the creation of an independent agency answerable directly to the court." ... ABA Standards Relating to Pretrial Release § 4.5 (Approved Draft 1968) commentary at 50.

Dike make clear our Supreme Court's willingness to limit the attorney's duty of confidentiality when the values protected by that duty are outweighed by other interests necessary to the administration of justice. The difficulty lies in framing a rule that will balance properly "the public interest in safety from violent attack" against the public interest in securing proper resolution of legal disputes without compromising a defendant's right to a loyal and zealous defense. We are persuaded by the position advanced by amicus "that the obligation to warn, when confidentiality would be compromised to the client's detriment, must be permissive at most, unless it appears beyond a reasonable doubt that the client has formed a firm intention to inflict serious personal injuries on an unknowing third person."

Because appellants rely to a great extent upon *Tarasoff* in arguing a common law duty to disclose, we will demonstrate that the *Tarasoff* decision is inapposite even though the facts are equally atypical and tragic. Tatiana Tarasoff was killed by one Prosenjit Poddar. The victim's parents alleged that 2 months earlier Poddar confided his intention to kill Tatiana to a defendant, Dr. Moore, a psychologist employed by the University of California. After a brief detention of Poddar by the police at Moore's request, Poddar was released pursuant to order of Dr. Moore's superior. No one warned Tatiana of her peril. The plaintiffs claimed the defendant psychologists had a duty to warn foreseeable victims. Defendants denied owing any duty of reasonable care to Tatiana. The trial court sustained a demurrer to the complaint which was reversed on appeal. The Supreme Court of California concluded that the complaint could be amended to state a cause of action against the psychologists by asserting that they had or should have determined Poddar presented a serious danger to Tatiana, pursuant to the standards of their profession, but had failed to exercise reasonable care for her safety.

In *Tarasoff*, the defendant psychologists had first-hand knowledge of Poddar's homicidal intention and knew it to be directed towards Tatiana Tarasoff, who was wholly unaware of her danger. The knowledge of the defendants in *Tarasoff* was gained from statements made to them in the course of treatment and not from statements transmitted by others. Further, the California court in *Tarasoff* did not establish a new duty to warn, but only held that psychologists must exercise such reasonable skill, knowledge, and care possessed and exercised by members of their profession under similar circumstances.

In the instant case Michael Hawkins' potential victims, his mother and sister, knew he might be dangerous and that he had been released from confinement, contrary to Tatiana Tarasoff's ignorance of any risk of harm. Thus, no duty befell Sanders to warn Frances Hawkins of a risk of which she was already fully cognizant. Further, it must not be overlooked that Sanders received no information that Hawkins planned to assault anyone, only that he was mentally ill and likely to be dangerous to himself and others. That Sanders received no information directly from Michael Hawkins is the final distinction between the two cases.

The common law duty to volunteer information about a client to a court considering pretrial release must be limited to situations where information gained convinces counsel that his client intends to commit a crime or inflict injury upon unknowing third persons. Such a duty cannot be extended to the facts before us.

In view of our disposition of this case, we do not reach the question of respondent Sanders' claimed immunity from civil liability.

The decision of the superior court granting summary judgment dismissing the respondents as party defendants is affirmed.

Hawkins' Malpractice Claim

Would the Model Code or Model Rules permit a lawyer to disclose Hawkins' state of mind? Does M.R. 1.14 or EC 7–12 help resolve this question?

The court points out that no questions on Hawkins' mental state were posed to Sanders in the bail hearing. Would Sanders have had a duty to answer such questions honestly? See M.R. 3.3. If Sanders had lied to or misled the court in response to questions at the bail hearing, would the result on the malpractice claim have been different?

A *Tarasoff* Duty for Lawyers?

Should the law impose civil liability on lawyers who fail to warn of a client's intent to endanger others? If so, what should be the scope of such a duty?

The *Hawkins* court would require lawyers to "volunteer information . . . to the court considering pretrial release where information gained convinces counsel that his client intends to commit a crime or inflict injury upon [specific and] *unknowing* third persons." The court apparently would impose such a duty only in cases of threatened physical injury. Should the court similarly require a lawyer to warn victims of a client's intended fraudulent schemes? Is physical injury so different?

Tarasoff v. Regents of University of California,[80] discussed in *Hawkins,* is the seminal case on a psychiatrist's duty to warn or otherwise protect others from patients whom a doctor knows or should know are dangerous. Although often referred to as a case establishing a duty to "warn," *Tarasoff* did not limit the duty described therein to warning:

> The discharge of this duty may require the therapist to take one or more of various steps, depending upon the nature of the case. Thus it may call for him to warn the intended victim or others

---

80. 17 Cal.3d 425, 431, 131 Cal.Rptr. 14, 20, 551 P.2d 334, 340 (1976).

likely to apprise the victim of the danger, to notify the police, or to take whatever other steps are reasonably necessary under the circumstances.[81]

Does *Hawkins* intimate a duty on the lawyer's part to do anything other than to volunteer information? [82]

Tort law generally accepts the principle that an affirmative duty to act to protect others may be imposed on a person in a special relationship with either a dangerous person or the dangerous person's victim.[83] The doctor-patient relationship, as evidenced by *Tarasoff*, exemplifies such a special relationship.

Recall the facts of Spaulding v. Zimmerman, printed in Chapter 1 above at p. 5. If David Spaulding had died a year after the settlement, should Zimmerman have been civilly liable for not disclosing the aneurysm to David or the court? Should Zimmerman's lawyers also have been liable for consequences flowing from nondisclosure?

Subsequent California cases to *Tarasoff*, generally followed in other states, limit the therapist's liability to specific identifiable victims on the theory that the scope of potential liability for professionals would be too broad if not so limited.[84] Recall the economic justification for such a limit given in *Greycas*, p. 75 above. Why doesn't Hawkins himself fall into the protected category? His mother? [85]

What standard of knowledge should trigger a duty to warn? Subjective or objective? If objective, should the standard be that the lawyer possessed information that would "convince a reasonable lawyer"? That would "cause a reasonable lawyer to believe"? Do such distinctions matter?

As of 1993, no case imposes liability on a lawyer for failing to warn of a client's intended dangerous conduct. At the same time, numerous cases since *Tarasoff* have recognized the liability of psychiatrists and

---

81.   131 Cal.Rptr. at 20.

82.   See Vanessa Merton, Confidentiality and the "Dangerous" Patient: Implications of Tarasoff for Psychiatrists and Lawyers, 31 Emory L.J. 263 (1982).

83.   The special relationship doctrine is a limited exception to the basic principle that tort law does not impose upon one person a duty to prevent another person from harming a third person. See Restatement (Second) of Torts § 314. The Restatement does not define a "special relationship," but § 314A provides examples. For a critique of the special relationship doctrine in tort law see, e.g., Note, Affirmative Duty After Tarasoff, 11 Hofstra L.Rev. 1013 (1983) (arguing that tort law should recognize a more general affirmative duty to act to protect others instead of a duty limited to special relationships); Note, Professional Obligation and the Duty to Rescue: When Must a Psychiatrist Protect His Patient's Intended Victim, 91 Yale L.J. 1430 (1982) (criticizing courts for failing to articulate components of the relationship that create affirmative duties).

84.   Thompson v. County of Alameda, 27 Cal.3d 741, 167 Cal.Rptr. 70, 614 P.2d 728 (1980). Also see Brady v. Hopper, 751 F.2d 329 (10th Cir.1984) (suit by James Brady, President Reagan's press secretary, against John Hinckley's psychiatrist). But see Schuster v. Altenberg, 144 Wis.2d 223, 424 N.W.2d 159 (1988) (under Wisconsin tort law, psychiatrists' duty to warn or protect third parties not limited to cases where victim is readily identifiable).

85.   See Jablonski by Pahls v. United States, 712 F.2d 391 (9th Cir.1983) (psychological profile indicating violence against women close to patient sufficiently "targeted").

psychologists either for failure to warn of a client's intent to harm others or for failure to take other appropriate steps.[86] The current conflict in this area involves state liability for releasing dangerous parolees or improperly supervising probationers.[87]

Why Impose a Duty on Psychotherapists and Not Others?

Why impose liability on therapists for failing to warn others about their dangerous clients and not impose similar liability on lawyers and other professionals with special access to a dangerous client's intent? Some therapists deny that they are able to predict dangerousness with any reliability.[88] Does the fact that mental health professionals (and probation boards) routinely make judgments about dangerousness, e.g., in civil commitment hearings, provide a reason for assuming they can predict dangerousness for purposes of tort liability?[89]

Unlike mental health professionals and probation boards, lawyers are not in the business of predicting dangerousness. Lawyers also believe they have limited capacity to make such predictions. Another argument advanced in favor of distinguishing lawyers from therapists and state correction authorities involves control: Probation boards, at least, may be in a better position than lawyers to control the conduct of a potential tortfeasor. Do therapists also exercise or possess greater control over their patients than lawyers over their clients?[90]

Two studies following *Tarasoff* have found that psychotherapists regard a duty to protect third parties from violent patients as consistent with their ethical obligations.[91] Consider this in light of the medical profession's general confidentiality provision, reprinted below. Another study has found that, contrary to predictions, *Tarasoff* has

86. See, e.g., Naidu v. Laird, 539 A.2d 1064 (Sup.Ct.Del.1988); Evans v. Morehead Clinic, 749 S.W.2d 696 (Ky.App.1988); Davis v. Lhim, 124 Mich.App. 291, 335 N.W.2d 481 (1983); McIntosh v. Milano, 168 N.J.Super. 466, 403 A.2d 500 (1979) and cases cited in the notes above.

87. See, e.g., Division of Corrections v. Neakok, 721 P.2d 1121 (Alaska 1986); Sterling v. Bloom, 111 Idaho 211, 723 P.2d 755 (1986).

88. See Task Force Report, Clinical Aspects of the Violent Individual (American Psychiatric Assn. 1974) at 28 (claiming that psychiatrists are no better than anyone else at predicting dangerousness). But see Daniel J. Givelber et al., *Tarasoff*, Myth and Reality: An Empirical Study of Private Law in Action, 1984 Wis.L.Rev. 443, 456–67 ("The task of assessing dangerousness is not viewed [by those therapists surveyed] as being beyond the competence of individual therapists or as a matter upon which therapists cannot agree.").

89. A prominent psychiatrist believes that psychiatrist-patient confidentiality is subject to more exceptions than that of other professional relationships because "psychiatrists have extensive civil authority, e.g., in circumstances involving abortions, personal injury suits, commitment procedures, and not-guilty-by-reason-of-insanity pleas." Dr. Eric A. Plaut, A Perspective on Client Confidentiality, 131 Am.J.Psych. 1021, 1022 (1974). What implications does this have for lawyer confidentiality?

90. See Davis v. Lhim, 124 Mich.App. 291, 335 N.W.2d 481 (1983), which makes control over the patient a key to the psychiatrist's tort liability for subsequent harmful acts.

91. See Daniel J. Givelber et al., supra, 1984 Wis.L.Rev. at 473–76, 486; and Mills, Sullivan & Eth, Protecting Third Parties: A Decade After *Tarasoff*, 144 Am.J.Psych. 68, 69–70 (Jan.1987).

neither discouraged therapists from treating dangerous patients nor apparently increased the use of involuntary commitment for those patients viewed as dangerous.[92] Do these latter findings suggest that psychotherapists already operate under a self-imposed duty to warn, based on their ethical obligations, and that the *Tarasoff* situation may have been unusual?

Confidentiality Obligations of Physicians

The American Medical Association's provision dealing with confidentiality reads:

§ 505. Confidentiality. The information disclosed to a physician during the course of the relationship between physician and patient is confidential to the greatest possible degree.... The physician should not reveal confidential communications or information without the express consent of the patient, unless required to do so by law

The obligation to safeguard patient confidences is subject to certain exceptions which are ethically and legally justified because of overriding social considerations. Where a patient threatens to inflict serious bodily harm to another person and there is a reasonable probability that the patient may carry out the threat, the physician should take reasonable precautions for the protection of the intended victim, including notification of law enforcement authorities. Also, communicable diseases, gun shot and knife wounds, should be reported as required by applicable statutes or ordinances.[93]

How does this compare with the rules governing lawyers?

In 1988, the American Medical Association amended its ethics rules to deal with the physician's responsibility to sexual partners of a patient carrying the AIDS virus:

Ideally, a physician should attempt to persuade the infected party to cease endangering the third party; if persuasion fails, the authorities should be notified; and if the authorities take no action, the physician should notify and counsel the endangered third party.

The AMA also urged that any state laws protecting doctor-patient confidences that would prevent such disclosure be amended to allow compliance with the amendment.[94]

4. Alternative Approaches to Confidentiality

Three broad approaches to the choice of values between client confidentiality and third-party and other social interests are discerni-

92. Givelber et al., supra.

93. Amer.Med.Ass'n Code of Medical Ethics and Annotated Current Opinions (1992). The Principles of Medical Ethics were substantially revised in 1990.

94. N.Y. Times, July 1, 1988, at p. A11.

ble.   The first approach views confidentiality as an overriding principle, requiring a lawyer always, or almost always, to protect a client's interests regardless of the consequences for others.[95]   A second, converse approach perceives prevention of harm to others as the dominant principle.   Philosopher Sissela Bok, for example, has argued that a moral duty exists to reveal client confidences in order to prevent serious harm that is likely to occur and even sometimes to reveal past crimes, the latter because of a policy interest in social justice and restitution.[96]   The third alternative suggests an intermediate approach *Balancing* by developing criteria or methods to balance competing interests either in particular cases or in categories of situations.

Any effort to balance competing interests involves fundamental choices between rule and discretion.   A rule-based approach would specify through more detailed rules situations in which disclosure is prohibited, permitted or required.   Alternatively, broad discretion can be delegated to individual lawyers to apply very general factors to particular situations.   Various combinations of rule and discretion are also possible.   Which approach is preferable?

Will recognition of more or broader exceptions to confidentiality undermine the effectiveness of representation?   In addition to common-sense arguments derived from fiduciary loyalty, the legal profession justifies confidentiality as essential to the preservation of individual rights and as serving the purposes of law enforcement by encouraging clients to come forward with information and plans that lawyers may then channel into lawful avenues.   Professor Harry Subin has summarized the premises of the rights-based defense of confidentiality:

> (a) [T]he primary objective of the legal system is the preservation of individual autonomy, through the protection of an individual's rights against encroachments by other individuals or the state; (b) in a complex society individuals can have meaningful access to the legal system, and therefore to the mechanism by which their rights can be protected, only if they are represented by attorneys who have the skill to guide them through the process; (c) attorneys can perform this function only if they are privy to all the client's information, because otherwise they would not be able to diagnose properly the legal problem or prescribe a resolution of it; (d) clients

95. See Monroe H. Freedman, Understanding Lawyers' Ethics c. 5 (1990). Freedman argues that, because confidentiality is a "fundamental" principle of the adversary system, the client's "sacred trust" should receive almost absolute protection. However, he favors a duty (not a permission) to disclose confidences in one situation: when human life is threatened. In this situation, Freedman would require disclosure even though no future crime is involved (thus he disagrees with the result in *Spaulding*) and the threatened action is by someone other than the client. The ALCC's confidentiality provisions (Rules 1.1—1.5) reject Freedman's advice (see proposed Rule 1.6). Illustration 1(g) to the ALCC presents the *Dead Bodies Case* facts, except that the woman "is seriously injured and unable to help herself or to get help"; the Illustration states that even if the lawyer discloses the woman's location anonymously, "[t]he lawyer has committed a disciplinary violation."

96. Sissela Bok, Secrets 127–131 (1982); see also, Alan Donagon, Justifying Legal Practice in an Adversary System, in The Good Lawyer 123, 139–45 (D. Luban, ed., 1984).

will not provide attorneys with all of the facts, including possibly embarrassing facts, if they believe that the attorney will disclose those facts; (e) therefore, confidentiality is essential to the preservation of individual autonomy.[97]

Critics of a requirement of confidentiality with few exceptions usually accept the general thrust of the rights-based argument, but argue that it justifies only good-faith client communications, not those in which a client wants to enlist an attorney as an accomplice in crime or fraud or to subvert the legal system by the use of false evidence. Preserving a client's autonomy, they insist, justifies the lawyer's assistance only when the client is pursuing lawful goals; the client has no legal right to subvert the legal system. In addition, they argue that even when a client is legitimately seeking legal advice, disclosure may be permissible or required when the client's past or future conduct will cause third persons serious harm that could be prevented.

Consider the following criticisms of the rights-based argument: First, the rights-based argument rests on assumptions about lawyer and client behavior that are dubious or wrong. If lawyers can perform their designated function only if clients tell their lawyers everything, perhaps lawyers can never perform their designated function. Few practicing lawyers would suggest that most or even many clients fully share all relevant information.[98] Moreover, it is not clear that most clients know or expect that confidentiality will have few or no exceptions.[9] Second, the current state of the law on prohibited assistance leads many lawyers to avoid learning things they would rather not "know." Edward Bennett Williams, a famous trial lawyer, frequently

97. Harry I. Subin, The Lawyer as Superego: Disclosure of Client Confidences to Prevent Harm, 70 Iowa L.Rev. 1091, 1160 (1985).

98. Professor Deborah Rhode says:

[M]any clients will withhold evidence of compromising conduct, regardless of the bar's formal rules or clients' perceptions of them. What knowledge their counsel acquires will often be the product of paper trails and external corroboration rather than voluntary revelations. In any event, concerns about personal as well as organizational liability frequently leave clients with no practical alternative but to consult attorneys, and it is unclear how often some risk of disclosure would materially alter the terms of counsel's involvement. From a historical and cross-cultural perspective, it appears that most professionals, including American lawyers, have managed to discharge confidential counseling functions without the absolute freedom from third-party obligations that the organized bar now claims.

Deborah L. Rhode, Ethical Perspectives on Legal Practice, 37 Stan.L.Rev. 589, 615 (1985).

99. The few empirical studies show that clients do not expect total confidentiality in the lawyer-client relationship but have expectations that parallel lay intuition concerning the morality of disclosure. A 1989 study of New York lawyers and clients reported that lawyers only rarely inform clients of the duty of confidentiality, that the clients believed the lawyers would be permitted or required to disclose in many situations in which professional rules require confidentiality and that most clients stated they would have confided the same information even if no duty of confidentiality existed. Fred C. Zacharias, Rethinking Confidentiality, 74 Iowa L.Rev. 351, 380–83 (1989). A 1962 survey concluded that "most people were either unaware of the attorney-client privilege or believed that it extended to other professional relationships as well." Note, Functional Overlap Between the Lawyer and Other Professionals: Its Implications for the Privileged Communications Doctrine, 71 Yale L.J. 1226, 1232 (1962).

stated "I never know whether my clients are guilty." [1]   Third, the rights-based defense proceeds as though ethics rules now accord confidences near-absolute protection from disclosure, but that is not so.   The ethics rules presently provide broad exceptions to confidentiality for collecting a lawyer's fee or defending a lawyer's own skin, and such exceptions are longstanding.   Would limited exceptions allowing disclosure to protect others make a critical difference.[2]   If so, how and why?

Confidentiality, Secrecy and Moral Choice

In her book, *Secrets,* moral philosopher Sissela Bok addresses the quandary of living in a society where secrets can both liberate and corrupt.[3]   Chapter 2, Secrecy and Moral Choice, opens with a description of four imaginary worlds.   In the first, neither Bok nor her reader can keep secrets, but others can.   In the second world, it is Bok and her reader who can keep secrets while others cannot.   In the third, no one can keep secrets.   And in the fourth, everyone can keep secrets.

The purpose of Bok's imaginary societies is not to offer idealized alternatives to the "real" world.   Rather, Bok suggests that even though our society struggles to balance secrecy and openness, an imperfect society in which the balance is sometimes weighed too heavily in favor of one or the other is preferable to any of the four imaginary worlds.   She offers a perspective on how the balance between secrecy and openness ought to be struck.

"Conflicts over secrecy," Bok writes, " ... are conflicts over power: the power that comes through controlling the flow of information."   She offers four defenses of secrecy.

The first defense is that control over information is necessary to protect the human identity.   By "identity" Bok refers to inner experience, including privacy, friendship, beliefs, feelings, memories and dreams.   That each person is unique flows from the fact that no one's identity is ever fully revealed.   And change—human growth—is possible, because our identity, our inner self, is never fully known at any one moment.

The second and third claims in defense of information control are inseparably entwined.   The second is that control is necessary to formulate plans, and the third is that control is necessary to execute those plans.   Plans to do something risky or unpopular may never

---

1. See Evan Thomas, The Man to See: Edward Bennett Williams 120–21 (1991). Recall Attorney Davis's comments about Attorney Hutner's attitude in the O.P.M. case, supra, p. 305.

2. Rhode, supra, at 616 (1985), states:

[N]othing in [the ethics rules] explains why disclosure to protect lay victims will erode client trust, while revelations to secure attorneys' financial interests will not.... Once one acknowledges that clients' general expectations of confidentiality can be maintained despite some limited risk of betrayal, it is unclear why the pecuniary concerns of lawyers should assume priority over the potentially more significant claims of third-party victims.

3. Sissela Bok, Secrets 15–28 (1982).

reach fruition if they are developed under the hot light of public scrutiny; but even after plans have been formulated, information control is necessary so that plans can be altered or abandoned easily. It is important to remember, however, that information control concerns not only secrecy but also disclosure. Planning and execution may ultimately require a well-timed disclosure for the plan to maximize its potential. For example, negotiations over a peace treaty may best be conducted in the shadows, but when an accord is reached, a blast of sudden publicity may be needed to persuade citizens to accept the treaty. If the negotiators cannot manipulate both secrecy and disclosure, the treaty may never be realized.

The final defense of control over information is that information is property. The claim has two prongs. The first is that we own our secrets in the same way one owns land. Bok points out, however, that this claim has limits. She cites the example of the school-bus driver with a severe heart condition. The bus driver cannot be said to own the knowledge of his disease; because the driver's secret endangers others, information concerning the heart condition should be revealed. The second prong is that information control is necessary to preserve what one owns. Bok uses the examples of hiding valuables from burglars or personal documents from busybodies.

Against these claims favoring control over secrecy and openness stand the dangers of information control. Secrecy, Bok contends, is primarily dangerous because it can "debilitate judgment ... [by s]hut[ting] out criticism and feedback, leading people to become mired down in stereotyped, unexamined, often erroneous beliefs and ways of thinking." Bok further asserts that a result of diminished judgment is corruption, the "deterioration from within." Because the dangers of secrecy have a natural tendency to spread, people or organizations wishing to hide scandal will shield themselves in increasing layers of secrecy.

Bok believes we should worry about secrecy not so much because of its impact on the keepers of secrets, but because of secrecy's impact on others:

> The power of ... secrecy can be immense. Because it bypasses inspection and eludes interference, secrecy is central to the planning of every form of injury to human beings. It cloaks the execution of these plans and wipes out all traces afterward. It enters into all prying and intrusion that cannot be carried out openly. While not all that is secret is meant to deceive ... all deceit does rely on keeping something secret.

Finally, secrecy confounds decision-making. When information is withheld, individuals and institutions make choices based on false or partial information. The result is not only irrational decisions, but also increasing secrecy. Those who are injured because of someone else's information control will themselves be more secretive next time.

Unlike lying, which is inherently bad, and honesty, which is inherently good, Bok concludes secrecy is neither inherently good nor bad. Although we may presume some uses of secrecy are good or bad, judgments about secrecy will generally depend on the setting in which it is exercised. Society must balance the freedom secrecy protects against the power of secrecy to infringe upon the freedom of others.

Chapter 5

DUTY TO THE COURT

Introductory Note

This chapter examines the advocate's special responsibilities to the court and how the legal norms governing the advocate differ from those governing the office lawyer. When a lawyer acts as an advocate rather than as a facilitator of transactions should she have different obligations when confronted with client fraud? Is there a difference in this respect between a criminal defense lawyer and a civil advocate?

The civil and criminal law relating to the lawyer's liability for assisting transactional fraud was considered in Chapter 2. This body of law demonstrates that a lawyer who lies to a third party while facilitating a fraudulent transaction may be liable under civil or criminal law for fraud.[1] The lawyer who acts *recklessly* in handling a transaction may also be liable for *civil* fraud, and one who acts carelessly may be liable for negligent misrepresentation.[2]

A lawyer who acts with indifference as to whether or not the client is committing fraud in a transaction, or as if incapable of discerning the truthfulness of the client's statements, therefore risks liability as an aider and abettor of the client's criminal and civil wrongs. The assertion that the lawyer must never be the judge of her client's cause is simply incorrect for out-of-court transactions.

These hard truths, however, are muddied by the uncertainty and incoherence of the ethics law dealing with prevention or rectification of client fraud. Transactional lawyers who rely on the black-letter text of Model Rule 1.6(b), for example, may be misled into believing that the lawyer's duties to client of loyalty and confidentiality override ordinary substantive fraud law and the law of prohibited assistance insofar as lawyers are concerned.

In studying the following materials, consider whether the tension apparent in transactional fraud between the state's law (the rules announced and enforced by the courts) and the profession's law and

---

1. A lawyer "lies" when she makes a false statement with the intent to deceive (or to aid a client in deceiving) another; when she omits material facts in circumstances where there is a duty to disclose those facts; or when she fails to correct the false statements or material omissions of a client while acting in a transaction based on those statements or omissions. Although a lawyer ordinarily is not guilty of *criminal* fraud unless she acted with the intent to deceive, acting with reckless disregard as to whether statements or omissions are false or misleading may be enough to satisfy the intent requirement. See, e.g., *United States v. Benjamin*, printed at p. 57 above.

2. See, e.g., *Greycas v. Proud*, printed at p. 75 above.

lore (the ethics codes and the profession's belief system) carries over to fraud on a tribunal. Does the lawyer as litigator have duties to client that permit action or inaction that impairs the integrity of adjudicatory process?

A. PERJURY

1. Creation or Use of False Evidence

Deliberate Corruption of Court Processes

A lawyer who deliberately corrupts court processes is subject to criminal prosecution and severe disciplinary sanctions. Advising another to testify falsely is a crime.[3] The offense of subornation of perjury, see, e.g., 18 U.S.C. § 1621, requires that perjury actually have been committed, but a lawyer may be convicted of obstructing justice for advising a client or witness to lie even if perjury does not result.[4] A lawyer may be held criminally liable for submitting false documents on behalf of a client,[5] and for conspiracy to suborn perjury or obstruct justice.[6] Knowingly presenting false evidence or destroying or concealing evidence may be punished as contempt.[7]

Monetary sanctions, including payment of the opposing side's attorneys' fees, may be imposed on lawyers who deliberately mislead the court or the opposing party. In addition to the inherent power of a court to award attorneys' fees for "bad faith" or frivolous conduct of cases,[8] statutes and procedural rules provide a battery of sanctions against both intentional and negligent misstatements and omissions that mislead the court or delay proceedings.[9]

Knowingly presenting or creating false evidence is also a violation

---

3. United States v. Vesich, 724 F.2d 451 (5th Cir.1984) (lawyer convicted of obstruction of justice, 18 U.S.C. § 1503, for advising a client to testify falsely before a grand jury).

4. See United States v. Silverman, 745 F.2d 1386 n. 7 at 1394 (11th Cir.1984) (citing cases).

5. For example, in United States v. Lopez, 728 F.2d 1359 (11th Cir.1984), a lawyer was convicted under 18 U.S.C. § 1001 for falsifying the dates on his client's application for permanent resident status. See also United States v. Vaughn, 797 F.2d 1485 (9th Cir.1986).

6. See 18 U.S.C. § 371.

7. See, e.g., United States v. Temple, 349 F.2d 116, 117 (4th Cir.1965) ("Lying to a judge is certainly misbehavior ... and therefore punishable [as contempt].").

8. See, e.g., Roadway Express v. Piper, 447 U.S. 752, 765–67 (1980); Chambers v. NASCO, Inc., 111 S.Ct. 2123 (1991), discussed at p. 436 below.

9. See, e.g., 28 U.S.C. § 1927 (monetary sanctions against lawyers who unreasonably and vexatiously multiply the proceedings); Fed.R.Civ.P. 26 and 37 (governing discovery); Fed.R.Civ.P. 11 (lies or misstatements in papers filed with the court). See, e.g., Carlucci v. Piper Aircraft, 775 F.2d 1440 (11th Cir.1985) (discussing the applicability of Rule 37 and § 1927 to deliberate misconduct). Cases discussed in the notes following *Golden Eagle,* below at p. 443, establish that negligent misstatements or omissions of material information may lead to monetary sanctions.

of ethical rules.[10]   Violation of these rules is frequently punished by disbarment.[11]   Unlike the ethics rules dealing with prevention or rectification of transactional fraud, the ethics rules concerning false evidence carry the same message as the civil and criminal law dealing with the same subject.

However, the line between impermissible and permissible activity is not always clear.   The metaphor of fight or battle for the adversary concept of a trial suggests that the trial lawyer is a champion or warrior who is not expected to act as a "civilian."   A trial would not be a trial—at least not as we know it—if the parties were expected merely to disclose the truth rather than to contest it.   But the trial lawyer is no more privileged to engage in fraud than a soldier is privileged to engage in torture.   When does the advocate cross the line?

Commentators have argued extensively about what the ethics rules require of the lawyer faced with client perjury.[12]   Professor Monroe Freedman's controversial views have been widely discussed.

MONROE H. FREEDMAN
"PERJURY: THE LAWYER'S TRILEMMA"

1 Litigation 26 (No. 1, Winter 1975).[13]

Is it ever proper for a lawyer to present perjured testimony?

10.   M.R. 3.4 and DR 7–102(A)(6) (creating false evidence); M.R. 3.3(a)(4) and DR 7–102(A)(4) (using/offering false evidence).   See also M.R. 3.4(a) and DR 7–102(A)(3), DR 7–109(A) (concealing or failing to reveal evidence required to be revealed by law).

11.   See, e.g., In the Matter of Benson, 431 N.W.2d 120 (Minn.1988) (disbarment for, among other violations, alteration of documents and conspiracy to present perjured testimony); Louisiana State Bar Ass'n v. Stewart, 500 So.2d 360 (La.1987) ("The appropriate penalty for ... suborning perjury is generally disbarment ..."); In re Sandground, 542 A.2d 1242 (D.C.App.1988) (assisting client to conceal information about funds in response to discovery requests); In the Matter of Ireland, 146 Ariz. 340, 706 P.2d 352 (1985) (misrepresenting client's assets to court and instructing client to testify falsely); Davis v. California, 33 Cal.3d 231, 188 Cal.Rptr. 441, 655 P.2d 1276 (1983) (wilful deception of the court).

12.   The following contributions to the debate are noteworthy: Charles P. Curtis, The Ethics of Advocacy, 4 Stan.L.Rev. 3 (1951); Henry S. Drinker, Some Remarks on Mr. Curtis' "The Ethics of Advocacy," 4 Stan.L.Rev. 349 (1952); John T. Noonan, Jr., The Purpose of Advocacy and the Limits of Confidentiality, 64 Mich.L.Rev. 1485 (1966); Marvin E. Frankel, The Search for Truth: An Umpireal View, 123 U.Pa.L.Rev. 1031 (1975); H. Richard Uviller, The Advocate, The Truth, and Judicial Hackles: A Reaction to Judge Frankel's Idea, 123 U.Pa.L.Rev. 1067 (1975); Monroe H. Freedman, Understanding Lawyers' Ethics (1990); Norman Lefstein, The Criminal Defendant Who Proposes Perjury: Rethinking the Defense Lawyer's Dilemma, 6 Hofstra L.Rev. 665 (1978); Wayne D. Brazil, Unanticipated Client Perjury and the Collision of Rules of Ethics, Evidence, and Constitutional Law, 44 Mo.L.Rev. 601 (1979); Charles W. Wolfram, Client Perjury, 50 S.Cal.L.Rev. 809 (1977).

13.   Copyright © 1975 by the American Bar Association, Section of Litigation.   Reprinted with permission.   Professor Freedman has expanded his views and modified them somewhat in his book, Lawyers' Ethics in an Adversary System (1975), and a subsequent book, Understanding Lawyers' Ethics (1990).   See also Freedman, Personal Responsibility in a Professional System, 27 Cath.U.L.Rev. 191 (1978); and Freedman, Legal Ethics and the Suffering Client, 36 Cath.U.L.Rev. 331 (1987).

One's instinctive response is in the negative. On analysis, however, it becomes apparent that the question is exceedingly perplexing. In at least one situation, that of the criminal defense lawyer, my own answer is in the affirmative.

... As an officer of the court, participating in a search for truth, what is the attorney obligated to do when faced with perjured testimony? That question cannot be answered properly without an appreciation of the fact that the attorney functions in an adversary system of justice which imposes three conflicting obligations upon the advocate. The difficulties presented by these obligations are particularly acute in the criminal defense area because of the presumption of innocence, the burden on the state to prove its case beyond a reasonable doubt, and the right to put the prosecution to its proof.

[The three conflicting obligations of the lawyer in the adversary system are: first, to learn everything the client knows about the case; second, to hold in strictest confidence what the client reveals; and third, to act with candor toward the tribunal.]

As soon as one begins to think about these responsibilities, it becomes apparent that the conscientious attorney is faced with what we may call a trilemma—that is, the lawyer is required to know everything, to keep it in confidence, and to reveal it to the court.

. . .

If we recognize that professional responsibility requires that an advocate have full knowledge of every pertinent fact, then the lawyer must seek the truth from the client, not shun it. That means that the attorney will have to dig and pry and cajole, and, even then, the lawyer will not be successful without convincing the client that full disclosure to the lawyer will never result in prejudice to the client by any word or action of the attorney. That is particularly true in the case of the indigent criminal defendant, who meets the lawyer for the first time in the cell block or the rotunda of the jail....

However, the inclination to mislead one's lawyer is not restricted to the indigent or even to the criminal defendant. Randolph Paul has observed a similar phenomenon among a wealthier class in a far more congenial atmosphere. The tax adviser, notes Mr. Paul, will sometimes have to "dynamite the facts of his case out of the unwilling witnesses on his own side—witnesses who are nervous, witnesses who are confused about their own interest, witnesses who try to be too smart for their own good, and witnesses who subconsciously do not want to understand what has happened despite the fact that they must if they are to testify coherently." Mr. Paul goes on to explain that the truth can be obtained only by persuading the client that it would be a violation of a sacred obligation for the lawyer ever to reveal a client's confidence. Of course, once the lawyer has thus persuaded the client of the obligation of confidentiality, that obligation must be respected scrupulously.

. . .

[A]nother way to resolve the difficulty ... [is] by "selective ignorance." The attorney can make it clear to the client from the outset that the attorney does not want to hear an admission of guilt or incriminating evidence from the client. According to the [ABA Criminal Defense] Standards, that tactic is "most egregious" and constitutes "professional impropriety." On a practical level, it also puts an unreasonable burden on the unsophisticated client to select what to tell and what to hold back, and it can seriously impair the attorney's effectiveness in counseling the client and trying the case.

. . .

... [T]he ABA Standards have chosen to resolve the trilemma by maintaining the requirements of complete knowledge and of candor to the court, and sacrificing confidentiality.... [But] the Standards ignore the issue of whether the lawyer should [warn the client at the outset of the relationship that incriminating facts may have to be revealed to the tribunal]. The Canadian Bar Association, for example, takes an extremely hard line against the presentation of perjury by the client, but it also explicitly requires that the client be put on notice of that fact. Obviously, any other course would be a gross betrayal of the client's trust, since everything else said by the attorney in attempting to obtain complete information about the case would indicate to the client that no information thus obtained would be used to the client's disadvantage.

On the other hand, the inevitable result of the position taken by the Canadian Bar Association would be to caution the client not to be completely candid with the attorney. That, of course, returns us to resolving the trilemma by maintaining confidentiality and candor, but sacrificing complete knowledge....

. . .

... I continue to stand with those lawyers who hold that the lawyer's obligation of confidentiality does not permit him to disclose the facts he has learned from his client which form the basis for his conclusion that the client intends to perjure himself. What that means—necessarily, it seems to me—is that, at least the criminal defense attorney, however unwillingly in terms of personal morality, has a professional responsibility as an advocate in an adversary system to examine the perjurious client in the ordinary way and to argue to the jury, as evidence in the case, the testimony presented by the defendant.

———

Freedman's Trilemma

Professor Freedman's argument is in part dependent on positing three duties—knowing all the facts, keeping confidences and candor to the court. What about the lawyer's responsibility under the criminal law and under the ethics rules to refrain from assisting criminal activity?

Freedman argues that "it is simply too much to expect of a human being ... facing loss of liberty and the horrors of imprisonment not to attempt to lie...." Do different considerations apply to lawyers in civil matters? If Freedman's central concern is the criminal defendant's right to tell her story, why is his argument not one for freeing the criminal defendant from the penalties of perjury or from the requirement of an oath? This is the path taken in Germany and other countries using nonadversarial procedural systems.[14]

At common law until the 19th century, a party, including a criminal accused, was disqualified from testifying on the ground that the temptation to falsify would put his soul in jeopardy. Today a criminal defendant has a due process right to testify in her own behalf.[15] If a state gives a defendant the option of testifying either on oath or unsworn, and the defendant elects an unsworn statement, should the jury be told by the judge or the prosecutor that this testimony is given without threat of penalty if found to be false?[16]

Is Assisting Perjury Like Assisting Other Crimes?

Professor Freedman's argument implicitly rests on the proposition that perjury is unlike other crimes that corrupt court processes. The American Lawyer's Code of Conduct [ALCC] adopts this distinction. The Comment to ALCC Chapter 1 explains:

> The corruption cases [i.e., cases where a judge or juror has been bribed or subject to extortion, see ALCC Rule 1.4] are an appropriate exception [to the confidentiality rule] because the corruption of the impartial judge or jury vitiates the adversary system itself. Since cases of corruption are infrequent, the exception should not have significant impact on the lawyer-client relationship. By contrast, cases of false testimony are more frequent, and the adversary

14. See, e.g., Mirjan R. Damaska, Presentation of Evidence and Fact Finding Precision, 123 U.Pa.L.Rev. 1083, 1088–90 (1975); and John H. Langbein, The German Advantage in Civil Procedure, 52 U.Chi.L.Rev. 823 (1985).

15. See Ferguson v. Georgia, 365 U.S. 570 (1961) (defendant may not be limited to giving unsworn testimony); and *Whiteside*, reprinted below, assuming that "a criminal defendant has a due process right to testify in his own behalf"). For a discussion of the historical transition from a rule of defendant's incompetency to testify to a rule of competency, see *Ferguson*, 365 U.S. 573–582.

16. Several cases have agreed with Justice Frankfurter, concurring in *Ferguson*, 365 U.S. at 599–600, who stated that giving a defendant the option of testifying under oath or making an unsworn statement is not a violation of constitutional rights. See, e.g., Bontempo v. Fenton, 692 F.2d 954, 959–61 (3d Cir.1982); and United States v. Robinson, 783 F.2d 64, 66 (7th Cir.1986).

system anticipates and is specifically designed to cope with false testimony through cross-examination, rebuttal, and observation of demeanor during testimony.

Freedman's position has been adopted in the District of Columbia. Its version of M.R. 3.3 gives the lawyer discretion to reveal a client's intent to bribe or intimidate judges, witnesses or jurors, but prohibits disclosure of intended client perjury of a criminal defendant or past fraud on the court when disclosure would reveal client confidences.[17]

In *Nix v. Whiteside*, reprinted below, the Court rejected the distinction:

> The crime of perjury in this setting is indistinguishable in substance from the crime of threatening or tampering with a witness or juror. A defendant who informed his counsel that he was arranging to bribe or threaten witnesses or members of the jury would have no "right" to insist on counsel's assistance or silence. Counsel would not be limited to advising against that conduct. An attorney's duty of confidentiality, which totally covers the client's admission of guilt, does not extend to a client's announced plans to engage in future criminal conduct.... [18]

Numerous commentators assert that perjury is pervasive and underprosecuted.[19] Other evidence suggests that when the crime of perjury is prosecuted it is taken very seriously by the courts. Courts are more likely to imprison a convicted perjurer than a defendant convicted of other white collar crimes.[20] Judges often express the view that perjury is a most serious crime because it thwarts and potentially destroys the search for truth.[21]

The failure to devote prosecutorial resources to prosecutions for perjury may reflect, in part, that prosecutors share Freedman's expectation that people charged with crimes will lie and that prosecutors have doubts, like his, about punishing defendants for doing so. Perjury is a difficult crime to prove. Many courts require that corroborating evidence be nearly indisputable.[22] Also, alternatives to prosecutions for perjury are seen as viable. One is to increase the sentence of a defendant who has perjured herself during trial. In United States v.

---

17. See D.C. R.Prof.Conduct, specifically Rules 1.6(c)(2); 3.3(b); 3.3(d).

18. Nix v. Whiteside, 475 U.S. 157, 174 (1986).

19. See, e.g., Stanley S. Arkin and Marc Bogatin, Perjury in Civil Litigation—The Unpunished Crime, N.Y.L.J., May 25, 1984, p. 1; Comment, Perjury: The Forgotten Offense, 65 J.Crim.L. & Criminology 361 (1974); Alfred D. Whitman, A Proposed Solution to the Problem of Perjury in Our Courts, 39 Dickinson L.Rev. 127 (1955); H. L. McClintock, What Happens to Perjurers, 24 Minn.L.Rev. 727 (1940).

20. See Sourcebook of Criminal Justice Statistics (1982), Tables 5.18 and 5.19, at 461 and 466.

21. See, e.g., United States v. Otto, 54 F.2d 277, 279 (2d Cir.1931); Edwards v. State, 577 P.2d 1380 (Wyo.1978).

22. See, e.g., United States v. Neff, 212 F.2d 297 (3d Cir.1954); United States v. Thompson, 379 F.2d 625 (6th Cir.1967).

Grayson,[23] the Supreme Court held that a judge's belief that the defendant had perjured herself is a valid sentencing consideration because it is seen as relevant to how likely the defendant is to be rehabilitated.[24]

In a subsequent article, Freedman returned to the question of how perjury can be distinguished from other crimes that corrupt court processes:

> [B]ribery is clandestine, usually not suspected when committed, and difficult to detect. Perjury, by contrast, takes place in the goldfish bowl of the courtroom, before a skeptical judge and jury, and is subject to immediate impeachment. Also, when perjury is detected by the court, the defendant faces the likelihood of an increased sentence.
>
> Further, as *Whiteside* illustrates, the lawyer ordinarily learns about the defendant's intended perjury as a result of a series of interviews with the client about the very offense that has been charged. That is, the lawyer's knowledge of the client's perjury is usually the direct outcome of lawyer-client communications about the crime that has been charged. Thus, knowledge of the "future crime" of perjury is inextricably interwoven with the crime that is the subject of the representation. A client's announcement of an intent to kill a witness, on the other hand, is a fact that stands separate and apart from communications about the crime that is the subject of the representation, such as what Whiteside did or did not see in the victim's hand just before he stabbed him.[25]

2. Client Perjury and the Whiteside Case

If the lawyer has advised and encouraged her client to testify truthfully and the client still insists upon lying, what should the lawyer do? The ethics rules require the lawyer to withdraw if necessary to avoid violating the rules or other law. M.R. 1.16(a)(1); DR 2–110(B)(2). Does withdrawal, assuming the trial has not begun and the court grants permission, end the problem?

What steps, if any, should the lawyer take before seeking to withdraw? What should the lawyer tell the court when asking permission to withdraw? Does it matter whether the case is civil or criminal? What should the lawyer do if the court denies permission to withdraw? Is it proper to seek withdrawal in the midst of a trial, if that is when the contemplated perjury is discovered? How certain should the lawyer be that the testimony will be perjurious before taking other action? What if the lawyer discovers the perjury after it has been offered?

---

23. 438 U.S. 41 (1978). Sentence enhancement as a consequence of false testimony continues under the sentencing guidelines. See United States v. Dunnigan, 113 S.Ct. 1111 (1993).

24. See also David W. Eagle, Civil Remedies for Perjury: A Proposal for a Tort Action, 19 Ariz.L.Rev. 349, 369–72 (1977); and the note on perjury as a tort, below at p. 412.

25. Monroe H. Freedman, Client Confidences and Client Perjury: Some Unanswered Questions, 136 U.Pa.L.Rev. 1939, 1951 (1988).

self defense + perjury

NIX v. WHITESIDE

Supreme Court of the United States, 1986.
475 U.S. 157, 106 S.Ct. 988, 89 L.Ed.2d 123.

CHIEF JUSTICE BURGER delivered the opinion of the Court.

Issue

We granted certiorari to decide whether the Sixth Amendment right of a criminal defendant to assistance of counsel is violated when an attorney refuses to cooperate with the defendant in presenting perjured testimony at his trial.[1]

I

A

murder conviction

Whiteside was convicted of second degree murder by a jury verdict which was affirmed by the Iowa courts. The killing took place on February 8, 1977 in Cedar Rapids, Iowa. Whiteside and two others went to one Calvin Love's apartment late that night, seeking marihuana. Love was in bed when Whiteside and his companions arrived; an argument between Whiteside and Love over the marihuana ensued. At one point, Love directed his girlfriend to get his "piece," and at another point got up, then returned to his bed. According to Whiteside's testimony, Love then started to reach under his pillow and moved toward Whiteside. Whiteside stabbed Love in the chest, inflicting a fatal wound.

Statement to Atty

Whiteside was charged with murder, and when counsel was appointed he objected to the lawyer initially appointed, claiming that he felt uncomfortable with a lawyer who had formerly been a prosecutor. Gary L. Robinson was then appointed and immediately began investigation. Whiteside gave him a statement that he had stabbed Love as the latter "was pulling a pistol from underneath the pillow on the bed." Upon questioning by Robinson, however, Whiteside indicated that he had not actually seen a gun, but that he was convinced that Love had a gun. No pistol was found on the premises; shortly after the police search following the stabbing, which had revealed no weapon, the victim's family had removed all of the victim's possessions from the apartment. Robinson interviewed Whiteside's companions who were present during the stabbing and none had seen a gun during the incident. Robinson advised Whiteside that the existence of a gun was

No gun found

1. Although courts universally condemn an attorney's assisting in presenting perjury, Courts of Appeals have taken varying approaches on how to deal with a client's insistence on presenting perjured testimony. The Seventh Circuit, for example, has held that an attorney's refusal to call the defendant as a witness did not render the conviction constitutionally infirm where the refusal to call the defendant was based on the attorney's belief that the defendant would commit perjury. United States v. Curtis, 742 F.2d 1070 (CA7 1984). The Third Circuit found a violation of the Sixth Amendment where the attorney could not state any basis for her belief that defendant's proposed alibi testimony was perjured. United States ex rel. Wilcox v. Johnson, 555 F.2d 115 (CA3 1977). See also Lowery v. Cardwell, 575 F.2d 727 (CA9 1978) (withdrawal request in the middle of a bench trial, immediately following defendant's testimony).

not necessary to establish the claim of self defense, and that only a reasonable belief that the victim had a gun nearby was necessary even though no gun was actually present.

Until shortly before trial, Whiteside consistently stated to Robinson that he had not actually seen a gun, but that he was convinced that Love had a gun in his hand. About a week before trial, during preparation for direct examination, Whiteside for the first time told Robinson and his associate Donna Paulsen that he had seen something "metallic" in Love's hand. When asked about this, Whiteside responded that

> "in Howard Cook's case there was a gun. If I don't say I saw a gun I'm dead."

Robinson told Whiteside that such testimony would be perjury and repeated that it was not necessary to prove that a gun was available but only that Whiteside reasonably believed that he was in danger. On Whiteside's insisting that he would testify that he saw "something-metallic" Robinson told him, according to Robinson's testimony,

> "we could not allow him to [testify falsely] because that would be perjury, and as officers of the court we would be suborning perjury if we allowed him to do it; ... I advised him that if he did do that it would be my duty to advise the Court of what he was doing and that I felt he was committing perjury; also, that I probably would be allowed to attempt to impeach that particular testimony."

Robinson also indicated he would seek to withdraw from the representation if Whiteside insisted on committing perjury.[2]

Whiteside testified in his own defense at trial and stated that he "knew" that Love had a gun and that he believed Love was reaching for a gun and he had acted swiftly in self defense. On cross examination, he admitted that he had not actually seen a gun in Love's hand. Robinson presented evidence that Love had been seen with a sawed-off shotgun on other occasions, that the police search of the apartment may have been careless, and that the victim's family had removed everything from the apartment shortly after the crime. Robinson presented this evidence to show a basis for Whiteside's asserted fear that Love had a gun.

The jury returned a verdict of second-degree murder and Whiteside moved for a new trial, claiming that he had been deprived of a fair trial by Robinson's admonitions not to state that he saw a gun or "something metallic." The trial court held a hearing, heard testimony by White-

---

2. Whiteside's version of the events at this pretrial meeting is considerably more cryptic:

"Q. And as you went over the questions, did the two of you come into conflict with regard to whether or not there was a weapon?

"A. I couldn't—I couldn't say a conflict. But I got the impression at one time that maybe if I didn't go along with—with what was happening, that it was no gun being involved, maybe that he will pull out of my trial."

side and Robinson, and denied the motion. The trial court made specific findings that the facts were as related by Robinson.

The Supreme Court of Iowa affirmed respondent's conviction. State v. Whiteside, 272 N.W.2d 468 (1978). That court held that the right to have counsel present all appropriate defenses does not extend to using perjury, and that an attorney's duty to a client does not extend to assisting a client in committing perjury. Relying on DR 7–102(A)(4) of the Iowa Code of Professional Responsibility for Lawyers, which expressly prohibits an attorney from using perjured testimony, and Iowa Code § 721.2 (now Iowa Code § 720.3 (1985)), which criminalizes subornation of perjury, the Iowa court concluded that not only were Robinson's actions permissible, but were required. The court commended "both Mr. Robinson and Ms. Paulsen for the high ethical manner in which this matter was handled."

B

Whiteside then petitioned for a writ of habeas corpus in the United States District Court for the Southern District of Iowa. In that petition Whiteside alleged that he had been denied effective assistance of counsel and of his right to present a defense by Robinson's refusal to allow him to testify as he had proposed. The District Court denied the writ. Accepting the State trial court's factual finding that Whiteside's intended testimony would have been perjurious, it concluded that there could be no grounds for habeas relief since there is no constitutional right to present a perjured defense.

The United States Court of Appeals for the Eighth Circuit reversed and directed that the writ of habeas corpus be granted. Whiteside v. Scurr, 744 F.2d 1323 (CA8 1984). The Court of Appeals accepted the findings of the trial judge, affirmed by the Iowa Supreme Court, that trial counsel believed with good cause that Whiteside would testify falsely and acknowledged that under Harris v. New York, 401 U.S. 222 (1971), a criminal defendant's privilege to testify in his own behalf does not include a right to commit perjury. Nevertheless, the court reasoned that an intent to commit perjury, communicated to counsel, does not alter a defendant's right to effective assistance of counsel and that Robinson's admonition to Whiteside that he would inform the court of Whiteside's perjury constituted a threat to violate the attorney's duty to preserve client confidences. According to the Court of Appeals, this threatened violation of client confidences breached the standards of effective representation set down in Strickland v. Washington, 466 U.S. 668 (1984). The court also concluded that *Strickland*'s prejudice requirement was satisfied by an implication of prejudice from the conflict between Robinson's duty of loyalty to his client and his ethical duties. A petition for rehearing en banc was denied.... We granted certiorari ... and we reverse.

U. S. S. Ct
Reversed

II

A

The right of an accused to testify in his defense is of relatively recent origin. Until the latter part of the preceding century, criminal defendants in this country, as at common law, were considered to be disqualified from giving sworn testimony at their own trial by reason of their interest as a party to the case....

By the end of the nineteenth century, however, the disqualification was finally abolished by statute in most states and in the federal courts.... Although this Court has never explicitly held that a criminal defendant has a due process right to testify in his own behalf, cases in several Circuits have so held and the right has long been assumed....

B

effective assistance of counsel

In *Strickland v. Washington,* we held that to obtain relief by way of federal habeas corpus on a claim of a deprivation of effective assistance of counsel under the Sixth Amendment, the movant must establish both serious attorney error and prejudice....

In *Strickland,* we acknowledged that the Sixth Amendment does not require any particular response by counsel to a problem that may arise. Rather, the Sixth Amendment inquiry is into whether the attorney's conduct was "reasonably effective." A court reviewing a claim of ineffective assistance must "indulge a strong presumption that counsel's conduct falls within the wide range of reasonable professional assistance." In giving shape to the perimeters of this range of reasonable professional assistance, *Strickland* mandates that

> "Prevailing norms of practice as reflected in American Bar Association Standards and the like, ... are guides to determining what is reasonable, but they are only guides."

Rol

Under the *Strickland* standard, breach of an ethical standard does not necessarily make out a denial of the Sixth Amendment guarantee of assistance of counsel. When examining attorney conduct, a court must be careful not to narrow the wide range of conduct acceptable under the Sixth Amendment so restrictively as to constitutionalize particular standards of professional conduct and thereby intrude into the State's proper authority to define and apply the standards of professional conduct applicable to those it admits to practice in its courts. In some future case challenging attorney conduct in the course of a state court trial, we may need to define with greater precision the weight to be given to recognized canons of ethics, the standards established by the State in statutes or professional codes, and the Sixth Amendment, in defining the proper scope and limits on that conduct. Here we need not face that question, since virtually all of the sources speak with one voice.

C

Issue

We turn next to the question presented: the definition of the range of "reasonable professional" responses to a criminal defendant client

what is reasonable professional response to criminal D who perjures?

who informs counsel that he will perjure himself on the stand. We must determine whether, in this setting, Robinson's conduct fell within the wide range of professional responses to threatened client perjury acceptable under the Sixth Amendment.

In *Strickland*, we recognized counsel's duty of loyalty and his "overarching duty to advocate the defendant's cause," Plainly, that duty is limited to legitimate, lawful conduct compatible with the very nature of a trial as a search for truth. Although counsel must take all reasonable lawful means to attain the objectives of the client, counsel is precluded from taking steps or in any way assisting the client in presenting false evidence or otherwise violating the law. This principle has consistently been recognized in most unequivocal terms by expositors of the norms of professional conduct since the first Canons of Professional Ethics were adopted by the American Bar Association in 1908. The 1908 Canon 32 provided that

> "No client, corporate or individual, however powerful, nor any cause, civil or political, however important, is entitled to receive nor should any lawyer render any service or advice involving disloyalty to the law whose ministers we are, or disrespect of the judicial office, which we are bound to uphold, or corruption of any person or persons exercising a public office or private trust, or deception or betrayal of the public.... He must ... observe and advise his client to observe the statute law...."

Of course, this Canon did no more than articulate centuries of accepted standards of conduct. Similarly, Canon 37, adopted in 1928, explicitly acknowledges as an exception to the attorney's duty of confidentiality a client's announced attention to commit a crime:

> "The announced intention of a client to commit a crime is not included within the confidences which [the attorney] is bound to respect."

These principles have been carried through to contemporary codifications of an attorney's professional responsibility. Disciplinary Rule 7–102 of the Model Code of Professional Responsibility (1980), entitled "Representing a Client Within the Bounds of the Law," provides that

> "(A) In his representation of a client, a lawyer shall not: ...
>
> > "(4) Knowingly use perjured testimony or false evidence....
> >
> > "(7) Counsel or assist his client in conduct that the lawyer knows to be illegal or fraudulent."

This provision has been adopted by Iowa, and is binding on all lawyers who appear in its courts. See Iowa Code of Professional Responsibility for Lawyers (1985). The more recent Model Rules of Professional Conduct (1983) similarly admonish attorneys to obey all laws in the course of representing a client:

"Rule 1.2 Scope of Representation

... "(d) A lawyer shall not counsel a client to engage, or assist a client, in conduct that the lawyer knows is criminal or fraudulent...."

Both the Model Code ... and the Model Rules ... also adopt the specific exception from the attorney-client privilege for disclosure of perjury that his client intends to commit or has committed. DR 4–101(C)(3) (intention of client to commit a crime); Rule 3.3 (lawyer has duty to disclose falsity of evidence even if disclosure compromises client confidences). Indeed, both the Model Code and the Model Rules do not merely *authorize* disclosure by counsel of client perjury; they *require* such disclosure. See Rule 3.3(a)(4); DR 7–102(B)(1); Committee on Professional Ethics and Conduct of Iowa State Bar Association v. Crary, 245 N.W.2d 298 (Iowa 1976).

These standards confirm that the legal profession has accepted that an attorney's ethical duty to advance the interests of his client is limited by an equally solemn duty to comply with the law and standards of professional conduct; it specifically ensures that the client may not use false evidence. This special duty of an attorney to prevent and disclose frauds upon the court derives from the recognition that perjury is as much a crime as tampering with witnesses or jurors by way of promises and threats, and undermines the administration of justice.

The offense of perjury was a crime recognized at common law, and has been made a felony in most states by statute, including Iowa. An attorney who aids false testimony by questioning a witness when perjurious responses can be anticipated, risks prosecution for suborntion of perjury under Iowa Code § 720.3 (1985).

It is universally agreed that at a minimum the attorney's first duty when confronted with a proposal for perjurious testimony is to attempt to dissuade the client from the unlawful course of conduct. Model Rules of Professional Conduct, Rule 3.3, Comment; Wolfram, Client Perjury, 50 S.Cal.L.Rev. 809, 846 (1977). A statement directly in point is found in the commentary to the Model Rules of Professional Conduct under the heading "False Evidence" [M.R. 3.3, Comment ¶ 5]:

"When false evidence is offered by the client, however, a conflict may arise between the lawyer's duty to keep the client's revelations confidential and the duty of candor to the court. Upon ascertaining that material evidence is false, the lawyer *should seek to persuade the client that the evidence should not be offered* or, if it has been offered, that its false character should immediately be disclosed." (emphasis added).

The commentary thus also suggests that an attorney's revelation of his client's perjury to the court is a professionally responsible and acceptable response to the conduct of a client who has actually given perjured testimony. Similarly, the Model Rules and the commentary, as well as the Code of Professional Responsibility adopted in Iowa expressly permit withdrawal from representation as an appropriate response of an attorney when the client threatens to commit perjury. Model Rules of Professional Conduct, Rule 1.16(a)(1), Rule 1.6, Comment (1983); Code of Professional Responsibility, DR 2–110(B), (C) (1980). Withdrawal of counsel when this situation arises at trial gives rise to many difficult questions including possible mistrial and claims of double jeopardy.[6]

The essence of the brief *amicus* of the American Bar Association reviewing practices long accepted by ethical lawyers, is that under no circumstance may a lawyer either advocate or passively tolerate a client's giving false testimony. This, of course, is consistent with the governance of trial conduct in what we have long called "a search for truth." The suggestion sometimes made that "a lawyer must believe his client not judge him" in no sense means a lawyer can honorably be a party to or in any way give aid to presenting known perjury.

D

Considering Robinson's representation of respondent in light of these accepted norms of professional conduct, we discern no failure to adhere to reasonable professional standards that would in any sense make out a deprivation of the Sixth Amendment right to counsel. Whether Robinson's conduct is seen as a successful attempt to dissuade his client from committing the crime of perjury, or whether seen as a "threat" to withdraw from representation and disclose the illegal scheme, Robinson's representation of Whiteside falls well within accepted standards of professional conduct and the range of reasonable professional conduct acceptable under *Strickland*.

. . .

The Court of Appeals' holding that Robinson's "action deprived [Whiteside] of due process and effective assistance of counsel" is not supported by the record since Robinson's action, at most, deprived Whiteside of his contemplated perjury. Nothing counsel did in any way undermined Whiteside's claim that he believed the victim was

---

6. In the evolution of the contemporary standards promulgated by the American Bar Association, an early draft reflects a compromise suggesting that when the disclosure of intended perjury is made during the course of trial, when withdrawal of counsel would raise difficult questions of a mistrial holding, counsel had the option to let the defendant take the stand but decline to affirmatively assist the presentation of perjury by traditional direct examination. Instead, counsel would stand mute while the defendant undertook to present the false version in narrative form in his own words unaided by any direct examination. This conduct was thought to be a signal at least to the presiding judge that the attorney considered the testimony to be false and was seeking to disassociate himself from that course. Additionally, counsel would not be permitted to discuss the known false testimony in closing arguments. See ABA Standards for Criminal Justice, 4–7.7 (2d ed. 1980). Most courts treating the subject rejected this approach and insisted on a more rigorous standard, see, e.g., United States v. Curtis, 742 F.2d 1070 (CA7 1984); McKissick v. United States, 379 F.2d 754 (CA5 1967), aff'd after remand, 398 F.2d 342 (CA5 1968); Dodd v. Florida Bar, 118 So.2d 17, 19 (Fla.1960). The Eighth Circuit in this case and the Ninth Circuit have expressed approval of the "free narrative" standards. Whiteside v. Scurr, 744 F.2d 1323, 1331 (CA8 1984); Lowery v. Cardwell, 575 F.2d 727 (CA9 1978).

The Rule finally promulgated in the current Model Rules of Professional Conduct rejects any participation or passive role whatever by counsel in allowing perjury to be presented without challenge.

reaching for a gun. Similarly, the record gives no support for holding that Robinson's action "also impermissibly compromised [Whiteside's] right to testify in his own defense by conditioning continued representation ... and confidentiality upon [Whiteside's] *restricted* testimony." The record in fact shows the contrary: (a) that Whiteside did testify, and (b) he was "restricted" or restrained only from testifying falsely and was aided by Robinson in developing the basis for the fear that Love was reaching for a gun. Robinson divulged no client communications until he was compelled to do so in response to Whiteside's posttrial challenge to the quality of his performance. We see this as a case in which the attorney successfully dissuaded the client from committing the crime of perjury.

Paradoxically, even while accepting the conclusion of the Iowa trial court that Whiteside's proposed testimony would have been a criminal act, the Court of Appeals held that Robinson's efforts to persuade Whiteside not to commit that crime were improper, *first*, as forcing an impermissible choice between the right to counsel and the right to testify; and *second*, as compromising client confidences because of Robinson's threat to disclose the contemplated perjury.

. . .

Whatever the scope of a constitutional right to testify, it is elementary that such a right does not extend to testifying *falsely*. In *Harris v. New York*, we assumed the right of an accused to testify "in his own defense, or to refuse to do so" and went on to hold that

> "that privilege cannot be construed to include the right to commit perjury. See United States v. Knox, 396 U.S. 77 (1969); cf. Dennis v. United States, 384 U.S. 855 (1966). Having voluntarily taken the stand, petitioner was under an obligation to speak truthfully...." 401 U.S., at 225.

In *Harris* we held the defendant could be impeached by prior contrary statements which had been ruled inadmissible under Miranda v. Arizona, 384 U.S. 436 (1966). *Harris* and other cases make it crystal clear that there is no right whatever—constitutional or otherwise—for a defendant to use false evidence. See also United States v. Havens, 446 U.S. 620, 626–627 (1980).

The paucity of authority on the subject of any such "right" may be explained by the fact that such a notion has never been responsibly advanced; the right to counsel includes no right to have a lawyer who will cooperate with planned perjury. A lawyer who would so cooperate would be at risk of prosecution for suborning perjury, and disciplinary proceedings, including suspension or disbarment.

Robinson's admonitions to his client can in no sense be said to have forced respondent into an *impermissible* choice between his right to counsel and his right to testify as he proposed for there was no *permissible* choice to testify falsely. For defense counsel to take steps to persuade a criminal defendant to testify truthfully, or to withdraw, deprives the defendant of neither his right to counsel nor the right to testify truthfully....

On this record, the accused enjoyed continued representation within the bounds of reasonable professional conduct and did in fact exercise his right to testify; at most he was denied the right to have the assistance of counsel in the presentation of false testimony. Similarly, we can discern no breach of professional duty in Robinson's admonition to respondent that he would disclose respondent's perjury to the court. The crime of perjury in this setting is indistinguishable in substance from the crime of threatening or tampering with a witness or a juror. A defendant who informed his counsel that he was arranging to bribe or threaten witnesses or members of the jury would have no "right" to insist on counsel's assistance or silence. Counsel would not be limited to advising against that conduct. An attorney's duty of confidentiality, which totally covers the client's admission of guilt, does not extend to a client's announced plans to engage in future criminal conduct.... In short, the responsibility of an ethical lawyer, as an officer of the court and a key component of a system of justice, dedicated to a search for truth, is essentially the same whether the client announces an intention to bribe or threaten witnesses or jurors or to commit or procure perjury. No system of justice worthy of the name can tolerate a lesser standard.

The rule adopted by the Court of Appeals, which seemingly would require an attorney to remain silent while his client committed perjury, is wholly incompatible with the established standards of ethical conduct and the laws of Iowa and contrary to professional standards promulgated by that State. The position advocated by petitioner, on the contrary, is wholly consistent with the Iowa standards of professional conduct and law, with the overwhelming majority of courts,[8] and with codes of professional ethics. Since there has been no breach of any recognized professional duty, it follows that there can be no deprivation of the right to assistance of counsel under the *Strickland* standard.

E

We hold that, as a matter of law, counsel's conduct complained of here cannot establish the prejudice required for relief under the second strand of the *Strickland* inquiry....

Whether he was persuaded or compelled to desist from perjury, Whiteside has no valid claim that confidence in the result of his trial has been diminished by his desisting from the contemplated perjury. Even if we were to assume that the jury might have believed his perjury, it does not follow that Whiteside was prejudiced.

---

8. See United States v. Curtis, 742 F.2d 1070 (CA7 1984); Committee on Professional Ethics v. Crary, 245 N.W.2d 298 (Iowa 1976); State v. Robinson, 290 N.C. 56, 224 S.E.2d 174 (1976); Thornton v. United States, 357 A.2d 429 (D.C.1976); State v. Henderson, 205 Kan. 231, 468 P.2d 136 (1970); McKissick v. United States, 379 F.2d 754 (CA5 1967); In re King, 7 Utah 2d 258, 322 P.2d 1095 (1958); In re Carroll, 244 S.W.2d 474 (Ky.1951); Hinds v. State Bar, 19 Cal.2d 87, 119 P.2d 134 (1941). Contra, Whiteside v. Scurr, 744 F.2d 1323 (CA8 1984); Lowery v. Cardwell, 575 F.2d 727 (CA9 1978).

In his attempt to evade the prejudice requirement of *Strickland*, Whiteside relies on cases involving conflicting loyalties of counsel. In Cuyler v. Sullivan, 446 U.S. 335 (1980), we held that a defendant could obtain relief without pointing to a specific prejudicial default on the part of his counsel, provided it is established that the attorney was "actively represent[ing] conflicting interests."

Here, there was indeed a "conflict," but of a quite different kind; it was one imposed on the attorney by the client's proposal to commit the crime of fabricating testimony without which, as he put it, "I'm dead." This is not remotely the kind of conflict of interests dealt with in *Cuyler v. Sullivan*. Even in that case we did not suggest that all multiple representations necessarily resulted in an active conflict rendering the representation constitutionally infirm. If a "conflict" between a client's proposal and counsel's ethical obligation gives rise to a presumption that counsel's assistance was prejudicially ineffective, every guilty criminal's conviction would be suspect if the defendant had sought to obtain an acquittal by illegal means. Can anyone doubt what practices and problems would be spawned by such a rule and what volumes of litigation it would generate?

Whiteside's attorney treated Whiteside's proposed perjury in accord with professional standards, and since Whiteside's truthful testimony could not have prejudiced the result of his trial, the Court of Appeals was in error to direct the issuance of a writ of habeas corpus and must be reversed.

JUSTICE BRENNAN, concurring in the judgment.

This Court has no constitutional authority to establish rules of ethical conduct for lawyers practicing in the state courts. Nor does the Court enjoy any statutory grant of jurisdiction over legal ethics.

Accordingly, it is not surprising that the Court emphasizes that it "must be careful not to narrow the wide range of professional conduct acceptable under the Sixth Amendment so restrictively as to constitutionalize particular standards of professional conduct and thereby intrude into the State's proper authority to define and apply the standards of professional conduct applicable to those it admits to practice in its courts." I read this as saying in another way that the Court *cannot* tell the states or the lawyers in the states how to behave in their courts, unless and until federal rights are violated.

Unfortunately, the Court seems unable to resist the temptation of sharing with the legal community its vision of ethical conduct. But let there be no mistake: the Court's essay regarding what constitutes the correct response to a criminal client's suggestion that he will perjure himself is pure discourse without force of law. As Justice Blackmun observes, *that* issue is a thorny one, but it is not an issue presented by this case. Lawyers, judges, bar associations, students and others should understand that the problem has not now been "decided."

I join Justice Blackmun's concurrence because I agree that respondent has failed to prove the kind of prejudice necessary to make out a claim under *Strickland.*

JUSTICE BLACKMUN, with whom JUSTICE BRENNAN, JUSTICE MARSHALL, and JUSTICE STEVENS join, concurring in the judgment.

How a defense attorney ought to act when faced with a client who intends to commit perjury at trial has long been a controversial issue.[1] But I do not believe that a federal habeas corpus case challenging a state criminal conviction is an appropriate vehicle for attempting to resolve this thorny problem. When a defendant argues that he was denied effective assistance of counsel because his lawyer dissuaded him from committing perjury, the only question properly presented to this Court is whether the lawyer's actions deprived the defendant of the fair trial which the Sixth Amendment is meant to guarantee. Since I believe that the respondent in this case suffered no injury justifying federal habeas relief, I concur in the Court's judgment.

. . .

B

The Court approaches this case as if the performance and prejudice standard requires us in every case to determine "the perimeters of [the] range of reasonable professional assistance," but Strickland v. Washington explicitly contemplates [that "a court need not determine whether counsel's performance was deficient before examining the prejudice suffered by the defendant as a result of the alleged deficiencies...."]

... In this case, respondent has failed to show any legally cognizable prejudice. Nor, as is discussed below, is this a case in which prejudice should be presumed.

The touchstone of a claim of prejudice is an allegation that counsel's behavior did something "to deprive the defendant of a fair trial, a trial whose result is reliable." *Strickland* .... The only effect Robinson's threat had on Whiteside's trial is that Whiteside did not testify, falsely, that he saw a gun in Love's hand.[4] Thus, this Court must ask whether its confidence in the outcome of Whiteside's trial is in any way

1. See, e.g., Callan and David, Professional Responsibility and the Duty of Confidentiality: Disclosure of Client Misconduct in an Adversary System, 29 Rutgers L.Rev. 332 (1976); Rieger, Client Perjury: A Proposed Resolution of the Constitutional and Ethical Issues, 70 Minn.L.Rev. 121 (1985); compare, e.g., Freedman, Professional Responsibility of the Criminal Defense Lawyer: The Three Hardest Questions, 64 Mich.L.Rev. 1469 (1966), and ABA Standards for Criminal Justice, Proposed Standard 4–7.7 (2d ed. 1980) (approved by the Standing Committing on Association Standards for Criminal Justice, but not yet submitted to the House of Delegates), with Noonan, The Purposes of Advocacy and the Limits of Confidentiality, 64 Mich.L.Rev. 1485 (1966), and ABA Model Rules of Professional Conduct, Rule 3.3 and comment, at 66–67 (1983).

4. This is not to say that a lawyer's threat to reveal his client's confidences may never have other effects on a defendant's trial. Cf. United States ex rel. Wilcox v. Johnson, 555 F.2d 115 (CA3 1977) (finding a violation of Sixth Amendment when an attorney's threat to reveal client's purported perjury caused defendant not to take the stand at all).

undermined by the knowledge that he refrained from presenting false testimony.

... [T]he Court has viewed a defendant's use of [perjured] testimony as so antithetical to our system of justice that it has permitted the prosecution to introduce otherwise inadmissible evidence to combat it.... The proposition that presenting false evidence could contribute to (or that withholding such evidence could detract from) the reliability of a criminal trial is simply untenable.

... [T]he privilege every criminal defendant has to testify in his own defense "cannot be construed to include the right to commit perjury." Harris v. New York, 401 U.S., at 225. To the extent that Whiteside's claim rests on the assertion that he would have been acquitted had he been able to testify falsely, Whiteside claims a right the law simply does not recognize. "A defendant has no entitlement to the luck of a lawless decisionmaker, even if a lawless decision cannot be reviewed." *Strickland* .... Since Whiteside was deprived of neither a fair trial nor any of the specific constitutional rights designed to guarantee a fair trial, he has suffered no prejudice.

The Court of Appeals erred in concluding that prejudice should have been presumed. Strickland v. Washington found such a presumption appropriate in a case where an attorney labored under " 'an actual conflict of interest [that] adversely affected his ... performance,' '.... In this case, however, no actual conflict existed. I have already discussed why Whiteside had no right to Robinson's help in presenting perjured testimony. Moreover, Whiteside has identified no right to insist that Robinson keep confidential a plan to commit perjury.... Here, Whiteside had no legitimate interest that conflicted with Robinson's obligations not to suborn perjury and to adhere to the Iowa Code of Professional Responsibility.

In addition, the lawyer's interest in not presenting perjured testimony was entirely consistent with Whiteside's best interest. If Whiteside had lied on the stand, he would have risked a future perjury prosecution. Moreover, his testimony would have been contradicted by the testimony of other eyewitnesses and by the fact that no gun was ever found. In light of that impeachment, the jury might have concluded that Whiteside lied as well about his lack of premeditation and thus might have convicted him of first-degree murder. And if the judge believed that Whiteside had lied, he could have taken Whiteside's perjury into account in setting the sentence. United States v. Grayson, 438 U.S. 41, 52–54 (1978). In the face of these dangers, an attorney could reasonably conclude that dissuading his client from committing perjury was in the client's best interest and comported with standards of professional responsibility.[7] In short, Whiteside failed to show the

---

7. This is not to say that an attorney's ethical obligations will never conflict with a defendant's right to effective assistance. For example, an attorney who has previously represented one of the State's witnesses has a continuing obligation to that former client not to reveal confidential information received during the course of the prior representa-

kind of conflict that poses a danger to the values of zealous and loyal representation embodied in the Sixth Amendment. A presumption of prejudice is therefore unwarranted.

C

In light of respondent's failure to show any cognizable prejudice, I see no need to "grade counsel's performance." *Strickland* .... The only federal issue in this case is whether Robinson's behavior deprived Whiteside of the effective assistance of counsel; it is not whether Robinson's behavior conformed to any particular code of legal ethics.

Whether an attorney's response to what he sees as a client's plan to commit perjury violates a defendant's Sixth Amendment rights may depend on many factors: how certain the attorney is that the proposed testimony is false, the stage of the proceedings at which the attorney discovers the plan, or the ways in which the attorney may be able to dissuade his client, to name just three. The complex interaction of factors, which is likely to vary from case to case, makes inappropriate a blanket rule that defense attorneys must reveal, or threaten to reveal, a client's anticipated perjury to the court. Except in the rarest of cases, attorneys who adopt "the role of the judge or jury to determine the facts," United States ex rel. Wilcox v. Johnson, 555 F.2d 115, 122 (CA3 1977), pose a danger of depriving their clients of the zealous and loyal advocacy required by the Sixth Amendment.[8]

I therefore am troubled by the Court's implicit adoption of a set of standards of professional responsibility for attorneys in state criminal proceedings. The States, of course, do have a compelling interest in the integrity of their criminal trials that can justify regulating the length to which an attorney may go in seeking his client's acquittal. But the American Bar Association's implicit suggestion in its brief *amicus curiae* that the Court find that the Association's Model Rules of Professional Conduct should govern an attorney's responsibilities is addressed to the wrong audience. It is for the States to decide how attorneys should conduct themselves in state criminal proceedings, and this Court's responsibility extends only to ensuring that the restrictions a State enacts do not infringe a defendant's federal constitutional rights. Thus, I would follow the suggestion made in the joint brief *amici curiae*

tion. That continuing duty could conflict with his obligation to his present client, the defendant, to cross-examine the State's witnesses zealously. See Lowenthal, Successive Representation by Criminal Lawyers, 93 Yale L.J. 1 (1983).

8. A comparison of this case with *Wilcox* is illustrative. Here, Robinson testified in detail to the factors that led him to conclude that respondent's assertion he had seen a gun was false. The Iowa Supreme Court found "good cause" and "strong support" for Robinson's conclusion. State v. Whiteside, 272 N.W.2d at 471. Moreover, Robinson gave credence to those parts of Whiteside's account which, although he found them implausible and unsubstantiated, were not clearly false. By contrast, in *Wilcox*, where defense counsel actually informed the judge that she believed her client intended to lie and where her threat to withdraw in the middle of the trial led the defendant not to take the stand at all, the Court of Appeals found "no evidence on the record of this case indicating that Mr. Wilcox intended to perjure himself," and characterized counsel's beliefs as "private conjectures about the guilt or innocence of [her] client." 522 F.2d at 122.

filed by 37 States at the certiorari stage that we allow the States to maintain their "differing approaches" to a complex ethical question. The signal merit of asking first whether a defendant has shown any adverse prejudicial effect before inquiring into his attorney's performance is that it avoids unnecessary federal interference in a State's regulation of its bar. Because I conclude that the respondent in this case failed to show such an effect, I join the Court's judgment that he is not entitled to federal habeas relief.

JUSTICE STEVENS, concurring in the judgment.

Justice Holmes taught us that a word is but the skin of a living thought. A "fact" may also have a life of its own. From the perspective of an appellate judge, after a case has been tried and the evidence has been sifted by another judge, a particular fact may be as clear and certain as a piece of crystal or a small diamond. A trial lawyer, however, must often deal with mixtures of sand and clay. Even a pebble that seems clear enough at first glance may take on a different hue in a handful of gravel.

As we view this case, it appears perfectly clear that respondent intended to commit perjury, that his lawyer knew it, and that the lawyer had a duty—both to the court and to his client, for perjured testimony can ruin an otherwise meritorious case—to take extreme measures to prevent the perjury from occurring. The lawyer was successful and, from our unanimous and remote perspective, it is now pellucidly clear that the client suffered no "legally cognizable prejudice."

Nevertheless, beneath the surface of this case there are areas of uncertainty that cannot be resolved today. A lawyer's certainty that a change in his client's recollection is a harbinger of intended perjury—as well as judicial review of such apparent certainty—should be tempered by the realization that, after reflection, the most honest witness may recall (or sincerely believe he recalls) details that he previously overlooked. Similarly, the post-trial review of a lawyer's pre-trial threat to expose perjury that had not yet been committed—and, indeed, may have been prevented by the threat—is by no means the same as review of the way in which such a threat may actually have been carried out. Thus, one can be convinced—as I am—that this lawyer's actions were a proper way to provide his client with effective representation without confronting the much more difficult questions of what a lawyer must, should, or may do after his client has given testimony that the lawyer does not believe. The answer to such questions may well be colored by the particular circumstances attending the actual event and its aftermath.

Because Justice Blackmun has preserved such questions for another day, and because I do not understand him to imply any adverse criticism of this lawyer's representation of his client, I join his opinion concurring in the judgment.

"Court Truth" and "Real Truth"

Did Whiteside see a metallic object in the victim's hand? How do we "know" what he did or didn't see? How did Robinson, Whiteside's lawyer, know that his client intended to perjure himself? How does the Court in *Whiteside* conclude that the testimony would have been perjurious? Justice Stevens' concurrence concentrates on the difficulty of being sure that a client intends to commit perjury. How can Justice Stevens be sure that Whiteside did not "after reflection ... sincerely believe" that he saw a metallic object?

What is the relationship between "court truth" and "real truth?" Although there were questions from the bench in *Whiteside* on how a lawyer is to "know" that the client intends to commit perjury, the opinions did not resolve the question of how certain a lawyer must be before acting on her judgment that the client will perjure herself.[26] This issue is discussed below at p. 375.

Persuading a Client not to Testify Falsely

What are the holdings in *Whiteside?* One holding, in which all nine justices concur, concerns the prejudice prong of the *Strickland* test; the other holding, in which five justices join, concerns the lawyer-performance aspect of that test. Is Justice Brennan correct in stating, in his concurrence, that "the Court's essay regarding what constitutes the correct response to a criminal client's suggestion that he will perjure himself is pure discourse without force of law?"

Whiteside itself does not say what a lawyer *must* do when faced with client perjury in a criminal case. It merely states what a lawyer may do, in conformity with the state's ethical standards, without unconstitutionally violating the defendant's rights. What action by a lawyer would run afoul of the defendant's constitutional rights?

Ethics Rules on False Evidence

Chief Justice Burger's statement that "both the Model Code and the Model Rules do not merely *authorize* disclosure by counsel of client perjury; they *require* such disclosure" has been severely criticized.[27] Is he correct? Does the answer under the Model Code depend upon the

---

26. See Monroe H. Freedman, Client Confidences and Client Perjury: Some Unanswered Questions, 136 U.Pa.L.Rev. 1939 (1988); and Brent Appel, The Limited Impact of *Nix v. Whiteside* on Attorney–Client Relations, 136 U.Pa.L.Rev. 1913 (1988) (both describing the oral argument in *Whiteside*).

27. See Carl A. Auerbach, What Are Law Clerks For?: Comments on *Nix v. Whiteside*, 23 San Diego L.Rev. 979, 982–87 (1986) (arguing that the statement is inaccurate and rests on an "unsupported dictum in a civil, not a criminal case"—the *Crary* case discussed below); and Monroe H. Freedman, The Aftermath of *Nix v. Whiteside*: Slamming the Lid on Pandora's Box, 23 Crim.L.Bull. 25, 26–27 (1987) (discussing the "manifest errors" in Chief Justice Burger's opinion).

assumption that is made concerning whether a state adopted the 1974 "except" clause? What would a fully accurate statement of current ethics law be? The Code provision on client fraud on the court is DR 7–102(B)(1), which also covers client fraud on third parties.[28] In Chapter 4, we discussed the ambiguity of DR 7–102(B)(1) as it applies to client fraud on third parties, see p. 295 above, and that discussion is equally applicable to DR 7–102(B)(1)'s treatment of client fraud on the court.

The ABA ethics opinions on fraud on the court, like the ethics opinions on fraud on third parties, have added to the confusion. Despite the language of DR 7–102(B)(1), i.e., "lawyer ... shall reveal ...", ABA ethics opinions took the position that when the lawyer learns of the client's false testimony after the fact, the lawyer may not disclose,[29] but has a duty to cease further representation of the client.[30] When the lawyer learns of the client's *intent* to commit perjury, the lawyer must advise the client that the lawyer is bound to take one of two courses of action: withdraw prior to submission of the false testimony, or, if the client persists in her plan, report the client's intent to the tribunal.[31] The perpetuation of ambiguity continues. See the material in Chapter 4 at pp. 294–300.

Commentators have argued extensively about what the Model Code requires of a lawyer faced with client perjury.[32] The courts, in contrast, have been clear that a lawyer has to take some action when she *knows* that a client or witness intends to lie. The cases are unanimous in requiring the lawyer at least to remonstrate with the client and to withdraw if the client insists on perjuring herself.[33] No court opinion suggests that it is proper for a lawyer to act as if testimony that she knows to be false is true. Not only the Supreme Court in *Whiteside* but the majority of courts state that at some point a lawyer has a duty to disclose client perjury so as to avoid assisting fraud on the tribunal.[34] The decisions base the obligation to disclose on a lawyer's duties not to assist criminal activity and not to offer false evidence.[35] A few cases, supported by a number of commentators, suggest that remonstration and withdrawal are a lawyer's only duties.[36]

28. Cf. DR 7–102(B)(2) covering fraud on the court committed by non-clients.

29. See Informal Op. 1314 (1975) and Formal Op. 341 (1975).

30. See Formal Op. 287 (1953) (interpreting the Canons).

31. See ABA Informal Op. 1314 (1975).

32. See, e.g., the articles cited above in note 12.

33. See, e.g., *Crary*, discussed below at p. 381, and *Long*, discussed below at p. 376.

34. See, e.g., *Doe*, discussed below at p. 381, and *Crary*, infra.

35. See DR 7–102(A)(7) and DR 7–102(A)(4).

36. State v. Lee, 142 Ariz. 210, 689 P.2d 153 (1984) (en banc) (criminal case: defense lawyer should move to withdraw but should not inform the court of the specific basis for the request; lawyer should state only that an "irreconcilable conflict" makes continued representation extremely difficult); In re A., 276 Or. 225, 554 P.2d 479, 486 (1976) (civil case: lawyer should encourage the client to permit the lawyer to disclose the fraud on the court, inform the client that the lawyer will have to withdraw if there is no disclosure and then withdraw if the client refuses to disclose). Cf. Norman Lefstein, Reflections on the Client Perjury Dilemma and *Nix v. Whiteside*, Crim.Just., Summer 1986, at 27, 28

Model Rule 3.3(a) specifies several situations in which the lawyer's duty of candor to the tribunal overrides the duty of confidentiality; M.R. 3.3(b) makes this hierarchy of duties explicit. Notice that the duty to take "remedial" measures, when one discovers after the fact that false evidence has been offered, extends only to evidence that is "material." When is perjured testimony not "material"?

Model Rule 3.3(b) states that a lawyer's duty to disclose that evidence she offered was false applies to any material evidence she learns is false while the proceeding is ongoing.[37] Should the rule also apply after the proceedings are over? How does the Comment justify the time limit? Is any statute of limitations justified?

Does a lawyer have discretion to disclose fraud she learns about after the proceedings are over? Clearly so if disclosure is necessary to establish a defense against an accusation that the lawyer participated in the fraud, M.R. 1.6(b)(2). The Comment to M.R. 1.6 also provides that nothing in 1.6 prevents a lawyer from withdrawing or disaffirming "any opinion, document, affirmation, or the like." Would this apply to a judgment or settlement procured by fraud?

M.R. 3.3(c) gives the lawyer discretion to refuse to offer evidence that the lawyer "reasonably believes is false." M.R. 3.3(d) requires the lawyer in an ex parte proceeding to inform the judge of "all material facts known to the lawyer" that, as the Comment explains, "the lawyer reasonably believes are necessary" for the judge to reach "an informed decision," "whether or not the facts are adverse."

In 1987, an ABA ethics opinion discussed the lawyer's duties under M.R. 3.3:

> If, prior to the conclusion of the proceedings, a lawyer learns that the client has given testimony the lawyer knows is false, and the lawyer cannot persuade the client to rectify the perjury, the lawyer must disclose the client's perjury to the tribunal, notwithstanding the fact that the information to be disclosed is information relating to the representation.
>
> If the lawyer learns that the client intends to testify falsely before a tribunal, the lawyer must advise the client against such course of action, informing the client of the consequences of giving false testimony including the lawyer's duty of disclosure to the tribunal. Ordinarily, the lawyer can reasonably believe that such advice will dissuade the client from giving false testimony and, therefore, may examine the client in the normal manner. However, if the lawyer knows, from the client's clearly stated intention, that the client will testify falsely, and the lawyer cannot effectively withdraw from the representation, the lawyer must either limit the examination of the client to subjects on which the lawyer believes

(accusing the majority opinion in *Whiteside* of "a shocking misstatement of the law pertaining to client perjury").

37. See M.R. 3.3(b) and the Comment to 3.3.

the client will testify truthfully; or, if there are none, not permit the client to testify; or, if this is not feasible, disclose the client's intention to testify falsely to the tribunal.[38]

Why is the ABA position on fraud on a tribunal so different from that on fraud involving financial harm to third persons? Doesn't the absence in the transactional context of the safeguards of the adversary process—impartial judge, jury as fact finder and testing of evidence by the opposing party's lawyer—suggest that more protection rather than less should be accorded when these protections are not present?

3. What Does a Lawyer "Know?"

Actual Knowledge

M.R. 3.3(a)(4) provides:

A lawyer shall not *knowingly*: ... (4) offer evidence that the lawyer *knows* to be false. If a lawyer has offered material evidence and comes to *know* of its falsity, the lawyer shall take reasonable remedial measures. (Emphasis added.)

The Terminology Section states that "Knowingly ... or Knows denotes actual knowledge," but adds that "a person's knowledge may be inferred from circumstances." Does this resolve the problem of the unusually credulous or deliberately blind lawyer? [39]

Judge Frankel has written that "[T]he sharp eye of the cynical lawyer becomes at strategic moments a demurely averted and filmy gaze," leaving him "unfettered by clear prohibitions that actual 'knowledge of the truth' might expose." [40] Does the "actual knowledge" standard include things the lawyer "should have known"? In *United States v. Benjamin*, printed in Chapter 2 at p. 57, the Second Circuit imposed criminal liability when a professional "deliberately closes his eyes to facts he has a duty to see." Is this standard inapplicable to client perjury?

Model Rule 3.3(c) gives the lawyer discretion to refuse to offer evidence that she *reasonably believes* is false. In exercising this discretion, the lawyer is not permitted to reveal client confidences. Only when the lawyer "knows" that the evidence is false does the duty in 3.3(a)(4) override the obligations of confidentiality, see M.R. 3.3(b). ABA Formal Op. 353 (1987) emphasizes that M.R. 3.3's obligation to disclose client perjury "is strictly limited" to situations when the

---

38. ABA Comm. on Prof. Ethics Formal Op. 353 (1987).

39. Consider ABA Formal Op. 353 n. 9 (1988), which states:

The Committee notes that some trial lawyers report that they have avoided the ethical dilemma posed by Rule 3.3 because they follow a practice of not questioning the client about the facts in the case and, therefore, never "know" that a client has given false testimony. Lawyers who engage in such practice may be violating their duties under Rule 3.3 and their obligation to provide competent representation under Rule 1.1. ABA Defense Function Standards 4–3.2(a) and (b) are also applicable.

40. Marvin E. Frankel, The Search for Truth: An Umpireal View, 123 U.Pa.L.Rev. 1031, 1039 (1975).

lawyer "knows" the testimony offered was false. "[O]rdinarily [this knowledge will be] based on admissions the client has made to the lawyer. The lawyer's suspicions are not enough."

After being reversed in *Whiteside*, the Eighth Circuit spoke again on the issue of client perjury in criminal trials in United States v. Long.[41] In *Long*, the lawyer told the trial judge, out of the presence of the jury, that his client wanted to testify but that the lawyer was "concerned about his testimony." The defense lawyer reiterated his concern "about the testimony that may come out" in an in camera meeting with the judge. The judge informed the defendant that he had a right to testify but that his lawyer had an obligation not to offer evidence "which he believed to be untrue. Although the judge stated that the defendant could take the stand and offer a narrative statement without questioning from his lawyer, the defendant did not testify.

The Eighth Circuit, reversing the conviction, distinguished *Long* from *Whiteside* in three respects, each of which required an evidentiary hearing. First, in this case, unlike *Whiteside,* the basis for the lawyer's belief that his client would perjure himself was unknown. Second, because the defendant did not testify, the court could not determine whether the lawyer's actions prevented his client from testifying *truthfully*. Third, in *Long* but not in *Whiteside* the lawyer "reveal[ed] his belief about his client's anticipated testimony to the trial court." The court stated that "a clear expression of intent to commit perjury is required before an attorney can reveal client confidences."[42] Does this mean that disclosure is permissible only when the defendant makes an explicit announcement that she intends to perjure herself? Is this consistent with *Whiteside*?

The Eighth Circuit considered two procedural mechanisms for resolving factual issues as to whether proposed testimony would be perjurious: (1) a hearing held by a judge other than the one presiding at trial, in which the defendant would get the benefit of the reasonable-doubt standard of proof;[43] and (2) establishment of a board of attorneys to decide the issue.[44] The Eighth Circuit implied, but did not hold, that some such safeguards might be constitutionally required.[45] Are there problems with implementing either of these solutions?

Can Trial Lawyers Ever "Know"? Radical Epistemology Revisited

St. Thomas Aquinas said concerning a confession to a priest:

---

41. 857 F.2d 436 (8th Cir.1988) (conviction for bank fraud affirmed on appeal, but opinion discusses the merits of one defendant's ineffective assistance of counsel claim and invites a collateral challenge to the conviction under 28 U.S.C. § 2255).

42. 857 F.2d at 445 (quoting from the Eighth Circuit opinion in *Whiteside*).

43. See Carol T. Rieger, Client Perjury: A Proposed Resolution of the Constitutional and Ethical Issues, 70 Minn.L.Rev. 121, 153 (1985).

44. See William H. Erickson, The Perjurious Defendant: A Proposed Solution to Defense Lawyer's Conflicting Ethical Obligations to the Court and to His Client, 59 Den.L.J. 75, 88 (1981).

45. 857 F.2d at 446–47 and n. 10.

Whatever the priest knows through confession he, in a sense, does not know, because he possesses this knowledge not as man, but as the representative of God. He may, therefore, without qualms of conscience, swear to his ignorance in court, because the obligation of a witness extends only to his human knowledge.[46]

At trial a lawyer acts in the fact finder's presence, and is expected to act, as if she were incapable of knowing that her client is guilty. Should this expectation of wilful blindness be extended to whether offered testimony is perjurious? Is the lawyer's ability to know things when inside the courtroom different than it is outside? Is the criminal defense lawyer "incapable" of "knowing" only when in the process of conducting the trial, but capable of knowing at side bar conferences or other exchanges outside the presence of the jury? What about the testimony of other defense witnesses? The authenticity of documents or other physical evidence? If we treat criminal defense lawyers as incapable of knowing whether evidence is false or not, should civil lawyers be treated the same in the interest of protecting their clients' due process rights?

4. Dealing With Client Perjury

Perjury Discovered During a Criminal Trial

When the client accedes to the lawyer's decision not to testify falsely, either before the trial as in *Whiteside* or during the trial, the courts have had little difficulty rejecting claims of interference with the right to counsel or to testify.[47] But what if the lawyer is initially unsuccessful in convincing the client not to testify falsely and some form of disclosure to the judge ensues?

In *Whiteside*, all steps occurred before the trial itself and within the attorney-client relationship (no third party was informed of the client's plans). If the client had continued to insist on testifying that he saw a gun or metallic object, what should the lawyer have done? Two decisions prior to *Whiteside* suggested that any action to prevent client perjury by a criminal defense lawyer, apart from confidentially trying to persuade the defendant to testify truthfully, would violate the defendant's constitutional rights.

In *Wilcox*[48] the lawyer believed that the defendant's proposed alibi testimony would be perjurious. She told the client she did not want to

---

46. Bertrand Kurtscheid, A History of the Seal of Confession 194–95 (F.A. Marks, transl., 1927). Acquinas' theory is not current official doctrine of the Catholic church.

47. For example, in United States v. Rantz, 862 F.2d 808 (10th Cir.1988), the court found that the lawyer's belief that the testimony would be false and ultimately detrimental to the defense was an adequate basis for the lawyer's refusal to call the defendant. The lawyer's belief was based on the overwhelming evidence offered by the prosecution, showing that the defendant was the initiator of the conspiracy. See also Williams v. Kemp, 846 F.2d 1276 (11th Cir.1988); and Commonwealth v. Blystone, 519 Pa. 450, 549 A.2d 81 (1988), aff'd on other grounds, 494 U.S. 299, (1990); State v. Fleck, 49 Wn.App. 584, 744 P.2d 628 (1987).

48. United States ex rel. Wilcox v. Johnson, 555 F.2d 115 (3d Cir.1977).

put him on the stand, but he insisted. The lawyer informed the trial judge in a side bar conference that her client insisted on testifying over her objection and that, if the judge permitted, she would make a motion to withdraw based on her belief that the testimony would be perjury. The court ruled that, if the client insisted on testifying, he would permit counsel to withdraw and the defendant would have to proceed without counsel for the remainder of the trial. The defendant then agreed not to testify. The Third Circuit held that the trial judge's ruling, threatening a loss of counsel, violated the defendant's right to counsel and his right to testify. The lawyer's behavior was criticized on two grounds. First, the lawyer requested to withdraw only if the defendant insisted on testifying. If there was an obligation to withdraw because of suspected future perjury, it applied whether or not the defendant continued to insist on testifying. Second, without a "firm factual basis" for her belief that the client intended to perjure himself, it was improper to disclose the intended perjury to the court.

In Lowery v. Cardwell [49] the defense lawyer was surprised during his client's testimony in a bench trial by what he was convinced was perjury. The lawyer immediately requested permission to withdraw. The lawyer offered no reason for his request and the judge sought none, but refused the request. The Ninth Circuit held that the lawyer's motion to withdraw was tantamount to an announcement to the trier of fact that his client had lied and thereby deprived the client of a fair trial. The court suggested that the lawyer could fulfill his obligation not to offer false evidence by letting the defendant testify in a narrative style without questioning from counsel.

> While a knowledgeable judge or juror, alert to the ethical problems faced by attorneys ... might infer perjury from [this procedure], counsel's belief [that the testimony was perjury] would not appear in the clear and unequivocal manner presented by the facts here.... The distinction we draw is between a passive refusal to lend aid to perjury and such direct action as we find here—the addressing of the court in pursuit of court order granting leave to withdraw. [50]

Is this a realistic distinction? *Whiteside* suggests that disclosure to the court in some circumstances is appropriate, but in *Whiteside* the court was not the fact-finder. [51]

Is a lawyer's request to withdraw essentially the same as informing the court of the lawyer's suspicions? May defense counsel in a criminal case seek to withdraw (or threaten to withdraw) only upon a "firm

49. 575 F.2d 727 (9th Cir.1978).

50. 575 F.2d at 731.

51. Compare Butler v. United States, 414 A.2d 844 (D.C.App.1980) (recusal of judge required where trial judge, sitting as trier of fact, learns from defense counsel that defendant plans to commit perjury).

factual basis" for her belief that the client will commit perjury? [52]

If the lawyer is obligated not to present false testimony, is the defendant denied effective assistance of counsel when the lawyer presents a defense based on perjury? [53]

Narrative Approach

The narrative solution endorsed in *Lowery* was proposed by the ABA's Criminal Justice Section in its draft of the ABA Standards of Criminal Justice. Defense Function Standard 4–7.7 provided that a defense lawyer should attempt to persuade the defendant to testify truthfully; if this attempt fails, the lawyer should seek to withdraw where feasible; if this fails, the lawyer should have the defendant tell her story in a narrative without further questioning by counsel. Before the defendant takes the stand, the lawyer should make a private record of the fact that the defendant is taking the stand against the lawyer's advice, presumably including a statement of why this advice was given. The lawyer may not argue the defendant's false version of the facts to the jury. What are the virtues of the narrative approach? The problems?

The ABA now firmly rejects the narrative approach. Standard 4–7.7 was omitted from the second edition of the Standards in 1979 and the "narrative" solution was rejected by the Model Rules for reasons stated in the Comment to M.R. 3.3. A subsequent ABA ethics opinion, interpreting the Model Rules, states: "[T]he lawyer can no longer rely on the narrative approach to insulate the lawyer from a charge of assisting the client's perjury." [54] The narrative approach, however, is embodied in the ethics rules in the District of Columbia [55] and endorsed in case law in some states, including California. [56] The narrative

52. See M.R. 1.16(a) requiring withdrawal if a violation of the rules *will* result; and M.R. 1.16(b)(1) permitting withdrawal if the lawyer *reasonably believes* the client's proposed course of action is criminal or fraudulent. See also M.R. 3.3(a)(4) and (c).

53. See People v. Avery, 129 A.D.2d 852, 513 N.Y.S.2d 883, 887 (1987) (defendant who "knowingly and willingly participated in an attempt to obstruct justice through perjured testimony ... is not in a position to ask this court to undo the consequences of [this wrongdoing]"); and North Dakota v. Skjonsby, 417 N.W.2d 818 (N.D.1987) (defendant, who had changed his story from time to time, claimed that he was denied effective assistance of counsel because his trial lawyer *failed* to stop him from offering a perjurious defense; the court held that evidence available to the trial lawyer was not sufficient to find that he knew that the fabricated defense was a lie). But compare State v. Lee, 142 Ariz. 210, 689 P.2d 153 (1984) (calling of perjurious witnesses on the client's demand fell below the standard of minimally competent representation; witnesses testified by narrative statement and lawyer made no closing argument to jury).

54. ABA Formal Op. 353 (1987).

55. The version of M.R. 3.3 adopted in the District of Columbia is similar to Standard 4–7.7. See D.C. Rule 3.3(b). Unlike M.R. 3.3, a D.C. lawyer may not disclose fraud on the tribunal if disclosure would reveal confidential client information protected by Rule 1.6.

56. People v. Guzman, 45 Cal.3d 915, 248 Cal.Rptr. 467, 755 P.2d 917 (1988), held that the narrative approach was neither inconsistent with the defendant's rights nor apparently a violation of the lawyer's duty to refrain from offering false evidence. In *Guzman* defense counsel informed the court, outside the jury's presence, that the defendant would testify against his advice and would use the narrative approach. The court advised the defendant to follow the lawyer's advice and not testify, but, when the defendant insisted,

approach may have more acceptance in actual practice than in formal recognition.

After *Whiteside*, the Supreme Court recognized the constitutional right of a criminal defendant to testify, but repeated the *Whiteside* statement that this does not include the right to testify falsely.[57]   Given the defendant's right to testify, what else can the trial court do, when informed by the defense counsel that she believes the defendant will lie, except let the defendant testify after proper warnings?   The only question then would be whether the court should permit a narrative statement or order defense counsel to question the witness in the regular fashion.[58]

Duty to Remonstrate With Client Before Taking Other Action

When a client proposes perjury, the lawyer should point out the dangers of being prosecuted for perjury.   In a criminal case, the lawyer should also point out the defendant's sentence may be increased if the court believes the defendant has perjured herself.[59]   When the lawyer discovers that the testimony was perjurious only after it has been offered, the lawyer should point out that recantation is a defense to perjury.   To make out a complete defense of recantation, however, the recantation must be made before (1) the prior false testimony has substantially affected the relevant proceeding, and (2) it has become manifest that the falsity of the prior testimony will be exposed.[60]

Government Use of Perjured Testimony to Obtain a Conviction

If the government knowingly uses perjured testimony to secure a conviction, the defendant is entitled to a new trial if "the false testimony could ... in any reasonable likelihood have affected the judgment of the jury...." [61] Even the government's *unwitting* use of perjured testimony violates due process if truthful testimony would "most likely change the outcome of the trial." [62]

permitted the defendant to testify in narrative format. Lead counsel made no mention of this testimony. The court found no violation of defendant's constitutional rights. Accord: State v. Fosnight, 235 Kan. 52, 679 P.2d 174 (1984); Coleman v. State, 621 P.2d 869 (Alaska 1980).

57.   Rock v. Arkansas, 483 U.S. 44 (1987).

58.   See United States v. Henkel, 799 F.2d 369 (7th Cir.1986) (lawyer moved to withdraw just before defendant's testimony; trial judge correctly understood this to mean counsel believed the defendant would commit perjury; the court offered the defendant the chance to testify through a narrative statement without assistance of counsel, which the client declined; held: no violation of defendant's rights because no right to have counsel's assistance to testify falsely).

59.   See United States v. Grayson, 438 U.S. 41 (1978) (perjury a legitimate sentencing consideration as it bears on the likelihood of the defendant being rehabilitated); United States v. Dunnigan, 113 S.Ct. 1111 (1993) (same result under sentencing guidelines).

60.   See, e.g., United States v. Scivola, 766 F.2d 37 (1st Cir.1985).

61.   Giglio v. United States, 405 U.S. 150, 154 (1972) (quoting Napue v. Illinois, 360 U.S. 264, 271 (1959)). See also Avery v. Procunier, 750 F.2d 444 (5th Cir.1985); United States v. Jones, 730 F.2d 593 (10th Cir.1984).

62.   Sanders v. Sullivan, 863 F.2d 218 (2d Cir.1988).

5. Perjury in Civil Cases

Lying at a Deposition

Testifying falsely in a sworn deposition is perjury.[63] In Committee on Professional Ethics v. Crary,[64] cited in *Whiteside*, the lawyer was found guilty of professional misconduct when he sat silently by while his client lied during a deposition; the court treated this as tantamount to assisting a client to lie at trial. The deposition was taken in a divorce action between Mrs. Curtis and her husband. Crary knew his client, Mrs. Curtis, was lying because her lie was that she was in Chicago with a woman friend when the truth was that she was with Crary, her lawyer, with whom she was having an affair.

> ... Assuming respondent did not know in advance that Mrs. Curtis was going to lie, his guilt was in failing to stop her or otherwise to call a halt when she started to lie....
>
> The attorney functions at the heart of the fact-finding process, both in trial and in pre- and post-trial proceedings. If he knowingly suffers a witness to lie, he undermines the integrity of the fact-finding system of which he himself is an integral part....
>
> ... We do not place the decision on [his] failure to inform opposing counsel or the court of the truth. In the present case no need really existed for this. Opposing counsel was not misled. His subsequent questions revealed he knew [where Mrs. Curtis had actually been]; he made [her] perjury patent. The vice ... was not in failing to reveal the truth but in participating in the corruption of the fact-finding system by knowingly permitting Mrs. Curtis to lie.... Contrast with respondent's conduct the acts of [his partner] Mr. Gray. When that attorney suspected on Friday that Mrs. Curtis was lying he confronted respondent and upon learning the truth said, "She can't sit there and tell this story." He thereupon recessed the deposition.[65]

The court also rejected Crary's contention that disclosure would have violated his duty to protect his client's confidences.[66]

False Evidence Offered by the Opposing Party

In Doe v. Federal Grievance Committee [67] the court addressed the lawyer's duty of candor to the court when the lawyer suspects an

---

63. See, e.g., 18 U.S.C. § 1623 ("Whoever under oath in any proceeding before or *ancillary* to any court ... knowingly makes any false material declaration ...); United States v. Moreno Morales, 815 F.2d 725 (1st Cir.1987) (prosecution for false deposition testimony in a civil action). Also see In Matter of Application of Charles M., 313 Md. 168, 545 A.2d 7 (1988) (denying bar admission to a person who as a layperson had lied in a deposition).

64. 245 N.W.2d 298 (Iowa 1976).

65. Id. at 305–06.

66. Accord: Attorney Grievance Committee v. Sperling, 296 Md. 558, 463 A.2d 868 (1983).

67. 847 F.2d 57 (2d Cir.1988).

adverse witness of perjury. During the course of civil litigation, the plaintiff's lawyer (the anonymous "Doe") had two conversations with his client concerning the deposition of a witness for the defendant. The client told Doe that the witness had reported that defendant's attorneys had instructed the witness to lie at an upcoming deposition. After the deposition, the client reported to Doe that the witness had told him he had, in fact, lied at the deposition.

At a hearing initiated by the trial judge into the behavior of lawyers for both sides, Doe testified that, regarding the first conversation, he did not believe defendant's counsel had instructed the witness to lie. He believed instead that the witness's impression was the result of a "layperson's [mis]interpretation of deposition preparation." Regarding the second conversation, Doe stated that he did *suspect* the witness had perjured himself. However, Doe testified that he based this conclusion not on his conversations with his client but on inconsistencies in documents and depositions. Doe asserted that he believed his conversations with his client were privileged communications and that he was therefore under a duty not to reveal their contents; Doe further stated that it was his intention to use the possibly perjured testimony to impeach the adverse witness at trial.

The district judge concluded Doe had violated his duty to reveal "information clearly establishing ... a fraud on the tribunal" [Disciplinary Rule 7-102(B)(2) of the Code of Professional Responsibility]. The court suspended Doe from practice in the district for six months. The court of appeals reversed, holding that "information clearly establishing" that someone has perpetrated a fraud on a tribunal requires actual knowledge, not just a belief and suspicion.

> [T]he only reasonable conclusion is that the drafters [of the Code of Professional Responsibility] intended disclosure of only that information which the attorney reasonably knows to be a fact.... [68]

> ... The proper forum for resolving [whether an adverse witness lied] is not a collateral proceeding, but is the trial itself. Determining credibility is unquestionably the hallmark of the adversarial system.[69]

Should an advocate have a duty to disclose to the tribunal the prospective or actual perjury of an adverse witness? Note that there is no counterpart to DR 7-102(B)(2) in the Model Rules. Rule 3.3(a)(2) imposes obligations when a lawyer's knowing failure to disclose a material fact will assist "a criminal or fraudulent act *by the client*." Rule 3.3(a)(4) and 3.3(c) deal with the lawyer *offering evidence* that the lawyer knows, or has reason to believe, is false. (Emphases added.)

68. 847 F.2d at 63. The court cited federal cases holding that attorneys may only reveal their clients' perjury if their suspicion of perjury is supported by a "firm factual basis," and noted that the Virginia Code of Professional Responsibility required attorneys to have "actual knowledge" before disclosing *client* perjury. The court also quoted Justice Stevens' comment in Nix v. Whiteside, 475 U.S. at 190, that "a pebble that seems clear enough at first glance may take on a different hue in a handful of gravel."

69. 847 F.2d at 63.

Thus the Model Rules permit the lawyer to attack the false testimony of an opposition witness by impeachment, preserving the strategic advantage that may be lost by advance disclosure to the tribunal.[70] Isn't disclosure to the tribunal likely to lead to a swearing match between opposing counsel?

The underlying matter in *Doe* was civil. The criminal cases requiring a high degree of certainty regarding client perjury are based on the constitutional rights of the accused. How does the court in *Doe* justify its standard? Fed.R.Civ.P. 11, discussed below, and similar rules in the states require a lawyer to conduct a reasonable investigation so that any paper filed with the court is "well grounded in fact . . .".[71] See also M.R. 3.1. Is reporting someone else's conduct different than initiating action?

False Evidence Offered by the Opposing Party

How important was it in *Doe* that the apparent fraud was perpetrated by a witness for the other side?

The Code provision at issue in *Doe*, DR 7–102(B)(2), covers fraud committed by anyone other than the client, which the court reads to include fraud by the opposing party. The court could have held that DR 7–102(B)(2) did not cover fraud committed by the opposing party; and that the only provision requiring a lawyer to report such conduct was DR 1–103(A), which imposes a duty to report professional misconduct only if this knowledge is "unprivileged."

Note that Model Rule 8.3, on reporting professional misconduct, applies only to non-confidential information, whereas M.R. 3.3(b) makes it clear that the obligation not to offer false evidence applies "even if compliance requires disclosure of information otherwise protected by Rule 1.6." Should a lawyer have a greater or lesser obligation to report perjury committed by her own witnesses than to report perjury by others?

Rule 60(b) and Fraud on the Court

"Fraud on the court" as used in DR 7–102(B) traditionally has been

---

70. Judge van Graafeiland, concurring in *Doe* stated:

[E]ven if appellant was convinced that an opposing witness had testified falsely during his deposition, DR 7–102(B)(2) did not require appellant to disclose this to the court. The drafters of the Rule must have realized that it is one thing to be convinced of something; it is another thing to prove it. I can think of no better way for a lawyer to damage his client's case than by making a pretrial accusation of perjury that he is unable to prove.

847 F.2d at 64.

71. See, e.g., Coburn Optical v. Cilco, 610 F.Supp. 656, 659 (M.D.N.C.1985) ("If all the attorney has is his client's assurance that facts exist or do not exist, when a reasonable inquiry would reveal otherwise, he has not satisfied his obligation [under Rule 11]."); and Kendrick v. Zanides, 609 F.Supp. 1162, 1172 (N.D.Cal.1985) (when the lawyer has a document refuting the client's allegations, she must investigate). Contrast In re Grand Jury Subpoena, 615 F.Supp. 958, 969 (D.Mass.1985) ("So long as the attorney does not have obvious indications of the client's fraud or perjury, the attorney is not obligated to undertake an independent investigation before advancing his client's position.").

interpreted to include the introduction of false evidence.[72] Judge van Graafeiland's concurrence in the *Doe v. Federal Grievance Committee*, summarized above at p. 381, argues for a more restrictive definition of fraud. He argues that "untruthful testimony, which has not been suborned by [a] lawyer, does not, standing alone, constitute fraud upon the court." [73] The cases cited in support, however, do not involve DR 7–102(B) or any counterpart; they all involve motions under Fed.R.Civ.P. 60(b) to set aside a judgment because of fraud on the court. Is Judge van Grafeiland wrong in assuming that cases dealing with reopening of judgments are relevant in interpreting what constitutes "fraud" for purposes of the ethics rules? [74]

6. What Should the Rules on Client Perjury Be?

Case law and ethics rules and opinions notwithstanding, at least in the case of a criminal defendant who intends to commit perjury, a substantial segment of the practicing bar believes the lawyer must present such testimony if the client insists.[75] In Kenneth Mann's revealing book, *Defending White Collar Criminals*, a lawyer tells Mann:

> It's my mission and obligation to defend the client, not to sit in moral, ethical or legal judgment of him. I cannot join him in transgressing the law, but whatever he does of his own impetus, whatever way he conducts himself in attempting to protect himself, is a decision he has to make independent of what I do. I must inform him of the consequences and significance of his action, but not punish him or sanction him or in other ways initiate law enforcement actions against him. My role in the adversary system is to protect him.[76]

Another lawyer admonishes an associate who believed that a client had lied to a government agency:

> What you are telling me is that the client is not telling the truth. What I am saying is that the response is credible. We are not law

72. See, e.g., Attorney Grievance Com'n v. Sperling, 296 Md. 558, 463 A.2d 868 (1983) (rejecting a narrow reading of "fraud on the court" and holding that "fraud" under DR 7–102(B) includes false swearing); *Nix v. Whiteside*, supra; ABA Formal Op. 341 (1975); Informal Op. 1314 (1975); and Formal Op. 287 (1953) (interpreting similar language in the Canons of Professional Ethics). See also ABA Formal Op. 353 (1987) (interpreting the words "criminal or fraudulent act by the client" in M.R. 3.3(a)(2) as including perjury and the introduction of false evidence because any other reading would be "irrational").

73. 847 F.2d at 64.

74. Rule 60(b)(3) permits setting aside a judgment procured on the basis of "fraud ...", misrepresentation, or other misconduct of an adverse party" by motion filed no later than one year after judgment; but motions for "fraud on the court" covered by Rule 60(b)(6) contain no time limit. Introduction of false evidence without the attorney's knowing involvement in the fraud is not considered "fraud on the court" under 60(b)(6), but it may constitute "fraud between the parties" under 60(b)(3). See, e.g., Great Coastal Express v. International Brotherhood of Teamsters, 675 F.2d 1349 (4th Cir.1982).

75. See the materials cited in note 12 above.

76. Kenneth Mann, Defending White Collar Criminals 121 (1985).

enforcement agents.[77]

Consider these statements in light of the earlier summary of what the rules now say, above at p. 350, and the case law already considered.

Assisting or Acquiescing in a Client's Lie

Professor Freedman's "trilemma," see p. 352 above, posits a defendant falsely accused of robbery whose truthful testimony about his whereabouts (i.e., that he was near the scene at the time of the crime) might lead the jury to convict him. By positing this case, Freedman presents us with a scenario in which lying seems not only reasonable but, perhaps more important, not a clear moral wrong. How is it "known" in Freedman's case, except hypothetically, that the client has been *falsely* accused? Would it indeed be reasonable for a defendant in this situation to lie? What dangers are there for the innocent defendant who lies and is thought by the fact-finder to have lied?

Assuming there are some circumstances in which it is reasonable for an innocent defendant to lie, a number of questions remain. First, does the moral justification for the defendant's lying extend to the lawyer, giving lawyers who represent defendants in these circumstances a moral justification for assisting the lie? Second, if some defendants are morally justified in lying, must the lawyer assist all defendants to lie because any other stance would distinguish between clients according to whether the lawyer believed them to be truly innocent? Third, if the lawyer is morally justified in assisting at least some defendants to lie, does that mean that the ethics rules should leave it to the lawyer's discretion when to assist perjury and when not? Does it mean that the rules should *require* lawyers to assist perjury?

These questions are posed and insightfully discussed by Professor Carl Selinger.[78] He concludes that an innocent defendant is morally justified in perjuring herself to avoid the greater wrong of unjustified imprisonment. Do you agree with Selinger's resolution of his first question? Should a lawyer advise the client that lying in court is unlawful but not immoral if she is innocent? Would that be counseling (assisting, encouraging) the client to commit criminal conduct? See M.R. 1.2(d).

Selinger argues that a lawyer's oath to uphold the law places her under a special obligation not to break the rules for adjudicating disputes; and that by voluntarily participating in the criminal justice system the lawyer assumes two special obligations: (1) to conduct herself in accordance with the rules for finding the facts; and (2) to accept the judgments reached by the system when reached in accordance with the system's own rules. Do you agree?

77. Id. at 110.

78. Carl M. Selinger, The Perry Mason Perspective and Others: A Critique of Reductionist Thinking about the Ethics of Untruthful Practices by Lawyers for "Innocent" Defendants, 6 Hofstra L.Rev. 631 (1978).

Selinger rejects a rule that would allow lawyers to assist "good" lying as opposed to "bad" lying because it would be difficult to administer such a rule in an evenhanded manner, and it would provide little guidance to lawyers trying to figure out what was prohibited.

An Outsider's Perspective on Secrecy and Disclosure

Philosopher Sissela Bok discusses the competing claims of secrecy and disclosure in professional relationships.[79] The duty to preserve professional confidences, Bok asserts, is " ... rooted in the most primeval tribal emotions: the loyalty to self [and] kin ... against ... the unrelated, the outsiders, the barbarians." Lying to protect clients and colleagues is the product of an age-old tradition of employing deceit to save family and tribe.

The duty to protect "kin and clan," however, must be "pitted against the restrictions on harming innocent persons." [80] Deceit that is legitimate must be distinguished from that which is circumscribed by law or morality. Bok explores this distinction by examining three justifications of lying to preserve confidences. The first is that a lie is justified if its purpose is avoiding harm to family or friends. The difficulty with this claim is that while a lie may protect a friend, it may cause harm—perhaps far greater harm—to third parties.

The second justification is lodged in the right to privacy. Some questions run to matters so personal that they do not deserve an honest answer. For example, questions about a presidential candidate's sexual practices may be regarded as illegitimate. Bok wonders, though, whether the right to privacy should bar a doctor from revealing a fiancee's syphilis. In balancing the right to privacy against harm to third parties, at what point do we reveal a confidence to protect an innocent person?

The third justification for confidentiality holds that a secret may be revealed to prevent harm, unless "a promise has been made not to reveal the information." Thus, a promise not to reveal a secret may not be violated even after it becomes known that the promise subverts the truth and harms innocent persons. Why afford so much deference to promises? First, people have a right to rely on our promises. Next, breaking a promise is itself a kind of lie. Finally, professional promises help ensure that those who need help will feel free to seek it. Still, there are limits to the inviolability of promises. In particular, Bok states that "a promise adds no justification at all to an undertaking ... that is in itself wrong." [81] The dilemma, then, is determining what may be rightly promised.

Bok then turns from general considerations of confidentiality to confidentiality in the professional setting. She quotes from Charles

79. Sissela Bok, Lying: Moral Choice in Public and Private Life 154–73 (1979), discussing lies protecting peers and clients.

80. Id. at 157.

81. Id. at 160.

Curtis, a Boston lawyer of a generation ago,[82] and Monroe Freedman, a prominent writer on legal ethics,[83] both of whom state that lying to defend clients is sometimes permitted. However, while Curtis would not lie in court, Freedman contends a lawyer may build on testimony he knows is perjured, asserting that a lawyer's paramount duty is to make the best possible case for the client. Bok discusses and rejects three justifications for the claim that lawyer confidentiality justifies lying.

First, everyone is entitled to sound advice and skilled advocacy; and these can only be realized if clients are able to discuss their problems openly. Bok accepts the premise that everyone is entitled to professional loyalty, but she rejects the conclusion that this loyalty should be "stretched to justify lies." To support her contention, Bok points to the Jewish and Christian traditions where perjury is regarded as the worst kind of falsehood.

The second and third arguments posit societal benefits from strict confidentiality. When clients, encouraged to confide fully in lawyers, receive proper representation, justice is served, thereby benefiting the whole society. Moreover, the adversary system, by eliciting relevant facts, encourages truthful outcomes. Bok's response is that these claims must be taken on faith because they are not supported by empirical evidence. And lying that takes the form of building on perjurious testimony cannot be viewed as "a mechanism for producing the truth."

Finally, Bok suggests that the law's response to lying should not be left to the profession alone to resolve. Rather, the public ought to be included in the debate, particularly if the practice of helping clients is to be justified on the claim that society as a whole is better off with

82. See Charles P. Curtis, The Ethics of Advocacy, 4 Stan.L.Rev. 3 (1951). Curtis discusses the following situations: (1) a meeting of lawyers and witnesses involved in a ship collision case in which the sea captain attempts to persuade the lookout, who had left his post in heavy fog to smoke, to lie, with the lawyers remaining silent; (2) a lawyer who, asked by the head of the grievance committee if he represents a lawyer suspected of blackmailing other lawyers, lies to protect that lawyer; and (3) a lawyer who knows where his fugitive client has gone, but who lies when asked by the police for information.

> [In these and similar situations a lawyer] lies. And why not? The relation between a lawyer and his client is one of the intimate relations. You would lie for your wife. You would lie for your child. There are others with whom you are intimate enough, close enough, to lie for them when you would not lie for yourself. At what point do you stop lying for them? I don't know and you are not sure.

4 Stan.L.Rev. at 8.

83. Monroe Freedman's initial assertion that it was proper under some circumstances for a criminal defense lawyer to present testimony that she knows is perjurious led to the filing of professional responsibility charges against him in the District of Columbia. His article, Professional Responsibility of the Criminal Defense Lawyer: The Three Hardest Questions, 64 Mich.L.Rev. 1469 (1966), generated widespread discussion. The adoption of Model Rule 3.3 and the Supreme Court's decision in *Nix v. Whiteside* indicate that the law promulgated by judges does not accept Freedman's position. In his latest book, Understanding Lawyers' Ethics 109–41 (1990), Freedman continues to assert that the lawyer's role in safeguarding the client's freedom and autonomy justifies the lawyer in offering and arguing perjured testimony when the client refuses to accept the lawyer's efforts to dissuade the client from doing so.

such a practice. If non-lawyers are included, the non-lawyers will likely reject many practices permitted by the lawyer codes. Bok offers an illustration:

> One effect of a public debate of these questions would inevitably be increased knowledge about deceptive professional practices in the law. And it can be argued that this knowledge ought to be shared with all who practice in trials—most especially judges and juries. Should juries perhaps then be instructed to take into account the fact that a number of lawyers believe it their right to build upon perjured testimony?

> It is clear that even those lawyers willing to support such a right for themselves would not wish juries to be thus instructed.... The most important reasons they might advance showing why juries should not have such knowledge are that it should remain easy to mislead them, that their trust in the legal profession and in courtroom procedures should remain whole.[84]

Bok urges that the question of confidentiality be resolved by the general public in accordance with general moral norms. "[P]rofessional insularity ... impoverishes [and] leads to a vacuum of genuine analysis."[85] Lawyers, Bok concludes, rate truth too low among the values that institutions of justice are meant to serve. Awareness of other perspectives would permit them to see, "not only the needs that press for perjury and lying, but the effect that such practices have upon the deceived and social trust."[86]

Would you support instructing juries that some lawyers believe it appropriate to present testimony they believe is false?

———

B. REMEDIES FOR ABUSIVE LITIGATION CONDUCT

Introductory Note

When ordinary people are confronted with formal process, such as a summons in a legal proceeding, their emotions and anxieties are powerfully engaged. They are commanded in the esoteric language of formal law to respond within a stated period of time and are threatened with serious consequences if they do not do so or if the merits of the case go against them. To protect their interests, they must procure a lawyer in whom they have confidence—a difficult task for those whose contact with the legal system is limited or non-existent—and put their fate in the hands of this professional. The costs and anxieties that flow

---

84. Id. at 172.

85. Id. at 170.

86. Id. at 173.

from being forced into the unwelcome role of a litigant are large, in psychic as well as economic terms. The loss of control over some aspects of one's future is itself a major problem; and if the litigation may result in serious losses, whether in money, reputation, marital status or personal freedom, the prospects are frightening. Lawyers often forget the truth stated by Judge Learned Hand: "After now some dozen years of experience, I must say that as a litigant I should dread a lawsuit beyond almost anything else short of sickness and death." [1]

The American Rule on legal fees, discussed in Chapter 6 at p. 539 below, requires each party to pay the costs incurred in pursuing or defending a legal proceeding.[2] The just claimant's recovery may be eroded or eliminated by the expense of vindicating the claim. The person forced to defend against an unfounded claim may be impoverished by a successful defense.

Given these realities, it is not surprising that criminal law, procedural law and ethics rules impose obligations on parties and their representatives not to abuse the judicial process. From the lawyer's point of view, the basic tension is between the lawyer's duties of loyalty to, and zeal for, a client and the battery of restraints that are imposed on a lawyer to protect the interests of the public, the courts and opposing parties. From the broader social point of view, the problem is one of devising social arrangements that permit the public expression of social norms while permitting efficient, accurate and fair resolution of disputes.[3]

1. Frivolity, Harassment and Delay: Professional Rules and Attitudes

Professional rules, in dealing with frivolity, harassment and delay, impose limits on the "warm zeal" with which a lawyer is to urge a client's interests. The rule provisions must be considered in light of widely-shared professional attitudes, which strongly influence the behavior of lawyers and the actions of disciplinary bodies. Both ethics

---

1. Learned Hand, The Deficiencies of Trials to Reach the Heart of the Matter (talk to ACBNY, Nov. 17, 1921), reprinted in 3 ACBNY Lectures on Legal Topics 1921–22 at 87, 105 (1926).

This focus on defendants should not obscure the fact that potential plaintiffs also face difficult emotional and practical problems. For example, a woman who has been the victim of sexual harassment by her superior in an employment setting must make a series of difficult choices: Would she be better off ignoring the incident than pursuing the matter? Are informal remedies provided by the employer available or promising? How does one find a trustworthy lawyer who has the requisite skills and judgment? Will a lawyer think the case is worth her time? What happens to one's life while a lawsuit is making its way through cumbersome court procedures? Etc.

2. The "court costs" often awarded to prevailing parties are typically small, fixed amounts that have no relationship to the real costs of litigating a matter. Attorneys' fees are the principal cost, but other litigation costs (investigations, expert witnesses, miscellaneous expenses) are often substantial.

3. See Roger C. Cramton, A Comment on Trial–Type Hearings in Nuclear Power Plant Siting, 58 Va.L.Rev. 585 (1972) (discussing criteria for evaluating hearing processes); and Robert S. Summers, Evaluating and Improving Legal Processes—A Plea for Process Values, 60 Cornell L.Rev. 1 (1974).

rules and professional attitudes are powerfully shaped by changes in procedural law.[4]

In re Solerwitz [5]

In 1982, shortly after 11,000 air traffic controllers were fired for participating in an illegal strike, Jack Solerwitz, a Long Island attorney, was retained by about 800 controllers to pursue reinstatement claims. When the Federal Merit System Protection Board rejected the claims, approximately 4600 petitions for review were filed in the United States Court of Appeals for the Federal Circuit. Because of the press of claims raising similar issues, the court designated twelve cases (including one of Solerwitz's) as "lead cases" that presented most of the common legal issues for review. These cases were given expedited hearing and review, and all others suspended. When the court decided the twelve lead cases (adversely to the controllers), it notified the petitioners and their lawyers in all of the other pending appeals, informed them that written notification was necessary to continue their appeals and warned them of the impropriety of maintaining frivolous appeals in cases that presented legal issues and fact patterns indistinguishable from those presented and decided in the lead cases.

Ignoring these warnings, Solerwitz filed or maintained appeals in 144 air traffic controller cases. The court directed Solerwitz to "show cause why he should not be suspended for two years from representing clients before this court." The show-cause order alleged that the briefs in Solerwitz's appeals (107 of which were virtually identical) were "devoid of any basis on which the precedents of this court could be distinguished in law or fact, and devoid of any effort to make such distinctions." At a hearing, there was evidence that Solerwitz pursued the appeals at the explicit request of his clients in the hope, which proved to be a vain one, that the Supreme Court would reverse the lead cases or that a political or legislative accommodation might come to the rescue of controllers whose cases were still pending.

According to the court's summary,

> Professor [Monroe] Freedman, [one of the ethics experts,] stated that "as long as counsel in good faith believes that his case is not frivolous, ... it is his duty to proceed with it notwithstanding any instructions to the contrary from the court" and that "the court is required to bend over backwards to defer to counsel's judgment

---

4. An example is the change in procedural rules relating to use of general denials. Some years ago the law of pleading made it customary and acceptable for a plaintiff to make allegations in broad terms and for a defendant to respond with a general denial requiring plaintiff to prove all elements of the claim. Today procedural law generally requires the plaintiff to provide the defendant with better notice of the facts relied on and the defendant to respond in a particularized manner. A defendant who knows that some of the facts stated in the complaint are true may no longer make a general denial. M.R. 3.1 implicitly reflects this change by carving out an exception for the lawyer for the criminal defendant or a person subject to incarceration, who by a general plea (e.g., "not guilty") may require the state to prove every element of the case.

5. In re Solerwitz, 848 F.2d 1573 (Fed. Cir.1988).

with regard to what is filed and what is argued...." [The trial judge] found Professor Freedman "regards as frivolous only a paper that is fallacious on its face as distinguished from sham pleading in which the argument is plausible but the lawyer knows or should know that the underlying facts are not there to support it." ... Professor Hellerstein [a second ethics expert in the case, expressed the] opinion that "a lawyer has an obligation to persist in making and remaking the same argument to an intermediate court at least until the Supreme Court foreclosed that court on the merits." ... [He] testified that in his entire practice he never once turned down a client's request to bring an appeal because he believed it was frivolous, if [he] felt there was anything that could be argued.... [6]

The court unanimously rejected these arguments:

> ... Mr. Solerwitz filed 107 briefs that ... merely repeated the same arguments that this court already had rejected in the lead cases. The purported fact distinctions he sought to draw between [these cases and the lead cases] ... were wholly unconvincing and did not provide any meaningful basis for distinguishing the lead cases.
>
> Mr. Solerwitz's briefs ... did not attempt to convince the court that the lead cases, decided only a short time earlier, had been incorrectly decided and should be overruled. Instead, he merely repeated the same basic arguments that the court had rejected in the lead cases.[7]

Solerwitz was suspended from practice before the Federal Circuit for a period of one year.[8]

Screening Out Frivolous Claims

Model Rule 3.1 states that a lawyer (other than one for a criminal defendant or a person subject to incarceration) "shall not bring or defend a proceeding, or assert or controvert an issue therein, unless there is a basis for doing so that is not frivolous, which includes a good

MR 1.3

---

6. 848 F.2d at 1576–77. A more colorful summary of the positions of the ethics experts appears in a news report:

> Three ethics experts rose to [Solerwitz's] defense. A lawyer should argue that the earth is flat if a client so demands, said Monroe Freedman of Hofstra Law School. "What is today's joke is tomorrow's constitutional principle," said William Hellerstein of Brooklyn Law School, who, as chief of appeals for the Legal Aid Society of New York, once lost 54 cases in a row. Harvey Silverglate, a Boston lawyer who has taught ethics at Harvard Law School, described his own test for what is "frivolous": if nobody in the office giggles, it passes muster.

David Margolick, N.Y.Times, Jan. 20, 1989, at p. B4.

7. 848 F.2d at 1579.

8. Solerwitz, who paid $100,000 in fines, $100,000 to his lawyers, Alan and Nathan Dershowitz, and $30,000 to expert witnesses, "is struggling to rebuild his practice and keep his spirits." " 'I was the only lawyer who kept the doors open for [the fired controllers], and I thought I'd get a medal for it,' he said. 'Instead, I was the one who drank the Kool–Aid.' " See David Margolick, N.Y. Times, Jan. 20, 1989, at p. B4.

faith argument for an extension, modification or reversal of existing law." [9]   M.R. 3.1 differs from its predecessor in the Model Code, DR 7–102(A)(1), in providing an objective rather than a largely subjective test for judging what is frivolous.   The Model Code limited disciplinary sanctions to situations in which the lawyer "*knows or it is obvious* that such action would serve *merely* to harass or maliciously injure another." (Emphasis added.)   Does the word "merely" make DR 7–102(A)(1) too lenient? Does the Model Code provision turn on whether a lawyer is clever enough to think up a plausible justification for the action that is non-harassing?

The Comment to M.R. 3.1 makes it clear that the Rule does not impose any duty on the lawyer to make a full inquiry about underlying facts before acting:

> The filing of an action or defense or similar action taken for a client is not frivolous merely because the facts have not first been fully substantiated or because the lawyer expects to develop vital evidence only by discovery.   Such action is not frivolous even though the lawyer believes that the client's position ultimately will not prevail.

What about colorable claims brought "merely to harass ..."?   See the Preamble to the Model Rules: "A lawyer should use the law's procedures only for legitimate purposes and not to harass or intimidate others."   M.R. 8.4(d) prohibits "conduct prejudicial to the administration of justice." [10]

Lawyers may be expected to screen out frivolous claims and defenses when it is in their self-interest to do so.   An unfounded claim or defense will result in legal fees that an unsuccessful client will be reluctant to pay and that may be unethical to exact. [11]   Abuses are more likely when lawyers are tempted by self-interest to pursue frivolous matters or cheat their clients.   When clients, unable to police their lawyers effectively or impelled by their own improper motivations, are able and willing to pay for unnecessary services, dishonest lawyers may be tempted to cheat them. [12]   Reports of bill padding and feather-bedding on the part of lawyers and law firms are encountered frequent-

---

9. A separate rule, M.R. 3.4(d), provides that a lawyer should not make "frivolous" discovery requests or fail to make "reasonably diligent" efforts to comply with proper discovery requests by another party.

10. See the discussion of this provision at p. 167 above.

11. Baranowski v. State Bar, 24 Cal.3d 153, 154 Cal.Rptr. 752, 593 P.2d 613 (1979) (lawyer disciplined where, without making any independent legal or factual investigation of the client's claim, he had made an overzealous assessment of the legal worth of the claim and had received a large retainer from the client).

12. Abuses may also result when a lawyer's incompetence leads to a gross misjudgment of the legal worth of the client's case, but a lawyer who does this frequently is likely to go out of business. Perhaps under-employed lawyers (e.g., a recent graduate whose time has low value because of lack of profitable work) will push marginal cases to an inappropriate degree.

ly in the popular and legal press.[13] In part to prevent such abuses, sophisticated clients monitor lawyer performance closely and require detailed fee statements.

The danger of litigation abuse is greatest, however, in situations in which the interests of both client and lawyer favor the use of abusive tactics. A lawyer, for example, may be tempted to file a damage action against a defendant solely to profit from a nuisance-value settlement entered into by a defendant to avoid the substantial costs of a successful defense. Or she may assert a legally insupportable defense to provide her client with a further period of use of the money sought at lower-than-market interest rates or to continue for a further period an illegal but profitable course of conduct.

What constitutes a "frivolous" claim or defense? Changes in the intellectual framework of American lawyers make this a more serious problem than it was in the past. Some streams of current legal theory, influenced by legal realism, critical legal studies and feminist and race theory, assert that law is culturally determined and highly contingent on existing social structures; that legal rules are themselves uncertain and legal outcomes indeterminate; and, consequently, that law is much more changeable than generally perceived. To the extent that law is uncertain and constantly changing, general agreement on whether a lawyer's action is "frivolous" will frequently be lacking. In *Solerwitz* the "ethics experts" appear to have urged these post-modern views, but the court was confident that it could distinguish frivolous from non-frivolous actions.

Enforcement of the code provisions presents practical difficulties apart from getting agreement on the standard of judgment. If the professional rule requires a finding of subjective bad faith, as may be the case under DR 7–102(A)(1), an evidentiary hearing may be required to probe the attorney's motives. If the rule examines the objective merit of the pleading or motion, as does M.R. 3.1, either expert testimony is required or a court must resolve the issue as a question of law. Does the application of either standard turn on whether the lawyer is clever enough to think up a supporting argument that is not wholly implausible? Professor Wolfram concludes, not surprisingly, that "discipline is rarely imposed for violations of the antiharassment rules ... [which] can very likely do little to restrain advocates from taking steps that, based on other calculations, seem in the best interests of clients."[14]

In addition to the chronic problems of disciplinary bodies, which are often understaffed, evenhandedness in enforcement is a problem.

13. See Lisa G. Lerman, Lying to Clients, 138 U.Pa.L.Rev. 659, 709–13 (1990) (reporting lawyer interviews detailing the frequency of bill padding and other forms of cheating on clients).

14. Wolfram, Modern Legal Ethics § 11.2.2, at 595 (1986). In 1988 the West Virginia Supreme Court sent a strong message to the state's disciplinary committee that the filing of frivolous litigation should be taken more seriously. Committee on Legal Ethics of the West Virginia State Bar v. Douglas, 179 W.Va. 490, 370 S.E.2d 325 (1988).

As a practical (or political) matter it is more likely that discipline for filing frivolous suits will be visited upon plaintiffs' lawyers than defendants' lawyers and upon sole and small firm practitioners than lawyers in large and prestigious firms or government attorneys.

Dilatory Tactics

Dilatory tactics are tempting to lawyers, especially when they serve interests of both the lawyer and the client. If the lawyer can earn additional fees while advancing the client's interest, delay becomes hard to resist. The legal profession has a schizophrenic attitude toward strategic use of delay, in part because its effective use involves professional skills that sometimes are admired. Bar leaders and professional codes speak out against the use of delay as a deliberate harassing tactic, but eminent lawyers often boast shamelessly at professional meetings of their skills in delaying cases. For example, Bruce Bromley of the Cravath firm, in a 1958 talk to an admiring audience of lawyers, said:

> Now I was born, I think, to be a protractor.... I quickly realized in my early days at the bar that I could take the simplest antitrust case that [the antitrust division] could think of and protract it for the defense almost to infinity.[15]

The point of Bromley's talk, aside from his amusing account of past exploits as a "protractor," was that procedural changes and more judicial control had made the life of the protractor much more difficult.

The Model Code's prohibition of lawyer delay, limited to delay that would "merely" serve to harass or maliciously injure another, implied that delay is permissible if it serves the client's interests. Model Rule 3.2, however, imposes on lawyers the affirmative obligation to "make reasonable efforts to expedite litigation consistent with the interests of the client." The test given in the comment to Rule 3.2 for resolving the tension between client interests and expeditious litigation is "whether a lawyer acting in good faith would regard the course of action as having some substantial purpose other than delay. Realizing financial or other benefit from otherwise improper delay in litigation is not a legitimate interest of the client." Would Bruce Bromley be subject to discipline under this standard?

Repetitive Harassment

Professional discipline is rarely imposed for violations of the anti-harassment rules. The occasional discipline case involves lawyer behavior, such as that in *Solerwitz*, that is repetitive, fraudulent or verges on the psychopathic.[16]

---

15. Bruce Bromley, Judicial Control of Antitrust Cases, 23 F.R.D. 417 (1959).

16. See In re Bithoney, 486 F.2d 319 (1st Cir.1973) (suspension for repeated filing of bad faith appeals in immigration cases to delay deportation of clients); In re Jafree, 93 Ill.2d 450, 67 Ill.Dec. 104, 444 N.E.2d 143 (1982) (disbarment for filing over forty frivolous suits and appeals with papers filled with scurrilous and defamatory statements about judges); In re Olkon, 299 N.W.2d 89 (Minn.1980) (filing false insurance claim for presumed client who was undercover police investigator).

2. Tort Remedies Against Lawyers for Litigation Conduct

a. *Civil Liability of Lawyers for Pursuing Unfounded Claims*

FRIEDMAN v. DOZORC

Supreme Court of Michigan, 1981.
412 Mich. 1, 312 N.W.2d 585.

LEVIN, JUSTICE.

The plaintiff is a physician who, after successfully defending in a medical malpractice action, brought this action against the attorneys who had represented the plaintiffs in the former action. Dr. Friedman sought under a number of theories to recover damages for being compelled to defend against an allegedly groundless medical malpractice action. The trial court granted the defendants' motions for summary and accelerated judgment.

The Court of Appeals affirmed in part and reversed in part. We granted leave to appeal to consider what remedies may be available to a physician who brings such a "countersuit".

We hold that:

(1) The plaintiff has failed to state an actionable claim on a theory of negligence because an attorney owes no duty of care to an adverse party in litigation;

(2) The plaintiff has failed to state an actionable claim on a theory of abuse of process because there is no allegation that defendants committed an irregular act in the use of the process issued in the prior case;

(3) The plaintiff has failed to state an actionable claim on a theory of malicious prosecution because his complaint did not allege interference with his person or property sufficient to constitute special injury under Michigan law.

. . .

I

Facts

Leona Serafin entered Outer Drive Hospital in May, 1970, for treatment of gynecological problems. A dilation and curettage was performed by her physician, Dr. Harold Krevsky. While in the hospital, Mrs. Serafin was referred to the present plaintiff, Dr. Friedman, for urological consultation. Dr. Friedman recommended surgical removal of a kidney stone which was too large to pass, and the operation was performed on May 20, 1970. During the surgery, the patient began to ooze blood uncontrollably. Although other physicians were consulted, Mrs. Serafin's condition continued to worsen and she died five days after the surgery. An autopsy was performed the next day; the report identified the cause of death as thrombotic thrombocytopenic purpura, a rare and uniformly fatal blood disease, the cause and cure of which are unknown.

On January 11, 1972, attorneys Dozorc and Golden, the defendants in this action, filed a malpractice action on behalf of Anthony Serafin, Jr., for himself and as administrator of the estate of Leona Serafin, against Peoples Community Hospital Authority, Outer Drive Hospital, Dr. Krevsky and Dr. Friedman, as well as another physician who was dismissed as a defendant before trial. In December, 1974, the case went to trial in Wayne Circuit Court. No expert testimony tending to show that any of the defendants had breached accepted professional standards in making the decision to perform the elective surgery or in the manner of its performance was presented as part of the plaintiff's case. The judge entered a directed verdict of no cause of action in favor of Dr. Friedman and the other defendants at the close of the plaintiff's proofs. The judge subsequently denied a motion for costs brought by codefendant Peoples Community Hospital Authority, pursuant to GCR 1963, 111.6. The Court of Appeals affirmed and this Court denied leave to appeal.

Dr. Friedman commenced the present action on March 17, 1976 in Oakland Circuit Court. The following excerpt from his complaint summarizes his theories of recovery and the injuries he allegedly sustained as a result of the initiation and prosecution of the malpractice action:

> "13. That as a direct and proximate result of the negligence, malicious prosecution and abuse of process of these Defendants, the Plaintiff, Seymour Friedman, M.D., has endured grievous damages, including, but not limited to, the following: the cost of defending the aforesaid cause and the appeal, an increase in his annual malpractice insurance premiums for so long as he practices medicine, the loss of two young associates from his office who could no longer afford to pay the increased malpractice insurance premiums thereby requiring him to work excessive hours without relief, damages to his reputation as a physician and surgeon, embarrassment and continued mental anguish."

[The trial court granted the defendants' motion for summary judgment and Dr. Friedman appealed. The case was viewed by the parties, amici curiae, and the Michigan appellate courts as a test case involving the liability of a lawyer for filing and pursuing unfounded claims.]

. . .

II [Negligence]

Plaintiff and amici in support urge this Court to hold that an attorney owes a present or prospective adverse party a duty of care, breach of which will give rise to a cause of action for negligence. We agree with the circuit judge and the Court of Appeals that an attorney owes no actionable duty to an adverse party.

Plaintiff and amici argue that an attorney who initiates a civil *theory of liab.* action owes a duty to his client's adversary and all other foreseeable third parties who may be affected by such an action to conduct a reasonable investigation and re-examination of the facts and law so that the attorney will have an adequate basis for a good-faith belief that the client has a tenable claim. Plaintiff contends that this duty is created by the Code of Professional Responsibility and by the Michigan General Court Rules.[6]

Plaintiff further argues that an attorney's separate duty under the Code of Professional Responsibility to zealously represent a client is limited by the requirement that the attorney perform within the bounds of the law. [Here the court quoted DR 7–102(A)(1) and (A)(2); EC 7–4; and EC 7–10.] Acting within the bounds of the law is said to encompass refraining from asserting frivolous claims; this charge upon the profession imposes upon counsel a duty to the public, the courts and the adverse party to conduct a reasonable investigation. Plaintiff contends that since the duty to investigate already arises from the attorney-client relationship under the code and court rules, recognition of a cause of action for negligence will impose no new obligation on the attorney.

. . .

In a negligence action the question whether the defendant owes an actionable legal duty to the plaintiff is one of law which the court decides after assessing the competing policy considerations for and against recognizing the asserted duty.

. . .

Analysis

Assuming that an attorney has an obligation to his client to conduct a reasonable investigation prior to bringing an action, that obligation is not the functional equivalent of a duty of care owed to the client's adversary. We decline to so transform the attorney's obligation because we view such a duty as inconsistent with basic precepts of the adversary system.

The duties, professional and actionable, owed to the client by the attorney acting as advocate and adviser are broader than the obligation of reasonable investigation. Those duties concern decisions which the attorney makes on behalf of, and often in consultation with, the client, regarding the manner of proceeding with the client's cause. A decision to proceed with a future course of action that involves litigation will necessarily adversely affect a legal opponent. If an attorney were held to owe a duty of due care to both the client and the client's adversary, the obligation owing to the adversary would extend beyond undertaking an investigation and would permeate all facets of the litigation. The attorney's decision-making and future conduct on behalf of both parties

---

6. Plaintiff's brief refers to Code of Professional Responsibility and Canons, Canon 1, DR 1–102(A), Canon 6, DR 6–101(A), Canon 7, DR 7–102(A), and various Ethical Considerations associated with Canon 7, especially EC 7–4 and EC 7–10, as well as to GCR 1963, 111.6 and 114.

would be shaped by the attorney's obligation to exercise due care as to both parties. Under such a rule an attorney is likely to be faced with a situation in which it would be in the client's best interest to proceed in one fashion and in the adversary's best interest to proceed contrariwise. However he chooses to proceed, the attorney could be accused of failing to exercise due care for the benefit of one of the parties.

. . .

In short, creation of a duty in favor of an adversary of the attorney's client would create an unacceptable conflict of interest [10] which would seriously hamper an attorney's effectiveness as counsel for his client. Not only would the adversary's interests interfere with the client's interests, the attorney's justifiable concern with being sued for negligence would detrimentally interfere with the attorney-client relationship. As the California Supreme Court observed in Goodman v. Kennedy, 18 Cal.3d 335, 344, 556 P.2d 737, 743, 134 Cal.Rptr. 375 (1976):

> "The attorney's preoccupation or concern with the possibility of claims based on mere negligence (as distinct from fraud or malice) by any with whom his client might deal 'would prevent him from devoting his entire energies to his client's interests' (Anderson v. Eaton, 211 Cal. 113, 116, 293 P. 788, 790 [1930]). The result would be both 'an undue burden on the profession' (Lucas v. Hamm, 56 Cal.2d 583, 589 [15 Cal.Rptr. 821, 824, 364 P.2d 685, 688 (1961)]) and a diminution in the quality of the legal services received by the client." (Footnote omitted.)

. . .

... We reiterate what this Court said in State Bar Grievance Administrator v. Corace, 390 Mich. 419, 434–435, 213 N.W.2d 124 (1973):

> "[O]ur adversary system 'intends, and expects, lawyers to probe the outer limits of the bounds of the law, ever searching for a more efficacious remedy, or a more successful defense'."

We agree with those courts in other jurisdictions which have relied on the policy of encouraging free access to the courts as a reason for

10. Under a section entitled Conflicts in Litigation, the comments to the Discussion Draft of ABA Model Rules of Professional Conduct, 48 USLW, No. 32, Supplement, p. 8 (February 19, 1980), most aptly identify the type of conflict of interest presented under the instant facts:

"Most if not all questions of conflict of interest are questions of degree. As noted above, minor and inevitable conflicts inherent in client-lawyer relationships necessarily must be tolerated. On the other hand, a conflict of interest may be so sharp as to preclude the lawyer from representing a particular client. For example, under no circumstances could a lawyer properly represent both the plaintiff and the defendant in contested litigation, or represent parties to a negotiation whose interests are fundamentally antagonistic to each other. When it is plain that prejudice to the client's interests is likely to result, the lawyer should not undertake the representation even with the consent of the client. A client's consent does not legitimate a lawyer's abuse of professional office."

declining to recognize a negligence cause of action in physician counter-suits.[12] No appellate court has yet approved such a cause of action.

. . .

III [Abuse of Process]

To recover upon a theory of abuse of process, a plaintiff must plead and prove (1) an ulterior purpose and (2) an act in the use of process which is improper in the regular prosecution of the proceeding. Spear v. Pendill, 164 Mich. 620, 623, 130 N.W. 343 (1911).[18]

Plaintiff contends he has pleaded that defendants' ulterior purpose in filing the former malpractice action was to coerce payments of large sums of money from plaintiff for defendants' financial gain by means of their contingent-fee arrangement with the former plaintiff. In addition, plaintiff alleges that irregular use of process was shown by defendants' filing of the complaint without adequate investigation.

Defendants counter that plaintiff's pleadings are deficient in failing to allege an act by the defendants beyond mere initiation of a lawsuit and an ulterior purpose other than settlement of a lawsuit.

We need not decide whether plaintiff's pleadings sufficiently allege that the defendants had an ulterior purpose in causing process to issue, since it is clear that the plaintiff has failed to allege that defendants committed some irregular act in the use of process. The only act in the use of process that plaintiff alleges is the issuance of a summons and complaint in the former malpractice action. However, a summons and complaint are properly employed when used to institute a civil action, and thus plaintiff has failed to satisfy the second element required in *Spear*, supra, 623, 130 N.W. 343, where the Court observed " '[t]his action for abuse of process lies for the improper use of process after it has been issued, not for maliciously causing it to issue.' "

. . .

IV [Malicious Prosecution]

Plaintiff relies upon the same allegations respecting defendants' conduct and their failure to meet professional standards which assertedly constitute negligence in contending that he has pled a cause of action for malicious prosecution. He argues that the question of

12. Weaver v. Superior Court of Orange County, 95 Cal.App.3d 166, 156 Cal.Rptr. 745 (1979); Berlin v. Nathan, 64 Ill.App.3d 940, 21 Ill.Dec. 682, 381 N.E.2d 1367 (1978); Lyddon v. Shaw, 56 Ill.App.3d 815, 14 Ill.Dec. 489, 372 N.E.2d 685 (1978); Brody v. Ruby, 267 N.W.2d 902 (Iowa, 1978); Spencer v. Burglass, 337 So.2d 596 (La.App., 1976); Hill v. Willmott, 561 S.W.2d 331 (Ky.App., 1978).

18. The Restatement Torts, 2d, explains the tort of abuse of process as follows:

"The gravamen of the misconduct for which the liability stated in this section is imposed is not the wrongful procurement of legal process or the wrongful initiation of criminal or civil proceedings; it is the misuse of process, no matter how properly obtained, for any purpose other than that which it was designed to accomplish.... The subsequent misuse of the process, though properly obtained, constitutes the misconduct for which the liability is imposed under the rule stated in this section." 3 Restatement Torts, 2d, § 682, comment a, p. 474.

probable cause in a malicious prosecution action against the attorney for an opposing party turns on whether the attorney fulfilled his duty to reasonably investigate the facts and law before initiating and continuing a lawsuit. If the attorney's investigation discloses that the claim is not tenable, then it is his obligation to discontinue the action.

Defendants respond that Michigan is among those jurisdictions that have not abandoned the special injury requirement in actions for the malicious prosecution of civil proceedings. They urge, in addition, that this Court adopt a rule that a successful motion pursuant to GCR 1963, 111.6 in the former lawsuit is a necessary condition precedent to institution of a subsequent malicious prosecution action by the former defendant.

[1. Special Injury]

We agree with defendants that under Michigan law special injury remains an essential element of the tort cause of action for malicious prosecution of civil proceedings....

The recognition of an action for malicious prosecution developed as an adjunct to the English practice of awarding costs to the prevailing party in certain aggravated cases where the costs remedy was thought to be inadequate and the defendant had suffered damages beyond the expense and travail normally incident to defending a lawsuit. In 1698 three categories of damage which would support an action for malicious prosecution were identified: injury to one's fame (as by a scandalous allegation), injury to one's person or liberty, and injury to one's property.[21] To this day the English courts do not recognize actions for malicious prosecution of either criminal or civil proceedings unless one of these types of injury, as narrowly defined by the cases, is present.[22]

A substantial number of American jurisdictions [perhaps 17] today follow some form of "English rule" to the effect that "in the absence of an arrest, seizure, or special damage, the successful civil defendant has no remedy, despite the fact that his antagonist proceeded against him maliciously and without probable cause." A larger number of jurisdictions, some say a majority, follow an "American rule" permitting actions for malicious prosecution of civil proceedings without requiring the plaintiff to show special injury.

The plaintiff's complaint does not allege special injury. We are satisfied that Michigan has not significantly departed from the English rule and we decline to do so today.

This Court heretofore has neither recognized the unrestricted availability of a tort cause of action, analogous to malicious prosecution, for the wrongful initiation or continuation of civil proceedings, nor abrogat-

21. Savile v. Roberts, 1 Ld.Raym. 374, 378, 91 Eng.Rep. 1147, 1149–1150 (1698).

22. For discussion of what will constitute the requisite injury, see Quartz Hill Consolidated Gold Mining Co. v. Eyre, L.R. 11 QBD 674, 689–693, 52 LJQB (NS) 488 (1883) (opinion of Bowen, L.J.); and Wiffen v. Bailey & Romford Urban Dist. Council, [1915] 1 KB 600.

ed the traditional requirement that a plaintiff alleging wrongful institution of civil proceedings have suffered special injury in the nature of an interference with person or property. . . .

. . .

Most commentators appear to favor abrogation of the special injury requirement to make the action more available and less difficult to maintain.[34] Their counsel should, however, be evaluated skeptically. The lawyer's remedy for a grievance is a lawsuit, and a law student or tort professor may be particularly predisposed by experience and training to see the preferred remedy for a wrongful tort action as another tort action. In seeking a remedy for the excessive litigiousness of our society, we would do well to cast off the limitations of a perspective which ascribes curative power only to lawsuits.

We turn to a consideration of Dean Prosser's criticisms of the three reasons commonly advanced by courts for adhering to the English rule. First, to the assertion that the costs awarded to the prevailing party are intended as the exclusive remedy for the damages incurred by virtue of the wrongful litigation, Prosser responds that "in the United States, where the costs are set by statute at trivial amounts, and no attorney's fees are allowed, there can be no pretense at compensation even for the expenses of the litigation itself." [35] This argument is compelling, but it does not necessarily justify an award of compensation absent the hardship of special injury or dictate that an award of compensation be assessed in a separate lawsuit. Second, to the arguments that an unrestricted tort of wrongful civil proceedings will deter honest litigants and that an innocent party must bear the costs of litigation as the price of a system which permits free access to the courts, Prosser answers that "there is no policy in favor of vexatious suits known to be groundless, which are a real and often a serious injury." [36] But a tort action is not the only means of deterring groundless litigation, and other devices may be less intimidating to good-faith litigants. Finally, in response to the claim that recognition of the tort action will produce interminable litigation, Prosser argues that the heavy burden of proof which the plaintiff bears in such actions will safeguard bona fide litigants and prevent an endless chain of countersuits. But if few plaintiffs will recover in the subsequent action, one may wonder whether there is any point in recognizing the expanded cause of action. If the subsequent action does not succeed, both parties are left to bear the expenses of two futile lawsuits, and court time has been wasted as well.

---

34. Prosser, supra, § 120, p. 851; Note, Promoting Recovery by Claimants in Iowa Malicious Prosecution Actions, 64 Iowa L.Rev. 408 (1979); Note, Malicious Prosecution: An Effective Attack on Spurious Medical Malpractice Claims?, 26 Case Western Reserve L.Rev. 653, 657–662 (1976); Birnbaum, Physicians Counterattack: Liability of Lawyers for Instituting Unjustified Medical Malpractice Actions, 45 Fordham L.Rev. 1003, 1090 (1977).

35. Prosser, supra, § 120, p. 851.

36. Id.

Although this case arises upon the plaintiff doctor's assertions that the defendant attorneys wrongfully prosecuted a medical malpractice action against him, if we were to eliminate the special injury requirement that expansion of the tort of malicious prosecution would not be limited to countersuits against attorneys by aggrieved physicians. An action for malicious prosecution of civil proceedings could be brought by *any* former defendant—person, firm or corporation, private or public— in whose favor a prior civil suit terminated, against the former plaintiff or the plaintiff's attorney or both. In expanding the availability of such an action the Court would not merely provide a remedy for those required to defend groundless medical malpractice actions, but would arm all prevailing defendants with an instrument of retaliation, whether the prior action sounded in tort, contract or an altogether different area of law.

This is strong medicine—too strong for the affliction it is intended to cure. To be sure, successful defense of the former action is no assurance of recovery in a subsequent tort action, but the unrestricted availability of such an action introduces a new strategic weapon into the arsenal of defense litigators, particularly those whose clients can afford to devote extensive resources to prophylactic intimidation.

· · ·

[2. Probable Cause]

Apart from special injury, elements of a tort action for malicious prosecution of civil proceedings are (1) prior proceedings terminated in favor of the present plaintiff, (2) absence of probable cause for those proceedings, and (3) "malice," more informatively described by the Restatement as "a purpose other than that of securing the proper adjudication of the claim in which the proceedings are based." [43]

· · ·

The absence of probable cause in bringing a civil action may not be established merely by showing that the action was successfully defended.[44] To require an attorney to advance only those claims that will ultimately be successful would place an intolerable burden on the right of access to the courts.

The Court of Appeals adopted, and plaintiff endorses, the standard for determining whether an attorney had probable cause to initiate and continue a lawsuit articulated in Tool Research & Engineering Corp. v. Henigson, 46 Cal.App.3d 675, 683–684, 120 Cal.Rptr. 291 (1975): ...

"An attorney has probable cause to represent a client in litigation when, after a reasonable investigation and industrious search of legal authority, he has an honest belief that his client's claim is tenable in the forum in which it is to be tried."

43. See, generally, Prosser, supra, § 120, pp. 850–856, and 3 Restatement Torts, 2d, §§ 674–681B, pp. 452–473. Propriety of purpose is discussed in § 676.

44. See Prosser, supra, § 120, p. 855. Cf. Drobczyk v. Great Lakes Steel Corp., 367 Mich. 318, 322, 116 N.W.2d 736 (1962).

In our view, this standard, while well-intentioned, is inconsistent with the role of the attorney in an adversary system.

Our legal system favors the representation of litigants by counsel. Yet the foregoing standard appears skewed in favor of non-representation; the lawyer risks being penalized for undertaking to present the client's claim to a court unless satisfied, after a potentially substantial investment in investigation and research, that the claim is tenable.

A lawyer may be confronted with the choice between allowing the statute of limitation to run upon a claim with which the client has only recently come forward, or promptly filing a lawsuit based on the information in hand. Such dilemmas are particularly likely to arise in connection with medical malpractice claims because a statute provides a six-month limitation period for bringing an action based on a belatedly discovered claim as an alternative to the normal two-year limitation period for malpractice actions. Time will not always permit "a reasonable investigation and industrious search of legal authority" before the lawyer must file a complaint to preserve the client's claim—and thus, perhaps, avoid an action by the client for legal malpractice.

In medical malpractice actions the facts relevant to an informed assessment of the defendant's liability may not emerge until well into the discovery process. Sometimes the relevant facts are not readily ascertainable. In the instant case, for example, defendants maintain that their efforts to acquire Mrs. Serafin's medical records were rebuffed until they commenced suit and thereupon became able to invoke established discovery procedures and the implicit power of the court to compel disclosure; it may be the practice of some doctors or hospitals to refuse to release medical records until a lawsuit has been commenced.

Moreover, the *Henigson* standard suggests rather ominously that every time a lawyer representing, say, a medical malpractice plaintiff encounters a fact adverse to the client's position or an expert opinion that there was no malpractice, he must immediately question whether to persevere in the action. An attorney's evaluation of the client's case should not be inhibited by the knowledge that perseverance may place the attorney personally at risk; the next fact or the next medical opinion may be the one that makes the case, and such developments may occur even on the eve of trial.

Indeed, a jury-submissible claim of medical malpractice may sometimes be presented even without specific testimony that the defendant physician violated the applicable standard of care. Thus, a lawyer may proceed in the good-faith belief that his proofs will establish a prima facie case of medical malpractice without expert testimony, only to find that the court disagrees. Such conduct is not the equivalent of proceeding without probable cause.

Indeed, whether an attorney acted without probable cause in initiating, defending or continuing proceedings on behalf of a client should not normally depend upon the extent of the investigation conducted. The Code of Professional Responsibility does not expressly impose any duty upon a lawyer to conduct an independent investigation of the merits of a client's claim. DR 7–102(A), upon which plaintiffs in the instant action rely, states only that a lawyer shall not:

"(1) File a suit, assert a position, conduct a defense, delay a trial, or take other action on behalf of his client *when he knows or when it is obvious that such action would serve merely to harass or maliciously injure another.*

"(2) *Knowingly* advance a claim or defense that is unwarranted under existing law, except that he may advance such claim or defense if it can be supported by good faith argument for an extension, modification, or reversal of existing law." (Emphasis supplied.)

DR 7–102(A) and the other professional standards to which plaintiff refers consistently incorporate a requirement of *scienter* as to groundlessness or vexatiousness, not a requirement that the lawyer take affirmative measures to verify the factual basis of his client's position. A lawyer is entitled to accept his client's version of the facts and to proceed on the assumption that they are true absent compelling evidence to the contrary.[53] The only general limitation on the lawyer's acceptance of employment is found in DR 2–109(A), the language of which parallels DR 7–102(A). And, although DR 6–101(A)(2) states that a lawyer shall not "[h]andle a legal matter without preparation adequate in the circumstances," that preparation need not entail verification of the facts related by the client.

Framed as it is in terms of "reasonableness", the *Henigson* standard is difficult to reconcile with the lawyer's obligation to represent his client's interests zealously. "Zealous representation" contemplates that the lawyer will go to the limits for his client, representing him loyally, tenaciously and single-mindedly. The question of whether a lawyer "abused that duty" is not a matter of what a hypothetical reasonable practitioner would have done in the same circumstances, but of whether the lawyer's conduct was beyond the limits of reason or the bounds of the law although another "reasonable" lawyer, or many such lawyers, might not have acted similarly.

The Restatement's definition of probable cause provides ample guidance whether damages are sought from a lawyer, his client or both:

"One who takes an active part in the initiation, continuation or procurement of civil proceedings against another has probable cause for doing so if he reasonably believes in the existence of the facts upon which the claim is based, and either

"(a) correctly or reasonably believes that under those facts the claim *may* be valid under the applicable law, or

53. Cf. Murdock v. Gerth, 65 Cal.App.2d 170, 179, 150 P.2d 489, 493 (1944): [lawyer "obligated to present" to a court any "fairly debateable" claim supported by "facts stated to him by his client" even though court subsequently determines that lawyer's "judgment was erroneous"].

"(b) believes to this effect in reliance upon the advice of counsel, sought in good faith and given after full disclosure of all relevant facts within his knowledge and information." [57] (Emphasis supplied.)

As applied to a plaintiff's lawyer, this standard would allow lack of probable cause to be found where the lawyer proceeded with knowledge that the claim had no factual or legal basis, but would impose no obligation to investigate if the lawyer could reasonably believe the facts to be as the client alleged.

[3. Malice]

This Court has said, in opinions addressed to the tort of malicious prosecution, that malice may be inferred from the facts that establish want of probable cause, although the jury is not required to draw that inference.[58] This rule, developed in cases where damages were sought from a lay person who initiated proceedings, fails to make sufficient allowance for the lawyer's role as advocate and should not be applied in determining whether a lawyer acted for an improper purpose.

A client's total lack of belief that the action he initiates or continues can succeed is persuasive evidence of intent to harass or injure the defendant by bringing the action. But a lawyer who is unaware of such a client's improper purpose may, despite a personal lack of belief in any possible success of the action, see the client and the claim through to an appropriate conclusion without risking liability. Restatement 2d, Torts, § 674, comment *d*, states:

"An attorney who initiates a civil proceeding on behalf of his client or one who takes any steps in the proceeding is not liable if he has probable cause for his action (see § 675); *and even if he has no probable cause and is convinced that his client's claim is unfounded, he is still not liable if he acts primarily for the purpose of aiding his client in obtaining a proper adjudication of his claim.* (See § 676). An attorney is not required or expected to prejudge his client's claim, and although he is fully aware that its chances of success are comparatively slight, it is his responsibility to present it to the court for adjudication if his client so insists after he has explained to the client the nature of the chances." (Emphasis supplied.)

While a client's decision to proceed with litigation although he knows that the facts are not as alleged, or that a proper application to the facts of existing law (or any modification thereof which can be advanced in good faith) will not support the claim, is indicative of the client's ulterior, malicious motive, that inference cannot so easily be drawn from conduct of a lawyer who owes his client a duty of represen-

---

57. 3 Restatement Torts, 2d, § 675, pp. 457–458.

58. Hamilton v. Smith, 39 Mich. 222 (1878); Drobczyk v. Great Lakes Steel Corp., supra; Renda v. International Union, UAW, 366 Mich. 58, 100–101, 114 N.W.2d 343 (1962).

tation and is unaware of the client's improper purpose. The lawyer who "acts primarily for the purpose of aiding his client in obtaining a proper adjudication of his claim," albeit with knowledge that the claim is not tenable, should not be subject to liability on the thesis that an inference of an improper purpose may be drawn from the lawyer's continuing to advance a claim which he knew to be untenable.[60]

The Restatement defines the mental element of the tort of wrongful civil proceedings as "a purpose other than that of securing the proper adjudication of the claim in which the proceedings are based." A finding of an improper purpose on the part of the unsuccessful attorney must be supported by evidence independent of the evidence establishing that the action was brought without probable cause.[61]

We affirm that portion of the Court of Appeals decision which upheld summary judgment in favor of defendants on plaintiff's claims sounding in negligence and abuse of process. With respect to plaintiff's claim for malicious prosecution, we reverse the decision of the Court of Appeals and affirm the trial court's grant of summary judgment; we do so on the ground that an action for malicious prosecution of a civil action may not be brought absent special injury and the plaintiff failed to plead special injury.

KAVANAGH, WILLIAMS and RYAN, JJ., concur.

LEVIN, JUSTICE (concurring).

Much of the discussion of the problem of unjustified litigation suffers from an undue focus upon the need to compensate the injury suffered by the defendant subjected to a groundless and malicious action. Groundless civil litigation is, however, more than an affliction visited upon a few scattered individuals; it besets the judicial system as a whole. It is, therefore, appropriate to think of it as a systemic problem and to fashion a remedy which preserves and strengthens the integrity of the civil litigation system rather than randomly providing a fortuitous amount of compensation in a handful of isolated cases.

. . .

... [T]his Court can appropriately devise an approach to wrongful litigation which is capable of providing both an appropriate measure of deterrence and reasonable compensation for wronged litigants without imperiling the right of free access to the courts. The remedy, quite simply, is to recognize the inadequacy of existing provisions for the taxation of costs and to adopt a new and distinct court rule authorizing

---

60. In, most if not, all attorney-client relationships, decision-making authority ultimately rests with the client. A client may, in apparent good faith, insist upon pressing the claim although the attorney has explained that it has no chance of succeeding. An attorney's ability to withdraw from representation is limited if the client objects.

61. A contingent fee arrangement or the expectation of the attorney that he will ultimately receive a fee for his services is not evidence of an improper purpose. In contrast, a purpose to secure an improper adjudication of the client's claim, as by coercing a settlement unrelated to the merits from an opponent who wishes to avoid the harassment, expense or delay of letting the lawsuit run its course, is an improper purpose. See 3 Restatement Torts, 2d, § 674, comment *d*, p. 453.

the judge to whom a civil action is assigned to order payment of the prevailing party's actual expenses, including reasonable attorneys' fees and limited consequential damages, where the action was wrongfully initiated, defended or continued.[5] Depending upon the circumstances, payment might be required of the attorney, the client or both. The factual questions implicit in such an evaluation of the losing side's conduct would be resolved by the judge after a prompt post-termination hearing at which the parties could call witnesses and they and their attorneys could testify.

The foundation for developing such a comprehensive structure for controlling vexatious litigation is already in place. GCR 1963, 111.6, [permits a court to impose sanctions on a party pleading facts unreasonably].

The principles of GCR 1963, 111.6, can readily be extended to wrongful litigation and defense as well as wrongful pleading and can be made applicable regardless of the stage at which the prior litigation terminates; the award of fees and expenses should be limited to those incurred after the point at which the action should have been discontinued or liability admitted.

The sum recoverable should include all fees and administrative charges incurred because of the litigation as well as reasonable attorney's fees. The judge could award a prevailing defendant in a professional malpractice case an additional sum for loss of income-producing time and injury to professional reputation or business resulting from the wrongful action if the amount is capable of being calculated with reasonable certainty.[6]

The rule could provide that the standard to be applied by the judge in determining whether such an award should be made is whether the losing party or his attorney had proceeded without probable cause and for an improper purpose. So defining the inquiry, in terms of the traditional elements of a cause of action for malicious prosecution of civil proceedings, allows the judge to consult existing precedent for guidance.

Having such a determination made by the judge to whom the original proceeding was assigned would have a number of advantages over assessment of these questions by judge and jury in a separate tort action:

First, a strategy for evaluating the propriety of litigation which is administered exclusively by judges is more susceptible of consistent application and careful supervision than a strategy which relies on a group of laymen chosen at random, often for one day and one trial.

5. Adoption of such a rule appears to be an appropriate exercise of this Court's plenary power over practice and procedure in Michigan courts. See Perin v. Peuler (On Rehearing), 373 Mich. 531, 540–541, 130 N.W.2d 4 (1964)....

6. The proposed procedure would not appear to violate a constitutional right of jury trial [because Michigan's right of jury trial applies only to common law claims existing prior to the adoption of the constitution in 1963].

Confiding the question solely to the judge avoids the bifurcation of function associated with jury trial on the critical issue of probable cause in an action for malicious prosecution of civil proceedings. Limiting recovery to actual pecuniary loss, thereby eliminating recovery for emotional distress, and relying on a judge to assess damages, combined with the greater control that appellate courts exercise over a judge's findings as compared to a jury's verdict, should tend to avoid awards which might intimidate good-faith litigants.

Second, the judge would usually be familiar with the history of the case; the necessary evidence could be adduced and the relevant findings made in far more efficient fashion than if a new action and a separate trial before a different judge were required.

Third, parties who might be reluctant to initiate further litigation although they felt themselves wronged would be more likely to avail themselves of internal sanctions than of the opportunity to start a separate action which would take its place on the crowded docket and which the defendants would be likely to resist with all available means.

... By adopting a court rule this Court would address the problem directly and in a manner compatible with its responsibility to exercise close control and supervision.

This is unmistakably a test case, brought primarily to secure a change in the law. If a court rule responsive to the problem of wrongful litigation is ultimately adopted, the plaintiff and others who have rallied to his cause may win the war even if they have lost this battle.

In pursuing this case, the plaintiff and his supporters have taken a leading role in directing our attention to a widely held concern that today the courts are burdened and innocent parties harassed by an epidemic of frivolous lawsuits. The measure proposed here will put the validity of that perception to the test. All those who feel that they have been made the victims of wrongful litigation would be able to seek a prompt remedy without facing the difficulties and delay inherent in a subsequent tort action.

The effectiveness of such a rule would depend upon the vigilance of the judges who would apply it. The opinion of the Court in the instant case describes certain instances in which sanctions should not be imposed against an attorney. Nothing in the opinion of the Court should, however, be understood as indicating that the Court is unwilling to commit itself to the imposition of sanctions against an attorney where it is appropriate.

[Chief Justice Coleman dissented from the portion of the majority opinion requiring an allegation of special injury to state a claim for malicious prosecution. He argued that the special-injury requirement was unrelated to whether the earlier suit was meritorious or frivolous; and that the court's concern for groundless malicious prosecution suits was "one-sided," demonstrating concern that such suits might cause legal malpractice insurance premiums to rise and ignoring the effect frivolous litigation has had on physicians' malpractice insurance premiums. Justice Moody's partial dissent also objected to the special-injury requirement as anachronistic. Formerly, most civil actions were accompanied either by civil arrest of the defendant or attachment or garnishment of the defendant's property. Thus the requirement of interference with the person or property of the defendant was routinely satisfied. Today, the requirement is a formidable obstacle to suit and is unrelated to the actual damage caused by a malicious suit.]

Was the Claim Against Dr. Friedman Frivolous?

The *Friedman* case was litigated in the Michigan courts on the assumption that lawyer Dozorc brought an unfounded medical malpractice claim against Dr. Friedman. Presumably this is why medical associations and bar associations treated the litigation as a major case and filed amici briefs. Did Dozorc violate M.R. 3.1 or DR 7–102(A)(1)? See the discussion of the professional rules dealing with pursuing frivolous matters at p. 389 above. Or do the limited facts suggest to the contrary that Dozorc was guilty of legal malpractice in failing to establish a prima facie case of medical practice against Dr. Friedman?

Negligence Claim

During the "medical malpractice crisis" of the 1970s, cases resembling *Friedman* were litigated in many states, with similar results.[17] The courts have uniformly rejected negligence claims brought against lawyers by people those lawyers had sued on behalf of a client.[18] The courts have likewise rejected the argument that the ethics rules, in particular the rules against maintaining frivolous suits, create a legal duty that extends to the opposing party.[19] Is there an inconsistency in relying on policies of "free access to the courts" to deny a civil recovery based on violations of M.R. 3.1 or DR 7–102(A)(1) when the purpose of those provisions is precisely to curtail frivolous filings?[20]

17. For discussion of Friedman v. Dozorc, see Gerald W. Boston, Liability of Attorneys to Nonclients in Michigan: A Re-examination of Friedman v. Dozorc and a Rule of Limited Liability, 68 U.Det.L.Rev. 307 (1991).

18. In addition to *Friedman* see: Morowitz v. Marvel, 423 A.2d 196 (D.C.App.1980); Drago v. Buonagurio, 46 N.Y.2d 778, 778–779, 413 N.Y.S.2d 910, 386 N.E.2d 821 (1978); Spencer v. Burglass, 337 So.2d 596, 600–601 (La.App.1976).

19. See Mozzochi v. Beck, 204 Conn. 490, 529 A.2d 171 (1987), discussed below.

20. Professor Wolfram argues that standards of lawyer performance in ethics codes should be treated in much the same way as criminal or regulatory standards are treated in tort litigation generally—as giving rise to a civil cause of action or as persuasive evidence of the standard of care. Because of the limited resources of disciplinary bodies, "judicial expansion of recoveries for professional civil liability may be necessary to achieve an acceptable level of attorney compliance with [professional codes]." Providing for civil liability for violation of professional rules prohibiting frivolous filings, Wolfram argues, would give bite to the professional rule. Charles W. Wolfram, The Code of

Do the reasons given in *Friedman* for rejecting the negligence claim apply with equal force to the type of claim allowed in *Greycas*, printed at p. 75 above? Why allow broader liability to third parties when the lawyer is acting as a facilitator of transactions than when the lawyer is acting as an advocate?

Abuse of Process

Why does the court in *Friedman* reject the abuse of process claim?

The Restatement states that a party is liable for abuse of process when it uses legal process primarily to accomplish a purpose for which it is not designed.[21] A Comment explains that the word "primarily" was added to exclude liability "when the process is used for the purpose for which it was intended, but there is an incidental motive of spite or an ulterior purpose of benefit to the defendant."[22] As explained in *Friedman*, the tort has two elements: (1) an ulterior purpose; and (2) a willful act that is improper in the regular conduct of the proceeding.[23]

Mozzochi v. Beck[24] involved an abuse of process claim against lawyers. The plaintiff alleged that the lawyers had maintained suit despite learning that the allegations were untrue and that the suit therefore was wholly without merit. The court concluded:

> [A]lthough attorneys have a duty to their clients and to the judicial system not to pursue litigation that is utterly groundless, that duty does not give rise to a third party action for abuse of process unless the third party can point to specific misconduct intended to cause specific injury outside of the normal contemplation of private litigation. Any other rule would ineluctably interfere with the attorney's primary duty of robust representation of the interests of his or her client.[25]

Implicitly, *Mozzochi* states that factually baseless claims are within the "normal contemplation of private litigation." Given M.R. 3.1, Fed. R.Civ.P. 11 and state counterparts to these rules, how can maintaining a factually baseless claim be regarded as "normal"? Do M.R. 3.1 and Rule 11 "ineluctably" interfere with the attorney's primary duty of "robust" representation? Compare Raine v. Drasin,[26] upholding a jury verdict against a lawyer, including punitive damages, for filing a complaint against two doctors when the lawyer had in his possession medical records showing the claim lacked substance.

Professional Responsibility as a Measure of Attorney Liability in Civil Litigation, 30 S.C.L.Rev. 281, 287–95, 310–314 (1979).

21. Restatement (Second) of Torts § 682.

22. Id., Comment b to § 682.

23. See W. Prosser and P. Keeton, Torts (5th Ed.1984) § 121.

24. 204 Conn. 490, 529 A.2d 171 (1987).

25. 529 A.2d at 174.

26. 621 S.W.2d 895 (Ky.1981).

Malicious Prosecution

The elements of a malicious prosecution cause of action are: (1) the defendant instituted a proceeding against the plaintiff; (2) the proceeding was terminated in favor of the plaintiff; (3) the absence of probable cause for the proceeding; [27] (4) the defendant acted out of malice or other improper purpose; and, in some jurisdictions, (5) the plaintiff suffered damage of the type required for this cause of action.

(i) Special injury requirement

Isn't the special injury requirement an anachronism that should be eliminated from today's common law? When nearly all civil actions were initiated by arrest of the defendant or an attachment or garnishment of property, the requirement was easily met. Today, when those summary remedies may be employed only in very special circumstances established after notice and hearing, the requirement has the effect of largely abolishing the malicious prosecution cause of action. Note that most American states have eliminated the special injury requirement.

(ii) Absence of probable cause

When, according to *Friedman*, does a lawyer's prior filing of a baseless suit satisfy the requirement that the suit was brought without probable cause?

In *Friedman*, the court rejects the standard for judging probable cause articulated by the California court in *Henigson*. Why? One reason given is that "[t]ime will not always permit 'a reasonable investigation and industrious search of legal authority."' How is this concern addressed in Rule 11 cases? Read the note on p. 433 below on what constitutes a reasonable investigation under Rule 11.

The California Supreme Court has partially disapproved of the standard articulated in *Henigson*. *Henigson* said that probable cause had an objective component (reasonable investigation and industrious legal research) and a subjective component (honest belief). In *Sheldon Appel* [28] the court (1) rejected the subjective component, holding that it was irrelevant to the issue of probable cause whether the lawyer actually believed the suit was tenable; (2) held that probable cause was ordinarily for the court to decide as a matter of law and not for the jury; and (3) held that if there was such probable cause, it is immaterial that the attorney may not have made an adequate investigation.

How is a court to judge whether the prior action was instituted with probable cause? The standard, according to *Sheldon Appel*, is whether, on the facts as known to the lawyer at the time she instituted suit, the suit was objectively tenable. Expert testimony on this ques-

---

27. The requirement of termination means that a malicious prosecution claim cannot be asserted as a counterclaim. A favorable termination does not include a settlement, but only a successful adjudication.

28. Sheldon Appel Co. v. Albert & Oliker, 47 Cal.3d 863, 254 Cal.Rptr. 336, 765 P.2d 498 (1989).

tion is not permitted.[29] How does the *Sheldon Appel* position on probable cause differ from that of the court in *Friedman*?

(iii) Malice

When does an attorney act with malice according to *Friedman*? In *Sheldon Appel*, the court held that once the judge finds that the prior action was *not* objectively tenable, then the fact that the lawyer never thought it tenable and the fact that she failed to do any research before filing become relevant to whether the suit was instituted with malice.

Note that when a *party* is sued for malicious prosecution, reliance on counsel's advice may serve to negate the element of malice.[30] However, reliance on counsel will not serve to negate malice when the client withholds facts from the lawyer.[31]

b. Other Tort Liability Issues

Immunity From Suit for Defamation

Lawyers and other participants in judicial proceedings are absolutely immune from suit for defamation based on statements made in the course of those proceedings or "reasonably related" thereto.[32] Some courts recognize only a qualified privilege for comments "preliminary to a proposed judicial proceeding."[33] Others recognize an absolute privilege for these comments.[34]

The broad reach of the privilege has been criticized:

> In the hands of some courts, the privilege has been reshaped into something very much like a privilege for a lawyer to be bumptious and unrestrained in all matters vaguely related to litigation and regardless of whether the communication is calculated to advance or to retard justice or the proceeding.... Courts have employed the privilege beyond defamation and have held that suits are barred by the same immunity if they are based on negligent misrepresentation, invasion of privacy, or intentional infliction of emotional distress.[35]

Perjury as a Tort

The common law rule followed in most jurisdictions is that, in the absence of a statute, it is not a tort to commit perjury or suborn

---

29. 765 P.2d at 510.

30. See, e.g., Noell v. Angle, 217 Va. 656, 231 S.E.2d 330 (1977).

31. See, e.g., Derby v. Jenkins, 32 Md.App. 386, 363 A.2d 967, 971 (1976).

32. See Restatement (Second) of Torts, § 586; W. Prosser and P. Keeton on Torts § 114 (5th Ed.1984).

33. See, e.g., Pinkston v. Lovell, 296 Ark. 543, 759 S.W.2d 20 (1988) (comments by lawyer in conversation with clients on advisability of malpractice action are privileged if the initiation of proceedings in good faith is being seriously considered).

34. See Arneja v. Gildar, 541 A.2d 621 (D.C.App.1988) (ethnic slurs).

35. Wolfram, Modern Legal Ethics (1986) at 231.

perjury.[36] There are a number of justifications given for this rule: (1) it protects society's interest in finality of judgments; (2) it prevents multiplication of litigation; and (3) it prevents the intimidation of witnesses and parties.[37] However, if the plaintiff otherwise states a cause of action, e.g., for malicious prosecution or conspiracy to defraud the plaintiff of property, proof of the use of perjury may establish other elements of the plaintiff's case.[38] In conspiracy cases, the courts usually require that the perjury be part of a larger scheme or plan to injure the plaintiff.[39]

Liability for perjury or suborning perjury may be predicated upon a statute. For example, N.Y. Jud. Law § 487 authorizes an injured person to recover treble damages in a civil action from an attorney "guilty of any deceit or collusion with intent to deceive the court or any party." This and similar statutes in other states, however, are interpreted narrowly and rarely invoked.

Tortious Spoliation of Evidence

A few states have imposed tort liability for the intentional or negligent destruction or loss of evidence. In cases involving the negligent destruction of evidence, the claim is usually that the defendant interfered with the plaintiff's efforts to sue some third party by negligently destroying or losing potential evidence. The plaintiff must show that the defendant had a special relationship to the plaintiff that entailed a duty to preserve the evidence, such as that of a health care provider to a patient.[40] The cases generally involve parties that the plaintiff would have sued had the evidence not been destroyed.[41] Other jurisdictions reject this tort on the ground, among other things, that other remedies are available.[42]

36. See W. Prosser and P. Keeton, Torts (5th Ed.1984) § 114; F. Harper, F. James and O. Gray, Torts § 5.22.

37. Shepherd v. Epps, 179 Ga.App. 685, 347 S.E.2d 289 (1986).

38. See, e.g., Snyder v. Faget, 295 Ala. 197, 326 So.2d 113 (1976) (perjury may be demonstrated to prove an overt act in furtherance of conspiracy to defraud).

39. See Stolte v. Blackstone, 213 Neb. 113, 328 N.W.2d 462 (1982) (collecting and discussing cases).

40. See, e.g., Bondu v. Gurvich, 473 So.2d 1307 (Fla.Dist.App.1984) (hospital failed to preserve certain medical records of the plaintiff; as a result plaintiff lost a medical malpractice lawsuit against doctors). See also Pirocchi v. Liberty Mutual Insurance Co., 365 F.Supp. 277 (E.D.Pa.1973) (action against claims adjuster for losing the chair that allegedly caused plaintiff's injuries, making it impossible for plaintiff to sue the chair's manufacturer). Compare, e.g., Parker v. Thyssen Min. Constr., Inc., 428 So.2d 615 (Ala.1983) (employer had no duty to preserve evidence for employee's potential civil action against third parties); Coley v. Arnot Ogden Mem. Hospital, 107 A.D.2d 67, 485 N.Y.S.2d 876 (1985) (same).

41. See, e.g., Smith v. Superior Court, 151 Cal.App.3d 491, 198 Cal.Rptr. 829 (1984) (dealer, who lost physical evidence of plaintiff's negligence claim against dealer after promising to keep it, held liable for tortious spoliation of evidence); Hazen v. Municipality of Anchorage, 718 P.2d 456 (Alaska 1986) (claim that police intentionally altered a record of favorable evidence concerning person charged with crime stated a claim for relief).

42. La Raia v. Superior Court, 150 Ariz. 118, 722 P.2d 286 (1986); and Miller v. Montgomery County, 64 Md.App. 202, 494 A.2d 761 (1985) (emphasizing that because

c. *Is Court Rule Better Than Tort Rule?* [43]

Courts have kept a tight rein on tort suits to redress frivolous litigation while enlarging the scope of court sanctions against lawyers who bring frivolous suits. Justice Levin, concurring in *Friedman*, argues for court rule instead of tort rule. Is a court rule preferable? Why?

After *Friedman* Michigan changed its rule on sanctions for frivolous litigation. M.C.R. 2.114 is substantially similar to Fed.R.Civ.P. 11 and is considerably more stringent than Michigan's old rule.[44]

3. Rule 11 Sanctions [45]

The Rule 11 Controversy

In actual effect on the practice of law, the single most important development in the law of professional responsibility in the 1980s was the 1983 amendment to Rule 11 of the Federal Rules of Civil Procedure.[46] Because many states adopted procedural rules modeled after the 1983 version of federal Rule 11, its effects reached beyond the federal courts. As amended in 1983, the rule provided that the lawyer's signature on any paper filed in federal court represented the lawyer's warranty that: (1) the lawyer had undertaken a reasonable inquiry as to the law and facts contained therein; (2) the lawyer believed, after such inquiry, that the paper was (a) well-grounded in fact and (b) warranted by existing law or a good faith argument for the extension, modification or reversal of existing law; and (3) the paper was not interposed for any improper purpose, such as to harass or to cause unnecessary delay or needless increase in the cost of litigation.

destruction was by opposing party, plaintiff had other remedies available, i.e., negative inferences would be drawn about what the material would have shown).

43. For a discussion of tort liability and court sanctions, see John W. Wade, On Frivolous Litigation: A Study of Tort Liability and Procedural Sanctions, 14 Hofstra L.Rev. 433 (1986).

44. Another mechanism for reducing the number of frivolous medical malpractice cases is the use of medical malpractice screening panels in these cases. Typically, a panel is composed of a judge, lawyer and physician. After filing a complaint, the parties to the suit are required to participate in an evidentiary hearing conducted by the panel to determine whether there is enough evidence to support a claim against the defendant. These panels have been criticized for adding time and expense to the settlement process, being generally biased toward the defendant and having lax standards for panel members and administration. See, e.g., Howard Bedlin and Paul Nejelski, Unsettling Issues About Settling Civil Litigation, 68 Judicature 9, 11 (1984) (which also cites, at n. 5, state cases finding the panel system unconstitutional).

45. This section has been prepared on the assumption that the amendments to Fed.R.Civ.P. 11 transmitted by the Supreme Court to the Congress on April 22, 1993 will go into effect on December 1, 1993. As of October 1993, when final changes were made on this manuscript, some congressional sentiment for postponing or rejecting proposed amendments to Rule 26 was evident, but little inclination to do so with respect to the Rule 11 amendments. The text of the Supreme Court's transmission is printed in 146 F.R.D. 402 (1993).

46. The full text of the rule as amended in 1983 is reproduced in the opening paragraphs of the *Golden Eagle* case, below at 417.

Unlike the original Rule 11, the 1983 rule required a lawyer to (1) make a reasonable inquiry before making a factual assertion or legal argument and (2) have an objective basis for a belief that an assertion or argument was warranted. The 1983 rule also made sanctions for violating the rule mandatory rather than discretionary: A district court was required to impose sanctions whenever the rule was violated.

The stiffening of Rule 11 in 1983 resulted in a large increase in the frequency of sanctions and provoked a heated controversy.[47] Many judges and some lawyers lauded the constraints it placed on assertion of unmeritorious claims and defenses and other abusive litigation tactics. A few judges and many trial lawyers complained that the cure was worse than the disease, arguing that tactical use of the rule and the cost of collateral proceedings outweighed any benefits.[48] The plaintiffs' and civil rights' bar, as well as some legal scholars, also argued that Rule 11 limited the growth of new legal interpretations because it was sometimes used to penalize lawyers who challenged existing doctrine.[49]

As you consider the materials that follow, think about the following questions: Did Rule 11 as amended in 1983 go too far? Not far enough? Was amendment desirable to address the concerns about chilling legitimate advocacy? When, if ever, does advocacy go too far? Would other deterrents be effective but less "chilling"?

The controversy over Rule 11 as amended in 1983 was fought out in courts and rules committees.[50] The *Golden Eagle* case, reprinted below, poses some of the major issues concerning the 1983 rule in the form of judicial interpretation of it. Many other judicial decisions, including nearly a half-dozen by the Supreme Court, gradually narrowed the interpretive uncertainties. Attention then shifted in the early 1990s to the rules committees of the Judicial Conference of the United States. After considering a large number of proposed amendments, some designed to broaden the rule and stiffen its requirements and others

47. Before the 1983 amendments Rule 11 motions had been filed in only nineteen reported cases; in the first four years after the rule was amended, there were more than 600 reported cases involving Rule 11 sanctions. See William W. Schwarzer, Rule 11 Revisited, 101 Harv.L.Rev. 1013 (1988); Georgene M. Vairo, Rule 11: A Critical Analysis, 118 F.R.D. 189 (1988).

48. See, e.g., Judge Jack B. Weinstein: "[Rule 11] has become another way of harassing the opponent and delaying the case. To date, the effects have been adverse." Tamar Lewin, A Legal Curb Raises Hackles, N.Y.Times, Oct. 2, 1986, pp. D1, D8 (quoting Judge Weinstein).

49. See, e.g., Melissa L. Nelken, Sanctions Under Amended Federal Rule 11—Some "Chilling" Problems in the Struggle Between Compensation and Punishment, 74 Geo.L.J. 1313, 1326 (1986). But see Jeffrey A. Parness, More Stringent Sanctions Under Federal Civil Rule 11: A Reply to Professor Nelken, 75 Geo.L.J. 1937 (1987).

50. For empirical study of experience under the 1983 rule, see, e.g., Thomas E. Willging, The Rule 11 Sanctioning Process (1989); Third Circuit Task Force on Federal Rule of Civil Procedure 11, Rule 11 in Transition (Stephen B. Burbank, Reporter) Amer.Judicature Soc'y, 1989; Elizabeth C. Wiggins, Thomas E. Willging, and Donna Stienstra, Report on Rule 11 (Federal Judicial Center 1991). Extended discussion of the case law involving Rule 11 may be found in George Joseph, Sanctions: The Federal Law of Litigation Abuse (1989); Georgene Vairo, Rule 11 Sanctions: Case Law Perspectives and Preventive Measures (1991).

designed to narrow and moderate it, the Supreme Court forwarded proposed amendments to the Congress in April 1993. The 1993 version of Rule 11 will become effective on December 1, 1993, unless Congress acts to postpone or reject the amended rule.

The rulemakers came up with an elaborate compromise that broadens the obligations of candor of Rule 11 in some respects but provides constraints and flexibility in dealing with infractions of the rule.[51] A "safe harbor" provision provides protection against sanctions if lawyers withdraw or correct contentions after a potential violation is called to their attention. In addition, imposition of sanctions is no longer mandatory but is in the discretion of the district court.

The text of the 1993 version of Rule 11(b) is as follows:

(b) *Representations to Court.* By presenting to the court (whether by signing, filing, submitting, or later advocating) a pleading, written motion, or other paper, an attorney or unrepresented party is certifying that to the best of the person's knowledge, information, and belief, formed after an inquiry reasonable under the circumstances,—

(1) it is not being presented for any improper purpose, such as to harass or to cause unnecessary delay or needless increase in the cost of litigation;

(2) the claims, defenses, and other legal contentions therein are warranted by existing law or by a nonfrivolous argument for the extension, modification, or reversal of existing law or the establishment of new law;

(3) the allegations and other factual contentions have evidentiary support or, if specifically so identified, are likely to have evidentiary support after a reasonable opportunity for further investigation or discovery; and

(4) the denials of factual contentions are warranted on the evidence or, if specifically so identified, are reasonably based on a lack of information or belief.

Justice Scalia expressed strong objections to the changes in the sanctions provisions of the amended rule, which are not reproduced here. Dissenting from the Court's adoption of the amended Rule 11, he stated, "The proposed revision would render the Rule toothless, by allowing judges to dispense with sanction, by disfavoring the compensation for litigation expenses, and by providing a 21–day 'safe harbor' within which, if the party accused of a frivolous filing withdraws the filing, he is entitled to escape with no sanction at all." [52]

Scalia argued that empirical evidence showed that the 1983 rule was effective in deterring frivolous pleadings and motions, an impor-

---

51. See 146 F.R.D. 577–92 (1993) for the text of the amended rule and the accompanying notes of the Advisory Committee on Civil Rules.

52. 146 F.R.D. at 507–08.

tant goal of the federal procedural system because it serves the fundamental purpose of the system—"just, speedy, and inexpensive determination of every action." Fed.R.Civ.P. 1. He cited data from a study by the Federal Judicial Center:

> [Eighty percent] of district judges believe Rule 11 has had an overall positive effect and should be retained in its present form, 95% believed the Rule had not impeded development of the law, and about 75% said the benefits justify the expenditure of judicial time.... True, many lawyers do not like Rule 11. It may cause them financial liability, it may damage their professional reputation in front of important clients, and the cost-of-litigation savings it produces are savings not to lawyers but to litigants. But the overwhelming approval of the Rule by the federal district judges who daily grapple with the problem of litigation abuse is enough to persuade me that it should not be gutted as the proposed revision suggests.[53]

GOLDEN EAGLE DISTRIBUTING CORP. v. BURROUGHS CORP.

United States Court of Appeals, Ninth Circuit, 1986.
801 F.2d 1531.

Before SCHROEDER, REINHARDT, and BEEZER, CIRCUIT JUDGES.

SCHROEDER, CIRCUIT JUDGE.

I. INTRODUCTION

This is an appeal from the imposition of sanctions under Rule 11 of the Federal Rules of Civil Procedure as amended in 1983. The appellant, a major national law firm, raises significant questions of first impression.

The relevant portions of the amended Rule provide:

> Every pleading, motion, and other paper of a party represented by an attorney shall be signed by at least one attorney of record in his individual name, whose address shall be stated. A party who is not represented by an attorney shall sign his pleading, motion, or other paper and state his address.... The signature of an attorney or party constitutes a certificate by him that he has read the pleading, motion, or other paper; that to the best of his knowledge, information, and belief formed after reasonable inquiry it is well grounded in fact and is warranted by existing law or a good faith argument for the extension, modification, or reversal of existing law, and that it is not interposed for any improper purpose, such as to harass or to cause unnecessary delay or needless increase in the cost of litigation. If a pleading, motion, or other paper is not signed, it shall be stricken unless it is signed promptly after the omission is called to the attention of the pleader or movant. If a

---

53. 146 F.R.D. at 509–10.

pleading, motion, or other paper is signed in violation of this rule, the court, upon motion or upon its own initiative, shall impose upon the person who signed it, a represented party, or both, an appropriate sanction, which may include an order to pay to the other party or parties the amount of the reasonable expenses incurred because of the filing of the pleading, motion, or other paper, including a reasonable attorney's fee.

The appellant Kirkland & Ellis is the law firm that represented the defendant Burroughs in the underlying litigation. The sanctions which we review here stemmed from an unsuccessful motion for summary judgment filed by appellant on Burroughs' behalf. . . .

.   .   .

The district court held that the positions taken by the appellant in its motions papers were supportable, both legally and factually. The district court concluded, however, . . . that the appellant should have stated that a position it was taking was grounded in a "good faith argument for the extension, modification, or reversal of existing law" rather than implying that its position was "warranted by existing law." Second, the court held that the appellant's moving papers had failed to cite contrary authority in violation of the ABA's Model Rules of Professional Conduct, and that this breach constituted a violation of Rule 11.

.   .   .

II. PROCEDURAL BACKGROUND OF THIS DISPUTE

Golden Eagle Distributing Corporation filed the underlying action in Minnesota state court for fraud, negligence, and breach of contract against Burroughs, because of an allegedly defective computer system. Burroughs removed the action to the federal district court in Minnesota. Burroughs then moved pursuant to 28 U.S.C. § 1404(a) to transfer the action to the Northern District of California. The district court granted the motion, noting that all of the sources of proof, including the relevant documents and the computer system at issue, and almost all of the witnesses, were located in California.

Burroughs next filed the motion for summary judgment which gave rise to the sanctions at issue here. It argued that the California, rather than the Minnesota, statute of limitations applied. . . .

.   .   .

A. The Statute of Limitations Argument

Kirkland & Ellis's opening memorandum argued that Golden Eagle's claims were barred by California's three-year statute of limitations. The question was whether the change of venue from Minnesota to California affected which law applied. Kirkland & Ellis essentially argued that under Van Dusen v. Barrack, 376 U.S. 612 (1964), California's law applied because a Minnesota court would have dismissed the action on forum non conveniens grounds. . . .

. . .

In imposing sanctions, the district court held that Kirkland & Ellis's argument was "misleading" because it suggested that there already exists a forum non conveniens exception to the general rule that the transferor's law applies. *Golden Eagle*, 103 F.R.D. at 126–28. *Van Dusen* raised the issue but did not decide it. 376 U.S. at 640.

Kirkland & Ellis's corollary argument, that a Minnesota court would have dismissed the case on forum non conveniens grounds, was found to be "misleading" because it failed to note that one prerequisite to such a dismissal is that an alternative forum be available. See Bongards' Creameries v. Alfa–Laval, Inc., 339 N.W.2d 561, 562 (Minn. 1983). Burroughs had pointed out in its Rule 11 memorandum, however, that the meaning of the term "available forum" is not settled. Compare Wasche v. Wasche, 268 N.W.2d 721, 723 (Minn.1978) (statute of limitations bar may affect dismissal) with Hill v. Upper Mississippi Towing Corp., 252 Minn. 165, 89 N.W.2d 654 (1958) (suggesting available forum is where defendant is amenable to process).

. . .

B. The Economic Damages Argument

Kirkland & Ellis also argued that Golden Eagle's claim for negligent manufacture lacked merit because Golden Eagle sought damages for economic loss, and such damages are not recoverable under California law. Kirkland & Ellis relied on Seely v. White Motor Co., 63 Cal.2d 9, 403 P.2d 145, 45 Cal.Rptr. 17 (1965). In *Seely*, the California Supreme Court limited recovery in negligence and strict liability tort actions to damages for personal injuries and harm to physical property.

The district court sanctioned Kirkland & Ellis for not citing three cases whose holdings it concluded were adverse to *Seely* : the California Supreme Court's opinion in J'Aire Corp. v. Gregory, 24 Cal.3d 799, 598 P.2d 60, 157 Cal.Rptr. 407 (1979), and two intermediate appellate court decisions interpreting *J'Aire's* effect on *Seely*, Pisano v. American Leasing, 146 Cal.App.3d 194, 194 Cal.Rptr. 77 (1983), and Huang v. Garner, 157 Cal.App.3d 404, 203 Cal.Rptr. 800 (1984).[1] The district court held that these omissions violated counsel's duty to disclose adverse authority, embodied in Model Rule 3.3, . . . which the court viewed as a "necessary corollary to Rule 11." *Golden Eagle*, 103 F.R.D. at 127.

Kirkland & Ellis continues to maintain vigorously that the cases are not directly adverse authority and that they are distinguishable. In this appeal we assume that they are directly contrary in order to

1. Kirkland & Ellis did cite and discuss *J'Aire* in its reply brief after the case was called to its attention in plaintiff's response.

reach the larger question of whether Kirkland & Ellis's failure to cite them was a violation of Rule 11.

III. THE BACKGROUND OF THE 1983 AMENDMENTS TO RULE 11 AND THEIR INTERPRETATION IN THE COURTS

Under the 1983 amendments to Rule 11, an attorney signing any motion in federal court warrants that the motion is well-grounded in fact, that it is warranted by existing law or a good faith argument for an extension, modification or reversal of existing law, and that it is not filed for an improper purpose....

The Advisory Committee Note to the amendments comments at length on their purpose. The members of the Advisory Committee, as well as its reporter, also commented extensively as individuals. All the comments make it clear that the amendments' major purposes were the deterrence of dilatory or abusive pretrial tactics and the streamlining of litigation. The Advisory Committee Note on the amendments to Rule 11, for example, states that the amended Rule will accomplish these purposes "by lessening frivolous claims or defenses." 97 F.R.D. 165, 198 (1983)....

. . .

Th[e] expansion [of Rule 11] gave rise to concerns that the new Rule might have unfortunate results in at least two respects. The first was that the amended Rule might tend to chill creativity in advocacy and impede the traditional ability of the common law to adjust to changing situations. The Advisory Committee responded....

> The rule is not intended to chill an attorney's enthusiasm or creativity in pursuing factual or legal theories. The court is expected to avoid using the wisdom of hindsight and should test the signer's conduct by inquiring what was reasonable to believe at the time the pleading, motion, or other paper was submitted.

Id. at 199

Another major concern was that the broadened availability of sanctions might lead to protracted and expensive satellite litigation over the appropriateness of sanctions....

... The leading decision in this circuit has identified the two major problems to which the amendments were directed as the problem of "frivolous filings" and the problem of "misusing judicial procedures as a weapon for personal or economic harassment." Zaldivar v. City of Los Angeles, 780 F.2d 823, 830 (9th Cir.1986). Along the same lines, the leading decision of the Second Circuit announced tests for the mandatory imposition of sanctions under both parts of the Rule. Sanctions should be imposed if (1) "after reasonable inquiry, a competent attorney could not form a reasonable belief that the pleading (or other paper) is well grounded in fact and is warranted by existing law or a good faith argument for the extension, modification or reversal of existing law" or if (2) "a pleading (or other paper) has been interposed for any improper purpose." Eastway [Construction Corp. v. City of New York] 762 F.2d [243] at 25 [(2d Cir.1985)]; see also McLaughlin v. Western Casualty & Surety Co., 603 F.Supp. 978, 981 (S.D.Ala.1985).

Courts have sanctioned attorneys for violating the first part of the Rule in a variety of circumstances. A legal position which is superficially plausible has been held sanctionable where it has no basis in the law and ignores relevant United States Supreme Court authority contrary to the position asserted. Rodgers v. Lincoln Towing Service, Inc., 771 F.2d 194, 205 (7th Cir.1985). A factually baseless contention that exigent circumstances justified a warrantless entry led to sanctions in Frazier v. Cast, 771 F.2d 259 (7th Cir.1985). A leading example of imposition of sanctions for violation of the second part of Rule 11 is Chevron, USA, Inc. v. Hand, 763 F.2d 1184 (10th Cir.1985), in which sanctions were upheld because the defendant had agreed to a stipulated settlement to dismiss the case and hired another attorney solely to delay the entry of the stipulated dismissal.

There is general agreement that whether the first of the two Rule 11 requirements has been satisfied is to be determined by use of an objective standard. . . .

As to the second, "not for improper purposes," part of Rule 11, we emphasized in *Zaldivar* the objective nature of the standard. We stated that a complaint which complies with the "well-grounded in fact and warranted by . . . law" clause cannot be sanctioned as harassment under Rule 11, regardless of the subjective intent of the attorney or litigant. *Zaldivar*, 780 F.2d at 832.

. . .

IV.   STANDARD OF REVIEW

[The court discussed Ninth Circuit decisions holding that the standard for appellate review in Rule 11 questions depended upon the issue involved and that de novo review was the appropriate standard when the issue, as in this case, involved "whether specific conduct violated the Rule." Subsequently, the Supreme Court in Cooter & Gell v. Hartmarx Corp., 496 U.S. 384 (1990), held that the standard of review for all issues arising under Rule 11 was whether the district court abused its discretion.]

V.   THE APPLICATION OF RULE 11 IN THIS CASE

The district court's application of Rule 11 in this case strikes a chord not otherwise heard in discussion of this Rule. The district court did not focus on whether a sound basis in law and in fact existed for the defendant's motion for summary judgment. Indeed it indicated that the motion itself was nonfrivolous. 103 F.R.D. at 126. Rather, the district court looked to the manner in which the motion was presented. The district court in this case held that Rule 11 imposes upon counsel an ethical "duty of candor." *Golden Eagle*, 103 F.R.D. at 127. The

[handwritten: motion ≠ frivolous]

court drew its principles from Rule 3.3 of the ABA's Model Rules and the accompanying comment. It said:

> The duty of candor is a necessary corollary of the certification required by Rule 11. A court has a right to expect that counsel will state the controlling law fairly and fully; indeed, unless that is done the court cannot perform its task properly. A lawyer must not misstate the law, fail to disclose adverse authority (not disclosed by his opponent), or omit facts critical to the application of the rule of law relied on.

Golden Eagle, 103 F.R.D. at 127.

. . .

We need not here definitively resolve the problems of the proper role of the courts in enforcing the ethical obligations of lawyers.[3] We must consider only whether Rule 11 requires the courts to enforce ethical standards of advocacy beyond the terms of the Rule itself.

The district court's invocation of Rule 11 has two aspects. The first, which we term "argument identification" is the holding that counsel should differentiate between an argument "warranted by existing law" and an argument for the "extension, modification, or reversal of existing law." The second is the conclusion that Rule 11 is violated when counsel fails to cite what the district court views to be directly contrary authority. We deal with each in turn, noting at the outset that many of our observations are applicable to both aspects of the court's interpretation of Rule 11.

A. "Argument Identification"

. . .

The text of the Rule does not require that counsel differentiate between a position which is supported by existing law and one that would extend it. The Rule on its face requires that the motion be either one or the other.... It is not always easy to decide whether an argument is based on established law or is an argument for the extension of existing law. Whether the case being litigated is or is not materially the same as earlier precedent is frequently the very issue which prompted the litigation in the first place. Such questions can be close.

Sanctions under Rule 11 are mandatory. See, e.g., *Eastway*, 762 F.2d at 254 n. 7. In even a close case, we think it extremely unlikely that a judge, who has already decided that the law is not as a lawyer argued it, will also decide that the loser's position was warranted by existing law. Attorneys who adopt an aggressive posture risk more than the loss of the motion if the district court decides that their argument is for an extension of the law which it declines to make.

---

3. Our judicial system reserves at least some role. See Roadway Express, Inc. v. Piper, 447 U.S. 752, 766–67 (1980); Eash v. Riggins Trucking Inc., 757 F.2d 557, 564–65 (3d Cir.1985) (en banc).

What is at stake is often not merely the monetary sanction but the lawyer's reputation.

The "argument identification" requirement adopted by the district court therefore tends to create a conflict between the lawyer's duty zealously to represent his client, Model Code of Professional Responsibility Canon 7, and the lawyer's own interest in avoiding rebuke. The concern on the part of the bar that this type of requirement will chill advocacy is understandable.[4] ...

Moreover, Rule 11 does not apply to the mere making of a frivolous argument. The Rule permits the imposition of sanctions only when the "pleading, motion, or other paper" itself is frivolous, not when one of the arguments in support of a pleading or motion is frivolous. Nothing in the language of the Rule or the Advisory Committee Notes supports the view that the Rule empowers the district court to impose sanctions on lawyers simply because a particular argument or ground for relief contained in a non-frivolous motion is found by the district court to be unjustified....

. . .

There is another risk when mandatory sanctions ride upon close judicial decisions. The danger of arbitrariness increases and the probability of uniform enforcement declines. The Federal Judicial Center recently studied the application of Rule 11 in fairly routine cases involving issues far less sophisticated than those involved in this case. The conclusion was as follows:

> Overall, we found that although the 1983 amendments appear to have increased judges' readiness to enforce the new certification requirements, their success thus far has been limited. Of specific concern are the findings that there is a good deal of interjudge disagreement over what actions constitute a violation of the rule, only partial compliance with the desired objective standard, inaccurate and systematically biased normative assumptions about other judges' reactions to frivolous actions, and a continued neglect of alternative, nonmonetary means of response.

. . .

B. The Failure to Cite Adverse Authority

. . .

Were the scope of the rule to be expanded as the district court suggests, mandatory sanctions would ride on close decisions concerning whether or not one case is or is not the same as another. We think Rule 11 should not impose the risk of sanctions in the event that the court later decides that the lawyer was wrong. The burdens of re-

---

4. The ABA's litigation section has commented, for example, that the *Golden Eagle* decision "caused complete consternation in the practicing bar which sees vigorous advocacy, seemingly without regard to its possible misrepresentations to the court, as the hallmark of aggressive and justified representation of the client."

search and briefing by a diligent lawyer anxious to avoid any possible rebuke would be great. And the burdens would not be merely on the lawyer. If the mandatory provisions of the Rule are to be interpreted literally, the court would have a duty to research authority beyond that provided by the parties to make sure that they have not omitted something.

· · ·

In rejecting the district court's broad interpretation of Rule 11, we do not suggest that the court is powerless to sanction lawyers who take positions which cannot be supported. A lawyer should not be able to proceed with impunity in real or feigned ignorance of authorities which render his argument meritless. See, e.g., Rodgers v. Lincoln Towing Service, Inc., 771 F.2d 194, 205 (7th Cir.1985). In addition, Rule 11 is not the only tool available to judges in imposing sanctions on lawyers. However, neither Rule 11 nor any other rule imposes a requirement that the lawyer, in addition to advocating the cause of his client, step first into the shoes of opposing counsel to find all potentially contrary authority, and finally into the robes of the judge to decide whether the authority is indeed contrary or whether it is distinguishable. It is not in the nature of our adversary system to require lawyers to demonstrate to the court that they have exhausted every theory, both for and against their client. Nor does that requirement further the interests of the court. It blurs the role of judge and advocate. The role of judges is not merely to

> match the colors of the case at hand against the colors of many sample cases spread out upon their desk.... It is when the colors do not match, when the references in the index fail, when there is no decisive precedent, that the serious business of the judge begins.

B. Cardozo, The Nature of the Judicial Process 21 (1922). In conducting this "serious business," the judge relies on each party to present his side of the dispute as forcefully as possible. The lawyers cannot adequately perform their role if they are required to make predeterminations of the kind the district court's approach to Rule 11 would necessitate.

[The Ninth Circuit denied a sua sponte request for an en banc hearing in *Golden Eagle*. Judge Noonan's dissent from that denial, joined by four other judges, follows:]

GOLDEN EAGLE DISTRIBUTING CORP. v. BURROUGHS CORP.

United States Court of Appeals, Ninth Circuit, 1987.
809 F.2d 584.

NOONAN, CIRCUIT JUDGE, with whom SNEED, ANDERSON, HALL, and KOZINSKI, CIRCUIT JUDGES, join dissenting from the denial of a sua sponte request for en banc hearing:

· · ·

... The district judge had in front of him a brief which did three things. The brief flatly misrepresented Minnesota law as having definitively decided the issue of forum non conveniens in a way favorable to the defendant. The brief insinuated that federal law on the same issue was definitively established the way the defendant would have liked. The brief set out California law without qualification and without mention of later authority which for purposes of the present opinion is assumed to have been "directly contrary." The court sanctioned Kirkland, Ellis for these three statements of law, each of which was not "warranted." The truth or falsity of a statement is not merely a matter of "the manner" in which a position is presented. A false statement presented as a true statement is simply a misstatement. It is not warranted. It should be sanctionable.

... The opinion substitutes extreme hypotheticals for the case at hand. It imagines close cases where a judge might sanction a lawyer because the judge disagrees with his argument. But close cases exist that test the workability of any rule, civil or criminal. They are not a reason for repealing the rule. Here, on the opinion's own admission, the case was not close. Kirkland, Ellis failed to cite "directly contrary" authority.

. . .

How can a brief be warranted by existing law if its argument goes in the face of "directly contrary" authority from the highest court of the jurisdiction whose law is being argued? How can a brief be warranted to be "a good faith argument for the extension, modification, or reversal of existing law" when there is not the slightest indication that the brief is arguing for extension, modification or reversal?

. . .

The opinion puts the question as one of "argument identification," treating Kirkland, Ellis' failure as a failure to identify correctly its argument as one for extension of existing law. But Kirkland, Ellis' failure was far greater. Kirkland, Ellis made no argument at all for extending existing law. It simply misrepresented the law it cited.

. . .

... The Rule mandates sanctions for any legal papers filed in federal court with *any* improper purpose. The opinion reads "any" out of the Rule.

. . .

... The opinion says that the signatory attorney "warrants." "Warrants" is a verb meaning "to assure a person of the truth of what is said." Webster's, Meaning 2b.

How can a lawyer offer testimony to the truth of what he has filed, how can he assure a person of its truth, if it is a misrepresentation?

. . .

... The opinion goes on to cite with apparent approval the view of the American Bar Association's Litigation Section that "the practicing bar" sees vigorous advocacy "seemingly without regard to its possible misrepresentations to the court" as the mark of "justified representation of the client."

This vision of vigorous advocacy "seemingly" indifferent to misrepresentations is cited by the opinion as "understandable" concern by the bar that vigorous advocacy not be chilled. Identification of vigorous advocacy with indifference to misrepresentation reflects a one-sided view. It is a view that has been repudiated by modern legal ethics. There is no reason to revive the old, discredited view, much less to incorporate the old view into an interpretation of Rule 11. Vigorous advocacy is, necessarily, truthful advocacy.

A distinct shift from the old view was made in a report by the Joint Conference on Professional Responsibility established by the American Bar Association and the Association of American Law Schools. "Confronted by the layman's charge" that the lawyer is "nothing but a hired brain and voice," this committee undertook to set out the duties of lawyers in terms of social functions that made the lawyer's role understandable, acceptable, and even necessary. See Introductory Statement of Co-chairmen Lon L. Fuller and John D. Randall, "Professional Responsibility: Report of the Joint Conference," 44 ABA Journal 1159 (1958). The report, in large measure, reflected the jurisprudence, the insights, and the wisdom of Professor Fuller. The report stressed that "the integrity of the adjudicative process itself" depends upon the participation of the advocate in order to hold in suspense the mind of the judge, prevent premature closure of the judge's mind, and make a wise decision possible. The function of the advocate defined his responsibilities and the limits of advocacy. The report concluded that a lawyer whose "desire to win leads him to muddy the headwaters of decision" and who "distorts and obscures" the true nature of a case "trespasses against the obligations of professional responsibility." Id. at 1161.

Modern codes of ethics have followed this line of thought. The American Bar Association's Model Code of Professional Responsibility invoked the report of the Joint Conference in stating that a lawyer today "stands in special need of a clear understanding of his obligations and of the vital connection between these obligations and the role his profession plays in society." Preamble, fn. 3, ABA Model Code of Professional Responsibility (1974). The first disciplinary rule of the Code is that "a lawyer shall not ... engage in conduct involving dishonesty, fraud, deceit or misrepresentation." DR 1–102(A)(4). The Disciplinary Rule does not distinguish misrepresentation of fact and misrepresentation of law.

More specifically, under the general heading, "Representing a Client Zealously", the Model Code provides that a lawyer "shall not ... knowingly advance a claim or defense that is unwarranted under existing law, except that he may advance such claim or defense if it can be supported by good faith argument for an extension, modification, or reversal of existing law." DR 7–102(A)(2). Ethical Consideration 7–23 in the same Code declares, "Where a lawyer knows of legal authority in the controlling jurisdiction directly adverse to the position of his client, he should inform the tribunal of its existence unless his adversary has done so ..." EC 7–23.

The standards of the Model Code are substantially followed in the Model Rules of Professional Conduct of the American Bar Association. Rule 3.3 under the heading, "Candor Toward the Tribunal" makes it a black letter rule that a lawyer should not knowingly "fail to disclose to the tribunal legal authority in the controlling jurisdiction known to the lawyer to be directly diverse to the position of the client and not disclosed by opposing counsel." Model Rules 3.3(a)(3). The note on this Rule goes on to say, "Legal argument based on a knowingly false representation of law constitutes dishonesty toward the tribunal ... The underlying concept is that legal argument is a discussion seeking to determine the legal premises properly applicable to the case."

In black letters the Model Rules also provide, "A lawyer shall not bring or defend a proceeding, or assert or controvert an issue therein unless there is a basis for doing so that is not frivolous, which includes a good faith argument for an extension, modification, or reversal of existing law." Model Rule 3.1. Commentary on this Rule explicitly links it to DR 7–102(A)(2) of the Model Code.

Amazingly, the opinion of the court fails to acknowledge the source for the language of Rule 11 that a paper should be "warranted by existing law or a good faith argument for the extension, modification or reversal of existing law." Both the ABA's Model Rules, adopted on August 2, 1983, and Rule 11, which became effective August 1, 1983, are properly seen as based on DR 7–102(A)(2) of the Model Code in their treatment of what a lawyer should not do. If the objective standard of Rule 11 is higher than the subjective standard of Model Rule 3.3, that is no reason for the court to ignore the link between Rule 11 and the ethical standards of the bar.

It is equally surprising that the opinion of the court does not acknowledge that in the ABA's Model Rules, frivolousness is specifically defined by the absence of "a good faith argument for an extension, modification or reversal of existing law." Frivolousness does not only consist, as the court appears to assume, in making a baseless claim. Frivolousness also consists in making a legal argument without a good faith foundation.

... Not only does the opinion suggest a view of unrestrained advocacy repudiated by modern authorities, it favors a type of analysis sponsored by the Eighth Circuit and overruled by the Supreme Court [in *Nix v. Whiteside,* supra p. 357]. The opinion takes the position that a requirement of truthful argumentation "tends to create a conflict between the lawyer's duty zealously to represent his client" and "the lawyer's own interest in avoiding rebuke."

Precisely such an analysis was offered by the Eighth Circuit in relieving the lawyer of an obligation not to present perjury. That court found "a conflict of interest" between the lawyer's duty to represent his client zealously and the lawyer's ethical duty not to present perjury. Whiteside v. Scurr, 744 F.2d 1323 (8th Cir.1984); rehearing en banc denied, 750 F.2d 713 (8th Cir.1984). Reversing the Eighth Circuit, the Supreme Court noted that there was no conflict of duties when the lawyer was asked by his client to assist "in the presentation of false testimony." . . .

A client has as little right to the presentation of false arguments as he has to the presentation of false testimony. No conflict exists when a lawyer confines his advocacy by his duty to the court. The opinion is insensitive and unresponsive to the teaching of the Supreme Court that a restraint on the freedom of a lawyer to present falsity as truth does not create any true conflict. The lawyer has a duty to work within the boundaries of professional responsibility. He is not free to suborn testimony, to perjure himself, to offer perjured testimony, or to misrepresent facts or law. . . .

[A concluding section of Judge Noonan's dissent from the denial of en banc rehearing summarized "alternative avenues" for dealing with lawyer misconduct, including discipline for violating the ethics rules adopted by the federal district court and the inherent judicial authority to punish bad faith litigating conduct. A lawyer who misstates the law, Noonan concluded, may be sanctioned under these discretionary powers if Rule 11 is interpreted so as not to reach this behavior. He suggested it was not to late to reach the conduct in this case:]

Where a court has applied sanctions on a basis which is subsequently held to be mistaken, and the case is remanded, the court retains the power to award sanctions on a proper basis, such as the inherent power of the court to sanction the bad faith of counsel. Roadway Express, Inc. v. Piper, 447 U.S. at 767.[54]

Notes on Golden Eagle

What, if anything, was wrong with Kirkland & Ellis' argument about *Van Dusen* in *Golden Eagle?* Its argument that the Minnesota court would have dismissed the case on forum non conveniens grounds? Its failure to cite *J'Aire?*

Do any of these arguments violate M.R. 3.3? Did Kirkland & Ellis' motion violate M.R. 3.1? How are Model Rules 3.3 and 3.1 or their

---

54. [Editors' note: Judge Schwarzer, the district judge, declined Judge Noonan's invitation when the case was remanded. Subsequently, a jury trial resulted in a substantial verdict in favor of Golden Eagle against Burroughs.]

Code counterparts, DR 7–102(A)(1), (2), (3), (5) and DR 7–106(B)(1), related to Rule 11 according to the panel in *Golden Eagle?* According to Judge Noonan?

Is the reference to the bar's view of "vigorous advocacy," see footnote 4 of the panel decision, cited with approval as Judge Noonan claims? For what purpose is it cited? How do the two opinions envision the role of the advocate? Are judicial applications of Rule 11 too heavily influenced by the predispositions of individual judges? [55]

Some decisions of other circuits were directly in conflict with *Golden Eagle* on two propositions: (1) that Rule 11 sanctions apply only if the *entire* paper is frivolous; [56] and (2) that the failure to characterize a misleading statement of existing law as a request for a change of law is not sanctionable. [57] The 1993 amendments to Rule 11 reject, as did the bulk of the case law, the Ninth Circuit's position that individual allegations or contentions are not sanctionable if the paper as a whole is nonfrivolous. On the second proposition, the "argument identification" problem, the committee notes to the 1993 amendments have this to say:

> Arguments for extensions, modifications, or reversals of existing law or for creation of new law do not violate subdivision (b)(2) provided they are "nonfrivolous." This establishes an objective standard, intended to eliminate any "empty-head pure-heart" justification for patently frivolous arguments. However, the extent to which a litigant has researched the issues and found some support for its theories even in minority opinions, in law review articles, or through consultation with other attorneys should certainly be taken into account in determining whether paragraph (2) has been violated. Although arguments for a change of law are not required to be specifically so identified, a contention that is so identified should be viewed with greater tolerance under the rule.

How would *Golden Eagle* be decided under the 1993 version of Rule 11?

---

55. Judge Schwarzer, the district judge in *Golden Eagle,* was a prominent exponent of the virtues of Rule 11. Judge Schroeder, who wrote the panel decision, was on record as an opponent of the adoption of Rule 11. See Mary M. Schroeder and John P. Frank, Discovery Reform: Long Road to Nowheresville, 68 A.B.A.J. 572 (1982) (any perceived advantages of requiring "reasonable inquiry" before filing a paper are vastly outweighed by increased delay and cost). Judge Noonan, who teaches legal ethics at Berkeley, has written that truthful outcomes should outweigh confidentiality in some situations. John T. Noonan, Jr., The Purposes of Advocacy and the Limits of Confidentiality, 64 Mich. L.Rev. 1485 (1966).

56. See, e.g., Szabo Food Service, Inc. v. Canteen Corp., 823 F.2d 1073, 1077 (7th Cir.1987) (each claim should be evaluated separately); and Frantz v. U.S. Powerlifting Federation, 836 F.2d 1063 (7th Cir.1987) (Rule 11 applies to every statement in every paper).

57. See, e.g., Szabo Food Service, Inc. v. Canteen Corp., 823 F.2d 1073 (7th Cir.1987) (a frivolous argument that failure to obtain a local government contract is a property right protected by the Due Process Clause must be identified as an argument for changed law to be treated as such); DeSisto College, Inc. v. Line, 888 F.2d 755 (11th Cir.1989) (before a lawyer can argue for a change in existing law, she must first state what the existing law is).

Duty to Reveal Adverse Legal Authority [58]

The earlier discussion of Spaulding v. Zimmerman, p. 5 above, concluded that a lawyer has a professional duty not to volunteer information adverse to her client to the opposing party. The information may only be proffered if properly requested pursuant to procedural rules, such as those governing pretrial discovery. Model Rule 3.3(a)(3), on the other hand, imposes an affirmative duty "to disclose to the tribunal legal authority in the controlling jurisdiction known to the lawyer to be directly adverse to the position of the client and not disclosed by opposing counsel." [59] Why the different treatment of "law" as distinct from "fact"? Did the Kirkland, Ellis brief in *Golden Eagle* violate M.R. 3.3(a)(3)? Does the professional rule in this instance require more or less candor than Rule 11?

Does Rule 11 Chill Creative Advocacy?

The tension between stability and change in the law is reflected in the arguments over Rule 11. One important question is whether courts can distinguish between a legal argument that is not well-grounded in law and not "a good faith argument for the extension, modification or reversal of existing law," on the one hand, and, on the other hand, innovative and creative lawyering that ensures that law can "adjust to changing situations." *Golden Eagle,* supra. [60] The contrasting opinions in *Golden Eagle* mount opposing arguments. Which approach is preferable?

A large body of information is available about the frequency, implications and effects of the 1983 version of Rule 11. A detailed study of Rule 11 motions in the Third Circuit included the following

58. The lawyer's obligation to disclose relevant authority that the opposing party has not cited is discussed in Geoffrey C. Hazard, Jr., Arguing the Law: The Advocate's Duty and Opportunity, 16 Ga.L.Rev. 821 (1982); Monroe H. Freedman, Arguing the Law in an Adversary System, 16 Ga.L.Rev. 833 (1982); and H. Richard Uviller, Zeal and Frivolity: The Ethical Duty of the Appellate Advocate to Tell the Truth about the Law, 6 Hofstra L.Rev. 729 (1977).

59. DR 7–106(B)(1) of the Model Code is substantially identical.

60. Professor Gilson argues that "the fear that too rigorous a requirement of legal support will chill the development of the law ... results in an underinclusive definition" of strategic litigation, defined as "litigation moves that are designed not to vindicate a substantive legal right, but as a strategic device to secure a business advantage by imposing costs on the other party." Ronald J. Gilson, The Devolution of the Legal Profession: A Demand Side Perspective, 49 Md.L.Rev. 869, 875, 908 (1990). Because judges will lean over backwards in a desire not to discourage plausible claims, Rule 11 "remains a poor [gatekeeping] substitute [for advance screening by lawyers], albeit better than nothing." Id. at 909. The problem is that the more promising alternative— screening by lawyers—has been undercut by changes in the market for legal services:

> The traditional structure of professionalism, dominated by elite outside counsel and sheltered by information asymmetry, has been rent by changes in the market.... [L]awyers functioning as private gatekeepers to enforce a Rawlsian agreement among clients—remains a desirable end which seemingly cannot be duplicated by public enforcement.... [T]he segment of the profession most likely empowered to play this role is inside counsel, individuals hardly representative of the profession's traditional elite.

findings and conclusions: [61]

First, application of Rule 11 is not uniform throughout the United States or within a judicial circuit. The variability is influenced not only by differing legal interpretations of the Rule, which presumably will diminish with time, but also by local legal culture and individual judicial attitudes towards sanctions as a case management device.

Second, counts of published decisions dealing with Rule 11 exaggerate the frequency of motions and sanctions. In the Third Circuit, Rule 11 sanctions were filed in less than 0.5% of all cases, and sanctions were imposed in 13.8% of cases in which motions were made.

Third, assertions that Rule 11 has a disproportionate impact on plaintiffs find some support, although the evidence is less striking than is sometimes asserted. In the Third Circuit, plaintiffs or their counsel are the target of two-thirds of Rule 11 motions, and they were sanctioned at a higher rate (15.9% of all cases in which motions were made) than defendants and their counsel (9.1%). Because defendants have only 20 days in which to file an answer and counterclaims generally must be included in the responsive pleading, judges may be more lenient in passing on their pleadings.

Fourth, civil rights plaintiffs or their counsel were sanctioned at a rate (47.1% of motions) that is considerably higher than the rate (8.5%) for plaintiffs in non-civil rights cases. The report suggests that this difference is due in part to the inclusion in the civil rights category of some special types of cases (prisoner cases, pro se cases and cases involving duplicative litigation). Yet the Third Circuit found the incidence of sanctions in § 1983 cases sufficiently troubling to recommend that judges should concentrate more on conduct (a lawyer acting with an improper purpose or failing to make a reasonable inquiry) and less on the legal merit of a filing.

Finally, the report concludes that the rule "has had widespread effects on conduct of the sort hoped for by the rulemakers." The rule has yielded benefits in terms of an increase in care in making filings and has contributed to case dismissal or settlement. The "directly associated costs (e.g., the costs of litigating Rule 11 issues to litigants and courts) do not appear to be clearly incommensurate with probable benefits"; "some other costs (e.g., chilling zealous but legitimate advocacy, poisoning attorney-client relations) are not presently a serious

---

61. Third Circuit Task Force on Federal Rule of Civil Procedure 11, Rule 11 in Transition (Stephen B. Burbank, Reporter) Amer.Judicature Soc'y, 1989. See also Stephen B. Burbank, The Transformation of American Civil Procedure: The Example of Rule 11, 137 U.Pa.L.Rev. 1925 (1989). Major studies of Rule 11, apart from the Third Circuit study and the most recent study by the Federal Judicial Center, discussed in the following footnote, include: Melissa L. Nelkin, The Impact of Fed.Rule 11 on Lawyers & Judges in the Northern District of California, 74 Judicature 147 (1990); Georgene Vairo, Rule 11: A Critical Analysis, 118 F.R.D. 189 (1988); Saul M. Kassin, An Empirical Study of Rule 11 (Fed.Jud.Center 1985).

problem in the Third Circuit, but ... some collateral consequences of Rule 11 (e.g., effect on insurance rates or availability) are imperfectly understood and may increase significantly in the future." [62]

The 1993 amendments to Rule 11 respond in part to concerns that the 1983 version of the rule "chills advocacy." [63] The revision requires that a Rule 11 motion be served separately from other motions and only after the targeted party has been given an opportunity to withdraw "the challenged claim, defense, contention, allegation, or denial" within 21 days of service of the notice.[64] This "safe harbor" requirement means that "a party will not be subject to sanctions on the basis of another party's motion unless, after receiving the motion, it refuses to withdraw that position or to acknowledge candidly that it does not currently have evidence to support a specified allegation." [65]

Should Certain Types of Claims Be Judged More Leniently?

Some judges and commentators have argued that courts should be more reluctant to sanction legal arguments in civil rights cases than in some other areas of law.[66] What justification is there for giving civil rights cases lenient treatment under Rule 11?

62. The Federal Judicial Center's Study of Rule 11, 2 FJC Directions (Nov. 1991), reaches many of the same conclusions as the Third Circuit study. In an examination of Rule 11 in the district courts for Arizona, the District of Columbia, Northern Georgia, Eastern Michigan and Western Texas, the Center examined case files, reviewed published opinions and surveyed judges' attitudes towards the Rule. The Center's report confirmed that Rule 11 activity is modest and that plaintiffs are the most frequent target of sanctions. However, contrary to the criticism that Rule 11 has a disproportionate impact on *represented* plaintiffs and their attorneys in civil rights cases, the Center's study "found that the percentage of motions/orders ... in civil rights cases was similar to ... that in other types of cases with substantial Rule 11 activity...." Id. at 22–23. The rate at which sanctions were imposed in civil rights cases was also "comparable to ... that for all other types of litigants and cases." Id. at 23. The Center concludes that the five district courts have not sanctioned civil rights plaintiffs' attorneys where their arguments have been reasonable. The Center's study also generated interesting data regarding the sanctioning practices of individual judges. For example, in Arizona one judge had imposed no sanctions, while another judge in the same district had imposed sanctions in 57 percent of his Rule 11 rulings. The Center did not explore the reasons for the discrepancy, but it suggested some possible explanations: Some judges are more receptive to Rule 11 motions than others; when lawyers perceive a judge as being open to Rule 11 sanctions they file more motions in that judge's court; and some judges delegate Rule 11 activity to magistrates.

63. 146 F.R.D. at 402.

64. See The Federal Judicial Center's Study of Rule 11, 2 FJC Directions 37 (Nov. 1991).

65. 146 F.R.D. at 591 (committee's notes explaining the amendment to Rule 11(c)).

66. E.g., Judge Cudahy, dissenting from the application of sanctions in Szabo Food Service, Inc. v. Canteen Corp., 823 F.2d 1073, 1086 (7th Cir.1987), stated: "Due process ... is an area where creativity and frivolity sometimes threaten to merge; I would be more restrained than my brethren in handing out sanctions for civil rights claims." Cf. Christiansburg Garment Co. v. EEOC, 434 U.S. 412, 422 (1978) (although fees are to be routinely awarded in favor of a prevailing plaintiff, attorney's fees may not be assessed against a plaintiff who fails to state a claim under 42 U.S.C. § 1988 or under Title VII of the Civil Rights Act of 1964 unless the complaint is frivolous).

Interpretation and Application of Rule 11

Factual Contentions Lacking Evidentiary Support

Many Rule 11 cases involve positively false factual assertions or assertions not supported by the underlying facts. The falsity need not be deliberate or even reckless. Under Rule 11 it is enough that the lawyer failed to make a reasonable pre-filing inquiry to ascertain what the facts were.[67] To determine whether an attorney or party made a reasonable inquiry into the facts, the trial court considers such factors as: how much time the signer had for the investigation; the extent to which the attorney had to rely on the client for factual foundation; whether the case was accepted from another attorney; the complexity of the facts; and the need for discovery to develop the claim.[68]

The duty to make reasonable inquiry carries considerable bite: "Blind reliance on the client is seldom a sufficient inquiry...."[69] The easier it is to verify the facts, such as when the information is publicly available, the greater the obligation to do so.[70] Although a lawyer is entitled to rely on client statements that are "objectively reasonable," relying on client statements without other pre-filing inquiry may be sanctionable conduct.[71] When there is no reasonable way to verify the client's statements through independent sources, the lawyer should question the client thoroughly, not simply accept the client's version on faith alone.[72]

The 1993 amendment of Rule 11 affects the required inquiry in several respects. First, the "safe harbor" provision allows a lawyer who has not made a reasonable inquiry in advance to avoid sanctions by providing support during the 21–day notice period or withdrawing the contention. Second, the amended rule protects a lawyer who, in making a factual allegation, states that the allegation is "likely to have evidentiary support after a reasonable opportunity for further investigation or discovery." Rule 11(b)(3). Finally, the 1993 rule protects a defendant who, in denying a factual contention, states that the denial is "reasonably based on a lack of information and belief." Rule 11(b)(4). The committee note states:

> [S]ometimes a litigant may have good reason to believe that a fact is true or false but may need discovery, formal or informal, from

67. See, e.g., King v. Idaho Funeral Service Association, 862 F.2d 744 (9th Cir.1988).

68. Thomas v. Capital Security Services, Inc., 836 F.2d 866, 988 (5th Cir.1988); Brown v. Federation of State Medical Bds., 830 F.2d 1429 (7th Cir.1987).

69. Southern Leasing Partners, Ltd. v. McMullan, 801 F.2d 783, 788 (5th Cir.1986); see Coburn Optical Industries v. Cilco, Inc., 610 F.Supp. 656, 659 (M.D.N.C.1985) (lawyer sanctioned for not verifying his client's claim that it did not do business in the jurisdiction).

70. See, e.g., Continental Air Lines, Inc. v. Group Systems International Far East, Ltd., 109 F.R.D. 594, 597 (C.D.Cal.1986) (when the information is publicly available, the lawyer must verify her client's version of the facts).

71. Calloway v. Marvel Entertainment Group, 854 F.2d 1452, 1470 (2d Cir.1988), rev'd on other grounds sub nom. Pavelic & LeFlore v. Marvel Entertainment Group, 493 U.S. 120 (1989).

72. See Nassau–Suffolk Ice Cream, Inc. v. Integrated Resources, Inc., 118 F.R.D. 45 (S.D.N.Y.1987).

opposing parties or third persons to gather and confirm the evidentiary basis for the allegation. Tolerance of factual contentions in initial pleadings ... does not relieve litigants from the obligation to conduct an appropriate investigation into the facts that is reasonable under the circumstances; it is not a license to join parties, make claims, or present defenses without any factual basis or justification.... [73]

A Continuing Duty to Comply With the Rule's Requirements?

Case law was divided as to whether the 1983 version of Rule 11 imposed a continuing duty to update or withdraw papers. The 1993 rule is explicit in imposing a continuing duty: Rule 11(b) specifies that any "later advocating" of an unsupported representation is sanctionable. If a lawyer learns that an assertion or argument, proper when made, is no longer supportable, and the lawyer continues to press the contention, the rule is violated unless that assertion or argument is withdrawn. The revised rule "emphasizes the duty of candor by subjecting litigants to potential sanctions for insisting upon a position after it is no longer tenable...." [74]

Papers Filed for an Improper Purpose

The "improper purpose" part of Rule 11 has been held to cover a variety of abusive litigation practices, including: filing repetitive papers; [75] pursuing harassing counterclaims; [76] and misstatements in papers as part of a persistent plan of discovery abuse. [77] Despite the word "purpose," courts have held that this part of Rule 11, like the rest of the rule, requires an objective determination of whether a reasonable lawyer acting as the lawyer did in this case would have been acting for improper purpose.

Sanction Issues

Under the 1993 version of Rule 11, sanctions are made discretionary with the district court. The incentive of parties to seek Rule 11 sanctions is dramatically lessened by a provision that monetary sanctions may not be awarded against a represented party for making unwarranted legal arguments (i.e., conduct violative of Rule 11(b)(2)),

---

73. 146 F.R.D. at 585.

74. 146 F.R.D. at 585. The committee's notes interpreting Rule 11(b) state, "[A] litigant's obligations with respect to the contents of [submitted] papers are not measured solely as of the time they are filed ..., but include reaffirming to the court and advocating positions contained in those pleadings and motions after learning that they cease to have any merit." Id.

75. See, e.g., Deere & Co. v. Deutsche Lufthansa, 855 F.2d 385 (7th Cir.1988) (filing repetitive papers that refuse to accept judge's ruling on an issue and fail to address remaining issues in the litigation).

76. Hudson v. Moore Business Forms, Inc., 836 F.2d 1156 (9th Cir.1987) (counterclaim brought for purpose of harassing plaintiff into dropping the case and deterring others from bringing suit).

77. Perkinson v. Gilbert/Robinson, Inc., 821 F.2d 686 (D.C.Cir.1987). The 1993 rule does not apply to conduct relating to discovery, which is governed by Rules 26–37.

and by a strong presumption against monetary compensation of a moving party. "Since the purpose of Rule 11 sanctions is to deter rather than to compensate, the rule provides that, if a monetary sanction is imposed, it should ordinarily be paid into court as a penalty." [78] Only in "unusual circumstances, particularly for (b)(1) violations [involving assertions or arguments made for an improper purpose]" will monetary compensation such as an award of attorney's fees be appropriate.[79] Is Justice Scalia right that these limits on sanctions have made the rule "toothless?"

Rule 11 provides for penalties against the lawyer, the client or both. Generally, courts seek to allocate sanctions between lawyer and client according to the relative responsibility of each for the Rule 11 violation.[80] The 1993 amendments permit a sanction to be imposed upon a law firm whose partner or associate has violated the rule.[81] Because Rule 11's central goal is to deter lawyer abuses, a federal court imposing a sanction on a lawyer may prohibit reimbursement from any source.[82]

Application to Habeas Proceedings and Government Lawyers

Rule 11 does not apply to criminal proceedings. Should habeas corpus proceedings, which are civil, be subject to Rule 11 sanctions? [83] Repetitive pro se petitioners may be ordered not to file any more petitions without court approval.

Read M.R. 3.1 and its comment. Should it have addressed the responsibilities of a lawyer representing a convicted person in a habeas proceeding? What should the standard be?

Should lawyers employed by state or federal agencies be subject to Rule 11 sanctions? In Taylor v. Commonwealth of Pennsylvania,[84] the court imposed Rule 11 sanctions on a state government lawyer for filing

---

78. 146 F.R.D. at 587–88.

79. 146 F.R.D. at 588.

80. See, e.g., Chevron, U.S.A., Inc. v. Hand, 763 F.2d 1184, 1187 (10th Cir.1985); In re Ruben, 825 F.2d 977, 986 (6th Cir.1987) (court reversed sanctions imposed on plaintiff for her bad faith in filing a suit, explaining that if any fault existed, it lay with the attorneys).

81. In Pavelic & LeFlore v. Marvel Entertainment Group, 493 U.S. 120 (1989), the Court interpreted the 1983 rule as permitting sanctions only upon a person who signed a paper violating the rule. A monetary sanction under the revised rule may be imposed on the law firm of the lawyer responsible for the violation.

82. Derechin v. State University of New York, 963 F.2d 513 (2d Cir.1992) (lawyer for state agency must pay $250 sanction personally even though state statute permits reimbursement).

83. Sanctions are rarely imposed in habeas proceedings absent special circumstances. See United States ex rel. Potts v. Chrans, 700 F.Supp. 1505, 1525 (N.D.Ill.1988) (spirit of habeas inconsistent with Rule 11 sanctions); United States v. Quin, 836 F.2d 654, 657 (1st Cir.1988) (sanctions appropriate when writ was used by retained counsel for "purely civil effect, the prevention of deportation").

84. 686 F.Supp. 492 (M.D.Pa.1988).

a frivolous motion to dismiss a habeas petition. A few cases hold that federal government lawyers are also subject to Rule 11 sanctions.[85]

4. Other Procedural Sanctions

Unreasonably and Vexatiously Multiplying Proceedings

28 U.S.C. § 1927 provides:

> Any attorney or other person admitted to conduct cases in any court of the United States or any Territory thereof who so multiplies the proceedings in any case unreasonably and vexatiously may be required by the court to satisfy personally the excess costs, expenses, and attorneys' fees reasonably incurred because of such conduct.

The decisions are in conflict whether § 1927 requires subjective bad faith on the part of counsel.[86] Recklessness in pursuing a frivolous claim or defense, however, constitutes subjective bad faith. Bad faith is established when a lawyer " 'knowingly *or* recklessly raises a frivolous argument *or* argues a meritorious claim for the purpose of harassing an opponent' ... [or undertakes t]actics ... with the intent to increase expenses.... Even if an attorney's arguments are meritorious, his conduct may be sanctionable if in bad faith." [87]

Inherent Judicial Authority to Sanction Bad Faith Conduct

The inherent authority of a federal court to impose sanctions, including an award of attorney fees, was upheld in Roadway Express, Inc. v. Piper.[88] This "inherent power" permits a federal district court to assess attorney fees when "the losing party has acted in bad faith, vexatiously, wantonly, or for oppressive reasons." Since the power of a court over members of its bar is "at least as great as its authority over litigants," a federal court can tax counsel fees "against counsel who wilfully abused judicial processes." [89]

In Chambers v. NASCO, Inc.,[90] the Supreme Court upheld a sanction of $996,645 against a party who had attempted to deprive the district court of jurisdiction, filed false and frivolous pleadings and tried to wear down the opposing party through delay. The district court, concluding that the first and last of these grounds were not sanctionable under Rule 11 and that 28 U.S.C. § 1927 only applied to attorneys, relied on its inherent power to impose a monetary sanction equivalent

---

85. See Adamson v. Bowen, 855 F.2d 668 (10th Cir.1988), holding that the Equal Access to Justice Act, 28 U.S.C. § 2412 (1981), waives the federal government's sovereign immunity as to Rule 11.

86. Compare, e.g., Haynie v. Ross Gear Div. of TRW, Inc., 799 F.2d 237, 243 (6th Cir.1986) (subjective bad faith not required), with e.g., Oliveri v. Thompson, 803 F.2d 1265, 1273 (2d Cir.1986) ("an award under § 1927 must be supported by a finding of bad faith ...").

87. New Alaska Development Corp. v. Guetschow, 869 F.2d 1298, 1306 (9th Cir.1989).

88. 447 U.S. 752 (1980).

89. 447 U.S. at 766.

90. 111 S.Ct. 2123 (1991).

to the total amount of the opposing party's litigation expenses, minus a contempt fee of $25,000 levied earlier.[91]　The Supreme Court, in a 5–4 decision, upheld the sanction: A federal court may use its "inherent power to police itself, thus serving the dual purpose of 'vindicating judicial authority ... and making the prevailing party whole for expenses caused by his opponent's obstinacy.'"[92]

Sanctions for Discovery Abuse

In 1976 the Court upheld a dismissal of an action under Fed. R.Civ.P. 37 upon a finding of failure in bad faith to comply with discovery.[1]　This policy was reinforced by amendments to Rules 26 and 37 in 1980 and 1983.　Rule 26(g) and Rule 37(b) provide that sanctions may include the award of attorneys fees.　In addition, Rule 37(b) provides that negative inferences may be drawn from a party's refusal to comply with discovery, that the party may be prevented from contesting certain matters and that the court may dismiss the claim or enter a default judgment for noncompliance.[2]

Sanctions at the Appellate Level

Sanctions for frivolous legal arguments at the appellate level are most often levied under Fed.R.App.P. 38:

> If a court of appeals shall determine that an appeal is frivolous, it may award just damages and single or double costs.

Rule 38 does not make the imposition of sanctions mandatory upon a finding that the appeal is frivolous.　Rule 38 sanctions require a determination that the appeal is frivolous and that sanctions are appropriate,[3] but a finding of subjective bad faith is not required.[4]　An argument with merit enough to escape Rule 11 sanctions at the trial level may be sanctionable under Rule 38 if pressed on appeal.[5]　On the other hand, appealing a Rule 11 sanction may result in additional sanctions under Rule 38.[6]　Blatantly mischaracterizing a court opinion

---

91. The district court and the court of appeals also imposed sanctions on others connected to the case.　In particular, one of Chamber's lawyers was disbarred, an issue the Supreme Court did not pass on.

92. 111 S.Ct. at 2133.

1. National Hockey League v. Metropolitan Hockey Club, Inc., 427 U.S. 639 (1976).

2. See Apex Oil Co. v. Belcher Co., 855 F.2d 1009 (2d Cir.1988), discussing the relationship between Rule 11 and Rule 26(g), Rule 37(c) and § 1927.　Also see Carlucci v. Piper Aircraft Corp., Inc., 775 F.2d 1440 (11th Cir.1985) (discussing statutes and rules authorizing sanctions for discovery abuse, including the court's inherent power).

3. Mays v. Chicago Sun–Times, 865 F.2d 134 (7th Cir.1989).

4. See, e.g., Sparks v. NLRB, 835 F.2d 705, 707 (7th Cir.1987) (subjective bad faith is not required).

5. See, e.g., Coghlan v. Starkey, 852 F.2d 806, 817 (5th Cir.1988) ("the unreasonableness of litigating [these] unsupported and meritless legal positions rose to a level appropriate for sanctions only after the opinion below elaborated why current law could not support the contention advanced").

6. See, e.g., Hale v. Harney, 786 F.2d 688, 692 (5th Cir.1986) (after Rule 11 sanctions were imposed counsel persisted by appealing a claim clearly barred by Supreme Court decisions).

in an appellate brief may also lead to sanctions. "We can think of no better example of a pleading not well grounded in fact or law than a brief that falsely imputes a particular position to this court." [7] Courts have also imposed sanctions against lawyers who file frivolous motions for Rule 38 sanctions. [8]

Rule 38 is not the only vehicle for sanctioning frivolous conduct on appeal. Although Rule 11 is not applicable on appeal unless incorporated into an appellate rule, [9] sanctions under 28 U.S.C. § 1927 and 42 U.S.C. § 1988 are available. [10] Sanctions on appeal may also be imposed under the court's inherent power. [11] See also 28 U.S.C. § 1912, which provides: "Where a judgment is affirmed by the Supreme Court or a court of appeals, the court in its discretion may adjudge to the prevailing party just damages for his delay, and single or double costs." [12]

The *Anders* Brief

Counsel should withdraw rather than pursue a frivolous appeal. But what about a court-appointed lawyer representing an indigent criminal defendant on appeal? In Anders v. California, [13] the Court held that counsel must accompany her request to withdraw with a brief setting forth "anything in the record that might arguably support the appeal." This brief is commonly referred to as an *Anders* brief. A Wisconsin Supreme Court rule that required that the *Anders* brief include "a discussion of why the issue lacks merit" was upheld in the *McCoy* case. [14] The defendant claimed that requiring his counsel to present the weaknesses in his cause deprived him of his Sixth Amendment right to effective assistance of counsel. The Court stated that the Wisconsin rule furthered the interest underlying *Anders*, i.e., protecting the defendant from counsel's mistaken conclusion that the appeal lacked merit, by assisting the court to make an independent determination. In dissent, Justice Brennan, joined by Justices Marshall and Blackmun, argued that the Wisconsin rule violated the lawyer's duty to advocate "the undivided interests of his client." The dissenters found this particularly troublesome because only indigent defendants would be affected by the rule. [15]

7. See, e.g., *Mays*, supra at 140.

8. See, e.g., Meeks v. Jewel Cos., 845 F.2d 1421 (7th Cir.1988).

9. Braley v. Campbell, 832 F.2d 1504, 1510 n. 4 (10th Cir.1987) (en banc) (Rule 11 not applicable on appeal); but see In re Disciplinary Action Curl, 803 F.2d 1004 (9th Cir.1986) (Rule 11 applies on appeal through Rule 5 of the Ninth Circuit rules).

10. See, e.g., Limerick v. Greenwald, 749 F.2d 97 (1st Cir.1984).

11. NASCO, Inc. v. Calcasieu Tel. & Radio, Inc., 894 F.2d 696 (5th Cir.1990), aff'd Chambers v. NASCO, Inc., 111 S.Ct. 2123 (1991); Trohimovich v. Commissioner, 776 F.2d 873, 876 (9th Cir.1985).

12. See Natasha, Inc. v. Evita Marine Charters, Inc., 763 F.2d 468, 472 (1st Cir.1985). 28 U.S.C. § 1912, however, is not interpreted to warrant fee shifting.

13. 386 U.S. 738, 744 (1967).

14. McCoy v. Court of Appeals of Wisconsin, 486 U.S. 429 (1988).

15. Apparently only one case has sanctioned a criminal defense lawyer for making frivolous arguments on appeal. See In re Becraft, 885 F.2d 547 (9th Cir.1989) (although

Given the *Anders* doctrine, lawyers taking an appeal on behalf of criminal defendants run little risk of Rule 38 sanctions.[16] Improper trial tactics by criminal defense lawyers are discussed later in this chapter.

5. Perspectives on Controlling Litigation Abuses

Lawyers often take a particularistic and perfectionist approach to issues relating to dispute resolution. Lawyers are trained to be distrustful of broad generalizations; their attention is focused on the detail of particular cases. A short-term perspective—to get the best result for a client in this case—often dominates. From that perspective, spending more on legal services is likely to improve marginally the prospects of a favorable result.[17] If the lawyer is working on an hourly-fee basis, that approach also furthers the lawyer's self-interest. "Winning the case" is a daily concern of the lawyer as litigator; systemic concerns of what is good for society generally move to the background.

Two views about litigation should be contrasted. Each rests on precepts and narratives that have large resonance in the American tradition. Each contains elements of larger truth.

The first draws on narratives central to the American political tradition. People came to these shores to escape tyranny, oppression and a fixed social order. America was a land of liberty and opportunity where individuals and groups could flourish. A long and arduous struggle, in which lawyers played principal roles, was required to achieve ordered liberty, and continuing effort is required to maintain it.

One of the tradition's central images—a "sacred story"—is that of the lawyer as champion who defends the individual against the political or economic power of the state or established institutions. Variations of this story are endlessly repeated in every context from early schooling to today's movies and television shows. Lawyers are bred on these narratives and they have a profound influence on attitudes toward law and litigation. Law is viewed as a contested product of hard-won fights to secure a vision of a more just social order; advocacy and litigation are the mechanisms that establish and maintain the rights on which freedom depends.

From this perspective, lawyers and litigation are not an evil to be deplored but a public good to be welcomed. First, litigation is essential to the maintenance of a social order not based on violence and self-help.

sanctions are generally inappropriate in criminal appeals, defense counsel was sanctioned under Rule 38 for arguing in a petition for rehearing that the federal tax laws did not apply to resident U.S. citizens).

16. For more on the lawyer's responsibilities on appeal in a criminal case, see Jones v. Barnes, 463 U.S. 745 (1983), and the notes following it, below at p. 505. Chapter 6 also addresses the allocation of authority between the defendant and the lawyer in the conduct of a criminal case.

17. A lawyer working on a contingent-fee basis may have an incentive to work fewer hours than the client would like. See the discussion of contingent fees in Chapter 6 at p. 530.

Second, litigation serves other public purposes—the testing, clarification and articulation of public norms through a highly visible and socially accepted process of deciding concrete cases. Since public norms cannot be left entirely to the play of market forces and legislation is a rough tool that cannot deal with all problems, the ideal of our republic—the ideal of a polity that chooses the rules under which it lives through a public process of deliberation and commitment—is dependent upon courts, lawyers and litigation.

Another view of litigation and lawyers also resonates in the American psyche: Litigation is costly, wasteful and often an instrument of selfish aggrandizement. This theme, from *Bleak House* to today's lawyer jokes, emphasizes the dark side of the partisan activities of lawyers in litigation. One aspect is that expressed by Judge Learned Hand earlier in this chapter: Litigation is a frightful ordeal to the individual caught up in it. A broader and more systemic critique flows from modern conceptions of political economy.

If clients are put behind a Rawlsian "veil of ignorance" and asked to devise social arrangements that are in their long-term best interests, they will emerge with arrangements that are designed to deter frivolous matters, avoid delay and arrive at reasonably accurate determinations of fact and law in an efficient manner, i.e., at costs that are moderate and proportionate to the interests at stake.[18] They would also recognize that litigation properly conducted is a public good: the declaration of public norms for future use serves interests of social cohesion and civil order.

The long-term shared interest of clients behind the veil often evaporates given the short-term advantages of using litigation as a strategic tool to gain benefits at the expense of others. Procedural law or ethics rules that attempt to protect parties and the public from abusive litigation tactics have to struggle against the incentives of particular litigants and their representatives to seek selfish advantage, even if that entails abuse of the justice system.

From an economic standpoint, the expenditure of resources on litigation is markedly different than such expenditures in the transactional context. Consensual transactions involve the creation of ar-

---

18. See Ronald J. Gilson, The Devolution of the Legal Profession: A Demand Side Perspective, 49 Md.L.Rev. 869, 876 (1990):

[a] Rawlsian assembly of clients would prohibit strategic use of litigation. Although such litigation can serve to redistribute wealth between the parties, behind the veil [of ignorance] a client could not predict whether he would be the perpetrator of such litigation or its object. And because such litigation imposes a pure dead weight loss, prohibition would be in everyone's interest.

From the perspective of those who value the role of litigation in the struggle for social justice, this abstract argument is criticized as defending things as they are. Real people have the particularity of a cultural identity. Views about the importance or means of deterring abusive litigation will be influenced by this particularity. In general, a group composed of people who identify with those who exercise or administer power is likely to support considerably more discretion for judges to determine what is frivolous and stronger sanctions for filing frivolous claims than a group composed of those who identify with the relatively powerless among us.

rangements in which everyone is better off: Benefits are conferred on all of the participants and opportunities for the creation of new wealth or satisfaction enrich the rest of society. Litigation, on the other hand, marks the breakdown of social peace. In the jargon of the game theorists, litigation is most often a zero-sum game in which there is a winner and a loser or, in many cases, because of the high costs of litigation, two losers. Consensual transactions have the capacity of making the social pie larger; litigation only divides a pie that itself is reduced by the high costs of litigation.[19]

An organization that expects to become involved in a certain number of disputes over a period of time will make arrangements, if it can, to control the expenditures involved in resolving those disputes. Thus in commercial settings, when manufacturers deal regularly with suppliers or buyers with the same sellers, contracts almost invariably provide for compulsory arbitration or other mode of dispute resolution more economical than litigation. Each participant can expect a certain number of disputes to arise, e.g., whether particular goods conform to contract specifications, and each has an incentive to resolve such disputes accurately, expeditiously and cheaply. Winning one or losing another is less important than maintaining good long-term relationships with business partners and minimizing the transaction costs of disputes.[20] Dispute resolution costs in such settings are relatively low.

When an organization's activities may result in litigation with an uncertain group of strangers, as in the product-liability context, and tort law prevents the organization from confining the claimant to a remedy provided in the contract, the organization is unable to control litigation expenditures. In a case involving a potential major liability, the organization has an incentive to spend additional amounts on legal services and other litigation costs as long as each expenditure marginally improves the overall outcome. Since it is known or suspected that the quality and extent of lawyering does affect the outcome of legal proceedings, the result is an escalation of expenditures on cases limited only by the magnitude of the stakes involved.

The social problem is that each party has the same incentive to maximize its position by increasing litigation expenditures. The private problem is that, when both sides spend more on litigation, the benefits of those expenditures to each are reduced or eliminated. The situation is a classic "prisoners' dilemma" problem in which rational

---

19. Again, however, one should keep in mind that arguments based on the economic paradigm, like most applications of Rawls' theory, tend to support the status quo. Any argument that proceeds by comparing costs and benefits has a built-in bias for existing conditions. Put simply, rearranging existing institutions is almost always going to involve an initial cost that is higher than leaving them alone. Thus, unless we assume some kind of natural justice is reflected by existing societal arrangements, including existing distributions of wealth, a solution may be economically efficient without being just.

20. See, e.g., Stewart Macaulay, Lawyers and Consumer Protection, 14 Law & Soc'y Rev. 115 (1979) (lawyers play a facilitating, mediating role in the consumer protection field, not the adversary role of the traditional professional model); Ian R. Macneil, The New Social Contract (1980).

behavior by each participant (increasing expenditures in order to win a case) produces unfortunate results both for the litigants and for society.[21] The total expenditures on litigation sharply diminish the benefits of winning and multiply the burdens of losing. Because each party invests heavily in litigation expenses that counterbalance each other, outcomes are much the same as they would be if each spent less. As in the prisoners' dilemma, the litigants are worse off than if they had agreed in advance to cooperate with one another (i.e., to limit expenditures on litigation.) From the social standpoint the outcome is even more unfortunate: Resources that might be devoted to more productive uses are wasted on excessive litigation expenditures.[22]

If the economists are correct, the only group that benefits from this arrangement are lawyers engaged in high-stakes litigation—cases in which the amount at stake is large enough to justify large expenditures on legal services. The market for legal services of this type is a "winner-take-all" market in which slight differences in the perceived or actual ability of lawyers result in large variations in income.[23] A corporation, for example, faced with a $100 million damage suit or a hostile merger that will eliminate the current management, has little incentive to economize on legal services. If lawyer X is perceived to have litigating abilities that are slightly better than Y or Z, thus increasing the probability of a successful outcome slightly, the corporation will bid up X's services. This type of market produces an income distribution which resembles those observed in other "winner-take-all" markets, e.g., the disparity of earnings between Michael Jordan and other very good basketball players (e.g., the average NBA guard or a very good semi-pro guard).[24]

---

21. For a good introduction, see Robert D. Luce and Howard Raiffa, Games and Decisions 94–102 (1957), and Robert M. Axelrod, The Evolution of Cooperation (1983). The prisoner's dilemma is a paradigm for situations in which no one wants to cooperate, yet all would benefit if they did. The name comes from an archetypal story: Two partners in crime are arrested and put into separate cells. If convicted, they will be sentenced to life imprisonment, but unless one agrees to turn state's evidence in exchange for probation, the prosecutor's evidence will not lead to conviction of a crime carrying more than, say, a two-year sentence. The two prisoners realize that if they both sit tight, they will be sentenced to only two years in prison. If one talks and the other sits tight, the informer goes free and his partner gets a life sentence. If both confess, both get 20–year sentences. What should each prisoner do? See also Robert H. Frank, Passions Within Reason: The Strategic Role of the Emotions c. 2 (1988).

22. Orley Ashenfelter and David Bloom, Lawyers as Agents of the Devil in a Prisoner's Dilemma Game (mimeographed working paper, 1991).

23. Robert H. Frank and Philip J. Cook, Winner–Take–All Markets (mimeographed working paper, 1992).

24. The distribution of lawyer incomes has the characteristics of a "winner-take-all" market. The partners of major law firms that handle high-stakes litigation may average as much as $1 million per year while the median income of all lawyers is less than $70,000 per year. See John J. Wright and Edward J. Dwyer, The American Almanac of Jobs and Salaries 253 (1990) (median annual income of U.S. lawyers in 1987 was $68,922). Because this type of high-stakes litigation requires large staffs of able younger lawyers who will work enormous hours under high pressure conditions to handle the voluminous documents and other complexities of such litigation, these firms bid up the beginning salaries of graduates of elite law schools to above the median salary for the profession as a whole. Similarly, on the plaintiffs' side, a relatively small number of plaintiffs' trial

This diagnosis suggests that segments of the bar have economic interests different from one another and that the interests of the profession are not fully congruent with those of the general public. This may explain why legislators and judges generally are more supportive of measures designed to deter lawyers from pursuing or defending frivolous matters than are trial lawyers generally.

These comments support a balance of the two contrasting views: Litigation is a vital aspect of the development of social norms and the struggle for a better social order. But litigation, like any other powerful medicine, is capable of abuse. Sanctions on lawyers who make unreasonable strategic use of litigation are therefore justified and necessary.

C. HOW FAR FOR A CLIENT?

As to the "art" of the advocate, there is no inherent reason why it should be respectable at all. On the contrary, a cynic ... might define it as "Spokesmanship; or the art of misleading an audience without actually telling lies."[25]

Cyril P. Harvey

1. Witness Preparation (Coaching)

There is very little law on the subject of witness preparation other than the criminal and ethical prohibitions on suborning perjury or using false evidence. Apparently the only ethics opinion is one responding to an inquiry concerning the proper level of lawyer involvement in preparing written testimony for regulatory proceedings. The committee, dealing more broadly with the subject, stated that "detailed, substantive consultations between lawyers and prospective witnesses are an expected part of trial preparation [and that] a lawyer's suggesting actual language to be used by a witness may be appropriate, as long as the ultimate testimony remains truthful and is not misleading." [26]

In *Anatomy of a Murder,*[27] a former prosecutor, Paul Biegler, defends a serviceman, Manion, accused of killing his wife's alleged rapist. At the initial interview with Manion, Biegler discovers that an hour elapsed between the time the serviceman learned of the assault on his wife and the time of the killing. The author of *Anatomy of a Murder*, then a justice of the Supreme Court of Michigan but writing

lawyers end up with most of the big-money cases and garner earnings that are the largest of any members of the legal profession.

25. Cyril P. Harvey, The Advocate's Devil 1–2 (1958) (Harvey was a prominent English barrister, 1923–1968).

26. John S. Applegate, Witness Preparation, 68 Tex. L. Rev. 277, 279 (1989), discussing D.C. Legal Ethics Comm.Op. 79 (1979).

27. Robert Traver's Anatomy of a Murder (1958), a best-selling novel, was later made into an award-winning movie by Otto Preminger.

under the pseudonym of Robert Traver, describes Biegler's thinking during the next meeting with his client:

> I paused and lit a cigar. I took my time. I had reached a point where a few wrong answers to a few right questions would leave me with a client—if I took his case—whose cause was legally defenseless. Either I stopped now and begged off ... or I asked him the few fatal questions and let him hang himself. Or else, like any smart lawyer, I went into the Lecture....

And what is the Lecture?

> The Lecture is an ancient device that lawyers use to coach their clients so that the client won't know he has been coached and his lawyer can still preserve the face-saving illusion that he hasn't done any coaching. For coaching clients, like robbing them, is not only frowned upon, it is downright unethical.... Hence the Lecture, an artful device as old as the law itself, and one used constantly by some of the nicest and most ethical lawyers in the land. "Who, me? I didn't tell him what to say," the lawyer can later comfort himself. "I merely explained the law, see." It is a good practice to scowl and shrug here and add virtuously: "That's my duty, isn't it?"

In the famous lecture scene, Biegler explains that there are four ways to defend murder under Michigan law, and then suggests that the client's only hope is to have a legal excuse for the killing. The responsive client, led step by step by the lawyer's discussion of controlling legal principles, begins to understand that a form of insanity, temporary impaired mental capacity, may be the only defense under the facts. At the close of the interview, Biegler advises his client, "See if you can remember just how crazy you were." [28]

Witness preparation does make a difference. [29] The most comprehensive recent discussion concludes:

> Witness preparation is not harmless. It provides opportunities for lawyers to encourage witnesses to adopt convenient, if not necessarily accurate, testimony. Even with the most honorable intentions, preparation may result in the distortion of witnesses' recollections. But witness preparation is integral to the lawyer's role in a judicial system that depends on partisan case development. Some preparatory activities are essential to a coherent and reasonably accurate factual presentation. More intensive prepara-

---

28. Another movie, *The Verdict,* presents a different picture of witness preparation: A defendant's lawyer prepares the doctors he is defending in a medical malpractice case to testify in a vivid and direct manner that will be more effective with the jury.

29. Criminal trials in England, where the barristers who are examining witnesses have had no contact with them prior to the trial and have prepared solely on the basis of written statements supplied by a solicitor, are marked by witness testimony that has, to an American legal observer, a startling spontaneity and tentativeness by contrast to that in American trials, which have a closer resemblance to staged dramatic presentations.

tion is required if the partisan advocate is to fulfill the ultimate responsibility to the client—presenting a persuasive case....[30]

Given current practice in the United States, does a lawyer commit malpractice by failing to prepare witnesses? The purpose of witness preparation, according to one manual for trial lawyers, is that of "shaping the testimony, focusing on the significant, emphasizing helpful points, and structuring the presentation to minimize the damage caused by adverse information." The adversary system, the manual counsels, means that "It is not your job to bring all the facts to the attention of jury [but to] present the facts in the light most favorable to your side."[31]

Marvin Frankel, a distinguished lawyer, law teacher, and judge, comments critically on the American practice of witness preparation:

> [E]very lawyer knows that the "preparing" of witnesses may embrace a multitude of ... measures [other than the ordering and refreshing of recollection], including some ethical lapses believed to be more common than we would wish. The process is labeled archly in lawyer's slang as "horseshedding" the witness, a term that may be traced to utterly respectable origins in circuit-riding and otherwise horsy days but still rings a bit knowingly in today's ear. Whatever word is used to describe it, the process often extends beyond helping organize what the witness knows, and moves in the direction of helping the witness to know new things. At its starkest, the effort is called subornation of perjury, which is a crime, and which we are permitted to hope is rare. Somewhat less stark, short of criminality but still to be condemned, is the device of telling the client "the law" before eliciting the facts—i.e., telling the client what facts would constitute a successful claim or defense, and only then asking the client what the facts happen perchance to be. The most famous recent instance is fictional but apt: Anatomy of a Murder, a 1958 novel by Robert Traver.... It is not unduly cynical to suspect that this, if not in such egregious forms, happens with some frequency.
>
> Moving away from palpably unsavory manifestations, we all know that the preparation of our witnesses is calculated, one way and another, to mock the solemn promise of the whole truth and nothing but. To be sure, reputable lawyers admonish their clients and witnesses to be truthful. At the same time, they often take infinite pains to prepare questions designed to make certain that the controlled flow of truth does not swell to an embarrassing flood. "Don't volunteer anything," the witnesses are cautioned. The

---

30. Applegate, supra, at 352. Applegate summarizes the large body of scientific studies to the effect that (1) witness preparation "intensifies the half-truth" problem by helping witnesses emphasize some facts and suppress others; and (2) distorts underlying memory both in terms of its content and the certainty with which the view is held. Applegate, supra, at 326–34.

31. Jeffrey L. Kestler, Questioning Techniques and Tactics § 9.14, at 332 (1988) (quoted in Applegate, supra, at 333).

concern is not that the volunteered contribution may be false. The concern is to avoid an excess of truth, where one spillover may prove hurtful to the case.... [32]

2. Fostering Falsity

A lawyer, faced with unfavorable evidence in a trial, may try to impeach the evidence or, alternatively or concurrently, she may draw on any ambiguities in the evidence in an effort to persuade the jury to draw a favorable inference. Impeachment seeks to persuade the jury that a witness is lying or mistaken; argument seeks to persuade the jury to draw favorable inferences. May she take either or both of these courses when she knows the witness is telling the truth and that the favorable inferences are in fact false?

Views of Commentators

Professor Monroe Freedman discusses a hypothetical in which a lawyer's client is charged with a street robbery. Freedman assumes that the lawyer knows her client is innocent even though the client concedes he was one block away within five minutes of the crime, where he was seen by an elderly woman who is somewhat nervous and wears glasses. The woman testifies truthfully and accurately that she saw the client at this time and place.

What should the lawyer do? Freedman argues that the lawyer's duty in the adversary system is to make the truthful witness "appear to be mistaken or lying." [33] Preservation of the client's autonomy under our system of individual rights requires this conduct "unless tactics dictate otherwise." [34]

> As soon as clients learned that confiding in their lawyers would result in less effective representation, such confidences [as the client's statement that he was near the scene of the crime] would rarely be given. The result would be selective ignorance, the practice in which the client is put on notice that he is not to tell his lawyer anything that might cause the lawyer to be less vigorous in her advocacy.[35]

But why do the interests of one human being justify a lawyer in inflicting harm on another, a well-meaning citizen who is cooperating in the pursuit of justice? [36] Why doesn't justice require that individuals bear the consequences of telling or not telling a lawyer truthful facts?

32. Marvin E. Frankel, Partisan Justice 15–16 (1980).

33. Monroe H. Freedman, Understanding Legal Ethics 167 (1990).

34. Id. at 168.

35. Id. at 167.

36. A news story reports that elderly victims of crime are reluctant to become witnesses in New York City in part because they are aware that defense lawyers will engage them in grueling cross-examinations designed to "give the impression of faulty memory, obtuseness and senility." In one case discussed, a lawyer engaged in a rapid-fire, detailed and repetitive examination designed to confuse an 89 year-old witness, whose former lawyer was charged with stealing $129,000 from her. A mistrial resulted

Professor Harry Subin has envisioned a role for defense lawyers (a "monitoring" role, he calls it) that is sharply less adversarial than Freedman's conception.[37]   In a criminal case, Professor Subin would make it "improper for an attorney who knows beyond a reasonable doubt the truth of a fact established in the state's case to attempt to refute that fact through the introduction of evidence, impeachment of evidence, or argument."   If the client nevertheless wants to go to trial, "the attorney would work to assure that all of the elements of the crime were proven beyond a reasonable doubt, on the basis of competent and admissible evidence."   The attorney could also argue to the jury that the evidence does not "sustain the burden of proof."

John B. Mitchell, an experienced criminal defense lawyer, disagrees, arguing that the attempt to raise a reasonable doubt usually involves challenging the persuasiveness of certain inferences from the testimony of witnesses.   Bringing out testimony, not itself false, to accredit a false theory, is not the same as arguing a false theory.[38]

Michigan Opinion CI–1164

A Michigan ethics opinion [39] provides a real-life situation to which these conflicting views may be applied:

> Client is charged with armed robbery. He proposes to call some friends as witnesses at trial, who will give truthful testimony that he was with them at the time of the crime. At the preliminary examination the victim had testified that the robbery occurred at the same hour and time to which the friends will testify. Client has confided to attorney that he robbed the victim; his theory on the time mix-up is that he stole the victim's watch and rendered him unconscious so that the victim's sense of time was incorrect when relating the circumstances of the robbery to the investigating detectives. Months later, at the preliminary examination, the victim relied on the detectives' notes to help him recall the time. Client and attorney have decided that client will not testify at trial. Would it be ethical for attorney to subpoena the friends to testify that client was with them at the alleged time of the crime?

The opinion concludes that the attorney may offer into evidence the testimony of the client's friends. The reasoning of the opinion runs as follows: The duty of zealous representation requires a criminal defense lawyer to use any truthful evidence that may help her client.

when the jury deadlocked 11–1 in favor of conviction. Although the victim died before the retrial, her testimony was provided by videotape. See In re Reisch, 101 A.D.2d 140, 474 N.Y.S.2d 741 (1st Dept.1984) (lawyer disbarred). E. R. Shipp, Fear and Confusion in Court Plague Elderly Crime Victims, N.Y. Times, Mar. 13, 1983, at p. A1.

37. Harry I. Subin, The Criminal Lawyer's "Different Mission": Reflections on the "Right" to Present a False Case, 1 Geo. J. Legal Ethics 125, 149–150 (1987).

38. John B. Mitchell, Reasonable Doubts Are Where You Find Them: A Response to Professor Subin's Position on the Criminal Lawyer's "Different Mission," 1 Geo.J.Legal Ethics 339, 343–46 (1987). See also Harry I. Subin, Is This Lie Necessary? Further Reflections on the Right to Present a False Defense, 1 Geo.J.Legal Ethics 689 (1988).

39. Michigan Ethics Op. CI–1164 (1987).

If the friends' testimony is truthful and it will help the client, then the lawyer must use it. Defense counsel is not permitted to inform the prosecution that its evidence is inaccurate. Nor must defense counsel ignore truthful evidence simply because counsel knows the client is guilty—the lawyer is a partisan advocate, not an impartial fact-finder.

Although DR 7–102(A)(4) [and M.R. 3.3(a)(4)] prohibit lawyers from introducing perjured testimony, in this fact situation the friends' testimony is truthful. A lawyer is not barred from using truthful testimony, even if that testimony will result in the acquittal of a defendant who has privately admitted his guilt to counsel. "One cannot suborn the truth." The burden is on the prosecution to prove the elements of the charge, and it must do so without the assistance of the defendant's lawyer.

Finally, the Opinion states that defense counsel should discuss with the client the decision of whether or not to use the testimony. Although the friends will testify truthfully, providing the defendant with an alibi, the prosecution may nonetheless have assembled overwhelming evidence against the defendant. If that is true, the testimony of the client's friends is unlikely to count for much with the jury. Under these circumstances, the defendant may be best advised to forego a trial and negotiate a plea bargain.

Is this reasoning sound? Is the conclusion just?

3. Dirty Tricks in Court

Deliberate Injection of Impermissible Matter

The professional codes mandate that a "lawyer shall not ... allude to any matter that the lawyer does not reasonably believe is relevant or that will not be supported by substantial evidence ...".[40] In real life as well as in the courtroom scenes portrayed in movies and television, however, trial lawyers frequently make statements or ask questions that assume irrelevant or inadmissible facts. Professor (now Judge) Keeton states:

> Some lawyers frankly state, and still more endorse by practice, the ethically indefensible proposition that this kind of improper question should be asked unless it is of such prejudicial character that the refusal of the trial court to declare a mistrial would be reversible error. This practice is sometimes used for the very purpose of confronting adverse counsel with the difficult choice of waiving objection by failing to make it, or else make an objection that may lead the jury to conclude that he is attempting to withhold information from them.[41]

---

40. M.R. 3.4(e). DR 7–106(C)(1) is substantially identical. For a decision upholding contempt sanctions for repeated violation of forensic rules by a lawyer in a criminal trial, see Hawk v. Superior Court, 42 Cal.App.3d 108, 116 Cal.Rptr. 713 (1974).

41. Robert E. Keeton, Trial Tactics and Methods 59 (2d ed. 1973).

Keeton implies, without so stating, that the threat of professional discipline is not an adequate deterrent: "Protection against the deliberate use of clearly improper questions is inadequate under existing rules of law, unless the trial judge uses his discretionary powers to deal with the practice sternly." The primary constraint is a tactical one: If the jury perceives the tactic is unfair, its use may have a negative effect on lawyer and client.

Some matters are viewed as so prejudicial that their introduction will result in a mistrial or other sanctions. For example, severe sanctions may be imposed when a lawyer refers to the other's side's liability insurance or to concessions made in settlement discussions.[42] What should the lawyer do in more equivocal situations in which evidence is of doubtful admissibility but has large persuasive value? Professor Keeton says:

> If you believe that the evidence of doubtful admissibility is likely to have a strong influence on the findings of the jury in the case, you may conclude that the chance of reversal is worth taking; the decision is based upon weighing the probable value of the evidence to you in its influence on the jury against the disadvantage of possible reversal of a favorable verdict and judgment.

Are you satisfied with this consequentialist approach?

A closely related issue involves the intentional use of leading questions to guide the witness.[43] The issue is complicated because under some circumstances leading questions may be employed. Leading questions, Professor Keeton states, are "tempting" because their effect cannot be erased by objection or instruction. Even if the leading question is stricken, the witness has been tipped off about how to respond to a properly phrased question. After implying that general provisions of ethics codes are unlikely to deter lawyers from using leading questions, Keeton discusses "tactical" reasons why they should be avoided in some situations.[44]

Deliberate and flagrant appeals to bias and prejudice are likely to result in a mistrial. Skilled advocates, however, are frequently successful in introducing issues of socio-economic status, wealth, race, religion or ethnicity by one means or another. On some occasions the issues may be framed so as to permit introduction of evidence of a defendant's

---

42. See, e.g., Fike v. Grant, 39 Ariz. 549, 8 P.2d 242 (1932) (liability insurance). See Richard H. Underwood and W. H. Fortune, Trial Ethics § 11.6 (1988).

43. Similar problems arise in connection with "speaking objections"—argumentative comments included in objections that are designed to put certain matter before the jury. Melvin Belli comments that a speaking objection "is not unethical if its purpose is further to emphasize, for example, the limited purpose of the introduction of certain testimony." Melvin M. Belli, Modern Trials 616 (Student ed. 1963).

44. Keeton, supra at 48–52. M.R. 3.4(c), providing that a lawyer "shall not ... knowingly disobey an obligation under the rules of a tribunal," is violated by deliberate use of leading questions objectionable under a jurisdiction's evidence rules. DR 7–106(A) is substantially identical.

wealth or character.[45] Indirect allusions or the use of code phrases in questions or argument may pass without objection or judicial reprimand. If all else fails, use of a "dumb show" technique may get a point across to the jury.[46]

Asserting Personal Knowledge, Belief or Opinion

M.R. 3.4(e) prohibits a lawyer from "assert[ing] personal knowledge of facts in issue except when testifying as a witness, or stat[ing] a personal opinion as to the justness of a cause, the credibility of a witness, the culpability of a civil litigant or the guilt or innocence of an accused." Professor Keeton offers advice on this subject to law students contemplating a career in advocacy:

> Probably you will be at your best as an advocate when you cause the judge and jury to believe that the decision you are urging them to reach is a decision you would reach yourself. Yet the Code of Professional Responsibility, in one of its Disciplinary Rules, prohibits any direct statement of belief in your cause. . . . It seems more consistent with the apparent objectives of the rule, as well as the prevailing practice, to treat it as a regulation of the form and manner of your conduct . . . rather than a regulation requiring that you not display, even indirectly, any appearance of commitment to your cause. Indeed, if interpreted as precluding even an indirect display of commitment to you cause, the rule could hardly be reconciled with your acknowledged duty as an advocate to bring "zeal" to your representation of your cause.[47]

Are you comfortable with this role of using non-verbal communication to portray your client as honest and her cause as just, without regard to your honest feelings and beliefs?

Intimidation and Harassment

Cross-examination of a witness that is harsh, unfair or oppressive carries its own deterrent. Even if the judge does not intervene, the jury may sympathize with the witness. For this reason, Professor Keeton suggests that

---

45. A punitive damage count may allow introduction of evidence of a defendant's wealth; character may become relevant if the subject is opened up by the adversary.

46. The most prevalent form of "dumb show" involves the dress and appearance of the client. The use of props, whether children or crutches, is frequent. Clarence Darrow, trying cases in a time when smoking was permitted in court, is reported to have distracted juries during the closing argument of his opponent by defying the law of gravity. A thin wire inserted in his cigar prevented the ash from falling.

Max Wildman, a well-known insurance defense lawyer in Chicago, used a creative strategy in a case in which his client, a widower, was suing Wildman's client for the wrongful death of his wife. Wildman employed a pretty young woman to sit immediately behind the plaintiff throughout the trial and to engage him in friendly conversation, in the presence of the jury, when the court was not in session. See Jeffrey O'Connell, The Lawsuit Lottery: Only the Lawyers Win c. 3 (1979) (discussing this and other "tricks of the trade" in tort cases).

47. Robert E. Keeton, Trial Tactics and Methods 2–3 (2d ed.1973).

[I]t is better not to make [an objection to oppressive or misleading cross-examination] if the witness is able to take care of himself.... If the substantive content of your witness' testimony is not being weakened and your witness is not responding with angry or sarcastic answers, you may as well let your adversary have the freedom to err; you may finally object, but not until you are certain that your adversary has gone so far that the court will sustain the objection and thus convict your adversary in the presence of the jury of trying to take unfair advantage of the witness.[48]

Other versions of harassment, however, do not have this self-limiting quality. They are often referred to as "blaming the victim." Examples are legion. Consider the following:

Dalkon Shield Depositions

Women who used the intrauterine birth control device known as Dalkon Shield reported serious harms from pelvic infections allegedly caused by the device. Thousands of lawsuits were eventually filed against the manufacturer, A. H. Robins Company, which reportedly engaged in litigation tactics designed to encourage women to withdraw their claims and to discourage others from filing claims. The tactics ultimately proved to be unsuccessful. Persistent plaintiffs' lawyers proved that "Robins had marketed the Dalkon Shield without investigating its safety and that, after they had learned of the propensity of the device to cause life-threatening pelvic infections, company officials had withheld and even destroyed this information while the Dalkon Shield was still being sold and used." [49] The result was a succession of punitive damage awards that led to withdrawal of the product in 1980 and bankruptcy for Robins in 1985.

Morton Mintz's book on the Dalkon Shield controversy describes the deposition tactics of Robins and its lawyers: [50]

No one disputes that certain sexual activities or unhygienic habits can enhance the environment for pelvic inflammatory disease [PID], even if they do not *cause* PID. This is why A. H. Robins had a right to make inquiries into highly private aspects of the lives of women who filed lawsuits blaming the Dalkon Shield for PID-related injuries. But it did not have a right to make *unreasonable and irrelevant* inquiries.

The record shows that Robins attorneys took depositions from Shield victims in which they asked not only intimate, but also demeaning and even intimidating questions. Although certain judges required defense-counsel to show a connection between the questions and women's injuries, others did not do so and allowed

---

48. Id. at 175.

49. Richard B. Sobol, Bending the Law: The Story of the Dalkon Shield Bankruptcy x (1991).

50. Morton Mintz, At Any Cost: Corporate Greed, Women and the Dalkon Shield 194–95 (1985).

Robins to ask at public trials what plaintiffs' lawyers call "dirty questions."

The following case is from the Shield suit of an Iowa mother of two children who had suffered PID and the consequent loss of her ovaries and womb. Robins's counsel took depositions from her and her husband, each in the presence of the other. To her, the company attorney put queries about her sexual relations before their marriage in 1963, *ten years before she was fitted with a Shield, and fifteen years before she was stricken with PID.* Her lawyer, Kenneth W. Green of Minneapolis, objected, calling such questions "disgusting as well as irrelevant."

Robins then submitted written questions, to her and also to her husband. These, Green said in an affidavit, were "even worse," partly because they returned to the premarital period. Two written questions to the wife were: "Prior to your marriage in 1963, did you have sexual relations with anybody else other than [your husband]? and "Who were these sexual partners?"

Green's own daughter had worn a Shield and suffered two episodes of PID, one of which almost killed her. But knowing of the invasions of privacy, he advised her not to sue Robins, and she didn't.

Panty hose can't cause PID; not even defense experts suggested they could. But in a case involving another Shield litigant, a Robins attorney made panty hose an issue. Among his questions was whether she wore them and what fabric was used in the crotch. To the latter query she replied, "I'll answer that, but this sounds more like an obscene phone call than anything else."

During a deposition in Minnesota in May 1982, lawyers for a Boston woman directed her not to answer questions by Robins counsel about which way she wiped, and whether, and how often she engaged in oral and anal intercourse and used so-called marital aids. Five months later, however, a judge compelled her to return to Twin Cities to answer the questions. As late as January 1984, a Midwestern woman was asked if before she was fitted with a Shield she had had any sexual partners in addition to her husband. By then the couple had adopted two children, her ability to bear a child of her own having been ruined by Shield-related PID.

Prego Cross–Examination

Dr. Veronica Prego brought suit against the public body operating a New York City hospital, claiming that she contracted AIDS by pricking a finger with a contaminated needle negligently left in a patient's bedding at defendant's hospital. Stanley Friedman, lawyer for the hospital authority, had the unenviable task of seeking to discredit Dr. Prego's testimony. He did so by challenging

her sincerity, her stamina, her character, her veracity and her memory. He examined her love life and discussed her abortions.

And as Dr. Prego, her mother and her sister sat nearby, he asked another witness to estimate her life expectancy.[51]

Columnists depicted Friedman as "an ogre, a sadist and a money-grubber," but he defended his cross-examination as only doing the job the adversary system required of him. Dr. Prego's pregnancies and love life were relevant because she might have contracted AIDs from transfusions or sexual contact; her life expectancy was relevant to damage issues. Lawyers for Dr. Prego predicted that Friedman's tactics would backfire. Perhaps they were right. Dr. Prego received a $1.35 million settlement award just before her case was to go to the jury.[52]

Countless other examples could be provided of tactics that some charge are improper: Tactics designed, it is said, to discourage or intimidate litigants or to prejudice the victim by blaming her for her harm. Is a lawyer required to use tactics that are harsh or repugnant if the inquiry is legally relevant? Or do professional rules permit the lawyer's moral conscience to come into play? If the latter, should a lawyer inform a client in advance of representation that she will not use "repugnant" tactics?

Trickery

Perry Mason may get away with tricking an expert witness, for example, with a fingerprint that is not the one that has been introduced into evidence. But the use of trickery in a real trial is ill-advised because judges may view it as dishonesty toward the court. In United States v. Thoreen,[53] defense counsel in a criminal case, without the trial court's knowledge and permission, seated someone who looked like the defendant at the counsel table while the defendant sat immediately behind in the public section. Predictably, two government witnesses misidentified the defendant. The trial court allowed the government to reopen its case, the defendant was convicted and the lawyer was charged with and convicted of criminal contempt. On appeal, the court, conceding that the "line between vigorous advocacy and actual obstruction is close," upheld the contempt finding.[54]

4. Special Responsibilities of Prosecutors [55]

M.R. 3.8 outlines the special responsibilities of a prosecutor. See also ABA Standards on the Administration of Criminal Justice (The

51. David Margolick, Defense Tactics in the AIDS Doctor's Suit, N.Y.Times, Jan. 23, 1990, at p. B1.

52. Arnold H. Lubasch, Judge, in Shift, Discloses that Prego Will Get $1.35 Million, N.Y.Times, Mar. 10, 1990, at pp. B27–B28.

53. 653 F.2d 1332 (9th Cir.1981).

54. Id. at 1339.

55. Criminal defense lawyers are subject to the general prohibitions against use of illegal means to gather evidence. For a revealing look at the ethics of white collar criminal defense lawyers, see Kenneth Mann, Defending White Collar Crime (1985). For reflections on the ethics of prosecutors, see Fred C. Zacharias, Structuring the Ethics of

Prosecution Function), particularly 3–3.9, Discretion in the Charging Decision.

In Brady v. Maryland,[56] the Supreme Court held that the prosecutor must reveal to the defense, upon request, exculpatory evidence "material either to guilt or to punishment." In United States v. Agurs,[57] the Court held that when the exculpatory evidence creates a reasonable doubt, the prosecution must disclose the evidence to the defense even if there is no request. However, the prosecution's failure to disclose evidence that could have effectively impeached government witnesses does not require automatic reversal; reversal is required only if nondisclosure might have affected the outcome.[58]

DR 7–103(B) requires the prosecutor to disclose to the defense, whether or not the defense makes a request, evidence "that tends to negate the guilt of the accused, mitigate the degree of the offense, or reduce the punishment." See also M.R. 3.8(d), which adopts the same standard as DR 7–103(B), except that in connection with sentencing the rule allows a prosecutor to withhold mitigating information that is privileged or is protected by order of a tribunal.

In People v. Jones,[59] the court held that the prosecutor did not violate the defendant's due process rights by failing to reveal during plea negotiations that the state's key witness had died. The court held that the prosecutor had neither a constitutional nor an ethical duty to reveal this information, as long as the prosecutor made no affirmative misrepresentation. The information was held to be outside the *Brady* rule because it was not exculpatory; the death of the witness merely made it difficult for the state to prove its case.

In Fambo v. Smith,[60] the court held that while the prosecutor did have a duty to disclose to the defendant that physical evidence critical to one of the counts of the indictment had been destroyed, the failure to do so did not affect the fairness of defendant's plea bargain.

Are these cases consistent with the *Brady* doctrine? With EC 7–13, which sets forth the justifications for the special responsibilities of a prosecutor? With ABA Standard 3–4.1, which says "[i]t is unprofessional conduct for a prosecutor knowingly to make false statements or representations in the course of plea discussion?"[61]

The prosecution also has a duty to preserve evidence.[62] In the *Trombetta* case, the Court held that the loss or destruction of evidence

Prosecutorial Trial Practice: Can Prosecutors Do Justice?, 44 Vand.L.Rev. 45 (1991); Stanley Z. Fisher, In Search of the Virtuous Prosecutor, 15 Am.J.Crim.Law 197 (1988).

56. 373 U.S. 83 (1963). See also Moore v. Illinois, 408 U.S. 786 (1972) (elaborating on the *Brady* rule).

57. 427 U.S. 97 (1976).

58. United States v. Bagley, 473 U.S. 667 (1985).

59. 44 N.Y.2d 76, 404 N.Y.S.2d 85, 375 N.E.2d 41 (1978).

60. 433 F.Supp. 590 (W.D.N.Y.1977), aff'd, 565 F.2d 233 (2d Cir.1977).

61. ABA Standards on the Administration of Justice (Prosecution Function), Standard 3–4.1.

62. California v. Trombetta, 467 U.S. 479 (1984).

does not violate the due process clause of the Constitution absent "official animus" or a "conscious effort to suppress exculpatory evidence." [63] In addition, the destroyed evidence must be "material" to the suspect's defense under a two-part test. First, the exculpatory value of the evidence has to have been apparent prior to the destruction of the evidence; and second, the evidence has to be such that the defendant would be unable to obtain comparable evidence by other reasonably available means.

5. Using Improper Means in Gathering Evidence

A lawyer may not use illegal means to gather evidence. The laws prohibiting fraud, burglary, theft, illegal use of the mail or wiretapping do not contain exceptions for lawyers. "It is unprofessional conduct for a lawyer knowingly to use illegal means to obtain evidence or information or to employ, instruct, or encourage others to do so." [64]

In addition, the ethics rules prohibiting "dishonesty, fraud, deceit or misrepresentation" may place more stringent limits on the ways in which lawyers may gather evidence. For example, ethics opinions and some disciplinary cases state that a lawyer should not record conversations without the consent or prior knowledge of all the parties to the conversation. [65]

United States v. Ofshe, [66] involved charges that improper means had been used in gathering evidence by then Assistant United States Attorney Scott Turow (the author of *One L*, *Presumed Innocent* and other books). A lawyer, Glass, who was under investigation for racketeering in the Northern District of Illinois, approached Turow and offered to inform on suspected drug merchants. One of the individuals on whom Glass informed was Ofshe, for whom Glass was co-counsel in a pending federal cocaine charge in Florida. Turow warned Glass not to report or record any privileged communications or anything relating to Ofshe's pending case. A "body bug" produced information concerning ongoing money laundering and drug conspiracies. Turow also told Glass that Glass would have to withdraw from his representation of Ofshe after providing information, and, when Glass refused to withdraw, Turow told the district court, in camera, of Glass's conflict of interest.

On appeal from conviction of the original cocaine charges, Ofshe argued that the invasion of his attorney-client relationship with Glass

---

63. 467 U.S. at 488.

64. ABA Standards Relating to the Administration of Criminal Justice: The Defense Function, Standard 4–4.2. See, e.g., Markham v. Markham, 272 So.2d 813 (Fla.1973); Lucas v. Ludwig, 313 So.2d 12 (La.App.1975); and Tennessee Bar Association v. Freemon, 50 Tenn.App. 567, 362 S.W.2d 828 (1961).

65. See, e.g., ABA Formal Op. 337 (1974) (lawyers should record conversations only with the consent or prior knowledge of all the parties to the conversation); ABA Informal Op. 1407 (1978) (in accord with 337). But see ABA Informal Op. 1357 (1975) (statements made at a public meeting may be recorded).

66. 817 F.2d 1508 (11th Cir.1987).

required dismissal of the indictment. A panel of the Eleventh Circuit refused the defendant's motion to dismiss the indictment, stating that the appropriate remedy was suppression of the evidence thus garnered. Nevertheless, the court called Turow's conduct "reprehensible" and suggested referral to the state's disciplinary commission. When Turow defended his conduct, which had been reviewed and upheld by the Department of Justice, the court wrote a further opinion suggesting that he should be prosecuted for obstruction of justice.[67] Turow later wrote an article identifying his struggle with the Eleventh Circuit as the most bitter experience of his life as a prosecutor: "I believed—and continue to believe—that neither clients nor lawyers have the right to plan crimes secure from government law enforcement efforts." [68]

Although prosecutors have an absolute immunity from tort liability for conduct "intimately associated with the judicial phase of the criminal process,"[69] they have only a qualified immunity while engaged in investigatory work or making out-of-court statements concerning an accused. Thus allegations that prosecutors fabricated evidence during the investigatory stage and made false statements at a press conference announcing an indictment stated claims for relief under 42 U.S.C. § 1983.[70] On aiding and abetting the destruction or concealment of evidence see the *Stenhach* case in Chapter 1 and the notes following it.

D. REFLECTIONS ON ADVERSARIAL ETHICS

SIMON H. RIFKIND
"THE LAWYER'S ROLE AND RESPONSIBILITY
IN MODERN SOCIETY"
30 The Record 534, 535–45 (1975).[1]

. . .

When I was first admitted to the bar, I was formally authorized to act as an attorney-at-law. The concept of attorneyship, of course, includes agency. An agent must have a principal; so must an attorney have a client. The lawyer's role and responsibility as attorney comes into being only when he is a member of a client-attorney, symbiotic team.

Once he becomes a member of such a team then, in the United States and in other countries having a common law tradition, he works

---

67. United States v. Ofshe, unpublished opinion, No. 96–5351 (11th Cir. Nov. 16, 1987).

68. Scott L. Turow, Law School vs. Reality, N.Y.Times Mag., Oct. 18, 1988, at p. 52. Professor Uviller agrees with Turow. Although Glass betrayed his client, he did so under circumstances in which the client was seeking his assistance in on-going criminal conspiracies. In any event, Uviller argues, Glass's misconduct is not attributable to Turow either under ethics rules or as an accessory to crime. H. Richard Uviller, Presumed Guilty: The Court of Appeals vs. Scott Turow, 136 U.Pa.L.Rev. 1879 (1988).

69. Imbler v. Pachtman, 424 U.S. 409, 430 (1976).

70. Buckley v. Fitzsimmons, 113 S.Ct. 2606 (1993).

1. Copyright © Association of the Bar of the City of New York. Reprinted with permission.

in an environment called the adversary system and engages in maneuvers called the adversary process.

Awareness of this fact is crucial to the understanding of the attorney's duty and responsibility. Failure to grasp the significance of the adversary system has given rise to much misunderstanding, both within and without the bar, and has, I suggest, led to some unproductive developments.

In an actual lawsuit, the operation of the adversary process becomes fully visible even to the uninitiated. As a matter of history and habit, we accept unquestioningly the bizarre arrangement by which the State hires one lawyer to prosecute a citizen for an alleged crime, another to defend him and a third to decide between them. A visitor from Mars might inquire, "Why not hire one to ascertain the truth?"

But it is not only for litigated matters that the adversary system constitutes the living ambience. Consensual arrangements may become the subject of litigation; the draftsman must, to the best of his ability, anticipate the vicissitudes his writing will experience during its voyage in the adversary process. Every will prepared in the privacy of a law office may be contested, every advice given may be challenged, every opinion given must be formulated in the light of the possibility of attack upon its validity and its subjection to the adversary process and judicial arbitrament.

Both the prospect of litigation and its actuality impose great restraint upon the attorney and challenge his learning, his wisdom and his capacity to prophesy. It also relieves him of much responsibility. In the course of his advocacy, he may urge propositions of which he is less than certain, because the lawyer is not the final arbiter. The final judgment will emerge out of the contest. In the collision of the two opposing forces, out of the cross-exposure by each of his adversary's weakness and out of the need to discover and articulate one's own virtues and advantages, in the fire of that antagonism a more refined truth is smeltered and a better judgement is filtered.

The adversary process is thus seen as a form of organized and institutionalized confrontation. Because organized confrontations also occur in many forms of sport, some have seized upon the superficial similarity to downgrade the adversary process as socially trivial. This contemnation would be appropriate if the object of the adversary process were to select the more skillful lawyer, as it is, for instance, to select the better boxer or tennis player. In the courtroom contest, the judge does not award prizes for skill. He uses the adversary process for illumination. And it is, I believe, the teaching of experience that the incentives generated by the adversary system do, indeed, tend to bring about a more thorough search for and evaluation of both the facts and the law.

. . .

So extensive is the pervasive effect of the adversary system in the resolution of controversies that, once grasped, it answers many questions frequently troubling the layman. It is like one of the great axioms of geometry from which flow many propositions and corollaries.

"How could you represent so-and-so?" is a question frequently put to me, ... The tone of voice which accompanies the question sufficiently discloses that the questioner has consigned the client to some subhuman category of untouchables.

As you know, there are fashions in untouchability. One season it is a sharecropper in Mississippi, the next season it is a multi-million share corporation in Detroit. From the viewpoint of the adversary system, the applicable principle is the same.

If only the lay public understood that if the outcasts, the rejected ones, the deviationists, the unpopular ones are to be unrepresented, the adversary system would fail for every one. If they comprehended how the engine of the adversary process is ignited and works, they would never ask to explain why a lawyer did take a particular case, but rather why he had rejected another. That indeed calls for justification.

Recently a group of law students picketed a prominent Washington lawyer [Lloyd Cutler of Wilmer, Cutler & Pickering] in order to give expression to their disapproval of his representation of a large corporation [opposing, on behalf of General Motors, proposed automobile safety regulations]. Had they mastered the meaning of the adversary system they would have known that their conduct was subversive of the central tenet of the profession they were about to enter.

. . .

... [O]ne of the roles of the lawyer is so to behave as to make the adversary process work. And one of his responsibilities is to teach each generation of laymen that, in so doing, the lawyer is fulfilling his assigned role.

From some of my philosophically oriented brethren I hear murmurs that the Anglo–American reliance on the adversary process may have exceeded the limits of its utility and that re-examination is now in order.... [T]o the logician, the adversary process will present many flaws. The inequality of resources between the contestants, the disparity in talent, are but two of many. But I recall the sage words of the Yankee from Olympus, "The life of the law has not been logic; it has been experience."

Experience tells me that the adversary system has been good for liberty, good for peaceful progress and good enough to have the public accept that system's capacity to resolve controversies and, generally, to acquiesce in the results.

And it has also accomplished something else. It has tended to reward most highly those lawyers who are best suited to the adversary process. In consequence, such lawyers have established the norms of performance. Any one who has worked with lawyers around the globe knows that those brought up in the Anglo–American tradition of adversary process devote themselves more comprehensively, more passionately, to the solution of their clients' problems than the lawyers reared under any other system.

... Some laymen have suggested that the very function the attorney presumes to discharge involves a conflict of interest between his duty to his client and his duty to society.

Those who have voiced such views have not taken account of the operation of the adversary process. The utility of that process is that it relieves the lawyer of the need, or indeed the right, to be his client's judge and thereby frees him to be the more effective advocate and champion. Since the same is true of his adversary, it should follow that the judge who will decide will be aided by greater illumination than otherwise would be available.

[As Johnson replied to Boswell's question: "But what do you think of supporting a cause which you know to be bad?"]

Johnson: "Sir, you do not know it to be good or bad till the judge determines it.... An argument which does not convince yourself may convince the judge to whom you urge it; and if it does convince him, why then, sir, you are wrong and he is right. It is his business to judge; and you are not to be confident in your opinion that a cause is bad, but to say all you can for your client, and then hear the court's opinion."

. . .

What I have said thus far ... [is radical doctrine today] because it rejects the notion which has gained considerable ground at the bar and very widespread allegiance on the campus that the lawyer should not be client-oriented and case-oriented.

This change in the professional wind has caused to bloom a body of lawyers who call themselves public interest lawyers. Instead of advancing the cause of a client who has selected the lawyer as his advocate, the public interest lawyer selects the client and advances his own cause. He pretends to serve an invisible client, the public interest.... Inevitably the lawyer is driven to identify his predilections with the public interest. That is unctuous.

... [T]he most baffling problem of substance is how to locate the public interest. It simply will not do to accept a set of simplistic labels and to decide, a priori, that in a contest between an employer and an employee the public interest demands that the employee shall always prevail; or that in a landlord-tenant controversy, the latter is always to be preferred.... Oh, if only life were that simple!

The traditional relationship of lawyer to client does not contemplate that the lawyer will be a hired hand or a hired gun. He is a professional counselor and not a menial servant. He takes instructions only in those areas in which it is appropriate for the client to give them. In other respect the lawyer is in command. To the client he owes loyalty, undivided and undiluted, zeal and devotion and some additional obligations which I shall mention. His object is to achieve for his client the best which is available within the law by means compatible with the canons of ethics.

I used the term, "best available," to distinguish it from the most readily available. The lawyer who contents himself with the latter in his effort to advance his client's interest is not fully discharging his duty. When necessary, he must make an effort at inventiveness. The Anglo–American system of law possesses a unique quality; the ability of any of its principles to grow and contract by judicial interpretation and legislative action.

The mother of such innovation is the proverbial necessity.

The client's necessity stimulates imagination and promotes the exercise of the lawyer's skill to discover the rule of law which is capable of that muscular stretch which will enable it to encompass the client's objective.

The role of inventor and innovator I regard as central for members of the profession and the exercise of that role fulfills a great responsibility of the lawyer. And it needs emphasis for this reason. Our journalists who report the news generally attribute these innovations to the courts which give them legitimacy. True, it is only after the courts had spoken that we knew that the indigent accused had right to counsel or that a dual school system was a denial of equal protection or that persons in custody must be instructed concerning their rights before they are questioned.

But in each case the court's judgment was the non-monopolistic patent issued to the lawyer-inventor who presented the innovation for approval.

. . .

One solution that has been proposed for the [ethical problems faced by lawyers] finds me in loud opposition. That is the attempt to convert the lawyer routinely into an informer against his client.

When it is stated in this simplistic form, our revulsion is instantaneous, if not instinctive. Our training, after all, has been in the western tradition of the confidentiality of the relationship between the lawyer and the client. The merest suggestion that the lawyer become a stool pigeon against his client fills us with abhorrence....

... Access between attorney and client, uncensored and uninhibited, is indispensable to the independence of the bar; and the independence of the bar is the condition precedent to a free society and a democratic government.

. . .

In general terms, truth commands a very high respect in our society. No one can be heard to challenge judges when they pay homage to truth.

With some trepidation I should like to tender the suggestion that in actual practice the ascertainment of the truth is not necessarily the target of the trial, that values other than truth frequently take precedence, and that, indeed, courtroom truth is a unique species of the genus truth, and that it is not necessarily congruent with objective or absolute truth, whatever that may be.

When I once casually expressed this notion to a group of laymen, they expressed shock and dismay as if I were a monk uttering some unutterable heresy to a Tenth Century congregation of bishops. But that reaction has not deterred me. On reflection, I have framed the hypothesis that courtroom truth is one of several varieties of truth and I have discovered that, consciously or unconsciously, the practicing trial lawyer behaves in a way compatible with that hypothesis. I have also formulated the conclusion that the object of a trial is not the ascertainment of truth but the resolution of a controversy by the principled application of the rules of the game. In a civilized society these rules should be designed to favor the just resolution of controversy; and in a progressive society they should change as the perception of justice evolves in response to greater ethical sophistication.

When the author of the Song of Solomon says, "I am the rose of Sharon and the lily of the valleys," no one believes that he is speaking of horticultural specimens. Nor is he suspected of suborning perjury when he causes a maiden to avow to her lover, "I have compared thee, o my love, to a company of horses in Pharaoh's chariots." Manifestly, a poet's perception of the truth is different from that of a speaker of prose. So, too I believe, the courtroom has developed its own version of truth.

The reception of information in most court proceedings is conducted through a complex filtering process. The filtering is designed in large measure to exclude information which is suspect or which experience has adjudged generally untrustworthy. In addition, there are baffles which exclude information, without reference to its truthbearing quality. These exclusions have been established to serve policies and to recognize values totally unrelated to truth.

It seems inescapable to me that the so-called truth which the trier of the facts, judge or jury, will discover at the end of the trial may, likely will, differ materially from the truth it might have found had no such barriers to information been in place. I make no assessment whether, measured by some standard not yet invented, such truth is of higher or lesser quality than courtroom truth. All I assert is that it may very well, and likely will, be different.

A few specific illustrations may help to flesh out the proposition I am asserting. [Rifkind then discusses: (1) the burden of proof, which resolves matters which science would leave unresolved; (2) evidence excluded as incompetent, such as one spouse's testimony against the other; (3) the privileges that protect communications made in confidential relationships or for public policy reasons; (4) the privacy interests protected by the Fourth and Fifth Amendments; (5) exclusionary rules based on lack of trustworthiness (including hearsay, parol evidence, and statute of frauds); and (6) exclusionary rules based on the apprehension that information will carry more persuasion than is warranted (e.g., evidence of prior convictions).]

It seems to me that were trials exposed to information utterly unfiltered by rules of the kind I have mentioned, the truth they would reveal would frequently be different from the truth presently ascertained. If I had to hazard a guess I would assert that the quality of our justice would suffer grievously were trials exposed to such unrestricted information.

Having over the years entertained these reflections, I have freed myself of the necessity of uttering the litany that the object of trials is to ascertain the truth and I have come to embrace the perhaps less exalted but more viable proposition that the office of a trial is to resolve a controversy.

This perception has more than academic significance. It affects the day to day work of the practicing trial lawyer. I have seen lawyers struggling like a butterfly beating its wings against an enveloping net when they find themselves caught in a contest between what they "know" of an event and the version of that event which emerges from the witness stand. Only the latter is the operative scenario. The effective lawyer must learn to deal with it even as an artist accommodates himself to the limitations of his pigments or playwright to the time frame of one evening on the stage.

. . .

Questions

Were the law students wrong in picketing attorney Cutler? If "public interest lawyer" is a ridiculous concept because the client is "invisible," what of the "corporation's lawyer" or "lawyer for a class?" Is the analogy between "court truth" and "poetry" a good one?

The Adversary System Excuse

The standard conception of the lawyer's role, David Luban argues, is encapsulated in a saying of Elihu Root: "The client never wants to be told he can't do what he wants to do; he wants to be told how to do it, and it is the lawyer's business to tell him how." [2] The "standard

2. David Luban is a moral philosopher and law professor at the University of Maryland. The fullest expression of his ideas is in David Luban, Lawyers and Justice: An Ethical Study (1988). This summary of his position is largely taken from a subsequent article replying to a critic of his book. See David Luban, Partisanship, Betrayal and Autonomy in the Lawyer–Client Relationship: A Reply to Stephen Ellmann, 90 Colum.L.Rev. 1004 (1990). Similar arguments have been made by other moral philosophers. See, e.g., Gerald J. Postema, Moral Responsibility in Professional Ethics, 55 N.Y.U.L. Rev. 63 (1980); Alvin H. Goldman, The Moral Foundations of Professional Ethics (1980); and the essays in David Luban (ed.), The Good Lawyer: Lawyers' Roles and Lawyers' Ethics (1984).

conception" rests on the two principles of partisanship and nonaccountability: [3]

> *Partisanship.* A lawyer must, within the established constraints on professional behavior, maximize the likelihood that the client's objectives will be attained.
>
> *Nonaccountability.* In representing a client, a lawyer is neither legally, professionally nor morally accountable for the means used or the ends achieved.

The first principle requires the lawyer to be a partisan for the client; the second excuses the lawyer, when acting in this prescribed role, from legal, professional and moral accountability for what the lawyer does on behalf of the client.

In his book, *Lawyers and Justice*, Luban attacks these premises.[4] First, the lawyer's one-sided partisan zeal is founded on professional obligations to the client, but these obligations are more ambiguous and uncertain than commonly recognized. Second, the obligations themselves—loyalty, confidentiality, competence, diligence and avoidance of conflicting interests—are justified as essential to the lawyer's role as the client's advocate-agent in legal proceedings; but lawyers do many things (e.g., planning, counseling, advising) that do not fit this model.

Third, the "adversary system excuse" is only as good as the adversary system.[5] The "standard conception" of adversarial ethics, Luban argues, is that the system justifies a lawyer doing everything that is legally permissible to advance a client's interest, notwithstanding how morally repugnant those things may be. But the system can justify immoral conduct only to the extent that it itself is morally justified.

Luban examines consequentialist and non-consequentialist arguments claiming that the adversary system is the best means of obtaining justice. The consequentialist claims are that the adversary system is the best method of getting at the truth in disputed matters and that, even if that is not the case, that it is the best way of advancing the dignity and autonomy of individuals. Empirical proof that the adversary system is better than other methods in ferreting out the truth is not available, and the argument that the adversary system mimics the scientific method by engaging in dialectical refutation is false. No real scientist tries to advance her cause by exploiting error and arguing what is false, as a trial lawyer is expected to do. Truth may result

3. The principles of advocacy were originally stated by Professor Murray Schwartz in slightly different words and have been discussed by a number of other authors. See Murray L. Schwartz, The Professionalism and Accountability of Lawyers, 66 Calif.L.Rev. 669, 673 (1978), and Schwartz, The Zeal of the Civil Advocate, 1983 Am.Bar Found. Research J. 543; and Gerald Postema, Moral Responsibility in Professional Ethics, 55 N.Y.U. L. Rev. 63 (1980).

4. David Luban, Lawyers and Justice: An Ethical Study (1988).

5. The "adversary system excuse" is Luban's term for the claim that the greater social good is served by lawyers performing the role assigned to them by the adversary system.

incidentally from this process but the trial lawyer who leaps to her feet to make spurious objections has little to do with it.

The consequentialist argument that the adversary system is the best way of defending individual legal rights, advanced by Professor Monroe Freedman and others,[6] confuses client desires with just results. Individuals are entitled only to their legal rights, not to the advocate's goal of "everything the law can be made to give." Prolonging discovery to exhaust an opponent's resources, for example, does not merely vindicate the client's rights; it infringes upon those of others.

One non-consequentialist justification of the adversary system holds that the traditional lawyer-client relation is an intrinsic moral good. If a lawyer's client is in fact a "man-in-trouble," [7] or a "special-purpose friend," [8] the autonomy argument has considerable force. But many lawyers employ adversarial wiles not for oppressed individuals but on behalf of large corporations and the rich and powerful. On many occasions clients of this sort are more aptly characterized as the "man [or organization]-who-troubles-others." Does this type of representation serve individual dignity and autonomy?

Luban's own justification of the adversary system is pragmatic. Despite its imperfections, the adversary system "seems to do as good a job as any [other set of institutions and practices] at finding truth and protecting legal rights".[9] None of its rivals, such as the inquisitorial system, seems demonstrably better, and others, such as trial by ordeal, are demonstrably worse. Furthermore, since some adjudicatory system is necessary, and this is the way in which we have always done things, a pragmatic argument justifies retaining the present system. "If a social system does a reasonable job, and the costs of replacing it outweigh the benefits, and the job needs to be done, we should stay with what we have." [10] That the system should not be replaced unless a morally superior alternative appears implies that, when professional and moral obligations conflict, moral obligation takes precedence; when they do not, professional obligations are primary. Luban's ulti-

---

6. Monroe H. Freedman, Understanding Lawyers' Ethics 14–65 (1990); Stephen L. Pepper, The Lawyer's Amoral Ethical Role, 1986 Amer. Bar Found. Research J. 613.

7. David Mellinkoff, The Conscience of a Lawyer 270–71 (1973):

The lawyer, as lawyer, is no sweet kind loving moralizer. He assumes he is needed, and that no one comes to see him to pass the time of day. He is a prober, an analyzer, a planner, a decision maker, a compromiser, eventually a scrapper, a man with a strange devotion to his client. Beautifully strange, or so it seems to the man-in-trouble; ugly strange to the untroubled onlooker.... The man-in-trouble finds in the lawyer the informed fortitude he himself lacks, the sturdy professionalism that lasts through reverses that long since exhausted both the client and his money.

This man-in-trouble ... is you, and I, and our neighbor, at the right moment. The lawyer, some lawyer, is there for each of us, with a lack of discrimination among clients and causes so disgusting to authoritarians of every stripe and stature....

8. Charles Fried, The Lawyer as Friend: The Moral Foundations of the Lawyer–Client Relation, 85 Yale L. J. 1060 (1976), discussed in Chapter 1 at p. 17. Fried argues that it is morally correct to represent even an obnoxious client, the "man-who-troubles-others."

9. Luban, The Adversary System Excuse, supra, at 112.

10. Id. at 112.

mate conclusion, then, is that, in light of the weakness of the institutional justification of the adversary system, lawyers are generally morally accountable for their actions on behalf of clients.

Luban, however, concedes that the adversary system is strongly justified in the "criminal defense paradigm"—a situation in which relatively powerless individual defendants confront the full weight of the state.

> In the criminal defense paradigm, adversary advocacy is a crucial device for protecting, and indeed overprotecting, the rights of individuals against a powerful and potentially dangerous bureaucratic institution. As the familiar argument of classical liberalism has it, states by their very nature pose a chronic threat to individual well-being even when they are currently benign, and thus we are fully warranted in creating prophylactic overprotections against the state.[11]

Is this true for all criminal defendants? What about a large corporation charged with criminal violations of a regulatory statute?[12]

Unlike other commentators, Luban extends his defense of zealous advocacy to any situation in which individuals face powerful bureaucratic organizations, even private ones, "since these too pose a chronic threat."[13] Given this extension, is it too simplistic to assume that the state is always more powerful than the criminal defendant? Should not the arguments that support "classical liberalism" be subject to the same examination as the arguments supporting the adversary system?

Are Luban's critique and proposal consistent with what we know about legal ethics and the behavior of lawyers? Professor Ted Schneyer has criticized Luban and others for overstating the legal profession's commitment to one-sided partisanship.[14] He argues that professional codes and underlying law require or permit the lawyer to recognize the interests of tribunals or third persons in many situations. The professional tradition is in fact more ambiguous and multi-faceted than the critics of adversary lawyering have asserted. The "standard conception of the lawyer's role" is an exaggerated hired-gun portrayal that fails to reflect the ambiguity and conflicting ideals embodied in the profession's rules and traditions, in which models of the lawyer as "officer of the court" and as gentleman-aristocrat compete with the total-commitment-to-client model. Luban now concedes the force of these observations and finds them heartening: The tradition of the morally activist lawyer

11. Luban, Partisanship, Betrayal and Autonomy in the Lawyer–Client Relation, supra, at 1019.

12. For a detailed description of how the state can be overwhelmed by the resources of a corporate defendant charged with criminal conduct, see Francis T. Cullen, Corporate Crime Under Attack: The Ford Pinto Case and Beyond (1987), which describes the Indiana state prosecutor's effort to convict Ford Motor Co. of criminally negligent homicide for recklessly designing and failing to recall the Pinto.

13. Id. at 1019.

14. Ted Schneyer, Moral Philosophy's Standard Misconception of Legal Ethics, 1984 Wis.L.Rev. 1529; and Some Sympathy for the Hired Gun, 41 J. Legal Educ. 11 (1991).

is not "a philosopher's pipe-dream; instead, it is a reaffirmation of one of the bar's vital traditions." [15]

In short, Schneyer argues, the philosophers' notion that there is some "standard conception" of legal ethics motivating the legal profession is false. The philosophers interpret the ethics codes as selectively as they choose the legal commentators on whom they rely. For every Lord Brougham advocating single-minded zeal in representing a client's interests, there is a Louis Brandeis suggesting that lawyers should sometimes act as "counsel for the situation" rather than serving the interests of only one party. The mistaken empirical assumptions underlying the "standard conception" oversimplify what real lawyers actually do. The philosophers' useful critique of *one* conception of the lawyer's role—that of a "hired gun"—will become even more useful when they abandon these assumptions. When lawyers do unduly favor their clients, "they often do so because of financial, psychological or organizational pressures and not because of professional ethics." [16] Because of this, Schneyer believes that studies by social scientists and journalists would be most useful in studying the actual, not hypothetical, constraints and incentives operating on lawyers in various settings, "and of measures that might be taken to alter those constraints and incentives." [17]

Schneyer is right about the ethics rules as adopted by state courts and even, although to a somewhat lesser extent, about the ethics codes drafted by the American Bar Association and recommended by state bars to the state courts for adoption: On their face those codes include important limitations on zeal in the pursuit of a client's interest. He is also right that we have little empirical data on the actual practices and attitudes of lawyers and that more would be instructive. Does his claim, however, that lawyers who demonstrate single-minded zeal do so not from an ethical sense but from financial, psychological or organizational pressures sufficiently reflect the ideological commitment of lawyers, individually and collectively, to zealous representation?

Luban argues that the hired-gun conception of lawyering continues to flourish, especially in areas of practice in which lawyers are privately retained. Criminal defense lawyers believe in zealous advocacy and do not accept moral accountability for putting guilty persons back onto the streets. Litigators in civil cases involving substantial stakes also tend to be imbued with the total-commitment approach, whether the field is personal injury, matrimonial property or commercial litigation.

> The true haven of the standard conception, however, is large-firm practice.... As corporations have taken more of their routine legal work in-house for reasons of economy, priorities have shifted from the genteel and relatively uncontentious paper-processing of the "classic" Wall Street-style firm, which frowned on

---

15. Id. at 1014.

16. Schneyer, Moral Philosophy's Standard Misconception, supra, at 1571.

17. Id.

the vulgarities of litigation practice, to mammoth and highly tense single transactions: mergers and acquisitions, major corporate litigation, big bankruptcies and restructurings.... [18]

[Increased competition among large law firms] provides a strong market incentive for success and performance. The result should be obvious: partisanship, "winning is everything," is the commodity large law firms sell. Taking on wheeler-dealers as clients without much regard to the externalities that their activities inflict on third parties ... is not simply an unfortunate part of the business. It *is* the business.[19]

Will the financial penalties imposed on a number of large law firms for their representation of wheeler-dealers in the thrift industry affect this trend? [20]

Social science studies of lawyers who handle minor criminal cases, simple divorces, minor personal injuries and many common legal transactions frequently find that lawyers act as "double agents": In addition to representing a client, lawyers cooperate with opposing lawyers and institutional actors to a high degree. The studies report, for example, the following common practices: a personal-injury lawyer "cooling the client off" to accept a low-end settlement involving very little work on the lawyer's part; [21] a criminal defense lawyer performing a similar function in pushing the client to accept a plea bargain; [22] and divorce lawyers seeking to dispose of cases with as little work as possible.[23]

Are these findings consistent with Luban's theory? Luban's response is that these situations involve small stakes rather than a rejection of the principle of partisanship. The lawyers are providing all

18. See Robert W. Gordon, The Ideal and the Actual in the Law: Fantasies and Practices of New York City Lawyers, 1870–1970, in Gerald W. Gawalt, ed., The New High Priests: Lawyers in Post–Civil War America (1984) (examining the transformation of corporate practice in the late 19th century).

19. Luban, Partisanship, Betrayal, and Autonomy in the Lawyer–Client Relation, supra, at 1016–17.

20. See *ACC/Lincoln*, p. 114 above, and the note at p. 789 below.

21. Douglas E. Rosenthal, Lawyer and Client: Who's In Charge? (1974) (study of plaintiffs' personal injury lawyers). The Rosenthal study is discussed in Chapter 6 below at p. 532.

22. Abraham S. Blumberg, The Practice of Law as Confidence Game: Organizational Cooptation of a Profession, 1 Law & Soc'y Rev. 15 (1967); Jerome H. Skolnick, Social Control in the Adversary System, 11 J. Conflict Resolution 52 (1967).

23. See Austin Sarat, Lawyers and Clients: Putting Professional Service on the Agenda of Legal Education, 41 J.Legal Educ. 43 (1991) (divorce lawyers, who desire to dispose of cases with as little effort as possible, treat their clients as nuisances or enemies). See also Austin Sarat and William Felstiner, Law and Social Relations: Vocabularies of Motive in Lawyer/Client Interaction, 22 Law & Soc'y Rev. 737 (1988) (lawyers, who are generally unresponsive to their clients' distress over their marital circumstances, will discuss the circumstances only for the self-interested reason of reinforcing wavering clients' initial decision to seek divorce rather than reconciliation); and Sarat and Felstiner, Lawyers and Legal Consciousness: Law Talk in the Divorce Lawyer's Office, 98 Yale L.J. 1663 (1989) (divorce lawyers portray themselves as insiders who can facilitate successful disposition and disparage the fairness and legitimacy of legal processes and officials).

the zeal that the client can reasonably expect for the relatively low fee that is being charged (e.g., a lawyer performing a $500 divorce cannot be expected to provide the service that Arnie Becker provides for $50,000). Lawyers in high-volume, low-fee practice, Luban says,

> accept the principle of partisanship, but (1) they understand that partisanship comes in degrees, and marginal units of zeal cost marginally more; and (2) they substitute for the "maximizing" conception of zeal in the principle of partisanship a "satisficing" conception of zeal. "Satisficing" is economists' jargon for strategies whereby an agent sometimes seeks less than the best, seeks (in other words) merely what is good enough: a good enough quarterly earning, a good enough price, etc.[24]

The Morally Activist Lawyer

The second half of David Luban's book, Lawyers and Justice, sketches an alternative vision of the good lawyer's role: the "morally activist lawyer." [25] Luban starts from the assumption that all lawyers, other than the criminal defense lawyer, are morally accountable for the means used and ends pursued in representing clients. The role obligations of partisanship are rebuttable presumptions which must be justified in specific situations. In many situations they will be overridden by the demands of common morality. Because the lawyer cannot hide behind the principle of nonaccountability, the lawyer is put in the demanding position of talking with the client about conflicts between the lawyer's considered moral judgments and the client's wishes. "If the client is unbending, the lawyer may have to refuse certain client requests. In desperate cases—cases, for example, in which the client will not be deflected from a course of action that will unjustifiably damage the interests of others—the lawyer may have to betray the client by blowing the whistle." Luban mentions the O.P.M. case, printed above at p. 300, as a situation in which betrayal would be appropriate.[26]

Louis Brandeis provides a model of Luban's "morally activist lawyer."

> ... Brandeis wrote the following advice (apparently) to himself: "Advise client what he should have—not what he wants." ... [Morally accountable lawyers, following the Brandeis example,] will sometimes find their consciences compelling them to disobey the principle of partisanship ... by refraining from morally improper tactics or by declining to pursue objectionable client ends. They may be forced to confront clients with moral objections to perfectly legal projects and their clients may regard this as unwarranted

---

24. Luban, Partisanship, Betrayal and Autonomy in the Lawyer–Client Relation, supra, at 1012.

25. For other statements of a similar moral vision on the part of lawyers, see, e.g., Robert W. Gordon, Corporate Law Practice as a Public Calling, 49 Md. L. Rev. 255 (1990); and William H. Simon, Ethical Discretion in Lawyering, 101 Harv. L. Rev. 1083 (1988).

26. Id. at 1022.

interference with autonomous choices or even as betrayal. The morally activist lawyer regrets this, but sees "advise client what he should have—not what he wants" as the minimum that legal ethics requires of her.[27]

Professor Stephen Ellmann attacks Luban's morally activist vision on a number of grounds: The burdens of deliberation with clients on the ends and means of representation are too onerous; the principles of common morality are too vague and controversial; the moral dialogue with clients involves too much paternalism; and selective refusal and betrayal amount to unjustifiable intrusions on the client's autonomy.[28] Are the burdens of deliberation significantly more onerous than the burdens of considering the economic consequences to the client of available legal approaches, which is deliberation most good lawyer-counselors would consider a necessary accompaniment to giving good legal advice? Is it necessary that the principles of common morality be clear to both lawyer and client before entering into dialogue? Is it less paternalistic to assume that the client cares not a whit for morality than it is to assume that the client might have moral concerns about a legal course of conduct? Does failing to raise these concerns discourage clients from raising them? If so, isn't that a form of exercising power over clients that should concern us?

How Adversarial Is the Adversary System?

Professional codes and ideology, reinforced by legal training and popular culture, portray lawyers as vigorous advocates for their clients. Does the real world conform to this model of adversarial behavior? Clearly there are some situations in which the model becomes reality: civil or criminal proceedings in which both parties are ably represented by well-funded counsel. Studies of lawyer behavior, however, suggest that the adversarial model may be more of a myth than a reality in many common settings.

First, nearly all civil and criminal cases (90–95 percent) are settled rather than tried.[29] The settlements are heavily influenced by lawyers' predictions of expected outcomes if the cases were to be fully litigated ("bargaining in the shadow of the court").[30] But factors other than the expected litigation outcome also have heavy influence on settlements: the resources or staying power of the litigants and their lawyers; their

---

27. Id. at 1004–05. See William H. Simon, The Ideology of Advocacy, discussed above at p. 28, for a critique of how lawyers decide what the client wants. Simon argues that lawyers impose a selfish persona on clients and act as if that represents the client's desires.

28. See Stephen J. Ellmann, Lawyering for Justice in a Flawed Democracy (Book Review), 90 Colum.L.Rev. 116 (1990).

29. See H. Laurence Ross, Settled Out of Court: The Social Process of Insurance Claims Adjustment 136 (1970) (90–95 percent of all civil damage cases settled without trial); James E. Bond, Plea Bargaining and Guilty Pleas 13–15 (1975) (estimating that plea bargaining dispositions occur in as many as 95 percent of criminal cases).

30. See Robert H. Mnookin and Lewis A. Kornhauser, Bargaining in the Shadow of the Law: The Case of Divorce, 88 Yale L. J. 950 (1979).

relative aggressiveness and risk-averseness; the differential effect on parties and lawyers of delay and increased cost; systemic matters such as multi-year delays for a civil jury trial or a crushing case load in the prosecutor's office or the fact that prisons are full; and many similar factors. The frequency of settlement suggests that cooperative modes of behavior, rather than purely adversarial ones, are dominant in many litigation contexts some or all of the time.

Second, empirical studies suggest that the "conflict" ethic is not the norm in routine matters handled on a high-volume basis, whether the setting is traffic court, criminal court or divorce court. Lawyers who are too compliant with opposing lawyers or judges are departing from the professional model of zealous and loyal representation, but the pressures on them to do so, especially in matters involving relatively small stakes, are large. Professor Skolnick's study comparing the performance of appointed counsel in criminal cases with that of privately retained counsel concludes that both "see greater advantage in cooperativeness than in conflict." [31] Defendants are pressured to accept guilty pleas because their lawyers predict that they will be found guilty and, if so, given a stiffer sentence. The fact that these expert predictions are frequently correct "leads to a system where the principal combatants are continually 'regressing' to a state of cooperation." [32] These tendencies, at odds with the adversarial ethic, become destructive "where cooperation may shade off into collusion, thereby subverting the ethical basis of the system." [33]

An even darker portrayal by Abraham Blumberg views the defense counsel in criminal cases as engaged in a "confidence game." [34] The confidence game starts with the fixing and collecting of a fee that will be as large as the defense lawyer can extract from the defendant by "playing upon his client's anxieties and establishing a seemingly causal relationship between the fee and the accused's extrication from his difficulties." [35] The second stage of the confidence game is to "prepare his client for defeat (a highly likely contingency) and then, if necessary, 'cool him out' [so that he will accept a plea bargain]." The third stage is that of "satisfy[ing] the court organization that he has adequately negotiated the plea so as to preclude an embarrassing incident which might invite 'outside' scrutiny." [36] In his role as "double agent"— working for both the defendant and the court system—

> the lawyer employs an air of professional confidence and "inside-dopesterism" to assuage anxieties on all sides. He makes the necessary bland assurances and in effect manipulates his client,

31. Jerome H. Skolnick, Social Control in the Adversary System, 11 J. Conflict Resolution 52, 68 (1967).

32. Id. at 68.

33. Id. at 69.

34. Abraham S. Blumberg, Criminal Justice: Issues and Ironies 242–46 (2d ed. 1979).

35. Id. at 243.

36. Id. at 244.

who is usually willing to do and say the things—true or not—that will help his attorney extricate him. Because what he is selling is not measurable, the lawyer can make extravagant claims of influence and secret knowledge with impunity. But, as in a genuine confidence game, the victim who has participated is loath to do anything that will upset the lesser plea which his lawyer has "conned" him into accepting.[37]

Kenneth Holland reports that the American court system is becoming more inquisitorial and bureaucratic.[38] Judges take the initiative to force settlements and to manage litigation. Courts have larger staffs and are surrounded by adjunct agencies that facilitate fact-determination and negotiation, such as magistrates, court-centered counseling agencies and the like. "Adversariness is declining ... because many of the disputes reaching courts are not being processed in the traditional manner."[39] The number of contested trials has stayed constant or declined even though total case volume has increased markedly.

In major cities, 75 percent of landlord-tenant and creditor-debtor cases end in default judgments. Divorce cases, originally adversarial, are now almost entirely uncontested and are resolved by the manipulation of the parties' consent. The procedures followed are better described as bureaucratic and cooperative than adversarial. Juvenile and civil-commitment proceedings typically lack key adversarial features, Supreme Court decisions notwithstanding. The evidence is that trial courts have come to do fewer formal dispute resolutions and a larger proportion of routine, cut-and-dried administration.[40]

Perhaps two trends are proceeding simultaneously: a more aggressive adversarial ethic in high-stakes litigation having a zero-sum character, and a more bureaucratic, cooperative mode of dispute resolution in many areas of law practice involving a high volume of fairly routine claims.

37. Id. at 245.

38. Kenneth M. Holland, The Twilight of Adversariness, in The Analysis of Judicial Reform 17, 22–27 (P. DuBois ed. 1982).

39. Id. at 22.

40. Ibid.

Chapter 6
LAWYER-CLIENT RELATIONSHIP
A. NATURE OF RELATIONSHIP
Introductory Note

The lawyer-client relationship is a complex one founded on contract and agency law but infused with professional ideals and governed in part by regulatory principles flowing from a lawyer's role as an officer of the court. Three simple models suggest facets of this complex relationship: (1) a fiduciary model, (2) a market model and (3) a regulatory or public utility model.[1]

The fiduciary model draws on a legal and professional tradition that views a client as dependent upon her lawyer's skill and knowledge. According to that tradition, because a client cannot evaluate the quality of legal services, she must make a leap of faith and trust her lawyer to provide loyal, competent and diligent service at reasonable cost. Ideally, each lawyer's professional values prevent abuse of the client's trust. The lawyer becomes a fiduciary expected to put the client's interest ahead of other interests, especially the lawyer's self-interest. When a client challenges a lawyer's actions, the courts thus look to agency and fiduciary principles to resolve the conflict.

The market model views the relationship between lawyer and client as a consensual exchange that benefits both lawyer and client: The client benefits from receiving services conforming to contract terms and market standards, and the lawyer benefits from receiving payment for services rendered. This approach presumes that a client can select an appropriate person to provide needed services, make satisfactory arrangements with that person and monitor the provision of service.[2] If either party seeks legal enforcement of the lawyer-client agreement, the courts look to contract law for governing principles. The market model suggests that the goal of such enforcement should be for clients

---

1. For useful discussion of various models of legal ethics, see John Leubsdorf, Three Models of Professional Reform, 67 Cornell L.Rev. 1021 (1982) (contrasting the approaches of market, public utility, and personal responsibility approaches to problems of professional reform); Anthony D'Amato and Edward J. Eberle, Three Models of Legal Ethics, 27 St. Louis U.L.Rev. 761 (1983) (applying autonomy, socialist and deontological models to the problem of confidentiality).

2. These assumptions are questioned by many people, including economists. See Kenneth Arrow, The Limits of Organization 61–79 (1974) (professional ethics are needed because patients lack information necessary to make the market model work in the health care field).

to receive the services they desire on terms and at prices and levels of quality set by market forces.

The regulatory or public utility model views lawyers as quasi-public officials performing important public functions. This approach perceives dispute resolution and other legal tasks as so vital to the community that they must be closely regulated in order to serve public objectives of legitimacy, finality, fairness and efficiency. Under this model, more pervasive abroad than in the United States, courts and legislatures provide detailed regulation of lawyers in the public interest.

The American legal system rarely involves institutions that have the simplicity and purity of these models. In the United States, the law and practice of the lawyer-client relationship has attributes of each model. The fiduciary approach triumphs on many issues, the market model on others (especially when clients are sophisticated repeat players in legal matters) and the public utility model prevails on some issues.

1. Perspectives on Lawyer–Client Relationship

What do ordinary Americans want from a lawyer? Empirical surveys performed by the American Bar Foundation indicate that the four principal qualities clients seek in their lawyers are commitment, integrity, competence and a fair and affordable fee.[3] Commitment demands that a lawyer should be concerned for her client and interested in the client's problem. Integrity embraces honesty, trustworthiness, candor, and moral and ethical standards. The survey data shows that the two sexes order these qualities somewhat differently: Women clients place somewhat more emphasis on a lawyer's commitment and integrity than men, who more often give competence a higher priority. Fairness in setting fees ranks equally important to both sexes.

Who's in Charge?

Douglas E. Rosenthal, focusing on the dynamics of power, has contrasted a "traditional model" of the lawyer-client relationship with a "participatory model."[4] Considering a professional to be someone who does something that requires expert knowledge and skill, the traditional model stresses respect for professional knowledge, competence and autonomy. Because lay persons lack the knowledge to evaluate adequately the quality of what a professional does, they must trust that professional's judgment and responsibility. The traditional model thus expects clients to be cooperative, deferential and obedient.

The participatory model, on the other hand, posits a client of equal status who participates actively in the professional relationship, shar-

---

3. Barbara A. Curran, Surveying the Legal Needs of the Public: What the Public Wants and Expects in the Lawyer–Client Relationship, in Gibson and Baldwin (eds.), Law in a Cynical Society: Opinion and Law in the 1980's 107–119 (1985).

4. Douglas E. Rosenthal, Lawyer and Client: Who's in Charge? 1–28 (1974).

ing control and decisional responsibility with the professional.[5] Rosenthal argues that the participatory model is preferable because it furthers client objectives and produces better results.[6] A lawyer, Rosenthal argues, "should be obligated to disclose to the client the relevant open choices involved in responding to his particular problem."[7] The lawyer should discuss with the client "the alternatives involved in identifying the problem, the alternatives for dealing with it, the professional's experience in employing these alternatives, and their anticipated difficulties and benefits. No action should be taken with respect to any of these choices until the client, aware of them, has given his consent."[8]

Paternalism and Manipulation

Lawyers, like physicians and other professionals, have passed through an arduous period of study and training. They view themselves, and are viewed by others, as a relatively elite group. They typically earn more than those who work with their hands and enjoy greater prestige and social status. Their knowledge appears esoteric to ordinary people, in part because it employs a special language inaccessible to many clients. These features of the professional role, Professor Richard Wasserstrom argues, "conspire to depersonalize the client in the eyes of the lawyer qua professional." As a result, lawyers tend to treat a "client as an object."[9]

> The lawyer qua professional is, of necessity, only centrally interested in that part of the client that lies within his or her special competency. And this leads any professional including the lawyer to respond to the client as an object—as a thing to be altered, corrected, or otherwise assisted by the professional rather than as a person. At best the client is viewed ... not as a whole person but as a segment or aspect of a person—an interesting kidney problem, a routine marijuana possession case, or another adolescent with an

5. Rosenthal argues that the two models take opposing positions on basic issues concerning the professional relationship and the provision of professional services. The traditional model posits a passive, trusting and obedient client; assumes that ineffective professional service is rare; views professional problems as routine and technical, having a best solution inaccessible to lay understanding; assumes that professionals can and do make a client's interests their own and that professions and courts set and maintain high professional standards; and posits that effective professional service is accessible to all paying clients. Rosenthal's participatory model provides opposing answers to these propositions.

6. The participatory model, Rosenthal found, produces larger awards in personal injury cases. In Rosenthal's study, a panel of experts evaluated the outcome of about 100 personal injury cases on the basis of a detailed workup of the facts, likely evidence, etc. The feature that most closely correlated with a good monetary outcome for a client was not the lawyer's education, experience, reputation, firm, professionalism or talent, but rather the aggressiveness of the client in monitoring the case.

7. Rosenthal, supra, at 155.

8. Id.

9. Richard Wasserstrom, Lawyers as Professionals: Some Moral Issues, 5 Human Rights 1 (1975). Another portion of this essay was reprinted in Chapter 1 at p. 18.

identity crisis.[10]

Professional training, status and role, combined with the vulnerability and inexperience of many clients, also "operate to make the relationship a paternalistic one." [11] Because a lawyer knows some "things that the client doesn't know, it is extremely easy to believe that one knows generally what is best for the client."

> Invested with all of this power both by the individual and the society, the lawyer qua professional responds to the client as though the client were an individual who needed to be looked after and controlled, and to have decisions made for him or her by the lawyer, with as little interference from the client as possible.... [12]

Such paternalism often leads, even if inadvertently, to a lawyer's manipulating a client. Such manipulation can run the gamut from serving what a lawyer perceives as a client's best interest to furthering the lawyer's own interest. At either end of this spectrum some manipulation may be inevitable. For example, in translating unfamiliar legal reality for a client, a lawyer necessarily alters the client's expectations to conform to that reality. Similarly, lawyers often deploy their authority and articulateness as professionals to persuade clients to undertake an alternate course of conduct more consistent with legal and moral realities—a course of conduct that is either in the client's best interest or "the right thing to do": "If you persist in your plan to perjure yourself, I will be forced to withdraw from representing you in this case;" "The subpoena asks for all relevant documents. Although this memorandum is damaging, the consequences of divulging it now are far less serious than the later discovery, which I consider probable, that we have concealed it." This kind of counseling—attempting to guide a less-informed client along a morally and legally acceptable

10. Id. at 21.

11. A large philosophical and legal literature exists on paternalism. See Gerald Dworkin, Paternalism, in Richard Wasserstrom (ed.), Morality and the Law 107 (1971); Dennis F. Thompson, Paternalism in Medicine, Law, and Public Policy, in Daniel Callahan and Sissela Bok (eds.), Ethics Teaching in Higher Education 245 (1980); David Luban, Paternalism and the Legal Profession, 1981 Wis.L.Rev. 454; Paul R. Tremblay, On Persuasion and Paternalism: Lawyer Decision–Making and the Questionably Competent Client, 1987 Utah L.Rev. 515. Paternalism, a continuing issue throughout this chapter, is discussed below at p. 511.

12. Id. at 22. Wasserstrom's argument that professionals dominate their clients or patients relies upon an image of professional role that is somewhat more characteristic of medicine than of law: The client or patient as an inexperienced and sick or troubled lay individual who must depend completely upon the professional. Many lawyers, however, serve relatively sophisticated business clients, some of whom have repeated encounters with the legal system. In addition, the medical profession encounters few analogs to in-house counsel, whose existence helps place many entity clients on a more even footing with their outside lawyers.

For discussion of the influence of images of professional role, see William F. May, The Physician's Covenant: Images of the Healer in Medical Ethics (1983). The medical profession is discussed in Eliot Freidson, Profession of Medicine: A Study of the Sociology of Applied Knowledge (1970) and Paul Starr, The Social Transformation of American Medicine (1982).

path—may demand of a lawyer extraordinary interpersonal skills, persuasiveness as an advocate and even courage.[13]

A less justifiable form of paternalism (perhaps "parentalism" is a better term) involves more extreme control of information, slanted advice and occasionally deceit. In this more suspect use of a lawyer's authority, the lawyer does not convince or persuade a client to follow the lawyer's advice, but instead diverts the client from something she wants and intends to do. A lawyer deprives the client of effective choice by controlling the flow of information: "The settlement offer isn't perfect, but it's the best one you're going to get and better than a 50 percent chance of losing at trial; you should take it;" "You can take the stand; but the jury won't believe you and the judge will hit you with a harder sentence." At the extreme, a lawyer may act without consulting the client, for example, rejecting a settlement offer or taking an important litigation step.

Another form of manipulation, clearly unjustifiable, involves situations in which a lawyer manipulates a client to serve the lawyer's self-interest. For example, a lawyer might pressure the client to accept a low settlement that provides the lawyer with a substantial fee on the basis of very little work.

Who Corrupts Whom?

Discussions of legal ethics are often predicated on opposing assumptions as to which side of the relationship poses danger to the other side or to the public interest. On the one hand, authors such as Rosenthal and Wasserstrom, focusing on the representation of injured or troubled individuals, view lawyers as dominant in the relationship and the locus of danger. These authors assume that ethics rules should prevent lawyers from abusing or corrupting clients.

Other authors, however, generally focusing on lawyers who serve corporate interests, view clients as the locus of danger—clients who exercise power over lawyers and bend those lawyers to the clients' will.[14] This view assumes implicitly that many clients are immoral, "bad" people who seek to use lawyers to further unjust causes by unjust means. Ethics rules thus should protect professional and public values, which are endangered when lawyers become merely "hired guns" or "mouthpieces" for clients.

Each of the competing stereotypes has some force in particular practice contexts, but both overlook the variety of law practice, individual variation and the powerful effects of the common culture shared by lawyers and clients. Assumptions that the morals of either lawyers or clients as a group are any worse (or any better) than the other are

---

13. This is particularly the case with a powerful client, such as a large corporation that generates and closely monitors a continuing volume of legal business, able to exercise control over the lawyer.

14. Robert W. Gordon, David Luban and William H. Simon are examples of writers taking this position.

dubious. Both groups include a highly diverse segment of humanity, with a sampling of saints and scoundrels amid many ordinary, decent people who only occasionally succumb to temptation. A corruptive force—or a moral insight—may flow in either direction, although economic, legal and institutional incentives or controls may push behavior in one direction or another.

Clients also have strong temptations to manipulate their lawyers, for example, by presenting a favorable version of the facts.[15] In a deeper sense, it is impossible for the relationship to be wholly free of manipulation.[16] In any case, when the client has limited capacity, as in the case of a child, full participation of the client is impossible. See M.R. 1.14.

Lawyer–Client Interaction

What actually occurs in the lawyer's office? Austin Sarat and William Felstiner observed, recorded and analyzed lawyer-client interaction in 40 divorce cases.[17] Among their findings were the following:

First, although the lawyers studied behaved adversarially in their negotiations with opposing parties, those same lawyers actively attempted to persuade their clients to reach negotiated settlements.

[L]awyers work hard to sell settlement to their clients and to avoid contested hearings and trials. The negotiation between lawyer and client over how to understand the nature of the divorce dispute and the nature of the legal process is, in most cases, intertwined with the efforts of lawyers to sell settlement.[18]

Second, Sarat and Felstiner learned that "lawyer/client interaction in divorce occurs against a background of mutual suspicion, if not antagonism, between lawyers and clients."[19] Clients, frustrated by the slowness of the process and their lawyers' unresponsiveness to the moral or emotional aspects of their cases, "worry that their lawyers will be inattentive or disloyal." On the other hand, lawyers view their clients as emotional, demanding and having unreasonable expectations. "For divorce lawyers, the client is ..., if not an enemy, an uncertain and unreliable partner and ally."[20]

15. Roy B. Fleming, Client Games: Defense Attorney Perspectives on Their Relations with Criminal Clients, 1986 Am.Bar Found.Research J. 253.

16. See Stephen J. Ellmann, Lawyer and Client, 34 UCLA L.Rev. 717 (1987). Compare Marcy Strauss, Toward a Revised Model of Attorney–Client Relationship: The Argument for Autonomy, 65 N.C.L.Rev. 315 (1987).

17. See Austin Sarat and William L.F. Felstiner, Law and Social Relations: Vocabularies of Motive in Lawyer/Client Interaction, 22 Law & Soc'y Rev. 737 (1988). The summary of their findings presented here is taken from Austin Sarat, Lawyers and Clients: Putting Professional Service on the Agenda of Legal Education, 41 J.Legal Educ. 43 (1991).

18. Sarat, supra, at 46.

19. Id. at 47.

20. Id.

Strains in the lawyer-client relationship in divorce cases, the study concluded, result from conflicting understandings about the nature of the dispute and the nature of the legal process. Clients view the underlying dispute from a retrospective and moral perspective. The failure of the marriage has left them feeling angry or hurt, victimized or guilty; and they attempt to enlist their lawyers in an effort to explain the marriage's failure and to assign blame. Their lawyers, viewing the question of who did what to whom and why as largely irrelevant in today's no-fault divorce regimes, tend to be emotionally unresponsive to their clients' concerns.[21] Yet the same lawyers engage in extensive counseling in efforts to fashion an appropriate "legal self" for the client. Divorce lawyers thus urge their clients not to trust their own feelings, not to be short-sighted and not to act on short-term emotions; the emphasis is on the financial, not emotional, aspects of the divorce.

> Thus, divorce lawyers can be seen as helping clients who will in the long run be more interested in the economics of settlement than in the vindication of immediate emotions.... [Lawyers] define their professional role so as to avoid assuming a sense of responsibility for the human consequences of being unresponsive to emotion. Clients, however, come to the divorce process expecting that their emotions will matter and that lawyers will care; they come away disappointed.[22]

Lawyers and clients have differing understandings of the legal process. Clients expect that the legal system will deal impartially with the facts, follow its own rules and arrive at fair and correct results. Divorce lawyers, however, "trash" the legal system and its rules, suggesting that judges and opponents will ignore the rules or find ways around them. The lawyers thus present law in action from the vantage point of legal realism, not in terms of idealized formal justice: "Lawyers suggest that what clients buy is knowledge of the ropes rather than knowledge of the rules; when they describe the legal system as idiosyncratic and personalistic, they endow themselves with the mystique of inside knowledge."[23]

Sarat concludes that a greater understanding of the emotional aspects of lawyer-client interaction should be a goal of legal education. "Learning how to identify and respond to the distinct problems and perspectives of clients is as important for the future securities lawyer as it is for the future divorce lawyer."[24]

---

21. "Client and lawyer are like performer and bored audience: although the lawyer will not interrupt the aria, she will not applaud too much either for fear of inviting an encore.... [W]hen lawyers refuse to engage with clients' efforts to give meaning to the past, clients often end up dissatisfied because they believe their lawyers do not understand or empathize with them." Id. at 48–49.

22. Id. at 50.

23. Id. at 52.

24. Id. at 53.

One Profession or Many?

Discussion of lawyers often proceeds on the assumption that the common characteristics of lawyers justify treating all lawyers the same—as members of a single profession governed by the same rules. But is that the case? Consider, for example, whether the ethical rules governing the practice of law should protect a lawyer's integrity against client overreaching (by permitting or requiring the lawyer to be something other than the client's "mouthpiece" or "hired gun") or, on the other hand, protect a client against lawyer overreaching.[25]

The mouthpiece characterization suggests a lawyer who is dependent upon or subservient to clients. Empirical studies of lawyer-client interaction conclude that large-firm corporate lawyers wield relatively little influence over their powerful and wealthy clients.[26] Lawyers in this sector of the profession tend to view themselves as technicians who do what their clients want. Corporate lawyers emphasize craft over counseling, allow their powerful business clients to set the agenda of corporate practice and "often seem to reject even the aspiration to serve as molders of corporate and public policy." [27]

On the other hand, studies of lawyers who deal with personal-plight practice (representation of individuals who face a legal problem and who have had little or no prior experience with lawyers or the legal system) emphasize the power and authority that lawyers exercise over clients.[28] Such studies imply or argue that personal-plight clients need to be protected against lawyer domination, manipulation and overreaching. One substantial study concluded that more participation by clients in this sector produces better results.[29]

25. Recall the discussion of "who corrupts whom," supra at p. 476.

26. See, e.g., John P. Heinz, The Power of Lawyers, 17 Ga.L.Rev. 891, 904 (1983):

On the present state of our knowledge, ... I do not find much evidence that the lawyers who serve corporations enjoy a highly independent, autonomous role, a role that would permit the lawyers' own values (as distinct from those of their clients) to determine the positions taken, with the lawyers thus having important, independent effects on the allocation of scarce resources. In short, it appears to me that corporate lawyers usually do their clients' bidding, rather than the other way around.

See also Robert L. Nelson, Partners with Power: The Social Transformation of the Large Law Firm (1988) (reporting that corporate lawyers very rarely refuse a potential assignment because it was contrary to their personal values); and Robert A. Kagan and Robert E. Rosen, On the Social Significance of Large Firm Law Practice, 37 Stan.L.Rev. 399 (1985) (the predominant role performed by lawyers in corporate law firms is that of "nonjudgmental conduits").

27. Kagan and Rosen, supra, at 440.

28. See, e.g., William L.F. Felstiner and Austin Sarat, Enactments of Power: Negotiating Reality and Responsibility in Lawyer–Client Interactions, 77 Cornell L.Rev. 1447 (1992) (matrimonial lawyers); Hubert O'Gorman, Lawyers in Matrimonial Cases (1963) (same); Douglas E. Rosenthal, Lawyer and Client: Who's in Charge? (1974) (personal injury lawyers); Abraham S. Blumberg, The Practice of Law as a Confidence Game: Organizational Cooptation of a Profession, 1 Law & Soc'y Rev. 15 (1967) (criminal defense lawyers); Gary Neustader, When Lawyer and Client Meet, 35 Buffalo L.Rev. 177 (1986) (consumer bankruptcy lawyers).

29. See the discussion of Rosenthal's study above at p. 473.

Should legal ethics differentiate between sectors of practice? Should the rules adopt a client-protective ethic for lawyers serving predominantly individuals and small businesses (unsophisticated clients) and a lawyer- and society-protective ethic for lawyers serving large corporations and their managers? [30]   In one hemisphere of the profession, where lawyers are dealing with informed, experienced and well-to-do clients,[31] ethics rules would seek to protect lawyer autonomy so that lawyers would be permitted or required to be something other than the client's "mouthpiece" or "hired gun." Simultaneously, ethics rules in the personal-plight sector would seek to protect clients against lawyer overreaching. Should ethics rules depart from the mythic premise that all lawyers are the same—a single profession governed by exactly the same rules?

Conflict and Mistrust Between Lawyer and Client

Lawyers and lawyer codes tend to view the lawyer-client relationship in romantic and idealized form: a relationship of trust and confidence between a responsible adult client and a competent lawyer who will vigorously and selflessly advance the client's goals. Some empirical study and much anecdotal evidence, however, describe a reality pervaded instead by fear, suspicion and mistrust: A relationship characterized from time to time and in varying degrees by hostility, anger and suspicion as well as by respect, confidence and trust.

Professor Robert Burt has considered the implications of this more realistic portrayal of the lawyer-client relationship.[32]   Although the legal profession emphasizes the necessity of mutual trust in the attorney-client relationship, Burt believes that an overabundance of mistrust exists between lawyers and their clients, whether those clients are private litigants, corporations or criminal defendants. The professional codes enhance mistrust between lawyer and client because a pretense of mutual trust discourages examination of the possible sources of mistrust and suppresses awareness of conflict. For example, because the limited disclosure provisions in the codes apply only when a lawyer has actual knowledge of a client's intent to commit a criminal act, clients have a powerful incentive to deceive their lawyers or withhold information from them; and lawyers, on the other hand, have equally powerful incentives to resist prying too closely into their clients' affairs. Lawyer and client thus acquiesce in a relationship of willful gullibility that is

---

30. This argument is made by Ted Schneyer, Some Sympathy for the Hired Gun, 41 J. Legal Educ. 11, 22–27 (1991). See also David B. Wilkins, Who Should Regulate Lawyers?, 105 Harv. L. Rev. 799 (1991) (arguing that different regulatory approaches and sanctions are required in different areas of legal practice to assure efficient compliance while protecting the independence of lawyers).

31. A major empirical study of the legal profession concludes that the legal profession is stratified, not by the type of legal services rendered, but by the socio-economic character of clients. The profession is divided into two hemispheres: those who serve corporate clients and those who serve individuals. John P. Heinz and Edward O. Laumann, Chicago Lawyers: The Social Structure of the Bar (1983).

32. See Robert A. Burt, Conflict and Trust Between Attorney and Client, 69 Geo.L.J. 1015 (1981).

founded on the pretense of mutual trust and the actuality of shared ignorance.[33]

Burt's controversial recommendation is that a duty of care be imposed on lawyers toward third persons injured by a client's wrongful conduct. Lawyers "who fail to act on their suspicions or who negligently fail to be reasonably suspicious of their clients [should] be held directly liable for consequent damages suffered by third parties."[34] Burt argues that clients would share more information with lawyers under his proposed legal regime than under current rules. To protect themselves from civil liability, lawyers would insist on honest conversations with their clients. The threat of disclosure would force clients to abandon illegal conduct. The hidden fears and suspicions of lawyers and clients in dealing with one another would be forced to the surface, and such revelation would ultimately yield a more confident and trusting relationship. Do you agree with Burt's proposal and argument?

2. Forming the Relationship

TOGSTAD v. VESELY, OTTO, MILLER & KEEFE
Supreme Court of Minnesota, 1980.
291 N.W.2d 686.

Per Curiam.

This is an appeal by the defendants from a judgment of the Hennepin County District Court involving an action for legal malpractice. The jury found that the defendant attorney Jerre Miller was negligent and that, as a direct result of such negligence, plaintiff John Togstad sustained damages in the amount of $610,500 and his wife, plaintiff Joan Togstad, in the amount of $39,000. Defendants (Miller and his law firm) appeal to this court from the denial of their motion for judgment notwithstanding the verdict or, alternatively, for a new trial. We affirm.

In August 1971, John Togstad began to experience severe headaches and on August 16, 1971, was admitted to Methodist Hospital where tests disclosed that the headaches were caused by a large aneurism[1] on the left internal carotid artery.[2] The attending physician, Dr. Paul Blake, a neurological surgeon, treated the problem by applying a Selverstone clamp to the left common carotid artery. The clamp was surgically implanted on August 27, 1971, in Togstad's neck to allow the gradual closure of the artery over a period of days.

33. Id. at 1027.

34. Id. at 1030.

1. An aneurism is a weakness or softening in an artery wall which expands and bulges out over a period of years.

2. The left internal carotid artery is one of the major vessels which supplies blood to the brain.

In the early morning hours of August 29, 1971, a nurse observed that Togstad was unable to speak or move. At the time, the clamp was one-half (50%) closed. Upon discovering Togstad's condition, the nurse called a resident physician, who did not adjust the clamp. Dr. Blake was also immediately informed of Togstad's condition and arrived about an hour later, at which time he opened the clamp. Togstad is now severely paralyzed in his right arm and leg, and is unable to speak.

Plaintiffs' expert, Dr. Ward Woods, testified that Togstad's paralysis and loss of speech was due to a lack of blood supply to his brain. Dr. Woods stated that the inadequate blood flow resulted from the clamp being 50% closed and that the negligence of Dr. Blake and the hospital precluded the clamp's being opened in time to avoid permanent brain damage....

About 14 months after her husband's hospitalization began, plaintiff Joan Togstad met with attorney Jerre Miller regarding her husband's condition. Neither she nor her husband was personally acquainted with Miller or his law firm prior to that time. John Togstad's former work supervisor, Ted Bucholz, made the appointment and accompanied Mrs. Togstad to Miller's office. Bucholz was present when Mrs. Togstad and Miller discussed the case.[3]

Mrs. Togstad had become suspicious of the circumstances surrounding her husband's tragic condition due to the conduct and statements of the hospital nurses shortly after the paralysis occurred. One nurse told Mrs. Togstad that she had checked Mr. Togstad at 2 a.m. and he was fine; that when she returned at 3 a.m., by mistake, to give him someone else's medication, he was unable to move or speak; and that if she hadn't accidentally entered the room no one would have discovered his condition until morning. Mrs. Togstad also noticed that the other nurses were upset and crying, and that Mr. Togstad's condition was a topic of conversation.

Mrs. Togstad testified that she told Miller "everything that happened at the hospital," including the nurses' statements and conduct which had raised a question in her mind. She stated that she "believed" she had told Miller "about the procedure and what was undertaken, what was done, and what happened." She brought no records with her. Miller took notes and asked questions during the meeting, which lasted 45 minutes to an hour. At its conclusion, according to Mrs. Togstad, Miller said that "he did not think we had a legal case, however, he was going to discuss this with his partner." She understood that if Miller changed his mind after talking to his partner, he would call her. Mrs. Togstad "gave it" a few days and, since she did not hear from Miller, decided "that they had come to the conclusion that there wasn't a case." No fee arrangements were discussed, no medical authorizations were requested, nor was Mrs. Togstad billed for the interview.

---

3. Bucholz, who knew Miller through a local luncheon club, died prior to the trial of the instant action.

Mrs. Togstad denied that Miller had told her his firm did not have expertise in the medical malpractice field, urged her to see another attorney, or related to her that the statute of limitations for medical malpractice actions was two years. She did not consult another attorney until one year after she talked to Miller. Mrs. Togstad indicated that she did not confer with another attorney earlier because of her reliance on Miller's "legal advice" that they "did not have a case."

On cross-examination, Mrs. Togstad was asked whether she went to Miller's office "to see if he would take the case of [her] husband...." She replied, "Well, I guess it was to go for legal advice, what to do, where shall we go from here? That is what we went for." Again in response to defense counsel's questions, Mrs. Togstad testified as follows:

Q   And it was clear to you, was it not, that what was taking place was a preliminary discussion between a prospective client and lawyer as to whether or not they wanted to enter into an attorney-client relationship?

A   I am not sure how to answer that. It was for legal advice as to what to do.

Q   And Mr. Miller was discussing with you your problem and indicating whether he, as a lawyer, wished to take the case, isn't that true?

A   Yes.

... Miller testified that "[t]he only thing I told her [Mrs. Togstad] after we had pretty much finished the conversation was that there was nothing related in her factual circumstances that told me that she had a case that our firm would be interested in undertaking."

Miller also claimed he related to Mrs. Togstad "that because of the grievous nature of the injuries sustained by her husband, that this was only my opinion and she was encouraged to ask another attorney if she wished for another opinion" and "she ought to do so promptly." He testified that he informed Mrs. Togstad that his firm "was not engaged as experts" in the area of medical malpractice, and that they associated with the Charles Hvass firm in cases of that nature. Miller stated that at the end of the conference he told Mrs. Togstad that he would consult with Charles Hvass and if Hvass's opinion differed from his, Miller would so inform her. Miller recollected that he called Hvass a "couple days" later and discussed the case with him. It was Miller's impression that Hvass thought there was no liability for malpractice in the case. Consequently, Miller did not communicate with Mrs. Togstad further.

told to get 2nd opinion

. . .

Kenneth Green, a Minneapolis attorney, was called as an expert by plaintiffs. He stated that in rendering legal advice regarding a claim of medical malpractice, the "minimum" an attorney should do would be to request medical authorizations from the client, review the hospital records, and consult with an expert in the field. John McNulty, a

π's xpert atty

Minneapolis attorney, and Charles Hvass testified as experts on behalf of the defendants. McNulty stated that when an attorney is consulted as to whether he will take a case, the lawyer's only responsibility in refusing it is to so inform the party. He testified, however, that when a lawyer is asked his legal opinion on the merits of a medical malpractice claim, community standards require that the attorney check hospital records and consult with an expert before rendering his opinion.

Hvass stated that he had no recollection of Miller's calling him in October 1972 relative to the Togstad matter. He testified that:

> A ... when a person comes in to me about a medical malpractice action, based upon what the individual has told me, I have to make a decision as to whether or not there probably is or probably is not, based upon that information, medical malpractice. And if, in my judgment, based upon what the client has told me, there is not medical malpractice, I will so inform the client.

Hvass stated, however, that he would never render a "categorical" opinion. In addition, Hvass acknowledged that if he were consulted for a "legal opinion" regarding medical malpractice and 14 months had expired since the incident in question, "ordinary care and diligence" would require him to inform the party of the two-year statute of limitations applicable to that type of action.

This case was submitted to the jury by way of a special verdict form. The jury found that Dr. Blake and the hospital were negligent and that Dr. Blake's negligence (but not the hospital's) was a direct cause of the injuries sustained by John Togstad; that there was an attorney-client contractual relationship between Mrs. Togstad and Miller; that Miller was negligent in rendering advice regarding the possible claims of Mr. and Mrs. Togstad; that, but for Miller's negligence, plaintiffs would have been successful in the prosecution of a legal action against Dr. Blake; and that neither Mr. nor Mrs. Togstad was negligent in pursuing their claims against Dr. Blake....

1. In a legal malpractice action of the type involved here, four elements must be shown: (1) that an attorney-client relationship existed; (2) that defendant acted negligently or in breach of contract; (3) that such acts were the proximate cause of the plaintiffs' damages; (4) that but for defendant's conduct the plaintiffs would have been successful in the prosecution of their medical malpractice claim. See, Christy v. Saliterman, 288 Minn. 144, 179 N.W.2d 288 (1970).

. . .

We believe it is unnecessary to decide whether a tort or contract theory is preferable for resolving the attorney-client relationship question raised by this appeal. The tort and contract analyses are very similar in a case such as the instant one,[4] and we conclude that under

---

4. Under a negligence approach it must essentially be shown that defendant rendered legal advice (not necessarily at someone's request) under circumstances which made it

either theory the evidence shows that a lawyer-client relationship is present here. The thrust of Mrs. Togstad's testimony is that she went to Miller for legal advice, was told there wasn't a case, and relied upon this advice in failing to pursue the claim for medical malpractice. In addition, according to Mrs. Togstad, Miller did not qualify his legal opinion by urging her to seek advice from another attorney, nor did Miller inform her that he lacked expertise in the medical malpractice area. Assuming this testimony is true, as this court must do, see, Cofran v. Swanman, 225 Minn. 40, 29 N.W.2d 448 (1947),[5] we believe a jury could properly find that Mrs. Togstad sought and received legal advice from Miller under circumstances which made it reasonably foreseeable to Miller that Mrs. Togstad would be injured if the advice were negligently given. Thus, under either a tort or contract analysis, there is sufficient evidence in the record to support the existence of an attorney-client relationship.

Defendants argue that even if an attorney-client relationship was established the evidence fails to show that Miller acted negligently in assessing the merits of the Togstads' case. They appear to contend that, at most, Miller was guilty of an error in judgment which does not give rise to legal malpractice. Meagher v. Kavli, 256 Minn. 54, 97 N.W.2d 370 (1959). However, this case does not involve a mere error of judgment. The gist of plaintiffs' claim is that Miller failed to perform the minimal research that an ordinarily prudent attorney would do before rendering legal advice in a case of this nature. The record, through the testimony of Kenneth Green and John McNulty, contains sufficient evidence to support plaintiffs' position.

In a related contention, defendants assert that a new trial should be awarded on the ground that the trial court erred by refusing to instruct the jury that Miller's failure to inform Mrs. Togstad of the two-year statute of limitations for medical malpractice could not constitute negligence. The argument continues that since it is unclear from the record on what theory or theories of negligence the jury based its decision, a new trial must be granted. Namchek v. Tulley, 259 Minn. 469, 107 N.W.2d 856 (1961).

The defect in defendants' reasoning is that there is adequate evidence supporting the claim that Miller was also negligent in failing

reasonably foreseeable to the attorney that if such advice was rendered negligently, the individual receiving the advice might be injured thereby. See, e.g., Palsgraf v. Long Island R. Co., 248 N.Y. 339, 162 N.E. 99, 59 A.L.R. 1253 (1928). Or, stated another way, under a tort theory, "[a]n attorney-client relationship is created whenever an individual seeks and receives legal advice from an attorney in circumstances in which a reasonable person would rely on such advice." 63 Minn.L.Rev. 751, 759 (1979). A contract analysis requires the rendering of legal advice pursuant to another's request and the reliance factor, in this case, where the advice was not paid for, need be shown in the form of promissory estoppel. See, 7 C.J.S., Attorney and Client, § 65; Restatement (Second) of Contracts, § 90.

5. As the *Cofran* court stated, in determining whether the jury's verdict is reasonably supported by the record a court must view the credibility of evidence and every inference which may fairly be drawn therefrom in a light most favorable to the prevailing party. 225 Minn. 42, 29 N.W.2d 450.

to advise Mrs. Togstad of the two-year medical malpractice limitations period and thus the trial court acted properly in refusing to instruct the jury in the manner urged by defendants. One of defendants' expert witnesses, Charles Hvass, testified:

Q   Now, Mr. Hvass, where you are consulted for a legal opinion and advice concerning malpractice and 14 months have elapsed [since the incident in question], wouldn't—and you hold yourself out as competent to give a legal opinion and advice to these people concerning their rights, wouldn't ordinary care and diligence require that you inform them that there is a two-year statute of limitations within which they have to act or lose their rights?

A   Yes. I believe I would have advised someone of the two-year period of limitation, yes.

Consequently, based on the testimony of Mrs. Togstad, i.e., that she requested and received legal advice from Miller concerning the malpractice claim, and the above testimony of Hvass, we must reject the defendants' contention, as it was reasonable for a jury to determine that Miller acted negligently in failing to inform Mrs. Togstad of the applicable limitations period.

———

Notes on *Togstad*

Was there an attorney-client relationship between the Togstads and lawyer Miller? *Togstad* demonstrates that a lawyer's interaction with a potential client may invoke some of the lawyer's duties to clients, such as confidentiality or due care, without becoming a full-fledged representation.[35]

What legal advice did lawyer Miller give the Togstads? How did that advice depart from the ordinary care standard? What should Miller have done instead? Should Miller have been disciplined professionally for his negligence?

May a lawyer require a client to sign a contract stating that in exchange for a free initial consultation the client waives the right to sue for any malpractice arising out of the initial interview? What if the contract stated that the initial interview was merely exploratory and did not create an attorney-client relationship? [36]

A lawyer often works intermittently over a period of time on various matters for a client. Does such intermittent work establish a

---

35. For further discussion of factors that trigger an obligation to people or entities with whom a lawyer has not established a full, formal client relationship, see Westinghouse Elec. Corp. v. Kerr–McGee Corp., 580 F.2d 1311 (7th Cir.1978), printed below in Chapter 7 at p. 627.

36. See M.R. 1.8(h) and DR 6–102(A), and the note on limiting one's liability for malpractice in Chapter 3 above at p. 191.

continuing attorney-client relationship? In North Carolina Bar v. Sheffield,[37] a lawyer who had worked intermittently for a person failed to file an answer to a complaint that that person left at his office. The court disciplined the lawyer for neglecting duties owned to a "client."

Limiting Liability by Limiting Scope of Employment

Model Rule 1.2(c) allows a lawyer to limit the objectives of representation with client consent. The Comment states: "The terms upon which the representation is undertaken may exclude specific objectives or means." But the Comment continues, such an agreement to limit the scope of employment

> must accord with the Rules of Professional Conduct and other law. Thus the client may not be asked to agree to representation so limited in scope as to violate M.R. 1.1, requiring competent representation, or to surrender the right to terminate the lawyer's services, or the right to settle litigation that the lawyer might wish to continue.

The Rule and Comment thus preclude an agreement limiting the scope of representation to a lawyer's off-the-cuff opinion based on no research or investigation, such as the advice provided by attorney Miller in *Togstad*. But could an agreement properly specify that a lawyer will provide only limited research in return for a reduced fee? Professor Wolfram argues that such an agreement is proper under M.R. 1.2.[38] Would such an agreement comport with M.R. 1.1?

B. SCOPE OF LAWYER'S AUTHORITY

Introductory Note

Who decides what in the lawyer-client relationship? This inquiry has an empirical dimension (how do lawyers and clients actually behave in various sectors of practice?), a normative dimension (how should authority be allocated between lawyer and client?), and a legal dimension (how do controlling principles of agency law, contract law and legal ethics allocate responsibility?).

The issue of decision-making authority is related to two matters already considered: (1) the scope of representation, discussed above, and (2) the duty of communication, see M.R. 1.4. The base line on scope of representation is the contractual agreement between a lawyer and her client: What have client and lawyer agreed that the lawyer should do? The contracting parties, however, do not have total freedom to shape the relationship. The client, for example, may not agree to a quality of service below the minimum standard required by the law-

---

37. North Carolina State Bar v. Sheffield, 73 N.C.App. 349, 326 S.E.2d 320 (1985). See also Jacobson v. Pitman–Moore, 624 F.Supp. 937 (D.Minn.1985), aff'd, 786 F.2d 1172 (8th Cir.1986) (mix-up in transfer of case from one firm to another).

38. Wolfram, Modern Legal Ethics § 5.6.7.

yer's duty to "provide competent representation." See M.R. 1.1. Some conflicts of interest are so extreme that they cannot be cured by client consent.[39] Nor is the client bound by a lawyer-client agreement that has the effect of "prospectively limiting the lawyer's liability to a client for malpractice." See M.R. 1.8(h). The lawyer cannot provide, nor the client seek, legal assistance "that the lawyer knows is criminal or fraudulent."[40] Moreover, the law, by delegating certain authority to lawyer or client—the issue discussed in this section—provides a structure for the relationship that removes certain matters from lawyer-client negotiation. The client's right to discharge a retained lawyer and the lawyer's opportunity to withdraw, when available, provide practical constraints on lawyer-client negotiations. Within these and other limitations on contractual choice, however, "[a] lawyer may limit the objectives of the representation if the client consents after consultation." M.R. 1.2(c).

Decision-making within the lawyer-client relationship depends upon two-way communication. A lawyer has a duty to provide a client with "sufficient information to participate intelligently in decisions concerning the objectives of the representation and the means by which they are to be pursued."[41] The duty of communication may not extend as far as the "informed consent" notion imposed on physicians by tort law, but the duty is now embodied in a weaker form in the text of M.R. 1.4.[42]

Model Rule 1.2(a), dealing with allocation of decision-making authority between lawyer and client, states:

> A lawyer shall abide by a client's decision concerning the objectives of representation, subject to paragraphs (c), (d) and (e), and shall consult with the client as to the means by which they are to be pursued. A lawyer shall abide by the client's decision whether to accept an offer of settlement of a matter. In a criminal case, the lawyer shall abide by the client's decision, after consultation with the lawyer, as to a plea to be entered, whether to waive jury trial and whether the client will testify.

The Model Code has no counterpart to M.R. 1.2.[43] The Comment to M.R. 1.2 should be read at this point.

39. The Comment to M.R. 1.7 states that "Paragraph (a) prohibits representation of opposing parties in litigation" and that "[o]rdinarily, a lawyer may not act as advocate against a client the lawyer represents in some other matter, even if the other matter is wholly unrelated."

40. M.R. 1.2(d) prohibits the lawyer from counseling or otherwise assisting a client to commit a fraud or crime; M.R. 1.2(e) states that if a client expects assistance prohibited by the rules of professional conduct, the lawyer should explain the limits imposed by the rules.

41. Comment to M.R. 1.4.

42. The only direct counterpart in the Model Code is EC 9–2, stating that "a lawyer should fully and promptly inform his client of material developments in the matters being handled for the client."

43. But see EC 7–7 (on the client's right to make decisions "affecting the merits of the cause or substantially prejudicing the rights of the client"); EC 7–8 (on the client's right

1. Allocation of Decision–Making Authority in Civil Cases

Decisions must be made at every point in the handling of a civil claim. Should a lawsuit be brought? What claims and legal theories should be asserted against whom? Should pretrial procedures be extensively used to gather information? Should settlement negotiations be undertaken and, if so, on what terms? What evidence should be presented at the trial and in what order and manner? Should the client testify? Should an opposing witness be cross-examined and, if so, with what purpose? What issues should be stressed in closing argument? The questions vary from small matters of technical detail (e.g., should an objection be made to a leading question by opposing counsel on a fairly insignificant matter?) to large issues of overall strategy (what remedies are sought on the basis of what legal theories and evidence?). Who is legally empowered to decide these and other questions? What prior consultation is required? Is the current allocation of authority sound?

One important variable is the context in which the issue arises. Suppose an advocate, without consulting her client, takes one of the actions mentioned above. By the time the client learns of it and objects, the tribunal and the opposing party have reacted to the action. Clients in civil cases generally are bound by the mistakes of their lawyers as well as their intended acts.

In holding that clients are bound by their lawyers' actions in a civil proceeding, courts are giving priority to concerns of judicial administration and to the interests of opposing parties. A mythic unity of lawyer and client is presumed, with the lawyer as the alter ego of the client. As Justice Harlan put it, "each party is deemed bound by the acts of his lawyer-agent and is considered to have 'notice of all facts, notice of which can be charged upon the attorney.' " [44] The presumption that the lawyer has communicated relevant information concerning the representation to the client is almost irrebuttable.

In Blanton v. Womancare, Inc.,[45] the court described the lawyer's authority to make decisions other than compromising or settling a client's claim:

> Considerations of procedural efficiency require ... that in the course of a trial there be but one captain per ship. An attorney must be able to make such tactical decisions as whether to call a particular witness, and the court and opposing counsel must be able to rely upon the decisions he makes, even when the client voices opposition in open court.... In such tactical matters, it

to decide whether to forego legally available means or objectives because of nonlegal factors); and DR 7–101 (lawyer shall not fail to seek the lawful objectives of the client except that she may avoid offensive tactics without violating this rule).

44. Link v. Wabash R.R. Co., 370 U.S. 626, 634 (1962) (upholding involuntary dismissal of an injured railroad worker's FELA claim for failure of his lawyer to attend a pretrial conference).

45. 38 Cal.3d 396, 403, 212 Cal.Rptr. 151, 155, 696 P.2d 645, 650 (1985).

may be said that the attorney's authority is implied in law, as a necessary incident to the function he is engaged to perform.

Is it essential that the lawyer have the right to decide which witnesses to call? What stipulations to enter into? What objections to make? Doctors know more than their clients, but we accept the principle that if there are alternate treatments available, the patient should decide after consultation (assuming she is conscious, sane and of legal age). Is the lawyer involved in litigation analogous to the surgeon in an operating room? Should it be assumed that the lawyer has not considered specific points of trial strategy until after the trial has actually begun? Is it possible to explain trial strategy choices to the client clearly enough so that she can make the decision?

The Comment to M.R. 1.2 states: "A clear distinction between objectives and means sometimes cannot be drawn, and in many cases the client-lawyer relationship partakes of a joint undertaking. In questions of means, the lawyer should assume responsibility for technical and legal tactical issues, but should defer to the client regarding such questions as the expense to be incurred and concern for third persons who might be adversely affected." Is this helpful?

If clients had the right to decide on tactics, would increased ethical violations by lawyers be the result? In medicine this does not seem to have happened. It is understood that a patient's right to decide on treatment is bounded by the law, e.g., a doctor cannot prescribe an illegal drug. Would a similar understanding work for lawyers and clients?

The analogy to medicine fails to capture that the lawyer, unlike the doctor, practices her craft through language and posture, i.e., means that appear intelligible to the client. The language of court (or of contract) resembles the language of the outside world. It is easy to imagine a client, armed with decision-making authority, who insists on speaking out for herself in court (or in negotiation). It is more difficult to imagine a patient wanting to give herself a blood test or any other medical procedure. Is it possible to explain how court-talk is different and thus convince the client that she is better off not interfering? Must legal institutions—through case law, court procedures and ethics rules—reinforce the client's subordinate role for her own good?

Does a lawyer have authority to waive the client's attorney-client privilege? The general rule is that a lawyer may not waive the privilege without the client's consent, but consent may be express or implied. See the Comment to M.R. 1.6: "A lawyer is impliedly authorized to make disclosures about a client when appropriate in carrying out the representation, except to the extent that the client's instructions or special circumstances limit that authority."

The principle that lawyers should have broad authority has been criticized by commentators, who argue that this gives the client too small a role in deciding her fate. If one purpose of trial is to affirm the individual's dignity and autonomy, that goal is ill-served by giving lawyers control over the process.[46] One major stream of academic commentary maintains that the lawyer's principal goal is to further the client's dignity and autonomy.[47] Lawyers who act upon a paternalistic model, Professor Judith Maute observes, may "disserve their clients when they pursue ends that they have imputed to their clients through means that they have not discussed with them." [48] Another group of commentators, sometimes associated with critical legal studies, urges "moral activism" on the lawyer.[49] Professor Simon, for example, urges lawyers to exercise more discretion in representing clients to avoid assisting the client in immoral acts; the lawyer should ask herself whether what the client wants the lawyer to do will further justice.[50]

Both groups of academics, those stressing client autonomy and those urging moral activism, argue that it is morally and legally important that the client fully participate in decisions involved in the representation. Nevertheless, an equal participatory model is difficult to reconcile with several considerations. First, typically the lawyer knows more about the legal aspects of the problem than the client, and more than the client practically can be told. Second, typically the lawyer is inured to the emotional distress of conflict and therefore can deal with it more steadily—this may be the other side of being "sensitive." Third, the decisions in carrying out a legal matter often require unabashed assertiveness: Should an impecunious widow take bankruptcy to avoid paying back rent to a landlord who may need the money almost as much as she? Lawyers are used to taking such measures, while ordinary people are not. Also, some clients expect the lawyer to

46. See, e.g., Susan R. Martyn, Informed Consent in the Practice of Law, 48 Geo.Wash. L.Rev. 307 (1980); Mark Spiegel, The New Model Rules of Professional Conduct: Lawyer–Client Decisionmaking and the Role of Rules in Structuring the Lawyer–Client Dialogue, 1980 Am.B.Found.Res.J. 1003; Vivian O. Berger, The Supreme Court and Defense Counsel: Old Roads, New Paths—A Dead End?, 86 Colum.L.Rev. 9 (1986); Marcy Strauss, Toward a Revised Model of Attorney–Client Relationship: The Argument for Autonomy, 65 N.C.L.Rev. 315 (1987).

47. See, e.g., Monroe H. Freedman, Understanding Legal Ethics 43–64 (1990) (assisting a client to maximize her autonomy, once a lawyer has undertaken a representation, is required professionally and morally); Charles J. Fried, The Lawyer as Friend: The Moral Foundations of the Lawyer–Client Relation, 85 Yale L.J. 1060, 1071 (1976) ("like a friend [the lawyer] acts in your interests, not his own; or rather he adopts your interests as his own"); and Stephen L. Pepper, The Lawyer's Amoral Ethical Role: A Defense, A Problem, and Some Possibilities, 1986 Am.Bar Found. Research J. 613 (defending the traditional conception that a lawyer may do immoral, but lawful, acts in furtherance of a client's interests).

48. Judith L. Maute, Allocation of Decisionmaking Authority Under the Model Rules of Professional Conduct, 17 U.C.Davis L.Rev. 1049, 1050 (1984). See also Roger W. Andersen, Informed Decision–Making in an Office Practice, 28 Bost.Coll.L.Rev. 225 (1987).

49. See, e.g., David Luban, Lawyers and Justice: An Ethical Study (1988) (arguing that the lawyer's traditional amoral role is only weakly justified and hence that lawyers should follow their own moral principles in assisting clients, even if this means disclosure of confidential information or betrayal of a client); Robert W. Gordon, Corporate Law Practice as a Public Calling, 49 Md.L.Rev. 255, 258 (1990): "lawyers [should] develop some vision of the common good or public interest, and try to realize it in their practices, if necessary against the immediate wishes of their clients"); and William W. Simon, Ethical Discretion in Lawyering, 101 Harv.L.Rev. 1083, 1113–19 (1988).

50. William H. Simon, Ethical Discretion in Lawyering, 101 Harv.L.Rev. 1083 (1988).

take responsibility for a difficult choice: "Tell me what I ought to do." Should such a wish be respected? These things said, lawyers often have strong inclinations and temptations to manipulate clients.

The studies discussed earlier suggest that the dynamics and problems of the attorney-client relationship vary with practice context. The danger in corporate practice is more likely to be client domination of and pressure on a lawyer to break legal norms; in divorce, personal injury and criminal defense work the greater danger is lawyer domination of the client and a consequent loss of autonomy by the client. Professor David Wilkins argues that the institutions that regulate lawyers should differ depending on the practice setting and the different dangers presented by those settings.[51] He suggests that administrative agencies and courts should exercise greater control over lawyers in corporate practice, to protect their professional independence and ensure compliance with legal norms, while professional discipline should play a stronger regulatory role in other settings, such as personal injury or criminal defense work.

Authority To Settle Civil Matters

INTERNATIONAL TELEMETER CORP.
v. TELEPROMPTER CORP. △

United States Court of Appeals, Second Circuit, 1979.
592 F.2d 49.

Before LUMBARD, FRIENDLY and OAKES, CIRCUIT JUDGES.

LUMBARD, CIRCUIT JUDGE:

In this case, originally brought as a suit for patent infringement, defendant Teleprompter Corporation appeals from a judgment of the district court, Motley, J., filed on February 21, 1978 after a bench trial and amended March 7, 1978, insofar as it (1) directs Teleprompter to pay plaintiff International Telemeter Corporation (ITC) $245,000 plus interest and costs for Teleprompter's breach of an agreement settling patent litigation, and (2) dismisses without prejudice Teleprompter's counterclaim for a declaration of the patent's invalidity.

The parties agree that New York law governs the enforceability of the settlement agreement, which was negotiated, consummated, and to be performed in New York, and which was explicitly made subject to New York law. The [issue is] whether there was a binding settlement agreement enforceable against Teleprompter.... As Teleprompter has not persuaded us that the district court erred in finding that the parties had consummated a binding settlement agreement, ... we affirm.

The relevant facts are undisputed. The present action arises from a suit for patent infringement commenced by ITC on March 15, 1968 against several defendants in the District Court for the Western Dis-

---

51. David B. Wilkins, Who Should Regulate Lawyers?, 105 Harv.L.Rev. 799 (1992).

trict of Washington. On September 1, 1970, Teleprompter intervened *procedure*
as a defendant and counterclaimant in the action, seeking, inter alia,
declarations of patent invalidity and noninfringement. Following the
dismissal of several claims and counterclaims, by 1973 the only parties
remaining in the litigation were ITC, Teleprompter, and [a group
referred to as the "Hamlin defendants"].

In February, 1973, William Bresnan, then President of Tele- *Negotiation*
prompter, wrote to Arthur Groman, a Los Angeles attorney, asking if
ITC wished to "discuss ... a [negotiated] resolution of the patent
litigation." On February 9, 1973, Groman responded by sending to
Bresnan a draft license agreement proposed by ITC as a basis for
settling the litigation. The draft agreement provided for minimum
royalties of $75,000 for the first three years and damages for past
infringement totalling $240,000. Bresnan turned down the proposed
agreement but suggested that a meeting be arranged to discuss possible
settlement.

The requested settlement meeting took place in New York City in
April, 1973. Present on behalf of Teleprompter were William K. Kerr,
Jules P. Kirsch, and Bresnan himself. Present on behalf of ITC were
Morton Amster, Thomas Harrison, and Kenneth Merklen. All but
Bresnan were acting as lawyers. The first meeting proved inconclu-
sive.

In early July, 1973, after a further settlement proposal of Bresnan
made on May 30 was found unacceptable by ITC, the parties met a
second time. According to Amster, at this meeting the parties "negotiated the terms of the settlement." The parties assigned to Amster the
task of preparing the initial drafts of the agreement, which included *settlement*
the following terms: an aggregate payment by Teleprompter of $245,- *proposal*
000 in settlement of all claims against Teleprompter and the Hamlin
defendants, the licensing of Teleprompter and the Hamlin defendants
under the disputed patent, the dismissal of the pending litigation, and
the issuance of a press release. These basic terms were never altered
during the subsequent negotiations.

On July 26, 1973, Amster sent Kerr a copy of the draft agreements
together with a proposed schedule for payments totalling $245,000.

There followed a series of minor revisions and exchanges of revised
drafts. Amster, as attorney for ITC, and Kirsch, as attorney for
Teleprompter, agreed to final changes at a meeting held on August 28
or September 7, 1973. Thereafter, on September 10, 1973, "clean
drafts" were forwarded by Amster to Kirsch. On September 26, 1973,
Amster sent to Kirsch copies of the Teleprompter and Hamlin license
agreements and copies of the stipulation and order of dismissal to be
filed in the patent lawsuit pending in the Western District of Washington. In his covering letter, Amster remarked, "Hopefully we have
attended to all the minor changes and the documents are in condition
for execution.... Perhaps upon a review of the papers, you would be
willing to advise your local counsel [in the Washington litigation] that

the case is settled so that he and [ITC's local counsel] can advise Judge Boldt that the case is settled and that a proposed stipulation and order will be filed shortly."

On October 3, 1973, Kirsch did so advise Teleprompter's Seattle counsel, Richard Williams. That same day, Williams wrote to Judge Boldt that "the final Settlement Agreement has been transmitted to all parties for the purpose of signature ... we should be in a position to present a Stipulation and Order of Stipulation to the Court for its consideration and entry." Williams further advised the court that the pending trial date "may be vacated." A copy of this letter was sent to Amster. If Williams overstated the parties' proximity to settlement, as Kirsch later claimed at trial, Kirsch failed to correct the allegedly mistaken impression conveyed to the trial court.

Just as the parties were finishing their work on the settlement documents, a dispute arose between Teleprompter and the Hamlin defendants over the Hamlin defendants' obligation to pay amounts claimed by Teleprompter pursuant to its intervention agreement with the Hamlin defendants. Rather than allow the settlement agreement to founder on this last minute disagreement between the defendants, Kirsch acted to secure a separate peace between Teleprompter and ITC. On October 25 and October 26, 1973, he telephoned and wrote to Amster to advise him of the falling out between Teleprompter and the Hamlin defendants and attempted to secure a settlement as to ITC and Teleprompter on precisely the same terms as those already agreed upon. In his October 26 letter, Kirsch wrote as follows to Amster:

Dear Mort:

As I advised you in our telephone discussions on Thursday and Friday, October 25 and 26, 1973, Mr. Hamlin is unwilling to pay Teleprompter the amounts due Teleprompter pursuant to the August 3, 1970 Intervention Agreement. As a consequence, Teleprompter now wishes to settle the litigation only with respect to Teleprompter on the terms which had been agreed upon with respect to Teleprompter in the Settlement Agreement and the License Agreement which accompanied your September 26, 1973 letter, and I understand that this is agreeable with ITC....

In our telephone conversation October 26, 1973, you and I agreed that I would revise the Settlement Agreement to limit its terms to Teleprompter only, that Teleprompter will make the payments specified in Schedule 1 to the original Settlement Agreement, that Teleprompter will execute the original ITC–Teleprompter License Agreement, and that I would revise the Stipulation and Order of Dismissal to limit dismissal of the action to Teleprompter only....

Sincerely,

Jules P. Kirsch

Thus Kirsch's letter committed Teleprompter to a settlement on the terms "which had been agreed upon" and which were already set forth in the draft settlement papers accompanying Amster's September 26, 1973 letter. At trial, Kirsch confirmed that he had Teleprompter's authorization to send this October 26, 1973 letter. In fact, Kirsch sent a copy of this letter to Teleprompter's general counsel, Barry Simon. If this letter inaccurately conveyed Teleprompter's intent to be bound, Simon made no effort to set the matter straight. All that remained to be done before a formal signed agreement could be executed was to eliminate mechanically all reference to the Hamlin defendants in the draft agreement.

Several important events occurred on October 29, 1973. Kirsch duly revised the settlement papers to delete all references to the Hamlin defendants and forwarded the revised documents to Amster on the morning of October 29.... Kirsch also sent a separate letter to Amster asking him to call as soon as he had finished reviewing the settlement papers "so that if there are any changes you wish to have made, we can discuss them. If necessary I can arrange for them to be made before I leave for Los Angeles this afternoon. In that way the final papers can be delivered promptly to Teleprompter for execution and returned to you." No changes were suggested by Amster. All that remained was to obtain the requisite signatures and make delivery. Consequently, that afternoon Kirsch wrote another letter to Amster, enclosing three copies of the stipulation and order of dismissal as to Teleprompter which Kirsch had signed and dated October 29, 1973. Amster also signed the stipulation and order of dismissal that afternoon, as requested by Kirsch. Kirsch also requested that Amster send a ribbon copy of the stipulation and order to ITC's Seattle, Washington counsel and return a signed electrostatic copy to Kirsch. Kirsch advised Amster that he had called Williams, Teleprompter's Seattle counsel, and that Williams would sign the stipulation upon receiving it from ITC's Seattle counsel and would then file it with the court.

That afternoon, October 29, Kirsch sent to Peter A. Gross, the assistant general counsel of Teleprompter, copies of the settlement agreement. Gross was to have these documents executed by Teleprompter and returned to Amster together with a certified check in the amount of $26,250.00 pursuant to Schedule 1 of the settlement agreement. Kirsch advised Gross that Amster would then arrange to have the signed agreements and the check delivered to ITC; duplicate signed copies of the settlement and license agreements would then be returned to Gross. Finally, Kirsch advised Gross that he was arranging to have the stipulation and order of dismissal filed in court by Teleprompter's Seattle counsel.

The following day, October 30, 1973, Teleprompter's president, Bresnan, signed the settlement agreement. Although plaintiff had demanded production of this document before trial, its existence came to light for the first time at trial during the testimony of Bresnan, after Judge Motley had overruled objections to questions concerning communications between Bresnan and Teleprompter's counsel. When the settlement agreement was first brought to him by Gross, Bresnan refused to sign without the approval of Jack Kent Cooke, Chairman of the Board and Chief Executive Officer of Teleprompter. At Gross' insistence, however, Bresnan signed the document "subject to the proviso that it would not be delivered until it had been reviewed with Mr. Cooke and also with Mr. Greene [Teleprompter's treasurer]."

That same day, October 30, Kirsch arrived in California as planned. That afternoon, he received a telephone message at his hotel, which read as follows: "Mr. Gross called. The settlement is O.K. Papers and check will go out tomorrow."

In what was apparently yet another reference to Bresnan's signing of the final agreement, on October 31, 1973, Kirsch wrote to Hamlin, advising him that "Teleprompter has decided to settle with ITC ... a revised Settlement Agreement as between ITC and Teleprompter only and a revised Stipulation of Dismissal of the Action as to Teleprompter only have been executed." Based on communications with Teleprompter, Kirsch believed these representations to be duly authorized and accurate when made. Indeed, Kirsch sent copies of this letter to Simon and to Gross, Teleprompter's in-house counsel, and to Amster and Harrison, ITC's counsel. If this letter inaccurately conveyed the impression that a settlement had been consummated, Teleprompter did not move to correct that impression.

Thereafter, new management at Teleprompter refused to proceed with the settlement agreement. Accordingly, on November 16, 1973, Kirsch called Amster to tell him that he had been mistaken in his earlier belief that Teleprompter had agreed to the settlement with ITC and had in fact executed the settlement. Kirsch confirmed the telephone conversation in a letter of the same date which reads as follows:

> Dear Mort:
>
> This letter will confirm that in my telephone conversation with you this afternoon I advised you that since I wrote a letter to Mr. Hamlin dated October 31, 1973, a copy of which was sent to you, in which I stated that the revised Settlement Agreement had been executed, I have learned that in fact the revised Settlement Agreement was not executed....
>
> Sincerely,
>
> Jules P. Kirsch

Kirsch's statement in this letter that the settlement agreement had never been executed conflicted not only with his prior statements, but also with Bresnan's later admission at trial that he had in fact signed the agreement. In any event, after sending this letter, Kirsch withdrew as Teleprompter's counsel in this dispute.

On November 28, 1973, Amster wrote to Kirsch stating that he had received Kirsch's November 16 letter but had nevertheless advised ITC that it had a legally enforceable agreement with Teleprompter.

. . .

The district court found that the parties had reached a final agreement as to the terms of the settlement and that both had manifested objective indications of their intent to be bound by October 29, 1973. . . .

As the district court found, the record strongly suggests that both parties would have signed prior to October 26, 1973 but for the disagreement between Teleprompter and the Hamlin defendants. The October 26 letter clearly indicates that all that remained to be done regarding the written agreement was to eliminate the now superfluous references to the Hamlin defendants. Kirsch's October 26 letter to Amster contains both an unequivocal expression of Teleprompter's intention to settle and a listing by incorporation of all the essential terms of the settlement. Although asked for his comments, Amster had none.

If there remained any doubt as to the nature of the parties' intent as of October 26, that doubt was dispelled by the events of October 29. On that day Kirsch sent to Amster for signing a complete set of settlement papers. All that remained was to have Bresnan sign the settlement agreement, to have local counsel in Seattle sign the stipulation and order of dismissal, and to file the necessary papers in court. Particularly significant, in our view, was the signing and transmittal to opposing counsel of the stipulation and order of dismissal. Teleprompter could have requested that the signed stipulation be held in escrow pending the signing and delivery of the other documents. It did not. Accordingly, Amster acted as any other reasonable person would have when he concluded that there was a binding agreement as of October 29, if not before. As the district court concluded, "these two lawyers would not have signed the stipulation unless they understood that both parties intended to be bound at that juncture and that all that remained to be done was the formalization of what had been agreed."

Subsequent communications by Teleprompter to ITC further support the district court's finding that the parties believed that a binding agreement had been consummated. On October 31, Kirsch stated in a letter to Amster that "Teleprompter had decided to settle with ITC as to Teleprompter only . . . a revised Settlement Agreement . . . and . . . Stipulation of Dismissal . . . have been executed." Teleprompter officials who authorized this communication received copies of this letter and did not disavow its contents.

. . . Teleprompter argues that Kirsch had no authority to bind Teleprompter to a settlement. Kirsch, however, was acting within the ambit of his apparent authority and ITC was entitled to rely upon Kirsch's authority so long as there was no reason to believe that he was exceeding it. Teleprompter knew that ITC believed that Kirsch had the requisite authority and did nothing to correct this impression. In fact, ITC had no reason to think that Kirsch was exceeding his authority and Teleprompter had no reason to correct any misimpression because, as the district court found, Kirsch had full authority to negotiate and consummate a settlement. That a lawyer should have such authority is not rare. In this case, moreover, Kirsch kept Teleprompter apprised at all times of what he was doing. Teleprompter officials were sent copies of all the correspondence which the district court relied upon in finding a binding agreement. Teleprompter officials failed to disavow Kirsch's actions even when Kirsch sent them copies of his October 31 letter announcing that the settlement was executed.

The district court's decision is consistent with New York case law dealing with similar situations.... See generally Restatement (Second) of Contracts § 26 (Tent.Draft # 1–7 1962) ("Manifestations of assent that are in themselves sufficient to conclude a contract will not be prevented from so operating by the fact that the parties also manifested an intention to prepare and adopt a written memorial thereof; but the circumstances may show that the agreements are preliminary negotiations").

... The cases relied upon by the appellant are distinguishable on their facts from the case at bar. In Scheck v. Francis, 26 N.Y.2d 466, 311 N.Y.S. 841, 260 N.E.2d 493 (1970) the Court of Appeals found that the parties did not intend to be bound before signing and delivery, and further, that there was no proof that the parties had ever reached an agreement on the terms of the disputed contract. Similarly, in Schwartz v. Greenberg, 304 N.Y. 250, 107 N.E.2d 65 (1952), the Court of Appeals held that the refusal to deliver a signed agreement defeated the contract because "the parties did not intend to be bound until a written agreement had been signed and delivered." Whether or not the parties have manifested an intent to be bound must depend in each case on all the circumstances. Here the district court specifically found an intent to be bound prior to signing and delivery of a written agreement.

. . .

FRIENDLY, CIRCUIT JUDGE, concurring:

The difficulty in deciding this case comes from the gap between the realities of the formation of complex business agreements and traditional contract formulation. The nature of the gap is well described in a passage in 2 Schlesinger (ed.), Formation of Contracts: A Study of the Common Core of Legal Systems 1584–86 (1968), ... which is reproduced in the margin.[1] Under a view conforming to the realities of business

---

1. "Especially when large deals are concluded among corporations and individuals of substance, the usual sequence of events is not that of offer and acceptance; on the contrary, the businessmen who originally conduct the negotiations, often will consciously refrain from ever making a binding offer, realizing as they do that a large deal tends to be complex and that its terms have to be formulated by lawyers before it can be permitted to become a legally enforceable transaction. Thus the original negotiators will merely attempt to ascertain whether they see eye to eye concerning those aspects of the deal which seem to be most important from a business point of view. Once they do, or think they do, the negotiation is then turned over to the lawyers, usually with instruc-

life, there would be no contract in such cases until the document is signed and delivered; until then either party would be free to bring up new points of form or substance, or even to withdraw altogether. However, I cannot conscientiously assert that the courts of New York or, to the extent they have not spoken, the Restatement of Contracts 2d § 26 and comment C (Tent.Drafts 1–7 Revised and Edited) have gone that far, nor can I find a fair basis for predicting that the New York Court of Appeals is yet prepared to do so.

On the other hand, it does seem to me that the New York cases cited by the majority can be read as holding, or at least as affording a fair basis for predicting a holding, that when the parties have manifested an intention that their relations should be embodied in an elaborate signed contract, clear and convincing proof is required to show that they meant to be bound before the contract is signed and delivered. Such a principle would accord with what I believe to be the intention of most such potential contractors; they view the signed written instrument that is in prospect as "the contract", not as a memorialization of an oral agreement previously reached. Also, from an instrumental standpoint, such a rule would save the courts from a certain amount of vexing litigation. The clear and convincing proof could consist in one party's allowing the other to begin performance ... or in unequivocal statements by the principals or authorized agents that a complete agreement had been reached and the writing was considered to be of merely evidentiary significance.

The facts forcefully marshalled by Judge Lumbard make a strong case for finding that the latter condition has been satisfied here. What weighs especially with me is Kirsch's letter of October 26, not claimed to have been unauthorized, saying that "Teleprompter now wishes to settle the litigation only with respect to Teleprompter on the terms which had been agreed upon with respect to Teleprompter" in the earlier three-party settlement "and I understand that this is agreeable with ITC". From then on the job of transforming the three-party agreement into a two-party one was largely scrivener's work and Teleprompter manifested no dissatisfaction with Kirsch's performance of this. Upon the understanding that our decision rests on the unique facts here presented and that we are not entering a brave new world where lawyers can commit their clients simply by communicating boldly with each other, I concur in the judgment of affirmance.

tions to produce a document which all participants will be willing to sign.... When the lawyers take over, again there is no sequence of offer and acceptance, but rather a sequence of successive drafts. These drafts usually will not be regarded as offers, for the reason, among others, that the lawyers acting as draftsmen have no authority to make offers on behalf of their clients. After a number of drafts have been exchanged and discussed, the lawyers may finally come up with a draft which meets the approval of all of them, and of their clients. It is only then that the parties will proceed to the actual formation of the contract, and often this will be done by way of a formal 'closing' ... or in any event by simultaneous execution or delivery in the course of a more or less ceremonial meeting, of the document or documents prepared by the lawyers."

Actual and Apparent Authority

Did Kirsch have *actual authority* (express or implied) to settle the case for his client, Teleprompter? Or is Teleprompter bound by the settlement because Kirsh had *apparent authority?* What is Judge Friendly's concern? Why did Kirsch resign after sending the "Dear Mort" letter (supra, at p. 500)? What could a lawyer do to ensure that the opposing party understood that there was no deal until a written settlement agreement was signed?

Actual authority of a lawyer may be either express or implied. Implied authority flows from legal rules delegating authority on some matter to the lawyer. Express authority exists when the principal (the client) through words or deeds causes *the agent* reasonably to believe that she has the authority to act.[52] Express authority to settle a dispute continues until and unless the client revokes the authority.[53] A client's grant of a general power to settle without specific limits or instructions is enough to constitute express authority to settle.[54] Does M.R. 1.2 or 1.4 require the lawyer to check with the client before entering into a settlement or may the lawyer proceed on the basis of the client's general direction "to settle the case?"[55]

Implied authority to take a lawful measure reasonably calculated to advance a client's objectives permits a lawyer, for example, to reveal confidential information when doing so will further the client's objectives in a settlement negotiation. See M.R. 1.6(a). But lawyers do not have implied authority to settle a client's disputed matter. Some jurisdictions, but not others, presume authority to settle from authority to negotiate.[56] This rebuttable presumption fosters the judicial policies

---

52. Restatement (Second) of Agency § 26.

53. The proposed Restatement of the Law Governing Lawyers, § 33 (Council Draft No. 7, Sept. 13, 1991), provides that the settlement decision is for the client and may not be "irrevocably delegated to the lawyer." Comment c states:

This Section allows a client to authorize a lawyer to enter a settlement, provided that the authorization is revocable. Thus, a client may authorize a lawyer to enter a settlement within a given range, or on the best terms possible. . . . Tribunals do not presume such an authorization. The authorization must be expressed by the client or fairly implied from the dealings of lawyer and client. An authorization to negotiate, for example, does not carry with it implied authority for the lawyer to approve a resulting agreement on behalf of the client.

54. Smedley v. Temple Drilling Co., 782 F.2d 1357, 1360 (5th Cir.1986) (general authorization sustained).

55. Close questions arise of what constitutes a settlement of a client's case. For example, is a lawyer's consent to the issuance of a preliminary injunction prohibiting any party from filing bankruptcy until a final judgment is issued a "compromise or settlement" of the client's case or a decision on tactics? See Hunt v. Bankers Trust Co., 799 F.2d 1060 (5th Cir.1986) (lawyer had implied authority).

56. See, e.g., St. Amand v. Marriott Hotel, Inc., 430 F.Supp. 488, 490 (E.D.La.1977), aff'd, 611 F.2d 881 (5th Cir.1980):

The law is settled that an attorney of record may not compromise, settle or consent to a final disposition of his client's case without express authority. . . . However, this

of encouraging settlements and supporting their finality.[57]   The client's knowing failure to disapprove of the settlement within a reasonable time will be construed as a ratification.[58]

Apparent Authority

As the *International Telemeter* case suggests, many jurisdictions hold that a client will be bound when the attorney has *apparent authority* to enter a settlement, even if she lacks actual authority. Apparent authority exists when the *principal* (i.e., the client) through words or deeds causes *a third party* reasonably to believe that the agent has the principal's authority to act.[59]   For apparent authority, courts generally require a showing of reliance and good faith on the part of the third party.[60]   Apparent authority, the cases hold, is created only by the representations of the principal to the third party and cannot be created by the agent's own actions or representations; authority to represent a client and appear at conferences does not create apparent authority to settle.[61]

Courts disagree sharply on whether apparent authority should be recognized and under what circumstances.   In Edwards v. Born, Inc.,[62] the court held that settlement authority could be found when the client repeatedly declined the lawyer's request to specify a settlement amount, saying that was the lawyer's job.   The "better rule," the court

general principal must be considered in connection with the rule that an attorney of record is *presumed* to have authority to compromise and settle litigation of his client, and a judgment entered upon an agreement by the attorney of record will be set aside only upon affirmative proof of the party seeking to vacate the judgment that the attorney had no right to consent to its entry.

57. See Surety Insurance Co. of California v. Williams, 729 F.2d 581, 582–583 (8th Cir.1984) (strong presumption that the lawyer acted within the scope of authority).   A lawyer's statement that she had authority is "highly probative" although not conclusive. An evidentiary hearing should be held.   *Mid–South Towing*, supra, 733 F.2d at 391.

58.   Cf. Capital Dredge and Dock Corp. v. Detroit, 800 F.2d 525 (6th Cir.1986) (no ratification when the client does not understand that the claim has been compromised).

59.   Restatement (Second) of Agency § 27.

60.   See Terrain Enterprises, Inc. v. Western Casualty and Surety Co., 774 F.2d 1320 (5th Cir.1985) (applying Mississippi law).

61.   Fennell v. TLB Kent Co., 865 F.2d 498 (2d Cir.1989).   In *Fennell* the client knew that his lawyers were engaged in settlement discussions with the opposing party, did not ask his lawyers to stop these discussions, would have accepted a higher settlement figure, and did not tell the opposing party's counsel that his lawyers' authority was limited in any way.   The Second Circuit held that these facts could not create apparent authority. But cf. Capital Dredge and Dock Corp. v. Detroit, 800 F.2d 525, 530–31 (6th Cir.1986), standing the traditional rule on its head by holding that

a third party who reaches a settlement agreement with an attorney employed to represent his client in regard to the settled claim is generally entitled to enforcement of the ... agreement even if the attorney was acting contrary to the client's express instructions.   In such a situation, the client's remedy is to sue his attorney for professional malpractice.   The third party may rely on the attorney's apparent authority unless he has reason to believe that the attorney has no authority to negotiate a settlement.

Compare the Sixth Circuit's concern about the power lawyers need to function in the real world of litigation with Judge Friendly's concurrence in *International Telemeter*.   Does the Sixth Circuit have a different type of lawyer in mind than Judge Friendly?   A different type of client?

62.   792 F.2d 387, 390–92 (3d Cir.1986).

said, was to consider whether "actual authority could be implied from the totality of the [lawyer-client] relationship. . . ." Other decisions criticize cases accepting apparent authority and hold that "compromise judgments depend on the actual authority of the person purporting to compromise the claim." [63]

Authority to Settle on Behalf of Government

Most of the cases dealing with the settlement authority of government lawyers hold that those dealing with the government "must turn square corners." Morgan v. South Bend,[64] holding that a governmental unit is not bound by a settlement entered into by its lawyer in the absence of express authority, is illustrative. In White v. United States Dept. of Interior,[65] the district court refused to enforce a $2 million settlement entered into by a United States attorney, holding that the lawyer had no apparent authority. "[P]arties who deal with a Government agent are charged with notice of the limits of the agent's authority. The government is not bound by agreements of agents beyond the scope of their authority in part because of this constructive knowledge." [66]

United States Department of Justice regulations provide that settlements over $2,000,000 can be entered only by the Deputy Attorney General on the Attorney General's behalf. The appropriate Assistant Attorney General generally is authorized to settle for amounts below this, and United States Attorneys are authorized to settle for $500,000 or less.[67]

In one well-known case, Delaware Valley Citizens' Council v. Pennsylvania,[68] the State of Pennsylvania was held bound by a consent decree entered by the state's lawyer agreeing to establish a system for testing vehicle emissions. The legislature's refusal to set up the system was upheld by the Supreme Court of Pennsylvania, which held that the consent decree was a "nullity" because the lawyer had no authority to enter it.[69] The Third Circuit, however, stating that federal courts determine the authority of litigants and their agents in federal court litigation, held that Pennsylvania was bound by its lawyer's action.[70] Is this case inconsistent with the general approach?

63. Morgan v. South Bend Community School Corp., 797 F.2d 471, 478 (7th Cir.1986).

64. 797 F.2d 471, 477 (7th Cir.1986).

65. 639 F.Supp. 82, 90 (M.D.Pa.1986), aff'd, 815 F.2d 697 (3d Cir.1987).

66. Id. at 90.

67. See 28 C.F.R. §§ 0.160–0.168, Appendix to Subpart Y.

68. 755 F.2d 38 (3d Cir.1985), reaffirming 678 F.2d 470 (1982).

69. Scanlon v. Commonwealth, Department of Transportation, 502 Pa. 577, 467 A.2d 1108, 1115 (1983).

70. 755 F.2d at 41. The Seventh Circuit criticized *Delaware Valley* in the *Morgan* case, 797 F.2d at 477–78:

Delaware Valley held that the entry of the consent decree was conclusive on the question of authority. We doubt that the Third Circuit meant to allow any employee of

2. Allocation of Decision–Making in Criminal Cases

Decisions a Client Has a Right to Make

The rule of thumb in criminal cases is similar to that in civil cases, i.e., questions on tactics and procedural matters are ones the lawyer may decide, questions on whether to compromise the client's cause are for the defendant. However, in criminal cases "procedural matters" are often matters of the defendant's fundamental rights, and it has long been recognized that at least four key matters should be decided by the defendant. "[T]he accused has the ultimate authority to make certain fundamental decisions regarding the case. . . . [They are] whether to plead guilty, waive a jury trial, testify in his or her own behalf, or take an appeal." [71]

Some jurisdictions add to the list of decisions that the defendant has a right to make: e.g., waiver of the right to speedy trial; [72] entry of an insanity plea; [73] and presentation of a diminished capacity defense in a death penalty case.[74] Are some of these cases merely ones where a trial strategy went wrong? Should the decision on whether to present a defense be one a criminal defendant always has a right to make? What if there is no credible evidence or the defense is legally frivolous? Who decides what is credible or frivolous?

If a lawyer, without the client's consent, makes any of the decisions that can be made only by a client, a new trial will be ordered. The converse is also true: A defendant who makes the decision against counsel's advice is held to it. In People v. Robles,[75] the defendant insisted on taking the stand over his lawyer's objection. On appeal, the defendant argued that the trial court had erred in allowing his testimony because the decision was tactical and within the province of the lawyer. The court upheld the conviction, stating that "where . . . a defendant insists that he wants to testify, he cannot be deprived of that opportunity." [76]

a state to bind the entire state just by signing his name to a consent decree, though this would be the logical consequence of the decision.

Also see Derrickson v. Danville, 845 F.2d 715 (7th Cir.1988) (again criticizing *Delaware Valley*).

  71.   Jones v. Barnes, 463 U.S. 745, 751 (1983), reproduced below. See M.R. 1.2(a); ABA Standards Relating to the Administration of Criminal Justice (Defense Function), Standards 4–5.2 and 4–8.2(a).

  72. See Townsend v. Superior Court, 15 Cal.3d 774, 126 Cal.Rptr. 251, 543 P.2d 619 (1975).

  73. People v. Gauze, 15 Cal.3d 709, 125 Cal.Rptr. 773, 542 P.2d 1365 (1975).

  74. People v. Frierson, 39 Cal.3d 803, 218 Cal.Rptr. 73, 705 P.2d 396, 403 (1985) (reversing a death penalty because decision to withhold presentation of any defense in guilt phase of a capital case, when defendant desires that a defense be presented and when there is some credible evidence to support it, is not one a lawyer may properly make).

  75. 2 Cal.3d 205, 85 Cal.Rptr. 166, 466 P.2d 710 (1970).

  76. 466 P.2d at 716.

Conduct by a lawyer that is the "practical equivalent" of entering a guilty plea over the client's objection has been considered ground for reversal.[77]   Generally see the notes following *Nix v. Whiteside* in Chapter 5 above.

Decisions a Lawyer May Make

ABA Defense Function Standard 4–5.2(b) and (c) provide:

(b) The decisions on what witnesses to call, whether and how to conduct cross-examination, what jurors to accept or strike, what trial motions should be made, and all other strategic and tactical decisions are the exclusive province of the lawyer after consultation with the client.

(c) If a disagreement on significant matters of tactics or strategy arises between the lawyer and the client, the lawyer should make a record of the circumstances, the lawyer's advice and reasons, and the conclusion reached.   The record should be made in a manner which protects the confidentiality of the lawyer-client relationship.

Outside the four areas entrusted to the client's control, courts have upheld the lawyer's authority to decide strategic matters in a criminal case, notwithstanding that the client has objected, that fundamental rights were waived or that the lawyer had ample opportunity to consult with the client but did not.[78]   How would courts monitor a requirement that counsel obtain the client's consent prior to waiving any constitutional rights?   Are the practical difficulties insurmountable?   How do courts monitor whether a defendant has freely agreed to waive the right to trial by jury, to testify or to plead guilty?

Decisions the lawyer may make without client consent include: which witnesses to call;[79] whether to agree to a mistrial;[80] whether a defense is plausible;[81] the nature of opening or closing argument or their waiver;[82] whether to waive objection to the racial composition of the grand jury;[83] and whether to seek a change of venue after extensive pretrial publicity.[84]

77.   See Brookhart v. Janis, 384 U.S. 1, 16 (1966) (lawyer's agreeing, over client's objection, that the trial should be conducted as a "prima facie trial," in which the defense would neither present evidence nor cross-examine witnesses, was "the practical equivalent of a plea of guilty").   But see People v. Ratliff, 41 Cal.3d 675, 224 Cal.Rptr. 705, 715 P.2d 665 (1986) (conceding client's guilt to a lesser charge without client's consent is a trial tactic, not tantamount to pleading guilty, and decision is properly vested in the lawyer).   Does *Ratliff* make sense?

78.   See People v. Ratliff, 41 Cal.3d 675, 224 Cal.Rptr. 705, 715 P.2d 665 (1986).

79.   Connecticut v. Davis, 199 Conn. 88, 506 A.2d 86 (1986).

80.   People v. Ferguson, 67 N.Y.2d 383, 502 N.Y.S.2d 972, 494 N.E.2d 77 (1986).

81.   Moreno v. Estelle, 717 F.2d 171 (5th Cir.1983).

82.   United States v. Mayo, 646 F.2d 369 (9th Cir.1981).

83.   Winters v. Cook, 489 F.2d 174 (5th Cir.1973).

84.   Curry v. Slansky, 637 F.Supp. 947 (D.Nev.1986).

Consider the following exchange from the trial record in Connecticut v. Davis: [85]

[Defense Counsel]: ... [B]efore the jury comes in, I'd like to make a statement for the record. My client ... has asked me to call one witness, who in my judgment, I do not think it would be wise to call, and under those circumstances, I have declined to follow [my client's] instructions ...

The Court: Well, I have to assume that the decision not to call this particular witness is a tactical decision that experienced trial counsel has made. He's the one who's lived with the case. He's been in attendance throughout and I respect this judgment. I have no basis or reason to make an independent judgment.[86]

JONES v. BARNES

Supreme Court of the United States, 1983.
463 U.S. 745, 103 S.Ct. 3308, 77 L.Ed.2d 987.

CHIEF JUSTICE BURGER delivered the opinion of the Court.

We granted certiorari to consider whether defense counsel assigned to prosecute an appeal from a criminal conviction has a constitutional duty to raise every non-frivolous issue requested by the defendants.... [David Barnes, who had been convicted of robbery and assault in a New York state court, asked his assigned counsel, Melinger, to raise a number of issues on appeal from the conviction. Melinger, after communicating with Barnes by letter, concentrated in his brief and oral argument on three of the issues, rejecting others because he believed they would not aid Barnes in obtaining a new trial or were not based on evidence in the record. Barnes' pro se brief presenting the other issues was submitted to the appellate court, which affirmed the conviction. When various post-conviction remedies proved unavailing, Barnes brought this federal habeas corpus action claiming that Melinger's failure to assert all the non-frivolous arguments Barnes had requested was a denial of his Sixth Amendment right to the effective assistance of counsel.]

. . .

This Court in holding that a State must provide counsel for an indigent appellant on his first appeal of right, recognized the superior ability of trained counsel in the "examination of the record, research of the law, and marshalling of arguments on [the appellant's] behalf," Douglas v. California [372 U.S. 353, 358 (1963)]. Yet by promulgating a per se rule that the client, not the professional advocate, must be allowed to decide what issues are to be pressed, the Court of Appeals [in this case] seriously undermines the ability of counsel to present the client's case in accord with counsel's professional evaluation.

85. 199 Conn. 88, 506 A.2d 86 (1986).
86. 506 A.2d at 87.

Experienced advocates since time beyond memory have emphasized the importance of winnowing out weaker arguments on appeal and focusing on one central issue if possible, or at most on a few key issues....

.   .   .

An authoritative work on appellate practice observes:

Most cases present only one, two, or three significant questions.... Usually ... if you cannot win on a few major points, the others are not likely to help, and to attempt to deal with a great many in the limited number of pages allowed for briefs will mean that none may receive adequate attention. The effect of adding weak arguments will be to dilute the force of the stronger ones. R. Stern, Appellate Practice in the United States, 266 (1981).

There can hardly be any question about the importance of having the appellate advocate examine the record with a view to selecting the most promising issues for review. This has assumed a greater importance in an era when oral argument is strictly limited in most courts—often to as little as 15 minutes—and when page limits on briefs are widely imposed.... Even in a court that imposes no time or page limits, however, the new per se rule laid down by the Court of Appeals is contrary to all experience and logic. A brief that raises every colorable issue runs the risk of burying good arguments—those that, in the words of the great advocate John W. Davis, "go for the jugular." Davis, The Argument of an Appeal, 26 A.B.A.J. 895, 897 (1940)—in a verbal mound made up of strong and weak contentions.... [6]

.   .   .

The Court's decision in Anders [v. California, 386 U.S. 738], far from giving support to the new per se rule announced by the Court of Appeals, is to the contrary. Anders recognized that the role of the advocate "requires that he support his client's appeal to the best of his ability." 386 U.S., at 744. Here the appointed counsel did that. For judges to second-guess reasonable professional judgments and impose on appointed counsel a duty to raise every "colorable" claim suggested by a client would disserve the very goal of vigorous and effective advocacy that underlies Anders. Nothing in the Constitution or our interpretation of that document requires such a standard....

Justice Brennan with whom Justice Marshall joins, dissenting.

6.   ... Respondent points to the ABA Standards for Criminal Appeals, which appear to indicate that counsel should accede to a client's insistence on pressing a particular contention on appeal, see ABA Standards for Criminal Justice 2–3.2, at 2–4.2 (2d ed.1980). The ABA Defense Function Standards provide, however, that, [with certain exceptions,] strategic and tactical decisions are the exclusive province of the defense counsel, after consultation with the client. See ABA Standards for Criminal Justice 4–5.2 (2d ed. 1980).... In any event, the fact that the ABA may have chosen to recognize a given practice as desirable or appropriate does not mean that that practice is required by the Constitution.

Dissent

The Sixth Amendment provides that "[i]n all criminal prosecutions, the accused shall enjoy the right ... to have the *Assistance of Counsel* " (emphasis added). I find myself in fundamental disagreement with the Court over what a right to "the assistance of counsel" means. The import of words like "assistance" and "counsel" seem inconsistent with a regime under which counsel appointed by the State to represent a criminal defendant can refuse to raise issues with arguable merit on appeal when the client, after hearing his assessment of the case and his advice, has directed him to raise them ...

. . .

... [I]n Faretta v. California, 422 U.S. 806 (1975) [holding a criminal defendant has a constitutional right to proceed without counsel] ... we observed:

> ... To force a lawyer on a defendant can only lead him to believe that the law contrives against him.... The right to defend is personal. The defendant, and not his lawyer or the State, will bear the personal consequences of a conviction. It is the defendant, therefore, who must be free personally to decide whether in his particular case counsel is to his advantage. And although he may conduct his own defense ultimately to his own detriment his choice must be honored out of that respect for the individual which is the lifeblood of the law. *Illinois v. Allen* (Brennan, J., concurring).

See DR 7-101(B)(1)

. . .

... [T]he Court argues that good appellate advocacy demands selectivity among arguments. That is certainly true-the Court's advice is good. It ought to be taken to heart by every lawyer called upon to argue an appeal ... and by his client. It should take little or no persuasion to get a wise client to understand that, if staying out of prison is what he values most, he should encourage his lawyer to raise only his two or three best arguments on appeal, and he should defer to his lawyer's advice as to which are the best arguments. The Constitution, however, does not require clients to be wise, and other policies should be weighed in the balance as well.

It is no secret that indigent clients often mistrust the lawyers appointed to represent them. There are many reasons for this, some perhaps unavoidable even under perfect conditions—differences in education, disposition, and socioeconomic class—and some that should (but may not always) be zealously avoided. A lawyer and his client do not always have the same interests. Even with paying clients, a lawyer may have a strong interest in having judges and prosecutors think well of him, and, if he is working for a flat fee—a common arrangement for criminal defense attorneys—or if his fees for court appointments are lower than he would receive for other work, he has an obvious financial incentive to conclude cases on his criminal docket swiftly. Good lawyers undoubtedly recognize these temptations and resist them, and they endeavor to convince their clients that they will. It would be naive, however, to suggest that they always succeed in either task. A constitutional rule that encourages lawyers to disregard their clients "wishes without compelling need can only exacerbate the clients" suspicions of their lawyers ...

. . .

... In many ways, having a lawyer becomes one of the many indignities visited upon someone who has the ill fortune to run afoul of the criminal justice system.

I cannot accept the notion that lawyers are one of the punishments a person receives merely for being accused of a crime. Clients, if they wish are capable of making informed judgments about which issues to appeal, and when they exercise that prerogative their choices should be respected unless they would require lawyers to violate their consciences, the law or their duties to the court.

Violation of Client Instructions as Ineffective Assistance

Was attorney Melinger's refusal to follow his client's instructions a violation of professional ethics? Justice Blackmun, concurring separately, stated that, as an ethical but not constitutional matter, a lawyer is bound to argue all nonfrivolous issues the appellant insists on.[87] Does the majority opinion rest on this distinction between unconstitutional lawyer conduct and unethical conduct? Or does it adopt a lawyer-centered view of the lawyer-client relationship in a criminal trial and appeal? What considerations support placing the defense lawyer so much in command? Does Justice Brennan's more client-centered approach impair the lawyer's sense of personal autonomy and professionalism by requiring the lawyer to play a "mouthpiece" role?

The backdrop of *Barnes* is the systemic problem of providing an appeal at public expense to each convicted indigent defendant. An indigent defendant has little incentive not to take an appeal, even if the prospects of success are low.[88] The *Anders* case attempted to make the right of appeal meaningful by requiring appointed counsel to discuss "anything in the record that might arguably support the appeal." [89] This constitutional requirement modifies the general ethics requirement that prohibits lawyers from pressing frivolous matters and requires them to withdraw rather than do so. *Anders* and its progeny suggest that the lawyer's advocacy function in this situation is infused with public responsibilities of assisting the court system in ensuring that a defendant's rights are adequately protected.

87. 463 U.S. at 754.

88. See Thomas Y. Davies, A Hard Look at What We Know (and Still Need to Know) About the "Costs" of the Exclusionary Rule, 1983 Am.Bar Found.Research J. 611 (only 26 of 544 criminal appeals in California's First District Court of Appeal, which includes San Francisco, were reversed in a one-year period; only four cases were accepted for review by the California Supreme Court).

89. Anders v. California, 386 U.S. 738 (1967), discussed in Chapter 5 above at p. 438.

The modification in counsel's role was itself modified in McCoy v. Wisconsin,[90] dealing with a Wisconsin rule requiring the lawyer to include an explanation of why the lawyer believes the appeal is frivolous in any brief filed pursuant to *Anders*. The Court held that the Wisconsin rule does not deprive the defendant of effective assistance of counsel. *McCoy* emphasizes a theme that pervades decisions on a lawyer's authority to make tactical decisions—the lawyer's role in assisting courts in handling the high volume of criminal appeals.

[handwritten margin note: atty cannot argue on appeal that 9 of 10 of his client's issues he wanted to raise = frivolous]

In People v. Vasquez,[91] the defendant asked his appointed counsel to raise ten points on appeal, but the lawyer decided to raise only one. The lawyer's appellate brief stated that the point raised had "substantial merit" but that the nine remaining points had been reviewed and "have been found to be without merit." The court ruled that counsel's gratuitous disparagement of his client's nine other arguments denied him effective assistance of counsel on the appeal. Appellate counsel should "argue the claim found meritorious and make no comment about claims considered frivolous", advising the client to submit a pro se brief "if he still thinks they should be addressed."[92] Doesn't this procedure also signal to the court counsel's view that some issues are frivolous?

Autonomy to Opt for Death

Does the autonomy argument made by Justice Brennan in his dissent in *Barnes* justify allowing a client to decide to forego legal tactics that might save her from the death penalty? In Gilmore v. Utah,[93] the Supreme Court affirmed the right of a person to refuse to appeal a death sentence. The court had previously granted the petition for a stay filed by Bessie Gilmore, the defendant's mother, which it now vacated, dismissing the action brought by his mother as "next friend" to stop the execution. In Lenhard v. Wolff,[94] the defendant's lawyers sought a writ of habeas corpus and a stay of their former client's execution, which the client refused to fight. They argued that in this case, unlike *Gilmore*, their client had never been shown to be competent to waive his rights. The Ninth Circuit refused to stay the execution because no evidence in the record raised a doubt about the client's competence.

If the defendant has the right to insist that a defense of diminished capacity be presented, as California has held, does he have the right to insist that such a defense not be presented? In People v. Deere the California Supreme Court held that the defendant does not control the defense in the penalty stage of a capital case.[95] The court described the penalty phase of the trial as follows:

90. 486 U.S. 429 (1988).
91. 70 N.Y.2d 1, 516 N.Y.S.2d 921, 509 N.E.2d 934 (1987).
92. 509 N.E.2d at 922.
93. 429 U.S. 1012 (1976).
94. 603 F.2d 91 (9th Cir.1979).
95. People v. Deere, 41 Cal.3d 353, 222 Cal.Rptr. 131, 710 P.2d 925 (1985).

Counsel first permitted his client to make a brief statement to the court ... "I know what I done was wrong" ... "I always believed [in] an eye for an eye. I feel I should die for the crimes I done...."

... [T]he defense attorney's honest but mistaken belief that he had "no right whatsoever to infringe upon his [client's] decisions about his own life" operated to deny defendant his right to the effective assistance of counsel. While counsel should of course endeavor to comply with his client's wishes to the maximum extent consistent with his legal and ethical responsibilities, he is not— contrary to a popular misconception—a mere "mouthpiece." As we recently found it necessary to reiterate, "Once an attorney is appointed to represent a client, he assumes the authority and duty to control the proceedings. The scope of this authority extends to matters such as deciding what witnesses to call, whether and how to conduct cross-examination, what jurors to accept or reject, what motions to make, and most other strategic and tactical determinations." [96]

Was the decision in *Deere* a "strategic or tactical" one? [97]

Accepting or Rejecting a Plea Bargain Offer

A guilty plea will be set aside and a new trial ordered if entered without client consent.[1] The defendant is given what she has lost: her right to a fair trial and all the other protections afforded by that process. But what happens when the defendant's lawyer *rejects* a plea bargain without client consent? When a defense lawyer rejects a plea without informing the client or without the client's consent, the defendant proceeds to trial. Would reversing that trial and ordering a new one be a sensible remedy? As the Iowa court has said: "One more fair trial, or even a series of them, would not necessarily revive the lost chance [for a plea bargain]."[2] Is the answer to provide no remedy?

Courts have had difficulty with this dilemma. Johnson v. Duckworth[3] held that a lawyer who rejects a plea bargain without client consent ordinarily violates the defendant's Sixth Amendment right to effective counsel; the lawyer's action was reasonable in this case,

---

96. 710 P.2d at 929, 931. The court stressed the state's interest in the reliable and fair administration of penalty decisions in capital cases, reasoning that a penalty trial at which available mitigating evidence is not presented is "no penalty trial at all." Id. at 934. But see In re Guzman, 45 Cal.3d 915, 248 Cal.Rptr. 467, 755 P.2d 917 (1988) (defense counsel's acquiescence in client's desire not to present mitigating evidence is not ineffective assistance of counsel).

97. On representing mentally impaired criminal defendants, see Rodney J. Uphoff, The Role of the Criminal Defense Lawyer in Representing The Mentally Impaired Defendant: Zealous Advocate or Officer of the Court?, 1988 Wis.L.Rev. 65. See also the discussion in the note on disabled clients at p. 511 below.

1. Boykin v. Alabama, 395 U.S. 238 (1969).

2. Iowa v. Kraus, 397 N.W.2d 671 (Iowa 1986). Other courts have noted the difference between accepting a plea and rejecting one. See, e.g., Johnson v. Duckworth, 793 F.2d 898 (7th Cir.1986).

3. 793 F.2d 898 (7th Cir.1986).

however, because the defendant was 17, confused and the lawyer talked
to the client's parents before deciding. The court also noted that the
defendant had made no showing that he would have accepted the
proffered plea, which would ordinarily be required before relief was
granted.[4]

Other courts have ordered new trials, perhaps to put the defendant
once again in the position where she can attempt to bargain with the
prosecutor.[5] The prosecutor, however, may not choose to repeat the
offer. This possibility was dealt with in Iowa v. Kraus: [6] The Iowa court
remanded the case, directing that the accused again be allowed to enter
a plea on the terms rejected by his lawyer (a plea to a lesser offense).
"If a guilty plea is entered judgment shall be pronounced accordingly
and defendant's conviction of second-degree murder shall stand as
reversed. If the defendant fails or refuses to enter such a plea his
conviction ... shall stand affirmed." [7]

Professor Albert Alschuler's discussion of the realities of the plea
bargaining process concludes that the client's right to decide whether to
plead guilty is realized only in a technical sense. Many defense
lawyers believe their judgment on the plea should prevail; if the client
resists, she should find a new lawyer.[8]

3. Disabled Clients

The normal adult client may be presumed capable of making or
participating in decisions concerning the scope, objectives or means of
representation. But many clients have impaired mental capacity (e.g.,
mentally retarded or senile clients), some are suffering from mental
disease and some are juveniles. How do these conditions or impairments affect what the lawyer should do? [9]

Model Rule 1.14 provides:

(a) When the client's ability to make adequately considered
decisions in connection with the representation is impaired, whether because of minority, mental disability or for some other reason,
the lawyer shall, as far as possible, maintain a normal client-
lawyer relationship with the client.

4. Also see Lloyd v. State, 258 Ga. 645, 373 S.E.2d 1 (1988) (failure to communicate
plea unreasonable but no prejudice where no evidence that defendant would have
accepted the offer).

5. E.g., State v. Simmons, 65 N.C.App. 294, 309 S.E.2d 493 (1983).

6. 397 N.W.2d 671 (Iowa 1986).

7. Id. at 676. Also see Turner v. Tennessee, 858 F.2d 1201 (6th Cir.1988) (state may
not withdraw plea offer unless it can show no vindictiveness in doing so). But see
Commonwealth v. Copeland, 381 Pa.Super. 382, 554 A.2d 54, 60 (1988) (court may only
order "imperfect relief" of new trial and cannot order the state to reinstate its plea offer).

8. Albert W. Alschuler, The Defense Attorney's Role in Plea Bargaining, 84 Yale L.J.
1179, 1306–7 (1975).

9. The lawyer's responsibilities when representing amorphous clients, such as a class
or a government, are considered below in chapter 8.

(b) A lawyer may seek the appointment of a guardian or take other protective action with respect to a client, only when the lawyer reasonably believes that the client cannot adequately act in the client's own interest.[10]

Paragraph (a) of M.R. 1.14 and the corresponding Comment remind the lawyer that a client under a disability may still be capable of participating in the representation, even if the client is unable to participate as fully as other clients. As the Comment states:

[A]n incapacitated person may have no power to make legally binding decisions. Nevertheless, a client lacking legal competence often has the ability to understand, deliberate upon, and reach conclusions about matters affecting the client's own well-being.... The fact that the client suffers a disability does not diminish the lawyer's obligation to treat the client with attention and respect.

A number of decisions, but not all, hold that the lawyer must ordinarily respect the client's decision to contest a civil commitment proceeding or to refrain from asserting an incompetency defense in a criminal case.[11]

When a legally incompetent client is adjudged unable to make a decision such as whether to dispose of property, the lawyer cannot act unless the lawyer has been legally appointed as guardian. If a guardian already exists, the lawyer "should ordinarily look to the representative for decisions on behalf of the client."[12] Why does the Comment qualify this statement with the word "ordinarily"?[13] A general analysis of the lawyer's relationship with the guardian of a disabled client or the fiduciary for any dependent client is considered in Chapter 8 below at p. 803. The presence of a guardian does not relieve the lawyer of the obligation to treat the disabled client as a client to the extent possible, particularly in maintaining communication. See the Comment to M.R. 1.14.

When there is no guardian M.R. 1.14(b) cautions that the lawyer should seek the appointment of a guardian "only when the lawyer

---

10. The Model Code has no rule on representing a client under a disability, although EC 7–12 does deal with the issue in less detail than is found in the Comment to M.R. 1.14.

11. See, e.g., In re Link, 713 S.W.2d 487 (Mo.1986) (in civil incompetency proceedings, where lawyer concludes that the client is capable of understanding the matter, the lawyer must abide by the client's decisions on whether to waive or exercise a right). See also Frendak v. United States, 408 A.2d 364 (D.C.App.1979) (defendant's decision to waive insanity defense should be respected). But see In re the Marriage of Beverly C. Rolfe, 216 Mont. 39, 699 P.2d 79 (1985) (although lawyer representing disabled client ordinarily should be guided by client, in custody proceedings lawyer should advocate a child's best interests even where they are at odds with child's expressed desires); Thompson v. Wainwright, 787 F.2d 1447 (11th Cir.1986) (lawyer who believed that his client had mental problems should not have relied on his client's request that he forego the investigation of mitigating evidence).

12. Comment to M.R. 1.14. See EC 7–12 to the same effect.

13. See Richard Neely, Handicapped Advocacy: Inherent Barriers and Partial Solutions in the Representation of Disabled Children, 33 Hastings L.J. 1359 (1982) (arguing that lawyers for a disabled client should not accept without critical examination decisions made by a guardian on behalf of the client).

reasonably believes that the client cannot adequately act in the client's own interests." But as the Comment suggests, even where the lawyer believes the standard of 1.14(b) has been met, seeking a guardian and thereby raising the question of incompetency may on balance do more harm to the client than good. The Comment says: "The lawyer's position in such cases is an unavoidably difficult one." It advises that the lawyer might seek guidance from a mental health professional.

When the lawyer decides that on balance a guardian should not be sought, the lawyer acts as de facto guardian, making certain decisions for the client and sometimes deciding to act against the client's express wishes. In State v. Aumann,[14] for example, the court held it proper, given the extent of the client's disability, for the lawyer to have decided against the client's wishes to take an appeal.

In an article on lawyer paternalism [15] Professor David Luban gives the following two hypotheticals, arguing that in the first the lawyer would be justified in overriding the client's decision, but not in the second where the client is able to articulate values for the decision:

> You are the court-appointed attorney representing the interests of a thirteen-year-old boy in a custody case. You must make a report to the court about who should get custody.... Your client, an inarticulate and unhappy looking boy in a faded jean jacket, is sullen and suspicious. He says he would rather live with his father, but falls silent when you try to find out why. The father is a glad-handing, sporadically employed alcoholic; the mother is a hard-working disciplinarian who lives with her mother in a tidy row-house. Both women appear concerned for your client's welfare. In your opinion, the boy prefers his father because his father lets him get away with more; the social worker on the case tells you that the boy is part of a drinking and doping crowd.

atty = Justified
In overriding ɔ

> . . .

> Your client is a teen-ager who was involved in a car accident in which his date was killed. He is charged with driving while intoxicated and vehicular homicide, but some of the circumstances are unclear, and the prosecutor offers to let him plead guilty to reckless operation of a vehicle. Client, however, insists that he will plead guilty to the greater charges, and in an emotional scene tells you that he cannot live with himself unless he publicly confesses what he knows to be his crime and expiates the guilt by going to jail.

Not Justified

How would you resolve the two situations? [16]

14. 265 N.W.2d 316 (Iowa 1978).

15. David Luban, Paternalism and the Legal Profession, 1981 Wis.L.Rev. 454, 455.

16. On representing children, see Stephen Wizner and Miriam Berkman, Being a Lawyer for a Child Too Young to be a Client: A Clinical Study, 68 Neb.L.Rev. 330 (1989); Robert H. Mnookin et al., In the Interest of Children: Advocacy, Law Reform and Public Policy (1985); Martin Guggenheim, The Right to be Represented But Not Heard: Reflections on Legal Representation of Children, 59 N.Y.U.L.Rev. 76 (1984) (concluding that

Professor Paul Tremblay, in another helpful article,[17] identifies six options available to the lawyer and finds that each one entails its own ethical problems: (1) follow the client's expressed wishes whatever the consequences; (2) seek a guardian; (3) allow the family of the disabled client to make the decisions usually reserved for the client; (4) act as a de facto guardian; (5) try to persuade the client to accept the lawyer's judgment on the appropriate course to follow; and (6) withdraw. He concludes that lawyer supersession of the client's right to make decisions is only warranted in emergencies, that only in extreme cases should the lawyer seek a guardian, that relying in part on the family is justifiable and that non-coercive persuasion is the appropriate course in moderate cases of disability.[18]

C. FEES

Introductory Note

Four types of fee arrangements are frequently encountered, separately or in combination: (1) a flat fee for a particular legal matter (e.g., $700 for a simple uncontested divorce or $150 for a simple will); (2) an hourly rate fee (e.g., $100 per hour for work on a particular matter); (3) a proportional fee (e.g., handling a real estate transaction for a percentage of the purchase price); and (4) a contingent fee (e.g., a fee of $10,000 to be paid if a particular result is obtained). Combinations of hourly rates with contingent features are common. And the classic contingent fee in the personal injury field is both contingent and proportional (e.g., one-third of any award after deduction of expenses).

Systematic studies of legal fees and the basis of their calculation are rare. Contingent fees, discussed below, have received some attention. The hourly rate fee is said to have become much more common during the last generation. The fee resulting from an hourly fee is the product of the hourly rate times the number of hours. Generally, the hourly rate is standard and calibrated to the lawyer's experience, while the number of hours is the product of the adversariness of the matter, the stakes, client goals and the relative complexity of the matter.[19]

"mature" children—the author suggests children over seven might be considered in this category—should be allowed to direct their lawyers' conduct; but that for children too young to direct the lawyer's conduct none of the existing models for the lawyer are adequate).

17. Paul R. Tremblay, On Persuasion and Paternalism: Lawyer Decisionmaking and the Questionably Competent Client, 1987 Utah L.Rev. 515.

18. Id. at 584. See also Rodney J. Uphoff, The Role of the Criminal Defense Lawyer in Representing The Mentally Impaired Defendant: Zealous Advocate or Officer of the Court?, 1988 Wis.L.Rev. 65 (exploring alternatives to raising competency for the lawyer representing a mentally impaired criminal defendant).

19. Herbert M. Kritzer et al., Understanding the Costs of Litigation: The Case of the Hourly–Fee Lawyer, 1985 Am. Bar Found. Research J. 559. The authors, in assessing how reform proposals might affect the costs of civil litigation, conclude that delay has relatively little effect on processing costs (though very costly to plaintiffs in other respects); that "the level of involvement and control exercised by the client can signifi-

However, as economic analysis would suggest, both the standard hourly rate and the number of hours committed are informed and constrained by the charges made by other lawyers in the same market.

Law firm bills sometimes are padded.[20] Many young lawyers report instances of recording more hours than were worked, recording lower echelon lawyers' hours as those of one with a higher hourly rate, billing personal time and the like. Disbursements may similarly be inflated. Various rationalizations, such as "the client is not a regular client of the firm" and the client is itself rapacious, provide informal support for those practices. Operating methods that elicit compliance with inflationary billing practices and prevent their disclosure are also prevalent, such as partner control of time sheets and work assignments and signals concerning the effect of "loyalty" to the firm on salary or promotion.[21]

1. Amount of the Fee

Model Rule 1.5(a) states simply: "A lawyer's fee shall be reasonable...." DR 2–106 defines a "clearly excessive" fee in terms of whether the fee is "reasonable." California Rule of Professional Conduct 4–200(A) prohibits "unconscionable" fees. This confusion over the standard is repeated in the cases. In addition, courts sometimes use words such as "fair" and "equitable" when judging the fee.[22]

BROBECK, PHLEGER & HARRISON v. TELEX CORP.

United States Court of Appeals, Ninth Circuit, 1979.
602 F.2d 866.

Before MOORE, SNEED and TANG, CIRCUIT JUDGES.

PER CURIAM:

This is a diversity action in which the plaintiff, the San Francisco law firm of Brobeck, Phleger & Harrison ("Brobeck"), sued the Telex Corporation and Telex Computer Products, Inc. ("Telex") to recover $1,000,000 in attorney's fees. Telex had engaged Brobeck on a contingency fee basis to prepare a petition for certiorari after the Tenth Circuit reversed a $259.5 million judgment in Telex's favor against International Business Machines Corporation ("IBM") and affirmed an

cantly reduce the amount of time the lawyer spends on the case"; that "lawyers who take cases because of the professional visibility they will gain appear to spend significantly more time per case (which then gets billed to the client)"; and that "clients with a strong desire to keep costs low should avoid the federal courts if they have the option." Id. at 592–93.

20. See Lisa G. Lerman, Lying to Clients, 138 U.Pa.L.Rev. 659, 705–20 (1990) (discussing lawyer dishonesty in billing).

21. For an economic analysis of a firm's basis for division of profits among partners, see Ronald J. Gilson and Robert H. Mnookin, Sharing Among the Human Capitalists: An Economic Inquiry into the Corporate Law Firm and How Partners Split Profits, 37 Stan.L.Rev. 313 (1985).

22. See, e.g., Ackermann v. Levine, 788 F.2d 830 (2d Cir.1986).

$18.5 million counterclaim judgment for IBM against Telex. Brobeck prepared and filed the petition, and after Telex entered a "wash settlement" with IBM in which both parties released their claims against the other, Brobeck sent Telex a bill for $1,000,000, that it claimed Telex owed it under their written contingency fee agreement. When Telex refused to pay, Brobeck brought this action. Both parties filed motions for summary judgment. The district court granted Brobeck's motion, awarding Brobeck $1,000,000 plus interest. Telex now appeals.

. . .

Having had reversed one of the largest antitrust judgments in history, Telex officials decided to press the Tenth Circuit's decision to the United States Supreme Court. To maximize Telex's chances for having its petition for certiorari granted, they decided to search for the best available lawyer. They compiled a list of the preeminent antitrust and Supreme Court lawyers in the country, and Roger Wheeler, Telex's Chairman of the Board, settled on Moses Lasky of the Brobeck firm as the best possibility.

Wheeler and his assistant made preliminary phone calls to Lasky on February 3, 4, and 13, 1975 to determine whether Lasky was willing to prepare the petition for certiorari. Lasky stated he would be interested if he was able to rearrange his workload. When asked about a fee, Lasky stated that, although he would want a retainer, it was the policy of the Brobeck firm to determine fees after the services were performed. Wheeler, however, wanted an agreement fixing fees in advance and arranged for Lasky to meet in San Francisco on February 10th to discuss the matter further with Telex's president, Stephen Jatras, and Floyd Walker, its attorney in the IBM litigation.

. . .

[After further discussion the following agreement was signed:]

MEMORANDUM

1. Retainer of $25,000.00 to be paid. If Writ of Certiorari is denied and no settlement has been effected in excess of the Counterclaim, then the $25,000.00 retainer shall be the total fee paid; provided however, that

2. If the case should be settled before a Petition for Writ of Certiorari is actually filed with the Clerk of the Supreme Court, then the Brobeck firm would bill for its services to the date of settlement at an hourly rate of $125.00 per hour for the lawyers who have worked on the case; the total amount of such billing will be limited to not more than $100,000.00, against which the $25,000.00 retainer will be applied, but no portion of the retainer will be returned in any event.

3. Once a Petition for Writ of Certiorari has been filed with the Clerk of the United States Supreme Court then Brobeck will be entitled to the payment of an additional fee in the event of a recovery by Telex

from IBM by way of settlement or judgment of its claims against IBM; and, such additional fee will be five percent (5%) of the first $100,000,-000.00 gross of such recovery, undiminished by any recovery by IBM on its counterclaims or cross-claims. The maximum contingent fee to be paid is $5,000,000.00 provided that if recovery by Telex from IBM in less than $40,000,000.00 gross, the five percent (5%) shall be based on the net recovery, i.e., the recovery after deducting the credit to IBM by virtue of IBM's recovery on counterclaims or cross-claims, but the contingent fee shall not then be less than $1,000,000.00.

4. Once a Writ of Certiorari has been granted, then Brobeck will receive an additional $15,000.00 retainer to cover briefing and arguing in the Supreme Court.

5. Telex will pay, in addition to the fees stated, all of the costs incurred with respect to the prosecution of the case in the United States Supreme Court.

. . .

Lasky, as agreed, prepared the petition for certiorari and filed it in July 1975. He also obtained a stay of mandate from the Tenth Circuit pending final disposition of the action by the Supreme Court. In the meantime Telex began to consider seriously the possibility of settlement with IBM by having Telex withdraw its petition in exchange for a discharge of the counterclaim judgment. Telex officials planned a meeting to discuss whether to settle on this basis, and Walker asked Lasky to attend in order to secure Lasky's advice on the chances that the petition for certiorari would be granted.

The meeting was held on September 5. Lasky told the assembled Telex's officials that the chances that the petition for certiorari would be granted were very good. Wheeler, however, was concerned that if the petition for certiorari was denied, the outstanding counterclaim judgment would threaten Telex with bankruptcy. Wheeler informed Lasky that Telex was seriously considering the possibility of a "wash settlement" in which neither side would recover anything and each would release their claims against the other. Lasky responded that in the event of such a settlement he would be entitled to a fee of $1,000,000. Wheeler, upon hearing this, became emotional and demanded to know from the others present whether this was what the agreement provided. Walker agreed that it had. Jatras said he didn't know and would have to read the correspondence.

. . .

Having returned to San Francisco, Lasky, at Telex's request, prepared a reply brief to IBM's opposition to the petition for certiorari, and sent it to the Supreme Court on September 17th for filing. In the meantime, Wheeler opened settlement discussions with IBM. He telephoned Lasky periodically for advice.

On October 2 IBM officials became aware that the Supreme Court's decision on the petition was imminent. They contacted Telex and the parties agreed that IBM would release its counterclaim judgment against Telex in exchange for Telex's dismissal of its petition for certiorari. On October 3, at the request of Wheeler and Jatras, Lasky had the petition for certiorari withdrawn. Thereafter, he sent a bill to Telex for $1,000,000. When Telex refused to pay, Brobeck filed its complaint. On the basis of depositions and exhibits, the district court granted Brobeck's motion for summary judgment.

Telex contends that, under California law,[2] if a client who has retained an attorney on a contingent fee basis discharges the attorney before the contingency has occurred, the attorney is limited to recovering the reasonable value of the services rendered. See Fracasse v. Brent, 6 Cal.3d 784, 100 Cal.Rptr. 385, 494 P.2d 9 (1972). Telex contends there is a factual dispute as to whether Brobeck was discharged, and summary judgment was therefore inappropriate.

This contention borders on frivolousness. As Telex concedes, it never formally discharged Brobeck. Nor did it say or do anything from which an intent to terminate Brobeck prematurely could be inferred.

. . .

Telex argues that, because it received no money by virtue of the wash settlement with IBM, there was "no recovery by Telex from IBM by way of settlement or judgment of its claims against IBM" [within paragraph three of the agreement], and therefore, the condition on which Brobeck would be paid was never fulfilled. Such a construction would create anomalies in the agreement that we cannot reasonably believe that the parties could have intended. First, Telex's requirement that it receive some cash by way of settlement of its claims against IBM could be satisfied by receipt of $1.00 from IBM. We agree with Brobeck that a construction of the contract that would condition the $1 million fee upon Telex's receipt of any amount of cash, no matter how slight, is untenable. Second, had Telex received $18.5 million from IBM in settlement of its antitrust claim, instead of receiving a discharge from its counterclaim judgment, it would have been in the same position as the wash settlement left it. Yet, Telex does not appear to dispute that in such a situation that Brobeck would be entitled to its $1 million fee. Telex's version of the agreement clearly exalts form over substance. Finally, Telex's construction of paragraph three is incompatible with paragraph two. Paragraph two provides that if the case is settled before the petition for a writ of certiorari is actually filed, then Brobeck could bill its services on an hourly basis not to exceed $100,-000. It makes no sense to interpret paragraph three such that Telex pays less in attorney's fees where the petition is filed than when it is not. Not only would Brobeck have expended more time and effort where it actually completes and files the petition, but it also would have conferred on Telex the ability to use the completed petition as bargaining leverage in its negotiations with IBM. The substantial

---

2. The parties have assumed throughout that California law should be applied. We make the same assumption here.

leverage that Telex gained by having filed a petition for certiorari is an explanation why Telex was willing to pay substantially more for a filed petition, and in fact, Telex appears to have benefitted significantly by having filed the petition.

Finally, Telex contends that the $1 million fee was so excessive as to render the contract unenforceable. Alternatively it argues that unconscionability depends on the contract's reasonableness, a question of fact that should be submitted to the jury.

Preliminarily, we note that whether a contract is fair or works an unconscionable hardship is determined with reference to the time when the contract was made and cannot be resolved by hindsight....

There is no dispute about the facts leading to Telex's engagement of the Brobeck firm. Telex was an enterprise threatened with bankruptcy. It had won one of the largest money judgments in history, but that judgment had been reversed in its entirety by the Tenth Circuit. In order to maximize its chances of gaining review by the United States Supreme Court, it sought to hire the most experienced and capable lawyer it could possibly find. After compiling a list of highly qualified lawyers, it settled on Lasky as the most able. Lasky was interested but wanted to bill Telex on hourly basis. After Telex insisted on a contingent fee arrangement, Lasky made it clear that he would consent to such an arrangement only if he would receive a sizable contingent fee in the event of success.

In these circumstances, the contract between Telex and Brobeck was not so unconscionable that "no man in his senses and not under a delusion would make on the one hand, and as no honest and fair man would accept on the other." Swanson v. Hempstead, 64 Cal.App.2d 681, 688, 149 P.2d 404, 407 (1944). This is not a case where one party took advantage of another's ignorance, exerted superior bargaining power, or disguised unfair terms in small print. Rather, Telex, a multi-million corporation, represented by able counsel, sought to secure the best attorney it could find to prepare its petition for certiorari, insisting on a contingent fee contract. Brobeck fulfilled its obligation to gain a stay of judgment and to prepare and file the petition for certiorari. Although the minimum fee was clearly high, Telex received substantial value from Brobeck's services. For, as Telex acknowledged, Brobeck's petition provided Telex with the leverage to secure a discharge of its counterclaim judgment, thereby saving it from possible bankruptcy in the event the Supreme Court denied its petition for certiorari. We conclude that such a contract was not unconscionable.

––––––

Compare *Brobeck* with the following cases:

1. *McKenzie Construction, Inc. v. Maynard,* 758 F.2d 97 (3d Cir. 1985). McKenzie Construction, after being discharged from a construc-

tion job for the Virgin Islands government, retained lawyer Maynard on a contingent-fee basis to collect the amount due for the work performed. Maynard's efforts resulted in a settlement of $195,000 for McKenzie, from which Maynard deducted his one-third contingency fee ($65,000) plus expenses. McKenzie brought suit to recover most of this amount on ground that the fee was clearly excessive. The trial court, although "uncomfortable" with the fee, which would have been about $5,000 if Maynard had charged his usual hourly rate, concluded that the client had not established that the fee was clearly excessive. The Third Circuit reversed, holding that the trial court erred in failing to consider circumstances arising after the agreement was entered into:

> [T]he district court had too narrow a view. Because courts have a special concern to supervise contingent attorney fee agreements, they are not to be enforced on the same basis as ordinary commercial contracts. Dunn v. H.K. Porter Co., Inc., 602 F.2d at 1108. This concern certainly extends to the performance of the attorney's contractual obligations as well as to the circumstances surrounding the engagement of the attorney. For example, the results obtained, the quality of the work, and whether the attorney's efforts substantially contributed to the result are all factors that have been used by courts in reviewing the reasonableness of contingent fees.... See also ABA Code of Professional Responsibility, DR 2–106 (1979). Further, events may occur after the fee arrangement was made so that "[a] contingent fee arrangement '[that] ... was in the first instance a fair contract becomes unfair in its enforcement.'" ... While the reasonableness at the time of contracting is a relevant consideration, it is not the only one. We, therefore, conclude that the rule announced by the district court contained legal error to the extent that it excluded relevant factors other than those existing at the time the fee agreement was executed.[23]

2. *Bushman* v. *State Bar of California*, 11 Cal.3d 558, 113 Cal. Rptr. 904, 522 P.2d 312 (1974). Bushman, a lawyer of seven years' experience at the time, was retained by Barbara Cox, aged 16, her parents and her current boy friend in a divorce and custody proceeding brought by her husband, Neal Cox. Barbara's parents, who were alleged to have physical custody of the child, were joined as defendants. The fee arrangements included a $5,000 promissory note signed by all the clients and a retainer agreement providing for an hourly rate of $60. The court awarded custody to Barbara on the basis of a stipulation of the parties, and the court ordered that the husband pay Bushman a fee of $300 and $60 in costs. Bushman, who did not inform the court of the promissory note or of the sums paid by his clients, had billed his clients for $2,800 plus $60 in costs, collected $600 from them

---

23. 758 F.2d, at 100–102. On remand, the district court held that the fee met the Third Circuit's reasonableness standard and, on a second appeal, the Third Circuit affirmed, stating that "no event occurred after the fee arrangement was entered into which rendered a contract admittedly fair when entered into unfair in its enforcement." McKenzie Construction Co. v. Maynard, 823 F.2d 43 (3d Cir.1987).

and claimed the full amount due under the promissory note. Bushman, who was also found guilty of prohibited solicitation, was suspended for one year. The Supreme Court accepted the State Bar's recommendation:

> [U]nder all the circumstances, the fee charged by Bushman was so exorbitant and wholly disproportionate to the services rendered to the defendants as to shock the conscience. An examination of the file in the Cox matter reveals that only a simple, almost routine series of documents was filed by Bushman on Barbara's behalf. Although he asserts that the case was "quite involved," he is unable to articulate any complex issues which required extensive research or specialized skills.... Aside from interviews with the defendants and a doctor, the only additional services performed by Bushman were two appearances in court for hearings on orders to show cause. He failed to substantiate his claim of 100 hours spent on the Cox case.... Cox's attorney spent slightly more than five hours on the case.

. . .

> Petitioner maintains that the board failed to consider the fact that his efforts on Barbara's behalf were successful in that she was ultimately awarded custody of the child, and that there was no element of concealment in his conduct since he revealed to the defendants why the fee would be so high; and they were free to consult another attorney. We do not deem these matters to be of sufficient significance to outweigh the clear showing set out above that Bushman was guilty of overreaching and unconscionable conduct.[24]

Excessive Fees

California lawyers were involved in both *Brobeck* and *Bushman* ? Why is a $1 million fee agreement for a certiorari petition enforceable while a $2,800 fee for a divorce and custody proceeding results in discipline? Do market principles control some lawyers and fiduciary principles others? After *Brobeck* there may be no fee that a court would consider excessive when the client is a sophisticated commercial player.[25] Reflecting the holding in *Brobeck*, Calif.R.Prof.Conduct 4–200(B)(2) provides that the client's "sophistication" is a factor to be considered in judging whether the fee is unconscionable.

24. 522 P.2d at 315–16.

25. See Ackermann v. Levine, 788 F.2d 830, 843 (2d Cir.1986) (" ... the American client was a sophisticated business person with competent American international legal counsel"). Martin Lipton of Wachtell, Lipton, one of the best-known specialists in merger-and-acquisition law, is reported to have earned a $20 million fee for representing Kraft Inc. in the Philip Morris–Kraft takeover negotiations—a fee of more than $5,000 an hour. Stephen Labaton, N.Y.Times, Nov. 4, 1988, at p. D1.

Should the standard applied in fee litigation between lawyer and client be the same as in a professional discipline case? In *McKenzie Construction,* supra, the court stated that "[W]e are convinced that in a civil action, a fee may be found to be 'unreasonable' and therefore subject to appropriate reduction by a court without necessarily being so 'clearly excessive' as to justify a finding of breach of ethics." [26] Is *McKenzie Construction* correct in stating that fee arrangements that may not warrant professional discipline may be unenforceable as between lawyer and client? In a dispute between lawyer and client over the fee, the lawyer generally has the burden of justifying the fee; the client, even when she is suing to recover part of the fee charged, does not bear the burden of proving that the fee was too high. "This allocation of the burden of proof is premised on the relationship of trust owed by a lawyer to his client.... This approach is at the very heart of the special relationship between attorney and client." [27]

The courts have power to scrutinize lawyer fee contracts to ensure that the fee charged is not excessive. The authority to examine lawyers' fees with greater care than ordinary commercial contracts is based on the courts' inherent and statutory power to regulate the profession.[28] In examining fee arrangements courts state that they are guided by the list of factors in M.R. 1.5(a) and DR 2–106. See discussion of the professional rules below.

In practice, court intervention concerning lawyers' fees is limited to situations where the court believes that the client is in need of special protection. Thus, courts are quick to find fees excessive and reduce them in cases where the client is a minor,[29] poor [30] or a class.[31]

Courts also protect middle-class clients who have had little or no prior experience with lawyers. In Jacobson v. Sassower,[32] for example, the agreement between client and lawyer to handle a divorce provided for an hourly fee of $100 and "a non-refundable retainer of $2,500 (which is not to be affected by any possible reconciliation between myself and my wife). Said retainer is to be credited against your charges...." After the lawyer had completed 10 hours of work on the matter, the client discharged her without cause. The client sued to recover the difference between the retainer of $2,500 and the hourly fee charge of $1,000. The court held for the client, stating:

26. 758 F.2d at 100.

27. Id.

28. See, e.g., Smitas v. Rickett, 102 A.D.2d 928, 477 N.Y.S.2d 752 (1984); Watson v. Cook, 427 So.2d 1312 (La.App.1983); In re LiVolsi, 85 N.J. 576, 428 A.2d 1268 (1981).

29. Hoffert v. General Motors Corp., 656 F.2d 161 (5th Cir.1981) (lawyer voluntarily reduced 40% contingency fee to 33%; court further reduced it to 20%).

30. United States v. Strawser, 800 F.2d 704 (7th Cir.1986) (criminal defense lawyer's fee so high that defendant rendered indigent and therefore unable to hire counsel to pursue appeal).

31. Dunn v. H.K. Porter Co., 602 F.2d 1105 (3d Cir.1979).

32. 66 N.Y.2d 991, 499 N.Y.S.2d 381, 489 N.E.2d 1283 (1985).

In cases of doubt or ambiguity, a contract must be construed most strongly against the party who prepared it, and favorably to a party who had no voice in the selection of its language. Additionally, and as a matter of public policy, courts pay particular attention to fee arrangements between attorneys and their clients. An attorney has the burden of showing that a fee contract is fair, reasonable, and fully known and understood by the client....

This retainer agreement was ambiguous because it did not state clearly that the "non-refundable retainer of $2,500" was intended to be a minimum fee and that the entire sum would be forfeited notwithstanding any event that terminated the attorney-client relationship prior to 25 hours of service. In the absence of such clear language, defendant was required to establish that plaintiff understood that those were the terms of the agreement and she failed to do so. Indeed, defendant does not claim that she explained the nature and consequences of the nonrefundable retainer clause to plaintiff before he executed the contract and the trial judge accepted plaintiff's evidence that he did not understand the payment to be a minimum fee.[33]

Most courts assert that they have a special obligation to scrutinize contingent fee arrangements with unsophisticated clients.[34] "The requirement that the client be fully informed applies especially to a contingent-fee contract.... Contracts for contingent fees generally have a greater potential for overreaching of clients than fixed-fee contracts [and] are closely scrutinized by the courts where there is a question as to their reasonableness." [35]

Professional Rules on Amount of Fee

DR 2–106(A) prohibits a lawyer from contracting, charging or collecting an "illegal or clearly excessive fee." Model Rule 1.5(a) eliminates mention of "excessive" and simply states that "[a] lawyer's fee shall be reasonable." Both DR 2–106 and M.R. 1.5(a) list multiple factors relevant in determining the reasonableness of a fee. The listed items include a smorgasbord of relevant factors. Do these make the criterion of "reasonableness" or "excessiveness" any more definite? For an even more extensive list of factors see Calif.R.Prof. Conduct 4–200(B).

One of the factors to be considered is the customary fee in the locality for similar services. See M.R. 1.5(a)(3) and DR 2–106(B)(3). Minimum fee schedules were once common.[36] In Goldfarb v. Virginia

---

33. 489 N.E.2d at 1284. In a subsequent case, a New York lawyer was disciplined for use of a nonrefundable retainer agreement in matrimonial cases. Matter of Cooperman, 187 A.D.2d 56, 591 N.Y.S.2d 855 (1993).

34. See, e.g., In re Teichner, 104 Ill.2d 150, 83 Ill.Dec. 552, 470 N.E.2d 972 (1984).

35. Committee on Legal Ethics of West Virginia Bar v. Tatterson, 177 W.Va. 356, 352 S.E.2d 107, 113–114 (1986).

36. See Note, A Critical Analysis of Bar Association Minimum Fee Schedules, 85 Harv.L.Rev. 971 (1972).

State Bar,[37] the Supreme Court held these schedules illegal under the antitrust laws.

Discipline for charging an excessive fee is rare but does occur.[38] When discipline is imposed, it is often in cases where the lawyer has engaged in some other misconduct as well, such as misleading the client on the difficulty of the legal matter involved.[39] In *Bushman*, for example, the lawyer was also charged with solicitation.

The necessarily vague criteria in DR 2–106 and M.R. 1.5 raise questions about the fairness of disciplining lawyers for "unreasonable" fees. In Attorney Grievance Commission v. Wright,[40] for example, three lawyers testified that the fee was reasonable and three that it was not. The court described all six lawyers as meeting the standard of DR 2–106, i.e., they were all "lawyer[s] of ordinary prudence." The court held that the disciplinary agency had failed to meet its burden of showing the fee was "clearly excessive."

How Fee Questions Come Before a Court

Whether the lawyer's fee is excessive may come before the court in several ways. The court may be required to approve the fee in connection with a settlement on behalf of a minor or a class. The lawyer may sue the client to recover a fee, as in *Brobeck*, or the client may sue to recover fees already paid, as in *Jacobson*. Fee questions may also be raised in disciplinary proceedings (see the note above), when one party is assessed the other's attorney's fee under a fee-shifting statute[41] or a court rule authorizing sanctions,[42] and in probate and bankruptcy proceedings where the court must approve the award of fees out of an estate or trust.

Beyond those situations, upon a client's complaint a court may review a lawyer's fee in a summary proceeding "without nice regard to jurisdictional, case or controversy, pleading, or other procedural requirements that normally govern suits."[43] In United States v. Vague,[44] however, summary proceedings on the court's own motion were disapproved. In *Vague*, the district judge, troubled by the amount a lawyer had charged a criminal defendant, held a hearing, found the fee excessive and ordered a partial refund. The Seventh Circuit reversed,

---

37. 421 U.S. 773 (1975).

38. See, e.g., Florida State Bar v. Moriber, 314 So.2d 145 (Fla.1975) (lawyer suspended for 45 days for charging an unreasonable and excessive fee).

39. See, e.g., Office of Disciplinary Counsel v. Stinson, 25 Ohio St.3d 130, 495 N.E.2d 434 (1986) (lawyer charged excessive fee, neglected a matter and created false evidence); Myers v. Virginia State Bar, 226 Va. 630, 312 S.E.2d 286 (1984) (lawyer charged excessive fee, misrepresented the amount to the court and misled the client into believing that the court had approved the fee).

40. 306 Md. 93, 507 A.2d 618 (1986).

41. See, e.g., 42 U.S.C. § 1988 (giving courts discretion to award the prevailing party reasonable attorney's fees in federal civil rights actions).

42. E.g., Fed.R.Civ.Proc. 11 (authorizing sanctions, including an award of attorneys' fees, for filing pleadings not supported by the facts or the law).

43. Wolfram, Modern Legal Ethics § 9.1 at 499 (1986). See, e.g., Coffelt v. Shell, 577 F.2d 30 (8th Cir.1978) (trial judge acted on his own motion to reduce lawyer's fee).

44. United States v. Vague, 697 F.2d 805 (7th Cir.1983).

stating it was "a mistake to graft onto a lawsuit an issue that the judge is neither asked nor required to resolve." [45] The trial court exceeded its power in ordering restitution; the judge should have referred the matter to the appropriate bar committee or instituted disciplinary proceedings pursuant to rules of court.

2. Illegal Fees

Illegal fees are prohibited explicitly by DR 2–106(A) and implicitly by Model Rules 1.5(a) and 8.4. Illegal fees include: fees collected by a public official when a statute prohibits the private practice of law while in office; [46] fees above those awarded by the court in cases where the court has exclusive power to decide fees; [47] fees collected for an illegal purpose; [48] and fees above the maximum amount allowed by a statute. Fees that the lawyer knows have been paid with the proceeds of criminal activity have also been considered illegal fees.[49] Whether a lawyer may be required to forfeit such funds under the federal forfeiture statutes is discussed above in Chapter 4 at p. 269.

Statutory Fee Limits

Various federal and state statutes limit the fees a lawyer can charge in particular types of legal work.[50] These limits generally have been upheld by the courts against contentions that they unconstitutionally interfere with the right to counsel and violate separation of powers by infringing upon the court's power to regulate the profession.

Walters v. National Association of Radiation Survivors [51] upheld the $10 fee limit for representing a veteran seeking benefits from the Veterans Administration (VA). The veterans claimed that the fee limit "denied them any realistic opportunity to obtain legal representation in presenting their claims to the VA and hence violated their rights under the Due Process Clause of the Fifth Amendment and under the First Amendment." [52] The Court said the limit furthered Congress' goal of fostering an informal, nonadversarial process that would allow veterans to get their benefits without lawyers. The veterans would have to show that the present lawyerless proceedings of the VA resulted in error in a significant number of cases and that lawyers would improve the pro-

45. Id. at 808. Other cases support the authority of a trial court to consider fee questions on its own initiative. See, e.g., Carlucci v. Piper Aircraft Corp., Inc., 775 F.2d 1440 (11th Cir.1985) (disapproving *Vague*).

46. See State v. Stakes, 227 Kan. 711, 608 P.2d 997 (1980).

47. See In re Crane, 96 Ill.2d 40, 70 Ill.Dec. 220, 449 N.E.2d 94 (1983).

48. In re Connaghan, 613 S.W.2d 626 (Mo.1981) (en banc) (lawyer collected fees to bribe state legislator).

49. See In re Prescott, 271 N.W.2d 822 (Minn.1978).

50. See, e.g., Federal Tort Claims Act, 28 U.S.C. § 2678 (as approved by court with a limit of 25 percent of an award); Social Security Act, 42 U.S.C. § 406 (as approved with a limit of 25 percent of retrospective benefits); and Veterans Benefit Act, 38 U.S.C. § 5904(c) ($10 fee limit).

51. 473 U.S. 305 (1985).

52. 473 U.S. at 308.

cess.[53] Justice Stevens, joined by Justices Brennan and Marshall, dissented, arguing that the "totalitarian" approach of the statute violated due process by denying claimants the "priceless" liberty of effective representation.

The limit was adopted by Congress in 1864 to prevent lawyers from taking advantage of Civil War veterans, but has been continued to maintain a less formal, less expensive, lawyer-free determination of these claims.[54] Efforts to eliminate the fee limit have been unsuccessful, in large part because of the political strength of the national veterans groups, which now provide volunteers to represent veterans before the VA. May Congress constitutionally make this choice? [55]

State statutes placing limits on attorneys fees are also common, for example, worker's compensation laws.[56] Lawyers may be disciplined for violating such limits.[57] Many states have general limits on the percentage lawyers may charge as contingency fees: Some provisions set ceilings on the percentage charged in all personal injury cases; others apply only in medical malpractice cases. See the note at p. 537 below. Exceeding those limits is charging an illegal fee.

Contracting With a Client for Rights to Client's Story

Another prohibited fee arrangement is a contract that gives a lawyer the literary or movie rights to a client's story. See M.R. 1.8(d) and DR 5–104(B). The reason for prohibiting such arrangements is that what makes "good copy" does not necessarily make a good defense. The movie rights, for example, may be worth more if the client receives the death penalty than if sentenced to a twenty-year term. Another problem with such arrangements is the broad advance waiver of client

---

53. On remand the trial court held that plaintiffs had met the required showing and that the $10 cap was unconstitutional as applied to this group of veterans; on appeal, the Ninth Circuit reversed, holding that the district court had misconstrued *Walters*. National Assn. of Radiation Survivors v. Derwinski, 994 F.2d 583, (9th Cir.1992), rev'g, 782 F.Supp. 1392 (N.D.Cal.1992). Statutory modifications of the VA legislation in 1988 permit limited judicial review of VA determinations and allow paid representation on appeal.

54. See Paul C. Weiler et al., Reporters' Study, Enterprise Responsibility for Personal Injury, v. 1, c. 13 (American Law Institute, Apr. 15, 1991) (about 95 percent of social security funds are paid out in benefits; 70–80 percent of workers' compensation costs are actually received by injured workers; but the tort system delivers less than 50 percent of insurance fund dollars to injured plaintiffs). Alternative dispute resolution is a fashionable topic and is relevant here. See Jethro Lieberman and James Henry, Lessons from the Alternate Dispute Resolution Movement, 53 U.Chi.L.Rev. 424 (1986).

55. The Black Lung Benefits Act is another federal law restricting legal fees in administrative proceedings. In Committee on Legal Ethics v. Triplett, 180 W.Va. 533, 378 S.E.2d 82 (1988), rev'd sub nom. United States Dep't of Labor v. Triplett, 494 U.S. 715 (1990), a lawyer was charged with engaging in conduct "involving dishonesty, fraud, deceit or misrepresentation," see DR 1–102(A)(4) and M.R. 8.4(c), for collecting a fee not authorized by the Act (collecting 25 percent of the award from clients although the Act requires request and administrative approval of fees). A West Virginia holding held that these provisions violated due process was reversed on appeal.

56. See Mack v. City of Minneapolis, 333 N.W.2d 744 (Minn.1983) (noting that almost all worker's compensation laws impose limits on attorney's fees).

57. Louisiana State Bar Association v. Thalheim, 504 So.2d 822 (La.1987); Hudock v. Virginia State Bar, 233 Va. 390, 355 S.E.2d 601 (1987).

confidences that they imply. See *von Bulow II*, discussed above in Chapter 4 at p. 277.

The reasons for prohibiting these contracts apply with equal force when the lawyer contracts with a third party to produce a book, movie or other portrayal based on information relating to the representation. M.R. 1.8(d) extends the prohibition to cover these third party contracts. Cases coming before the courts have involved convicted defendants seeking to have their convictions overturned. The claim is that the contract created a conflict of interest for the lawyer that resulted in ineffective assistance of counsel. Courts usually respond by criticizing the contract but upholding the conviction.[58]

In Maxwell v. Superior Court of Los Angeles,[59] however, the California Supreme Court held that the defendant's constitutional right to counsel gave him the right to transfer the rights to his story to his lawyer in exchange for legal representation as long as he did so knowingly, voluntarily and after full disclosure by counsel of the risks and benefits involved in such a deal. Many of the laws that limit the extent to which a criminal defendant may profit from the story of her crime were struck down as violative of the first amendment in the "Son of Sam" case.[60]

3. Fee Disputes

Fee Division and Referral Fees

Consider the following situation: A person seriously injured by a manufactured product consults a lawyer acquaintance, a general practitioner, and signs a one-third contingency fee agreement in which the lawyer agrees to handle the client's product liability claim against the manufacturer. The lawyer has had no prior experience in product liability litigation but has represented the client's family on other matters in the past. When the lawyer's efforts to negotiate an adequate settlement fail, she obtains the client's agreement to a new retainer agreement providing that the one-third contingency fee will be split between the lawyer and a products-liability trial specialist who will handle the trial. The trial lawyer obtains a substantial verdict and then refuses to split it with the forwarding lawyer on the grounds that he performed the bulk of the work and that the fee-splitting arrangement is unenforceable because it violates the ethics rules. In an action to enforce the fee agreement, what result?

---

58. See, e.g., United States v. Marrera, 768 F.2d 201 (7th Cir.1985) (the contract alone is insufficient to show ineffective assistance of counsel); Dumond v. State, 294 Ark. 379, 743 S.W.2d 779 (1988). Cf. People v. Corona, 80 Cal.App.3d 684, 145 Cal.Rptr. 894 (1978) (conviction reversed because of counsel's gross neglect of basic duties and failure to develop key defenses; an alternate ground for reversal was that the literary contract between lawyer and client created an impermissible conflict of interest).

59. 30 Cal.3d 606, 180 Cal.Rptr. 177, 639 P.2d 248 (1982).

60. Simon & Schuster, Inc. v. Members of New York State Crime Victims Bd., 112 S.Ct. 501 (1991).

Fee splitting is an issue on which the legal profession tends to say one thing and to do something else. DR 2–107(A) of the Model Code permits fee sharing only if: (1) the client consents to employment of the other lawyer after a disclosure that the client's fee payment will be split; (2) the fee is divided "in proportion to the services performed and responsibilities assumed" by each lawyer; and (3) the total amount of the fee is not unreasonable for the total amount of legal services rendered. The hypothetical, based on the facts of McNeary v. American Cyanamid Co.,[61] satisfies (1) and (3) but not (2), unless the forwarding lawyer has performed roughly one-half of the total work. Perhaps because forwarding arrangements such as that in the *McNeary* case are extremely common, professional discipline for violation of the fee-sharing prohibition is very rare and most courts enforce the fee agreement against arguments that it is an illegal contract violative of public policy.[62] Some courts, taking the restrictions on fee sharing more seriously, enforce the fee-sharing agreement only if the forwarding lawyer has performed work substantially proportionate to the share provided by the fee agreement.[63]

Plaintiffs' trial lawyers support broad enforcement of fee-sharing arrangements. At a 1978 ATLA conference, the conferees, finding that DR 2–107(A)'s prohibition was "flagrantly violated" by lawyers and "does little good," concluded that fee splitting "work[s] in a client's best interest by giving lawyers the incentive to refer their contingent fee clients to the most competent attorneys." [64]

Model Rule 1.5(e) subsequently relaxed the procedures for fee splitting. First, the share of each lawyer need not reflect the respective amounts of services performed if "by written agreement with the client, each lawyer assumes joint responsibility for the representation." Second, the provision for client disclosure and consent is more perfunctory than under DR 2–107(A)(1). The client need be advised only of "the participation of all the lawyers involved" and "not object." M.R. 1.5(e) does not require that the client be informed of the fact of fee splitting or its size, nor, as in the Model Code, a disclosure of how work is to be shared.

Professor Wolfram argues that "[f]orwarding is justifiable on public policy grounds only if it enhances the ability of a client to receive

---

61. 105 Wn.2d 136, 712 P.2d 845 (1986).

62. See, e.g., Oberman v. Reilly, 66 A.D.2d 686, 687, 411 N.Y.S.2d 23, 25 (1978) ("an agreement between attorneys for division of a legal fee is valid and is enforceable ... provided that the attorney who seeks his share of the fee contributed some work, labor or service toward the earning of the fee"—a circumstance that is almost invariably the case).

63. See, e.g., Belli v. Shaw, 98 Wn.2d 569, 657 P.2d 315 (1983) (a fee forwarding agreement that violates DR 2–107(A), because the bulk of the work was performed by the lawyer who tried the case, was unenforceable as against public policy). But compare *McNeary*, supra, holding that when both lawyers perform very substantial amounts of work the fee agreement should be enforced as written.

64. Roscoe Pound–American Trial Lawyers Foundation, Annual Chief Justice Earl Warren Conference on Advocacy in the United States, Ethics and Advocacy 16–18 (1978).

superior legal service." [65] He argues that clients should be given full information about who will handle their matters and how the fees will be divided, permitting clients "to shop for a better division of fees and responsibilities among other lawyers." [66]

Fee Arbitration [67]

The Comment to Model Rule 1.5 provides: "If a procedure has been established for resolution of fee disputes, such as an arbitration or mediation procedure established by the bar, the lawyer should conscientiously consider submitting to it."

No state requires a client to arbitrate a fee dispute, presumably because such a rule would violate the client's constitutional right to a jury trial. But some require the lawyer to arbitrate if the client requests it. Anderson v. Elliott [68] upheld a Maine bar rule requiring lawyers to arbitrate fee claims at the client's request. The court rejected the claim that the rule violated the lawyer's right to a jury trial, stressing "the uniqueness of the attorney's relation to the court and to the client." [69]

Should the courts enforce a contract between lawyer and client that requires the client to submit to arbitration in the event of a fee dispute? Once a lawyer and client submit to arbitration should the result be binding? In California neither party is bound if either appeals the decision, unless there is a prior agreement to be bound. In New Jersey both parties are bound.

A Massachusetts decision considers a client's attack on a bar-sponsored arbitration procedure.[70] The client appeared without counsel before an arbitration board composed only of lawyers. In going without a lawyer, the client had relied on information provided by bar association staff and publications stating that "these proceedings are informal." The court reversed the board's award of the total fee claimed by the lawyer on two grounds: The information provided the client did not adequately inform her of her rights to appeal; and the arbitration proceedings were not adequately described to her. The court stated:

> There is nothing inherently wrong with encouraging self-representation by clients. Nevertheless, a client who is unsophisticated in legal proceedings and is not given an adequate advance understanding of the hearing may well be intimidated by being virtually the only nonattorney present. Since such a person also lacks the

---

65. Wolfram, Modern Legal Ethics 513 (1986).

66. Id. at 511.

67. See James R. Devine, Mandatory Arbitration of Attorney–Client Fee Dispute: A Concept Whose Time Has Come, 14 U.Toledo L.Rev. 1205 (1986) (summarizing the various state procedures and enforcement mechanisms).

68. 555 A.2d 1042 (Me.1989).

69. Id. at 1047. Also see In re LiVolsi, 85 N.J. 576, 428 A.2d 1268 (1981); and Kelley Drye & Warren v. Murray Indus., Inc., 623 F.Supp. 522 (D.N.J.1985) (both upholding New Jersey's client-initiated mandatory fee arbitration system).

70. Marino v. Tagaris, 395 Mass. 397, 480 N.E.2d 286 (1985).

legal background to know the factors relevant in mounting a successful challenge to the ... fee, this might lead to a *perception* by the client that she is on an unequal footing with the attorney.[71]

These problems, the court concluded, could be cured by fully informing the client in advance of the nature of the proceedings. What information should be provided? Does the client need to be told that bringing a lawyer would be helpful? If so, what is the advantage that arbitration has for the client over a lawsuit? Can the proceedings be made "informal" in a lay person's understanding of that word? Would non-lawyers on the panel cure the problem? Is the disparity of the parties' positions in bar-sponsored arbitration "a perception" problem or a reality? Some bar associations include lay persons on their arbitration panels.

Client Confidentiality in Fee Disputes

A lawyer may reveal client confidences to collect a fee or establish a defense in a dispute with the client over the fee. See M.R. 1.6(b)(2) and DR 4–101(C)(4) and the discussion of this issue in Chapter 4 above. The Comment to M.R. 1.6 explains:

> A lawyer entitled to a fee is permitted by paragraph (b)(2) to prove the services rendered in an action to collect it. This aspect of the rule expresses the principle that the beneficiary of a fiduciary relationship may not exploit it to the detriment of the fiducia-ry.... [T]he lawyer must make every effort practicable to avoid unnecessary disclosure of information relating to a representation, to limit disclosure to those having the need to know it, and to obtain protective orders or make other arrangements minimizing the risk of disclosure.

Should a lawyer advise a client that confidential information may be disclosed if the client proceeds to challenge the lawyer's fee?[72]

4. Contingent Fees

In a contingent fee arrangement the lawyer is compensated only if a positive result is obtained for the client—the fee is contingent on the result. A contingent fee is usually calculated as a percentage of the client's recovery, but a contract calling for the lawyer to receive a fixed amount if the client prevailed is also a contingent fee contract. In most personal injury cases, the plaintiff's lawyer's fee is contingent, but contingent fees are not limited to personal injury work.[73] Contingent fees are common in tax refund practice, condemnation proceedings, suits challenging wills, debt collection cases and class action suits for damages.

---

71. 480 N.E.2d at 289–90. (Emphasis in original.)

72. See Lindenbaum v. State Bar, 26 Cal.2d 565, 160 P.2d 9 (1945) (improper to threaten client with disclosure).

73. See Boston & Maine Corp. v. Sheehan, Phinney, Bass & Green, 778 F.2d 890 (1st Cir.1985) (contingent fee in an eminent domain case).

Although contingent fee arrangements are common for a plaintiff, they are sometimes used in civil cases by a defendant. In *Brobeck*, supra, p. 531, for example, Telex was in the position of a defendant with respect to the counterclaims against it.[74] In Wunschel Law Firm P.C. v. Clabaugh,[75] the court held invalid a contingent fee contract by a defendant in a tort damages case that calculated the defense lawyer's fee as a percentage of the difference between the amount of the plaintiff's prayer for relief and the amount actually recovered by the plaintiff. The court reasoned that a prayer is often exaggerated for strategic purposes; that it is misleading to suggest that the difference between the prayer and actual recovery is due to the defense lawyer's skills; and that a reasonable client adequately informed would not agree to a fee calculated on this basis.

Contingent fees in this country originally were considered illegal as a form of champerty.[76] They are still prohibited in Great Britain and many other countries, although in 1991 the Lord Chancellor put forward a "cautious" proposal for the introduction of contingent fees. The proposal would permit a contingent fee of 10 percent in personal injury cases only.[77] In the United States, contingent fees are now universally accepted; Maine, the last state to accept contingent fees, lifted its prohibition in 1965. At first, acceptance was grudging—contingent fees were disreputable although not illegal.[78] The disrepute was based on two fears: that lawyers would be tempted to use illegal or unethical means to win judgments, for example, manufacturing evidence or bringing frivolous suits in the hopes of coercing a settlement; and that lawyers would put their own interests before those of the client, e.g., settling a case early, thereby guaranteeing the lawyer the greatest return for the smallest amount of work, when the client would be better served by pursuing the matter through trial. Contingent fees are still prohibited in some types of cases, notably divorce and criminal work. See the notes below at p. 534.

Contingent fees are most often justified as a necessary means of broadening access to justice, allowing those otherwise unable to afford counsel to obtain representation in the courts. They are often referred

74. See also Dunham v. Bentley, 103 Iowa 136, 72 N.W. 437 (1897) (defendant agreed to pay 30 percent of her interest in any estate property that the lawyer successfully protected from creditor's claims).

75. 291 N.W.2d 331 (Iowa 1980).

76. See Note, Lawyer's Tight Rope—Use and Abuse of Fees, 41 Cornell L.Q. 683, 685–6 (1956); and Max Radin, Maintenance by Champerty, 24 Calif.L.Rev. 48 (1935).

77. See David Pannick, "No Win, No Fee," No Case Against, London Times, July 9, 1991. The Lord Chancellor's 1989 green paper, "Contingency Fees," noted that such fees had been permitted in Scotland without abuse and recommended their use in personal injury actions in England and Wales. Legislation in 1990 made conditional fees lawful subject to an implementing order by the Lord Chancellor. Permission to use a 10 percent fee in personal injury cases became effective in October 1992. Other types of cases, such as libel actions and commercial cases, may be added in the future, the Lord Chancellor has said, "depending on the outcome of the initial working of this section."

78. See, e.g., Rooney v. Second Avenue R.R., 18 N.Y. 368 (1858). See generally Frederick B. MacKinnon, Contingent Fees (1964).

to as "the poor man's key to the courthouse door." [79]   In countries that prohibit contingent fees, lawyers are paid by public funds to represent indigent civil litigants.   What is wrong with that solution?

The courts generally will enforce a contingent-fee agreement in customary form between parties who bargained and contracted. Unusual agreements, however, are scrutinized and those thought to be unfair are not enforced. Compare *Brobeck* with *McKenzie Construction,* discussed above at p. 519.

The courts give closer scrutiny to contingent fee arrangements when the client is unsophisticated, particularly if the contingent fee is substantial and the work legally elementary.[80] The court on its own motion may review a contingent fee arrangement, at least if the client is entitled to special protection of the court.[81]

Continuing Criticism of Contingent Fees

Criticism of contingent fees continues. The argument that they encourage frivolous suits is still used: "The legislature may also have imposed limits on contingency fees in [medical malpractice cases] as a means of deterring attorneys from either instituting frivolous suits or encouraging their clients to hold out for unrealistically high settlements." [82] The court found such a rationale reasonable and upheld the limits.

Another criticism is that contingency fees create inevitable conflicts between the interests of lawyer and client. The rationale for this criticism is that a plaintiff's lawyer has an economic incentive to settle a claim relatively quickly on the basis of a limited amount of work. Because a lawyer cannot be indifferent to the amount of time spent on a case, the interests of the lawyer and client diverge to a degree.[83] Douglas Rosenthal states:

> Faced with an economic crunch, even after weeding out the thin cases and utilizing economies of specialization, the ethical and competent attorney has four realistic options for proceeding with the claim: (1) He can cut corners in preparing the case. (2) He can build his fee by charging disbursements to the client. (3) He can

79. See, e.g., Arnold v. Northern Trust Co., 116 Ill. 157, 107 Ill.Dec. 224, 506 N.E.2d 1279, 1281 (1987); Matter of Swartz, 141 Ariz. 266, 686 P.2d 1236, 1242 (1984).

80. See, e.g., Randolph v. Schuyler, 284 N.C. 496, 201 S.E.2d 833 (1974).

81. See, e.g., Schlesinger v. Teitelbaum, 475 F.2d 137 (3d Cir.1973) (client was a seaman); Cappel v. Adams, 434 F.2d 1278 (5th Cir.1970) (clients were children); Dunn v. H.K. Porter Co., 602 F.2d 1105 (3d Cir.1979) (class action suits).

82. Roa v. Lodi Medical Group, Inc., 37 Cal.3d 920, 211 Cal.Rptr. 77, 695 P.2d 164, 170–71 (1985).

83. See Douglas E. Rosenthal, Lawyer and Client: Who's in Charge? 96–112 (1974): "The widespread assumption that the contingent fee makes the lawyer a 'partner' of the client in his claim with complete mutuality of interest in the ultimate case disposition is, in dollars and cents, simply not true." See also Kevin M. Clermont and John D. Currivan, Improving on the Contingent Fee, 63 Cornell L.Rev. 529 (1987) (proposing a fee agreement contingent on a positive recovery but including an hourly rate component as a way to align the economic interests of lawyer and client).

persuade the client that a discounted early settlement is in his best interest. (4) He can bring the existing interest conflict to the client's attention and negotiate a compromise claims strategy. . . . The first three of these options for making the economics of representation feasible put the lawyer in direct conflict with his client's interest—without making the client aware of the fact.[84]

Rosenthal concludes that "most attorneys employ the device of preparing the client to accept less than he anticipates and persuading him that it is in his best interest to do so—'cooling the client out.'" The actual behavior of lawyers in frequently sacrificing client interests for self-interest is concealed by the profession's rhetoric. Rosenthal quotes Erving Goffman:

> Performers often foster the impression that they have ideal motives . . . and ideal qualifications for the role and that it was not necessary for them to suffer any indignities, insults, and humiliations, or make any tacitly understood "deals" in order to acquire the role. . . . Reinforcing these ideal impressions there is a kind of "rhetoric of training" whereby . . . licensing bodies require practitioners to absorb a mystical range and period of training, in part to maintain a monopoly, but in part to foster the impression that the licensed practitioner is someone who has been reconstituted by his learning experience and is now set apart from other men.[85]

Do the provisions of Model Rule 1.7(b), which require consent after full disclosure, adequately deal with the problems raised by Rosenthal? What information should a lawyer provide under M.R. 1.7(b) before advising the client to accept an early settlement of a claim covered by a contingent fee contract?

Contingent fees are also criticized as a means to charge excessive fees to unwitting clients. The theory of a contingent fee is that a lawyer will agree to assume the risk of no fee in exchange for the chance to make more than in a fixed fee situation, assuming the client prevails. The problem is that lawyers have superior knowledge of the risks involved. Critics contend that many of the cases in which lawyers charge the customary one-third of recovery are cases where recovery is for all practical purposes assured.[86]

Judicial decisions set aside contingent fee agreements in those situations in which the facts indicate a lawyer faces no risk, such as

---

84. Rosenthal, supra, at 106.

85. Erving Goffman, The Presentation of Self in Everyday Life 46 (1959), quoted in Rosenthal, supra, at 112.

86. Rosenthal's study finds that personal injury lawyers screen their cases carefully and that "[l]awyers at the top of their profession . . . can afford to turn down all cases in which the liability is not near-perfect and in which the anticipated recovery at trial is less than five figures." Rosenthal, supra, at 99. Judge Grady, for example, says: "[A]t least 95 percent of the total claims handled by lawyers are settled before trial, and many of these settlements involve very little work on the part of the lawyer. . . . Many lawyers handle a large volume of personal injury claims without ever trying one. They have no losers to balance because they settle every case." John Grady, Some Ethical Questions About Percentage Fees, Litigation (Summer 1976) at 24–25.

when a client is clearly due a sum under an insurance policy.[87] In West Virginia State Bar v. Tatterson,[88] the court upheld discipline of a lawyer who had charged a one-third contingency fee for settling a claim to life insurance proceeds due a client upon her husband's death: "In the absence of any real risk, an attorney's purportedly contingent fee which is grossly disproportionate to the amount of work required is a 'clearly excessive fee'...."

Professional Rules on Contingent Fees

Model Rule 1.5(c) specifically authorizes contingency fees where not prohibited by 1.5(d) or other law, but requires that all contingency fees be in writing.[89] Under M.R. 1.5(c), the writing must include:

> the method by which the fee is to be determined, including the percentage or percentages that shall accrue to the lawyer in the event of settlement, trial or appeal, litigation, and other expenses to be deducted from the recovery, and whether such expenses are to be deducted before or after the contingent fee is calculated.

M.R. 1.5(c) also requires the lawyer to provide the client with a written statement upon completion of the representation detailing the outcome, the client's share, the lawyer's share and how the division of proceeds was calculated

Should the rules require that all fee contracts be in writing? That the lawyer relate the proposed fee to the factors specified in M.R. 1.5(a)? As proposed by the Kutak Commission and as adopted in some states, Rule 1.5(b) provides: "When the lawyer has not regularly represented the client, the basis or rate of the fee shall be communicated to the client in writing, before or within a reasonable time after commencing the representation." The ABA's version of M.R. 1.5(b) says such an agreement shall be "preferably in writing."

Divorce Cases

The rationale for prohibiting contingent fees in divorce cases is that it contravenes the strong public interest in preserving marriages because such a fee may interfere with reconciliation.[90] Divorce itself used to be regarded as against public policy except in very limited situations and in many states could be obtained only upon proof of criminal misconduct or adultery. A contingent fee was considered an

---

87. See, e.g., Harmon v. Pugh, 38 N.C.App. 438, 248 S.E.2d 421 (1978) (20 percent of life insurance payment is excessive when lawyer's service consisted of writing to get medical information and autopsy report).

88. 177 W.Va. 356, 352 S.E.2d 107, 113–14 (1986).

89. Contingent fees are given little specific attention by the Model Code. DR 5–103(A)(2) allows them as an exception to the general prohibition to acquiring a propriety interest in litigation; DR 2–106(B)(8) says that whether a fee is contingent or fixed should be a factor in considering its reasonableness; and DR 2–106(C) prohibits them in criminal defense work. EC 2–20 states that they are "rarely justified" in domestic relations cases.

90. See, e.g., Florida Bar v. Winn, 208 So.2d 809 (Fla.1968); In re Fisher, 15 Ill.2d 139, 153 N.E.2d 832 (1958); Baskerville v. Baskerville, 246 Minn. 496, 75 N.W.2d 762 (1956); McCarthy v. Santangelo, 137 Conn. 410, 78 A.2d 240 (1951).

unduly dangerous inducement to legal dissolution of marriage. The prohibition undoubtedly worked to the detriment of women, who in the typical marriage held little property or income-producing capacity and therefore lacked means to pay a fixed fee. In most marriages, this meant the male partner had greater freedom to dissolve the relationship and was at less financial risk in doing so than he would otherwise have been. On the other hand, a contingent fee deters the lawyer from facilitating reconciliation, for that would eliminate the division of property from which the fee could be paid. Moreover, in most jurisdictions the impecunious spouse, still usually the wife, can require the other party to pay attorneys' fees, including a part payment at the beginning of the litigation.[91] Is reconciliation generally a good to be encouraged?

The interest in encouraging reconciliation does not explain cases that disallow contingent fees in actions to modify or enforce divorce agreements.[92] If a lawyer takes a divorce case on a contingent basis, most states allow the lawyer to recover on the basis of quantum meruit.[93] A number of commentators have criticized the prohibition of contingent fees in divorce cases.[94]

Criminal Defense Work

Contingent fees for defending criminal cases have traditionally been prohibited, although the reasons for doing so have been criticized.[95] Because a damage award is not created by a defense lawyer's efforts and winning a criminal case does not ordinarily increase the client's assets, a fee contingent on success would rarely be a necessary means to employ private counsel. Unless carefully drafted, a contingent-fee agreement for criminal representation might affect the client's choice in accepting a plea bargain or risking a trial. Defense lawyers, who generally prefer advance payment of a flat fee, have not pushed for permission to employ contingent fees. Finally, some fear that contingent fees would promote unscrupulous representation. Is overzealous misconduct more likely in criminal than in civil cases?

All states prohibit contingent fees for the defense of a criminal case. If a defense lawyer employs a contingent fee, the fee agreement is unenforceable but the illegality of the fee arrangement is not enough

91. See Wolfram, Modern Legal Ethics § 9.4.4 (1986). Compare Marriage of Gonzales, 51 Cal.App.3d 340, 124 Cal.Rptr. 278 (1975).

92. See, e.g., Licciardi v. Collins, 180 Ill.App.3d 1051, 129 Ill.Dec. 790, 536 N.E.2d 840 (1989) (contingent fee unethical and therefore void in action to modify a divorce decree seven years after its entry).

93. See *Baskerville* supra. But see *Licciardi*, supra (no *quantum meruit* recovery).

94. For an argument that contingent fees should be allowed in divorce cases, see Comment, Professional Responsibility—Contingent Fees in Domestic Relations Actions: Equal Freedom to Contract for the Domestic Relations Bar, 62 N.C.L.Rev. 381 (1984).

95. See, e.g., ALI Proposed Restatement of the Law Governing Lawyers, § 47, Comment c(i), Tent. Draft No. 4, Apr. 10, 1991, at 219–20 (although black-letter rule continues the traditional ban on contingent fees in criminal cases, the comment states that "the reasons for doing so are on balance unpersuasive" and argues that permitting contingent fee arrangements "would promote effective assistance of counsel").

to establish a claim for ineffective assistance of counsel in a postconviction proceeding for a new trial.[96]   In Schoonover v. Kansas,[97] although the trial judge refused the defendant a new trial, he referred the lawyer to the state bar, which imposed discipline.[98]

Stronger arguments support a ban on financial arrangements that would make the compensation of prosecutors dependent upon success. A lawyer whose pay depends on securing a conviction will be tempted to prize convictions more than justice.[99]   A prosecutor has special obligations to see that justice is done.[1]   Does a similar argument justify prohibiting contingent fees for defense lawyers?

Public Litigation

Should contingent fees be prohibited for lawyers retained by governmental bodies to enforce civil claims?   Does this situation invoke the same policies that lead to prohibition of contingent fees in criminal cases?   Government employment of lawyers on a contingent fee basis has generated few cases, probably because full-time government lawyers are compensated on a salary basis so the issue of contingent fees does not arise.   But the practice of hiring private lawyers to prosecute governmental claims may be growing.   The federal agencies seeking to recover from those responsible for savings-and-loan failures have employed numerous private law firms, paying out million of dollars per year in fees.   A contingent-fee arrangement with the Cravath firm, calling for premium billing of up to $600 per hour in successful cases, has been criticized.[2]

The California Supreme Court held that a contingent fee is improper in any category of government civil cases "that demands the representative of the government be absolutely neutral."[3]   The category

96.   See, e.g., People v. Winkler, 71 N.Y.2d 592, 528 N.Y.S.2d 360, 523 N.E.2d 485 (1988); Downs v. Florida, 453 So.2d 1102 (Fla.1984); Schoonover v. Kansas, 218 Kan. 377, 543 P.2d 881 (1975).   But see United States ex rel. Simon v. Murphy, 349 F.Supp. 818 (E.D.Pa.1972) (new trial granted where counsel represented defendant on contingent fee basis, which provided no fee if a guilty plea was entered, and counsel failed to communicate in a timely fashion to defendant the prosecutor's offer of a plea bargain to a lesser offense and persistently advised defendant not to plead guilty).

97.   218 Kan. 377, 543 P.2d 881 (1975).

98.   In re Steere, 217 Kan. 271, 536 P.2d 54 (1975).

99.   See Young v. United States ex rel. Vuitton et Fils S.A., 481 U.S. 787 (1987) (appointment of lawyers who represented plaintiffs in the private action from which this contempt prosecution emerged was improper because of their interest in the matter).

1.   See Model Rule 3.8 on the Special Responsibilities of a Prosecutor and the Comment; and Standard 3–1.1, ABA Standards Relating to the Administration of Criminal Justice (Prosecution Function).   Contingent fees encourage prosecutions based on the likelihood of conviction regardless of whether the conviction would be just.

2.   See Marianne Lavelle, Cravath S & L Fees Under Fire, Nat'l L.J., Apr. 20, 1992, at p. 3: "[Six Democratic senators calling for renegotiation of the fee arrangement] say that Cravath stands to earn more than $80 million under its current agreement with the Federal Deposit Insurance Corp., under which senior partners will earn bonus compensation amounting to $600 per hour."

3.   People ex rel. Clancy v. Superior Court of Riverside County, 39 Cal.3d 740, 218 Cal.Rptr. 24, 705 P.2d 347, 352 (1985).

includes eminent domain actions and actions to abate a public nuisance.[4] Is the same policy applicable to "private attorney general" actions brought under fee-shifting statutes, such as those applicable to civil rights, consumer and environmental claims?

Contingent Fee Schedules

A number of states have enacted so-called "tort reform legislation" as a means of curbing tort suits. These statutes typically prescribe maximum fee schedules for lawyers. In some states, for example New Jersey and New York, the maximum fee schedules apply to all personal injury cases handled on a contingent basis; in others, the fee schedules are limited to a particular type of suit, most commonly medical malpractice.

The fee schedules vary in detail but generally provide a descending sliding scale. For example, in California the plaintiff's lawyer in a medical malpractice case may charge no more than: 40 percent of the first $50,000 of client's recovery; 33 1/3 percent of the next $50,000; 25 percent of the next $500,000; and 15 percent of any amount exceeding $600,000.[5] Florida's limits on attorney's fees in medical malpractice actions permit a larger percentage in later stages of pursuing a claim (e.g., 40 percent after the jury is sworn), but restrict the contingency fee to 15 percent of any recovery in excess of $2 million.[6]

Some federal laws specify a single maximum percentage fee no matter how large the client's recovery. For example, the Federal Tort Claims Act allows fees no greater than 25 percent of any recovery once a case has been filed and 20 percent of any recovery prior to filing. The schedule encourages lawyers to file suit to gain a greater part of the recovery. What incentives do the California and Florida systems provide?

The courts generally have upheld these fee schedules whether they apply only to medical malpractice cases or more broadly.[7] But some decisions have struck down legislative fee arrangements applicable only to medical malpractice.[8]

---

4. 39 Cal.3d at 749.

5. California Medical Injury Compensation Reform Act of 1975 (MICRA), Calif.Bus. and Prof.Code § 6146.

6. Fla.Stat. § 766.109 (1988 Supp.).

7. See, e.g., Bernier v. Burris, 113 Ill.2d 219, 100 Ill.Dec. 585, 497 N.E.2d 763 (1986) (medical malpractice only); Roa v. Lodi Medical Group, Inc., 37 Cal.3d 920, 211 Cal.Rptr. 77, 695 P.2d 164 (1985) (same); Johnson v. St. Vincent Hospital, Inc., 273 Ind. 374, 404 N.E.2d 585 (1980) (same); American Trial Lawyers v. New Jersey Supreme Court, 66 N.J. 258, 330 A.2d 350 (1974) (all personal injury cases); and Gair v. Peck, 6 N.Y.2d 97, 188 N.Y.S.2d 491, 160 N.E.2d 43 (1959) (same).

8. See Carson v. Maurer, 120 N.H. 925, 424 A.2d 825 (1980) (statute limiting plaintiffs' rights in medical malpractice cases and imposing a fee schedule for such actions held unconstitutional); Heller v. Frankston, 504 Pa. 528, 475 A.2d 1291 (1984) (statute requiring arbitration of medical malpractice claims and limiting attorney's fees in such cases unconstitutional).

In sustaining a maximum fee schedule, the Florida court in In re Florida Bar,[9] also provided that a client may cancel any contingent contract within three days of its execution and required lawyers to provide clients with an elaborate statement of their rights:

STATEMENT OF CLIENT'S RIGHTS

Before you, the prospective client, arrange a contingency fee agreement with a lawyer, you should understand this Statement of your rights as a client. This Statement is not part of the actual contract between you and your lawyer, but as a prospective client, you should be aware of these rights:

1.   There is no legal requirement that a lawyer charge a client a set fee or percentage of money recovered in a case. You, the client, have the right to talk with the lawyer about the proposed fee and to bargain about the rate or percentage as in any other contract. If you do not reach an agreement with one lawyer you may talk with other lawyers. . . .

3.   Before hiring a lawyer, you, the client, have the right to know about the lawyer's education, training and experience. If you ask, the lawyer should tell you specifically about his or her actual experience dealing with cases similar to yours. If you ask, the lawyer should provide information about special training or knowledge and give you this information in writing if you request it.

4.   Before signing a contingency fee contract with you, a lawyer must advise you whether he or she intends to handle your case alone or whether other lawyers will be helping with the case. If your lawyer intends to refer the case to other lawyers he or she should tell you what kind of fee sharing arrangement will be made with the other lawyers. If lawyers from different law firms will represent you, at least one lawyer from each firm must sign the contingency fee contract. . . .

7.   You, the client, have the right to be told by your lawyer about possible adverse consequences if you lose the case. Those adverse consequences might include money which you might have to pay to your lawyer for costs, and liability you might have for attorney's fees to the other side. . . .

10.   You, the client, have the right to make the final decision regarding settlement of a case. Your lawyer must notify you of all offers of settlement before and after the trial. Offers during the trial must be immediately communicated and you should consult with your lawyer regarding whether to accept a settlement. However, you must make the final decision to accept or reject a settlement. . . .

9.   494 So.2d 960, 964 (Fla.1986).

Why is such a statement required only in contingent fee cases? Compare M.R. 1.5. The Florida statement has 11 paragraphs. Would it be more understandable if it covered fewer eventualities and were a lot shorter? Does a client need a lawyer to deal with her lawyer? Why not?

Structured Settlements

Large personal injury claims may be resolved by a "structured settlement." Essentially, this is a plan of payments over time instead of full cash payment. Typically, the plan calls for substantial cash up front, in contemplation that this will be used to pay the lawyer's contingent fee share, and an annuity to provide periodic payments to the claimant over a term of years. A structured settlement involves a major investment decision and inherent conflict between the lawyer and the client. Questions can arise whether the lawyer adequately counselled the client about the investment aspects of a settlement and about the existence and implications of the conflict between them.[10]

D. WHO SHOULD PAY FOR LITIGATION?

1. The American Rule and Its Alternatives [11]

The American rule is that each litigant must absorb her own litigation expenses, including attorney's fees. The "costs" typically awarded to prevailing parties do not begin to cover the actual costs of litigation, of which attorney's fees are the largest component. The origins of the American rule are obscure but apparently were a reaction by lawyers and judges to legislative fee limitations in the nineteenth century.[12]

Throughout most of the civilized world a prevailing litigant, whether plaintiff or defendant, recovers reasonable legal fees and other litigation expenses. This position on litigation expenses, referred to in the United States as the English rule, has origins in Roman law. The English rule (two-way fee shifting in favor of the prevailing party, or "loser pays") rests primarily on considerations of reparative justice: A successful party should be made whole by recovering the expenses necessarily entailed in vindicating a just claim or defense. This indemnity argument is supported in some instances by a punishment argument: A losing party who, by failing to settle a just claim or abandon a meritless one, has caused the winning party to spend money on legal

---

10. For a case involving malpractice liability in mishandling a structured settlement, see Perez v. Pappas, 98 Wn.2d 835, 659 P.2d 475 (1983). See also Larry R. Meyer, Settling in Your Client's Interest, Calif.Lawyer, July, 1988, at p. 53.

11. See Wolfram, Modern Legal Ethics § 16.6 (1986), for a good introduction to this topic.

12. John Leubsdorf, Toward a History of the American Rule on Attorney Fee Recovery, 47 Law & Contemp.Probs. 9 (1984) (arguing that anti-lawyer sentiment expressed in limitations on awardable "costs" gave rise to the rule that parties were liable for their own attorney fees, thus separating fees from the award of costs).

fees should be punished by reimbursing the costs of the opposing party. Utilitarian arguments are also advanced on behalf of two-way fee shifting: Frivolous or vexatious litigation should be discouraged (a deterrence argument) and dilatory tactics should be penalized.

The American rule, however, is deeply entrenched and efforts to dislodge it on rightness or consequentialist grounds have failed repeatedly.[13] Arguments in favor of the American rule include the following:

- *Fairness.* The outcome of litigation is highly uncertain, especially in the United States, where law is more malleable and the application of law to fact more unpredictable than it is in England and many other countries. If a jury trial can be characterized as a "lottery," as some torts scholars argue,[14] it may be unfair to penalize the party who loses.

- *Reduced access to justice.* Saddling the loser with the winner's fees may discourage those with little means or large caution from using the judicial system. Risk-averse individuals generally will be more reluctant to bring lawsuits when there is some chance of losing.[15]

- *Administrative convenience.* Determining attorney's fees is difficult and tends to be hotly contested. A great deal of wasted effort—peripheral litigation not involving the merits—is involved in making an attorney fee award in every case unless, as in most foreign countries, relatively arbitrary amounts are awarded automatically.[16]

One-way fee shifting—the award of attorney fees to a prevailing plaintiff—is yet another alternative to the American rule, an alternative that has been embodied in more than 100 federal statutes and thousands of state laws.[17] The major federal enactment, on which

---

13. The report of the Quayle Commission in 1991 is the latest of these efforts. President's Council on Competitiveness, Agenda for Civil Justice Reform in America (1991) (favoring two-way fee shifting, as in the English rule).

14. See, e.g., Jeffrey O'Connell, The Lawsuit Lottery: Only the Lawyers Win (1979).

15. Aversion to the risks of being required to pay an opponent's litigation expenses varies with individuals and with types of litigants. In general, a one-time participant in litigation is likely to be more risk-averse than a "repeat player." See Mark Galanter, Why the "Haves" Come Out Ahead: Speculation on the Limits of Legal Change, 9 Law & Soc'y Rev. 95 (1974). An institutional litigant, such as a liability insurer, a large corporation or a government agency, is likely to be risk-neutral; it can predict the costs on the basis of past experience and can spread them over a portfolio of cases. See Charles W. Wolfram, The Second Set of Players: Lawyers, Fee Shifting, and the Limits of Professional Discipline, 47 Law & Contemp.Probs. 293 (1984).

16. See Werner Pfennigstorf, The European Experience with Fee Shifting, 47 Law & Contemp.Probs. 37 (1984) (reporting the fixed amounts of attorney's fees awarded, for example, in Germany).

17. In his dissent in Marek v. Chesny, 473 U.S. 1, 42–51 (1985), Justice Brennan listed more than 100 federal fee-shifting statutes. A survey of all fee-shifting legislation at the state level reported almost two thousand statutes; see Note, State Attorney Fee Shifting Statutes: Are We Quietly Repealing the American Rule?, 47 Law & Contemp.Probs. 321 (1984).

others have been modeled, is the Civil Rights Attorney's Fees Act of 1976 (Fees Act), 42 U.S.C. § 1988, which provides:

> In any action or proceeding to enforce [certain listed civil rights statutes], the court, in its discretion, may allow the prevailing party, other than the United States, a reasonable attorney's fee as part of the costs.

On its face, this provision might be viewed as adopting the English rule ("loser pays" or two-way fee shifting). The legislative purpose, however, was to ensure that civil rights plaintiffs are provided with competent representation. The Supreme Court, relying heavily on the legislative history, interpreted the Fees Act as *requiring* a fee award for a prevailing plaintiff and as *permitting* one for a prevailing defendant only under very limited conditions.[18] Hence the Fees Act as construed is an example of one-way fee shifting to prevailing plaintiffs.

The economic effects of fee-shifting statutes have been studied extensively. Some things are clear, such as that a one-way fee shifting statute, providing a fee award to prevailing plaintiffs, stimulates the enforcement of the underlying right. The risk of having to pay the injured party's fees encourages the calculating actor to conform to the law rather than to risk liability.[19] Presumably legislators are acting on this insight in adopting discrete fee-shifting statutes in consumer, environmental, civil rights and other areas. One-way fee shifting provisions have other predictable effects.[20]

On other issues relevant to social policy, however, the effects of the various alternative fee provisions are less predictable. Simplistic assertions that adoption of the English rule would discourage litigation, increase the settlement rate, reduce total litigation expenditures and the like have been rejected by most scholars.[21] The subject is a very complex one, requiring consideration of a number of variables. The scholarly consensus, contrary to common understanding, is that the English rule, if transplanted to the United States, might result in more

[handwritten: civil rights]

---

18. Newman v. Piggie Park Enterprises, 390 U.S. 400, 402 (1968), held that prevailing plaintiffs in civil rights actions are entitled to fee awards as a matter of course even though the losing defendant acted in good faith. Christiansburg Garment Co. v. Equal Employment Opportunity Comm'n, 434 U.S. 412 (1978), held that a prevailing defendant should not ordinarily be awarded fees unless the plaintiff's case was or became groundless or frivolous, or was pursued in bad faith.

19. See Richard Posner, Economic Analysis of Law 143 (2d ed. 1977).

20. More claims will be asserted if a one-way fee shifting statute applies to a particular right. It is not clear, however, whether the rate of settlement will be affected. A great deal of party and judicial effort will go into the fee-setting process, discussed below. To the extent that governmental units bear the costs, they are shifted to taxpayers, and this may lead to downward pressure on fees that may make certain areas unattractive to many lawyers (e.g., low rates of compensation under the Criminal Justice Act of $20–$30 per hour). The frequency of situations in which a normal lawyer-client relation does not exist will multiply, e.g., when a public interest lawyer acts as "private attorney general" and defines the cause and the ways to further it.

21. The best source is the symposium on Attorney Fee Shifting, 47 Law & Contemp.Probs. 1 (1984), especially the article by Thomas D. Rowe, Jr., Predicting the Effects of Attorney Fee Shifting, id. at 39, which summarizes the economic findings in nontechnical language.

litigation and greater total legal expenditures than the American rule. Given the difficulties of comparative analysis, in which so many other things affect results, uncertainty remains. Perhaps, given other societal and legal differences, the English rule is best for England and the American rule for the United States. Displacement of the American rule in discrete areas, resting upon the importance of vindicating certain legal rights or the desirability of deterring certain misconduct or both, has been the choice of American legislators.

What are the effects of the different rules on the frequency, results and costs of litigation? This question can be viewed either from the posture of a participant with a particular interest (e.g., a plaintiffs' contingent fee lawyer) or from a broader social dimension. Is one fee rule more just in some types of cases? All types of cases?

Some of the more important variables are:

- *Type of client.* Three important variables here are: (1) posture in litigation (claimant or defendant); (2) economic status (poor or rich); and (3) frequency of participation (a one-shot participant or institutional litigant). For example, a poor client is deterred by any arrangement that requires payment in advance of litigation costs, including attorney fees, but a poor person is not likely to be the target of loser-pays fee shifting because the resources for paying an award are not available. The contingent fee provides access to the courts to plaintiffs with limited or no resources, but is unlikely to assist claims that are small, nonmonetary, or unlikely to succeed (with the possible exception of a claim that will produce an extremely large recovery in the unlikely event it is successful). The possibility of bearing the other side's fees is a more substantial constraint with respect to clients with resources. Repeat players are presumably risk-neutral, while one-shot participants (especially injured accident victims) are likely to be risk-averse.

- *Type of lawyer.* A privately retained lawyer must earn her living from fees that are generated; a publicly funded lawyer receives a salary, in general, regardless of the outcome of the litigation or the time spent on it. Although there is great demand for the services of publicly funded lawyers (creating an allocation or rationing problem), in theory such lawyers are able to give a matter, even a small one, the time it requires without regard to economic considerations. A lawyer retained to pursue a $1,000 commercial claim cannot act in this manner; she cannot charge a fee that is disproportionate to the amount at stake.

- *Nature of claim.* Important variables here are: (1) the amount at stake (varying from a small sum to a huge stake); (2) the indeterminacy of recovery (varying from a claim with a highly certain recovery to one that is highly problematic); and (3) the type of relief sought (money damages or specific relief). Litigants who must pay their own lawyers will not incur litigation expenses that are disproportionate to the amount at stake, but those who are being provided with a lawyer at someone else's expense will not necessarily be deterred by expense considerations.

2. Court Awarded Attorney's Fees

Common law exceptions to the American rule that parties bear their litigation expenses include: (1) situations in which the parties have provided for fee shifting by contract; (2) when the losing party has litigated in bad faith; [22] and (3) the common fund doctrine, applicable when a litigant expends attorney fees in creating a common fund from which others—such as a class of shareholders, trust beneficiaries or the like—may benefit. [23] The last doctrine has its source in federal equity jurisprudence but has been generalized in some states to a broader "doctrine that permits an award of fees to a party who has prevailed in an action in a way that benefits many other litigants." [24] One example is litigation establishing a scenic easement that significantly increases the value of neighboring properties.

Statutes Authorizing Award of Attorney's Fees

As previously indicated, many statutes now provide that a losing party may be required to pay the other side's attorney's fees. Two-way fee shifting occasionally is provided, but usually the statutes, as in the Fees Act, prefer plaintiffs (one-way fee shifting to prevailing plaintiffs). Calculation of a "reasonable fee" under such statutes has consumed innumerable hours at the trial court level, generated a formidable number of appellate court decisions and occasioned much comment in the journals. [25]

For some years a multi-factor approach stemming from the Fifth Circuit's *Johnson* case was followed by a number of federal courts. [26] A

---

22. See the discussion of Roadway Express, Inc. v. Piper, 447 U.S. 752 (1980) (inherent federal judicial authority to require a litigant, or a litigant's lawyer or both, who litigates in bad faith to pay the attorney fees of an opposing party) in Chapter 5 supra at p. 436.

23. See generally Wolfram, Modern Legal Ethics § 16.6.2 (1986).

24. Id. at 924.

25. See, e.g., Dan B. Dobbs, Awarding Attorney Fees Against Adversaries: Introducing the Problem, 1986 Duke L.J. 435; Thomas D. Rowe, Jr., The Legal Theory of Attorney Fee Shifting: A Critical Overview, 1982 Duke L.J. 651; John Leubsdorf, The Contingency Factor in Attorney Fee Awards, 90 Yale L.J. 473 (1981); Samuel R. Berger, Court Awarded Attorneys' Fees: What is "Reasonable?," 126 U.Pa.L.Rev. 281 (1977). Current information on attorney-fee awards is reported in Inside Litigation, a monthly newsletter published by Prentice–Hall. See also Mary F. Derfner and Arthur D. Wolf's looseleaf service on attorney fee awards (since 1983). Books include E. Richard Larson, Federal Court Awards of Attorney's Fees (1981); and Stuart M. Speiser, Attorneys' Fees (1973).

26. Johnson v. Georgia Highway Express, Inc., 488 F.2d 714 (5th Cir.1974), listed twelve factors the trial court should consider in setting a fee, including all those listed in ethics rules (see M.R. 1.5(a); DR 2–106(B)). The Senate Report on the Civil Rights Attorney's Fees Awards Act of 1976 approved the *Johnson* formula. S.Rep. No. 94–1011, 94th Cong., 2d Sess. 4, reprinted in 1976 U.S.Code Cong. & Admin.News 5908, 5912. However, Supreme Court decisions appear to require lower courts to follow the lodestar method. See City of Burlington v. Dague, 112 S.Ct. 2638 (1992) (stating that the lodestar fee is "*the* 'reasonable fee' " and rejecting one of the *Johnson* factors—the contingency of

second major method for setting attorney fees, commonly referred to as the "lodestar" method, was developed by the Third Circuit in *Lindy I* and clarified in *Lindy II*.[27]   Under this approach a basic figure or lodestar was derived by multiplying the number of hours reasonably expended by a reasonable hourly rate for the attorney's services. The "lodestar" sum would then be adjusted upward or downward to reflect the contingent nature of the case or the unusual quality (good or bad) of the legal service in the particular case.

In Pennsylvania v. Delaware Valley Citizens' Council for Clean Air,[28] the Court noted the advantages of the *Lindy*-lodestar approach, stating that it "provided a more analytical framework ... than the unguided 'factors' [in] *Johnson*."   Other Supreme Court cases have approved the lodestar approach[29] and City of Burlington v. Dague[30] appears to require it.

Problems in Implementing One–Way Fee Shifting

Problems in interpreting the Fees Act, 42 U.S.C. § 1988, and other one-way fee-shifting provisions have largely been resolved. Some of the major issues in application of federal fee-shifting statutes are:

When does a plaintiff "prevail?" For example, suppose a civil rights plaintiff wins on one of six claims against one of five defendants. Is a plaintiff entitled to a fee award under these circumstances? In general, the plaintiff receives an award of reasonable attorney's fees on any prevailing claim for which fee shifting is allowed if the claim meets a substantiality threshold.[31]

What is a "reasonable attorney's fee?" The lodestar method (hours reasonably expended multiplied by a reasonable hourly rate) has become "the guiding light" of the Court's fee-shifting jurisprudence.[32] The "reasonable hourly rate" turns out to be a community standard rather than an actual hourly rate in many cases. In Blum v. Stenson,[33] the Court held that the reasonable hourly rate for attorneys' fees is the prevailing rate in the community for the type of work performed, even where the attorneys are employed by a non-profit legal services organi-

recovery); Pennsylvania v. Delaware Valley Citizens' Council for Clean Air, 478 U.S. 546, 563 (1986) (Delaware Valley I).

27. See, Lindy Bros. v. American Radiator & Stan.San.Corp., 487 F.2d 161 (3d Cir.1973) (Lindy I), 540 F.2d 102 (3d Cir.1976) (Lindy II).

28. 478 U.S. 546, 563 (1986) (Delaware Valley I).

29. In Blum v. Stenson, 465 U.S. 886 (1984), Justice Powell, for a unanimous court, declared that the lodestar generally is "presumed to be a reasonable fee." The lodestar approach was also approved in Hensley v. Eckerhart, 461 U.S. 424 (1983).

30. 112 S.Ct. 2638 (1992).

31. Smith v. Robinson, 468 U.S. 992, 1006 (1984) (plaintiff not entitled to attorney's fees under Fees Act for successful claim under another federal statute); Maher v. Gagne, 448 U.S. 122 (1980) (plaintiff is a "prevailing party" when rights are vindicated by consent judgment or settlement).

32. City of Burlington v. Dague, 112 S.Ct. 2638 (1992) (stating "a 'strong presumption' that the lodestar represents *the* 'reasonable' fee."). (Emphasis added.)

33. 465 U.S. 886 (1984).

zation.[34] A lawyer who customarily charges below the prevailing market rate in serving particular types of clients may nonetheless recover attorneys' fees based on the prevailing rate.[35] The work of paralegals and law clerks may be compensated at market rates rather than the actual cost to the lawyer.[36] But compensation paid to the prevailing plaintiff's expert witnesses may not be included in a "reasonable attorney's fee." [37]

May the lodestar fee be multiplied or enhanced when the plaintiff's lawyer has taken a case on a contingent-fee basis or when the case is novel or difficult? After wobbling on the issue for a number of years, the Court held that federal fee-shifting statutes do not permit contingency enhancement of a lodestar award.[38] The Court reasoned that one of the factors that might justify a fee enhancement—the relative difficulty of the case—was already included in the number of hours or the hourly rate that make up the lodestar fee. A contingency enhancement would involve double-counting. To reward the other factor—the relative merits of the claim—would come "at the social cost of indiscriminately encouraging nonmeritorious claims to be brought...." [39]

May the "reasonable attorney's fee" greatly exceed the money damages awarded to a prevailing plaintiff? In City of Riverside v. Rivera,[40] the Court dealt somewhat inconclusively with the proportionality question. Police in Riverside, California, broke up a private party of Chicanos and arrested some of them in violation of state and federal law. A lengthy lawsuit resulted in a jury award of $33,350 followed by the trial court's award of almost $279,000 as a "reasonable attorney's fee." The fee award was upheld in a no-clear majority decision.

Four members of the Court in an opinion by Justice Brennan argued that the purposes of the Fees Act are served by including all hours reasonably expended. Measuring the award by the work actually done, Brennan said, serves the "private attorney general" policies underlying the Fees Act, which include provision of competent counsel in cases in which damages are relatively small. Four other justices, in an opinion by Justice Rehnquist, argued that a fee award 7.4 times as

34. A prevailing plaintiff represented by a legal services organization is entitled to a fee award even though legal services lawyers work on a salary and are prohibited by law from charging a fee. See Evans v. Jeff D., 475 U.S. 717 (1986).

35. Save Our Cumberland Mountains, Inc. v. Hodel, 857 F.2d 1516 (D.C.Cir.1988) (en banc).

36. Missouri v. Jenkins, 491 U.S. 274 (1989).

37. West Virginia University Hosp., Inc. v. Casey, 499 U.S. 83 (1991).

38. City of Burlington v. Dague, 112 S.Ct. 2638 (1992) (a "reasonable" attorney's fee can never include an enhancement for cases taken on contingency). In an earlier case, Pennsylvania v. Delaware Valley Citizens' Council for Clean Air, 483 U.S. 711 (1987), the Court divided 4–1–4 on the question, with Justice O'Connor, who stated that sometimes an enhancement might be permissible, providing the decisive vote. *City of Burlington* rejects *Delaware Valley II* by a 6–3 vote.

39. 112 S.Ct. at 2642.

40. 477 U.S. 561 (1986).

large as the award on the merits was unreasonable under the Fees Act. The Rehnquist opinion included this analogy:

> Suppose that A offers to sell Blackacre to B for $10,000 [a fair market value].... B consults an attorney and requests a determination whether A can convey good title to Blackacre. The attorney writes an elaborate memorandum concluding that A's title to Blackacre is defective, and submits a bill to B for $25,000. B refuses to pay the bill, the attorney sues, and the parties stipulate that the attorney spent 200 hours researching the title issue because of an extraordinarily complex legal and factual situation, and that the prevailing rate at which the attorney billed, which was also a "reasonable" rate, was $125. Does anyone seriously think that a court should award the attorney the full $25,000 which he claims? Surely a court would start from the proposition that ... a "reasonable" attorney's fee for researching the title to a piece of property worth $10,000 could not exceed the value of the property. Otherwise the client would have been far better off never going to an attorney in the first place, and simply giving A $10,000 for a worthless deed. The client thereby would have saved himself $15,000.[41]

Is Rehnquist's analogy a fair one? Justice Rehnquist concluded that a fee award that exceeds the damage award is unreasonable. Justice Powell, who cast the controlling vote upholding the fee award, agreed with both sides. His opinion emphasized the discretion of the district court and the special findings in this case of the public aspects of the litigation.[42]

The *Rivera* case raises important and troublesome issues. First, small claims or those in which outcomes are highly uncertain will be discouraged by the Rehnquist approach (especially when combined with *City of Burlington*'s prohibition of a risk-enhancement multiplier), but helped by the Brennan approach. If the fee award must be a proportion of or no larger than the damage award, lawyers will be unwilling to undertake civil rights actions that involve relatively small or uncertain claims. Note that in areas where the contingent fee subsidizes litigation, such as personal injury law, lawyers generally will not undertake claims unless the plaintiff has sustained serious damage and there is a good chance of recovery. The Rehnquist approach also rewards defendants who fiercely resist meritorious claims.

A second issue involves the dilemma of defendants who are facing a litigant who is not restrained by the practical consideration of keeping the costs of litigation in proportion to what is at stake. Is it unfair to defendants to require them both to pay a fee award that may be greater than the amount at stake if they lose, in addition to their own defense costs, without any realistic possibility of recovering their own costs if

---

41. 477 U.S. at 592–93.

42. 477 U.S. at 584–85. Given the subsequent changes in the personnel of the Court, the status of *Rivera* is unclear.

they win? Does this asymmetry give plaintiffs' lawyers unfair leverage to coerce settlements? Marek v. Chesny [43] protects defendants who make a lump-sum settlement offer when a plaintiff, after rejecting the offer, fails to obtain a larger amount.

Should statutory awards of attorneys' fees be limited to the amount provided in a plaintiff's contingent-fee arrangement with her lawyer? The Court has held that the lawyer's compensation is determined by the fee contract, which may provide either a higher or lower amount than the statutory fee awarded to the plaintiff.[44] For example, if a lawyer takes a civil rights damage action on a one-third contingent-fee basis and the award on the merits is $90,000, the lawyer receives the contract amount ($30,000) from the client whether the reasonable attorney's fee found by the court is $10,000 or $50,000. The statutory fee award is the plaintiff's, not the lawyer's.

Criticism of Lodestar Approach [45]

Scholars and judicial bodies have criticized prevailing fee-setting standards and methods.[46] The administrative costs of setting fees in each individual case are heavy, especially because both parties have an incentive to litigate the fee question extensively. Although the lodestar method has an appearance of objectivity, the resulting awards are highly variable and appear to reflect the attitudes of individual judges more than anything else.[47] Even more serious, the lodestar method "encourages lawyers to expend excessive hours, and, in the case of attorneys presenting fee petitions, engage in duplicative and unjustified work, inflate their 'normal' billing rate, and include fictitious hours or hours already billed on other matters, perhaps in the hope of offsetting any hours the court may disallow." [48] Judges are not in a position to police the hours expended as they occur and after-the-fact scrutiny is difficult and time-consuming. A further concern is that the lodestar method discourages early settlement of cases because lawyers on both sides have an incentive to keep the litigation alive to log more hours. Finally, the public interest bar charges that lodestar fees in securities and antitrust cases are set higher than those under the civil rights Fees Act, with discouraging effect on the willingness of lawyers to take those cases.

43. 473 U.S. 1 (1985) (upholding defendant's lump sum settlement offer in a civil rights case, including any liability for fees and costs).

44. Blanchard v. Bergeron, 489 U.S. 87 (1989) (attorney's fee under 42 U.S.C. § 1988 not limited to private fee arrangement); Venegas v. Mitchell, 495 U.S. 82 (1990) (private fee arrangement can coexist with statutory fee award).

45. For more on court awarded fees see the discussion of plaintiffs' class actions in Chapter 8 below, p. 852.

46. See, e.g., Report of the Third Circuit Task Force on Court Awarded Attorney Fees, 108 F.R.D. 237 (1985).

47. The Third Circuit study states that the claim that judges "manipulate" the fee-setting process to achieve a pre-determined overall result "appears to be supported" by some empirical evidence. Id. at 247 and n. 32.

48. Id. at 247–48.

The Third Circuit report discusses these concerns at length and concludes with recommendations that a standardized table of hourly rates, applicable to all lawyers within a judicial district, be uniformly applied to all lawyers in all statutory fee cases. Judges should attempt to control hours by providing estimates of the maximum hours that will be compensated "so that the attorneys understand that excessive discovery or any other lawyer hyperactivity will not be tolerated or compensated." [49] These recommendations, especially standardized fees and recognition of a contingency element, are also intended to reduce the bias in fee setting against public interest lawyers.

The Third Circuit report, as do some judicial decisions,[50] distinguishes sharply between "common fund" cases and statutory fee-shifting cases. In common fund cases, in which a lawyer's efforts produce a fund to be distributed to certain claimants or beneficiaries, the court should require the opposing parties to negotiate a percentage fee agreement, subject to the court's approval, at the outset of the case. The lodestar approach would be continued in statutory fee cases. Risk enhancement in statutory fee cases penalizes the defendant with a strong case, whereas this is not a problem in common fund cases because the fee is charged against the plaintiffs' recovery, not to the defendant. Other factors, however, such as the incentives to the plaintiff's lawyer and the interests of the justice system, must also be considered.

3. Settlement Conditioned Upon Fee Waiver

EVANS v. JEFF D.

Supreme Court of the United States, 1986.
475 U.S. 717, 106 S.Ct. 1531, 89 L.Ed.2d 747.

JUSTICE STEVENS delivered the opinion of the Court.

The Civil Rights Attorney's Fees Awards Act of 1976 (Fees Act) provides that "the court, in its discretion, may allow the prevailing party ... a reasonable attorney's fee" in enumerated civil rights actions. 90 Stat. 2641, 42 U.S.C. § 1988. In Maher v. Gagne, 448 U.S. 122 (1980), we held that fees *may* be assessed against state officials after a case has been settled by the entry of a consent decree. In this case, we consider the question whether attorney's fees *must* be assessed when the case has been settled by a consent decree granting prospective relief to the plaintiff class but providing that the defendants shall not pay any part of the prevailing party's fees or costs. We hold that the District Court has the power, in its sound discretion, to refuse to award fees.

---

49. Id. at 263.

50. See, e.g., Skelton v. General Motors Corp., 860 F.2d 250 (7th Cir.1988) (fee enhancement easier to qualify for in common fund cases than in statutory fee cases).

I

The petitioners are the Governor and other public officials of the State of Idaho responsible for the education and treatment of children who suffer from emotional and mental handicaps. Respondents are a class of such children who have been or will be placed in petitioners' care.[1]

On August 4, 1980, respondents commenced this action by filing a complaint against petitioners in the United States District Court for the District of Idaho. The factual allegations in the complaint described deficiencies in both the educational programs and the health care services provided respondents. These deficiencies allegedly violated the United States Constitution, the Idaho Constitution, four federal statutes, and certain provisions of the Idaho Code. The complaint prayed for injunctive relief and for an award of costs and attorney's fees, but it did not seek damages.

On the day the complaint was filed, the District Court entered two orders, one granting the respondents leave to proceed in *forma pauperis,* and a second appointing Charles Johnson as their next friend for the sole purpose of instituting and prosecuting the action. At that time Johnson was employed by the Idaho Legal Aid Society, Inc., a private, nonprofit corporation that provides free legal services to qualified low-income persons.[2] Because the Idaho Legal Aid Society is prohibited from representing clients who are capable of paying their own fees,[3] it made no agreement requiring any of the respondents to pay for the costs of litigation or the legal services it provided through Johnson. Moreover, the special character of both the class and its attorney-client relationship with Johnson explains why it did not enter into any agreement covering the various contingencies that might arise during the course of settlement negotiations of a class action of this kind.

Shortly after petitioners filed their answer, and before substantial work had been done on the case, the parties entered into settlement negotiations. They were able to reach agreement concerning that part of the complaint relating to educational services with relative ease and, on October 14, 1981, entered into a stipulation disposing of that part of the case. The stipulation provided that each party would bear its "own attorney's fees and costs thus far incurred." The District Court promptly entered an order approving the partial settlement.

Negotiations concerning the treatment claims broke down, however, and the parties filed cross-motions for summary judgment. Although the District Court dismissed several of respondents' claims, it

---

1. ... Although ... only 40 or 50 children are in custody at any one moment, the membership in respondents' class is apparently well over 2,000.

2. Although Johnson subsequently entered private practice and apparently bore some of the financial burden of the litigation himself, any award of costs or fees would inure to the benefit of Idaho Legal Aid.

3. Idaho Legal Aid receives grants under the Legal Services Corporation Act, 42 U.S.C. §§ 2996–2996*l*, and is not allowed to represent clients who are capable of paying their own legal fees, see § 2996f(b)(1); 45 CFR § 1609 (1984).

Constitutional Issues went to Trial prep.

Settlement proposal

Dist. Ct.

held that the federal constitutional claims raised genuine issues of fact to be resolved at trial. Thereafter, the parties stipulated to the entry of a class certification order, engaged in discovery, and otherwise prepared to try the case in the spring of 1983.

In March 1983, one week before trial, petitioners presented respondents with a new settlement proposal. As respondents themselves characterize it, the proposal "offered virtually all of the injunctive relief [they] had sought in their complaint." The Court of Appeals agreed with this characterization, and further noted that the proposed relief was "more than the district court in earlier hearings had indicated it was willing to grant." 743 F.2d 648, 650 (CA9 1984). As was true of the earlier partial settlement, however, petitioners' offer included a provision for a waiver by respondents of any claim to fees or costs.[4] Originally, this waiver was unacceptable to the Idaho Legal Aid Society, which had instructed Johnson to reject any settlement offer conditioned upon a waiver of fees, but Johnson ultimately determined that his ethical obligation to his clients mandated acceptance of the proposal. The parties conditioned the waiver on approval by the District Court.

After the stipulation was signed, Johnson filed a written motion requesting the District Court to approve the settlement "except for the provision on costs and attorney's fees," and to allow respondents to present a bill of costs and fees for consideration by the court. At the oral argument on that motion, Johnson contended that petitioners' offer had exploited his ethical duty to his clients—that he was "forced," by an offer giving his clients "the best result [they] could have gotten in this court or any other court," to waive his attorney's fees. The District Court, however, evaluated the waiver in the context of the entire settlement and rejected the ethical underpinnings of Johnson's argument. Explaining that although petitioners were "not willing to concede that they were obligated to [make the changes in their practices required by the stipulation], ... they were willing to do them as long as their costs were outlined and they didn't face additional costs," it concluded that "it doesn't violate any ethical considerations for an attorney to give up his attorney fees in the interest of getting a better bargain for his client[s]." Accordingly, the District Court approved the settlement and denied the motion to submit a costs bill.

When respondents appealed from the order denying attorney's fees and costs, petitioners filed a motion requesting the District Court to suspend or stay their obligation to comply with the substantive terms of the settlement. Because the District Court regarded the fee waiver as a material term of the complete settlement, it granted the motion. The Court of Appeals, however, granted two emergency motions for stays requiring enforcement of the substantive terms of the consent decree pending the appeal. More dramatically, after ordering preliminary

4. ... [T]he parties' correspondence setting forth their respective positions on settlement [indicates] that petitioners' proposals uniformly included fee waivers while respondents' almost always did not.

relief, it invalidated the fee waiver and left standing the remainder of the settlement; it then instructed the District Court to "make its own determination of the fees that are reasonable" and remanded for that limited purpose. 743 F.2d, at 652.

In explaining its holding, the Court of Appeals emphasized that Rule 23(e) of the Federal Rules of Civil Procedure gives the court the power to approve the terms of all settlements of class actions,[8] and that the strong federal policy embodied in the Fees Act normally requires an award of fees to prevailing plaintiffs in civil rights actions, including those who have prevailed through settlement. The court added that "[w]hen attorney's fees are negotiated as part of a class action settlement, a conflict frequently exists between the class lawyers' interest in compensation and the class members' interest in relief." 743 F.2d, at 651–652. "To avoid this conflict," the Court of Appeals relied on Circuit precedent which had "disapproved simultaneous negotiation of settlements and attorney's fees" absent a showing of "unusual circumstances." Id., at 652.[10] In this case, the Court of Appeals found no such "unusual circumstances" and therefore held that an agreement on fees "should not have been a part of the settlement of the claims of the class." Ibid. It concluded:

> "The historical background of both Rule 23 and section 1988, as well as our experience since their enactment, compel the conclusion that a stipulated waiver of all attorney's fees obtained solely as a condition for obtaining relief for the class should not be accepted by the court." Ibid.

The importance of the question decided by the Court of Appeals, together with the conflict between its decision and the decisions of other Courts of Appeals, led us to grant certiorari. We now reverse.

II

The disagreement between the parties and *amici* as to what exactly is at issue in this case makes it appropriate to put certain aspects of the case to one side in order to state precisely the question that the case does present.

To begin with, the Court of Appeals' decision rested on an erroneous view of the District Court's power to approve settlements in class actions. Rule 23(e) wisely requires court approval of the terms of any settlement of a class action, but the power to approve or reject a

8. "Dismissal or Compromise. A class action shall not be dismissed or compromised without the approval of the court, and notice of the proposed dismissal or compromise shall be given to all members of the class in such manner as the court directs." Fed.Rules Civ.Proc. 23(e).

10. That precedent, Mendoza v. United States, 623 F.2d 1338 (CA9 1980), like the Third Circuit decision in Prandini v. National Tea Co., 557 F.2d 1015 (1977), ... instituted a ban on simultaneous negotiations of merits and attorney's fees issues to prevent attorneys from trading relief benefiting the class for a more generous fee for themselves. See Mendoza v. United States, supra, at 1352–1353; Prandini v. National Tea Co., 557 F.2d, at 1020–1021. In neither of those cases had the court rejected a part of the settlement and enforced the remainder.

settlement negotiated by the parties before trial does not authorize the court to require the parties to accept a settlement to which they have not agreed. . . .   The options available to the District Court were essentially the same as those available to respondents: it could have accepted the proposed settlement; it could have rejected the proposal and postponed the trial to see if a different settlement could be achieved; or it could have decided to try the case. The District Court could not enforce the settlement on the merits and award attorney's fees anymore than it could, in a situation in which the attorney had negotiated a large fee at the expense of the plaintiff class, preserve the fee award and order greater relief on the merits. The question we must decide, therefore, is whether the District Court had a duty to reject the proposed settlement because it included a waiver of statutorily authorized attorney's fees.

That duty, whether it takes the form of a general prophylactic rule or arises out of the special circumstances of this case, derives ultimately from the Fees Act rather than from the strictures of professional ethics. Although respondents contend that Johnson, as counsel for the class, was faced with an "ethical dilemma" when petitioners offered him relief greater than that which he could reasonably have expected to obtain for his clients at trial (if only he would stipulate to a waiver of the statutory fee award), and although we recognize Johnson's conflicting interests between pursuing relief for the class and a fee for the Idaho Legal Aid Society, we do not believe that the "dilemma" was an "ethical" one in the sense that Johnson had to choose between conflicting duties under the prevailing norms of professional conduct. Plainly, Johnson had no *ethical* obligation to seek a statutory fee award. His ethical duty was to serve his clients loyally and competently.[14] Since the proposal to settle the merits was more favorable than the probable outcome of the trial, Johnson's decision to recommend acceptance was consistent with the highest standards of our profession. The District Court, therefore, correctly concluded that approval of the settlement involved no breach of ethics in this case.

The defect, if any, in the negotiated fee waiver must be traced not to the rules of ethics but to the Fees Act.[15] Following this tack,

14. Generally speaking, a lawyer is under an ethical obligation to exercise independent professional judgment on behalf of his client; he must not allow his own interests, financial or otherwise, to influence his professional advice. ABA, Model Code of Professional Responsibility EC 5–1, 5–2 (as amended 1980); ABA, Model Rules of Professional Conduct 1.7(b), 2.1 (as amended 1984). Accordingly, it is argued that an attorney is required to evaluate a settlement offer on the basis of his client's interest, without considering his own interest in obtaining a fee; upon recommending settlement, he must abide by the client's decision whether or not to accept the offer, see Model Code of Professional Responsibility EC 7–7 to EC 7–9; Model Rules of Professional Conduct 1.2(a).

15. Even state bar opinions holding it unethical for defendants to request fee waivers in exchange for relief on the merits of plaintiffs' claims are bottomed ultimately on § 1988. . . .   For the sake of completeness, it should be mentioned that the bar is not of one mind on this ethical judgment. See Final Subcommittee Report of the Committee on Attorney's Fees of the Judicial Conference of the United States Court of Appeals for the District of Columbia Circuit, reprinted in 13 Bar Rep. 4, 6 (1984) (declining to adopt flat rule forbidding waivers of statutory fees). . . .

Coercion

respondents argue that the statute must be construed to forbid a fee waiver that is the product of "coercion." They submit that a "coercive waiver" results when the defendant in a civil rights action (1) offers a settlement on the merits of equal or greater value than that which plaintiffs could reasonably expect to achieve at trial but (2) conditions the offer on a waiver of plaintiffs' statutory eligibility for attorney's fees. Such an offer, they claim, exploits the ethical obligation of plaintiffs' counsel to recommend settlement in order to avoid defendant's statutory liability for its opponents' fees and costs.[16]

The question this case presents, then, is whether the Fees Act requires a district court to disapprove a stipulation seeking to settle a civil rights class action under Rule 23 when the offered relief equals or exceeds the probable outcome at trial but is expressly conditioned on waiver of statutory eligibility for attorney's fees. For reasons set out below, we are not persuaded that Congress has commanded that all such settlements must be rejected by the District Court. Moreover, on the facts of record in this case, we are satisfied that the District Court did not abuse its discretion by approving the fee waiver.

III

The text of the Fees Act provides no support for the proposition that Congress intended to ban all fee waivers offered in connection with substantial relief on the merits.[17] On the contrary, the language of the Act, as well as its legislative history, indicates that Congress bestowed on the "prevailing *party*" (generally plaintiffs) a statutory eligibility for a discretionary award of attorney's fees in specified civil rights actions.[19] It did not prevent the party from waiving this eligibility anymore than it legislated against assignment of this right to an attorney, such as effectively occurred here. Instead, Congress enacted the fee-shifting provision as "an integral part of the remedies necessary to obtain" compliance with civil rights laws, S.Rep. No. 94–1011, p. 5 (1976), U.S.Code Cong. & Admin.News 1976, p. 5912, to further the same general purpose—promotion of respect for civil rights—that led it to provide damages and injunctive relief. The statute and its legisla-

---

16. See Committee on Professional and Judicial Ethics of the New York City Bar Association, Op. No. 80–94, reprinted in 36 Record of N.Y.C.B.A., at 508 ("Defense counsel thus are in a uniquely favorable position when they condition settlement on the waiver of the statutory fee: they make a demand for a benefit which the plaintiff's lawyer cannot resist as a matter of ethics and which the plaintiff will not resist due to lack of interest"). Accord, District of Columbia Bar Legal Ethics Committee, Op. No. 147, reprinted in 113 Daily Wash.L.Rep., at 394.

17. The operative language of the Fees Act provides, in its entirety:

"In any action or proceeding to enforce a provision of sections 1977, 1978, 1979, 1980, and 1981 of the Revised Statutes, title IX of Public Law 92–318, or in any civil action or proceeding, by or on behalf of the United States of America, to enforce, or charging a violation of, a provision of the United States Internal Revenue Code, or title VI of the Civil Rights Act of 1964, the court, in its discretion, may allow the prevailing party, other than the United States, a reasonable attorney's fee as part of the costs." 90 Stat. 2641, 42 U.S.C. § 1988.

19. This straightforward reading of § 1988 accords with the view held by the majority of the Courts of Appeals. [Citing cases.]

(handwritten margin note: D sought to waiver P's Fix P's Liability)

tive history nowhere suggest that Congress intended to forbid *all* waivers of attorney's fees—even those insisted upon by a civil rights plaintiff in exchange for some other relief to which he is indisputably not entitled [20]—anymore than it intended to bar a concession on damages to secure broader injunctive relief. Thus, while it is undoubtedly true that Congress expected fee shifting to attract competent counsel to represent citizens deprived of their civil rights, it neither bestowed fee awards upon attorneys nor rendered them nonwaivable or nonnegotiable; instead, it added them to the arsenal of remedies available to combat violations of civil rights, a goal not invariably inconsistent with conditioning settlement on the merits on a waiver of statutory attorney's fees.[22]

In fact, we believe that a general proscription against negotiated waiver of attorney's fees in exchange for a settlement on the merits would itself impede vindication of civil rights, at least in some cases, by reducing the attractiveness of settlement. . . .

Most defendants are unlikely to settle unless the cost of the predicted judgment, discounted by its probability, plus the transaction costs of further litigation, are greater than the cost of the settlement package. If fee waivers cannot be negotiated, the settlement package must either contain an attorney's fee component of potentially large and typically uncertain magnitude, or else the parties must agree to have the fee fixed by the court. Although either of these alternatives may well be acceptable in many cases, there surely is a significant number in which neither alternative will be as satisfactory as a

---

20. Judge Wald has described the use of attorney's fees as a "bargaining chip" useful to plaintiffs as well as defendants. In her opinion concurring in the judgment in Moore v. National Assn. of Security Dealers, Inc., she wrote:

"On the other hand, the *Jeff D.* approach probably means that a defendant who is willing to grant immediate prospective relief to a plaintiff case, but would rather gamble on the outcome at trial than pay attorneys' fees and costs up front, will never settle. In short, removing attorneys' fees as a 'bargaining chip' cuts both ways. It prevents defendants, who in Title VII cases are likely to have greater economic power than plaintiffs, from exploiting that power in a particularly objectionable way; but it also deprives plaintiffs of the use of that chip, even when without it settlement may be impossible and the prospect of winning at trial may be very doubtful." 762 F.2d at 1112.

22. Indeed, Congress specifically rejected a mandatory fee-shifting provision, see H.R.Rep. No. 94–1558, supra, at 3, 5, 8; 122 Cong.Rec. 35123 (1976) (remarks of Rep. Drinan), a proposal which the dissent would virtually reinstate under the guise of carrying out the legislative will. Even proponents of nonwaivable fee awards under § 1988 concede that "one would have to strain principles of statutory interpretation to conclude that Congress intended to utilize fee non-negotiability to achieve the purposes of section 1988." Calhoun, Attorney–Client Conflicts of Interest and the Concept of Non–Negotiable Fee Awards under 42 U.S.C. § 1988, 55 U.Colo.L.Rev. 341, 385 (1984). This conclusion is buttressed by Congress' decision to emulate the "over fifty" fee-shifting provisions that had been successful in enlisting the aid of "private attorneys general" in the prosecution of other federal statutes that had been on the books for decades. H.R.Rep. No. 94–1558, supra, at 3, 5. Accord, S.Rep. No. 94–1011, supra, at 3. See also 122 Cong.Rec., supra, at 35123 (appendix to remarks of Rep. Drinan) (listing more than 50 fee-shifting statutes). No one has suggested that the purpose of any of those fee-shifting provisions has been frustrated by the absence of a prohibition against fee waivers.

decision to try the entire case.[23]

The adverse impact of removing attorney's fees and costs from bargaining might be tolerable if the uncertainty introduced into settlement negotiations were small. But it is not. The defendants' potential liability for fees in this kind of litigation can be as significant as, and sometimes even more significant than, their potential liability on the merits. This proposition is most dramatically illustrated by the fee awards of district courts in actions seeking only monetary relief.[24] Although it is more difficult to compare fee awards with the cost of injunctive relief, in part because the cost of such relief is seldom reported in written opinions, here too attorney's fees awarded by district courts have "frequently outrun the economic benefits ultimately obtained by successful litigants." 122 Cong.Rec. 31472 (1976) (remarks of Sen. Kennedy).[25] Indeed, in this very case "[c]ounsel for defendants view[ed] the risk of an attorney's fees award as the most significant liability in the case." Brief for Defendants in Support of Approval of Compromise in Jeff D. v. Evans, No. 80–4091 (D.Idaho), p. 5. Undoubtedly there are many other civil rights actions in which potential liability for attorney's fees may overshadow the potential cost of relief on the merits and darken prospects for settlement if fees cannot be negotiated.

The unpredictability of attorney's fees may be just as important as their magnitude when a defendant is striving to fix its liability. Unlike a determination of costs, which ordinarily involve smaller outlays and are more susceptible of calculation, see Marek v. Chesny, 473 U.S. [1] at 7 (1985), "[t]here is no precise rule or formula" for determining attorney's fees, Hensley v. Eckerhart, 461 U.S. 424, 436 (1983).[26] Among

23. It is unrealistic to assume that the defendant's offer on the merits would be unchanged by redaction of the provision waiving fees. If it were, the defendant's incentive to settle would be diminished because of the risk that attorney's fees, when added to the original merits offer, will exceed the discounted value of the expected judgment plus litigation costs. If, as is more likely, the defendant lowered the value of its offer on the merits to provide a cushion against the possibility of a large fee award, the defendant's offer on the merits will in many cases be less than the amount to which the plaintiff feels himself entitled, thereby inclining him to reject the settlement. Of course, to the extent that the merits offer is somewhere between these two extremes the incentive of both sides to settle is dampened, albeit to a lesser degree with respect to each party.

24. See, e.g., Rivera v. Riverside, 763 F.2d 1580, 1581–1583 (CA9 1985) (city ordered to pay victorious civil rights plaintiffs $245,456.25 following a trial in which they recovered a total of $33,350 in damages), cert. granted, 474 U.S. 917 (1985); Cunningham v. City of McKeesport, 753 F.2d 262, 269 (CA3 1985) (city ordered to pay some $35,000 in attorney's fees in a case in which judgment for the plaintiff was entered in the amount of $17,000); Copeland v. Marshall, 641 F.2d 880, 891 (1980) (en banc) ($160,000 attorney's fees awarded for obtaining $33,000 judgment); Skoda v. Fontani, 646 F.2d 1193, 1194 (CA7), on remand, 519 F.Supp. 309, 310 (ND Ill.1981) ($6,086.12 attorney's fees awarded to obtain $1 recovery). Cf. Marek v. Chesny, 473 U.S. [1] at 7 ($171,692.47 in claimed attorney's fees and costs to obtain $60,000 damages judgment).

25. See, e.g., Grendel's Den, Inc. v. Larkin, 749 F.2d 945, 960 (CA1 1984) (awarding $113,640.85 in fees and expenses for successful challenge to law zoning liquor establishments in Larkin v. Grendel's Den, 459 U.S. 116 (1982)).

26. While this Court has identified "the number of hours reasonably expended on the litigation multiplied by a reasonable hourly rate" as "[t]he most useful starting point for

other considerations, the district court must determine what hours were reasonably expended on what claims, whether that expenditure was reasonable in light of the success obtained, see id., at 436, 440, and what is an appropriate hourly rate for the services rendered. Some District Courts have also considered whether a "multiplier" or other adjustment is appropriate. The consequence of this succession of necessarily judgmental decisions for the ultimate fee award is inescapable: a defendant's liability for his opponent's attorney's fees in a civil rights action cannot be fixed with a sufficient degree of confidence to make defendants indifferent to their exclusion from negotiation.[27] It is therefore not implausible to anticipate that parties to a significant number of civil rights cases will refuse to settle if liability for attorney's fees remains open,[28] thereby forcing more cases to trial, unnecessarily burdening the judicial system, and disserving civil rights litigants. Respondents' own waiver of attorney's fees and costs to obtain settlement of their educational claims is eloquent testimony to the utility of fee waivers in vindicating civil rights claims.[29] We conclude, therefore, that it is not necessary to construe the Fees Act as embodying a general rule prohibiting settlements conditioned on the waiver of fees in order to be faithful to the purposes of that Act.[30]

determining the amount of a reasonable fee," Hensley v. Eckerhart, 461 U.S., at 433, the "product of reasonable hours times a reasonable rate does not end the inquiry," id., at 434, for "there may be circumstances in which the basic standard of reasonable rates multiplied by reasonably expended hours results in a fee that is either unreasonably low or unreasonably high." Blum v. Stenson, 465 U.S. 886, 897 (1984). "A district court is expressly empowered to exercise discretion in determining whether an award is to be made and if so its reasonableness." Id., at 902, n. 19. See Hensley v. Eckerhart, 461 U.S., at 437. The district court's calculation is thus anything but an arithmetical exercise.

27. The variability in fee awards is discussed in, for example, Berger, Court Awarded Attorneys' Fees: What is "Reasonable"?, 126 U.Pa.L.Rev. 281, 283–284 (1977); Diamond, The Firestorm over Attorney Fee Awards, 69 A.B.A.J. 1420, 1420 (1983); . . . .

28. This is the experience of every judge and a majority of the members of a Third Circuit Task Force which concluded that that Circuit's ban on fee negotiations "tends to discourage settlement in some cases and, on occasion, makes it impossible." Report of the Third Circuit Task Force: Court Awarded Fees 38 (1985). . . .

29. Respondents implicitly acknowledge a defendant's need to fix his total liability when they suggest that the parties to a civil rights action should "exchange information" regarding plaintiff's attorney's fees. . . . If this exchange is confined to time records and customary billing rates, the information provides an insufficient basis for forecasting the fee award for the reasons stated above. If the "exchange" is more in the nature of an "assurance" that attorney's fees will not exceed a specified amount, the rule against waiving fees to obtain a favorable settlement on the merits is to that extent breached. Apparently, some parties have circumvented the rule against simultaneous negotiation in one Circuit by means of tacit agreements of this kind. See El Club Del Barrio, Inc. v. United Community Corps., 735 F.2d, at 101, n. 3 (defendants' counsel suggest that the Third Circuit's ban on simultaneous negotiations is " 'more honored in the breach' "); . . . .

30. The Court is unanimous in concluding that the Fees Act should not be interpreted to prohibit all simultaneous negotiations of a defendant's liability on the merits and his liability for his opponent's attorney's fees. See opinion of Brennan, J., dissenting. We agree that when the parties find such negotiations conducive to settlement, the public interest, as well as that of the parties, is served by simultaneous negotiations. This reasoning applies not only to individual civil rights actions, but to civil rights class actions as well.

IV

The question remains whether the District Court abused its discretion in this case by approving a settlement which included a complete fee waiver. As noted earlier, Rule 23(e) wisely requires court approval of the terms of any settlement of a class action. The potential conflict among members of the class—in this case, for example, the possible conflict between children primarily interested in better educational programs and those primarily interested in improved health care—fully justifies the requirement of court approval.

The Court of Appeals, respondents, and various *amici* supporting their position, however, suggest that the court's authority to pass on settlements, typically invoked to ensure fair treatment of class members, must be exercised in accordance with the Fees Act to promote the availability of attorneys in civil rights cases. Specifically, respondents assert that the State of Idaho could not pass a valid statute precluding the payment of attorney's fees in settlements of civil rights cases to which the Fees Act applies. From this they reason that the Fees Act must equally preclude the adoption of a uniform state-wide policy that serves the same end, and accordingly contend that a consistent practice of insisting on a fee waiver as a condition of settlement in civil rights litigation is in conflict with the federal statute authorizing fees for prevailing parties, including those who prevail by way of settlement.[31] Remarkably, there seems little disagreement on these points. Petitioners and the *amici* who support them never suggest that the district court is obligated to place its stamp of approval on every settlement in which the plaintiffs' attorneys have agreed to a fee waiver. The Solicitor General, for example, has suggested that a fee waiver need not be approved when the defendant had "no realistic defense on the merits," Brief for United States as *Amicus Curiae* Supporting Reversal 23, n. 9; see id., at 26–27, or if the waiver was part of a "vindictive effort ... to teach counsel that they had better not bring such cases,".

Although the dissent would allow simultaneous negotiations, it would require that "whatever fee the parties agree to" be "found by the court to be a 'reasonable' one under the Fees Act." The dissent's proposal is imaginative, but not very practical. Of the 10,757 "other civil rights" cases filed in federal court last year—most of which were 42 U.S.C. § 1983 actions for which § 1988 authorizes an award of fees—only 111 sought class relief.... Assuming that of the approximately 99% of these civil rights actions that are not class actions, a further 90% would settle rather than go to trial, the dissent's proposal would require district courts to evaluate the reasonableness of fee agreements in several thousand civil rights cases annually while they make that determination in slightly over 100 civil rights class actions now. Moreover, if this novel procedure really is necessary to carry out the purposes of the Fees Act, presumably it should be applied to all cases arising under federal statutes that provide for fee shifting. But see n. 22, supra.

31. See Committee on Professional and Judicial Ethics of the New York City Bar Association, Op. No. 80–94 (1981) ("[T]he long term effect of persistent demands for the waiver of statutory fees is to ... undermine efforts to make counsel available to those who cannot afford it"). Accord, District of Columbia Bar Legal Ethics Committee, Op. No. 147 (1985). National staff counsel for the American Civil Liberties Union estimates that requests for fee waivers are made in more than half of all civil rights cases litigated. See Winter, Fee Waiver Requests Unethical: Bar Opinion, 68 A.B.A.J. 23 (1982).

We find it unnecessary to evaluate this argument, however, because the record in this case does not indicate that Idaho has adopted such a statute, policy, or practice. Nor does the record support the narrower proposition that petitioners' request to waive fees was a vindictive effort to deter attorneys from representing plaintiffs in civil rights suits against Idaho. It is true that a fee waiver was requested and obtained as a part of the early settlement of the education claims, but we do not understand respondents to be challenging that waiver, and they have not offered to prove that petitioners' tactics in this case merely implemented a routine state policy designed to frustrate the objectives of the Fees Act. Our own examination of the record reveals no such policy.

In light of the record, respondents must—to sustain the judgment in their favor—confront the District Court's finding that the extensive structural relief they obtained constituted an adequate *quid pro quo* for their waiver of attorney's fees. The Court of Appeals did not overturn this finding....

What the outcome of this settlement illustrates is that the Fees Act has given the victims of civil rights violations a powerful weapon that improves their ability to employ counsel, to obtain access to the courts, and thereafter to vindicate their rights by means of settlement or trial. For aught that appears, it was the "coercive" effect of respondents' statutory right to seek a fee award that motivated petitioners' exceptionally generous offer. Whether this weapon might be even more powerful if fee waivers were prohibited in cases like this is another question,[34] but it is in any event a question that Congress is best equipped to answer. Thus far, the Legislature has not commanded that fees be paid whenever a case is settled. Unless it issues such a command, we shall rely primarily on the sound discretion of the district courts to appraise the reasonableness of particular class-action settlements on a case-by-case basis, in the light of all the relevant circumstances. In this case, the District Court did not abuse its discretion in upholding a fee waiver which secured broad injunctive relief, relief greater than that which plaintiffs could reasonably have expected to achieve at trial.

The judgment of the Court of Appeals is reversed.

JUSTICE BRENNAN, with whom JUSTICE MARSHALL and JUSTICE BLACKMUN join, dissenting.

34. We are cognizant of the possibility that decisions by individual clients to bargain away fee awards may, in the aggregate and in the long run, diminish lawyers' expectations of statutory fees in civil rights cases. If this occurred, the pool of lawyers willing to represent plaintiffs in such cases might shrink, constricting the "effective access to the judicial process" for persons with civil rights grievances which the Fees Act was intended to provide. H.R.Rep. No. 94–1558, p. 1 (1976). That the "tyranny of small decisions" may operate in this fashion is not to say that there is any reason or documentation to support such a concern at the present time. Comment on this issue is therefore premature at this juncture. We believe, however, that as a practical matter the likelihood of this circumstance arising is remote. See Moore v. National Assn. of Securities Dealers, Inc., 762 F.2d, at 1112, n. 1 (Wald, J., concurring in judgment).

Ultimately, enforcement of the laws is what really counts. It was with this in mind that Congress enacted the Civil Rights Attorney's Fees Awards Act of 1976, 42 U.S.C. § 1988 (Act or Fees Act). Congress authorized fee shifting to improve enforcement of civil rights legislation by making it easier for victims of civil rights violations to find lawyers willing to take their cases. Because today's decision will make it more difficult for civil rights plaintiffs to obtain legal assistance, a result plainly contrary to Congress' purpose, I dissent.

I

The Court begins its analysis by emphasizing that neither the language nor the legislative history of the Fees Act supports "the proposition that Congress intended to ban all fee waivers offered in connection with substantial relief on the merits." I agree. There is no evidence that Congress gave the question of fee waivers any thought at all. However, the Court mistakenly assumes that this omission some-how supports the conclusion that fee waivers are permissible. On the contrary, that Congress did not specifically consider the issue of fee waivers tells us absolutely nothing about whether such waivers ought to be permitted. It is black-letter law that "[i]n the absence of specific evidence of Congressional intent, it becomes necessary to resort to a broader consideration of the legislative policy behind th[e] provision...."

[handwritten margin note: No indication by Congress that fee waivers should/should not be allowed.]

II

. . .

... In theory, Congress might have awarded attorney's fees as simply an additional form of make-whole relief, the threat of which would "promote respect for civil rights" by deterring potential civil rights violators. If this were the case, the Court's equation of attor-ney's fees with damages would not be wholly inaccurate. However, the legislative history of the Fees Act discloses that this is not the case. Rather, Congress provided fee awards to ensure that there would be lawyers available to plaintiffs who could not otherwise afford counsel, so that these plaintiffs could fulfill their role in the federal enforcement scheme as "private attorneys general," vindicating the public interest.[1]

. . .

[handwritten margin note: Reasons why should/not]

III

As this review of the legislative history makes clear, then, by awarding attorney's fees Congress sought to attract competent counsel

---

1. This is not to deny that the threat of liability for attorney's fees contributes to compliance with civil rights laws and that this is a desirable effect.... My point is simply that this effect was not what led Congress to enact the Fees Act. Significantly, the Court cites nothing from the legislative history—or anywhere else for that matter—to support its argument that, in awarding attorney's fees to prevailing parties, Congress thought it was merely adding one more remedy to the plaintiff's existing "arsenal." As the discussion which follows clearly establishes, this is because Congress viewed attor-ney's fees as a special kind of remedy designed to serve a specific purpose.

to represent victims of civil rights violations. Congress' primary purpose was to enable "private attorneys general" to protect the public interest by creating economic incentives for lawyers to represent them. The Court's assertion that the Fees Act was intended to do nothing more than give individual victims of civil rights violations another remedy is thus at odds with the whole thrust of the legislation. Congress determined that the public as a whole has an interest in the vindication of the rights conferred by the civil rights statutes over and above the value of a civil rights remedy to a particular plaintiff.[4]

I have gone to great lengths to show how the Court mischaracterizes the purpose of the Fees Act because the Court's error leads it to ask the wrong question. Having concluded that the Fees Act merely creates another remedy to vindicate the rights of individual plaintiffs, the Court asks whether negotiated waivers of statutory attorney's fees are "invariably inconsistent" with the availability of such fees as a remedy for individual plaintiffs. Not surprisingly, the Court has little difficulty knocking down this frail straw man. But the *proper* question is whether permitting negotiated fee waivers is consistent with Congress' goal of attracting competent counsel. It is therefore necessary to consider the effect on *this* goal of allowing individual plaintiffs to negotiate fee waivers.

A

Permitting plaintiffs to negotiate fee waivers in exchange for relief on the merits actually raises two related but distinct questions. First, is it permissible under the Fees Act to negotiate a settlement of attorney's fees simultaneously with the merits? Second, can the "reasonable attorney's fee" guaranteed in the Act be waived? ... [T]he Court's discussion conflates the different effects of these practices, and its opinion is of little use in coming to a fair resolution of this case. An independent examination leads me to conclude: (1) that plaintiffs should not be permitted to waive the "reasonable fee" provided by the Fees Act; but (2) that parties may undertake to negotiate their fee claims simultaneously with the merits so long as whatever fee the parties agree to is found by the court to be a "reasonable" one under the Fees Act.

---

4. The Court seems to view the options as limited to two: either the Fees Act confers a benefit on attorneys, a conclusion which is contrary to both the language and the legislative history of the Act; or the Fees Act confers a benefit on individual plaintiffs, who may freely exploit the statutory fee award to their own best advantage. It apparently has not occurred to the Court that Congress might have made a remedy available to individual plaintiffs primarily for the benefit of the *public* .... As long as the interests of individual plaintiffs coincide with those of the public, it does not matter whether Congress intended primarily to benefit the individual or primarily to benefit the public. However, when individual and public interests diverge, as they may in particular situations, we must interpret the legislation so as not to frustrate Congress' intentions. See Brooklyn Savings Bank v. O'Neil, 324 U.S. 697, 704 (1945).

B

1

It seems obvious that allowing defendants in civil rights cases to condition settlement of the merits on a waiver of statutory attorney's fees will diminish lawyers' expectations of receiving fees and decrease the willingness of lawyers to accept civil rights cases. Even the Court acknowledges this possibility [in its footnote 34].…

I must say that I find the Court's assertions somewhat difficult to understand.… [7] [C]ommentators have recognized that permitting fee waivers creates disincentives for lawyers to take civil rights cases and thus makes it more difficult for civil rights plaintiffs to obtain legal assistance.…

… [I]t does not require a sociological study to see that permitting fee waivers will make it more difficult for civil rights plaintiffs to obtain legal assistance. It requires only common sense. Assume that a civil rights defendant makes a settlement offer that includes a demand for waiver of statutory attorney's fees. The decision whether to accept or reject the offer is the plaintiff's alone, and the lawyer must abide by the plaintiff's decision. See, e.g., ABA, Model Rules of Professional Conduct 1.2(a) (1984); ABA, Model Code of Professional Responsibility EC 7-7 to EC 7-9 (1982).[8] As a formal matter, of course, the statutory fee belongs to the plaintiff, and thus technically the decision to waive entails a sacrifice only by the plaintiff. As a practical matter, however, waiver affects only the lawyer. Because "a vast majority of the victims of civil rights violations" have no resources to pay attorney's fees, H.R.Rep. 1,[9] lawyers cannot hope to recover fees from the plaintiff and must depend entirely on the Fees Act for compensation.[10] The plaintiff

7. It is especially important to keep in mind the fragile nature of the civil rights bar. Even when attorney's fees are awarded, they do not approach the large sums which can be earned in ordinary commercial litigation. See Berger, Court Awarded Attorneys' Fees: What is "Reasonable"?, 126 U.Pa.L.Rev. 281, 310–315 (1977). It is therefore cost inefficient for private practitioners to devote much time to civil rights cases. Consequently, there are very few civil rights practitioners, and most of these devote only a small part of their time to such cases.… Instead, civil rights plaintiffs must depend largely on legal aid organizations for assistance. These organizations, however, are short of resources and also depend heavily on statutory fees.…

8. The attorney is, in fact, obliged to advise the plaintiff whether to accept or reject the settlement offer based on his independent professional judgment, and the lawyer's duty of undivided loyalty requires that he render such advice free from the influence of his or his organization's interest in a fee. See, e.g., ABA, Model Code of Professional Responsibility EC 5–1, EC 5–2, DR 5–101(A) (1982); ABA, Model Rules of Professional Conduct 1.7(b), 2.1 (1984). Thus, counsel must advise a client to accept an offer which includes waiver of the plaintiff's right to recover attorney's fees if, on the whole, the offer is an advantageous one.…

9. … Indeed, legal aid organizations receiving funds under the Legal Services Corporation Act, 42 U.S.C. §§ 2996–2996 *l*, are prohibited from representing individuals who are capable of paying their own legal fees. See § 2996f(b)(1); 45 CFR § 1609 (1985).

10. Nor can attorneys protect themselves by requiring plaintiffs to sign contingency agreements or retainers at the outset of the representation.… [L]egal aid societies … are prohibited by statute, court rule, or Internal Revenue Service regulation from entering into fee agreements with their clients.… Moreover, even if such agreements could be negotiated, the possibility of obtaining protection through contingency fee arrangements is unavailable in the very large proportion of civil rights cases which, like this case, seek only injunctive relief. In addition, the Court's misconceived doctrine of

thus has no real stake in the statutory fee and is unaffected by its waiver. See Lipscomb v. Wise, 643 F.2d 319, 320 (CA5 1981) (per curiam). Consequently, plaintiffs will readily agree to waive fees if this will help them to obtain other relief they desire.[11] As summed up by the Legal Ethics Committee of the District of Columbia Bar:

> "Defense counsel ... are in a uniquely favorable position when they condition settlement on the waiver of the statutory fee: They make a demand for a benefit that the plaintiff's lawyer cannot resist as a matter of ethics and one in which the plaintiff has no interest and therefore will not resist." Op. No. 147, reprinted in 113 Daily Washington Reporter, supra n. 8, at 394.

Of course, from the lawyer's standpoint, things could scarcely have turned out worse. He or she invested considerable time and effort in the case, won, and has exactly nothing to show for it. Is the Court really serious in suggesting that it takes a study to prove that this lawyer will be reluctant when, the following week, another civil rights plaintiff enters his office and asks for representation? Does it truly require that somebody conduct a test to see that legal aid services, having invested scarce resources on a case, will feel the pinch when they do not recover a statutory fee?

And, of course, once fee waivers are permitted, defendants will seek them as a matter of course, since this is a logical way to minimize liability. Indeed, defense counsel would be remiss *not* to demand that the plaintiff waive statutory attorney's fees. A lawyer who proposes to have his client pay more than is necessary to end litigation has failed to fulfill his fundamental duty zealously to represent the best interests of his client. Because waiver of fees does not affect the plaintiff, a settlement offer is not made less attractive to the plaintiff if it includes a demand that statutory fees be waived. Thus, in the future, we must expect settlement offers routinely to contain demands for waivers of statutory fees.

The cumulative effect this practice will have on the civil rights bar is evident. It does not denigrate the high ideals that motivate many civil rights practitioners to recognize that lawyers are in the business of practicing law, and that, like other business people, they are and must be concerned with earning a living. The conclusion that permitting fee waivers will seriously impair the ability of civil rights plaintiffs to obtain legal assistance is embarrassingly obvious.

---

state sovereign immunity, see Atascadero State Hospital v. Scanlon, 473 U.S. 234, 247 (1985) (Brennan, J., dissenting), precludes damages suits against governmental bodies, the most frequent civil rights defendants. Finally, even when a suit is for damages, many civil rights actions concern amounts that are too small to provide real compensation through a contingency fee arrangement....

11. This result is virtually inevitable in class actions where, even if the class representative feels sympathy for the lawyer's plight, the obligation to represent the interests of absent class members precludes altruistic sacrifice. In class actions on behalf of incompetents, like this one, it is the lawyer himself who must agree to sacrifice his own interests for those of the class he represents. See, e.g., ABA, Model Code of Professional Responsibility EC 7–12 (1982).

Because making it more difficult for civil rights plaintiffs to obtain legal assistance is precisely the opposite of what Congress sought to achieve by enacting the Fees Act, fee waivers should be prohibited. We have on numerous prior occasions held that "a statutory right conferred on a private party, but affecting the public interest, may not be waived or released if such waiver or release contravenes the statutory policy." [Cites omitted]. This is simply straightforward application of the well-established principle that an agreement which is contrary to public policy is void and unenforceable. See Restatement (Second) of Contracts § 178.... [14]

This all seems so obvious that it is puzzling that the Court reaches a different result. The Court's rationale is that, unless fee waivers are permitted, "parties to a significant number of civil rights cases will refuse to settle...." This is a wholly inadequate justification for the Court's result.

.   .   .

In an attempt to justify its decision to elevate settlement concerns, the Court argues that settlement "provides benefits for civil rights plaintiffs as well as defendants and is consistent with the purposes of the Fees Act" because " '[s]ome plaintiffs will receive compensation in settlement where, on trial, they might not have recovered, or would have recovered less than what was offered." ' ...

... The fact that fee waivers may produce some settlement offers that are beneficial to a few individual plaintiffs is hardly "consistent with the purposes of the Fees Act," if permitting fee waivers fundamentally undermines what Congress sought to achieve. Each individual plaintiff who waives his right to statutory fees in order to obtain additional relief for himself makes it that much more difficult for the next victim of a civil rights violation to find a lawyer willing or able to bring *his* case. As obtaining legal assistance becomes more difficult, the "benefit" the Court so magnanimously preserves for civil rights plaintiffs becomes available to fewer and fewer individuals, exactly the opposite result from that intended by Congress....

.   .   .

... [E]ven assuming that settlement practices are relevant, the Court greatly exaggerates the effect that prohibiting fee waivers will have on defendants' willingness to make settlement offers. This is largely due to the Court's failure to distinguish the fee waiver issue from the issue of simultaneous negotiation of fees and merits claims.

14. To be sure, prohibiting fee waivers will require federal courts to make a determination they would not have to make if fees could be waived. However, this additional chore will not impose a significant burden.... [I]f the parties have agreed to a fee (or a range of acceptable fees) as part of a settlement, the court will not be required to hear testimony or engage in judicial factfinding in order to resolve disputes over hours reasonably spent, hourly rates, and the like.... The court's simple task will be to review the parties' raw billing data in order to determine whether the court itself *could* reasonably have made a fee award of the amount agreed to by the parties. Such calculations will, in the vast majority of cases, require little time or effort.

The Court's discussion mixes concerns over a defendant's reluctance to settle because total liability remains uncertain with reluctance to settle because the cost of settling is too high. However, it is a prohibition on simultaneous negotiation, not a prohibition on fee waivers, that makes it difficult for the defendant to ascertain his total liability at the time he agrees to settle the merits. Thus, while prohibiting fee waivers may deter settlement offers simply because requiring the defendant to pay a "reasonable attorney's fee" increases the total cost of settlement, this is a separate issue altogether, and the Court's numerous arguments about why defendants will not settle unless they can determine their total liability at the time of settlement, are simply beside the point.... [17]

. . .

C

I would, on the other hand, permit simultaneous negotiation of fees and merits claims, since this would not contravene the purposes of the Fees Act. Congress determined that awarding prevailing parties a "reasonable" fee would create necessary—and sufficient—incentives for attorneys to work on civil rights cases. Prohibiting plaintiffs from waiving statutory fees ensures that lawyers will receive this "reasonable" statutory fee. Thus, if fee waivers are prohibited, permitting simultaneous fees and merits negotiations will not interfere with the Act; the lawyer will still be entitled to and will still receive a reasonable attorney's fee....

IV

Although today's decision will undoubtedly impair the effectiveness of the private enforcement scheme Congress established for civil rights legislation, I do not believe that it will bring about the total disappearance of "private attorneys general." It is to be hoped that Congress will repair this Court's mistake. In the meantime, other avenues of relief are available. The Court's decision in no way limits the power of state and local bar associations to regulate the ethical conduct of lawyers. Indeed, several Bar Associations have already declared it unethical for defense counsel to seek fee waivers.... Such efforts are to be commended and, it is to be hoped, will be followed by other state and local organizations concerned with respecting the intent of Congress and with protecting civil rights.

In addition, it may be that civil rights attorneys can obtain agreements from their clients not to waive attorney's fees.[20] Such agree-

17. For the reasons stated in Part III–C, I would permit simultaneous negotiation of fees and merits. The parties could agree upon a reasonable fee which would be subject to judicial approval under the Fees Act. Any settlement on the merits could be made contingent upon such approval. By permitting defendants to ascertain their total liability prior to settling, this approach fully alleviates the Court's concerns in this regard.

20. Since Congress has not sought to regulate ethical concerns either in the Fees Act or elsewhere, the legality of such arguments is purely a matter of local law. See Nix v. Whiteside, 475 U.S. 157, 176 (1986) (Brennan, J., concurring in judgment).

ments simply replicate the private market for legal services (in which attorneys are not ordinarily required to contribute to their client's recovery), and thus will enable civil rights practitioners to make it economically feasible—as Congress hoped—to expend time and effort litigating civil rights claims.

Client Waiver of a Statutory Fee Award

What is a lawyer's proper course when offered a more-than-generous settlement for her client on the condition that she waive her attorney's fee? Was part of the problem in *Jeff D.* that the lawyer, not anticipating such an offer from the defendant, had not reached an understanding with the client as to what the response should be? Given the nature of the client in *Jeff D.*, with whom would such an understanding have been made?

As both the opinions in *Jeff D.* note, several bar associations had issued opinions holding it to be unethical for defendants to request fee waivers in exchange for relief on the merits. The majority emphasizes that these opinions were based on interpretations of the Fees Act and its purposes. In large measure that is true. Are these opinions vitiated by the decision in *Jeff D.*? [51]

The New York ethics opinion cited in *Jeff D.* was withdrawn and replaced by a different opinion after *Jeff D.* [52] The later opinion says that whether a defendant may offer settlement conditioned on waiver of attorneys' fees is to be determined on a case-by-case basis, and lists nine factors to be considered in determining whether such an offer is ethical. It further states that plaintiffs' counsel is not ethically bound to accept a waiver of attorneys' fees. Why not?

What are the effects of *Jeff D.* on the availability of competent counsel in civil rights cases? Is *Jeff D.* consistent with the purposes of the Fees Act as described by the Court? Does *Jeff D.* undermine the Fees Act? [53]

In most personal injury cases, the plaintiff's lawyer has a contingent fee arrangement. If the defendant offers the plaintiff $50,000 on the condition that plaintiff not pay the lawyer, presumably the plaintiff would have no incentive to accept because the lawyer could later sue for the fee due under the contract. In suits based on fee-shifting statutes, a lawyer could likewise sue her client to recover any agreed upon fee, but there are two problems with this remedy: (1) as in *Jeff D.*,

----

51. A law review note argues that *Jeff D.* should be taken as superseding state ethics decisions on this matter. See Comment, *Evans v. Jeff D.* and the Proper Scope of State Ethics Decisions, 73 Va.L.Rev. 783 (1987).

52. Ass'n Bar City of N.Y.Comm.Prof.Ethics Op. 80–94 (1984); withdrawn and replaced by Op. 87–4 (1987).

53. See The Supreme Court, 1985 Term: Leading Case, 100 Harv.L.Rev. 258 (1986).

the plaintiff may have no monetary award from which to pay counsel, having sued or settled for injunctive relief; and (2) the governing bodies and granting agencies that control and support public interest law firms may prohibit or strongly protest the firm (or agency) bringing suit against the disadvantaged clients, whom it is dedicated to serve.

If a plaintiff's lawyer is serving on a contingent fee basis, is defense counsel making a fee-waiver offer liable for tortious interference with contract? [54] If civil rights lawyers had contracts with their clients requiring the client to pay a contingent fee whether or not the court awarded fees, they could sue for tortious interference with contract. However, there is usually no such contract. Could a lawyer sue for tortious interference with a contract in which the client promises not to accept any settlement that was conditioned on a fee waiver? Should courts uphold such contracts?

Contracts Purporting to Restrict a Client's Right to Settle

Justice Brennan's dissent suggests that civil rights lawyers might find a way to live with *Jeff D.* by asking their clients to agree not to accept any settlement conditioned on a fee waiver or that would result in the lawyer's receiving less than a "reasonable fee," noting that it is a matter of local law whether such agreements would be allowed. What if "local law" consists of Model Rule 1.2? The comment to M.R. 1.2 states, "[T]he client may not be asked to agree ... to surrender ... the right to settle litigation that the lawyer might wish to continue." [55] What is wrong with agreements that limit the client's right to settle? [56]

Negotiating Attorney's Fees

In *Jeff D.* the Supreme Court rejected the ban on simultaneous negotiations articulated in Prandini v. National Tea Co.[57] The Court emphasized the need for the defendant to know what its ultimate liability would be before settling. Can this need be satisfied without permitting simultaneous negotiation of fees? The defendant's need for certainty on its maximum exposure might be satisfied by having the plaintiff's lawyer supply information on the firm's hourly charge and the number of hours worked, as the dissent in *Jeff D.* argues. This

---

54. See, e.g., State Farm Mutual Insurance Co. v. St. Joseph's Hospital, 107 Ariz. 498, 489 P.2d 837 (1971) (holding that a lawyer may bring an action for tortious interference with contract against a third party who, for her own benefit, interferes with the lawyer-client relationship). Accord: Sharrow, Chartered v. State Farm Mut.Auto.Ins. Co., 306 Md. 754, 511 A.2d 492 (1986); Edwards v. Travelers Insurance, 563 F.2d 105 (6th Cir.1977) (applying Tennessee law); Weiss v. Marcus, 51 Cal.App.3d 590, 124 Cal.Rptr. 297 (1975).

55. See Lewis v. S.S. Baune, 534 F.2d 1115, reh'g den., 545 F.2d 1299 (5th Cir.1976) (clauses in contract between lawyer and client prohibiting a settlement without lawyer's consent are void as against public policy). But see La.Rev.Stat.Ann. § 37–218 (Supp.1976) (permits a lawyer by contract to prohibit client from settling without lawyer's written consent).

56. For a discussion of this question see Emily M. Calhoun, Attorney–Client Conflicts of Interest and the Concept of Non–Negotiable Fee Awards under 42 U.S.C. § 1988, 55 U.Colo.L.Rev. 341 (1984).

57. 557 F.2d 1015 (3d Cir.1977) (lawyers' fees may not be negotiated until the parties have reached settlement on the damage award of the underlying claim).

approach is more plausible now that the Court in *City of Burlington*, supra, has rejected the possibility of the court awarding a multiplier to the basic "lodestar" calculation (lodestar is hours times hourly rate).

4. Lawyer Financing of Class Actions

DR 5–103(B) of the Model Code provides that a lawyer may advance court costs and litigation expenses "provided the client remains ultimately liable for such expenses." Model Rule 1.8(e) removes the requirement that the client remain liable, allowing the lawyer to advance costs that can be recouped only if the client is successful on the merits. The major reason for this change was to permit "private attorney general" class actions, in which no single member of the class can fund the action but the lawyer would be willing to do so when there is a strong enough probability of success.[58]

Some commentators approve of M.R. 1.8(e), arguing that it vindicates the enforcement of law and results in greater access to courts, and suggest that the rules should allow the lawyer to acquire property interests in class litigation.[59] But the following case suggests a much more restrictive approach to the financing of class action litigation.

IN RE "AGENT ORANGE" PRODUCT LIABILITY LITIGATION

United States Court of Appeals, Second Circuit, 1987.
818 F.2d 216.

Before VAN GRAAFEILAND, WINTER and MINER, CIRCUIT JUDGES.

MINER, CIRCUIT JUDGE:

[During the Vietnam War a defoliant herbicide known as Agent Orange was used by United States military forces to clear away foliage to deprive enemy forces of protective cover near highways, power lines and military bases. It was also used to destroy crops available to the enemy. The plaintiffs in this massive litigation—military personnel who served in Vietnam—claimed that they had been exposed to Agent Orange while serving in Vietnam and that this exposure had caused a wide range of injuries to them and their families. Defendants—the chemical companies who had supplied Agent Orange to the military—raised a number of defenses: If anyone was responsible it was the United States government; the companies shared in the government's immunity from tort liability as government contractors; valid scientific evidence that Agent Orange had caused the injuries alleged, which occur frequently from natural and other causes, was not available; and allocating responsibility among the companies, whose products con-

---

58. See Mark Lynch, Ethical Rules in Flux: Advancing Costs of Litigation, 7 Litigation 19 (1981). For criticism of the change see Janet E. Findlater, The Proposed Revision of DR 5–103(B): Champerty and Class Actions, 36 Bus.Law 1667 (1981).

59. See the discussion of plaintiffs' class actions in Chapter 8 below at p. 836. On the funding of mass tort litigation, see Vincent R. Johnson, Ethical Limitations on Creative Financing of Mass Tort Class Actions, 54 Brooklyn L.Rev. 539 (1988).

tained differing amounts of dioxin and were used in differing amounts, could not be done in a reasonable manner.

[The initial lawsuit, begun in 1978 by an individual veteran, was later transformed into an extraordinary class-action mass-tort case in the United States District Court for the Eastern District of New York by action of the multijurisdictional litigation panel. In the following years, the class was certified, the United States was eliminated as a defendant and Yannacone & Associates, a consortium of lawyers who banded together for purposes of the litigation, was designated lead counsel for the representatives of the plaintiff class. In September 1983, internal disputes and a critical lack of funding led to the removal of Yannacone and the formation of a new consortium: the Plaintiffs' Management Committee ("PMC"), which was approved as new class counsel.

[PMC included nine members. One of its members, David Dean, who had been closely involved in the case from its inception, was appointed by Judge Weinstein as the lawyer responsible for preparation and trial of the plaintiffs' case. A written fee-sharing agreement signed by the nine members, as later revised, provided that five members would advance $250,000 each to cover litigation expenses, a sixth would advance $200,000. The investing members would be reimbursed threefold from a potential fee award. The remainder would be distributed pro rata to each PMC member "in the proportion the individual's and/or firm's fee award bears to the total fees awarded." The district court was not informed of the fee-sharing agreement.]

[After the case was settled,[60] Judge Weinstein awarded $4.7 million in fees to the nine members of the PMC in accordance with the lodestar method (the time and contribution that each had made to the successful conclusion of the case). Dean was awarded over 30 percent of the total (about $1.4 million); the six investing members were awarded much lower amounts, ranging from $41,886 to $515,163. Once the fee-sharing agreement was applied to these awards, however, Dean's share was reduced to $542,310, while the smallest share of an investor was $513,026. Dean then challenged the fee-sharing agreement, claiming that it violated professional ethics and did not protect the rights of the class. Judge Weinstein, with some reluctance, upheld the agreement.]

Dean's appeal presents an issue of first impression: whether an undisclosed, consensual fee sharing agreement, which adjusts the distribution of court awarded fees in amounts which represent a multiple of

---

60. [Editors' note:] In May 1984 a settlement between the class representatives and the chemical companies, providing for a total fund of $180 million for payment to veterans and other litigation-related purposes, was fashioned and then approved by Judge Weinstein. The substantive portions of the settlement were largely upheld by the Second Circuit in a number of decisions which fill about one hundred pages in the federal reporter. See In re "Agent Orange" Product Liability Litigation, 818 F.2d 145 (2d Cir.1986), the first of nine opinions disposing of the case. The case ended, except for continuing efforts to obtain further relief from either the Veterans Administration or Congress, when the Supreme Court denied petitions of certiorari by various objectors, e.g., veterans who had opted out of the plaintiff class.

the sums advanced by attorneys to a class for litigation expenses, satisfies the principles governing fee awards and is consistent with the interests of the class.

. . .

At the outset, we note that the fees in this case were awarded pursuant to the equitable fund doctrine, first set forth in Trustees v. Greenough, 105 U.S. 527 (1982).... The underlying rationale for the doctrine is the belief that an attorney who creates a fund for the benefit of a class should receive reasonable compensation from the fund for his efforts.... Because the calculation of fees necessarily will affect the funds available to the class, this circuit has adopted a lodestar formula for fee computation [which] seeks to protect the interests of the class by tying fees to the "actual effort made by the attorney to benefit the class." Grinnell II, 560 F.2d at 1099.

. . .

The ultimate inquiry, therefore, in examining fee agreements and setting fee awards under the equitable fund doctrine and Fed.R.Civ.P. 23(e) [requiring court approval of any settlement of a class action suit in order to protect the interests of the class], is the effect an agreement could have on the rights of a class. Because we find that the agreement here conflicts substantially with the principles of reasonable compensation in common fund actions set forth in Grinnell I and Grinnell II, and that it places class counsel in a potentially conflicting position in relation to the interests of the class, we reverse.

[handwritten margin note: Holding places class counsel in conflicting position]

... [T]he agreement, by tying the fee to be received by individual PMC members to the amounts each advanced for expenses, completely distorted the lodestar approach to fee awards. In setting fees here, the district judge meticulously examined counsel's fee petitions in accordance with the Grinnell decisions and arrived at individual awards for each PMC member based upon the services that each had provided for the class. By providing for threefold returns of advanced expenses, however, the agreement vitiated these principles. The distortion was so substantial as to increase the fees awarded to one investor by over twelve times that which the district judge had determined to be just and reasonable, and, in a second case, to decrease the otherwise just and reasonable compensation of a non-investor by nearly two-thirds.

There is authority for a court, under certain circumstances, to award a lump sum fee to class counsel in an equitable fund action under the lodestar approach and then to permit counsel to divide this lode-star-based fee among themselves under the terms of a private fee sharing agreement.... We reject this authority, however, to the extent it allows counsel to divide the award among themselves in any manner they deem satisfactory under a private fee sharing agreement. Such a division overlooks the district court's role as protector of class interests under Fed.R.Civ.P. 23(e) and its role of assuring reasonableness in the awarding of fees in equitable fund cases....

[handwritten margin note: Authority for such fee Agreement = Rejected]

A careful examination of those decisions permitting internal fee sharing agreements to govern the distribution of fees reveals no case where return on investment was a factor. More important, in a number of those cases the courts apparently assumed that the internal fee sharing agreement would be based substantially on services rendered by individual counsel....

Accordingly, while the practice of allowing class counsel to distribute a general fee award in an equitable fund case among themselves pursuant to a fee sharing agreement is unexceptional, we find that any such agreement must comport essentially with those principles of fee distribution set forth in Grinnell I and Grinnell II. This does not mean that a fee sharing agreement must replicate the individual awards made to PMC members under the district court's lodestar analysis. Even after the court makes the allocation, the attorneys may be in a better position to judge the relative input of their brethren and the value of their services to the class.... Nor does this mean that class counsel need follow, line by line, the lodestar formula in arriving at an agreement as to fee distribution. Obviously, the needs of large class litigation may at times require class counsel, in assessing the relative value of an individual attorney's contribution, to turn to factors more subjective than a mere hourly fee analysis. It does mean that the distribution of fees must bear some relationship to the services rendered.

In our view, fees that include a return on investment present the clear potential for a conflict of interest between class counsel and those whom they have undertaken to represent. "[W]henever an attorney is confronted with a potential for choosing between actions which may benefit himself financially and an action which may benefit the class which he represents there is a reasonable possibility that some specifically identifiable impropriety will occur." Zylstra v. Safeway Stores, Inc., 578 F.2d 102, 104 (5th Cir.1978). The concern is not necessarily in isolating instances of major abuse, but rather is "for those situations, short of actual abuse, in which the client's interests are somewhat encroached upon by the attorney's interests." Court Awarded Attorney Fees, Report of the Third Circuit Task Force, 108 F.R.D. 237, 266 (Oct. 8, 1985). Such conflicts are not only difficult to discern from the terms of a particular settlement, but "even the parties may not be aware that [they exist] at the time of their [settlement] discussions," id. This risk is magnified in the class action context, where full disclosure and consent are many times difficult and frequently impractical to obtain....

The district court recognized that the agreement provided an incentive for the PMC to accept an early settlement offer not in the best interests of the class, because "[a]n attorney who is promised a multiple of funds advanced will receive the same return whether the case is settled today or five years from now." Agent Orange I, 611 F.Supp. at 1460. Given the size and complexity of the litigation, it seems apparent that the potential for abuse was real and should have been discouraged. Unlike the district court, however, we conclude that the risk of such an adverse effect on the settlement process provides adequate grounds for invalidating the agreement as being inconsistent with the interests of the class.... The conflict was especially egregious here, since six of the nine PMC members were investing parties to the agreement.

The district court's factual finding, that the adequacy of the settlement demonstrated that the agreement had no effect on the PMC's conduct, is not dispositive.... The test to be applied is whether, at the time a fee sharing agreement is reached, class counsel are placed in a position that might endanger the fair representation of their clients and whether they will be compensated on some basis other than for legal services performed. Review based on a fairness of settlement test would not ensure the protection of the class against potential conflicts of interest, and, more important, would simply reward counsel for failing to inform the court of the existence of such an agreement until after a settlement.

We also reject the district court's finding that its authority to approve settlement offers under Fed.R.Civ.P. 23(e) acts to limit the threat to the class from a potential conflict of interest. At this late stage of the litigation, both class counsel and defendants seek approval of the settlement. The court's attention properly is directed toward the overall reasonableness of the offer and not necessarily to whether class counsel have placed themselves in a potentially conflicting position with the class.... See Allegheny Corp. v. Kirby, 333 F.2d 327, 347 (2d Cir.1964) (Friendly, J., dissenting) (at this stage of litigation, "[a]ll the dynamics conduce to judicial approval of such settlements"); ... Coffee, The Unfaithful Champion: The Plaintiff As Monitor In Shareholder Litigation, 48 Law & Contemp. Probs. 5, 26–27 (Summer 1985) (judicial review not a significant barrier to collusive settlements).

Equally unpersuasive is the district court's determination that the potential incentive to settle early is offset by an incentive, fostered by the lodestar formula, to prolong the litigation. While a number of commentators have asserted that use of the lodestar formula encourages counsel to prolong litigation for the purpose of billing more hours, e.g., Wolfram, The Second Set of Players: Lawyers, Fee Shifting, and the Limit of Proportional Discipline, 47 Law & Contemp. Probs. 293, 302 (Winter 1984), the formula's effect in this regard is far from clear, see Coffee, supra, at 34–35 ("the claim that the lodestar formula results in excessive fees is nonetheless a red herring").... Consequently, we do not view the lodestar system as countervailing the clear interest in early settlement created by the private agreement.

. . .

We find the various additional rationales for approving the fee sharing agreement set out in the district court's decision equally unpersuasive. First, the fact that the returns on the advanced expenses did not directly affect the class fund is of little consequence, since we have already determined that the district court's responsibility under Grinnell I and Grinnell II, as well as under Fed.R.Civ.P. 23(e), goes beyond concern for only the overall amount of fees awarded and requires attention to the fees allocated to individual class counsel. Second, while we sympathize with counsel regarding the business decisions they must make in operating an efficient and manageable practice and agree that a certain flexibility on the court's part is essential, we are not inclined to extend this flexibility to encompass situations in which the bases for awarding fees in an equitable fund action are so clearly distorted. Third, whether this class action would have collapsed without an agreement calling for a threefold return is a matter of speculation. Any such collapse, however, would have been due to the pervasive weaknesses in the plaintiffs' case. Fourth, we find wholly unconvincing the district court's suggestion that the investors could have made a sizeable return on their funds if they had invested them in other ventures. We take notice of the fact that a threefold return on one's money is a rather generous return in any market over a short period of time. Fifth, while the effect of this fee sharing agreement might have been dwarfed to the point of insignificance if the fees awarded to counsel had been much greater, this simply is too speculative to defend the agreement as to affecting the interests of the class. Finally, we do not find class counsel to have formed an ad hoc partnership. They merely are a group of individual lawyers and law firms associated in the prosecution of a single lawsuit, and they lack the ongoing relationship that is the essential element of attorneys practicing as partners.

We do agree with the district court's ruling that in all future class actions counsel must inform the court of the existence of a fee sharing agreement at the time it is formulated.... Only by reviewing the agreement prospectively will the district courts be able to prevent potential conflicts from arising....

Having determined that the fee sharing agreement violates the principles for awarding fees in an equitable fund action and places class counsel in a position potentially in conflict with the interests of the class which they represent, we reverse. We award all the PMC members the fees to which the district court determined they were entitled.

Fee Sharing Agreements

The *Agent Orange* fee litigation raises a number of important questions about fees and their relationship to the financing of litigation. Did the fee-sharing agreement violate DR 2–107(A) and DR 2–103 of the Model Code, which was in effect in New York and most states at the time of the agreement? Would it violate Model Rules 1.5(e) and 1.8(j)? Are you persuaded that the danger of an early settlement, pushed by lawyer-investors who would treble their investment in a short time without contributing any work, outweighed the very real likelihood that the lawsuit would have had to be abandoned for lack of resources if the investors had not come to the rescue?

Peter Schuck's extensive analysis of the *Agent Orange* litigation has this to say about the controversy over the fee agreement:[61]

> The legal system cannot have it both ways.... If it wishes to encourage so-called public interest tort litigation on behalf of diffuse, poorly financed interests over extremely complex issues of scientific or technical uncertainty, then it must either transform the government into a tort litigator on behalf of these interests (a solution with enormous problems of its own), or it must countenance, indeed welcome, private arrangements for securing the resources necessary for effectively prosecuting such cases. The truth is that in the fall of 1983, if the Agent Orange litigation was to go forward, the resources of the financiers were desperately needed; it is no exaggeration to say that at that critical moment and thereafter, they were needed far more than the services of the chief trial counsel, valuable as his services were.... [62]

Why doesn't the PMC count as a law firm for purposes of M.R. 1.5(e) or DR 2–107(A)? If a large firm with wealthy partners had been counsel for the class, the fee award could be distributed among the firm's partners in accordance with the partnership agreement, which might lead to rainmakers and capital contributors receiving a large share of the profits. If entrepreneurial lawyers are not able to make binding agreements like that in the *Agent Orange* case, will lawyers be available for expensive and risky class-action litigation of this kind? Doesn't the decision favor established business interests by denying plaintiffs meaningful access to the justice system?

Did plaintiffs' lawyers in *Agent Orange* receive adequate compensation? More than 100 plaintiffs' lawyers devoted thousands of unreimbursed hours over an extended period of time and advanced more than $1 million in litigation expenses. Although the lawyers' efforts produced a settlement fund of $180 million for the plaintiff class, Judge Weinstein awarded them fees and expenses of less than $10.8 million (less than 5 percent of the award). This (meager?) fee award was affirmed by the Second Circuit in a separate opinion.[63] By contrast, the lawyers for the chemical companies had earned an estimated $100 million in hourly fees in defending the litigation. Judge Weinstein's "lodestar" fee award, which used a national hourly rate of $150 for partners and $100 for associates, provided only a few of the lawyers with a small multiplier.[64]

---

61. Peter H. Schuck, Agent Orange on Trial: Mass Toxic Disasters in the Courts 204 (1986).

62. Id. at 204.

63. 818 F.2d 226 (2d Cir.1987).

64. According to Schuck, Weinstein's low fee award reflected "his conviction that plaintiffs had no case, that such cases should be discouraged in the future, and that he, and not the PMC, had really effected the settlement." Even the lawyer who received the

E.　LAWYER'S RELATIONSHIP WITH NON-CLIENTS

1.　Communicating With Another Lawyer's Client

Anti-Contact Rule

Model Rule 4.2 and DR 7–104(A)(1), referred to here as the "anti-contact rule," require that lawyers communicate with other represented parties through those parties' lawyers and not by speaking to the parties directly. Both rules allow for direct communication where the other party's lawyer has consented or the law otherwise authorizes direct communication. An example of the latter situation is when the other party is the government; the First Amendment's right to petition for grievances allows some direct communication with the government itself.[1]

The anti-contact rule does not, and indeed could not, prevent one client from communicating with another. May a lawyer circumvent the rule by getting a nonlawyer to communicate with the party in the lawyer's stead?[2]

Does the anti-contact rule continue to apply even if a lawyer knows or believes that the other lawyer is violating a duty owed to her client? In *The Verdict,* a movie based on an actual medical malpractice case, the plaintiff's lawyer, played by Paul Newman, receives a substantial settlement offer from the liability insurer for the hospital and doctors accused of malpractice. Newman allows the settlement offer to expire without informing his client's guardian, who is outraged when she hears what he has done. What steps may the defendants' lawyer take to bring a settlement offer to the attention of the plaintiff?[3] Direct communication is prohibited by the anti-contact rule, even if it takes the relatively non-obtrusive form of a copy of a letter sent to the plaintiff's lawyer. But what if the plaintiff calls the defendants' lawyer and states: "My lawyer tells me nothing and does not return my phone calls. Have you made a settlement offer?" May the lawyer handle the problem by asking his client to talk directly with the opposing party? An earlier position that a lawyer cannot advise a client to deal directly

---

largest amount complained: "Dean, pointing out that he had lost his marriage, his health, and at least $40,000 in undocumented expenses, remarked, 'But how can you tell the man on the street that $1.34 million isn't a lot of money?' " Schuck, supra, at 201.

　1.　Vega v. Bloomsburgh, 427 F.Supp. 593 (D.Mass.1977).

　2.　M.R. 8.4(a); People v. Hobson, 39 N.Y.2d 479, 384 N.Y.S.2d 419, 348 N.E.2d 894 (1976) (police officer obtained incriminating statements from criminal defendant in police custody without notice to or presence of defendant's lawyer); Schantz v. Eyman, 418 F.2d 11 (9th Cir.1969) (prosecutor sent psychiatrist to interview criminal defendant without prior notice to defendant or his lawyer). But compare ABA Formal Op. 92–362 (1992), discussed infra, note 4.

　3.　A lawyer may urge the other party's lawyer to have her client present at the next settlement conference, seek the lawyer's consent to make direct contact with the client and report the lawyer's failure to communicate the settlement offer to the state disciplinary agency.

with the opposing party is now contradicted by a 1992 ABA ethics opinion reaching the contrary conclusion.[4]

The purpose of the anti-contact rule is to protect the lawyer-client relationship from outside interference. The fear is that an unsophisticated client, such as the personal injury claimant in *The Verdict,* may lose confidence in her lawyer or relinquish legal rights if a skilled professional representing an opposing interest is free to make direct contact. But does that policy extend to situations in which the lawyer who is being bypassed is violating duties to her client and the client initiates the contact? What effect does the rule have on the dynamics of power and control in the lawyer-client relationship?

Professor Leubsdorf argues that the anti-contact rule is given too broad an application.[5] He proposes that a lawyer be allowed to communicate with any person by letter with a simultaneous copy to the person's lawyer or directly as long as that person's lawyer is informed prior to the contact.

_____

NIESIG v. TEAM I

Court of Appeals of New York, 1990.
76 N.Y.2d 363, 559 N.Y.S.2d 493, 558 N.E.2d 1030.

KAYE, JUDGE.

Plaintiff in this personal injury litigation, wishing to have his counsel privately interview a corporate defendant's employees who witnessed the accident, puts before us a question that has generated wide interest: are the employees of a corporate party also considered "parties" under Disciplinary Rule 7–104(A)(1) of the Code of Professional Responsibility, which prohibits a lawyer from communicating directly with a "party" known to have counsel in the matter?[1] The trial court and the Appellate Division both answered that an employee of a counseled corporate party in litigation is by definition also a "party" within the rule, and prohibited the interviews. For reasons of policy, we disagree.

As alleged in the complaint, plaintiff was injured when he fell from scaffolding at a building construction site. At the time of the accident he was employed by DeTrae Enterprises, Inc.; defendant J.M. Freder-

4. Compare In re Marietta, 223 Kan. 11, 569 P.2d 921 (1977) (discipline for having "caused" client-client contact) and ABA Formal Op. 92–362 (1992) (lawyer may advise her client to communicate directly with the opposing party).

5. John Leubsdorf, Communicating with Another Lawyer's Client: The Lawyer's Veto and the Client's Interest, 127 U.Pa.L.Rev. 683 (1979).

1. ... Employees individually named as parties in the litigation, and employees individually represented by counsel, are not within the ambit of the question presented by this appeal. Nor, obviously, are direct interviews on consent of counsel, or those authorized by law, or communications by the client himself (unless instigated by counsel).

ick was the general contractor, and defendant Team I the property owner. Plaintiff thereafter commenced a damages action against defendants, asserting two causes of action centering on Labor Law § 240, and defendants brought a third-party action against DeTrae.

Plaintiff moved for permission to have his counsel conduct ex parte interviews of all DeTrae employees who were on the site at the time of the accident, arguing that these witnesses to the event were neither managerial nor controlling employees and could not therefore be considered "personal synonyms for DeTrae." DeTrae opposed the application, asserting that the disciplinary rule barred unapproved contact by plaintiff's lawyer with any of its employees. Supreme Court denied plaintiff's request, and the Appellate Division modified by limiting the ban to DeTrae's current employees.

. . .

We begin our analysis by noting that what is at issue is a disciplinary rule, not a statute. In interpreting statutes, which are the enactments of a coequal branch of government and an expression of the public policy of this State, we are of course bound to implement the will of the Legislature; statutes are to be applied as they are written or interpreted to effectuate the legislative intention. The disciplinary rules have a different provenance and purpose. Approved by the New York State Bar Association and then enacted by the Appellate Divisions, the Code of Professional Responsibility is essentially the legal profession's document of self-governance, embodying principles of ethical conduct for attorneys as well as rules for professional discipline (see, Code of Professional Responsibility, Preliminary Statement, McKinney's Cons.Law of N.Y., Book 29, at 355). While unquestionably important, and respected by the courts, the code does not have the force of law (see, Matter of Weinstock, 40 N.Y.2d 1, 6, 386 N.Y.S.2d 1, 351 N.E.2d 647).

That distinction is particularly significant when a disciplinary rule is invoked in litigation, which in addition to matters of professional conduct by attorneys, implicates the interests of nonlawyers (see, S & S Hotel Ventures Ltd. Partnership v. 777 S.H. Corp., 69 N.Y.2d 437, 443, 515 N.Y. S.2d 735, 508 N.E.2d 647.) In such instances, we are not constrained to read the rules literally or effectuate the intent of the drafters, but look to the rules as guidelines to be applied with due regard for the broad range of interests at stake. . . .

DR 7–104(A)(1), which can be traced to the American Bar Association Canons of 1908, fundamentally embodies principles of fairness. "The general thrust of the rule is to prevent situations in which a represented party may be taken advantage of by adverse counsel; the presence of the party's attorney theoretically neutralizes the contact." (Wright v. Group Health Hosp., 103 Wash.2d 192, 197, 691 P.2d 564, 567.) By preventing lawyers from deliberately dodging adversary counsel to reach—and exploit—the client alone, DR 7–104(A)(1) safeguards against clients making improvident settlements, ill-advised disclosures and unwarranted concessions (see, 1 Hazard & Hodes, Lawyering, at 434–435 [1989 Supp.]; Wolfram, Modern Legal Ethics § 11.6, at 613 [Practitioner's ed. 1986]; Leubsdorf, Communicating with Another Lawyer's Client: The Lawyer's Veto and the Client's Interests, 127 U.Pa. L.Rev. 683, 686 [1979]).

There is little problem applying DR 7–104(A)(1) to individuals in civil cases. In that context, and meaning of "party" is ordinarily plain enough: it refers to the individuals, not to their agents and employees (see, Gillers & Dorsen, Regulation of Lawyers: Problems of Law and Ethics, at 433 [2d ed 1989]). The question, however, becomes more difficult when the parties are corporations—as evidenced by a wealth of commentary, and controversy, on the issue [citing numerous articles].

The difficulty is not in whether DR 7–104(A)(1) applies to corporations. It unquestionably covers corporate parties, who are as much served by the rule's fundamental principles of fairness as individual parties. But the rule does not define "party," and its reach in this context is unclear. In litigation only the entity, not its employee, is the actual named party; on the other hand, corporations act solely through natural persons, and unless some employees are also considered parties, corporations are effectively read out of the rule. The issue therefore distills to *which* corporate employees should be deemed parties for purposes of DR 7–104(A)(1), and that choice is one of policy. The broader the definition of "party" in the interests of fairness to the corporation, the greater the cost in terms of foreclosing vital informal access to facts.

The many courts, bar associations and commentators that have balanced the competing considerations have evolved various tests, each claiming some adherents, each with some imperfection (see generally, Annotation, Right of Attorney to Conduct Ex Parte Interviews with Corporate Party's Nonmanagement Employees, 50 ALR4th 652 [1986] [collecting cases]). At one extreme is the blanket rule adopted by the Appellate Division and urged by defendants, and at the other is the "control group" test—both of which we reject. The first is too broad and the second too narrow.

Defendants' principal argument for the blanket rule [3]—correlating the corporate "party" and all of its employees—rests on Upjohn v. United States (449 U.S. 383). As the Supreme Court recognized, a corporation's attorney-client privilege includes communications with low- and mid-level employees; defendants argue that the existence of

---

3. This rule was adopted only in one formerly reported decision and three bar association ethics committee opinions (see, Committee on Professional Ethics, Bar Ass'n of Nassau County Opn. No.2–89 [1989]; Los Angeles County Formal Ethics Opn. No. 410 [1983]; New York County Lawyers' Ass'n, Opn. No. 528 [1964]). The formerly reported decision, Hewlett–Packard Co. v. Superior Ct. (Jensen) (205 Cal.App.3d 43, 252 Cal.Rptr. 14), was "depublished" by the California Supreme Court and thus is without precedential significance. Moreover, on November 28, 1989, the California Supreme Court approved a new disciplinary rule which permits attorneys to initiate ex parte interviews with certain employees of a corporation (see, Cal. Rules Prof. Conduct, rule 2–100; Triple A Mach. Shop v. State of California, 213 Cal.App.3d 131, 261 Cal.Rptr. 493).

an attorney-client *privilege* also signifies an attorney-client *relationship* for purposes of DR 7–104(A)(1).

Upjohn, however, addresses an entirely different subject with policy objectives that have little relation to the question whether a corporate employee should be considered a "party" for purposes of the disciplinary rule. First, the privilege applies only to *confidential communications* with counsel (see, CPLR 4503), it does not immunize the underlying factual information—which is in issue here—from disclosure to an adversary (see also, Upjohn v. United States, 449 U.S. at 395–396 supra). Second, the attorney-client privilege serves the societal objective of encouraging open communication between client and counsel (see, Rossi v. Blue Cross & Blue Shield, 73 N.Y.2d 588, 592, 542 N.Y.S.2d 508, 540 N.E.2d 703), a benefit not present in denying informal access to factual information. Thus, a corporate employee who may be a "client" for purposes of the attorney-client privilege is not necessarily a "party" for purposes of DR 7–104(A)(1).

The single indisputable advantage of a blanket preclusion—as with every absolute rule—is that it is clear. No lawyer need ever risk disqualification or discipline because of uncertainty as to which employees are covered by the rule and which not. The problem, however, is that a ban of this nature exacts a high price in terms of other values, and is unnecessary to achieve the objectives of DR 7–104(A)(1).

Most significantly, the Appellate Division's blanket rule closes off avenues of informal discovery of information that may serve both the litigants and the entire justice system by uncovering relevant facts, thus promoting the expeditious resolution of disputes. Foreclosing all direct, informal interviews of employees of the corporate party unnecessarily sacrifices the long-recognized potential value of such sessions. "A lawyer talks to a witness to ascertain what, if any, information the witness may have relevant to his theory of the case, and to explore the witness' knowledge, memory and opinion—frequently in light of information counsel may have developed from other sources. This is part of an attorney's so-called work product." (International Business Machs. Corp. v. Edelstein, 526 F.2d 37, 41 [citing Hickman v. Taylor, 329 U.S. 495]. Costly formal depositions that may deter litigants with limited resources, or even somewhat less formal and costly interviews attended by adversary counsel, are no substitute for such off-the-record private efforts to learn and assemble, rather than perpetuate, information.

Nor, in our view, is it necessary to shield all employees from informal interviews in order to safeguard the corporation's interest. Informal encounters between a lawyer and an employee-witness are not—as a blanket ban assumes—invariably calculated to elicit unwitting admissions; they serve long-recognized values in the litigation process. Moreover, the corporate party has significant protection at hand. It has possession of its own information and unique access to its documents and employees; the corporation's lawyer thus has the earliest and best opportunity to gather the facts, to elicit information from employees, and to counsel and prepare them so that they will not make the feared improvident disclosures that engendered the rule.

We fully recognize that, as the Appellate Division observed, every rule short of the absolute poses practical difficulties as to where to draw the line, and leaves some uncertainty as to which employees fall on either side of it. Nonetheless, we conclude that the values served by permitting access to relevant information require that an effort be made to strike a balance, and that uncertainty can be minimized if not eliminated by a clear test that will become even clearer in practice.

We are not persuaded, however, that the "control group" test— defining "party" to include only the most senior management exercising substantial control over the corporation—achieves that goal. Unquestionably, that narrow (though still uncertain) definition of corporate "party" better serves the policy of promoting open access to relevant information. But that test gives insufficient regard to the principles motivating DR 7–104(A)(1), and wholly overlooks the fact that corporate employees other than senior management also can bind the corporation. The "control group" test all but "nullifies the benefits of the disciplinary rule to corporations." ... Given the practical and theoretical problems posed by the "control group" test, it is hardly surprising that few courts or bar associations have ever embraced it.[4]

By the same token, we find unsatisfactory several of the proposed intermediate tests, because they give too little guidance, or otherwise seem unworkable. In this category are the case-by-case balancing test (see, B.H. v. Johnson, 128 F.R.D. 659 [N.D.Ill.]; Morrison v. Brandeis Univ. [125 F.R.D. 312 [D. Mass]]), and a test that defines "party" to mean corporate employees only when they are interviewed about matters within the scope of their employment (Committee on Professional Ethics, Ass'n of Bar of City of N.Y., Opn. No. 80–46 [1980]; Committee on Professional Ethics, Massachusetts Bar Ass'n, Formal Opn. No. 82–7 [1982]). The latter approach is based on rule 801(d)(2)(D) of the Federal Rules of Evidence, a hearsay exception for statements concerning matters within the scope of employment, which is different from the New York State rule....

The test that best balances the competing interests, and incorporates the most desirable elements of the other approaches, is one that defines "party" to include corporate employees whose acts or omissions in the matter under inquiry are binding on the corporation (in effect, the corporation's "alter egos") or imputed to the corporation for purposes of its liability, or employees implementing the advice of counsel. All other employees may be interviewed informally.

4. A "control group" test was adopted in Fair Automotive Repair v. Car–X Serv. Sys. (128 Ill.App.3d 763, 84 Ill.Dec. 25, 471 N.E.2d 554), Maxwell v. Southwestern Bell Tel. Co. (No. 80–4239 [D.Kan., Oct. 28, 1980]), and three bar association opinions (Los angeles County Bar Ass'n Opn. No. 369 [1977]; Arizona State Bar Ass'n Opn. No. 303 [1966]; Idaho State Bar Ass'n Opn. No. 21 [1960]).

How does court's test fit č DR7-104

Unlike a blanket ban or a "control group" test, this solution is specifically targeted at the problem addressed by DR 7–104(A)(1). The potential unfair advantage of extracting concessions and admissions from those who will bind the corporation is negated when employees with "speaking authority" for the corporation, and employees who are so closely identified with the interests of the corporate party as to be indistinguishable from it, are deemed "parties" for purposes of DR 7–104(A)(1). Concern for the protection of the attorney-client privilege prompts us also to include in the definition of "party" the corporate employees responsible for actually effectuating the advice of counsel in the matter (see, Polycast Technology Corp. v. Uniroyal, Inc., 129 F.R.D. 621, 625, 628, 629 [S.D.N.Y.]; 1 Hazard & Hodes, op. cit., at 436–437).

Court's RoC

In practical application, the test we adopt thus would prohibit direct communication by adversary counsel "with those officials, but only those, who have the legal power to bind the corporation in the matter or who are responsible for implementing the advice of the corporation's lawyer, or any member of the organization whose own interests are directly at stake in a representation." (Wolfram, op. cit., § 11.6, at 613.) This test would permit direct access to all other employees, and specifically—as in the present case—it would clearly permit direct access to employees who were merely witnesses to an event for which the corporate employer is sued.

Apart from striking the correct balance, this test should also become relatively clear in application. It is rooted in developed concepts of the law of evidence and the law of agency, thereby minimizing the uncertainty facing lawyers about to embark on employee interviews. A similar test, moreover, is the one overwhelmingly adopted by courts and bar associations [5] throughout the country, whose long practical experience persuades us that—in day-to-day operation—it is workable.[6]

... Defendants' assertions that ex parte interviews should not be permitted because of the dangers of overreaching ... impel us to add the cautionary note that, while we have not been called upon to consider questions relating to the actual conduct of such interviews, it is of course assumed that attorneys would make their identity and interest known to interviewees and comport themselves ethically.

---

5. See, e.g., Wright v. Group Health Hosp., 103 Wash.2d 192, 691 P.2d 564; Bey v. Village of Arlington Hgts., 50 Fair Empl.Prac.Cas. (BNA) 1375 (N.D.Ill.); Chancellor v. Boeing Co., 678 F.Supp. 250 [D.Kan.]; Porter v. Arco Metals Co., 642 F.Supp. 1116 (D.Mont.); Frey v. Department of Health & Human Servs., 106 F.R.D. 32 (E.D.N.Y.); Shealy v. Laidlaw Bros., 34 Fair Empl. Prac.Cas. (BNA) 1223 (D.S.C.); Sobel v. Yeshiva Univ., 28 Empl.Prac.Dec. (CCH) ¶ 32,479 (S.D.N.Y.); see also, ABA/BNA Lawyers' Manual on Professional Conduct, at 71:303–71:304 (1984)....

6. Given the nationwide experience with the test we now adopt, we find no basis for the assertion made in the concurrence that the test will unnecessarily curtail informal factgathering or itself generate litigation.... [W]e are reversing the Appellate Division's [blanket] prohibition and permitting interviews of employee-witnesses to an accident, which would not be allowed under a blanket ban. In order to put to rest any possible confusion, we make clear that the definition of "party" we adopt for the purposes of DR 7–104(A)(1) is not derived from the Official Comment to ABA Model Rule 4.2....

[Judge Bellacosa, concurring in the result, argued that the "control group" test was preferable as a matter of policy and because it was more easily applied:]

[T]he "control group" definition better balances the respective interests by allowing the maximum number of informal interviews among persons with potentially relevant information, while safe-guarding the attorney protections afforded the men and women whose protection may well be of paramount concern—those at the corporate helm and the fictional entity itself, the corporation. Also, this approach is more consistent with the ordinary understanding and meaning of "party", and more reasonably fits the purpose for which the disciplinary rule exists; a professional responsibility purpose quite distinct from enactments in public law prescribing the rights and protections of parties to litigation.

Who Is an Opposing Party for Purposes of Anti–Contact Rule? [6]

What difference does it make whether the plaintiff's lawyer may interview employees who were at the injury site? How will conversations with these possible witnesses interfere with the relationship between DeTrae and its lawyer?

The court in *Niesig* describes the various interpretations that might be given to the term "party" as used in M.R. 4.2 and DR 7–104(A)(1). These interpretations range from prohibiting ex parte contact with any agents of the opposing party to prohibiting contact only with the control group of the corporation. What reasons does the court give for defining "party" as it does? Why does the court reject the definition of "client" provided in *Upjohn*, printed above at p. 226.

May a lawyer apply the *Niesig* test with ease and confidence that an informal interview will not lead to charges of misconduct, a disqualification motion or possible exclusion of the resulting evidence? *Niesig* places the responsibility on each lawyer to apply the court's rule; some other decisions ask the lawyer to seek judicial approval before talking with witnesses. In Mills Land and Water Co. v. Golden West Refining Co.,[7] the court held that the lawyer could not make a unilateral decision about who was to be considered the opposing party for purposes of the communication rule: The court, not the attorney, must decide the issue. Lawyers opposing the Mills company conducted an ex parte interview with a director of company who had formerly served as its president; the court held that his position as a director and majority shareholder made him a constituent of the company. The court specifi-

6. In addition to Leubsdorf, supra, see Samuel R. Miller and Angelo J. Calfo, Ex Parte Contact with Employees and Former Employees of a Corporate Adversary: Is it Ethical?, 42 Bus.Law. 1053 (1987).

7. 186 Cal.App.3d 116, 230 Cal.Rptr. 461 (1986).

cally reserved the question of whether a shareholder, who was not also a director, might qualify as a constituent of the opposing corporation.

In Morrison v. Brandeis University,[8] the court adopted a case-by-case balancing approach, emphasizing that lawyers were bound by the strictures of M.R. 4.2 or DR 7–104(A)(1) unless authorized by a court to make direct contact otherwise prohibited by the ethics rules.[9] *Morrison* involved a civil rights suit brought by an instructor against Brandeis University alleging racial and gender discrimination in its denial of her tenure. Under the court's balancing approach, plaintiff's counsel was allowed to contact University professors who participated in the tenure decision. The court found that these people were in the "control group" or were persons whose statements might be admitted against the university, but that this was outweighed by the plaintiff's need for the information and the unlikelihood that these people would speak freely in front of university counsel.[10] Consider the implications of this case-by-case balancing approach, requiring the judge to decide in every case who a lawyer may interview, on the cost of litigation and the possibility of making the pre-filing investigation of facts called for by Fed.Civ.R.Proc. 11.

When Opposing Party Is a Class

In Kleiner v. First National Bank,[11] the bank's counsel tried to get members of the opposing class to opt out of the suit. The bank claimed that the First Amendment protected these communications with the members of the class, citing Gulf Oil Corp. v. Bernard.[12] The court distinguished *Gulf* on the ground that the speech in that case, between class counsel and the class, was associational and thus entitled to more protection under the First Amendment than the speech in *Kleiner*, which was commercially-motivated and thus subject to greater regulation. Is this distinction persuasive? [13]

In Haffer v. Temple University,[14] a class of women students brought an action against Temple University alleging sex discrimination in the intercollegiate athletic program. Temple's counsel and an associate director in its athletic department distributed a memo to class members at Temple attempting to dissuade women athletes from taking part in the suit. The memo argued the importance of loyalty to the school. Temple's lawyer also telephoned two class members to dissuade

---

8.   125 F.R.D. 14 (D.Mass.1989).

9.   Id. at 18 n. 1.

10.   Compare Chancellor v. Boeing Co., 678 F.Supp. 250 (D.Kan.1988) (citing *Upjohn*, the court denied plaintiff's counsel ex parte contact with employees involved in denying plaintiff's promotion).

11.   751 F.2d 1193 (11th Cir.1985).

12.   452 U.S. 89 (1981). The *Bernard* case is discussed below at p. 853.

13.   Contrast In re School Asbestos Litigation, 842 F.2d 671 (3d Cir.1988) (applying *Gulf* to hold that an order which restricted defendants' communications on school asbestos matters with any group reasonably believed to include a member of the plaintiff class was overbroad).

14.   115 F.R.D. 506 (E.D.Pa.1987).

them from meeting with class counsel. The court sanctioned Temple and its counsel for communicating with members of the class directly and for attempting to discourage them from cooperating with class counsel.[15]

When Opposing Party Is a Government Agency *Exception*

M.R. 4.2 and DR 7–104(A)(1), prohibiting communication with the opposing party unless that party's lawyer consents, both provide that such communication is permissible when "authorized by law". The Comment to M.R. 4.2 explains: "Communications authorized by law include, for example, the right of a party to a controversy with a government agency to speak with government officials about the matter." [16] The First Amendment protects the right to petition the government for a redress of grievances.

Does this mean that a government lawyer has no right to control access to her client's agents to prevent them from making adverse disclosures? See M.R. 3.4(f). Contacts with high policy-making officials are clearly protected by the right of petition, unless they are improper ex parte contacts in an adjudicatory matter. Contacts with government employees who have non-privileged information (e.g., occurrence witnesses) are also permissible because they are not the "client" of the government lawyer. But direct contacts with government agents who are within the managing/speaking category of agency law are treated as if they were the government lawyer's client. In Frey v. Department of Health and Human Services,[17] for example, the court held that the opposing party must be allowed direct access to all government employees except those "who are the 'alter egos' of the entity, that is, those individuals who can bind it to a decision or settle controversies on its behalf." [18] The court observed that "while for most litigation purpose the law treats a government entity just like any other party, . . unlike a corporate party, the government also has a duty to advance the public's interest in achieving justice, an ultimate obligation that outweighs its narrower interest in prevailing in a law suit." [19]

---

15. Also see Tedesco v. Mishkin, 629 F.Supp. 1474 (S.D.N.Y.1986) (sanctioning lawyer for communicating directly with opposing class members and for communicating in a misleading and coercive manner).

16. Also see Cal.Rule of Prof.Cond. 2–100(C)(1) (expressly excepting from the rule against direct communication, "communication with a public officer, board, committee or body").

17. 106 F.R.D. 32, 35 (E.D.N.Y.1985).

18. Id. at 35.

19. Id. at 36. See also Vega v. Bloomsburgh, 427 F.Supp. 593, 595 (D.Mass.1977) (state's attempt to bar its employees from communicating with opposing counsel impermissibly infringed on the state employee's First Amendment rights where there was no showing that any of the employees' "interests are adverse to those of the plaintiffs, or for that matter consistent with those of the defendants"). Also see Fusco v. City of Albany, 134 Misc.2d 98, 509 N.Y.S.2d 763 (1986) (state freedom of information law authorized direct contact with government employees without prior consent of the government's lawyers).

Application of Anti–Contact Rule to Prosecutors [20]

A heated controversy between bar groups, on the one hand, and federal and state prosecutors, on the other, concerns the application of the anti-contact rule to criminal investigations and prosecutions. It is generally agreed that the rule applies once a formal charge has been made against a represented defendant, but three other questions are disputed: (1) Does the anti-contact rule apply to contacts at the investigatory, pre-indictment stage? (2) May a prosecutor communicate with a represented defendant at the latter's initiative and request? And (3) what remedies are appropriate for violation of the anti-contact rule?

These issues involving the anti-contact rule are complicated by the rule's interrelation with the large body of law dealing with the accused's Sixth Amendment right to counsel. After a formal charge has been made, law enforcement officers may not question a criminal defendant in the absence of counsel unless the accused knowingly and intelligently waives her right to have defense counsel present.[21] Nor is violation of the anti-contact rule itself a constitutional violation that leads to the exclusion of resulting evidence.[22] The questions, then, are whether questioning permissible under the Sixth Amendment violates the anti-contact rule and, if so, what is the appropriate remedy. Does the defendant's informed consent waive the anti-contact rule as well as the Sixth Amendment right to counsel? Does the body of federal law dealing with waiver by the accused bring the contact within the "authorized by law" exception of the anti-contact rule?

Pre-indictment contacts. Does the anti-contact rule apply at the investigatory stage? When Ivan Boesky and Dennis Levine agreed to cooperate with federal law enforcement officials engaged in a wide-ranging grand jury investigation of securities fraud, other potential targets quickly retained counsel, who in turn wrote federal prosecutors that their clients were represented and all communication should be through counsel. Are their clients now immune from routine inquiries by FBI agents? M.R. 4.2 prohibits communication "about the *subject matter of the representation* with a *party* " whom the lawyer making the contact knows is represented by another lawyer in the "*matter.*" When does a proceeding take on the concrete form suggested by the words "party" and "matter?"[23] Does the anti-contact rule apply to investiga-

---

20. For comprehensive discussion see Roger C. Cramton and Lisa K. Udell, State Ethics Rules and Federal Prosecutors: The Controversies over the Anti–Contact and Subpoena Rules, 53 U.Pitt.L.Rev. 291 (1992).

21. Patterson v. Illinois, 487 U.S. 285 (1988).

22. The Court has declined to hold that violation of the anti-contact rule is a violation of an accused's Sixth Amendment right to counsel. Patterson v. Illinois, 487 U.S. 285 (1988), and Michigan v. Harvey, 494 U.S. 344 (1990). Justice Stevens, dissenting in both cases, argued that the constitutional standard should incorporate the fairness aspect of the ethics rule—the danger of overreaching when an accused, even with adequate consent, communicates with law enforcement officials in the absence of appointed counsel.

23. Compare United States v. Ryans, 903 F.2d 731 (10th Cir.1990) (because the anti-contact rule contemplates "an adversarial relationship between litigants," it is inapplica-

tory personnel such as the FBI, who may have legal training but are not acting as lawyers? Or is it sufficient that another lawyer, the federal prosecutor, is providing supervision and direction? [24] The decisions are in a state of confusion.

In United States v. Hammad,[25] the prosecutor furnished an informant with a false subpoena and a hidden tape recorder whereby the informant recorded conversations with the defendant. The prosecutor knew the defendant was represented by counsel in the matter under investigation. The Sixth Amendment was not at issue because the incident took place as part of an investigation, not after criminal proceedings had been instituted. The court held that the anti-contact rule applies to prosecutors, but that the legitimate use of informants in an investigation was within the "authorized by law" exception to the rule. Here, however, the use of the informant was held not legitimate because the prosecutor engaged in "egregious misconduct" in using a "specious and contrived subpoena" and hence violated DR 7–104(A)(1). The court further held that exclusion of the evidence would be an appropriate remedy.

Post-indictment contacts with defendant's consent. United States v. Lopez [26] involved contact between an indicted defendant represented by counsel and a federal prosecutor who, after obtaining approval of a magistrate, held several conversations with the defendant without the consent or presence of defendant's lawyer. The defendant, stymied by his lawyer's refusal to assist him in plea bargaining, initiated the contacts and waived his lawyer's presence, stating that his lawyer was not acting in his best interests. After the plea negotiations failed, the defendant's successor counsel moved to dismiss the indictment for violation of California's version of the anti-contact ethics rule (also adopted by local rule of the federal district court). The district court dismissed the indictment on the ground that the prosecutor's communications with the represented defendant violated the "widely accepted and time-honored" anti-contact rule. The Ninth Circuit upheld the application of the anti-contact rule, relying on facts suggesting that the prosecutor had misled the magistrate by not informing her of facts that

ble to investigative contacts occurring before the proceedings become accusatory), and United States v. Guerrerio, 675 F.Supp. 1430 (S.D.N.Y.1987) (evidence obtained at investigatory stage not subject to suppression because the subject of representation "is nebulous until the time of the formal initiation of the prosecution"), with United States v. Hammad, 858 F.2d 834 (2d Cir.1988) (the anti-contact rule applies at the investigatory stage, but ordinary investigative activity is generally within the rule's "authorized by law" exception).

24. Compare United States v. Thomas, 474 F.2d 110, 112 (10th Cir.1973) (enforcement officials are agents of the prosecuting party), and United States v. Jamil, 707 F.2d 638, 646 (2d Cir.1983) (no ethics violations where prosecutor was neither involved in nor aware of surreptitious contact with represented defendant), with United States v. Scarpelli, 713 F.Supp. 1144, 1159 n.25 (N.D.Ill.1989) (rule does not apply to FBI agents).

25. 858 F.2d 834 (2d Cir.1988).

26. 765 F.Supp. 1433 (N.D. Cal.1991), rev'd in part and aff'd in part, 989 F.2d 1032 (9th Cir.1993).

she failed to elicit from the defendant in an in camera hearing.[27]

Does the holding in *Lopez* deprive the defendant of her right to petition the government in a situation in which she may believe that her interests are not being served by her lawyer? Why doesn't judicial approval of the conversations bring the case within the "authorized by law" exception to the anti-contact rule? Why can't a client consent to waiver of the anti-contact rule? Do some applications of the rule increase the dependence of clients on lawyers?

Remedying violations. What remedies are appropriate if a prosecutor violates the anti-contact rule? Ethics rules provide standards for professional discipline, yet prosecutors are rarely disciplined for violations of the anti-contact rule.[28] The preamble to the Model Rules states that the rules govern professional discipline but do not create rights enforceable in other contexts. Nevertheless, courts refer and rely on the rules in deciding disqualification motions, fee controversies and a variety of other matters.[29] Should evidence be excluded in civil or criminal proceedings because of violation of the rule?[30] *Lopez* held that dismissal of a criminal indictment was normally inappropriate as a remedy for violation of the anti-contact rule, but scattered decisions have excluded evidence obtained by contacts violating the rule.[31]

2. Fairness to Persons Not Represented by Counsel

Model Rule 4.3 provides that when the other person is not represented, "the lawyer shall not state or imply that the lawyer is disinterested." Further, if the lawyer "knows or reasonably should know that

27. The anti-contact rule, the court held, bars direct prosecutorial communication with represented defendants after indictment and the general statutory authority of federal prosecutors does not override the rule. Although a magistrate's approval of contact would normally bring it within the "authorized by law" exception, the magistrate in this case was misled by the prosecutor. However, because defendant was able to secure competent replacement counsel, the district court erred in dismissing the indictment.

28. Prosecutors who bypass defense counsel are rarely disciplined. See In re Burrows, 291 Or. 135, 629 P.2d 820 (1981). For imposition of discipline for direct communication in civil litigation, see, e.g., Toledo Bar Ass'n v. Westmeyer, 35 Ohio St.3d 261, 520 N.E.2d 223 (1988); Florida Bar v. Shapiro, 413 So.2d 1184 (Fla.1982).

29. See the discussion of the relevance and authority of ethics rules in other legal contexts at p. 190 above.

30. In Mills Land & Water Co. v. Golden West Refining Co., 186 Cal.App.3d 116, 230 Cal.Rptr. 461 (1986), discussed above, the court refused to suppress any information gained in the improper conversation that was otherwise discoverable, stating that the exclusionary rule was inappropriate in *civil* litigation. In criminal prosecutions evidence obtained through direct communication with the accused would not be discoverable. Should this make a difference in fashioning a remedy?

31. United States v. Hammad, 858 F.2d 834, 837 (2d Cir.1988) (prosecutor's use of a sham subpoena was egregious misconduct justifying exclusion of informant's secret recording); United States v. Thomas, 474 F.2d 110 (10th Cir.1973) (violation of anti-contact rule may justify exclusion of resulting evidence); People v. Hobson, 39 N.Y.2d 479, 384 N.Y.S.2d 419, 348 N.E.2d 894 (1976) (same). Contra: Gentry v. Texas, 770 S.W.2d 780, 791 (Tex.Crim.App.1988) (en banc) (disciplinary action against the prosecution, not exclusion of evidence, is the appropriate remedy); Suarez v. Florida, 481 So.2d 1201 (Fla.1985) (same); People v. Green, 405 Mich. 273, 274 N.W.2d 448, 454 (1979) (same).

the unrepresented person misunderstands the lawyer's role in the matter, the lawyer shall make reasonable efforts to correct the misunderstanding." DR 7–104(A)(2) provides that a lawyer shall not give advice to someone not represented by counsel "other than the advice to seek a lawyer". Note too that M.R. 8.4(d) and DR 1–102(A)(4) prohibit "conduct involving dishonesty, fraud, deceit or misrepresentation."

Ethics opinions state that before interviewing a potential defendant, a lawyer must advise her that the lawyer is counsel for the plaintiff,[32] and that a lawyer who interviews an employee of an opposing party or a nonparty witness must disclose the lawyer-client relationship.[33]

In mass disaster situations, such as an air crash or a hotel fire, plaintiffs' lawyers who attempt to bring their services to the attention of potential claimants are criticized by bar groups and the public for improper solicitation. What about the lawyer representatives of potential defendants or their liability insurers, who interview accident victims or their relatives to obtain information or to settle claims? Assuming that the lawyer is careful to identify her role, may a lawyer seek to get a release of liability or ask the potential claimant to accept a settlement offer? What if the contact is carried on by a non-lawyer insurance adjuster carrying forms and instructions prepared by the insurer's legal counsel? Is any effort at persuasion appropriate, even truthful statements that "hiring a lawyer and bringing a court proceeding will take much longer, and you will have to pay an attorney fee"?

In W.T. Grant, Inc. v. Haines,[34] a lawyer for a retail chain was conducting an internal investigation of company employees who were suspected of taking kickbacks and bribes in making store leases. Haines, one of the employees, was called to New York for a meeting scheduled as a ruse to get him to New York, and was then interviewed for five and one-half hours by the company's lawyer, who, with Haines' consent, recorded the conversation and later obtained Haines' consent for a lie detector test. The lawyer told Haines that he had been retained by the employer to look into commercial dealings with shopping centers, but did not inform Haines that a fraud case naming Haines as a defendant had been filed that morning. In that proceeding, Haines later moved to disqualify the lawyer's law firm on ground that the lawyer gave legal advice to Haines, who was an unrepresented person. The court was troubled by this sequence of events but thought that DR 7–104(A)(2) was not violated by statements to Haines that "candid answers to the inquiry might clear his name 'if that [was] possible.' " [35] Asking Haines to sign authorizations consenting to access to his tax, credit cards and financial accounts, however, presented a

32. ABA Informal Op. 908 (1966).

33. ABA Formal Op. 117 (1934).

34. 531 F.2d 671 (2d Cir.1976).

35. Id. at 675.

"close question." [36] Didn't the lawyer give "advice" by urging that cooperation might help alleviate Haines' legal problems? [37]

Model Rule 3.8(c) prohibits a prosecutor from seeking "to obtain from an unrepresented accused a waiver of important pretrial rights, such as the right to a preliminary hearing." Should this rule be limited to prosecutors?

Model Rule 3.4(f) provides that a lawyer shall not request a person, other than the client, "to refrain from voluntarily giving relevant information to another party." However, the lawyer can so advise a person who is a relative, employee or agent of the client, *if* "the lawyer reasonably believes that the person's interests will not be adversely affected by refraining from giving such information." A lawyer may not advise another to refrain from cooperating if that advice is in furtherance of the client's illegal activity.[38]

F. LAWYER-CLIENT TRANSACTIONS

1. Handling Client Property

Commingling Funds

David Hoffman, the father of American legal ethics, stated in 1836:

I will on no occasion blend with my own my client's money. If kept *distinctly as his*, it will be less liable to be considered *as my own.*[39]

Although this simple rule has been recognized as fundamental for long before lawyers had written ethics codes, it is still one of the most frequent bases of lawyer disbarment.[40]

The Code provision on safeguarding client property is DR 9–102. Professor Brickman provides a summary of the provisions of this rule:

36. See ABA Formal Op. 84–350 (1984) (withdrawing two previous ABA Informal opinions, Op. 1140 (1970) and Op. 1255 (1940), both of which prohibited lawyers from presenting documents to adverse parties who were not represented by counsel).

37. See 2 Hazard & Hodes, Law of Lawyering 752 (2d ed.1990) (arguing that the lawyer's conduct violated both DR 7–104(A)(2) and M.R. 4.3). The court in *Haines* went on to hold that, even if the ethics rule was violated, disqualification was an inappropriate remedy where the violation did not "taint" the trial of the case and would deprive the other party of its counsel of choice. Professional discipline was the only appropriate remedy.

38. See In re Blatt, 65 N.J. 539, 324 A.2d 15 (1974) (lawyer urged witnesses not to cooperate with federal investigation); In re Russell, 59 N.J. 315, 282 A.2d 42 (1971) (lawyer advised witnesses, who were represented by another lawyer, to plead the Fifth Amendment to help lawyer's client).

39. David Hoffman (1784–1854) wrote the first statement of professional ethics for American lawyers. His fifty "Resolutions in Regard to Professional Deportment" were first published in 1817 and in a revised form in 1836. See Thomas L. Shaffer, American Legal Ethics 59 (1985); and Maxwell Bloomfield, David Hoffman and the Shaping of a Republican Legal Culture, 38 Md. L. Rev. 673 (1979).

40. See Matter of Hessler, 549 A.2d 700 n. 1 (D.C.App.1988), citing Annotation, Attorney's Commingling of Client's Funds with His Own as Grounds for Disciplinary Action—Modern Status, 94 A.L.R.3d 846, 850 (1979).

[Its] design ... can be best gleaned if the protections are listed in the chronological order in which they come to apply to client property. The birth of fiduciary concern occurs when the attorney comes into possession of client property in any of its various forms; for example securities or funds. At that point, if it did not come directly from the client he is to notify the client of its receipt. The attorney must initiate careful record keeping procedures for all client property in his possession regardless of whether it came to him directly from the client or was paid or delivered by a third party, and is to render an accounting to the client whenever appropriate. If the property is in the form of securities or other valuable items, it is to be safeguarded by placement in a safe deposit box (or other safe place) as quickly as possible. If the property is in the form of "funds of clients paid to a lawyer" including "funds belonging in part to a client and in part presently or potentially to the lawyer," it is to be safeguarded by segregating it from the lawyer's personal funds and depositing it to a client security account.[41]

M.R. 1.15, Safekeeping Property, is substantially similar to DR 9–102, but it applies also to property of a third person that is in the lawyer's possession in connection with the representation.

As to funds partly or potentially belonging to the lawyer, the lawyer may withdraw funds from the trust account when payment from the client is due *unless* the client disputes the lawyer's claim, in which case the disputed portion "shall be kept separate by the lawyer until the dispute is resolved." M.R. 1.15(c); DR 9–102(A)(2) is substantially identical. Most jurisdictions read these provisions as requiring the lawyer to deposit money received as a general retainer in a trust account and allowing withdrawal only as the fee is earned.[42] A minority of jurisdictions permit the lawyer to deposit advance fee payments in the general office account.[43]

The prohibition against commingling is violated whether the lawyer deposits the client's money in the lawyer's account or the lawyer's money is deposited in the client's trust account. A violation occurs even if the lawyer was merely negligent. "[I]t is essentially a per se offense."[44] Courts treat violations of the ban against commingling of funds very seriously;[45] in some jurisdictions a violation results in

---

41. Lester Brickman, The Advance Fee Payment Dilemma, 10 Cardozo L.Rev. 647, 656 (1989).

42. See, e.g., In re Aronson, 352 N.W.2d 17 (Minn.1984); and Miele v. Commissioner, 72 T.C. 284 (1979) (interpreting Pennsylvania code to require segregation of retainer fees). For a more complete list see Brickman, The Advance Fee Dilemma, supra, at 655.

43. See, e.g., N.Y. State Bar Assn.Comm. Prof.Ethics, Op. 570 (1985); and D.C. Bar Op. 113 (1982).

44. In re Hessler, 549 A.2d 700 n. 3 (D.C.App.1988); Fitzsimmons v. State Bar, 34 Cal.3d 327, 193 Cal.Rptr. 896, 667 P.2d 700, 702 (1983).

45. See, e.g., In re Pierson, 280 Or. 513, 571 P.2d 907, 908–09 (1977) (a single conversion of client funds will result in disbarment); Akron Bar Ass'n v. Hughes, 46 Ohio

automatic disbarment. In New Jersey, for example, the court will not consider a lawyer's inexperience, an otherwise outstanding career or the lawyer's restitution of the funds as mitigating factors in cases of intentional commingling: [46]

> [The lawyer] knowingly used his client's money as if it were his own. We hold that disbarment is the only appropriate discipline [and] . . . use this occasion to state that generally all such cases shall result in disbarment.

> Like many rules governing the behavior of lawyers, this one has its roots in the confidence and trust which clients place in their attorneys. Having sought his advice and relying on his expertise, the client entrusts the lawyer with the transaction—including the handling of the client's funds. . . .

> It is a trust built on centuries of honesty and faithfulness. Sometimes it is reinforced by personal knowledge of a particular lawyer's integrity or a firm's reputation. The underlying faith, however, is in the legal profession, the bar as an institution. No other explanation can account for clients' customary willingness to entrust their funds to relative strangers simply because they are lawyers.

> . . .

> What are the merits of these cases? The attorney has stolen the client's money. No clearer wrong suffered by a client at the hands of one he had every reason to trust can be imagined. The public is entitled, not as a matter of satisfying unjustifiable expectations, but as a simple matter of maintaining confidence, to know that never again will that person be a lawyer. . . . [47]

In discussing whether restitution should matter in determining the appropriate discipline, the court said:

> When restitution is used to support the contention that the lawyer intended to "borrow" rather than steal, it simply cloaks the mistaken premise that unauthorized use of clients' funds is excusable when accompanied by an intent to return them. The act is no less a crime. . . . Banks do not rehire tellers who "borrow" depositors' funds. Our professional standards, if anything, should be higher. . . . [48]

Record Keeping   *MR 1.15(a) must keep records for 5 yrs.*

Both the Model Code and the Model Rules require that the lawyer maintain complete records of all funds and property maintained by the lawyer for another. M.R. 1.15(a) specifies that the records be kept for

St.2d 369, 348 N.E.2d 712, 715 (1976) (penalty for commingling of funds is either indefinite suspension or disbarment).

46. In Matter of Wilson, 81 N.J. 451, 409 A.2d 1153 (1979).

47. 409 A.2d at 1154–55.

48. Id. at 1156.

five years following the termination of the representation. New Jersey, which generally has stricter regulations for the legal profession than most other jurisdictions, has detailed requirements for law office bookkeeping, including provisions on recording the flow of all entrusted funds, billing the client, paying others on behalf of the client, and reconciling ledger and bank statements. The records must be kept "in accordance with generally accepted accounting practice" and retained for seven years, along with "copies of those portions of each client's case file reasonably necessary for a complete understanding of the financial transactions pertaining thereto." [49] Some other states have adopted requirements going beyond those in the Code and Rules.[50]

The American Bar Association is considering a proposal that would subject a lawyer's financial accounts to random inspection by the bar regulatory agency. A number of jurisdictions, in addition to New Jersey, have adopted audit procedures.[51]

Client Security Funds

Many jurisdictions have set up client security funds to provide some reimbursement for clients whose assets have been misappropriated by a lawyer admitted to the state bar. These funds are often maintained by mandatory contributions from lawyers in the state or by state bar dues money. They are woefully inadequate as a means of providing restitution for victims of lawyer dishonesty. The amount maintained in such accounts is far below the amount lawyers actually misappropriate each year. To qualify for funds, the client must show that all avenues of relief against the lawyer have been exhausted to no avail. Further, there are usually other demanding showings that the client must make to obtain compensation. Assuming the client makes it over those hurdles, ceilings in the state plans generally restrict the amount each client may recover and the amount paid out per lawyer who violates the rule no matter how many clients are injured and the amount per transaction.

Why shouldn't lawyers be required to obtain a fidelity bond covering loss or embezzlement of client funds?

Keeping Money of Multiple Clients in One Account

The rules allow a lawyer to use one trust account to deposit the funds of multiple clients. This is necessary because for many clients the lawyer may hold amounts too small or too briefly to justify the maintenance of separate trust accounts. If, on the other hand, the client's funds are great enough and the time the lawyer is to hold those funds is long enough, or the funds are held in a separate capacity, the lawyer should put the money in a separate interest bearing account.[52]

---

49. N.J.Court Rules 1:21–6.

50. See, e.g., N.H. Rule 37 § 7 (specifying accounting system, including separate ledger pages for each client and an index to all trust accounts).

51. As of March 1992 eight states had adopted random audit procedures.

52. See, e.g., In re Petition of Minn. State Bar Ass'n, 332 N.W.2d 151, 157 (Minn.1982).

The Comment to M.R. 1.15 states that "[s]eparate trust accounts may be warranted when administering estate monies or acting in similar fiduciary capacities." A state statute or case law may require the maintenance of a separate account in those and other situations.[53]

IOLTA Funds

IOLTA stands for Interest On Lawyers' Trust Accounts. Trust accounts containing the funds of multiple clients were traditionally non-interest bearing accounts because the lawyer has no right to the interest, and calculating and distributing the interest to each client was not administratively feasible. Today, almost all states have IOLTA plans. Under these plans the funds of multiple clients are kept in interest bearing "IOLTA accounts." The state either requires the lawyer to maintain the money of multiple clients in these accounts or allows the lawyer to do so. When an IOLTA account has been established, the bank pays the aggregate interest on the account to the state bar's IOLTA program. The money is used primarily to fund legal services for the poor, but other uses include funding of client security accounts or projects relating to the administration of justice.

Where lawyers are required to participate, the funds raised by IOLTA programs are substantial, but fluctuate with changes in interest rates. Florida, the state where IOLTA began, raised almost $1 million in the first year that its mandatory plan was in operation. In less than five years, California's mandatory program raised $40 million. Where the plans are voluntary, lawyer participation is generally low perhaps due to the fact that lawyers who keep client funds in non-interest bearing accounts are favored customers of banks. Is it ethical to accept benefits from a bank in exchange for keeping a non-interest bearing account?

After the cutbacks in federal funding for legal services programs for the poor in the early 1980s (see Chapter 11), IOLTA programs were expected to help make up the shortfall. Revenue has, however, been far below expectations where IOLTA programs are voluntary. In 1988, responding to the great difference in effectiveness between mandatory and voluntary programs, the ABA House of Delegates adopted a resolution urging states to make their voluntary IOLTA programs mandatory. Thus far, mandatory IOLTA programs have withstood constitutional challenges.[54]

The biggest threat to the continued vitality of IOLTA plans is technological innovation. Banks are developing software that makes it cost effective to keep track of the interest earned by relatively small

---

53. See, e.g., Attorney Grievance Commission v. Boehm, 293 Md. 476, 446 A.2d 52 (1982) (separate account necessary when administering an estate).

54. In Cone v. State Bar of Florida, 819 F.2d 1002 (11th Cir.1987), Florida's mandatory IOLTA program was upheld against a challenge that it constituted an unconstitutional taking of property without just compensation. See also Carroll v. State Bar of California, 166 Cal.App.3d 1193, 213 Cal.Rptr. 305 (1985) (upholding the California mandatory program against various constitutional challenges).

amounts of money deposited within larger accounts. A few banks have already made these subaccounting services available to lawyers. If the interest can be returned to the client, are IOLTA plans justified?

2. Transactions With Clients

Business Transactions [55]

Lawyer-client business dealings are addressed by Model Rule 1.8(a) and DR 5–104(A) of the Model Code.

Rule 1.8(a) provides that:

A lawyer shall not enter into a business transaction with a client *MR 1.8(a)* ... unless:

> (1) the transaction and terms ... are fair and reasonable to the client and are fully disclosed and transmitted in writing to the client ...;

> (2) the client is given reasonable opportunity to seek the advice of independent counsel in the transaction; and

> (3) the client consents in writing thereto.

The rules governing business transactions with a client apply whether or not the lawyer is actually representing the client in the transaction, but do not apply to standard business transactions made on the same terms available to other customers (e.g., a bank account or a purchase of a car). The focus is whether an ordinary person in the circumstances would look to the lawyer as a protector rather than an adversary or a person dealing at arms length.[56] A violation may be established whether or not the client suffers economic loss.[57] Even where the terms of the transaction are reasonable, failure to make full disclosure of the potential conflict of interest is a violation.[58] The requirement that a client be given a reasonable opportunity to seek the advice of independent counsel is taken seriously. The New Jersey court, interpreting Rule 1.8(a)(2), stated that a "passing suggestion" that a client consult a second attorney does not discharge the lawyer's duty to carefully explain to the client the need for independent legal advice upon entry into business transactions in which the lawyer and client have different interests.[59]

when does it apply? (see pg. 595)

Under common law, a lawyer in a transaction with a client is treated as a fiduciary. As such the lawyer has the burden of proving that the transaction is "fair and equitable" to the client. In some

---

55. See generally 1 Hazard & Hodes, Law of Lawyering 262–68 (2d ed. 1990); Wolfram, Modern Legal Ethics § 8.11 (1986). See also Restatement of Law Governing Lawyers § 207 (Tent. Draft No. 4, Apr. 10, 1991).

56. Sexton v. Arkansas Supreme Court Committee on Professional Conduct, 299 Ark. 439, 774 S.W.2d 114 (1989); Matter of Spear, 160 Ariz. 545, 774 P.2d 1335 (1989).

57. Committee on Professional Ethics and Conduct v. Baker, 269 N.W.2d 463, 466 (Iowa 1978).

58. See In re Appeal of Panel's Affirmance, 425 N.W.2d 824 (Minn.1988).

59. Matter of Smyzer, 108 N.J. 47, 527 A.2d 857, 862 (1987).

jurisdictions this requirement is augmented by a "presumption" that such a transaction is tainted by fraud. It is not always clear whether the presumption means more than imposing on the lawyer the burden of proof. Remedies include rescission of a transaction, civil liability, professional discipline and others.

The reported cases usually involve one of the following common situations: (1) lawyer buying estate property from estate beneficiaries; (2) lawyer investing funds awarded in settlement of personal injury or wrongful death action; (3) loan from client to lawyer; (4) secured loan from lawyer to client. In most cases the client was not an experienced business person. Little wonder the cases make hard law.[60]

The following cases illustrate lawyer-client business transactions that resulted in discipline of a lawyer:

- Lawyer convinced client to invest proceeds from the sale of her home in a holding company without disclosing his interest in the company;[61]

- Client loaned money to her lawyer on terms found to be usurious; the lawyer failed to disclose risks of nonpayment;[62]

- Lawyer advised a widow to invest $10,000 of her inheritance in a second mortgage on property worth one-half that amount which was owned by a company in which the lawyer owned a 25 percent interest, concealing from her the recent purchase price of the property, its real value and that the taxes on it were unpaid.[63]

In light of this sad experience, it would be defensible to prohibit any business transaction with a client except transactions in the client's ordinary course of business, such as buying a car from a client in the automobile business. Some court decisions come close to having this practical effect. In Matter of Neville,[64] for example, the client was an experienced real estate trader who had been represented by the lawyer in various real estate deals over a period of ten years. Dispute arose concerning certain deals in which the lawyer participated. The court said:

> The policy expressed by DR 5–104 is based on the realization that those who consider themselves clients come to depend upon the confidentiality and fairness arising from their relationships with their attorneys. They do not take a transactional approach to

---

60. See Roy R. Anderson and Walter W. Steele, Jr., Ethics and the Law of Contract Juxtaposed: A Jaundiced View of Professional Responsibility Considerations in the Attorney–Client Relationship, 4 Geo.J.Legal Ethics 791 (1991) (arguing that "outmoded, unrealistic concepts" impose responsibilities on lawyers that are far more restrictive than those to which other professions or even other kinds of fiduciaries are subject).

61. Matter of Smyzser, 108 N.J. 47, 527 A.2d 857 (1987).

62. Sexton v. Arkansas Supreme Court Committee on Professional Conduct, 299 Ark. 439, 774 S.W.2d 114 (1989).

63. Matter of Wolk, 82 N.J. 326, 413 A.2d 317 (1980).

64. 147 Ariz. 106, 708 P.2d 1297 (1985).

these relationships, turning their confidence on and off at the end of each transaction....

We hold ... that ... DR 5–104(A) ... applies ... to transactions in which ... an ordinary person would look to the lawyer as a protector rather than as an adversary....

The lawyer must give the client that information which he would have been obliged to give if he had been counsel rather than interested party....

If this statement of the law applies to a client who had long experience in the very type of transaction, would any substantial transaction between lawyer and client in effect be voidable at the client's option? Should a lawyer deal with a client on that assumption? Should a lawyer deal with a client at all?

A number of opinions state that the only safe course is for a lawyer to avoid all business transactions with a client.[65] Consider the following statements from courts in Arizona, Iowa and New Jersey:

The better rule may be to prohibit entirely lawyer-client business dealings.... As a general rule ... no lawyer should allow a client to invest or otherwise participate in the lawyer's business ventures unless the client obtains independent legal advice. Nothing else will protect our profession's integrity and the public interest.[66]

[W]e have done our best to discourage business ventures between attorneys and their clients.... [The lawyer has] three alternatives when [the client proposes a deal]. The safest and perhaps best course [is] to refuse to participate.... Alternatively, he [can] recommend ... the client obtain independent advice. Finally ... he [can make] the least desirable choice ... he [can] attempt ... to meet the high standard of disclosure.... [67]

As a general rule, an attorney should refrain from engaging in transactions with a client or former client who has not obtained independent legal advice on the matter.[68]

Acquiring an Interest in Litigation *prohibited*

Both the Model Rules and the Model Code prohibit the lawyer from acquiring a proprietary interest in litigation. M.R. 1.8(j) and DR 5–103(A). Important exceptions are the contingent fee, considered above, *Exception*

65. On the risks of participating in a business venture with a client, see Vanessa Merton, The Evils of Lawyer–Client Deals, Calif.Lawyer, Dec. 1987, at p. 53; and Timothy R. Benevino, Attorney–Client Business Transactions: An Analysis of the Ethical Problems, 6 J.Law & Com. 443 (1986).

66. Matter of Spear, 160 Ariz. 545, 774 P.2d 1335, 1344 (1989).

67. Committee on Professional Ethics v. Postma, 430 N.W.2d 387, 391–92 (Iowa 1988).

68. Matter of Pascoe, 113 N.J. 229, 549 A.2d 1247, 1248 (1988) (holding that client's long experience in transactions of this type does not exonerate the lawyer who otherwise violates the rule). Cf. Alala v. Peachtree Plantations, Inc., 292 S.C. 160, 355 S.E.2d 286 (1987) (after carefully scrutinizing lawyer/client transaction court found that it was acceptable given that the clients were three experienced land developers and the terms of the contract were fair).

and attorney's liens. A lawyer may acquire a lien against the client's property to secure the lawyer's fee or expenses when other law so provides.[69] Further, a lawyer may advance litigation costs when and to the extent that the rules allow. See M.R. 1.8(e) and DR 5–103(B).

An attorney's retaining lien allows a lawyer to keep possession of a client's property, but not to sell it, until the client pays what is owed to the lawyer.[70] The major issue here is the opportunity that a lawyer has to coerce a dissatisfied client into paying a fee the client does not believe the lawyer has earned by retaining client documents that are needed by successor counsel.[71] A charging lien attaches to the legal proceeding and allows the lawyer to recover expenses and fees incurred in that litigation from the proceeds. Lawyers may be disciplined for asserting charging liens that are the equivalent of illegal contingent fees.[72]

Advancing Funds to a Client

Lawyers subsidize litigation on an extensive basis. The contingent fee has the effect of loaning the value of the lawyer's services to the client, to be repaid only if and when the lawyer produces a substantial award from which the interest-free loan may be repaid. In addition, professional rules and longstanding practice permit the lawyer to advance litigation expenses (e.g., filing fees, investigation costs, fees for expert witnesses). DR 5–103(B) provides:

> While representing a client in connection with contemplated or pending litigation, a lawyer shall not advance or guarantee financial assistance to his client, except that a lawyer may advance or guarantee the expenses of litigation, including court costs, expenses of investigation, expenses of medical examination, and costs of obtaining and presenting evidence, provided that the client remains ultimately liable for such expenses.

Although the Model Code requires that "the client remains ultimately liable" for litigation expenses, lawyers are not required to press clients to recover these expenses. In most situations in which lawyers advance litigation expenses—usually where the retainer is on a contingent-fee

69. On attorneys' liens generally, see Wolfram, Modern Legal Ethics § 9.6.3, pp. 558–562 (1986).

70. For guidelines on whether to invoke a retaining lien, see ABA Inf.Op. 1461 (1980). See also Rubel v. Brimacombe & Schlecte, P.C., 86 B.R. 81 (E.D.Mich.1988) (using the guidelines to decide whether to allow an attorney's charging lien).

71. The proposed Restatement of Law Governing Lawyers § 57 (Tent. Draft No. 4, Apr. 10, 1991) states that a lawyer ordinarily may not retain a client's property or documents against the client's wishes, but Comment b concedes that "the law of all but a few jurisdictions" is to the contrary. The majority position "protects the lawyer's legitimate interest in compensation," but the use of papers entrusted to the lawyer by the client to gain help "conflicts with the fiduciary responsibilities of lawyers ... [and] may also motivate clients to keep important papers out of the hands of their lawyers, and thus foster uninformed legal services."

72. See, e.g., State ex rel. Nebraska Bar Ass'n v. Jensen, 171 Neb. 1, 105 N.W.2d 459 (1960) (attorney's lien upon 15 percent of wife's alimony was in effect a contingent fee contract).

basis for a person of moderate or limited means—the possibilities of recovery if the case fails are remote and are rarely pursued.

Model Rule 1.8(e) recognizes this reality by providing that the lawyer's investment in litigation expenses may also be contingent upon the result of the litigation. It provides:

> A lawyer shall not provide financial assistance to a client in connection with pending or contemplated litigation, except that:
>
> > (1) a lawyer may advance court costs and expenses of litigation, the repayment of which may be contingent on the outcome of the matter; and
> >
> > (2) a lawyer representing an indigent client may pay court costs and expenses of litigation on behalf of the client.

What purposes are served by these rules? Given that contingent fees are allowed in some cases, why not allow other means of acquiring an interest in litigation?

Both rules implicitly prohibit a lawyer from advancing money to a client for anything other than litigation expenses. The prohibition on advancing funds for living expenses or health care bills while litigation is pending raises a substantial issue of policy. An injured person, out of work and desperate for living and medical expenses, may be forced to settle a meritorious claim at a fraction of its real worth because the defendant, by claiming its right to jury trial and engaging in pretrial procedures, can postpone a recovery for a number of years. Under such circumstances, why shouldn't lawyers advance funds so that the plaintiff may obtain a more adequate award?

In Louisiana State Bar Ass'n v. Edwins,[73] the court held that a lawyer could provide financial assistance to a client under certain circumstances, provided that the advances were not used to solicit clients. The problems engendered by this approach are discussed in Sims v. Selvage,[74] In *Sims* the client discharged his lawyer, testifying that he did so because the lawyer refused to provide money to pay his medical fees. The court said of the *Edwins* rule:

> The obviously well intended interpretation of [DR] 5–103(B) in [*Edwins*] ..., to allow "a lawyer's guarantee of necessary medical treatment for his client, even for a non-litigation related illness ... if the lawyer for reasons of humanity can afford to do so", and to authorize as expenses of litigation, "the advance or guarantee by a lawyer to a client (who has already retained him) of minimal living expenses, of minor sums necessary to prevent foreclosures, or of necessary medical treatment" ... has created problems within the profession that override any benefit to the client. *Edwins*, in conjunction with [case law] allowing the client to withdraw from the contingency fee contract with relative impunity, pretty well

73. 329 So.2d 437 (La.1976).

74. 499 So.2d 325 (La.App.1986).

guarantees that clients will not remain with the attorney who does not gear his practice to providing this type of service. No attorney solicitation is necessary. The reputation of providing these services is enough to draw the client.... The profession is demeaned [by this situation]. Surely, it is time to reconsider this whole area.[75]

Is the "problem" discussed in *Sims* one that should concern clients or only one of increased competition for lawyers? What is it that "demeans" the profession? Why not permit a market in claims, so that able lawyers could buy up prospective claims and combine them for purposes of litigation?[76] A few other states allow lawyers to advance funds in situations prohibited under the Model Rules and Model Code.[77]

Gifts From Clients [78] *No Rule - ct looks @ EC 5-5*

Courts have always looked at substantial gifts from clients, especially those solicited by the lawyer or conferred by means of an instrument drafted by the lawyer, with a highly skeptical eye and have invalidated them on a theory of presumptive fraud unless the lawyer has clearly demonstrated that the gift was not the result of undue influence or overreaching.[79]

The problem is one of distinguishing between a Christmas present of a bottle of expensive wine from a grateful client who has become the lawyer's friend and situations in which the lawyer has used her influence with the client to induce a substantial gift. The cases record the sad reality that temptation seduces intelligent and successful lawyers who clearly knew better.[80]

Although the Model Code lacks a disciplinary rule on the subject, the courts read the strictures of EC 5–5 into general disciplinary provisions to provide a basis for disciplinary sanctions.[81] The underly-

---

75. Id. at 329.

76. For a critical view of the prohibition against acquiring an interest in litigation as it applies to plaintiffs' lawyers in class action suits, see the discussion of proposals by Professors Macey, Miller and Coffee supporting the creation of a market in claims (Chapter 8 below at p. 837).

77. See, e.g., Calif.Ct.R. 4–210. Also see M.R. 1.8(e) as amended in Minnesota and North Dakota.

78. For a thorough examination of the legality and propriety of an estate lawyer writing a will that names the lawyer as a beneficiary, executor or as attorney for the estate, see Gerald P. Johnston, An Ethical Analysis of Common Estate Planning Practices—Is Good Business Bad Ethics?, 45 Ohio State L.J. 57 (1984).

79. See, e.g., Matter of Putnam's Will, 257 N.Y. 140, 177 N.E. 399 (1931); McDonald v. Hewlett, 102 Cal.App.2d 680, 228 P.2d 83 (1951); Laspy v. Anderson, 361 S.W.2d 680 (Mo.1962); Klaskin v. Klepak, 126 Ill. 376, 128 Ill.Dec. 526, 534 N.E.2d 971 (1989); In re Mapes, 738 S.W.2d 853 (Mo.1987).

80. See Committee on Professional Ethics v. Randall, 285 N.W.2d 161 (Iowa 1979) (former ABA president disbarred for drafting a client's will making him sole beneficiary); In re Cohn, 118 A.D.2d 15, 503 N.Y.S.2d 759 (1st Dept.1986) (Roy Cohn disbarred for assisting an elderly, bedridden and probably incompetent client in signing his name to an instrument giving Cohn a substantial property interest).

81. EC 5–5 provides that: "[a] lawyer should not suggest to his client that a gift be made" to the lawyer; and that before accepting any gift from the client the lawyer should urge the client to obtain advice from an independent person. EC 5–5 concludes: "Other

[handwritten margin notes: "Pol under E-C"]

ing transaction is voidable under decisional law that presumes over-reaching and undue influence when a lawyer solicits a valuable gift or prepares an instrument effectuating it.[82]

Model Rule 1.8(c) states: *[handwritten: "can't draft Instrument giving atty/Relative any gift. –"]*

> A lawyer shall not prepare an instrument giving the lawyer or a person related to the lawyer as parent, child, sibling, or spouse any substantial gift from a client including a testamentary gift, except where the client is related to the donee.

This absolute prohibition goes beyond pre-Rules case law, which permitted a lawyer to draft such an instrument, if the lawyer had urged the client to seek independent legal assistance, provided full disclosure and the client continued to insist that the lawyer do so.[83] The Rule, however, is narrower than the cases in that the Rule only applies to substantial gifts transferred by instruments drafted by the lawyer/beneficiary. What about gifts transferred without papers?

The Comment to M.R. 1.8 assumes that any substantial gift will require the preparation of documents and thus will fall under 1.8(c). As for smaller gifts, the Comment states that these may be accepted as long as "the transaction meets general standards of fairness." When a lawyer is disqualified under M.R. 1.8(c), those in practice with the lawyer are likewise disqualified. See M.R. 1.10, discussed in Chapter 7 below.

Model Rule 1.8(c) provides an exception for instruments drafted by a lawyer for people to whom the lawyer is related. This exception, however, does not apply to friends of the lawyer. Lawyers must insist that friends who wish to make a gift to the lawyer retain other counsel to draft the documents of transfer. Even relatives of the lawyer (and the lawyer herself) are well advised to have independent counsel draft any documents of transfer whenever possible, the exception in 1.8(c) notwithstanding. If the relative wishes to make a substantial gift to

[handwritten margin note: "Exception where = client related to Donee (?)"]

---

than in exceptional circumstances, a lawyer should insist that an instrument in which [the client names the lawyer as a beneficiary] be prepared by another lawyer selected by the client." Discipline has been imposed under DR 5–101(A), the general conflict of interest provision, and under DR 1–102(A)(4) and (A)(6), prohibiting conduct that adversely reflects on the lawyer's fitness to practice, which have been read to incorporate the provisions of EC 5–5. See, e.g., Matter of Rentiers, 297 S.C. 33, 374 S.E.2d 672 (1988) (public reprimand under DR 5–101(A) for drafting a will in which the lawyer/draftsman was named as executor, trustee of a testamentary trust and given an option to purchase real estate at below market value; lawyer failed to disclose that the will would be vulnerable to attack upon grounds of undue influence); Mahoning County Bar Association v. Theofilos, 36 Ohio St.3d 43, 521 N.E.2d 797 (1988) (lawyer disciplined under DR 1–102(A)(6) for drafting a will that provided a $200,000 bequest for lawyer and his son and provided nothing for the client's relatives; lawyer failed to insist that independent counsel draft the will).

82. See, e.g., Radin v. Opperman, 64 A.D.2d 820, 407 N.Y.S.2d 303 (1978) (lawyer forced to give up Totten Trust accounts opened by client for lawyer's benefit, where no evidence of independent advice overcomes presumption of undue influence).

83. The proposed Restatement of the Law Governing Lawyers § 208(3) follows the case law rather than M.R. 1.8 in validating client gifts if the lawyer has not unduly influenced or overreached the client and has urged and given the client a reasonable opportunity to seek competent, independent advice, which need not be from another lawyer.

the lawyer or there is any chance that the gift will be challenged, independent counsel should be obtained.

Sexual Relationship With Client [84]

A growing body of case law deals with sexual relations between a lawyer and an individual client during the course of representation. In Drucker's Case [85] a lawyer was suspended for two years for sexual relations with a divorce client who suffered from an anxiety disorder; the court held that the lawyer's conduct violated M.R. 1.7(b) (conflict with the lawyer's own interests), M.R. 1.8(b) (use of client information to disadvantage the client), and M.R. 1.14(a) (failure to maintain a normal lawyer-client relationship with an impaired client). In re Marriage of Kantar [86] required a hearing of a divorce client's charges that her lawyer's $15,000 bill for services rendered included time spent in sexual liaisons. In People v. Gibbons [87] a criminal defense lawyer, who represented both a woman and her husband, initiated a sexual relationship with the female client; the lawyer, who had also engaged in other misconduct, was disbarred on conflict of interest grounds.

Although the number of reported discipline complaints involving sexual contact is relatively small,[88] a low report rate is characteristic of sexual harassment. Studies of psychotherapists' sexual involvement with patients reveal that 12 percent of psychotherapists nationwide report sexual contact with patients despite a flat professional prohibition.[89] Although Arnold Becker, the philandering divorce lawyer of *L.A. Law*, may not be typical, accumulating evidence suggests that sexual relationships between lawyers and divorce clients occur quite frequently. Manipulation and exploitation are especially probable when a client is vulnerable or in distress.

A 1992 ABA ethics opinion reviews the ethics rules that may be violated by a sexual relationship with an individual client during the course of representation.[90] First, the lawyer may breach fiduciary obligations to the client if the sexual relationship results from the client's dependence and vulnerability or the lawyer's manipulation of the client's trust.[91] Second, a lawyer's independent professional judgment may be lost due to sexual involvement with a client. M.R. 2.1. Third, a prohibited conflict with the lawyer's own interest results if

---

84. See generally Note, Keeping Sex Out of the Attorney–Client Relationship: A Proposed Rule, 92 Colum.L.Rev. 887 (1992) (discussing and proposing a per se rule banning lawyer-client sexual relationships with limited exceptions).

85. 133 N.H. 326, 577 A.2d 1198 (1990).

86. 220 Ill.App.3d 323, 163 Ill.Dec. 55, 581 N.E.2d 6 (1991).

87. 685 P.2d 168 (Colo.1984).

88. See Linda M. Jorgenson and Pamela K. Sutherland, Lawyer–Client Contact: State Bars Polled, Nat'l L. J., June 15, 1991, at p. 26 (only 90 complaints filed in 47 responding states).

89. Id. at 27.

90. ABA Standing Comm. on Ethics and Prof.Resp., Formal Op. 92–364 (July 6, 1992).

91. See M.R. 1.7(b), 1.8(a), (b), and 1.14(a).

that interest impairs or materially limits the representation. M.R. 1.7(b). Finally, client confidences are protected by the attorney-client privilege only when communications are made for the purpose of receiving legal advice, imperiling statements made during a sexual relationship. The opinion advises lawyers to refrain from sexual relationships with clients. If such a relationship occurs and actually impairs the lawyer's representation, a disciplinary violation has occurred.

Many lawyers and legislators argue that requiring a client to prove that the sexual relationship impaired the lawyer's representation poses too high a burden on the client.[92] Proposals for per bans on sexual relationships with individual clients are under consideration in several states. California is the only state thus far to have adopted a rule. As proposed by the state bar, the rule contained a rebuttable presumption that lawyers who have sexual relations with clients have received impaired representation. However, the presumption was removed by the California Supreme Court when it adopted the rule. As adopted Rule 3–120(B) of the California Rules of Professional Conduct provides that members of the California bar shall not:

> (1) Require or demand sexual relations with a client incident to or as a condition of any professional representation; or (2) Employ coercion, intimidation, or undue influence in entering into sexual relations with a client; or (3) Continue representation of a client with whom the member has sexual relations if such sexual relations cause the member to perform legal services incompetently in violation of rule 3–110.

Does the rule as adopted add anything that is not already in the ethics codes?

Should a per se rule impose discipline whenever a lawyer has sex during the course of the relationship with an individual client?[93] Opponents of a per se rule argue that existing ethics provisions deal satisfactorily with the problem, sexual harassment charges and damage actions against lawyers will be encouraged, and privacy and autonomy interests of lawyers will be impaired.[94] Does the constitutional right of privacy stand in the way of regulation of lawyer-client sexual relationships?[95] Note that a professional rule would not restrict a lawyer's

92. Legislative resolutions in California and Illinois have requested the state supreme court to adopt a professional rule dealing with lawyer-client sexual relationships. A proposed rule in Oregon was defeated by a close vote of the Oregon state bar in May 1991. See A.B.A.J. 24 (Feb. 1992).

93. The proposed rules generally provide exceptions for sexual relationships with spouses or that preexisted the representation. Some would apply only to non-business clients and most would have limited or no application to sexual relationships with agents of a corporate or organizational client.

94. See Philip Corboy, No, It's Already Covered, A.B.A.J., Jan. 1992, at p. 35; William C. Barker and C. Harker Rhodes, Jr., Draconian Sex Rules Premature, Nat'l L.J., June 29, 1992, at p. 17.

95. See Carey v. Population Services International, 431 U.S. 678, 684 (1977) (one aspect of the "liberty" protected by the due process clause of the Fourteenth Amendment

sexual relationships, but only require that she withdraw from representation before commencing a sexual relationship.

G. TERMINATING THE LAWYER-CLIENT RELATIONSHIP

1. Withdrawal

Mandatory Withdrawal

Model Rule 1.16 and DR 2–110 cover withdrawal, mandatory and permissive. The Model Code provision differs from the Rule in that it seems not to require withdrawal except in a case before a tribunal. See DR 2–110(B). The better and common reading is that withdrawal is required under the Code in any of the situations listed in DR 2–110(B) whether or not the lawyer is before a tribunal.

Both the Rules and the Code require withdrawal when the client discharges the lawyer. Withdrawal also is required if the lawyer is too ill to continue the representation.[1] Finally and perhaps most important, withdrawal is required when the continuing representation will result in a violation of ethics rules or other law.[2]

How sure must the lawyer be that the representation will result in a violation of other law or the rules before withdrawal is mandatory? Do M.R. 1.16(b)(2) and DR 2–110(C)(2) help answer the question? Also see DR 2–110(C)(1)(a), (b) and (c).

As the *Balla* case makes clear, the provisions on withdrawal are part of the package of ethical rules dealing with client crime or fraud. They should be read in conjunction with other provisions of the codes: (1) the prohibition against lawyer participation in criminal or fraudulent conduct;[3] (2) provisions requiring or permitting disclosure of client fraud;[4] and (3) provisions requiring disclosure of fraud on the court.[5]

M.R. 1.16 covers declining to undertake representation as well as withdrawal. Therefore, the provisions in M.R. 1.16(a) would require a lawyer not to accept employment in any of the situations outlined in

is the right to certain zones of privacy); but cf. Bowers v. Hardwick, 478 U.S. 186 (1986) (state may regulate sodomy).

1. M.R. 1.16(a)(2) and DR 2–110(B)(3). See also M.R. 1.1 and 1.3 and DR 6–101(A)(3) (dealing with lawyer competence and diligence).

2. M.R. 1.16(a)(1) and DR 2–110(B)(2). Note that while DR 2–110(B)(2) does not mention "other law," it is a violation of the Code to violate other law in the course of the representation, DR 7–102(B)(7), and thus withdrawal is required under DR 2–110(B)(2).

3. M.R. 1.2(d) and DR 7–102(A)(7); see the discussion of prohibited assistance at p. 57 above.

4. DR 4–101(C)(3); DR 7–102(B)(1); M.R. 1.6(b); and the Comment to 1.6(b) on giving notice of withdrawal (regulating the disclosure of client confidences to prevent or rectify criminal or fraudulent conduct); see the discussion of client fraud at p. 294 above.

5. M.R. 3.3 and DR 7–102(B)(1) (on disclosing fraud on the court); see the discussion of client perjury at p. 357 above. See also M.R. 2.3 (evaluations conducted for third parties); and M.R. 4.1 (honesty in dealing with nonclients).

that section. The Model Code deals with the decision to accept employment in a separate provision, DR 2–109.

Permissive Withdrawal

Model Rule 1.16(b) and DR 2–110(C) state the circumstances under which a lawyer *may* withdraw from representation, in effect, "fire" the client. Lawyers do not have the same freedom as clients to withdraw from the relationship. If the matter is before a tribunal, withdrawal must be with the court's permission. In Kriegsman v. Kriegsman,[6] for example, a law firm agreed to represent a client in a divorce action, eventually receiving $2,000 from her in fees. Billings and disbursements on the case, however, had exceeded $7,500 because the opposing spouse, acting pro se, was totally uncooperative and refused to comply with some court orders. The client, who was on welfare and unable to pay further charges, successfully opposed her lawyers' motion's to withdraw. The court stated:

> When a firm accepts a retainer to conduct a legal proceeding, it impliedly agrees to prosecute the matter to a conclusion. The firm is not at liberty to abandon the case without justifiable or reasonable cause, or the consent of its client....
>
> ... The firm should not be relieved at this stage of the litigation merely because plaintiff is unable to pay them all of the fees they have demanded.... [An attorney's] obligations do not evaporate because the case becomes more complicated or the work more arduous or the retainer not as profitable as first contemplated or imagined....[7]

M.R. 1.16(b) is clearer than DR 2–110(C) in differentiating between withdrawal for cause and withdrawal without cause. A lawyer may withdraw (or decline to undertake representation) for any reason or no reason as long as withdrawal can be accomplished without "material adverse effect" on the client. A lawyer may withdraw even if there is harm to the client if the withdrawal is for any of the six reasons listed in 1.16(b). DR 2–110(C), permissive withdrawal before a tribunal, also list six reasons, but the reasons listed in the Code and Rules differ. Compare DR 2–110(C) and M.R. 1.16(b). In some sense, all of the items in the Code's list deal with client misconduct. On the other hand, M.R. 1.16(b)(5) and (6) do not necessarily involve client conduct at all. Do they give the lawyer too much latitude to abandon a client such as the one in *Kriegsman*? Is M.R. 1.16(b)(6) so broad that it swallows the rest of 1.16(b)?

In Picker Int'l v. Varian Associates,[8] the court held that a lawyer could not withdraw from representation, regardless of actual prejudice, if the purpose was to take on representation in a matter hostile to the client but nonrelated to the prior matter. Does this rule—prohibiting a

---

6. 150 N.J.Super. 474, 375 A.2d 1253 (1977).

7. 375 A.2d at 1255–56.

8. 869 F.2d 578 (Fed.Cir.1989).

lawyer from "dropping a client like a hot potato"—extend the duty of loyalty or merely state a corollary? Compare M.R. 1.7 and 1.9. See Chapter 7 generally.

Protecting a Client Upon Withdrawal

Under the Model Code, whether a lawyer is required to withdraw or permitted to withdraw, it must be accomplished in accordance with DR 2–110(A). Compare M.R. 1.16(c) and (d). In addition to M.R. 1.16, other Model Rules regulate a lawyer's actions after withdrawal. For example, the Comment to M.R. 1.6 discusses giving notice of withdrawal, see Chapter 4 above; and M.R. 1.9 prohibits future representations that are materially adverse to a former client unless the former client consents, see Chapter 7 below, and requires a lawyer to keep in confidence the former client's secrets.

2. Discharge and Its Consequences

Terminating Inside Counsel

BALLA v. GAMBRO, INC.

Supreme Court of Illinois, 1991.
145 Ill.2d 492, 164 Ill.Dec. 892, 584 N.E.2d 104.

*atty dischArGed
Because told
Pres. he would
do anything
he could to
stop shipment*

JUSTICE CLARK delivered the opinion of the court:

The issue in this case is whether in-house counsel should be allowed the remedy of an action for retaliatory discharge.

Appellee, Roger Balla, formerly in-house counsel for Gambro, Inc. (Gambro), filed a retaliatory discharge action against Gambro, its affiliate ... (Gambro Germany), [and] its parent company ... (Gambro Sweden) ... in the circuit court of Cook County (Gambro, Gambro Germany and Gambro Sweden [are] collectively referred to as appellants). Appellee alleged that he was fired in contravention of Illinois public policy and sought damages for the discharge. The trial court dismissed the action on appellants' motion for summary judgment. The appellate court reversed. (203 Ill.App.3d 57, 560 N.E.2d 1043.) We granted appellant's petition for leave to appeal and allowed amicus curiae briefs from the American Corporate Counsel Association and Illinois State Bar Association.

Gambro is a distributor of kidney dialysis equipment manufactured by Gambro Germany. Among the products distributed by Gambro are dialyzers which filter excess fluid and toxic substances from the blood of patients with no or impaired kidney function. The manufacture and sale of dialyzers is regulated by the United States Food and Drug Administration (FDA)....

Appellee, Roger J. Balla, is and was at all times throughout this controversy an attorney licensed to practice law in the State of Illinois. On March 17, 1980, appellee executed an employment agreement with

Gambro which contained the terms of appellee's employment.... [Balla's duties included assuring "compliance with applicable laws and regulations." He supervised the manager of regulatory affairs and in 1983, when the person holding that position left the company, Balla also assumed the specific duties of that position. Gambro's corporate organizational chart referred to appellee's positions as "Dir. of Admin./Personnel; General Counsel; Mgr. of Regulatory Affairs."]

In July 1985 Gambro Germany informed Gambro in a letter that certain dialyzers it had manufactured, the clearances of which varied from the package insert, were about to be shipped to Gambro. Referring to these dialyzers, Gambro Germany advised Gambro:

> "For acute patients risk is that the acute uremic situation will not be improved in spite of the treatment, giving continuous high levels of potassium, phosphate and urea/creatine. The chronic patient may note the effect as a slow progression of the uremic situation and depending on the interval between medical check-ups the medical risk may not be overlooked."

Appellee told the president of Gambro to reject the shipment because the dialyzers did not comply with FDA regulations. The president notified Gambro Germany of its decision to reject the shipment on July 12, 1985.

However, one week later the president informed Gambro Germany that Gambro would accept the dialyzers and "sell [them] to a unit that is not currently our customer but who buys only on price." Appellee contends that he was not informed by the president of the decision to accept the dialyzers but became aware of it through other Gambro employees. Appellee maintains that he spoke with the president in August regarding the company's decision to accept the dialyzers and told the president that he would do whatever necessary to stop the sale of the dialyzers.

On September 4, 1985, appellee was discharged from Gambro's employment by its president. The following day, appellee reported the shipment of the dialyzers to the FDA. The FDA seized the shipment and determined the product to be "adulterated within the meaning of section 501(h) of the [Federal Act]."

On March 19, 1986, appellee filed a four-count complaint in tort for retaliatory discharge seeking $22 million in damages....

. . .

We agree with the trial court that appellee does not have a cause of action against Gambro for retaliatory discharge under the facts of the case at bar. Generally, this court adheres to the proposition that " 'an employer may discharge an employee-at-will for any reason or for no reason [at all].' " (Fellhauer v. City of Geneva (1991), 142 Ill.2d 495, 505, quoting Barr v. Kelso–Burnett Co. (1985), 106 Ill.2d 520, 525, 478 N.E.2d 1354.) However, in Kelsay v. Motorola, Inc. (1978), 74 Ill.2d 172, 384 N.E.2d 353, this court first recognized the limited and narrow tort of retaliatory discharge. In *Kelsay*, an at-will employee was fired for filing a worker's compensation claim against her employer. After examining the history and purpose behind the Workers' Compensation Act to determine the public policy behind its enactment, this court held that the employee should have a cause of action for retaliatory discharge. This court stressed that if employers could fire employees for filing workers' compensation claims, the public policy behind the enactment of the Workers' Compensation Act would be frustrated.

Subsequently, in Palmateer v. International Harvester Co. (1981), 85 Ill.2d 124, 421 N.E.2d 876, this court again examined the tort of retaliatory discharge. In *Palmateer*, an employee was discharged for informing the police of suspected criminal activities of a co-employee, and because he agreed to provide assistance in any investigation and trial of the matter. Based on the public policy favoring the investigation and prosecution of crime, this court held that the employee had a cause of action for retaliatory discharge. Further, we stated:

> "All that is required [to bring a cause of action for retaliatory discharge] is that the employer discharge the employee in retaliation for the employee's activities, and that the discharge be in contravention of a clearly mandated public policy." 85 Ill.2d at 134.

In this case it appears that Gambro discharged appellee, an employee of Gambro, in retaliation for his activities, and this discharge was in contravention of a clearly mandated public policy. Appellee allegedly told the president of Gambro that he would do whatever was necessary to stop the sale of the "misbranded and/or adulterated" dialyzers. In appellee's eyes, the use of these dialyzers could cause death or serious bodily harm to patients. As we have stated before, "[t]here is no public policy more important or more fundamental than the one favoring the effective protection of the lives and property of citizens." (85 Ill.2d at 132 ...). However, in this case, appellee was not just an employee of Gambro, but also general counsel for Gambro.

... [I]n Herbster v. North American Co. for Life & Health Insurance (1986), 150 Ill.App.3d 21, 501 N.E.2d 343, our appellate court held that the plaintiff, an employee and chief legal counsel for the defendant company, did not have a claim for retaliatory discharge against the company due to the presence of the attorney-client relationship. Under the facts of that case, the defendant company allegedly requested the plaintiff to destroy or remove discovery information which had been requested in lawsuits pending against the company. The plaintiff refused arguing that such conduct would constitute fraud and violate several provisions of the Illinois Code of Professional Responsibility. Subsequently, the defendant company discharged the plaintiff.

The appellate court refused to extend the tort of retaliatory discharge to the plaintiff in *Herbster* primarily because of the special relationship between an attorney and client. The court stated:

"The mutual trust, exchanges of confidence, reliance on judgment, and personal nature of the attorney-client relationship demonstrate the unique position attorneys occupy in our society." (150 Ill. App.3d at 29.)

The appellate court recited a list of factors which make the attorney-client relationship special such as: the attorney-client privilege regarding confidential communications, the fiduciary duty an attorney owes to a client, the right of the client to terminate the relationship with or without cause, and the fact that a client has exclusive control over the subject matter of the litigation and a client may dismiss or settle a cause of action regardless of the attorney's advice. Thus, in *Herbster*, since the plaintiff's duties pertained strictly to legal matters, the appellate court determined that the plaintiff did not have a claim for retaliatory discharge.

We agree with the conclusion reached in *Herbster* that, generally, in-house counsel do not have a claim under the tort of retaliatory discharge. However, we base our decision as much on the nature and purpose of the tort of retaliatory discharge, as on the effect on the attorney-client relationship that extending the tort would have. In addition, at this time, we caution that our holding is confined by the fact that appellee is and was at all times throughout this controversy an attorney licensed to practice law in the State of Illinois. Appellee is and was subject to the Illinois Code of Professional Responsibility (see the Rules of Professional Conduct which replaced the Code of Professional Responsibility, effective August 1, 1990), adopted by this court. The tort of retaliatory discharge is a limited and narrow exception to the general rule of at-will employment. (See *Fellhauer*, 142 Ill.2d at 505.) The tort seeks to achieve " 'a proper balance ... among the employer's interest in operating a business efficiently and profitably, the employee's interest in earning a livelihood, and society's interest in seeing its public policies carried out.' " Further, as stated in *Palmateer*, "*[t]he foundation of the tort of retaliatory discharge lies in the protection of public policy ....*" (Emphasis added.)

In this case, the public policy to be protected, that of protecting the lives and property of citizens, is adequately safeguarded without extending the tort of retaliatory discharge to in-house counsel. Appellee was required under the Rules of Professional Conduct to report Gambro's intention to sell the "misbranded and/or adulterated" dialyzers. Rule 1.6(b) of the Rules of Professional Conduct reads:

> "A lawyer *shall* reveal information about a client to the extent it appears necessary to prevent the client from committing an act that would result in death or serious bodily injury." (Emphasis added.) (134 Ill.2d R. 1.6(b).)

Appellee alleges, and the FDA's seizure of the dialyzers indicates, that the use of the dialyzers would cause death or serious bodily injury. Thus, under the above-cited rule, appellee was under the mandate of this court to report the sale of these dialyzers.

*π = there are
2 bad
choices
if tell
or not
tell*

... [A]ppellee argues that not extending the tort of retaliatory discharge to in-house counsel would present attorneys with a "Hobson's choice." According to appellee, in-house counsel would face two alternatives: either comply with the client/employer's wishes and risk both the loss of a professional license and exposure to criminal sanctions, or decline to comply with client/employer's wishes and risk the loss of a full-time job and the attendant benefits. We disagree. Unlike the employees in *Kelsay* which this court recognized would be left with the difficult decision of choosing between whether to file a workers' compensation claim and risk being fired, or retaining their jobs and losing their right to a remedy (see *Kelsay*, 74 Ill.2d at 182, 384 N.E.2d 353), in-house counsel plainly are not confronted with such a dilemma. In-house counsel do not have a choice of whether to follow their ethical obligations as attorneys licensed to practice law, or follow the illegal and unethical demands of their clients. In-house counsel must abide by the Rules of Professional Conduct. Appellee had no choice but to report to the FDA Gambro's intention to sell or distribute these dialyzers, and consequently protect the aforementioned public policy.

*Would
contravene
client's ability
to discharge
atty ī or s̄
cause –*

In addition, we believe that extending the tort of retaliatory discharge to in-house counsel would have an undesirable effect on the attorney-client relationship that exists between these employers and their in-house counsel. Generally, a client may discharge his attorney at any time, with or without cause.... This rule applies equally to in-house counsel as it does to outside counsel. Further, this rule "recognizes that the relationship between an attorney and client is based on trust and that the client must have confidence in his attorney in order to ensure that the relationship will function properly." (78 Ill.2d at 228;....) As stated in *Herbster*, "the attorney is placed in the unique position of maintaining a close relationship with a client where the attorney receives secrets, disclosures, and information that otherwise would not be divulged to intimate friends." (150 Ill.App.3d at 27.) We believe that if in-house counsel are granted the right to sue their employers for retaliatory discharge, employers might be less willing to be forthright and candid with their in-house counsel. Employers might be hesitant to turn to their in-house counsel for advice regarding potentially questionable corporate conduct knowing that their in-house counsel could use this information in a retaliatory discharge suit.

*Employers
might
limit
communication
ī counsel.*

We recognize that under the Illinois Rules of Professional Conduct, attorneys shall reveal client confidences or secrets in certain situations (see 134 Ill.2d Rules 1.6(a), (b), (c)), and thus one might expect employers/clients to be naturally hesitant to rely on in-house counsel for advice regarding this potentially questionable conduct. However, the danger exists that if in-house counsel are granted a right to sue their employers in tort for retaliatory discharge, employers might further limit their communication with their in-house counsel. As stated in Upjohn Co. v. United States (1981), 449 U.S. 383, 389, regarding the attorney-client privilege:

"Its purpose is to encourage full and frank communication between attorneys and their clients and thereby promote broader public interests in the observance of law and administration of justice. The privilege recognizes that sound legal advice or advocacy serves public ends and that *such advice or advocacy depends upon the lawyer being fully informed by the client.*" (Emphasis added.)

If extending the tort of retaliatory discharge might have a chilling effect on the communications between the employer/client and the in-house counsel, we believe that it is more wise to refrain from doing so.

Our decision not to extend the tort of retaliatory discharge to in-house counsel also is based on other ethical considerations. Under the Rules of Professional Conduct, appellee was required to withdraw from representing Gambro if continued representation would result in the violation of the Rules of Professional Conduct by which appellee was bound, or if Gambro discharged the appellee. (See 134 Ill.2d Rules 1.16(a)(2), (a)(4).) In this case, Gambro did discharge appellee, and according to appellee's claims herein, his continued representation of Gambro would have resulted in a violation of the Rules of Professional Conduct. Appellee argues that such a choice of withdrawal is "simplistic and uncompassionate, and is completely at odds with contemporary realities facing in-house attorneys." These contemporary realities apparently are the economic ramifications of losing his position as in-house counsel. However difficult economically and perhaps emotionally it is for in-house counsel to discontinue representing an employer/client, we refuse to allow in-house counsel to sue their employer/client for damages because they obeyed their ethical obligations. In this case, appellee, in addition to being an employee at Gambro, is first and foremost an attorney bound by the Rules of Professional Conduct. These Rules of Professional Conduct hope to articulate in a concrete fashion certain values and goals such as defending the integrity of the judicial system, promoting the administration of justice and protecting the integrity of the legal profession. (See Ill. Const.1970, Preamble.) An attorney's obligation to follow these Rules of Professional Conduct should not be the foundation for a claim of retaliatory discharge.

We also believe that it would be inappropriate for the employer/client to bear the economic costs and burdens of their in-house counsel's adhering to their ethical obligations under the Rules of Professional Conduct. Presumably, in situations where an in-house counsel obeys his or her ethical obligations and reveals certain information regarding the employer/client, the attorney-client relationship will be irreversibly strained and the client will more than likely discharge its in-house counsel. In this scenario, if we were to grant the in-house counsel the right to sue the client for retaliatory discharge, we would be shifting the burden and costs of obeying the Rules of Professional Conduct from the attorney to the employer/client. The employer/client would be forced to pay damages to its former in-house counsel to essentially mitigate the financial harm the attorney suffered for having to abide by Rules of Professional Conduct. This, we believe, is impermissible for all attorneys know or should know that at certain times in their professional career, they will have to forgo economic gains in order to protect the integrity of the legal profession.

Our review of cases from other jurisdictions dealing with this issue does not persuade us to hold otherwise. In Willy v. Coastal Corp. (S.D.Tex.1986), 647 F.Supp. 116, the district court declined to extend the tort of retaliatory discharge to the wrongful termination of in-house counsel. In that case, the plaintiff, in-house counsel for the defendant company, alleged that he was fired because he required the defendant to comply with environmental laws. The court held that the ethical canons and disciplinary rules set forth the standards for attorneys to follow and that they require an attorney presented with ethical conflicts to withdraw from representation. Further, once the client elects to terminate the relationship, "the attorney is required *mandatorily* to withdraw from any further representation of that client." (Emphasis in original.) 647 F.Supp. at 118.

Also, in Nordling v. Northern States Power Co. (Minn.App.1991), 465 N.W.2d 81, the appellate court of Minnesota, relying exclusively on our appellate court's decision in *Herbster*, held that the plaintiff's status as in-house counsel precluded not only a breach-of-contract claim against the defendant company, but also the plaintiff's retaliatory discharge claim. (465 N.W.2d at 86 n. 1.) ... Since the relationship between the plaintiff and the defendant company required an atmosphere of continued mutual trust, the breakdown of that trust allowed the defendant to discharge the plaintiff without liability.

In contrast to the two cases discussed above which specifically held that in-house counsel do not have a right to sue for retaliatory discharge, two other cases have allowed in-house counsel to sue their employer for wrongful termination. However, both cases are distinguishable from our holding. In Parker v. M & T Chemicals, Inc. (1989), 236 N.J.Super. 451, 566 A.2d 215, the superior court of New Jersey construed that State's "Whistleblowers Act" as compelling "a retaliating employer to pay damages to an employee-attorney who is wrongfully discharged or mistreated ... for any reason which is violative of law, fraudulent, criminal, or incompatible with a clear mandate of New Jersey's public policy concerning public health, safety or welfare." (566 A.2d at 220.) The court also noted in distinguishing the aforementioned *Herbster* and *Willy* opinions that they did not involve "whistleblower" statutes, only the right of in-house counsel to maintain a cause of action for retaliatory discharge at common law. (566 A.2d at 220.)

In Mourad v. Automobile Club Insurance Association (1991), 186 Mich.App. 715, 465 N.W.2d 395, the plaintiff, as in-house counsel for the defendant company, sued the defendant for, *inter alia*, breach of employment contract and retaliatory demotion. The appellate court of Michigan determined that the plaintiff had a cause of action for breach of a just-cause contract, but not for retaliatory demotion. The court distinguished the aforementioned *Herbster*, *Willy* and *Parker* cases as involving the issue of whether the "state will recognize a public policy exception to the typical employment-at-will contract." (465 N.W.2d at 399.) In this case, however, the Michigan court stated that the defendant company's policy manual and pamphlets had created a contract to terminate for just cause. Thus, plaintiff's claim for retaliatory demotion was an alternative theory of recovery from a breach of a just-cause contract, and could not be sustained as an independent claim for recovery. The Michigan court made no statements regarding the propriety of in-house counsel's bringing claims for retaliatory discharge.

[The court considered and rejected Balla's factual claim that he was acting in a lay capacity, and not as corporate counsel, in his role as manager of regulatory affairs. Balla's job description and deposition testimony established that "the two roles ... were so intertwined" that he was "inescapably engaged in the practice of law" as corporate general counsel.]

For the foregoing reasons, the decision of the appellate court is reversed, and the decision of the trial court is affirmed.

JUSTICE FREEMAN, dissenting:

... [T]he majority first reasons that the public policy implicated in this case, i.e., protecting the lives and property of Illinois citizens, is adequately safeguarded by the lawyer's ethical obligation to reveal information about a client as necessary to prevent acts that would result in death or serious bodily harm (134 Ill.2d R. 1.6(b)). I find this reasoning fatally flawed.

... [T]o say that the categorical nature of ethical obligations is sufficient to ensure that the ethical obligations will be satisfied simply ignores reality. Specifically, it ignores that, as unfortunate for society as it may be, attorneys are no less human than nonattorneys and, thus, no less given to the temptation to either ignore or rationalize away their ethical obligations when complying therewith may render them unable to feed and support their families.

I would like to believe, as my colleagues apparently conclude, that attorneys will always "do the right thing" because the law says that they must. However, my knowledge of human nature, which is not much greater than the average layman's, and, sadly, the recent scandals involving the bench and bar of Illinois are more than sufficient to dispel such a belief. Just as the ethical obligations of the lawyers and judges involved in those scandals were inadequate to ensure that they would not break the law, I am afraid that the lawyer's ethical obligation to "blow the whistle" is likewise an inadequate safeguard for the public policy of protecting lives and property of Illinois citizens.

... [T]his court must take whatever steps it can, within the bounds of the law, to give lawyers incentives to abide by their ethical obligations, beyond the satisfaction inherent in their doing so. We cannot continue to delude ourselves and the people of the State of Illinois that attorneys' ethical duties, alone, are always sufficient to guarantee that lawyers will "do the right thing." In the context of this case, where doing "the right thing" will often result in termination by an employer bent on doing the "wrong thing," I believe that the incentive needed is recognition of a cause of action for retaliatory discharge, in the appropriate case.

The majority also bases its holding upon the reasoning that allowing in-house counsel a cause of action for retaliatory discharge will have a chilling effect on the attorney-client relationship and the free flow of information necessary to that relationship. . . .

One of the basic purposes of the attorney-client relationship, especially in the corporate client-in-house counsel setting, is for the attorney to advise the client as to, exactly, what conduct the law requires so that the client can then comply with that advice. Given that purpose, allowing in-house counsel a cause of action for retaliatory discharge would chill the attorney-client relationship and discourage a corporate client from communicating freely with the attorney only where, as here, the employer decides to go forward with particular conduct, regardless of advice that it is contrary to law. I believe that, just as in-house counsel might reasonably so assume, this court is entitled to assume that corporate clients will rarely so decide. As such, to allow a corporate employer to discharge its in-house counsel under such circumstances, without fear of any sanction, is truly to give the assistance and protection of the courts to scoundrels.

. . .

In holding as it does, the majority also reasons that an attorney's obligation to follow the Rules of Professional Conduct should not be the basis for a claim of retaliatory discharge. . . . It is incontrovertible that the law binds all men, kings and paupers alike. . . . An attorney should not be punished simply because he has ethical obligations imposed upon him over and above the general obligation to obey the law which all men have. Nor should a corporate employer be protected simply because the employee it has discharged for "blowing the whistle" happens to be an attorney.

. . . [T]he majority ignores the employer's decision to persist in the questionable conduct which its in-house counsel advised was illegal. It is that conduct, not the attorney's ethical obligations, which is the predicate of the retaliatory discharge claim. . . . [G]ranting the attorney a claim for retaliatory discharge simply allows recovery against the party bent on breaking the law, rather than rewarding an attorney for complying with his ethical obligations.

. . .

[T]his case involves an attorney discharged from his employment, not one who has voluntarily resigned due to his ethical obligations. . . . [T]e majority overlooks the very real possibility that in-house counsel who is discharged, rather than allowed to resign in accordance with his ethical obligations once the employer's persistence in illegal conduct is evident to him, will be stigmatized within the legal profession. That stigma and its apparent consequences, economic and otherwise, in addition to the immediate economic consequences of a discharge, also militate strongly in favor of allowing the attorney a claim for retaliatory discharge.

Retaliatory Discharge Claims by Lawyers [9]

Why should a lawyer employed by an organization receive less protection against retaliatory discharge that violates a state's public policy than other employees of the organization? The *Balla* case links issues considered throughout this book: the lawyer's duties not to assist a client in violating the law (Chapter 2 on Conformity to Law), to maintain client confidentiality (Chapter 4 on Confidentiality), to withdraw if continued representation will violate law or a professional rule (Chapters 4 and 6, dealing with the obligation to withdraw) and the economic consequences of withdrawal for good cause (considered here). Does the Illinois court correctly balance the competing interests involved? What might attorney Balla have done differently? See the discussion of Model Rule 1.13 in connection with the *Carter and Johnson* case, printed below at p. 779.

The Illinois version of the confidentiality rule, M.R. 1.6(b), unlike that adopted by the ABA, does not limit a lawyer's disclosure authority to situations in which the client's conduct is "criminal" and threatens "*imminent* death or substantial bodily harm." Further, Illinois imposes a mandatory duty of disclosure ("shall reveal") rather than a permission to disclose as in M.R. 1.6(b). If Illinois had adopted M.R. 1.6(b) as proposed by the ABA, would Balla have been under a professional duty to disclose? Suppose Gambro, Inc. had been engaged in a continuing fraud and the professional rule *prohibits* disclosure (Illinois also permits disclosure of "the intention of a client to commit a crime"). What result? Does the *Balla* court take the position that the ethics rule trumps other law?

Suppose lawyer Balla had been asked by his employer to forge a document or falsify a statement to a governmental body, both constituting criminal acts. Is a refusal to act in those situations more deserving of protection than the reporting issue in *Balla*, which involves a lawyer taking the initiative to "betray" a client's confidences?

In Wieder v. Skala,[10] a breach-of-contract claim was upheld in a different context of lawyer employment—an associate alleged he was fired by his law firm because he insisted that the firm report the

9. See Stephen Gillers, Protecting Lawyers Who Just Say No, 5 Georgia St.L.Rev. 1 (1988) (critique of the *Herbster* decision discussed in *Balla*). Also see Daniel S. Reynolds, Wrongful Discharge of Employed Counsel, 1 Geo.J.Legal Ethics 553 (1988).

10. 80 N.Y.2d 628, 593 N.Y.S.2d 752, 609 N.E.2d 105 (1992).

professional misconduct of another lawyer in the firm.[11] The New York court relied on the disciplinary rule requiring any lawyer knowing about another lawyer's misconduct to report such conduct to the disciplinary authorities. Because of the disciplinary rule, the relationship between a lawyer and a legal employer is not merely that of employer and employee. Lawyers are also "independent officers of the court responsible in a broader public sense for their professional obligations." The disciplinary rules created an "implied understanding", on both sides, that neither will do anything to prevent the other from upholding the rule. Firing a lawyer for acting ethically breaches this implied term of the law firm's employment contract with an associate. Is *Wieder* inconsistent with *Balla*? Perhaps the answer will turn on whether a lawyer's ethical "duty to report" is an implied term of an employment contract only when the contract is between lawyers, as in *Wieder*, or includes contracts between a lawyer and a non-lawyer, as in *Balla*.

Suppose Balla had been an outside lawyer whose principal client was Gambro, Inc.? Does a discharged outside lawyer have any remedy against the former client? The retaliatory discharge tort is a common law development arising out of termination of employment. The agency relationship of a client with an independent contractor presumably is outside its purview. Because outside lawyers generally work for a number of clients, discharge by one client does not involve the same degree of economic dependency. The economic consequences of discharge of lawyers who undertake a case on a contingent fee basis are discussed in *Plaza Shoe*, reprinted below, and its accompanying notes. To the extent that Balla's employment contract provides vested rights (e.g., employment for a term of years, pension rights), Gambro, Inc. cannot eliminate them by discharging him without cause.

Fees on Termination

PLAZA SHOE STORE v. HERMEL

Supreme Court of Missouri, en banc, 1982.
636 S.W.2d 53.

MORGAN, JUDGE.

[Plaintiff, Plaza Shoe Store, suffered damages, apparently from water leakage, because of allegedly negligent design or construction of shopping center premises which it had rented under a long-term lease. Represented by predecessor counsel, it brought suit for $43,441 in damages against the owner of the shopping center. After discharging those lawyers, Plaza Shoe entered into a one-third contingency fee agreement with the law firm of Greene, Cassity to press the claim. Greene, Cassity corrected the pleadings shortly before the statute of

---

11. The court rejected the tort theory of retaliatory discharge, which has been construed in New York as limited to situations covered by a relatively narrow statute.

limitations would have run to name the proper plaintiffs, added claims against the architect and builder, defeated a motion by defendants for summary judgment and prepared the case for trial.

[The firm recommended rejection of settlement offers of $25,000 and $47,500, but later advised acceptance of a $50,000 offer including a long-term reduction in rent. Plaza Shoe rejected all three offers and on the occasion of the third offer "accused [the firm] of being crooks and selling them out to defendants." The antagonism was so severe that the firm withdrew, a withdrawal that the court treated as a discharge by the client without cause. After withdrawal Greene, Cassity filed notice of a charging lien <u>on any proceeds</u> awarded in the proceeding. A third set of lawyers then took over the litigation and eventually obtained a $58,000 settlement, which the court held in escrow.

[Greene, Cassity then sought to enforce the charging lien against the proceeds, asking for the contract amount of one-third plus expenses. The trial court, after considering evidence of the hours worked, expenses incurred and services performed, found that Greene, Cassity was entitled to the contract amount. In the alternative, the trial court found that the reasonable value of the law firm's services and expenses was $15,190.]

. . .

This case comes before us upon transfer from the Court of Appeals, Southern District, with an opportunity to consider again the proper recovery to be made available to an attorney discharged without cause by a client after legal services have been rendered pursuant to a contingent fee contract but before judgment or settlement has been reached. Prior decisions in this state have held that an attorney may treat the contract as rescinded and sue for the reasonable value of services rendered until the time of discharge; or, at his or her option treat the cause of action as liquidated by reduction to judgment (or settlement) and proceed upon the contingent fee contract.... Appellants [defendants below] invite this court to review the above holdings, taking into account the modern trend toward limiting the discharged attorney's recovery to the reasonable value of services rendered up to the time of discharge.

. . .

... Missouri has been among those states that adhere to the so-called "contract rule" with the employment agreement between attorney and client being treated as any other employment contract. However, there are persuasive reasons why the contract between attorney and client should not be lumped together with those of ordinary trades....

The Florida Supreme Court recently found need to reevaluate its policy with reference to the recovery an attorney employed under a contingent fee contract may have, after discharge without cause, in Rosenberg v. Levin, 409 So.2d 1016 (Fla.1982). After recognizing the differing theories, discussed later herein, with respect to alternative means of recovery available to the discharged attorney, the court enunciated the public policy which must guide the Court throughout any discussion: "The attorney-client relationship is one of special trust and confidence. The client must rely entirely on the good faith efforts of the attorney in representing his interests. This reliance requires that the client have complete confidence in the integrity and ability of the attorney and that absolute fairness and candor characterize all dealings between them." 409 So.2d at 1021. From this premise, the court logically reasoned that the unique aspects of the attorney-client relationship dictate that the client be given greater freedom to change legal representation than might be tolerated in other employment relationships. With this, the court overruled prior holdings which followed the majority or "contract rule," and adheres now to the growing minority or "modern rule", which limits the discharged attorney's recovery to the reasonable value of services rendered (quantum meruit). Id. at 1022....

The so-called modern rule is built upon the foundation of the special confidence and trust which should set the attorney-client relationship apart from other employment relationships. As stated in Martin v. Camp, 219 N.Y. 170, 114 N.E. 46 (1916), at p. 47, "the peculiar relation of trust and confidence that such a relationship implies injects into the contract certain special and unique features." Taking into account this special relationship, and the greater freedom to change legal representation mandated thereby, the courts which observe the modern rule allow a client to discharge his attorney, with or without cause, at any time.... [1] To quote again from the *Martin* case:

> The discharge of the attorney by his client does not constitute a breach of the contract, because it is a term of such contract, implied from the peculiar relationship which the contract calls into existence, that the client may terminate the contract at any time with or without cause.

114 N.E. at 48.

Besides being in the best interests of both the clients and the legal profession as a whole, *Rosenberg*, supra, at 1021, it can be said that the modern rule strikes a better balance between the client's power to discharge his attorney without undue restrictions and the attorney's right to fair compensation for services rendered. The majority-contract rule, which contemplates requiring payment of the contracted contingent fee regardless of the posture of the case at the time of discharge, was and continues to be patently unfair to clients, particularly where the client truly has lost faith in the attorney. See 41 Cincinnati Law Review 1003 (1972). As the Florida court correctly observed, the contract rule can "have a chilling effect on the client's power to discharge his attorney." *Rosenberg*, supra, at 1021. The economics of

---

1. E.g., Martin v. Camp, 219 N.Y. 170, 114 N.E. 46, 47 (1916); Rosenberg v. Levin, slip op. June 11, 1981; Fracasse v. Brent, 6 Cal.3d 784, 494 P.2d 9, 100 Cal.Rptr. 385 (1972).

paying a discharged attorney the full contract price, and then hiring another attorney to continue his work, may be prohibitive. This danger is especially apparent in contingency fee situations, where "each" attorney may receive a large percentage of the client's final recovery. The consequences of the contract rule, in practical terms, may be that clients are forced to continue in their service attorneys in whose integrity, judgment or capacity they have lost confidence. See Salopek v. Schoemann, 20 Cal.2d 150, 124 P.2d 21 (1942) (Gibson, C.J., concurring).

Notwithstanding the logic and public policy which support the more modern view, there remain several problems under either theory....

[One] problem arises within the issue of "how much" the discharged attorney may recover....

The better rule, undoubtedly, would be to use the contract price as an upper limit or ceiling on the amount the discharged attorney could recover....

Our adoption of the modern rule limiting the recovery of the attorney to the reasonable value of services rendered, not to exceed the contracted fee, and payable only upon the occurrence of the contingency, makes the case at bar easily disposed of. Paragraph 15 of the trial court's findings of fact anticipated that the contingency fee contract approach could be overruled, and, in the alternative, found from the evidence that the reasonable value of the services rendered by the attorneys, including proper out-of-pocket expenses, equaled $15,-190.35....

The "Modern" Rule

Plaza Shoe seeks to reconcile two competing principles: a client's freedom to discharge a retained lawyer at will and a lawyer's right to be compensated for work performed. Why not enforce the contingent-fee contract agreed to by the parties? Does the "modern rule"—as it is called in *Plaza Shoe*—make it too easy for a client to change counsel without cause? What happens if the quantum meruit amount is more than the contract amount? What happens if the contingency never occurs because a trial on the merits results in a defendant's verdict or the plaintiff decides to abandon the claim? [12]

The "modern rule" is now the majority rule. All recent cases have agreed that recovery in quantum meruit should replace recovery on the

12. Two leading cases, Fracasse v. Brent, 6 Cal.3d 784, 100 Cal.Rptr. 385, 494 P.2d 9 (1972), and Rosenberg v. Levin, 409 So.2d 1016 (Fla.1982), hold that a discharged contingency-fee lawyer recovers nothing until and unless the contingency happens. There is some authority to the contrary.

contract.[13] When the lawyer has committed a clear and serious violation of a duty owed to the client, the lawyer forfeits any right to compensation whether discharged by the client or not.[14]

Should retainer agreements be subject to the quantum meruit theory? Should a contract making a retainer agreement nonrefundable be honored? See Jacobson v. Sassower,[15] where a "nonrefundable retainer of $2,500" in a matrimonial case was "to be credited against [the client's] charges." The court construed the clause against the lawyer who had drafted it, holding that she was only entitled to compensation in quantum meruit.

Under M.R. 1.16(a)(3) and DR 2–110(B)(4) the lawyer is required to withdraw when the client dismisses her. If, however, the case is before a court, court permission is necessary before withdrawing and the court may withhold its permission. Courts are reluctant to allow indigent defendants to switch appointed counsel because judges suspect that this is merely a tactic to delay the proceedings. When the request is made after the trial has begun, the defendant "must show good cause, such as an actual conflict of interest, a complete breakdown in communication or an irreconcilable conflict with his attorney." [16] In Ogala Sioux Tribe v. United States,[17] the tribe sought to fire lawyers who had handled a complex case for thirty years. The court had awarded the tribe over $40 million dollars for land ceded under an 1868 treaty and the sole remaining issue was the amount of government offsets. The court upheld the trial court's refusal to terminate the authority of the lawyers to stipulate to this amount, emphasizing that the tribe had not found substitute counsel who could handle the case without significant delay.

13. See, e.g., Fox & Associates Co. v. Purdon, 44 Ohio St.3d 69, 541 N.E.2d 448 (1989) (adopting quantum meruit rule when client discharges lawyer retained on a contingent fee).

14. See proposed Restatement of the Law Governing Lawyers § 49 (Tent. Draft No. 4, Apr. 10, 1991).

15. 66 N.Y.2d 991, 499 N.Y.S.2d 381, 489 N.E.2d 1283 (1985), discussed above at p. 522.

16. Wilson v. Mintzes, 761 F.2d 275, 280 (6th Cir.1985).

17. 862 F.2d 275 (Fed.Cir.1988).

Chapter 7

CONFLICTS OF INTEREST

A. INTRODUCTION

Underlying Concerns in Conflict Cases

An early statement by Justice Joseph Story (1779–1845) suggests the concerns underlying the law of conflicts of interest:

> An attorney is bound to disclose to his client every adverse retainer, and even every prior retainer, which may affect the discretion of the latter. No man can be supposed to be indifferent to the knowledge of facts, which work directly on his interests, or bear on the freedom of his choice of counsel. When a client employs an attorney, he has a right to presume, if the latter be silent on the point, that he has no engagements, which interfere, in any degree, with his exclusive devotion to the cause confided to him; that he has no interest, which may betray his judgment, or endanger his fidelity.[1]

The rules on conflicts of interest do not aim at elimination of all possible conflicts; this is impossible. Even if we envisioned lawyers as ascetics, renouncing all self interest, devoted only to their calling—we have no such vision—even if our notion of a lawyer was someone who served one client for the entirety of her career—and, of course, it is not—conflicting interests would be present: The client's interest would still sometimes conflict with the interests of third parties or with the law itself. Dealing with conflicting interests is inherent in a lawyer's life.

Conflicting interests are not unique to the lawyer-client relationship. The practice of law is a social relationship comparable to partnership, a joint venture or friendship. Any such relationship between two people carries the potential for a conflict of interest: Each party has her own interests, which may conflict with the interests of the other person.

Although everyone faces similar questions, the conflicts questions faced by lawyers are perhaps greater in number and intensity than those faced by most other people. Nor are the conflicts rules in non-lawyer relationships (e.g., a business partnership) a sure guide in analyzing lawyer conflicts of interest. The lawyer-client relationship is

1. Williams v. Reed, 3 Mason 405, 418, 29 F.Cas. 1386, Fed.Case No. 17,733 (C.C.Me. 1824).

unique by definition, i.e., it is a relationship whose object is the rendering of legal advice and counsel. The most striking implication of this fact is that the rendering of illegal aid is, by definition, outside the bounds of the relationship. This is not true in the same sense for other relationships. In addition, a lawyer has a special legal duty of confidentiality to the client, recognized in importance by a corresponding attorney-client privilege protecting client confidences in court.

All voluntary social relations are based on some measure of loyalty, commitment and trust. Loyalty stands in opposition to betrayal. The measure of loyalty required to sustain the relation depends on the purpose of the relation itself and the stakes. Less commitment is required to have a viable or satisfactory employment relationship than a satisfactory marriage. It is therefore necessary to speak of loyalty and trust specifically between lawyer and client. We are not here addressing the general question of whether clients ever "really" do or should trust their lawyers: about mistrust engendered by stereotypes (true or false) about the profession; about mistrust that might arise from difference between the lawyer's class, economic status or race and that of the client. These are important issues.[2] Here we are talking only about mistrust created when a lawyer acts as the client's agent in the face of serious conflicting interests. Ideal lawyer-client relationships in this respect may be impossible, but "reasonable loyalty" is not.

Questions of loyalty, commitment and trust speak both to the quality of the lawyer-client *relationship* and to the quality of the *representation*. If the client does not see the conflict as a betrayal, i.e., fails to appreciate the conflict or chooses to disregard it, the representation might nevertheless suffer. That is, there is a good chance that the lawyer with a serious conflict will shortchange her client, even if inadvertently. This aspect of conflicts of interest rules reinforces competency in representation.

The Several Faces of Conflicts

Lawyers are exposed to two primary categories of conflicts: conflicts between clients and conflicts between lawyer and client. The latter category was considered in Chapter 6 above.

"Conflicts between clients" generally are analyzed in two major aspects: concurrent and successive representation. Conflict in concurrent representation involves conflict between two present or two prospective clients or between one present and one prospective client. Conflict in successive representation involves conflict between a former client and a present or prospective client. Concurrent representation is taken up first, followed by successive representation. Some more complex situations are considered in Chapter 8.

"Adversity" and Relationship Between "Matters"

A client seeks representation but her interests are adverse to those of an existing client or a former client. A key question is whether the

---

2. They are discussed in Chapter 6 at p. 480.

"matter" involved is the "same or substantially related to" the matter in which the other client is being represented or was represented.

Suppose persons with adverse or potentially adverse interests seek representation by the same lawyer or law firm in matters totally unrelated to the matter in which their interests differ. May the lawyer undertake both representations? In the case of *concurrent* representation, if the matters are related, a conflict problem necessarily is presented because of the potential adversity of interest. If the matters are *unrelated*, the key question is whether this adversity amounts to antagonism. Both "relatedness" and the extent of "adversity" are questions of degree.

In *successive representation*, when matters are unrelated the lawyer ordinarily can proceed without the former client's permission. When the two matters in the successive representations are "the same or substantially related," on the other hand, a conflict generally is presented. Most successive representation cases turn on whether two matters are substantially related. A lawyer has a continuing duty of confidentiality concerning a former client's affairs. See M.R. 1.9(c). The conflicts rules, primarily to protect this confidential information, give the former client priority over a potential client if the two matters are substantially related.

A lawyer is allowed to sue a former client on behalf of a new client where the matter of the lawsuit is unrelated to the matter in which the former client was represented. However, a lawyer generally cannot directly oppose a present client even in a totally unrelated matter. Does this distinction make sense?

The established answer is that the lawyer owes her former client a duty of confidentiality that continues after the termination of the relationship, but the lawyer does not owe the former client a duty of eternal loyalty. Hence if matters are unrelated, a lawyer will be able to represent a new client against a former client without exploiting her former client's confidences. In contrast, if the matters are related, the risk of exploiting the former client's confidences is always present. And since the duty of confidentiality is a continuing one, this risk must be avoided.

If there is little risk of disclosing confidences when matters are totally unrelated, why not permit concurrent representation of adverse interests in unrelated matters? The answer is that a present client is entitled not only to protection of confidences but to the kind of loyal relationship that makes confiding possible.

What if two or more clients seek joint representation? Should they be barred from making this choice in all situations where their interests are adverse? Potentially adverse? The more adverse the clients' interests are, the more likely it becomes that one of them will be shortchanged in the loyalty she receives and the protection her confidences are given. Determining when interests are so adverse that the concurrent representation should not be permitted is often a difficult question.

Conflicts Between Clients and Others to Whom a Lawyer Owes a Duty

Akin to conflicts in concurrent representation are conflicts between a client's interests and some third party who is not a client but to whom the lawyer owes some duty nevertheless. These include: officers of a corporation where, as is usually the case, a lawyer represents the corporation as such and not the officers; an insurance company or other third party who is paying for a lawyer's services to the client; and a person for whom a lawyer prepares an evaluation of a client's affairs with the understanding that person can rely on the lawyer's evaluation, e.g., a person who receives the lawyer's opinion letter on the legality of a client's securities registration. Some of these problems are dealt with later in this chapter; others are considered in Chapter 8 below. Preparing an evaluation for a third party was discussed in Chapter 2.

Imputed Conflicts

A further question is whether lawyers in the same firm with a lawyer who is disqualified because of a conflict are themselves also disqualified. Conflicts-of-interest questions are especially troubling in large law firms because the usual answer is affirmative: One personally disqualified lawyer may taint a whole firm. See M.R. 1.10.

Does the taint of a disqualified lawyer travel with that lawyer if she moves from one firm to another? If you are disqualified because you are in a firm with a disqualified lawyer, do you stay disqualified when you move to a new firm? If you go to a new firm, is everyone in that firm now disqualified? If you are disqualified because one of your partners is disqualified, when that partner leaves the firm are you still disqualified? These questions of imputed or vicarious conflicts are considered below at p. 705.

Who Is the Client?

In conflicts between clients, concurrent and successive, as well as in conflicts between the lawyer and the client, the problem may turn on who it is, among various candidates, the lawyer represents. This is particularly true when a group or organization is involved.

This question of client identity arises as well in contexts other than conflicts. For example, when the client is an organization, to whom does the lawyer owe the duty of communication? From whom shall she take instruction on settlement? To whom does she owe the duty to keep confidences? The question of client identity where the lawyer represents an organization will be examined in all these aspects in Chapter 8.

———

B. CONCURRENT REPRESENTATION IN LITIGATION

Introduction: Diverging Interests and Antagonism

The rules governing conflicts of interest in concurrent representation address two problems: (1) the problem of diverging interests: the effect on adequacy of representation when a lawyer represents two clients, interested in the same matter, whose interests diverge; and (2) the problem of antagonism: the effect on a client's trust when the client's lawyer also represents the client's opponent.

When a lawyer seeks to represent two clients in matters that are related, the lawyer confronts both diverging interests and the potential for antagonism. When the two matters are unrelated, no problem of diverging interests is presented. For example, suppose a lawyer is representing Bob in an eviction suit against Mark and then is asked by Hector to sue Bob for defamation. The lawyer could present each cause without deflection of effort in deference to the other cause.

But the problem of antagonism would remain. From Bob's perspective, what counts is that his lawyer is aligned with his adversary. The breach of loyalty and the concomitant loss of trust will be hardly less than if the two matters were related. In Bodily v. Intermountain Health Care Corp.,[3] for example, "Bob" fired the firm when he learned that it was suing him on behalf of "Hector" in an unrelated matter. "Bob" then moved to disqualify the firm from representing "Hector." The court held that the firm had violated DR 5–105 of the Model Code, discussed below, but refused to disqualify the firm because its ethical misconduct had not prejudiced "Bob" in the litigation brought by "Hector." The standard in judging whether to disqualify a lawyer in ongoing litigation may be more lenient than the standard applied in judging whether the lawyer has violated the ethics rules, a question considered later in these materials.

The degree to which interests diverge and antagonism develops depends on the degree of adversity between clients and the relationship between the two matters. If one is suing the other, their interests are directly opposed in the same matter and the antagonism between A and B is at its legal maximum. In a joint venture A and B can entirely share common goals or see themselves as allies in a common fight; if so, their interests largely coincide and there may be little or no antagonism between them.

3. 649 F.Supp. 468 (D.Utah 1986).

1. Professional Rules on Concurrent Representation

Canons and Model Code of Professional Responsibility

Canon 6 of Canons of Professional Ethics provides:

It is unprofessional to represent conflicting interests, except by express consent of all concerned given after a full disclosure of the facts. Within the meaning of this canon, a lawyer represents conflicting interests when in behalf of one client, it is his duty to contend for that which duty to another client requires him to oppose.

Canon 6 seems to say that consent would permit a lawyer to proceed no matter what the conflict, but the courts did not interpret it this way.[4] Client consent, however, allowed a lawyer to proceed in the face of a conflict that would have precluded dual representation in the absence of consent.[5] This distinction between "consentable" and "unconsentable" conflicts remains a basic conflicts concept.

The key conflicts provision of the Model Code of Professional Responsibility is DR 5–105. DR 5–105(C) provides that a lawyer may not concurrently represent clients with "differing interests," unless (1) the lawyer obtains consent after full disclosure and (2) it is "obvious" that the lawyer can "adequately represent" both clients.

The term "obvious" implies an objective standard. Hence, it is not enough that the client actually consents. The circumstances must satisfy an independent authority, such as a court or a disciplinary board, that the lawyer properly proceeded with the multiple representation.

When is it "obvious" that a lawyer can "adequately represent" both clients? In Unified Sewerage Agency v. Jelco Inc.,[6] a leading case, the court specified several factors in deciding whether two clients can be adequately represented: the nature of the litigation or other matter; the information to which the lawyer has access; the client's ability to recognize her vulnerability and protect her interests; and the questions in dispute.

Many cases attempt to avoid the difficulties of "obvious" by concentrating on consent and the client's "right" to choose her own counsel. But the client's right to choose her own counsel is not unqualifiedly paramount. In serious conflicts, the client may have only the right to get another lawyer.[7]

Model Rules of Professional Conduct

Case law on conflicts issues filled the gaps left by the Canons and the Model Code. To a large extent, Model Rules 1.7 through 1.15, and

---

4. See, e.g., Kelly v. Greason, 23 N.Y.2d 368, 296 N.Y.S.2d 937, 244 N.E.2d 456 (1968); In re A. and B., 44 N.J. 331, 209 A.2d 101 (1965).

5. See, e.g., Arden v. State Bar of California, 52 Cal.2d 310, 341 P.2d 6 (1959).

6. 646 F.2d 1339 (9th Cir.1981).

7. See, e.g., Rice v. Baron, 456 F.Supp. 1361, 1374 (S.D.N.Y.1978) (even with consent the representation might not have been proper; lawyer represented plaintiffs with possible counterclaims against one another); also Sapienza v. New York News, 481 F.Supp. 676 (S.D.N.Y.1979).

2.2 and 2.3 codify that case law.   M.R. 1.16, Declining and Terminating the Representation, and M.R. 2.1, Advisor, are also relevant to conflicts problems.   A conflict of interest is presented whenever a lawyer wants to withdraw and her client wants her to continue or would be harmed by her withdrawal.   Similarly, M.R. 2.1 speaks of professional judgment that is unaffected by conflicting interests.   Consideration of conflicts problems also raises issues of confidentiality under M.R. 1.6, such as when a lawyer wants to communicate a client's confidence to a prospective client to obtain consent to a concurrent or successive representation that would otherwise be prohibited, but the client does not agree.

Interests "Directly Adverse"

Model Rule 1.7(a) prohibits the representation of a client whose interests are directly adverse to another client's interests, unless:

> 1) the lawyer reasonably believes that the representation will not adversely affect the *relationship* with the other client; and

> 2) each client consents after consultation.   (Emphasis added.)

When can a lawyer "reasonably believe" that the *relationship* will not be adversely affected?   The use of the word "relationship" here instead of "representation" is significant.   It is difficult to represent interests directly adverse to an individual client without the relationship with that client being "adversely affected", even if the matters are wholly unrelated.   Is the client consent proviso empty?

As the Comment to M.R. 1.7 points out, the proviso permits the adverse representation in some situations, particularly where the clients are organizations.   For example, a lawyer represents Corporation X in all its securities matters; Company Y, a bakery, is one of 30 subsidiaries of Corporation X; the lawyer is hired by Z who wants to sue Company Y for breaching a delivery contract.   The lawyer may reasonably believe that this suit will not have any adverse effect on the relationship with Corporation X. The lawyer would then be able to proceed, if after explaining the potential problems (consultation), Corporation X gave its consent.   That is, the lawyer would be able to proceed assuming that it is reasonable to believe that neither the relationship with X nor that with Z would be adversely affected and consent is obtained from *both* clients after consultation.

Another example of when the proviso to M.R. 1.7(a) might apply is as follows: A lawyer working for the Securities and Exchange Commission wants to represent a pro bono client whose welfare benefits are about to be revoked.   The adverse party in the welfare case is the Department of Health and Human Services, an agency of the federal government.   Would it not be reasonable for the SEC lawyer to believe that her relationship with the SEC will not be adversely affected by her representing the welfare recipient before HHS, even though both are agencies of the federal government?   This example assumes no other law prohibits the lawyer from representing the pro bono client. In this instance, however, a federal statute prohibits the representation.[8]

Representation "Materially Limited"

The paradigm of direct adversity is one client suing another: A lawyer may not, without consent, represent her client's opponent in any matter, no matter how unrelated to the client's suit. Apart from litigation, it seems clear that when two clients are involved in a hostile negotiation their interests are also directly adverse. Further along the continuum situations become more difficult to assess: How adverse are the interests of two parties in friendly negotiations? The parties always have some divergent aims, for example, one wants to buy for the least amount of money and the other wants to sell for the greatest. The interests here do not seem directly adverse, but are they nevertheless adverse enough to preclude one lawyer representing both parties? Consider Model Rule 1.7(b).

M.R. 1.7(b) provides that a lawyer shall not represent a client if the representation may be "materially limited" by the lawyer's responsibilities to another client or to a third person, or by the lawyer's own interests. The lawyer may, however, proceed in such situations if: (1) she reasonably believes the *representation* will not be affected; and (2) the client consents after consultation.

Under M.R. 1.7(b) the emphasis is on the quality of the representation to be provided. The rule does not use the term "adverse" to describe the other interests that might trigger the rule. This is because responsibilities of a lawyer to another client might interfere with a concurrent representation even where the clients' interests are not so opposed as to be called "adverse." Thus, the duty of loyalty might cause the lawyer to be less committed to a client with a different interest in the matter; the duty of confidentiality might result in hesitancy to discuss related issues with a second client; and the duty of due diligence might cause the lawyer to neglect one matter in favor of another that is more demanding of her time or more lucrative.

Model Rule 2.2

Model Rule 2.2 deals with the lawyer who acts as an intermediary between two clients who have adverse interests, but who share a common purpose that may transcend their differences. M.R. 2.2 may be considered a specific application of 1.7(b). It gives the lawyer who contemplates acting as an intermediary between two clients more specific guidance than 1.7 alone provides.

---

8.   18 U.S.C. § 205 prohibits an employee of the federal government from representing anyone before any department, agency or court in any matter in which the government is a party or has a direct and substantial interest. The ABA has proposed that § 205 be amended to allow pro bono representation in situations as in the example; the federal government actively opposed this legislative proposal, which failed to pass. For a case allowing lawyers representing a state agency to proceed against the state in an unrelated matter, see Aerojet Properties, Inc. v. New York, 138 A.D.2d 39, 530 N.Y.S.2d 624 (1988).

Per Se Bans on Concurrent Representation

Although courts are quick to disapprove "unconsented" concurrent representation, they are reluctant to overrule client consent to the representation of conflicting interests. Respect for client consent recognizes the importance of a client's right to select counsel of her own choosing and, within limits, to select the kind of representation as between full-blown partisanship and intermediation.

The Supreme Court of New Jersey, for example, refused to approve a New Jersey ethics committee opinion that would have imposed an absolute ban on the joint representation of a government entity and individual government officials as defendants in § 1983 actions.[9] The ethics committee was concerned that a case-by-case approach was too uncertain. The court thought the absolute ban was overinclusive, i.e., that there are some situations where the dual representation does not present an actual conflict:

> Only in the most sensitive circumstances have we imposed a per se rule of disqualification. In the past we have by administrative directive prohibited the joint representation of driver and passenger in automobile negligence cases (other than those involving husband and wife or parent and child).[10]

Why is the driver-passenger situation "sensitive" enough to adopt a per se rule and not the § 1983 situation?[11]

2. Concurrent Representation in Civil Litigation

WESTINGHOUSE ELEC. CORP. v. KERR-McGEE CORP.

United States Court of Appeals, Seventh Circuit, 1978.
580 F.2d 1311.

Before FAIRCHILD, CHIEF JUDGE, and SPRECHER and BAUER, CIRCUIT JUDGES.

SPRECHER, CIRCUIT JUDGE.

The novel issues on this appeal are (1) whether an attorney-client relationship arises only when both parties consent to its formation or can it also occur when the lay party submits confidential information to the law party with reasonable belief that the latter is acting as the former's attorney and (2) whether the size and geographical scope of a law firm exempt it from the ordinary ethical considerations applicable to lawyers generally.

The four separate appellants are some of the defendants in this antitrust case who were each denied their motions to disqualify the law

---

9. In the Matter of Opinion 552 of Advisory Committee on Professional Ethics, 102 N.J. 194, 507 A.2d 233 (1986).

10. Id. at 239, n. 3.

11. See also Fleming v. State, 246 Ga. 90, 270 S.E.2d 185 (1980) (absolute ban on representing more than one defendant in death penalty cases).

firm of Kirkland and Ellis ("Kirkland") from further representing the plaintiff Westinghouse Electric Corporation ("Westinghouse"). Whether fortuitously or by design, on the same day, October 15, 1976, Kirkland, while representing the American Petroleum Institute ("API"), of which three of the appellants, Gulf Oil Corporation ("Gulf"), Kerr–McGee Corporation ("Kerr–McGee") and Getty Oil Company ("Getty"), were members, released a report which took an affirmative position on the subject of competition in the uranium industry, while simultaneously filing this lawsuit, representing Westinghouse, seeking to establish an illegal conspiracy in restraint of trade in the uranium industry.

The fourth appellant, Noranda Mines Limited ("Noranda"), asserts a different conflict of interest in Kirkland resulting from its prior representation of Noranda from 1965 to 1967 in several matters.... [This part of the opinion is omitted. The court held that Kirkland's earlier representation of Noranda did not warrant disqualification because it was not substantially related to the current litigation.]

I

On September 8, 1975, Westinghouse, a major manufacturer of nuclear reactors, notified utility companies that 17 of its long-term uranium supply contracts had become "commercially impracticable" under § 2–615 of the Uniform Commercial Code. In response, the affected utilities filed 13 federal actions, one state action, and three foreign actions against Westinghouse, alleging breach of contract and challenging Westinghouse's invocation of § 2–615. The federal actions were consolidated for trial in the Eastern District of Virginia at Richmond....

As an outgrowth of its defense of these contract actions, Westinghouse on October 15, 1976, filed the present antitrust action against 12 foreign and 17 domestic corporations engaged in various aspects of the uranium industry.

Kirkland's representation of Westinghouse's uranium litigation has required the efforts of 8 to 14 of its attorneys and has generated some $2.5 million in legal fees.

Contemporaneously with its Westinghouse representation in the uranium cases, Kirkland represented API, using six of its lawyers in that project.

In October, 1975, Congress was presented with legislative proposals to break up the oil companies, both vertically by separating their control over production, transportation, refining and marketing entities, and horizontally by prohibiting cross-ownership of alternative energy resources in addition to oil and gas. Since this proposed legislation threatened oil companies with a potential divestiture of millions of dollars of assets, in November, 1975, the API launched a Committee on Industrial Organization to lobby against the proposals. On December 10, 1975, API's president requested that each company designate one of its senior executives to facilitate coordination of the Committee's activities with the individual companies.

The Committee was organized into five task forces. The Legal Task Force was headed by L. Bates Lea, General Counsel of Standard Oil of Indiana, assisted by Stark Ritchie, API's General Counsel.

On February 25, 1976, Ritchie wrote to Frederick M. Rowe, a partner in Kirkland's Washington office, retaining the firm to review the divestiture hearings and "prepare arguments for use in opposition to this type of legislation." On May 4, 1976, Ritchie added that the Kirkland firm's work for API "should include the preparation of possible testimony, analyzing the probable legal consequences and antitrust considerations of the proposed legislation" and "you should make an objective survey and study of the probable effects of the pending legislation, specifically including probable effects on oil companies that would have to divest assets." Ritchie noted that "[a]s a part of this study, we will arrange for interviews by your firm with a cross-section of industry personnel." The May 4 letter to Rowe concluded with:

> Your firm will, of course, act as an independent expert counsel and hold any company information learned through these interviews in strict confidence, not to be disclosed to any other company, or even to API, except in aggregated or such other form as will preclude identifying the source company with its data.

On May 25, 1976, Ritchie sent to 59 API member companies a survey questionnaire seeking data to be used by Kirkland in connection with its engagement by API. In the introductory memorandum to the questionnaire, Ritchie advised the 59 companies that Kirkland had "ascertained that certain types of data pertinent to the pending anti-diversification legislation are not now publicly available" and the API "would appreciate your help in providing this information to Kirkland...." The memorandum included the following:

> Kirkland, Ellis & Rowe is acting as an independent special counsel for API, and will hold any company information in strict confidence, *not to be disclosed to any other company, or even to API,* except in aggregated or such other form as will preclude identifying the source company with its data. (Emphasis in original).

The data sought was to assist Kirkland "in preparing positions, arguments and testimony in opposition to this type of legislative [divestiture]" and was not to be sent to API but rather to Kirkland.

Pursuant to the provision in Ritchie's May 4, 1976 letter to Rowe that interviews would be arranged with a cross-section of industry personnel, Nolan Clark, a Kirkland partner, interviewed representatives of eight oil companies between April 29 and June 15, 1976.

After going through several drafts, the final Kirkland report to API was released on October 15, 1976. The final report contains 230 pages of text and 82 pages of exhibits. References to uranium appear throughout the report and uranium is the primary subject of about 25 pages of text and 11 pages of exhibits. The report marshalls a large number of facts and arguments to show that oil company diversification does not threaten overall energy competition. In particular the report asserts that the relatively high concentration ratios in the uranium industry can be expected to decline, that current increases in uranium prices are a result of increasing demand, that oil company entry into uranium production has stimulated competition and diminished concentration, that oil companies have no incentive to act in concert to restrict coal or uranium production and that the historical record refutes any charge that oil companies have restricted uranium output. The report concludes that "the energy industries, both individually and collectively, are competitive today and are likely to remain so." 448 F.Supp. at 1296.

As noted at the outset of this opinion, the API report was issued on the same day as the present antitrust suit was filed against several defendants, including Gulf, Kerr–McGee and Getty.

The district court concluded that "[a] comparison of the two documents reveals a rather basic conflict in their contentions and underlying theories." 448 F.Supp. at 1295. The court also observed that "[p]erhaps in recognition of the diametrically opposing theories of the API report and the Westinghouse complaint, Kirkland does not attempt to rebut the oil companies' charges that it has simultaneously taken inconsistent positions on competition in the uranium industry." 448 F.Supp. at 1296.

Gulf, Kerr–McGee and Getty are substantial dues-paying members of API. Kerr–McGee and Getty are also represented on API's board of directors.

At Ritchie's request, the cross-section interviews were mainly arranged by Gerald Thurmond, Washington Counsel of Gulf Oil Company and a member of API's Antitrust Strategy Group. On May 11, 1976, Thurmond advised Gulf officials that Nolan Clark of Kirkland planned to visit them. Attached to Thurmond's letter were the questions "which will be covered" in the meeting.[2]

The meeting was held on May 28, 1976 in Denver. Nolan Clark represented Kirkland. In attendance for Gulf were six vice presidents, a comptroller and a regional attorney. Also present was a Harvard professor who "also is working with API on the same subject." The meeting lasted more than two hours followed by lunch, during which discussions continued. After the meeting and in three letters from Gulf vice president Mingee to Clark dated August 10, 11 and 13, Gulf submitted specific information sought by Clark through the question-

2. [The questions, prepared by Nolan Clark as "the kinds of questions I might want to ask", are included in a lengthy footnote to the court's opinion. They sought detailed information about "alternative energy businesses" and a number of them referred specifically to uranium. E.g., "Do you expect the same rate of return for oil drilling, coal production, uranium exploration?" "Do you attempt to sell oil, natural gas, coal and uranium at BTU equivalent prices?"]

naire and other written questions and in each letter Mingee stressed the confidential basis upon which the information was supplied.

Nolan Clark's interview with two Kerr–McGee vice presidents took place in Oklahoma City on June 9, 1976 and lasted about three hours. Clark was given considerable background information on Kerr–McGee's uranium industry, including mining locations, uranium conversion process, and pellet fabrication. On the subject of uranium marketing and pricing, one of the Kerr–McGee vice presidents described the escalating prices and tightening supplies in the current market, and the reasons behind the trends. Kerr–McGee sent its completed questionnaire to Clark on August 25, 1976.

Kirkland did not interview any Getty personnel. However, Getty received the confidential API questionnaire which requested it to estimate the value of its assets subject to proposed divestiture and its research and development outlays in alternative energy fields. Getty completed the questionnaire and mailed its data sheets to Nolan Clark on June 4, 1976, with the understanding that the data would be held in confidence.

II

The crux of the district court's determination was based upon its view that an "attorney-client relationship is one of agency to which the general rules of agency apply" and "arises *only* when the parties have given their consent, either express or implied, to its formation." 448 F.Supp. at 1300 (emphasis supplied). Although some courts have stated that the attorney-client relation is one of agency and that the general rules of law applicable to agencies apply, in none of those cases was an agency principle applied to assist an attorney to avoid what would otherwise be an obligation to his client....

. . .

The district court first determined that there existed no explicit or express attorney-client relationship in that no oil company representative requested Kirkland to act as its attorney orally or in writing and Kirkland did not accept such employment orally or in writing. The district court found that "Kirkland sent its legal bills to the API, and was compensated only by the API." 448 F.Supp. at 1301. A professional relationship is not dependent upon the payment of fees [6] nor, as we

6. Allman v. Winkelman, 106 F.2d 663, 665 (9th Cir.1939), cert. denied, 309 U.S. 668 (1940) ("lawyer's advice to his client establishes a professional relationship though it be gratis"); Fort Meyers Seafood Packers, Inc. v. Steptoe and Johnson, 381 F.2d 261, 262 (D.C.1967), cert. denied, 390 U.S. 946 (1968) (attorney's fees paid by third party "If appellant is not obligated to pay appellees for their services, it does not follow that there was no attorney-and-client relation"); Dresden v. Willock, 518 F.2d 281, 286 (3d Cir.1975) ("The fact that Dresden was to be paid by receiving stock in the enterprise did not change the nature of the [attorney-client] relationship"); E.F. Hutton & Co. v. Brown, 305 F.Supp. 371, 388 (S.D.Tex.1969) (Relation of attorney and client "is not dependent on the payment of a fee").

have noted, upon the execution of a formal contract.[7]

The court then purported to determine whether the professional relationship "may be implied from the conduct of the parties." First, it found no "indicia" such as "the preparation of a legally-binding document like a contract or a will, or the attorney's appearance in a judicial or quasi-judicial proceeding." 448 F.Supp. at 1301. Second, the court searched for evidence of three fundamental characteristics of an agency relationship the power to affect the legal relations of the principal and others; a fiduciary who works on behalf of his principal and primarily for his benefit; and a principal who has the right to control the conduct of the agent. 448 F.Supp. at 1301–03. Using these tests, the court concluded that "[v]iewed in its totality, we believe that the evidence shows that no attorney-client relationship has existed between Kirkland and the oil companies." As we have indicated, to apply only the agency tests is too narrow an approach for determining whether a lawyer's fiduciary obligation has arisen.

The district court also erroneously permitted itself to be influenced by the size of the law firm involved. In addition to identifying Kirkland as one of the largest law firms in Chicago with a two-city operation including 130 lawyers in the Chicago office and 40 lawyers in the Washington, D.C. office, the court observed that "[w]ith the modern-day proliferation of large law firms representing multi-billion dollar corporations in all segments of the economy and the governmental process, it is becoming increasingly difficult to insist upon absolute fidelity to rules prohibiting attorneys from representing overlapping legal interests." 448 F.Supp. at 1287–88.

Although the court recognized that "where courts have found a disclosure of client information to one member of a law firm, such knowledge has traditionally been imputed to all members of his firm," it opted in this case to reject "this rigid approach, in recognition of the changing realities of modern legal practice." 448 F.Supp. at 1304.

The district court abused its discretion in applying a narrow, formal agency approach to determining the attorney-client relation and in applying a different imputation of knowledge principle in the case of a large law firm than that "traditionally" and recently applied by this circuit to sole practitioners and smaller firms. Schloetter v. Railoc of Indiana, Inc., 456 F.2d 706, 710 (7th Cir.1976).

III

. . .

Three district courts have held that each individual member of an *unincorporated* association is a client of the association's lawyer. In Halverson v. Convenient Food Mart, Inc., 458 F.2d 927, 930 (7th Cir.1972), we held that a lawyer who had represented an informal group of 75 franchisees "[b]ecause ... [he] in effect had represented and

---

7. Udall v. Littell, 366 F.2d 668, 676 (D.C.Cir.1966), cert. denied, 385 U.S. 1007 (1967); E.F. Hutton & Co. v. Brown, supra note 6, at 388.

benefitted every franchisee, ... could reasonably believe that each one of them was his client."

Here we are faced with neither an ordinary commercial corporation nor with an informal or unincorporated association, but instead with a nation-wide trade association with 350 corporate and 7,500 individual members (448 F.Supp. at 1290) and doing business as a non-profit corporation.

We need not make any generalized pronouncements of whether an attorney for such an organization represents every member because this case can and should be decided on a much more narrow ground.

There are several fairly common situations where, although there is no express attorney-client relationship, there exists nevertheless a fiduciary obligation or an implied professional relation:

(1) The fiduciary relationship existing between lawyer and client extends to preliminary consultation by a prospective client with a view to retention of the lawyer, although actual employment does not result.[12]

(2) When information is exchanged between co-defendants and their attorneys in a criminal case, an attorney who is the recipient of such information breaches his fiduciary duty if he later, in his representation of another client, is able to use this information to the detriment of one of the co-defendants, even though that co-defendant is not the one which he represented in the criminal case. Wilson P. Abraham Const. Corp. v. Armco Steel Corp., 559 F.2d 250 (5th Cir.1977) (disqualification case).

(3) When an insurer retains an attorney to investigate the circumstances of a claim and the insured, pursuant to a cooperation clause in the policy, cooperates with the attorney, the attorney may not thereafter represent a third party suing the insured nor indeed continue to represent the insurer once a conflict of interest surfaces.[13]

(4) In a recent case, where an auditor's regional counsel was instrumental in hiring a second law firm to represent some plaintiffs suing the auditor and where the second firm through such relationship was in a position to receive privileged information, the second law firm, although having no direct attorney-client relationship with the auditor,

---

12. ABA Code of Professional Responsibility, EC 4 1: "Both the fiduciary relationship existing between lawyer and client and the proper functioning of the legal system require the presentation by the lawyer of confidences and secrets of one who has employed or sought to employ him." Cf. McCormick on Evidence (2d ed.1972), § 88, p. 179: "Communications in the course of preliminary discussion with a view to employing the lawyer are privileged though the employment is in the upshot not accepted." See also, Taylor v. Sheldon, 172 Ohio St. 118, 173 N.E.2d 892, 895 (1961).

13. ABA, Opinions of the Committee on Professional Ethics (1967 ed.), Formal Op. 247 (1942). See also, State Farm Mutual Automobile Ins. Co. v. Walker, 382 F.2d 548 (7th Cir.1967), cert. denied, 389 U.S. 1045 (1968). For general discussion of conflicts inherent in insurance matters, see H. Drinker, Legal Ethics (1953) 114–18; L. Patterson and F. Cheatham, The Profession of the Law (1971) 237–40.

was disqualified from representing the plaintiffs. Fund of Funds, Ltd. v. Arthur Andersen & Co., 567 F.2d 225 (2d Cir.1977).

(5) In a recent case in this circuit, a law firm who represented for many years both the plaintiff in an action and also a corporation which owned 20% of the outstanding stock of the defendant corporation, was permitted to continue its representation of the plaintiff but was directed to disassociate itself from representing or advising the corporation owning 20% of defendant's stock. Whiting Corp. v. White Machinery Corp., 567 F.2d 713 (7th Cir.1977).

In none of the above categories or situations did the disqualified or disadvantaged lawyer or law firm actually represent the "client" in the sense of a formal or even express attorney-client relation. In each of those categories either an implied relation was found or at least the lawyer was found to owe a fiduciary obligation to the laymen.

The professional relationship for purposes of the privilege for attorney-client communications "hinges upon the client's belief that he is consulting a lawyer in that capacity and his manifested intention to seek professional legal advice." [14] The affidavits before the district court established that: the Washington counsel for Gulf "was given to believe that the Kirkland firm was representing both API and Gulf;" Kerr–McGee's vice president understood a Kirkland partner to explain that Kirkland was working on behalf of API and also its members such as Kerr–McGee; and Getty's vice president stated that in submitting data to Kirkland he "acted upon the belief and expectation that such submission was made in order to enable [Kirkland] to render legal service to Getty in furtherance of Getty's interests."

A fiduciary relationship may result because of the nature of the work performed and the circumstances under which confidential information is divulged.[18] The Supreme Court approved and transmitted to Congress in 1972 the Federal Rules of Evidence,[19] which included among the lawyer-client privilege rules eventually eliminated by Congress, the following definition: [20]

> A "client" is a person, public officer, or corporation, association, or other organization or entity, either public or private, who is rendered professional legal services by a lawyer, or who consults a lawyer with a view to obtaining professional legal services from him.

· · ·

14. McCormick on Evidence (2d ed.1972), § 88, p. 179. See also R. Wise, Legal Ethics (1970) 284: "The deciding factor is what the prospective client thought when he made the disclosure, not what the lawyer thought."

18. Note Attorney's Conflict of Interests: Representation of Interest Adverse to That of Former Client, 55 Bost.U.L.Rev. 61, 66 (1975).

19. Supreme Court Order, November 20, 1972.

20. Rules of Evidence for the United States Courts and Magistrates as approved by Supreme Court (West Pub. Co.1972). Rule 503(a)(1).

Although Kirkland asserted, and the district court agreed, that it constructed a "Chinese wall" between the 8 to 14 Chicago-based attorneys working for Westinghouse and the 6 D.C.-based attorneys working for API, both conceded that William Jentes, one of Kirkland's lead attorneys working on the Westinghouse antitrust complaint, in August 1976 agreed with API task force head Lea, to prepare a legal memorandum analyzing arguments which had been advanced to broaden the scope of existing antitrust laws to outlaw interlocking directorates. Lea forwarded the Kirkland memorandum to the API, which mailed it to its member-company contact officers on September 23, 1976. Despite this breach of the "wall," we do not recognize the wall theory as modifying the presumption that actual knowledge of one or more lawyers in a firm is imputed to each member of that firm.[27] Here there exists a very reasonable possibility of improper professional conduct despite all efforts to segregate the two sizeable groups of lawyers.[28]

Kirkland has argued that the oil companies were aware that Kirkland was representing Westinghouse while it was also representing API, inasmuch as Kirkland sought discovery from Kerr–McGee, Getty and abortively from Gulf, relating to the Richmond litigation, in the way of voluntary interviews, depositions and the production of documents. The point, however, is not that the oil companies were aware that Kirkland represented Westinghouse but whether the oil companies were aware that such representation would lead to Kirkland representing Westinghouse in a lawsuit in which the oil companies would be defendants. As the district court noted, "none of the [Kirkland] Washington attorneys working on the API divestiture assignment knew of the separate Westinghouse antitrust complaint until it was filed in court on October 15 [1976], after the stock exchanges closed on that day." 448 F.Supp. at 1296. If some of Kirkland's own partners were not aware of the Westinghouse antitrust complaint until it was filed, the oil companies can scarcely be presumed to have greater knowledge that it was impending with themselves as some of the defendants. It was Kirkland's duty to keep the oil companies advised of actual or potential conflicts of interest, not the oil companies' burden to divine those conflicts.

Gulf, Kerr–McGee and Getty each entertained a reasonable belief that it was submitting confidential information regarding its involvement in the uranium industry to a law firm which had solicited the

27. Schloetter v. Railoc of Indiana, Inc., 546 F.2d 706, 710 (7th Cir.1976). See also, Fund of Funds, Ltd. v. Arthur Andersen & Co., 435 F.Supp. 84, 96 (S.D.N.Y.), rev'd in part and aff'd in part, 567 F.2d 225, 229, n. 10 (2d Cir.1977).

28. Judge Fairchild notes that he has a different view on this point. It is his understanding that on appeal, Kirkland does not rely on a Chinese wall theory. In his opinion, if it had been established that there was real insulation in all relevant particulars between the lawyers working in the Washington office on the API Report and those working in the Chicago office on the antitrust action, imputation of knowledge to all partners would be eliminated from consideration and a different result may have been appropriate.

information upon a representation that the firm was acting in the undivided interest of each company....

The fact that the two contrary undertakings by Kirkland occurred contemporaneously, with each involving substantial stakes and substantially related to the other, outbalances the client's interest in continuing with its chosen attorney. However, we believe that Westinghouse should have the option and choice of dismissing Gulf, Kerr–McGee and Getty from the antitrust case or discharging Kirkland as its attorney in the case. Substitute counsel has represented Westinghouse in the case since February 17, 1978, so that the impact of any change-over has been somewhat eased.

. . .

When Is a Person a "Client" for Conflicts Purposes?

What were the possible consequences to the law firm (Kirkland) and its client (Westinghouse) of the court's holding in *Westinghouse?*[12] Were the three oil companies (Getty, Gulf, and Kerr–McGee) "clients" of Kirkland or "quasi-clients" who are owed certain duties but are not full clients? Why was screening (creation of a wall of separation of the lawyers and files concerned with the two matters) insufficient?

How would *Westinghouse* have been decided under the Model Rules? Would the outcome have been the same if the lobbying effort for the trade association had no relationship to the uranium antitrust litigation? For example, if Kirkland's Washington office had been engaged in opposing legislative changes in oil depreciation allowances, rather than legislation involving the energy activities of oil companies, including uranium. Would the outcome have been different if the trade association had gathered data on uranium activities by interviewing the oil companies and had supplied Kirkland only aggregated data for the industry as a whole?

In IBM v. Levin,[13] a law firm was disqualified from representing a computer leasing firm in an antitrust action against IBM because the firm had represented IBM on various labor matters over a number of years. The court held that IBM was a present client of the firm, despite the fact that the firm "had no specific assignment from IBM on hand on the day that [the firm filed suit against IBM] and even though

12. James B. Stewart, The Partners: Inside America's Most Powerful Law Firms c. 4 (1983), includes a fascinating discussion of Kirkland's representation of Westinghouse. Stewart reports that Westinghouse retained the Wall Street firm of Donovan, Leisure to take over the uranium antitrust litigation. The antitrust case was later settled for about $100 million in cash plus various options to acquire uranium ore. Id. at 199. An internal investigation by Westinghouse resulted in a decision not to seek to recover approximately $3 million in fees from Kirkland. A shareholders' suit to force Westinghouse to pursue this claim was subsequently abandoned. Id.

13. 579 F.2d 271 (3d Cir.1978).

[the firm] performed services for IBM on a fee for services basis rather than pursuant to a retainer agreement." [14]   The court found that "the pattern of repeated retainers, both before and after the filing of the complaint, supports the finding of a continuous relationship." [15]

Is initial contact with a person seeking representation enough to establish an attorney-client relationship for purposes of the conflicts rules? Can a person "taint" a lawyer by interviewing her? In Hughes v. Paine, Webber, Jackson and Curtis Inc.,[16] one of the defendants met with a partner in the law firm that was representing the plaintiffs. The defendant talked with the lawyer about the possibility of the lawyer representing him in an SEC investigation arising out of the acts at the heart of the plaintiffs' case against the defendant. But the defendant did not then seek to hire the firm; instead, he sought other counsel. The court refused to disqualify the firm from continuing to represent the plaintiffs. At the time the defendant consulted the plaintiffs' law firm, he had every reason to know that the firm was handling the case against him, having received a letter about the case written on behalf of the plaintiffs by the law firm on its stationery.

The court, citing *Westinghouse*, found that there had been an attorney-client relationship between the lawyer consulted and the defendant and that consequently an irrebuttable presumption arose that confidential information had been passed to that lawyer. But the court also held, contrary to *Westinghouse*, that the defendant had never been a client of the "firm", only of the lawyer consulted. Since the client had never been a "firm" client, the court held that the presumption that the lawyer passed information on to his partners could be rebutted.

Is *Hughes* the best analysis of the "taint shopping" problem? The Scope section of the Model Rules states that the client-lawyer relationship does not exist until the client has asked the lawyer to render service and the lawyer has agreed, but that "some duties, such as the duty of confidentiality ... may attach when the lawyer agrees to consider whether a client-lawyer relationship shall be established." Does this help? In situations in which a corporation is shopping for a law firm to handle a major case, both sides must exercise care.[17]   A lawyer must be careful not to receive confidential information relating to the merits, but inquire only as to matters concerning potential conflicts and suitability of the firm for the case. The potential client must also act with caution, lest a court come to the conclusion that it is

14. Id. at 281.

15. Id. See also Fund of Funds, Ltd. v. Arthur Andersen & Co., 435 F.Supp. 84, 95 (S.D.N.Y.), aff'd in part, rev'd in part on other grounds, 567 F.2d 225 (2d Cir.1977) (representation should be treated as concurrent even if the firm, in an effort to avoid the conflict, ceases representation of one of the clients before the motion to disqualify is filed).

16. 565 F.Supp. 663 (N.D.Ill.1983).

17. See ABA Formal Op. 90–358 (1990) (discussing the measures a lawyer should take in initial conversations with a would-be client in order to avoid conflicts of interest problems arising from the firm's representation of other clients).

engaged in an effort to disqualify law firms from representing the adversary.[18]

May firms utilize waiver agreements providing that anything told to them in an initial interview is not confidential? What about provisions that waive, not the right to confidentiality, but the right to complain of future conflicts? See the discussion of these provisions in the note on advance waiver of conflicts, p. 639 below.

Adversity in Unrelated Matters

In *Westinghouse*, the court points to the substantial relationship between the two matters as a factor justifying disqualification. Why? Would the firm have been disqualified if it had been representing the two clients in totally unrelated matters?

In Cinema 5, Ltd. v. Cinerama, Inc.,[19] a leading case on concurrent representation, the firm argued that it should be allowed to proceed against a present client because the matter in which it represented the client bore no "substantial relationship" to that in which it was suing the client. The court said:

> Putting it as mildly as we can, we think it would be questionable conduct for an attorney to participate in any lawsuit against his own client without the knowledge and consent of all concerned....

> Whether such adverse representation, without more, requires disqualification in every case, is a matter we need not now decide. We do hold, however, that the 'substantial relationship' test does not set a sufficiently high standard by which the necessity for disqualification should be determined. That test may properly be applied only where the representation of a former client has been terminated.... Where the relationship is a continuing one, adverse representation is prima facie improper ... and the attorney must be prepared to show, at the very least, that there will be no actual or *apparent* conflict in loyalties or diminution in the vigor of his representation.[20]

18. See B.F. Goodrich v. Formosa Plastics Corp., 638 F.Supp. 1050, 1052–53 (S.D.Tex. 1986) (attorney-client relationship not established in preliminary interview when firm was but one of five interviewed, demonstrating interviewing company did not intend attorney-client relationship; firm would only be disqualified if confidences were actually communicated).

19. 528 F.2d 1384 (2d Cir.1976).

20. Id. at 1386–1387. The new Texas ethics rules permit a lawyer to engage in concurrent representation for and against a current client, without the consent of both clients, if the matters are not substantially related and the lawyer's responsibilities to one client do not "reasonably appear to be or become adversely limited by the lawyer's ... responsibilities to another client." Tex.R.Prof.Conduct 1.06(b). When a district court, following the Texas rule, permitted a law firm to represent a class in an antitrust case against a company the firm was currently representing in other litigation, the Fifth Circuit granted mandamus and reversed. In re Dresser Industries, Inc., 972 F.2d 540 (5th Cir.1992). The applicable conflicts law governing disqualification in a federal court, the court said, is not the state ethics rule, whether or not it is adopted as a local rule by the district court, but the national law of professional responsibility interpreted and applied in Fifth Circuit decisions. Under that law "a law firm may [not] sue its own client, which

The court in *Westinghouse* may have found the relationship between the two matters important because it was balancing the rights of one client against the right of another to continue with counsel of its choice. Should a different standard be used in deciding whether to discipline a lawyer for a conflict, as distinct from the standard in disqualification cases? [21] The law codified in M.R. 1.7 and M.R. 1.9 by and large developed not in disciplinary cases but in court cases on motions to disqualify. Is this portion of the Model Rules then uniquely applicable to conflicts questions arising outside the disciplinary process?

Advance Waiver of Conflicts

To avoid disqualifications, firms increasingly employ provisions in retainer agreements whereby the client agrees to waive certain future conflicts should they arise. These provisions usually relate to successive conflicts, i.e., conflicts that might occur after the firm has concluded representing the client who signs the waiver. But the provisions sometimes apply to concurrent representation.

An early case dealing with such a provision, In re Boone,[22] refused to enforce a release permitting the lawyer subsequently to represent his client's opponent in the same matter. The court said,

> the client may waive a privilege which the relation of attorney and client confers upon him, but he cannot enter into an agreement whereby he consents that the attorney may be released from all the duties, burdens, obligations and privileges pertaining to the duty of attorney and client. . . . Courts owe a duty to themselves, to the public, and to the profession which the temerity or improvidence of clients cannot supersede.[23]

In another aspect of the *Westinghouse* case,[24] Gulf sought to disqualify a law firm representing a co-defendant, which firm had formerly represented Gulf in a matter held to be substantially related. Gulf had agreed that the firm could continue to represent another client even if a conflict developed between the two clients' interests. The court, citing *In re Boone*, disqualified the firm despite the agreement, holding that the agreement could not give the firm permission to use the client's confidences against its own interests in favor of another client.[25] What if the consent agreement provided for screening within the firm?

it concurrently represents in other matters ... and most certainly not here, where the motivation appears only to be the law firm's self-interest."

21. See, e.g., Bodily v. Intermountain Health Care Corp., 649 F.Supp. 468 (D.Utah 1986), described on p. 623 above.

22. 83 Fed. 944, 957 (N.D.Cal.1897).

23. Id. at 957.

24. Westinghouse Elec. Corp. v. Gulf Oil Corp., 588 F.2d 221 (7th Cir.1978).

25. See also Kennecott Copper Corp. v. Curtiss–Wright Corp., 584 F.2d 1195 (2d Cir.1978).

Procedures to Discover Conflicts

The court in Hughes v. Paine, Webber, Jackson and Curtis, Inc., discussed above at p. 637, criticized the law firm's procedures for discovering conflicts. The procedure involved a clerk's survey of the current matter file titles to determine clients and matters represented by the firm. The court said that "it should be noted that a files check may not reveal even the most obvious conflict, e.g., a new client seeks to sue a person who, it later turns out, is the chief executive officer of a corporate client." [26] The court recommended that in addition to a files check, a "new cases" memorandum be circulated within the firm "briefly describing the subject matter and the parties" before finally accepting any new case. Would this be adequate? What about affiliated corporations? Recall that Gulf Oil was not an immediate client of the firm in the *Westinghouse* case but was a member of the trade association, the American Petroleum Institute, which was the client. What about adverse parties in non-litigation matters, such as contentious negotiations? What about the addition of new parties in litigation? See the Comment to M.R. 1.7 (calling on lawyers to adopt "reasonable procedures, appropriate for the size and type of firm and practice" to discover conflicts).

Definition of "Firm"

The law generally has treated lawyers in the same firm as a single lawyer for purposes of conflict of interest. Is this fiction too far from the reality of contemporary law practice, frequently involving large firms with offices in a number of cities? How much information is really shared? Would an office in one city be any less vigorous in presenting a case against a client represented in an unrelated matter by a branch office in another city than against the client of a firm two floors above it in an office complex? Would client confidentiality be less respected?

The rule of decisions such as *Westinghouse* effectively limits the size of firms. At some point, expansion does not pay if it excessively multiplies the number of cases in which the firm will be disqualified. Can firms avoid this problem by forming relationships with "corresponding firms" in different cities rather than opening branch offices? [27] How close a relationship between one firm and another would signify that they are de facto the same firm for purposes of the conflicts rules?

With respect to lawyers who share office space but not fees, the Comment to M.R. 1.10 says:

> Whether two or more lawyers constitute a firm [for purposes of the conflicts rules] can depend on the specific facts. For example, two practitioners who share office space and occasionally consult or assist each other ordinarily would not be regarded as constituting a firm. However, if they present themselves to the public in a way

26. 565 F.Supp. at 673.

27. See ABA Formal Op. 84–351 (1984) ("affiliated" firms are treated as one firm for conflicts purposes).

suggesting that they are a firm or conduct themselves as a firm, they should be regarded as a firm for the purposes of the Rules. . . .

Much will depend on factual details, especially those concerning how the lawyers' relationship has been presented to potential clients.[28] An ABA ethics opinion states that lawyers who share office space may represent conflicting interests if they "exercise reasonable care" to protect their clients' confidences.[29]

Lawyers Related to Other Lawyers

Model Rule 1.8(i) states:

A lawyer related to another lawyer as parent, child, sibling or spouse shall not represent a client in a representation directly adverse to a person who the lawyer knows is represented by the other lawyer except upon consent by the client after consultation regarding the relationship.

A lawyer disqualified under M.R. 1.8(i) does not taint other lawyers in the firm.

M.R. 1.8(i) has no counterpart in the Model Code. DR 5–101(A) and DR 5–105(D), the general provisions on conflicts and imputed disqualification give no specific guidance in this situation and would seem to require the disqualification of the entire firm whenever a lawyer in it is disqualified because married or otherwise closely related to an opposing lawyer. This was not, however, the reading given by the ABA ethics committee. The committee's opinion rejected a per se rule of imputed disqualification, but emphasized the need for the related lawyers to take special precautions to preserve client confidences.[30]

The reported decisions deal primarily with lawyers who are married to each other.[31] The cases on spouses generally accord with the Model Rules approach of requiring disqualification when interests are directly adverse but not insisting on imputed disqualification.[32] In Jones v. Jones,[33] the court refused to find impropriety even though the married lawyers represented clients whose interests were directly adverse.

M.R. 1.8(i) does not apply by its terms to people who are dating on a regular basis, but M.R. 1.7(a) would apply and would yield the same

---

28. See Shelton v. Shelton, 151 A.D.2d 659, 542 N.Y.S.2d 719 (1989) (lawyer who sublet office space within a firm not member of the firm for purposes of conflicts rules). Cf. United States v. Cheshire, 707 F.Supp. 235 (M.D.La.1989) (lawyers who maintained separate practice but shared office space and letterhead, which described them as an "Association of Attorneys," treated as one firm under conflicts rules).

29. ABA Informal Op. 1486 (1982).

30. ABA Formal Op. 340 (1975).

31. For a case involving a father and son representing opposing interests, see Peek v. Harvey, 599 S.W.2d 674 (Tex.Civ.App.1980) (disqualification would have been proper but reversal not required because no showing of harm).

32. See generally: John J. Cross, III, Ethical Issues Facing Lawyer–Spouses and Their Employers, 34 Vand.L.Rev. 1435 (1981); James C. Word, Risk and Knowledge in Interspousal Conflicts of Interest, 7 Whittier L.Rev. 943 (1985).

33. 258 Ga. 353, 369 S.E.2d 478 (1988).

result as M.R. 1.8(i). As for imputed disqualification of dating lawyers disqualified under 1.7(a), the more sensible reading of M.R. 1.10 would be to treat those lawyers in the same way that 1.8(i) treats related lawyers, i.e., not requiring that the whole firm be disqualified. In People v. Jackson,[34] the question was whether the defendant was denied effective assistance of counsel because his lawyer was involved in an ongoing romantic relationship with the prosecutor that she did not disclose to the defendant. The court reversed the conviction.[35]

Lawyers for Government [36]

Professional rules adopted by a state may apply to government as well as private lawyers admitted or practicing in that jurisdiction. Government attorneys are, in general, bound to follow the rules in the bar with jurisdiction over their conduct. Federal preemption, however, may abrogate a state standard inconsistent with federal law.[37] In addition, various ethics codes have been promulgated by various federal, state and local agencies, and agencies may also provide that their lawyers should be guided by the Model Code or Model Rules.[38]

The Model Rules provide that government lawyers are bound by the conflicts rules that bind other lawyers, including M.R. 1.7,[39] with the following exceptions: When one government lawyer is disqualified because of a former representation in private practice, whether those working in the government with that lawyer are disqualified is controlled by M.R. 1.11, not M.R. 1.10. When a lawyer is disqualified because of prior representation of the government, whether those in private practice with that lawyer are likewise disqualified is again governed by M.R. 1.11 and not 1.10. These matters, as well as the other provisions of 1.11, will be explored later in this chapter. The special rules provided for government lawyers in M.R. 1.11 primarily deal with conflicts caused by successive representation.[40]

In Young v. United States ex rel. Vuitton et Fils, S.A.,[41] the defendants violated a settlement order enjoining them from further

---

34. 167 Cal.App.3d 829, 213 Cal.Rptr. 521 (1985).

35. See also Gregori v. Bank of America, 207 Cal.App.3d 291, 254 Cal.Rptr. 853 (1989) (disqualification of firm not warranted when lawyer in firm dated secretary in opponent's firm unless confidences were likely disclosed).

36. The special conflicts problems faced by present and former government lawyers are taken up in more depth later in this chapter and in Chapter 8.

37. Sperry v. Florida ex rel. Florida State Bar, 373 U.S. 379 (1963) (federal law permitting practice by nonlawyers in Patent Office proceedings overrides state unauthorized practice law); Baylson v. Disciplinary Board of Supreme Court of Pennsylvania, 975 F.2d 102 (3d Cir.1992) (state ethics rule requiring judicial approval of a subpoena to a lawyer cannot be applied to federal prosecutors), discussed in Chapter 4 at pp. 131 and 268.

38. See, e.g., the regulations for Department of Justice lawyers, 28 C.F.R. § 45.735–1(b) (to be guided by Model Code).

39. See the Comment to M.R. 1.10.

40. The exception is M.R. 1.11(c)(2), covering negotiating for private employment while working for the government.

41. 481 U.S. 787 (1987).

infringing on Vuitton's trademark. The judge appointed Vuitton's lawyers as special prosecutors to prosecute the defendants for contempt. The Supreme Court upheld the court's power to appoint private lawyers to prosecute contempt charges. Appointing Vuitton's lawyers, however, was improper because of their interest in the matter. Because a prosecutor's job is to seek justice and not merely to convict, "federal prosecutors are prohibited from representing the government in any matter in which they, their family, or their business associates have any interest, 18 U.S.C. § 208(a)." The private lawyer's duty to private clients conflicted with the government's interest "in dispassionate assessment of the propriety of criminal charges." [42]

Lawyers Supplied by Government

The government not only employs lawyers to represent itself (whoever or whatever that is), it also pays lawyers to represent others, e.g., public defenders. These lawyers face many of the problems of vicarious conflicts encountered by lawyers in firms. For example, are all public defenders under one organizational umbrella members of a single firm, no matter how many different offices the public defender "firm" has, perhaps even in different cities? An ABA ethics opinion concludes that a public defender office in one city cannot represent a defendant whose interests conflict with a defendant represented by a public defender office in another city when both offices are under the control of the state's chief public defender. [43]

Some courts, perhaps influenced by the unavailability of other representation for the indigent clients served by legal services offices and public defenders, take a more relaxed position on this issue. New Jersey v. Bell [44] holds that multiple representation by a public defender office does not in itself give rise to a presumption of prejudice. The reasons for presuming prejudice when a private law firm is involved have less application to government lawyers working on a salary: (1) in a private firm all firm members usually have access to confidential information; (2) the entire firm shares an economic interest in the clients of each attorney; and (3) public confidence in the integrity of the bar would be eroded if a lawyer's partner were allowed to do what the lawyer herself could not. Are these considerations less applicable

42. Id. at 803. Accord: People ex rel. Clancy v. Superior Court, 39 Cal.3d 740, 218 Cal.Rptr. 24, 705 P.2d 347 (1985) (impermissible conflict created by government hiring of private lawyer on a contingent basis in civil abatement proceedings because of the affinity between such proceedings and criminal prosecutions and the incompatibility of the prosecution function and payment based on whether a conviction is obtained). See also Federal Trade Commission v. American National Cellular, 868 F.2d 315 (9th Cir.1989) (*Vuitton* distinguished where question was whether full-time government lawyers involved in civil litigation against a party on behalf of the government could be involved in prosecuting the party for criminal contempt arising out of the civil case).

43. See ABA Informal Op. 1418 (1978). See also Commonwealth v. Westbrook, 484 Pa. 534, 400 A.2d 160 (1979) (lawyers working for public defender organization are members of the same firm).

44. 90 N.J. 163, 447 A.2d 525 (1982). Accord: People v. Free, 112 Ill.2d 154, 97 Ill.Dec. 396, 492 N.E.2d 1269 (1986).

to government offices that provide services to poor people? Is the court merely trying to facilitate economical representation of indigents? [45]

In Flores v. Flores,[46] the court said that the state's legal services organization, Alaska Legal Services Corporation (ALSC), need not be treated as a private law firm for conflict of interest purposes. The court encouraged ALSC to develop regulations on "recordkeeping, access to files, supervision and physical separation of offices which would be sufficient to ensure that two attorneys employed by ALSC could represent conflicting positions in litigation, each having undivided loyalty to his client and fully able to exercise ... independent professional judgment." [47] Compare the case printed below.

FIANDACA v. CUNNINGHAM

United States Court of Appeals, First Circuit, 1987.
827 F.2d 825.

Before COFFIN, DAVIS and SELYA, CIRCUIT JUDGES.

COFFIN, CIRCUIT JUDGE.

This opinion discusses two consolidated appeals related to a class action brought by twenty-three female prison inmates sentenced to the custody of the warden of the New Hampshire State Prison. The suit challenges the state of New Hampshire's failure to establish a facility for the incarceration of female inmates with programs and services equivalent to those provided to male inmates at the state prison. After a bench trial on the merits, the district court held that the state had violated plaintiffs' right to equal protection of the laws and ordered the construction of a permanent in-state facility for plaintiffs no later than July 1, 1989. It also required the state to provide a temporary facility for plaintiffs on or before November 1, 1987, but prohibited the state from establishing this facility on the grounds of the Laconia State School and Training Center ("Laconia State School" or "LSS"), New Hampshire's lone institution for the care and treatment of mentally retarded citizens.

One set of appellants consists of Michael Cunningham, warden of the New Hampshire State Prison, and various executive branch officials responsible for the operation of the New Hampshire Department of Corrections ("state"). They challenge the district court's refusal to disqualify plaintiffs' class counsel, New Hampshire Legal Assistance ("NHLA"), due to an unresolvable conflict of interest. See N.H.Rules of Professional Conduct, Rule 1.7(b). They also seek to overturn that portion of the district court's decision barring the establishment of an interim facility for female inmates at LSS, arguing that this prohibition

---

45. ABA Informal Op. 1474 (1982) deals with conflicts problems of military lawyers assigned to represent service people in court martials.

46. 598 P.2d 893 (Alaska 1979).

47. Id. at 896–897.

is unsupported either by relevant factual findings, see Fed.R.Civ.P. 52(a), or by evidence contained in the record.

The other group of appellants is comprised of the plaintiffs in a separate class action challenging the conditions and practices at the Laconia State School, Garrity v. Sununu, No. 78–116–D (D.N.H. filed April 12, 1978), including the New Hampshire Association for Retarded Citizens ("NHARC") and the mentally retarded citizens who currently reside at LSS (the "*Garrity* class"). This group sought unsuccessfully to intervene in the relief phase of the instant litigation after the conclusion of the trial, but prior to the issuance of the court's final memorandum order. See Fed.R.Civ.P. 24. On appeal, these prospective intervenors argue that the district court abused its discretion in denying their motion.

We begin by presenting the relevant facts and then turn to our analysis of the legal issues raised by each of these appeals.

I. Factual Setting.

This case began in June, 1983, when plaintiffs' appellate counsel, Bertram Astles, filed a complaint on behalf of several female inmates sentenced to the custody of the state prison warden and incarcerated at the Rockingham County House of Corrections. NHLA subsequently became co-counsel for plaintiffs and filed an amended complaint expanding the plaintiff class to include all female inmates who are or will be incarcerated in the custody of the warden. In the years that followed, NHLA assumed the role of lead counsel for the class, engaging in extensive discovery and performing all other legal tasks through the completion of the trial before the district court. Among other things, NHLA attorneys and their trial expert, Dr. Edyth Flynn, twice toured and examined potential facilities at which to house plaintiffs, including buildings at the Laconia State School, the New Hampshire Hospital in Concord, and the Youth Development Center in Manchester.

Pursuant to Fed.R.Civ.P. 68, the state offered to settle the litigation on August 1, 1986, in exchange for the establishment of a facility for female inmates at the current Hillsborough County House of Corrections in Goffstown. The state had already negotiated an agreement with Hillsborough County to lease this facility and expected to have it ready for use by the end of 1989. Plaintiffs rejected this offer, however, primarily because the relief would not be available for over three years and because the plan was contingent on Hillsborough County's ability to complete construction of a new facility for the relocation of its prisoners. Plaintiffs desired an in-state facility within six to nine months at the latest and apparently would not settle for less.

The state extended a second offer of judgment to plaintiffs on October 21, 1986. This offer proposed to establish an in-state facility for the incarceration of female inmates at an existing state building by June 1, 1987. Although the formal offer of judgment did not specify a particular location for this facility, the state informed NHLA that it planned to use the Speare Cottage at the Laconia State School. NHLA, which also represented the plaintiff class in the ongoing *Garrity* litigation, rejected the offer on November 10, stating in part that "plaintiffs do not want to agree to an offer which is against the stated interests of the plaintiffs in the *Garrity* class." The state countered by moving immediately for the disqualification of NHLA as class counsel in the case at bar due to the unresolvable conflict of interest inherent in NHLA's representation of two classes with directly adverse interests. The court, despite recognizing that a conflict of interest probably existed, denied the state's motion on November 20 because NHLA's disqualification would further delay the trial of an important matter that had been pending for over three years. It began to try the case four days later.

The *Garrity* class filed its motion to intervene on December 11, ten days after the conclusion of the trial on the merits. The group alleged that it had only recently learned of the state's proposal to develop a correctional facility for women at the Laconia State School. The members of the class were concerned that the establishment of this facility at the school's Speare Cottage, which they understood to be the primary building under consideration, would displace 28 residents of the school and violate the remedial orders issued by Chief Judge Devine in *Garrity*, 522 F.Supp. at 239–44, as well as N.H.Rev.Stat.Ann. ch. 171–A. The district court denied the motion to intervene on December 23, assuring the applicant-intervenors that it would "never approve a settlement which in any way disenfranchises patients of LSS or contravenes the letter or intent of [Chief Judge] Devine's order in *Garrity*."

Meanwhile, the court agreed to hold up its decision on the merits pending the conclusion of ongoing settlement negotiations, permitting the principal parties to spend the month of December, 1986, engaged in further efforts to settle the case. Within approximately one week after the conclusion of the trial, the parties reached an understanding with regard to a settlement agreement which called for the establishment of a "fully operational facility at the present site of the Laconia State School for the incarceration of female inmates by November 1, 1987." The agreement also provided that all affected residents of LSS would receive appropriate placements at least two months prior to the opening of the correctional facility. After negotiating this agreement, NHLA moved to withdraw as class co-counsel on December 11 and attorney Astles signed the settlement agreement on plaintiffs' behalf. The state, however, refused to sign the agreement.

This collapse of the post-trial settlement efforts prompted Judge Loughlin, the district judge in the instant case, and Chief Judge Devine, the *Garrity* trial judge, to convene a joint settlement conference on December 22, 1986. At this conference, plaintiffs formally withdrew their consent to the original settlement agreement in light of the state's refusal to abide by the agreement. Both parties agreed, nevertheless, to try once again to settle the matter in a manner acceptable to all concerned and to report to the en banc court by January 12, 1987.

Judge Loughlin, apparently believing that NHLA's conflict of interest prevented its effective performance as plaintiffs' class counsel, granted NHLA's pending motion to withdraw the day after the joint settlement conference. NHLA, however, had reconsidered its withdrawal from the case in light of the state's failure to sign the settlement agreement and it immediately petitioned the court to be reinstated as class counsel. The court denied the motion for reinstatement, reasoning that the "doctrine of necessity," its purported justification for denying the state's earlier disqualification motion in the face of NHLA's conflict of interest, no longer had force because the case had been tried to a conclusion.

The district court finally announced its decision on the merits on January 13, 1987. Finding that the conditions of confinement, programs, and services available to New Hampshire female prisoners are not on par with the conditions, programs, and services afforded male inmates at the New Hampshire State Prison, the court held that such gender-based, inferior treatment violates the Equal Protection clause of the Fourteenth Amendment. As a primary remedy, it ordered the state to establish "a permanent facility comparable to all of the facilities encompassed at the New Hampshire State Prison ... to be inhabited no later than July 1, 1989." In crafting a temporary remedy, it reiterated that "there shall not be a scintilla of infringement upon the rights and privileges of the *Garrity* class," and proceeded to rule that the state had to provide plaintiffs with "a building comparable to the Speare Building," but that such facility "shall not be located at the Laconia State School or its environs." This appeal resulted.

II. Appeal of State Department of Corrections.

. . .

A. Refusal to Disqualify for Conflict of Interest.

The state's first argument is that the district court erred in permitting NHLA to represent the plaintiff class at trial after its conflict of interest had become apparent. As we recognized in Kevlik v. Goldstein, 724 F.2d 844 (1st Cir.1984), a district court is vested with broad power and responsibility to supervise the professional conduct of the attorneys appearing before it. Id. at 847. It follows from this premise that "[w]e will not disturb the district court['s] finding unless there is no reasonable basis for the court's determination." Id. We must determine, therefore, whether the court's denial of the state's disqualification motion amounts to an abuse of discretion in this instance.

The state's theory is that NHLA faced an unresolvable conflict because the interests of two of its clients were directly adverse after the state extended its second offer of judgment on October 21, 1986. The relevant portion of New Hampshire's Rules of Professional Conduct states:

A lawyer shall not represent a client if the representation of that client may be materially limited by the lawyer's responsibilities to another client ... unless:

(1) the lawyer reasonably believes the representation will not be adversely affected; and

(2) the client consents after consultation and with knowledge of the consequences.

. . .

N.H.Rules of Professional Conduct, Rule 1.7(b). The comment to Rule 1.7 prepared by the ABA goes on to state:

Loyalty to a client is also impaired when a lawyer cannot consider, recommend or carry out an appropriate course of action for the client because of the lawyer's other responsibilities or interests. The conflict in effect forecloses alternatives that would otherwise be available to the client.

N.H.Rules of Professional Conduct, Rule 1.7, comment. In this case, it is the state's contention that the court should have disqualified NHLA as class counsel pursuant to Rule 1.7 because, at least with respect to the state's second offer of judgment, NHLA's representation of the plaintiff class in this litigation was materially limited by its responsibilities to the *Garrity* class.

We find considerable merit in this argument. The state's offer to establish a facility for the incarceration of female inmates at the Laconia State School, and to use its "best efforts" to make such a facility available for occupancy by June 1, 1987, presented plaintiffs with a legitimate opportunity to settle a protracted legal dispute on highly favorable terms. As class counsel, NHLA owed plaintiffs a duty of undivided loyalty: it was obligated to present the offer to plaintiffs, to explain its costs and benefits, and to ensure that the offer received full and fair consideration by the members of the class. Beyond all else, NHLA had an ethical duty to prevent its loyalties to other clients from coloring its representation of the plaintiffs in this action and from infringing upon the exercise of its professional judgment and responsibilities.[4]

NHLA, however, also represents the residents of the Laconia State School who are members of the plaintiff class in *Garrity*. Quite understandably, this group vehemently opposes the idea of establishing a correctional facility for female inmates anywhere on the grounds of LSS. As counsel for the *Garrity* class, NHLA had an ethical duty to advance the interests of the class to the fullest possible extent and to

---

4. The fact that the conflict arose due to the nature of the state's settlement offer, rather than due to the subject matter of the litigation or the parties involved, does not render the ethical implications of NHLA's multiple representation any less troublesome. Among other things, courts have a duty to "ensur[e] that at all stages of litigation ... counsel are as a general rule available to advise each client as to the particular, individualized benefits or costs of a proposed settlement." Smith v. City of New York, 611 F.Supp. 1080, 1090 (S.D.N.Y.1985).

oppose any settlement of the instant case that would compromise those interests. In short, the combination of clients and circumstances placed NHLA in the untenable position of being simultaneously obligated to represent vigorously the interests of two conflicting clients. It is inconceivable that NHLA, or any other counsel, could have properly performed the role of "advocate" for both plaintiffs and the *Garrity* class, regardless of its good faith or high intentions. Indeed, this is precisely the sort of situation that Rule 1.7 is designed to prevent.

Plaintiffs argue on appeal that there really was no conflict of interest for NHLA because the state's second offer of judgment was unlikely to lead to a completed settlement for reasons other than NHLA's loyalties to the *Garrity* class. We acknowledge that the record contains strong indications that settlement would not have occurred even if plaintiffs had been represented by another counsel. For instance, in ruling on the intervention motion, the district court stated that, pursuant to its duties under Fed.R.Civ.P. 23(e), it would not approve a settlement that infringed in any way on the rights of the LSS residents. Furthermore, as plaintiffs contend, the second offer of judgment was unattractive because it was phrased in "best efforts" language and did not set a firm date for establishment of the facility. The question, however, is not whether the state's second offer of judgment would have resulted in a settlement had plaintiffs' counsel not been encumbered by a conflict of interest. Rather, the inquiry we must make is whether plaintiffs' counsel was able to represent the plaintiff class unaffected by divided loyalties, or as stated in Rule 1.7(b), whether NHLA could have reasonably believed that its representation would not be adversely affected by the conflict. Our review of the record and the history of this litigation—especially NHLA's response to the state's second offer, in which it stated that "plaintiffs do not want to agree to an offer which is against the stated interests of plaintiffs in the *Garrity* case"—persuade us that NHLA's representation of plaintiffs could not escape the adverse effects of NHLA's loyalties to the *Garrity* class.

Both the district court and plaintiffs on appeal have also advanced the belief that "necessity" outweighed the adverse effects of NHLA's conflict of interest in this instance and justified the denial of the state's pre-trial disqualification motion. See United States v. Will, 449 U.S. 200, 213–17 (1980)....

While it is surely laudable that the court was anxious to resolve a lingering dispute concerning an unfortunate state of affairs, we fail to see how the doctrine of *necessity* is implicated in a case such as this. As plaintiffs' counsel admitted at oral argument, there was no particular emergency at the time of the court's decision to ignore the conflict of interest and proceed to trial. Plaintiffs simply continued to suffer the effects of the same inequitable treatment that had persisted for many years. While it would have been desirable to avoid delaying the trial for up to a year or more, it certainly was not "necessary" in the sense of limiting the court to but one potential course of action. We realize that other courts occasionally consider the possible effects of delay in ruling on disqualification motions, see, e.g., Laker Airways Ltd. v. Pan American World Airways, 103 F.R.D. 22, 27–28 (D.D.C.1984) ("Were the motion to disqualify to be granted, the resulting additional delay might well be crippling."), but in this circuit, arguments premised on delay have been less availing. As we held in *Kevlik*, 724 F.2d at 844, "we cannot, in the face of a breach of professional duty, ignore the wrong because appellees' counsel neglected to discern the conflict earlier, *or even opted to delay litigation by raising the motion ....*" Id. at 848 (emphasis supplied).

Absent some evidence of *true* necessity, we will not permit a meritorious disqualification motion to be denied in the interest of expediency unless it can be shown that the movant strategically sought disqualification in an effort to advance some improper purpose. Thus, the state's motivation in bringing the motion is not irrelevant; as we recognized in *Kevlik*, "disqualification motions can be tactical in nature, designed to harass opposing counsel." Id. However, the mere fact that the state moved for NHLA's disqualification just prior to the commencement of the trial is not, without more, cause for denying its motion. See id. There is simply no evidence to support plaintiffs' suggestion that the state "created" the conflict by intentionally offering plaintiffs a building at LSS in an effort "to dodge the bullet again" with regard to its "failure to provide instate housing for the plaintiff class." We do not believe, therefore, that the state's second offer of judgment and subsequent disqualification motion were intended to harass plaintiffs. Rather, our reading of the record indicates that a more benign scenario is more probable: the state made a good faith attempt to accommodate plaintiffs by offering to establish a correctional facility in an existing building at the Laconia State School and, once NHLA's conflict of interest with regard to this offer became apparent, the state moved for NHLA's disqualification to preserve this settlement option.

· · ·

B. Proper Remedy.

In light of the district court's error in ignoring NHLA's conflict of interest, we believe it necessary to remand the case for further proceedings. We must consider a further question, however: must the district court now start from scratch in resolving this dispute? The state argues that the court's failure to disqualify NHLA is plain reversible error, and therefore requires the court to try the matter anew. We subscribe to the view, however, that merely "conducting [a] trial with counsel that should have been disqualified does not 'indelibl[y] stamp or taint' the proceedings." Warpar Manufacturing Corp. v. Ashland Oil, Inc., 606 F.Supp. 866, 867 (N.D.Ohio, E.D.1985) (quoting Firestone Tire & Rubber Co. v. Risjord, 449 U.S. 368, 376 (1981)). With this in mind, we look to the actual adverse effects caused by the court's error in refusing to disqualify NHLA as class counsel to determine the nature of the proceedings on remand. Cf. Board of Education of New York v.

Nyquist, 590 F.2d 1241, 1246 (2d Cir.1979) (courts should be hesitant to disqualify an attorney unless trial will be tainted); Smith v. City of New York, 611 F.Supp. at 1091–92 (same); SMI Industries Canada Ltd. v. Caelter Industries, Inc., 586 F.Supp. 808, 814 (N.D.N.Y.1984) (same).

We do not doubt that NHLA's conflict of interest potentially influenced the course of the proceedings in at least one regard: NHLA could not fairly advocate the remedial option—namely, the alternative of settling for a site at the Laconia State School—offered by the state prior to trial. The conflict, therefore, had the potential to ensure that the case would go to trial, a route the state likely wished to avoid by achieving an acceptable settlement. Nevertheless, we do not see how a trial on the merits could have been avoided given the manner in which the case developed below. Judge Loughlin stated on the record that he would not approve a settlement infringing on the rights of LSS residents, and under Rule 23(e), any settlement of this class action required his approval to be effective. It seems to us, therefore, that even if some other counsel had advised plaintiffs to accept the state's offer for a building at LSS, a trial on the merits would have been inevitable.

With respect to the merits of the equal protection issue, the state has been unable to identify any way in which the court's error adversely affected its substantial rights at trial. The state admits that it had long recognized the need to establish an in-state facility for female inmates comparable to the state prison and that it had already taken steps in this direction by negotiating an agreement for the use of the present Hillsborough County House of Correction beginning in 1989. The evidence adduced at trial confirmed what both parties had known all along—that female state inmates do not enjoy services, programs, and conditions of confinement similar to those afforded the male inmates at the state prison—and this evidence led the court to conclude that the state had violated plaintiffs' right to equal protection of the laws.

The state has not directly challenged any of the district court's findings, which were based on the overwhelming evidence of inequitable treatment, and there has been no suggestion that the proceedings on the merits and the court's holding on the issue of liability were tarnished in any way by NHLA's participation. Indeed, as the state had to concede at oral argument, if the trial had been bifurcated into liability and remedy phases, NHLA's conflict of interest would have tainted its representation of plaintiffs—and required disqualification—only in the second, remedial phase of the trial. It seems plain to us, therefore, that at least with regard to the court's determination on the merits of the equal protection issue, the error in refusing to disqualify NHLA as class counsel is not inconsistent with substantial justice and should not require retrial of this issue. For these reasons, we hold that, with regard to the merits of the case, the district court's failure to disqualify NHLA constitutes harmless error at most, Fed.R.Civ.P. 61, and we affirm the district court's holding that the state violated plaintiffs' rights to equal protection of the laws.

The situation is different, however, with respect to the remedy designed by the district court. We believe that it would be inappropriate to permit the court's remedial order—which includes a specific prohibition on the use of LSS—to stand in light of the court's refusal to disqualify NHLA. The ban on the use of buildings located on the grounds of LSS is exactly the sort of remedy preferred by NHLA's *other* clients, the members of the *Garrity* class, and therefore has at least the appearance of having been tainted by NHLA's conflict of interest. Consequently, we hold that the district court's remedial order must be vacated and the case remanded for a new trial on the issue of the proper remedy for this constitutional deprivation. This determination leads us to the question of which parties should be permitted to participate in this new trial, an issue that forms the heart of the appeal brought by NHARC and the other members of the *Garrity* class as prospective intervenors. [The court allowed the intervention].

Notes on *Fiandaca*

How did the interests of the two client classes conflict? Will consent of each client class solve the problem or does the court hold that the conflict is so severe that it is nonconsentable? How does a class of mentally retarded persons who are institutionalized consent to a conflict? Who acts on their behalf? Does M.R. 1.14 help answer this question?

Should the court have paid more attention to the fact that a legal services organization represented both classes? To the reality that alternate counsel might not have been available to either class? Should this be a factor in judging "true necessity?" Does the court too lightly dismiss the harm to the female prisoners caused by delay?

What about the state's motives in proposing the Laconia site? Why would the state have persisted in offering the Laconia site given the judge's statement that he would not approve it? Why did the state refuse to sign the settlement agreement? What other evidence could plaintiffs have offered to show the state acted with improper motives?

What about the remedy? Is it too harsh or too lenient? How important should deterring lawyer misconduct be in fashioning a conflicts remedy? Discipline for violating the conflicts rules is rare unless there are other ethical violations, such as self-dealing or dishonesty.[48]

Should the court have held the state lacked standing to raise the conflict? Most courts do not require any special showing of standing before entertaining a motion to disqualify based on a conflict of inter-

---

48. See, e.g., Lake County Bar Assn. v. Gargiulo, 62 Ohio St.2d 239, 404 N.E.2d 1343 (1980) (simultaneous conflict and self-dealing); Codiga v. State Bar, 20 Cal.3d 788, 144 Cal.Rptr. 404, 575 P.2d 1186 (1978) (lying to conceal conflict).

est.[49]   Typically, a motion to disqualify is made by an opposing party or interest.

Estoppel or Previous Consent

Earlier decisions holding that "mere delay or laches" is not a defense to a motion to disqualify [50] have been rejected by most courts. As disqualification motions became widely used, often for tactical purposes, judges increasingly applied delay and estoppel arguments in ruling on them.[51] In United Sewerage Agency v. Jelco, Inc.,[52] disqualification was denied on the basis of client consent, coupled with delay and the finding that it was "obvious" that the firm could adequately conduct the present representation. The two disputes involved the same contract, but different contract provisions were in issue.

Positional Conflicts

May a lawyer argue in one case for one client that a particular law is valid, while at the same time arguing for another that the same law is invalid? This type of conflict is often referred to as a "positional conflict." The professional tradition flowing from English barristers to present-day lawyers accords a lawyer great freedom to assert whatever reasonable legal arguments will advance a client's clause, leaving it to the tribunal to reach an appropriate result. But many lawyers under today's conditions are concerned about arguing inconsistent positions or even those that a major client may believe are opposed to its interests.

The Comment to M.R. 1.7 states:

> A lawyer may represent parties having antagonistic positions on a legal question that has arisen in different cases, unless representation of either client would be adversely affected. Thus, it is ordinarily not improper to assert such positions in cases pending in different trial courts, but it may be improper to do so in cases pending at the same time in an appellate court.

Does this mean that you should not assert contrary legal positions in unrelated cases in the same trial court? Be clear that the conflict is not cured by foregoing a particular argument on behalf of one client so as not to end up asserting contrary positions before the same court. The decision to forego the argument is tainted because it is influenced by obligations to another client. *Fiandaca* involves this principle.

49. See, e.g., Kevlik v. Goldstein, 724 F.2d 844, 847–48 (1st Cir.1984) (standing to raise a disqualification motion based on ethical responsibility of all lawyers to bring to the court's attention possible ethical violations).

50. See, e.g., Emle Industries, Inc. v. Patentex, Inc., 478 F.2d 562, 573–74 (2d Cir.1973) (three-year delay did not bar disqualification motion because it is in the public interest to enforce lawyers' ethical obligations).

51. See, e.g., Cox v. American Cast Iron Pipe Co., 847 F.2d 725, 729 (11th Cir.1988); Trust Corp. of Montana v. Piper Aircraft Corp., 701 F.2d 85, 87 (9th Cir.1983); MacArthur v. Bank of New York, 524 F.Supp. 1205, 1209 (S.D.N.Y.1981) ("the burden on the party seeking disqualification may be greater as a result of his undue delay").

52. 646 F.2d 1339 (9th Cir.1981).

Appealability of Disqualification Rulings

Are disqualification rulings immediately appealable? In 1981 the Supreme Court held that orders denying disqualification of lawyers in civil cases are not immediately appealable under 28 U.S.C. § 1291 prior to judgment on the merits.[53] Several years later the Court held that orders granting disqualification motions in civil cases were not final orders under § 1291.[54] A third case [55] holds that in a criminal case the granting of a disqualification motion is not immediately appealable. The rule is different in some state courts.[56]

The courts' impatience with disqualification motions underlies these holdings. In discussing the potential for frivolous appeals of motions to disqualify, the Supreme Court said, "Given an attorney's personal and financial interest in the disqualification decision, orders disqualifying counsel may be more likely to lead to an interlocutory appeal than other pretrial rulings, whether those rulings are correct or otherwise." [57] And the Court rejected the argument that the disqualified lawyer's desire for vindication was a valid ground for interlocutory appeal. "As a matter of professional ethics ... the appeal should turn entirely on the client's interest." [58]

Thus disqualification orders are not generally reviewable in the federal courts prior to judgment on the merits.[59] Hence most of the law on this subject is now made by district courts, not the federal courts of appeals, because a ruling on disqualification is rarely grounds for reversing a subsequent judgment on the merits. Occasionally, a disqualification ruling may be certified for interlocutory appeal pursuant to 28 U.S.C. § 1292(b) or satisfy the demanding conditions for issuance of a writ of mandamus from the court of appeals.[60]

When a client appeals after final judgment, claiming that the grant or denial of a disqualification motion was reversible error, what is the standard by which this claim should be judged? Must the client show

53. Firestone Tire & Rubber Co. v. Risjord, 449 U.S. 368 (1981).

54. Richardson–Merrell Inc. v. Koller, 472 U.S. 424 (1985).

55. Flanagan v. United States, 465 U.S. 259 (1984).

56. See, e.g., Maddocks v. Ricker, 403 Mass. 592, 531 N.E.2d 583 (1988) (order granting disqualification motion appealable); Russell v. Mercy Hospital, 15 Ohio St.3d 37, 472 N.E.2d 695 (1984) (same); Gregori v. Bank of America, 207 Cal.App.3d 291, 254 Cal.Rptr. 853 (Ct.App.1989) (denial of motion to disqualify appealable).

57. Richardson–Merrell, 472 U.S. at 434.

58. Id. at 435.

59. *Richardson–Merrell*, 472 U.S. at 435, suggested that disqualified lawyers whose reputations are "egregiously injured" by the disqualification order, but whose clients are satisfied by substitute counsel, "might be able to obtain relief from the Circuit Judicial Council pursuant to 28 U.S.C. § 332(d)(1)." See also Matter of Grand Jury Subpoena of Rochon, 873 F.2d 170 (7th Cir.1989) (order disqualifying Attorney General of the United States from participating in a criminal investigation is immediately appealable).

60. See Firestone Tire & Rubber Co. v. Risjord, 449 U.S. 368, 373 n. 13 (1981); Matter of Sandahl, 980 F.2d 1118 (7th Cir.1992) (order disqualifying a law firm cannot be reviewed by mandamus unless patently erroneous, requiring a showing of both irreparable harm and the existence of a demonstrable injustice).

prejudice resulted? How can a client show that it was prejudiced when competent successor counsel tried the case? The Supreme Court in *Firestone* and *Richardson–Merrell* expressly reserved the question of whether a client in a civil case would have to show prejudice resulting from the disqualification order when appealing after judgment on the merits. For discussion of what a criminal defendant must show on appeal, see the notes following *Cuyler v. Sullivan,* printed below at p. 661.

    Disciplinary action for filing or resisting disqualification motions for strategic purposes is extremely rare. Rule 11 sanctions, however, are imposed against a lawyer who files a frivolous motion to disqualify or defends against a motion to disqualify when there is no legal or factual basis for doing so.[61] State courts are also concerned about the increased use of disqualification motions for strategic purposes: "Court resources are sorely taxed by the increasing use of disqualification motions as harassment or dilatory tactics." [62]

Curing a Simultaneous Conflict

    EC 5–19 suggests that a lawyer who represents multiple clients with potentially differing interests may cure the problem by deferring to the judgment of the client who objects to the multiple representation and withdrawing from representing that client. Courts have recognized that the ex ante prohibitions on conflicts should not always be imposed ex post to disqualify.[63] But a number of decisions hold that a concurrent conflict cannot be converted into a successive conflict by firing an objecting or unwanted client. In Picker International, Inc. v. Varian Associates, Inc.,[64] for example, a newly merged law firm found itself representing clients directly adverse in unrelated matters. The court held that the conflict could not be cured by dropping one client. Had the lawyers successfully withdrawn from the litigation prior to the merger, the case would be analyzed as one of successive representation: Because a lawyer may oppose *former* clients in matters *unrelated* to the previous representation, the newly merged firm would have been allowed to proceed.[65]

61. See, e.g., Optyl Eyeware Fashion Int'l Corp. v. Style Companies, Ltd., 760 F.2d 1045 (9th Cir.1985) (sanctions for filing frivolous motion to disqualify); Analytica v. NPD Research, Inc., 708 F.2d 1263 (7th Cir.1983) (sanctions for defending against a motion to disqualify). The court may also sanction a lawyer under 28 U.S.C. § 1927 for vexatiously multiplying the proceedings by bringing a groundless motion to disqualify.

62. Gorovitz v. Planning Board of Nantucket, 394 Mass. 246, 475 N.E.2d 377, 380 n. 7 (1985). See also Alexander v. Superior Court, 141 Ariz. 157, 685 P.2d 1309, 1317 (1984).

63. See, e.g., Bodily v. Intermountain Health Care Corp., 649 F.Supp. 468 (D.Utah 1986); and Pennwalt Corp. v. Plough, Inc., 85 F.R.D. 264 (D.Del.1980) (both involving simultaneous representation in unrelated matters).

64. 869 F.2d 578 (Fed.Cir. 1989).

65. See the discussion of successive conflicts below at p. 692. For another case involving conflicts created by law firm merger, see Harte Biltmore Ltd. v. First Pennsylvania Bank, N.A., 655 F.Supp. 419, 421 (S.D.Fla.1987).

The question of whether successor counsel may use the work product of disqualified counsel is considered in the *First Wisconsin* case, reprinted below.

3. Remedies for Conflicts of Interest

Conflict of interest violations may lead to a number of sanctions and remedies. Lawyers may be disciplined for violation of professional rules.[66] A conflict of interest is a breach of duty that may provide the basis for a malpractice action.[67] Fee forfeiture is also an available remedy—a lawyer may not be entitled to fees for work performed after the conflict arose.[68] A conflict of interest may also be the basis for setting aside a contract or gift, especially one between a lawyer and client.[69] Federal and state statutes impose criminal penalties for conflict of interest violations on the part of government employees, former government employees and those dealing with the government.[70] In situations in which a lawyer seeks to use as evidence information obtained from a former client, the evidence may be excluded to protect that client's confidentiality interests. Other remedies may also be appropriate.[71]

The most common sanction for conflicts of interest in litigation is disqualification of the client's lawyer, as in *Westinghouse* and *Fiandaca,* considered above.[72] "The sanction assures both that the case is well presented in court, that confidential information of present or former clients is not misused, and, where appropriate, that a client's interest in a lawyer's loyalty is not violated." [73]

Sometimes, as in *Westinghouse,* a lawyer or law firm is disqualified in the middle of a transaction or litigation. May successor counsel make use of the work of the disqualified lawyers?

66. See, e.g., In re Banks, 283 Or. 459, 584 P.2d 284 (1978) (lawyer reprimanded for representing a corporation and its president after their interests became conflicting). For general discussion of conflicts remedies, see C. Wolfram, Modern Legal Ethics § 7.1.7 (1986).

67. See, e.g., Woodruff v. Tomlin, 616 F.2d 924 (6th Cir.1980) (lawyer held liable for malpractice for representing insurer, driver, owner and passenger in an accident case and not telling passenger that she might have a claim against the driver and owner on which insurer would be liable).

68. See, e.g., Financial General Bankshares, Inc. v. Metzger, 523 F.Supp. 744 (D.D.C. 1981) (corporate lawyer who also secretly advised dissident shareholder denied fees for the period in question), rev'd on other grounds, 680 F.2d 768 (D.C. Cir.1982).

69. See the discussion of this question in Chapter 6 beginning at p. 593.

70. These issues are discussed below at p. 725.

71. For general discussion of remedies for conflicts of interest, see the proposed Restatement of the Law Governing Lawyers § 201, Comment e and Reporter's Note (Tent. Draft No. 4, Apr. 10, 1991). Other remedies include dismissal of an action. See, e.g., Doe v. A. Corp., 330 F.Supp. 1352 (S.D.N.Y.1971), aff'd sub nom. Hall v. A. Corp., 453 F.2d 1375 (2d Cir.1972) (facts in shareholders' suit against corporation were derived entirely from information acquired by lawyer while employed by the corporation).

72. See generally James Lindgren, Toward a New Standard of Attorney Disqualification, 1982 Am.Bar Found. Research J. 419.

73. Restatement of Law Governing Lawyers § 201, Comment e, at 11.

FIRST WISCONSIN MORTGAGE TRUST
v. FIRST WISCONSIN CORP.

United States Court of Appeals, Seventh Circuit, 1978, En Banc.
584 F.2d 201.

PELL, CIRCUIT JUDGE.

The ultimate, and apparently first impression, issue in this appeal, stated as simply as possible is whether, when attorneys are judicially determined to have been disqualified to represent a client because of prior simultaneous representation of that client's adversary in litigation, the written product of lawyer work [1] performed during the period of disqualification may be made available to successor counsel. The answer to this issue, in our opinion, is not a per se preclusion but must be a flexible one based upon an examination of the particular facts of the case under consideration.

[First Wisconsin Corp.(FWC), a bank holding company, established a subsidiary, Mortgage Trust (Trust), in 1971 to manage and sell real estate investment trust certificates (REITs) to individuals who wanted tax-sheltered real estate investments. Other FWC subsidiaries made loans and provided investment advice to Trust. Foley & Lardner, a large Milwaukee firm, jointly represented FWC, Trust and other FWC subsidiaries. The sale of the REITs was subject to federal securities laws.

[The underlying investments did poorly and Trust experienced a series of loan defaults in 1973 and 1974. The Foley firm at that time recommended that Trust retain separate counsel to negotiate disputes arising out of the defaults. The Sonnenschein firm of Chicago was then engaged by Trust. After negotiations began and Trust threatened to file suit, Foley resigned as general counsel to Trust. In March 1975 Trust filed suit against FWC and two of its subsidiaries for federal securities law violations. Foley then sought Trust's consent to its continued representation of FWC and the other defendants. Trust refused its consent and moved to disqualify Foley. The district court disqualified Foley fifteen months later on November 16, 1976.

[Defendants' new counsel, the Mayer firm of Chicago, moved for authorization to obtain Foley's work product from 1974 and early 1975, primarily consisting of the analysis by fifteen Foley lawyers of approximately 300 real estate investment transactions. Defendants' motion was denied and a panel of the Court of Appeals affirmed by a 2–1 vote. A rehearing en banc was granted, resulting in reversal. The merits of

---

1. Throughout this litigation, the parties and the district court have used the generic term "work product" to describe the written work which the defendants desire their present counsel to receive and which the plaintiff contends should not be delivered, a position accepted by the district court. While "work product" as a term probably encompasses substantially broader and more legally sophisticated writings than the routine analyses here in controversy, see Hickman v. Taylor, 329 U.S. 495 (1947), we shall use the term here for convenience of reference.

the disqualification motion were not considered because the court holds, as did the Supreme Court later in Richardson–Merrell Inc. v. Koller, 472 U.S. 424 (1985), that an order granting disqualification is not separately appealable.]

Turning to the merits of this appeal, we do so with the underlying assumption that the disqualification of Foley was correct, the appeal having been dismissed.

That which the defendants seek to secure from the attorneys formerly representing them in the present litigation is, as described by the defendants, the "written work product, consisting essentially of summaries of loan files relating to more than 300 complex transactions, and an explanation limited to an identification of the documents reviewed."

Beginning in 1974 a number of Foley attorneys were engaged in analyzing the various claims being asserted on behalf of Trust and analyzing the loan files regarding such claims. This work continued after suit was filed. The analysis of the loan files was conducted by a team of 15 Foley lawyers for more than a year prior to the ultimate disqualification of that firm in November 1976.

Neither the district court in its opinion, nor the plaintiff in its brief or at oral argument has contradicted the defendants' contention that the loan file summaries are the result of routine lawyer work of a type which any competent lawyer, by spending the substantial time which would be required, could accomplish just as well as did Foley. The work product came into being for the benefit of the defendants. It may be safely assumed that the work was not performed gratuitously by Foley but rather on a compensated fee basis. There is no challenge to the defendants' assertion that the preparation of the loan file summaries was not aided by any confidential information acquired by the Foley lawyers through their prior relationship with Trust. Indeed, it appears that the summaries are no different than they would have been if made in their entirety by lawyers who were strangers to all of the parties.

The district court in its opinion under review here, while noting the contention that no confidential information was involved, in effect found this to be of no significance....

As we read the district court's opinion in this respect, it is saying that because the Foley firm was disqualified from the time litigation was instituted, and in all probability from the very beginning of its representation of the defendants on the matter which ultimately went into litigation, any work performed during this entire period is automatically tainted by the disqualification and is unavailable to the party for whom the work was performed. This, of course, constitutes a sanction for representation subsequently determined to be improper without any independent basis therefor related to the work itself.

In our opinion, such an automatic or per se equation of denial of the work product to the disqualification of representation is not good law and the application of such a rule without more requires reversal. No doubt it will frequently be that the lawyer who is unfortunate enough to become involved in the Goodwin Sands of simultaneously representing clients whose interests either are or thereafter come into conflict, and who ceases representation of one of the clients, will find that the work performed during the period subject to disqualification will have aspects of confidentiality or other unfair detriment to the former client arising from the very fact of the knowledge and acquaintanceship acquired during the period of the prior representation. This does not mean, however, that this is always the situation, or even that it is frequently so. We see no reason for an irrebuttable presumption merely from dual representation in the conflict context to the effect that whenever cause of disqualification exists any lawyer work thereafter is lost work irrespective of its nature or any other pertinent factors.

The present case presents a particularly strong case for justifying a flexible rule in that the order of disqualification did not occur until 15 months after the motion for that purpose. The practical effect of this time frame is that once a motion of disqualification is filed the work performed thereafter is subject to the risk of automatically being wasted work to the detriment of the client.... Unfortunately the practical effect might well be to impose a moratorium upon trial preparation for such period of time as it might take to rule upon a motion for disqualification.

A secondary aspect of this matter is that litigation must be ongoing, and the counsel representing the party prior to an ultimate disqualification is confronted with other aspects of the litigation as it proceeds, such as filing responsive pleadings, answering interrogatories, addressing requests for admissions, and production of documents, and in taking part in depositions. In the present case, all of these procedures, other than the work product, which were performed by Foley on behalf of the defendants have been left extant without challenge by Trust.

. . .

With this background in mind, we deem it appropriate to observe that in our opinion a lawyer who is charged with impropriety, here a disqualifying conflict of interest, should not, if he or she reasonably and in good conscience denies the charge, be expected forthwith to withdraw from the representation. Indeed, proper representation of the client might seem to militate against such precipitous action, suggesting instead a vigorous resistance where in good faith it is believed that impropriety does not exist. Leveling the charge of impropriety at opposing counsel, which if sustained would require withdrawal, should not be a standard part of counsel's offensive armament to be used routinely or without reasonable and good faith belief in its necessity. In the present case, we must also observe that we have no basis for discerning lack of good faith on the part of either charging or resisting counsel.

. . .

In the present case the raw materials which Foley had examined and analyzed were loan files which were equally available to the plaintiff for examination and analysis. The work product, the analyses, if "tainted" in the present case are only so by virtue of the application of a per se sanction flowing from the disqualification, and relating back in extent to the beginning of the cause for disqualification. They are not "tainted" by virtue of having been based upon confidential knowledge or other advantage gained during or from the dual representation.

. . .

. . . [W]e have no particular quarrel with the test proposed by the dissent that the cases would "turn upon whether there exists a reasonable possibility of confidential information being used in the formation of, or being passed to substitute counsel through, the work product in question." The dissent after stating this test then proceeds in part II. C., although first asserting that the possibility of Foley's using confidential information in its work on this case is "inescapable," to engage in speculation as to confidential information which "possibly," or as a "possibility," or even as "a distinct possibility," and finally as "highly probable," could have tainted the work product in question.

The difficulty here, however, is that this contention is made only in the dissenting opinion. Trust was in a position to know whether such possibilities existed, but the argument advanced by the concededly competent counsel now representing Trust contains no such contentions. The record in the case before us, and that is the only case we now need to decide, is devoid of any showing, either directly or by necessary implication, that the routine lawyer work bore the imprint of confidentially acquired or secret information.

. . .

Use of a Disqualified Lawyer's Work [74]

Should the trial court in *First Wisconsin* have disqualified the Foley firm? On what basis? Should Foley have seen the conflict coming and acted sooner to avoid or lessen its impact? Should Foley have been more cautious in getting into the situation of representing related corporations with significant and diverse public ownership?

[74]. On access to a disqualified lawyer's work see also: Developments in the Law— Conflicts of Interests in the Legal Profession, 94 Harv.L.Rev. 1244, 1484–86 (1981); Comment, The Availability of the Work–Product of a Disqualified Attorney: What Standard?, 127 U.Pa.L.Rev. 1607 (1979); Comment, Access to Work Product of Disqualified Counsel, 46 U.Chi.L.Rev. 443 (1979).

Given the disqualification of Foley, should its work be available to FWC's successor counsel? If the loan workups had not been made available, would Foley risk disgorging all fees earned in producing them? Consider the same issue with respect to the millions of dollars in fees Kirkland & Ellis charged to Westinghouse in that litigation.

Does the functional or utilitarian approach of *First Wisconsin* mean that disqualified counsel's work will be made available if and to the extent the work is not based on confidential information of the former client? If the conflict is severe and obvious, should a prophylactic rule be applied denying the use of the lawyer's work?

In EZ Paintr Corp. v. Padco, Inc.,[75] two lawyers of the law firm representing Padco had formerly been members of the firm representing EZ Paintr. The court disqualified Padco's firm and limited the turn-over of work product from the disqualified law firm to successor counsel to that prepared before the two tainted lawyers joined the firm.[76]

What about consultation between the disqualified firm and substitute counsel? The emerging rule is that a disqualified lawyer may consult with successor counsel concerning work that may be turned over but not as to other matters.[77]

4. Concurrent Representation in Criminal Litigation

CUYLER v. SULLIVAN

Supreme Court of the United States, 1980.
446 U.S. 335, 100 S.Ct. 1708, 64 L.Ed.2d 333.

MR. JUSTICE POWELL delivered the opinion of the Court.

The question presented is whether a state prisoner may obtain a federal writ of habeas corpus by showing that his retained defense counsel represented potentially conflicting interests.

I

Respondent John Sullivan was indicted with Gregory Carchidi and Anthony DiPasquale for the first-degree murders of John Gorey and Rita Janda. The victims, a labor official and his companion, were shot to death in Gorey's second-story office at the Philadelphia headquarters of Teamsters' Local 107. Francis McGrath, a janitor, saw the three defendants in the building just before the shooting. They appeared to be awaiting someone, and they encouraged McGrath to do his work on

---

75. 746 F.2d 1459 (Fed.Cir.1984).

76. See also Capital City Publishing Co. v. Trenton Times Corp., 1983 WL 1958, 1984–1 Trade Cas.(CCH) ¶ 65,955 (D.N.J.1983) (not reported in F.Supp.).

77. IBM v. Levin, 579 F.2d 271, 281 (3d Cir.1978) (disqualified counsel permitted to turn over work to and consult with new counsel concerning it); Williams v. TWA, 588 F.Supp. 1037, 1610 (W.D.Mo.1984) (portions of the disqualified firm's work made available to new counsel but consultation limited to that necessary to explain the work).

another day. McGrath ignored their suggestions. Shortly afterward, Gorey arrived and went to his office. McGrath then heard what sounded like firecrackers exploding in rapid succession. Carchidi, who was in the room where McGrath was working, abruptly directed McGrath to leave the building and to say nothing. McGrath hastily complied. When he returned to the building about 15 minutes later, the defendants were gone. The victims' bodies were discovered the next morning.

Two privately retained lawyers, G. Fred DiBona and A. Charles Peruto, represented all three defendants throughout the state proceedings that followed the indictment. Sullivan had different counsel at the medical examiner's inquest, but he thereafter accepted representation from the two lawyers retained by his codefendants because he could not afford to pay his own lawyer.[1] At no time did Sullivan or his lawyers object to the multiple representation. Sullivan was the first defendant to come to trial. The evidence against him was entirely circumstantial, consisting primarily of McGrath's testimony. At the close of the Commonwealth's case, the defense rested without presenting any evidence. The jury found Sullivan guilty and fixed his penalty at life imprisonment. Sullivan's post-trial motions failed, and the Pennsylvania Supreme Court affirmed his conviction by an equally divided vote. Commonwealth v. Sullivan, 446 Pa. 419, 286 A.2d 898 (1971). Sullivan's codefendants, Carchidi and DiPasquale, were acquitted at separate trials.

Sullivan then petitioned for collateral relief under the Pennsylvania Post Conviction Hearing Act. He alleged, among other claims, that he had been denied effective assistance of counsel because his defense lawyers represented conflicting interests. In five days of hearings, the Court of Common Pleas heard evidence from Sullivan, Carchidi, Sullivan's lawyers, and the judge who presided at Sullivan's trial.

DiBona and Peruto had different recollections of their roles at the trials of the three defendants. DiBona testified that he and Peruto had been "associate counsel" at each trial. Peruto recalled that he had been chief counsel for Carchidi and DePasquale, but that he merely had assisted DiBona in Sullivan's trial. DiBona and Peruto also gave conflicting accounts of the decision to rest Sullivan's defense. DiBona said he had encouraged Sullivan to testify even though the Commonwealth had presented a very weak case. Peruto remembered that he had not "want[ed] the defense to go on because I thought we would only be exposing the [defense] witnesses for the other two trials that were coming up." Sullivan testified that he had deferred to his lawyers' decision not to present evidence for the defense. But other testimony suggested that Sullivan preferred not to take the stand because cross-examination might have disclosed an extramarital affair. Finally,

---

1. DiBona and Peruto were paid in part with funds raised by friends of the three defendants. The record does not disclose the source of the balance of their fee, but no part of the money came from either Sullivan or his family. See United States ex rel. Sullivan v. Cuyler, 593 F.2d 512, 518, and n. 7 (CA3 1979).

Carchidi claimed he would have appeared at Sullivan's trial to rebut McGrath's testimony about Carchidi's statement at the time of the murders.

. . .

The Pennsylvania Supreme Court affirmed both Sullivan's original conviction and the denial of collateral relief. Commonwealth v. Sullivan, 472 Pa. 129, 371 A.2d 468 (1977). The court saw no basis for Sullivan's claim that he had been denied effective assistance of counsel at trial. It found that Peruto merely assisted DiBona in the Sullivan trial and that DiBona merely assisted Peruto in the trials of the other two defendants. Thus, the court concluded, there was "no dual representation in the true sense of the term." Id., at 161, 371 A.2d, at 483. The court also found that resting the defense was a reasonable tactic which had not denied Sullivan the effective assistance of counsel. Id., at 162, 371 A.2d, at 483–484.

Having exhausted his state remedies, Sullivan sought habeas corpus relief in the United States District Court for the Eastern District of Pennsylvania....

. . .

The Court of Appeals ... held that the participation by DiBona and Peruto in the trials of Sullivan and his codefendants established, as a matter of law, that both lawyers had represented all three defendants. The court recognized that multiple representation " 'is not tantamount to the denial of effective assistance of counsel....' " But it held that a criminal defendant is entitled to reversal of his conviction whenever he makes " 'some showing of a possible conflict of interest or prejudice, however remote....' " ... The court acknowledged that resting at the close of the prosecutor's case "would have been a legitimate tactical decision if made by independent counsel." Nevertheless, the court thought that action alone raised a possibility of conflict sufficient to prove a violation of Sullivan's Sixth Amendment rights. The court found support for its conclusion in Peruto's admission that concern for Sullivan's codefendants had affected his judgment that Sullivan should not present a defense. To give weight to DiBona's contrary testimony, the court held, "would be to ... require a showing of actual prejudice." 593 F.2d at 522.

[The Court considered in part II the scope of federal judicial review of state findings of fact in a federal habeas proceeding; part III rejected the argument that ineffectiveness of counsel claims were inapplicable when a criminal defendant was represented by privately retained counsel rather than appointed counsel.]

IV

We come [now] to Sullivan's claim that he was denied the effective assistance of counsel guaranteed by the Sixth Amendment because his lawyers had a conflict of interest. The claim raises two issues expressly reserved in Holloway v. Arkansas, 435 U.S. [475] at 483–484 [(1978)].

The first is whether a state trial judge must inquire into the propriety of multiple representation even though no party lodges an objection. The second is whether the mere possibility of a conflict of interest warrants the conclusion that the defendant was deprived of his right to counsel.

A

In *Holloway*, a single public defender represented three defendants at the same trial. The trial court refused to consider the appointment of separate counsel despite the defense lawyer's timely and repeated assertions that the interests of his clients conflicted. This Court recognized that a lawyer forced to represent codefendants whose interests conflict cannot provide the adequate legal assistance required by the Sixth Amendment. Id., at 481–482. Given the trial court's failure to respond to timely objections, however, the Court did not consider whether the alleged conflict actually existed. It simply held that the trial court's error unconstitutionally endangered the right to counsel. Id., at 483–487.

Holloway requires state trial courts to investigate timely objections to multiple representation. But nothing in our precedents suggests that the Sixth Amendment requires state courts themselves to initiate inquiries into the propriety of multiple representation in every case.[10] Defense counsel have an ethical obligation to avoid conflicting representations and to advise the court promptly when a conflict of interest arises during the course of trial.[11] Absent special circumstances, therefore, trial courts may assume either that multiple representation entails no conflict or that the lawyer and his clients knowingly accept such risk of conflict as may exist. Indeed, as the Court noted in *Holloway*, trial courts necessarily rely in large measure upon the good faith and good judgment of defense counsel. "An 'attorney represent-

---

10. In certain cases, proposed Federal Rule of Criminal Procedure 44(c) provides that the federal district courts "shall promptly inquire with respect to ... joint representation and shall personally advise each defendant of his right to the effective assistance of counsel, including separate representation." See also ABA Project on Standards for Criminal Justice, Function of the Trial Judge § 3.4(b) (App.Draft 1972).

Several Courts of Appeals already invoke their supervisory power to require similar inquiries.... As our promulgation of Rule 44(c) suggests, we view such an exercise of the supervisory power as a desirable practice. See generally Schwarzer, Dealing with Incompetent Counsel—The Trial Judge's Role, 93 Harv.L.Rev. 633, 653–654 (1980).

Although some Circuits have said explicitly that the Sixth Amendment does not require an inquiry into the possibility of conflicts ..., a recent opinion in the Second Circuit held otherwise.

11. ABA Code of Professional Responsibility, DR 5–105, EC 5–15 (1976); ABA Project on Standards for Criminal Justice, Defense Function § 3.5(b) (App.Draft 1971).

Seventy percent of the public defender offices responding to a recent survey reported a strong policy against undertaking multiple representation in criminal cases. Forty-nine percent of the offices responding never undertake such representation. Lowenthal, Joint Representation in Criminal Cases: A Critical Appraisal, 64 Va.L.Rev. 939, 950, and n. 40 (1978). The private bar may be less alert to the importance of avoiding multiple representation in criminal cases. See Geer, Representation of Multiple Criminal Defendants: Conflicts of Interest and the Professional Responsibilities of the Defense Attorney, 62 Minn.L.Rev. 119, 152–157 (1978); Lowenthal, supra, at 961–963.

ing two defendants in a criminal matter is in the best position professionally and ethically to determine when a conflict of interest exists or will probably develop in the course of a trial." ' 435 U.S., at 485, quoting State v. Davis, 110 Ariz. 29, 31, 514 P.2d 1025, 1027 (1973). Unless the trial court knows or reasonably should know that a particular conflict exists, the court need not initiate an inquiry.

Nothing in the circumstances of this case indicates that the trial court had a duty to inquire whether there was a conflict of interest. The provision of separate trials for Sullivan and his codefendants significantly reduced the potential for a divergence in their interests. No participant in Sullivan's trial ever objected to the multiple representation. DiBona's opening argument for Sullivan outlined a defense compatible with the view that none of the defendants was connected with the murders. The opening argument also suggested that counsel was not afraid to call witnesses whose testimony might be needed at the trials of Sullivan's codefendants. Finally, as the Court of Appeals noted, counsel's critical decision to rest Sullivan's defense was on its face a reasonable tactical response to the weakness of the circumstantial evidence presented by the prosecutor. On these facts, we conclude that the Sixth Amendment imposed upon the trial court no affirmative duty to inquire into the propriety of multiple representation.

B

Holloway reaffirmed that multiple representation does not violate the Sixth Amendment unless it gives rise to a conflict of interest. See 435 U.S., at 482. Since a possible conflict inheres in almost every instance of multiple representation, a defendant who objects to multiple representation must have the opportunity to show that potential conflicts impermissibly imperil his right to a fair trial. But unless the trial court fails to afford such an opportunity, a reviewing court cannot presume that the possibility for conflict has resulted in ineffective assistance of counsel. Such a presumption would preclude multiple representation even in cases where " '[a] common defense ... gives strength against a common attack." ' Id., at 482–483, quoting Glasser v. United States, 315 U.S. 60 (1942) (Frankfurter, J., dissenting).

In order to establish a violation of the Sixth Amendment, a defendant who raised no objection at trial must demonstrate that an actual conflict of interest adversely affected his lawyer's performance. In Glasser v. United States, for example, the record showed that defense counsel failed to cross-examine a prosecution witness whose testimony linked Glasser with the crime and failed to resist the presentation of arguably inadmissible evidence. Id., at 72–75. The Court found that both omissions resulted from counsel's desire to diminish the jury's perception of a codefendant's guilt. Indeed, the evidence of counsel's "struggle to serve two masters [could not] seriously be doubted." Id., at 75. Since this actual conflict of interest impaired Glasser's defense, the Court reversed his conviction.

Dukes v. Warden, 406 U.S. 250 (1972), presented a contrasting situation. Dukes pleaded guilty on the advice of two lawyers, one of whom also represented Dukes' codefendants on an unrelated charge. Dukes later learned that this lawyer had sought leniency for the codefendants by arguing that their cooperation with the police induced Dukes to plead guilty. Dukes argued in this Court that his lawyer's conflict of interest had infected his plea. We found " 'nothing in the record ... which would indicate that the alleged conflict resulted in ineffective assistance of counsel and did in fact render the plea in question involuntary and unintelligent." ' Id., at 256, quoting Dukes v. Warden, 161 Conn. 337, 344, 288 A.2d 58, 62 (1971). Since Dukes did not identify an actual lapse in representation, we affirmed the denial of the habeas corpus relief.

Glasser established that unconstitutional multiple representation is never harmless error. Once the Court concluded that Glasser's lawyer had an actual conflict of interest, it refused "to indulge in nice calculations as to the amount of prejudice" attributable to the conflict. The conflict itself demonstrated a denial of the "right to have the effective assistance of counsel." 315 U.S., at 76. Thus, a defendant who shows that a conflict of interest actually affected the adequacy of his representation need not demonstrate prejudice in order to obtain relief. See *Holloway*, supra, 435 U.S., at 487–491. But until a defendant shows that his counsel actively represented conflicting interests, he has not established the constitutional predicate for his claim of ineffective assistance. See *Glasser*, supra, 315 U.S., at 72–75.[15]

C

The Court of Appeals granted Sullivan relief because he had shown that the multiple representation in this case involved a possible conflict of interest. We hold that the possibility of conflict is insufficient to impugn a criminal conviction. In order to demonstrate a violation of his Sixth Amendment rights, a defendant must establish that an actual conflict of interest adversely affected his lawyer's performance. Sullivan believes he should prevail even under this standard. He emphasizes Peruto's admission that the decision to rest Sullivan's defense reflected a reluctance to expose witnesses who later might have testified for the other defendants. The petitioner, on the other hand, points to DiBona's contrary testimony and to evidence that Sullivan himself wished to avoid taking the stand. Since the Court of Appeals did not weigh these conflicting contentions under the proper legal standard, its judgment is vacated and the case is remanded for further proceedings consistent with this opinion.

[Justices Brennan and Marshall, in separate partial dissents, argued that the Sixth Amendment required a state court on its own initiative to inquire in every case of joint representation, to warn

---

15. See Comment, Conflict of Interests in Multiple Representation of Criminal Co-Defendants, 68 J.Crim.L. & C. 226, 231–232 (1977).

defendants of the possible risks and to ascertain that the representation is the result of the defendants' informed choice.]

Notes on the *Cuyler* Standard

Cuyler requires a defendant to show both that counsel actively represented conflicting interests, and that the conflict "adversely affected" counsel's performance. The defendant need not show "prejudice," i.e., that the result would have been different but for the conflict. Contrast this to the rule in *Strickland v. Washington* discussed in Chapter 3 above at p. 194. What is the difference between "adversely affected" and "prejudice"? Contrast *Cuyler* with the standard in civil cases. *Westinghouse*, for example, did not require proof of adverse effect from the conflict.

The Third Circuit on remand in *Cuyler* held that the representation was adversely affected in that the lawyer did not call the codefendant to testify because doing so would have been against that defendant's interest.[78]

What does it take to show an "actual conflict" that "adversely affected" the defense lawyer's conduct? Should a showing that defense counsel simultaneously represents an important prosecution witness suffice? The cases turn on their facts, but many do not find an actual conflict resulting in an adverse effect when a prosecution witness is a former client of the defense counsel.[79]

The *Cuyler* standard has been found satisfied where, at the trial, a prosecution witness represented by defense counsel accused defense counsel of involvement in the defendant's crime,[80] and where collusion between the defense attorney and the prosecutor has been found.[81] How much more protection is actually afforded the defendant under *Cuyler* than under *Strickland*?

Some courts do not require a showing of adverse effect, reasoning that such an effect is likely to consist of an omission by the lawyer— options passed by, strategies neglected, etc. Proving a negative is difficult and should be unnecessary if the defendant can show an actual conflict existed. On this basis the Massachusetts court, interpreting the state constitution's guarantee of effective assistance of counsel, held

78. Cuyler, 631F.2d 14 (3d Cir.1980).

79. See, e.g., Castillo v. Estelle, 504 F.2d 1243 (5th Cir.1974) (conviction reversed). But see Wycoff v. Nix, 869 F.2d 1111 (8th Cir.1989) (concurrent representation of defendant and potential prosecution witness not an actual conflict because witness was not called and matters in representation were unrelated); and United States v. Gambino, 864 F.2d 1064 (3d Cir.1988) (no reversal under *Cuyler* despite fact that defense counsel, without defendant's knowledge, was representing a third party and failed to advance argument for defendant that third party and not defendant was source of heroin).

80. Mannhalt v. Reed, 847 F.2d 576 (9th Cir.1988).

81. United States ex rel. Duncan v. O'Leary, 806 F.2d 1307 (7th Cir.1986).

that adverse effect will be presumed even if the defendant knew of the potential conflict before the trial began.[82] The defendant's lawyer also represented one of the prosecution's witnesses in an unrelated civil case. The court held that the possibility that the lawyer might go easy when cross-examining this witness warranted reversal without a showing of actual adverse effect.[83]

Disfavoring Multiple Representation in Criminal Cases

Multiple representation in criminal cases is strongly discouraged by ethics rules and case law.[84] The cases hold that any doubts as to potential conflict should be resolved in favor of separate counsel.[85] A number of commentators urge a complete ban on dual representation in criminal cases.[86]

Why is the predisposition against dual representation so strong? First, of course, a conflict in a criminal case may result in a defendant being convicted who should be acquitted. A co-defendant with more money (e.g., a higher-up in a criminal ring) may pay the lawyer's fee and call the shots. Whenever a third person pays the lawyer's fee there is a potential conflict between that person's interests and the client's.[87]

Second, the courts and commentators may be worried about the possibility of cooperative perjury. Should that be a factor in considering the legitimacy of joint representation?

Finally, the issue arises in the context of what game theory refers to as the "prisoner's dilemma." Assume two prisoners are co-defendants. Each can either inform on the other to the prosecutor or keep quiet. The prosecutor promises each that if either informs she will be sentenced to no more than one year, but if one informs and the other remains silent, the one who keeps quiet will receive between 5 and 10 years. The best choice for each individual, acting alone, is to inform on the other (providing the other does not also do so). An even better result, however, is imaginable. If they could cooperate with each other they might both go free for lack of evidence. But cooperation as a practical matter may be impossible.

---

82. Commonwealth v. Hodge, 386 Mass. 165, 434 N.E.2d 1246 (1982).

83. Also see People v. Spreitzer, 123 Ill.2d 1, 121 Ill.Dec. 224, 525 N.E.2d 30, 34 (1988) (describing categories of cases in which Illinois courts will presume adverse effect).

84. See the Comment to M.R. 1.7; ABA Standards for Criminal Justice, The Defense Function 3.5(b); Fed.Rule Crim.Proc. 44(c).

85. See, e.g., Lollar v. United States, 376 F.2d 243 (D.C.Cir.1967); State v. Bush, 108 Ariz. 148, 493 P.2d 1205 (1972). Also see Fleming v. State, 246 Ga. 90, 270 S.E.2d 185 (1980) (imposing an absolute ban on a lawyer representing more than one defendant in death penalty cases).

86. John S. Geer, Representation of Multiple Criminal Defendants, 62 Minn.L.Rev. 119 (1978); Gary T. Lowenthal, Joint Representation in Criminal Cases, 64 Va.L.Rev. 939 (1978); Peter W. Tague, Multiple Representation and Conflicts of Interest in Criminal Cases, 67 Geo.L.J. 1075 (1979).

87. For rules on third parties paying for a lawyer's representation of a client, see Model Rules 1.7(b), 1.8(f) and 5.4(c); DR 5–107(A) and (B).

Prosecutors use divide-and-conquer tactics in plea-bargaining. A common defense strategy by a single defense lawyer can counter this tactic. But co-defendants in the real world are never in equal positions; the degree of their culpability and the penalties each faces are different. A lawyer who tries to counsel co-defendants in the real world, given their unequal position, cannot counsel the same course for both. Yet the choices made by one—particularly, whether to accept the prosecutor's offer—are crucial to the fate of the other.[88]

Denial of Defense Counsel of Choice

When a criminal defendant is denied counsel of her choice, the defendant's Sixth Amendment right to counsel is implicated.[89] In a federal criminal trial, the defendant must await appeal upon final judgment to pursue the claim that she was denied counsel of her choice.[90] Must prejudice be shown when a defendant is wrongly denied counsel of her choice, i.e., when the trial judge's order of disqualification was erroneous? The emerging case law is that "A defendant who is arbitrarily deprived of the right to select his own counsel need not demonstrate prejudice." [91]

This leaves the question of when it is wrong, because of a conflict, to disqualify counsel over defendant's protest. In Wheat v. United States,[92] the district court denied Wheat's request to be represented by the same lawyer who was representing two other people charged with involvement in the drug distribution conspiracy that formed the basis for the charges against Wheat. Wheat, who was to be tried separately from the other parties, expressed his willingness to waive the conflict, as the other defendants had done, and asserted that the Sixth Amendment gave him the right to counsel of his choice. Nevertheless, the district court, citing the likelihood that the co-defendants would be witnesses at one another's trials, held that counsel would be operating with an irreconcilable conflict and thus refused to allow counsel to represent Wheat. Wheat appealed from a subsequent conviction, claiming that the court's rejection of his counsel of choice violated his Sixth Amendment rights. The Court (5–4) upheld the conviction:

88. See, e.g., Thomas v. Foltz, 818 F.2d 476 (6th Cir.1987) (one lawyer represented three co-defendants; the prosecutor offered to reduce the charges to second degree murder if all three would plead guilty; defendant Thomas was quite resistant but eventually decided to plead guilty; held: counsel was operating under an actual conflict of interest that adversely affected his representation of Thomas).

89. United States v. Curcio, 680 F.2d 881 (2d Cir.1982) (government's interest in disqualifying defendant's counsel does not override defendant's choice of counsel where defendant's waiver of the right to separate representation was knowing and voluntary).

90. Flanagan v. United States, 465 U.S. 259 (1984), held that an order disqualifying defense counsel is not immediately appealable under 28 U.S.C. § 1291.

91. United States v. Rankin, 779 F.2d 956, 960 (3d Cir.1986) (convicted defendant, erroneously deprived of counsel of choice, need not show that substitute counsel's performance harmed the defendant). In accord: Anaya v. Colorado, 764 P.2d 779 (Colo.1988).

92. 486 U.S. 153 (1988).

Unfortunately for all concerned, a district court must pass on the issue of whether or not to allow a waiver of a conflict of interest by a criminal defendant not with the wisdom of hindsight after the trial has taken place, but in the murkier pre-trial context when relationships between parties are seen through a glass, darkly. The likelihood and dimensions of nascent conflicts of interest are notoriously hard to predict, even for those thoroughly familiar with criminal trials. It is a rare attorney who will be fortunate enough to learn the entire truth from his own client, much less be fully apprised before trial of what each of the Government's witnesses will say on the stand. A few bits of unforeseen testimony or a single previously unknown or unnoticed document may significantly shift the relationship between multiple defendants. These imponderables are difficult enough for a lawyer to assess, and even more difficult to convey by way of explanation to a criminal defendant untutored in the niceties of legal ethics. Nor is it amiss to observe that the willingness of an attorney to obtain such waivers from his clients may bear an inverse relation to the care with which he conveys all the necessary information to them.

For these reasons we think the District Court must be allowed substantial latitude in refusing waivers of conflicts of interest not only in those rare cases where an actual conflict may be demonstrated before trial, but in the more common cases where a potential for conflict exists which may or may not burgeon into an actual conflict as the trial progresses.[93]

Compare the concern in *Wheat* for potential conflicts of interest with the showing the defendant has to make under *Cuyler*. Justice Marshall, dissenting in *Wheat*, criticized the majority for its unwarranted deference to the district court's decision, given the importance of the Sixth Amendment right involved. Justice Stevens' dissent emphasized the voluntary nature of defendant's waiver of the conflict.

Should the defendant be allowed to waive any conflict, no matter how serious? If she makes the waiver for strategic purposes?[94] Should voluntary waiver bar any future claim of ineffective counsel based on the conflict? How would courts determine whether a waiver is voluntary or informed?[95] The Court in *Wheat* stated: "Nor does a waiver by the defendant necessarily solve the problem, for we note, without passing judgment on, the apparent willingness of Courts of Appeals to entertain ineffective assistance claims from defendants who have specif-

---

93. 486 U.S. at 162–63.

94. See United States v. Bradshaw, 719 F.2d 907 (7th Cir.1983) (co-defendants had strategic purposes in presenting a common defense).

95. See Duncan v. Alabama, 881 F.2d 1013 (11th Cir.1989) (one of defendant's court-appointed lawyers had represented the murder victim in her efforts to stop the defendant from harassing her; defendant's other lawyer had represented the district attorney in a divorce action and could foresee continuing to represent him; the court held that defendant's waiver of these conflicts barred him from raising them after conviction).

ically waived the right to conflict-free counsel." [96]   This statement does not sound particularly approving of the practice described, does it?   Is the Court suggesting that waiver should cure all conflicts for post-conviction purposes?

A California decision holds that under the California Constitution, trial courts do not have the same wide latitude to disqualify defendant's counsel of choice that the federal courts have under *Wheat*.[97] "A court abridges a defendant's right to counsel when it removes retained defense counsel in the face of a defendant's willingness to make an informed and intelligent waiver of his right to ... conflict-free counsel." [98]   The court rejected any other rule as "paternalistic", quoting from John Stuart Mill's *On Liberty* and writing itself that "[a] right that is imposed, as compared to a right that is chosen, is an impoverished right." [99]   Is the line between what is "chosen" and what "imposed" easy to discern in this context?

Judicial Inquiry to Determine Whether a Conflict Exists

In federal cases when one lawyer proposes to represent multiple defendants, the judge must hold a hearing to advise each defendant of her right to separate counsel. Fed.R.Crim.P. 44(c). Rule 44(c) further states that "[u]nless there is good cause to believe no conflict of interest is likely to arise, the court shall take such measures as may be appropriate to protect each defendant's right to counsel."   The presumption is clearly against joint representation.

How can a court adequately satisfy itself that a defendant's waiver is voluntary and appropriate without breaching client confidences? [100]   When one counsel represents multiple defendants, should a failure to conduct a Rule 44(c) inquiry constitute per se reversible error? [101]

State courts are not bound to follow the procedure specified in Rule 44(c). However, when a defendant objects to representation on the basis of a conflict, the court must inquire into it and appoint independent counsel if there is a potential conflict.

C. CONCURRENT REPRESENTATION IN TRANSACTIONS

1. Representing Both Parties to a Transaction

Imagine a contract renewal negotiation between a ballet dancer and the New York City Ballet. The ballet company hires Law Firm Y

---

96.   486 U.S. at 161–62.

97.   Alcocer v. Superior Court, 206 Cal.App.3d 951, 254 Cal.Rptr. 72 (1988).

98.   254 Cal.Rptr. at 75.

99.   Id. at 74.

100.   See In re Paradyne Corp., 803 F.2d 604 (11th Cir.1986) (granting mandamus against a proposed in camera inquiry by the trial court). Also see United States v. Roth, 860 F.2d 1382 (7th Cir.1988) (trial court's failure to probe possible conflicts does not invalidate defendant's waiver).

101.   See United States v. Colonia, 870 F.2d 1319 (7th Cir.1989) (no reversal in absence of showing of actual conflict).

to represent it in the negotiation with the dancer and you represent the dancer. Should you simultaneously represent the ballet company in a real estate negotiation with the City of New York? Does Model Rule 1.7(b) apply? 1.7(a)? What more would you like to know before deciding?

What if the New York City Ballet, whom you have helped with real estate matters, wants you to represent it in the negotiation with the dancer, and the dancer wants you to represent her too. Should you undertake to represent both the ballet dancer and the ballet company in working out the best contract for both?

What if instead of an employment contract, it is two or more people who want to start up a business? Or two people who want amicably to work out a divorce settlement? Should the clients' desire to use one lawyer, either to save money or to keep the negotiation friendly, be decisive? Model Rule 2.2, as well as Rule 1.7(b) may be helpful in an analysis of these and other common situations.

STATE v. CALLAHAN

Supreme Court of Kansas, 1982.
232 Kan. 136, 652 P.2d 708.

PER CURIAM:

This is an original proceeding in discipline. The proceeding is the result of a complaint filed on behalf of Mrs. Ruth Fulton.

Ruth Fulton, an elderly lady, owned 320 acres of land in Butler County which she had inherited from her father. Although she was born in Kansas, she has been a resident of California for over 60 years, and the land had been leased to a neighboring landowner for a number of years.

In 1974, Mrs. Fulton decided to sell her land. She first offered it to her tenant who declined the offer. He advised, however, that a Lowell Lygrisse was in the market for such property and offered to contact him.

Subsequently, Lygrisse called Mrs. Fulton by phone and a tentative agreement was reached. During this conversation, Lygrisse suggested that the respondent, John Callahan, handle the transaction for both of them. Mrs. Fulton agreed, and later called respondent and retained his services.

The interpretation of the parties as to respondent's scope of employment differed. Mrs. Fulton stated that she believed respondent would act as a California escrow officer would and protect the interests of both parties. Respondent testified that he believed that he represented both parties as a scrivener to draw the papers and close the sale only after the terms of the purchase agreement had been negotiated between the parties.

Respondent prepared two contracts controlling the sale in accordance with the terms provided by Lygrisse and without consulting Mrs. Fulton. The first contract was entitled "Real Estate Purchase Contract." It provided for a sale price of $96,000.00, to be paid $24,000.00 at the time of closing and the balance in three annual installments of $24,000.00 each. The first annual installment was to be secured by a certificate of deposit.

The contract was unusual, however, in that it provided that the seller would execute and deliver a deed to the buyer at closing, and that the land would be included with other land in a mortgage to the Federal Land Bank. Although Mrs. Fulton did not fully understand the transaction, she signed the contract on November 14, 1974, in reliance upon respondent.

On December 11, 1974, respondent wrote to Mrs. Fulton enclosing a deed for her to sign and informed her that he would hold the deed until the first $24,000.00 was paid. He also informed her that when Lygrisse secured his loan from the Federal Land Bank, respondent would purchase a certificate of deposit in the amount of $24,000.00 and pledge it as security for the second payment, and that he would then formalize the agreement on the balance owing. Mrs. Fulton signed the deed and returned it to respondent.

Thereafter, respondent filed and conducted the necessary legal action to quiet title to the land and obtained inheritance tax clearance. He also advised Mrs. Fulton as to certain tax consequences of the sale. He billed Mrs. Fulton on March 14, 1975, for his services in clearing the title and was paid.

The second contract was entitled "Pledge, Escrow and Agreement." It recited the schedule of payments on the unpaid balance and set up an escrow of the certificate of deposit securing the first annual payment due April 1, 1976.

It differed from the first contract of sale in that Paragraph 7 provided for acceleration of the unpaid balance upon default and provided:

"In the event of default and nonpayment of any judgment therefore the Fulton's shall have a specific lien on the real estate covered hereby subject only to the Federal Land Bank first mortgage of record."

Mrs. Fulton signed the agreement on May 21, 1975, in reliance on respondent's request as her attorney, without independent legal advice, believing that the provisions of paragraph 7 would effectively place her in the position of a second mortgagee. She further assumed respondent would record anything necessary to perfect her "specific lien." No such other documents were prepared or recorded by respondent.

For several years before and after 1974, respondent was Lygrisse's personal attorney, and they were each owners of 50% of the common stock of L–C Farm Co., Inc., a corporation engaged in buying and selling farms and other real estate. Respondent was required to and did personally guarantee some or all of the debts of the corporation which at times exceeded $500,000.00. The Fulton farm was not purchased for the account of L–C Farms Co., Inc., however, and no claim is made that respondent personally acquired any interest therein. Respondent admits that he did not disclose to Mrs. Fulton his business relationship with Lygrisse.

No problems arose until Lygrisse defaulted on the final payment due April 1, 1978. Mrs. Fulton called respondent several times for advice. He told her that Lygrisse had suffered some business reversals but that he was sure Lygrisse would make the final payment. Sometime in late 1978, she contacted respondent again and asked how long she had to file for foreclosure. Respondent advised her that she had five years from the date of default, but suggested again that she didn't need to foreclose, that he was sure Lygrisse would pay.

In May of 1979, Mrs. Fulton and her husband traveled to Wichita and met with respondent for the first time in person. They asked respondent to file a foreclosure action on what they perceived to be their second mortgage. Respondent declined, citing as his reason a conflict of interest, but he agreed to refer them to another attorney. He did not advise them at that time that they did not have a secured interest in the real estate.

The Fultons then went to see Lygrisse who promised to pay them within a few weeks. When the payment was not forthcoming, Mrs. Fulton again phoned respondent who again assured them that he believed Lygrisse would pay and advised them not to foreclose.

Finally, on March 1, 1980, Mr. Fulton called respondent and again asked for the name of an attorney to file foreclosure proceedings. During this conversation, respondent for the first time advised the Fultons that they had no mortgage and that all they had was a promissory note.

The Fultons were subsequently referred to Jim Lawing of Wichita who prepared and filed a malpractice action against respondent. Shortly thereafter respondent filed a voluntary petition in bankruptcy and was ultimately discharged.

In the spring of 1980, the Federal Land Bank foreclosed its mortgage against the Fulton farm. Mrs. Fulton was not a party to the action and learned of the action through independent inquiry. Included in the action was a second mortgage given to an El Dorado bank by Lygrisse around the time the down payment to Mrs. Fulton was made. She has never received the final payment of $24,000.00.

Following a letter of complaint from Jim Lawing to the disciplinary administrator, a formal complaint with Lawing's letter attached was filed by the disciplinary administrator before the Board for Discipline of Attorneys. A hearing was held on November 18, 1981, and the hearing panel found that respondent had violated disciplinary rules DR 5–105(B), DR 6–101(A)(3), and DR 1–102(A)(4). It recommended indefinite suspension of respondent. Respondent has taken exception to the report.

The hearing panel found that respondent had violated DR 5–105(B) in that he represented both the sellers and the buyer when a conflict of interest existed by failing to warn the sellers that they did not have a perfected second mortgage or security interest.

[The court quoted DR 5–105(B) and (C).]

It is respondent's contention that the terms of the sale were agreed upon between the parties before he was employed and that he only represented the parties, insofar as the contract of sale was concerned, as a scrivener to write up the contract and close the sale in accordance with the prior agreement of the parties. He asserts further that he was under no duty to suggest "better terms" for the seller or to make and record a second mortgage not called for by the terms of the contract.

Under the circumstances here, however, we fail to see how respondent could have been unaware that he was not exercising his independent professional judgment in behalf of the Fultons in preparing the contract solely on the terms dictated by Lygrisse without consulting the Fultons, or at least advising them of the risk inherent in not taking a second mortgage to secure the balance of the purchase price.

Furthermore, respondent did not make a full disclosure to the Fultons of his close business and professional associations with the buyer.

This court, in State v. Hilton, 217 Kan. 694, 698, 538 P.2d 977 (1975), stated:

> "The unmistakable intent of DR 5–105(C) is exemplified in 'Ethical Considerations' [EC] 5–15 (ABA Standards, Code of Professional Responsibility). It reads in pertinent part:
>
> > " 'If a lawyer is requested to undertake or to continue representation of multiple clients having potentially differing interests, he must weigh carefully the possibility that his judgment may be impaired or his loyalty divided if he accepts or continues the employment. He should resolve all doubts against the propriety of the representation. . . .' "

The panel also found respondent guilty of violating DR 1–102(A)(4) in that he misrepresented to the sellers that they had a specific lien on the property sold, subject only to a first mortgage to the Federal Land Bank, when in fact they had no such lien.

DR 1–102(A)(4) provides [that a lawyer shall not] "Engage in conduct involving dishonesty, fraud, deceit, or misrepresentation."

Respondent contends that nothing in the pledge agreement provides for a second mortgage. Paragraph 7, he argues, refers only to a lien given to a judgment under K.S.A. 60–2202 (Corrick), and when considered with other provisions of the contract amounts to no more than a warranty that Lygrisse would not allow a subsequent lien or mortgage to attach.

Again, under the circumstances here, we fail to see how the Fultons could reasonably have given such an interpretation to this provision. They believed that they had a "specific lien," and on several occasions when the Fultons inquired of respondent about foreclosure proceedings, he failed to disclose to them that there was no valid foreclosable interest and advised them not to foreclose. He finally offered to give them the name of another attorney to handle such an action. They were not advised that they had no security interest to foreclose until almost two years after the final payment was due.

The duty of good faith imposed upon an attorney does not always cease immediately upon termination of his employment. It continues as long as the influence created by the relationship continues. Alexander v. Russo, 1 Kan.App.2d 546, 571 P.2d 350, rev. denied 222 Kan. 749 (1977). The Fultons still looked to respondent for aid, and his conduct in failing to disclose to them that they had no lien on the property to secure the balance due them clearly rises to the level of deceit and dishonesty.

"Full Disclosure" as Predicate of Consent [1]

Lawyer Callahan helped a California woman sell her Kansas farm land to a Kansas dealer in such land. What did Callahan do that violated the disciplinary rules? What should he have done? Do your responses assume the answer to the question whether a lawyer may represent both the buyer and seller in a real estate transaction? [2]

Suppose Callahan revealed his long-term connection with Lygrisse and fully disclosed that the transaction, as proposed by Lygrisse, constituted an unsecured, interest-free loan of part of the purchase price. Will Mrs. Fulton's consent be adequate or is this a nonconsentable conflict? Can Callahan make the full disclosure required by M.R. 1.7 and D.R. 5–105(C) without violating his duties to his other client, Lygrisse?

1. See generally Wolfram, Modern Legal Ethics § 7.2 (1986); and Nancy J. Moore, Conflicts of Interest in the Simultaneous Representation of Multiple Clients, 61 Tex. L.Rev. 211 (1982).

2. This question is considered below at p. 677.

In Financial General Bankshares v. Metzger,[3] the court said full disclosure means "[an] affirmative revelation by the attorney of all the facts, legal implications, possible effects, and other circumstances relating to the proposed representation." The fact that the client knows the lawyer represents another client whose interests are adverse does not constitute full disclosure.

California Rule 3–310 requires the *written* consent of the parties before a lawyer may proceed to represent conflicting interests. In practice this is interpreted not to require that the predicate disclosure also be in writing.

Providing full disclosure is not easy and sometimes is impossible. The reasons include:

- The rules on confidentiality: How is a lawyer to make full disclosure without breaching the other client's confidences? The lawyer must have each client's permission to share confidential information with the other client.

- Uncertainty about the facts: The lawyer is supposed to detail the facts relating to the proposed representations. But facts are often uncertain or undiscovered, especially at early stages of a transaction. Uncertainty about what the lawyer has been retained to do on behalf of either client is also often uncertain.

- Change of facts: Facts change as transactions move forward. Consequently, disclosure must be an ongoing process. Cycles of continuing disclosure and renewed consent may be required.

Must a client get another lawyer's advice before consenting to representation by a lawyer with a conflict? In Aetna Cas. & Sur. Co. v. United States,[4] the court held that consent given without the advice of independent counsel may still be informed consent.

Representing Buyer and Seller

The *Callahan* case is premised on the implicit assumption that a lawyer may represent a buyer and seller in at least some situations. In most states a lawyer may represent a buyer and seller in a residential real estate transaction if certain conditions are met. For example, a Colorado ethics opinion[5] permits joint representation if the material terms of the agreement have been agreed upon by the parties (e.g., price, time and manner of payment, status of title upon transfer, inclusion of personal property, status of any present leases or tenancies, amount of earnest money deposit and the treatment of amounts so deposited upon the default of either party). The lawyer must disclose to the parties the risks of joint representation, including a warning that if litigation develops the lawyer cannot represent either party and that

---

3. 523 F.Supp. 744, 771 (D.D.C.1981), rev'd on other grounds, 680 F.2d 768 (D.C.Cir. 1982), discussed further in Chapter 8 below at p. 796.

4. 570 F.2d 1197 (4th Cir.1978), rev'g, 438 F.Supp. 886 (W.D.N.C.1977).

5. Colo. Bar Ass'n Ethics Op. 68, Resolving Multiple Representation Conflicts (Apr. 20, 1985).

the attorney-client privilege may not apply to their communications to the lawyer. Both parties must consent and the lawyer must determine that she can provide adequate representation to each. If the lawyer has represented one party in the past, this must be revealed and its effect on the representation considered. The lawyer may not serve as a mere scrivener, but must fulfill the full obligations of the attorney-client relationship.

Even if it is permissible to undertake the representation, the Colorado opinion warns that difficulties may arise during its course: First, material issues may arise that the parties have not considered. The lawyer must inform the parties of the available alternatives and leave the decision to them. Second, if a title defect is discovered, the lawyer must raise the matter for the mutual consideration of the parties.

The case law is to much the same effect. In re Kamp [6] holds that a lawyer seeking to represent both the seller and buyer in a real estate or similar transaction must disclose to each his relationship to the other, the pitfalls of dual representation which might make it desirable for each party to have separate counsel, and "[t]he full significance of the representation of conflicting interests."

> If the attorney cannot properly represent the buyer in all aspects of the transaction because of his relationship to the seller, full disclosure requires that he inform the buyer of the limited scope of his intended representation of the buyer's interests and point out the advantages of the buyer's retaining independent counsel.[7]

Can a lawyer be sure this formula has been fulfilled?

Although concurrent representation of buyers and sellers has been conventional in many localities, it is risky and should not be undertaken without carefully examining the circumstances surrounding the proposed representation, including the lawyer's past relationships with both clients and the attitude of both clients towards the proposed representation and each other. In In re Banta,[8] for example, a lawyer was reprimanded for having relayed to the buyer inaccurate facts given to the lawyer by the seller.

It is proper in some circumstances for a lawyer to bring two clients together to facilitate a deal between them.[9] But when the lawyer has a longstanding relationship with one party and a new relationship with the other, it may be unreasonable to believe that she can be impartial between them.[10]

6. 40 N.J. 588, 194 A.2d 236 (1963).

7. 199 A.2d at 240.

8. 412 N.E.2d 221 (Ind.1980).

9. See, e.g., Atlantic Richfield Co. v. Sybert, 295 Md. 347, 456 A.2d 20 (1983).

10. See Comment to M.R. 2.2; Attorney Grievance Commission v. Collins, 295 Md. 532, 457 A.2d 1134 (1983); In re Lanza, 65 N.J. 347, 322 A.2d 445 (1974); In re Nelson, 112 Wis.2d 292, 332 N.W.2d 811 (1983). For a case where, despite differences in

Ethics Rules on Lawyer as Intermediary

Model Rule 2.2 has a complex set of provisions on the lawyer as intermediary.[11] Subparagraph (a)(1) specifies issues the lawyer should discuss with the clients before obtaining their consent. Subparagraphs (a)(2) and (a)(3) require that the lawyer reasonably believe the following: the matter can be resolved on terms compatible with the clients' best interests; each client will be able to make informed decisions; material prejudice to either client's interests should the contemplated resolution fail is unlikely; and the common representation can be undertaken impartially and without improper effect on the responsibilities the lawyer has to either client.

M.R. 2.2(b) prescribes how the lawyer should proceed while acting as an intermediary. M.R. 2.2(c) requires the lawyer to withdraw if either client requests or if the lawyer can no longer meet the requirements of paragraph (a). After withdrawing, the lawyer may not represent any of the clients in the matter that was the subject of the intermediation.

A lawyer who decides to act as an intermediary faces serious risks. In Klemm v. Superior Court,[12] the court identified some of these risks:

- If the lawyer fails fully to inform the clients of the facts, risks and potential disadvantages of the joint representation, the lawyer may be civilly liable to those clients for any loss suffered;

- The lawyer lays herself open to charges, whether well founded or not, of unethical and unprofessional conduct;

- The validity of any agreement negotiated without independent representation of each of the parties is vulnerable to easy attack as having been procured by misrepresentation, fraud and overreaching.

The court concluded that "[i]t thus behooves counsel to cogitate carefully and proceed cautiously before placing himself/herself in such a position." [13] Wouldn't a lawyer seeking to adjust a matter between clients be better off to call it "adjustment" and be governed by M.R. 1.7? Or do both rules require the same things?

2. Lawyer's Role in Matrimonial Cases

Joint Representation in Matrimonial Dissolution

When a lawyer represents both spouses in some stage of matrimonial dissolution, the context suggests difficulties not encountered in

relationships, the court found a joint representation acceptable, see Dillard v. Broyles, 633 S.W.2d 636 (Tex.Ct.App.1982).

11. EC 5–20 of the Model Code states "[a] lawyer is often asked to serve as an impartial arbitrator or mediator in matters which involve present or former clients." Little guidance is given for performing such a role. EC 5–20 says only that the lawyer "may serve in either capacity if he first discloses such present or former relationships." A lawyer must look to DR 5–105, the Code's general rule on conflicts of interest.

12. 75 Cal.App.3d 893, 142 Cal.Rptr. 509, 514 (1977).

13. 142 Cal.Rptr. at 514.

friendly negotiations of potential contracts or startup of business ventures. First, the existence of marital difficulties suggests some degree of antagonism between the spouses, even if they concur in a preference for an "amicable" and inexpensive parting of the ways. Second, if a contract negotiation fails the parties may walk away, but spouses are legally bound to each other in "holy deadlock." If agreement is not possible, they can either continue their marriage or resort to litigation to end it. Third, in many marital situations one spouse is a dominant figure who may have greater experience in dealing with property or contentiousness or both.

The latter factor, one spouse's undue influence over the other, is a serious impediment to representing both husband and wife in domestic relations cases. Matrimonial agreements can all be challenged on the ground of overreaching. Representation of both spouses by one lawyer is an invitation to such a challenge. On the other hand, presuming an incapacity on the part of one spouse, usually the wife, to make an informed consent to a cheaper and possibly more amicable parting of the ways is itself demeaning and paternalistic.

State courts agree that a single lawyer cannot represent both spouses in the courtroom phase of divorce cases. But there is disagreement on whether a lawyer, with the informed consent of both spouses, may negotiate a separation arrangement and draft other papers dealing with property division or child custody for subsequent submission to the divorce court. In some states it is permissible for a lawyer, after negotiating an agreement on these matters, to represent the moving spouse in an uncontested court proceeding. In other states the parties must act pro se in the divorce court or obtain other representation.

In Levine v. Levine,[14] a former wife sought to rescind a separation agreement prepared by a lawyer who jointly represented both spouses. Despite the presence of factors suggesting overreaching—the lawyer was related to the husband by marriage and had previously represented the husband's business—the separation agreement was upheld on the basis of findings that the agreement was fair, the lawyer acted in a neutral capacity and the lawyer made full disclosure of relevant facts:

> ... While the potential conflict of interests inherent in such joint representation suggests that the husband and wife should retain separate counsel, the parties have an absolute right to be represented by the same attorney provided "there has been a full disclosure between the parties, not only of all relevant facts but also of their contextual significance, and there has been an absence of inequitable conduct or other infirmity which vitiate the execution of the agreement."

. . .

Contrary to the determination below, the fact that the same attorney represented both parties in the preparation of the separa-

14. 56 N.Y.2d 42, 451 N.Y.S.2d 26, 436 N.E.2d 476 (1982).

tion agreement does not, without more, establish overreaching on the part of the husband.... [15]

Although the separation agreement was upheld, the lawyer's clients were put to considerable trouble and expense litigating its validity. Was the joint representation worth the risks entailed?

Some states prohibit a single lawyer from representing both spouses in matrimonial mediation, negotiation or litigation. These jurisdictions reason that divorce actions are inherently adversarial and involve great potential of opposing interests on such issues as support, child custody, visitation, ownership and division of property; consequently, one attorney should not represent both the husband and the wife at either the negotiation or litigation stage.[16] If one or both spouses cannot afford to retain a lawyer, and publicly-funded civil legal assistance is not available, as is likely to be the case, one or both must go unrepresented.

Divorce Mediation

Model Rule 2.2 is consistent with a number of ethics opinions in permitting a lawyer to play an intermediary role in some marital situations.[17] An opinion of the Association of the Bar of the City of New York,[18] for example, considers a structured divorce mediation service in which a trained therapist consults with a separating couple to aid them in working out aspects of the separation or divorce (e.g., property division, child custody, visitation and support). The opinion gives somewhat grudging approval to participation of a lawyer as part of the mediating team to give impartial legal advice to the parties and to draft a divorce or separation agreement approved by them.

Mediation, the opinion states, has a range of meanings from relatively passive listening and questioning to active involvement in framing a comprehensive resolution. Dangers in performing the mediation function arise because of: the divergent interests of parties, doubt as to whether one or both of the parties understand the risks and give an informed consent, inequalities of bargaining power of the parties and the potential for misunderstandings and later recrimination against the lawyer. On the other hand, the adversary process has legal, emotional

15. 436 N.E.2d at 479. Compare Klemm v. Superior Court, 75 Cal.App.3d 893, 142 Cal.Rptr. 509 (1977). In *Klemm*, one factor that may have led the court to sustain the dual representation was that the challenge to the support agreement was brought not by either spouse but by the County of Fresno, which wanted the husband to pay child support to offset the AFDC payments being made to the mother. The wife asserted that she was content with the agreement for no support.

16. Blum v. Blum, 59 Md.App. 584, 477 A.2d 289 (1984) (facts relating to separation agreement prepared by a lawyer representing both parties should be examined for possible duress; even where separating parties appear in full accord, lawyer may not represent them both due to seriousness of potential conflict).

17. For a review of bar association opinions on use of mediation in matrimonial dissolution, see Note, Model Rule 2.2 and Divorce Mediation: Ethics Guideline or Ethics Gap?, 65 Wash.U.L.Q. 223 (1987). The opinions in a number of states reflect hostility to mediatory representation in divorce proceedings.

18. Ass'n of Bar of City of New York, Comm. on Prof. Ethics No. 80–23 (1980).

and economic costs that may outweigh its advantages in some situations. If the parties are antagonistic or troubled, or there is inequality of bargaining position, the lawyer cannot serve as a mediator. If there are complex and difficult legal questions (e.g., tax consequences), separate representation is required.

In appropriate situations, the opinion concludes, a lawyer may participate in the non-legal aspects of mediation, provide impartial legal advice and assist in reducing the parties' agreement to writing if: (1) the parties are fully advised of the risks (including the sharing of confidences); (2) the lawyer is satisfied the parties understand the risks; (3) legal advice is given only to both parties in each others' presence; (4) the parties are advised of the advantages of seeking independent legal counsel before executing any agreement; and (5) the lawyer does not represent either party in any subsequent legal proceedings relating to the divorce. The opinion also warns that the lawyer must take care not to assist non-lawyers on the mediation team in the unauthorized practice of law.

3. Joint Representation in Business Ventures

Suppose a lawyer represents a partnership whose two members are friends or siblings. Trouble erupts between the business associates. They have sharp differences about the course that the business should take, or one accuses the other of malfeasance or neglect in business performance. They come to the lawyer and ask her to work out a fair dissolution. What are the risks to the lawyer? To the clients? How is this case different from the case of a marriage that is in serious difficulty? Under the standards stated in the New York City ethics opinion, supra, should the lawyer insist that the parties obtain separate representation?

Is starting a business venture an easier situation for joint representation? Suppose a lawyer is asked by Tom, Dick and Harriet, three acquaintances that she has never previously represented, to assist them in setting up a new business venture. Tom (age 30 and unmarried) has specialized expertise in the field; he will be the full-time manager providing much of the know-how. Dick (age 45 and married with two teenage children) will handle marketing and sales. Harriet (age 60, a retired businesswoman) will participate as the principal investor. Tom and Dick will work full-time for the new venture, Tom on a modest salary and Dick on salary plus commissions. Harriet will receive no salary but a share of the profits. The three clients ask the lawyer to set up a corporation, to help them work out the detailed terms of the venture (investment understandings, employment contracts, stock holdings, buy-out arrangements, etc.) and to prepare necessary documents. May the lawyer undertake the representation?

When this hypothetical was posed to two experienced business lawyers, they reached opposing conclusions.[19]   Richard H. Levin approved the lawyer's undertaking the joint representation: She should help the parties work out a happy future together.   Concededly, the undertaking is a difficult one because representation of the differing interests of each client requires a good deal of disclosure of the risks, care in dealing with the personalities and problems as they arise and a sensitive awareness to developing conflicts.   Joint representation, however, has many advantages: It focuses everyone on the promise of the future and getting the job done; it downplays conflict and accentuates agreement and cooperation; and it is less expensive.   In many situations, if one lawyer cannot serve, parties will get along with non-lawyers.   Separate lawyers can create controversy and break deals.   In negotiation, Levin says, "defining a problem tends to establish it and discussing it tends to arouse fears, belligerence, and obstinacy." [20]

> Most transactions should be viewed primarily as to their opportunities, and only secondarily as to their problems.   The lawyer is most useful in affirmative planning, and adding cooks does not necessarily improve the broth.[21]

Another experienced lawyer, Meyer J. Myer, concluded that the present and potential differences are so large that separate representation is required.   The clients have not resolved many critical issues.   How can the lawyer resolve them?   For example, the allocation of shares is a difficult problem when the participation of money and energy of each of the three is different; the facts suggest the desirability, in Harriet's interest, of providing a preferred debt interest for at least part of her investment but that may not be in the interest of the other two participants; given the different ages and family situations of the parties, working out buy-out arrangements and current income payments is problematic.   Given these and other divergent interests, the lawyer cannot adequately represent each client:

> Experience has shown that when more than slight differences in interest, present or potential, exist, a full explanation by the lawyer of their implications, and a firm stand against the representation, will not only dissolve the criticism of unnecessary duplication of legal services but in the long run will enhance respect for the lawyer and the profession.[22]

May a lawyer represent both the buyer and seller of a business? The general rule is that the divergent interests of the parties are such that a lawyer cannot be on both sides of the termination of a business. These transactions are too complex and the parties will not have considered all of the complexities even if they come to the lawyer with what they think is a completed deal.

19.   Stanley A. Kaplan (ed.), Legal Ethics Forum: Representation of Multiple Clients, 62 A.B.A.J. 648 (1976).

20.   Id. at 650.

21.   Id.

22.   Id. at 652.

4. "Lawyer for the Situation"

Louis D. Brandeis (1848–1941)

Justice Louis D. Brandeis, one of the great American lawyers of the first half of the 20th century, provides an inspiring example of living a great life in the law. His piercing intellect, passionate social commitment and enormous accomplishments continue to inspire many American lawyers. The focus here is on a less well-known aspect of Brandeis' life: His conception of the appropriate role of a lawyer during his years as a practicing attorney in Boston. Because Brandeis often preferred to facilitate a comprehensive resolution to a dispute rather than represent a single party in adversarial negotiations, he described his role on occasion as "lawyer for the situation." Acting in this role involves either joint representation or an intermediary role, both a departure from advocacy of a single client's interest—the role primarily envisioned by the lawyer codes.

Our knowledge of these matters comes primarily from the Senate confirmation hearings on President Wilson's nomination of Brandeis in 1916 as an associate justice of the U.S. Supreme Court.[23] At the hearing, prominent members of the bar charged Brandeis with unethical behavior in several instances where he acted as lawyer for the situation. The Warren case is illustrative.[24]

Brandeis had served as lawyer for the family of Samuel Warren, his law partner. Sam Warren's father had owned a substantial paper manufacturing company. When the father died, he left an estate of some $2 million to his wife and children. Brandeis sought to dispose of the estate appropriately and represented both members of the family and the estate. Sam Warren wished to keep the family business going but the other children did not desire an active role in the business. To satisfy all the children's wishes, Brandeis created a trust from which Sam could lease and continue operating the business. Brandeis transferred the mills to an inter vivos trust with Sam, his mother and a Mr. Mason (superintendent of the mills) as trustees. The trust then leased the property to Sam, his brother Fiske and Mr. Mason, who operated the business. As the mills prospered, the lessees were entitled to keep some of the profits as compensation for their services. Another portion of profits passed to the trustees and eventually to all the Warren children as beneficiaries.

This arrangement worked well for nineteen years until Ned Warren (one of the beneficiaries) became unhappy with Sam's management of the mills. In 1909, Ned brought an action to void the lease and to secure an accounting. He alleged fraud and collusion on the part of Sam Warren and Brandeis, arguing the arrangement with Sam as both

23. See Alpheus T. Mason, Brandeis: A Free Man's Life 465–508 (1946) (discussing the confirmation fight).

24. The Warren case is discussed in John P. Frank, The Legal Ethics of Louis D. Brandeis, 17 Stan. L. Rev. 683, 694–98 (1965).

lessee and trustee gave Sam an unjust financial gain at the expense of Ned and other family members. In the litigation, Brandeis represented the lessees. Before trial, Sam Warren died, Ned sold his interest in the trust to other family members and the litigation was abandoned.

The Warren case came back to haunt Brandeis at his confirmation hearings. Why did he represent both lessees and trustees at the drafting stage of the trust? Why did he represent only the lessees when Ned filed suit? Why did he continue to accept annual retainers from both trustees and lessees while the trust arrangement was working successfully?

Another representation explored in the confirmation hearings was Brandeis' handling of a debtor-creditor relationship.[25] Brandeis was approached by the owners of a tannery business which was in financial difficulties. The tanners thought Brandeis undertook to represent them but Brandeis eventually helped the creditors of the tannery, who drove the tannery into bankruptcy. When pressed to identify for whom he was actually working, Brandeis replied, "I should say that I was counsel for the situation." This misty response has caught the attention of legal commentators. What exactly are the characteristics of a lawyer for the situation? Is such behavior ethical?

After five months of investigation of this and other alleged improprieties in Brandeis' law practice, the Senate judiciary committee approved his nomination by a narrow 10 to 8 vote. He was confirmed by the Senate by a 47–22 vote.[26]

Professor Geoffrey Hazard describes a lawyer for the situation as follows:

> [N]o other lawyer is involved. Hence, the lawyer is no one's partisan and, at least up to a point, everyone's confidant. He can be the only person who knows the whole situation. He is an analyst of the relationship between the clients, in that he undertakes to discern the needs, fears, and expectations of each and to discover the concordances among them. He is an interpreter, translating inarticulate or exaggerated claims and forewarnings into temperate and mutually intelligible terms of communication. He can contribute historical perspective, objectivity, and foresight into the parties' assessment of the situation. He can discourage escalation of conflict and recruitment of outside allies. He can articulate general principles and common custom as standards by which the parties can examine their respective claims. He is advocate, mediator, entrepreneur, and judge, all in one. He could be said to be playing God.[27]

25. This matter, referred to as the Lennox Case, is discussed in Frank, supra, at 698–703.

26. Mason, supra, at 505.

27. Geoffrey C. Hazard, Jr., Ethics in the Practice of Law 64–65 (1978).

The role of lawyer for the situation requires skill, detachment and the capacity to sustain confidence. If mishandled, it generates bitterness that a deep trust has been betrayed. Brandeis encountered mixed results in its application. Though it may promote efficient resolution of disputes, it clouds traditional notions of lawyers as advocates for single clients with discrete interests. The balance of this note presents three varying interpretations of the propriety of serving as "lawyer for the situation."

John P. Frank

John P. Frank's analysis of Brandeis's ethics, published in 1965, offers a straight-forward rejection of lawyering for the situation. Frank's thesis is simple: "Lawyers are not retained by situations, and the adversary system assumes that they faithfully represent one interest at a time." [28] A "situation" is too vague for intelligible representation. Only specific clients, who can articulate particular interests in particular matters, are proper "units" of representation. Frank concludes:

> ... [T]he greatest caution to be gained from study of the Brandeis record is, never be "counsel for a situation." A lawyer is constantly confronted with conflicts which he is frequently urged to somehow try to work out.... Particularly when old clients are at odds, counsel may feel the most extreme pressure to solve their problems for them. It is a time-consuming, costly, unsuccessful mistake, which results in disaffecting both sides.[29]

Despite his rejection of the notion of acting as a lawyer for the situation, Frank does not find any ethical impropriety in Brandeis' handling of the Warren matter. First, Ned Warren, a beneficiary of the trust arrangement, never retained Brandeis as counsel. Thus, when Ned sued the lessees, Brandeis had no conflict in representing the lessees. Is the argument sound? Did Brandeis, while representing the trustee, owe duties to the trust beneficiaries? [30]

Assuming a conflict of interest did exist between Ned and the lessees and that Brandeis eventually argued against Ned's interests, Frank offers Ned's consent as a second justification for the conduct. This second defense relies on a cloudy factual record: Did Brandeis, acting as lawyer for the trustees, fully disclose all relevant information to Ned Warren, who lived in England?

Frank concedes that generally it is a conflict of interest to represent both a trust and someone leasing property from a trust. Trustees inherently want to maximize their profit from property while lessees want to pay as little as possible. Nevertheless, Frank justifies Brandeis

---

28. John P. Frank, The Legal Ethics of Louis D. Brandeis, 17 Stan. L. Rev. 683, 702 (1965).

29. Id. at 708.

30. See the *Fickett* case printed below at p. 804.

by distinguishing the normal lessor-lessee relationship from the special familial nature of the Warren transaction:

> When the elder Warren died, the Warren family faced a problem together.... [N]o canon of legal ethics ... requires each of the relatives of the deceased to take different counsel to the funeral. If a half-dozen heirs were required to pay a half-dozen counsel, they would indeed have additional grounds for grief.[31]

Is this argument, absolving Brandeis because of the understanding and internal accord of the Warren family regarding their father's estate, consistent with Frank's premise that ethics rules contemplate the representation of individuals, not amorphous groups such as a "family"?

Thomas L. Shaffer

Professor Thomas L. Shaffer writes approvingly of Brandeis' "disagreement with the profession's elaborate concern for conflicts of interest." [32]   He defends the concept and the practice of acting as lawyer for the situation:

> The lawyer-for-the situation claim involves ... saying that the situation has reality.... [Married couples and other family groups] have reality; they are *something*; and it is possible for a lawyer to recognize the reality of such situations (units) and then to accord professional representation and defense to such situations (units).... The situation might be a married couple who want, together, to arrange for the disposition of their wealth after the survivor of them dies, or a married couple who have decided to seek divorce and have agreed on how to unravel their lives together; or an owner of property and someone who wants to rent it, who have agreed on the terms of the deal and need a *lawyer—a* lawyer—to reduce the deal to formal terms for the protection of *both* of them.... [T]o recognize the risks and to acknowledge that there are in such representation opportunities for self-deception is not to say that "situations" lack reality.... If human associations have reality, then it is not the case that the typical lawyer's client is always a (lonely) individual.[33]

In Shaffer's world view, the ancient bonds of family properly subordinate individual interests; professional responsibility rules are corrupting, he argues, if they do not temper zealous advocacy for the individual with a healthy measure of respect for organic communities of persons.

To what extent do current professional rules recognize interests broader than those of a discrete individual or legal entity? Even if lawyers may represent situations, do not ethical dilemmas arise when

31. Id. at 697.

32. Thomas L. Shaffer, American Legal Ethics 302 (1985).

33. Id. at 302–03. See also Thomas L. Shaffer, The Legal Ethics of Radical Individualism, 65 Tex.L.Rev. 963 (1987).

divorcing couples disagree on terms of settlement or when lessors and lessees clash over a provision? How is a lawyer to determine her ultimate responsibilities if she is not directly reporting to a client with a discrete interest?

Geoffrey C. Hazard, Jr.

Professor Geoffrey C. Hazard, Jr., takes an intermediate position between Frank's rejection of lawyering for the situation and Shaffer's acceptance of it.[34] Hazard sees lawyers for the situation as playing a constructive role in certain situations, but sounds loud warnings about the potential for abuse, alienation of clients and confused professional responsibilities. Hazard begins by noting that professional codes recognize lawyering for the situation to some extent. EC 5–20 of the Model Code, for example, allows a lawyer to serve as "an impartial arbitrator or mediator," terms that "can imply that the lawyer is actively involved, indeed aggressively involved, in exploring alternative arrangements by which the positions of the parties can be accommodated in a comprehensive resolution of the matter at hand." [35]

The Model Rules deal more explicitly and in greater detail with the lawyer's roles in counseling clients. M.R. 2.1, 2.2 and 2.3 should be reviewed at this point.

The active and creative role of lawyer of the situation, Hazard writes, can be

> ... perhaps the best service a lawyer can render to anyone. It approximates the ideal forms of intercession suggested by the models of wise parent or village elder. It provides adjustment of difference upon a wholistic view of the situation, rather than bilaterally opposing ones. It rests on implicit principles of decision that express commonly shared ideals in behavior rather than strict legal right. The basis of decision is mutual assent and not external compulsion. The orientation in time tends to be a hopeful view of the future rather than an angry view of the past. It avoids the loss of personal autonomy that results when each side commits his cause to his own advocate. It is the opposite of going to law.[36]

But the role has many dangers. First, the lawyer for the situation undertakes an amorphous function: representing the best interests of all. Second, the degree to which the attorney is an active participant in a situation may become worrisome. Unlike representation of a single interest, a lawyer for the situation has no structure of goals and constraints imposed from the outside. Third, lawyering for the situation strains client trust: Clients must accept the lawyer's actions and judgments without being able to verify their soundness. Fourth, the lawyer for a situation faces much harder moral choices than an attorney in an adversarial system. Short of violating law, the tradi-

---

34. Geoffrey C. Hazard, Jr., Ethics in the Practice of Law 58–63 (1978).

35. Id. at 63.

36. Id. at 65.

tional role permits a lawyer to leave hard choices to the client. Reliance on the premises of the profession allows the lawyer to occupy a simplified moral universe. A lawyer for the situation, on the other hand, has "choices to make that obviously can go against the interest of one client or another...." [37] The existence of these hard choices may explain why many lawyers are reluctant to become lawyers for the situation and why professional rules give little recognition of the propriety of such practice.

In the end, Hazard retreats to a cautious middle ground. If lawyering for the situation works, the rewards are plentiful. Lawyers can and do perform this role. Yet the difficulties and dangers are inescapable:

> A person may be entrusted with [lawyering for the situation] only if he knows that in the event of miscarriage he will have no protection from the law. In this respect, acting as lawyer for the situation can be thought of as similar to a doctor's "authority" to terminate the life of a hopeless patient: It can be undertaken only if it will not be questioned afterwards. To this extent Brandeis' critics may have been right. [38]

5. Representing an Insured Person Upon Request of an Insurer

In General [39]

For many years the ABA waffled on the lawyer's responsibility in representing an insured through retainer by an insurer. A 1942 ethics opinion declined to say whether information given by the insured to the lawyer is confidential as against the insurer. [40] The opinion stated that this "is a question of law and not of ethics," a question on which the courts were divided. [41]

In 1950, however, the ethics committee took the position that "[t]he essential point of ethics involved is that the lawyer so employed shall represent the insured as his client with undivided fidelity...." [42] This is the accepted rule today. A leading case, Parsons v. Continental National American Group, [43] states:

37. Ibid.

38. Ibid.

39. For general commentary, see Robert E. O'Malley, Ethics Principles for the Insurer, the Insured, and Defense Counsel: The Eternal Triangle Reformed, 66 Tulane L.Rev. 511 (1991); Allan D. Windt, Insurance Claims and Disputes: Representation of Insurance Companies and Insureds (1982); and Brooke Wunnicke, The Eternal Triangle: Standards of Ethical Representation by the Insurance Defense Lawyer, For the Defense, Feb.1989, p. 7.

40. ABA Formal Opinion 247 (1942).

41. See Annot., 108 A.L.R. 505, for court decisions on this issue contemporaneous with Opinion 247.

42. ABA Formal Opinion 282 (1950).

43. 112 Ariz. 223, 550 P.2d 94 (1976).

When an attorney who is an insurance company's agent uses the confidential relationship between an attorney and a client to gather information so as to deny the insured coverage under the policy in the garnishment proceeding, we hold that such conduct constitutes a waiver of any policy defense, and is so contrary to public policy that the insurance company is estopped as a matter of law from disclaiming liability under an exclusionary clause in the policy.[44]

Model Rule 1.8(f) provides that a lawyer shall not accept payment from another for legal services to a client unless: (1) the client consents after consultation; (2) there is no interference with the lawyer's independence or professional judgment or with the client-lawyer relationship; and (3) information relating to representation of the client is protected as required by M.R. 1.6 (the rule on confidentiality). In addition, M.R. 1.8(b) provides that "[a] lawyer shall not use information relating to representation of a client to the disadvantage of the client unless the client consents after consultation." Observe that "use" of information may be made without disclosure of such information.[45]

Coverage Questions

A liability insurer may assign a case to a defense lawyer believing that the event is within policy coverage. The defense attorney subsequently may discover facts indicating that the insured's liability falls outside the policy (e.g., the insured acted intentionally rather than negligently). May the defense attorney reveal that information to the insurance company? The cases hold that defense counsel's duty of loyalty to the insured bars her from taking any action that may be adverse to her clients' interests.[46] Thus, if an investigating defense lawyer discovers defendant's wrongful act was intentional, the lawyer may not reveal that information to the insurance company. Liability insurers often protect themselves against this possibility by undertaking the defense under a reservation of rights, leaving open the possibility of litigating coverage in a separate proceeding against the insured. The insurer's reservation of rights warns the insured that it may be in the latter's best interest to obtain separate representation.

Settling an Insurance Claim

In Crisci v. Security Insurance Co.,[47] the court said: "When there is a great risk of a recovery beyond the policy limits so that the most reasonable manner of disposing of the claim is a settlement which can

44. 550 P.2d at 99. Accord: State Farm Mutual Automobile Ins. Co. v. Walker, 382 F.2d 548 (7th Cir.1967) (en banc) (lawyer cannot disclose the information and must withdraw from representing both the insurer and the insured).

45. DR 5–107(B) provides that "A lawyer shall not permit a person who recommends, employs, or pays him to render legal services for another to direct or regulate his professional judgment in rendering such legal services."

46. See Parsons v. Continental National American Group, 113 Ariz. 223, 550 P.2d 94 (1976).

47. 66 Cal.2d 425, 58 Cal.Rptr. 13, 426 P.2d 173 (1967).

be made within those limits, a consideration in good faith of the insured's interest requires the insurer to settle the claim." [48]   The duty-to-settle doctrine poses dangers for insurance defense counsel who reject offers of settlement within policy limits. In Lysick v. Walcom,[49] the insurer authorized counsel to settle for the policy limit, $10,000. Defense counsel offered plaintiff $9,500, which plaintiff refused. When defense counsel finally tendered the policy limit, plaintiff rejected the offer. At trial, the jury returned a plaintiff's verdict of $225,000. The insured settled its bad faith claim against the insurer for $89,000. The insurer, in turn, sued defense counsel for malpractice. The court found for the carrier, holding counsel liable for the excess.[50]

May the insurer settle without the insured's consent? This fact pattern commonly arises in the malpractice setting, when a professional is interested in protecting her reputation. In Rogers v. Robson, Masters, Ryan, Brumund & Belom,[51] the court held that, even though the insurance policy authorized the insurer to settle without the insured physician's consent, the insured had a cause of action against the lawyer who settled against the physician's instructions and without fully disclosing to him the intent to settle. The lawyer's duty concerning settlement without the client's consent stemmed from the attorney-client relationship, not the policy.[52] Other states, however, treat the language of the insurance policy as a binding waiver by the insured.[53] Courts in these jurisdictions may be influenced by the fact that policies generally are available at a higher premium if an insured desires to control settlement.

A lawyer representing insurer and insured during settlement negotiations faces difficult choices; one court states that "the ethical dilemma ... would tax Socrates, and no decision or authority we have studied furnishes a completely satisfactory answer." [54] The ABA negotiated a detailed set of "guiding principles" with major casualty and

48. 426 P.2d at 176.

49. 258 Cal.App.2d 136, 65 Cal.Rptr. 406 (1968).

50. If the insurance company was responsible for refusing the settlement offer, neither the insured nor the insurer can recover from the lawyer. See Purdy v. Pacific Automobile Ins. Co., 157 Cal.App.3d 59, 203 Cal.Rptr. 524 (1984) (lawyer's actions were not the proximate cause of the insured's loss when the insurer, not the lawyer, rejected the settlement offer).

51. 81 Ill.2d 201, 40 Ill.Dec. 816, 407 N.E.2d 47 (1980). The court absolved the insurer from liability on contract grounds even though it had instructed defense counsel to settle.

52. See M.R. 1.8(g), M.R. 1.2(a); DR 5–106. Accord: L & S Roofing Supply Co. v. St. Paul Fire & Marine Ins. Co., 521 So.2d 1298 (Ala.1987); Lieberman v. Employers Insurance of Wausau, 84 N.J. 325, 419 A.2d 417 (1980).

53. See Mitchum v. Hudgens, 533 So.2d 194 (Ala.1988) (lawyer not liable to insured for malpractice for settling without insured's consent when policy gave insurer exclusive power to handle settlement matters; the court distinguished *L & S Roofing,* supra, by noting that here the insurer had not reserved rights against the insured, who therefore had no financial stake in the settlement).

54. Hartford Accident & Indemnity Co. v. Foster, 528 So.2d 255, 270–273 (Miss.1988). See also Moritz v. The Medical Protective Co. of Fort Wayne, Indiana, 428 F.Supp. 865 (W.D.Wis.1977); Hamilton v. State Farm Insurance Co., 83 Wn.2d 787, 523 P.2d 193 (1974).

liability insurance companies during the 1970s.[55] Although later rescinded, apparently to avoid antitrust concerns, the principles continue to provide informal guidance to lawyers and insurers in some situations. In some respects they are in conflict with more recent court decisions holding that the lawyer retained by the insurer to represent an insured must treat the insured as the client when a conflict arises.[56]

D. SUCCESSIVE REPRESENTATION

1. Substantial Relationship Test

The substantial relationship test, important in concurrent representation cases, is central in successive representation cases. In successive representation, if the matters are not the "same or substantially related," the lawyer may proceed without even consulting the former client. If the matters are substantially related, the former client's consent must be obtained before going forward.

Oddly enough, the Model Code has no provision specifying whether, and if so when, it is proper for a lawyer to oppose a former client on behalf of a present client. The courts filled the gap, relying on pre-Code common law principles. The case law on this subject has multiplied in recent decades, largely in connection with motions to disqualify.[57]

Lacking a specific Code provision on conflicts with former clients, courts relied on Canon 4 (preserving client confidences), Canon 5 (exercising independent judgment) and Canon 9 (avoiding the appearance of impropriety) in fashioning the law on this subject. The basic test, which antedated the Code, was first enunciated by Judge Weinfeld in T.C. Theatre Corp. v. Warner Brothers Pictures, Inc.: [58]

> [T]he former client need show no more than that matters embraced within the pending suit wherein his former attorney appears on behalf of his adversary are substantially related to the matters or cause of action wherein the attorney previously represented him, the former client. The court will assume that during the course of the former representation confidences were disclosed to the attorney bearing on the subject matter of the representation. It will not inquire into their nature and extent. Only in this manner can the lawyer's duty of absolute fidelity be enforced and the spirit of the rule relating to privileged communications be maintained.

55. Guiding Principles, reprinted in 20 Fed.Ins.Couns.Q. 95 (1972).

56. For example, the principles provide that if the lawyer discovers a question of coverage he must notify both the company and the insured, and the insured should be invited to retain her own counsel at her own expense to represent her separate interest, Paragraph IV. But if the lawyer's information is a confidential communication from the insured, the lawyer should neither disclose the coverage question to the insurer or discuss the issue with the insured, Paragraph VI.

57. See the discussion above at p. 654 of the misuse of motions to disqualify counsel.

58. 113 F.Supp. 265, 268–269 (S.D.N.Y.1953).

2. Model Rule 1.9

The Model Rules, unlike the Model Code, specifically deal with the question of successive representation. M.R. 1.9(a) provides that a lawyer shall not: "represent another person in the same or a substantially related matter in which that person's interests are materially adverse to the interests of the former client unless the former client consents after consultation."

The rule, which applies only when the new client's interests are *materially adverse* to those of the former client, adopts the substantial relationship test. In requiring material adversity of interests, it is a rule against "switching sides." Finally, the former client's consent (after consultation) is enough to cure the conflict. M.R. 1.9 is not a "consent plus" rule like M.R. 1.7, which requires that the representation be objectively reasonable.

M.R. 1.9(c), originally adopted by the ABA and adopted in many states as M.R. 1.9(b), is a reminder that the lawyer also has a continuing duty of confidentiality to a former client. Even if the former client consents under M.R. 1.9(a) to the new representation, that consent does not obviate the lawyer's continuing duty of confidentiality. M.R. 1.9(b), as amended in 1989, is concerned with imputed disqualification and will be addressed later in this chapter.

M.R. 1.9 applies to all lawyers, including those whose former client was the government. Lawyers who formerly worked for the government, however, are bound by M.R. 1.11 *in addition* to M.R. 1.9. As we will see later in this chapter, M.R. 1.11 restricts a lawyer's representation of new clients in the same or substantially related matters, even when the new client's interests are in harmony with that of the former government client.

A "Former Client"?

Under the rule limiting representation adverse to a former client, it first must be shown that an attorney-client relationship previously existed between the objecting party and the lawyer. Whether a person previously was a client involves essentially the same issues as determining whether a person presently has become a client.[59] The alleged relationship can be considered "objectively," i.e., whether a reasonable observer would conclude that a lawyer-client relationship had existed. It can also be considered "subjectively," i.e., whether the alleged erstwhile client supposed that the lawyer was representing her. The court in *Westinghouse* adopted a combined standard: If the *client reasonably believed* that the relationship existed then the client had a right to believe the information communicated was confidential, and an attorney-client relationship will be held to have existed for purposes of conflict questions.

---

59. See the *Togstad* case printed in Chapter 6 above at p. 481, and the *Westinghouse* case printed earlier in this chapter at p. 627.

The distinction among the tests may be purely conceptual, even for a client who "taint shops," i.e., tries to create objective manifestations of consulting the lawyer with no real intention of retaining her. The tactic of "taint shopping" has been recognized as a problem by the courts.[60]

What Are the "Matters"?

Assuming a past attorney-client relationship, is the present "matter" substantially related to the "matter" in which the lawyer represented the former client? This requires specification of the two things to be compared. Where both representations were of private clients, each "matter" usually is a lawsuit or a negotiation, in either case with more or less discernible identity. Where the prior or present client is a government agency, the definition of "matter" is often more amorphous. In that context the debate centers on whether tasks like drafting legislation or regulations are to be considered "matters" for purposes of the conflicts rules. For example, can a lawyer who drafts legislation later challenge its validity or argue a particular interpretation?

Are the Matters "Substantially Related"?

The courts have employed different formulas for "substantially related." Some decisions adopt what seems a broad definition. For example, the Fifth Circuit in Kraft, Inc. v. Alton Box Board Co.[61] held that the prior representation "need only be akin to the present action in a way reasonable persons would understand as important to the issues involved." The broad term "akin," however, was narrowed by the use of an objective standard, "reasonable persons," and the requirement that the matters be related in a manner *"important* to the *issues."* What makes the relationship "important" is a combination of at least two factors: how divergent are the interests of the two clients in the two matters; and how relevant to the present matter is the information the lawyer would have received in the former representation, i.e., how potentially harmful that information might be.

Perhaps the broadest formula was suggested in Chugach Electric Association v. United States District Court.[62] The case involved a former corporate general counsel, hence a lawyer who probably knew everything about the client's legal affairs. But the court said of the lawyer's former association with the opposing party that it "would provide him with greater insight and understanding of the significance of subsequent events ... and offer a promising source of discovery." [63]

---

60. See, e.g., Hughes v. Paine, Webber, Jackson and Curtis, Inc., 565 F.Supp. 663 (N.D.Ill.1983) (discussed in the notes to *Westinghouse* at p. 637. See also Levin v. Ripple Twist Mills, Inc., 416 F.Supp. 876 (E.D.Pa.1976), appeal dism'd, 549 F.2d 795 (3d Cir.1977).

61. 659 F.2d 1341, 1346 (5th Cir.1981).

62. 370 F.2d 441 (9th Cir.1966).

63. 370 F.2d at 443.

A narrower formula has been adopted by the Second Circuit. In *Government of India v. Cook Industries, Inc.*,[64] the court said that the relationship between the two matters must be "patently clear," the issues "identical" or "essentially the same".[65]

The broad interpretation of "substantially related" in *Chugach Electric*, supra, has not been followed by other circuits and the Ninth Circuit appears to have abandoned it.[66] But it stands on the opposite end of the spectrum from the Second Circuit's view of "identity of issues." *Chugach Electric* could be said to stand for a "till death do us part" approach, while the Second Circuit cases adopt a "here today, gone tomorrow" attitude. Perhaps the differing verbal formulations are influenced or controlled by the facts of individual cases. It should make a difference, should it not, whether the first representation concerned an isolated transaction, as distinct from long-term general counseling? Few cases have involved the latter, which unmistakably would implicate disloyalty. Is that what the court in *Chugach Electric* had in mind?

Notwithstanding the confusion over how loyalty should figure into the analysis, it seems clear that the central concern in the "substantial relation" test is the likelihood that confidential information relevant to the present case is possessed by the lawyer by virtue of her former relationship with the objecting party.

The risk to confidences must be assessed without revealing the confidences that the test seeks to protect. The problem is one of drawing inferences from the circumstances. This in turn involves a heavy interjection of the judge's experience in practice and her attitude toward loyalty to clients. A judge whose practice has been general counseling is likely, other things being equal, to have a different attitude from one whose practice was litigation or other "here today, gone tomorrow" transactions.

Another source of uncertainty is that the test seeks to protect competing interests. While the former client must be reasonably protected, the present client has a right to the counsel of its choice.

Presumption That Confidential Information Was Received

If the court finds that the two matters are substantially related, it will presume that the lawyer possesses confidential information and that the information will be used, even if inadvertently, to the detriment of the former client. The presumption is ordinarily irrebutta-

---

64. 569 F.2d 737, 739–740 (2d Cir.1978).

65. Also see Federal Deposit Insurance Corp. Co. v. Amundson, 682 F.Supp. 981, 988 (D.Minn.1988). But see Anchor Packing Co. v. Pro–Seal, 688 F.Supp. 1215, 1220 (E.D.Mich.1988) (Sixth Circuit rejects this narrow view, citing General Electric Co. v. Valeron Corp., 608 F.2d 265, 267 (6th Cir.1979)).

66. See United Sewerage Agency v. Jelco Inc., 646 F.2d 1339, 1351 (9th Cir.1981); Merle Norman Cosmetics, Inc. v. United States District Court, 856 F.2d 98, 100–101 (9th Cir.1988).

ble.[67] The function of the substantial relationship test is considered further in notes following *Brennan's*.[68]

3. Successive Representation of Joint Clients

BRENNAN'S INC. v. BRENNAN'S RESTAURANTS, INC.

United States Court of Appeals, Fifth Circuit, 1979.
590 F.2d 168.

Before BROWN, CHIEF JUDGE, and GEWIN and TJOFLAT, CIRCUIT JUDGES.

TJOFLAT, CIRCUIT JUDGE:

This is an action for trademark infringement and unfair competition. This appeal, however, concerns the disqualification of attorneys. The district court barred the appellants' attorneys from further representing them on grounds of conflict of interest. The correctness of this order is the only issue before us.

I

The underlying dispute in this case arises out of the business affairs of the Brennan family of New Orleans, Louisiana, who have been in the restaurant business for many years. All of the corporate parties are owned and closely held by various members of the Brennan family. Appellee Brennan's, Inc., the plaintiff below, owns and operates Brennan's restaurant at 417 Royal Street in New Orleans. The corporate appellants own and operate other restaurants in Louisiana, Texas, and Georgia. . . .

Prior to 1974, all the members of the Brennan family were stockholders and directors of plaintiff, and some of them were stockholders and directors of the corporate defendants. All the corporations were independent legal entities in the sense that none held any of the stock of another, but they were all owned by members of the Brennan family and had interlocking boards of directors. In 1971, Edward F. Wegmann became general counsel for the family businesses, and his retainer was paid pro rata by all the corporations. He continued this joint representation until November 1973.

As part of his services, Mr. Wegmann, in close cooperation with trademark counsel in Washington, D.C., prosecuted applications for the federal registration of three service marks: "Brennan's," "Breakfast at Brennan's," and a distinctive rooster design. A registration for the rooster design was issued in February 1972, but the applications for the other two marks were initially denied on the ground that they were primarily a surname. On the advice of Washington trademark counsel,

---

67. See, e.g., Fred Weber, Inc. v. Shell Oil Co., 566 F.2d 602, 608 (8th Cir.1977); Schloetter v. Railoc, Inc., 546 F.2d 706, 710 (7th Cir.1976).

68. For a comprehensive review of the test, see U.S. Football League v. National Football League, 605 F.Supp. 1448 (S.D.N.Y.1985). Compare Satellite Financial Planning Corp. v. First Nat. Bank of Wilmington, 652 F.Supp. 1281 (D.Del.1987).

Mr. Wegmann collected data supporting a demonstration that the marks had acquired a secondary meaning,[2] and the applications were amended to include this material. Registrations were subsequently issued in plaintiff's name in March 1973. These registered service marks are the subject of this lawsuit.

Later in 1973 a dispute developed within the Brennan family over the operation and management of the family businesses. This dispute was resolved in November 1974 by dividing the corporations' stock between the two opposing family groups. Plaintiff became 100% owned by one group and the corporate defendants became 100% owned by the second group, composed of the individual defendants. Mr. Wegmann elected to continue to represent defendants and severed his connections with plaintiff and its shareholders.

At no time during the negotiations which culminated in the November 1974 settlement was there any discussion of who would have the right to use the registered service marks. Both sides claimed ownership of the marks and continued to use them after the settlement. Attempts to negotiate a license or concurrent registration were unsuccessful. Plaintiff filed this suit for trademark infringement and unfair competition on May 21, 1976. In their answer and counterclaim defendants alleged that the marks were registered in plaintiff's name for convenience only, and, "in truth and actuality, the applications were filed and the registrations issued for the benefit and ownership of all of the Brennan family restaurants, including the corporate defendants." Defendants also alleged that the marks and registrations are invalid.

Upon the filing of this suit, Mr. Wegmann, on behalf of the defendants, retained the services of Arnold Sprung, a New York patent and trademark attorney, to assist him in the defense of the case. On October 22, 1976, plaintiff moved for the disqualification of both attorneys: Mr. Wegmann on the ground that his present representation was at odds with the interests of plaintiff, his former client, and Mr. Sprung by imputation of Mr. Wegmann's conflict. After a hearing, the district court granted the motion. It found that the subject matter of the present suit is substantially related to matters in which Mr. Wegmann formerly represented plaintiff, and to allow him now to represent an interest adverse to his former client creates the appearance of impropriety. It also found that "the close working relationship which has been shown to exist between Mr. Wegmann and Mr. Sprung creates a significant likelihood that Mr. Sprung would have had access to or been informed of confidential disclosures made to Mr. Wegmann by his former client."

II

. . .

---

2. This supporting data included numerous local and national advertisements, articles from several publications and letters commending the quality of Brennan's, and statements of the dollar volume of sales and advertising.

Defendants argue that the district court failed to consider that in his prior representation of plaintiff, Mr. Wegmann also represented defendants. This fact of joint representation is crucial, they assert, since no confidences can arise as between joint clients. Hence, the argument goes, Mr. Wegmann violates no ethical duty in his present representation.

We have not addressed this precise question before. In Wilson P. Abraham Construction Corp. v. Armco Steel Corp., [559 F.2d 250 (5th Cir.1977)] we reaffirmed the standard that "a former client seeking to disqualify an attorney who appears on behalf of his adversary, need only to show that the matters embraced within the pending suit are *substantially related* to the matters or cause of action wherein the attorney previously represented him," 559 F.2d at 252 (emphasis in original),[4] but we acknowledged that "[t]his rule rests upon the presumption that confidences potentially damaging to the client have been disclosed to the attorney during the former period of representation," id. Defendants contend that this presumption cannot apply in this case. This argument, in our view, interprets too narrowly an attorney's duty to "preserve the confidences and secrets of a client." ABA Code of Professional Responsibility, Canon 4 (1970).[5] The fundamental flaw in defendants' position is a confusion of the attorney-client evidentiary privilege with the ethical duty to preserve a client's confidences. Assuming the prior representation was joint, defendants are quite correct that neither of the parties to this suit can assert the attorney-client privilege against the other as to matters comprehended by that joint representation. Garner v. Wolfinbarger, 430 F.2d 1093, 1103 (5th Cir.1970). But the ethical duty is broader than the evidentiary privilege: "This ethical precept, unlike the evidentiary privilege, exists without regard to the nature or source of information or the fact that others share the knowledge." ABA Code of Professional Responsibility, EC 4–4 (1970). "A lawyer should not use information acquired in the course of the representation of a client to the disadvantage of the client...." Id. EC 4–5. The use of the word "information" in these Ethical Considerations as opposed to "confidence" or "secret" is particularly revealing of the drafters' intent to protect all knowledge acquired from a client, since the latter two are defined terms. See id., DR 4–101(A).[6] Information so acquired is sheltered from use by the attorney

4. Accord, Celanese Corp. v. Leesona Corp. (In re Yarn Processing Patent Validity Litigation), 530 F.2d 83, 89 (5th Cir.1976); American Can Co. v. Citrus Feed Co., 436 F.2d 1125, 1128 (5th Cir.1971); T.C. Theater Corp. v. Warner Bros. Pictures, 113 F.Supp. 265, 268 (S.D.N.Y.1953).

5. As the profession's own expression of its ethical standards, the Code of Professional Responsibility, Ethical Considerations, and Disciplinary Rules provide substantial guidance to federal courts in evaluating the conduct of attorneys appearing before them. See NCK Organization v. Bregman, 542 F.2d 128, 129 (2d Cir.1976); Woods v. Covington County Bank, 537 F.2d 804, 810 (5th Cir.1976).

6. *DR 4–101 Preservation of Confidences and Secrets of a Client.*

(A) "Confidence" refers to information protected by the attorney-client privilege under applicable law, and "secret" refers to other information gained in the profession-

against his client by virtue of the existence of the attorney-client relationship. This is true without regard to whether someone else may be privy to it. NCK Organization v. Bregman, 542 F.2d 128, 133 (2d Cir.1976). The obligation of an attorney not to misuse information acquired in the course of representation serves to vindicate the trust and reliance that clients place in their attorneys. A client would feel wronged if an opponent prevailed against him with the aid of an attorney who formerly represented the client in the same matter. As the court recognized in E.F. Hutton & Co. v. Brown, 305 F.Supp. 371, 395 (S.D.Tex.1969), this would undermine public confidence in the legal system as a means for adjudicating disputes. We recognize that this concern implicates the principle embodied in Canon 9 that attorneys "should avoid even the appearance of professional impropriety." ABA Code of Professional Responsibility, Canon 9 (1970). We have said that under this canon there must be a showing of a reasonable possibility that some specifically identifiable impropriety in fact occurred and that the likelihood of public suspicion must be weighed against the interest in retaining counsel of one's choice. Woods v. Covington County Bank, 537 F.2d 804, 812–13 (5th Cir.1976). The conflict of interest is readily apparent here, however, and we think that the balance weighs in favor of disqualification. See Zylstra v. Safeway Stores, Inc., 578 F.2d 102 (5th Cir.1978) (adopting per se rule of disqualification in class action cases for attorneys who are members of the class or partners or spouses of named plaintiffs). The need to safeguard the attorney-client relationship is not diminished by the fact that the prior representation was joint with the attorney's present client. Accordingly, we find the rule of Wilson P. Abraham Construction Corp. v. Armco Steel Corp. fully applicable to this case. Since the district court's findings of prior representation and substantial relationship are not disputed, we affirm the disqualification of Mr. Wegmann.

III

Whether Mr. Sprung should be disqualified presents a more difficult case. He has never had an attorney-client relationship with plaintiff; the district court disqualified him by imputation of Mr. Wegmann's conflict. Up to this point we have accepted, for the sake of argument, defendants' assertion that they were formerly joint clients with plaintiff of Mr. Wegmann. There is no dispute that plaintiff and defendants were previously represented by Mr. Wegmann simultaneously, but plaintiff maintains that, at least with respect to the registration of the service marks, Mr. Wegmann was representing plaintiff alone. The district court made no findings on the issue. Because we think that the disqualification of Mr. Sprung may turn on this fact and others not found by the court below, we vacate that part of the court's order relating to Mr. Sprung and remand the cause for

---

al relationship that the client has requested be held inviolate or the disclosure of which would be embarrassing or would be likely to be detrimental to the client.

further proceedings. For the guidance of the court on remand, we set forth our view of the applicable ethical standards.

If the court finds that Mr. Wegmann previously represented plaintiff and defendants jointly, we can see no reason why Mr. Sprung should be disqualified. As between joint clients there can be no "confidences" or "secrets" unless one client manifests a contrary intent. See Garner v. Wolfinbarger, 430 F.2d 1093, 1103 (5th Cir.1970); ABA Code of Professional Responsibility, DR 4–101 (1970). Thus, Mr. Sprung could not have learned anything from Mr. Wegmann that defendants did not already know or have a right to know. Plaintiff argues that this permits the defendants indirectly to gain the benefit of Mr. Wegmann's services when they could not do so directly. If the representation was joint, however, defendants possess no information as to which plaintiff could have had any expectation of privacy in relation to the defendants. The only remaining ground for disqualification then would be an appearance of impropriety. In Part II of this opinion, we decided there is such an appearance when an attorney represents an interest adverse to that of a former client in a matter substantially related to the subject of the prior representation. Mr. Sprung has never been plaintiff's counsel, however; he is only the co-counsel of one who was. We are enjoined not to give Canon 9 an overly broad application and to maintain "a reasonable balance between the need to ensure ethical conduct on the part of lawyers ... and other social interests, which include the litigant's right to freely chosen counsel." Woods v. Covington County Bank, 537 F.2d 804, 810 (5th Cir.1976). In the case of Mr. Sprung, we think the balance weighs against disqualification.... [7]

If the district court finds that Mr. Wegmann did not previously represent these parties jointly, it does not necessarily follow that Mr. Sprung should be disqualified. The courts have abjured a per se approach to the disqualification of co-counsel of disqualified counsel. Akerly v. Red Barn System, Inc., 551 F.2d 539 (3rd Cir.1977); American Can Co. v. Citrus Feed Co., 436 F.2d 1125 (5th Cir.1971). In the absence of an attorney-client relationship between Mr. Sprung and plaintiff, a presumption of disclosure of confidences is inappropriate. Wilson P. Abraham Construction Corp. v. Armco Steel Corp., 559 F.2d 250, 253 (5th Cir.1977). Mr. Sprung should not be disqualified unless he has learned from Mr. Wegmann information the plaintiff had intended not be disclosed to the defendants. See id.

---

7. It is very likely that Mr. Wegmann will be a witness in this case. He handled the registrations for the service marks which are the subject of this suit. Moreover, he prepared and notarized two affidavits that were executed at the time the registrations were issued. Defendants rely on these affidavits in support of their claim of ownership of the marks. The circumstances of their execution and the facts to which these affidavits purport to attest will undoubtedly be a subject of dispute at trial and Mr. Wegmann's knowledge may be relevant. If he represented all the family corporations at the time, however, none of his knowledge is privileged and his testimony could freely be sought by either side.

Loyalty and Successive Representation

Identify the two matters in *Brennan's*. Were the elements of a successive conflict satisfied: a former client? material adversity of interest? the same or a substantially related matter? absence of consent of the former client? If these elements are met, why does the court consider other issues?

One can agree with the holding in *Brennan's* without agreeing with the court's articulation of reasons. Isn't the explanation in part II that the duty of confidentiality is broader than the attorney-client privilege inconsistent with the holding of part III that Sprung need not be disqualified if both parties were joint clients in the 1973 trademark registration matter? Are successive conflicts of interest based solely on the protection of confidential client information or do they also involve a loyalty aspect? See the discussion of the duty of loyalty below. How would *Brennan's* be decided under Model Rule 1.9?

A few cases recognize a distinction between primary and secondary clients, and hold that when a joint representation terminates, the lawyer may continue representing the primary client against the secondary one. The genesis of the "primary client" analysis is Allegaert v. Perot.[69] In *Allegaert*, the court said "before the substantial relationship test is even implicated, it must be shown that the attorney was in a position where he could have received information which his former client might reasonably have assumed the attorney would withhold from his present client."[70] The court held that because the moving party "necessarily knew that information given to [the law firm] would certainly be conveyed to [its] primary clients ..., the substantial relationship test is inapposite," and the law firm need not now be disqualified.[71]

While the language of *Allegaert* would seem to contradict *Brennan's*, its facts suggest an important distinction. In *Allegaert* the law firm representing Perot had represented him for some time. Perot and Walston entered into an agreement for joint operation of a business. The firm represented both Walston and Perot's interests in a substantially related matter affecting that business—a stockholder derivative action which involved challenges to the business. Thereafter, Walston went into bankruptcy and its trustee in bankruptcy asserted a claim against Perot. With the exception of the stockholder derivative suit, Walston was independently represented. The trustee in bankruptcy for Walston moved to disqualify the firm because of the firm's prior representation of Walston in the stockholder action.

69. 565 F.2d 246 (2d Cir.1977).

70. Id. at 250.

71. Id.

In refusing to disqualify Perot's counsel, the *Allegaert* court said:

> Integral to our conclusion that [Perot's lawyers] were not in a position to receive information intended to be withheld from [Perot] is the [lawyers'] continuous and unbroken legal relationship with their primary client [Perot]. In contrast with our earlier cases, the attorneys sought to be disqualified here have not changed sides from a former client to a current, adverse client.[72]

Allegaert and *Brennan's* are similar in that the former representation was not one in which client communications were protected from disclosure to the other party. Joint clients were involved in *Brennan's* and cooperating litigants sharing pooled information in *Allegaert*. In neither case did the party moving to disqualify the common lawyer have a reasonable expectation that information provided by that party would be withheld from the other party. The two cases are different, however, with respect to the duty of loyalty. In *Brennan's* the lawyer had an intimate professional relationship with each branch of the family prior to their breakup. In *Allegaert*, however, Walston knew that counsel's primary loyalty was to Perot. Indeed, in defending the stockholder suit (the prior "matter") Walston was essentially a free rider on the Perot representation.[73] Cf. M.R. 2.2.

Conventional doctrine is that a lawyer owes "equal" loyalty to every client. Does the notion of a "primary client" contradict this proposition? Compare the Comment to M.R. 2.2 which says that "intermediation is improper when ... impartiality cannot be maintained. For example, a lawyer who has represented one of the clients for a long period and in a variety of matters might have difficulty being impartial between that client and one to whom the lawyer has only recently been introduced."

Whatever the problems with the primary client theory, some courts rely on *Allegaert* for the proposition that there is no expectation of confidentiality between joint clients and hence no basis for subsequent disqualification of a lawyer representing one client against the other in a related transaction. For example, in American Special Risk Insurance Co. v. Delta America Re Insurance Co.,[74] the district court, citing *Allegaert*, said:

> This Circuit has held, however, that the substantial relationship test is inapplicable where a law firm's alleged disqualification arises out of simultaneous representation of two clients if each

---

72. Id. at 251.

73. See also C.A.M. v. E.B. Marks Music, Inc., 558 F.Supp. 57, 59 (S.D.N.Y.1983) (motion to disqualify denied where the prior representation had been joint and, as in *Allegaert*, "the attorneys ... had a long-standing relationship with a primary client and briefly represented both parties when their interests apparently coincided.... [T]he later representation of the primary client against the interests of the former joint client could not cause the disclosure of any secrets—there was no expectation that information would be concealed from the primary client."). See also Anderson v. Pryor, 537 F.Supp. 890, 895 (W.D.Mo.1982).

74. 634 F.Supp. 112, 121 (S.D.N.Y.1986).

client was aware of the other's relationship to the firm and had no reason to believe that confidences of one party would be withheld from the other.[75]

"Sophisticated Clients" Beware

Another factor noted by the *Allegaert* court was the sophistication of the parties involved: "[T]he parties were not only aware of their mutual relationship, but also were as sophisticated, perhaps, as the American corporate community can be." [76] Should the former client's sophistication be considered? Would the *Brennan's* court have given weight to that factor?

Duty of Loyalty to a Former Client

Brennan's recognizes two underlying concerns of the substantial relationship test: the duty to preserve confidences and the duty of loyalty to a former client. Lawyer Sprung is treated differently from Lawyer Wegmann because he has no duty of loyalty to clients whom he never represented.

Nevertheless, some courts seem to reduce the substantial relationship test to one designed solely to protect the former client's confidences. The opinion in Analytica v. NPD Research,[77] for example, stated that two matters are considered to be substantially related "if the lawyer could have obtained confidential information in the first representation that would be relevant to the second." But other courts still recognize a duty of loyalty apart from the duty of confidentiality in two types of cases: when the lawyer switches sides (attacking the former client) or launches an attack on the lawyer's own prior work ("fouling one's nest").

The standard stated in *Analytica*, supra, would seem to apply whether or not the matters are substantially related and hence could be read as *broader* than the "substantial relationship" test. That is, if the question is as *Analytica* states it, namely whether the lawyer "*could have*" obtained confidential information relevant to the second matter, does not that possibility exist no matter what the first matter involved? At the same time, the *Analytica* standard seems to require greater risk that confidences will be disclosed to prove that they might be used against the client. The Seventh Circuit cases are notable for this inversion of the substantial relationship test.[78]

75. 634 F.Supp. at 121. See also Christensen v. FSLIC, 844 F.2d 694, 698 (9th Cir.1988) (collecting cases); Kempner v. Oppenheimer & Co., Inc., 662 F.Supp. 1271, 1277 (S.D.N.Y.1987) (collecting cases). But see Anchor Packing Co. v. Pro–Seal, 688 F.Supp. 1215, 1217 (E.D.Mich.1988) (disapproving of this line of cases and adopting *Brennan's* approach); and United States Co. v. Moscony, 697 F.Supp. 888, 891 (E.D.Pa.1988) (*Brennan's* approach is appropriate in criminal cases especially when parties are not sophisticated).

76. 565 F.2d at 251.

77. 708 F.2d 1263, 1266 (7th Cir.1983).

78. For another example, see LaSalle Nat'l Bank v. County of Lake, 703 F.2d 252 (7th Cir.1983).

The underlying reason for reducing the successive conflict question to one of protecting confidences may be the courts' growing impatience with disqualification motions used for tactical purposes. This impatience also has led to more frequent use of sanctions for frivolous motions to disqualify.[79]

A still deeper problem is that the courts are not of one mind on whether to demand relatively strict loyalty to a former client, at the cost of requiring one or both parties to get new lawyers if they have a falling out, or to avoid that cost through a more relaxed standard of loyalty. M.R. 2.2 is clear that, if intermediation fails, "the lawyer shall not continue to represent any of the clients in the matter that was the subject of the intermediation." One of the risks of joint representation is inability to represent either joint client if there is a falling-out between them.

Competition as an Adverse Interest

Suppose a lawyer has worked in the past for a software manufacturer on intellectual property problems. She is now asked to perform similar work for another software manufacturer, an economic competitor. The former client is not a party to the second matter, but the representation involves many of the same skills and legal principles. Is the lawyer barred from undertaking the representation? M.R. 1.9 does not deal with the issue directly, but the Comment of M.R. 1.7, in discussing adversity of interest, states: "representation in unrelated matters of clients whose interests are only generally adverse, such as competing economic enterprises, does not require consent of the respective clients."

In Maritrans GP Inc. v. Pepper, Hamilton & Scheetz,[80] a law firm dropped one client, a large maritime operator, and undertook representation of a number of its major competitors. Although Maritrans had consented to joint representation of a few minor competitors, provided effective screening was put in place, it sought an injunction and damages against the firm when the firm discharged Maritrans and undertook a broader representation of its major competitors. The trial court found that the firm, in handling Maritrans' labor work, became "intimately familiar with Maritrans' operations" and "gained detailed financial information, including Maritrans' financial goals and projections, labor cost savings, crew costs, and operating costs." An injunction was granted and the case remanded for consideration of damages even though Pennsylvania's version of the Model Rules permits screening in this situation. A lawyer's duty under common-law fiduciary principles to protect client confidences, the court held, is not displaced by the ethics rule provision:

79. See, for example, Optyl Eyewear Fashion Int'l Corp. v. Style Companies, Ltd., 760 F.2d 1045 (9th Cir.1985), where the court imposed sanctions against the lawyer after finding that the disqualification motion was brought in bad faith. In *Analytica* the Seventh Circuit imposed sanctions for frivolously resisting a motion to disqualify.

80. 529 Pa. 241, 602 A.2d 1277 (1992).

[W]hether a law firm can later represent competitors of its former client is a matter that must be decided from case to case and depends on a number of factors. One factor is the extent to which the fiduciary was involved in its client's affairs.... We do *not* wish to establish a blanket rule that a law firm may not later represent the economic competitor of a former client in matters in which the former client is not also a party to a suit. But situations may well exist when the danger of revelation of the confidences of a former client is so great that injunctive relief is warranted.... There is a substantial relationship here between [the law firm's] former representation of Maritrans and their current representation of Maritrans' competitors such that the injunctive relief here was justified.[81]

Will Maritrans' damage recovery from Pepper, Hamilton, include all fees paid since the conflict arose?

E. IMPUTED CONFLICTS

1. Rules and Problems

DR 5–105(D) of the Model Code provides that if any lawyer in a firm is disqualified from representing a client or being involved in a case, all the lawyers in the firm are disqualified. This rule proceeds on the legal fiction that those who practice together are "one lawyer." No matter how large the firm or how far away the offices, no matter how tangential the first lawyer's involvement, DR 5–105 specifies that if one lawyer is out, the firm is out. See, for example, the *Westinghouse* case printed above at p. 627. The broad sweep of the Code's imputed disqualification rule led courts to create limited exceptions.

What is the rationale for the imputation rule? First, lawyers who practice together talk to one another about their cases, and in doing so share client confidences. This collegial interchange is one of the benefits and enjoyments of group practice. To protect confidences from being revealed or used in an improper manner, all lawyers who have had access to them are disqualified. The rule carries this possibility further, and presumes that confidences have been shared. Second, lawyers who practice together share professional and financial interests and are concerned with furthering each other's interest. Where a lawyer's interests suggest that her loyalty to a client will be impaired, her colleagues' loyalty can be similarly affected. Third, whether or not the first and second dangers are real in a particular case, their specter could cause clients and the public to lose confidence in the system of legal representation were the firm of a disqualified lawyer allowed to proceed.

The merit of the Code approach is that it is simple and easily applied. But its problems are apparent in a world in which lawyers

---

81. 602 A.2d 1286–87.

move with increasing frequency from firm to firm. A strict operation of the rule in this world creates what more than one commentator has called legal "Typhoid Marys." Consider the following problems:

Mr. Gulliver is with First & First. Ms. First, a partner in the firm, represented Sewer Corp. in its suit against Bland Construction. Motor Corp. comes to the First firm wanting to sue Sewer in a substantially related matter. The firm must turn down the case: Ms. First is disqualified so everyone in the firm is disqualified, including Mr. Gulliver who never worked on the Sewer trial.

Now Gulliver leaves First. He joins Second & Second, but when Motor was turned down by First, it went to the Second firm which is now representing it against Sewer. Is the disqualification imputed to Gulliver when he was at First to be imputed to all the lawyers at Second? Must Second now drop the Motor case?

The first question to be answered in this problem is whether Gulliver remains disqualified after leaving First. The applicable rule is that a lawyer may not be involved in suing a former client in a substantially related matter. But is that rule engaged in this situation? Was Sewer Gulliver's client? The Model Code did not address this question.

The original conflicts provisions in the Model Rules and the provisions as amended in 1989 are somewhat ambiguous on whether and under what circumstances Gulliver would remain personally disqualified when he moved to the Second firm. Under M.R. 1.9(a), Gulliver would be disqualified from opposing Sewer in the same or a substantially related matter if Sewer can be considered Gulliver's former client. But is Sewer to be considered to have been Gulliver's client? At one extreme, M.R. 1.9(b), as amended, [M.R. 1.10(b) as originally adopted] [1] makes it clear that Sewer would be considered Gulliver's former client if Gulliver had "acquired information material to the matter" when at First. In this situation neither Gulliver nor any other lawyer at Second could proceed against Sewer in this matter; Second would have to drop the Motor case. But what if Gulliver while at First had learned no material confidences about Sewer or for that matter no confidences at all?

One reading of the Model Rules is that Gulliver is not considered as having represented Sewer at all or in a substantially related matter if no material confidences were learned. Another reading, however, is suggested by the original Comment to M.R. 1.10, now included in the Comment to M.R. 1.9. The Comment discusses the lawyer's duty of

---

1. In 1989, the ABA House of Delegates amended the conflicts provisions of the Model Rules. In effect, the amendments moved old M.R. 1.10(b) to new M.R. 1.9(b); made old M.R. 1.9(b) into new M.R. 1.9(c); and made old M.R. 1.10(c) into new M.R. 1.10(b). Because many states based their rule sections on the original numbering, we will indicate the original Model Rule section in brackets after the Model Rule section number as amended. Thus, new M.R. 1.9(b), will be referred to as M.R. 1.9(b) [1.10(b)]. The corresponding sections are not identical, but they are close enough that the analysis presented here is the same under either version of the Model Rules.

loyalty to the client (her obligation to avoid adverse representation in a related matter) separately from the duty to preserve confidences. It explains that this loyalty interest, while not requiring the new firm's disqualification, may nonetheless require that the individual lawyer refrain from opposing a former client even in cases where 1.9(b) [1.10(b)] would allow the firm to proceed, i.e., in cases where the lawyer had not actually acquired material confidences. Does this mean Gulliver is disqualified no matter how insignificant his involvement with the Sewer matter was while at First? According to the Comment to M.R. 1.9 [Comment to 1.10] the answer is no. The Comment specifically states that when the lawyer has acquired "no knowledge of information relating to a particular client of the firm" then that lawyer is not personally disqualified. The best reading of these provisions, then, is that Gulliver may be disqualified in some instances when Second is not, i.e., when he has been involved enough in the case to have been considered Sewer's lawyer but not enough to have learned any material confidences that he could pass on to Second. On the other hand, Gulliver may have had no contact or such insignificant contact with the Sewer matter while at First that he may work on the very same matter on behalf of Motor. The size of First and Gulliver's position at First would be two important factors in determining whether to allow him to proceed. Other factors are discussed in the *Nemours* case printed below.

This resolution is in accordance with the case law. In Silver Chrysler Plymouth, Inc. v. Chrysler Motors Corp.,[2] the tainted lawyer had been an associate while at the first firm. The court, evaluating the level of work by the associate, concluded that there was little or no possibility that the associate would have been privy to client confidences.[3]

M.R. 1.10(b) [1.10(c)] is exemplified by the next problem. While Gulliver was at First, he defended Landlord in a suit brought by a tenant, charging that the building was unsafe. After Gulliver leaves First, the city housing department asks First to represent it in a suit against Landlord for violating the housing code, which provides for civil penalties. Can First take the suit now that Gulliver is gone?

While Gulliver was at First, the firm would have had to turn down the suit whether or not Gulliver had ever talked about the case to any of the lawyers at First, M.R. 1.10(a). However, after Gulliver has gone, whether First remains disqualified is decided under M.R. 1.10(b) [1.10(c)]. Under these provisions, First can take the case, even though it is substantially related to a case in which Gulliver represented the

2. 518 F.2d 751 (2d Cir.1975).

3. A similar holding is Gas–A–Tron of Arizona v. Union Oil Co. of California, 534 F.2d 1322 (9th Cir.1976). See also Freeman v. Chicago Musical Instrument, 689 F.2d 715, 722 (7th Cir.1982) (factors to be considered include the size of the firm, lawyer's area of specialization and the lawyer's position in the firm).

other side, if none of the lawyers still with the firm has acquired confidential information about Landlord from Gulliver.[4]

2. Imputed Disqualification and Migratory Lawyers

NEMOURS FOUNDATION v. GILBANE, AETNA FEDERAL INS. CO.

United States District Court, District of Delaware, 1986.
632 F.Supp. 418.

FARNAN, DISTRICT JUDGE.

At this late juncture in a long and complicated proceeding the plaintiff, The Nemours Foundation ("Nemours"), has filed a motion to disqualify counsel for the defendant in this case, Pierce Associates, Inc. ("Pierce").... In Nemours' motion to disqualify, filed on October 4, 1985, Nemours requests the disqualification of the entire firm of Biggs & Battaglia ("Biggs"), Pierce's local Wilmington counsel, from further representation of their client. Nemours alleges that Biggs has a conflict of interest due to the former involvement of one of its present associates in this litigation as a former associate of Howard M. Berg & Associates ("Berg"), counsel for Furlow [a co-party of Nemours'] and co-counsel for Nemours at the time. [The litigation concerned a dispute arising out of construction of an addition to a hospital. Nemours was the architectural firm, Gilbane the general contractor, Pierce a subcontractor of Gilbane, and Furlow was the firm responsible for mechanical engineering. Furlow and Nemours were aligned in interest in the litigation against Pierce.]

BACKGROUND

Much of the factual background is not in dispute. Paul A. Bradley, the attorney whose former representation of Furlow has raised the issue of disqualification in this case, was admitted to the practice of law in February 1983 while he was employed at Berg. He began his employment there on September 7, 1982. Bradley became involved in the litigation in April 1984, when he assisted Howard M. Berg, who "made all decisions regarding the representation of Furlow." Bradley's responsibilities as a low-level associate involved preparing for a "mini-trial" among the parties in efforts to reach a settlement agreement. Bradley prepared the materials for a set of books to be distributed to the party participants and the arbitrator. Most of his consultation with experts concerned these materials. Bradley also reviewed documents for Berg's client, Furlow, which included documents produced by Nemours, the party moving for the disqualification of Biggs in this case. Bradley further attested in his affidavit submitted to the Court that, having reviewed thousands of documents, he presently (November 1, 1985) has no recollection of the content or existence of any documents

---

4. See Novo Terapeutisk Laboratorium A/S v. Baxter Travenol Laboratories, 607 F.2d 186 (7th Cir.1979).

that potentially were covered either by the work product doctrine or attorney-client privilege. To the best of his knowledge, Bradley's involvement in the Furlow case terminated after the end of the mini-trial.[3]

Bradley subsequently did not follow the litigation, review any discovery materials, or attend depositions concerning Furlow. He stated that he had no way to determine if any conversation he had while representing Furlow or any document involved in that case has been disclosed beyond the purview of the attorney-client privilege or work product doctrine. When he interviewed for a position with Biggs, he did not know of its involvement in the present litigation and had no conversation with anyone concerning his work for Furlow before being hired.[4]

It is apparent that Biggs was completely innocent of any knowledge of Bradley's involvement in the litigation, as was Bradley of Biggs' until Bradley met Jack Rephan, an attorney for Braude, Margulies, Sacks & Rephan ("Braude, Margulies"), Pierce's main counsel, when Rephan visited Biggs' offices approximately in May 1985. Bradley and his superiors at Biggs immediately decided that Bradley would have no contact with the Pierce litigation whatsoever and would not discuss it. Bradley himself resolved that he would not discuss the litigation or prior representation of Furlow "in any way with anyone" at Biggs. He further attested that he has never been asked by anyone at Biggs or Braude, Margulies concerning his Furlow representation. He does not [know] nor ... has [he ever] known the location of the Pierce files at Biggs.

Victor Battaglia described his firm's procedure of "screening" Bradley from the litigation. All attorneys in the Pierce litigation must report to him. Biggs has a central file room, but since the actions of the litigation were consolidated, and long before Bradley was hired, all Pierce files have been kept directly adjacent to Robert Beste's offices. Furthermore, the only documents in the file are pleadings and other documents filed and of record with the Court, and previous drafts of filed documents.

3. Bradley stated that to the best of his knowledge he did not meet with Nemours' attorneys or their clients at any time after the mini-trial. He did attend a brief meeting to discuss settlement, but no attorneys from Nemours, Pierce, or other clients were present. Finally, he did some research on the proper form of Release and Stipulation of Dismissal to be filed with the Court.

4. Since then, Bradley's contacts with anyone involved in the litigation were limited to the following. He became aware that Biggs represented Pierce when he met Jack Rephan, of Braude, Margulies, Sacks & Rephan, at Biggs' offices, probably in May 1985. He merely greeted him and helped him carry several sealed boxes to an elevator; they did not discuss the litigation. On the same day, Victor F. Battaglia and Robert Beste, attorneys at Biggs, also became aware of Bradley's prior involvement. They briefly discussed only the fact of his representation of Furlow. All agreed, and Bradley was so advised, that he should not discuss the litigation with anyone. Finally, he walked a Pierce employee to a federal grand jury hearing after gaining permission from Victor Battaglia. To the best of his knowledge, the hearing had nothing to do with the Nemours and Pierce litigation.

ANALYSIS

On this motion for disqualification of Biggs, this Court is faced with two major issues. The first question is whether Bradley's previous involvement on behalf of Furlow in this litigation calls for his disqualification. Pierce argues that an attorney-client relationship never existed between Bradley and Nemours and contends therefore that there is no conflict of interest. The Court must address this issue first to determine the extent of Bradley's own involvement in the litigation, a necessary step in addressing the second issue. The essential discordance between Nemours' and Pierce's positions centers on whether this involvement of Bradley, now associated with Biggs, requires the disqualification of the entire firm of Biggs, as Nemours argues it should. Biggs contends that it has effectively "screened off" Bradley from any involvement or contacts with the Nemours litigation. This defense has been commonly termed the "Chinese Wall" * defense. In ruling on this motion, the Court has coined the term "cone of silence" as a more accurate description of the ethical commands involved and the policies at stake.

. . .

A. Disqualification of Bradley

Nemours alleges that the conflict of interest originates with Bradley, thus leading ultimately to the disqualification of Bradley and his firm. Bradley, as an associate at Berg, worked on the current litigation as counsel for Furlow. At that time, Furlow was a co-defendant of Nemours. As counsel for Furlow, Bradley was privy to confidences of both Furlow and Nemours as both planned "strategy sessions" in concert against Gilbane. This "commonality of interest" necessitated a sharing of work product, attorney-client privileges, and other confidential information. . . . After intense negotiations, Gilbane, Furlow, and Nemours entered a series of agreements to settle or to dismiss claims. During this entire period, according to Nemours, the interests of Pierce—whose counsel is Biggs, Bradley's new employer—were adverse to those of Furlow. Applying the Rules to this set of facts, specifically Rule 1.6 on confidentiality, Bradley is disqualified because the information he gained from Nemours was confidential information which must be protected, because Nemours must be considered a "client" of Bradley. Under Rule 1.9, Bradley cannot represent a client whose interests are "materially adverse" to the interest of the former client.

Pierce argues that Nemours cannot be considered a former client of Bradley for purposes of Rules 1.6 and 1.9. Nemours was merely a co-party of Furlow. The presumption that confidential information has passed to an attorney, which arises in the context of the attorney-client relationship, therefore does not apply. Nemours must prove that

---

* Editor's note: The term "Chinese Wall" can be interpreted as having an ethnic connotation, notwithstanding that it refers to an architectural phenomenon. References to "walls" may be avoided by referring to the issue as one of "screening."

confidential information actually did pass from Nemours to Bradley, which it has been unable to do. (D.I. 730 at 15.)

Analysis must begin with the Rules. Rule 1.9, which deals with conflict of interest, reads as follows: [The court then quoted M.R. 1.9 as it was in 1986, which is substantially identical to present M.R. 1.9(a) and (c)(1).]

Several requirements arise from this provision. First, the lawyer must have had an attorney-client relationship with the former client. Second, the present client's matter must either be the same as the matter the lawyer worked on for the first client, or a "substantially related" matter. Third, the interests of the second client must be materially adverse to the interests of the former client. Fourth, the former client must not have consented to the representation after consultation. The second part of the provision lists the conditions on the use of the information relating to representation of the former client.

Rule 1.7, which Rule 1.9 references, provides guidance for determining when the interests of two clients are adverse: [The court quoted M.R. 1.7 at this point.]

This provision applies to both simultaneous representation of two clients, or successive representation, where the attorney-client relationship has been formally terminated, which characterizes the case at hand. The duty involved is one of loyalty to the client.

[The court then discussed Third Circuit and other decisions under the Canons and Model Code dealing with conflict of interest.]

Resolving the question of whether to disqualify counsel cannot be accomplished through mechanical means, but requires a careful balancing of the goals and objectives of professional conduct. "The chosen mode of analysis is to carefully sift 'all the facts and circumstances'." *Pennwalt Corp. v. Plough, Inc.*, 85 F.R.D. 264, 269 (D.Del.1980); *Akerly v. Red Barn System, Inc.*, 551 F.2d 539, 543 (3d Cir.1977). The Third Circuit has long refused to adopt a per se rule in questions of disqualification. *Akerly*, 551 F.2d at 543.

There is no doubt that Nemours must be considered a former "client" of Bradley for the purpose of determining whether a conflict of interest exists. Bradley himself stated that he reviewed confidential documents of Nemours when he represented Furlow in the litigation. Although there was no express attorney-client relationship, a fiduciary obligation, or "implied professional relation" existed nevertheless because Nemours disclosed information acting on the belief and expectation that such submission was made in order for Berg to render legal service to Nemours in furtherance of Nemours' interests. *Westinghouse Elec. Corp. v. Kerr–McGee Corp.*, 580 F.2d 1311, 1319–20 (7th

Cir.1978).[7]

Regarding the second requirement, under the old Code the Third Circuit adopted the "substantial relationship" test, now formally incorporated into the Rules, in determining when an attorney is prohibited from accepting a subsequent representation. Disqualification of counsel is required "where it appears that the subject matter of a pending suit in which the attorney represents an interest adverse to a prior employer is such that during the course of the former representation the attorney 'might have acquired substantially related material.' " . . .

There is no doubt that the Pierce litigation in which the Biggs' firm is involved is substantially related to the matter in which Bradley was involved when he was representing Furlow; indeed, the matter is one and the same.

The third requirement of Rule 1.9 is also met: Pierce's interests are adverse to Nemours'. Finally, Nemours, the "former client," now moving for disqualification of Biggs, certainly has not consented to the continued representation of Pierce. Bradley is thus clearly disqualified from representing Pierce in this litigation.

B. Disqualification of Biggs & Battaglia

The next issue is whether the entire law firm of Biggs must be disqualified, given the disqualification of one of its associates. Pierce argues that an effective screening mechanism is an acceptable alternative to disqualification of an entire law firm when one of its associates formerly represented a client whose interests are "substantially related," and adverse, to those of a present client of the law firm.

An attorneys' disqualification is normally "imputed" to the other attorneys in his law firm. [The court quoted M.R. 1.10(a) and (b), which are substantially the same as current M.R. 1.10(a) and 1.9(b).]

There is now an explicit exception to imputed disqualification. The Rules, unlike the Code, sanction the use of a screening mechanism in appropriate circumstances, specifically referring to former government attorneys. Rule 1.11 states: "A firm with which that lawyer is associated may undertake or continue representation in the matter only if the disqualified lawyer is screened from any participation in the matter and is apportioned no part of the fee therefrom." Rule 1.11(b). The policy supporting this rule is to enable the government to attract qualified lawyers and to prevent the disqualification rule from imposing too severe a deterrent against entering public service. Comment to Rule 1.11.

7. There is no doubt that as far as Bradley's formal client, Furlow, was concerned, the confidences relayed to him from Furlow's co-party, Nemours, were "confidential" within this primary attorney-client relationship.

. . . Rule 1.6 which deals with confidentiality . . . "applies not merely to matters communicated in confidence by the client but also to all information relating to the representation, whatever its source." Such a source would certainly include a co-party such as Nemours.

The Comment to Rule 1.10 indicates the firm intention of its draftsmen that a pragmatic approach is necessary to the question of vicarious disqualification. The Comment also extends the analysis of Rule 1.10 to disqualified lawyers in law firms generally, not only former government attorneys. In the section "Lawyers Moving Between Firms," the authors of the Rules adopt a "functional analysis" in determining questions of vicarious disqualification. The rigid formalism underlying Canon 9's injunction against an "appearance of impropriety" is strongly rejected in favor of a new philosophy of pragmatism which balances the expectations of confidentiality of a former client against the importance of allowing a client the representation of his choice and promoting the mobility of attorneys, particularly associates, from one private law firm to another. The language of the Comment merits extensive quotation:

Functional Analysis ↓

[The court then quoted the comments to current M.R.1.9(b) (formerly 1.10(b)), which appear under the heading "Lawyers Moving Between Forms." The student should read these paragraphs at this time.]

. . .

... In INA Underwriters Insurance Co. v. Rubin, 635 F.Supp. 1 (E.D.Pa.1983), the "Chinese Wall" defense was raised against a motion to disqualify a law firm. In that case, a client contacted a partner of the law firm Wolf, Block & Schorr ("Wolf, Block"). The client confided certain confidential information to the partner, but the partner subsequently refused to represent the client because he found that a conflict of interest existed. The court refused to apply an irrebuttable presumption that confidences were shared by the partners of Wolf, Block, and to impute the disqualification firm-wide. Id. at 3. There was no question that the partner who had met with the client was disqualified. The court approved of the screening of secret documents and firm members possessing knowledge of secrets and confidences in order to avoid disqualification of an entire firm. Id. at 4. The partner had never discussed the substantive content of his meeting with the client with any of the attorneys inside or outside the Wolf, Block firm. Id. at 5. A refusal to disqualify Wolf, Block in this case would not only maintain public confidence and integrity of the legal system, but also promote the policies of respecting a litigant's right to retain counsel of its choice and of enabling attorneys to practice without excessive restrictions. Id. at 5–6.

Case Law

Before the adoption of the Rules, case law in other circuits[8] and

8. See Fred Weber, Inc. v. Shell Oil Co., 566 F.2d 602, 609 (8th Cir.1977) (holding that every representation against a former client's co-defendant in a related matter raises an appearance of impropriety would unnecessarily restrict choice of counsel available to litigants); Woods v. Covington County Bank, 537 F.2d 804, 813 n. 12 (5th Cir.1976) (test is whether likelihood of public suspicion or obloquy outweighs social interests served by lawyer's continued participation in a particular case); Silver Chrysler Plymouth, Inc. v. Chrysler Motors Corp., 518 F.2d 751, 757 (2d Cir.1975) (underscoring importance of public's right to counsel of its choice and economic mobility).

scholarly commentary[9] had already adopted a liberalized approach based on a functional analysis. In the Second Circuit, where this approach has received its most extensive development, the test is whether the conduct of the disqualified attorney taints the underlying trial. Armstrong v. McAlpin, 625 F.2d 433, 444 (2d Cir.1980) (en banc), vacated on other grounds and remanded, 449 U.S. 1106 (1981). Disqualification if based solely on the appearance of impropriety cannot be justified as long as a firm's representation does not pose a threat to the integrity of the trial process. Id. As the court in *McAlpin* stated:

> We recognize that a rule that concentrates on the threat of taint fails to correct all possible ethical conflicts.... However, absent a threat of taint to the trial, we continue to believe that possible ethical conflicts surfacing during a litigation are generally better addressed by the "comprehensive disciplinary machinery" of the state and federal bar [citation omitted] or possibly by legislation.

Id. at 445–46; Board of Education of New York City v. Nyquist, 590 F.2d 1241, 1246 (2d Cir.1979). A court should only reluctantly order disqualification because of the immediate adverse effect on the client of separating him from counsel of his choice. *Nyquist*, 590 F.2d at 1246. Such motions for disqualification are often made for tactical reasons, and even when made in the best of faith, inevitably cause delay.

Several circuits have extended this functional analysis to create a rebuttable presumption of shared confidences among attorneys in a law firm in order to avoid vicarious disqualification....

The factual circumstances of Lemaire v. Texaco, Inc., 496 F.Supp. 1308 (E.D.Tex.1980), closely resemble those of the case at bar. In that case, an attorney switched law firms after having represented one party in a lawsuit to the limited extent of filing initial pleadings. His new law firm represented the opposite side in the *same* litigation. The screening was established immediately, even before the attorney accepted the position with the new firm. The attorney went to great lengths to insure that he would have no connection with any facet of the lawsuit. He also made certain he would receive no part of any attorneys' fees collected in the case or share in its expenses.[10]

The lawsuit was complex and very expensive to prepare. There was no other law firm in the area qualified or willing to take on the litigation. Id. at 1309. The court found that any appearance of impropriety was greatly outweighed by the plaintiffs' right to have counsel of their choice. Id. at 1310.

9. See Liebman, The Changing Law of Disqualification: The Role of Presumption and Policy, 73 Nw.U.L.Rev. 996 (1979); Lindgren, Toward a New Standard of Attorney Disqualification, 1982 A.B.A. Found.Research J. 419 (1982); Comment, The Ethics of Moving to Disqualify Opposing Counsel for Conflict of Interest, 1979 Duke L.J. 1310 (1979); Note, The Chinese Wall Defense to Law–Firm Disqualification, 128 U.Pa.L.Rev. 677 (1980); Note, A Dilemma in Professional Responsibility: The Subsequent Representation Problem, 50 UMKC L.Rev. 165 (1982).

10. See Rule 1.11(b).

There is no substantial reason against extending the exception to vicarious disqualification from the case of a former government attorney to private attorneys generally although the complex of policy factors differs somewhat in the two situations:

> Once it is admitted that a Chinese Wall can rebut the presumption of imputed knowledge in former government attorney cases, it becomes difficult to insist that the presumption is irrebuttable when the disqualified attorney's previous employment was private and not public. To hold fast to such a proposition would logically require a belief that privately employed attorneys are inherently incapable of being effectively screened, as though they were less trustworthy or more voluble than their ex-Government counterparts. If former government attorneys can be screened effectively, it follows that former private attorneys can be too.

INA Underwriters Insurance Co. v. Rubin, 635 F.Supp. at 5 (quoting Note, The Chinese Wall Defense To Law–Firm Disqualification, 128 U.Pa.L.Rev. 677, 701 (1980)).

The Court holds that an appropriate screening mechanism, in the proper circumstances, may rebut the presumption of shared confidences that arises under Rule 1.10 in cases where the disqualified attorney's conflict of interest originated in private practice. The Court prefers to refer to this screening procedure figuratively as a "cone of silence" [11] rather than a "Chinese Wall." The conical image, a metaphor adopted from popular television, more appropriately describes the responsibility of the *individual* attorney to guard the secrets of his former client. He is commanded by the ethical rules to seal, or encase, these particular confidences within his own conscience. The term "Chinese Wall" is suggestive of attempts in the context of a large law firm to physically cordon off attorneys possessing information from the other members of the firm who represent clients whose interests are adverse to interests of these attorneys' former clients. See Analytica, Inc. v. NPD Research, Inc., 708 F.2d 1263, 1269 (7th Cir.1983). Such an approach tends to cast a shadow of disrepute on attorneys separated in this manner from their professional colleagues. The implicit assumption is that the wall, if high and thick enough, will resist an errant attorney's lack of discretion, and calm public mistrust through prophylaxis. A firm of more moderate size must therefore erect a wall of greater impenetrability. Instead, the Court believes that the more logically consistent, honest, and straightforward approach is to credit members of the legal profession with a certain level of integrity. This emphasis on the ethical rules themselves, rather than a presumption that they will be circumvented, should more effectively promote public respect for the bar. In effect, the Rules enjoin the attorney to guard his client's secrets in an affirmative and deliberate manner, through self-

---

11. As explained at greater length later in this opinion, in this case, Bradley determined on his own initiative not to speak to anyone concerning the Furlow–Nemours representation. This self-imposed silence began immediately upon his gaining knowledge of the adverse representation at Biggs.

imposed silence. Canon 4 and Rule 1.6, which mandate maintenance of a client's confidences, have an independent significance. *Baglini v. Pullman*, 412 F.Supp. 1060, 1064 n. 11 (E.D.Pa.), aff'd, 547 F.2d 1158 (3d Cir.1976). Moreover, the trend among courts now to rule out an "appearance of impropriety" as the sole basis for disqualification strongly supports this increased emphasis on the ethical rule of confidentiality. *McAlpin*, 625 F.2d at 444; *Silver Chrysler Plymouth*, 518 F.2d at 757.

On the other hand, certain objective circumstances, including the timing and physical characteristics of the screening, will in many cases require disqualification of an entire firm. The evidence of faithfulness to Rule 1.6 is only one factor in a balancing of the policy factors identified above against the likelihood that confidences will be violated. The size of the firm remains an important consideration, as well as the nature of the prior involvement of the tainted attorney and the extensiveness of the screening. The test is one that integrates subjective reliance on the Rules manifested by the attorney's "cone of silence," with objective evidence that the Rules are being followed.

As in *Rubin* and *Lemaire*, Biggs' and Bradley's deliberateness and speed in establishing a "cone of silence" in the instant case similarly help support denial of the motion to disqualify. The circumstances of this case strongly support such a finding. Bradley himself is required by Rule 1.6 to maintain the confidences of his former client. The Court harbors no doubt based on the present affidavits that he thus far has not violated this ethical norm. If he should disclose any information, although he claims that he has no recollection of any substantive confidences, he can be subject to the disciplinary machinery of the state bar. *McAlpin*, 625 F.2d at 446. The Court's primary task at this juncture is to ensure a fair and just trial. Id. at 445–46; *Nyquist*, 590 F.2d at 1246. Following Rule 1.6, Bradley immediately sealed himself in a "cone of silence," resolving not to say anything concerning the substance of any communication, documents, or information to which he may have had access. In addition, Bradley's present lack of access to the information helps to reinforce his fidelity to Rule 1.6. When he changed firms, Bradley did not personally retain any notes or documents with which to refresh his recollection. (Id. at ¶ 6.) Furthermore, the information he reviewed when he was with the Berg firm was primarily non-confidential and his memory of this information is now fading. The importance of the ethical precept against disclosure of client confidences as a prophylactic safeguard in instances where violation of confidences is possible was recognized by the district court in *Baglini v. Pullman*, 412 F.Supp. at 1064 n. 11. See Silver Chrysler Plymouth, Inc. Chrysler Motors Corp., 518 F.2d 751, 757 (2d Cir.1975) (Canon 9 should not override delicate balance created by Canon 4).

Supplementing Bradley's own self-imposed silence, Biggs has established an effective screening mechanism which has been in place ever since Bradley's former involvement was discovered. No information was disclosed to other Biggs attorneys up to that time or since then.

Bradley does not know where the Pierce files are located at Biggs. These files are not contained in Biggs' central filing system but are segregated in separate file cabinets, all adjacent to one partner's office. Only pleadings and correspondence are located in Biggs' offices. Although Biggs would be considered a medium-size firm by Wilmington standards, the limited nature of Bradley's contact with his "former client" and knowledge of the litigation effectively counterbalance this factor.[12]

Another factor indicating that the confidences and secrets of Nemours will remain inviolate is the extent of Bradley's previous involvement in the litigation. Bradley was not the lead counsel in this litigation when he was at Berg. He had only recently joined Berg after becoming a member of the Delaware Bar,[13] and was assigned the duties which typically characterize the life of a young associate in his position. In addition, his involvement was brief, lasting only about four months, and ended approximately eight months before he changed firms. The attorney's degree of prior involvement, whether he controlled strategy, whether he was an associate or partner, and whether he shared legal fees from his firm's representation are all important factors in evaluating the effectiveness of a "cone."[14]

Furthermore, the policies identified in the Comment to Rule 1.10 would be promoted by a decision denying disqualification in this case. As of October 1985, in the entire State of Delaware there were currently 856 attorneys in private practice, 710 of whom practice in New Castle County. Of the 710 attorneys, over 280, or over forty percent, work for only ten Wilmington law firms. Eleven different law firms have been involved directly in this case and eight of these are in the "top ten." Attorney mobility, especially among young associates, would be severely restricted if a per se rule against a "cone of silence" were adopted. The small number of private firms in Wilmington of substantial size, combined with the facts and circumstances of this case, cry out for a flexible approach to vicarious disqualification.

In addition, Pierce would be considerably prejudiced by the disqualification of Biggs at this point in the litigation, shortly before trial is scheduled to begin on March 31, 1986. When Pierce attempted to obtain local counsel in Wilmington, all the major law firms in Wilmington either were already representing parties or believed that a conflict existed. Jack Rephan, attorney for Braude, Margulies, stated that he was not aware of any other office in Delaware of "sufficient abilities or facilities equipped to represent Pierce" in this litigation other than Biggs, after the other firms were found to have a conflict of interest. This large, complex litigation requires a large law office locally located

---

12. As reported by the law firms themselves, as of March 1986, Biggs & Battaglia had 16 attorneys; Richards, Layton & Finger and Morris, Nichols, Arsht & Tunnell, two of Wilmington's largest law firms, had 52 and 43 attorneys, respectively, in Wilmington.

13. Bradley became a member of the Delaware Bar in 1983, having graduated from law school in 1981. 1 Martindale–Hubbell Law Directory 3408B (1985).

14. As an associate, Bradley would receive only his fixed, annual salary.

with sufficient facilities and manpower to adequately represent Pierce's interests. The Court has scheduled three full months for the trial. Moreover, an "excellent working relationship" has developed between Pierce and its local counsel. An abrupt withdrawal by Biggs would substantially prejudice Pierce in this litigation.[19]

In contrast, Nemours fails to adduce any convincing evidence of prejudice to its interests resulting from Biggs' continued representation of Pierce. Nowhere in presenting its argument does Nemours allege the slightest disadvantage or harm. Certainly, the fact that Nemours was only a co-party of Bradley's primary client has some significance. Furthermore, this is not the case of a partner who, as a major strategist, must be quarantined from contact with other members of his firm who are involved in a case from which he is disqualified. This representation of Pierce by Biggs therefore has no tendency to "taint the underlying trial." *McAlpin*, 625 at 444; *Nyquist*, 590 at 1246. This fact, in combination with the harm that would accrue to Pierce should Biggs be required to withdraw, and the other powerful arguments of policy, all support denial of Nemours' motion to disqualify.

In addendum, the Court takes note of a factor weighing against Nemours' motion involving possible delay. Courts have been extremely reluctant to disqualify attorneys when there is a possibility that a motion was made primarily for strategic purposes in a litigation. Even when made in the best of faith, such motions inevitably cause delay. *McAlpin* at 444. It is possible—but by no means proven—that counsel for Nemours knew already in April 1985 that Bradley had joined Biggs.[20] Nemours raised this issue five months later, in September. Shortly before that, Nemours had lost a motion to compel. The total absence of any prejudice to Nemours of Bradley's association with Biggs . . . tends to strengthen the appearance of mere delay and harassment as the overriding motive for the plaintiff's motion to disqualify. Nevertheless, the evidence is not sufficient to show that delay was an intentional element. The other factors standing alone are sufficient to withstand a motion to disqualify.

---

19. Indeed, if Biggs & Battaglia were to be disqualified in the circumstances of this case, it is quite possible that in view of the realignment of the parties which resulted in the disqualification of Bradley, other firms should be disqualified, including counsel for the moving party on this motion.

Gilbane and Pierce were originally aligned together and shared confidential information. Through settlement, Gilbane is now aligned with Nemours. The technical disqualifications resulting from this realignment would rapidly cause this litigation to become unmanageable.

20. In April 1985, notices were sent to all members of the Delaware Bar that Bradley had joined the Biggs firm.

Notes on *Nemours*

Suppose Bradley had not worked on the *Nemours* matter while an associate with the Berg firm. After moving to the Biggs firm, would he be personally disqualified from participating in the case?

Why was Bradley personally disqualified in *Nemours*? Why wasn't the Biggs firm disqualified? Why was it necessary for Bradley to maintain a "cone of silence"? Why did the court substitute this metaphor for "Chinese Wall?"[5] Does the court place too much emphasis on Bradley's personal integrity? Does the "cone" metaphor give insufficient emphasis to the responsibilities of other lawyers in the firm? See M.R. 5.1 and M.R. 5.2

In Atasi Corp. v. Seagate Technology,[6] the court held that neither, in its words, a "Chinese Wall" nor a "cone of silence" could allow the firm to proceed. In the process of so holding the court described the "cone of silence" as a screening method in which "the attorney switching firms, but not the other members of the [new] firm, agrees not to share confidences of prior clients with his new associates." Is this what the *Nemours* court had in mind? Screening is discussed further in subsequent notes.

A novel approach to the reimputation problem was invoked in City of Cleveland v. Cleveland Electric Illuminating Co.[7] The case involved imputed disqualification of a second firm by a "tainted" lawyer who had been vicariously disqualified because one of his former partners had handled a particular matter. The court held that the presumption that the lawyer had access to confidential information about the client should apply only when the lawyer's practice was in the same area of concentration as that of the former partner who handled the case.

The *City of Cleveland* approach dispenses with inquiry into whether the disqualified lawyer has actual knowledge of confidences or not. But it is both too broad and too narrow. It is too broad in that a litigation department in a large firm may be organized in such a way that makes communications between lawyers on different litigation "teams" highly unlikely. It is too narrow in that the corporate department in a firm might have its offices right next to those of the litigators and information on cases might be routinely exchanged in the halls. Furthermore, the managing partner or other senior partners might routinely be apprised of the developments in all cases, whatever department is handling the case.

To avoid the disclosure of confidences during the inquiry into whether the tainted lawyer has knowledge, courts look at such factors

5. See Employers Insurance of Wausau v. Albert D. Seeno Construction Co., 692 F.Supp. 1150, 1165 (N.D.Cal.1988) (using "ethical wall," noting that some find "Chinese Wall" offensive and others confuse it with a flimsy paper structure instead of the Great Wall of China).

6. 847 F.2d 826, 831–832 (Fed.Cir. 1988) (interpreting the law in the Ninth Circuit).

7. 440 F.Supp. 193, 211 (N.D.Ohio 1976), aff'd without opinion, 573 F.2d 1310 (6th Cir.1977).

as: the firm's size, the lawyer's position in the firm (partners are judged more likely than associates to have actual confidences on the cases of others in the firm), the formal and informal patterns of communication among those who work at the firm, the procedures on access to client files, the number of the firm's lawyers involved in the original matter, and the testimony of lawyers, both the lawyers involved in the original case as to whether they discussed it with the tainted lawyer, and the testimony of the tainted lawyer as to whether she has any information about the original matter. Outcomes depend to an important extent on the judge's own prior experience in practice and her sensitivity to "purity" versus "mobility".

Screening [8]

Formal screening, otherwise known as building an "insulation wall" or establishing a "cone of silence," refers to physical and procedural barriers established in a firm to prevent the tainted lawyer from transmitting or receiving information on a particular matter, which that lawyer is disqualified from handling.

The messy reality of life is rarely as straightforward as our logical concepts. Screening was instituted by the Biggs firm in *Nemours* but not until some months after Bradley joined the firm. He also, the court says in note 4, "walked a Pierce employee to a federal grand jury hearing."

In Schiessle v. Stephens,[9] the Seventh Circuit stated that the question to be asked when a tainted lawyer moves to a new firm is: "[W]hether the knowledge of the 'confidences and secrets' of [the client of the first firm] which [the attorney] brought with him has been passed on to or is likely to be passed on to the members of the [second] firm." [10] How is this question different from the question to be asked under the Model Rules? Is the *Schiessle* formulation of the test better than that in the Model Rules?

In Panduit Corp. v. All States Plastic Mfg. Co., Inc.,[11] a patent lawyer who had handled Panduit's foreign patent work later joined a firm that represented a company that Panduit was suing for infringing a related patent. The tainted lawyer worked briefly on the case, observing one deposition, before screening was instituted. Following Seventh Circuit law, see *Schiessle,* supra, the court reversed a disqualification order. The standard is likelihood that confidences have passed, not certainty that this had occurred; and the presumption that confidences have been shared may be rebutted by the testimony of the lawyers involved.

---

8. For general discussion of screening in conflicts cases, see Wolfram, Modern Legal Ethics § 7.6.4 (1986); and Thomas D. Morgan, Screening the Disqualified Lawyer: The Wrong Solution to the Wrong Problem, 10 U. Ark. (Little Rock) L. J. 37 (1987).

9. 717 F.2d 417 (7th Cir.1983).

10. 717 F.2d at 421.

11. 744 F.2d 1564 (Fed. Cir.1984) (applying Seventh Circuit law).

If the Seventh Circuit is right that the question is whether information has been transferred, why not use screening to cure all conflicts within a firm? Isn't the logic of screening to prevent taint as expansive as imputation is to attribute taint? Why couldn't a firm establish "screens" between all matters being worked on by different lawyers in the firm?

Why was screening rejected in *Westinghouse*? See p. 635 above. A 1993 survey indicates that the overwhelming majority of jurisdictions (all but eight) *do not* recognize screening of a tainted lawyer as a cure for imputed disqualification of the entire firm.[12]

Screening has been accepted in cases of lawyers moving between government and private practice, see *Armstrong*, discussed below at p. 729, and M.R. 1.11(a). Where the conflict arises between private clients, the prevailing rule is that screening will not prevent imputed disqualification unless the lawyer joining the firm is disqualified vicariously rather than through personal contact with the former client's representation.[13]

[handwritten margin note: MR 1.11(a) gov't to private]

The difficulties created by the imputation rule have led to much dissatisfaction with it, especially on the part of large law firms. These difficulties are especially significant for young lawyers, who are more likely to move than their older colleagues. A lawyer seeking to move from one firm to another will have to account for all her prior involvements in representation and have those checked against the prospective firm's list of pending clients and matters. This makes it important for young lawyers to keep an accurate record of the matters on which they have worked. It also suggests that young lawyers should keep their noses out of cases being handled by their firms in which they have no direct involvement.

Nemours and a number of other cases depart from the general rule of imputed disqualification. Where do the courts get authority to permit screening in situations in which the ethical rules do not permit it? Courts may more readily permit screening where the opposing party acquiesces or the conflict arose from an unusual or unforeseeable chain of events.[14] Most courts continue the rigorous stance against screening.[15] The proposed Restatement of the Law Governing Lawyers "permits screening as a remedy in appropriate, limited situations in which the personally-prohibited lawyer possesses relevant, but not

---

12. See the table prepared by Attorneys Liability Assurance Society (ALAS) and reprinted in T. Morgan and R. Rotunda, 1993 Selected Standards on Professional Responsibility 138.

13. See, e.g., Schiessle v. Stephens, 717 F.2d 417 (7th Cir.1983); Cheng v. GAF Corp., 631 F.2d 1052 (2d Cir.1980) vac'd, 450 U.S. 903 (1981).

14. See, e.g., Manning v. Waring, Cox, James, Sklar and Allen, 849 F.2d 222 (6th Cir.1988); Cox v. American Cast Iron Pipe Co., 847 F.2d 725 (11th Cir.1988).

15. See, e.g., Atasi Corp. v. Seagate Technology, 847 F.2d 826, 831–832 (Fed.Cir.1988) (interpreting Ninth Circuit law).

significant, confidential information of the former client." [16]   The accompanying illustrations indicate that preparing a legal memorandum on facts stated in pleadings would not give rise to significant, confidential information, but that preparing an expert witness who was to give important testimony in a case would involve such significant information that screening would not cure the problem if the lawyer moves to the firm representing the opposing party.[17]

The versions of M.R. 1.10 adopted in a handful of states also permit screening.[18]   The District of Columbia ethics rules specifically address the problems of law students moving between firms. The rules provide that law students are bound to keep the former client's confidences,[19] but that the new firm is not disqualified.[20]   The D.C. Rules do not explicitly require that the firm implement screening procedures in this situation, but it would seem the prudent course.

Conflicts When Law Firms Merge

The conflicts problems arising when a lawyer moves from one firm to another are compounded when two firms merge. In a merger, all the current clients of each firm become the current clients of the surviving firm under M.R. 1.7, and the former clients of both firms come within the purview of M.R. 1.9. In dealing with law firm mergers, the courts have refused to allow a firm simply to dump one of the clients who will not consent to a conflict and indeed have said that notice to the affected clients should be given when the negotiations reach the stage that merger has "reasonable likelihood." [21]

Conflicts Created by Paralegals and Secretaries Moving Between Firms

In *Kapco Mfg. Co. v. C & O Enterprises, Inc.*,[22] a secretary from one law firm moved to the opponent's law firm. Kapco moved to disqualify C & O's lawyers based on this secretary's move. The court held that the same conflict rules and tests applied when the conflict was created by a non-lawyer changing firms as those that apply when lawyers move. Note that the litigation was ongoing in *Kapco*, so the tainted person would have been disqualified under M.R. 1.7, not 1.9. Little case law deals with the conflicts issues posed by secretaries or paralegals migrating from one law firm to another. According to the court in

16. Restatement of the Law Governing Lawyers § 204(2), comment d, p. 69 (Tent. Draft No. 4, Apr. 10, 1991).

17. Id. at 70–71.

18. For example, Pennsylvania's version of M.R. 1.10 permits screening of lawyers moving between private firms in the same way as M.R. 1.11(a) permits screening of former government lawyers entering private practice.

19. D.C. Rule 1.6(g).

20. D.C. Rule 1.10(b).

21. See, e.g., In re Eastern Sugar Antitrust Litigation, 697 F.2d 524 (3d Cir.1982); Picker International v. Varian Associates, 869 F.2d 578 (Fed.Cir.1989). Also see the discussion of curing simultaneous conflicts in Chapter 7 above.

22. 637 F.Supp. 1231 (N.D.Ill.1985).

Kapco, "the courts in both [prior] cases took the disqualification motions seriously and applied analysis similar to those applied in attorney-transfer cases." [23]

F. GOVERNMENT LAWYERS AND THE REVOLVING DOOR

Introduction

A large and complicated body of law deals with the ethics, including conflicts of interest, of government lawyers.[24] Criminal statutes at the federal and state level are supplemented by agency regulations that duplicate some requirements and impose additional ones. Judicial decisions interpreting and applying these provisions are a third source of law. Finally, the lawyer codes include provisions that treat the lawyer moving in or out of government somewhat differently than other lawyers who change their employment.[25]

What are the opposing concerns that influence the shape of this body of law? The traditional concerns that infuse the law of conflicts of interest applicable to lawyers in the private sector also apply, but with modified force, to the government lawyer. First, confidentiality interests are at stake even though the special characteristics of government legal practice give these interests somewhat different contours. A government agency's confidential information, like that of a private client, must be kept in confidence by the agency's lawyer. Information concerning material prepared in anticipation of litigation (e.g., strategy in litigation, settlement objectives and other work product) is protected client information. Much information possessed by the government, however, is publicly available under laws dealing with public records, open meetings and freedom of information. Moreover, other categories of material possessed by the government are specially protected by law, such as information obtained from private persons by required submission or compulsory process. Thus the tax, health and social security records of individuals, along with grand jury minutes and transcripts, are given special protection by law: It is ordinarily a crime to divulge them unless there is statutory authorization for doing so.

23. 637 F.Supp. at 1236. The two prior cases dealing with secretaries and paralegals who change law firms, both discussed in *Kapco,* are: Williams v. Trans World Airlines, Inc., 588 F.Supp. 1037 (W.D.Mo.1984); and Swanson v. Wabash, Inc., 585 F.Supp. 1094 (N.D.Ill.1984).

24. Most of this law does not deal with lawyers as such but is applicable to government officers and employees, whether acting in a legal or some other capacity. The professional rules, of course, apply only to persons admitted to practice, but extend to activities of a lawyer acting in a non-legal capacity (e.g., as an elected official or a political appointee of the executive branch).

25. For general discussion of conflicts of former government lawyers, see Wolfram, Modern Legal Ethics § 8.10 (1986); Robert H. Mundheim, Conflict of Interest and the Former Government Employer: Rethinking the Revolving Door, 14 Creighton L. Rev. 707 (1981).

Second, a government lawyer must be loyal to her client but loyalty has a somewhat different meaning in this setting. The role of a government lawyer is different from that of an advocate who seeks to win for a client: "[T]he duty of the public prosecutor [is] to seek justice, not merely to convict, and the duty of all government lawyers [is] to seek just results rather than the result desired by a client." [26] Nor does the normal lawyer-client relationship prevail: The "client" is often amorphous and hard to define, whether it be viewed as the employing agency or the executive branch or "we, the people." [27] A government lawyer may shape and define the interests of her amorphous client more than the typical lawyer in private practice. Nevertheless, a government agency is entitled to protection against side-switching because loyalty continues to be a concern and because side-switching may contribute to a public impression that government decision-making is neither fair nor impartial.

Some additional concerns are operative when dealing with governmental ethics. The metaphor of the "revolving door" conveys at least two special concerns. First, a government official may make decisions not in the public interest to advance the official's future career in private life. She may, for example, shape her positions to favor potential private employers or use governmental power to obtain information helpful to future private clients. Some special constraints are appropriate in order to assure the public that government decision-makers exercise public authority for public and not private purposes.

Second, the image of the revolving door suggests undue influence, favoritism and possibly corruption. A lawyer spends a number of years in a government agency acquiring specialized knowledge, skills and experience. They become part of the human capital that makes that person's services more valuable in the private sector. So far, so good.[28] The lawyer also may have acquired inside information, not available to the public or even to other lawyers in the specialty, concerning internal policies and procedures of the agency or leanings on pending matters. She may have personal friendships with agency staff that lead to special treatment in the handling or timing of matters. At the extreme she may have "connections" or "influence" with agency staff who worked for her or with her that shade off into outright corruption. The public is properly concerned with combatting favoritism of this type, which affects the legitimacy of governmental action.

26. ABA Formal Opinion 342, reprinted in 62 A.B.A.J. 517, 521 (1976), discussed below at p. 728.

27. See the discussion of "who is the government lawyer's client" in Chapter 8 at p. 820.

28. ABA Formal Op. 342, 62 A.B.A.J. at 519, n. 21, states: "Many a lawyer who has served with the government has an advantage when he enters private practice because he has acquired a working knowledge of the department in which he was employed, has learned the procedures, the governing substantive and statutory law and is to a greater or lesser degree an expert in the field in which he was engaged. Certainly this is perfectly proper and ethical...."

The dangers of the revolving door must be weighed against the advantages to government and to the public of able lawyers moving in and out of public service. A strong theme of American democracy involves citizen participation in and control of government. The American experience has been hostile to the notion of a permanent civil service that dominates the executive branch. The flux of democratic political change and electoral upheavals is thought best served by private citizens moving in and out of governmental service.

In addition, federal and state governments have become dependent upon recruiting young lawyers some of whom do not plan to make government service a lifetime career. The government benefits by hiring a cadre of able young lawyers who carry out a substantial proportion of the government's total legal work. Not all of them could be promoted to leadership roles within the government legal service. Policies that narrowed prospects of private employment would adversely affect the recruitment and quality of new government lawyers. Such policies would also affect the career mobility of lawyers and diminish the opportunity of clients to obtain counsel of choice, particularly in specialized areas of practice.

1.   Sources of Law on Government Lawyer's Conflicts

Statutes and Regulations

Federal statutes regulating conflicts of interest fall into two categories: (1) restrictions governing activities during federal employment; and (2) restrictions on post-government activities. Examples of the former include: A government employee may not, with limited exceptions, "participate personally or substantially" in any matter in which she or her immediate family or business associates has a financial interest; receive compensation outside of government salary; make or retain certain investments; and receive certain gifts and entertainment.[29] Extensive financial reporting requirements enforce these and other restrictions.

The federal conflict of interest statute, 18 U.S.C. § 207, deals with disqualification of former officers and employees. Knowing violations are punishable by a fine of not more than $10,000 or imprisonment for not more than two years or both. Any effort to summarize the act's complex provisions is a hazardous undertaking, but three separate bases of disqualification "of a former officer or employee of the executive branch of the United States" are provided:

- A *permanent bar* of the former employee from representing any client before a federal agency or court in "a particular matter" in which "the United States ... is a party or has a direct and substantial interest" when the employee "participated personally and substantially" in the matter while with the government.

---

29.   See also the conflicts rules in the Integrity in Procurement Act, 41 U.S.C. § 423.

Official Responsibility ②
- A *two-year bar* of the former employee from representing another in connection with "a particular matter" in which "the United States ... is a party or has a direct and substantial interest" when the employee had "official responsibility" over the matter during the employee's final year with the government.[30]

High-level Executive ③
- A *one-year bar* *("cooling-off period")* against any appearances before the same agency or department for any client if the employee was a high-level executive officer.

Regulations promulgated by federal departments and agencies mirror the statutory provisions and frequently add further requirements. For example, 28 C.F.R. § 45.735 et seq. governs employees and former employees of the Department of Justice.[31]

The Federal Lobbying Act[32] requires that anyone "receiving any contributions" in order to "influence, directly or indirectly, the passage or defeat of any legislation" by Congress must register and file quarterly reports of receipts and expenditures. Persons who act as "agent of a foreign principal" are also subject to the Foreign Agents Registration Act and its implementing regulations.[33] Such an agent must register with the Department of Justice, thereafter file reports every six months and comply with record-keeping requirements.

Virtually every state has statutory provisions governing conflicts of interest on the part of state and municipal employees and those acting on behalf of government agencies.[34]

Conflicts of interest statutes raise many difficult interpretive questions. For example, in United States v. Nofziger,[35] a former top assistant to President Reagan challenged his conviction for violating the one-year bar applicable to high-level government executives. Nofziger, who had established a political consulting firm after leaving his White House post, lobbied White House officials on behalf of three clients within the one-year period. Nofziger claimed that, while he knowingly lobbied the White House, the government had not proved

30. In 1993 the Clinton administration announced a new policy of extending this bar to five years.

31. 28 C.F.R. § 45.735–2(a) requires all Department of Justice employees to "conduct themselves in a manner that creates and maintains respect for" the Department and the government. Following provisions prohibit certain activities during government service and impose restrictions on activities after leaving public service. Many of the provisions, such as those dealing with receipt of gifts and entertainment, are highly detailed. Other agencies have similar regulations, see, e.g. 17 C.F.R. § 200.735 (SEC); 16 C.F.R. § 4.1 (FTC); 31 C.F.R. § 10.26 (IRS).

32. 2 U.S.C. §§ 261–270. The Act was construed, and a First Amendment challenge to its constitutionality rejected, in United States v. Harriss, 347 U.S. 612 (1954).

33. 22 U.S.C. §§ 611–621; 28 C.F.R. § 5.100 (implementing regulations). In Meese v. Keene, 481 U.S. 465 (1987), the Court upheld the Foreign Registration Act against a challenge that its use of the term "political propaganda" to trigger its requirements violated the First Amendment.

34. See, e.g., Ariz.Rev.Stat.Ann. § 38–504; Fla.Stat.Ann. § 112.313; Iowa Code Ann. § 68B.7; N.J.Stat.Ann. § 52:13D–12; N.Y. Pub.Off.Law § 73. See also Council of State Governments, Campaign Finance, Ethics and Lobby Law Blue Book 1986–87 (1986).

35. 878 F.2d 442 (D.C.Cir.1989).

that he did so with the requisite intent—*knowledge* that the White House had a "direct and substantial interest" in the matters. The court reversed Nofziger's conviction, stating that the government's view that intent to influence the White House violated the statute "would impose strict liability on a lobbyist who is misinformed." Doesn't the court's interpretation put a premium on staying misinformed? Why would Nofziger be communicating with the White House with the intent to influence it if he did not think it had a "direct and substantial interest" in the matter?

In addition to statutes and regulations governing members of the executive branch, legislatures have rules that govern their members with restrictions that may implicate lawyer members or lawyers who have dealings with legislators.[36] The principal provisions of the rules governing the U.S. Senate and House of Representatives seem remarkably porous compared to the rules governing the executive branch. For example, the House rules provide that "A Member . . . shall conduct himself at all times in a manner which shall reflect creditably on the House of Representatives." [37] On other matters, however, such as outside income and receipt of gifts, the rules are more detailed and specific.

Model Code of Professional Responsibility

The profession's ethics rules apply on their face to all lawyers, including government lawyers. Their provisions become enforceable against government lawyers when adopted by a state in which a government lawyer is admitted to or engaged in practice; when adopted by a federal court before which the lawyer makes an appearance; and when adopted by an agency by which the lawyer is employed. More specific requirements of state or federal law, however, may displace an ethics rule.

DR 9–101 of the Model Code provides that a lawyer shall not accept employment in a private matter upon which she acted as a judge or in which she had substantial responsibility while a public employee. This rule disqualifies a lawyer from subsequent representation of a private party in a matter in which the lawyer had substantial responsibility while with the government, *even if the private party is on the "same side" as the government.* The prohibition is broader than the general rule on subsequent representation of private clients developed in the case law and codified in M.R. 1.9(a), which applies only when the present client's interests are *adverse* to the interests of the former client, i.e., when the lawyer has "switched sides." Why the broader rule for government lawyers?

---

36. The 1990–91 Senate inquiry into the conduct of the "Keating Five"—five Senators who simultaneously received major campaign contributions from the savings-and-loan mogul and intervened on his behalf with federal regulatory authorities—raised novel questions concerning senatorial ethics. See Richard L. Berke, Appearances Worry Congress as S. & L. Shadow Lengthens, N.Y. Times, July 29, 1990, at p. 1.

37. House Rule XLIII—Code of Official Conduct, Rule 1.

In 1975 an influential ethics opinion, ABA Formal Opinion 342,[38] summarized "the policy considerations underlying DR 9–101(B):"

> the treachery of switching sides; the safeguarding of confidential governmental information from future use against the government; the need to discourage government lawyers from handling particular assignments in such a way as to encourage their own future employment in regard to those particular matters after leaving government service; and the professional benefit derived from avoiding the appearance of evil.

DR 5–105(D) provides that when one lawyer is disqualified the whole firm is disqualified. When read together with DR 9–101, this would require the disqualification of the entire firm in any case in which the former government lawyer had substantial responsibility. Moreover, neither provision provides for removal of the disqualification by waiver, i.e., consent of the appropriate government agency. However, the ABA, the courts and state ethics committees interpreted these rules to allow firms to proceed if the disqualified former government lawyer was screened from participation.

ABA Formal Opinion 342 led the way in rejecting the imputed disqualification of a firm employing a former government lawyer:

> There are, however, weighty policy considerations in support of the view that a special disciplinary rule relating only to former government lawyers should not broadly limit the lawyer's employment after he leaves government service. Some of the underlying considerations favoring a construction of the rule in a manner not to restrict unduly the lawyer's future employment are the following: the ability of government to recruit young professionals and competent lawyers should not be interfered with by imposition of harsh restraints upon future practice nor should too great a sacrifice be demanded of the lawyers willing to enter government service; the rule serves no worthwhile public interest if it becomes a mere tool enabling a litigant to improve his prospects by depriving his opponent of competent counsel; and the rule should not be permitted to interfere needlessly with the right of litigants to obtain competent counsel of their own choosing, particularly in specialized areas requiring special technical training and experience.[39]

The opinion noted that a literal reading of DR 5–105(D) would disqualify a government agency from handling a matter in the reverse situation of a private lawyer joining the government. "Necessity dictates that government action not be hampered by such a construction of DR 5–105(D).... Likewise, DR 9–101(B)'s command of refusal of employment by an individual lawyer does not necessarily activate

---

38. ABA Comm. on Prof. Ethics, Formal Op. 342 (Nov. 24, 1975), reprinted in 62 A.B.A. J. 517, 518 (1976).

39. Id. at 518–19.

DR 5–105(D)'s extension of that disqualification." [40]   The opinion concluded, "whenever the government agency is satisfied that screening measures will effectively isolate the individual lawyer from participating in the particular matter and sharing in the fees attributable to it, and that there is no appearance of significant impropriety affecting the interests of the government, the government may waive the disqualification of the firm." [41]   Shortly thereafter, Kesselhaut v. United States [42] went further in holding that the government agency's consent was not required.

✗   Armstrong v. McAlpin [43] is the leading decision on screening of the former government lawyer under the Model Code.   In 1974 Altman, while at the SEC, had supervised an SEC investigation growing out of the collapse of the Capital Growth investment companies, in which McAlpin was a principal figure.   When the bubble burst, McAlpin fled to Costa Rica.   In 1975 Altman left the SEC and joined the Gordon firm in New York City.   Armstrong, the receiver of the corporation victimized by the fraud, had originally retained his own law firm (Barrett) in an effort to track down assets and claims of the bankrupt company against McAlpin and others.   The SEC turned over its investigatory files to the receiver.   When a conflict of interest problem required withdrawal of the Barrett firm, the receiver then sought to employ the Gordon firm because some of its lawyers had the specialized competencies required.   Because Altman was personally disqualified, his presence in the Gordon firm was a problem but Armstrong and the firm, with the approval of the district court and the consent of the SEC, went ahead after screening Altman from the case.

leading code decision on screening

The majority of the en banc panel upheld the district court's refusal to disqualify the Gordon firm under these circumstances.   Although "reasonable minds may and do differ on the ethical propriety of screening in this context," imputed disqualification is not required absent a threat of taint to the trial.   Because disqualification motions affect a client's choice of counsel, are used for tactical purposes and result in delay in reaching the merits, disciplinary standards should not be applied inflexibly.   Unfair use of privileged government information was not involved since the SEC had made its files available to the receiver.   Concerns about the "appearance of impropriety" are "disserved by an order of disqualification in a case such as this, where no

40.   Id. at 521.

41.   Id. at 521.

42.   555 F.2d 791 (Ct.Cl.1977) (rejecting an inflexible rule of imputed disqualification of the former government lawyer's new firm and also rejecting a requirement of government consent to the representation).   See also Comm. on Prof. and Jud. Ethics of the Ass'n of Bar of City of New York, Op. 889, 31 Record 552 (1976).

43.   625 F.2d 433 (en banc, 2d Cir.1980), vacated 449 U.S. 1106 (1981).   *Armstrong* is frequently cited even though the decision was vacated on jurisdictional grounds on the basis of Firestone Tire & Rubber Co. v. Risjord, discussed above at p. 654, holding denial of disqualification motions nonappealable.   See, e.g., Telectronics Proprietary, Ltd. v. Medtronic, Inc., 836 F.2d 1332, 1335 (Fed.Cir.1988).

threat of taint exists and where appellants' motion to disqualify opposing counsel has successfully crippled the efforts of a receiver, appointed at the request of a public agency, to obtain redress for alleged serious frauds on the investing public." [44]

Judge Newman, dissenting to the rejection of imputed disqualification, argued that "[t]he purposes of DR 9–101(B) cannot be fully achieved unless there is no possibility that the government attorney can be (or seem to be) influenced by the prospect of later private employment." [45] Disqualification of the former government lawyer's firm was required to prevent unfair use of information unavailable to the other side and because of public fears that screening would be ineffective. "[T]he public will not believe ... [that] Altman will not in fact disclose to his partners anything he learned while exercising substantial government responsibilities for related matters." [46]

Armstrong's approval of screening is much more tentative than that of ABA Formal Opinion 342. First, the case does not involve side-switching—the private action is a follow-up of the SEC enforcement effort and consistent with it. Second, according to the majority, no confidential government information was involved. Third, the decision states that "reasonable minds can differ" on the question involved and emphasizes the special circumstances and facts of the particular case.

1982 amendments to the District of Columbia's ethics rules anticipated provisions of the 1983 Model Rules of Professional Conduct. The former government lawyer's firm was not disqualified if the personally disqualified lawyer was screened from participation and fees. Prompt and elaborate notice to the government of the screening was required, but consent was not. [47]

Model Rules of Professional Conduct

Under the Model Rules, lawyers who move between the government and private practice are bound by the conflicts rules applicable to all lawyers. Thus, M.R. 1.7 applies not only to private lawyers but to government and former government lawyers, as does M.R. 1.9, as

---

44. 625 F.2d at 446.

45. 625 F.2d at 453.

46. 625 F.2d at 453.

47. See D.C. R. Prof.Conduct, Rule 1.11 (1990). The form of notice in the D.C. rule is elaborate: The personally disqualified lawyer is required to file with the government agency involved and serve on all other parties to the proceeding a signed document attesting that she will not participate in or discuss the matter with any other lawyer in the firm and will not share in any fees attributable to the matter. In addition, at least one other lawyer from the disqualified lawyer's firm must file with the government and serve on all other parties to the proceeding a signed document attesting that all affiliated lawyers are aware that the disqualified lawyer must be screened and describing the screening procedures which the firm is implementing. Should these notice provisions have been included in the Model Rules' provision? Where screening is allowed in cases involving private clients, see e.g., *Nemours*, supra at p. 708, should the courts require that similar documents be filed with the court or the opposing party?

originally adopted, and M.R. 1.9(a) and (c), as amended in 1989.[48] In addition, the special provisions in M.R. 1.11 apply to lawyers moving between private and government practice.

Model Rule 1.11(a) does two things: first, for an individual lawyer formerly with the government and now in private practice, the rule augments the prohibitions on subsequent representation found in M.R. 1.9; second, for a firm hiring a lawyer formerly with the government, it limits disqualification by imputation.

As to the individual lawyer now in private practice, who formerly worked for the government, M.R. 1.11(a) provides that where a lawyer participated in a matter *personally and substantially* while working for the government, the lawyer may not later represent a private client in connection with that matter unless the government agency consents or other law expressly permits the representation. Like its predecessor provision in the Code, M.R. 1.11(a) applies whether or not the present client's interests are adverse to the former client (the government).

Even though the lawyer's present involvement may not be prohibited by M.R. 1.11(a), the former government lawyer must also make sure that M.R. 1.9(a) does not prohibit the representation. M.R. 1.9(a) does not require "personal and substantial" involvement in the former representation before it is triggered. Thus, when a present client's interests are adverse to those of the government, the former government lawyer's disqualification in a substantially related matter is broader than the limitation of M.R. 1.11(a) alone.

Consent from the appropriate government agency (the former client) allows the individual lawyer to proceed under M.R. 1.11(a). As with consent under M.R. 1.9(a), the government's consent under M.R. 1.11(a) does not waive the government's right to preservation of its confidences. The lawyer's duty to preserve the government's confidences under M.R. 1.9(c) and M.R. 1.6 remains in effect unless expressly waived.

M.R. 1.11(a) provides that when a lawyer is disqualified under this subsection (because she participated personally and substantially in the matter while with the government), the lawyer's entire firm is disqualified unless:

    (1) the disqualified lawyer is screened from any participation in the matter and is apportioned no part of the fee therefrom; and

    (2) written notice is promptly given to the appropriate government agency to enable it to ascertain compliance with the provisions of this rule.[49]

---

48. See the Comments to these rules, which make it clear that while M.R. 1.11 only applies to former and present government lawyers, rules 1.6, 1.7 and 1.9 apply to all lawyers, government and former government lawyers included.

49. New Jersey's version of 1.11 provides two separate bases for disqualifying the former government lawyer. The first tracks M.R. 1.11(a): the lawyer is disqualified if she was personally and substantially involved in the matter while with the government. If the lawyer is disqualified on these grounds, the entire firm is disqualified, i.e., screening

Notice to, not consent of, the government agency is required before the firm may proceed. The government's consent is necessary for the *individual lawyer* to participate (to avoid screening) but is unnecessary for representation by the *lawyer's firm* once the firm screens the lawyer. Why this distinction? Bear in mind that some governmental bodies may lack authority to waive a conflict of interest objection and others prefer a notification procedure that does not require formal agency action.

2. Disqualification of Former Government Lawyers

SECURITIES INVESTOR PROTECTION CORP. (SIPC) v. VIGMAN

United States District Court, Central District of California, 1984.
587 F.Supp. 1358.

TASHIMA, DISTRICT JUDGE.

This is an action brought by the Securities Investor Protection Corporation ("SIPC").... The complaint names seventy-five individual and corporate defendants and alleges numerous violations of § 10(b) of the Securities Exchange Act of 1934 (the "Exchange Act"), 15 U.S.C. §§ 78a et seq., and Rule 10b–5 promulgated thereunder, the Racketeer Influenced and Corrupt Organizations Act, 18 U.S.C. §§ 1961 et seq. ("RICO"), fraud and breaches of fiduciary duty under California common law.... I address here, the motion of defendant Isadore Diamond, joined in by five other defendants, to disqualify SIPC's counsel.

BACKGROUND

Gerald E. Boltz and Charles R. Hartman are members of the law firm of Rogers & Wells and counsel of record for plaintiff SIPC in this action. Both attorneys formerly were employed by the Securities and Exchange Commission ("SEC" or the "Commission"). Boltz was employed as an attorney by the SEC for approximately 20 years, from 1959 until 1979. From 1972 until 1979, he was Regional Administrator of the SEC's Los Angeles Regional Office. Hartman was employed as an attorney by the SEC for approximately 11 years, from 1969 to 1980. From 1972 until 1980, he was assigned to the SEC's Los Angeles Regional Office, where he held the position of regional counsel from 1976 to 1980.

During the early 1970s, two related proceedings were instituted by the SEC against, among others, certain of the defendants named in this action. The first was a Commission administrative proceeding brought by the SEC's Washington Office in March, 1971.... The second was a civil injunctive action filed in this court by the SEC's Los Angeles Regional Office [in 1973].... The gravamen of the complaint in that

will not cure the conflict. The second basis for disqualification, N.J. Rule 1.11(b), is "appearance of impropriety." If the lawyer is disqualified on this ground, the firm may proceed with the representation provided the lawyer is screened and written notice is given to the government.

action was the alleged fraudulent manipulation of the common stock of DCS Financial Corporation ("DCS"). Although the scope of the responsibilities and actions of Boltz and Hartman in those proceedings is in dispute, it is uncontested that Boltz signed the complaint and trial brief in the 1973 civil action and that Hartman appeared as trial counsel for the SEC in that action.

The complaint in the instant action, filed July 22, 1983, was signed by Boltz and lists Rogers & Wells and, among others, Hartman as attorneys, for plaintiff SIPC. Like the 1973 civil action and the 1971 administrative proceeding, plaintiff alleges the manipulation of a number of securities. The instant action, however, alleges an extremely elaborate scheme, encompassing the manipulation of seven securities on the over-the-counter market, including the securities of Bunnington Corp. ("Bunnington"), the company into which DCS had merged. As stated, the complaint charges numerous violations of the anti-manipulative provisions of the Exchange Act and RICO, as well as other violations of law. Certain of the claimed violations are based on asserted securities manipulations which occurred prior to the 1971 administrative proceeding and the 1973 civil action.

Defendants seek to disqualify Boltz, Hartman and Rogers & Wells from further representing SIPC in this action on the ground that continued representation by these former government attorneys in a matter connected to their government work contravenes the ethical standards of the legal profession.

I. THE APPLICABLE STANDARD OF PROFESSIONAL RESPONSIBILITY

Defendants contend that Boltz and Hartman's representation of SIPC in this action violates Rule 1.11(a) of the American Bar Association's ("ABA") recently adopted Model Rules of Professional Conduct (1983) ("Model Rules"). [The court quoted the text of Rule 1.11(a).][1] Since SIPC does not contend that Boltz and Hartman have been screened from participation in this action, disqualification of either of these attorneys would require that Rogers & Wells also be disqualified. Model Rule 1.11(a)(1).

The district court has primary responsibility for controlling the conduct of attorneys practicing before it. Trone v. Smith, 621 F.2d 994, 999 (9th Cir.1980). Although the ABA does not establish rules of law that are binding on this Court, it is the Court's prerogative to disqualify counsel based on contravention of the ABA Model Rules.... This is true, despite the fact that neither this Court's Local Rules nor the Rules of Professional Conduct of the State Bar of California expressly

---

1. Except for the provision allowing representation when "the appropriate government agency consents after consultation," Rule 1.11(a) is similar to former Disciplinary Rule ("DR") 9–101(B), which provided that "[a] lawyer shall not accept private employment in a matter in which he had substantial responsibility while he was a public employee." Model Code of Professional Responsibility DR 9–101(B) (1979). See also footnote 9, ante.

refers to the ABA Model Rules. As the Ninth Circuit has recently stated:

> Despite the deletion in 1975 of a reference to the ABA Model Code in the Rules of Professional Conduct of the State Bar of California ... the California courts continue to rely on the Model Code in addressing issues not covered precisely by the Rules of Professional Conduct of the State Bar of California.

... But see People v. Ballard, 104 Cal.App.3d 757, 761, 164 Cal.Rptr. 81 (1980) (dictum) ("conduct of California attorneys is governed by California Rules of Professional Conduct" not ABA Model Code).

Because California courts have consistently looked to the Model Code, the predecessor of the Model Rules, as a source of ethical principles governing the conduct of California lawyers, I conclude that Rule 1.11(a) is an appropriate standard to apply in this case. See Local Rule 2.5.1 (requiring lawyers to comply with "decisions of any court applicable" to "standards of professional conduct required of members of the State Bar of California"). As noted, Rule 1.11(a) is substantially similar to former DR 9–101(B). Thus, California attorneys are, or should be, apprised of the standard of responsibility encompassed by the rule, from decisions of California and federal courts applying former DR 9–101(B).[2]

SIPC contends that Rule 1.11(a) was meant to apply only to "switching sides" cases, that is, situations where a former government attorney seeks to represent a private litigant whose interests are adverse to the government. SIPC argues that such a limitation is supported by the rule's allowance of an otherwise prohibited representation when "the appropriate government agency consents after consultation." I disagree. Nowhere in the Model Rules, the Comments, or the ABA draft proposals is there support for limiting Rule 1.11(a) to switching sides cases....

Neither *Woods* [v. Covington County Bank, 537 F.2d 804 (5th Cir.1976)] nor *General Motors* [v. City of New York, 501 F.2d 639 (2d Cir.1974)—two cases cited in notes to the 1981 draft of the Model Rules—] involved an attorney switching sides. In fact, the focus in both of these cases was not on whether or not an attorney had switched sides, but instead, was on avoiding the "appearance of impropriety." In *General Motors*, the City of New York brought an action against a bus manufacturer alleging an unlawful nationwide monopoly. One of the City's attorneys formerly had been employed by the Department of Justice and during that time had substantial responsibility in the investigatory and preparatory stages of a similar antitrust action against the same manufacturer. The court, in disqualifying the attorney from further representation of the City, noted that the purpose

---

2. Although the ABA Model Rules were not adopted until Aug. 2, 1983, 11 days after this action was commenced, they are the appropriate standard against which to test the *continued* representation of SIPC. Moreover, as the ensuing discussion will indicate, the outcome of the analysis under former Canon 9 and DR 9–101(B) would not differ.

behind former Canon 9 and DR 9–101(B), as stated in ABA Formal Opinion No. 37 (1931), was to avoid:

> the manifest possibility ... [that a former government lawyer's] action as a public legal official might be influenced (or open to the charge that it had been influenced) by the hope of later being employed privately to *uphold* or *upset* what he had done.

501 F.2d at 649 (emphasis in the original). The court further recognized that its responsibility was:

> to preserve a balance, delicate though it may be, between an individual's right to his own freely chosen counsel ... and the need to maintain the highest ethical standards of professional responsibility. This balance is essential if the public's trust in the integrity of the Bar is to be preserved.

Id., quoting Emle Indus., Inc. v. Patentex, Inc., 478 F.2d 562, 564–65 (2d Cir.1973). The disqualification was not based on actual impropriety, but in order to avoid the appearance of impropriety and to safeguard the "public's trust." Id.

In *Woods*, the Fifth Circuit found no such danger of public mistrust. There, a former naval reserve attorney, during service, had investigated a securities fraud allegedly perpetrated on returning ex-prisoners of war ("POWs") on behalf of the POWs. He later represented the POWs in a private fraud action. The district court's disqualification order was reversed because, the court concluded, the attorney's conduct could not conceivably impugn the public's trust in the Navy or the legal profession. This was due, in large part, to the fact that

> as a legal assistance officer ... [the attorney] did not possess any investigative authority beyond that available to a private lawyer....   Neither is there any allegation that [the attorney] ever held himself out to be an investigating officer acting on behalf of the United States Navy or as having any special governmental authority.

537 F.2d at 817.

... SIPC's contention that the "government consent" provision was meant to limit the application of Rule 1.11(a) to switching sides cases is contrary to the drafters' reliance on *Woods* and *General Motors* and, therefore, must be rejected. I now turn to an examination of the substantive aspects of the rule.[3]

---

3. SIPC argues that this motion is governed by Model Rule 1.11(b), rather than Rule 1.11(a). [The court then quoted M.R. 1.11(b).] Possible disqualification under this rule is independent of and in addition to any basis for disqualification under Rule 1.11(a). Because I conclude that disqualification is required under Rule 1.11(a), I do not reach the question of whether Rule 1.11(b) also applies.

II. APPLICATION OF RULE 1.11(a)

A. Agency Consent

As indicated, Rule 1.11(a) appears to allow an otherwise prohibited representation by a former government attorney when "the appropriate government agency consents after consultation." When, at the hearing on the motion, the Court confirmed that agency consent had not been sought, SIPC was directed to consult with the Commission to ascertain whether it would consent to the continued representation of SIPC by Boltz and Hartman. The SEC was then contacted by Rogers & Wells, as well as a number of other counsel in this action. The Commission has declined to give its consent, stating:

> [T]he Commission believes that as a general matter, a policy of waiving the personal disqualification of former Commission law-yers to permit them to participate in the matters which they handled while on the staff could undermine the public's confidence in the activities of the Commission's lawyers. After reviewing the factors relevant to this case, the Commission sees nothing unique in this situation which would warrant deviating from that general principle. Therefore, the Commission has determined that it would not waive any disqualification personal to Messrs. Boltz and Hartman, pursuant to Rule 1.11(a).[4]

The Commission's declination to waive personal disqualification in this case must be accepted as that agency's discretionary determination, as contemplated by the rule, that this is not a situation where waiver of disqualification would be in the public interest. However, it remains to be considered whether the predicate requirements for the application of Rule 1.11(a) are here present.[5]

B. Same Matter

Although the ABA Model Rules do not define the term "matter" as used in Rule 1.11(a), it can be said that a matter includes a "discrete, identifiable transaction or conduct involving a particular situation and specific parties." See ABA Formal Opinion No. 342 (1975). Opinion No. 342 provides the following examples:

> The same lawsuit or litigation is the same matter. The same issue of fact involving the same parties and the same situation or conduct is the same matter. . . . [T]he same "matter" is not in-volved [when] . . . there is lacking the discrete, identifiable transac-tion or conduct involving a particular situation and specific parties.

SIPC contends that, under this definition, the 1973 civil action is not the same matter as the instant action. However, examination of the instant complaint belies this contention. In paragraph 200 of the

---

4. The Commission's determination was communicated to counsel in a letter signed by its General Counsel. A copy of that letter, dated February 28, 1984, is appended hereto.

5. As explained in the SEC's letter, the Commission has "made no determination" that this action and the 1973 civil action "are the same particular matter and that Messrs. Boltz and Hartman had personal and substantial responsibility for both mat-ters."

complaint, in support of the first claim for violation of RICO, plaintiffs allege:

> that at various times prior to November, 1967, *and thereafter, Vigman ... and Diamond* participated in a fraudulent scheme to manipulate the prices of various securities, including ... *DCS Corporation (a corporation subsequently merged with Bunnington)....   Said conduct violated Section 10(b) of the Exchange Act and Rule 10b–5.*

(Emphasis added.) In paragraph 211 of the complaint, plaintiffs further allege:

> that between November, 1967 and January, 1971, in furtherance of the racketeering enterprise, Vigman, Diamond, and others engaged in a scheme to defraud the public in violation of the Securities Act, the Exchange Act and Rule 10b–5. This scheme involved the placement of unregistered securities into the marketplace and the subsequent manipulation of the price of those securities for the benefit of the RICO Defendants.

The complaint also alleges that defendant Vigman, despite being barred from the securities business on November 1, 1967, "continued to exercise control over Newport Securities Corp.", as well as a number of issuers, including Bunnington, and that the racketeering enterprise was carried out through, inter alia, Newport Securities.

It must be remembered that the subject of the 1973 civil action was the alleged manipulation of DCS stock by, among others, Vigman and Diamond (defendants here) in violation of, inter alia, § 10(b) of the Exchange Act and Rule 10b–5. Although the subject of the 1973 civil action largely was alleged manipulations occurring in 1972, the complaint in the 1973 civil action also alleged fraudulent manipulation of securities "since about September 15, 1970."

It is evident that paragraphs 200, 208, 211 and 212 of the instant complaint refer to the same matter that was the subject of the 1973 civil action. Although this is not a situation where the subsequent complaint was "lifted ad haec verba" from the SEC complaint, *General Motors*, 501 F.2d at 650, I find that a discrete series of transactions involving a specific situation and specific parties in the 1973 civil action is part and parcel of a subsequent, broader allegation of widespread securities fraud and racketeering in the case at bench. The essence of the complaint here is that, since 1967, Vigman, Diamond and others have engaged in a sophisticated conspiracy to manipulate the price of securities. Thus, the complaint includes among its allegations, the alleged manipulation of the price of DCS stock by, among others, Diamond and Vigman, which allegation was the precise subject of the 1973 civil action. Therefore, I find that Boltz and Hartman are representing SIPC "in connection with a matter" which the SEC prosecuted in the 1973 civil action, within the meaning of Rule 1.11(a).[7]

C. Personal and Substantial Participation   yes, Boltz & Hartman

SIPC argues that neither Boltz nor Hartman personally and substantially participated in the 1973 civil action. However, it is uncontroverted that Boltz signed both the complaint and the trial brief in that action. Although in his declaration Boltz states that his signatures "merely reflect a general SEC practice and policy that a Regional Administrator should personally sign the initial complaint in any action filed by that office," his argument ignores that plain requirement of F.R.Civ.P. 11. At the time Boltz signed the complaint and trial brief, Rule 11 provided that "[t]he signature of an attorney constitutes a certificate by him that he has read the pleading; that to the best of his knowledge, information, and belief there is good ground to support it." The Ninth Circuit has interpreted this language to require an attorney, before filing a civil action, "to make an investigation to ascertain that it has at least some merit, and further to ascertain that the damages sought appear to bear a reasonable relation to the injuries actually sustained." ... Therefore, when Boltz, as Regional Administrator, signed the complaint and trial brief, he assumed, as a matter of law, the personal and substantial responsibility of ensuring that there existed good ground to support the SEC's case and that it had, at least, some merit.[9] The assumption and proper discharge of that responsibility required his personal and substantial participation in the action. That Boltz had such responsibility under law is further indicated by former Rule 11's provision that an attorney who violated the rule "may be subjected to appropriate disciplinary action." I, thus, find that Boltz had personal and substantial responsibility over and participation in the 1973 civil action within the meaning of Rule 1.11(a).[10] Cf. Telos, Inc. v. Hawaiian Tel. Co., 397 F.Supp. 1314, 1316 n. 11 (D.Haw.1975) ("Signing a complaint, is, ... by itself, except in rare circumstances, the exercise of substantial responsibility" under former DR 9–101(B).).

7. Because of this finding, it is unnecessary to and I do not reach the question of whether this action also involves the same matter as the 1971 administrative proceeding.

9. One reason the Model Rule employs the term "participated personally and substantially" is because the term "substantial responsibility" used in former DR 9–101(B), "could disqualify the former head of a large governmental agency from private employment with respect to any matter arising during his tenure. See Cleveland v. Cleveland Elec. Illum. Co., 440 F.Supp. 193 (N.D.Ohio 1977); ABA Formal Opinion 342 (1975) [other citations omitted]." Boltz's disqualification here is not based on his "substantial responsibility" as Regional Administrator of the SEC's Los Angeles Regional Office, but on his personal substantial responsibility and participation in the 1973 civil action as an attorney who, by signing the complaint and trial brief and other actions personally participated substantially in the 1973 civil action. An attorney who personally signs the pleadings in an action is not immunized from Rule 11's imposition of personal responsibility because he also happens to be the head of a governmental office.

10. Further evidence of Boltz's personal participation in the 1973 civil action is found in the response of the SEC staff attorney who deposed defendant Diamond to Diamond's request for a copy of his deposition transcript: "Mr. Boltz has asked me to assure you on behalf of the [SEC] staff" that such a copy would be provided.

With respect to Hartman, it is not contested that he appeared at the trial as counsel of record on each day of the three-day trial in the 1973 civil action. However, Hartman contends that his role at the trial merely was to supervise an attorney-colleague at the SEC, who had no prior trial experience. Hartman further declares that all of the legal work in the 1973 civil action, "including both the actual preparation and the trial itself, was performed by" the other trial attorney.

Be that as it may, it is unlikely that an experienced attorney would or could effectively and properly supervise an inexperienced colleague without familiarizing himself with the facts of the case and the applicable law. To this end, Hartman no doubt had access to records, both public and confidential, relating to the case. It is difficult to conceive how an experienced attorney could carry out the type of supervisory role assigned to Hartman without becoming familiar with the evidence to be presented both by and against the SEC and conferring with and advising his less-experienced colleague during the course of the three-day trial. Therefore, I find that Hartman also had personal and substantial responsibility over and participation in the 1973 civil action within the meaning of Rule 1.11(a).

III.   CONCLUSION

Because courts have differed as to whether the somewhat subjective standard of the "appearance of impropriety" under former Canon 9 and DR 9–101 was an appropriate one to guide the conduct of lawyers, Model Rule 1.11(a) "sets forth more specifically the circumstances in which concern for public confidence in government necessitates disqualification of a government lawyer." 1981 Draft Notes at 304. The concerns addressed, however, remain the same. The specific circumstances requiring disqualification under Rule 1.11(a) have been met here. Because I find that Boltz and Hartman are representing a private client in connection with a matter in which both of them participated personally and substantially while employed by the SEC, and because the Commission has declined to consent to such representation, these attorneys and Rogers & Wells must be disqualified from further representation of SIPC in this action. Of course, this ruling is intended in no way to suggest any actual wrongdoing on the part of the attorneys involved or their law firm. Rather, this ruling is intended to effectuate the prophylactic purpose of Rule 1.11(a). See *General Motors Corp.*, 501 F.2d at 649.

[The letter from the SEC, declining to consent to any personal disqualification of Boltz and Hartman, included the following footnote:

While Model Rule 1.11(a) permits a government agency to waive the personal disqualification of its former lawyers, 18 U.S.C. § 207, the federal post-employment statute would, if applicable, presumably eliminate any such discretionary action by a federal agency. While authoritative interpretations of Section 207 are the province of the Office of Government Ethics and the Department of Justice, it appears that Section 207 does not apply in this instance.]

SIPC and Model Rule 1.11

Boltz and Hartman are prohibited from representing SIPC under M.R. 1.11(a) if the representation involves the same "matter," they "participated personally and substantially" in the government's handling of it, and the government has not consented to the representation.[50] Consider each of these elements of Model Rule 1.11(a).

What Is the Same "Matter"?

The court in *SIPC* says that the Model Rules do not define the word "matter" as used in M.R. 1.11(a). The court is in error in this respect. M.R. 1.11(d) defines "matter" "as used in this rule" as including:

[handwritten margin note: MR 1.11(d) does define "matter"]

> (1) any judicial or other proceeding, application, request for a ruling or other determination, contract, claim, controversy, investigation, charge, accusation, arrest or other particular matter involving a specific party or parties; and

> (2) any other matter covered by the conflict of interest rules of the appropriate government agency.

ABA Formal Opinion 342, discussed above at p. 728, gave some examples of government lawyering that did not constitute the "same matter":

> [W]ork as a government employee in drafting, enforcing or interpreting government or agency procedures, regulations, or laws, or in briefing abstract principles of law, does not disqualify the lawyer under DR 9–101(B) from subsequent private employment involving the same regulations, procedures, or points of law; the same "matter" is not involved because there is lacking the discrete, identifiable transactions or conduct involving a particular situation and specific parties.[51]

Are these examples consistent with "matter" as defined in M.R. 1.11(d)?

The Department of Justice, in its comments to the Kutak Commission's draft of the Model Rules, argued that the final version of the Model Rules should make clear that the definition of "matter" does not include "such prior government activities as drafting proposed legislation, participation in rulemaking, or reviewing government contracts [because an] overly broad categorization of disqualifying activity could

---

50. Recall the facts of *ACC/Lincoln*, above at p. 114, for another example of "revolving door" representation by a former government lawyer. Lawyer Schilling, who as a government bank regulator had expressed concerns about Lincoln's "serious regulatory violations," was engaged six months later in soliciting Lincoln's business on behalf of his new employer, Jones, Day. Settlement of the government's claims against Jones, Day and Schilling included provisions barring Schilling from representing thrifts or holding positions in the banking industry. See Wade Lambert, Jones Day Settles Claim at Lincoln Thrift, Wall St.J., Apr. 20, 1993, at p. B12.

51. ABA Formal Opinion 342, 62 A.B.A.J. at 599.

impede government hiring significantly." [52]   Are these activities included in the definition of "matter" in M.R. 1.11(d)?

Suppose the lawyers involved in *SIPC* had participated only in an effort by the SEC to issue guidelines for prohibited forms of stock manipulation?   An effort to issue formal regulations on this subject?

Participated "Personally and Substantially"

ABA Formal Opinion 342, interpreting the Model Code language, stressed the government lawyer's participation in "investigative or deliberative processes:"

> "[S]ubstantial responsibility" envisages a much closer and more direct relationship than that of mere perfunctory approval or disapproval of the matter in question.   It contemplates a responsibility requiring the official to become personally involved to an important, material degree, in the investigative or deliberative processes regarding the transactions or facts in question.   Thus, being the chief official in some vast office or organization does not *ipso facto* give that government official or employee the "substantial responsibility" contemplated by the rule in regard to all the minutiae of facts lodged within that office.   Yet it is not necessary that the public employee or official shall have personally and in a substantial manner investigated or passed upon the particular matter, for it is sufficient that he had such a heavy responsibility for the matter in question that it is unlikely he did not become personally and substantially involved in the investigative or deliberative processes regarding that matter. . . .

The Model Rules' provision, unlike the Model Code, adds the adverb "personally" to describe the kind of involvement that will trigger the rule.   What difference does this make?

Suppose Boltz had been a commissioner of the SEC at the time of the Commission's investigation of Vigman and others.   He had been briefed about the matter at a Commission meeting, but no formal agency action was required.   Suppose, alternatively, that he had been head of the SEC's enforcement division and had signed papers permitting the investigation and formal proceeding to go forward, but without acquiring detailed familiarity with the facts.   Do these constitute the requisite degree of participation?

Government Consent and Screening

M.R. 1.11(a) permits the government to waive the individual lawyer's disqualification.   If consent is either not requested or not granted, the firm may still continue the representation provided the disqualified lawyer is isolated from all involvement in the case.   Unlike Formal Opinion 342, however, M.R. 1.11(a) does not require the government's consent to continued representation and screening.   The firm's only

52.   Letter from Ass't Att'y Gen. Jonathan C. Rose to Robert J. Kutak, July 23, 1982, p. 2.

obligation is promptly to notify the government agency involved so that it may monitor the firm's compliance with the rule's dictates on screening the lawyer. Is Opinion 342's requirement of consent to the screening a better rule?

If the lawyers for SIPC had formerly represented another private party against Vigman, they could represent SIPC now because M.R. 1.9 only applies when interests of the former and present clients are adverse. When consent was requested in *SIPC*, the SEC refused on the basis of its general policy. Is the SEC's general policy wise? What would be wrong with a policy to grant consent, absent special circumstances, whenever the lawyer was on the same side of the matter in the private case as she was when she worked for the government?

If the SEC had consented to participation by Boltz and Hartman in *SIPC*, the question whether they were barred by M.R. 1.11(b) would need to be faced. How should it be resolved? See the discussion of "confidential government information" below.

Was the *SIPC* court correct in stating that a "prophylactic" disqualification does not "suggest any actual wrongdoing on the part of the attorneys or their law firm"? Doesn't violation of a "prophylactic" ethics rule subject a lawyer to potential discipline? And what about the criminal law? Did Boltz and Hartman violate the criminal prohibitions of 18 U.S.C. § 207, discussed above at p. 725? Why does the SEC say in its letter that the statute "appears" to be inapplicable?

Confidential Government Information

As used in M.R. 1.11(b), the phrase "confidential government information" protects the confidences of persons about whom the government has acquired information.[53] The confidences of the government itself are protected by M.R. 1.6.

M.R. 1.11(b) provides that a lawyer who, by virtue of her former government employment, has "confidential government information about a person ... may not represent a private client whose interests are adverse to that person in a matter in which the information could be used to the material disadvantage of that person." The government has no power to waive this provision. The trigger for M.R. 1.11(b) is not whether the matters are the same, but whether the lawyer has "confidential government information" about a third party.

In light of M.R. 1.11(b), consider again the question of whether one level of government should be treated as a private client with respect to 1.11(a)'s prohibitions. Should one agency of government be considered a private client with respect to former employment by a different agency of the same government? Bear in mind that government agencies are not free to share information gathered about private

---

53. M.R. 1.11(e) defines "confidential government information" as "information which has been obtained under governmental authority and which, at the time this rule is applied, the government is prohibited by law from disclosing to the public or has a legal privilege not to disclose, and which is not otherwise available to the public."

parties with other agencies at their own discretion. Other law may restrict the transfer of information between government agencies. See, e.g., Fed.R.Crim.P. 6(e) (dealing with grand jury and other protected material).

Complicated ethical questions arise when the government changes its position in a lawsuit, moving from one side of the controversy to another—usually due to a change in administrations.[54] This question is considered in Chapter 8 below at p. 830.

Why Limit Screening to Cases Involving Former Government Lawyers?

In *Nemours,* above at p. 708, the court argued that migratory lawyer situations involving movement between private law firms should be treated the same as movement from government to private employment. Private lawyers, the court said, are as trustworthy as government lawyers. Yet the Model Rules and most of the case law reject this view, permitting screening to remove the imputed disqualification in the case of former government lawyers but not in that of migratory private lawyers.[55]

Why allow screening in the case of the tainted former government lawyer but not in the case of the tainted private lawyer who moves from one firm to another? Consider the following arguments (and unstated counter-arguments): First, a government lawyer's obligation to seek just results departs somewhat from the traditional adversarial model. Second, the boundaries of many government matters, which often involve expansive issues of law, policy or formulation of general rules, are more difficult to determine than those involved in private representation. Practical problems of administration and, perhaps, a reduced level of loyalty are suggested when interests of government are diffuse and widely shared. The government, unlike private persons, deals with everyone. Third, confidentiality is less of a concern when the government is involved because so much government information is available to the public. The confidentiality concern involves litigation strategy on the part of the government and flow of information about private persons held by government, an issue dealt with separately by criminal statutes and in M.R. 1.11(b). Fourth, government lawyers work on a fixed salary; they do not have the same economic incentive to use confidential information to win cases. Finally, the consistent position of the federal government (and most state governments) has favored the use of screening, arguing that the public interest in able, mobile lawyers is more important than the danger that government information will be used against the government. In a sense, the government has consented in advance to screening procedures.

54. See Note, Professional Ethics in Government Side–Switching, 96 Harv.L.Rev. 1914 (1983).

55. Most commentators support the distinction. See, e.g., C. Wolfram, Modern Legal Ethics § 7.6.4 at 403–04 (1986). Most of the cases also limit screening to cases involving former government lawyers.

Can Government Be Disqualified by Imputation?

If one lawyer in a government agency is disqualified because of prior representation of a private client (or for any other reason), is the entire office disqualified? M.R. 1.11(c) is silent on the question. M.R. 1.10 is inapplicable to government law departments. See M.R. 1.10 and the definition of "firm" in Terminology. Hence, no rule prohibits a government law department (e.g., a prosecutor's office or a city counsel's office) from proceeding when one of its lawyers is disqualified. Nor does any rule prescribe the manner in which such an office could proceed in this situation, e.g., by screening. Would it nevertheless be prudent for a government law office to screen a lawyer who had formerly represented a private client against whom the office is now engaged?

The case law in this area arises primarily out of criminal trials. Typically, the defendant seeks to disqualify the state prosecutor's office (or the U.S. Attorney's office) on the ground that one of the lawyers in that office formerly represented the accused or a co-defendant or a witness in connection with the same case. Most state courts hold that the government should be allowed to proceed as long as the disqualified lawyer is not personally involved.[56] Where the state prosecutor has multiple offices, courts sometimes require that the case be handled by an office in a different location.

Some cases suggest that the entire government might be disqualified. In People v. Shinkle,[57] for example, the Chief Assistant District Attorney in Sullivan County, the prosecuting office, had formerly been with the Legal Aid Society, where he had been actively involved with the representation of the defendant in the same matter. In vacating the conviction, the New York Court of Appeals implied that a special prosecutor would have to be appointed to reprosecute.

The federal courts have refused to require that an entire United States Attorney's office be disqualified because of one disqualified lawyer.[58] If the disqualified prosecutor has not been properly screened, the whole office may be disqualified.[59] But disqualification of one unit of government will not extend to another.[60]

56. See, e.g., Florida v. Cote, 538 So.2d 1356 (Fla.App.1989); People v. Lopez, 155 Cal.App.3d 813, 202 Cal.Rptr. 333 (1984); State v. Laughlin, 232 Kan. 110, 652 P.2d 690 (1982); Pisa v. Commonwealth, 378 Mass. 724, 393 N.E.2d 386 (1979).

57. 51 N.Y.2d 417, 415 N.E.2d 909 (1980). See also Collier v. Legakes, 98 Nev. 307, 646 P.2d 1219 (1982).

58. See, e.g., United States v. Caggiano, 660 F.2d 184 (6th Cir.1981); In re Grand Jury Proceedings, 700 F.Supp. 626 (D.P.R.1988); United States v. Newman, 534 F.Supp. 1113 (S.D.N.Y.1982).

59. For example, in Arkansas v. Dean Foods Prods. Inc., 605 F.2d 380 (8th Cir.1979), the state's entire antitrust division was disqualified from prosecuting an individual who had been the client of the division's new chief when the chief was in private practice.

60. See United States v. Weiner, 578 F.2d 757 (9th Cir.1978), where defendant moved to disqualify the U.S. Attorney's Office in a securities case because his former lawyer was now working for the SEC. The court denied the motion, finding that the size and

3. Other Issues of Government Lawyer Conflicts

When the Former Client Is Another Level of Government

An oft-cited case involving "same side" representation by a former government lawyer is General Motors Corp. v. City of New York.[61] In that case the lawyer while working for the federal government helped develop an antitrust case against General Motors involving alleged monopolization of bus manufacturing. Later, in private practice, he was retained on a contingent-fee basis by New York City to handle a private damage case against General Motors involving the same charges. The Justice Department consented to this representation. The court held that the lawyer was disqualified because his prior involvement in the matter was substantial and his arrangement with New York City was private employment. The fact that New York City was on the "same side" as the federal government was not enough to eliminate the "appearance of impropriety". "[T]here lurks great potential for lucrative returns in following into private practice the course already charted with the aid of government resources." [62]

ABA Opinion 342 states that the restrictions on former government lawyers should not apply if the new employer is another government agency.[63] The Comment to M.R. 1.11, however, rejects this view:

> When the client is an agency of one government, that agency should be treated as a private client for purposes of this Rule if the lawyer thereafter represents an agency of another government, as when a lawyer represents a city and subsequently is employed by a federal agency.

What about a lawyer who transfers from one agency of government to another agency of the same government? Should one agency of government be treated as the same client as another agency of government—thereby mooting conflict questions? Would your answer change if the first "agency" was the Congress and the second "agency" was the White House legal team?

Moving From Private Practice Into Government Service

Model Rule 1.11(c)(1) governs situations where a lawyer moves from private practice into government service. It is a counterpart to M.R. 1.11(a) and like that provision applies even if the present client (the government) is on the "same side" as the former client. The exception in M.R. 1.11(c) allows the present government lawyer to proceed in the same matter if law expressly allows *or* if "no one is, or by lawful delegation may be, authorized to act in the lawyer's stead in the

complexity of the two government offices made any imputation of knowledge inappropriate.

61. 501 F.2d 639 (2d Cir.1974). The case is discussed in *SIPC* at p. 734.

62. 501 F.2d 650.

63. See ABA Formal Op. 342, n. 18., stating that this construction is consistent with *General Motors* because in that case the court found that the lawyer's employment by the city constituted private employment.

matter." This exception prevents the conflicts rules from paralyzing the government in those rare cases where the only person able to handle the matter for the government has a conflict.

M.R. 1.11(c)(1) has no consent provision. Whether the government lawyer can proceed on the *same side* of a matter in which she worked for a private client is not determined by whether the private client consents. Whether a government lawyer can proceed in a matter in which her former private client's interests are *adverse* to the government, is governed by M.R. 1.9(a). Moreover, whenever a government lawyer proceeds in a matter she handled while in private practice M.R. 1.9(c) and M.R. 1.6 protect the former private client's confidences.[64]

Other Conflicts Rules for Those in Public Service

Model Rule 1.11(c)(2) prohibits government lawyers from negotiating "with any person who is involved as a party or as attorney for a party in a matter in which the lawyer is participating personally and substantially." M.R. 1.12 governs the conflicts faced by former judges or arbitrators. Law clerks, of course, have substantial ethical responsibilities.[65]

---

64. Generally see Ronald D. Rotunda, Ethical Problems in Federal Agency Hiring of Private Attorneys, 1 Geo.J.Legal Ethics 85 (1987).

65. On the ethical responsibilities of law clerks, see Note, The Law Clerk's Duty of Confidentiality, 129 U.Pa.L.Rev. 1230 (1981).

Chapter 8

WHO IS THE CLIENT?

A. INDIVIDUAL OR ENTERPRISE

Introductory Note

A lawyer is required to communicate and confer with a client, to keep the client's secrets and to abide by the client's decision on whether to accept a settlement offer.[1] When a lawyer represents an entity rather than an individual, to whom are these and other professional duties owed?

- When a lawyer represents a corporation, is communicating with the chief executive officer always sufficient? Should the lawyer ever insist on communicating with the board of directors? The shareholders?

- When the CEO communicates with the lawyer, is the attorney-client privilege personally held by the CEO or may the corporation waive it against the CEO's wishes? Who may waive the privilege on the corporation's behalf?

A lawyer for an organization constantly faces these and other delicate questions. Similar issues confront lawyers for partnerships, lawyers for trustees and other fiduciaries, and lawyers for a government agency. This chapter deals with those questions.

When organizational peace reigns and all the organization's agents lawfully fulfill their responsibilities to the entity, deciding who personifies the client is not difficult: The person designated by the organization's powers-that-be to deal with the lawyer personifies the client. This is so not because it is the right answer but because harmony prevails within the organization. When no one within the organization will contradict the designee, the lawyer may safely rely upon that person's instructions. But harmony in large or small organizations is a sometime thing that can be fractured by economic hard times, problems of succession, changes in ownership and such chancy events as deterioration in personal relationships. Problems arise when there is infighting over control of an entity and when the person designated to speak for the entity acts in a way that may harm it. Who personifies the client then? What duties does the lawyer for the organization owe to whom? Will conflict among constituents of the organization inevitably

---

1. M.R. 1.4 (duty of communication); M.R. 1.6 (duty of confidentiality); and M.R. 1.2(a) (client makes settlement decision).

result in termination of the lawyer's employment because of conflicts of interest?

The Model Code's primary provision on this subject, EC 5–18, provides little guidance on these difficult questions:

> A lawyer employed or retained by a corporation or similar entity owes his allegiance to the entity and not to a stockholder, director, officer, employee, representative, or other person connected with the entity. In advising the entity, a lawyer should keep paramount its interests and his professional judgment should not be influenced by the personal desires of any person or organization. Occasionally, a lawyer for an entity is requested by a stockholder, director, officer, employee, representative, or other person connected with the entity to represent him in an individual capacity; in such case the lawyer may serve the individual only if the lawyer is convinced that differing interests are not present.

The Model Rules contain a more elaborate provision, M.R. 1.13, but it also leaves many questions unanswered.

1. Representing an Organization

MEEHAN v. HOPPS

District Court of Appeal, First District, Division 1, California, 1956.
144 Cal.App.2d 284, 301 P.2d 10.

BRAY, JUSTICE.

This is an appeal from a certain order in an action brought by respondents as plaintiffs, against appellants as defendants, for an accounting and other relief on behalf of the policyholders, creditors and stockholders of the Rhode Island Insurance Company, in which it is charged that Stewart B. Hopps, former director, member of the executive committee and chairman of the board of the company, dominated and managed the company's affairs for his own personal gain in violation of his fiduciary duties. Defendants moved the trial court to restrain and enjoin the Providence, Rhode Island, law firm of Edwards & Angell, ... from further participation in the case and from disclosing information pertaining thereto. The motion was based upon the alleged dual relationship of Edwards & Angell towards Hopps and a claim that Hopps had turned over to that firm as his lawyers certain files, documents and other information which plaintiffs have used and have threatened to use against him in the present action. After a hearing the motion was denied. Defendants appeal.

. . .

With legislative authority the Board of Governors of the State Bar of California have formulated rules of professional conduct approved by the Supreme Court. These rules are binding upon all members of the

State Bar. Bus. and Prof.Code § 6077.[4] Applicable here are Rule 5: "A member of the State Bar shall not accept employment adverse to a client or former client, without the consent of the client or former client, relating to a matter in reference to which he has obtained confidential information by reason of or in the course of his employment by such client or former client"; Rule 7: "A member of the State Bar shall not represent conflicting interests, except with the consent of all parties concerned." Section 6068, Business and Professions Code, provides: It is the duty of an attorney "(e) To maintain inviolate the confidence, and at every peril to himself to preserve the secrets, of his client."

As the law is clear, we deem it unnecessary to cite the many cases holding that an attorney who attempts to use against the interests of his former client information gained while the attorney-client relationship existed, may be enjoined from so doing.

The question first to be determined is:

1. Had There Been an Attorney–Client Relationship Between Counsel and Hopps?

The determination of that question is one of law. De Long v. Miller, 133 Cal.App.2d 175, 178, 283 P.2d 762. However, where there is a conflict in the evidence the factual basis for the determination must first be determined, and it is for the trial court to evaluate the evidence. Id., 133 Cal.App.2d at page 179, 283 P.2d at page 764.

On the question of whether counsel ever represented Hopps as his attorney, the evidence is directly conflicting. Concededly the firm never charged nor received payment from Hopps for any services whatever. The services which Hopps claims were for him personally were paid for by Rhode Island. Soon after Hopps became connected with the company, counsel ceased to act as general counsel for it. Thereafter they were employed on special matters from time to time. At the time counsel first met Hopps they were working for Rhode Island on a merger of the Merchants Insurance Company into the former. Rhode Island's chairman asked counsel to draw a contract for the employment of Hopps, which was done. Hopps claims that the attorney drawing the contract advised him as well as the company. The attorney denied this and claimed that Hopps consulted his own lawyer, Farber, exclusively concerning the contract. Hopps testified that he confided in and was advised by counsel concerning his personal involvement in the affairs of Rhode Island; that he turned over to counsel his personal files; that Attorney Winsor of the firm was a friendly advisor and legal confidant and familiar with Hopps' personal affairs; that the firm undertook to represent Hopps' personal interest

Hopps' allegation [handwritten annotation]

---

4. The firm of Edwards & Angell are the attorneys for the receiver, and the attorneys of that firm representing the receiver in the action were admitted by the trial court to the California State Bar for the purpose of participating in this case. None of them appear of record on this appeal.

in the California controversy [5] and in a number of other matters. We deem it unnecessary to detail the evidence concerning the matters testified to by Hopps as showing a personal attorney and client relationship between him and counsel. Suffice it to say that evidence to the contrary on all matters was presented by Edwards & Angell. The question is primarily one of credibility. The trial court obviously disbelieved Hopps.

There are four matters in which appellants particularly claim that counsel acted personally for Hopps.

(1) The preparation of the employment contract between Rhode Island and Hopps. While Hopps does not claim that he employed counsel in this behalf but that Gilman, of counsel, advised him personally, Gilman denied this. Gilman had been handling for Rhode Island a proposed merger of Merchants Insurance Company with it. Watson, Rhode Island's chairman, asked Gilman to draw the employment contract. Gilman conferred with both Hopps and Watson, sending copies of the contract when prepared to both. In the letter to Hopps accompanying the proposed contract Gilman stated that if it was not satisfactory to Hopps Gilman would take up with Watson any proposed changes. It frequently happens that one retained by a client to draft an agreement between him and another, will send such agreement to the other, asking for the latter's suggestions concerning it, which suggestions the drafter will take up with his client. This statement did not convert Gilman's relationship from attorney for Rhode Island to attorney for Hopps in any respect. The agreement was not to become effective unless the merger was made, and provided that Hopps was to have the right to be interested in the Merchants Insurance Company's dealing with Rhode Island and was only required to give part of his time to the latter. Winsor, of counsel, called on Hopps in New York in connection with the merger. None of these matters changed counsel's relationship as attorney for Rhode Island into attorney for Hopps as well. In his deposition Hopps stated that the work done by counsel on the employment contract was done for Rhode Island. At the trial he retracted that statement....

(2) Approximately nine years after the contract was drawn, counsel were employed by Rhode Island in connection with a controversy with Cuban interests. It involved nine companies and individuals including Hopps and Rhode Island on the American side, and seven on the Cuban side. It was actually a fight for control. Although the controversy had been going on for approximately seven years, counsel had nothing to do with it until approximately three months prior to its settlement. At Watson's request, counsel were employed to represent Rhode Island. At counsel's request Hopps prepared and gave them data concerning the background and history of the controversy and his interest in it. One of the most important problems was whether a proxy held by

---

5. This was a conflict between the Insurance Commissioner of California and Rhode Island, see Rhode Island Ins. Co. v. Downey, 95 Cal.App.2d 220, 212 P.2d 965, in which the actions of Hopps were looked upon with disfavor by the commissioner.

Hopps or those held by the Cuban interests should prevail. Hopps prepared memoranda concerning these, sending copies to Rhode Island's executive committee as well as to counsel. Counsel advised Rhode Island that only Hopps' proxy could be considered. The fact that counsel so advised, and the other matters they did in connection with the controversy, did not make them attorneys for Hopps.

(3)   (3) The Pioneer Equitable Settlement. This involved a dispute between Rhode Island on one side, the Pioneer Equitable and other companies and an individual on the other. Hopps had interests on both sides. There were a number of lawyers representing Rhode Island in this matter including counsel, who were employed by Rhode Island as special counsel in connection with a suit over custodian funds included in the controversy. Counsel denied Hopps' assertion that their special duty in the controversy involved any consideration by them of Hopps' personal interests nor any advice to him concerning them.

Special counsel over custodial funds.

(4)   (4) The California controversy. [T]his was a controversy between Rhode Island and the Insurance Commissioner of California.... In addition to proceedings in the federal court, counsel endeavored to work out a settlement of the controversy with the commissioner. Richards, of counsel, after consultation with Hopps and the obtaining of data from Hopps and other company officers, went to California for that purpose. Richards was told by the California authorities that the commissioner objected to Hopps' association with the company. Richards testified that he told them that he would not discuss personalities, but wanted to work out an arrangement by which the company could continue in business in California. During the negotiations in California, Hopps came out as well as other members of counsel, and together they prepared memoranda to be submitted to the commissioner's counsel. Here again there was nothing done by counsel or information received by them, which in any way made them attorneys for Hopps. While they refused to agree to Hopps' removal from a position of authority in the company, or even to discuss such a change, they were not representing Hopps in so doing, but as attorneys for the company were refusing to discuss the matter of the removal of its president.

Appellants point out that the "contemporaneous record" is replete with instances where Hopps presented memoranda and material to counsel and spent considerable time in conference with counsel, all to assist them in the preparation of the various proceedings in which they were engaged for the corporation. These are matters which Hopps' position as an officer of the corporation, and particularly one who dictated, or at least was instrumental in determining, the policy of the corporation in the particular matter, required him to give the corporation.

Disregarding the testimony of Hopps, as we are required to do on this appeal, we can find nothing in the record to show any relationship of attorney and client between Hopps and counsel, nor that he gave them any data, or disclosed to them any information which he as an officer of the company was not required by his position to do, nor which they as attorneys for the company in the matters entrusted to them, were not entitled to receive.

2. Effect of Representation of the Company

Appellant has not cited, nor have we found, any case holding that an attorney for a corporation is disqualified from representing it in an action brought by it against one of its officers, nor that in such an action the attorney may not use information received from such officer in connection with company matters. The attorney for a corporation represents it, its stockholders and its officers in their representative capacity. He in nowise represents the officers personally. It would be a sorry state of affairs if when a controversy arises between an attorney's corporate client and one of its officers he could not use on behalf of his client information which that officer was required by reason of his position with the corporation to give to the attorney.

Kingman, of counsel, testified that on May 26, 1950, White, the then president of the company, came to counsel's office and informed him that the company would have to go into receivership and that Hopps stated that he was going to get counsel appointed as co-counsel for the receiver with another firm of attorneys.... The fact that counsel, as attorney for the receiver, requested and received Hopps' cooperation in certain receivership matters, that prior to their appointment as receiver, counsel on behalf of the company had prepared an answer in which it alleged that the officers, directors and agents of the company were not at fault, in nowise affected their right to represent the receiver, nor to participate in an action in which the receiver claims that Hopps, one of the officers, was at fault. If Hopps' action in arranging for the appointment did not constitute a consent to counsel being appointed attorneys for the receiver and acting in all respects as their duty as attorneys for the receiver required, such action indicates at least that Hopps originally did not consider that counsel had been his personal attorneys nor that he had disclosed to them any information over and above what his position with the company required him to disclose.

Cases cited by appellants where attorneys were enjoined from proceeding against former clients are easily distinguishable from our case. In all of them the relationship of attorney and client actually had existed between the attorney and the party against whom the attorney was now acting.... Consolidated Theatres v. Warner Bros., 2 Cir., 1954, 216 F.2d 920: An attorney who had been in the office of the law firm defending a motion picture producer in anti-trust litigation attempted to represent an exhibitor's anti-trust damage suit against the producer. United States v. Bishop, 6 Cir., 1937, 90 F.2d 65: An attorney represented the government on the first trial of an action by a veteran on a war risk policy. On the second trial of the same issue he attempted to represent the veteran. Watson v. Watson, 1939, 171 Misc. 175, 11 N.Y.S.2d 537: A wife sued to annul a marriage on the ground of the husband's previous conviction of a crime. The attorneys who had defended the husband in the criminal proceeding and who had obtained from him the history of his life attempted to represent the wife in the annulment action. The other cases cited by appellants relate to situations where the attorney either had represented the person whom he was now appearing against in the same matter or one connected with it or had advised other counsel representing the person he was now proceeding against. In none of the cases was there a situation where the attorney for a corporation was appearing for the corporation adversely to a former officer thereof.

Assuming that some of the information obtained from Hopps by counsel as representative of the corporation is that upon which the receiver's contention that Hopps dominated the corporation, its officers and companies, to its damage, is partially based, nevertheless such fact would not prevent counsel from representing either the corporation or the receiver in a controversy with Hopps nor from using that information against him.... If this were true, then the attorney representing a corporation in any given matter becomes the personal attorney of each stockholder because the attorney's actions benefiting the corporation likewise benefit the stockholder. Such relationship would disqualify the attorney from acting adversely to the stockholder concerning that particular matter in any controversy between the stockholder and a third party, but obviously would not prevent the attorney from representing the corporation in any controversy between it and the stockholder. As attorneys for the corporation, counsel's first duty is to it. Likewise, as an officer of the corporation, it was Hopps' duty to disclose to it all information necessary for its purposes. To hold that the giving of such information in that more or less intimate relationship which necessarily must exist between an officer of the corporation and its attorneys would prevent the corporation attorneys from thereafter using it in favor of the corporation in litigation against the officer, would be unfair to the corporation and its stockholders, and would violate the above mentioned very important precept, namely, that the attorney's first duty is to his client....

Notes on *Meehan*

What was the alleged conflict of interest in *Meehan?* Does the opinion rest on an implicit assumption that, if Hopps had been represented individually by the Edwards firm, the firm could not represent the corporation in the accounting proceeding?

Is the court's holding that no lawyer-client relationship existed between the Edwards firm and Hopps, the former head of the company it represented, consistent with cases like *Togstad* and *Westinghouse*[1] where a relationship giving rise to fiduciary duties was found between a lawyer and persons who reasonably believed that an attorney-client relationship had been established? Might Hopps, after dealing with the Edwards firm on a number of matters over a long period of time, have felt betrayed when the firm attacked him in the accounting proceeding? Why wasn't his belief that the Edwards firm were "his lawyers" a reasonable one?

When the Edwards firm negotiated the employment contract between Hopps and the corporation, was it acting as lawyer for both parties? What must an officer show to prove that an organization's lawyer also represented him as an individual? Does the lawyer have a duty to warn the officer from time to time that she represents the corporation and not the officer personally?

The rule in *Meehan* that a lawyer for a corporation represents the corporation and not the individual officers, directors or shareholders is the general rule followed by American courts. See M.R. 1.13(a) and EC 5–18. As the court notes in *Meehan*, the working relationship between counsel and the managing officers of a company can easily blur the distinction (in the mind and actions of lawyer and corporate official alike) between representing the company and representing the individual. M.R. 1.13(d) requires that a lawyer for an organization provide corporate officers or other constituents something like a Miranda warning about who it is the lawyer represents whenever "it is apparent that the organization's interests are adverse to those of the constituents with whom the lawyer is dealing." Would this have helped in the *Meehan* case?

Representing Both an Organization and Its Officer

In E.F. Hutton & Co. v. Brown,[2] the court disqualified the firm representing Hutton on the ground that previously the firm had jointly represented Hutton's former officer, Brown, in a personal capacity while serving as corporate counsel. The firm claimed that it had represented only the company and that its dealings with Brown were in his official capacity as an officer of Hutton.

As vice-president of Hutton, Brown had authorized a loan to a third person to be secured by Westec common stock. Shortly after the loan was made the SEC suspended trading in Westec stock because of suspected trading illegalities. One issue in a subsequent SEC investigation was whether Brown knew that the loan would be used to purchase stock. Brown was twice called to testify about this matter in the SEC investigation. Hutton's lawyers discussed with him his forthcoming testimony and told him that they would accompany him to the hearings. At both hearings, Brown was asked if the lawyers with him were

1. *Togstad* is printed in chapter 6 above at p. 481; *Westinghouse* is printed in chapter 7 above at p. 627.

2. 305 F.Supp. 371 (S.D.Tex.1969).

his lawyers, and he responded that they were. Thereafter, Hutton fired Brown and sued him for negligence in authorizing the loan. When Brown claimed that his communications with Hutton's lawyers were privileged, the lawyers argued that his testimony at the hearings surprised them because they had previously explained to Brown that they represented Hutton and not him individually. (Brown disputed this.) The lawyers had not corrected Brown's assertion at either hearing.

The court placed great emphasis on these facts, stating:

> An attorney's appearance in a judicial or semi-judicial proceeding creates a presumption that an attorney-client relationship exists between the attorney and the person with whom he appears. This presumption shifts to Hutton, the party denying the existence of the relationship, the burden of persuasion. When the relationship is also evidenced by the entry of a formal appearance by the attorney on behalf of the person with whom he appears, the presumption becomes almost irrebuttable.... [3]

The fact that Brown had not paid the lawyers' fee and that he had never asked the firm to represent him were held not to overcome the relationship implied by the conduct of the lawyers at the hearings.

The court rejected arguments that the lawyers represented Brown only in his official capacity at a time when the interests of Hutton and Brown were perceived as identical. The SEC was investigating both Hutton and Brown, hence his interests as well as Hutton's were at stake. Brown's assertions that the lawyers represented him, therefore, meant Brown as an individual. Brown's belief that he was represented individually was reasonable, given the failure of counsel to correct the record and the fact that Hutton faced civil penalties, but Brown faced a potential prison term. Corporate counsel, the court observed, have "an obligation to ensure that there is no misunderstanding by the officer." Fears of adverse effects on corporate representation were unjustified: "Only those counsel who permit the officer to believe that they represent him individually will disable themselves from appearing in subsequent litigation against him." [4]

In *Hutton* the court said that a corporate lawyer who becomes aware that a corporate officer might misconstrue the lawyer's participation as individual representation has two options: (1) joint representation of the officer and the corporation after obtaining the informed consent of both clients; or (2) representing the corporation's separate interest after informing the officer that she did not represent him and that his interest would go unprotected unless he employed personal counsel. [5] If joint representation had been chosen in *Hutton*, would

3. Id. at 387.
4. Id. at 398.
5. 305 F.Supp. 396–97.

Hutton's lawyers have been disqualified from suing Brown? [6]

The underlying issue in cases like *Meehan* and *Hutton* is whether the putative client had a reasonable belief that a lawyer-client relationship existed. In United States v. Keplinger,[7] a corporate officer who had been convicted of mail and wire fraud claimed that evidence admitted against him should have been excluded under the attorney-client privilege. The corporation's lawyers had accompanied him to a meeting with the Food and Drug Administration (FDA), and FDA officials had referred to the lawyers as "your counsel." The court distinguished *Hutton* on the grounds that the lawyers had not entered a formal appearance as counsel and that the officer's subjective belief that counsel was representing him as an individual was not sufficient to demonstrate that an attorney-client relationship existed: "[N]o individual attorney-client relationship can be inferred without some finding that the potential client's subjective belief is minimally reasonable." [8]

Who Controls a Corporation's Attorney–Client Privilege?

Corporations like natural persons may claim an attorney-client privilege. See Upjohn Co. v. United States.[9] The privilege belongs to the corporation, not individual corporate officers.[10] But who speaks for the corporation? Corporate law generally provides that the board of directors or a person authorized by the board to act may act for the corporation, if approval of shareholders on the particular matter is not required. In general, decisions concerning routine litigation are delegated to particular officers, but settlement of a major litigation that threatens the continuance or profitability of a corporation (e.g., the Pennzoil litigation in the case of Texaco) requires board action.

In Commodity Futures Trading Commission v. Weintraub,[11] the issue was whether the trustee for a bankrupt corporation could waive the privilege on the corporation's behalf and against the wishes of the former directors of the debtor. Weintraub had been counsel to the now-bankrupt company. When called before the Commodity Commission to testify about the company's transactions, Weintraub refused, citing attorney-client privilege. The trustee in bankruptcy then waived the privilege on the corporation's behalf, but former officers intervened and attempted to assert it.

6. See M.R. 1.9 and *Brennan's* case, p. 696. See also Cooke v. Laidlaw, Adams & Peck, 126 A.D.2d 453, 510 N.Y.S.2d 597 (1987) (firm that had jointly represented corporation and officer disqualified from representing corporation against the now-former officer involving matter substantially related to joint representation even if no confidences were in fact communicated to lawyer by officer).

7. 776 F.2d 678 (7th Cir.1985).

8. 776 F.2d at 701. See also Bernstein v. Crazy Eddie, Inc., 702 F.Supp. 962, 988 (E.D.N.Y.1988).

9. 449 U.S. 383 (1981), printed in Chapter 4 above at p. 226.

10. See Citibank, N.A. v. Andros, 666 F.2d 1192, 1195 (8th Cir.1981); In re Grand Jury Proceedings, 434 F.Supp. 648, 650 (E.D.Mich.1977), aff'd, 570 F.2d 562 (6th Cir.1978); United States v. Piccini, 412 F.2d 591, 593 (2d Cir.1969).

11. 471 U.S. 343 (1985).

The Supreme Court held that the trustee, as the company's current management, controlled the privilege on the company's behalf. The former directors argued that vesting control of the privilege with the trustee would leave shareholders' interests unprotected or at least always subservient to the interests of creditors. The Court stated that the trustee had fiduciary duties that ran to both creditors and shareholders. Although the privilege could be used by trustees in favor of creditors at the expense of shareholders, this posture was "in keeping with the hierarchy of interests created by the bankruptcy laws." [12]

Weintraub involved communications made in the ordinary course of business prior to bankruptcy. What about communications between corporate management and bankruptcy counsel relating to the filing of bankruptcy? Can the bankruptcy trustee subsequently waive the privilege as to those communications?

A Privilege for Individual Corporate Officers?

Unlike the court in *Meehan*, the court in *Hutton* found an attorney-client relationship between the corporate officer and corporate counsel. Nevertheless, *Hutton* also held that the officer had no privilege to assert against the company:

> Brown gave information to counsel concerning the ... loan transaction long before counsel appeared with him at the SEC and bankruptcy hearings. As a corporate officer, Brown's duty to his corporate employer required him to furnish this information to counsel at Hutton's request. In fact, because Brown obtained his knowledge within the scope of his position as an officer of Hutton, the information which he conveyed to counsel was, as a matter of law, already known to Hutton. The attorney-client privilege is therefore not available to Brown against Hutton, since all information he gave to counsel already was known to Hutton, and since Brown gave the information to counsel knowing that counsel, in turn, would convey it to Hutton's New York management. [13]

The grounds for denying Brown the privilege—the timing of communications, the status of information possessed by a corporate agent and his duty as an officer to communicate information relating to corporate business—suggest that a corporate officer, who has been represented as an individual and joint client with the corporation, may never be able to assert a privilege against the corporation itself. Several courts have so held. [14]

Other courts have stated that an officer sometimes may assert the privilege against the corporation, but only as to personal matters not related to the officer's duties or the corporation's business (e.g., drafting

---

12. 471 U.S. at 344.

13. 305 F.Supp. at 400–01.

14. See, e.g., *Piccini*, supra, 412 F.2d at 593; Polycast Technology Corp. v. Uniroyal, Inc., 125 F.R.D. 47, 49 (S.D.N.Y.1989); In re O.P.M. Leasing Services, Inc., 13 B.R. 64, 67–68 & n. 11 (S.D.N.Y.1981), aff'd, 670 F.2d 383 (2d Cir.1982).

an officer's personal will). In In re Grand Jury,[15] the court held that a corporate officer who claims a personal privilege must show, in addition to all the usual elements of the attorney-client privilege, "that the substance of their conversation did not concern matters within the company or the general affairs of the company." [16] In Matter of Bevill, Bresler & Schulman Asset Management Corp.,[17] the court held that a personal attorney-client privilege could not be asserted against the corporation as to communications made by the officer about matters within the officer's "roles and functions" within the corporation. Corporate officers could have a personal attorney-client privilege only as to communications "not related to their role as officers of the corporation." [18] Is the *Bevill/Grand Jury* test consistent with the general rules on privilege between joint clients? Review the note on this subject in Chapter 4 above at p. 225.

2. Representing an Organization and Its Agents in Derivative Actions

YABLONSKI v. UNITED MINE WORKERS OF AMERICA

United States Court of Appeals, District of Columbia Circuit, 1971.
448 F.2d 1175.

Before McGOWAN, ROBINSON and WILKEY, Circuit Judges.

PER CURIAM:

This is an action under § 501 of the Labor–Management Reporting and Disclosure Act[1] brought by the late Joseph A. Yablonski and 48 other members of the United Mine Workers of America against the UMWA and three named officers—Boyle, President; Titler, Vice President; Owens, Secretary–Treasurer—asking for an accounting of UMWA funds disbursed by them and for restitution of funds allegedly misappropriated and misspent.

No trial on the merits has been had. The issue on this appeal is whether the law firm regularly representing the UMWA [Williams & Connolly of Washington, D.C.], who originally entered an appearance for the UMWA and the three individual officer-defendants, should be allowed to continue its representation of the UMWA after it withdrew as counsel for the individual defendants. The District Court found that the regular UMWA outside counsel was not disqualified from continuing its representation in this action, but for reasons enunciated infra

15. In re Grand Jury Investigation No. 83–30557, 575 F.Supp. 777 (N.D.Ga.1983).

16. 575 F.Supp. at 780.

17. 805 F.2d 120, 123 (3d Cir.1986) (relying on *In re Grand Jury*).

18. Id. at 125.

1. 29 U.S.C. § 501(b) (1964) provides [that a union member may bring an action in a federal or state court against a union officer who has violated fiduciary duties owed to the union "to recover damages or secure an accounting or other appropriate relief for the benefit of the labor organization."]

we hold that in the particular circumstances of this case such representation should be discontinued.

After the action was filed in December 1969, appellant-plaintiffs filed in May 1970 a motion to disqualify counsel on the grounds (1) that the compensation of the regular UMWA counsel would continue to come from the UMWA treasury and (2) that there existed a conflict between the UMWA and the individual defendant officers. A month later the UMWA counsel withdrew as counsel for the individual defendants but remained as counsel for the UMWA, which the District Court sustained as proper.

At the outset of the lawsuit the then counsel for all defendants set about with commendable diligence to delineate the real issues of the lawsuit, filing in behalf of the UMWA and the three individual defendants answers setting forth all customary general defenses, and filing 34 pages of interrogatories to develop more fully the scope of the case.

The appellants argue that this period of six months' prior representation in this same suit disqualifies the regular union outside counsel to continue its representation of the UMWA, even after its withdrawal as counsel for the three individual officer-defendants. With this we do not agree. It has been inferentially held that one lawyer can properly represent all defendants if a suit appears groundless, and that separate counsel is required only in a situation where there is a potential conflict between the interests of the union and those of its officers. We regard the actions of the regular UMWA counsel during its six-month representation of both the union and its officers as an effort to ascertain the exact nature of the lawsuit and protect the interests of all defendants, and by our ruling herein do not imply any censure of counsel's action during this period of joint representation. But there does exist in our judgment a more serious barrier to the continued representation of the UMWA by its regular outside counsel in this particular lawsuit.

I. Effect of Other Litigation in Which Regular UMWA-Counsel Represent Defendant President Boyle

Of far more concern is the existence of other litigation in which the regular UMWA counsel is representing Boyle, sometimes in conjunction with representation of the union, at other times not.

(1) The "reinstatement" or "reprisal" case—one of four "election" cases brought by Joseph A. Yablonski against the UMWA and its officers, alleging that the reassignment or severance of plaintiff Yablonski from certain union duties was a reprisal for his running for president against the incumbent Boyle. After the death of Yablonski the trial court dismissed the case as moot, and this action is on appeal in this court. Appellants here claim that if this court should hold that the trial court was wrong in dismissing the reprisal case as moot, then appellee Boyle may subsequently be required to pay substantial punitive damages to the estate of Yablonski, and thus Boyle has a personal,

as distinguished from a union, interest in that appeal. Although initially the union and its officers were represented by the union general counsel in the District Court, the regular UMWA outside counsel represented both the UMWA and Boyle personally on the motion to dismiss as moot, and continues such representation on appeal in this court.

(2) Denial of attorney's fees—as an outgrowth of the UMWA election cases, attorneys for "the Yablonski group" applied for attorney's fees to be paid by the union, which the District Court denied, finding that "no malfeasance on the part of the officers has yet been established." These four cases are now on appeal. The regular UMWA counsel represents both the union and the individual officer-defendants here and did so on the merits in two of the cases in the District Court (the "*Journal*" and "fair election" cases, paragraph 3 infra) and on the motions to dismiss in all four cases, where the issue originally was the compliance of the incumbent officers with the Labor–Management Reporting and Disclosure Act. This series of cases is alleged to be related to the case at bar, inasmuch as paragraph 13 of the complaint herein alleges that Boyle and the other individual officer-defendants employed counsel to defend them on charges of breach of trust and paid such counsel from UMWA funds, the regular outside UMWA counsel here involved being one of those whose representation and compensation is being challenged in this present suit.

(3) The "*Journal*" and "fair election" cases—during the UMWA election campaign candidate Yablonski claimed that the union newspaper was being used to promote the candidacy of incumbent President Boyle. On appeals in this court the regular UMWA counsel represented Boyle and the union, although in one aspect in the District Court which was severed and consolidated with the instant case, whether Boyle should be made to pay for some of the costs of printing of the *Journal*, the regular UMWA counsel does not represent Boyle.

(4) Blankenship v. Boyle—a group of retired miners sued the Trustees of the UMWA Welfare and Retirement Fund of 1950, one of the Three Trustees being Boyle, alleging that the Fund had been mismanaged by the Trustees. Boyle was charged with using his position as a Trustee to increase pension benefits to assist his re-election campaign. The District Court ordered his removal as Trustee and this court has recently refused to stay the effectiveness of that order, although not deciding the appeal on the merits. Regular UMWA counsel represents Boyle individually in all three of the capacities in which he is sued, as Trustee of the Fund, President of the UMWA, and Director of the National Bank of Washington, as well as representing the union.

We have listed and briefly described the above actions of record in which the regular UMWA counsel represents Boyle individually. Each of these has been minutely examined by appellees' counsel to demonstrate that in no instance is the representation of Boyle individually in conflict with the good faith representation of the UMWA in this case;

in effect, that the interests of the UMWA and of Boyle individually are the same. We are assured that if any conflict should arise appellees' counsel would be prompt to withdraw as counsel to the UMWA in this case.

While the issues involved in each of the individual cases, and the past or present existence or nonexistence of any conflict, are relevant to the propriety of the regular UMWA counsel continuing its representation of the union in the case at bar, yet we do not think that this analysis is determinative of the real problem here. It is undeniable that the regular UMWA counsel have undertaken the representation of Boyle individually in many facets of his activities as a UMWA official, as a Trustee of the Fund, as a Director of the Bank owned 74% by the union. With strict fidelity to this client, such counsel could not undertake action on behalf of another client which would undermine his position personally. Yet, in this particular litigation, counsel for the UMWA should be diligent in analyzing objectively the true interests of the UMWA as an institution without being hindered by allegiance to any individual concerned.

We are not required to accept at this point the charge of the appellants that the "true interest" of the union is aligned with those of the individual appellants here; this may or may not turn out to be the fact. But in the exploration and the determination of the truth or falsity of the charges brought by these individual appellants against the incumbent officers of the union and the union itself as a defendant, the UMWA needs the most objective counsel obtainable. Even if we assume the accuracy of the appellee's position at the present time that there is no visible conflict of interest, yet we cannot be sure that such will not arise in the future.

Whether facts are discovered and legal positions taken which would create such a conflict of interest between the UMWA position and the position of the individual defendant Boyle may well be determined by the approach which counsel for the UMWA takes in this case. We think that the objectives of the Labor–Management Reporting and Disclosure Act [8] would be much better served by having an unquestion-

8. 29 U.S.C. § 401 (1964) sets forth the congressional declaration of findings, purposes and policy of the LMRDA, including *inter alia* the statement that "in order to accomplish the objective of a free flow of commerce it is essential that labor organizations, employers, and their officials adhere to the highest standards of responsibility and ethical conduct in administering the affairs of their organizations...." The legislative history of the Act makes plain that a major congressional objective was to provide union members, as well as the Government in the public interest, with a variety of means to ensure that officials of labor organizations perform their duties in accordance with fiduciary standards.... The House Committee strongly expressed its concern that:

Some trade unions have acquired bureaucratic tendencies and characteristics. The relationship of the leaders of such unions to their members has in some instances become impersonal and autocratic. In some cases men who have acquired positions of power and responsibility within unions have abused their power and forsaken their responsibilities to the membership and to the public. The power and control of the affairs of a trade union by leaders who abuse their power and forsake their responsibilities inevitably leads to the elimination of efficient, honest and democratic practices

ably independent new counsel in this particular case. The public interest requires that the validity of appellants' charges against the UMWA management of breach of its fiduciary responsibilities be determined in a context which is as free as possible from the appearance of any potential for conflict of interest in the representation of the union itself.

II. Objective Determination of the UMWA's Institutional Interest

Counsel for the appellees here have stressed the "institutional interest" of the UMWA in all of the issues raised, and particularly the institutional interest of the union in "repose." Counsel's interpretation of the "institutional interest" of the union appears to have been broad enough to authorize UMWA counsel to undertake practically everything worthwhile in the defense of this lawsuit. After the withdrawal of the regular union counsel from representation of Boyle individually in this case, the individual practitioner selected to represent Boyle has apparently contributed little to the defense.

By far the strongest laboring oar has been stroked by the regular UMWA counsel on behalf of the union. On oral argument appellees' counsel stated that it had prepared 94 pages of answers to interrogatories, that the individual practitioner representing Boyle had agreed they should do this, as the UMWA had a definite interest that all questions as to the conduct of union affairs previously were accurately answered and that the accurate answers were to be found in the union records. We can see the UMWA interest in having such interrogatories answered accurately, but we would think that since it is the individual defendants who are charged with the misconduct, their counsel would be the one to initiate and to carry the burden....

In the crucial area of discovery matters, clearly representing the vast bulk of the effort expended by the parties defendant at this stage of the litigation, UMWA counsel have prepared 174 pages of answers to plaintiffs' initial interrogatories which were directed to all defendants, while counsel for the individual defendants, until 2 April 1971, some 7 months after the interrogatories were originally served, had contented himself with filing 2 pages of answers for each individual defendant, a total of 6 pages. On 2 April 1971 counsel finally filed additional answers on behalf of defendant Boyle; however, as of the date of argument of this appeal, answers on behalf of the other individual defendants had not been filed.

. . .

... It appears that in 18 months of representation (6 months for both the UMWA and Boyle individually, and 12 months for the UMWA

within such union, and often results in irresponsible actions which are detrimental to the public interest. (H.R. No. 741, 86th Cong., 1st Sess. 6 (1959).

Appellants' complaint in the instant case alleges a state of affairs existing within the leadership of the UMWA of the magnitude of that which the House Report condemned.

alone), the regular UMWA counsel has not brought forth a single issue on which the UMWA and the Boyle individual interest have diverged.

We think the analogy of the position of a corporation and its individual officers when confronted by a stockholder derivative suit is illuminating here.[10]   We believe it is well established that when one group of stockholders brings a derivative suit, with the corporation as the nominal defendant and the individual officers accused of malfeasance of one sort or another, the role of both the corporate house counsel and the regular outside counsel for the corporation becomes usually a passive one.   Certainly no corporate counsel purports to represent the individual officers involved, neither in the particular derivative suit nor in other litigation by virtue of which counsel necessarily must create ties of loyalty and confidentiality to the individual officers, which might preclude counsel from the most effective representation of the corporation itself.   The corporation has certain definite institutional interests to be protected, and the counsel charged with this responsibility should have ties on a personal basis with neither the dissident stockholders nor the incumbent officeholders.

Purportedly a stockholder derivative suit is for the benefit of the corporation, even though the corporation is a nominal defendant, just as the appellants here assert (yet to be proved) that their action is for the benefit of the UMWA and that the individual incumbent officers are liable to the union itself for their alleged misdeeds.   And, under established corporate law, if the individual officers are successful in the defense of a suit arising out of the performance of their duties as corporate officers, then they may justifiably seek reimbursement from the corporation for the costs of their successful defense.

In the ordinary case the action taken here by the regular UMWA counsel in the District Court might well have been the proper one, i.e., after establishing the nature of the lawsuit by interrogatories and filing answers on behalf of both the union and the individual officers in order fully to protect the position of all parties, then to step aside as counsel for the individual defendants and continue the representation of the union.   But this particular case is a derivative action for the benefit of the union, and furthermore must be viewed in its relationship to this entire complex of numerous cases already pending or decided in this and the District Courts in which the regular UMWA counsel has already undertaken the representation of Boyle individually.   Each and every one of these cases either directly arises out of or is directly connected with the struggle for power in the UMWA being waged by the Yablonski group on one side and the incumbent officers headed by President Boyle on the other.   In this situation, the best interests of the UMWA and the purposes of the Labor–Management Reporting and Disclosure Act will be much better served by the disqualification of the

10. See Phillips v. Osborne, 403 F.2d 826, 831 (9th Cir.1968); Int'l Brotherhood of Teamsters, etc. v. Hoffa, 242 F.Supp. 246, 251 (D.D.C.1965).   Indeed, as appellees themselves noted in a motion filed in the court below "The action by Mr. Yablonski and others is a derivative action on behalf of the union...."

regular union counsel in this particular suit and its continued representation of the individual Boyle in the other lawsuits.

We are cognizant that any counsel to represent the UMWA selected by President Boyle will be to some degree under his control. But
such counsel will still only have one client—the UMWA—to represent
in matters growing out of the union's affairs. Such counsel would
never be professionally obligated to consider Boyle's personal interests,
because they would not be representing him individually in related
matters. And the extent of their labors would be gauged by the need to
protect the UMWA position in this litigation. . . .

―――――

The fight for control of the United Mine Workers union began in
the late 1960s when a group of dissidents led by Yablonski challenged
the corrupt leadership of Boyle. The Boyle faction and the union itself
were represented by Williams & Connolly; the Yablonski faction was
represented by Joseph Rauh.[19]

Following the decision printed above, the Williams & Connolly firm
withdrew from representation of the union, and the union's in-house
general counsel and his staff attorneys entered appearances on behalf
of the union. The Yablonski group immediately moved to disqualify
these lawyers, but the District Court denied the motion. The Court of
Appeals in a sharply critical opinion overturned the ruling and disqualified counsel.[20] In this second opinion, the court said:

> The record now reveals a new arrangement for union counsel
> which in final analysis does not differ essentially from the older
> [one]. . . . UMWA general counsel and three members of his staff
> are representing or have represented to some extent union officers
> who are accused of wrongdoing in this case. One staff member is
> the son of one of such officers, and another is the son of a nonparty
> officer whom the charges conceivably could implicate. Atop that,
> three of the five attorneys are themselves named in appellants'
> complaint as recipients of payments allegedly made by officers in
> breach of fiduciary duties.

> Considerably more is both charged and largely denied, but
> merely to recite only these several uncontested circumstances is to
> demonstrate satisfactorily that house counsel as a group do not fit
> the specifications we previously laid down for those who would
> undertake representation of UMWA in this cause. They simply
> are not "unquestionably independent new counsel" whose contem-
> plated appearance would enable resolution of the issues "in a
> context which is as free as possible from the appearance of any
> potential for conflict of interests in the representation of the union
> itself." It follows that the license the District Court gave them to

19. See Evan Thomas, The Man to See: Edward Bennett Williams 308–309 (1991).
20. Yablonski v. United Mine Workers, 454 F.2d 1036 (D.C.Cir.1971).

remain union counsel is a grave departure from the terms of our prior mandate....

The district court's ruling [was apparently based on its] belief that "a passive role" was in store for UMWA in this case....

... [T]here is no predicate for a present assumption that UMWA must or will remain an inactive party. UMWA may, but is not inexorably bound to, take and maintain a detached position on the merits....

Much of appellees' presentation is devoted to attempted justification of UMWA's representation by its house counsel on the ground that its institutional interests as a union coincide with the individual defensive interests of the officers who are sued. That approach puts the cart before the horse....

. . .

... [A] sine qua non of permissible union representation ... is the absence of any duty to another that might detract from a full measure of loyalty to the welfare of the union. House counsel no less than outside counsel must survive that test.... [21]

In December 1969, Yablonski and his wife and daughter were murdered by gunmen who broke into their home. After the Williams & Connolly firm was disqualified from representing the union in the *Yablonski* case, the firm continued to represent Boyle and the other officers in other matters. Boyle and others were eventually convicted of conspiring to murder Yablonski. [22]

Notes on *Yablonski*

An action under the Labor–Management Reporting and Disclosure Act is analogous to a shareholder derivative suit: Union members are seeking, on behalf of the union, to enforce the fiduciary duties of union officers to the entity. The union is a nominal defendant in a suit brought on its behalf.

Suppose the Williams & Connolly firm had not been representing Boyle in other cases involving the same parties and many of the same issues, i.e., breach of fiduciary duties owed by union officers to union members. Would the firm have been disqualified from representing the union? On the actual facts of *Yablonski*, what conflict prevents continued representation of the union?

Role of Corporate Counsel in Shareholder Derivative Suits

The relationship between a corporation's shareholders, directors and officers is usually orderly and harmonious. In *Yablonski* and in all

---

21. Id. at 1040–42.

22. See Prater v. United States Parole Commission, 802 F.2d 948, 949 (7th Cir.1986). Prater, a union official, pled guilty to conspiracy to deprive a citizen of civil rights for his role in transferring union pension funds to those who killed Yablonski and his family.

situations resulting in a shareholder derivative suit, this harmony has broken down: Shareholders, or some of them, are suing members of the control group in the name of the corporation to enforce an obligation allegedly due the corporation.[23]   Somewhere in the fray stands counsel to the corporation, either an outside law firm, "inside" lawyers employed by the corporation on a full-time basis or both.   What is the position of the corporation's lawyer when a derivative suit is brought, and what difference does that position make?

In a derivative suit, shareholders formally place themselves in the shoes of the corporation to enforce a corporate right.   As the court points out in *Yablonski*, the corporation is a defendant in name only;[24] the real defendants are the named persons, usually one or more of the corporation's officers, directors and majority shareholders, i.e., those with control of the corporation.

Corporate law, supplemented by the procedural law governing class actions, generally permits a derivative action only if the following conditions are satisfied:[25] (1) The shareholder was such both at the time of the wrong and at the time of suit.   (2) If not excused as futile, a demand is made on the board of directors to pursue the action, and the board's response does not have the effect of terminating the action. The board may respond either by (a) taking over the suit, (b) permitting the derivative suit to proceed, or (c), more likely in today's world, filing a motion to dismiss or stay the action.   The last response flows from a

---

23.   A derivative action brought by a shareholder to redress an injury to the corporation must be distinguished from a direct action by a shareholder to redress an injury sustained by, or a duty owed to, the shareholder. See ALI, Principles of Corporate Governance: Analysis and Recommendations § 7.01 and comments (Proposed Final Draft, Mar. 31, 1992). For example, a claim that seeks to enforce a shareholder's right to vote is direct, not derivative, as is the claim of a shareholder who bought shares on the basis of misleading or false statements in a prospectus. On the other hand, if an officer or director injures the corporation by a violation of the duty of fair dealing, the action is derivative. Some situations are difficult to classify or may lead to an overlap of the two remedies.

What difference does it make whether the claim is direct or derivative? A direct action is exempt from special procedural requirements generally applicable to a derivative action: e.g., demand, security for expenses, verification of the complaint. See note 25 below. In addition, a direct action, unlike a derivative action, may not be terminated on the basis of a board recommendation or shareholder action. Unless a direct claim is subject to a statutory fee-shifting provision, the plaintiff's lawyer must be compensated out of the award either on a contingent-fee or common-fund basis. Corporate law provides for the payment by the corporation of litigation expenses of a successful derivative suit. The application of the *Garner* exception to the attorney-client privilege, see p. 774 below, may also depend on whether the action is a direct or derivative one.

24.   See Ross v. Bernhard, 396 U.S. 531 (1970).

25.   See ALI, Principles of Corporate Governance: Analysis and Recommendations § 7.02 (Proposed Final Draft, Mar. 31, 1992) (standing to commence and maintain a derivative action only if the owner of an equity security has been a contemporaneous and continuing owner and is "able to represent fairly and adequately the interests of the shareholders"); id. at § 7.03 (intracorporate remedies must be exhausted by a demand requesting the board to prosecute the action or take suitable corrective measures); id. at § 7.04 (special pleading and procedural rules applicable to derivative actions including verification of facts pleaded in the complaint and, in a minority of states, provision of security-for-expense bond by the plaintiff shareholder).

determination, made by vote of a disinterested board or a special litigation committee composed of disinterested directors, that prosecution of the derivative action is not in the best interests of the corporation.[26]   (3) Security for the corporation's expenses in defending the action is provided, usually in the form of an indemnity bond.[27]   And (4) the plaintiff shareholders are representative of the class and are adequately represented by counsel. A further degree of judicial control is provided by the requirement that any settlement of a derivative suit must be approved by the court.

Yablonski states that corporate counsel's proper role in a derivative suit is to protect the corporation's interests, as distinct from the interests of either the director-defendants or the plaintiff-shareholders. Following this approach, corporate counsel should not jointly represent the corporation and either the director-defendants or the plaintiff-shareholders; the corporation is entitled to "independent counsel." Nevertheless, the court approves counsel's having jointly represented all defendants in the initial stages of the lawsuit. Why?

Many courts allow joint representation when the plaintiffs' suit appears to lack merit. This is seen as necessary to handle nuisance suits.[28] Representation during preliminary stages when the interests of the corporation and the officers either coincide or are being defined also may be proper.[29] Other courts, however, have questioned the "meritless" lawsuit standard.[30]

26. See ALI, Principles of Corporate Governance § 7.05 (Proposed Final Draft, Mar. 31, 1992) (authorizing delegation of board authority to seek dismissal of a derivative action, approve a settlement, or seek a stay to a special litigating committee of disinterested directors even if a majority of the board is interested); and id. at § 1.10 (providing for court dismissal of a derivative claim if the board has so recommended and the claim is subject to the business judgment rule, but subjecting the board's action to more scrutiny when the claim may involve a knowing and culpable violation of law or a violation of the duty of fair dealing).

27. An indemnity bond is required only in a minority of states. The cost of providing a bond that will reimburse the corporation or individual defendants for legal expenses incurred in defending an action determined to be lacking in merit is considerable: It may cost $30,000 to provide a bond of $100,000. ALI, Principles of Corporate Governance: Analysis and Recommendations § 7.04, comment g (Proposed Final Draft, Mar. 31, 1992), opposes the "security-for-expenses" requirement because it chills meritorious actions and discriminates unfairly against small shareholders. The problem of irresponsible derivative actions, the ALI concludes, is dealt with more directly and effectively by other legal devices: (1) award of costs against a lawyer who brings a derivative action without legal cause, and (2) use of litigation committee reports to terminate suits.

28. See, e.g., Schwartz v. Guterman, 109 Misc.2d 1004, 441 N.Y.S.2d 597, 598 (1981), ("In a meritless ... suit [retaining] separate counsel for the corporation ... may delay the matter and cause a needless expense, ultimately borne by the shareholders."); In re Conduct of Kinsey, 294 Or. 544, 660 P.2d 660, 669 (1983) (counsel may represent all defendants if the suit is "patently sham or patently frivolous").

29. See Hausman v. Buckley, 299 F.2d 696, 699 (2d Cir.1962).

30. In Lewis v. Shaffer Stores Company, 218 F.Supp. 238, 240 (S.D.N.Y.1963), the court stated, "I have no doubt that ... [the law firm for the defendants believes] in good faith that there is no merit to this action. Plaintiff, of course, vigorously contends to the contrary. The court cannot and should not attempt to pass upon the merits at this stage." The court held the corporation should retain independent counsel for the litigation.

In Cannon v. United States Acoustics Corporation,[31] a leading case on the issue of joint representation, the court concluded that a lawyer should be disqualified from simultaneously representing the corporation and the individual officer defendants:

> [T]his is a derivative shareholder action against four officer-directors and two corporations. The complaint alleges that certain directors misappropriated monies of the corporation and violated federal and state securities laws. These are serious charges. If they are proved, the corporations stand to gain substantially. The [Code of Professional Responsibility] unquestionably prohibits one lawyer from representing multiple clients when their interests are in conflict. The Code goes so far as to say that if the clients' interests are potentially differing, the preferable course is for the lawyer to refuse the employment initially....
>
> ... Nevertheless, defendants' counsel argue there is no present conflict and should one arise they will withdraw their representation of the individual defendants and represent only the corporations. There are a number of problems with this solution. First, the complaint on its face establishes a conflict that cannot be ignored despite counsel's good faith representations. Second, counsel overlooks the hardship on the court and the parties if in the middle of this litigation new counsel must be obtained because a conflict arises. Lastly, although counsel offers to withdraw its representation of the individual defendants and remain counsel for the corporations if a conflict should arise, the appropriate course ... is for the corporation to retain independent counsel. Under this procedure, once counsel has examined the evidence, a decision can be made regarding the role the corporation will play in the litigation. This decision will be made without the possibility of any influence emanating from the representation of the individual defendants, and will also eliminate the potential problem of confidences and secrets reposed by the individual defendants being used adverse to their interests by former counsel should new counsel have had to have been selected under the approach suggested by defense counsel. This solution, concededly, is not without its disabilities. The corporations' rights to counsel of their choice are infringed and in a closely held corporation, as here, the financial burden is increased. Nevertheless, on balance, the corporations must obtain independent counsel.... [32]

In contrast to *Cannon*, the Comment to M.R. 1.13 suggests that joint representation is presumptively valid:

---

31. 398 F.Supp. 209 (N.D.Ill.1975), aff'd in relevant part, 532 F.2d 1118 (7th Cir.1976).

32. 398 F.Supp. at 220. See also Messing v. FDI, Inc., 439 F.Supp. 776, 772 (D.N.J. 1977); Murphy v. Washington American League Base Ball Club, Inc., 324 F.2d 394 (D.C.Cir.1963); Harry G. Henn, Corporations § 370 (2d ed. 1970); Developments in the Law: Conflicts of Interest in the Legal Profession, 94 Harv.L.Rev. 1244, 1339–40 (1981).

The question can arise [in a shareholder derivative suit] whether counsel for the organization may defend such an action. The proposition that the organization is the lawyer's client does not alone resolve the issue. Most derivative actions are a normal incident of an organization's affairs, to be defended by the organization's lawyer like any other suit. However, if the claim involves serious charges of wrongdoing by those in control of the organization, a conflict may arise between the lawyer's duty to the organization and the lawyer's relationship with the board. In those circumstances, Rule 1.7 governs who should represent the directors and the organization.

Under corporate law, however, a derivative suit is predicated on failure of the board to take legal action appropriate to protect the corporation. Such inaction, if it occurred, necessarily involves at least serious neglect. Isn't that "wrongdoing?"

The older case law provides some support for the Comment's approach.[33] But almost all of the more recent cases find joint representation improper, except in cases involving claims that clearly lack merit on their face.[34] One case, citing M.R. 1.13, holds that corporate counsel may represent the officers who are charged with harming the corporation because counsel for the plaintiff shareholder represents the interests of the corporation.[35] Does this analysis make sense?

The Comment to M.R. 1.13 may reflect the more relaxed practice of lawyers representing small corporations, usually closely held, a setting in which joint representation and serving as "lawyer for the situation" have been common in the past. Because of greater awareness of conflicts problems and concerns about malpractice, joint representation of both the corporation and officer defendants is rare today in situations involving large publicly held corporations. The corporation's regular counsel arranges for separate representation of any independent litigation committee. Officers and directors who are targeted by the action are usually represented independently. Corporate counsel remains involved on behalf of the corporate entity, but the representation is independent of that of the officer defendants. The view expressed in *Yablonski*, that the corporation has an "institutional interest" not voiced by a specific "constituent," either stockholder, officer or director, now largely prevails.

33. See Selama–Dindings Plantations, Ltd. v. Durham, 216 F.Supp. 104 (S.D.Ohio 1963), aff'd, 337 F.2d 949 (6th Cir.1964); Otis & Co. v. Pennsylvania R. Co., 57 F.Supp. 680 (E.D.Pa.1944), aff'd, 155 F.2d 522 (3d Cir.1946) (per curiam).

34. See, e.g., In re Conduct of Kinsey, 294 Or. 544, 660 P.2d 660 (1983), and the cases cited in *Cannon*, 398 F.Supp. at 218–19.

35. Robinson v. Snell's Limbs and Braces, 538 So.2d 1045, 1048 (La.App.1989). Another variant is representation of officers and directors by the corporation's regular counsel, whose advice may be in issue in the derivative action, with independent counsel representing the corporation. See Morgan Shipman, Professional Responsibilities of the Corporation's Lawyer, in ABA, Professional Responsibility, A Guide for Attorneys, p. 280 (1978). Does the fact that the corporation's lawyer may be defending her own work make this arrangement better or worse?

Should an Organization's Lawyer Serve as Officer or Director?

The Comment to Model Rule 1.7 reads in part:

A lawyer for a corporation or other organization who is a member of its board of directors should determine whether the responsibilities of the two roles may conflict. The lawyer may be called on to advise the corporation in matters involving actions of the directors. Consideration should be given to the frequency with which such situations may arise, the potential intensity of the conflict, the effect of the lawyer's resignation from the board and the possibility of the corporation's obtaining legal advice from another lawyer for such situations. If there is material risk that the dual role will compromise the lawyer's independence of professional judgment the lawyer should not serve as a director.

In an informal opinion in 1966,[36] the ABA stated that it was not an ethical violation for a lawyer for a bank also to serve on the bank's board of directors. The brief opinion stated that the dual role is a common practice "which to our knowledge has not been criticized" and that it did not involve the representation of conflicting interests. Since then, commentators have argued that the dual role is risky, unsound and should be prohibited by law.[37]

Lawyers who serve in dual roles as outside counsel and member of the client's board of directors may jeopardize the attorney-client privilege. The privilege is not available for information communicated to or learned by counsel through membership on the board.[38] Some law firms prohibit their members from sitting on the boards of client corporations; others have lawyers on the boards of almost all clients. Malpractice insurers oppose the practice, arguing that it greatly increases a law firm's risk of civil liability.

"Switching Sides" in a Derivative Suit: Representing Shareholders Against Management

Because shareholder derivative suits are brought on behalf of the corporation, it has been argued that a lawyer formerly engaged in representing the corporation would not be switching sides, i.e., opposing a former client, if she subsequently represented shareholders in a derivative suit. Most courts considering this argument have rejected it.[39] How would the Model Rules resolve this question? How would the corporate bar do so?

---

36. ABA Informal Op. 930 (1966).

37. See, e.g., Wolfram, Modern Legal Ethics 738–40 (1986); Simon Lorne, The Corporate and Securities Adviser, the Public Interest, and Professional Ethics, 76 Mich.L.Rev. 423, 490–95 (1978).

38. See, e.g., Securities and Exchange Commission v. Gulf & Western Industries, Inc., 518 F.Supp. 675 (D.D.C.1981).

39. See, e.g., Richardson v. Hamilton International Corporation, 469 F.2d 1382 (3d Cir.1972); Doe v. A. Corp., 330 F.Supp. 1352 (S.D.N.Y.1971), aff'd sub nom. Hall v. A. Corp., 453 F.2d 1375 (2d Cir.1972). But see Jacuzzi v. Jacuzzi Bros., Inc., 218 Cal.App.2d 24, 32 Cal.Rptr. 188, 191 (Dist.Ct.App.1963) (former attorney for the Jacuzzi company

May an Organization's Lawyer Be Plaintiff?

May an organization's lawyer, who also owns shares in the corporation, sue the corporation as a plaintiff-shareholder after terminating representation of the company?

In Doe v. A. Corp.,[40] Doe had been an attorney with the law firm that represented the A. Corporation; he had worked on the corporation's business and had access to its confidential files. Two weeks before he left the firm, he bought one share of A. Corporation stock. He admitted that he bought this stock for the purpose of trying to oust current management by initiating a shareholder-derivative suit. He further conceded that "every fact alleged in the complaint" was acquired by him through his employment as A.'s lawyer. The court held: "[I]f an attorney believes that executives of a corporate client are engaging in wrongful conduct, he may disclose this to the corporation's board of directors; but he infringes Canon 4 [of the Code of Professional Responsibility] if he himself institutes suit." [41]

In Hull v. Celanese Corp.,[42] Hull, an employee of Celanese, brought suit against the company alleging sex-based discrimination under Title VII of the Civil Rights Act of 1964. Delulio was a member of Celanese's in-house counsel staff, who had done some work on the Hull suit for Celanese. Delulio contacted Hull's lawyers and asked them to represent her in the lawsuit as another plaintiff. Celanese sought to disqualify the firm based on the risk that confidential information received by Delulio in her role as one of the corporation's lawyers would be used by the firm against Celanese. The firm argued that in its dealings with Delulio it had "cautioned [her] not to reveal any information received in confidence as an attorney for Celanese, but rather to confine her revelations ... to the facts of her own case." [43] The court, after commending the firm for the care it had taken, disqualified it from representing either plaintiff, and then added that its decision "should not be read to imply that either Hull or Delulio cannot pursue her claim of employment discrimination." [44]

How should Delulio's new lawyer proceed?

Choosing Independent Counsel for a Corporation

After the first *Yablonski* case, the president of the union, Boyle, selected new counsel for the union who were no more independent of his influence than the counsel they were replacing. Should the court

could represent shareholders in a derivative suit that sought to restore assets to the corporation; attorney acted "for the benefit of the corporation he previously represented" and, therefore, "is not representing an interest adverse to the corporation").

40. 330 F.Supp. 1352 (S.D.N.Y.1971), aff'd sub nom. Hall v. A. Corp., 453 F.2d 1375 (2d Cir.1972).

41. 330 F.Supp. at 1355, citing ABA Formal Op. 202 (1940).

42. 513 F.2d 568 (2d Cir.1975).

43. Id. at 571.

44. Id. at 572.

have appointed successor counsel instead of leaving it to Boyle? Should the court have ordered the board of the corporate defendant (here, the union) to delegate to a group of independent directors, i.e., directors not implicated in the present action, the power to appoint and work with corporate counsel?

Although there is some authority for court appointment of counsel on behalf of the organization-client,[45] most courts agree with the court in *Yablonski* that this is too great an interference in the corporation's governance.[46] In Messing v. FDI,[47] after regular corporate counsel was disqualified, the court declined either to appoint counsel, as requested by the plaintiff shareholders, or approve a plan proposed by the board for selection of counsel. "It is for [the board], in the first instance, to devise a method to accommodate the need to continue the corporate enterprise while refraining from participating in any corporate decision in which they might have a personal interest. They act, or fail to act, at their peril." [48]

Should a board, the majority of whose members are named as defendants in a derivative suit, be permitted to appoint a committee to direct the litigation for the corporation, usually referred to as a "special litigation committee"? Almost all courts have approved this solution because a contrary rule would permit one shareholder to incapacitate the entire board by leveling charges against a majority of its members.[49]

Court decisions differ on the deference to be given the judgments of special litigation committees. The leading Delaware case, Zapata Corp. v. Maldonado,[50] takes an intermediate position of modest judicial review; New York takes an approach of extreme judicial deference; and most courts describe the choice as one between the New York approach and the somewhat more interventionist *Zapata* approach.[51] The ALI also recommends an intermediate position: The board's conclusion is

45. See Rowen v. LeMars Mutual Insurance Co., 230 N.W.2d 905 (Iowa 1975); Niedermeyer v. Niedermeyer, 1973 WL 419, CCH Fed.Sec.L.Rep. ¶ 94,123 (D.Or.1973).

46. See, e.g., *Cannon* supra, and Lewis v. Shaffer Stores Company, 218 F.Supp. 238 (S.D.N.Y.1963).

47. 439 F.Supp. 776 (D.N.J.1977).

48. Id. at 783–84.

49. See, e.g., Hasan v. CleveTrust Realty Investors, 729 F.2d 372 (6th Cir.1984) (applying Massachusetts law); Joy v. North, 692 F.2d 880 (2d Cir.1982) (applying Connecticut law); Lewis v. Anderson, 615 F.2d 778 (9th Cir.1979) (applying California law); Abbey v. Control Data Corp., 603 F.2d 724 (8th Cir.1979) (applying Delaware law); Zapata Corp. v. Maldonado, 430 A.2d 779 (Del.1981). See also Principles of Corporate Governance: Analysis and Recommendations, § 7.10 Comment f (Tent. Draft No. 9, April 14, 1989).

50. 430 A.2d 779 (Del.1981).

51. For the New York approach, see Auerbach v. Bennett, 47 N.Y.2d 619, 419 N.Y.S.2d 920, 393 N.E.2d 994 (1979). See Abella v. Universal Leaf Tobacco Co., 546 F.Supp. 795, 799 (E.D.Va.1982) ("*Zapata* approach adequately safeguards the competing interests at stake"); Alford v. Shaw, 320 N.C. 465, 358 S.E.2d 323, 325–26 (1987) ("recent trend among courts faced with [a] choice ... is away from" the deferential approach and toward *Zapata*). Commentators have also been critical of the deferential approach. See, e.g., Victor Brudney, The Independent Director: Heavenly City or Potemkin Village, 95 Harv.L.Rev. 597 (1982); George W. Dent, The Power of Directors to Terminate Shareholder Litigation: The Death of the Derivative Suit?, 75 Nw.U.L.Rev. 96 (1980).

given great deference on duty-of-care matters subject to the business judgment rule, but statutory violations and violations of the duty of loyalty (such as self-dealing by officers or directors) receive somewhat greater judicial scrutiny.[52]

Protections for Corporate Officers and Agents [53]

Arrangements for protecting corporate directors and other top corporate officials from the legal risks of their decisions affect the decisions of lawyers engaged in suing and representing corporations. Corporate officials have two basic protections: First, the judicially developed "business judgment rule" shields directors from liability based on mere bad judgment.[54] Second, a complicated array of law and practice provides for indemnification from the corporation, for liability insurance or for both in many situations.

An officer or director who incurs expenses or liabilities while acting in good faith on the corporation's behalf has a strong claim to indemnification. On the other hand, the deterrent effect of legal sanctions is undercut and illegal conduct furthered if law permits officers and directors who have breached their fiduciary obligations to be indemnified at the expense of the corporation.

State statutes govern a corporation's authority to make advance arrangements or after-the-fact decisions to indemnify officers and directors.[55] In Delaware, the leading jurisdiction, a statute provides for indemnification of litigation expenses if a corporate official is "successful on the merits or otherwise in defense." On the other hand, the corporation is not permitted to indemnify an officer held liable on the merits. If litigation against an officer is settled, the Delaware code permits corporations to pay defense expenses providing the corporation, through specified procedures, determines that the official "acted in good faith and in a manner he reasonably believed to be in or not opposed to the best interests of the corporation." [56] But the statute expressly limits indemnification in litigation to expenses incurred, precluding indemnification of judgments or amounts paid in settling the merits.[57]

52. ALI, Principles of Corporate Governance: Analysis and Recommendations § 7.10 (Proposed Final Draft, Mar. 31, 1992).

53. For discussions of director and officer liability, see Reinier H. Kraakman, Corporate Liability Strategies and the Cost of Legal Controls, 93 Yale L.J. 857 (1984); John C. Coffee, Jr., Beyond the Shut–Eyed Sentry: Toward a Theoretical View of Corporate Misconduct and an Effective Response, 63 Va.L.Rev. 1099 (1977); and Corporate Governance and Directors' Liabilities: The Legal, Economic, and Sociological Analysis of Corporate Social Responsibility (K. Hopt & G. Teubner eds. 1984).

54. See generally ALI, Principles of Corporate Governance § 4.01 (Proposed Final Draft, Mar. 31, 1992).

55. See Dale A. Oesterle, Limits on a Corporation's Protection of Its Directors and Officers from Personal Liability, 1983 Wis.L.Rev. 513, 520–21 (with footnotes containing citations to statutory provisions).

56. 8 Del.Code § 145(a); see also Model Business Corp. Act § 5(b) (1982).

57. See ALI, Principles of Corporate Governance § 7.20, reporter's note at 925 (Proposed Final Draft, Mar. 31, 1992), stating that the Delaware pattern is followed in 28

The indemnification arrangements affect the incentives of parties and their lawyers in bringing and settling derivative suits. If the plaintiff's lawyer, who usually finances the litigation, loses on the merits, a fee-shifting provision may impose the defendants' costs on the plaintiff's lawyer. On the other hand, if the case is settled, the settlement may provide for an attorney's fee award. From the defendants' point of view, in a jurisdiction following the Delaware pattern, a settlement that includes no award on the merits but is limited to a fee award is also advantageous, because expenses may be indemnified or covered by insurance while a judgment on the merits cannot. Thus both sides have an incentive to agree on a settlement that limits relief to prospective procedural changes on the part of the corporation combined with a handsome fee award to the plaintiff's lawyer. Is this a form of collusion that violates professional ethics? [58]

Another protection available to corporate officers and agents is the "reliance on counsel" defense. Good faith reliance on advice of counsel allows corporate officers to escape liability for acts taken in their official capacity if such reliance negates relevant intent. On the other hand, permitting this defense puts a premium on an opinion that shields the officer and may encourage "opinion shopping." [59]

Attorney–Client Privilege in Derivative Suits: *Garner* Doctrine

As *Weintraub*, p. 756 above, makes clear, a corporation's current management controls the privilege and may waive it despite the objections of present or former constituents. But can current management assert the privilege against constituents, e.g., shareholders?

In Garner v. Wolfinbarger,[60] the Fifth Circuit recognized an exception to the corporation's attorney-client privilege, holding that shareholder-plaintiffs in derivative suits may gain access to information protected by the corporation's attorney-client privilege if they can "show cause why [the privilege] should not be invoked in the particular instance." [61] The *Garner* court reasoned that where management is charged with a breach of fiduciary responsibility, accountability to shareholders justifies interference with confidentiality. The court also analogized shareholders, as constituents of the corporation, to joint

states. Statutes in 15 states permit indemnification of settlement awards, but court approval is required in some of them.

58. Settlement patterns suggest the possibility of collusive settlements in which the plaintiff's lawyer recovers generous attorney's fees in return for a settlement that permits the defendants to be indemnified by the corporation for their expenses. See Janet Cooper Alexander, Do the Merits Matter? A Study of Settlements in Securities Class Actions, 43 Stan.L.Rev. 497 (1991). ALI, Principles of Corporate Governance 587–602 (Proposed Final Draft, Mar. 31, 1991), discusses policy arguments concerning the derivative action and summarizes available empirical studies.

59. See Douglas W. Hawes and Thomas J. Sherrard, Reliance on Advice of Counsel as a Defense in Corporate and Securities Cases, 62 Va.L.Rev. 1 (1976).

60. 430 F.2d 1093 (5th Cir.1970), on remand, 56 F.R.D. 499 (S.D.Ala.1972).

61. 430 F.2d at 1103–04.

clients of the lawyer, noting that the privilege is unavailable among joint clients.

The *Garner* exception rests on common law precedent: If a plausible showing is made of serious breach of fiduciary duty, the privilege may not be claimed by the fiduciary against the beneficiary for whose benefit the legal relationship exists. By extension, corporate officers, who are also fiduciaries, should not be able to claim the privilege to protect themselves at the expense of the entity. To determine what counts as "good cause" for shareholder access to corporate information, *Garner* listed various factors.[62] Those factors reflect exceptions to the attorney-client privilege and whether the shareholder-plaintiffs have made a plausible showing that the derivative claim seeks to remedy a serious, possibly meritorious, breach of duty that defendant agents of the corporation owed to the corporation.

Although widely recognized,[63] the *Garner* "good cause" standard has been criticized as vague and overbroad.[64] One commentator has urged that the *Garner* exception to the attorney-client privilege be abandoned entirely, with its office performed by the crime-fraud exception.[65] But how would shareholders demonstrate defendant officers acted with a criminal or fraudulent intent? The crime-fraud exception may be too narrow for the purposes envisioned by *Garner*, which seeks to ensure the attorney-client privilege is asserted in the best interests of the organization rather than for the benefit of management. *Garner* is concerned with bad faith in asserting the privilege, not bad faith in communicating with counsel for an illegal purpose.

After the Supreme Court's decision in *Upjohn*, p. 226 above, affirming the corporation's strong interest in frank and confidential communications with counsel, some commentators predicted the demise of

62. The listed factors are: the number of shareholders bringing the claim against the corporation and the percentage of stock they represent; the bona fides of the shareholders; the nature of the shareholders' claim and whether it is obviously colorable; whether the information is vital to the shareholders and whether it is available from other sources; whether the shareholders' claim alleges that corporate officers acted criminally, or illegally but not criminally, or in a way that is of doubtful legality; whether the communication related to past or to future actions, i.e., whether the communications might have been part of an ongoing fraud; whether the communication concerns advice about the litigation itself; the extent to which the shareholders are fishing for information; and the risk of revelation of trade secrets or other information in whose confidentiality the corporation has an interest beyond the present litigation. 430 F.2d at 1104.

63. See, e.g., Quintel Corp. v. Citibank, N.A., 567 F.Supp. 1357, 1363–64 (S.D.N.Y. 1983); Panter v. Marshall Field & Co., 80 F.R.D. 718, 722–23 (N.D.Ill.1978); Cohen v. Uniroyal, Inc., 80 F.R.D. 480, 482–85 (E.D.Pa.1978); In re Transocean Tender Offer Sec. Litig., 78 F.R.D. 692, 695–97 (N.D.Ill.1978); Valente v. Pepsico, 68 F.R.D. 361, 366–68 (D.Del.1975).

64. Note, The Attorney–Client Privilege in Shareholder Litigation: The Need for a Predictable Standard, 9 Loy.U.Chi.L.J. 731 (1978) (arguing that the criteria in *Garner* for determining good cause are vague and overbroad).

65. Developments in the Law—Privileged Communication: III. Attorney–Client Privilege, 98 Harv.L.Rev. 1501 (1985) (arguing that instead of using the *Garner* exception, courts should rely exclusively on the crime-fraud exception to get at those communications that corporate managers should not be allowed to shield from shareholders or others).

Garner,[66] yet the *Garner* exception has survived and prospered.[67] Analogous principles have long been applied outside the shareholder/corporation context to allow others to whom a fiduciary duty is owed to gain access to communications between a fiduciary and her counsel.[68] This case law is discussed in the notes to *Fickett* below at p. 807. *Garner* is inapplicable to communications with counsel about the derivative suit itself.[69]

The *Garner* rule was developed by federal courts as part of the federal common law of evidentiary privileges applicable to federal questions in a federal court under Fed.R.Evid. 501. Some state courts have used their general common law power to adopt *Garner* as state law.[70] California, however, has refused to follow *Garner*, holding the California statute on the attorney-client privilege does not empower the courts to carve out exceptions.[71]

3. Duties of Corporation's Lawyer Faced With Corporate Wrongdoing

Consider the following situation: A lawyer for a corporation learns that the corporation, under the direction of incumbent management, is planning or is engaged in serious wrongdoing. The officers in control refuse to recognize the problem or to do anything about it. What should the lawyer do? The alternatives include: remaining silent while continuing to represent the corporation, withdrawing from representation but remaining silent, seeking review within the corporate structure and, finally, making a "noisy withdrawal," one which discloses the problem to affected persons or the public.

66. See, e.g., Thomas Kirby, New Life for the Corporate Attorney–Client Privilege in Shareholder Litigation, 69 A.B.A.J. 174 (1983); John E. Sexton, A Post–Upjohn Consideration of Corporate Attorney–Client Privilege, 57 N.Y.U.L.Rev. 443 (1982).

67. See Ward v. Succession of Freeman, 854 F.2d 780, 785 (5th Cir.1988) ("*Upjohn* does not undermine . . . *Garner* "); Donald B. Lewis, Garner is Alive and Well in Securities Litigation, 69 A.B.A.J. 903 (1983).

68. Should the *Garner* doctrine be applied to direct actions by shareholders? Some courts have so held. See, e.g., *Cohen v. Uniroyal*, supra (following *Garner* approach in federal securities lawsuit brought by individual plaintiff on his own behalf). But other decisions hold the policy rationale of *Garner* does not apply where the plaintiff seeks a damage recovery for an injury to her own interests rather than a recovery for the benefit of the corporation. See Weil v. Investment/Indicators, Research & Management, Inc., 647 F.2d 18, 23 (9th Cir.1981) ("*Garner's* holding and policy rationale simply do not apply [when plaintiff is seeking damages for herself]").

69. In re LTV Securities Litigation, 89 F.R.D. 595 (N.D.Tex.1981) (*Garner* exception inapplicable to "after-the-fact" communications concerning offenses already completed). See also In re International Sys. & Controls Corp., 693 F.2d 1235 (5th Cir.1982) (refusing to apply *Garner* to the lawyer's work-product concerning the pending litigation).

70. See, e.g., Hoopes v. Carota, 74 N.Y.2d 716, 544 N.Y.S.2d 808, 543 N.E.2d 73 (1989) (adopting *Garner* approach to determine whether beneficiaries of a trust plan may gain access to communications between the plan's trustee and his attorney); Neusteter v. The District Court of Denver, 675 P.2d 1 (Colo.1984) (adopting the "good cause" exception of *Garner* and applying it to accountant-client privilege).

71. See Dickerson v. Superior Court of Santa Clara County, 135 Cal.App.3d 93, 185 Cal.Rptr. 97 (1982); and Hoiles v. Superior Court of Orange County, 157 Cal.App.3d 1192, 204 Cal.Rptr. 111, 114–15 (1984).

Model Rule 1.13: Organization as Client [72]

Model Rule 1.13(a) states that a lawyer for an organization represents the organization not its constituents. M.R. 1.13(b) addresses what a lawyer should do when a constituent, e.g., an officer or employee, is acting in a way that may legally harm the organization:

> (b) If a lawyer for an organization knows that an officer, employee or other person associated with the organization is engaged in action, intends to act or refuses to act in a matter related to the organization that is a violation of a legal obligation to the organization, or a violation of law which reasonably might be imputed to the organization, the lawyer shall proceed as is reasonably necessary in the best interest of the organization....

Note that only those acts harmful to the *organization* trigger the rule: An act must either be a violation of a legal obligation owed to the organization, such as a fiduciary duty or contractual obligation, or a violation of law that might reasonably be imputed to the organization.

Assuming the rule is triggered, M.R. 1.13(b) continues:

> In determining how to proceed, the lawyer shall give due consideration to the seriousness of the violation and its consequences, the scope and nature of the lawyer's representation, the responsibility in the organization and the apparent motivation of the person involved, the policies of the organization concerning such matters and any other relevant considerations....

The rule further requires that "[a]ny measure taken shall be designed to minimize disruption of the organization and the risk of revealing information relating to the representation to persons outside the organization."

What may the lawyer do? The rule has a non-exhaustive list ("such measures may include among others"): (1) asking reconsideration of the matter; (2) advising that a separate legal opinion on the matter be sought for presentation to appropriate authority in the organization; and (3) referring the matter to higher authority in the organization, including, if warranted by the seriousness of the matter, referral to the highest authority that can act in behalf of the organization as determined by applicable law.

What should the lawyer do if the highest authority (which, in the case of a corporation, is usually the board of directors) refuses to act in the best interests of the corporation to prevent the harm? Should the lawyer inform the shareholders? A government agency? A proposal of

---

72. See Stephen Gillers, Model Rule 1.13(c) Gives the Wrong Answer to the Question of Corporate Counsel Disclosure, 1 Geo.J.Legal Ethics 289 (1987). For a step-by-step analysis of the rules governing corporate internal investigations, see Drew L. Kershen, Ethical Issues for Corporate Counsel in Internal Investigations: A Problem Analyzed, 13 Okla.City U.L.Rev. 1 (1988). For an exploration of various models of the lawyer's role in an internal investigation, see Samuel H. Gruenebaum and Martin A. Oppenheimer, Special Investigative Counsel: Conflicts and Roles, 33 Rutgers L.Rev. 865 (1981).

the Kutak Commission [73] provided that the lawyer's options "may include revealing information, otherwise protected by Rule 1.6 *only if* the lawyer reasonably believes that:"

> (1) the highest authority in the organization has acted to further the personal or financial interests of members of that authority which are in conflict with the interest of the organization; *and*

> (2) revealing the information is necessary in the best interest of the organization.

The Kutak Commission proposal was rejected by the ABA House of Delegates, and M.R. 1.13(c) as adopted reads:

> If, despite the lawyer's efforts in accordance with paragraph (b), the highest authority that can act on behalf of the organization insists upon action, or a refusal to act, that is clearly a violation of law, and is likely to result in substantial injury to the organization, the lawyer may resign in accordance with Rule 1.16.

Does this rule sufficiently protect the lawyer from liability under other law? Recall the standards in *Benjamin, Greycas* and *ACC/Lincoln* printed in Chapter 2 above, and the *O.P.M.* case in Chapter 4. Consider this question in reading the *Carter and Johnson* case, printed below, and the notes that follow it. For discussion of the special problems of lawyers employed by an organization, see the *Balla* case, p. 604 above.

Relationship of Organization's Lawyers to Board of Directors

Is M.R. 1.13 as adopted a "board as client" concept more than one of "organization as client"? Compare the approach suggested by the American Trial Lawyers Association (ATLA) in the American Lawyer's Code of Conduct (ALCC), Rule 2.5, with M.R. 1.13.

ALCC Rule 2.5 provides:

> A lawyer representing a corporation shall, as early as possible in the lawyer-client relationship, inform the board of directors of potential conflicts that might develop among the interests of the board, corporate officers, and shareholders. The lawyer shall receive from the board of directors instructions in advance as to how to resolve such conflicts, and shall take reasonable steps to ensure that officers with whom the lawyer deals, and the shareholders, are made aware of how the lawyer has been instructed to resolve conflicts of interest.

The Comment explains that the lawyer's "conundrum"—protecting an officer's confidence or informing the board—arises only when the lawyer has not obtained advance instructions from the board as to which course the board desires the lawyer to take:

---

73. Revised Final Draft M.R. 1.13(c), June 30, 1982 (emphasis added).

... On the basis of the board's instructions, the lawyer can then make sure that each interested party is informed in advance and is thereby in a position to seek adequate protection.

For example, one board might prefer to maximize candor between its officers and the lawyer, and therefore, instruct the lawyer to honor the officers' confidences, even in reporting to the board. The shareholders would then be in a position to approve or disapprove that policy, or to relinquish their shares. Another board might prefer to know everything the lawyer knows. In that event the officers would be on notice that they might want to consult personal counsel before disclosing certain information to corporate counsel....

Is this Comment consistent with the principle that as fiduciaries of the corporation, corporate officers have a duty to reveal "awkward" information to counsel or the board of directors?

The ALCC approach suggests that it would be appropriate for the board of directors to agree to be kept uninformed. Would such an agreement be consistent with the directors' duties under corporation law? Consistent with regulatory law in such fields as banking and securities?

IN RE CARTER AND JOHNSON

Securities and Exchange Commission, 1981.
[1981 Transfer Binder] Fed.Sec.L.Rep. (CCH) ¶ 82,847.

William R. Carter and Charles J. Johnson, Jr., respondents, appeal from the initial decision of the Administrative Law Judge in this proceeding brought under Rule 2(e) of the Commission's Rules of Practice. In an opinion dated March 7, 1979, the Administrative Law Judge found that, in connection with their representation of National Telephone Company, Inc. during the period from May 1974 to May 1975, Carter and Johnson willfully violated and willfully aided and abetted violations of Sections 10(b) and 13(a) of the Securities Exchange Act of 1934 ... and Rules 10b–5, 12b–20 and 13a–11 thereunder and that they engaged in unethical and improper professional conduct. In light of these findings, the Administrative Law Judge concluded that Carter and Johnson should be suspended from appearing or practicing before the Commission for periods of one year and nine months, respectively.

For the reasons stated more fully below, we reverse the decision of the Administrative Law Judge with respect to both respondents. We have concluded that the record does not adequately support the Administrative Law Judge's findings of violative conduct by respondents. Moreover, we conclude that certain concepts of proper ethical and professional conduct were not sufficiently developed, at the time of the conduct here at issue, to permit a finding that either respondent breached applicable ethical or professional standards. In addition, we are today giving notice of an interpretation by the Commission of the term "unethical or improper professional conduct," as that term is used in Rule 2(e)(1)(ii). This interpretation will be applied prospectively in cases of this kind.

[The Commission first rejected challenges to its authority to promulgate or enforce Rule 2(e), noting that federal courts had consistently upheld the Commission's authority to discipline professionals appearing before it. See, e.g., Touche Ross & Co. v. S.E.C., 609 F.2d 570, 582 (2d Cir.1979). It then discussed the background of Rule 2(e), stating:]

[Rule 2(e) is addressed to] professional misconduct—and its sanction is limited to that necessary to protect the investing public and the Commission from the future impact on its processes of professional misconduct.

Rule 2(e) represents a balancing of public benefits. It rests upon the recognition that the privilege of practicing before the Commission is a mechanism that generates great leverage—for good or evil—in the administration of the securities laws.[21] A significant failure to perform properly the professional's role has implications extending beyond the particular transaction involved, for wrongdoing by a lawyer or an accountant raises the specter of a replication of that conduct with other clients.

Recognition of the public implications of the securities professional's role does not mean that the Commission has, by rule, imposed duties to the public on lawyers where such duties would not otherwise exist.... [T]he traditional role of the lawyer as counselor is to advise his client, not the public, about the law. Rule 2(e) does not change the nature of that obligation. Nevertheless, if a lawyer violates ethical or professional standards, or becomes a conscious participant in violations of the securities laws, or performs his professional function without regard to the consequences, it will not do to say that because the lawyer's duty is to his client alone, this Commission must stand helplessly by while the lawyer carries his privilege of appearing and practicing before the Commission on to the next client.

. . .

Against that background, we turn to an analysis of respondents' conduct. In our judgment, that conduct presents difficult questions under the applicable legal and professional standards.

21. We have previously noted

the peculiarly strategic and especially central place of the private practicing lawyer in the investment process and in the enforcement of the body of federal law aimed at keeping that process fair....

In the Matter of Emanuel Fields, 45 S.E.C. 262, 266, n. 20 (1973), aff'd without opinion, 495 F.2d 1075 (C.A.D.C. 1974). See also S.E.C. v. Spectrum, Ltd., 489 F.2d 535, 541–42 (2d Cir.1973); United States v. Benjamin, 328 F.2d 854, 863 (C.A.2) (Friendly, J.) ("In our complex society the accountants' certificate and the lawyer's opinion can be instruments for inflicting pecuniary loss more potent than the chisel or the crowbar").

... The conduct at issue in these proceedings occurred in connec- *Conduct* tion with respondents' legal representation of National Telephone Co. ("National") during the period from mid–1974 through mid–1975....

The architect of National's meteoric rise was Sheldon L. Hart, one of its founders and ... its controlling stockholder.... Hart was National's chief executive officer, chairman of the board of directors, president and treasurer. National's chief in-house counsel was Mark I. Lurie, who ... was one of respondents' principal contacts with the company.

[An S.E.C. investigation into the circumstances of National's insolvency in 1975 led to an injunction proceeding, alleging securities violations, against Hart and other officers and directors of National. A permanent injunction was granted.]

... Carter, an attorney admitted to practice in the State of New York, ... received his law degree from Harvard Law School and has been working for the law firm now known as Brown, Wood, Ivey, Mitchell & Perry ("Brown, Wood") since 1945, having become a partner of the firm in 1954. Carter's principal areas of practice have been securities, general corporate and antitrust law.

Johnson, also admitted to practice as an attorney in the State of New York, as well as in the State of Connecticut, ... received his legal education at Harvard Law School and joined Brown, Wood's predecessor firm in 1956, becoming a partner in 1967. Johnson's principal areas of practice have been corporate and securities law.

Kenneth M. Socha [who was not named as a respondent in these proceedings] worked with Carter and Johnson on a variety of legal matters affecting National, including all of the matters which are the basis of these proceedings. Socha joined Brown, Wood as an associate in 1970 and continued in that capacity during all periods relevant to these proceedings.

. . .

During 1974 and 1975, Brown, Wood, principally through Carter, Johnson and Socha, provided a wide range of legal services to National.... Johnson was charged with the overall coordination of Brown, Wood's legal efforts on National's behalf and was generally kept aware of progress on all significant projects....

[The chronology of National's final year, May 1974 to May 1975, is described in great detail in the Commission's opinion.

[National was engaged in the business of installing and leasing telephone systems that interface with AT & T equipment. While National presented an outward picture of continued growth and profits, it was faced increasingly with liquidity problems. In an attempt to rectify this problem, in the spring of 1974, the company arranged for a $15 million loan from a consortium of banks. Before the loan could be finalized, however, National began taking short term advances on the loan and, by September 1974, had used up almost the entire line of credit. In an attempt to placate the banks, National agreed to enter into a "lease maintenance program" (LMP) if the company continued to experience financial difficulties. Under the terms of the LMP, National would wind down its business by restricting sales and only maintaining leases which it had already sold. Under the terms of the company's agreement with the banks, if National sought to borrow additional funds from the banks or if certain liquidity ratios were not satisfied, National would be required to institute the LMP.

[During this period of financial crisis, National's president, Sheldon Hart, failed to disclose the financial problems that the company was facing and continued to issue optimistic reports to National's shareholders and the financial community. Specifically, the particulars of the loan agreement, the existence of the LMP and the potential consequences of both for National were not disclosed in a December 20 press notice released by National, a December 23 letter to the company's shareholders or in National's Form 8–K for December 1974. The press release and the Form 8–K were prepared by Hart with the assistance of attorneys Carter and Johnson.

[By March 1975, National's financial situation had deteriorated to such an extent that the company was required under the terms of the loan agreement to implement the LMP. In response to this situation, Hart, without knowledge of counsel, falsely certified to the banks that compliance with the LMP had been initiated. Later in March and again in April, Carter and Johnson advised Hart that National should publicly disclose its obligation to implement the LMP. Hart, however, refused to follow the attorneys' advice. In fact, the terms of the loan agreement, including National's obligation to implement the LMP were not disclosed until May 27, 1975, three days after Hart was forced to resign as National's president. On July 2, 1975, National initiated Chapter XI bankruptcy proceedings.

[The Rule 2(e) proceedings against Carter and Johnson charged them with aiding and abetting violations of the securities laws by assisting Hart in the preparation of the misleading news release and Form 8–K and by failing to disclose material facts concerning National's financial condition between May 1974 and May 1975. The SEC staff also charged that the attorneys had engaged in unethical and unprofessional conduct during their representation of National. After conducting a hearing, the Administrative Law Judge found that the evidence supported the charges and suspended Carter from appearing before the Commission for one year and Johnson for nine months.

[After determining that National's failure to disclose the nature of the LMP in the December 20 press release and the December Form 8–K constituted primary violations of the securities laws, the Commission turned to respondents' conduct.]

... Our primary concern, however, is with the respondents' relationship to these violations of the securities laws. Although "[t]he elements of an aiding and abetting claim have not yet crystallized into a set pattern," we have examined the decisions of the various circuits and conclude that certain legal principles are common to all the decisions.

[The Commission recited the three-part test for aiding and abetting liability: (1) a securities law violation by the principal; (2) the agent's knowledge of that violation; and (3) conduct of the agent that knowingly and substantially assists the violation. See *ACC/Lincoln*, p. 114 above.]

As noted above, we have no difficulty in finding that National committed numerous substantial securities law violations. The [third] element—substantial assistance—is generally satisfied in the context of a securities lawyer performing professional duties, for he is inevitably deeply involved in his client's disclosure activities and often participates in the drafting of the documents, as was the case with Carter. And he does so knowing that he is participating in the preparation of disclosure documents—that is his job.

. . .

... [T]he crucial inquiry in a Rule 2(e) proceeding against a lawyer inevitably tends to focus on the awareness or the intent element of the offense of aiding and abetting. It is that element which has been the source of the most disagreement among commentators and the courts....

. . .

Although it is a close judgment, after careful review, we conclude that the available evidence is insufficient to establish that either respondent acted with sufficient knowledge and awareness or recklessness to satisfy the test for willful aiding and abetting liability....

. . .

Our review of the record, which includes respondents' periodic exhortations to Hart to improve the quality of National's disclosure, leads us to believe that respondents did not intend to assist the violations by their inaction or silence. Rather, they seemed to be at a loss for how to deal with a difficult client.

Association of a law firm with a client lends an air of legitimacy and authority to the actions of a client. There are occasions when, but for the law firm's association, a violation could not have occurred. Under those circumstances, if the firm were cognizant of how it was being used and acquiesced, or if it gained some benefit from the violation beyond that normally obtained in a legal relationship, inaction would probably give rise to an inference of intent. This, however, is not such a case, and we find that respondents did not intend to assist the violation by their inaction.

. . .

Our concern focuses on the professional obligations of the lawyer who gives essentially correct disclosure advice to a client that does not follow that advice and as a result violates the federal securities laws. The subject of our inquiry is not a new one by any means and has received extensive scholarly treatment [66] as well as consideration by a number of local bar ethics committees and disciplinary bodies.[67] Similar issues are also presently under consideration by the ABA's Commission on Evaluation of Professional Standards in connection with the review and proposed revision of the ABA's Code of Professional Responsibility.[68]

While precise standards have not yet emerged, it is fair to say that there exists considerable acceptance of the proposition that a lawyer must, in order to discharge his professional responsibilities, make all efforts within reason to persuade his client to avoid or terminate proposed illegal action. Such efforts could include, where appropriate, notification to the board of directors of a corporate client....

. . .

The problems of professional conduct that arise in this relationship are well-illustrated by the facts of this case. In rejecting Brown, Wood's advice to include the assumptions underlying its projections in its 1974 Annual Report, in declining to issue two draft stockholders letters offered by respondents and in ignoring the numerous more informal urgings by both respondents and Socha to make disclosure, Hart and Lurie indicated that they were inclined to resist any public pronouncements that were at odds with the rapid growth which had been projected and reported for the company.

If the record ended there, we would be hesitant to suggest that any unprofessional conduct might be involved. Hart and Lurie were, in effect, pressing the company's lawyers hard for the minimum disclosure required by law. That fact alone is not an appropriate basis for a finding that a lawyer must resign or take some extraordinary action. Such a finding would inevitably drive a wedge between reporting companies and their outside lawyers; and more sophisticated members of management would soon realize that there is nothing to gain in consulting outside lawyers.

However, much more was involved in this case. In sending out a patently misleading letter to stockholders on December 23 in contra-

---

66. E.g., Hoffman, On Learning of a Corporate Client's Crime or Fraud—The Lawyer's Dilemma, 33 Bus. Lawyer 1389 (1978); Association of the Bar of The City of New York, Report by Special Committee on The Lawyers Role in Securities Transactions, 32 Bus. Lawyer 1879 (1977); Cooney, The Registration Process: The Role of the Lawyer in Disclosure, 33 Bus. Lawyer 1329 (1978); Cutler, The Role of the Private Law Firm, 33 Bus. Lawyer 1549 (1978); Sonde, The Responsibility of Professionals Under the Federal Securities Laws—Some Observations, 68 Nw. U.L. Rev. 1 (1973); New York Law Journal, "Expanding Responsibilities Under the Securities Law" (1972), 29 (remarks of Manuel F. Cohen, Esq.).

67. E.g., Ethics Committee of the State Bar of Texas, Op. No. 387 (April 1977); Los Angeles County Bar Association, Op. No. 353 (Feb. 12, 1976); ABA Informal Op. No. 1349 (Oct. 8, 1975); ABA Op. No. 202 (May 25, 1940).

68. See ABA Commission on Evaluation of Professional Standards, Model Rules of Professional Conduct (Discussion Draft, Jan. 30, 1980) Rule 1.13.

vention of Socha's plain and express advice to clear all such disclosure with Brown, Wood, in deceiving respondents about Johnson's approval of the company's quarterly report to its stockholders in early December and in dissembling in response to respondents' questions about the implementation of the LMP, the company's management erected a wall between National and its outside lawyers—a wall apparently designed to keep out good legal advice in conflict with management's improper disclosure plans.

Any ambiguity in the situation plainly evaporated in late April and early May of 1975 when Hart first asked Johnson for a legal opinion flatly contrary to the express disclosure advice Johnson had given Hart only five days earlier, and when Lurie soon thereafter prohibited [a subordinate] from delivering a copy of the company's April 1975 Form 8–K to Brown, Wood.

These actions reveal a conscious desire on the part of National's management no longer to look to Brown, Wood for independent disclosure advice, but rather to embrace the firm within Hart's fraud and use it as a shield to avoid the pressures exerted by the banks toward disclosure. Such a role is a perversion of the normal lawyer-client relationship, and no lawyer may claim that, in these circumstances, he need do no more than stubbornly continue to suggest disclosure when he knows his suggestions are falling on deaf ears.

... The Commission is of the view that a lawyer engages in "unethical or improper professional conduct" under the following circumstances: When a lawyer with significant responsibilities in the effectuation of a company's compliance with the disclosure requirements of the federal securities law becomes aware that his client is engaged in a substantial and continuing failure to satisfy those disclosure requirements, his continued participation violates professional standards unless he takes prompt steps to end the client's noncompliance. The Commission has determined that this interpretation will be applicable only to conduct occurring after the date of this opinion.

We do not imply that a lawyer is obliged, at the risk of being held to have violated Rule 2(e), to seek to correct every isolated disclosure action or inaction which he believes to be at variance with applicable disclosure standards, although there may be isolated disclosure failures that are so serious that their connection becomes a matter of primary professional concern. It is also clear, however, that a lawyer is not privileged to unthinkingly permit himself to be co-opted into an ongoing fraud and cast as a dupe or a shield for a wrong-doing client.

Initially, counselling accurate disclosure is sufficient, even if his advice is not accepted. But there comes a point at which a reasonable lawyer must conclude that his advice is not being followed, or even sought in good faith, and that his client is involved in a continuing course of violating the securities laws. At this critical juncture, the lawyer must take further, more affirmative steps in order to avoid the inference that he has been co-opted, willingly or unwillingly, into the scheme of non-disclosure.

The lawyer is in the best position to choose his next step. Resignation is one option, although we recognize that other considerations, including the protection of the client against foreseeable prejudice, must be taken into account in the case of withdrawal.[76] A direct approach to the board of directors or one or more individual directors or officers may be appropriate; or he may choose to try to enlist the aid of other members of the firm's management. What is required, in short, is some prompt action [77] that leads to the conclusion that the lawyer is engaged in efforts to correct the underlying problem, rather than having capitulated to the desires of a strong-willed, but misguided client.

Some have argued that resignation is the only permissible course when a client chooses not to comply with disclosure advice. We do not agree. Premature resignation serves neither the end of an effective lawyer-client relationship nor, in most cases, the effective administration of the securities laws. The lawyer's continued interaction with his client will ordinarily hold the greatest promise of corrective action. So long as a lawyer is acting in good faith and exerting reasonable efforts to prevent violations of the law by his client, his professional obligations have been met. In general, the best result is that which promotes the continued, strong-minded and independent participation by the lawyer.

We recognize, however, that the "best result" is not always obtainable, and that there may occur situations where the lawyer must conclude that the misconduct is so extreme or irretrievable, or the involvement of his client's management and board of directors in the misconduct is so thorough-going and pervasive that any action short of resignation would be futile. We would anticipate that cases where a lawyer has no choice but to resign would be rare and of an egregious nature.

... As noted above, because the Commission has never adopted or endorsed standards of professional conduct which would have applied to respondents' activities during the period here in question, and since generally accepted norms of professional conduct which existed outside the scope of Rule 2(e) did not, during the relevant time period, unambiguously cover the situation in which respondents found themselves in 1974–75, no finding of unethical or unprofessional conduct would be appropriate. That being the case, we reverse the findings of the Administrative Law Judge under Rule 2(e)(1)(ii). In future proceedings

---

76. See, e.g., ABA D.R. 2–110; ABA E.C. 2–32, 2–33.

77. In those cases where resignation is not the only alternative, should a lawyer choose not to resign, we do not believe the action taken *must be successful* to avoid the inference that the lawyer had improperly participated in his client's fraud. Rather, the acceptability of the action must be considered in the light of all relevant surrounding circumstances. Similarly, what is "prompt" in any one case depends on the situation then facing the lawyer.

of this nature, however, the Commission will apply the interpretation of subparagraph (ii) of Rule 2(e)(1) set forth in this opinion.

Aftermath of *Carter and Johnson*

The SEC staff had hoped for a stronger ruling from the Commission, perhaps one imposing an affirmative duty of disclosure on lawyers faced with client intransigence.[74] The SEC issued a request for comments on the rule laid down in *Carter and Johnson*,[75] in which it stated that the following rule taken from *Carter and Johnson* would apply for all conduct occurring after February 28, 1981 and would remain the rule unless modified by the SEC: "What is required, in short, is some prompt action that leads to the conclusion that the lawyer is engaged in efforts to correct the underlying problem, rather than having capitulated to the desires of a strong-willed, but misguided client."

The ABA's response challenged the SEC's authority to discipline lawyers under Rule 2(e) and the standard of conduct in the *Carter and Johnson* case.[76] After the comment period, the SEC took no further official action on the release.

Many commentators were critical of the SEC's use of 2(e) in cases like *Carter and Johnson*, arguing that lawyers would become over-cautious in order to protect themselves from liability, which would in turn result in clients keeping more and more information from their lawyers.[77]

The SEC continues to assert that it has the authority to issue and enforce 2(e), but it has brought very few cases against lawyers and has refrained from articulating standards of conduct for securities lawyers. "[T]he SEC has done virtually nothing to articulate its position ... since it decided the *Carter and Johnson* case".[78]

74. SEC Commissioner A. A. Sommer startled the securities bar in 1973 by stating that "in securities matters (other than those where advocacy is clearly proper) the attorney will have to function in a manner more akin to that of the auditor than to that of the advocate." Sommer, Emerging Responsibilities of the Securities Lawyer, [1973–74 Transfer Binder] Fed.Sec.L.Rep. (CCH) ¶ 79,631 (Jan.1974). This and other statements suggested a duty of disclosure.

75. Sec. Act Release No. 6344, Sec. Exchange Act Release No. 18106 (Sept. 21, 1981).

76. ABA Section of Corporation, Banking and Business Law, 37 Bus.Law. 915 (1982).

77. See, e.g., Richard L. Miller, The Distortion and Misuse of Rule 2(e), 7 Sec.Reg.L.J. 54, 59 n. 13 (1979); Steven C. Krane, The Attorney Unshackled: SEC Rule 2(e) Violates Clients' Sixth Amendment Right to Counsel, 57 Notre Dame Lawyer 50 (1981); Note, SEC Disciplinary Proceedings Against Attorneys Under Rule 2(e), 79 Mich.L.Rev. 1270, 1275–77, 1285 (1981). SEC Commissioner Roberta Karmel, who had recused herself in *Carter and Johnson* because she formerly had been a partner with the law firm that had represented some of the directors of National Telephone, attacked the Commission's position in a series of dissenting opinions and articles. See, e.g., Joseph C. Daley and Roberta S. Karmel, Attorneys' Responsibilities: Adversaries at the Bar of the SEC, 24 Emory L.J. 747 (1975).

78. See Steve Nelson, Hushed SEC Voice Adds Little to Legal Ethics Debate, Legal Times, May 16, 1983, at p. 13. In 1991 the Commission ruled that it did not have

Carter and Johnson Standard

The *Carter and Johnson* standard does not obligate a securities lawyer to blow the whistle on a client but only to take some action consistent with the law and ethics of lawyering. But what action and under what circumstances?

When does a lawyer have "significant responsibilities" in a client's compliance program? Presumably, the senior partner in charge of the client's affairs would fall within this definition. What about a senior associate working extensively on the client's securities matters? Note that the five-year associate involved in *Carter and Johnson* was not charged with misconduct.

A second variable is what constitutes a "substantial and continuing failure" to satisfy disclosure requirements. The SEC says that a lawyer is not obliged to correct "every isolated" failure to disclose by a client. However, "there may be isolated disclosure failures that are *so serious* that their correction becomes a matter of primary professional concern." Some action by the lawyer is required, apparently, after more than one occurrence of inaccurate disclosure.

The critical variable in the *Carter and Johnson* standard is what "prompt steps" should be taken to end a client's noncompliance. The SEC states that while "counselling accurate disclosure" may be sufficient for awhile, "there comes a point at which a reasonable lawyer must conclude that his advice is not being followed, or even sought in good faith, and that his client is involved in a continuing course of violating the securities laws." At that point, the SEC requires that an attorney "take further, more affirmative steps" to clear herself of an inference of participation in the client's scheme. What steps will satisfy this obligation?

The ABA and the securities bar, which often mischaracterize the SEC action as converting a lawyer into a law enforcement officer required to betray her client, apparently are concerned about having a federal agency, the SEC, make judgments about what lawyer conduct satisfies professional standards. Why are lawyers so hostile to these judgments being made by someone other than a state court or disciplinary body?

Duties of Directors and Their Lawyers

After the collapse of the company in *Carter and Johnson*, the SEC brought charges against all of its directors, including non-officer or "outside" directors. An SEC release stated:

authority to order a prominent New York City securities lawyer, George C. Kern, Jr., to comply with SEC rules requiring timely disclosure of developments that could affect the price of publicly traded securities. Kern, who served both as lawyer to and director of a company, failed promptly to disclose the company's talks with a third party during a takeover contest. See S.E.C. Drops Merger Case, N.Y.Times, June 22, 1991, at p. 45; Gregory A. Robb, S.E.C. Hears Arguments in Lawyer Case, N.Y.Times, June 9, 1989, at p. D1.

The outside directors of National were aware during the fall of 1974 and the winter and spring of 1975 of significant facts concerning National's troubled financial condition. Moreover they were aware of the optimistic nature of the company's public disclosures, disclosures which were in direct contrast with the true state of the company's affairs. Under these circumstances the company's outside directors had an affirmative duty to see to it that proper disclosures were made.[79]

As former SEC Director of Enforcement Stanley Sporkin put it:

The Commission was not saying that the directors of a company are responsible for proofreading every line of every press release and periodic filing made by the company. Rather, the Commission was cautioning that at a time of distress in a company's existence, the directors have an affirmative duty to ensure that the marketplace is provided accurate and full disclosures concerning the basic liability of the company and the continuity of its operations. *Directors cannot play the role of the ostrich.* Directors cannot simply say, "We are not going to do anything." They have a duty and a responsibility [to take some action].[80]

What were the responsibilities of the law firm in *Carter and Johnson* to the non-officer directors? Did the law firm have a fiduciary relationship with these directors? What if a law firm represented such a director as a client? See the *Fassihi* case printed below.

Lawyers for Thrifts and the "S & L Mess"

The real estate binge of the 1980s combined with partial deregulation of federally-insured savings and loan institutions, along with other factors, resulted in the failure of hundreds of thrifts. Meeting the national obligation to stand behind deposits will cost hundreds of billions of dollars. Federal agencies have brought civil and criminal proceedings against a large number of managers of thrifts that failed and their professional advisers, including the lawyers who represented the thrifts. Investors in and creditors of the thrifts have brought civil suits that presented many of the same issues.

The *ACC/Lincoln* case, p. 114, involved three fairly traditional claims against lawyers who represented the managers of a thrift that subsequently was found to have been engaged in ongoing fraud: (1) aiding and abetting client fraud or negligent misrepresentation, (2) giving a legal opinion that negligently misrepresented law or fact and (3) malpractice liability for breaching fiduciary duties to the entity by providing advice, at the request of thrift managers, that sacrificed the interests of other constituents. If one assumes that the lawyers knew

---

79. See Report of Investigation in the Matter of National Telephone Co., Inc. Relating to Activities of the Outside Directors ... [1977–78 Transfer Binder] Fed.Sec.L.Rep. (CCH) ¶¶ 81,410, 88,878.

80. Stanley Sporkin, Symposium: Southeastern Conference on Corporate and Securities Law I. SEC Enforcement and Corporate Responsibility: SEC Enforcement and the Corporate Board Room, 61 N.C.L.Rev. 455, 458 (1983). (Emphasis added.)

that the thrift's manager was engaged in illegal, self-dealing conduct that was likely to defraud other constituents and third persons, cases like *ACC/Lincoln* are neither novel nor challenging.

If, however, one assumes that an honest lawyer is trying to provide professional assistance to a careless client who is in trouble with regulatory authorities, an important question arises: What may a lawyer do in helping such a client?

Suppose that a lawyer is retained by the manager of a thrift after the real estate bubble has burst. The manager reports that the decline in real estate values has resulted in a number of unproductive loans, worsening the thrift's financial situation. Moreover, the thrift was sloppy in its loan practices and may have violated some banking regulations (referred to by the client as "technical" violations). The lawyer, who has no reason to suspect the manager of more egregious conduct,[81] agrees to assist the thrift in working out prospective regulatory problems. A detailed examination of the thrift's loan transactions reveals several things. Documentation that shows the value of mortgaged property or that the borrower is credit-worthy is lacking in a substantial number of loan transactions. Minutes of board meetings showing formal board approval in advance of the loan also are missing in a number of these transactions. The manager explains that the loans were made hurriedly and that the board gave oral approval that was not recorded in official minutes. In addition, the lawyer discovers a small number of loan transactions that may be illegal (e.g., linked transactions that may together exceed regulatory limits on the amount that may be loaned to a single borrower). Assume the bank examiners are scheduled to arrive in a few weeks. What advice should the lawyer give? What actions may the lawyer advise the manager to take to minimize the adverse consequences to the thrift of the regulatory violations described above?

Consider the following possible courses of action: Remonstrate with the officers who were involved in the loan transactions and who control the thrift? Go to the board of directors or its outside members? Withdraw from the representation? Send a letter to the investors and depositors withdrawing a legal opinion relating to a prior loan transaction in which the firm had been involved? Inform the banking regulators or state and federal securities agencies? Does it make a difference that the banking regulatory agency, under the law, would succeed to the management of the thrift and to claims that the thrift entity might have against its officers and attorneys for negligence and other wrongs toward the thrift?

The next set of questions arises when the thrift's manager rejects the lawyer's advice and embarks on a course of deliberate illegality. Assume the lawyer knows that the client has refused to follow her advice and believes that the manager is removing documents from some

---

81. The lawyer's responsibilities change when she has reasons to suspect the manager of illegal conduct. See discussion of *O'Melveny & Meyers*, infra.

loan files, inserting backdated documents in other loan files, etc.—
conduct that is not only illegal but harmful to the long-term interests of
the thrift's shareholders and depositors. Should the lawyer also consider the interests of the thrift's creditors and of the United States as
guarantor of deposits? What steps may or must the lawyer take to
prevent the manager from causing further harm to the thrift, its
constituents and outside interests? Is silent withdrawal, one of the
choices under M.R. 1.13, a sufficient response? May or must the lawyer
go to the thrift's board of directors? Make a "noisy withdrawal"?
These questions are the same as those raised by *Carter and Johnson*.

What inquiry concerning underlying circumstances must be made
by a law firm that handles a transaction for the thrift during a period
in which its financial situation is deteriorating? In Federal Deposit
Insurance Corp. v. O'Melveny & Meyers,[82] the receiver of a failed thrift
was held to have stated a claim for relief against a law firm that had
assisted the thrift in two real estate syndications offered to investors.
When the private placements were made, the thrift was in unsound
financial condition; its officers had fraudulently overvalued assets and
generally "cooked the books." [83] The complaint alleged that O'Melveny
did not question the thrift's prior auditors, its prior law firm, federal or
state regulators or the thrift's chief financial officer about the thrift's
financial status before assisting the thrift in soliciting investors. After
the thrift failed, the FDIC, acting as conservator, rescinded the investments and was assigned the investors' claims against O'Melveny. The
receiver then brought suit against O'Melveny for professional negligence and negligent misrepresentation.

The Ninth Circuit held that, under these circumstances, allegations
that the law firm "failed to make a reasonable, independent investigation" established a claim of professional negligence:

> Part and parcel of effectively protecting a client, and thus
> discharging the attorney's duty of care, is to protect the client from
> liability which may flow from promulgating a false or misleading
> offering to investors. An important duty of securities counsel is to
> make a "reasonable independent investigation to detect and correct
> false or misleading materials." . . . This is what is meant by a due
> diligence investigation. . . . The Firm had a duty to guide the
> thrift as to its obligations and protect it against liability. In its
> high specialty field, O'Melveny owed a duty of care not only to the
> investors, but also to its client. . . . [84]

82. 969 F.2d 744 (9th Cir.1992) (the case incorrectly refers to O'Melveny & Myers as
"O'Melveny and Meyers").

83. 969 F.2d at 746.

84. 969 F.2d at 749. The opinion in *O'Melveny* states in dicta that a lawyer's duty of
due care in connection with a public offering of securities, owed to *both* the client and to
investors, requires the lawyer "to make a reasonable, independent investigation" of
underlying facts. Quoting a commentator, the court stated:

[A]ttorneys, in rendering opinions relating to the securities laws, are not justified in
assuming facts as represented to them by their clients [are correct]. Rather . . . the

The *Kaye, Scholer* case [85] raises a further set of questions, many of which concern the interpretation and validity of FIRREA and other banking regulation.[86] But major issues concerning the role of lawyers for regulated entities are also presented, as well as issues involving the use of coercive governmental authority in situations in which legal requirements may be unclear or uncertain.[87]

Kaye, Scholer served as an outside counsel for Lincoln, the thrift involved in *ACC/Lincoln*, p. 114, in various matters from 1984 until shortly before it was seized by the government in 1989. In June 1986 the firm was retained by Lincoln to assist it through what was expected to be a difficult, perhaps hostile, bank examination. Treating the bank examination as "litigation," Fishbein, the partner in charge, instructed bank examiners to channel all inquiries through Kaye, Scholer rather than dealing directly with Lincoln. Kaye, Scholer's aggressive representation of Lincoln during this bank examination led the Office of Thrift Supervision (OTS) in March 1992 to file administrative charges against the firm and three of its partners.[88] Six of the ten charges alleged that Kaye, Scholer had knowledge of, but failed to disclose to the bank examiners, material facts, thereby making false and misleading other factual representations that were made to the bank board by the firm as Lincoln's agent.[89] By making such representations, OTS alleged, Kaye, Scholer violated regulations prohibiting false and misleading statements and omissions of material facts that have the effect of making a factual representation misleading. OTS sought "restitution" of losses of at least $275 million (Kaye, Scholer had been paid about $13 million in fees); the administrative proceeding was accompanied by an asset preservation ("freeze") order that sought to prevent the law firm's assets from being dissipated while permitting it to carry on its law practice. Kaye, Scholer settled the matter for $41 million

attorney must make a reasonable effort to independently verify the facts on which the opinion is based.

Id.

85. The reader should know that Geoffrey C. Hazard, Jr., one of the co-authors of this book, provided legal advice and a favorable legal opinion to the Kaye, Scholer firm in connection with the charges made against it.

86. The Financial Institutions Reform, Recovery, and Enforcement Act of 1989 ("FIRREA"), Pub.L. No. 101–73, 103 Stat. 183. FIRREA issues are discussed in the ABA Report, supra.

87. For a collection of articles on the OTS action against Kaye, Scholer, see Symposium, 66 S.Cal.L.Rev. 977 (1993) (including articles by Susan P. Koniak and David B. Wilkins).

88. This Office of Thrift Supervision administrative proceeding is not reported. For discussion and citation of relevant materials, see ABA Working Group on Lawyers' Representation of Regulated Clients, "Laborers in Different Vineyards?"—The Banking Regulators and the Legal Profession 24–30, 197–212 (Jan.1993). Also see Note, Administrative Watchdogs or Zealous Advocates? Implications for Legal Ethics in the Face of Expanded Attorney Liability, 45 Stan.L.Rev. 645 (1993).

89. For one version of the factual basis of the charges against Kaye, Scholer, see Susan Beck and Michael Orey, They Got What They Deserved, The American Lawyer 68 (May 1992).

within a week without contesting the freeze order or admitting or denying the allegations.[90]

One feature of *Kaye, Scholer* is unique and is unlikely to recur: OTS argued that the law firm, by interposing itself between Lincoln and the bank examiners, had become an alter ego of its client, Lincoln, and was not acting merely as a lawyer.

A second feature of *Kaye, Scholer*, however, is of great continuing importance: the scope of a lawyer's duty to disclose facts adverse to the lawyer's client to a regulatory agency.[91] Although a lawyer must not make false or misleading statements in representing a client, when, if ever, may or must a lawyer come forward with information? Consider (1) the attorney-client privilege, (2) the work-product immunity, (3) the lawyer's duty not to disclose information adverse to a client except when required by law or when doing so would further the client's interest (see *Spaulding v. Zimmerman*, p. 5 above), (4) the lawyer's duty not to commit a crime or fraud and (5) the lawyer's duty not to assist a client in crime or fraud. *Upjohn*, p. 226 above, establishes that information gathered by a lawyer "in anticipation of litigation" is ordinarily protected from government investigators by the corporation's attorney-client privilege and the work-product doctrine. When does a bank examination become sufficiently hostile or investigatory that a thrift may consider it to be a prelude to adversary litigation? Does the climate of a regulatory examination affect the candor required of the thrift's lawyer in dealing with bank examiners?

Kaye, Scholer also provides a repeat of the *Carter and Johnson* disagreement between federal regulators and the organized bar concerning a lawyer's duty when she discovers that her corporate client is engaged in an illegal or fraudulent course of conduct. Must the lawyer, as the SEC said in *Carter and Johnson* and OTS argued in *Kaye, Scholer*, take "some action" to prevent the continuing non-compliance with law? Must the lawyer climb the corporate ladder to the board of directors? Or, as stated by M.R. 1.13, is the lawyer's action permissive and triggered only by substantial injury to the corporation? Does a possibility that the corporation may be held liable in the future constitute "substantial injury" to the corporation?

Finally, *Kaye, Scholer* raised questions about the proper use of summary and extraordinary governmental authority. Unlike Jones,

---

90. See Amy Stevens and Paulette Thomas, How a Big Firm Was Brought to Knees by Zealous Regulators: At Kaye, Scholer, Survival Prevailed Over Principle as Partnership Panicked, Redefining a Lawyer's Duty, Wall St.J., Mar. 13, 1992, at A1, A5.

91. Why weren't the charges against Kaye, Scholer limited to the more well-established theories involved in other S & L cases, such as *ACC/Lincoln* ? The available facts, disputed by Kaye, Scholer, were at least as strong as those in the case involving Jones, Day, and would probably have established a prima facie case against Kaye, Scholer of professional negligence, breach of fiduciary obligations to the entity client and aiding and abetting client illegalities. See Beck and Orey, supra, American Lawyer 68 (May 1992) (summarizing the available evidence). Harris Weinstein, then general counsel for OTS, has emphasized the unusual action of Kaye, Scholer in placing itself between the banking regulators and Lincoln.

Day in *ACC/Lincoln*, the charge against Kaye, Scholer was not brought in a federal court where a defendant would have the right to a jury trial before an Article III judge. Kaye, Scholer's fate was to be decided in an administrative proceeding before the agency that had brought the charges, with subsequent opportunity for limited judicial review of the administrative determination. Although summary provisional remedies in other contexts are now generally unconstitutional,[92] the asset preservation order had the effect, along with the size and plausibility of the OTS damage claim, of depriving Kaye, Scholer of working capital and bringing it quickly to settlement. Law firms and the organized bar worry that the bar's independence may be threatened by governmental exercise of such extraordinary powers.[93]

Realities of Practice and Alternatives to Entity Theory

In the real world of corporate practice, lawyers often see the client as management (the real-life people who run the company), not some abstract entity. Does M.R. 1.13 and its Comment adequately deal with this reality?

Two alternatives to the "organization as client" approach are worth considering.[94] The first treats the constituents, not the organization, as joint clients of the lawyer. If the lawyer perceives a conflict among the constituents, e.g., the board and the shareholders or the board and the CEO, the lawyer is to withdraw and may not represent any of the constituents in subsequent matters substantially related to the work done on behalf of the joint clients. Given the reality of corporate infighting and shareholder derivative suits, this theory could result in a succession of lawyers for any one corporation, which would deprive the corporation of the benefit of sustained representation over time. It would also undercut whatever autonomy a lawyer might have as corporate counsel. It might also mean the end of the institution of in-house counsel.

The second theory conceives of corporate counsel as "lawyer for the situation," empowered to act to further the best interests of all concerned as the lawyer perceives those interests. The lawyer would function as a mediator among the various factions, ultimately deciding on the legal course that best serves the corporation, conceived as the embodiment of those various interests. This approach, if taken to its

---

92. See Connecticut v. Doehr, 111 S.Ct. 2105 (1991) (invalidating a state law that permitted prejudgment attachment of a defendant's assets without a hearing to determine whether the plaintiff established "probable cause"); but see United States v. Monsanto, Inc., 924 F.2d 1186 (2d Cir.1991) (pretrial forfeiture of attorney's fees on government's ex parte application permissible providing an opportunity for an adversary hearing providing prior to trial).

93. A number of the recommendations of the ABA Report, supra, are concerned with restraint on the part of regulatory agencies in use of their broad authority against lawyers.

94. See generally Scott T. FitzGibbon, Professional Ethics, Organizing Corporations 7–8 (ABA Problems in Professional Responsibility Monograph No. 3, 1982).

conclusion, divests management of control of the corporation's legal actions and places enormous power in the hands of "disinterested" lawyers. Its conception of the corporate lawyer as sage seems at odds with the real world.

The "organization as client" approach embodied in Rule 1.13 may conflict with the real corporate world as experienced by the lawyer and in some cases is difficult to translate into action. However, it is grounded in both the law of corporations and the law of agency. The law of corporations recognizes the corporation as a "person" capable of holding privileges and entering into relationships;[95] the law of agency describes and delineates the relationships among agents that serve a common principal (the lawyer, the CEO, the directors, etc. and the corporation).[96] This grounding in substantive law apart from the ethics rules provides a structure of legal relationships in which to locate the lawyer's role. Second, corporate and agency law bridge between theory and fact in corporate functions in the same way that the corporate lawyer must bridge between theory and action in professional responsibility.

Reality's intrusion on the idea of "organization as client" is perhaps most acute when one person dominates the organization. In *Carter and Johnson,* for example, Hart was controlling stockholder, CEO, chairman of the board, president and treasurer of National Telephone. Should this make a difference in the lawyer's analysis of who the client is? If not, what can the lawyer who is faced with such a dominant figure do to ensure some measure of independence? The *O.P.M.* case, p. 300, is another instance of dominant figures in an organization acting to harm it. Would M.R. 1.13 have suggested a different course of conduct for the lawyers in that case?

Mediating Among Competing Interests Within an Organization

Corporations and other organizations may become battlefields of conflicting interests. How much involvement by the lawyer is appropriate? For example, is it proper for corporation counsel to advise the president of the corporation on how to conduct an upcoming election of directors so as to frustrate a minority attempt to gain representation on the board? An ABA ethics opinion,[97] advising that such advice was appropriate, said:

> In acting as counsel for a corporation a lawyer not only may but should give legal advice to its officers in all matters relating to the

95. See Dartmouth College v. Woodward, 17 U.S. (4 Wheat.) 518, 636 (1819); New Colonial Ice Co. v. Helvering, 292 U.S. 435, 442 (1933).

96. See Restatement (Second) of Agency generally and § 1 Comment e (on the lawyer as agent) (1958); Floyd R. Mechem, Outlines of the Law on the Law of Agency, particularly § 12(a), 76 (4th ed.1952). See also William M. Fletcher, Cyclopedia of the Law of Private Corporations, §§ 275, 437, 466.3, 483 (rev.perm.ed.1982).

97. ABA Informal Op. 1056 (1968).

corporation as long as they are in office, except in situations where to his knowledge the interests of the officers are adverse to the interests of the corporation and the giving of the advice would be contrary to the interests of the corporation.

Would M.R. 1.13 or its Comment suggest a different conclusion? How is a lawyer to judge when the "giving of such advice would be contrary to the interests of the corporation?"

Questions such as those just discussed are infrequently presented to courts or disciplinary boards. Something has to go very wrong before a lawyer's decisions on such matters are reviewed in a formal setting. Even then, the lawyer's decisions are unlikely to be second-guessed except in egregious cases. Courts and disciplinary boards justifiably perceive that they cannot recreate the inner workings of organizations and their relationships with counsel. The reality that confronts corporate counsel is ordinarily too idiosyncratic, amorphous and dynamic to dissect in an adversary proceeding.[98]

This is not to suggest that courts should ignore gross misconduct. If the courts will not examine gross misconduct by lawyers, who will? In Financial General Bankshares, Inc. v. Metzger,[99] the district court found that attorney Metzger had breached his fiduciary and ethical duties to his corporate client by secretly engaging in attempts to seize or sell control of the company. The court held that Metzger's involvement with a group of minority shareholders who were plotting to take over the corporation with the aid of outside investors violated "the requirement that a corporate advisor remain neutral when confronted with an internecine conflict."[100] The court rejected Metzger's claim that his status as a shareholder gave him the right "to express his views on the management of the company." The court of appeals reversed, holding that the district court abused its discretion in exercising pendent jurisdiction over the local claim of lawyer misconduct after the federal securities law claims had been settled or dismissed.

---

98. On the inner workings of corporate bureaucracies, see Robert Jackall, Moral Mazes: The World of Corporate Managers (1988) (focusing on mid-level management); and Geoffrey C. Hazard, Jr., Ethics and Politics in the Corporate World, 6 Yale J.Reg. 155 (1989) (reviewing Jackall's book).

99. 523 F.Supp. 744 (D.D.C.1981), rev'd for lack of jurisdiction, 680 F.2d 768 (D.C.Cir. 1982).

100. Id. at 765. The court cited Canon 5 of the Model Code; several ABA opinions, including 1056 supra; and *Yablonski*, supra.

B. ALMOST CLIENTS

1. Representing a Closely–Held Corporation

R Adiologist

FASSIHI v. SOMMERS, SCHWARTZ, SILVER, SCHWARTZ AND TYLER, P.C.   *Epstein*

Court of Appeals of Michigan, 1981.
107 Mich.App. 509, 309 N.W.2d 645.

PER CURIAM.

... In his complaint, plaintiff asserted that he was a 50% share-holder, officer, and director of Livonia Physicians X–Ray, P.C., a professional medical corporation. The various allegations included breach of *Action* the attorney-client relationship, breach of fiduciary, legal, and ethical duties, fraud, and legal malpractice. Defendant [law firm] filed a motion for summary judgment on the basis that ... no attorney-client relationship existed with plaintiff. This motion was denied....

Following the trial court's order denying defendant's motion for summary judgment, plaintiff deposed attorney Donald Epstein. How- *atty refused to answer?* ever, during the deposition Epstein repeatedly refused to answer questions, claiming an attorney-client privilege. Plaintiff moved for an order compelling discovery, but the trial court denied the motion.... This order also extended to both parties the opportunity to take an interlocutory appeal from the denial of their respective motion.

This Court granted leave to take the interlocutory appeals....

The following factual recitation comes from plaintiff's complaint and the statement of facts appearing in his brief. Since we are obligated to consider the facts in the light most favorable to the nonmoving party when passing on a motion for summary judgment....

In the summer of 1973, plaintiff, a radiologist practicing medicine in Ohio, was asked by Dr. Rudolfo Lopez to come to Michigan and join him in the practice of radiology at St. Mary's Hospital in Livonia. In August, 1973, the doctors formed a professional corporation known as Livonia Physicians X–Ray. Each doctor owned 50% of the stock, was an employee of the corporation, and received an identical salary. Plaintiff contends that the by-laws adopted by the two shareholders made each of them a member of the Board of Directors and that the two of them constituted the entirety of the board. Dr. Lopez was president of the corporation, and Dr. Fassihi was the secretary-treasurer.

Shortly after the corporation was organized, plaintiff sought and obtained medical staff privileges at St. Mary's [Hospital]. For a period of approximately 18 months, the doctors practiced together at the hospital in the radiology department.

Some time on or before June 4, 1975, Dr. Lopez decided that he no longer desired to be associated with plaintiff. Consequently, Lopez requested that the attorney for the professional corporation, the defendant, ascertain how plaintiff could be ousted from Livonia Physicians X–Ray.

Lopez wanted π out of practice + discussed c̄ the Corp. Counsel

On or about June 6, 1975, defendant's agent, Donald Epstein, Esquire, personally delivered to plaintiff a letter dated June 4, 1975, purporting to terminate his interest in the professional corporation. The letter stated that this termination followed a meeting of the board of directors.[2] Plaintiff denies that any such meeting ever occurred. On June 9, 1975, plaintiff went to St. Mary's to perform his duties as a staff radiologist. At this time officials at the hospital told him that, due to his "termination" from the professional corporation, he was no longer eligible to practice at St. Mary's.

Dr. Lopez had an agreement with St. Mary's Hospital prior to plaintiff's association with Livonia Physicians X–Ray giving him personal and sole responsibility for staffing the radiology department. This agreement necessitated membership in Livonia Physicians X–Ray, P.C.

Defendant was responsible for drafting all the agreements pertaining to membership in the professional corporation. Defendant, and specifically Donald Epstein, had knowledge of the arrangements between Dr. Lopez and the hospital but never disclosed these facts to plaintiff. Plaintiff finally states that defendant has represented both Lopez individually and the professional corporation without disclosing to him this dual representation.

This case presents us with the difficult question of what duties, if any, an attorney representing a closely held corporation has to a 50% owner of the entity, individually.[3] This is a problem of first impression in Michigan.

We start our analysis by examining whether an attorney-client relationship exists between plaintiff and defendant....

A corporation exists as an entity apart from its shareholders, even where the corporation has but one shareholder.... While no Michigan case has addressed whether a corporation's attorney has an attorney-client relationship with the entity's shareholders, the general proposition of corporate identity apart from its shareholders leads us to conclude, in accordance with decisions from other jurisdictions, that the attorney's client is the corporation and not the shareholders....

Although we conclude that no attorney-client relationship exists between plaintiff and defendant, this does not necessarily mean that defendant had no fiduciary duty to plaintiff. The existence of an

---

2. Whether or not the by-laws of the professional corporation made Drs. Fassihi and Lopez the sole directors of the organization, Donald Epstein in a deposition contended that a Joseph Carolan was a third director. Mr. Carolan was apparently the business manager of Livonia Physicians X–Ray. We assume that at least defendant considers him a proper director. Otherwise, it would have been impossible for Lopez to effect his scheme of terminating Fassihi's association with the professional corporation as Fassihi would have undoubtedly opposed the plan. In any case, a corporate arrangement whereby one 50% shareholder can oust the other 50% shareholder—whether individually or with the assistance of a third director—seems highly unusual and comes to us on a stipulated hypothetical for purposes of this appeal.

3. See L. Greenhouse, In Corporate Law, Who's the Client? The New York Times, Sunday, February 15, 1981, p. 20 E.

attorney-client relationship merely establishes a per se rule that the lawyer owes fiduciary duties to the client.

A fiduciary relationship arises when one reposes faith, confidence, and trust in another's judgment and advice. Where a confidence has been betrayed by the party in the position of influence, this betrayal is actionable, and the origin of the confidence is immaterial.... Furthermore, whether there exists a confidential relationship apart from a well defined fiduciary category is a question of fact.... Based upon the pleadings, we cannot say that plaintiff's claim is clearly unenforceable as a matter of law.

Plaintiff asserts that he reposed in defendant his trust and confidence and believed that, as a 50% shareholder in Livonia Physicians X–Ray, defendant would treat him with the same degree of loyalty and impartiality extended to the other shareholder, Dr. Lopez. In his complaint plaintiff states that he was betrayed in this respect. Specifically, plaintiff asserts that he was not advised of defendant's dual representation of the corporate entity and Dr. Lopez personally.[5] Plaintiff also alleges that he was never informed of the contract between Lopez and St. Mary's which gave Lopez sole responsibility in the staffing of the radiology department and, more importantly, that defendant actively participated with Lopez in terminating plaintiff's association with the corporation and using the Lopez–St. Mary's contract to his detriment.

In support of his position that he has an attorney-client relationship with defendant, plaintiff cites a number of cases standing for the proposition that the corporate veil will be pierced where the corporate identity is being used to further fraud or injustice.... These cases are not factually similar to the instant matter as they involve claims against a corporate principal attempting to protect himself from personal liability through the corporate entity. At the same time, these cases are instructive as they point out the difficulties in treating a closely held corporation with few shareholders as an entity distinct from the shareholders. Instances in which the corporation attorneys stand in a fiduciary relationship to individual shareholders are obviously more likely to arise where the number of shareholders is small. In such cases it is not really a matter of the courts piercing the corporate entity. Instead, the corporate attorneys, because of their close interaction with a shareholder or shareholders, simply stand in confidential relationships in respect to both the corporation and individual shareholders.[6]

---

5. The Code of Professional Responsibility and Canons DR 5–105 requires full disclosure of dual representation of parties to the clients involved and forbids dual representation in some circumstances.

6. Although factually different, Prescott v. Coppage, 266 Md. 562, 296 A.2d 150 (1972), is illuminating in its discussion of an attorney's obligations to third parties apart from a specific attorney-client relationship. In *Prescott*, the Maryland court found that the attorney owed a duty to a preferred creditor on a third-party beneficiary theory. The question in any given case is whether, irrespective of an actual attorney-client relation-

In addition to the claim for breach of fiduciary duties, plaintiff contends that his complaint states a cause of action for fraud. The elements of fraud are: (1) a material representation which is false; (2) known by defendant to be false, or made recklessly without knowledge of its truth or falsity; (3) that defendant intended plaintiff to rely upon the representation; (4) that, in fact, plaintiff acted in reliance upon it; and (5) thereby suffered injury. Hyma v. Lee, 338 Mich. 31, 37, 60 N.W.2d 920 (1953); Cormack v. American Underwriters Corp., 94 Mich.App. 379, 385, 288 N.W.2d 634 (1979). The false material representation needed to establish fraud may be satisfied by the failure to divulge a fact or facts the defendant has a duty to disclose. An action based on the failure to disclose facts is one for fraudulent concealment....

Plaintiff's fraudulent concealment claim is premised on defendant's failure to divulge its dual representation of Livonia Physicians X–Ray and the failure of defendant to disclose the existence of the contract between Dr. Lopez and St. Mary's Hospital. We agree with plaintiff that, irrespective of any other duty, defendant would have an obligation to divulge its dual representation of the corporation and Dr. Lopez individually. The failure to divulge this fact might serve as the basis for a fraudulent concealment action. We cannot agree, however, that defendant had an obligation to divulge the existence or contents of the Lopez–St. Mary's Hospital contract to plaintiff. Defendant's knowledge of this contract arose out of a confidential attorney-client relationship between [it] and Dr. Lopez.[7] This attorney-client relationship prohibited defendant from divulging facts learned during the course of representation of Dr. Lopez unless Lopez waived his right to the attorney-client privilege. While defendant should have, and likely did, consider the effect that its relationship with Lopez might have on the representation of the corporation and incidentally plaintiff, as a 50% shareholder, officer, and director, it was not prohibited from representing both if its employees' independent professional judgment on behalf of either would not likely be adversely affected by representation of the other. Code of Professional Responsibility and Canons DR 5–105(C).

. . .

We now turn to the issue of whether defendant has a privilege to refuse to answer questions relative to communications concerning the ouster of plaintiff from the corporation. Defendant contends that these communications are privileged because they were made on behalf of the majority of the board of directors and the attorney-client privilege belongs to the control group.

ship, plaintiff has pled sufficient allegations tending to show some legal duty on the part of the attorney to him personally.

    7. This is not to say that Dr. Lopez's personal failure to divulge the existence of his contract with St. Mary's Hospital could not serve as the basis for a fraudulent concealment claim.

We hold that under defendant's own argument, the attorney-client privilege may not be asserted against plaintiff. As a member of the board of directors, plaintiff was a member of the corporate control group. See Diversified Industries, Inc. v. Meredith, 572 F.2d 596 (CA 8, 1977). Thus, with respect to any communications defendant had with Dr. Lopez while representing the corporation, as opposed to Lopez personally, plaintiff, as a member of the control group, is equally entitled to this information.

Additionally, defendant acknowledges that the attorney-client privilege does not protect communications made for the purpose of perpetrating a fraud. See Garner v. Wolfinbarger, 430 F.2d 1093 (CA 5, 1970). Although plaintiff's complaint does not use the magic word "fraud", the gist of his complaint rests on a species of fraud. Plaintiff asserts that defendant, while under the guise of representing the corporation, conspired to withhold information from him which he had a right to have as a 50% shareholder and member of the board of directors and to wrongfully deprive him of the benefits of a business opportunity. These allegations were sufficient to defeat the invocation of the attorney-client relationship pursuant to the fraud exception.

. . .

Notes on *Fassihi*

Who is suing whom for what in *Fassihi?* Compare *Fassihi* to *Meehan.* Would the *Fassihi* court have found on the facts in *Meehan* that the corporation's law firm in *Meehan* owed fiduciary duties to Hopps during Hopps' tenure as chairman of the board? After the bankruptcy? Does not the CEO of a large publicly-held corporation "repose faith, confidence, and trust in [corporate counsel's] judgment and advice" as Fassihi did? Is a fiduciary relationship thus created between corporate counsel and the CEO? Between corporate counsel and the shareholders? A Massachusetts decision,[1] commenting on *Fassihi,* states:

> [T]here is logic in the proposition that, even though counsel for a closely held corporation does not by virtue of that relationship alone have an attorney-client relationship with the individual shareholders, counsel nevertheless owes each shareholder a fiduciary duty. See *Fassihi,* ... for a well-reasoned opinion supporting that view. Just as an attorney for a partnership owes a fiduciary duty to each partner, it is fairly arguable that an attorney for a close corporation owes a fiduciary duty to the individual shareholders.[2]

Does the same logic extend to lawyers for publicly owned corporations?

1. See Schaeffer v. Cohen, Rosenthal, Price, 405 Mass. 506, 541 N.E.2d 997 (1989).
2. 541 N.E.2d at 1002.

The court in *Fassihi* found no attorney-client relationship between Fassihi and the corporation's law firm, but held that the firm nevertheless owed this 50–percent shareholder fiduciary duties, which presumably it breached by helping to oust him from the corporation and keeping important information from him.[3] This is doctrinally consistent with the proposition that a lawyer for a corporation represents it and not any of its constituents, but is unclear as to the extent of the lawyer's responsibility to constituents. If the lawyer's duties are essentially the same as those owed a client, would it not be clearer to call it a client relationship? Or do the duties owed to a "client" differ from those owed to an "almost client?"

Co–Clients or Almost Clients?

A number of courts simply hold that a lawyer representing a closely-held corporation also represents the individual shareholders as joint clients. In re Banks[4] involved a closely-held family corporation that had been dominated by one family member during most of its history. Other family members subsequently wrested control of the corporation from that one family member, and the corporation's lawyers brought suit against him on their behalf. The court held that "in closely held ... corporations where the operator of the corporation either owns or controls the stock in such a manner that it is reasonable to assume that there is no real reason for him to differentiate in his mind between his own and corporate interests," the lawyer for the corporation owes that person the same duty not to represent conflicting interests that she would owe a client.[5] In a subsequent case[6] the Oregon court went one step further:

> Where a small, closely held corporation is involved, and in the absence of a clear understanding with the corporate owners that the attorney represents solely the corporation and not their individual interests, it is improper for the attorney thereafter to represent a third party whose interests are adverse to those of the stockholders and which arise out of a transaction which the attorney handled for the corporation. In actuality, the attorney in such a situation represents the corporate owners in their individual capacities as well as the corporation unless other arrangements are clearly made.[7]

In Rosman v. Shapiro,[8] the court held that it is reasonable for a 50 percent shareholder in a closely-held corporation, where there is only one other shareholder, to believe that the lawyer for the corporation "is

---

3. Also see Adell v. Sommers, Schwartz, Silver and Schwartz, P.C., 170 Mich.App. 196, 428 N.W.2d 26, 29 (1988) (lawyers for partnership owe fiduciary duties to limited partners).

4. 283 Or. 459, 584 P.2d 284 (1978).

5. 584 P.2d at 292.

6. In re Brownstein, 288 Or. 83, 602 P.2d 655 (1979).

7. 602 P.2d at 657.

8. 653 F.Supp. 1441, 1445 (S.D.N.Y.1987).

in effect his own individual attorney." [9] Are these cases consistent with *Meehan*? [10]

Should the courts find "joint clients" in some circumstances and a fiduciary relationship in others? What facts should be important in making this determination? [11] These questions are examined further in the notes following the next case and in the Hazard article on triangular relationships printed below at p. 809.

As *Fassihi* demonstrates, the question of "whistleblowing" can readily arise in a partnership, business or closely-held corporation when one of the entrepreneurs seeks to defraud or otherwise exploit another. An ABA ethics opinion [12] states that a lawyer representing a general or limited partnership normally represents the entity, not individual partners; that dual representation of the partnership and individual partners raises serious problems of conflict of interest and confidentiality; and that "information received by a lawyer in the course of representing the partnership ... normally may not be withheld from individual partners." An earlier New York ethics opinion concluded that a lawyer representing a limited partnership, upon discovering that a general partner has committed acts adversely affecting the interests of limited partners, may disclose those facts to the limited partners: The lawyer "may disclose his knowledge of the general partner's actions to the limited partners so that they will be able to take steps to protect their interests." [13]

Although the New York opinion is cast in terms of a permission to disclose wrongdoing of a general partner to limited partners, the fiduciary principles on which it is based suggest that a failure to disclose may make the lawyer liable for resulting damages.[14]

---

9. 653 F.Supp. at 1445.

10. See also Margulies v. Upchurch, 696 P.2d 1195 (Utah 1985) (lawyer for partnership may be found to have an attorney-client relationship with limited partners that would preclude him from suing them as individuals). See also Woods v. Superior Court of Tulare County, 149 Cal.App.3d 931, 197 Cal.Rptr. 185 (1983); In re Bowman Trading Co., Inc., 99 A.D.2d 459, 471 N.Y.S.2d 289 (1984); In the Matter of Nulle, 127 Ariz. 299, 620 P.2d 214 (1980); Opdyke v. Kent Liquor Mart, Inc., 40 Del.Ch. 316, 181 A.2d 579 (1962).

11. Cf. Stainton v. Tarantino, 637 F.Supp. 1051, 1077 (E.D.Pa.1986) (in deciding whether attorney-client relationship exists with individual partners, jury should consider whether individual partners confided in, relied on and had partnership counsel perform legal services for them as individuals; if no attorney-client relationship existed, no fiduciary duty exists either).

12. ABA Formal Op. 91–361 (July 12, 1991).

13. Ass'n Bar City of New York Op. No. 1986–2.

14. See Roberts v. Heim, 123 F.R.D. 614, 625 (N.D.Cal.1988) (limited partners are clients of the partnership's counsel for purposes of the attorney-client privilege because both counsel and the general partners have a fiduciary duty to make full disclosure of material facts to their beneficiaries, the limited partners, and withholding such information would constitute fraud).

2. Representing a Fiduciary

FICKETT v. SUPERIOR COURT OF PIMA COUNTY

Court of Appeals of Arizona, Division 2, 1976.
27 Ariz.App. 793, 558 P.2d 988.

HOWARD, CHIEF JUDGE.

Suit filed by Conservator of Guardianship of estate.

Petitioners are defendants in a pending superior court action filed by the present conservator (formerly guardian) of an incompetent's estate against the former guardian and petitioners, attorneys for the former guardian. The gravamen of the complaint was that petitioner Fickett, as attorney for the former guardian, was negligent in failing to *Complaint* discover that the guardian had embarked upon a scheme to liquidate the guardianship estate by misappropriation and conversion of the funds to his own use and making improper investments for his personal benefit.[1]

[The surcharge case cited in note 1 reports that Herbert Schwager, the former guardian, was an investment adviser with a "well-known" brokerage house. He had befriended Mrs. Styer, who was old and had failing eyesight. Schwager was appointed guardian of Mrs. Styer's $1.3 *How spent* million estate, consisting almost entirely of common stock. Within little more than a year, Schwager had sold most of the stock to build a two-unit business building. The two tenants were Schwager's wife, who ran a beauty salon, and another business in which Schwager had an interest. Both businesses became bankrupt. A separate corporation, wholly owned by Schwager, managed the building. It paid large salaries to Schwager and other family members for "management services." Schwager also extensively commingled funds in his personal *Atty. represented Schwager (Conservator)* account. Within three years most of Mrs. Styer's assets were gone and those that remained had large liens for loans or taxes. The plaintiff, a successor conservator, was able to recover little for the estate from Schwager or third parties. The conservator then brought this proceeding against the law firm which had represented Schwager as guardian.]

Petitioners filed a motion for summary judgment contending that, as a matter of law, since there was no fraud or collusion between the guardian and his attorney, the attorney was not liable for the guardian's misappropriation of the assets of the guardianship estate. In opposing the motion for summary judgment, the present conservator conceded that no fraud or collusion existed. His position, however, was that one could not say as a matter of law that the guardian's attorney owed no duty to the ward. The respondent court denied the motion for summary judgment and petitioners challenge this ruling by special action.

Rule The general rule for many years has been that an attorney could not be liable to one other than his client in an action arising out of his professional duties, in the absence of fraud or collusion. 7 Am.Jur.2d, Attorneys at Law, § 167. In denying liability of the attorney to one not

---

1. The facts of the guardian's misconduct can be found in the case of In Re Guardianship of Styer, 24 Ariz.App. 148, 536 P.2d 717 (1975). There we affirmed a judgment surcharging the guardian in the sum of $378,789.62.

in privity of contract for the consequences of professional negligence, the courts have relied principally on two arguments: (1) That to allow such liability would deprive the parties to the contract of control of their own agreement; and (2) that a duty to the general public would impose a huge potential burden of liability on the contracting parties. An annotation of cases dealing with an attorney's liability to one other than his immediate client for the consequences of negligence in carrying out his professional duties may be found in Annot., 45 A.L.R.3d 1181 et seq.

We cannot agree with petitioners that they owed no duty to the ward and that her conservator could not maintain an action because of lack of privity of contract. We are of the opinion that the better view is that the determination of whether, in a specific case, the attorney will be held liable to a third person not in privity is a matter of policy and involves the balancing of various factors, among which are the extent to which the transaction was intended to affect the plaintiff, the foreseeability of harm to him, the degree of certainty that the plaintiff suffered injury, the closeness of the connection between the defendant's conduct and the injuries suffered, the moral blame attached to the defendant's conduct, and the policy of preventing future harm. Biakanja v. Irving, 49 Cal.2d 647, 320 P.2d 16 (1958); Lucas v. Hamm, 56 Cal.2d 583, 15 Cal.Rptr. 821, 364 P.2d 685 (1961); ...

We believe that the public policy of this state permits the imposition of a duty under the circumstances presented here. In the case of In re Fraser, 83 Wash.2d 884, 523 P.2d 921 (1974), the Supreme Court of Washington in considering a complaint concerning an attorney's refusal to withdraw as attorney for a client-guardian, stated:

> "The respondent maintains and we agree that under the circumstances he would not have been justified in withdrawing as counsel until such time as the guardian had secured the agreement of some other attorney to take over the handling of the guardianship. As the respondent suggests, *the attorney owes a duty to the ward, as well as to the guardian.* Since the guardian in this case manifested a greater interest in obtaining money for herself than in serving the interest of the ward, it would have been hazardous to the interest of the ward to turn the assets of her small estate over to the guardian.

> In re Michelson, 8 Wash.2d 327, 335, 111 P.2d 1011, 1015 (1941), we said:

> 'It must be borne in mind that the real object and purpose of a guardianship is to preserve and conserve the ward's property for his own use, as distinguished from the benefit of others.'

> We think that under the circumstances of this case, the respondent cannot be faulted for refusing to abandon the ward at the guardian's request." 523 P.2d at 928. (Emphasis ours)

Relationship is Established w the WARD

We are of the opinion that when an attorney undertakes to represent the guardian of an incompetent, he assumes a relationship not only with the guardian but also with the ward. If, as is contended here, petitioners knew or should have known that the guardian was acting adversely to his ward's interests, the possibility of frustrating the whole purpose of the guardianship became foreseeable as did the possibility of injury to the ward. In fact, we conceive that the ward's interests overshadow those of the guardian. We believe the following statement in *Heyer v. Flaig*, supra, as to an attorney's duty to an intended testamentary beneficiary is equally appropriate here:

> "The duty thus recognized in *Lucas* stems from the attorney's undertaking to perform legal services for the client but reaches out to protect the intended beneficiary. We impose this duty because of the relationship between the attorney and the intended beneficiary; public policy requires that the attorney exercise his position of trust and superior knowledge responsibly so as not to affect adversely persons whose rights and interests are certain and foreseeable.

> "Although the duty accrues directly in favor of the intended testamentary beneficiary, the scope of the duty is determined by reference to the attorney-client context. Out of the agreement to provide legal services to a client, the prospective testator, arises the duty to act with due care as to the interests of the intended beneficiary. We do not mean to say that the attorney-client contract for legal services serves as the fundamental touchstone to fix the scope of this direct tort duty to the third party. The actual circumstances under which the attorney undertakes to perform his legal services, however, will bear on a judicial assessment of the care with which he performs his services." 74 Cal.Rptr. at 229, 449 P.2d at 165.

We, therefore, uphold the respondent court's denial of petitioners' motion for summary judgment since they failed to establish the absence of a legal relationship and concomitant duty to the ward.

. . .

Notes on *Fickett*

Fickett imposes a duty on a lawyer who learns that a fiduciary whom the lawyer represents is violating fiduciary duties to the beneficiary to prevent such violations. What should a lawyer do upon discovering such a breach? [15]

Corporate directors and officers have fiduciary responsibilities to shareholders. May a lawyer for a corporation be sued by shareholders

---

15. See Joel C. Dobris, Ethical Problems for Lawyers Upon Trust Terminations: Conflicts of Interests, 38 U.Miami L.Rev. 1 (1983), for a thoughtful analysis of conflicts where the lawyer represents the trustee.

for failing to discover (and stop) corporate fraud? Does *Fickett* provide additional guidance to the lawyer for a corporation that is dominated by one person?

In *Carter and Johnson,* p. 779 above, the outside directors retained counsel of their own as the situation at the company grew worse. What obligation, if any, would that lawyer have to the company?

Attorney–Client Privilege of Fiduciary

As discussed in the notes after *Yablonski,* a corporation's attorney-client privilege may be pierced on a showing of good cause by shareholders suing on behalf of the corporation. See the discussion of Garner v. Wolfinbarger above at p. 774. Even before *Garner* the case law dealing with beneficiary/fiduciary situations allowed beneficiaries in suits alleging breach of fiduciary duties access to information otherwise protected by the attorney-client privilege. Today the *Garner* exception is applied whenever there is a fiduciary, rather than an arm's-length, relationship between the litigants. Consider the following cases:

In Valente v. Pepsico, Inc.,[16] the minority shareholders in Wilson Co. brought suit against Pepsico, which was the majority shareholder, alleging violations of the securities laws. The court found that *Garner* was relevant because a majority shareholder owes fiduciary responsibilities, just as a corporation does, to minority shareholders. The court held that the minority shareholders could gain access to communications between Pepsico and its lawyers that touched upon the interests of the minority and the duties owed to them. "A fiduciary owes the obligation to his beneficiaries to go about his duties without obscuring his reasons from the legitimate inquiries of the beneficiaries." [17] The court stated that the purpose of the privilege to encourage frank communication between lawyer and client was outweighed by the "more general and important right of those who look to fiduciaries to safeguard their interests to be able to determine the proper functioning of the fiduciary." [18]

In Quintel Corp., N.V. v. Citibank, N.A.,[19] Gajria contracted with Citibank to be his agent in acquiring certain investment property. His suit alleged that Citibank breached its fiduciary duties to him in acquiring the property. The court, in applying *Garner* to allow Gajria access to communications between Citibank and its lawyers, said:

> ... Here as in *Garner,* Citibank and Gajria had a mutuality of interest in the consummation of the acquisition on the most advantageous terms. Citibank acted not for itself but for Gajria, in similar fashion to corporate management's actions taken on behalf of the corporation's shareholders. Here as in *Garner* ..., the

16. 68 F.R.D. 361 (D.Del.1975).

17. Id. at 370.

18. Id. n. 16.

19. 567 F.Supp. 1357 (S.D.N.Y.1983).

fiduciary's duty to exercise its authority without veiling its reasons from the grantor of that authority outweighs the fiduciary's interest in the confidentiality of its attorney's communications. The *Garner* rule stems not only from the general proposition that a beneficiary is entitled to know how the authority he has granted has been exercised but on the recognition that because of the mutuality of interest between the parties, the faithful fiduciary has nothing to hide from his beneficiary.[20]

Should *Garner* allow individuals who allege the government has violated its trust to discover communications of government lawyers upon a showing of good cause? Should a similar rule permit members of a class to obtain communications between class representatives and the lawyer for the class? [21]

Commentators have argued that a broad interpretation of *Garner* "effectively swallows the [attorney-client privilege]." [22] What are the dangers of allowing beneficiaries access to their fiduciaries' conversations with counsel? If the faithful fiduciary has "nothing to hide" from his beneficiary, why must the beneficiary show good cause before gaining access to the confidential communications between lawyer and fiduciary?

Some courts have held that the fiduciary does not have a privilege to assert against the beneficiary, i.e., that the beneficiary is a joint client for purposes of the privilege.[23] In California, as indicated earlier, the courts have held that they are precluded by statute from adopting *Garner*. Hence, in that state, beneficiaries are denied access to fiduciary-lawyer communications unless the court finds that beneficiaries are joint clients, whereupon the joint client exception to the privilege

20. Id. at 1363. See also Aguinaga v. John Morrell & Co., 112 F.R.D. 671, 681 (D.Kan.1986) (*Garner* applies to allow union members access to communications between union counsel and union leadership); Donovan v. Fitzsimmons, 90 F.R.D. 583 (N.D.Ill. 1981) (*Garner* rule allows the Secretary of Labor, suing a pension fund on behalf of the fund's beneficiaries, access to communications between the pension fund trustee and its lawyers). Compare In re Atlantic Financial Management Securities Litigation, 121 F.R.D. 141, 146 (D.Mass.1988) ("Without a showing of a fiduciary relationship, the *Garner* exception does not apply."); and In re Colocotronis Tanker Securities Litigation, 449 F.Supp. 828 (S.D.N.Y.1978) (*Garner* exception inapplicable between parties to an arm's-length contract).

21. See Note, The Attorney–Client Privilege in Class Actions: Fashioning an Exception to Promote Adequacy of Representation, 94 Harv.L.Rev. 947 (1984) (arguing that a *Garner*-like exception be created for class members who seek access to communication between class representatives and counsel).

22. See Developments in the Law—Privileged Communication: III. Attorney–Client Privilege, 98 Harv.L.Rev. 1501, 1527 (1985) (arguing that *Garner* be abandoned altogether in favor of the crime-fraud exception to the attorney-client privilege).

23. See, e.g., Roberts v. Heim, 123 F.R.D. 614 (N.D.Cal.1988) (limited partners are joint clients of lawyer for partnership for purposes of the privilege); United States v. Evans, 796 F.2d 264, 265–66 (9th Cir.1986) (pension trustee may not assert privilege against pension plan beneficiaries because "trustee is not the real client in the sense that he is personally being served"); Washington–Baltimore Newspaper Guild v. Washington Star Co., 543 F.Supp. 906 (D.D.C.1982) (beneficiaries of an employees' benefit plan granted access to communications between the plan's administrators and their lawyers without requiring a showing of good cause).

provides free access. California courts may be moved to find a co-client relationship in situations involving fiduciaries because the *Garner* doctrine is not available to penetrate the attorney-client privilege.[24]

In *Valente,* supra, the court shifted the burden to the fiduciary, requiring that it show why the privilege should not yield. Is this middle position between *Garner* and no privilege a better alternative?

The privilege still protects communications between fiduciary and lawyer that do not relate to the fiduciary relationship or that occur after the fiduciary relationship has been terminated. What about communications between the fiduciary and counsel about forming the fiduciary relationship, which by definition occurred before the fiduciary relationship actually began.[25] Should communications between the fiduciary and its lawyers about the extent of its obligations to the beneficiary be available to the beneficiary under *Garner*? The court in *Quintel* said yes, stating that such communications were made "as part of and in furtherance of ... fiduciary obligations." [26]

3. Triangular Lawyer Relationships

GEOFFREY C. HAZARD, JR.
"TRIANGULAR LAWYER RELATIONSHIPS:
AN EXPLORATORY ANALYSIS
1 Georgetown Journal of Legal Ethics 15 (1987).[27]

I. Introduction

This article examines the nature of a lawyer's responsibilities where the lawyer's client has a special legal relationship with another party that modifies the lawyer's "normal" professional responsibilities. This legal relationship is termed "triangular," denoting the coexistence of a linkage of legal responsibility between the lawyer's client and a third person along with a linkage of professional responsibility between the lawyer and the client. The combination results in a special legal relationship between the lawyer and the third person.

. . .

This exploration focuses on two types of triangular relationships. The first involves a client in a fiduciary relationship to a third party.

---

24. See Roberts v. Heim, 123 F.R.D. 614 (N.D.Cal.1988) (limited partners are joint clients; decided under federal common law, but court notes that result would be the same under California law); and Hoiles v. Superior Court of Orange County, 157 Cal.App.3d 1192, 204 Cal.Rptr. 111, 115 n. 4 (1984).

25. Compare *Quintel,* 567 F.Supp. at 1364 ("Prior to the investor's entry on the scene the important mutuality of interest is absent since Citibank's interest is in putting together a proposal that it can sell to the investor, an interest not shared by the investor"; therefore, the privilege holds); with *Roberts v. Heim,* supra (limited partners may later gain free access to general partner's communications with lawyer for partnership).

26. 567 F.Supp. at 1357.

27. Copyright © 1987 by the Georgetown Journal of Legal Ethics.

The classic example is that of a lawyer representing a guardian in matters relating to the guardian's responsibilities to a ward. In that relationship, the client-guardian has a set of strong and well defined legal obligations. Given these obligations, what are the legal obligations of the lawyer to the ward?

The lawyer → guardian → ward triangular relationship can be diagrammed:

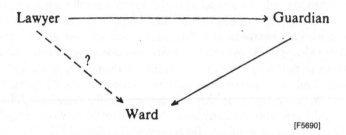

[F5690]

The second type of triangular relationship involves a third party who owes fiduciary duties to the lawyer's client, and the third party rather than the client is the one with whom the lawyer deals ordinarily. The classic situation is that of a lawyer who represents a corporation but who, in the ordinary course of professional service, deals with the corporation's officers, directors, and employees. To simplify terminology, we can treat the corporate officers, directors, and employees as a single category, even though important differences exist in their legal relationships to the corporation. Thus simplified, the corporate lawyer triangular relationship can be designated as lawyer → corporation ← officer.

The lawyer-corporation-officer triangular relationship can be diagrammed:

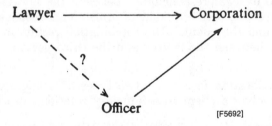

[F5692]

The difference in the vectors of obligation in these two triangular relationships is important. In the lawyer → guardian → ward triangular relationship, the ward is the dependent person and the obligee of the guardian, but the guardian is the dependent person and the primary obligee of the lawyer. In the lawyer → corporation ← officer triangular relationship, the corporation is the dependent entity and the obligee of both the lawyer and the corporate officer. This structural difference in obligations can help identify and define the lawyer's role in the two triangular relationships....

Other triangular relationships can be classified into the two basic types:

I.	II.
Classic	*Classic*
Lawyer → Guardian → Ward	Lawyer → Corporation ← Officer
Others	*Others*
Lawyer → General Partner → Partnership	Lawyer → Partnership ← General Partner
Lawyer → Govt. Employee → Govt.	Lawyer → Govt. ← Govt. Employee
Lawyer → Union Officer → Union	Lawyer → Union ← Union Officer
Lawyer → Director → Corp.	Lawyer → Ward ← Guardian

As the foregoing chart depicts, whether a triangular relationship falls into one or the other of the two basic categories depends on which party is the lawyer's client. If the lawyer represents the *guardian*, for example, the relationship is lawyer → guardian → ward and is of the first basic type. On the other hand, if the lawyer represents the *ward*, the relationship is lawyer → ward ← guardian and is of the second basic type. Similarly, a lawyer retained to represent a corporate officer or director rather than the corporation falls under the first basic type, whereas the normal corporate lawyer relationship is lawyer → corporation ← director and falls under the second basic type.

. . .

II.　Traditional Concepts for Defining a Lawyer's Responsibilities

A.　Three Possible Relationships

Part of the difficulty posed by triangular lawyer relationships lies in the traditional limitations in the definition of a lawyer's responsibilities. Generally, those responsibilities recognize only three relationships that a lawyer may have. One is with a client; the second is with the court; and the third is with a third party. In substance and orientation, these relationships differ from each other radically. In moral and existential quality, they are strangely alike in their radical simplicity. They characterize the lawyer's "relevant other" respectively as something like friend, father, and foe.

1.　Clients

[Professor Hazard describes the lawyer's relationship with a client as legally both amorphous and secret. The lawyer's primary duty to the client is loyalty and the relationship may be analogized to that of limited-purpose "friendship." [17] Beyond the duty of loyalty, however, the lawyer-client relationship is largely unstructured, the only real limit being the "bounds of the law."]

17. Charles Fried, The Lawyer as Friend: The Moral Foundations of the Lawyer–Client Relationship, 85 Yale L.J. 1060 (1976).

2. Courts

[Starting with the basic proposition that "a lawyer is an officer of the court," Hazard suggests a lawyer owes the court only a minimal duty of diligence and candor. But while the lawyer's substantive responsibility to the court is minimal, the formal aspects of that relationship—the law of procedure and the rules of evidence—are highly detailed and exacting. Thus, where the lawyer's relationship with a client is legally unstructured and secret, the lawyer's relationship with the court is legally structured and visible.]

3. Third Party

The third kind of lawyer's relationship is that with a third party. In general, a third party is entitled to very little from the lawyer. If Brougham's dictum about the duty of the advocate is taken as the measure of the lawyer's legal duty to anyone but the client, a lawyer owes a third party nothing. The law concerning a lawyer's obligations to others is hard indeed, but not quite that hard. Against a lawyer, a third party is entitled to the protection of the criminal law and the law of fraud.... Rules against abusive litigation, such as rule 11 of the Federal Rules of Civil Procedure are essentially corollaries of the rule against fraud.

B. Inadequacy of Conceptual Premises

The established conceptual system thus allows for only three parties with whom the lawyer may have a professional relationship: client, court, third party. As we shall see, the most difficult problems in triangular relationships are those in which the lawyer is performing a counseling function as distinct from the function of advocate. In counseling situations one thing is clear: none of the relevant others is a judge. Under the established scheme, that reduces the conceptual possibilities from three to two. The lawyer's relationship to the other person—the ward or the corporate office—must be characterized as either that between lawyer and client or that between lawyer and third party.

This is a stark choice. If the relationship is characterized as that with a client, then the duties of loyalty, zealous partisanship, and confidentiality are fully engaged. To say that when the lawyer represents a guardian he or she thereby also represents the ward, or that when a lawyer represents a corporation he or she also represents its corporate officers, is to implicate very serious practical and conceptual difficulties, indeed contradictions.

[Hazard describes four problems that would arise if we were to accept that guardian and ward were co-clients or that corporation and corporate officer were co-clients: (1) because potential conflict between the two clients (guardian and ward or corporation and corporate officer) is always present, concurrent representation of both would involve an impermissible conflict of interest; (2) similarly, the rules prohibiting representation adverse to a former client in the "same or a substantially related" matter would prevent a lawyer who was deemed to represent both from representing either the guardian or the ward if a subsequent dispute arose; and (3) confidential communications between the joint clients would not be protected either by professional rules or by the attorney-client privilege.]

. . .

The courts have rightly hesitated to embrace the foregoing implications. They have been confused, however, in knowing where to stop or even where to start. They evidently recognize that the lawyer in these triangular relationships has special protective responsibilities to the person who is not the client, but they do not wish to say that these responsibilities include the whole package owed to a client. Under the conventional conceptual system, the alternative is to say that the lawyer's relationship to the other person is that of lawyer and third party. In the guardian-ward situation, this would mean that the ward is merely a stranger. The same would be true of the corporate lawyer's responsibility to a corporate director, officer, or employee.

To treat the ward or the corporate officer as a mere stranger is unappealing and incoherent. It is unappealing because it affords the ward or the corporate employee, insofar as the lawyer is concerned, only the cold comfort provided by the laws of crime and fraud. It is incoherent in the guardianship situation because it calls for the lawyer as agent of the guardian to have an arm's length relationship with one to whom the guardian has an intimate and exacting fiduciary duty. That makes no sense under basic principles of the law of agency. Under the law of agency, the duty of an agent of the principal (i.e., the lawyer representing the guardian) to a third person (i.e., the ward) is a function of the duty of the principal (i.e., the guardian) to that person. To treat the ward as a stranger vis-á-vis the lawyer disregards that interconnection.

In the corporate situation an even more complicated set of difficulties is presented if the corporate officer is treated as a mere stranger. For one thing, the corporate officer is effectively the personification of the corporate client for most ordinary legal purposes. Corporate counsel and the corporate officer must maintain an intimacy that substantially replicates that between counsel and a flesh and blood client. It is simply impossible to hold that a person who is, in fact, a confidential intimate shall nevertheless be regarded in law as a total stranger. Moreover, under the law of agency, some kind of protective responsibility is owed by the principal to the agent in matters within the scope of the agency. A corporation owes a responsibility to its employees, sometimes something like that of guardian to ward. Thus, whatever the relationship between a corporation and its director, officer, or employee, it is not that of one stranger to another.

[Hazard argues that the unmodulated and polarized character of the alternative relationships (lawyer-client and lawyer-third party) are inappropriate when one of the two persons the lawyer is dealing with owes fiduciary duties to the other. The polar notions of friend or foe—

the client as friend and the third party as foe) do not reflect the accommodation of competing values required by the situation. "The complex interdependencies in the[se] ... situations do not lend themselves to analysis in terms of friend or foe."]

The inadequacy of these premises no doubt explains why the responses of courts and scholars to lawyer triangular relationships have been so baffled and baffling. Lacking an adequate conceptual system to address the problem, the courts have done what courts always do in such circumstances: They adhere to bad concepts and get poor results, or, as in the *Fickett* and *Yablonski* cases, they reach what may be good results but improvise on concepts. A variation of this technique is to marshal miscellaneous "factors," factors found in all the problematic situations, and then to maintain that the correct solution depends on "all the factors." ... [See, e.g., the list of factors to be considered in deciding whether shareholders may gain access to the corporation's confidential communications with counsel. *Garner v. Wolfinbarger*.]

. . .

IV. Toward Better Conceptualizations

. . .

Neither the concept of "client" nor that of "third party" appropriately engages the complexities of triangular relationships, even a simple one such as that of guardian and ward involved in *Fickett v. Superior Court*. The client in such a triangular situation is not a person alone—the *A* of classical legal hypotheticals, where "*A*, the owner of Blackacre" does something to or is done something by *B*. One who has become another's guardian is no longer *A* but has become "*A* encumbered by duties to *B*." So long as the relationship between *A* and *B* exists, and for some purposes even after it ends, *A* is not a legal monad. Rather *A* is a member of an "institution," (as said in *Yablonski v. United Mine Workers*), that has a "whole purpose," (as said in *Fickett*). In legal terms, a guardian as such is an officeholder constituted by law, by court appointment as in the *Fickett* case or by private contractual designation. So also, and more obviously, the corporate director, officer, or employee is an officeholder constituted by legally sanctioned private ordering, and is a member of an "institution" that has a "whole purpose." As a matter of law, both guardian and corporate officer are not persons but personages, individuals who act in legal capacities.

. . .

The vocabulary and metaphorical geometry used in analyzing the "normal" lawyer-client relationship contemplate an intimate dyad of lawyer and client, facing outward toward an alien and presumptively hostile world of third parties. That vocabulary and geometry misdescribes relationships between a lawyer, a client who is a legal personage, and a third person whose very existence defines that personage. The problem is to develop concepts and vocabulary that intelligibly address relationships where the lawyer must care about two parties.

. . .

A. Client Openly Adverse to the "Other"

There are cases where a lawyer in a triangular situation has the same "arm's length" position vis-á-vis the "relevant other" as a lawyer "normally" should have on behalf of a client. The clearest is where the lawyer, not having been involved previously, is retained to represent a guardian or a corporate officer in litigation concerning that person's performance of duties. The specification that the lawyer has *no* previous involvement with the guardian or corporate officer indicates that the lawyer has not incurred any responsibility in the transaction prior to the litigation.

In the case of a guardianship, litigation could involve a proceeding initiated by the ward against the guardian, either an independent suit or a motion in the guardianship proceeding to surcharge or remove the guardian. Litigation could involve an objection by the ward to a periodic accounting submitted by the guardian; such an accounting is essentially a request by the guardian for a declaratory judgment of exoneration and is therefore a surcharge proceeding with the parties reversed. The guardian risks legal condemnation, financial loss, civic disgrace, and moral obloquy. This being the guardian's legal exposure, the guardian is entitled to vigorous marshalling of evidence tending to show he did not violate his trust, and he is entitled to vigorous argument for a favorable definition of his legal obligations. By the same token, the lawyer is obliged to make zealous efforts on the guardian's behalf; hold in confidence information garnered for the representation; and abstain from conflicting representation in the matter.

There should be no equivocation or confusion about the nature of lawyer-client relationship and the lawyer's duties in this situation. An action for surcharge is a legal claim against the guardian in his or her individual capacity for alleged wrong committed in the course of an official capacity. The potential financial loss, moral obloquy, and civic disgrace faced by the guardian are real individual interests. Persons with that kind of exposure are entitled to legal representation, which means full service advocacy.

The same analysis applies where a lawyer, not previously involved, is retained to represent a corporate director, officer, or employee. Ordinarily, that kind of representation is arranged only when there is a significant possibility that the interests of the director, officer, or employee may diverge from the corporation's interests. When this possibility exists, there is also a risk that there will be legal or informal recrimination on behalf of the corporation. Persons with that kind of exposure are likewise entitled to full service advocacy.

The same analysis again applies where a lawyer, not previously involved, is retained to represent the corporation against a corporate director, officer, or employee to redress malfeasance in office. That was the situation in *Yablonski,* where the derivative suit sought to redress the officer's misspending of organization funds. The holding in *Yablonski* that the organization is entitled to the zeal of an uncompromised advocate is correct....

[Hazard discusses two additional cases of "arm's length" relationships. One involves a lawyer retained to represent someone nominated as guardian or corporate officer in negotiating the terms of the office. The other concerns a lawyer with no prior involvement who is brought into negotiations for termination or reformation of the special relationship. In both instances the lawyer is not involved in the conduct of the relationship, but only in negotiations concerning the creation, reformation, or termination of the relationship. In both cases the fiduciary is dealing at arm's length with a beneficiary, and the role of the lawyer becomes the typical one of negotiation or advocacy on behalf of the fiduciary-client.]

B. Normal Protective Relationship

While the positions of the fiduciary and the "relevant other" are openly adverse in some situations, normally the fiduciary's protective responsibility is unambiguous. In the normal legal relationship between guardian and ward, or between corporation and corporate director, officer, or employee, the legal purpose of the relationship is being fulfilled and the fiduciary is conforming his or her conduct to legal requirements.

The lawyer's task in this normal situation is to assist the fiduciary in meeting his or her legal obligations, and to help minimize legal risks to the relationship from outside forces, such as persons with competing claims on the assets or the tax collector. Toward these ends the lawyer supplies advice and employs legally recognized techniques that further the undertaking. Thus, the lawyer provides the forms and procedures for board action in the corporation, for the proprieties where a director has a conflict of interest that disqualifies him or her from voting on a corporate matter, etc. In the guardianship, the lawyer similarly safeguards the proprieties. The lawyer represents the guardian *in taking care* of the ward—the "whole purpose of the relationship," to use the phrase from *Fickett.* In the corporate situation, the corporate counsel works with the corporate director, officer, or employee *in taking care* of the corporation's "institutional interests," to use the phrase from *Yablonski.* Neither a "guardianship" nor a "corporation" has material existence or autonomous identity. They are legal events, artifacts of the lawyer's endeavors in the representation. The relationship itself is an evolving legal event that the lawyer's services continuously create.

. . .

[T]he lawyer's responsibilities may well be analogized to multiple representation. The key rules are those of confidentiality and loyalty. In multiple representation, the rule of confidentiality includes all within the group and excludes all outside it. In the corporate situation, the rule of confidentiality applies to information the corporate lawyer obtains from corporate "constituents" in the course of the representation, as does the corresponding rule of attorney-client privilege.[51] The same principle would apply to information provided to a lawyer for a partnership and ought to apply to information received from a ward by a lawyer or a guardian.

Concerning the principle of loyalty, a lawyer may serve two or more clients in the same matter if they do not have adverse interests. In a triangular relationship in the normal state, the interests of the nonlawyer participants are not adverse; both, therefore, may be considered to be clients.

Conceptualizing both the "relevant others" as clients, and the lawyer as engaged in multiple representation, seems entirely natural when the triangular relationship is in its normal state. The question is whether there are reasons for refusing to conceptualize it in this way. Only one reason exists for such hesitancy: the implications that follow if the triangular relationship ceases to be normal and instead becomes antagonistic.

... Under standard doctrine, in multiple representation each client has the full rights of a client, including the power over confidentiality and the right to enforce the conflict of interest rules against the lawyer. Thus, if the corporate officer is treated in all respects as a client, then confidences he or she has imparted to the lawyer would not be usable against him or her *after* the normal triangular relationship has collapsed and the corporation and its officers become legal antagonists.[54] If the corporate officer is treated as a client in all respects, upon the collapse of his or her relationship with the corporation, the officer could then insist that the corporate lawyer not represent the corporation against him or her.[55] These are undesirable corollaries and their specter is a weighty objection.

This weighty objection indicates that the multiple representation concept should not operate fully once the triangular relationship has collapsed; indeed, that is the recognized rule. Ordinarily upon collapse of the relationship, the lawyer may continue to represent the person or entity that was his client in the full and formal sense, even though

51. Upjohn Co. v. United States, 449 U.S. 383 (1981) (attorney-client privilege covers employee responses to questionnaires and interview notes of counsel).

54. The corporate officer does not have that right. E.g., Lane v. Chowning, 610 F.2d 1385 (8th Cir.1979) (defendant bank's attorney has no obligation to plaintiff-officer to refrain from using information acquired in representing bank).

55. The corporate officer does not have that right either. E.g., Meehan v. Hopps, 144 Cal.App.2d 284, 301 P.2d 10 (1956) (attorney not precluded from representing client-corporation against officer where no prior attorney-client relationship existed between counsel and officer).

representation entails a position adverse to the other member of the triangle.[56] If both were treated as clients in the strict sense, that option would not be available.[57] The law should continue to recognize the lawyer's authority to continue representation of a guardian or a corporation after the relationship with the other party becomes antagonistic. On the other hand, the possibility that a triangular relationship might collapse into antagonism is an insufficient reason for rejecting the multiple representation analogy while the triangular relationship is still intact. It is also insufficient reason for denying the "relevant other" some of the rights of a full-fledged former client if the relationship does collapse, particularly where the lawyer had not made the ground rules clear earlier.[59]

C. Ambivalent and Unstable Situations

A triangular relationship may, then, be analyzed in two ways regarding the lawyer. One of the parties can be regarded as the client and the other as the third party, or both can be regarded as clients. Each interpretation fits traditional concepts and terminology, and each implies a firm set of legal consequences. While both interpretations are plausible, they result in radically different definitions of the lawyer's responsibilities. Under one interpretation the "relevant other" is like a friend, under the second the "relevant other" is like a foe.

.   .   .

The difference between a "normal" triangular relationship and one contaminated by antagonism does not lie in the *structure* of the relationship. Until finally resolved or dissolved, the structure is ambiguously triangular, with the nonlawyer parties being fellow clients, or antipodal, with the nonlawyer parties being antagonists. The proper interpretation depends not on structure but on process—what has happened within the relationship. The relevant set of happenings include, above all, what the lawyer has done in the relationship.

---

56. E.g., Commodity Futures Trading Comm'n v. Weintraub, 471 U.S. 343 (1985) (trustee of corporation in bankruptcy has power to waive corporation's attorney-client privilege with respect to communications that took place before filing petition in bankruptcy); Lane v. Chowning, 610 F.2d 1385 (8th Cir.1979); Meehan v. Hopps, 144 Cal. App.2d 284, 301 P.2d 10 (1956).

57. E.g., Opdyke v. Kent Liquor Market, Inc., 40 Del.Ch. 316, 181 A.2d 579 (1962) (attorney who organized and was retained by three man corporation owed fiduciary duty to stockholders, breached fiduciary duty to minority stockholder by buying majority stock to which minority shareholder had claim, and held stock as constructive trustee for minority stockholder).

59. Compare Model Rule 1.13 (Organization as Client), ... with E.F. Hutton & Co. v. Brown, 305 F.Supp. 371 (S.D.Tex.1969) (in-house counsel who had represented corporate officer in his individual capacity in prior separate litigation disqualified from representing corporation in negligence action against officer); see G. Hazard & W. Hodes, The Law of Lawyering 243–244, 262–264 (1985) (discussing fairness to nonclients within an organization and the *Miranda*-type warning required by rule 1.13(d)); but cf. W.T. Grant Co. v. Haines, 531 F.2d 671 (2d Cir.1976) (court has discretion to allow outside counsel to represent corporation in antitrust action against former employee even if counsel has had allegedly improper communication with employee unrepresented by counsel).

In *Fickett,* the lawyer had done nothing when he should have been doing something. The "something" he should have been doing was neither mysterious nor extraordinary. If he had adhered to normal lawyer practice followed in a normal guardian representation, he would have satisfied himself that the guardian had at least some idea of the responsibilities concerning investments and of the requirements for periodic accounting, and would have activated the procedure for submitting such accounts. If the guardian had approached him to confide that some of the investments were irregular, normal lawyer practice would suggest that the lawyer should have said something like, "That could involve very serious difficulties." The lawyer would thereby not commit himself to representing the guardian versus the ward, or vice versa; the lawyer would only be suggesting the urgent need for redefinition of the relationship between the guardian and the ward. He or she should do nothing to further or conceal the guardian's misfeasance, because the law provides that doing so would constitute fraudulent conduct on the lawyer's part. If the guardian persisted in misconduct, under accepted standards of practice the lawyer could withdraw and advise the ward of the fact of withdrawal.

In *Yablonski,* the organization's lawyer did things when the situation was such that "the role of ... counsel ... becomes usually a passive one." [61] The lawyer should not have assisted the president in defending colorable claims of malfeasance toward the organization. If the lawyer had adhered to proper practice in this abnormal situation, he or she would have advised the president to get independent legal representation and perhaps have advised the board to get other independent representation for the organization. Indeed, as the law has now evolved, any other course by the lawyer could be regarded as furthering or concealing the president's malfeasance.

V. Conclusion

The critical problem the lawyer faces in triangular relationships is that his or her professional responsibilities depend unavoidably on what the other two parties do for and to each other. The lawyer's duty cannot adequately be defined, as it normally is, by specifying *ex ante* the identity of "the client." Neither of the "relevant others" is a legally freestanding person in the standard conceptual sense of "client." The guardian is not an individual alone but a person whose legal identity is expressed in terms of legal responsibilities ex officio. The corporation is not an individual at all, but exists only in law and through personification by others who act ex officio. If the other parties to the relationship conduct themselves as the law contemplates they should, then all the "relevant others" collectively can be considered "the client." That principle is already well established for corporations,[62] and there seems to be no reason not to think of guardianships and other triangular relationships in the same way. On the other

---

61. *Yablonski,* 448 F.2d at 1179.
62. Upjohn Co. v. United States, 449 U.S. 383 (1981).

hand, if the dominant party is guilty of misconduct toward the dependent one and if the lawyer behaves as though everything were still normal, the lawyer would then have at least an ethical problem and quite possibly legal liability.

. . .

The lawyer can see and act. Depending on what he or she sees and does, the dominant actor may have to be treated as something less than a client simpliciter and the lawyer himself or herself as something different from one who "knows no other duty." That definition of role entails being an active, visible participant in the transaction and exercising independent judgment. Such deportment does not fit the conventional mold.

C. LAWYERS FOR THE GOVERNMENT

Introductory Note

Who is the client of the government lawyer? Possible contenders include the agency head, the chief executive officer (e.g., the governor or president), the legislature as the elected representatives of the public and the "public."

One way to begin the analysis is to ask who is the counterpart for the government lawyer of the constituents of organizational clients that make up a corporate lawyer's world. What government counterpart takes the place of the chief executive officer (CEO), the board of directors or the shareholders? For a lawyer in the United States Department of Justice is the Attorney General analogous to the CEO? Does the answer depend on whether or not the lawyer is concerned about illegal acts on the part of the Attorney General? Is the "public" comparable to shareholders? What duties, if any, does the lawyer owe to Congress? For a lawyer at the Securities and Exchange Commission, is the Commission akin to a board of directors?

As these questions demonstrate, the analogy to corporations is imperfect. Corporations are private organizations subject to public law and usually have a limited purpose (e.g., making money) and a limited ultimate constituency (e.g., the shareholders). Governments are themselves instruments of public law whose purpose cannot be expressed in a single formula. Further, the federal government, state governments and many local governments are organized on the basis of separation of powers, not integrated under one "board of directors." Finally, the public's interest is more amorphous than the shareholders' interest. While the law artificially reduces shareholders' interest to law-abiding profitability, reduction of the public's interest to a corruption-free, law-abiding government is simplistic.

1. Identifying a Government Lawyer's Client

ROGER C. CRAMTON
"THE LAWYER AS WHISTLEBLOWER: CONFIDENTIALITY AND THE GOVERNMENT LAWYER"

5 Georgetown J. Legal Ethics 291, 292–306 (1991).[28]

The United States government employs more than 22,000 lawyers to handle its legal problems (two to three percent of all U.S. lawyers). Most of these lawyers are employed full-time by one or another of the myriad departments or agencies of the executive branch. The variety of legal work performed by government lawyers is nearly as broad as the breadth of legal activity generally. Lawyers for the federal government are advisors, counselors and litigators; and they deal in virtually every legal specialty, although for obvious reasons administrative law and federal specialties have special prominence in their work.

. . .

The government lawyer's duty of confidentiality differs from that of a lawyer in private practice in two significant ways. First, pervasive regulations govern much of the information with which a government lawyer must necessarily deal. A large portion of the information in the hands of the federal government consists of public records or information available upon request to the public. Recent legislation, in particular the Freedom of Information Act, provides citizens with access to a wide range of government documents. An obvious corollary to such legislation is that a government lawyer's duty of confidentiality does not extend to information that the government has made available upon request to the public. In terms of the professional ethics rules, the government in effect has consented to disclosure. Government lawyers also deal with more sensitive and more protected information than lawyers in the private sector. For example, government lawyers have access to military secrets, sensitive negotiations with foreign governments, grand jury minutes dealing with investigation of federal crimes and millions of records dealing with the most private matters of individuals and corporations. Information in the last category includes income tax records, medical records, and trade secrets. Not surprisingly, a detailed regulatory scheme limits the government lawyer's use of this information and prohibits its improper dissemination. Protection of information of this character is not dependent solely on the attorney-client privilege or the lawyer's professional duty of confidentiality.

Second, the government lawyer functions within a complex federal system based on the principle of separation of powers.[22] It is an untidy structure of incredible complexity in which the President provides the

---

28. Copyright © 1991 Georgetown Journal of Legal Ethics.

22. See generally Geoffrey P. Miller, Government Lawyers' Ethics in a System of Checks and Balances, 54 U.Chi.L.Rev. 1293 (1987).

principal focus of cohesion and unity while Congress, responding to interest groups, tends to further the centrifugal tendencies of a pluralistic society. The Constitution vests "executive power" in the President and legislative authority in the Congress, but in practice the functions are mixed, with independent agencies created by Congress having varying degrees of independence from presidential control and, conversely, the executive branch exercising delegated and inherent legislative authority in the form of executive orders, agency rules, and interpretive guidelines.... [A]lthough the President has broad power within the executive branch, there are independent agencies, officers with specific delegated functions and quasi-governmental corporations each operating within their own spheres of authority.

The Attorney General's control of litigation in which the United States is a party follows a similar pattern. Although the Attorney General has broad control over government litigation, Congress has passed more than one hundred statutes giving particular agencies separate litigating authority. The government lawyer in such a federal system must necessarily conform his conduct to statutes and regulations that do not apply to a lawyer in the private sector.[25]

In this unusual world, who is the government lawyer's client? The question has vexed decision-makers and commentators for many years. The possibilities include: (1) the public, (2) the government as a whole, (3) the branch of government in which the lawyer is employed, (4) the particular agency or department in which the lawyer works and (5) the responsible officers who make decisions for the agency. Although a scattering of support can be found for each possibility, the dispute has been primarily between a broader loyalty to "the public interest" or the government as a whole, on the one hand, and a more restricted vision of the government lawyer as the employee of a particular agency, on the other. With rare exceptions, the discussion has not taken full account of the array of constitutional and statutory obligations that override the simple issue of "who is the client?" ...

. . .

Even more so than the lawyer who represents a large, publicly held corporation, the government lawyer must deal with a wide range of interests, constituencies and competing values. "A government lawyer serves the interests of many different entities: his supervisor in the department or agency, the agency itself, the statutory mission of the agency, the entire government of which that agency is part, and the public interest."[31] These interests are not inchoate but are expressed in constitutional structure and duties, statutory command and regulatory obligations. The professional rules are drafted on the assumption

25. See, e.g., 18 U.S.C. § 205 (1982) (prohibiting government employees from representing parties in actions against the United States or the District of Columbia); 18 U.S.C. § 207 (1982) (placing restrictions on successive government and private employment); and 18 U.S.C. § 208 (financial conflict of interest statute).

31. Note, Developments in the Law—Conflicts of Interest in the Legal Profession, 94 Harv.L.Rev. 1244, 1414 (1981).

that the normal case is one in which a lawyer is representing an individual client or an uncomplicated organization. Only in recent years has specific attention been given to the special problems that arise when a lawyer represents a complex organization.

For day-to-day operating purposes, the government lawyer may properly view as his or her client the particular agency by which the lawyer is employed. The Federal Bar Association proposed this rule of thumb in 1973, but immediately qualified it to include "those charged with [the agency's] administration insofar as they are engaged in the conduct of the public business." [33] The inquiry then turns to when the responsible officers are no longer "engaged in the conduct of the public business." [34]

Some years ago, Judge Fahy argued that "because the Government is a composite of the people[,] Government counsel therefore has as a client the people as a whole." [36] Under this approach, the government lawyer becomes "the maker of the conscience of the government." [37] This approach has several serious drawbacks. First, the public interest approach would interfere with the government lawyer's ability to function effectively as counselor and adviser to government officials. Second, conceptions of the "public interest" vary significantly from one person to the next. Third, the public interest approach raises separation of powers concerns. In short, defining the government lawyer's client as the public interest would fail to provide any real guidance in regulating lawyers' conduct.

... Suppose, for example, that a government lawyer refuses to participate in the creation of a program on the grounds that it violates Supreme Court precedent and lacks congressional authorization. He bases his refusal on a belief that he represents the government as a whole, and that his participation in such a program would disserve the judicial and legislative branches of government. The government lawyer's assumption, however, fails to take into account the fact that he operates "within a system of separation of powers and checks and balances." [52] In such a system, "it is not the responsibility of an agency attorney to represent the interests of Congress or the Court." [53] Instead, the constitutional system places a premium on "the institutional loyalty of its lawyers." [54] The public interest approach threatens the

33. Federal Bar Ass'n Professional Ethics Comm., Op. 73–1 (1973) ("The Government Client and Confidentiality"), reprinted in 32 Fed.B.J. 71, 72 (1973). [For a critique of Opinion 73–1, see Robert P. Lawry, Who Is the Client of the Federal Government Lawyer? An Analysis of the Wrong Question, 37 Fed.Bar.J. 61 (1979). Also see William Josephson and Russell Pearce, To Whom Does the Government Lawyer Owe the Duty of Loyalty When the Clients are in Conflict, 29 Howard L.J. 539 (1986).]

34. Id.

36. Charles Fahy, Special Ethical Problems of Counsel for the Government, 33 Fed.B.J. 331, 332 (1974) (lecture delivered at Columbia Law School, April 11, 1950)....

37. Fahy, supra note 36, at 335.

52. [Miller, supra, note 22, at 1296.]

53. Id.

54. Id.

separation of powers and fails to adequately protect this constitutional
system.

. . .

The simple rule of thumb that "the employing agency should in
normal circumstances be considered the client of the government
lawyer" [67] offers useful guidance to government attorneys. For most
day-to-day purposes, a government lawyer properly may consider the
employing agency as the client. Responsible officials of that agency
hire the lawyer, provide instructions and supervision, and make decisions concerning change or termination of employment. But the agency approach does not reflect the complex web of institutional arrangements, regulations, statutes, and constitutional commands that shape
the government lawyer's actions in those situations in which they come
into play. On some occasions, the general litigating authority of the
Department of Justice may alter the responsibilities of the agency
lawyer. Obligations to report wrongdoing to officials within and without the agency may override normal duties of confidentiality owed to
the agency and its responsible officials. If the particular activity is
subject to the direction of the President, and the President chooses to
exercise authority, the head of the executive branch displaces the
agency head as the authoritative architect of government policy. Discussion of some illustrative situations will clarify these points.

Assume that Charles Hughes works on the legal staff of a federal
agency that administers a major federal program subsidizing private
activity. In the course of providing legal advice on subsidy applications, he learns from the head of the agency that a particular application was approved ahead of many others because the applicant had
plied the official with special favors, including an all-expenses paid trip
to last year's Super Bowl.

Do duties of confidentiality prevent Hughes from disclosing this
information to an appropriate law enforcement official within or outside his agency? The intuition that tells one that the answer must be
"no" is correct. But reflect a minute on some potential difficulties in
reaching this conclusion. If Hughes was a lawyer in private practice
and an individual client, in seeking legal advice from him, had revealed
information indicating the commission of a past crime, Hughes could
not disclose the information without violating his professional obligations. A voluntary disclosure would violate the professional duty of
confidentiality, and the attorney-client privilege would prevent the
forced disclosure of the information by a tribunal authorized to sum-

67. D.C. Report, *supra*, at 54. [A special committee of the District of Columbia Bar
recommended that some additional provisions and commentary be added to the District's
version of the Model Rules to provide clarification and guidance to government lawyers;
the District of Columbia Court of Appeals adopted most of the recommended changes.
Report by the District of Columbia Bar Special Committee of Government Lawyers and
the Model Rules of Professional Conduct, reprinted in The Washington Lawyer, at 53
(Sept.-Oct. 1988). See also Keith W. Donahoe, The Model Rules and the Government
Lawyer, A Sword or Shield?, 2 Geo.J.Legal Ethics 987 (1989).]

mon evidence. If Hughes represented a private client who had bribed an official (other than the tribunal before whom the lawyer is representing the client), and this information was communicated to the lawyer during the course of representation, one of the stronger cases for confidentiality would forever seal the lawyer's lips (except to the extent that disclosure was in the client's interest and with the client's consent). Why is the situation different when Hughes receives the information as a government lawyer?

The short answer, of course, is that Hughes doesn't represent the officer in the latter's individual capacity. True, he may have been hired by the officer and be supervised by and somewhat dependent upon the officer. Yet Hughes works for an agency of the executive branch of the Government of the United States, not for an individual who temporarily occupies one of its offices. The officer should understand that; if he does not, Hughes should take early steps to relieve the officer of the false impression that Hughes is his personal lawyer.* The situation is not unlike that of in-house counsel for a public corporation who learns from an officer of the corporation that the officer has violated duties owed to the corporation. . . .

As a federal lawyer, Hughes has statutory duties [74] to report criminal misconduct to the head of his agency, and, if the agency head is involved, to the Attorney General. These duties would preempt the District of Columbia professional code if the latter purported to prohibit Hughes from disclosing the communication outside the agency in which he is employed (assuming that Hughes practices in the Washington, D.C., headquarters of his agency). There is no conflict, however, if the executive branch is viewed as the client when corrupt official behavior is involved. The duty of disclosure inside the organization does not stop at the boundaries of the agency. Federal law requires that illegality be reported to appropriate law enforcement officials, who are ultimately

---

* [Eds. note.] The Federal Ethical Considerations promulgated by the Federal Bar Association for the guidance of federal government lawyers include the following provisions dealing with confidentiality:

F.E.C. 4–1. If, in the conduct of official business of his department or agency, it appears that a fellow employee of the department or agency is revealing or about to reveal information concerning his own illegal or unethical conduct to a federal lawyer acting in his official capacity the lawyer should inform the employee that a federal lawyer is responsible to the department or agency concerned and not the individual employee and, therefore, the information being discussed is not privileged.

F.E.C. 4–2. If a fellow employee volunteers information concerning himself which appears to involve illegal or unethical conduct or is violative of department or agency rules and regulations which would be pertinent to that department's or agency's consideration of disciplinary action, the federal lawyer should inform the individual that the lawyer is responsible to the department or agency concerned and not the individual employee.

F.E.C. 4–3. The federal lawyer has the ethical responsibility to disclose to his supervisor or other appropriate departmental or agency official any unprivileged information of the type discussed above in F.E.C. 4–1 and 2.

Reprinted in C. Normand Poirer, The Federal Government Lawyer and Professional Ethics, 60 A.B.A.J. 1541, 1543 (1974).

74. See 28 U.S.C. § 535(b) (1968).

subject to presidential authority as head of the executive branch. Under this view, however, disclosure other than to appropriate law enforcement officers would not be professionally appropriate.

Consider, however, a second scenario. In this one Hughes is asked to assist the responsible agency officials in a course of action suggested or determined by a new administration. The proposed action—it could be promulgation of a legislative rule, a change of position in ongoing or frequent litigation or the major alteration or abandonment of a current federal program—is politically sensitive and raises substantial legal issues. At one end of the spectrum, the proposed action, in Hughes's view, is clearly illegal: unauthorized by statute, directly contrary to controlling court decisions or violative of well-established constitutional rights. At midpoint on the spectrum, it is of uncertain legality, but plausible legal arguments can be made on its behalf. Toward the other end of the spectrum, it is a legal option available to the agency, but strong policy arguments can be made against it. Should Hughes, who shares the policy objections against the proposed action, do legal work on the proposal? May he seek to mobilize political support against the proposal by disclosing the agency's plans or its legal strategy?

If an individual client asked Hughes to do legal work under these varying circumstances, Hughes's professional obligations would be fairly clear. Hughes could exercise his choice as to whether to undertake the representation, and his dislike for the cause could be an important or controlling factor in his decision.[76] If the proposed action was clearly illegal (one end of the spectrum), or the lawsuit involved a frivolous claim or defense and the client did not have a good faith basis for arguing for a change in the law, Hughes would be required to refuse assistance.[77] If the proposal is not clearly illegal, however, Hughes would be free to undertake representation. Having done so, he would be required to put his personal feelings aside except as they might be brought to bear to persuade the client to alter the goals of representation or to assist in achieving the client's goals.

What difference does it make that Hughes is a full-time staff attorney for the agency undertaking the proposed action? Unless the agency accommodates a request to be assigned to other work, a request that in itself may have adverse effects on Hughes's future, Hughes is faced with a starker choice. If ordered to proceed, he must do so or resign. Even if the case of illegality is strong, the proposal was unlikely to be advanced unless there was something to be said for its legality. The reinterpretation of old law and the development of new law often flow from executive initiative founded on an electoral mandate. The leeway of a new President, armed with a victory at the polls, to argue for a change in the law, either by a reinterpretation of a statute or the distinguishing or overruling of prior court decisions, is

76. Model Code DR 7–102(A)(1) and (2); Model Rules Rule 3.1. See also Wolfram, [Modern Legal Ethics], § 4.1.

77. Model Code DR 7–102(A)(1); Model Rules 1.2(d); 3.1 . . . .

substantial. American history is studded with instances in which Presidents attempted, often successfully, to move the law in a new direction.

If Hughes does undertake to work on the matter, to whom does he owe loyalty and confidentiality? Normally, unless the action is clearly illegal, Hughes is obliged to advance the goals of the agency and the executive branch. Only in the extreme case, where the proposal is indisputably illegal, do the professional rules and statutory obligations prohibit Hughes from providing legal assistance. Lawyers, as well as other federal employees, are obligated to uphold the Constitution and the laws of the United States. In addition, as a lawyer, Hughes may not assist in pursuing frivolous claims or defenses in litigation or assist in carrying out a crime or fraud. If clear illegality is involved, he may neither undertake representation nor continue after it is discovered. But a legal rule or litigation posture for which a good faith argument exists, even though there is some likelihood that it will be found to be illegal, is not a crime or fraud. And there are strong arguments in support of the position that the appropriate government policy-maker, not Hughes, should make the decision whether to test the legitimacy of the proposed action.... The decision should be made by officials who are elected and appointed for that purpose rather than by staff lawyers.**

More detail is needed about the particular problem and agency before a confident response can be given as to who is the appropriate decision-maker. If rule-making or litigating authority has been delegated to an independent agency or to an officer who is substantially immunized from executive branch control, the agency or officer is Hughes's client. In the more usual situation in which ultimate policy in the executive branch is determined by the President, disclosure beyond the agency for which Hughes works should not be a problem. Assuming the (unlikely) situation in which an agency is secretly working against the policy approach of the President, disclosure of the agency's position to the White House is appropriate. Another variant of the same problem is a case in which the Attorney General has statutory authority over the litigation, but several agencies or departments have strong and divergent interests. The Department of Justice, for example, may represent the Environmental Protection Administration (EPA) in the action, but the responsibilities of the Departments of Energy and Transportation are affected and they take positions contrary to that of EPA. Lawyers in the Environmental Division of Justice who are working on the case should be free to communicate

---

** [Eds. note.] F.E.C. 8–2 of the Federal Ethical Considerations states that a government lawyer "may reasonably be expected to abide, without public criticism, with certain policies or rulings closely allied to his sphere of responsibility even if he disagrees with the position taken by the agency." He "should be prepared to resign before [publicly attacking a decision which is contrary to his professional, ethical or moral judgment,] and he is not free to abuse professional confidences reposed in him in the process leading to the decision." Reprinted in C. Normand Poirer, The Federal Government Lawyer and Professional Ethics, 60 A.B.A.J. 1541, 1544 (1974).

with each of the three agencies in an effort to formulate a common policy, obtain information or improve the Government's overall litigating position. If the policy disagreement is a major political issue, the President may properly seek to make the decision. Any notion that a lawyer working for EPA would breach confidentiality by communicating facts, work product or litigating strategy to officials in any of the agencies or officials involved in the matter is unfounded. Only disclosure beyond the Executive Branch, or out of proper channels, would be violative of the professional duty of confidentiality. In this type of situation, and for this purpose, the executive branch, headed by the President, is best viewed as the lawyer's client.

State Judicial Decisions

Case law on the identity of the government lawyer's client is sparse. In Humphrey v. McLaren,[29] the Minnesota Attorney General's office brought suit against the former executive director of a state agency, the Public Employees Retirement Association (PERA), to recover state funds the director allegedly misappropriated. The former executive director, McLaren, sought to disqualify the Attorney General's office on the ground that it had represented him during his tenure at PERA. A state statute made the attorney general's office legal counsel to PERA. The court refused to disqualify the Attorney General's office, stating that even the individual lawyer who had advised PERA during McLaren's tenure would have been free to sue him now. The court, citing Minnesota's version of M.R. 1.13 and its Comment, held that the agency (and in some cases the entire government) was the client, not the individual head of the agency. This opinion is consistent with the holding in *Meehan,* above at p. 748.[30] But is it a satisfactory resolution?

The authority of a state attorney general turns on state constitutional arrangements that vary considerably from state to state. In People ex rel. Deukmejian v. Brown,[31] the California Attorney General sought a writ of mandamus to prevent the Governor from enforcing an employee relations statute which the Attorney General alleged was unconstitutional. The Governor moved to enjoin the litigation. The court granted the Governor's motion, holding that the Attorney General could not bring such a case on his own authority. A Massachusetts decision,[32] however, holds that the Massachusetts Attorney General could seek review against the objections of the head of the affected

29. 402 N.W.2d 535 (Minn.1987).

30. Also see United States v. Troutman, 814 F.2d 1428 (10th Cir.1987) (no impermissible conflict when state attorney general assisted United States attorneys in prosecution of state official).

31. 29 Cal.3d 150, 172 Cal.Rptr. 478, 624 P.2d 1206 (1981).

32. Feeney v. Commonwealth, 373 Mass. 359, 366 N.E.2d 1262 (1977).

agency, the Governor, and the Massachusetts legislature (both houses of which passed resolutions asking that review not be sought) of a lower court decision holding that the state's civil service preference for veterans unconstitutionally discriminated against women.[33]

Several factors contribute to the sparsity of case law. First, whereas in the corporate context the issue of final authority usually arises when various constituents are fighting for control of the corporation, in government such a struggle normally plays out politically rather than through litigation. Second, standing requirements and requirements of justiciability, e.g., the political question doctrine, may bar a suit to challenge whether the government as an entity is being adequately represented. Third, under prevailing state administrative law, litigation in other forms is readily available to resolve disputed substantive questions of official authority, for example a taxpayers' or citizens' suit. Suits in this form ordinarily would not expose conflict between the agency and the lawyer representing it. If the lawyer agrees with the agency, she will defend the suit; otherwise either the suit will be acquiesced in or some other government lawyer will be assigned to defend the agency position.

Federal Law

The Cramton excerpt, printed above at p. 821, provides an overview of the bearing of structural considerations and federal statutes on the loyalty of the federal government lawyer. Eric Schnapper takes an opposing view, arguing that a government lawyer may sometimes take a course of action or accept a settlement contrary to the wishes of agency heads: [34]

> The relationship of agency officials to government counsel is not that of client and attorney in any ordinary sense, for the identities and desires of those officials may vary with popular opinion, the vote of the electorate, or the whims of their superiors, while the law to which both officials and counsel owe their allegiance remains unaltered.[35]

33. For cases in accord with *Deukmejian*, see Manchin v. Browning, 170 W.Va. 779, 296 S.E.2d 909 (1982); and Arizona State Land Dept. v. McFate, 87 Ariz. 139, 348 P.2d 912 (1960). In accord with *Feeney* are State ex rel. Howard v. Oklahoma Corp. Commission, 614 P.2d 45 (Okl.1980); Connecticut Commission on Special Revenue v. Connecticut Freedom of Information Commission, 174 Conn. 308, 387 A.2d 533 (1978). Also see Ann B. Stevens, Can the State Attorney General Represent Two Agencies Opposed in Litigation? 2 Geo.J.Legal Ethics 757 (1989).

34. Eric Schnapper, Legal Ethics and the Government Lawyer, 32 The Record 649 (1977). Other materials on the government lawyer's responsibilities include: Geoffrey P. Miller, Ethics in a System of Checks and Balances, 54 U.Chi.L.Rev. 1293 (1987); Comment, Government Employee Disclosure of Agency Wrongdoing: Protecting the Right to Blow the Whistle, 42 U.Chi.L.Rev. 530 (1975); Charles Fahy, Special Ethical Problems of Counsel for the Government, 33 Fed.Bar J. 331 (1974); Jack B. Weinstein, Some Ethical and Political Problems of a Government Lawyer, 18 Me.L.Rev. 155 (1966); Luther A. Huston, Arthur S. Miller, Samuel Krislov & Robert G. Dixon, Jr., Roles of the Attorney General of the United States (1968); and Charles A. Horsky, The Washington Lawyer (1952).

35. Id. at 649.

Schnapper rejects the usual arguments in support of deferring to the legal and policy decisions of agency heads. Government officials, he argues, are entitled to the free representation of government lawyers only when "they are right." When the disputed conduct does not "in fact represent public policy," it is burdensome to opposing parties and the courts for government lawyers to advance positions that do not represent sound public policy.[36]

Does Schnapper assume that legal and policy questions faced by government agencies have a single, unambiguous answer? Are his views applicable to the many situations in which law and policy are contested or uncertain? Why should a lawyer's view prevail over that of elected or appointed officials?

By statute, 28 U.S.C. § 518, the Solicitor General of the United States has authority to decide whether to petition the U.S. Supreme Court to review decisions in lower courts ruling against agencies and departments of the United States. A long tradition has vested substantial but not total discretion in the Solicitor General to control access to the Supreme Court and to determine the positions taken in cases before the Court.[37] But the President may give directions to the Solicitor General or remove the Solicitor General from office.

The litigating position of "the United States" may change as a consequence of a presidential election. In 1979, for example, the Justice Department's Civil Rights Division intervened on behalf of the plaintiffs in an action against the Birmingham fire department to compel the city to implement an affirmative action hiring plan to correct past discrimination against blacks and hispanics. In 1981, after President Carter was defeated by President Reagan, while the suit was still in the discovery stage, the new head of the Civil Rights Division ordered a staff lawyer to seek court permission to withdraw the government's brief on behalf of the plaintiffs and to intervene instead on behalf of the fire department. What should such a lawyer do if she believes that "truth, justice, and the law" are with the plaintiffs? [38]

Does government side-switching raise conflict-of-interest or confidentiality concerns? In Washington v. Seattle School District No. 1,[39] the Supreme Court noted that the government had changed its position

---

36. Id. at 650–51.

37. See United States v. Providence Journal Co., 485 U.S. 693 (1988) (attorney appointed by district court to prosecute criminal contempt charges cannot represent the United States before the Supreme Court without authorization from the Solicitor General, who declined to give such authorization). See generally Lincoln Caplan, The Tenth Justice: The Solicitor General and the Rule of Law (1987) (arguing the importance to the Supreme Court and "the rule of law" of the independent authority of the Solicitor General to define the interests of the United States in bringing and arguing cases in the Supreme Court). Cf. Ethics in Government Act, 28 U.S.C. § 594(a)(9) (authorizing independent counsel to appear before "any court of competent jurisdiction ... in the name of the United States").

38. See Stuart Taylor, Jr., Second–Class Citizens, American Lawyer, Sept. 1989, at p. 42, discussing the Birmingham fire department litigation.

39. 458 U.S. 457, 471 (1982).

during the course of the litigation, but did not address the ethical or legal issues raised. The Department of Justice, on behalf of the United States, intervened on the side of the local school district in support of a voluntary school busing plan but, after a change in administrations, fought the plan. The school district argued that the Justice Department should be disqualified from further representation of the government because the government lawyers had access to the school district's confidences during the time of cooperation.[40] Should disqualification of individual government lawyers be limited to those cases in which the government has been aligned with another party that it now seeks to oppose?

The Watergate cover-up led to the creation of the institution of the "special prosecutor." President Nixon had promised Archibald Cox independence to conduct an investigation into whether members of the executive branch had been involved in the break-in at Democratic headquarters at the Watergate Building and had further broken the law by trying to cover-up their involvement. When it was learned that President Nixon had taped conversations in the Oval Office, Cox sought access to these tapes. Judge John Sirica ordered the tapes turned over to the court for in camera review, after which the court would transmit unprivileged portions to Cox for use before the grand jury. The Court of Appeals sustained Sirica's order.[41]

> [The President] decided to avoid a "constitutional crisis" by declining to appeal the decision and ordered Cox, as "an employee of the executive branch," not to pursue the matter further. Declining to follow the court's order, he proposed instead to provide White House "summaries" of the tapes. Cox rejected the offer, and on October 20, in what has become known as the "Saturday Night Massacre," the President accepted the resignation of Attorney General Elliot Richardson when he refused to fire Cox, then fired Deputy Attorney General Ruckelshaus when he refused to fire Cox, and finally persuaded Solicitor General Robert H. Bork to fire Cox and [some] of his staff of ninety investigators.[42]

The outcry over these events compelled President Nixon to appoint a new special prosecutor, Leon Jaworski. The tapes were turned over to the new special prosecutor after the Supreme Court rejected President Nixon's claim of executive privilege.[43] Shortly thereafter, President Nixon resigned.

----

40. See Note, Professional Ethics in Government Side–Switching, 96 Harv.L.Rev. 1914 (1983), arguing that government lawyers should be disqualified when the government cooperates with one party and then switches sides to cooperate with that party's adversary. The Note urges use of presumptions to prevent misuse of confidential information shared with the government by a former ally.

41. Nixon v. Sirica, 487 F.2d 700 (D.C.Cir.1973).

42. Robert E. Cushman, Cases in Constitutional Law (7th ed. 1989) at 79.

43. United States v. Nixon, 418 U.S. 683 (1974) (ordering President Nixon to turn over the Watergate tapes).

To ensure the independence of future prosecutors investigating the executive branch, Congress passed the Ethics in Government Act, 28 U.S.C. § 591 et seq. This statute gives a three-judge panel the power to appoint an independent counsel to investigate and prosecute members of the executive branch in lieu of the Department of Justice and further provides that the Attorney General may remove a special prosecutor only by "personal action ... and only for good cause, physical disability, mental incapacity, or any other condition that substantially impairs the performance of such independent counsel's duties." Upon such removal, the Attorney General must submit a report to the three-judge panel and to the Judiciary Committees of the House and Senate.[44]

Renewed controversy over the independent counsel statute has arisen because of the length, cost and tenacity of special counsel investigations. Who is the client of the independent counsel? Is a lawyer whose only function is to identify and prosecute a target likely to pursue a matter well beyond the pragmatic bounds faced by ordinary prosecutors?[45]

The Model Rules

The Scope section of the Model Rules states:

Under various legal provisions, including constitutional, statutory and common law, the responsibilities of government lawyers may include authority concerning legal matters that ordinarily reposes in the client in private client-lawyer relationships. For example, a lawyer for a government agency may have authority on behalf of the government to decide upon settlement or whether to appeal from an adverse judgment. Such authority in various respects is generally vested in the attorney general and the state's attorney in state government, and their federal counterparts, and the same may be true of other government law officers. Also, lawyers under supervision of these officers may be authorized to represent several government agencies in intragovernmental legal controversies in circumstances where a private lawyer could not represent multiple private clients. They also may have authority to represent the "public interest" in circumstances where a private lawyer would not be authorized to do so. These Rules do not abrogate any such authority.

---

44. See Morrison v. Olson, 487 U.S. 654 (1988) (holding that the independent counsel provisions of this statute are constitutional).

45. The Iran–Contra probe headed by special counsel Lawrence Walsh was in its sixth year, with expenditures of $32 million, when Casper Weinberger—the former secretary of defense who opposed the 1985 arms-for-hostages deal with Iran within the Reagan Administration—was indicted for lying to Congress (President Bush later pardoned Weinberger and other Iran–Contra figures). Critics charge that the special prosecutor's independent status "creates a lack of accountability that is worrisome given the potentially oppressive nature of the prosecutorial power." Stuart Taylor, Jr., Who Handles the Next Scandal?, Amer. Lawyer, Sept. 1992, pp. 5, 82–84 (considering arguments that the president's appointees who are the targets of independent counsel "come under scrutiny more sustained and merciless (and legal fees more crushing) than are faced by members of Congress, corporate chieftains, or ordinary citizens").

The Comment to Rule 1.13 states:

> The duty defined in this Rule applies to governmental organiza-
> tions. However, when the client is a governmental organization, a
> different balance may be appropriate between maintaining confi-
> dentiality and assuring that the wrongful official act is prevented
> or rectified, for public business is involved.... Therefore, defining
> precisely the identity of the client and prescribing the resulting
> obligations of such lawyers may be more difficult in the govern-
> ment context. Although in some circumstances the client may be a
> specific agency, it is generally the government as a whole. For
> example, if the action or failure to act involves the head of a
> bureau, either the department of which the bureau is a part or the
> government as a whole may be the client for purpose of this Rule.
> Moreover, in a matter involving the conduct of government offi-
> cials, a government lawyer may have authority to question such
> conduct more extensively than that of a lawyer for a private
> organization in similar circumstances. This Rule does not limit
> that authority.

2. Government Lawyer as Whistleblower

"Whistleblower" is the modern term for an employee who makes
public charges of wrongdoing against officials of that person's agency or
organization. The dissent, accusation and disloyalty of whistleblowers
often lead to job retaliation by those in control of the organization.
Federal and state statutes seek to protect whistleblowers from such job
retaliation, but moral issues remain: [46] What circumstances and what
degree of certainty justify the breach of loyalty involved in "going
public?" Should avenues of change within the organization be first
exhausted? Must a whistleblower who is a lawyer also resign? How
important is the whistleblower's intent in judging the propriety of her
disclosure?

Many states have enacted laws protecting government-employee
whistleblowers from retaliatory action. [47] Does a whistleblower statute
supersede or nullify the ethical obligations otherwise governing a
government lawyer?

At the federal level, the Civil Service Reform Act of 1978, as
amended by the Whistleblower Protection Act of 1989, [48] prohibits a
federal agency from taking an adverse personnel action against an
employee's disclosure of information, not "specifically prohibited by
law," that evidences: (1) a violation of law, rule or regulation, (2) gross
mismanagement, (3) a gross waste of funds, (4) an abuse of authority, or
(5) a specific and substantial danger to public health and safety. The

46. See Sissela Bok, Secrets 212–27 (1982) (discussing moral aspects of whistleblowing).

47. See, e.g., Cal.Gov.Code § 10543; Colo.Rev.Stat. 24–50.5–101; Me.Rev.Stat.Ann. tit.
26, § 831; N.Y. Labor Law § 740; Ohio Rev.Code Ann. § 4113.51; 43 Pa.Cons.Stat.
§ 1421.

48. See especially 5 U.S.C. § 3202(b).

disclosure, which may be made to anyone, including a journalist or a congressional staffer, is protected if the employee "reasonably believes" that the information "evidences" the specified wrongdoing.   Government lawyers are covered by the Act, and the general prohibitions of disclosures of client information in ethics rules (e.g., M.R. 1.6) apparently do not fall within the Act's exception protecting information that Congress, by statute, has specifically protected, such as classified information.

Suppose a government lawyer, believing that waste will result if the government settles a case that might be won after a full trial, sabotages the settlement by revealing the government's settlement position.   Or an EPA lawyer who believes that EPA regulations under the Clean Air Act are inconsistent with the Act or will endanger public health leaks internal memoranda to the press.   Are these actions protected by the Whistleblower Act?   Does the Act have the effect, at least in some circumstances, of eliminating the government's right to discharge a lawyer for breach of confidentiality? [49]

In addition to the whistleblower statutes, the First Amendment protects the speech of federal, state and local government employees. In Pickering v. Board of Education,[50] the Supreme Court held that an individual's exercise of his "right to speak on issues of public importance may not furnish the basis for his dismissal from public employment." [51]   In Connick v. Myers,[52] the Court discussed the limits on this doctrine.   Myers was a deputy district attorney who had circulated a questionnaire about internal office procedures regarding transfers and office morale; she was about to be transferred.   The Court emphasized that the questionnaire focused not on "evaluat[ing] the performance of the office but rather [on] gather[ing] ammunition for another round of controversy with [Myers'] superiors." [53]   Had the questionnaire involved the office's conduct of a particular case, could the prosecutor have been disciplined under M.R. 3.6?   See the *Gentile* case, reprinted in Chapter 11 below.

3.   Government Lawyers Representing Individual Government Employees

In Dunton v. County of Suffolk,[54] Dunton brought a suit under 42 U.S.C. § 1983 against a Suffolk County police officer and the county.

---

49. Roger C. Cramton, The Lawyer as Whistleblower: Confidentiality and the Government Lawyer, 5 Geo.J. Legal Ethics 291, 315 (1991), concludes: "Until and unless [federal government] lawyers avail themselves of the whistleblower provisions, forcing agency heads and the courts to wrestle with [the Act's uncertainties and] complexities, we will not have authoritative answers to these vexing questions."

50. 391 U.S. 563, 574 (1968).

51. Also see Rankin v. McPherson, 483 U.S. 378, 383 (1987) (government employer may not discipline an "employee on a basis that infringes that employee's constitutionally protected interest in freedom of speech").

52. 461 U.S. 138 (1983).

53. Id. at 148.

54. 729 F.2d 903 (2d Cir.1984), modified, 748 F.2d 69 (1984).

Dunton charged that the officer had beaten him after having found him in a car with the officer's wife. The county attorney represented both defendants. At trial, the lawyer argued that the county was not liable because the officer was not acting within the scope of his employment but was an "irate husband." This argument apparently prevailed; the county was found not liable and the officer liable. The Second Circuit remanded for a new trial based on an impermissible conflict of interest on the part of the county attorney. While the Court of Appeals refused to ban all joint representation in such situations, it emphasized that the "district court is under a duty to ensure that the client fully appreciates his situation." [55]

Under Monell v. New York City Department of Social Services, [56] liability may be imposed on a municipality under 42 U.S.C. § 1983 for a violation of civil rights resulting from the "execution of a government's policy or custom, whether made by its lawmakers or by those whose edicts or acts may fairly be said to represent official policy." [57] When city employees are sued as individuals along with the city, the city can avoid liability by arguing that the employees' conduct was not city "policy or custom" but individual misconduct, and individual employees may avoid liability by arguing that their actions were taken pursuant to official policy, giving such employees qualified immunity.

Where employees may raise qualified immunity as a defense, courts generally have allowed joint representation only when the municipality embraces the employees' acts as municipal policy. Even in those situations, the court may require proof that the individual defendants have been adequately and fully informed of the potential conflict and its effect on the representation. [58] Within these contours, municipalities still rely on joint representation. [59]

None of these cases address whether the government, as opposed to the employee, could adequately consent to the joint representation; whether the decision to embrace the employee's acts, i.e., to waive a defense, was made free from conflict; or whether the government would be adequately defended. Who would have standing to challenge the government's consent to the joint representation? Do these concerns justify a per se rule?

55. Id. at 908. See also Clay v. Doherty, 608 F.Supp. 295, 305 (N.D.Ill.1985) ("[B]oth lawyer and judge must guard against any threatened interests … in the *Dunton*-type cases.").

56. 436 U.S. 658 (1978).

57. Id. at 693.

58. See, e.g., Manganella v. Keyes, 613 F.Supp. 795 (D.C.Conn.1985).

59. Compare Shadid v. Jackson, 521 F.Supp. 87 (E.D.Tex.1981) (disqualifying government lawyer from representing individual defendants without inquiring whether defenses would be incompatible), with Coleman v. Smith, 814 F.2d 1142, 1147–48 (7th Cir.1987) (expressing reservations about the broad language condemning joint representation in *Dunton*). Also see Suffolk County Patrolmen's Benevolent Association, Inc. v. County of Suffolk, 751 F.2d 550 (2d Cir.1985) (upholding procedure creating panel of three independent lawyers from which police officers who were co-defendants with the county in civil rights actions had to choose counsel in order to get the county to reimburse their attorneys' fees).

D. LAWYERS FOR A CLASS

Introductory Note

"Experience teaches that it is counsel for the class representatives, and not the named parties, who direct and manage [class] actions. Every experienced federal judge knows that any statement to the contrary is sheer sophistry." [60]

Lawyer-client relationships can be arrayed according to how closely they resemble the paradigm of the individual client who defines the objectives of the representative: Lawyers for partnerships and small businesses are closest to the paradigm, then corporation lawyers, then government lawyers and finally lawyers for a class.[61]

As the Model Rules acknowledge, the lawyer for the government often acts as both client and lawyer at least in the office of state's attorney. However, the government lawyer is not free to make choices for the client because political constraints mean that public policies— the objectives of the representation—are never solely matters for the lawyer. Within accepted policy limits the government lawyer may have free rein, but at the limits the government lawyer still has a client.

Lawyers for a class, on the other hand, often construct the client by defining the objectives of the representation. A class often is defined in terms of a legal theory formulated by the lawyer. While the lawyer for a class appears in the mask of agent, the client may be solely the lawyer's creation and may exist only to serve the lawyer's ends.

When the lawyer is engaged in social advocacy or institutional reform, such as a lawyer for a public interest group or a legal services organization, the principal problem is that of paternalism—a lawyer shaping a dispute and making decisions on behalf of an otherwise unrepresented class of persons. Law reform litigation of this type is considered in Chapter 11 below at p. 1060.

A second major type of class action lawyer is considered at this point: A lawyer acting as a "private attorney general" who is engaged in enforcing the legal rights of a class but who is also strongly motivated by the hope of a substantial attorney's fee. Examples include a class derivative action brought by the shareholders of a

---

60. Greenfield v. Villager Industries, Inc., 483 F.2d 824, 832 n. 9 (3d Cir.1973).

61. A different ordering would prevail if the client's ability to monitor the lawyer's performance were also considered. Experienced clients who regularly use the legal system ("repeat players") are now in the best position. Liability insurers and large corporations have the greatest ability to control their lawyers directly and indirectly through the funneling of repeat business. Individuals, especially those who face a personal plight requiring a lawyer, normally encounter more substantial "agency costs" in selecting, supervising and monitoring a lawyer.

company or a mass tort suit such as that by the victims of the chemical leak in Bhopal, India.[62]

Lawyers engaged in social advocacy and institutional reform (the lawyer as "social advocate") are both similar to and different from lawyers engaged in making a living from the attorney fees generated by successful class actions (the lawyer as "bounty hunter" or "legal mercenary"). Solicitation, financing of litigation and conflict of interest problems (conflicts within the represented class and conflicts between the interests of the lawyer and those of the class) are problems shared by both types of lawyers. A valuable empirical study finds important differences, however, between the "social advocate" and the "legal mercenary."[63] They differ in terms of creativity in legal strategy (the mercenary prefers not to experiment), mobilization of the class (the mercenary prefers it to be inert), obtaining certification of the class (the mercenary may not be interested in certification unless it will increase settlement value), and settlement approach (the mercenary is interested in the fee, the social advocate in the decree).

Does it matter that the lawyer is hoping to make a profit out of the proceeds of the suit? Should we be more or less concerned with the lawyer's interest in making a profit than her interest in seeing ideological goals realized?

1. Role of Plaintiffs' Lawyer in Class Action and Derivative Litigation

JONATHAN R. MACEY AND GEOFFREY P. MILLER
"THE PLAINTIFFS' ATTORNEY'S ROLE IN CLASS ACTION AND DERIVATIVE LITIGATION"
58 U. Chi. L. Rev. 1, 3–19, 116–118 (1991).*

[T]he single most salient characteristic of class and derivative litigation is the existence of "entrepreneurial" plaintiffs' attorneys. Because these attorneys are not subject to monitoring by their putative clients, they operate largely according to their own self-interest, subject only to whatever constraints might be imposed by bar discipline, judicial oversight, and their own sense of ethics and fiduciary responsibilities....

... In both the class action and the shareholder's derivative suit, the attorney's client is not actively involved in the conduct of the

---

62. See Deborah L. Rhode, Solicitation, 36 J.Legal Educ. 317, 319 (1986) (discussing the Bhopal incident and others).

63. See Bryant Garth, Ilene H. Nagel and S. Jay Plager, The Institution of the Private Attorney General: Perspectives from an Empirical Study of Class Action Litigation, 61 S.Cal.L.Rev. 353 (1988).

* Copyright © 1991 The University of Chicago Law Review. Reprinted with permission.

litigation on the plaintiff's side. But in other respects these devices are quite different in theory and rationale.

The class action is a tool for overcoming the free-rider and other collective action problems that impair any attempt to organize a large number of discrete individuals in any common project. These kinds of problems are prevalent in situations when a large number of people have been injured by another person's conduct, but when the injury to many of these individuals is small. In the absence of a class action device, such injuries would often go unremedied because most individual plaintiffs would not themselves have a sufficient economic stake in the litigation to incur the litigation costs....

The class action procedure partially overcomes these difficulties by providing an effective and inexpensive procedure for joining large numbers of individual plaintiffs. A representative plaintiff can file an action and seek class certification, which has several prerequisites. Among other things, the class must be "so numerous that joinder of all members is impracticable"; there must be "questions of law or fact common to the class"; the claims or defenses of the representative parties must be "typical of the claims or defenses of the class"; and the representative party must "fairly and adequately protect the interests of the class." [9] In addition, the representative plaintiff must establish the prerequisites for one of three separate subcategories of class action. The role of the entrepreneurial attorney is most prominent in the so-called "(b)(3)" class action, in which "questions of law or fact common to the members of the class predominate over any questions affecting only individual members, and ... a class action is superior to other available methods for the fair and efficient adjudication of the controversy."

The economic rationale for the (b)(3) class action—as a method for overcoming free-rider and other collective action problems—stands in sharp contrast to the rationale for the shareholder's derivative suit. Shareholder's derivative actions are not premised on collective action problems in the *litigation*. On the contrary, they presuppose the existence of a corporate form that is already organized to overcome such collective action problems. The corporation has standing and is fully competent to bring legal actions to redress injuries to its rights. The problem, rather, is with collective action *within* the corporate form itself. As scholars since Berle and Means have observed, corporate managers typically have only a small ownership stake in the firms they manage. Thus, their interests deviate from those of shareholders: they may prefer to consume excessive perquisites or practice their golf whereas shareholders would want them to work diligently at maximizing profits.

The shareholder's derivative suit is one of many devices in corporate law for controlling these conflicts between managers and shareholders.... The classic case is the action for breach of fiduciary duty

---

9. FRCP 23(a). The rule also permits class actions in which many individual *defendants* are joined; these cases are uncommon, however.

against corporate directors. Obviously the directors cannot be trusted to cause the corporation to sue themselves. The derivative action allows a representative shareholder in such circumstances to take over the litigation from recalcitrant managers and prosecute it on behalf of the corporation. Unlike the class action, in which the relief is given to the plaintiff class members, any relief recovered in a derivative action (net of expenses including attorneys' fees) is returned to the corporation.

. . .

Both the class action and the shareholder's derivative lawsuit can thus be explained and rationalized in terms of modern economic theory.... The following discussion assumes that private enforcement of the applicable substantive laws represents sound social policy, or at least a policy preferred by those charged with making and enforcing the laws.

The role of the entrepreneurial attorney in class and derivative litigation can best be understood in terms of the economic theory of agency costs....

The attorney in litigation is, in theory and legal form, the agent of the client. As agent, the attorney is charged with the duty to advance the client's interests "zealously within the bounds of the law." Yet attorneys do not always fulfill this responsibility, because their interests are rarely perfectly aligned with those of the client. The client pays the bill; the lawyer does the work. Many of the regulatory structures applicable to lawyers are designed to ensure that lawyers act as faithful agents of clients and do not abuse the client's trust.

... [From an economic perspective] the agency relationship [is] "a contract under which one or more persons (the principal(s)) engage another person (the agent) to perform some service on their behalf which involves delegating some decision making authority to the agent." [24] In such cases, as Jensen and Meckling observe, the interests of the agent are likely to deviate from those of the principal. This deviation of interests may not serve either principal or agent ex ante, and both, accordingly, may expend resources to overcome it. Jensen and Meckling identify two principal means for reducing agency costs: monitoring by the principal and bonding by the agent. To these we might add a third, namely devices that align the incentives of the agent more closely with those of the principal.

[Monitoring of a lawyer's performance by a client is likely to be "costly and therefore incomplete" because the client cannot observe the lawyer's efforts taking place outside of the client's presence and, even if

---

24. Michael C. Jensen and William H. Meckling, Theory of the Firm: Managerial Behavior, Agency Costs and Ownership Structure, 3 J Fin Econ 305, 308 (1976). Although Jensen and Meckling restrict their agency cost theory to analysis of corporate financial structure, they recognize that the basic elements of the theory are applicable to a much broader range of economic transactions. Id at 309. See also Kenneth J.Arrow, The Economics of Agency, in John W. Pratt and Richard J. Zeckhauser, eds, Principals and Agents: The Structure of Business 37 (Harvard Business School Press, 1985).

observed, lacks the expertise to determine whether the lawyer is doing a good job. Bar admission requirements may have some value in assuring that lawyers are competent and faithful fiduciaries; and some ethics rules, such as the duty to keep a client informed and to abide by the client's settlement decision, "reduce agency costs by enhancing monitoring."

[Bonding refers to contractual arrangements or structural features of the lawyer-client relationship that tend "to assure the principal that the agent will carry out her duty to the principal faithfully even in the absence of effective monitoring." Loss of repute or professional license flowing from abuse of the client's trust may provide assurance that lawyers "will observe at least minimal fiduciary standards." In particular, a "firm that has built up a reputation has a strong interest in maintaining that reputation by continuing to observe high ethical and quality standards."

[Incentive structures that align the interests of lawyer and client also reduce agency costs. Fee arrangements, whether hourly fee or contingent fee, align the interests of lawyer and client partially but imperfectly. The professional ideal of "zealous service of the client's interest" may "play a role in influencing behavior, at least at the margin." Conflicts of interest rules prevent "egregious misalignments of attorney-client interests."]

Plaintiffs' attorneys in class action and derivative suits occupy an uneasy place in the American legal system. The traditional image of the lawyer is of an independent professional providing advice and advocacy on behalf of a client. The attorney, in this view, is an agent of the client and subject to the client's control in all important matters. Plaintiffs' class action and derivative attorneys do not fit this mold. They are subject to only minimal monitoring by their ostensible "clients," who are either dispersed and disorganized (in the case of class action litigation) or under the control of hostile forces (in the case of derivative litigation). Accordingly, plaintiffs' class and derivative attorneys function essentially as entrepreneurs who bear a substantial amount of the litigation risk and exercise nearly plenary control over all important decisions in the lawsuit.

The absence of client monitoring raises the specter that the entrepreneurial attorney will serve her own interest at the expense of the client. The existing regulatory system attempts to prevent such abuse—and to reduce what have been termed "agency costs"—in three principal ways. First, it allocates certain elements of litigating authority to persons other than the plaintiffs' attorney—absent class members, managers of corporations involved in derivative suits, representative plaintiffs, and the courts themselves. Second, it contains a number of special features ostensibly designed to weed out inappropriate representative plaintiffs. The representative plaintiff must assert claims that are typical of the claims being asserted, and must represent the class or corporation adequately. Third, plaintiffs' attorneys are subject to applicable rules of legal ethics that purport to constrain the attorneys' behavior in order to safeguard clients' interests.

We believe this regulatory structure is poorly designed in a number of respects, particularly when applied to "large-scale, small-claim" litigation in which the overall liability is large but the individual interests of the class members or corporate shareholders are small. The existing regulations are extraordinarily ineffective at aligning the interests of attorney and client; indeed, they often impair the interests of the clients they are ostensibly designed to protect. Many regulatory shortfalls can be traced ultimately to a single fundamental error: the inappropriate attempt to treat entrepreneurial litigation as if it were essentially the same as standard litigation, in which the client exercises substantial influence. Even when the regulatory system acknowledges that entrepreneurial litigation poses special problems, it frequently attempts to resolve those problems by forcing class action and derivative litigation back into a standard model. The inevitable result is regulatory failure, simply because entrepreneurial litigation cannot be transformed into the traditional model even by brute regulatory force.

We propose revising the regulatory system in a number of ways. Our proposals have a common goal: to control agency costs with sensible rules that take into account the fact that the plaintiffs' attorney—not the client—controls the litigation. For example, the existing regulatory regime requires that all absent class members be given notice of a pending damages action and an opportunity to opt out of the suit—regardless of the size of the claim.[1] The high cost of notifying absent class members when potential recovery is very small deters entrepreneurial attorneys from bringing meritorious suits. Thus, the rule harms, rather than protects, absent class members. We suggest that notice of class action in such cases should not be required for small claimants in advance of some authoritative disposition on the merits.

Another problem area is judicial review of settlements and fee requests, which is often haphazard, unreliable, and lacking in administrable standards. Although review of settlements is necessary so long as the entrepreneurial attorney's interests differ from those of the client, we suggest that review could be improved by the use of guardians ad litem to represent the interest of the class in large-scale, small-claim cases. As to fee requests, we join other recent commentators in finding that, despite serious drawbacks, a percentage-of-recovery method (in which the plaintiffs' attorneys are awarded some percentage of the class recovery as fees, either on a fixed percentage basis or according to some more complex sliding scale) is superior to the currently favored lodestar approach (which allows attorneys to recover according to the number of hours they spend on a case). The lodestar approach has three principal, related defects: it involves enormously burdensome

---

1. See Phillips Petroleum Co. v. Shutts, 472 U.S. 797, 812 (1985); Eisen v. Carlisle & Jacquelin, 417 U.S. 156, 173–77 (1974).

calculation costs; it encourages attorneys to exaggerate their hours; and, because it guarantees that the attorneys will receive their fees if successful, it fails to give plaintiffs' attorneys the proper incentive to strike a settlement agreement that maximizes recovery for the plaintiff class.

We also criticize the current system for regulating the identity of the named plaintiff. The existing requirements of typicality (under which the named plaintiff's claim must be similar to that of the other class members or shareholders) and adequacy (under which the named plaintiff must be capable of competently and adequately representing the absent class members or the corporation) often exclude appropriate representative plaintiffs and reduce artificially the supply of attorneys able to serve the class or corporation. Given that the named plaintiff has little control over how the suit is conducted, the analysis should focus not on the appropriateness of the named plaintiff but rather on the reliability and competence of the plaintiffs' attorney.

Further, the regulatory system should acknowledge explicitly what is already the case, namely that ethics rules on solicitation, maintenance, fee-splitting and the acceptance of impropriety have virtually no current force or rationale in the large-scale, small-claim setting and are routinely circumvented with only the thinnest veneer of compliance. We recommend that these ethics rules be jettisoned in this group of cases. Instead of the current attempt to force the ethics analysis into standard, but inappropriate, doctrinal categories, the regulatory system should investigate whether the attorney's behavior poses real dangers to the interests of the class or corporation.

Underlying many of these observations is a more basic critique of the existing regulatory system's requirement that there be an actual identified individual plaintiff in large-scale, small-claim cases. Because these cases are dominated by entrepreneurial attorneys, the identified plaintiff operates almost always as a mere figurehead. The named plaintiff does little—indeed, usually does nothing—to monitor the attorney in order to ensure that representation is competent and zealous, or to align the interests of the attorney with those of the class or corporation. On the other hand, the requirement that there be an actual named plaintiff artificially limits the supply of attorneys able to bring large-scale, small-claim cases because in many cases "appropriate" representative plaintiffs are hard to find. The quality of representation is thereby diminished, and the private enforcement of law impaired. Further, attorneys are routinely forced to circumvent ethical restrictions on solicitation and maintenance in order to obtain named plaintiffs as their ticket into profitable litigation. We believe that the costs of requiring an actual named plaintiff greatly outweigh the benefits. Accordingly, we recommend that actual, identified named plaintiffs not be required in large-scale, small-claim litigation. Instead, a plaintiffs' attorney should be allowed to bring "Jane Doe" or "Richard Roe" complaints on behalf of a class or corporation.

Although we make several recommendations for ways in which the existing regulatory structure could be changed to deal more effectively with the unique problems posed by entrepreneurial litigation, we believe that a more fundamental change may be in order. We draw on the economic theory of agency costs to suggest that the special problems of entrepreneurial litigation could be substantially overcome if the legal system were to allow some form of auction for plaintiffs' claims, under which attorneys (and others) could bid for the right to bring the litigation and gain the benefits, if any, that flow from success. A pure form of auction would simply sell the plaintiffs' claims outright to the winning bidder, with the proceeds to be distributed immediately to the class or corporation. Under such an approach, the winner of the auction would have litigation incentives that are very similar to those which a claimholder would have in traditional, two-party litigation. There would be no need for any rules on typicality or adequacy of representation or for judicial scrutiny of settlements and fee awards. Class members would receive a certain and quick recovery rather than an uncertain and delayed one. The result would be more effective private enforcement of the law. Other possibilities we discuss involve partial bids or bids for lead counsel rights based on the percentage of the recovery that the attorney would be willing to take as a fee; these may be more feasible to implement, although they retain some of the problems of misalignment between the interests of the attorney and client.[3]

We do not advocate the auction approach as a panacea to the problem of attorney-client conflicts in class and derivative suits. There are a number of problems with an auction approach, including difficulties in defining the claim to be sold, the possibility that adequate financing will not be available to bidders, the problem of obtaining the cooperation of class members whose claims have been sold, and issues of consolidation of cases brought in different jurisdictions. Although we recognize these problems as serious, we believe there is considerable merit to the auction approach.

————

JULIE AMPARANO
"A LAWYER FLOURISHES BY SUING CORPORATIONS
FOR THEIR SHAREHOLDERS"
Wall Street Journal, pp. 1, 19 (April 28, 1987).[64]

Richard D. Greenfield specializes in giving corporate executives sleepless nights.

3. District Judge Vaughn Walker of the Northern District of California has recently conducted an auction of lead counsel rights based on fee percentages. See In re Oracle Securities Litigation, 131 F.R.D. 688 (N.D.Cal.1990) (setting up the bidding process); In re Oracle Securities Litigation, 132 F.R.D. 538 (N.D.Cal.1990) (awarding lead counsel rights to one of four bidders ...).

64. Copyright © 1987 Wall Street Journal. Reprinted with permission.

He does that partly by staying up late himself to clip newspaper and magazine articles about corporations. By the time he turns off the light, the clippings often cover his entire bed—and his sleeping wife. At breakfast he scours the morning papers. Then he heads off for another day of suing corporations.

Mr. Greenfield is one of the most active practitioners of the burgeoning legal sub-specialty of shareholder-rights litigation. As probably every corporate director in the nation knows, the number of shareholder-rights suits filed has quadrupled over the past decade.

Mr. Greenfield has ridden the crest of that tidal wave: Of the 15 most prominent shareholder suits filed last year, according to Wyatt Co., a corporate consulting concern, Mr. Greenfield handled seven. "That's more than any other firm or attorney," notes Warren Brock-meier, a Wyatt vice president who advises corporations on shareholder litigation.

For top attorneys such as Mr. Greenfield, shareholder-rights work has become a surprisingly lucrative legal niche. Mr Greenfield says he wins or settles for payment about 85% of all suits he brings. He estimates that since 1970 his law firm has squeezed some $500 million out of corporations, including a hefty $70 million payment arising from Midland Bank PLC's purchase of Crocker National Corp. He won't disclose his own income, but other attorneys reckon he makes more than $300,000 a year.

Getting to the Core

Obscure just a decade ago, Mr. Greenfield now commands attention, if not always respect, from his potential adversaries. "He's being taken very seriously by the corporate world. He's bright and tough," says Stephen Harmelin, who, when he was the chairman of Publicker Industries Inc., was sued by Mr. Greenfield for alleged mismanagement. (Publicker settled the case by agreeing to change certain management practices.)

"A lot of boards act properly because they fear what Richard Greenfield might do," adds Alan Fellheimer, the chairman of Equimark Corp., which Mr. Greenfield sued for alleged securities fraud in 1983. Equimark denied the charge and settled the suit for $3 million. "He knows how to get to the core of a corporation," Mr. Fellheimer says with some admiration.

. . .

In recent years Mr. Greenfield has made a kind of micro-specialty of bringing shareholder suits against financial concerns. In 1985, when Midland Bank offered to buy out Crocker National for stock with an indicated value of $247.6 million, Mr. Greenfield sued on behalf of Crocker shareholders, alleging that they weren't getting adequate compensation. A judge agreed, and awarded them an additional $70 million.

Similarly, when certain Chase Manhattan Corp. shareholders felt they had suffered from the company's lending practices, he sued a group of Chase's directors and executives and won a settlement of $32.5 million. (A Chase spokesman declines to comment on the matter.)

Long before Bank America Corp. reported $388 million in loan losses last summer, Mr. Greenfield says, he had spotted disturbing inconsistencies in the banking concern's financial disclosures. Thus, he was prepared when BankAmerica reported a $640 million loss for its second quarter—its biggest quarterly loss ever. Within days, Mr. Greenfield filed a suit alleging inadequate disclosure and asking for an unspecified amount of damages. (A BankAmerica spokesman declines to comment on the suit.)

But Mr. Greenfield doesn't restrict himself to banks. Earlier this month the Nuclear Regulatory Commission found that control-room operators in Philadelphia Electric Co.'s Peach Bottom nuclear power plant had slept on the job. Mr. Greenfield soon accused the utility's entire board of mismanagement. (Company officials decline to discuss the charge.) Two years ago, Mr. Greenfield wandered even further afield and sued the city of Philadelphia after a confrontation between police and the radical group MOVE resulted in the fiery destruction of a neighborhood.

Two Criticisms

In court documents, attorneys for the city raised two criticisms of Mr. Greenfield that usually are made only in executive suites: his possible solicitation of clients and his speed in bringing suit. One city legal brief noted that Mr. Greenfield's pro bono filing was in the court "almost before . . . the embers were cold." Another suggested that Mr. Greenfield may not have played a completely passive role in finding a plaintiff.

Corporate executives and attorneys aren't so bold. Most of those asked decline to discuss Mr. Greenfield on the record. In private, however, many question his ethics and techniques. One lawyer, for example, notes that the plaintiff in Mr. Greenfield's Crocker–Midland suit was Mr. Greenfield's wife.

Mr. Greenfield shrugs off such criticism. After all, there is a solid economic reason to rush to the courthouse: It's not uncommon for several shareholder suits to be filed almost simultaneously, and judges usually name the first attorney to file as the lead counsel for the plaintiffs. Lead counsel, of course, generally get the biggest fees. So like many other attorneys, Mr. Greenfield keeps "fill in the blanks" legal briefs standing by in his firm's word processors.

Mr. Greenfield denies that he solicits cases. Some are brought to him by disgruntled shareholders, he says, while others are referred by law firms. As for the Crocker case, he says, it was simply coincidence that his wife was a shareholder. Nonetheless, his firm maintains a list of clients and their stockholdings in order to be able to file quickly when the occasion arises.

Bearding Big Business

Most of all, Mr. Greenfield gives the impression that he really doesn't care what corporate executives think of him. As he sees it, his job is to defend the little guy against the excesses of Big Business. His cable address is "WHITEHAT." Growing up in Brooklyn, he says, conditioned him to "standing up to bullies." The bloody noses of his youth, he claims, prepared him for taking on the swarms of expensive lawyers a big outfit such as CBS Inc. hires when it is sued by him.

As part of his anti-corporate posture, Mr. Greenfield takes pains to distinguish himself from the typical Philadelphia lawyer. Instead of the standard corporate lawyer's uniform of a three-piece pin-striped suit, yellow or red tie, and wing-tip shoes, the tall, bearded lawyer often comes to work in blue jeans and a flannel shirt. He has been known to sport a Western-style leather vest. At least once, he says, he has shown up dressed that way to meet with opposing bankers, "just to be ornery." Mr. Greenfield's partners and staff are similarly casual, sometimes leading visitors to confuse attorneys with delivery boys.

. . .

———

Entrepreneurial Lawyers

Suppose a lawyer such as Richard Greenfield learns from a newspaper story or an amendment to an SEC filing about a previously unknown transaction between Empire Corp. and its principal manager and shareholder. This hypothetical Greenfield immediately calls Freeman, who owns a thin but widely diversified portfolio of stocks in American companies, asks him whether he owns Empire (Freeman does) and whether he is willing to act as the representative shareholder in a class or derivative action against Empire and its controlling stockholder challenging the transaction. Freeman, who has acted frequently in this capacity for Greenfield in the past, consents to the representation and litigation. Greenfield then investigates the case just enough to overcome a Rule 11 sanctions problem and files suit. (In a derivative suit the demand requirement must first be satisfied unless excused as futile.) Discovery is then employed to ferret out the details of the transaction. Settlement negotiations result in an agreement providing for a prospective change in the company's procedures designed to prevent a recurrence of the problem and an award of substantial attorney's fees to Greenfield. The court approves the settlement, which is supported by all represented parties. The corporation reimburses the individual defendant for the costs of defending the suit and pays Greenfield a substantial attorney's fee award.

This scenario, which may or may not be typical, suggests that current arrangements may result in the under-enforcement of some legal rights, some situations of wasteful or excessive over-enforcement and problems of collusion in which the interests of the entity are sacrificed to those of the plaintiffs' lawyer and the individual defendants.

Professor John C. Coffee, Jr., has examined these problems in several influential articles.[65] He describes the plaintiffs' lawyer as an entrepreneur who performs the socially useful function of deterring undesirable conduct. Existing arrangements permit the plaintiffs' lawyer (1) to acquire a financial interest in the case and to perform a risk-taking function (i.e., to advance expenses and receive reimbursement and an attorney's fee only if the litigation is successful); (2) to settle a class or derivative action over the objections of class representatives, with court approval; and (3) to obtain compensation, if successful, under fee formulas that view "the lawyer as a calculating entrepreneur regulated by calculating judges." [66]

These arrangements encourage vindication of publicly-created rights that otherwise would not be enforced, but run the risk of two problems: (1) pursuit of some claims where the total social costs (including costs to the public as well as to the defendants) are greater than any social benefits (a type of undesirable over-enforcement, often characterized as "greymail" or extortion); and (2) collusive settlements that are in the interest of the plaintiffs' lawyer and the individual defendants but which sacrifice the interests of the plaintiff class (a type of undesirable under-enforcement of law).

Coffee, contrary to other analysts, concludes that collusion is a greater problem than extortion, but suggests that current legal arrangements provide opportunities for both. The following paragraphs summarize a portion of his argument.

In mercenary actions the lawyer finds the client rather than the client finding the lawyer. Lawyers inexpensively search out potential claims by, for example, piggy-backing on public enforcement in antitrust or securities fields or following up publicized occurrences, such as a mass tort or a financial event involving a corporation. Identification of nominal plaintiffs is then a relatively simple matter. Thinking about this type of lawyer as a fiduciary is unrealistic. Behavior is controlled by the lawyer's interests as an entrepreneur: Litigation is a risky asset that requires continuing investment decisions.

Private and social incentives to litigate bear no necessary relationship to each other. Because the public bears a substantial portion of the costs of litigation, an excessive incentive to litigate may exist under

65. See, e.g., John C. Coffee, Jr., Understanding the Plaintiff's Attorney: The Implications of Economic Theory for Private Enforcement of Law Through Class and Derivative Suits, 86 Colum.L.Rev. 669 (1986).

66. Id. at 678, quoting from John Leubsdorf, The Contingency Factor in Attorney Fee Awards, 90 Yale L.J. 473, 481 (1982).

some circumstances. But empirical evidence indicates that this is probably not the case in class and derivative actions. Fee awards in these cases range between 20–30 percent of recoveries, but they decrease in percentage as the recovery increases. Thus plaintiffs' lawyers have an incentive to settle more cheaply as the damages involved increase. Litigation stakes are asymmetric, with the defendant focusing on the total award and the plaintiff's attorney focusing on the fee, which is a declining percentage of the recovery.

By severing the fee award from the amount of the settlement or judgment, the lodestar method of determining the attorney's fee has unfortunate consequences. It provides incentive and opportunity for defendants and plaintiffs' attorneys to "arrange collusive settlements that exchange a low recovery for a high fee award." [67] Coffee suggests that alternatives to the lodestar approach may be desirable: (1) allowing lawyers to buy claims and pursue them (lawyers would then have an incentive to expend effort up to the socially optimal position); (2) awarding damages that are a multiple of actual harm (dangers of over-deterrence are offset by the low risk of detection that accompanies many forms of illegal behavior); and (3) providing for an increasing percentage of fee as the recovery increases.

Coffee examines and rejects the argument that, because costs to defendants are higher than those to plaintiffs, even frivolous actions have some settlement value. In theory, a plaintiffs' lawyer, by bringing an action, can require a defendant to bear substantial costs in order to dismiss it (much larger than those required on the part of plaintiffs); if this is the case, the lawyer can extort a fee award from the defendant as a way of avoiding the larger expense of defending on the merits. Coffee argues that in practice the low and decreasing percentage of fee to recovery, by creating a high risk that the award will not cover the plaintiffs' lawyer's opportunity costs, results in asymmetric stakes that favor defendants. Defendants, by forcing plaintiffs to make a larger investment in a case, are in a position to reduce the rate of return of the plaintiffs' attorney.

Plaintiffs' lawyers in derivative actions should be viewed as risk-preferring repeat players who hold a diversified portfolio of cases, whereas officers and directors are risk-averse one-time players. "The contrast is similar to that between a fully diversified investor and an investor who holds only a single speculative asset." [68] Coffee concludes that the best strategy for a plaintiff's lawyer in this field is to bring a substantial number of actions, but devote relatively little time to any of them. This behavior is "less an extortionate attempt to exploit the cost differential that favors plaintiffs' attorneys than a means of achieving the only form of risk spreading available to plaintiffs' attorneys in small firms." [69]

67. Id. at 691.

68. Id. at 705.

69. Id. at 711–12.

Coffee also argues that the strategic behavior of plaintiffs' lawyers (bringing a substantial number of cases and succeeding in a very small portion of them) is also a function of establishing a reputation as someone who has to be taken seriously by defendants. Bringing in a few wins provides the reputation that then permits a pattern of collusive settlements. Reputation also affects a lawyer's role in the team of ad hoc lawyers that jockey for control of good class action cases. The lawyer's share of the fee award is largely determined by her role on the litigating team.

Coffee concludes that collusive settlements are the serious problem in the area, not extortion. One set of interests (that of plaintiff classes) is systematically sacrificed for the benefit of the other two (plaintiffs' lawyers and defendants). Courts are both unable and unwilling to prevent the "covert exchange of a cheap settlement for a high award of attorney's fees." [70] In shareholder derivative suits, for example, the fact that the officers and directors receive indemnification only if wrongdoing is not found provides a strong incentive for the control group to settle cases for a juicy fee award wholly apart from litigation merits. Officers and directors also have an incentive to pay an award on securities charges against the corporation in order to get off the hook on personal liability; and plaintiffs' attorneys have an incentive to go along with this strategy. "[S]ettlements that shift these costs from officers to their corporations both rob the law of its deterrent impact and, paradoxically, force shareholders, who are the intended beneficiaries of the substantive legal standard, to bear the costs of the actions." [71]

Two devices to deter nuisance actions (the bond requirement in derivative actions and the judicial reliance on the report of a special litigation committee) shift the odds against plaintiffs, but the latter has had the paradoxical effect of increasing the number of derivative suits. Because the special report procedure is extremely costly and time-consuming—often requiring two years and a cost of $1 million—its effect is to reduce the effort a plaintiffs' lawyer devotes to cases while increasing their number. The cost of the process facilitates collusive settlements: The plaintiffs' lawyer can underbid the cost of the committee procedure.

Coffee concludes that "good intentions"—the profession's and courts' desire to regulate the bounty hunter as a fiduciary—have had bad results. The lodestar fee encourages collusive settlements; other reforms (such as the litigation committee approach) may encourage the extortion of nuisance suits. Reforms that will be effective must operate on the incentives of the plaintiffs' attorney and be self-policing. Coffee favors a "deregulatory" approach: fee awards that are stated in terms of percentage of recovery and that provide either for multiple damages, prejudgment interest, or a marginally increasing percentage. Sensible

70. Id. at 714.
71. Id. at 720.

policy-making, Coffee concludes, has to reflect the fact that the derivative and class-action lawyer is different from other attorneys. In derivative and class actions, unlike other lawyer-client relationships, the lawyer controls the client, systemic conflict with clients is built into the relationship, and the lawyer has an incentive for opportunistic conduct at the expense of social interests. A "fixation" on the "nostalgic lens of fiduciary analysis," according to Coffee, "is likely to blind us to the real issues relating to the incentives and misincentives that the law today creates for the plaintiff's attorney." [72]

What about defendants' lawyers and their incentives? Is there substantial churning and fee-padding on their part at the expense of defendants? Are the substantive areas in which entrepreneurial lawyers operate fields in which lawyers for the adversaries are the principal beneficiaries?

Do you favor the reform proposals of Macey and Miller, on the one hand, or Coffee, on the other? Would the reforms of either or both result in an increased number of frivolous filings? Would their reforms reduce the number or frequency of collusive settlements? What assumptions do these authors make about the legal ethics of lawyers in class and derivative actions?

2. Regulating Class Action Lawyers

Professor Deborah Rhode, addressing class actions in which a public interest lawyer seeks structural reform of public and private institutions, argues that the fiduciary approach to regulating the class-action lawyer is an unrealistic but nevertheless useful fiction.[73] *Fiandaca*, p. 644 above, and *Jeff D.*, p. 548 above, are illustrative of class actions involving structural reform of public institutions.

Rhode states that disagreements in preferences among members of an unstable and inchoate class of persons are inevitable when broad relief is sought in a context that is political in character. She urges the lawyer for the class to inquire about class preferences concerning relief and settlement, but not necessarily to defer to them. The utility of the class-action device as a mechanism for social advocacy justifies the "white lie" that imposes vague obligations on class counsel but leaves her free to make paternalistic judgments. Other alternatives such as "pluralism" (separate representation of discrete interests) or democratic participation (direct class participation through plebiscites and public hearings) would cripple the effectiveness of class actions, according to Rhode.

Rule 23(a)(4) of the Federal Rules of Civil Procedure provides, inter alia, that the parties representing the class must "fairly and adequately protect the interests of the class." This provision has been applied to class counsel as well as the named representatives of the class. In

---

72. Id. at 727.

73. Deborah L. Rhode, Class Conflicts in Class Actions, 34 Stan.L.Rev. 1183 (1982).

Wagner v. Lehman Brothers Kuhn Loeb Inc.,[74] counsel for the class engaged in unethical conduct: offering to pay a witness a percentage of any recovery in exchange for favorable testimony and interviewing the opposing party without informing that party's counsel. The court held that this unethical conduct barred the lawyer from representing the class:

> ... An inquiry into the character of counsel for the class-representative is also necessary because he stands in a fiduciary relationship with the absent class. See, e.g., Greenfield v. Villager Industries, Inc., 483 F.2d 824, 832 (3d Cir.1973); Stavrides v. Mellon National Bank & Trust Co., 60 F.R.D. 634, 637 (W.D.Pa.1973)....

"Unethical and improper actions" by counsel for the plaintiff class, *Wagner* holds, result in a determination that "he cannot adequately represent the putative class in accordance with his fiduciary duties." [75]

Should the court make this kind of inquiry in every class action— acting as guardian for the absent class in deciding whether to "hire" the particular lawyer? The court's failure to inquire in every class action may be partly justified by the assumption that deficiencies in the class counsel's competence or integrity will be brought out by the opposing party in the class certification process, which is an adversary proceeding.[76] But is it always in the opposing party's interest to challenge class counsel?

One commentator has suggested that a *Garner*-like exception to the attorney-client privilege be adopted to protect the interests of absentee class members.[77] Would this proposal meet the problems addressed by Rhode? If the *Garner* exception were available in class actions before the case had been resolved on the merits, how would the court ensure that the opposing party did not become the primary beneficiary of the invasion of the class' confidences? Should the exception be limited to class members challenging a settlement or attorney's fees?

For a case of shareholder class members challenging the class lawyer's claim for attorney fees, see In re Fine Paper Antitrust Litigation.[78] This case is infamous for the patronage system that developed among the scores of plaintiffs' lawyers for the various classes represented, for the scale of the alleged padding of fees and expenses and for the animosity that developed between the two lead counsel.[79]

74. 646 F.Supp. 643 (N.D.Ill.1986).

75. 646 F.Supp. at 661–62.

76. For an example of the court allowing the opposing party to inquire into the class lawyer's character, see Stavrides v. Mellon National Bank & Trust Co., 60 F.R.D. 634 (W.D.Pa.1973).

77. See Note, The Attorney–Client Privilege in Class Actions: Fashioning an Exception to Promote Adequacy of Representation, 97 Harv.L.Rev. 947 (1984).

78. 98 F.R.D. 48 (E.D.Pa.1983), rev'd, 751 F.2d 562 (3d Cir.1984).

79. A good discussion of this case can be found in John C. Coffee, Jr., Rescuing the Private Attorney General: Why the Model of the Lawyer as Bounty Hunter Is Not Working, 42 Md.L.Rev. 215 (1983).

Costs of Monitoring a Lawyer's Conduct

Class counsel who generates a monetary recovery for the class—a "common fund"—is entitled to attorney's fees from the fund, subject to court approval.[80]

> In these situations, the plaintiffs' attorney's role changes from one of a fiduciary for the clients to that of a claimant against the fund created for the clients' benefit. The perspective of the judge also changes because the court now must monitor the disbursement of the fund and act as a fiduciary for those who are supposed to benefit from it, since typically no one else is available to perform that function—the defendant has no interest in how the fund is distributed and the plaintiff class members rarely become involved. Note that neither of these concerns arise in the statutory fee context, which continues to be an adversary proceeding until resolution, except when a statutory fee case is 'converted' into a fund case by settlement.[81]

Protection of the class in fee awards imposes an enormous burden on the courts in reviewing the hourly rates, hourly activities and expenditures of the lawyers on behalf of the class.[82] To impose on courts a duty of still closer scrutiny would transform the adversary process and might push the judiciary beyond its effective capability.

In In re Oracle Securities Litigation,[83] more than 25 law firms sought the role of lead counsel in a securities class action. The court stated that the lodestar approach to "common fund" fee awards "is now thoroughly discredited by experience."

> The lodestar approach is unworkable because, among other things, it abandons the adversary process ...; requires judges to assess, *after* the litigation is over, strategic and other decisions made by plaintiffs' lawyers in the midst of litigation ...; [and] delays the recovery of class members still longer.... [84]

The court decided to adopt a contingent fee approach and ordered the contesting law firms to submit sealed bids from which the court would pick lead counsel.

Would more or less statutory or judicial regulation be desirable? [85] Can courts or disciplinary boards monitor the "market" in named representatives? Adopt an auction approach that attempts to replicate a market?

---

80. See Boeing Co. v. Van Gemert, 444 U.S. 472, 478 (1980).

81. Report of the Third Circuit Task Force on Court Awarded Attorney Fees, 108 F.R.D. 237, 255 (1985).

82. See also the discussion of attorney's fee awards in "common fund" cases at p. 548 above.

83. 131 F.R.D. 688 (N.D.Cal.1990).

84. 131 F.R.D. at 689.

85. See Brian J. Waid, Ethical Problems of the Class Action Practitioner: Continued Neglect by the Drafters of the Proposed Model Rules of Professional Conduct, 27 Loy.L.Rev. 1047 (1981).

Value of Myth

Professors Rhode and Coffee agree that the legal concept that considers a lawyer for a class as a fiduciary has an unrealistic, mythic quality. Rhode, however, argues that the myth of the lawyer as fiduciary for the class has some value at least in institutional reform litigation. Coffee, on the other hand, argues that the myth leads to faulty analysis of the problem of conflicts in entrepreneurial class actions and spawns misguided "reform" proposals, which, if enacted, might worsen the problems they are designed to cure. Does Coffee's critique of the fiduciary myth apply to "public interest" lawyers and their clients? See the *Jeff D.* case, printed above at p. 548.

Class Counsel Communicating With the Class

As soon as a class action is filed, the lawyer for the class usually wishes to solicit potential class members to increase the likelihood of certification. Before and after certification, the lawyer has an interest in contacting class members to gather evidence and to discourage opting-out, for once a class is certified eligible members are counted "in" unless they opt out. See Fed.R.Civ.P. 23(c)(2)(a). By such contacts the lawyer strengthens the class' case, which in turn maximizes the potential award and increases the lawyer's fee. The Comment to M.R. 7.2 on advertising states that "[n]either this Rule nor Rule 7.3 [on direct solicitation] prohibits communications authorized by law, such as notice to members of a class in class action litigation." May the court, however, prohibit such solicitation?

Gulf Oil Co. v. Bernard[86] was a class action brought by black employees charging race discrimination. Gulf was hoping that employees would opt out of the class action and instead accept a back-pay award which Gulf had negotiated with the EEOC in a conciliation agreement. Gulf petitioned the court for an order limiting the named plaintiffs and their lawyers from communicating with potential class members, alleging that counsel was telling potential class members that they could double their recovery by joining the suit and rejecting the back-pay offer. Without corroborating Gulf's allegations, the district court issued an order barring both the parties and their lawyers from communicating with the class without court approval.

The Supreme Court, while acknowledging the potential for abuse, held that the trial court had abused its discretion: "[A]n order limiting communications between parties and potential class members should be based on a clear record and specific findings that reflect a weighing of the need for a limitation and the potential interference with the rights of the parties."[87] The order in this case had thwarted the plaintiff's ability to form a class and maintain the action, thereby violating Rule 23. The Court did not decide the case on First Amendment grounds, as

---

86. 452 U.S. 89 (1981).

87. 452 U.S. at 101.

the Court of Appeals had done,[88] but said that any order limiting communications should be "carefully drawn ... to limit speech as little as possible...."[89]

3. Settlement Conditioned Upon Fee Waiver

EVANS v. JEFF D.

Supreme Court of the United States, 1986.
475 U.S. 717, 106 S.Ct. 1531, 89 L.Ed.2d 747.

[This case is reprinted and discussed in Chapter 6 at p. 548.]

88. 604 F.2d 449 (5th Cir.1979).

89. Id. at 102. See also Rossini v. Ogilvy & Mather, Inc., 798 F.2d 590 (2d Cir.1986) (upholding an order restricting communications between class counsel and the class against a challenge under *Gulf Oil v. Bernard*).

Chapter 9

THE BAR AS A LEGAL AND
SOCIAL INSTITUTION

Introduction: Historical Sketch of
American Legal Profession

In their beginnings, the colonies had few trained lawyers, and their citizens dealt with legal formalities as best they could. In the absence of a regulatory system, anyone could be a lawyer who could use a set of legal forms and maintain a position in argument. Someone who did so more or less regularly for money could call himself a practicing lawyer. So much the better if one had, or pretended to have had, some kind of practice experience in the mother country, for example, serving as a justice of the peace.[1]

The practice of law, however, has been a regulated vocation almost from the time that an identifiable legal profession emerged in this country. As the political economy of the colonies expanded from 1620 to 1776, a legal profession evolved, concentrated in the wealthier and more populous colonies. The skills of practice were acquired primarily by the same means by which technical knowledge was usually transmitted in those days—apprenticeship with an established practitioner. Apprenticeship was essentially a contract whereby tutelage was provided by the master in return for scut work by the apprentice, such as scrivening documents and running errands. The apprenticeship system could accommodate only a limited number of new entrants, restraining competition within the profession. Quality of training necessarily varied widely. The system undoubtedly favored sons and relatives of existing practitioners. In time, weight was given to years of college education in place of apprenticeship years.

Concerning the colonial period, historian Michael Burrage says:

Seven colonies required periods of apprenticeship, ranging from three years in Delaware to seven in New York and New Jersey. New York and Massachusetts granted some exemption for college education and also set additional requirements for those wishing to practice as barristers in the higher courts. New Jersey, imitating

---

1. For history of the beginnings of the English legal profession in the 12th century, see Symposium, 5 Law and History Rev. 1 (1987). For a review of historical sources on the American legal profession, see Olavi Maru, Research on the Legal Profession c. 1 (2d ed. 1986).

the English bar, had a third, higher coopted order of serjeants.[2] Virginia and South Carolina, with sizable number of lawyers, had no formal training requirements, probably because a large proportion of lawyers in both colonies qualified at the Inns of Court in London. Virginia seems to have expected those not trained in London, and certainly those who wished to appear in the higher courts, to serve a four-year apprenticeship. In sum, the principle of a specialist, trained, select bar seems to have been accepted in the majority of the colonies. However, it is not always clear whether the bar admission rules were imposed by the governor and the courts or by the practitioners themselves. Only in Massachusetts do we know for certain that the bar devised, administered, and enforced its own admission rules.[3]

Attempts to practice by those who lacked the requisite training, what is today called unauthorized practice of law, were little noticed or recorded. Although someone who represented himself as a lawyer, but who was not, would be subject to an action for deceit or perhaps malpractice,[4] such remedies were costly and worth pursuing only if damages could be both proved and collected. An alternative to a deceit action by the client might have been a suit by the bar to enjoin unauthorized practice by the unlicensed practitioner. As the law of unfair competition stood until the 20th century, however, members of the bar probably would have had no right of action against someone pretending to be qualified as a lawyer.[5]

Prior to enactment of statutes prohibiting the practice of law by unlicensed persons, the bar could do little to prevent untrained people from doing law office work, such as conveyancing and giving legal advice. The bar also could not prevent informal practice in the justice of the peace courts. However, those trained in law practice had two effective controls on law practice by those not admitted to the bar. One was ostracism. Thus, nonlawyers would be excluded from the formal and informal associations of practitioners, hence would be shut out from professional lore and professional gossip. Then as now this kind of access—being a member of "the club"—is important. Second, and relatedly, courts of general jurisdiction had control over the right to appear before them on behalf of others. Admission before the court in turn would be granted only to those recognized by their professional peers who had passed through the apprenticeship process. From an early date the key to entry into the profession was admission before the

2. [Editors' note:] "Serjeants" refers to serjeants at law, a small order of highest level barristers that originated in medieval times and became obsolescent in the 18th century.

3. Michael Burrage, Revolution and the Collective Action of the French, American, and English Legal Professions, 13 Law & Social Inquiry 225, 243 (1988) (containing an excellent summary of the history of the American legal profession).

4. See C. Wolfram, Modern Legal Ethics § 5.6.1 (1986).

5. See Milton Handler, False and Misleading Advertising, 39 Yale L.J. 22, 29 (1929). In the 20th century it was made a statutory offense for a person not a lawyer to engage in law practice. That prohibition is in turn a basis for injunctive proceedings by the bar to prevent such practice. See Florida Bar v. Brumbaugh, p. 938 below.

trial court of general jurisdiction under the auspices of the apprentice-ship system. This system apparently was fairly effective at the time the Constitution was adopted in 1787.

At the time of the Revolution, a hardy class of lawyers had established themselves in each of the original colonies. This generation of lawyers played an extraordinary role in creating the new republic (33 of the 55 participating members of the Constitutional Convention in 1787 were lawyers), molding the constitutional structure during the Federalist and Jeffersonian periods and expounding a vision of the "republican" lawyer-gentleman that two hundred years later remains at the heart of professional ideology.

Efforts to "do away with the lawyers" are often an aftermath of a successful revolution. Populist sentiment emanating from the American and French Revolutions culminated in the early 19th century in what was subsequently called the Jacksonian revolution.[6] Measures to abolish any special lawyer prerogatives arose in a few states and spread to others beginning as early as 1801.[7] Deregulation gained momentum over the next four decades:

> In one way or another, therefore, most states reduced or eliminated mandatory requirements for admission to the bar dur-ing the first half of the 19th century....
>
> The reduction or elimination of bar admission requirements had a disastrous effect on professional organization, leading to the collapse of all existing bar associations. The Suffolk County Bar Association, the leading organization in Massachusetts, dissolved in 1836.... The only exception was the Philadelphia Bar Associa-tion, which originated in 1802 as a law library but later became a professional body. However, it exercised these functions only among an elite, never seeking to extend its authority over all lawyers in the city or county....
>
> The repeal of bar admission rules and the collapse of bar associations prevented the American profession from remaining as a small, closed, aloof, and largely self-recruiting status group....
>
> This process of opening legal practice to members of lower socioeconomic classes ... must have accelerated everywhere with the mushrooming of university and private commercial night schools after the Civil War. As a result, the American legal profession ... became a heterogeneous occupational category whose "members," if that is the right word, were stratified by their social and ethnic origins, law schools they attended, and places of work. Since they could no longer look to practitioners' organiza-tions to confer distinctive professional honors or titles, they were obliged to earn their status like everyone else in American society

6. See Murray L. Schwartz, Lawyers and the Legal Profession 328–29 (2d ed.1985).

7. Georgia in 1801 required that admission to practice law be allowed simply on application to court; Ohio in 1802 abrogated all requirements for admission, Tennessee in 1809 and South Carolina in 1812.

by their educational qualifications, their incomes, and their life-styles.[8]

Does the American legal profession continue to be a "heterogeneous occupational category" today?

Throughout most of the 19th century the practice of law, like the practice of medicine, was not an especially notable, highly rewarded or high-status endeavor.[9]   There were no law schools similar to those of today; many lawyers did not have a college degree.[10]   Some years later, during the last decade of the 19th century, 88 percent of newly admitted Chicago lawyers had attended law school, and more than one-half of this group also had a college degree.[11]   A major change in the "professionalism" of the bar had occurred gradually throughout the century, resulting in its last decades in changes that some scholars refer to as the "transformation" of the profession.[12]

> [T]he critical developments [in the evolution of the bar from a weak, corporate guild to a powerful, individualistic profession] came in the late nineteenth century as the forces of industrialization posed increasingly complex legal issues that only trained professionals could solve.   Like the other [learned] professions, lawyers during these years fashioned a monopoly sanctioned by the state.   This monopoly meant that lawyers set the standards for training and admission to the bar, the proper forms of practice, and code of conduct that practitioners were to follow.[13]

The three institutions central to the shaping of the professional ideology and practice environment of the modern legal profession were (1) the law school, (2) the large law firm and (3) the bar association. The American law school as we know it today dates from 1870 when Christopher Langdell became dean of the Harvard Law School.   Entrance requirements were imposed (a college degree and competence in Latin); three years of instruction rather than two were required for graduation; and the case method of dialectical teaching replaced lectures and rote memorization of legal texts.   This method encouraged the scientific study of law; systematization and rationalization provided an answer to the explosion of knowledge and waning cultural authority of traditional beliefs.

8.   Burrage, supra, 13 Law & Social Inquiry at 249, 252.

9.   The classic discussion is J. Willard Hurst, The Growth of American Law: The Law Makers (1950).   See also Maxwell Bloomfield, Lawyers and Public Criticism: Challenge and Response in Nineteenth–Century America, 15 Am. J. of Legal History 269 (1971); Bloomfield, The Texas Bar in the Nineteenth Century, 32 Vand. L. Rev. 261 (1979).

10.   Terence C. Halliday and Mark W. Granfors, Class, Status, and Education in the Transition to Modern Professionalism, 1830–1900 at Table I.

11.   Id.

12.   See Gerard W. Gawalt (ed.), The New High Priests: Lawyers in Post Civil War America (1984); Wayne K. Hobson, The American Legal Profession and the Organizational Society, 1890–1930 (1986).

13.   Kermit L. Hall (ed.), The Legal Profession: Major Historical Interpretations xi-xii (1987).

The graduates of the new law schools were largely responsible for another turn-of-the century innovation—the large law firm. The division of legal labor in a larger organization met the specialized needs of corporate clients. Counseling by senior lawyers assisted by the careful research of junior lawyers resulted in a new organizational form of practice, very different from the "oratory and showmanship" of the pre-Civil War generation.[14]

Bar associations as formal and powerful organizations flowed from the desire of relatively elite lawyers to respond to social change and to improve the profession and its standing. Local bar associations were first organized in the 1870s, beginning with the Association of the Bar of the City of New York in 1877. The number of local and state bar associations grew rapidly at the end of the century, but their activities were primarily social in character until the 1920s. Only 15 percent of all lawyers in 1915 belonged to state bars. The American Bar Association (ABA), formed in 1878, was a small and selective group of lawyers from across the country with a shared concern over preparation and admission to the bar. Its annual meetings at resort hotels in Saratoga, New York were pleasant social events attended by several hundred lawyers. Only after 1921 did the ABA, gradually growing in numbers and influence, begin to have a substantial effect on preparation for and admission to the bar.

Beginning in the 1920s the requirements for entry into the profession were increased.[15] Bar exams, which began in the late 19th century, were improved; requirements of prelegal college education were gradually put in place; and graduation from an ABA-approved law school became a prerequisite for bar admission. Alternatives, such as apprenticeship or study at unapproved schools, most of which were proprietary in character, were eliminated entirely in most states and drastically narrowed in the remainder. These developments were not completed until the 1950s.

A. ADMISSION TO PRACTICE

1. Modern Admission Standards

Admission to the practice of law today takes the form of admission before the highest court of the state, except in New York, where it takes the form of admission to a lower court. Admission to the court carries with it the right of audience (i.e., to present matters on behalf of clients) in all courts of the jurisdiction, and to engage in law office practice.

14. Hall, supra, at xiv. The structure of the large law firm owes much to Paul D. Cravath's organizing principles, which spread to other firms. See Robert T. Swaine, The Cravath Firm (3 vols., 1946–48). For contemporary discussion of the growth of large law firms, see Marc Galanter and Thomas Palay, Tournament of Lawyers (1991).

15. See Richard L. Abel, American Lawyers 40–73 (1989) (discussing control of the production of lawyers); and Robert B. Stevens, Law School: Legal Education in America from the 1850s to the 1980s (1983).

A parallel procedure governs admission to practice in federal courts. Admission to practice in a state does not of itself result in admission to practice in the federal courts in that state. Rather, a motion for admission to the federal court must be made. Separate admission is required to each United States district court, to each United States court of appeals and to the Supreme Court of the United States. The basic requirement for admission to federal court is that the applicant have been admitted in a state. However, local federal court rules often require in addition a period of practice experience, participation in a number of trials, proof of familiarity with federal procedure or a combination of such requirements.[16]

Today, admission to practice in a state generally entails three requirements: (1) completion of the curriculum at a law school approved by the ABA; (2) passing a bar examination; and (3) meeting a requirement of "good character." Until invention of the bar examination in the latter half of the 19th century, admission required satisfying a judge that the applicant was conversant with the law, providing proof of good character and, in some states, fulfilling an apprenticeship requirement. As noted in the historical sketch, the apprenticeship system yielded uneven products under the best of circumstances. "Good character" was often interpreted to mean acceptability to the local establishment in the bench and bar. The requirement that the applicant demonstrate knowledge of the law could mean almost anything. One 19th century lawyer, who later was a member of the California Supreme Court, recalled that in 1836 the judge administered his rite of passage by "asking not a single legal question."[17] The modern admissions process may leave much to be desired, but it displaced a system that was uneven, frequently indifferent to any matters of qualification and often discriminatory against newcomers in society.

Accredited Law Schools [18]

Three national organizations participate in setting standards and procedures that govern law schools. The ABA, acting through its Section of Legal Education and Admissions to the Bar, has promulgated standards for "approved law schools" and applies these standards through extensive scrutiny of new schools and sabbatical inspections (once every seven years) of previously approved law schools. The ABA is recognized by the U.S. Department of Education as the only accreditation agency for degrees in law.

---

16. See C. Wolfram, Modern Legal Ethics §§ 15.2 et seq. (1986).

17. Joseph G. Baldwin, The Flush Times of Alabama and Mississippi: A Series of Sketches (1858; 1957 ed.).

18. Comprehensive data on law schools, law school enrollments and bar admissions requirements are published annually by the ABA Section of Legal Education and Admissions to the Bar (entitled "A Review of Legal Education in the United States, Law Schools and Bar Admissions Requirements). Bar admission requirements are compiled in an annual publication of the ABA section and the National Conference of Bar Examiners (NCBE) (entitled "Comprehensive Guide to Bar Admission Requirements").

The Association of American Law Schools (AALS) has as its purpose "the improvement of the legal profession through legal education." [19] The AALS is an association of law schools; of the 176 ABA-approved J.D.-granting law schools, 158 are AALS members. The AALS participates in ABA inspection of those law schools that are AALS members and applies membership standards through an accreditation committee. The AALS annual meeting in the first week of January features a large array of scholarly programs and other activities of interest to law teachers, librarians and administrators. The AALS also provides a faculty recruitment service to assist law schools and those desiring to enter law teaching. The AALS also publishes the *Journal of Legal Education* and carries on many other activities.

The Law School Admission Council (LSAC) participates in selecting individuals for law practice through its administration of the Law School Admission Test (LSAT). An ABA standard provides that approved law schools require applicants to submit an LSAT score (with some limited exceptions).

Accreditation by the ABA requires maintenance of specified standards as to curriculum, law library, classroom facilities and faculty. Compliance is enforced by periodic inspections and by the sanction of withdrawal of accreditation. The standards permit a substantial range in faculty-student ratio (but no more than 30 students per full-time faculty member), pedagogical procedure (e.g., "lecture" versus "Socratic method"), clinical instruction, training in legal writing and research, subject matter of courses and relative balance between theory and "nuts and bolts." [20]

According to the rules in every state, accreditation of a law school by the ABA constitutes accreditation for purposes of fulfilling that state's requirement of graduation from an approved law school. A few states such as California separately accredit law schools, so that a law school may be accredited for purposes of admission by a state such as California but not for purposes of admission in other states. A handful of states still permit completion of study in a law office instead of completion of law school. However, this alternative, essentially an apprenticeship, pursued by Justice Robert Jackson (Supreme Court of the United States, 1941 to 1954) and a good many others in his generation, is pursued by few people today. As a practical matter, graduation from an accredited law school is a requirement for admission to the bar.

19. See generally Robert B. Stevens, Law School: Legal Education in America from the 1850s to the 1980s (1983); AALS, Report of the AALS Long Range Planning Committee—May 1989.

20. See Symposium, The Regulation of Legal Education, 32 J. Legal Educ. 159–271 (1982); Barry B. Boyer and Roger C. Cramton, American Legal Education: An Agenda for Research and Reform, 59 Cornell L.Rev. 221 (1974); Note, ABA Approval of Law Schools, 72 Mich.L.Rev. 1134 (1974); and James P. White, Legal Education in the Era of Change: Law School Autonomy, 1987 Duke L.J. 292.

Bar Examination

With very limited exceptions, a second requirement for admission to practice is passing the bar examination. One or two states recognize a "diploma privilege" under which graduation from a law school in the state fulfills the requirement of legal knowledge.

The legitimacy of the bar examination has often been disputed but remains generally accepted. It is acknowledged that the examination tests only part of the skills required to be a lawyer, and may test those skills imperfectly. However, the bar examination produces documentary evidence that can be reviewed without revealing the applicant's identity and compared with the performance of other applicants. The alternatives are an interview system, in which personal identity would be important, or an apprenticeship system, in which personal identity and family connections would heavily influence selection for the limited number of places, or no qualifications test at all. In modern times the latter has been considered unacceptable.

State bar examinations have encountered two sometimes related legal challenges: One was that the grading of essays was subjective and therefore arbitrary and therefore required judicial review; the other was that the bar examination results were systematically adverse to blacks, Hispanics and other racial minorities.[21] The courts have uniformly rejected these challenges, once satisfied that examinations have been graded anonymously and conducted by a structured procedure. Charges of subjectivity in grading, even where grading is "blind," have been answered by giving an applicant who fails the right to repeat the examination. The theory is that any subjectivity is unlikely as a statistical matter to repeat itself against the same applicant. In Lucero v. Ogden,[22] for example, where an applicant challenged the Colorado bar examination, the court stated:

> Although the plaintiff asks for "an adversary hearing, an unbiased judge or hearing examiner, the opportunity to argue the facts and cross examine the other party, and the right to present evidence", ... there is nothing to indicate that any of these procedures would be any more effective in detecting grading errors than the absolute right to retake the examination.[23]

Poats v. Givan[24] sustained an Indiana rule limiting an applicant to four attempts to pass the bar examination.

---

21. Claims that the general "fail" rate on the bar examination had been raised in order to restrain competitive entry into the profession arose in the 1930s and again in California in the 1950s and in Arizona in the 1970s. See Hoover v. Ronwin, 466 U.S. 558 (1984) (denied applicant alleged that Arizona's bar admissions committee had reduced the pass rate to restrain competition; complaint did not state a violation of federal antitrust law because of "state action" exemption).

22. 718 F.2d 355 (10th Cir.1983).

23. 718 F.2d at 358.

24. 651 F.2d 495 (7th Cir.1981).

The problem of disparate impact of the bar examination on blacks and Hispanics has been raised in a number of states, including California, New York and Pennsylvania. The most systematic challenge appears to have been that litigated in Delgado v. McTighe,[25] involving the Pennsylvania bar examination. The court's extensive opinion recited earlier investigations of the Pennsylvania bar examination and the procedures for administering the examination in the years 1972–1976.

The Pennsylvania examination, like that in many other states, included one day of multiple-choice questions (the Multistate Bar Examination) and one day of essay questions formulated and graded by the state's bar examiners. The court found that the essay questions were graded "blind," that errors in grammar and spelling were not counted negatively and that the examiners had established adequate procedures for reviewing initial grades. The court placed heavy reliance on an outside study commissioned by the Pennsylvania Board of Bar Examiners, based on the 1972 examination. The study found that the lower pass rate for black candidates would have occurred at whatever combination of scores on the Multistate and essay portions were designated as a passing score. "[A]s groups, the blacks and whites had different distribution of scores on both [portions of the examination]." Because the distribution of white scores was higher than that of blacks, "[n]o matter where the passing point is set, except at the very bottom, more blacks than whites will be failed." The court noted:

> The remedy for this situation is beyond the scope of the present inquiry. It seems clear, however, that further improvement in the Bar examination itself, through further increasing the reliability and the validity of the test, will not change the situation.[26]

The court in *Delgado* found that the disproportionate failure rate was not due to purposeful discrimination or to any invidious standards or grading procedures. *Delgado* appears to be the last court challenge to bar examinations on the ground of discriminatory impact. The constitutional legitimacy of the current type of bar examination thus seems beyond serious legal challenge.

Character and Fitness

In addition to meeting educational requirements and passing a written bar examination, admission to the bar requires fulfillment of a "character and fitness" requirement.[27] Traditionally, proof was supplied through affidavits from people personally acquainted with the applicant, a mechanism still used. Although "character and fitness" are meaningful standards in extreme cases (e.g., prior convictions for

---

25. 522 F.Supp. 886 (E.D.Pa.1981).

26. 522 F.Supp. at 893–894.

27. See generally Deborah L. Rhode, Moral Character as a Professional Credential, 94 Yale L.J. 491 (1985).

embezzling money or mental incompetency), the terms are indeterminate and vague in other contexts. At some places and times, examiners
may have applied the standards to assure that only individuals of
proven upright character would be admitted. It was unclear how
someone, especially a young person, who had not yet undergone the
strain of practice could show the capacity to handle such strain, but to
character committees "good background" was always propitious. In
the late 19th century, the requirement was sometimes employed to
screen out applications by blacks and women; during the first decades
of the 20th century, at least in some localities, the requirement effectively was employed to deter applications by Jews and those of immigrant origin.

From time to time the character and fitness requirement also has
provided a basis for inquiring into an applicant's political beliefs,
particularly Communism during the period from 1947 to 1970. Many
serious people thought such inquiry within limits made sense, on the
ground that it would be difficult to be "an officer of the court" if one
believed that law was inherently oppressive. Other serious people
thought that there was no correlation between political radicalism,
including membership in the Communist Party, and predisposition to
violate standards of professional conduct. Moreover, some believed
that excluding political radicals from law practice would change the
pool of lawyers available to take various types of cases, particularly
cases involving political radicals. That in turn would also change the
kinds of causes and arguments that would be taken to the courts. At
all events, inquiries into radical political beliefs were often administered with high anxiety and were resisted on constitutional grounds.

The confrontation of views resulted in a series of decisions by a
closely divided Supreme Court that have imposed some restraints on
the subject matter and procedure of inquiries into political beliefs and
associations. Schware v. Board of Bar Examiners of New Mexico [28]
involved an applicant who was denied admission because of prior
membership in the Communist Party and related activities, including
participation in the 1930s in shipyard strikes that became embittered
and violent; numerous arrests; use of aliases; and recruiting volunteers for the anti-Franco forces in the Spanish Civil War. Schware quit
the Communist Party in 1940, served honorably in the Army and
entered the state university law school in 1950, graduating in 1953. In
support of his application he offered testimony of his rabbi, his attorney
and the faculty, fellow students and staff at the law school. No
witnesses contradicted this testimony of current good character. The
bar committee nevertheless denied him admission: "Taking into consideration the use of aliases by the applicant, his former connection with
subversive organizations, and his record of arrests, he has failed to
satisfy the Board as to the requisite moral character." The U.S.
Supreme Court reversed the state court's denial of admission, saying:

28. 353 U.S. 232 (1957).

Any qualification must have a rational connection with the applicant's fitness or capacity to practice law.... There is nothing in the record which suggests that Schware has engaged in any conduct during the past 15 years which reflects adversely on his character.... During the period when Schware was a member, the Communist Party was a lawful political party.... Assuming that some members of the Communist Party during the period from 1932 to 1940 had illegal aims and engaged in illegal activities, it cannot automatically be inferred that all members shared their evil purposes or participated in their illegal conduct.... There is no evidence in the record which rationally justifies a finding that Schware was morally unfit to practice law.[29]

The "rational connection" rule remains the law.

A more difficult issue was the constitutionality of questioning that sought to establish a connection between membership in the Communist Party and fitness to practice law. This issue first arose in Konigsberg v. State Bar of California (*Konigsberg I*),[30] decided the same day as *Schware*. In the hearing on his application for admission, Konigsberg presented favorable character evidence by law teachers, friends, a rabbi and a monsignor. He was asked whether he had been a member of the Communist Party, but refused to answer on First Amendment grounds. The Bar Examiners declined to approve his application, grounding their decision on Konigsberg's failure affirmatively to establish his good character as distinct from his refusal to answer questions about his Party membership. The Supreme Court in a 5–4 decision reversed the denial of his application:

Serious questions of elemental fairness would be raised if the Committee had excluded Konigsberg simply because he failed to answer questions without first explicitly warning him that he could be barred for this reason alone....

If ... the Board had barred Konigsberg solely because of his refusal to respond to its inquiries into his political associations and his opinions about matters of public interest, then we would be compelled to decide far-reaching and complex questions relating to freedom of speech, press and assembly.[31]

The Court's opinion interweaves inquiries into three questions: (1) the burden of proof—whether Konigsberg had to show that there was no substantial doubt as to his character or the bar examiners had to show there was such doubt; (2) the constitutional propriety of the bar examiners asking about Konigsberg's membership in the Communist Party; and (3) the significance of such membership as proof of deficient moral character.

29. 353 U.S. at 239, 244, 246–47.
30. 353 U.S. 252 (1957).
31. 353 U.S. at 261.

These questions could have been asked in this order: (1) Is present membership in the Communist Party, as of the early 1950s, evidence of deficient moral character? (2) Assuming present membership is such evidence, can the bar examiners ask the applicant whether he presently holds such membership? (3) If the applicant is asked the question and refuses to answer, has he failed to carry his burden of proof?

Resolution of the second and third questions seems not very difficult if the first question is resolved affirmatively—that membership in the Communist Party in the 1950s was probative of indifference to a lawyer's professional obligations. The argument for this affirmative was as follows: The Communist Party was committed to violent overthrow of capitalist regimes; membership in the Party constituted an affirmation of that commitment; and a person making that affirmation probably could not be relied on to represent clients "within the limits of the law." However, opposing considerations were weighty: First, it does not follow that membership in an organization involves affirmation of all of the organization's purposes, nor does it follow that affirmation of a general political purpose (to overthrow capitalist regimes) signifies indifference to immediate legal obligations imposed by such a regime. Second, even if membership in the Communist Party is probative of a predisposition to ignore a lawyer's professional obligations, the fact of membership is constitutionally privileged information of group or associational activity that the government cannot inquire into without violating the First Amendment.[32] That is, the bar examiners could no more ask an applicant to disclose membership in organizations than they could require him to incriminate himself.[33] Third, disclosure of membership in the Communist Party, even if it did not preclude admission to the bar, could have disastrous effect on the applicant's professional career, a consideration not to be ignored.

The Court in *Konigsberg I* did not address these issues, but Justice Harlan in dissent said:

> The Court decides the case as if the issue were whether the record contains evidence demonstrating as a factual matter that Konigsberg had a bad moral character. I do not think that is the issue. The question before us ... is whether it violates the Fourteenth Amendment for a state bar committee to decline to certify ... an applicant who ... [refuses] to answer questions relevant to his fitness under valid standards, and who is therefore deemed ... to have failed to carry his burden of proof to establish that he is qualified.[34]

On remand, the California bar examiners asked Konigsberg whether he was presently a member of the Communist Party, indicating clearly that refusal to answer would be regarded as obstruction of

32. Cf. NAACP v. Alabama, 357 U.S. 449 (1958).

33. See Matter of Anonymous Attorneys v. Bar Association, 41 N.Y.2d 506, 393 N.Y.S.2d 961, 362 N.E.2d 592 (1977), p. 888 below.

34. 353 U.S. at 279–280.

necessary inquiry into his fitness to practice law. Konigsberg refused to answer on the ground that the question was impermissible under the First Amendment. The Supreme Court by 5–4 vote affirmed the bar's denial of his admission (*Konigsberg II*).[35] In an opinion by Justice Harlan, the Court held that the question of Communist Party membership was legitimate even if its being asked might have some chilling effect on speech:

> General regulatory statutes, not intended to control the content of speech but incidentally limiting its unfettered exercise, have not been regarded as the type of law the First or Fourteenth Amendment forbade Congress or the States to pass, when they have been found justified by subordinating valid governmental interests, a prerequisite to constitutionality which has necessarily involved a weighing of the governmental interest involved....

> It would indeed be difficult to argue that a belief, firm enough to be carried over into advocacy, in the use of illegal means to change the form of the State or Federal Government is an unimportant consideration in determining the fitness of applicants for membership in a profession in whose hands so largely lies the safekeeping of this country's legal and political institutions.[36]

A case involving essentially the same issue, decided the same day as *Konigsberg II* by the same 5–4 vote, was In re Anastaplo.[37] Justice Harlan there stated for the Court:

> Where, as with membership in the bar, the State may withhold a privilege available only to those possessing the requisite qualifications, it is of no constitutional significance whether the State's interrogation of an applicant on matters relevant to these qualifications—in this case Communist Party membership—is prompted by information which it already has about him from other sources, or arises merely from a good faith belief in the need for exploratory or testing questioning of the applicant.[38]

Justice Black, along with Chief Justice Warren and Justices Douglas and Brennan, bitterly dissented in both cases, stating in *Anastaplo*:

> Consider ... the following remarks of Anastaplo to the Committee—remarks the sincerity of which the majority does not deny:

>> "I speak of a need to remind the bar of its traditions and to keep alive the spirit of dignified but determined advocacy and opposition. This is not only for the good of the bar, of course, but also because of what the bar means to American republican government. The bar when it exercises self-control is in a peculiar position to mediate between popular passions and informed and principled men, thereby upholding republican

35. Konigsberg v. State Bar of California, 366 U.S. 36 (1961).

36. 366 U.S. at 50–52.

37. 366 U.S. 82 (1961).

38. 366 U.S. at 90.

government. Unless there is this mediation, intelligent and responsible government is unlikely. The bar, furthermore, is in a peculiar position to apply to our daily lives the constitutional principles which nourish for this country its inner life. Unless there is this nourishment, a just and humane people is impossible. The bar is, in short, in a position to train and lead by precept and example the American people."

These are not the words of a man who lacks devotion to "the law in its broadest sense."

... If I had ever doubted that the "balancing test" comes close to being a doctrine of governmental absolutism—that to "balance" an interest in individual liberty means almost inevitably to destroy that liberty—those doubts would have been dissipated by this case. For this so-called "balancing test" ... here proves pitifully and pathetically inadequate to cope with an invasion of individual liberty so plainly unjustified that even the majority apparently feels compelled expressly to disclaim "any view upon the wisdom of the State's action." [39]

The issue came up for reconsideration in a set of three cases in 1971: *Baird, Stolar,* and *Wadmond.*[40] All three cases were decided 5–4, with Justice Stewart being the decisive vote. In *Wadmond* the Court upheld a New York character and fitness inquiry into whether the applicant was a "knowing member" of an organization advocating violent overthrow of government. Stewart's opinion stated:

It is ... well settled that Bar examiners may ask about Communist affiliations as a preliminary to further inquiry into the nature of the association and may exclude an applicant for refusal to answer.[41]

The relationship between organizational membership and fitness to practice law remains complicated today. Consider, for example, whether it would be proper for the bar examiners to inquire into, or to attach significance to, membership in an anti-abortion organization that publicly professes "direct action" against abortion clinics.

No subsequent Supreme Court decisions have considered the "rational connection" standard in character and fitness determinations. State courts, however, have considered such questions as homosexuality[42] and psychological abnormalities.[43] Clearly proper subjects of inquiry include previous criminal convictions, financial dealings that have been legally questioned and involvement in litigation.

---

39. 366 U.S. at 110–111 (Black, J., dissenting).

40. Baird v. State Bar of Arizona, 401 U.S. 1 (1971); In re Stolar, 401 U.S. 23 (1971); and Law Students Civil Rights Research Council, Inc. v. Wadmond, 401 U.S. 154 (1971).

41. 401 U.S. at 165–166.

42. Florida Board of Bar Examiners Re N.R.S., 403 So.2d 1315 (Fla.1981) (impermissible to inquire into sexual preference).

43. In re Florida Board of Bar Examiners, 443 So.2d 77 (Fla.1983) (inquiry proper).

Professor Deborah Rhode has made a comprehensive empirical study that documents the character and fitness inquiry in operation. The following matters are considered significant but not decisive and hence a basis for more intensive inquiry: criminal record, drug or alcohol abuse, repeated traffic offenses, dishonesty in business transactions, plagiarism and other cheating in school, unauthorized practice of law, psychiatric treatment and nondisclosure or false statements on the bar admission questionnaire.[44] These would all seem to comport with the "rational connection" standard. Professor Rhode's findings suggest that the character and fitness inquiry is invoked fairly rarely, but with exasperating detail and troublesome policy implications in a number of cases. The inquiry into character for admission to practice is far more rigorous than the standards used for disciplining those already inside the bar.[45] Should it be?

2. Women, Blacks and Other Minorities in the Profession

Women

The history of women in the legal profession through the 19th century is essentially a story of frustration and exclusion.[46] The socio-legal attitude sustaining exclusion was stated in the high Victorian age by Justice Bradley, concurring in Bradwell v. State.[47] That decision affirmed denial of admission to the Illinois bar of Myra Bradwell, who surely was better qualified than most of her contemporaries. Justice Bradley said:

[T]he civil law, as well as nature herself, has always recognized a wide difference in the respective spheres and destinies of man and woman.... The natural and proper timidity and delicacy which belongs to the female sex evidently unfits it for many of the occupations of civil life. The constitution of the family organization, which is founded in the divine ordinance, as well as in the nature of things, indicates the domestic sphere as that which properly belongs to the domain and functions of womanhood.... So firmly fixed was this sentiment in the founders of the common law that it became a maxim of that system of jurisprudence that a woman had no legal existence separate from her husband, who was regarded as her head and representative in the social state; and, notwithstanding some recent modifications of this civil status, many of the special rules of law flowing from and dependent upon this cardinal principle still exist in full force in most States.... This very incapacity was one circumstance which the Supreme

44. See Deborah L. Rhode, Moral Character as a Professional Credential, 94 Yale L.J. 491, 533–36 (1985).

45. Id. at 546.

46. The story is recounted in Karen B. Morello, The Invisible Bar: The Woman Lawyer in America, 1638 to the Present (1986).

47. 83 U.S. (16 Wall.) 130 (1873).

Court of Illinois deemed important in rendering a married woman incompetent fully to perform the duties and trusts that belong to the office of an attorney and counsellor.[48]

The available data indicate that the number of women lawyers rose from less than a dozen in 1870 to about 1,000 in 1910 but was still less than 10,000 by 1960, when women were about 3 percent of law students.[49] The increase in numbers whereby women have become a significant proportion of the profession has occurred since the 1960s. From 1973 to 1983, the size of the profession doubled; the number of women lawyers increased seven-fold.[50] As of 1991 about 22 percent of American lawyers were women.[51]

A 1985 ABF study[52] provides a breakdown of employment data indicating that a higher fraction of women than of men have law jobs in government (other than the judiciary) and in legal education and that the fraction in private law firms is lower for women than men. Within private firm settings, women are somewhat more heavily concentrated in sole practice and in very large firms (51 lawyers and more). Correlatively, women are disproportionately fewer in small and middle-sized firms. This pattern may reflect that engaging in sole practice does not depend so much on others, and that big firms tend to be more self-conscious about their hiring practices. Solo practice may allow greater control over one's life or constitute the residual form of professional employment when other possibilities are unsatisfactory or both. Judge Judith Kaye states that large law firms "are in fact a superb example of our halting progress toward general equality in the workforce. The big firms cast a giant shadow, in terms of public perceptions of the profession, parallels in other fields, and standards within the legal community."[53]

Annual surveys conducted by the National Law Journal indicate that women and minority lawyers are making slow but measurable

48. 83 U.S. (16 Wall.) at 141 (Bradley, J., concurring).

49. For an analysis of long-term demographic trends in the legal profession, giving special attention to gender, see Terence Halliday, Six Score Years and Ten: Demographic Transitions in the American Legal Profession, 1950–1980, 20 Law & Soc'y Review 53 (1986).

50. Donna Fossum, Women in the Law: A Reflection on Portia, 69 A.B.A.J. 1389 (1983).

51. ABA Section of Legal Education and Admissions to the Bar, Task Force Report on Law Schools and the Profession, Legal Education and Professional Development—An Educational Continuum 18–22 (1992). The proportion of women among the law school population rose from 3 percent in 1960 to 9 percent in 1970 to 34 percent in 1980 to 42 percent in 1992. As women have entered the profession in larger numbers, the proportion of women in the total lawyer population has grown from 2 percent in 1950 to 22 percent in 1991. Women lawyers, as a group, were substantially younger than men: In 1988 the median age for women lawyers was 34 and the median age for men lawyers 42.

52. Barbara A. Curran et al., Supplement to the Lawyer Statistical Report: The U.S. Legal Profession in 1985, Am.Bar Foundation (1986).

53. Judith S. Kaye, Women Lawyers in Big Firms: A Study in Progress Toward Gender Equality, 57 Fordham L.Rev. 111, 113 (1988).

gains in the nation's largest law firms.[54] The 1991 survey of the 250 largest firms found that women made up 26.3 percent of all lawyers and minorities 4.9 percent. Partners, however, remained overwhelmingly white and male. Women increased their share of partnerships to 11 percent from 9 percent in 1989; minorities claimed 2.4 percent of partnerships, up from 1.9 percent in 1989.[55] White males suffered the bulk of recession cutbacks in these firms, which cut the total number of associates by nearly 1,700 (4.4 percent) from 1989 to 1991.

The number of women on law school faculties in tenured or tenure-track position increased by about 50 percent in the six years between 1980 and 1986, from 10.8 percent of all teachers to 15.9 percent.[56] In evaluating this increase several caveats are in order. According to Professor Richard Chused, "[a]bout one-fifth of the reporting law schools currently maintain faculties in which the proportion of women remains below the national average of six years ago. The 'high prestige' institutions are heavily represented among these laggard institutions. Legal writing, moreover, may be on its way to becoming a 'woman's job'." [57] Anecdotal and other evidence indicates that women have experienced difficulties in receiving tenure.[58] Chused's study showed that although tenure and departure rates "were almost identical for men and women," women gain tenure more frequently in schools that already have a larger number of tenured women faculty members. The presence of tenured women faculty member may result in "mentoring" relationships, provide a bloc of supporters or change the perceptions of male faculty members.[59] The presence of senior women and the number of such women in firms and other practice settings may similarly affect the career progression of junior women and undoubtedly has an effect on how sensitive others in the workplace are to sexist attitudes and practices.[60]

54. The data in this paragraph are from Progress Glacial for Women, Minorities, Nat'l L.J., Jan. 27, 1991, at p. 1.

55. Forty-four firms had no minority partners; 61 more had only one minority partner. Only one of the large firms had no women partners. Firms in San Francisco had the highest percentage of both women and minority partners.

56. Richard H. Chused, The Hiring and Retention of Minorities and Women on American Law School Faculties, 137 U.Pa.L.Rev. 537, 548 (1988) (study sponsored by the Society of American Law Teachers (SALT); faculty members at 149 schools, over 85 percent of those American Association of Law School (AALS) member institutions, returned survey questionnaires).

57. Id.

58. See, e.g., Marina Angel, Women in Legal Education: What It's Like to be Part of a Perpetual First Wave or the Case of the Disappearing Women, 61 Temp.L.Q. 799 (1988); Women Face Hurdles as Professors, Nat'l L.J., Oct. 24, 1988, at p. 1; and Richard H. Chused, Faculty Parenthood: Law School Treatment of Pregnancy and Child Care, 35 J.Legal Educ. 568, 584 (1985).

59. Id. at 550–52.

60. On women in legal academia, see Carrie J. Menkel–Meadow, Women as Law Teachers: Toward the Feminization of Legal Education, in Essays on the Application of a Humanistic Perspective to Law Teaching (1981); Symposium on Women in Legal Education, 38 J. Legal Educ. 1–194 (1988).

Gender bias in the courtroom against women lawyers and women litigants has received attention by state court judges and state, local and women bar associations.[61]   In 1984, New Jersey became the first state to issue a report on gender bias in the courts.   Many other states have since undertaken studies of the problem.   New York issued a report in 1986 which concluded that "gender bias," defined as "[d]ecisions made or actions taken because of weight given to preconceived notions of sexual roles rather than upon a fair and unswayed appraisal of merit as to each person or situation," is "pervasive."   It operates against not only women lawyers but women litigants and court personnel.   "[P]roblems are perpetuated by some attorneys' and judges' misinformed belief that complaints by women are contrivances of overwrought imaginations and hypersensitivities.   More was found ... than bruised feelings resulting from rude and callous behavior.   Real hardships are borne by women."   Is suffering callous behavior not a real hardship?   What audience is addressed by such terms as "bruised feelings?"   Is this characterization itself a problem or merely a response to political realities?

As shown in the New York report, women litigants are accorded less credibility because of their gender and face a judiciary poorly informed and in many cases misinformed about matters integral to the welfare of women.   As to women lawyers, the study found that they must brave a "verbal and psychological obstacle course" in the courtroom.   Examples of overt sexism include: being ordered not to use Ms. and to use her husband's last name, not her own, under threat of "sleep[ing] in the county jail tonight;" [62] being told by a judge "I don't think ladies should be lawyers" and being asked what "her husband thought of her working here;" [63] and being referred to as "lawyerette" and "attorney generalette." [64]

---

61.   Generally see Note, Gender Bias in the Judicial System, 61 So.Calif.L.Rev. 2193 (1988).   In 1980 the NOW Legal Defense Fund in cooperation with the National Association of Women Judges created the National Judicial Education Program to Promote Equality for Women and Men in the Courts.

62.   See N.Y. Times, July 14, 1988, at p. A23 (comments made by United States District Court Judge Teitelbaum to attorney Barbara Wolvowitz who was trying a race discrimination case in federal court).

63.   Nancy Blodgett, I Don't Think that Ladies Should be Lawyers, 72 A.B.A.J. 48 (1986) (reporting comments made by a Illinois state court judge to a woman lawyer from Mayer, Brown & Platt of Chicago in 1986).

64.   Complaint Concerning the Honorable John J. Kirby, 354 N.W.2d 410 (Minn.1984) (censuring state court judge for these remarks).

DEBORAH L. RHODE
"PERSPECTIVES ON PROFESSIONAL WOMEN"
40 Stan.L.Rev. 1163 (1988).[65]

In a variety of studies, female students have also expressed lower expectations for occupational success than males and have attached greater priority to relational aspects of employment such as opportunities for helping others than to opportunities for money, status and power. Family and peer pressure can also skew vocational choices and discourage career decisions that would compete with domestic responsibilities, require geographic mobility, or bring wives greater prestige and income than their husbands. Such pressures can be particularly intense within certain class, race, and ethnic groups.

Disparities between traits associated with femininity and traits associated with vocational achievement further reinforce these gender socialization processes. A wide array of experiential and clinical evidence indicates that profiles of successful professionals conflict with profiles of normal or ideal women. The aggressiveness, competitiveness, dedication, and emotional detachment traditionally presumed necessary for advancement in the most prestigious and well-paid occupations are incompatible with traits commonly viewed as attractive in women: cooperativeness, deference, sensitivity, and self-sacrifice. Despite substantial progress toward gender equality over the last several decades, these gender stereotypes remain remarkably resilient. Females aspiring to nontraditional or high-status positions remain subject to a familiar double bind. Those conforming to traditional characteristics of femininity are often thought lacking in the requisite assertiveness and initiative, yet those conforming to a masculine model of success may be ostracized in work settings as bitchy, aggressive, and uncooperative. As long as aspiring women are found wanting either as professionals or as women, they face substantial disincentives to aspire. . . .

Of particular significance are the sexes' different priorities concerning family responsibilities. Although cultural commitments to equal opportunity in vocational spheres have steadily increased, these sentiments have not translated into equal obligations in domestic spheres. Most studies have indicated that women still perform about 70 percent of the family tasks in an average household. Employed wives spend about twice as much time on homemaking demands as employed husbands; men married to women with full-time jobs devote only 1.4 hours a week more to domestic duties than other husbands. When time spent in paid labor and domestic labor is combined, employed males average two hours less per day than employed females, and a disproportionate amount of male homemaking contributions involve relatively enjoyable activities such as playing with the children. . . . Women, particularly social and ethnic minorities, are also

65. Copyright © 1988 by the Board of Trustees of the Leland Stanford Junior University. Reprinted with permission.

far more likely to become single parents, with all the associated demands. In the late 1980s, females headed 90 percent of the nation's single-parent households, and women of color were disproportionately likely to have such responsibilities....

Not only do women bear the vast majority of family obligations, they do so in occupational environments designed by and for men. As a result, career success has often meant compromise of caretaking values.

Female employees unwilling to make that sacrifice have paid a demanding professional price....

... [E]lite professionals also tend to impose longer and more unpredictable working hours, and are particularly resistant to extended leaves, part-time or flexible-time shifts, and home work. That resistance springs from a variety of sources. Many clients and colleagues object to the inconveniences and the apparent lack of commitment among employees working nonconventional hours....

Extended hours, unpredictable schedules, and frequent travel mesh poorly with childrearing responsibilities. Yet for women "on the road to success," no detours from standard workplace obligations are advisable....

The self, it appears, should conform to a male model with a vengeance....

Unconscious gender bias can operate on three levels: (1) prototypes, the images associated with members of a particular occupation; (2) schema, the personal characteristics and situational factors that are used to explain conduct; and (3) scripts, definitions of appropriate behavior in a given situation. Thus, when a female applicant for a given position (e.g., litigator) does not fit the evaluator's prototype (e.g., aggressive male), her credentials will be judged with greater skepticism. Many explanatory schema embody similar stereotypes: Men's success is more likely to be explained in terms of ability and their failure in terms of luck, while women's achievement is more often attributed to luck or effort and their failures ascribed to inability. Since evaluations of ability are most crucial in hiring and promotion decisions, these attribution biases entrench gender hierarchies. So too, the scripts defining appropriate social behavior often reflect patterns of gender dominance, deference, and accommodation. For example, in group conversation, male participants tend to speak and interrupt more often, and to hold the floor for longer periods than females. Women are expected not only to talk less but also to allow more interruptions, and those who deviate from their accustomed role provoke negative evaluations. Once again, these perceptual prejudices create a double bind: Women who conform to accepted stereotypes will appear to have less to contribute and less leadership potential than the male colleagues, while women who take a more assertive stance risk appearing arrogant, aggressive, and abrasive. How to seem "demure but tough" is particularly difficult when standards vary among those whose opinions are most critical. In male-dominated cultures, women are subject to criticism for being "too feminine" and not "feminine enough."

Unconscious gender prejudices affect not only the evaluation of individual performance, they also affect the performance itself. As both experimental and longitudinal studies have repeatedly demonstrated, low expectations of achievement frequently become self-fulfilling prophecies. Individuals often signal their assumptions in subtle or not so subtle ways. These forms of negative feedback, including lower salaries and less demanding assignments, can adversely affect self-confidence and job performance. Such consequences then reinforce the initial expectations, and a self-perpetuating cycle continues....

Effect of Women on Professional Norms

The problems encountered by women lawyers and the responses to these problems are mirrored in the experience of women in other fields, such as medicine and college teaching.[66] Women in the professions and women in academia have changed the focus in many substantive legal areas, in some areas have changed what is considered worthy of debate in law and have challenged the ground rules of traditional legal debate itself.[67] A large literature by and about women in the profession is now available, ranging from statistical demographics to narratives recounting personal experience.[68]

Women's situation in the contemporary legal profession has greatly enlarged the matters considered relevant to lawyers' social roles and personal psychology, not only for women but for men as well. Among women and among men, as well as between women and men, there is a great deal of variance concerning "prototypes," "schema" and "scripts."

66. See Penina Glazer and Miriam Slater, Unequal Colleagues: The Entrance of Women into the Professions (1987).

67. See, e.g., Judith Resnik, On the Bias: Feminist Reconsiderations of the Aspirations for our Judges, 61 So.Calif.L.Rev. 1877 (1988); Martha L. Minow, Foreword: Justice Engendered, 101 Harv.L.Rev. 10 (1987); Susan R. Estrich, Rape, 95 Yale L.J. 1087 (1986); Lucinda M. Finley, Transcending Equality Theory: A Way Out of the Maternity and the Workplace Debate, 86 Colum.L.Rev. 1118 (1986); Sylvia Ann Law, Rethinking Sex and the Constitution, 132 U.Pa.L.Rev. 955 (1984); Martha L. Minow, "Forming Underneath Everything that Grows:" Toward a History of Family Law, 1985 Wis.L.Rev. 819; Frances Olsen, Statutory Rape: A Feminist Critique of Rights Analysis, 63 Tex.L.Rev. 387 (1984); Catherine A. MacKinnon, Sexual Harassment of Working Women: A Case of Sex Discrimination (1979). Generally see Carrie J. Menkel–Meadow, Excluded Voices: New Voices in the Legal Profession Making New Voices in the Law, 42 U.Miami L.Rev. 29 (1987); Ann C. Scales, The Emergence of Feminist Jurisprudence: An Essay, 95 Yale L.J. 1373 (1986); and Rand Jack and Dana C. Jack, Moral Vision and Professional Decisions: The Changing Values of Women and Men Lawyers (1989).

68. For a comprehensive bibliography, see Anthony P. Grech and Daniel J. Jacobs, Women and the Legal Profession: A Bibliography of Current Literature, 44 The Record 215 (March 1989), covering the following subheadings: General, Bar Association Participation, Biographies, History, Networking, Part–Time Lawyering, Rise to Partnership, Studies and Reports, Surveys and Statistics, Women in the Study of Law, Women Judges.

Any universal description of lawyers of either gender unavoidably approaches a stereotype. Many men, even among those who have become lawyers, give a larger priority to their families than to their careers. For example, one of the attractions of certain staff legal jobs—areas of the profession in which women are somewhat overrepresented—is that they do not involve irregular hours, unpredictable schedules and heavy travel and allow more time for nonprofessional life. So also many men are much more concerned with maintenance of group cohesion than fully articulating differences of opinion. Men so inclined may be better "deal makers" and law firm managing partners than "hired gun" types. Despite the stereotype of aggressive talkativeness, many male lawyers are actually good listeners.

With respect to women lawyers, many are intensely interested in legal and philosophical ideas, are attracted to the excitement of competitive interaction and are uninterested in most or all aspects of domestic life and nurturing children. These differences among women appear to have more fully emerged in the discussions about women in the legal profession than have the corresponding differences among men. The relative silence of and about men in this respect is partly the product of male prototypes, schema and scripts. Males from an early age, we are told, learn to talk less about matters of feeling and identity. When they do talk about such matters, many males tend to speak indirectly, facetiously and in cliches, punctuated by occasional outbursts of feeling from the depths. However, male lawyers would resist being described as coy or emotional.

Do these generalizations about variation in characteristics within each gender make any sense? Which of the authors of this book do you think had primary responsibility for writing the section you have just read?

———

History of Blacks in Law

The history of blacks in the law essentially parallels that of women, except that the pattern of events since the 1960s has been morally more equivocal and far less encouraging to those who believe in "natural progress" toward human equality in opportunity and life realization. The history of other minorities in the legal profession, particularly Hispanics and Asians, has not been as well-developed.

Geraldine Segal's history is the basic work on blacks in the legal profession.

GERALDINE R. SEGAL
BLACKS IN THE LAW
Pp. 1–7, 16–19, 28–33, 76–77 (1985). [69]

Throughout the first half of the twentieth century, and even beyond, to become a black lawyer in America required an extraordinary measure of courage, determination, and vision. To most blacks it was a goal that seemed to defy social and economic realities. Indeed, at the turn of the century W.E.B. DuBois found that physicians and lawyers together comprised only 1.5 percent of the black population. According to the 1910 United States census, there were then only 798 black lawyers in the country, and by 1940 there were a mere 1,925—one black lawyer for every 13,000 blacks in America.

During those years blacks who did manage to become lawyers found themselves in a profession that was pervaded by racism and fundamentally segregated. Until 1937 there was no black federal judge in the nation, and even then it was a term appointment in the Virgin Islands; until 1949, none on a United States Circuit Court; until 1961, none on a United States District Court; and until 1967, none on the United States Supreme Court. Until 1936, blacks were not admitted to "white" law schools. Until 1943 color had to be stated on applications to the American Bar Association. Until 1946 there was no black teacher on the faculty of predominantly white law schools....

Legal Education

Between 1877 and 1935 Howard [University Law School] was the only substantial source of legal education for blacks in the United States. During this period no black could obtain a legal education in an approved law school anywhere south of Washington, D.C.

During the next twelve years three other currently functioning accredited black law schools, all state institutions and all in the South, came into existence. The first of these was North Carolina Central University Law School in Durham, North Carolina, founded in 1939. The next two, both founded in 1947, were Texas Southern University Law School in Houston, Texas, and Southern University Law School in Baton Rouge, Louisiana. Howard and these three state black law schools have trained the majority of black lawyers in the nation.

Not content with the perpetuation of a situation that limited blacks to black law schools, skilled black advocates instituted suits beginning in the middle 1930s on the reasoning that blacks were entitled to a common education forum with whites if they were to practice the same law. Under the leadership of Charles H. Houston, and later Thurgood Marshall, and under the auspices of the NAACP Legal Defense and Educational Fund, a series of lawsuits were filed to obtain for blacks the right to attend predominantly white southern law schools. When

69. Copyright © 1985 by Geraldine Segal. Published by the University of Pennsylvania Press. Reprinted with permission.

Houston and Marshall took up the fight to enable Donald Murray, a 1934 black graduate of Amherst College, to enter the University of Maryland Law School, legal barriers restricting admission of blacks to white law schools began to fall, but only after persistent and effective advocacy produced court orders mandating this result....

Undoubtedly, the decision of the United States Supreme Court in *Brown v. Board of Education,* handed down in 1954, had some significant impact on the thinking of white law schools....

After this milestone was reached, changes came more rapidly. By the late 1960s most law schools, spurred on by the civil rights legislation and by the argument that minority leaders could benefit the country in numerous ways, had initiated minority recruitment and admissions programs....

Overt policies of racial discrimination in admissions were not the only barriers that potential black law students had to overcome. Many blacks grew up in deprived environments and did not receive in early life the educational opportunities that would allow them to compete in higher education....

Parents deliberately discouraged their children from entering the legal profession. They were skeptical of the black lawyer's ability to obtain justice in the courts; they realized that a large proportion of the black community chose white lawyers to represent them; and they knew that black lawyers frequently had to associate themselves with white lawyers and split fees if they wanted clients.

The discouragement facing potential black lawyers graphically appears in the advice given to Malcolm X when he discussed his career plans with his high school teacher and adviser:

" ... Malcolm, you ought to be thinking about a career. Have you been giving it thought?"

" ... I've been thinking I'd like to be a lawyer."

" ... Malcolm, one of life's first needs is for us to be realistic ... You've got to be realistic about being a nigger. A lawyer— that's no realistic goal for a nigger."

In addition to family opposition, educational handicaps, and humiliating conditions diverting blacks from a career in the law, there was the problem of the high costs of both undergraduate and law school education....

In the mid–1960s a number of philanthropic organizations attempted to spur the interest of blacks in becoming lawyers by making grants to reduce the financial barriers to their entering law school....

That the increased financial aid and remedial programs detailed above were successful to a significant degree is clear from the dramatic increases in black enrollment in law schools all over the country during the late 1960s and early 1970s. In 1965, Harvard Law School estimated that of the approximately 65,000 law students in accredited law schools in the nation, there were no more than 700 black students, or approximately 1 percent. By 1972 the 4,423 black students constituted 4.3 percent of all students attending accredited law schools in the country, and by the 1976–77 school year there were 5,503 black students, or about 4.7 percent of the total, in approved law schools.

In the succeeding three school years, however, black enrollment leveled off instead of continuing in its prior record of steady growth....

Professional Associations

Although blacks have not yet achieved anything near proportional representation in the legal profession, the situation has improved markedly since Brown v. Board of Education (1954). Before that legal turning point, black attorneys were virtually isolated professionally. Opportunities to work with white colleagues or to represent white clients were almost nonexistent. Moreover, many blacks who needed legal representation feared that black lawyers would be unsuccessful against a white lawyer and before a white judge, regardless of the ability or the quality of the performance of the black lawyers. Those blacks who did retain black lawyers were usually too poor to furnish a lucrative practice. Black lawyers were largely confined to petty criminal cases and were rarely given the opportunity to prove their ability in other areas of the law.

In varying degrees this problem of professional segregation has beset black lawyers throughout the century. In 1912, racism within the legal community was so rampant that a storm arose over the "inadvertent" election of the first three black attorneys to the American Bar Association by its Executive Committee. When the Executive Committee discovered that it had unknowingly elected three members "of the colored race," the committee rescinded its prior action, stating that "the settled practice of the Association has been to elect only white men to membership." ...

In 1925, twelve black lawyers from around the nation (eleven men and one woman) met in Des Moines, Iowa, to organize and incorporate the National Bar Association (NBA). Although not restricting its membership to race, the NBA was designed to be, and became, the chief professional association of black lawyers....

In 1981, the NBA estimated that there were 12,000 black lawyers, of whom about 8,000 belonged to the NBA. From an American Bar Foundation estimate of a total of 535,000 lawyers in the United States in 1980, it appears that black lawyers comprise a little more than 2.2 percent of the American lawyer population....

[As Segal's study demonstrates, a "black lawyer," like all lawyers, lives and practices in a specific practice setting, in a specific community, during a specific historical period. Law practice tends to be highly localized, being bound up in an immediate socio-political context and tied to specific economic possibilities. Segal accordingly has subchapters on individual black lawyers and on several cities in which black lawyers have concentrated, including Atlanta, New York, Philadelphia and Washington, D.C. Of Philadelphia, for example, she writes:]

Aaron Mossell was the first black to graduate from the University of Pennsylvania Law School. Born in Hamilton, Ontario, the son of a free Black who migrated to Canada to avoid having his children reared in a slave state, he returned to Philadelphia after the Emancipation. He entered Lincoln University (situated near) as an undergraduate and then matriculated at the University of Pennsylvania Law School, from which he graduated in 1888. After he was admitted to the Philadelphia Bar on February 18, 1893, he began the practice of law. He and John Wesley Parks later formed a partnership and practiced law together, apparently successfully. Mossell was the father of the distinguished lawyer, Sadie Tanner Mossell Alexander....

The 1910 census reported that there were thirteen black lawyers in Philadelphia.... [F]rom 1909 to 1945, a period of thirty-six years, only twenty black lawyers (nineteen males and one female) were admitted to the Philadelphia Bar.

A remarkable number of these twenty lawyers went on to achieve success in the profession and to attain judgeships and other public offices, thereby doing a great deal to enhance the standing of the black lawyer in Philadelphia.

Herbert E. Millen had the distinction of being the first black judge in Philadelphia when he became judge of the Municipal Court in 1948. Raymond Pace Alexander, husband of Sadie T.M. Alexander, gave up a lucrative law practice in 1958 to become the first black judge on the Court of Common Pleas, the trial court of general jurisdiction.... He was also Chief Counsel for the NAACP and was elected and reelected to the Philadelphia City Council in the 1950s. Robert N.C. Nix, Sr. was elected to fill the unexpired term of a Philadelphia Congressman in 1958 and served in the House of Representatives until January 1, 1979. J. Austin Norris, after a successful career as a newspaper publisher in Pittsburgh, returned to the practice of law in Philadelphia and started a law firm that produced its own corps of talented black lawyers, several of whom became judges and high-level public officials. Among these are: A. Leon Higginbotham, Jr., United States Court of Appeals for the Third Circuit; Clifford Scott Green, United States District Court for the Eastern District of Pennsylvania; Robert W. Williams, Jr., Commonwealth Court of Pennsylvania; Doris M. Harris and Harvey N. Schmidt, Court of Common Pleas of Philadelphia; William F. Hall, United States Magistrate; and William H. Brown, III....

As the times and circumstances changed, a different occupational picture developed. Offers from white sole practitioners, from law firms and corporations, and from federal and state governments, which were unknown to the oldest cohort, became routine for the youngest cohort. Offers from black practitioners and black firms, which were the major employers of the oldest cohort, decreased proportionately in the youngest cohort, while white law firms and corporations vied for the services of the outstanding black law school graduates....

But what happened to the black lawyers in Philadelphia who received no offers from major firms? ...

Of the seventeen who had received no offers, seven became sole practitioners; seven took posts with government (three city, one state, and three federal); one went with a black sole practitioner; and one with a white firm....

Lingering Racism

Despite the greater opportunity that blacks now have for entry into the legal profession, their life chances in the profession remain precarious.[70] In particular, the number of blacks making partner in predominantly white firms is small and increasing very slowly. The black experience in legal academia has been equally bleak. According to the Chused study, supra, "[in] 1986–87, a typical law school faculty had thirty-one members.... Of these ... thirty were white, one was black, Hispanic or other minority...."[71] In 1980, blacks constituted 2.8 percent of the faculty at other than the few traditionally black law schools. By 1986, the figure had risen only to 3.7 percent.[72] Compare the increase in the same period for women, discussed earlier; for Hispanics the percentage went from 0.5 to 0.7 percent; and for other minorities from 0.5 to 1.0 percent. "The data ... demonstrate that minority professors in general, and black professors in particular, tend to be tokens if they are present at all.... In sheer numbers, the increase has been very small ... only thirty-five more tenured black professors ... than there were in 1981."[73]

An adequate explanation of the precarious situation of black lawyers in the white-controlled institutions of the legal profession would cover American social history for the last three decades. In the final

---

70. For more general background, see also John Preston Davis, The American Negro Reference Book (1966); Marion S. Goldman, A Portrait of the Black Attorney in Chicago (1972); Richard Kluger, Simple Justice (1977). Also see Edward J. Littlejohn and Donald L. Hobson, Black Lawyers, Law Practice, and Bar Associations—1844 to 1970: A Michigan History, 33 Wayne L.Rev. 1625 (1987).

71. Richard H. Chused, Hiring and Retention, supra, 137 U.Pa.L.Rev. at 538.

72. Id.

73. Id. at 539–40. On the experience of blacks in legal academia, see Andrew W. Haines, Minority Law Professors and the Myth of Sisyphus: Consciousness and Praxis Within the Special Teaching Challenge in American Law Schools, 10 Nat'l Black L.J. 247 (1988); Richard Delgado, Minority Law Professors' Lives: The Bell–Delgado Survey (Institute for Legal Studies Working Papers Series 39, Oct. 1988); Charles R. Lawrence, Minority Hiring in AALS Law Schools: The Need for Voluntary Quotas, 20 U.S.F.L.Rev. 429 (1986); Derrick A. Bell, Jr., Application of the "Tipping Point" Principle to Law Faculty Hiring Policies, 10 Nova L.J. 319 (1986); Derrick A. Bell, Jr., Strangers in Academic Paradise: Law Teachers of Color in Still White Law Schools, 20 U.S.F.L.Rev. 385 (1986).

analysis, however, racism remains a potent force. Consider the following two statements:

I

Simply put, while most Americans avow and genuinely believe in the principle of equality, most white Americans still consider black people as such to be obnoxious and socially inferior. This prevalent attitude is generally and appropriately called racism. "Racism" is to be distinguished from "racists." These days only a small discredited minority of Americans are willing to say explicitly that they regard blacks as inherently obnoxious and inferior. We have no racists in this country, or only a handful of them, because being a self-acknowledged racist has become socially and politically impermissible. To be sure, many white Americans will acknowledge that "everyone has his prejudices" or that "every individual is different." Most white Americans know individual blacks with whom they get along and some whom they like and some whom they respect. Most white Americans, in my observation, try to be fair and try to do the right thing in specific dealings with blacks, at least where they do not feel threatened. Nevertheless, most white Americans do not have the same positive attitude toward blacks that they have to others in general, or even that they have toward whites who are quite different from themselves in respects other than race.

The attitude of American whites toward racial minorities other than blacks has often been similarly negative. I refer particularly to the attitude of white Anglo–Saxon Protestants toward Native Americans, Asians, and Hispanics, and in different degree toward Jews and Southern and Eastern European ethnics. Viewed in broad historical and social perspectives, however, the attitude toward blacks has been qualitatively different—more persistent, more manifest, and more resistant to eradication. From one individual white to another this negative attitude is more or less intense, more or less repressed psychologically, and more or less consistently suppressed in behavior. But it is there.[74]

II

It is 1948. I am sitting in a kindergarten classroom at the Dalton School, a fashionable and progressive New York City private school. My parents, both products of a segregated Mississippi school system, have come to New York to attend graduate and professional school. They have enrolled me and my sisters here at Dalton to avoid sending us to public school in our neighborhood where the vast majority of the students are black and poor. They want us to escape the ravages of segregation, New York style.

---

74. Geoffrey C. Hazard, Jr., *Permissive Affirmative Action for the Benefit of Blacks*, 1987 U.Ill. L.Rev. 379, 385 (1987).

It is circle time in the five-year-old group, and the teacher is reading us a book. As she reads, she passes the book around the circle so that each of us can see the illustrations. The book's title is *Little Black Sambo*. Looking back, I remember only one part of the story, one illustration: Little Black Sambo is running around a stack of pancakes with a tiger chasing him. He is very black and has a minstrel's white mouth. His hair is tied up in many pigtails, each pigtail tied with a different color ribbon. I have seen the picture before the book reaches my place in the circle. I have heard the teacher read the "comical" text describing Sambo's plight and have heard the laughter of my classmates. There is a knot in the pit of my stomach. I feel panic and shame. I do not have the words to articulate my feelings—words like "stereotype" and "stigma" that might help cathart the shame and place it outside of me where it began.

But I am slowly realizing that, as the only black child in the circle, I have some kinship with the tragic and ugly hero of this story—that my classmates are laughing at me as well as at him. I wish I could laugh along with my friends. I wish I could disappear.

I am in a vacant lot next to my house with black friends from the neighborhood. We are listening to *Amos and Andy* on a small radio and laughing uproariously. My father comes out and turns off the radio. He reminds me that he disapproves of this show that pokes fun at Negroes. I feel bad—less from my father's reprimand than from a sense that I have betrayed him and myself, that I have joined my classmates in laughing at us.

I am certain that my kindergarten teacher was not intentionally racist in choosing *Little Black Sambo*. I knew even then, from a child's intuitive sense, that she was a good, well-meaning person. A less benign combination of racial mockery and profit motivated the white men who produced the radio show and played the roles of Amos and Andy. But we who had joined their conspiracy by our laughter had not intended to demean our race.

A dozen years later I am a student at Haverford College. Again, I am a token black presence in a white world. A companion whose face and name I can't remember seeks to compliment me by saying, "I don't think of you as a Negro." I understand his benign intention and accept the compliment. But the knot is in my stomach again. Once again, I have betrayed myself.

This happened to me more than a few times. Each time my interlocutor was a good, liberal, white person who intended to express feelings of shared humanity. I did not yet understand the racist implications of the way in which the feelings were conceptualized. I am certain that my white friends did not either. We had not yet grasped the compliment's underlying premise: To be thought of as a Negro is to be thought of as less than human. We were all victims of our culture's racism. We had all grown up on *Little Black Sambo* and *Amos and Andy.*

Another ten years pass. I am thirty-three. My daughter, Maia, is three. I greet a pink-faced, four-year-old boy on the steps of her nursery school. He proudly presents me with a book he has brought for his teacher to read to the class. "It's my favorite," he says. The book is a new edition of *Little Black Sambo.*[75]

Other Minorities

Discrimination on grounds of race, sex and ethnicity have affected many groups. Although discrimination against Jews has markedly eased in the last generation, it was a serious problem earlier. Jews in small number have been members of the American legal profession since the 19th century. Beginning with the large immigration from central and eastern Europe at the end of the 19th century, a substantial fraction of whom were Jews, the established legal profession became uneasy, widely hostile and discriminatory. Similar attitudes were manifested toward Catholics on religious grounds and toward Irish, Italians and Poles on ethnic grounds, but with less intensity. The same holds for all ethnic minorities in one degree or another.[76] At least since the mid–1970s, however, discrimination appears to have sharply declined in the legal profession, as much or more than in other vocational groups, as against people of European heritage.

Discrimination and differentials in opportunity evidently persist as against Hispanics, Asians and other ethnic minorities. Lawyers who are physically disabled and gay and lesbian lawyers also confront discrimination and barriers to entry into the "establishment" legal institutions in the United States. The high academic achievement of many Asians has improved their competitive position, but also engenders fear of competition. The moral challenge remains.

In 1986 the ABA adopted a ninth goal: "To promote full and equal participation in the profession by minorities and women."[77] A Commission on Minorities in the legal profession was created to carry out recommendations of the 1986 report.

---

75. Charles R. Lawrence, III, The Id, the Ego, and Equal Protection: Reckoning with Unconscious Racism, 39 Stan.L.Rev. 317–318 (1987).

76. See generally Jerold S. Auerbach, Unequal Justice: Lawyers and Social Change in Modern America (1976).

77. See Report of ABA Task Force on Minorities in the Legal Profession (Jan.10, 1986).

B. DISCIPLINARY ENFORCEMENT

1. Disciplinary Procedure

Evolution of Disciplinary Procedure

The old regime of disciplinary procedure was relatively informal.[78]

Since the beginning of the nineteenth century, most American jurisdictions have required one who acts as a lawyer for others to be licensed. In the older parlance, and in the Hohfeldian sense, the practice of law is a "privilege," i.e., a capacity that is not an incident of citizenship but is conferred by law on a limited number of people who meet specified requirements....

The term "privilege" has long been used as a predicate in analysis of the rules governing both admission to practice and lawyer discipline. The leading treatise on law practice of the early twentieth century ... stated:

> The right to practice law is not a natural inherent right, but one which may be exercised only upon proof of fitness, through evidence of the possession of satisfactory legal attainments and fair character. The privilege of practicing law is not open to all, but is a special personal franchise limited to persons of good moral character, with special qualifications.... [Edward M. Thornton, A Treatise on Attorneys at Law 22–23 (1914)].

Under traditional legal doctrine, this characterization implied that constitutional law would require only a modicum of procedural formality for revocation of an attorney's license....

According to Thornton, a petition for disbarment was to set forth verified allegations specifying with reasonable particularity the misconduct for which disbarment was sought. If the court found the allegations sufficient in law, it would ordinarily issue an order against the lawyer in question, directing him to show cause why he should not be disbarred. The burden of proof thus was on the attorney to prove his innocence. There was little or no pretrial discovery. Appellate review was nominally available, but the tenor of the decisions suggests that a lawyer found guilty of an offense warranting disbarment had little chance of obtaining reversal on either substantive or procedural grounds.[79]

The Supreme Court has considered remarkably few cases involving lawyer disciplinary proceedings, particularly compared with the number of bar admission cases it has considered. This suggests that the bar itself supports protective procedural standards in disciplinary matters, whatever its views might be on the rights of new applicants. The principal Supreme Court cases are In re Ruffalo and Spevack v. Klein.

In re Ruffalo[80] involved charges that the respondent lawyer solicited personal injury claims to be brought under the Federal Employers Liability Act and hired a railroad employee to investigate claims

---

78. Geoffrey C. Hazard, Jr. and Cameron Beard, A Lawyer's Privilege Against Self–Incrimination in Professional Disciplinary Proceedings, 96 Yale L.J. 1060, 1063–65 (1987).

79. Id. at 1063–65.

80. 390 U.S. 544 (1968).

against his employer railroad. The Court invalidated a disbarment based on a charge that was added only after the evidence had been received at the disciplinary hearing:

> [The lawyer] is entitled to procedural due process, which includes fair notice of the charge.... These are adversary proceedings of a quasi-criminal nature.... The charge must be known before the proceedings commence. They become a trap when ... the charges are amended on the basis of testimony of the accused. He can then be given no opportunity to expunge the earlier statements and start afresh.[81]

Spevack v. Klein [82] held that a lawyer could not be disbarred for refusing to produce records in a disciplinary proceeding concerning solicitation of personal injury cases. The decision rested on the ground that the Fifth Amendment's privilege against self-incrimination protected the lawyer against being compelled to give evidence in a disciplinary matter that could expose him to incrimination in a criminal prosecution. The premise was that the Fifth Amendment protects against being compelled to produce records because producing records is in effect being "compelled ... to be a witness against himself" within the meaning of the Amendment. That premise, however, has since been overruled by Fisher v. United States,[83] p. 243 above. Two propositions stated in *Spevack* are still apparently sound, however: (1) A lawyer cannot be disciplined for failure to respond in a disciplinary proceeding when the failure consists of invoking a constitutional privilege, and (2) the Fifth Amendment may be invoked in a disciplinary proceeding to avoid giving incriminating testimony.

Lawyer disciplinary procedure now adheres to a "due process" model. In most jurisdictions, the procedure is similar to a civil proceeding tried to a judge rather than a jury, with a preliminary prosecutorial review to determine probable cause: [84]

> First, there is a required screening by the disciplinary agency to determine whether lodging a formal charge would be warranted. Functionally, this resembles the probable cause hearing in criminal procedure. It screens out those complaints for which the evidence is insufficient to get to a trier of fact, and synthesizes the evidence when it meets the sufficiency test, in the latter case laying the foundation for possible "plea bargaining." The second variation from the civil procedure model concerns discovery. In some jurisdictions, the accused lawyer has the same rights of discovery as are available in civil actions in the trial court of general jurisdiction, but the prevailing pattern gives the accused only informal access to the prosecution's dossier. Third, except in Texas and Georgia, there is no right to a jury trial.

81. 390 U.S. at 550–551.
82. 385 U.S. 511 (1967).
83. 425 U.S. 391 (1976).
84. Hazard and Beard, supra, 96 Yale L.J. at 1066–67.

The prevailing model thus may be described as a relatively formal version of administrative law procedure. Its elements include:

- The benefit of pre-charge screening by the disciplinary enforcement agency;

- The right to notice and a statement of the charge or grievance;

- The right to formal or informal discovery;

- The right to assistance of counsel;

- The rights to subpoena witnesses and evidence, to cross-examine adverse witnesses, and to exclude evidence inadmissible under the rules of evidence;

- The requirement of proof by a preponderance of the evidence or, in some cases, by clear and convincing evidence; and

- The right to judicial review.

A model procedure recommended by the American Bar Association has been widely adopted, with relatively minor variations from state to state.[85] A description of a fairly typical disciplinary process, that of the District of Columbia, was included in Chapter 2 above at p. 155.

Jurisdiction to Impose Discipline

Model Rule 8.5 provides that "[a] lawyer admitted to practice in this jurisdiction is subject to the disciplinary authority of this jurisdiction although engaged in practice elsewhere." Thus, state courts assert disciplinary authority over lawyers admitted to practice before a federal court although one case has held that a federal prosecutor charged with a state disciplinary violation growing out of prosecutorial activities may remove the proceeding to a federal court.[86]

Obligation to Report Misconduct

Model Rule 8.3(a) of the Rules of Professional Conduct requires a lawyer to report to appropriate disciplinary authority "a violation of the rules of professional conduct that raises a substantial question as to that lawyer's honesty, trustworthiness or fitness as a lawyer in other respects." M.R. 8.3(b) imposes a counterpart obligation regarding misconduct by a judge. DR 1–103(A) goes further, requiring report of any violation by another lawyer.

These obligations are not generally observed. When a lawyer is representing a client in seeking redress against another lawyer for malpractice and reporting the violation would inhibit reaching a settle-

---

85. See Am.Bar Ass'n, Standards for Lawyer Discipline and Disability Proceedings (1979).

86. Compare Waters v. Barr, 103 Nev. 694, 747 P.2d 900 (1987) (state court asserting disciplinary authority over federal prosecutors), with Kolibash v. Committee on Legal Ethics of the West Virginia Bar, 872 F.2d 571 (4th Cir.1989) (disciplinary proceeding of federal prosecutor commenced in state tribunal removable to federal court under 28 U.S.C. § 1442). See also Theard v. United States, 354 U.S. 278 (1957); Comment, Disbarment in the Federal Courts, 85 Yale L.J. 975 (1977).

ment, failure to report is understandable and perhaps justified. For a lawyer to agree not to report another lawyer's violation, however, is clearly a violation. Such an agreement could constitute or approximate extortion if it is done in connection with exacting a payment from the second lawyer.[87]

2. Discipline and the Fifth Amendment

ANONYMOUS ATTORNEYS v. BAR ASSN. OF ERIE COUNTY
Court of Appeals of New York, 1977.
41 N.Y.2d 506, 393 N.Y.S.2d 961, 362 N.E.2d 592.

PER CURIAM.

The sole issue before the court is whether incriminating testimony given by an attorney, following a grant of immunity, may be used as evidence against him in a disciplinary proceeding.

The appellants, attorneys admitted to practice in the State of New York, were called to testify before a Grand Jury investigating alleged irregularities in the fixing of traffic tickets in the City Court of Buffalo. The District Attorney requested that they execute waivers of immunity which they declined to do, and the Grand Jury then voted them full immunity pursuant to CPL 50.10. The Grand Jury probe resulted in an indictment against certain officials and, subsequently, the appellants, still retaining immunity, testified at the trial of these officials. Thereafter, they were served with a petition and notice of motion instituted by the respondent Bar Association seeking to have them disciplined for their involvement in the activity concerning which they had testified. After service of the petitions, the appellants commenced an action in the Federal District Court seeking an injunction against prosecution of these disciplinary proceedings. The respondent's motion to dismiss the Federal action was granted on the ground of insufficiency under the abstention doctrine of Younger v. Harris, 401 U.S. 37, and that dismissal was affirmed (Anonymous J. v. Bar Assn. of Erie County, 2 Cir., 515 F.2d 435). Thereafter, appellants moved in the Appellate Division for an order dismissing the petitions on the ground that they had been granted immunity from any penalties or forfeitures arising out of the transactions concerning which they had testified. The Appellate Division denied the motion to dismiss and granted leave to appeal to this court on a certified question. We affirm the order of the Appellate Division and answer the certified question in the affirmative.

Initially, we confront the question of statutory construction of the immunity statute.... The appellants strongly urge that the possible sanctions flowing from the disciplinary proceeding constitute a "penalty or forfeiture" within the meaning of the statute. Without doubt the sanctions which may be imposed in such proceedings may have serious

---

87. The ethical duty to report misconduct and the *Himmel* case are considered more fully in Chapter 2 above at p. 158.

consequences resulting in impairment of repute, loss of clientele, or, in the case of disbarment, loss of license to practice a profession which is their very source of livelihood. Although serious in consequence, these sanctions are not penalties or forfeitures within the meaning of the Criminal Procedure Law. The penalties and forfeitures encompassed by this immunity are those imposed or sought to be imposed as punishment upon conviction for a criminal offense committed in violation of the Penal Law or other statute of the State.... We hold that disciplinary sanctions are not punishment within the meaning of section 50.10. As Judge Cardozo explained in Matter of Rouss (supra, 221 N.Y. pp. 84–85, 116 N.E. p. 783): "Membership in the bar is a privilege burdened with conditions. A fair private and professional character is one of them. Compliance with that condition is essential at the moment of admission; but it is equally essential afterwards [citations omitted]. Whenever the condition is broken, the privilege is lost. To refuse admission to an unworthy applicant is not to punish him for past offenses. The examination into character, like the examination into learning is merely a test of fitness. To strike the unworthy lawyer from the roll is not to add to the pains and penalties of crime." Whether the practice of law is termed a privilege (*Matter of Rouss,* supra) or a right (Matter of Levy, 37 N.Y.2d 279, 282, 372 N.Y.S.2d 41, 44, 333 N.E.2d 350, 352) disciplinary sanctions imposed for misconduct are not criminal penalties under the statute.

Immunity does not protect against all private consequences of the facts or involvement revealed by testimony given under its shelter. And some people, because of their relationship with government, may suffer governmentally imposed consequences of a serious nature (see Uniformed Sanitation Men Assn. v. Commissioner of Sanitation, 2 Cir., 426 F.2d 619, Note, Immunity Statutes and the Constitution, 68 Col. L.Rev. 959). The criterion is whether the sanctions are imposed in the context of a criminal proceeding, covered by immunity, or whether such subsequent proceedings are civil in nature where immunity does not necessarily extend. Disciplinary proceedings against an attorney for professional misconduct have consistently been held not to be criminal proceedings but rather are those which serve to protect the court and society from the practice of law by persons who fail to maintain the necessary standards of integrity and probity (..., Chilingirian, State Disbarment Proceedings and the Privilege Against Self–Incrimination, 18 Buffalo L.Rev. 489). The immunity statute, prohibiting use of covered testimonial evidence in criminal proceedings, does not bar the use of such evidence in disciplinary proceedings brought against an attorney on the grounds of misconduct; and this has been the established law in this State for over 40 years (Matter of Solovei, 250 App.Div. 117, 121, 293 N.Y.S. 640, 644, affd., 276 N.Y. 647, 12 N.E.2d 802).

The appellants also contend that the Fifth Amendment privilege against self incrimination precludes the use of any immunity-clothed statements in a disciplinary proceeding. The appellants were concededly granted transactional immunity in return for their Grand Jury and trial testimony. They assert that their testimony was compelled by the grant of immunity arguing that subsequent refusal would result in contempt charges and as such must be coextensive with the privilege against self incrimination which it replaced and that privilege must be deemed to protect against the use of compelled self-incriminating statements in disciplinary proceedings. This argument has a surface attractiveness that dissipates under analysis.

The Fifth Amendment provides that no person "shall be compelled *in any criminal case* to be a witness against himself" (emphasis added), and the State Constitution assures this privilege in the very same language (N.Y. Const., art. I, § 6). These constitutional protections forbid the State from compelling incriminating answers which may be used in any criminal proceedings but they permit "that very testimony to be compelled if neither it nor its fruits are available for such use" (Lefkowitz v. Turley, 414 U.S. 70, 84; Kastigar v. United States, 406 U.S. 441). Where immunity coextensive with the privilege against self incrimination is granted, the courts have the power to compel testimony by the use of civil contempt and coerced imprisonment.... The Supreme Court has held that "immunity from use and derivative use is coextensive with the scope of the privilege against self incrimination, and therefore is sufficient to compel testimony over a claim of the privilege" (Kastigar v. United States, supra, 406 U.S. p. 453). The New York Statute goes further and provides full transactional immunity.... Thus, the appellants are clothed with full transactional immunity which immunizes them against prosecutions for any and all *crimes* to which their testimony might relate.

The constitutional protection does not, however, extend to its use in other than criminal proceedings. It is certain that the privilege against self incrimination may be asserted in any situation where the testimony may ultimately be used in a criminal proceeding against the person testifying (Matter of Gault, 387 U.S. 1, 47–48), but where immunity bars such use the testimony is nonetheless admissible in other noncriminal hearings such as those involving disciplinary charges. The salient question is whether that proceeding is a criminal case within the purview of the Fifth Amendment. A criminal case is "one which may result in sanctions being imposed upon a person as a result of his conduct being adjudged violative of the criminal law. The essence of state bar disciplinary proceedings, however, is not a resolution regarding the alleged criminality of a person's acts, but rather a determination of the moral fitness of an attorney to continue in the practice of law. Although conduct which could form the basis for a criminal prosecution might also underlie the institution of disciplinary proceedings, the focus is upon gauging an individual's character and fitness, and not upon adjudging the criminality of his prior acts or inflicting punishment for them" (Matter of Daley, 7 Cir., 549 F.2d 469, 474). In urging a contrary position, appellants rely on cases which are not here applicable. In Spevack v. Klein, 385 U.S. 511, the Supreme Court held that an attorney could not be disciplined solely on the ground that he had asserted his privilege against self incrimination. The threat of disbarment for the mere exercise of the privilege was viewed as an unconstitutional compulsion to waive the privilege without a coextensive protection against the ultimate use of those statements in a criminal proceeding. Likewise in Garrity v. New Jersey, 385 U.S. 493, certain police officers made incriminating statements during an inquiry concerning the fixing of traffic tickets. The statements were made under the threat that if they refused to respond to the questions put to them, they would be removed from office. Since no immunity was granted, the Supreme Court considered those threats coercive, negating any apparent waiver of the privilege against self incrimination and the statements were thus declared inadmissible in a later criminal action against them. Further, in Gardner v. Broderick, 392 U.S. 273, the court held that refusal to waive the privilege could not be grounds for termination of a police officer's employment. In all of these cases testimony was being compelled by threats of disbarment or the loss of employment without a guarantee that the statements would not later be used in criminal proceedings. The Fifth Amendment and our State Constitution prohibit such coercion. But these decisions in no way imply that once immunity coextensive with the privilege is granted, the statements may not be used in a disciplinary hearing. When assurance is made that the statements cannot be used in a related criminal action, the constitutional privilege is satisfied and no more is required. Further use of the information does not offend the essential purposes of the privilege but guarantees the proper opportunity for the pursuit of other public values.

The State has a compelling interest in regulating our system of justice to assure high standards of professional conduct. Sanctions imposed in that capacity are distinct and apart from penalties and forfeitures stemming from criminal proceedings. Once the constitutional guarantee that no person "shall be compelled in any criminal case to be a witness against himself" is assured by a grant of immunity, the State may act, and indeed must act, in its supervisory capacity to assure that those standards are maintained.

Accordingly, the order of the Appellate Division should be affirmed and the certified question answered in the affirmative.

---

3. Effectiveness of Disciplinary Enforcement

The procedural protections afforded lawyers in disciplinary proceedings are substantial. The effectiveness of the enforcement process, however, has been repeated criticized. In 1970, the ABA sponsored a study of lawyer discipline by a special committee headed by former Supreme Court Justice Tom C. Clark. The Clark Report, as it is commonly called, found that the disciplinary machinery in most jurisdictions was in poor shape: inadequate staff, poor record keeping, feeble prosecution, erratically functioning grievance committees and other defects. It also found that the sanctions were unequal and generally mild relative to the heinousness of offenses. The report called for comprehensive reform, including enlarged staff resources, more hospitable concern for complainants, speedier preliminary investigations and trial and better calibrated sanctions.[88]

The course of events since the Clark Report has not been smooth. Most jurisdictions have introduced reforms along the lines recommended in the report. At the same time, the volume and backlog of disciplinary cases has rapidly increased in many jurisdictions, sometimes overwhelming the disciplinary system, as in California in the 1980s. The bar takes some satisfaction in its efforts to improve disciplinary enforcement, but many people within the bar and in the general public remain profoundly dissatisfied.

In 1992, the ABA adopted in amended form the recommendations of the Commission on Evaluation of Disciplinary Enforcement, which had spent three years studying lawyer disciplinary enforcement.[89] The Commission's study concluded:

> It is no exaggeration to say that revolutionary changes have occurred. Twenty years ago, most states conducted lawyer discipline at the local level with no professional staff. Lawyer discipline was a secretive procedural labyrinth of multiple hearings and reviews....
>
> Today almost all states have professional disciplinary staff with statewide jurisdiction. Most have eliminated duplicative procedures. In over half the states, disciplinary hearings are public.... In the two decades since the Clark Report, most states and the ABA have adopted most of its recommendations.[90]

The ABA recommendations deal with a number of recurring issues concerning the lawyer disciplinary system:

Who should control the disciplinary process? The ABA Commission accepted the view of consumer groups that control of the lawyer discipline system by state bar associations creates an appearance of conflicts of interest and of impropriety. In many states, including Florida, New York and Texas, bar officials investigate, prosecute and adjudicate disciplinary cases, subject to judicial review. The Commission's recommendation that the state high court, and not some other governmental authority, should exclusively control the disciplinary

---

88. See ABA, Special Committee on Evaluation of Disciplinary Enforcement (1970) (often referred to as the McKay Commission after its initial chairman).

89. ABA, Lawyer Regulation for a New Century: Report of the Commission on Evaluation of Disciplinary Enforcement (1992).

90. Id. at xiv.

process was adopted by the ABA House of Delegates in 1993 in a close vote.[91]

Should disciplinary proceedings be open to the public? The ABA Commission concluded that the effort to shield honest lawyers' reputations by holding disciplinary hearings behind closed doors contributed to public distrust of lawyer discipline. The Commission initially recommended that lawyer disciplinary records be open to the public from the time of the complainant's initial communication with the disciplinary agency (the procedure followed in Oregon). In the face of opposition, however, the Commission retreated to the position that records be kept confidential until a complaint has been dismissed or until a determination has been made that "probable cause" exists to believe that misconduct has occurred. The ABA House of Delegates rejected the view that dismissed complaints should be open to the public, resolving that a disciplinary matter should go public only upon a finding of probable cause. Should the disciplinary process be fully open to public view?

What can be done to make professional discipline a more effective remedy for clients? Clients are largely unaware of the existence and details of disciplinary procedure.[92] Moreover, up to 90 percent of all complaints against lawyers are dismissed, and only a very small percentage of complaints result in significant sanctions.[93] Although a large number of complaints are properly dismissed as frivolous (e.g., client is unhappy with the outcome of litigation), a gap between client expectations and regulatory performance is responsible for a substantial portion of dismissals. The most common client grievances involve fee disputes, neglect and negligence. Clients expect that these matters will be taken seriously by disciplinary bodies, but disciplinary agencies view most such complaints as not within their jurisdiction[94] or lack resources to pursue them. The ABA endorses a system of expedited procedures for minor misconduct that is not subject to suspension or disbarment. It also has dealt with public concerns by recommending that states adopt a client protection fund, mandatory arbitration of fee disputes, voluntary arbitration of lawyer malpractice claims and ran-

91. The ABA rejected proposals that regulation of the legal profession should be turned over to state legislatures. The Commission report, while urging that lawyers be regulated exclusively by state high courts, warned that "failure of the profession and the judiciary to act [to protect clients] imperils the inherent power of the court to regulate its officers [and] threatens the independence of counsel." Id. at xvi. For an argument that greater legislative participation in the regulation of lawyers would be desirable, see Deborah L. Rhode, The Rhetoric of Professional Reform, 45 Md.L.Rev. 274 (1986).

92. See Richard Abel, American Lawyers 144 (1989) (only 13 percent of clients found to be aware of disciplinary process); Eric H. Steel and Raymond T. Nimmer, Lawyers, Clients, and Professional Regulation, 1976 Am.Bar Found.Res.J. 917, 959–60 (individual clients aggrieved by lawyers do not know how to obtain redress; business clients pursue other options).

93. Lawyer Regulation for a New Century, supra, at xv: "Some jurisdictions dismiss up to ninety percent of all complaints."

94. Many fee disputes involves fees that are high but not so "unreasonable" or "clearly excessive" that they are disciplinary violations. Single instances of neglect and incompetence are generally viewed as not within the jurisdiction of the disciplinary system. See the discussion at p. 172.

dom audits of lawyer trust accounts (the latter is in place in eight states as of 1992).

Where will the needed resources come from? Everyone concedes that disciplinary agencies are understaffed and underfunded. Bar dues are now substantial in many states (e.g., $200–500 per year), and lawyers resist substantial further increases to finance disciplinary staff. Placing lawyer discipline under the court system rather than the legislature requires that government funding come through budgets for the judicial branch, many of which are experiencing serious funding problems.

As currently structured, the disciplinary process is largely invisible and reactive. Should it be made more visible and proactive? Should fee disputes, neglect and negligence be made disciplinary offenses? The disciplinary process would be more visible to clients if lawyers were required to include information concerning how to file a disciplinary complaint in fee retainer agreements. If adequately funded and authorized, disciplinary staff could initiate disciplinary proceedings on the basis of malpractice filings, judicial sanctions and random audits of trust funds. Subjecting law firms to discipline might increase incentives of firms to maintain quality control of firm lawyers.[95]

The volume and vehemence of public criticism of lawyer ethics is hard to overestimate, as is the frustration and outrage of many clients at being unable to get recourse against misconduct and mistreatment by their lawyers, including overcharging, procrastination, refusal to respond, evasion and lying. Consider the following excerpt:

GEOFFREY C. HAZARD, JR.
"DISCIPLINARY PROCESS NEEDS MAJOR REFORMING"
National Law Journal, August 1, 1988, p. 13.[96]

HALT [Help Abolish Legal Tyranny] is a non-profit activist organization whose aim is improving the quality and integrity of the legal profession. That description would also fit the American Bar Association, so it is important to note that HALT is not quite the same as the ABA. Although concerned about the legal profession, and having lawyers as part of its constituency, HALT seeks to improve the profession from the outside rather than the inside.

Recently HALT issued a report on the state of disciplinary enforcement throughout the country. Its primary findings were:

- In many jurisdictions there is prolonged delay between a grievance and a disposition. Serious cases usually take a couple of years. Meanwhile, the lawyer continues to practice.

---

95. See Ted Schneyer, Professional Discipline for Law Firms?, 71 Cornell L.Rev. 1 (1991) (professional discipline system should be extended to law firms).

96. Copyright © 1988 by the National Law Journal.

- Investigatory and prosecutorial resources are in short supply compared with the demand. If enforcement were made more rigorous, the imbalance would be worse.

- Complainants are not given an encouraging reception nor moral support. The button for the disciplinary machinery often is difficult to locate. The proceedings themselves are invisible to the general public, owing to the requirement that they be kept confidential until a sanction is imposed.

- Sanctions generally are mild. Many cases get plea-bargained down to minor dispositions. Even in serious cases the authorities, including the reviewing courts, are sympathetic to lawyer infirmities. Lawyers who have cheated and lied to clients, including lying about their cheating, may get off with a short suspension if they can prove they were alcoholics, or were having marital problems, or other mitigating circumstances.

The total effect, according to HALT, is a system that is overburdened, more or less fortuitous in its outcomes, cool toward the rage and frustration of victims, and lenient when measured by the premise that professional misconduct is a serious matter.

Sound familiar? The conclusions drawn by HALT are not greatly different from those of the Clark Committee twenty years ago.

The uncertain condition of disciplinary enforcement thus persists. This, despite the fact that almost all jurisdictions have substantially expanded and improved their disciplinary machinery over the years since the Clark Report. What is happening?

A partial explanation is that the number of lawyers has greatly increased over the same period, at a rate paralleling the increase in disciplinary resources. Moreover, the expansion of the bar has been at the low end of the professional population in terms of age and experience. Younger and more inexperienced lawyers are probably no more prone to misbehavior than older ones. However, they probably are more vulnerable to temptation and to being caught if they succumb.

Another factor is the "due process explosion" in disciplinary procedure. Disciplinary procedure used to be drum-head justice, partly because it was invoked only in clearcut cases. However, the procedure has become elaborate—preliminary investigation, probable cause hearing, adversarial trial in contested cases, and judicial review where serious sanctions were involved.... In short, the typical case unit in disciplinary matters has become larger than it used to be.

Another likely factor in the disciplinary crunch is that lawyers are now more willing to report miscreant colleagues and to testify against them. In the old days, they usually just turned their backs, a powerful sanction when the bar was an intimate group.

Still another factor may be that more lawyers are willing to take ethical risks than they used to be. Many people nowadays see pervasive decline in conformity to legal standards throughout our society. There is no reason to think lawyers are immune from this tendency.

Finally, improvement in the disciplinary machinery itself probably contributes to the problem. When disciplinary enforcement was largely nominal so were the enforcement statistics. This phenomenon mirrors the truism in criminal justice that improvement in law enforcement results in higher reported crime rates.

In all these respects, the disciplinary system is eerily similar to the criminal justice system as it operates in white collar offenses. Indeed, perhaps we should analyze the disciplinary system as if it were a quasi-criminal system involving a special category of white collar law enforcement. Such a characterization is implicit in one of HALT's principal recommendations, that administration of the disciplinary system be moved outside the bar and be placed in a public agency, like other regulatory enforcement.

The HALT report implies that relocating enforcement jurisdiction from the bar to a public agency would substantially improve the machinery's performance. Such a change could make for some improvement. It seems likely that reviewing judges could then recognize that lawyer discipline deals with white-collar crime and miscreancy instead of simple waywardness within a fraternity. Moreover, legislatures might provide more financial resources to an agency under their scrutiny than one under the aegis of the legal profession. Perhaps a public agency would incline toward more publicity and show more solicitude toward victims. If these influences combined, the result could be substantial strengthening of the disciplinary process and enhancement of its deterrent effects.

There would be little loss to the bar in such a reallocation of disciplinary jurisdiction. The disciplinary system is already beyond the direct supervision of the organized bar, except in the few jurisdictions where the profession is still an essentially fraternal group. On a day-to-day basis the disciplinary machinery is in the hands of the professional staff, who do the investigations, make the charging decisions, and prosecute the cases that have to go the whole route. A change in jurisdiction would not much affect those routines, and the system would remain remote from the daily concerns of the large majority of the practicing bar....

Perhaps there is need to reexamine basic premises and to consider more radical reforms. For example, lawyers could be required to be members of associations that would themselves be answerable in some way for misconduct of their members. There is now a rule that members of firms must monitor ethical performance within the firm. Model Rule 5.1 provides: "A partner in a law firm shall make reasonable efforts to ensure that the firm has in effect measures giving reasonable assurance that all lawyers in the firm conform to the rules of professional conduct." What if every lawyer had to maintain membership in an association that had such a responsibility?

Policing Incompetence

A thoughtful study by Professor Susan Martyn focuses on the problem of enforcing competence by punishing incompetence.[97] Martyn concludes that the bar has not been successful in dealing with incompetence and is unlikely to be so, and hence that either the remedy of civil malpractice suits or more pervasive public regulation will be needed. This is much the same conclusion as in the HALT report, summarized above. The malpractice remedy, however, operates more or less randomly, and more intensive public regulation seems an unlikely prospect. If the principal justification for licensure is protection against incompetence (as distinct from lawyer dishonesty, which is covered by criminal law in any event), and if effective policing against incompetency remains unattainable, what is the justification for licensure?[98]

A specific problem of great seriousness in the legal profession is incompetence and other misconduct resulting from substance abuse.[99] The impaired lawyer has given rise to peer review programs, rehabilitative arrangements and special disciplinary procedures and remedies.

C. LEGAL EDUCATION

1. Criticism of Legal Education

The legal profession in the United States is large, heterogeneous and fragmented. Law practice, which is increasingly specialized in character, is influenced by the nature of client needs and by the context of practice. Thus lawyers do very different things that require very different knowledge, skills and experience. Aside from the bar examination, the major shared experience of American lawyers is law school. To the extent that all lawyers, whatever work they do, share a common culture and ideology, legal education is a critical aspect of the common socialization of the bar.

Criticism of legal education has been constant and repetitious for many years.[1] The four principal categories of criticism, considered briefly below, are: (1) Law school does not adequately prepare its

97. Susan R. Martyn, Lawyer Competence and Lawyer Discipline: Beyond the Bar?, 69 Geo.L.J. 705 (1981).

98. For a descriptive survey of studies of regulation of the legal profession, see Olavi Maru, Research on the Legal Profession: A Review of Work Done, c. 4 (2d ed. 1986). Also see Bryant G. Garth, Rethinking the Legal Profession's Approach to Collective Self-Improvement: Competence and the Consumer Perspective, 1983 Wis.L.Rev. 639.

99. For a review of the alcohol problem, see Michael A. Bloom and Carol L. Wallinger, Lawyers and Alcoholism: Is It Time for a New Approach?, 61 Temple L.Rev. 1409 (1988), which includes references to the related problem of drug abuse.

1. Robert B. Stevens, Law School: Legal Education in America from the 1850s to the 1980s 278 (1983):

graduates for the practice of law; (2) the educational experience has a destructive effect upon the character or values of students; (3) law school fails to produce public-spirited and socially responsible lawyers; and (4) legal education is not accessible to all sectors of American society.

The lament that law school does not provide adequate preparation for the realities of practice is an old one that takes a number of forms. Critics charge that law school is too theoretical, too removed from the day-to-day context in which lawyers do their work. Academics respond that the distinction between theory and practice is meaningless (any good practice rests on a decent theory) and that learning how to learn throughout a long career is more important than memorizing information that will soon become outdated. Another form of the inadequate-preparation charge is that legal education concentrates too exclusively on cognitive analysis of appellate cases and manipulation of legal doctrine, providing insufficient exposure to other capacities required in lawyering, such as complex problem-solving skills (e.g., fact investigation, interviewing, negotiation, drafting, litigating).[2] Clinical legal education responds in part to this concern.[3] A related criticism is that law school omits development of the interpersonal skills that are so vital in lawyer-client relations, in working with other professionals and in persuading those with whom one is negotiating or dealing.[4]

The second charge, that law school has a destructive effect upon the character or values of students, also takes a variety of forms. One frequently expressed concern is that the teaching method—questions and answers based on appellate judicial decisions—is either too narrow, too stultifying or too humiliating.[5] Legal education reaches its height of interest and involvement in the first year, followed by a long downhill slide.[6] The decline of student interest, referred to by Professor Anthony Amsterdam as the MOPIE Syndrome (Maximum Obtain-

Students will continue to reiterate the complaints about law schools that have been mouthed with remarkable regularity since ... the 1930s.... In practice, that remarkable and resilient vehicle, the case method, will continue to dominate legal education.

2. Two major studies have compared what practicing lawyers state are the skills needed in practice with those learned by these lawyers in law school. Leonard L. Baird, A Survey of the Relevance of Legal Training to Law School Graduates, 29 J.Legal Educ. 264 (1978); and Frances K. Zemans and Victor G. Rosenblum, The Making of a Public Profession, 55 et seq. (1981).

3. For discussion of the potential and problems of clinical legal education, see the articles in symposium, Clinical Legal Education, 33 J.Legal Educ. 604 et seq. (1983) (articles by Robert J. Condlin, Norman Redlich, Gary Bellow, Michael Meltsner and David Luban).

4. See, e.g., Thomas L. Shaffer and Robert S. Redmount, Lawyers, Law Students and People (1977).

5. Critics charge that the controlled dialogue erodes students' self-respect, encourages cynicism and conveys an erroneous impression of the lawyer's role. See Paul N. Savoy, Toward a New Politics of Legal Education, 79 Yale L.J. 444 (1970).

6. In this respect it differs sharply from medical education, in which student interest and involvement increases as medical students become involved in patient care. See Roger C. Cramton, Professional Education in Medicine and Law: Structural Differences, Common Failings, Possible Opportunities, 34 Cleve.St.L.Rev. 349 (1985).

able Passivity in Education), means that the whole of the curriculum is less than the sum of its parts, many of which are excellent.[7] Students, Amsterdam argues, coping with an instructor's surprise questions concerning judicial opinions, become solution-critics rather than problem-solvers. A variant of the same concern relies on humanistic, psychological or feminist arguments in concluding that law school narrows or warps law students.[8]

The effect of law school in shaping student values has been extensively studied, but the studies reach differing conclusions. Law students enter law school with strong commitments to social justice, it is said, but leave talking of jobs and choosing to serve as apologists of things as they are.[9] The bulk of the careful empirical studies, however, conclude that law school has only limited effect on student attitudes and values, but that market forces and contact with the practicing profession play a substantial role.[10]

Do law schools fail to produce public-spirited and responsible lawyers? This third deficiency is value-laden since it requires assumptions as to what constitutes a "good lawyer." Law graduates, if educated soundly and well, Richard Wasserstrom has said,

> would have and display a deep and abiding attachment to and concern for the moral worthiness and rightness of all that they do, of whatever they choose to do as lawyers, and a corresponding sense of responsibility for the justness and goodness of the legal

7. Anthony G. Amsterdam, Talk to SALT Annual Meeting (1989).

8. See Francis A. Allen, Law, Intellect, and Education (1979) (essays stressing the importance of a broad humanistic approach in legal education); Roger C. Cramton, The Ordinary Religion of the Law School Classroom, 29 J.Legal Educ. 247 (1978) (discussing the assumed value framework of contemporary legal education); J. B. Taylor, Law School Stress and the "Deformation Professionelle," 27 J.Legal Educ. 251 (1975) (psychological approach); Alan Stone, Legal Education on the Couch, 85 Harv.L.Rev. 392 (1971) (same); Andrew S. Watson, Some Psychological Aspects of Teaching Professional Responsibility, 16 J.Legal Educ. 1 (1963) (same); and Carrie Menkel–Meadow, Feminist Legal Theory, Critical Legal Studies, and Legal Education, or "The Fem–Crits Go to Law School," 38 J.Legal Educ. 61 (1988).

9. See Robert V. Stover, Making and Breaking It: The Fate of Public Interest Commitment During Law School (Howard S. Erlanger, ed., 1989) (law students' interest in public interest law declines significantly during law school; they become less interested in helping others and more interested in professional advancement); James C. Foster, The "Cooling Out" of Law Students, 3 Law & Policy Q. 243 (1981). But compare Murray L. Schwartz, The Reach and Limits of Legal Education, 32 J. Legal Educ. 543, 547 (1982), concluding on the basis of a number of studies that:

> Reasons for attending law school have not varied significantly over time. By far the most important are prestige, financial reward, and the achievement of a stable, secure future—all indices of upward social mobility.... Legal education has little effect on personal attitudes of lawyers. Ethnic and religious backgrounds and type of practice far outweigh legal education in affecting their political and social values.

10. See E. Gordon Gee and Donald W. Jackson, Current Studies of Legal Education: Findings and Recommendations, 32 J.Legal Educ. 471, 494–501 (1982) (reviewing the studies and concluding: "law-school socialization operates within the constraints of the market for law graduates, where preferences meet hard realities"); Lawrence K. Hellman, The Effects of Law Office Work on the Formation of Law Students' Professional Values: Observation, Explanation, Optimization, 4 Geo.J.Legal Ethics 537 (1991) (law office intern experiences, which may involve contact with unprofessional conduct, have a powerful effect on students).

system that their skills and training equip them to understand and
to utilize.[11]

These graduates would care for their clients, treating them fairly and
decently; they would also be concerned about persons affected by the
client and with the justness and goodness of the actions and choices
made on behalf of the client; and, finally, they would be interested and
concerned for the justness and goodness of existing systems of law.
Forming habits and dispositions of this character would be a fundamental aim of legal education.

Do any American law schools fulfill a grand vision of this type?
The excerpts from Duncan Kennedy and Stewart Macaulay that follow
shed some light on this question and provide other perspectives on the
goals and performance of law schools.

The fourth major criticism is that legal education is not accessible
to all sectors of American society. Changes since 1960—growth in the
demand for legal education, opening of opportunities for women and
minorities and the increased cost of a legal education—have resulted in
a major shift in the demographics of law students and lawyers. Paradoxically, these changes probably have reduced opportunities of non-
minority individuals of lower socio-economic status to attend law
school. As the number of applicants has grown, most law schools have
become increasingly selective in admissions. Reliance on standard
academic credentials, such as college grades, quality of college and
LSAT score, favors applicants of higher socio-economic status because
of the substantial correlation between those factors and socio-economic
status. Similarly, the women who now take up 42 percent of the seats
in American law schools generally are drawn from higher socio-economic backgrounds than the males they replaced. Given these constraints,
the diversity of the law school population compares well with that of
other fields of graduate and professional study. In few if any fields
does the student population include 42 percent women, 6 percent
blacks, and 14 percent total minorities, as was the case in law as of
1991.

The cost of legal education, however, is a substantial barrier.
Including the opportunity costs of foregoing employment during three
academic years, the total cost ranges from $100,000 to $200,000 per
student, depending on the school and other factors.[12] This is a major
investment in human capital that graduates expect to recoup from
earnings after law school. This fact, coupled with the need to borrow
extensively to pay the costs, clearly has a powerful effect on choice of
initial employment. Because these costs must be repaid from income

11. Richard Wasserstrom, Legal Education and the Good Lawyer, 34 J.Legal Educ. 155
(1984).

12. For discussion of the costs of legal education, see John R. Kramer, Proceedings of
the National Conference on Legal Education for a Changing Profession 93–114 (March
25–27, 1988) (law school tuition has increased much faster than the consumer price index;
most of the increased revenues have gone to increased faculty salaries and expanded
administrative staffs rather than to new faculty or the educational program).

generated in practice, lawyers become too expensive for some tasks and more expensive for all.[13]

This array of criticisms suggests that legal education is in serious trouble. Yet the dominant fact is that legal education, despite the constant drumbeat of criticism, is somewhat of an American success story in terms of its growth, resources and prestige. It must be doing something reasonably well. For several generations law schools have prepared individuals who then exercised power and influence in American private and public life. The demand for legal education has grown steadily with the result that the number of college graduates who desire to attend law school has grown from about 12,000 per year in the 1950s to more than seven times that figure today. This number includes a major portion of college graduates who are the most highly qualified in academic credentials (academic achievement, test scores, membership in Phi Beta Kappa, Rhodes scholars and the like). Law schools have steadily garnered new resources and often occupy the newest or grandest physical facilities on university campuses. The law curriculum may be disorganized, the education inadequate in a number of ways, but somehow legal education has not only survived but prospered. Its characteristic structure, curriculum and teaching method have been highly resistant to change. For better or worse, it has muddled through.

Consider the excerpts that follow in light of the foregoing criticisms of legal education and your own experience.

2. Perspectives on Legal Education

DUNCAN KENNEDY
LEGAL EDUCATION AND THE REPRODUCTION OF HIERARCHY
i, ii, 3, 5–7, 16–17, 20–22, 58, 65, 68, 70, 101–03 (1983).[14]

This is an essay about the role of legal education in American social life. It is a description of the ways in which legal education contributes to the reproduction of illegitimate hierarchy in the bar and in society. And it suggests ways in which left students and teachers who are determined not to let law school demobilize them can make the experience part of a left activist practice of social transformation.

The general thesis is that law schools are intensely *political* places, in spite of the fact that they seem intellectually unpretentious, barren

13. Judge Richard A. Posner argues that state requirements that require graduation from an ABA-approved law school as a prerequisite to admission to the bar provide law schools with a "captive audience, insulating [them] from a true market test of the value of the services they provide." He urges deregulation: If individuals could sit for the bar examination without law school training, law schools would have to convince them and their legal employers that the education was worth the time and money spent on it. Ken Myers, At Conference, Posner Lambasts Academics for Weak Scholarship, Nat'l L.J., Jan. 21, 1991, at p. 4.

14. Copyright © Duncan Kennedy. Reprinted with permission.

of theoretical ambition or practical vision of what social life might be. The trade school mentality, the endless attention to trees at the expense of forests, the alternating grimness and chumminess of focus on the limited task at hand, all these are only a part of what is going on. The other part is ideological training for willing service in the hierarchies of the corporate welfare state.

To say that law school is ideological is to say that what teachers teach along with basic skills is wrong, is nonsense about what law is and how it works. It is to say that the message about the nature of legal competence, and its distribution among students, is wrong, is nonsense. It is to say that the ideas about the possibilities of life as a lawyer that students pick up from legal education are wrong, are nonsense. But all this is nonsense with a tilt, it is biased and motivated rather than random error. What it says is that it is natural, efficient and fair for law firms, the bar as a whole, and the society the bar services to be organized in their actual patterns of hierarchy and domination.

· · ·

The First Year Experience

· · ·

The initial classroom experience sustains rather than dissipates ambivalence. The teachers are overwhelmingly white, male, and deadeningly straight and middle class in manner. The classroom is hierarchical with a vengeance, the teacher receiving a degree of deference and arousing fears that remind one of high schools rather than college. The sense of autonomy one has in a lecture, with the rule that you must let teacher drone on without interruption balanced by the rule that teacher can't *do* anything to you, is gone. In its place is a demand for a pseudo-participation in which you struggle desperately, in front of a large audience, to read a mind determined to elude you.

· · ·

The actual intellectual content of the law seems to consist of learning rules, what they are and why they have to be the way they are, while rooting for the occasional judge who seems willing to make them marginally more humane. The basic experience is of double surrender: to a passivizing classroom experience and to a passive attitude toward the content of the legal system.

The first step toward this sense of the irrelevance of liberal or left thinking is the opposition in the first year curriculum between the technical, boring, difficult, obscure legal case, and the occasional case with outrageous facts and a piggish judicial opinion endorsing or tolerating the outrage. The first kind of case—call it a cold case—is a challenge to interest, understanding, even to wakefulness. It can be on any subject, so long as it is of no political or moral or emotional significance. Just to understand what happened and what's being said about it, you have to learn a lot of new terms, a little potted legal history, and lots of rules, none of which is carefully explained by the casebook or the teacher. It is difficult to figure out why the case is there in the first place, difficult to figure out whether one has grasped it, and difficult to anticipate what the teacher will ask and what one should respond.

The other kind of case usually involves a sympathetic plaintiff, say an Appalachian farm family, and an unsympathetic defendant, say a coal company. On first reading, it appears that the coal company has screwed the farm family, say by renting their land for strip mining, with a promise to restore it to its original condition once the coal has been extracted, and then reneging on the promise. And the case should include a judicial opinion that does something like awarding a meaningless couple of hundred dollars to the farm family, rather than making the coal company do the restoration work.

The point of the class discussion will be that your initial reaction of outrage is naive, non-legal, irrelevant to what you're supposed to be learning, and maybe substantively wrong into the bargain. There are good reasons for the awful result, when you take a legal and logical view, as opposed to a knee-jerk passionate view, and if you can't muster those reasons, maybe you aren't cut out to be a lawyer.

. . .

The Ideological Content of Legal Education

... Law schools teach ... rather rudimentary, essentially instrumental skills in a way that almost completely mystifies them for almost all law students. The mystification has three parts. First, the schools teach skills through class discussions of cases in which it is asserted that law emerges from a rigorous analytical procedure called "legal reasoning," which is unintelligible to the layman, but somehow both explains and validates the great majority of the rules in force in our system. At the same time, the class context and the materials present every legal issue as distinct from every other, as a tub on its own bottom, so to speak, with no hope or even any reason to hope that from law study one might derive an integrating vision of what law is, how it works, or how it might be changed (other than in an incremental, case by case, reformist way).

Second, the teaching of skills in the mystified context of legal reasoning about utterly unconnected legal problems means that skills are taught badly, unself-consciously, to be absorbed by osmosis as one picks up the knack of "thinking like a lawyer." Bad or only randomly good teaching generates and then accentuates real differences and imagined differences in student capabilities. But it does so in such a way that students don't know when they are learning and when they aren't, and have no way of improving or even understanding their own learning processes. They experience skills training as the gradual emergence of differences among themselves, as a process of ranking that reflects something that is just "there" inside them.

Third, the schools teach skills in isolation from actual lawyering experience. "Legal reasoning" is sharply distinguished from law practice, and one learns nothing about practice. This procedure disables students from any future role but that of apprentice in a law firm organized in the same manner as a law school, with older lawyers controlling the content and pace of depoliticized craft training in a setting of intense competition and no feedback.

. . .

This whole body of implicit messages is nonsense. Legal reasoning is not distinct, *as a method for reaching correct results*, from ethical and political discourse in general (i.e., from policy analysis). It is true that there is a distinctive lawyers' body of knowledge of the rules in force. It is true that there are distinctive lawyers' argumentative techniques for spotting gaps, conflicts and ambiguities in the rules, for arguing broad and narrow holdings of cases, and for generating pro and con policy arguments. But these are *only* argumentative techniques. There is never a "correct legal solution" that is other than the correct ethical and political solution to that legal problem.

Put another way, everything taught, except the formal rules themselves and the argumentative techniques for manipulating them, is policy and nothing more. It follows that the classroom distinction between the unproblematic legal case and the policy oriented case is a mere artifact: each could as well be taught in the opposite way. And the curricular distinction between the "nature" of contract law as highly legal and technical by contrast, say, with environmental law, is equally a mystification.

These errors have a bias in favor of the center-liberal program of limited reform of the market economy and pro forma gestures toward racial and sexual equality. The bias arises because law school teaching makes the choice of hierarchy and domination, which is implicit in the adoption of the rules of property, contract and tort, look as though it flows from legal reasoning, rather than from politics and economics. The bias is reenforced when the center-liberal reformist program of regulation is presented as equally authoritative, but somehow more policy oriented, and therefore less fundamental.

The message is that the system is basically OK, since we have patched up the few areas open to abuse, and that it has a limited but important place for value-oriented debate about further change and improvement. If there is to be more fundamental questioning, it is relegated to the periphery of history or philosophy. The real world is kept at bay by treating clinical legal education, which might bring in a lot of information threatening to the cozy liberal consensus, as free legal drudge work for the local bar or as mere skills training.

. . .

The Modeling of Hierarchical Relationships

Yet another way in which legal education contributes causally to the hierarchies of the bar is through ... law teachers that model for students how they are supposed to think, feel and act in their future professional roles. Some of this is a matter of teaching by example, some of it a matter of more active learning from interactions that are a kind of clinical education for lawyer-like behavior.

. . .

Often, it boils down to law review. At first, everyone claims they aren't interested, wouldn't want to put in the time, don't work hard enough to make it, can't stand the elitism of the whole thing. But most students give about equal time to fantasies of flunking out and fantasies of grabbing the brass ring. And even though the class has been together for a semester or a year, everything is still different after the lightning of grades. An instant converts jerks into statesmen; honored spokespeople retire to the margins, shamed. Try proposing that law review should be open to anyone who will do the work. Within a week or two, the new members have a dozen arguments for competitive selection. Likewise at the hour of partnership.

. . .

The culmination of law school as training for professional hierarchy is the placement process, with the form of the culmination depending on where your school fits in the pecking order.

. . .

By dangling the bait, making clear the rules of the game, and then subjecting almost everyone to intense anxiety about their acceptability, firms structure entry into the profession so as to maximize acceptance of hierarchy. If you feel you've succeeded, you're forever grateful, and you have a vested interest. If you feel you've failed, you blame yourself, when you aren't busy feeling envy. When you get to be the hiring partner, you'll have a visceral understanding of what's at stake, but it will be hard even to imagine why someone might want to change it.

. . .

Strategy

In the absence of a mass movement of the left, the way to organize a left intelligentsia is in the workplace, around ideas and around the concrete issues that arise within the bourgeois corporate institutions where the potential members of such an intelligentsia live their lives.

. . .

... Organizing around ideas means developing a practice of left study, left literature and left debate about philosophy, social theory, and public policy that would give professional, technical and managerial workers the sense of participating in a left community.

Along with workplace organization around ideas there goes organization around the specific issues of hierarchy that are important in the experience of people in these institutions. This has to do with the authoritarian character of day-to-day work organization—with the use of supervisory power.... Selection, promotion and pay policies, along with a whole universe of smaller interventions, many of which are merely "social," maintain class/sex/race and also generational and meritocratic stratification within the cells of the hierarchy, while at the same time disciplining everyone to participate in the complex of hierarchical attitudes and behaviors.

. . .

What this means is that lawyers can have and should have workplace struggles, no matter where they are situated in the hierarchy of the bar, and whether or not they are actively engaged in political law practice. For law students, it means that it is important to have a law school struggle, even if they are spending most of their time on extracurricular activities that support oppressed people.

STEWART MACAULAY
"LAW SCHOOLS AND THE WORLD OUTSIDE THEIR DOORS II: SOME NOTES ON TWO RECENT STUDIES OF THE CHICAGO BAR"

32 Journal of Legal Education 506, 511–12, 521–25, 527 (1982).[15]

[The initial portion of Macaulay's article discusses two empirical studies of Chicago lawyers: (1) John P. Heinz and Edward O. Laumann, Chicago Lawyers: The Social Structure of the Bar (1982), discussed further at p. 922; and (2) Frances K. Zemans and Victor G. Rosenblum, The Making of a Public Profession (1981). Zemans and Rosenblum's book reports an appraisal of legal education by a sample drawn from the Chicago bar. Zemans and Rosenblum asked these lawyers to rank 21 skills and areas of knowledge related to the practice of law. They also asked where their respondents had gained these skills, what law schools tell their students about the importance of these skills and what they perceived as the goals of their law school. Zemans and Rosenblum found that lawyers see legal education as valuing and teaching "the ideal symbolic work of the legal profession." However, lawyers also thought that what was neglected in the law schools' self-defined mission were "the very competencies that practitioners find most important to the actual practice of law."]

... Those skills most closely identified with law school education [were considered surprisingly unimportant] when the responses of all of the lawyers are considered together. For example, "ability to understand and interpret opinions, regulations, and statutes" ranked fifth,

---

15. Copyright © 1982 Association of American Law Schools. Reprinted by permission.

trailing "fact gathering," "capacity to marshal facts and order them so that concepts can be applied," "instilling others' confidence in you," and "effective oral expression." 86.6 percent did rate such understanding and interpretive skill as important, but only 50 percent rated it extremely important. 77 percent said they learned this skill "essentially in law school." "Knowledge of theory underlying law" may seem critically important to law professors, but Zemans and Rosenblum's Chicago lawyers ranked it only thirteenth out of the twenty-one skills and areas of knowledge. 61.1 percent rated it as important but only 23 percent saw it as extremely important. 84 percent said they gained this knowledge in law school rather than in practice. 76.9 percent of the graduates of national law schools saw "providing the theoretical basis of law" as being a major goal of their school, while only 34.5 percent of the graduates of local law schools characterized such theoretical knowledge as a major goal of their education.

As might be expected, evaluations of skills and knowledge are not randomly distributed among lawyers. Zemans and Rosenblum conclude that the "lower prestige specialties seem to involve more interpersonal skills, while the higher prestige specialties are more likely to rate more purely 'analytic' skills as important to their practice." ...

The lawyers acknowledged that many skills could not be taught easily in law school, but they criticized law schools for failing even to make their students aware of the importance of these parts of practice....

. . .

[The concluding portion of Macaulay's article places empirical studies of legal education in the light of Duncan Kennedy's critique.]

What, then, are we to conclude? Few law professors, in all likelihood, would take their Duncan Kennedy neat; most would dilute his position greatly before they accepted it or, more likely, they would ignore it.[51] Most law professors probably would accept the picture

---

51. Those offended by Kennedy's position might consider Roger Cramton's The Ordinary Religion of the Law School Classroom, 29 J. Legal Educ. 247 (1978) which avoids Kennedy's "radical" or "left" vocabulary. Cramton finds the unarticulated fundamental assumptions of the American law school classroom to be: "a skeptical attitude toward generalizations; an instrumental approach to law and lawyering; a 'tough minded and analytical attitude toward legal tasks and professional roles; and a faith that man, by the application of his reason and the use of democratic processes, can make the world a better place." Id. at 248. He makes observations such as "The law teacher must stress cognitive rationality along with 'hard' facts and 'cold' logic and 'concrete' realities. Emotion, imagination, sentiments of affection and trust, a sense of wonder or awe at the inexplicable—these soft and mushy domains of the 'tender minded' are off limits for law students and lawyers." Id. at 250. "Instead of transforming society, the functional approach tends to become dominated by society, to become an apologist and technician for established institutions and things as they are, to view change as a form of tinkering rather than a reexamination of basic premises. Surface goals such as 'efficiency,' 'progress,' and 'the democratic way' are taken at face value and more ultimate questions of value submerged." Id. at 254. "Modern dogmas entangle education—amoral relativism tending toward nihilism, a pragmatism tending toward an amoral instrumentalism, a realism tending toward cynicism, an individualism tending toward atomism, and a faith in reason and democratic processes tending toward mere credulity, and idolatry. We will

painted by the two studies of the Chicago bar—perhaps quarreling about a detail here and there—and acknowledge that there is a gap between what lawyers do and what law schools teach. Some, at least, would not be too troubled by this gap, seeing law school as properly specializing in teaching legal analysis. In essence, their reply to Zemans and Rosenblum would be that their lawyer respondents were wrong in rating the importance of analytical skill. These law teachers might see a division of labor, with law school teaching legal analysis while other skills are best learned elsewhere. Many law professors would be pleased by Francis Allen's view of legal education as one of the humanities, as a discipline concerned with the realization of the core values of the society through legal institutions.

My own view is what might be called a liberal straddle.... Duncan Kennedy's views must be faced. In many ways, legal education always risks being a kind of con game—an exercise in mystification, or a process of transforming idealistic students into hired guns. Allen's portrait flatters the subject greatly. His humanistic claim for legal education states an ideal while the reality—at least in others' classrooms—often is lip service to liberal values coupled with little concern for their realization in everyday affairs. Of course, all institutions have a kind of official picture of themselves, a version of their functions that gives them legitimacy. And given the nature of the world, there always is likely to be a gap between promise and performance. It also may be that legal education is trapped in a contradiction between the high ideals it sometimes considers and the inability of its subject matter—appellate cases—to tell us much about whether those ideals have any meaning within society. Whatever the source of the problem, we are unlikely to move much beyond empty symbolism if we are unwilling to reconsider many of our presuppositions and look beyond reported decisions.

Law school, for some students at least, does involve an important transformation of outlook. Some students still come into law school with "rhetorical visions, fantasy chains or organizational frames" concerning the profession they want to enter. They see lawyers as well paid in money and status. Moreover, their work is seen as involving defending core American values....

Most of these idealistic students are transformed into apprentice lawyers who will find it acceptable to represent those who are likely to

neither understand nor transform these modern dogmas unless we abandon our unconcern for value premises. The beliefs and attitudes that anchor our lives must be examined and revealed." Id. at 262. Recognizing that Cramton and Kennedy are starting from such very different positions, I find the similarity in their views remarkable. But see William Stanmeyer, On Legal Education: The Selection of Faculty, 6 Law & Liberty—A Project on the Legal Framework of A Free Society 1–3 (Winter 1981) (describing legal education similarly but arguing students are indoctrinated against property and freedom). I think if one examined the "beliefs and attitudes that anchor our lives" as law teachers *in light of the two Chicago bar studies*, one would have to grant much of Kennedy's case....

be the best customers of their services.[54] Kennedy certainly is right
that the first year of law school will be hard on students who question
capitalism, liberal pluralism, or the existing distributions of wealth,
privilege, and status in the society. The curriculum usually begins
with a heavy dose of common law and ignores the many statutory
rejections of its answers. The discussion in the classroom frequently
celebrates individualism, efficiency, an incremental process, and protection of zones of freedom within which those with power can exercise it.
A slightly idealistic first-year student often makes a statement in class
which the professor can push into the form of "it is just to equalize
wealth; X is the poorer of the parties and Y is a large corporation with
a deep pocket; therefore X ought to win." When a master teacher is
through, the student or one of his susceptible classmates will have
asserted the virtues of rewards to the efficient who create wealth for all
of us, the virtues of holding individuals responsible for their actions,
and the evils of paternalism which robs the weaker of their choice and
substitutes that of a purported expert. In a well-run class, all will see
visions of grass growing in the streets if courts were to yield to
softhearted sentiment. Other skilled teachers will drive home the
message that the redistribution of wealth may be an appropriate
function of legislatures in a pluralistic society but falls out of bounds
for courts; however, they seldom examine seriously the likely consequences of this position. While such conclusions may flow from our
political outlook, it would be hard to call them neutral or scientific with
a straight face.

Even when the message of a first-year classroom is not so openly
political, there is another message which is part of the process of
transforming entering students into apprentice lawyers. A strong
lesson is that there is always an argument the other way, and the Devil
usually has a very good case. Heffernan has pointed out that law
teaching tends to be Sophist rather than Socratic. Socrates asked
questions in search of an understanding of justice. The Sophists, in
contrast, played intellectual games and sought to make the weaker
argument the stronger. Many law professors are famous for their skill
in responding to whatever their students say by leaping to the other
side. When a naive student thinks he can gain favor by joining the
professor, the professor turns the argument on its head and leaps back
to the original argument, perhaps stating it more persuasively. The
successful student learns that there are no answers but just arguments.
Of course, the really successful student learns that, as was true of
Orwell's pigs, some arguments are more equal than others; indeed, the
point may be that while there are few right arguments, there are many
wrong ones. Nonetheless, the process is not a Socratic search for
justice but a Sophist game. And if one is paid to play a game, it does
not make much difference whether he plays for the Yankees, Brewers,

---

54. See James C. Foster, The "Cooling Out" of Law Students, 3 Law & Pol'y Q. 243
(1981). Some students, of course, do not get cooled out and are willing and able to find
jobs involving idealistic elements.

Red Sox, or Orioles—or for IBM, General Motors, ITT, or the Department of Justice.

However, for many it would go too far to see lawyering as only a game. Part of the answer for them is supplied by comforting assumptions and ideas about the adversary system. Everyone involved in a controversy will have a lawyer pressing his case; the excesses of one will be canceled out by the zeal of another; thus, the unseen hand of competition in the marketplace of ideas will yield truth. If opposing lawyers play the intellectual game, nothing should be overlooked. A wise judge will be able to put aside bias and see all that is involved before making a decision. Thus, one who works for *any* client is serving an important social process, and, indeed, one has an obligation not to pull punches out of a misguided sense of social responsibility.

Kennedy certainly is right that law school tends to celebrate only part of the work and skills of attorneys and in this way reinforces the status hierarchies of the profession. However, when one looks at the two studies of the Chicago bar and other reports about the top end of the profession, one has to wonder if something else is not also involved. Law school does not track perfectly with the needs of the largest law firms; it offers little training for much of their work.... General corporate practice also has high status, and occupies far more lawyers' time than corporate litigation. Nonetheless, law school tends to neglect training in planning transactions and drafting the needed legal documents to carry out the plan....

To a great extent, legal education has attempted to be all things to all people in order to claim status and rewards from both inside and outside the academy. However it is not easy to have it both ways....

------

3. Legal Profession's Messages About Professional Responsibility

Professor Ronald Pipkin, on the basis of a substantial empirical study, argues that many law school courses in professional responsibility actually "desensitize students to legal ethics." [16] He begins by identifying the manifest and latent hierarchy of courses in law schools. The manifest hierarchy identifies important courses by such official indicators as the number of credits assigned to each course and whether a course is required or elective. The latent hierarchy is "less visible, less explicitly rationalized, and may either reinforce or work at cross-purposes to the official ... manifest structure. The latent hierarchies are communicated to students through the content of instruction, cues from the faculty, advice from practitioners and other students, feedback from the job market, bar exams and so forth." [17] Pipkin argues that

16. Ronald Pipkin, Law School Instruction in Professional Responsibility: A Curricular Paradox, 1979 Amer.Bar Found.Research J. 247.

17. Id. at 252–53.

the latent hierarchy works to undercut whatever importance the manifest hierarchy assigns to courses in professional responsibility.

Pipkin interviewed students at seven law schools in the academic year 1975–76. His data showed that students perceived courses in professional responsibility as requiring less time, as substantially easier, as less well-taught and as a less valuable use of class time. His data further suggested that courses in professional responsibility were held in low intellectual esteem in large measure because they were more likely to be taught by discussion method than by either lecture or the socratic method. Generally, courses taught by the Socratic method were considered by students to be the most intellectually demanding, with courses taught by lecture coming in second and courses, no matter what the subject, taught by discussion coming in a poor third. Although students perceived professional responsibility as highly relevant to their later careers as practicing lawyers, a course's perceived relevance to life as a lawyer was irrelevant to how much time students expended on the course or whether or not they saw the course as intellectually challenging.

How does law school communicate messages about the importance of professional responsibility? If professional responsibility issues have come up in other courses, how has the subject been treated by the professor? Is professional responsibility a theme that runs through your law school career? How do legal employers treat the subject? Fellow students? How have these messages affected your attitude toward professional responsibility?

D. THE ORGANIZED BAR

1. Bar Associations [18]

CHARLES W. WOLFRAM
MODERN LEGAL ETHICS
33–38 (1986).[19]

Bar Organizations as Bar Regulators

One whose reading about the legal profession was confined to appellate court reports might be led to believe that state supreme courts exercise both power and initiative in its regulation. In fact, courts serve as the largely passive sounding boards and official approvers or disapprovers of initiatives that are taken by lawyers operating

---

18. For a description of studies of the organized bar, see Olivi Maru, Research on the Legal Profession c. 5 (2d ed. 1986). See also John A. Flood, The Legal Profession in the United States (3d ed., 1985, American Bar Foundation) (containing an annotated bibliography).

19. Copyright © 1986 West Publishing Co. Reprinted by permission.

through bar associations. Bar associations set and execute the agenda of business of the organized bar. Their power can be much the same regardless of the particular form or official status of the bar association. Formal and, to an extent, functional differences do exist between unofficial bar associations and those, called "integrated" or mandatory bars, that every lawyer must join as a condition of being eligible to practice law. At the end of the day, however, bar associations exercise pervasive influence over bar admission and discipline, whatever the form of their organization.

Bar Associations

Bar associations arose in the American colonies as eating clubs or similar social gatherings of lawyers.[91] Lawyer business was also their object, and early rules setting uniform fees and regulating the admission of lawyers to practice came from the bar associations. Bar associations fell into decline and ceased to exist during the early part of the nineteenth century. Little formal organization characterized the American bar until after the Civil War, although the groups of lawyers that accompanied judges on circuit undoubtedly had some cohesion and exercised some collective power.

The American Bar Association

Among the earliest groups of lawyers to band together in the orgy of occupational organization that swept the industrial world in the last third of the nineteenth century was the American Bar Association.[92] The ABA was organized in the late summer of 1878 in Saratoga Springs, New York, a popular summering spot for the well-to-do.... The ABA started, and continues, as a private organization that controls its own membership and other affairs and is accountable to no public body for action it might take on organizational or policy matters.

The ABA can advance several reasons in support of a claim that it speaks for the entire legal profession. The ABA is the only national organization with significant lawyer membership from all areas of practice. It operates primarily through sections that are devoted to many fields of law or law practice.... Its membership in recent decades has averaged 45 to 55 percent of the nation's licensed lawyers. The ABA House of Delegates, its chief legislative arm, consists in large part of lawyers appointed from several sections or other parts of the ABA or elected from state and local bar associations that, in turn, exercise varying degrees of control over local lawyers. Historically, the leadership of the ABA and officials of both national and state govern-

91. Among histories of bar associations, see, e.g., R. Pound, The Lawyer from Antiquity to Modern Times (1953); C. Warren, A History of the American Bar (2d ed. 1966). Pound and, to an extent, Warren give laudatory, and largely uncritical, acceptance to the notion that the most highly organized and powerful forms of bar associations are the best.

92. Accounts of the founding of the ABA are given in E. Sunderland, History of the American Bar Association and Its Work (1953); C. Goetsch, Essays on Simeon E. Baldwin (1981). See generally Brockman, The History of the American Bar Association: A Bibliographic Essay, 6 Am.J.Leg.Hist. 269 (1962).

ments have worked in harmony on a variety of projects, including many in the area of lawyer regulation.

. . .

Other Bar Associations

The ABA has several fellow and sister bar associations, but none compares in size or power. Most state and local bar associations are aligned with the ABA but some have no connections. Most other bar associations are devoted to the interests of lawyer specialists or to a particular issue, cause, or ethnic group. For example, the Federal Bar Association consists primarily of lawyers employed by the federal government. Lawyers are eligible for membership in the Association of Trial Lawyers of America (ATLA) only if they represent claimants in personal injury, products liability, or worker compensation claims. Lawyers who belong to the American College of Trial Lawyers, by contrast, predominantly defend large businesses and insurance companies. The National Bar Association is an organization of black lawyers. The National Lawyers Guild is primarily an organization of leftist lawyers interested in civil rights, civil liberties, and poverty issues.... Both in membership and in power, all other special-interest bar associations taken together cannot equal the power of the ABA.

State and local bar associations historically have operated much as the ABA—as autonomous, private organizations of largely like-minded lawyers within a state, county, city judicial district, or other geographical area.... Even as purely private organizations, state and local bar associations gained considerable power in the early decades of this century. With growing influence they began to lead more ambitious campaigns to influence the education and admission of lawyers, to restrict nonlawyer competition through the creation of unauthorized-practice barriers, and to deal with disfavored practices such as solicitation and advertising by small-firm lawyers. Their power on those and other professional issues was exerted through public and private pressure on courts and legislatures to cede a wider regulatory role to bar associations.

The Operation of Bar Associations

While bar associations retained the formal status of private clubs, their legal powers widened increasingly as they came to gain political power over the profession. In recent decades, bar associations have turned to explicitly political activity such as legislative and administrative lobbying, public relations efforts, and the support of positions on issues. Some of those efforts relate to law reform, some relate to more controversial political issues, and much does not relate directly to the economic or professional status of bar members. Bar associations do not, however, overtly support candidates for political office, aside from the practice of some associations of expressing approval or regret concerning candidates for judicial offices.

As is true of other professional organizations, the majority of the members of bar associations are inactive on most organizational projects.... Most bar association business is conducted in private meetings of committees or boards. The general membership becomes simply the ratifier of predetermined menus of issues and proposals for their resolution. Of course, the general membership must remain content enough not to resign or to vote out a leadership that has struck off too far on its own. Such membership revolts are known among bar associations and serve to instill conservatism and timidity in bar leaders and executives.[5]

Mandatory Bars

The striving by local bars for more effective control of the legal profession resulted in an effort beginning in the early 1920s to "integrate"[7] the bars of the various states. The term does not refer to racial or gender diversity, which, at that time, was rejected by most bar associations and their members. Instead, integration referred to an organized bar effort to enact court rules or statutes to require every lawyer who actively practiced law to belong to the state bar association. Among other things, making bar membership mandatory would permit the bar association to exercise greater control over the admission and particularly the discipline of lawyers.

Typically the bar was made mandatory by an order issued by the state supreme court under its inherent power to regulate the practice of law, although several mandatory bars have been created by statute. Courts have uniformly upheld the power of the courts themselves or of bar associations to exact mandatory bar fees from lawyers and threaten suspension from practice as a penalty for a lawyer who, without excuse, does not pay.[10] In 1961 a divided Supreme Court in Lathrop v. Donohue[11] rejected federal constitutional attacks on mandatory lawyer membership in state bars. By the early 1980s thirty-three states and the District of Columbia had mandatory bars.

... Because courts lack the time, staff, funds, or means of information gathering, they probably are not intimately aware of the actual operation of mandatory bars and supervise them only in a passive and

---

5. The widely held lawyer belief is that bar associations tend to be conservative groups heavily dominated by large-firm lawyers unsympathetic to social change. A sociologist has argued, however, that the history of the positions taken by various bar groups on controversial social and political issues since the Second World War suggests that liberal as well as conservative causes are often espoused. Halliday, The Idiom of Legalism in Bar Politics: Lawyers, McCarthyism, and the Civil Rights Era, 1982 Am.B.Found.Research J. 913.

7. Mandatory bars were originally referred to as "integrated" bars and are now more commonly called "unified." The term "mandatory" is less euphemistic and more descriptive of their salient characteristic.

10. Petition of Florida State Bar Ass'n, 40 So.2d 902 (Fla.1949); In re Unification of New Hampshire Bar, 109 N.H. 260, 248 A.2d 709 (1968); Petition of Rhode Island Bar Ass'n, 118 R.I. 489, 374 A.2d 802 (1977)....

11. 367 U.S. 820 (1961). ...

reactive capacity by passing upon initiatives that are generated and shaped in detail elsewhere....

Although mandatory bars have existed since 1921, they continue to generate controversy.[16] The concept of mandatory bar associations has been resisted for a number of reasons by many lawyers, primarily those in solo practice or small firms. Opponents have feared that annual dues would become too high and that funds taken from members' dues would be used to support projects opposed by a majority of members or to support political causes....

----

2. Compulsory Membership in the Bar

KELLER v. STATE BAR OF CALIFORNIA

Supreme Court of the United States, 1990.
496 U.S. 1, 110 S.Ct. 2228, 110 L.Ed.2d 1.

CHIEF JUSTICE REHNQUIST delivered the opinion of the Court.

Petitioners, members of the State Bar of California, sued that body claiming its use of their membership dues to finance certain ideological or political activities to which they were opposed violated their rights under the First Amendment of the United States Constitution. The Supreme Court of California rejected this challenge on the grounds that respondent State Bar is a state agency and, as such, may use the dues for any purpose within its broad statutory authority. We agree that lawyers admitted to practice in the State may be required to join and pay dues to the State Bar, but disagree as to the scope of permissible dues-financed activities in which respondent may engage.

Respondent State Bar is an organization created under California law to regulate the State's legal profession. It is an entity commonly referred to as an "integrated bar"—an association of attorneys in which membership and dues are required as a condition of practicing law in a State. Respondent's broad statutory mission is to "promote 'the improvement of the administration of justice.'" 767 P.2d 1020, 1021 (1989) (quoting Cal.Bus. & Prof.Code Ann. § 6031(a) (West Supp.1990)). The association performs a variety of functions such as "examining applicants for admission, formulating rules of professional conduct, disciplining members for misconduct, preventing unlawful practice of the law, and engaging in study and recommendation of changes in procedural law and improvement of the administration of justice." 767 P.2d, at 1023–1024. Respondent also engages in a number of other activities

----

16. See generally Schneyer, The Incoherence of the Unified Bar Concept: Generalizing from the Wisconsin Experience, 1983 Am.B.Found. Research J. 1. Professor Schneyer concludes that the contradictions inherent in the concept of a mandatory bar association should lead to their demise, with their functions taken over by voluntary bar associations or, if necessary, by special-purpose agencies for bar discipline and the like that are financed by court assessment of dues on all lawyers.

which are the subject of the dispute in this case.   "[T]he State Bar for many years has lobbied the Legislature and other governmental agencies, filed amicus curiae briefs in pending cases, held an annual conference of delegates at which issues of current interest are debated and resolutions approved, and engaged in a variety of education programs." 767 P.2d, at 1021–1022.   These activities are financed principally through the use of membership dues.

Petitioners, 21 members of the State Bar, sued in state court claiming that through these activities respondent expends mandatory dues payments to advance political and ideological causes to which they do not subscribe.   Asserting that their compelled financial support of such activities violates their First and Fourteenth Amendment rights to freedom of speech and association, petitioners requested, inter alia, an injunction restraining respondent from using mandatory bar dues or the name of the State Bar of California to advance political and ideological causes or beliefs.

. . .

In Lathrop v. Donohue, 367 U.S. 820 (1961), a Wisconsin lawyer claimed that he could not constitutionally be compelled to join and financially support a state bar association which expressed opinions on, and attempted to influence, legislation.   Six Members of this Court . . . rejected this claim.

. . .

In Abood v. Detroit Board of Education, 431 U.S. 209 (1977), the Court confronted the issue whether, consistent with the First Amendment, agency-shop dues of nonunion public employees could be used to support political and ideological causes of the union which were unrelated to collective-bargaining activities.   We held that while the Constitution did not prohibit a union from spending "funds for the expression of political views . . . or toward the advancement of other ideological causes not germane to its duties as collective-bargaining representative," the Constitution did require that such expenditures be "financed from charges, dues, or assessments paid by employees who [did] not object to advancing those ideas and who [were] not coerced into doing so against their will by the threat of loss of governmental employment." Id., at 235–236. . . .   The Court acknowledged Thomas Jefferson's view that " 'to compel a man to furnish contributions of money for the propagation of opinions which he disbelieves, is sinful and tyrannical.' " 431 U.S., at 234–235, n. 31. . . .   [I]n the later case of Ellis v. Railway Clerks, 466 U.S. 435 (1984), the Court made it clear that the principles of Abood apply equally to employees in the private sector.   See 466 U.S., at 455–457. . . .   [T]he California Supreme Court in this case held that respondent's status as a regulated state agency exempted it from any constitutional constraints on the use of its dues.   "If the bar is considered a governmental agency, then the distinction between revenue derived from mandatory dues and revenue from other sources is immaterial.   A governmental agency may use unrestricted revenue, whether derived from taxes, dues, fees, tolls, tuition, donation, or other sources, for any purposes within its authority." 767 P.2d, at 1029.

Of course the Supreme Court of California is the final authority on the "governmental" status of the State Bar of California for purposes of state law. But its determination ... is not binding on us when such a determination is essential to the decision of a federal question. The State Bar of California is a good deal different from most other entities that would be regarded in common parlance as "governmental agencies." Its principal funding comes not from appropriations made to it by the legislature, but from dues levied on its members by the board of governors. Only lawyers admitted to practice in the State of California are members of the State Bar, and all 122,000 lawyers admitted to practice in the State must be members. Respondent undoubtedly performs important and valuable services for the State by way of governance of the profession, but those services are essentially advisory in nature. The State Bar does not admit anyone to the practice of law, it does not finally disbar or suspend anyone, and it does not ultimately establish ethical codes of conduct. All of those functions are reserved by California law to the State Supreme Court....

There is, by contrast, a substantial analogy between the relationship of the State Bar and its members, on the one hand, and the relation of the employee unions and their members, on the other. The reason behind the legislative enactment of "agency shop" laws is to prevent "free riders"—those who receive the benefit of union negotiation with their employers, but who do not choose to join the union and pay dues—from avoiding their fair share of the cost of a process from which they benefit. The members of the State Bar concededly do not benefit as directly from respondent's activities as do employees from union negotiations with management, but the position of the organized bars has generally been that they prefer a large measure of self-regulation to regulation conducted by a government body which has little or no connection with the profession. The plan established by California for the regulation of the profession is for recommendations as to admission to practice, the disciplining of lawyers, codes of conduct, and the like to be made to the courts or the legislature by the organized bar. It is entirely appropriate that all of the lawyers who derive benefit from the unique status of being among those admitted to practice before the courts should be called upon to pay a fair share of the cost of the professional involvement in this effort.

But the very specialized characteristics of the State Bar of California discussed above served to distinguish it from the role of the typical government official or agency.... If every citizen were to have a right to insist that no one paid by public funds express a view with which he disagreed, debate over issues of great concern to the public would be limited to those in the private sector, and the process of government as we know it radically transformed. Cf. United States v. Lee, 455 U.S. 252, 260 (1982) ("The tax system could not function if denominations were allowed to challenge the tax system because tax payments were spent in a manner that violates their religious belief").

The State Bar of California was created, not to participate in the general government of the State, but to provide specialized professional advice to those with the ultimate responsibility of governing the legal profession. Its members and officers are such not because they are citizens or voters, but because they are lawyers. We think that these differences between the State Bar, on the one hand, and traditional government agencies and officials, on the other hand, render unavailing respondent's argument that it is not subject to the same constitutional rule with respect to the use of compulsory dues as are labor unions representing public and private employees.

. . .

Petitioners assert that the State Bar has engaged in, inter alia, lobbying for or against state legislation (1) prohibiting state and local agency employers from requiring employees to take polygraph tests; (2) prohibiting possession of armor-piercing handgun ammunition; (3) creating an unlimited right of action to sue anybody causing air pollution; and (4) requesting Congress to refrain from enacting a guest worker program or from permitting the importation of workers from other countries. Petitioners' complaint also alleges that the conference of delegates funded and sponsored by the State Bar endorsed a gun control initiative, disapproved statements of a United States senatorial candidate regarding court review of a victim's bill of rights, endorsed a nuclear weapons freeze initiative, and opposed federal legislation limiting federal court jurisdiction over abortions, public school prayer, and busing.

Precisely where the line falls between those State Bar activities in which the officials and members of the Bar are acting essentially as professional advisors to those ultimately charged with the regulation of the legal profession, on the one hand, and those activities having political or ideological coloration which are not reasonably related to the advancement of such goals, on the other, will not always be easy to discern. But the extreme ends of the spectrum are clear: Compulsory dues may not be expended to endorse or advance a gun control or nuclear weapons freeze initiative; at the other end of the spectrum petitioners have no valid constitutional objection to their compulsory dues being spent for activities connected with disciplining members of the Bar or proposing ethical codes for the profession.

. . .

The judgment of the Supreme Court of California is reversed, and the case is remanded for further proceedings not inconsistent with this opinion.

Notes on *Keller*

What state bar activities are "political or ideological" as distinct from those that are "necessarily or reasonably incurred" for the purpose of regulating the legal profession or improving the quality of legal services? Which of the following activities are permissible under *Keller*: Resolutions or lobbying activities concerning the appointment rather than election of judges? Greater public funding of civil legal assistance for the poor? Longer periods of maternity leave for employees, including fathers? Extension of anti-discrimination laws to protect homosexuals against discrimination in housing, employment, education and public accommodations? Termination of China's "most favored nation" trade status because of that nation's departures from "the rule of law?"

On remand in *Keller,* the California State Bar reexamined its expenditures and determined that only $3 of the typical 1991 dues of $478 were not germane to the bar's central purposes. Members who did not want to underwrite non-chargeable activities were permitted to take a $3 deduction. In Michigan, however, a similar evaluation resulted in an $18 rebate from total annual dues of $200.[20]

3. Future of Self–Regulation

When lawyers refer to "self-regulation," they usually have in mind the fact that by and large, only lawyers regulate lawyers. Leaders of the bar identify self-regulation as an essential component of "professionalism." The traditional view is that the responsible lawyer internalizes appropriate standards of conduct and supports institutional arrangements by which the profession implements and enforces these standards. The special expertise of the profession with respect to legal services, it is argued, permits it to perform this function better than an external regulatory body. Freedom of lawyers from oppressive state regulation permits the profession to maintain a degree of independence that supports challenges of official authority, a predicate of ordered liberty.[21]

Others challenge the profession's traditional view. The extreme claim is that professional rhetoric is a mask for self-interested activity that enhances lawyer status and earnings.[22] A more modest version of the same criticism notes the propensity of groups to view the world

20. Where Are the Big Savings?, A.B.A. J. 36–37 (March 1991).

21. See, e.g., the report of the ABA Commission on Professionalism, " . . . In the Spirit of Public Service:" A Blueprint for the Rekindling of Lawyer Professionalism, 112 F.R.D. 243, 261–62 (1986), which includes in one of its definitions of "professionalism" the following: "That the occupation is self-regulating—that is, organized in such a way as to assure the public and the court that its members are competent, do not violate their client's trust, and transcend their own self-interest."

22. See, e.g., Richard Abel, American Lawyers 226–33 (1989), arguing that the evidence supports the "cynical view" that lawyers have sought to control the supply and demand for legal services "in order to enhance both their earning power and their collective status." In Abel's view, the legal profession has "[sought] regulatory powers largely to immunize [itself] from external scrutiny." Id. at 232.

from a special perspective influenced by experience and sometimes by self-interest.[23]   Developments since the 1960s, especially the rise of the consumer movement and the Watergate cover-up, have generated skepticism about authority, including that exercised by the organized bar. The response is a modern trend for greater openness, broadened participation and enlarged accountability.   As applied to the legal profession, these developments involve a gradual shift from regulation by bar associations to judicial regulation, the use of notice-and-comment procedures in rulemaking, decreased secrecy in professional discipline and inclusion of nonlawyers on the official bodies responsible for admission and discipline.   Yet the process remains a distinctive one in that legislative authority is either excluded entirely or rarely exercised, with the regulation of the profession largely committed to state high courts. Should state and federal legislatures play a larger role in regulation of the legal profession than they have in the past?

E.   REGULATION OF THE PROFESSION BY INSTITUTIONAL CONTROLS

1.   Legal Structure of Law Practice

Introductory Note

As Justice O'Connor suggests in her dissent in Shapero v. Kentucky State Bar, p. 968, being a "lawyer" is a distinct social identity.   A practitioner of law is someone who: (1) graduated from an accredited law school and thus underwent the socialization process of legal education;   (2) successfully passed the bar admission requirements and has a certificate to prove it, thereby marking herself off from the large majority of the white collar workforce that does not have such a certificate;   (3) primarily is engaged in work that is done exclusively or primarily by lawyers, including preparing and conducting various kinds of litigation and negotiating and documenting various kinds of transactions;   (4) spends her day in lawyer work settings, particularly independent law firms and the law departments of government agencies and business corporations;   and (5) talks and thinks "law" in shop talk, at professional meetings, in schmoozing with peers after work, and in response to conversational gambits at cocktail parties.

Being a lawyer is sustained and influenced by complex institutional structures, far beyond admission requirements and the disciplinary

---

23.   See, e.g., Thomas D. Morgan, The Evolving Concept of Professional Responsibility, 90 Harv. L. Rev. 702 (1977) (bar's ethical codes favor professional over public interests); and Deborah L. Rhode, Why the ABA Bothers: A Functional Perspective on Professional Codes, 59 Tex. L. Rev. 689 (1981) (same).

system. Even in the absence of admission requirements and the disciplinary system, the practice of law would still be subject to general legal controls that operate on lawyers along with everyone else. These controls include criminal law, contract law and tort law, including the law of malpractice. Throughout this book we have seen these general legal controls applied to lawyers.[24] Indeed, many of the central provisions in the Model Rules of Professional Conduct and the Model Code of Professional Responsibility reflect or correspond to general rules of common law, particularly the law of agency. These rules of law would continue to operate in the absence of specific regulation of the legal profession and would protect clients and third persons even if there were no restrictions on admission to practice law and no disciplinary machinery.

The common law position, however, is that trades and businesses generally are open to competition. Statutes prohibiting the unauthorized practice of law, i.e., doing what lawyers generally do without being admitted to the bar, have displaced this common law rule insofar as law practice is concerned. The regulation of competition in the delivery of legal services is considered in Chapter 10, but the topic is highly relevant also to matters considered here.

Indirect Legal Controls on the Lawyer's Workplace

Law practice is also subject to indirect controls that have legal foundations. Particularly influential on the lawyer's environment are the atmosphere and routines in the law firm or law department in which the lawyer works day-to-day; in other law firms and law departments with which the lawyer interacts in her day-to-day work and by whom she might be employed if she changes jobs; in the courts and the government agencies with whom the lawyer interacts; and in the bar associations in which the lawyer participates. These institutions—the firms, the government agencies and the bar associations—all have political structures and agendas and are subject to economic incentives and constraints. They all have cultural characteristics. For example, some law firms are high pressure and earn high incomes; others are not. Some are very "pro bono" oriented; others are not. Some courts where lawyers appear are well-managed and on top of their calendars; others are bogged down and chaotic. Some government agencies with which lawyers deal have high technical competence and high esprit de corps; others are sluggish and incompetent. Together, these institutions are the matrix of life in which a lawyer tries to accomplish professional tasks, adjusts to the realities of practice and takes on her professional identity.

Systematic studies of careers in law are relatively few. One can imagine studies that take samples from cohorts of graduates from a cross-section of law schools ("elite," "national," state university, "local," etc.) at various years (1960, 1970, 1980, for example) and track their

---

24. See, e.g., United States v. Benjamin, p. 57 (lawyer's criminal liability for mail fraud and securities fraud); Fassihi v. Sommers, p. 797 (fiduciary duty).

employment patterns over the years.   Such studies would show what kinds of jobs graduates begin with (firms, prosecutor offices, sharing office space, etc.), when and where they shift jobs, and when they more or less settle into a permanent career.   In 1985, seven law schools cooperated in such a study but only on the condition that the data not correlate the schools with their graduates.[25]   Key findings were the following: 70 percent remain in the same metropolitan area in which they took their first law job; about 80 percent of law school graduates remain in law practice or a law-related vocation such as government; 40 percent were in a work setting other than a private law firm; 75 percent of those who had been out 25 years had made at least one job change.   Lawyers more than 15 years out of law school will have had on the average two or three different jobs.   Those most likely to remain in the same work setting for long periods of time are large law firm lawyers and solo practitioners.

A study of Chicago lawyers by Professors Heinz and Laumann provides the best conceptual formulation of lawyer employment in terms of the structure of contemporary law practice.[26]   They conclude that the legal profession is highly stratified and has a relatively clear status hierarchy.   Variation within the profession is best accounted for, not by the type of legal services rendered, but by the social and economic character of clients.   The profession is organized in two hemispheres: lawyers who serve corporate clients and those who serve individuals.   Corporate lawyers, who have fewer clients each year than those representing individuals, are often engaged in "symbol manipulation"; those who represent individuals are more often involved in "people persuasion."[27]   Because lawyers respond to the interests and demands of their clients, "the nature of the clients served ... primarily determines the structure of social differentiation...."[28] Fields of practice that serve large corporate clients, such as securities, corporate tax, antitrust and banking, are at the top of the profession's prestige structure while those serving individual clients in fields such as divorce, landlord and tenant, debt collection and criminal defense are at the bottom.   Lawyers who serve the core economic values of American society are accorded more prestige than those who are people-oriented or cause-oriented.[29]

25. See Leona M. Vogt, From Law School to Career: Where Do Graduates Go and What Do They Do?, Harvard Law School Program on the Legal Profession (May 1986) ("Career Paths Study") The schools were Boston College, Boston University, Columbia, University of Connecticut, Harvard, Northeastern and Suffolk.

26. John P. Heinz and Edward O. Laumann, Chicago Lawyers: The Social Structure of the Bar (1982). The study is based on structured interviews of a random sample of 777 Chicago lawyers in 1975. The Heinz and Laumann study is discussed in Stewart Macaulay, Law Schools and the World Outside Their Doors II: Some Notes on Two Recent Studies of the Chicago Bar, 32 J.Legal Educ. 506 (1982), p. 906 above.

27. Id. at 61.

28. Id. at 83.

29. Id. at 127–34.

A growing body of literature discusses one or another aspect of today's legal profession.[30] In most of these studies there is a tendency to treat all lawyers with similar backgrounds as more or less the same, disregarding differences within various "sectors" of the legal profession and among individuals. That there are sharp individual differences is suggested by recalling the backgrounds of some Supreme Court Justices. For example, Chief Justice Earl Warren was a graduate of the law school of the University of California, Berkeley, and Justice William Brennan was a graduate of Harvard Law School, while Chief Justice Warren Burger was a graduate of William Mitchell Law School and Governors Cuomo of New York and Deukmejian of California went to St. Johns at the same time. This diversity probably proves something, but exactly what?

A full account of the lawyer's vocational matrix would have to include a political, economic, sociological and historical analysis of American legal institutions. This is not possible here. An adequate account of the vocation of "lawyer," however, would extend that far, and the student should incorporate by reference whatever she has come to know about those aspects of the law.

The institutions constituting the lawyer's vocational matrix also have legal structures. Institutions such as law firms, courts and bar associations do not simply exist. They have been created by law or with the authority of law; they have legal powers that can impinge on lawyers; and they are legally accountable in one way or another. See, e.g., Hishon v. King & Spalding (law firm), printed below; Shapero v. Kentucky State Bar (bar association), p. 962. See Model Rules 5.1 to 5.3, dealing with the roles and responsibilities of partners, subordinate lawyers and legal assistants.

The legal aspects of this institutional structure are as much a part of the system of professional regulation as are the rules governing admission to practice or those of professional discipline. For example, among the important institutional influences on law practice is the character of the courts in which a litigation lawyer practices and in which a transaction lawyer has to anticipate the transaction may

---

30. Valuable studies focusing on large law firms are Robert L. Nelson, Partners with Power: The Social Transformation of the Large Law Firm (1988), and Robert L. Nelson, The Changing Structure of Opportunity: Recruitment and Careers in Large Law Firms, 1983 Am. Bar Found.Research J. 109. See also James M. Hedegard, Causes of Career–Relevant Interest Changes Among First–Year Law Students: Some Research Data, 1982 Am.Bar Found.Research J. 789 (effect of law school on attitudes and career choices); Ronald L. Hirsch, Are You on Target?, 12 Barrister 17 (1985) (survey of lawyers' job satisfaction); Richard H. Sander and E. Douglass Williams, Why Are There So Many Lawyers? Perspectives on a Turbulent Market, 14 Law & Social Inquiry 431 (1989) (analyzing factors that have led to a spiraling demand for legal services, large increases in the number of lawyers and growing inequality of incomes between lawyers in elite firms and solo practitioners). Compare Duncan Kennedy, Legal Education and the Reproduction of Hierarchy: A Polemic Against the System (1983) (critical legal theory perspective); Richard L. Abel, American Lawyers (1989), and Abel, Lawyers, in Leon Lipson and Stanton Wheeler, eds., Law and the Social Sciences (1988) (same); and Joel F. Handler, The Lawyer and His Community: The Practicing Bar in a Middle–Sized City (1967).

ultimately be litigated. Contrast in this respect the Supreme Court of the United States, whose opinions make up a large part of today's law school curriculum, and the trial court in a state where judges are elected by popular vote.

Suppose, for example, a lawyer had a case involving the publishability of a literary work alleged to be pornographic. Would she handle the matter differently if she took it over after certiorari had been granted by the Supreme Court, as compared with the situation of a client who could not afford to litigate beyond a preliminary injunction in front of the local trial court? It would, of course, make all the difference in the world, or at least all the difference in the United States. Among the differences: The Supreme Court is the Supreme Court, not a one-person local trial judge; the Supreme Court is an instrument of the United States Government, and its judges have tenure effectively for life; the state trial judge faces an election in the near future, and has to worry about the local news media and being able to raise campaign funding if necessary; the Supreme Court will have amicus briefs from all sectors of the national intelligentsia while the state trial judge may have nothing more than poorly drafted briefs by practitioners who have never before handled a First Amendment case. All these aspects of the case are "legal"—the rules governing tenure of the judges, the rules defining the participants in the litigation and the character of the forum that determines the kinds of argument that are submitted.

The institutions most directly influencing the lawyer are her situation of employment and her relationship to professional colleagues. Consider, first, the lawyer's employment situation: Although a lawyer's relationship with a client can be terminated by the client at any time and without reason, M.R. 1.16, it does not necessarily follow that the lawyer's employment relationship with a firm or law department similarly is merely "at will." See Hishon v. King & Spalding, printed below. Did the court in Balla v. Gambro, Inc., p. 604, recognize the complexities of the situation before it?

2. General Statutory Regulation of Lawyers

Gender Discrimination in Partnership Decisions

HISHON v. KING & SPALDING

Supreme Court of the United States, 1984.
467 U.S. 69, 104 S.Ct. 2229, 81 L.Ed.2d 59.

CHIEF JUSTICE BURGER delivered the opinion of the Court.

We granted certiorari to determine whether the District Court properly dismissed a Title VII complaint alleging that a law partnership discriminated against petitioner, a woman lawyer employed as an associate, when it failed to invite her to become a partner.

I

A

In 1972 petitioner Elizabeth Anderson Hishon accepted a position as an associate with respondent, a large Atlanta law firm established as a general partnership. When this suit was filed in 1980, the firm had more than 50 partners and employed approximately 50 attorneys as associates. Up to that time, no woman had ever served as a partner at the firm.

Petitioner alleges that the prospect of partnership was an important factor in her initial decision to accept employment with respondent. She alleges that respondent used the possibility of ultimate partnership as a recruiting device to induce petitioner and other young lawyers to become associates at the firm. According to the complaint, respondent represented that advancement to partnership after five or six years was "a matter of course" for associates "who receive[d] satisfactory evaluations" and that associates were promoted to partnership "on a fair and equal basis." Petitioner alleges that she relied on these representations when she accepted employment with respondent. The complaint further alleges that respondent's promise to consider her on a "fair and equal basis" created a binding employment contract.

In May 1978 the partnership considered and rejected Hishon for admission to the partnership; one year later, the partners again declined to invite her to become a partner. Once an associate is passed over for partnership at respondent's firm, the associate is notified to begin seeking employment elsewhere. Petitioner's employment as an associate terminated on December 31, 1979.

B

Hishon filed a charge with the Equal Employment Opportunity Commission on November 19, 1979, claiming that respondent had discriminated against her on the basis of her sex in violation of Title VII of the Civil Rights Act of 1964, 78 Stat. 241, as amended, 42 U.S.C. § 2000e et seq. Ten days later the Commission issued a notice of right to sue, and on February 27, 1980, Hishon brought this action in the United States District Court for the Northern District of Georgia. She sought declaratory and injunctive relief, backpay, and compensatory damages "in lieu of reinstatement and promotion to partnership." This, of course, negates any claim for specific performance of the contract alleged.

The District Court dismissed the complaint on the ground that Title VII was inapplicable to the selection of partners by a partnership. 24 FEP Cases 1303 (1980). A divided panel of the United States Court of Appeals for the Eleventh Circuit affirmed. 678 F.2d 1022 (1982)....

II

At this stage of the litigation, we must accept petitioner's allegations as true. A court may dismiss a complaint only if it is clear that no relief could be granted under any set of facts that could be proved consistent with the allegations. Conley v. Gibson, 355 U.S. 41, 45–46 (1957). The issue before us is whether petitioner's allegations state a claim under Title VII, the relevant portion of which provides as follows:

"(a) *It shall be an unlawful employment practice for an employer—*

"(1) to fail or refuse to hire or to discharge any individual, or otherwise *to discriminate against any individual with respect to his* compensation, *terms, conditions, or privileges of employment, because of such individual's* race, color, religion, *sex,* or national origin." 42 U.S.C. § 2000e–2(a) (emphasis added).

A

Petitioner alleges that respondent is an "employer" to whom Title VII is addressed.[3] She then asserts that consideration for partnership was one of the "terms, conditions, or privileges of employment" as an associate with respondent.[4] See § 2000e–2(a)(1). If this is correct, respondent could not base an adverse partnership decision on "race, color, religion, sex, or national origin."

Once a contractual relationship of employment is established, the provisions of Title VII attach and govern certain aspects of that relationship.[5] In the context of Title VII, the contract of employment may be written or oral, formal or informal; an informal contract of employment may arise by the simple act of handing a job applicant a shovel and providing a workplace. The contractual relationship of employment triggers the provision of Title VII governing "terms, conditions, or privileges of employment." Title VII in turn forbids discrimination on the basis of "race, color, religion, sex, or national origin."

Because the underlying employment relationship is contractual, it follows that the "terms, conditions, or privileges of employment" clearly include benefits that are part of an employment contract. Here, petitioner in essence alleges that respondent made a contract to consider her for partnership.[6] Indeed, this promise was allegedly a key

3. The statute defines an "employer" as a "person engaged in an industry affecting commerce who has fifteen or more employees for each working day in each of twenty or more calendar weeks in the current or preceding calendar year," § 2000e(b), and a "person" is explicitly defined to include "partnerships," § 2000e(a). The complaint alleges that respondent's partnership satisfies these requirements.

4. Petitioner has raised other theories of Title VII liability which, in light of our disposition, need not be addressed.

5. Title VII also may be relevant in the absence of an existing employment relationship, as when an employer *refuses* to hire someone. See § 2000e–2(a)(1). However, discrimination in that circumstance does not concern the "terms, conditions, or privileges of employment," which is the focus of the present case.

6. Petitioner alleges not only that respondent promised to consider her for partnership, but also that it promised to consider her on a "fair and equal basis." This latter promise is not necessary to petitioner's Title VII claim. Even if the employment contract did not afford a basis for an implied condition that the ultimate decision would be fairly made on the merits, Title VII itself would impose such a requirement. If the promised consideration for partnership is a term, condition, or privilege of employment, then the

contractual provision which induced her to accept employment. If the evidence at trial establishes that the parties contracted to have petitioner considered for partnership, that promise clearly was a term, condition, or privilege of her employment. Title VII would then bind respondent to consider petitioner for partnership as the statute provides, i.e., without regard to petitioner's sex. The contract she alleges would lead to the same result.

Petitioner's claim that a contract was made, however, is not the only allegation that would qualify respondent's consideration of petitioner for partnership as a term, condition, or privilege of employment. An employer may provide its employees with many benefits that it is under no obligation to furnish by any express or implied contract. Such a benefit, though not a contractual *right* of employment, may qualify as a "privileg[e]" of employment under Title VII. A benefit that is part and parcel of the employment relationship may not be doled out in a discriminatory fashion, even if the employer would be free under the employment contract simply not to provide the benefit at all. Those benefits that comprise the "incidents of employment," S.Rep. No. 867, 88th Cong., 2d Sess., 11 (1964),[7] or that form "an aspect of the relationship between the employer and employees," Chemical & Alkali Workers v. Pittsburgh Plate Glass Co., 404 U.S. 157, 178 (1971),[8] may not be afforded in a manner contrary to Title VII.

Several allegations in petitioner's complaint would support the conclusion that the opportunity to become a partner was part and parcel of an associate's status as an employee at respondent's firm, independent of any allegation that such an opportunity was included in associates' employment contracts. Petitioner alleges that respondent's associates could regularly expect to be considered for partnership at the end of their "apprenticeships," and it appears that lawyers outside the firm were not routinely so considered.[9] Thus, the benefit of partnership consideration was allegedly linked directly with an associate's

partnership decision must be without regard to "race, color, religion, sex, or national origin."

7. Senate Report No. 867 concerned S.1937, which the Senate postponed indefinitely after it amended a House version of what ultimately became the Civil Rights Act of 1964. See 110 Cong.Rec. 14602 (1964). The Report is relevant here because S.1937 contained language similar to that ultimately found in the Civil Rights Act. It guaranteed "equal employment opportunity," which was defined to "include all the compensation, terms, conditions, and privileges of employment." S.Rep. No. 867, 88th Cong., 2d Sess., 24 (1964).

8. *Chemical & Alkali Workers* pertains to § 8(d) of the National Labor Relations Act (NLRA), which describes the obligation of employers and unions to meet and confer regarding "wages, hours, and other terms and conditions of employment." 61 Stat. 142, as amended, 29 U.S.C. § 158(d). The meaning of this analogous language sheds light on the Title VII provision at issue here. We have drawn analogies to the NLRA in other Title VII contexts, see Franks v. Bowman Transportation Co., 424 U.S. 747, 768–770 (1976), and have noted that certain sections of Title VII were expressly patterned after the NLRA, see Albemarle Paper Co. v. Moody, 422 U.S. 405, 419 (1975).

9. Respondent's own submissions indicate that most of respondent's partners in fact were selected from the ranks of associates who had spent their entire prepartnership legal careers (excluding judicial clerkships) with the firm.

status as an employee, and this linkage was far more than coincidental: petitioner alleges that respondent explicitly used the prospect of ultimate partnership to induce young lawyers to join the firm. Indeed, the importance of the partnership decision to a lawyer's status as an associate is underscored by the allegation that associates' employment is terminated if they are not elected to become partners. These allegations, if proved at trial, would suffice to show that partnership consideration was a term, condition, or privilege of an associate's employment at respondent's firm, and accordingly that partnership consideration must be without regard to sex.

B

Respondent contends that advancement to partnership may never qualify as a term, condition, or privilege of employment for purposes of Title VII. First, respondent asserts that elevation to partnership entails a change in status from an "employee" to an "employer." However, even if respondent is correct that a partnership invitation is not itself an offer of employment, Title VII would nonetheless apply and preclude discrimination on the basis of sex. The benefit a plaintiff is denied need not *be* employment to fall within Title VII's protection; it need only be a term, condition, or privilege *of* employment. It is also of no consequence that employment as an associate necessarily ends when an associate becomes a partner. A benefit need not accrue before a person's employment is completed to be a term, condition, or privilege of that employment relationship. Pension benefits, for example, qualify as terms, conditions, or privileges of employment even though they are received only after employment terminates. Arizona Governing Committee for Tax Deferred Annuity & Deferred Compensation Plans v. Norris, 463 U.S. 1079 (1983) (opinion of Marshall, J.). Accordingly, nothing in the change in status that advancement to partnership might entail means that partnership consideration falls outside the terms of the statute. See Lucido v. Cravath, Swaine & Moore, 425 F.Supp. 123, 128–129 (SDNY 1977).

Second, respondent argues that Title VII categorically exempts partnership decisions from scrutiny. However, respondent points to nothing in the statute or the legislative history that would support such a per se exemption.[10] When Congress wanted to grant an employer

---

10. The only legislative history respondent offers to support its position is Senator Cotton's defense of an unsuccessful amendment to limit Title VII to businesses with 100 or more employees. In this connection the Senator stated:

"[W]hen a small businessman who employs 30 or 25 or 26 persons selects an employee, he comes very close to selecting a partner; and when a businessman selects a partner, he comes dangerously close to the situation he faces when he selects a wife." 110 Cong.Rec. 13085 (1964); accord, 118 Cong.Rec. 1524, 2391 (1972).

Because Senator Cotton's amendment failed, it is unclear to what extent Congress shared his concerns about selecting partners. In any event, his views hardly conflict with our narrow holding today: that in appropriate circumstances partnership consideration may qualify as a term, condition, or privilege of a person's employment with an employer large enough to be covered by Title VII.

complete immunity, it expressly did so.[11]

Third, respondent argues that application of Title VII in this case would infringe constitutional rights of expression or association. Although we have recognized that the activities of lawyers may make a "distinctive contribution ... to the ideas and beliefs of our society," NAACP v. Button, 371 U.S. 415, 431 (1963), respondent has not shown how its ability to fulfill such a function would be inhibited by a requirement that it consider petitioner for partnership on her merits. Moreover, as we have held in another context, "[i]nvidious private discrimination may be characterized as a form of exercising freedom of association protected by the First Amendment, but it has never been accorded affirmative constitutional protections." Norwood v. Harrison, 413 U.S. 455, 470 (1973). There is no constitutional right, for example, to discriminate in the selection of who may attend a private school or join a labor union. Runyon v. McCrary, 427 U.S. 160 (1976); Railway Mail Assn. v. Corsi, 326 U.S. 88, 93–94 (1945).

III

We conclude that petitioner's complaint states a claim cognizable under Title VII. Petitioner therefore is entitled to her day in court to prove her allegations. The judgment of the Court of Appeals is reversed, and the case is remanded for further proceedings consistent with this opinion.

JUSTICE POWELL, concurring.

I join the Court's opinion holding that petitioner's complaint alleges a violation of Title VII and that the motion to dismiss should not have been granted. Petitioner's complaint avers that the law firm violated its promise that she would be considered for partnership on a "fair and equal basis" within the time span that associates generally are so considered. Petitioner is entitled to the opportunity to prove these averments.

I write to make clear my understanding that the Court's opinion should not be read as extending Title VII to the management of a law firm by its partners. The reasoning of the Court's opinion does not require that the relationship among partners be characterized as an "employment" relationship to which Title VII would apply. The relationship among law partners differs markedly from that between employer and employee—including that between the partnership and its associates.[2] The judgmental and sensitive decisions that must be made

11. For example, Congress expressly exempted Indian tribes and certain agencies of the District of Columbia, 42 U.S.C. § 2000e(b)(1), small businesses and bona fide private membership clubs, § 2000e(b)(2), and certain employees of religious organizations, § 2000e–1. Congress initially exempted certain employees of educational institutions, § 702, 78 Stat. 255, but later revoked that exemption, Equal Employment Opportunity Act of 1972, § 3, 86 Stat. 103.

2. Of course, an employer may not evade the strictures of Title VII simply by labeling its employees as "partners." Law partnerships usually have many of the characteristics that I describe generally here.

among the partners embrace a wide range of subjects.[3] The essence of the law partnership is the common conduct of a shared enterprise. The relationship among law partners contemplates that decisions important to the partnership normally will be made by common agreement, see, e.g., Memorandum of Agreement, King & Spalding, App. 153–164 (respondent's partnership agreement), or consent among the partners.

Respondent contends that for these reasons application of Title VII to the decision whether to admit petitioner to the firm implicates the constitutional right to association. But here it is alleged that respondent as an employer is obligated by contract to consider petitioner for partnership on equal terms without regard to sex. I agree that enforcement of this obligation, voluntarily assumed, would impair no right of association....

Notes on *Hishon*

Ms. Hishon, who consulted nearly a dozen Atlanta lawyers before finding one who would take her case, subsequently settled her case against King & Spalding for a damage award. She is now practicing real estate law part-time in Atlanta.[31]

Hishon did not seek an order directing the firm to make her a partner. Why? Price Waterhouse v. Hopkins,[32] discussed below, suggests that specific performance—an order requiring a firm to elect an employee to partnership—is an available remedy. A lower court decision subsequent to *Hishon* has held that the court has authority to award tenure to a college professor in an appropriate case.[33] But reported cases involving law firms have been limited to money damages;[34] none as yet has ordered specific relief in the form of partnership status.

Why did a large Atlanta firm, King & Spalding, which boasted Jimmy Carter's attorney general as one of its partners, fight so hard to

3. These decisions concern such matters as participation in profits and other types of compensation; work assignments; approval of commitments in bar association, civic, or political activities; questions of billing; acceptance of new clients; questions of conflicts of interest; retirement programs; and expansion policies. Such decisions may affect each partner of the firm. Divisions of partnership profits, unlike shareholders' rights to dividends, involve judgments as to each partner's contribution to the reputation and success of the firm. This is true whether the partner's participation in profits is measured in terms of points or percentages, combinations of salaries and points, salaries and bonuses, and possibly in other ways.

31. See Elizabeth A. Hishon: Unlikely Plaintiff, Nat'l L.J., Aug. 22, 1983, at p. 28; and Order Bares Partnership Process, Nat'l L.J., Dec. 10, 1990, at pp. 3, 15.

32. 490 U.S. 228 (1989).

33. Pyo v. Stockton State College, 603 F.Supp. 1278 (D.N.J.1985).

34. See, e.g., Ezold v. Wolf, Block, Schorr and Solis–Cohen, 983 F.2d 509 (3d Cir.1992) (law firm, not the trial judge, determines weight to be given to particular performance criteria; trial court erred in awarding damages based on its own criteria when law firm regularly emphasized legal analytical ability in making partnership decisions), rev'g, 751 F.Supp. 1175 (E.D.Pa.1990).

avoid the application of Title VII to partnership decisions? Is there anything to its free speech-free association argument? Is law firm autonomy related to the professional independence that is a celebrated ingredient of "professionalism?"

Three major questions were left unanswered by *Hishon* : (1) Does Title VII regulate the relationship among partners? (2) Who is a partner for Title VII purposes? (3) Will the courts grant specific performance in a Title VII partnership case?

As to the first question, Justice Powell's concurrence in *Hishon* states that the case does not speak to the relationship among partners. Powell's dictum has importance, but its significance is limited by an emerging restrictive definition of "partner."

A person called a "partner" may nevertheless be an employee for purposes of fair employment practices. In EEOC v. Peat, Marwick, Mitchell & Co.,[35] the court ruled that the EEOC might subpoena records of Peat Marwick to determine whether or not nominal partners really were employees. Hyland v. New Haven Radiology Associates, P.C.[36] held that a professional corporation has no partners, only employees; hence New Haven Radiology, having taken the corporate form for tax purposes, could not assert that it was a partnership for Title VII purposes.[37]

Suppose a group of lawyers are considering the possibility of setting up a new firm; they want to restrict it on gender, ethnic or religious grounds (e.g., women who want to establish a "feminist" law firm or Mormons who want to practice with co-religionists). Is Title VII violated? What about state anti-discrimination statutes?

Reports of gender bias in the courts have led to studies and reports in a number of states. In California, for example, the state's judicial council adopted 67 recommendations in 1990 to redress gender discrimination in the operation of the courts and corrections facilities. They include a requirement that juries be instructed in gender-neutral language, a recruitment program to correct lopsided court appointments of lawyers and an ethics prohibition against judges belonging to discriminatory private clubs.[38] The allegations of sexual harassment in the work place by Anita Hill in the confirmation hearings of Clarence Thomas in 1991 focused professional and public attention on this issue.[39]

35. 775 F.2d 928 (8th Cir.1985).

36. 794 F.2d 793 (2d Cir.1986).

37. See also Reiver v. Murdoch and Walsh, P.A., 625 F.Supp. 998 (D.Del.1985), holding that whether a member of the board of directors of a professional corporation (law firm) is an employee is a triable question of fact. Compare EEOC v. Dowd and Dowd, Ltd., 736 F.2d 1177 (7th Cir.1984), which held that a professional corporation (law firm) was, in economic reality, a partnership for purposes of Title VII.

38. See California Judiciary Acts in Effort To Redress Gender Bias in System, Wall St.J., Nov. 19, 1990, p. B8.

39. For discussion of the Thomas hearing, see David B. Wilkins, Presumed Crazy: The Structure of Argument in the Hill/Thomas Hearings, 65 So.Cal.L. Rev. 1517 (1992). For

Causation and Burden of Proof

Causation and burden of proof in Title VII cases were considered in Price Waterhouse v. Hopkins.[40] Hopkins, described by partners at Price Waterhouse as "an outstanding professional ... with strong character, independence, and integrity," was denied partnership in the accounting firm. Virtually all of the criticism of Hopkins had to do with her "interpersonal skills." She was described as "sometimes overly aggressive" and "macho" and as someone who "overcompensated for being a women." One partner advised her to take a course in "charm school," and another objected to "a lady using foul language." The Court held that the evidence was sufficient to establish that sexual stereotyping played a part in evaluating Hopkins' candidacy for partnership. The plurality opinion held that once a plaintiff establishes that her gender played a part in the employment decision, the burden shifts to the employer to show by a preponderance of evidence that it would have made the same decision had it not taken gender into account. Justices O'Connor and White, who provided the concurring votes, stated that the plaintiff must demonstrate that gender was a substantial factor in the employment decision.

Other Applicable General Laws

Consistent with *Hishon* a number of decisions hold that general legislation regulating employers or service-providers or protecting consumers applies to lawyers. In Debakey v. Staggs,[41] the court held that the treble-damage and fee-shifting provisions of the Texas Deceptive Trade Practices Act applied when a lawyer acted unconscionably in botching a name change and refusing to return an advance fee payment. The statute sought to protect consumers by regulating "services" as well as the sale of goods. Are these decisions consistent with those holding that the highest court of a state has exclusive authority to regulate the practice of law (see Chapter 10 below at p. 954? The Connecticut court, in upholding the application of the state's unfair trade practices act to lawyers, stated that the emphasis of disciplinary rules is ethical and regulatory, whereas that of general regulation is on the prevention of injury to consumers.[42] At least four states, including Massachusetts, have extended their sales taxes to legal services.[43] Federal legislation has also been applied to lawyers despite strong

general discussion of sexual harassment, see Marina Angel, Sexual Harassment by Judges, 45 U. Miami L.Rev. 817 (1991) (sexual harassment by judges is more widespread than most lawyers believe and little has been done to punish it).

40. 490 U.S. 228 (1989).

41. 605 S.W.2d 631 (Tex.Civ.App.1980), aff'd, 612 S.W.2d 924 (Tex.1981).

42. Heslin v. Connecticut Law Clinic of Trantolo, 190 Conn. 510, 461 A.2d 938 (1983).

43. See Massachusetts Imposes 5% Levy on Range of Services, Wall St. J., July 9, 1990, at p. A2.

claims that failure to imply an exception for lawyers would undermine the lawyer-client relationship and reveal client identity.[44]

44. See, e.g., United States v. Goldberger & Dubin,P.C, 935 F.2d 501 (2d Cir.1991) (lawyers must report cash receipts of more than $10,000 under Federal Money Laundering Act even though client identity will be revealed); Attorney General of U.S. v. Covington & Burling, 411 F.Supp. 371 (D.D.C.1976) (Federal Foreign Agents Registration Act requires any "agent" of a foreign government, including a law firm, to register with the Attorney General even though some threat to confidentiality is involved).

Chapter 10

REGULATION OF COMPETITION IN LEGAL SERVICES

Introduction: Production and Distribution of Legal Services

The legal profession is a service industry engaged in the production and distribution of legal services. An economic analysis of factors affecting the availability, cost and quality of legal services in the United States must consider both the demand for and the supply of legal services.

Demand for Legal Services

Major corporations encounter few problems in obtaining adequate legal services. They are experienced users of legal services and may choose who and how service is provided from a wide array of individual lawyers, outside law firms and inside staff counsel. Market forces operate fairly well in this sector of the legal services industry although corporations may complain about legal costs and others may complain that too many legal resources are devoted to corporations.

Ordinary Americans, however, face more difficulties. A major study, conducted in 1974 by the American Bar Foundation (ABF), reports that about two-thirds of the adult population consult a lawyer at least once in a lifetime.[1] For most Americans the exposure to lawyers is very infrequent: one-third have never consulted a lawyer, and more than another third have consulted a lawyer on only one matter. Only about 10 percent of Americans report professional exposure to three or more lawyers during their lifetimes.

The ABF study also attempts to explore the prevailing conception of an unfilled need for legal services. Is there a vast, untapped demand for legal services that is not being handled for one reason or another? Some of the possible reasons for unserved need are: (1) Individuals lack information about the legal character of a problem or the value of a lawyer's help in dealing with it. (2) They do not know how to find a lawyer qualified to handle the problem at a cost they can afford. (3) They lack the resources to pay even a small or reasonable legal fee. And (4) lay persons fear lawyers and legal proceedings, with attendant loss of control over their own lives.

The ABF study provides some confirmation of the hypothesis of unfilled need. Individuals report that only a portion of their "legal

1. Barbara A. Curran and Francis O. Spaulding, The Legal Needs of the Public 79–81 (1974).

problems" are taken to lawyers, a percentage that is highly variable. For example, 1 percent of job discrimination problems are taken to a lawyer; 10 percent of tort problems; 36 percent of real property problems; and 73 percent of estate planning problems (wills). The four largest categories of work actually taken to lawyers by individuals involve real property, estate planning, marital problems and torts, in that order. Variations in lawyer use are affected by demographic factors such as income (those of higher income report more property and estate planning problems), sex (incidence of torts is greater for men, but women are somewhat more likely to consult a lawyer), and race (minorities are more likely to consult lawyers for tort problems but in general use lawyers less than whites).

The social fairness of current patterns in the distribution of legal services has attracted criticism. President Jimmy Carter, speaking to the Los Angeles County Bar Association in 1978, stated themes that have now become cliches from frequent repetition:

> We have the heaviest concentration of lawyers on earth ..., three times as many as are in England; four times as many as are in West Germany; twenty-one times as many as there are in Japan. We have more litigation; but I am not sure that we have more justice.

> No resources of talent and training in our own society, even including medical care, are more wastefully or unfairly distributed than legal skills. Ninety percent of our lawyers serve 10 percent of our people. We are overlawyered and underrepresented.

> Excessive litigation and legal featherbedding are encouraged. [T]he organized bar ... has fought innovations [that would make legal services more competitive and more widely available].

> Too often the amount of justice that a person gets depends on the amount of money that he or she can pay. Access to justice must not depend on economic status, and it must not be thwarted by arbitrary procedural rules.

> [We must] make the adversary system less necessary for the daily lives of most Americans—and more efficient when it must be used. By resorting to litigation at the drop of a hat, by regarding the adversary system as an end in itself, we have made justice more cumbersome, more expensive, and less equal that it ought to be.

> Those of us—presidents and lawyers—who enjoy privilege, power, and influence in our society can be called to a harsh account for the ways we are using this power. Our hierarchy of privilege in this nation, based not on birth but on social and economic status, tends to insulate us from the problems faced by the average American. The natural tendency for all of us is to ignore what

does not touch us directly. The natural temptation when dealing with the law is to assume that whatever is legal is just.[2]

Supply of Legal Services

Regulation of the supply of legal services takes a number of forms. This chapter considers: (1) the prohibition on the practice of law by nonlawyers (unauthorized practice); (2) restraints on the flow of information about legal services (restrictions on lawyer advertising and solicitation of legal business); (3) restrictions on the form of delivery, such as limitations on group legal services, nonlawyer participation in or ownership of law firms and dual practice restrictions; and, finally, (4) the local counsel requirement that limits multistate practice. Direct regulation of access to the profession in the form of admission requirements—legal education, bar examination and character and fitness requirements—was considered in Chapter 9, but efforts to exclude nonresidents by residency requirements are considered here.

A. THE PROFESSIONAL MONOPOLY: UNAUTHORIZED PRACTICE OF LAW

Introduction

In the United States many tasks of a more or less legal nature may be undertaken only by a lawyer. Statutes, court rules and judicial decisions restrict "the practice of law" to lawyers duly admitted in the jurisdiction. The only general exception to the professional monopoly of law practice is that persons who are directly affected may undertake to handle their own legal problems by arguing their own cases, writing their own wills or copying out their own deeds—a right of self-representation.[3] The law of unauthorized practice and its current status and justification are examined here.[4]

Until the 20th century, the doctrine of unauthorized practice of law meant only that a nonlawyer could not appear in court to represent

---

2. Public Papers of the Presidents of the United States, Jimmy Carter, Book I, 834. Carter's speech to the Los Angeles County Bar Association on May 4, 1978, focused public attention on complaints about lawyers and the legal system that had been building for a number of years: cost, delay, unfairness in distribution and lack of access. Similar themes were expressed in a widely discussed and reprinted report of Derek Bell, then president of Harvard University but formerly dean of its law school. Derek C. Bok, A Flawed System of Law Practice and Training, 33 J.Legal Educ. 570 (1983).

3. See Faretta v. California, 422 U.S. 806 (1975) (criminal defendant who made a "knowing and intelligent" waiver of the constitutional right to the assistance of counsel had a constitutional right to self-representation).

4. The best general accounts of the bar's attempts to suppress unauthorized practice of law are Barlow F. Christensen, The Unauthorized Practice of Law: Do Good Fences Really Make Good Neighbors—Or Even Good Sense, 1980 Am.Bar Found.Research J. 159, primarily an historical analysis, and Deborah L. Rhode, Policing the Professional Monopoly: A Constitutional and Empirical Analysis of Unauthorized Practice Prohibitions, 34 Stan.L.Rev. 1 (1981), primarily an empirical study of contemporary bar association enforcement practice.

another person.   Courts enforced the doctrine mainly by regulating who could enter an appearance in litigation.   Outside the courthouse, nonlawyers freely performed tasks that today would be called the unauthorized practice of law.   Late in the 19th century, for example, title guaranty companies and debt collection agencies performed legal work as part of their services.   Trust companies often drafted wills, and accountants gave tax advice.   These and other activities on the part of nonlawyers encountered increasing resistance from the organized bar during the first half of the 20th century.

A vigorous and expansive doctrine of unauthorized practice did not appear upon the American scene until sometime after the First World War.   During the Depression, economic pressures on the bar and a social environment that was more hospitable to occupational licensing led to more vigorous enforcement of the expanded doctrine by unauthorized practice committees in virtually every state.   During this period the present scope of unauthorized practice became embodied in judicial decisions stating the modern rationale of the doctrine.

After judicial decisions had established broad parameters of unauthorized practice, the organized bar, beginning in the 1930s, negotiated treaties with organized groups of competitors.   The agreements had the effect of dividing the market for services in areas reserved for lawyers, on the one hand, and accountants, architects, claims adjusters, collection agencies, liability insurance companies, lawbook publishers, professional engineers, realtors, title companies, trust companies and social workers, on the other.   The growth of the consumer movement and the evolution of federal antitrust law brought an end to this market division strategy.   The *Goldfarb* decision in 1975,[5] striking down the bar's suggested minimum fee schedules, made it clear that anticompetitive activity by bar associations was subject to the federal antitrust laws.   Subsequently, lower court decisions and the initiation of a federal challenge led to retrenchment and reorganization of unauthorized practice activity.   The interprofessional treaties were abandoned because of fears of antitrust liability, a number of states disbanded their unauthorized practice committees and, in other states, regulatory activity was narrowed and channeled through the state supreme court.   The statutory prohibitions against unauthorized practice, however, continue in force.

1.   Unauthorized Practice of Law

Legal Remedies Against Unauthorized Law Practice

A nonlawyer who provides legal assistance to others may be subject to legal consequences.   If the unlicensed person holds herself out as a lawyer, the law of fraud is violated.[6]   A further legal consequence is that an unlicensed person rendering legal services is held to a licensed

5.   Goldfarb v. Virginia State Bar, 421 U.S. 773 (1975) (bar association's minimum fee schedules violate federal antitrust laws).

6.   See, e.g., People v. Schreiber, 250 Ill. 345, 95 N.E. 189 (1911).

lawyer's standard of care and competence.[7] Another possible consequence is that fee contracts made by an unlicensed person may not be
legally enforceable.[8] The unlicensed person also could be enjoined from
practicing law on the principle supporting injunction against a public
nuisance.[9] Practicing law without a license has been treated as contempt of court.[10] Finally, it is defined as a crime in most states.[11] The
quality of the services provided by an unlicensed practitioner is an issue
only in the malpractice case.

FLORIDA BAR v. BRUMBAUGH
Supreme Court of Florida, 1978.
355 So.2d 1186.

Per Curiam.

The Florida Bar has filed a petition charging Marilyn Brumbaugh
with engaging in the unauthorized practice of law, and seeking a
permanent injunction prohibiting her from further engaging in these
allegedly unlawful acts. . . . We now issue an injunction, delineating in
this opinion those acts of respondent which we deem to constitute the
unauthorized practice of law, and ordering her to stop such activities.

Respondent, Marilyn Brumbaugh, is not and has never been a
member of the Florida Bar, and is, therefore, not licensed to practice
law within this state. She has advertised in various local newspapers
as "Marilyn's Secretarial Service" offering to perform typing services
for "Do–It–Yourself" divorces, wills, resumes, and bankruptcies. The
Florida Bar charges that she performed unauthorized legal services by
preparing for her customers those legal documents necessary in an
uncontested dissolution of marriage proceeding and by advising her
customers as to the costs involved and the procedures which should be
followed in order to obtain a dissolution of marriage. For this service,
Ms. Brumbaugh charges a fee of $50.

. . . [I]n cases such as this, the Florida Supreme Court is not
confined to act solely in its judicial capacity. In addition, it acts in its
administrative capacity as chief policy maker, regulating the administration of the court system and supervising all persons who are engaged
in rendering legal advice to members of the general public. Such
authority carries with it the responsibility to perform this task in a way
responsive to the needs and desires of our citizens. This principle has

7. See Biakanja v. Irving, 49 Cal.2d 647, 320 P.2d 16 (1958) (will drafting by notary
public).

8. See, e.g., Ames v. Gilman, 51 Mass. (10 Metc.) 239 (1845); cf. Gesellschaft Fur
Drahtlose Telegraphie M.B.H. v. Brown, 78 F.2d 410 (D.C.App.1935) (lawyer barred from
recovering fees for services rendered in violation of ethical standards).

9. See, e.g., State v. Scopel, 316 S.W.2d 515 (Mo.1958) (injunction against unlicensed
practice of medicine); W. Prosser and P. Keeton on Torts § 90 (5th ed. 1984).

10. See, e.g., In re Root, 173 Kan. 512, 249 P.2d 628 (1952).

11. See Deborah L. Rhode, Policing the Professional Monopoly, 34 Stan.L.Rev. 1, 11 n.
39 (1981) (collection of state statutes).

long been our goal.   In State v. Sperry, 140 So.2d 587, 595 (Fla.1962), we noted:

> The reason for prohibiting the practice of law by those who have not been examined and found qualified to practice is frequently misunderstood.   It is not done to aid or protect the members of the legal profession either in creating or maintaining a monopoly or closed shop.   It is done to protect the public from being advised and represented in legal matters by unqualified persons over whom the judicial department can exercise little, if any, control in the matter of infractions of the code of conduct which, in the public interest, lawyers are bound to observe.

The Florida Bar as an agent of this Court, plays a large role in the enforcement of court policies and rules and has been active in regulating and disciplining unethical conduct by its members.   Because of the natural tendency of all professions to act in their own self interest, however, this Court must closely scrutinize all regulations tending to limit competition in the delivery of legal services to the public, and determine whether or not such regulations are truly in the public interest.   Indeed, the active role of state supreme courts in the regulation of the practice of law (when such regulation is subject to pointed reexamination by the state court as policy maker) is accorded great deference and exemption from federal interference under the Sherman Act.   Bates v. State Bar of Arizona, 433 U.S. 350 (1977).

The United States Supreme Court has recently decided issues which may drastically change the practice of law throughout the country, especially with regards to advertising and price competition among attorneys.   Bates v. State Bar of Arizona, supra; Goldfarb, et al. v. Virginia State Bar, 421 U.S. 773 (1975).   In addition, the Supreme Court has affirmed the fundamental constitutional right of all persons to represent themselves in court proceedings, Faretta v. California, 422 U.S. 806 (1975).   In *Faretta,* the Supreme Court emphasized that an attorney is merely an assistant who helps a citizen protect his legal rights and present his case to the courts.   A person should not be forced to have an attorney represent his legal interests if he does not consent to such representation.   It is imperative for us to analyze these cases and determine how their holdings and the policies behind them affect our regulation of the legal profession in this state.

With regard to the charges made against Marilyn Brumbaugh, this Court appointed a referee to receive evidence and to make findings of fact, conclusions of law, and recommendations as to the disposition of the case.   The referee found that respondent, under the guise of a "secretarial" or "typing" service prepares, for a fee, all papers deemed by her to be needed for the pleading, filing, and securing of a dissolution of marriage, as well as detailed instructions as to how the suit should be filed, notice served, hearings set, trial conducted, and the final decree secured.   The referee also found that in one instance, respondent prepared a quit claim deed in reference to the marital property of the parties. The referee determined that respondent's contention that she merely operates a typing service is rebutted by numerous facts in evidence. Ms. Brumbaugh has no blank forms either to sell or to fill out. Rather, she types up the documents for her customers after they have asked her to prepare a petition or an entire set of dissolution of marriage papers. Prior to typing up the papers, respondent asks her customers whether custody, child support, or alimony is involved. Respondent has four sets of dissolution of marriage papers, and she chooses which set is appropriate for the particular customer. She then types out those papers, filling in the blank spaces with the appropriate information. Respondent instructs her customers how the papers are to be signed, where they are to be filed, and how the customer should arrange for a final hearing.

Marilyn Brumbaugh, who is representing herself in proceedings before this Court, has made various objections to the procedure and findings of fact of the referee. Respondent alleges that the referee has an inherent conflict of interest because he is a lawyer and a member of The Florida Bar. She asserts that "all lawyers have a property interest in this case, because they have been making money, running typing services, without proper licenses." She further alleges that the referee did not provide her with a proper hearing, that he threw her in jail for pleading the Fifth Amendment, and denied her constitutional right to a jury trial. Respondent argues that she has never held herself out as an attorney, and has never professed to have legal skills. She does not give advice, but acts merely as a secretary. She is a licensed counselor, and asserts the right to talk to people and to let her customers make decisions for themselves. Finally, respondent contends that her civil rights have been violated, and that she has been denied the right to make an honest living.

This case does not arise out of a complaint by any of Ms. Brumbaugh's customers as to improper advice or unethical conduct. It has been initiated by members of The Florida Bar who believe her to be practicing law without a license. The evidence introduced at the hearing below shows that none of respondent's customers believed that she was an attorney, or that she was acting as an attorney in their behalf. Respondent's advertisements clearly addressed themselves to people who wish to do their own divorces. These customers knew that they had to have "some type of papers" to file in order to obtain their dissolution of marriage. Respondent never handled contested divorces. During the past two years respondent has assisted several hundred customers in obtaining their own divorces. The record shows that while some of her customers told respondent exactly what they wanted, generally respondent would ask her customers for the necessary information needed to fill out the divorce papers, such as the names and addresses of the parties, the place and duration of residency in this state, whether there was any property settlement to be resolved, or any determination as to custody and support of children. Finally, each petition contained the bare allegation that the marriage was irretrievably broken. Respondent would then inform the parties as to which documents needed to be signed, by whom, how many copies of each paper should be filed, where and when they should be filed, the costs involved, and what witness testimony is necessary at the court hearing. Apparently, Ms. Brumbaugh no longer informs the parties verbally as to the proper procedures for the filing of the papers, but offers to let them copy papers described as "suggested procedural education."

The Florida Bar argues that the above activities of respondent violate the rulings of this Court in The Florida Bar v. American Legal and Business Forms, Inc., 274 So.2d 225 (Fla.1973), and The Florida Bar v. Stupica, 300 So.2d 683 (Fla.1974). In those decisions we held that it is lawful to sell to the public printed legal forms, provided they do not carry with them what purports to be instructions on how to fill out such forms or how to use them. We stated that legal advice is inextricably involved in the filling out and advice as to how to use such legal forms, and therein lies the danger of injury or damage to the public if not properly performed in accordance with law. In *Stupica,* supra, this Court rejected the rationale of the New York courts in New York County Lawyer's Association v. Dacey, 28 A.D.2d 161, 283 N.Y.S.2d 984, reversed and dissenting opinion adopted 21 N.Y.2d 694, 287 N.Y.S.2d 422, 234 N.E.2d 459 (N.Y.1967), which held that the publication of forms and instructions on their use does not constitute the unauthorized practice of law if these instructions are addressed to the public in general rather than to a specific individual legal problem. The Court in *Dacey* stated that the possibility that the principles or rules set forth in the text may be accepted by a particular reader as solution to his problem, does not mean that the publisher is practicing law. Other states have adopted the principle of law set forth in *Dacey,* holding that the sale of legal forms with instructions for their use does not constitute unauthorized practice of law. See State Bar of Michigan v. Cramer, 399 Mich. 116, 249 N.W.2d 1 (1976); Oregon State Bar v. Gilchrist, 272 Or. 552, 538 P.2d 913 (1975). However, these courts have prohibited all personal contact between the service providing such forms and the customer, in the nature of consultation, explanation, recommendation, advice, or other assistance in selecting particular forms, in filling out any part of the forms, suggesting or advising how the forms should be used in solving the particular problems.

Although persons not licensed as attorneys are prohibited from practicing law within this state, it is somewhat difficult to define exactly what constitutes the practice of law in all instances. This Court has previously stated that:

> . . . if the giving of such advice and performance of such services affect important rights of a person under the law, and if the reasonable protection of the rights and property of those advised and served requires that the persons giving such advice possess legal skill and a knowledge of the law greater than that possessed by the average citizen, then the giving of such advice and the

performance of such services by one for another as a course of conduct constitute the practice of law.

Sperry, supra, 140 So.2d at 591.

This definition is broad and is given content by this Court only as it applies to specific circumstances of each case. We agree that "any attempt to formulate a lasting, all encompassing definition of 'practice of law' is doomed to failure 'for the reason that under our system of jurisprudence such practice must necessarily change with the ever-changing business and social order.'" State Bar of Michigan v. Cramer, supra, 399 Mich. 116, 249 N.W.2d at 7.

In determining whether a particular act constitutes the practice of law, our primary goal is the protection of the public. However, any limitations on the free practice of law by all persons necessarily affects important constitutional rights. Our decision here certainly affects the constitutional rights of Marilyn Brumbaugh to pursue a lawful occupation or business.... Our decision also affects respondent's First Amendment rights to speak and print what she chooses. In addition, her customers and potential customers have the constitutional right of self representation, *Faretta,* supra, and the right of privacy inherent in the marriage relationship, Roe v. Wade, 410 U.S. 113 (1973); Boddie v. Connecticut, 401 U.S. 371 (1971). All citizens in our state are also guaranteed access to our courts by Article I, Section 21, Florida Constitution (1968). Although it is not necessary for us to provide affirmative assistance in order to ensure meaningful access to the courts to our citizens, as it is necessary for us to do for those incarcerated in our state prison system, Bounds v. Smith, 430 U.S. 817 (1977), we should not place any unnecessary restrictions upon that right. We should not deny persons who wish to represent themselves access to any source of information which might be relevant in the preparation of their cases. There are numerous texts in our state law libraries which describe our substantive and procedural law, purport to give legal advice to the reader as to choices that should be made in various situations, and which also contain sample legal forms which a reader may use as an example. We generally do not restrict the access of the public to these law libraries, although many of the legal texts are not authored by attorneys licensed to practice in this state. These texts do not carry with them any guarantees of accuracy, and only some of them purport to update statements which have been modified by subsequently enacted statutes and recent case law.

The policy of this Court should continue to be one of encouraging persons who are unsure of their legal rights and remedies to seek legal assistance from persons licensed by us to practice law in this state. However, in order to make an intelligent decision as whether or not to engage the assistance of an attorney, a citizen must be allowed access to information which will help determine the complexity of the legal problem. Once a person has made the decision to represent himself, we should not enforce any unnecessary regulation which might tend to hinder the exercise of this constitutionally protected right. However, any restriction of constitutional rights must be "narrowly drawn to express only the legitimate state interests at stake." *Roe v. Wade,* supra, NAACP v. Button, 371 U.S. 415, 438 (1963). "And if there are other reasonable ways to achieve those goals with a lesser burden on constitutionally protected activity, a state may not choose the way of greater interference. If it acts at all, it must choose less drastic means. Shelton v. Tucker, 364 U.S. 479, 488 (1960).

[The opinion then considered Florida's no-fault divorce legislation which "clearly has the remedial purpose of simplifying the dissolution of marriage whenever possible."]

Families usually undergo tremendous financial hardship when they decide to dissolve their marital relationships. The Legislature simplified procedures so that parties would not need to bear the additional burden of expensive legal fees where they have agreed to the settlement of their property and the custody of their children. This Court should not place unreasonable burdens upon the obtaining of such divorces, especially where both parties consent to the dissolution.

Present dissolution procedures in uncontested situations involve a very simplified method of asserting certain facts required by statute, notice to the other parties affected, and a simple hearing where the trial court may hear proof and make inquiries as to the facts asserted in those pleadings.

The legal forms necessary to obtain such an uncontested dissolution of marriage are susceptible of standardization. This Court has allowed the sale of legal forms on this and other subjects, provided that they do not carry with them what purports to be instructions on how to fill out such forms or how they are to be used. *The Florida Bar v. American Legal and Business Forms, Inc.,* supra; *The Florida Bar v. Stupica,* supra. These decisions should be reevaluated in light of those recent decisions in other states which have held that the sale of forms necessary to obtain a divorce, together with any related textual instructions directed towards the general public, does not constitute the practice of law. The reasons for allowing the sale of such legal publications which contain sample forms to be used by individuals who wish to represent themselves are persuasive. *State Bar of Michigan v. Cramer,* supra, reasoned that such instructional material should be no more objectionable than any other publication placed into the stream of commerce which purports to offer general advice on common problems and does not purport to give a person advice on a specific problem particular to a designated or readily identified person. In Bates v. State Bar of Arizona, 433 U.S. 350, 364 (1977), the Supreme Court discussed at length the substantial interests in the free flow of commercial speech. The Court said that the choice between the dangers of suppressing information and the dangers arising from its free flow is precisely the choice "that the First Amendment makes for us." There the Court, in approving legal advertising, reasoned that the state cannot assume a paternalistic approach which rests in large part on its citizens being kept in ignorance. The Court stated that we must assume that this information is not in itself harmful, and "that people will perceive their own best interests if only they are well enough informed, and that the best means to that end is to open the channels of communication rather than to close them."

Although there is a danger that some published material might give false or misleading information, that is not a sufficient reason to justify its total ban. We must assume that our citizens will generally use such publications for what they are worth in the preparation of their cases, and further assume that most persons will not rely on these materials in the same way they would rely on the advice of an attorney or other persons holding themselves out as having expertise in the area. The tendency of persons seeking legal assistance to place their trust in the individual purporting to have expertise in the area necessitates this Court's regulation of such attorney-client relationships, so as to require that persons giving such advice have at least a minimal amount of legal training and experience. Although Marilyn Brumbaugh never held herself out as an attorney, it is clear that her clients placed some reliance upon her to properly prepare the necessary legal forms for their dissolution proceedings. To this extent we believe that Ms. Brumbaugh overstepped proper bounds and engaged in the unauthorized practice of law. We hold that Ms. Brumbaugh, and others in similar situations, may sell printed material purporting to explain legal practice and procedure to the public in general and she may sell sample legal forms. To this extent we limit our prior holdings in *Stupica* and *American Legal and Business Forms, Inc.* Further, we hold that it is not improper for Marilyn Brumbaugh to engage in a secretarial service, typing such forms for her clients, provided that she only copy the information given to her in writing by her clients. In addition, Ms. Brumbaugh may advertise her business activities of providing secretarial and notary services and selling legal forms and general printed information. However, Marilyn Brumbaugh must not, in conjunction with her business, engage in advising clients as to the various remedies available to them, or otherwise assist them in preparing those forms necessary for a dissolution proceeding. More specifically, Marilyn Brumbaugh may not make inquiries nor answer questions from her clients as to the particular forms which might be necessary, how best to fill out such forms, where to properly file such forms, and how to present necessary evidence at the court hearings. Our specific holding with regard to the dissolution of marriage also applies to other unauthorized legal assistance such as the preparation of wills or real estate transaction documents. While Marilyn Brumbaugh may legally sell forms in these areas, and type up instruments which have been completed by clients, she must not engage in personal legal assistance in conjunction with her business activities, including the correction of errors and omissions.

Accordingly, having defined the limits within which Ms. Brumbaugh and those engaged in similar activities may conduct their business without engaging in the unauthorized practice of law, the rule to show cause is dissolved.

[Justice Karl, concurring specially, responded to the charge that restrictions on unauthorized practice are "nothing more than a method of providing economic protection for lawyers." "Just as the public must be protected from physical harm inflicted by those who would prescribe drugs and perform surgery without proper training, so must we provide protection from financial and other damage inflicted by pseudo-lawyers."]

Personalized Assistance in Filling Out Legal Forms

What services did Marilyn Brumbaugh provide to whom? If she cannot render these services, what alternatives do her customers have? Who was complaining about her activities? What dangers does she pose to Florida's polity? What does the Florida court say that Ms. Brumbaugh can and cannot do? Thus restricted, will her services be helpful to anyone?

Brumbaugh did not present herself as a lawyer, quite the contrary. Nor was it established that her services fell below the standard of care and competence of lawyers performing services in similar matters. So far as appears, her customers were satisfied enough to pay her for her services. No evidence was produced that her customers had complained or that the average quality of her services was lower than that of Florida's general practitioners. Although the court does not say so, Florida makes practicing law without a license a criminal offense.[12] Legislative proscription of unauthorized practice, according to general legal principles, is an adequate basis for injunctive relief.[13]

The *Brumbaugh* case was replicated a few years later when Rosemary Furman was ordered not to provide oral advice in connection with her provision of divorce forms to persons seeking an uncontested divorce. Furman, who had had 30 years of legal experience as a court reporter and legal secretary, charged $50 for her services; at the time the usual charges of Florida lawyers for a simple uncontested divorce were $350–$500. When Furman continued to provide oral advice, the bar sought to punish her for contempt. The Florida Supreme Court found that she had wilfully violated its prior order and imposed a fine and prison sentence.[14] Consumer groups rallied to Furman's support, and the bar's attempt to deprive willing customers of her services was

12. West's Fla.Stat.Ann. § 454.23.

13. See W. Prosser and P. Keeton on Torts § 90 (5th ed. 1984).

14. Florida Bar v. Furman, 451 So.2d 808 (1984). The case is more fully discussed in Deborah L. Rhode and David Luban, Legal Ethics 734–38 (1992).

featured in national newsmagazines and on television. Although Furman's constitutional claims were rejected by the U.S. Supreme Court and she ultimately closed her business, the adverse publicity had a restraining effect on bar efforts to enforce unauthorized practice restrictions. Furman was pardoned by the Florida governor, and the Florida court created a simplified dissolution procedure for childless couples who had agreed on property division and payment of debts. A new court rule also permitted nonlawyers to give advice regarding "routine administrative procedures" related to the completion of court-approved legal forms.[15]

What Is the "Practice of Law"?

The difficult question concerning unauthorized practice of law is that of defining the activities that constitute the "practice of law," not of fashioning remedies against it. The Model Rules and the Model Code prohibit a lawyer from assisting the unauthorized practice of law. See M.R. 5.5; DR 3–101(A). These provisions, however, do not define the phrase. As the opinion in *Brumbaugh* indicates, such definition has been a matter of ad hoc decision. The most common formulation is the "professional judgment" test: Is the activity one in which a lawyer's presumed special training and skills are relevant?[16] Does this test involve circular reasoning?

Case law has said that a matter having legal ramifications requires a lawyer's involvement only when it involves "difficult or doubtful legal questions."[17] Suppose Brumbaugh had made an arrangement with a lawyer under which any of her clients who had questions about filling out the forms could call the lawyer. Would the lawyer violate M.R. 5.5 by participating in such an arrangement? M.R. 5.5 provides that a lawyer may not assist a person who is not a member of the bar in the performance of an activity that constitutes the unauthorized practice of law.

The boundaries of "practice of law" for purposes of enforcing the licensure requirement remain indistinct and vary from one state to another. The location of the boundaries is the product of interaction between the organized bar and competing service-providers, state law as formulated by state courts, constitutional law as formulated by the Supreme Court, inter-professional detente and market forces. In Florida and Colorado, for example, the bar associations have been fairly aggressive, whereas in some other jurisdictions they have been nearly

15. Rhode and Luban, supra, at 736.

16. EC 3–5, after stating that "[i]t is neither necessary nor desirable to attempt the formulation of a single, specific definition of what constitutes the practice of law," provides a functional (but circular?) one: It is the practice of law when the "professional judgment of a lawyer" is involved in relating "the general body and philosophy of law to a specific legal problem of a client." The context suggests that this determination is to be made in the light of public interest considerations, i.e., the sphere of exclusion is to be determined by the purposes to be served.

17. Gardner v. Conway, 234 Minn. 468, 48 N.W.2d 788 (1951); Agran v. Shapiro, 127 Cal.App.2d Supp. 807, 273 P.2d 619 (1954).

dormant. In general, the state courts act only in response to bar association initiatives, as in *Brumbaugh*. When the state courts have been asked to suppress activity as unauthorized practice of law, they have in general sided with the bar's position. As the *Brumbaugh* opinion recognizes, however, the scope of state proscription of unauthorized practice had been significantly limited by Supreme Court decisions applying the First Amendment to provision of legal services.

Deference to First Amendment concerns led the court in *Brumbaugh* to recognize that a nonlawyer could disseminate written "how to" materials, including not only legal forms but also instructions about using the forms. However, she may not give oral advice. Is oral utterance not protected by the First Amendment? What if Brumbaugh had made videotapes of "instructions"? Interestingly, concerning the problem of lawyer solicitation of clients, the Supreme Court has drawn a line between sending out written materials to prospective clients, which is protected by the First Amendment, and personal contact with clients, which is not. See the *Shapero* case, p. 962 below.

Professor Deborah Rhode and some other commentators argue that the current enforcement of unauthorized practice law raises significant due process and First Amendment questions.[18] The prohibition, she argues, is unduly vague and threatens in an overbroad fashion self-representation and other First Amendment interests. To date, the Supreme Court has rejected such claims.[19] In the typical injunction proceeding, the vagueness problem is reduced because the initial order is one that enjoins specific behavior. The injunction remedy, of course, also deprives the nonlawyer of a lay jury that might be more sympathetic than a lawyer-judge to lay competition.

Legal Assistants and Paralegals

Could a lawyer operate a service like that which Brumbaugh provided, calling it a "People's Law Center" or the like, having all intake and basic work done by paralegals such as Brumbaugh, and having a lawyer involved only when the paralegal considers such involvement necessary? Many law firms operate a high-volume practice in such matters as divorce, real estate closings, worker's compensation claims and personal bankruptcy.[20] In these firms, and in legal services organizations representing the poor, intake and basic work is done by paralegals, with the lawyers involved only as necessary.

Nonlawyer competitors of lawyers frequently complain that law firms engaged in the same counseling activities do so with extensive use

18. Rhode, Policing the Professional Monopoly, supra.

19. See Furman v. Florida, 444 U.S. 1061 (1980) (appeal in a divorce-advice case dismissed for want of a substantial federal question).

20. See the detailed description of Raul Lovett's worker's compensation and personal injury practice in Philip B. Heymann and Lance Liebman (eds.), The Social Responsibilities of Lawyers: Case Studies 258 (1988). A description of the high-volume practice of a legal clinic relying on extensive advertising is also included in the same volume. Id. at 49.

of nonlawyers (legal secretaries, legal assistants and paralegals) who are given very limited supervision by lawyers. The bar's response is that professional codes require supervision and make the supervising lawyer responsible for an employee's breach of fiduciary or other obligations. See M.R. 5.3 and EC 3–6.[21] Is this a satisfactory response?

The dramatic growth in the use of legal assistants and paralegals in recent decades has given rise to proposals that these individuals should be licensed by the state after demonstration of competence through education, examination or other entry requirements. The ABA has developed standards for legal assistant training programs and accredits particular programs as complying with its standards. A few states have developed licensing programs that are related to bar admission activities. Is it desirable to extend credentialing into this area? Should these developments be under the control of the legal profession or independent from the bar? The issues are not dissimilar to those involving the relationship of physicians to other health care occupations, such as nursing.

The most controversial aspect of the 1986 report of the ABA Commission on Professionalism was some language dealing with paraprofessional competition under the innocuous heading that lawyers should "encourage innovative methods which simplify and make less expensive the rendering of legal services." Lawyers, the report stated, "should have to compete with properly licensed paraprofessionals" in "certain real estate closings, the drafting of simple wills, and selected tax services" if "clients of ordinary means are to be served at all." [22]

> [I]t can no longer be claimed that lawyers have the exclusive possession of the esoteric knowledge required and are therefore the only ones able to advise clients on any matter concerning the law.... Lawyer resistance to [inroads on lawyer exclusivity] for selfish reasons only brings discredit on the profession.[23]

These sentences in the Commission's report provoked a violent, critical reaction from lawyers and local bar groups.[24]

Potential clients, particularly those of lower and middle socio-economic status, often fear lawyers and are unsure how to deal with them. That fear may have been one reason why Brumbaugh's service appealed to her customers. Does the Florida court take that possibility into account? What could be done to respond to that kind of fear?

---

21. The Comment to M.R. 5.3 states:

Lawyers generally employ assistants in their practice, including secretaries, law student interns, and paraprofessionals. Such assistants, whether employees or independent contractors, act for the lawyer in rendition of the lawyer's professional services.

22. ABA Commission on Professionalism, " ... In the Spirit of Public Service:" A Blueprint for the Rekindling of Lawyer Professionalism, 112 F.R.D. 243, 301 (1986).

23. Id. at 301.

24. In California, where lay persons have been actively engaged in providing services in a number of these areas, proposals to license paralegals have been considered but not adopted. See Deborah L. Rhode, The Delivery of Legal Services by Non-lawyers, 4 Geo.J.Legal Ethics 209, 222–28 (1990) (discussing the California situation).

Nonlawyer Representation in Adjudicatory Proceedings

Representation of parties in proceedings in courts of general jurisdiction is the strongest case for the lawyer's professional monopoly. Here there is an unbroken tradition, flowing from the exclusive right of the English barrister to represent parties in high courts. Arguments of special skill and competence (the intricacies of court procedure and trial tactics), essential to protect clients from serious harm, are bolstered in this context by concerns about the efficient functioning of the legal system. The settlement and disposition of cases in an orderly and efficient manner is facilitated when a relatively small group of professional representatives deal with judges and each other on a regular basis.

> The possibility of permitting anyone to represent another before a tribunal poses more difficulties than does permitting anyone to draft a document. The hypothesized deliberate choice by a client of a nonlawyer for advice whether to sign a lease may result in economic loss to the client through improper counseling, but in most instances it will be loss to the client alone. However, the choice of one not trained to appear before a tribunal involves costs that must be borne by others—costs to the tribunal itself and to the other litigants. At a time when many are calling for a specialized trial bar because of allegedly inadequate lawyer performance, a move in the opposite direction to permit anyone to try cases for others seems of dubious viability.[25]

Even in the adjudicatory realm, however, statutes or custom carve out some exceptions for lower tribunals (e.g., justice of the peace courts, small claims courts) and some administrative tribunals. In most of these situations, the losing party is entitled to a de novo trial or further hearing before a constitutional court, in which nonlawyers will be forbidden from appearing on behalf of others.

Representation before tribunals has been an area of lively contest between interests such as consumer groups and lawyers. State statutes or agency rules that have attempted to broaden the power of nonlawyers to represent others in agency proceedings have been struck down as a violation of the exclusive inherent power of the state's highest court to regulate the practice of law.[26] Is the integrity of "judicial power" really threatened by legislative choices of this type?

Restrictions on Law Practice by Corporations

Most states prohibit the practice of law by corporations (other than "professional corporations" composed solely of lawyers). The prohibi-

---

25. Thomas Ehrlich and Murray L. Schwartz, Reducing the Costs of Legal Service: Possible Approaches by the Federal Government, Subcomm. on Representation of Citizen Interests of the Comm. on the Judiciary, U.S. Senate, 93d Cong., 2d Sess. 3 (1974).

26. See, e.g., Idaho St. Bar Ass'n v. Idaho Pub. Utilities Comm'n, 102 Idaho 672, 637 P.2d 1168 (1981) (agency rule authorizing representation in utility commission proceedings by nonlawyer representatives of consumer groups and trade associations held invalid).

tion prevents competition from banks, insurance companies, title insurance companies and others. It also forestalls attempts by national marketing chains to make law practice a true consumer product for the national market by installing law offices in retail stores.

The prohibition against law practice by corporations also prevents a corporation from appearing pro se in litigation; the corporation must always be represented by a lawyer who is properly admitted to practice. Do corporations, like individual consumers, need to be protected against their own ignorance? Or is the problem that, when non-lawyer agents represent a corporation, those agents may not provide a lawyer's independent judgment? Although corporations may be represented by lawyers in their employ (house counsel), the organized bar and some state courts take a dim view of efforts by liability insurers to handle the defense of insured tortfeasors through salaried lawyers.

"Unauthorized" Practice of Business Law

All large accounting firms have large in-house legal staffs. These lawyers help in the services that accounting firms provide their clients. Similarly, all large banks have legal departments that help in the financial services that banks provide their customers. Further, all large corporations have legal departments that help in corporate operations. All these forms of legal service give legal shape to transactions involving the clients or customers of these organizations.

Are these business organizations involved in the "unauthorized practice of law"? The technical answer has been that the corporation is engaged in unauthorized practice if its lawyers provide legal assistance to *others*, such as the corporation's customers. However, the corporation can provide legal assistance to *itself* without thereby engaging in practice of law. This conclusion has never been fully reconciled with the proposition that a corporation's law department lawyers are treated as full-fledged practitioners for purposes of the attorney-client privilege. That is, corporate law department attorneys are regarded as rendering legal advice to someone (the corporation) for purposes of the attorney-client privilege,[27] but are not regarded as providing legal services to that someone for purposes of the unauthorized practice of law prohibition.

Why are accounting firms, banks and corporations allowed to employ lawyers as they do? A political explanation is that in-house legal services are regarded as more efficient by the businesses that pay for them and that these businesses have enough political clout to block the bar from interfering. Until the 1950s, the bar maintained substantial influence in defining what is "the practice of law." However, in the early 1960s the bar suffered defeats from which lessons could be learned. A well-publicized instance of conflict between realtors and lawyers arose in Arizona in 1962. The state bar succeeded in persuading the Arizona Supreme Court that the existing practice in which

---

27. See Upjohn Co. v. United States, 449 U.S. 383 (1981), p. 226 above.

realtors, in conjunction with title insurance companies, prepared legal documents in real estate transactions, was unauthorized practice of law.[28] The realtors reacted with a petition campaign to reverse the court's decision by means of a constitutional amendment. The realtors won a resounding victory when the constitutional amendment was adopted by an overwhelming vote.

Substantial conflict of interest problems are generated when commercial entities such as insurers, trust companies or realtors perform legal services for their customers. The principal business of each is to sell something to the public, such as insurance in the case of insurance companies or trust services in the case of trust companies. If staff lawyers deal with customers in this setting, they might not provide the independent judgment expected of an outside lawyer. Fiduciary or malpractice law may provide some protection against extreme instances of impartial advice. Is it sufficient? If not, does prohibiting corporations from engaging in law practice provide needed protections to consumers that fiduciary and malpractice law cannot?

Policy Choices

The American law of unauthorized practice goes well beyond that of the remainder of the common law world in extending the prohibition to out-of-court legal services. Because law is such an omnipresent reality in today's world, it is impossible for individuals in hundreds of endeavors to carry on their work without dealing with "the law." Consider the police officer patrolling a neighborhood beat, the small business filing its tax return, the buyer or seller of a residential home, the consumer dealing with an aggressive finance company or collection agency, or the spouse considering a no-fault divorce. Each of these individuals may consult a lawyer, but many of them may seek or get advice from nonlawyers: the police officer from a nonlawyer supervisor, the small business from an accountant, the home buyer from a realtor, the consumer from a consumer group, and the spouse from a self-help kit or a Rosemary Furman. In which of these situations, if any, should sound public policy attempt to protect consumers from competitive services provided by nonlawyers? Why? Do these people need to be protected against their own inability to judge the quality of the services offered? Does the organized bar provide assurance that the lawyers whom the consumers will otherwise be required to consult have the necessary competence and integrity? Will the requirement that some or all of these activities be provided by lawyers with seven years of higher education involve costs that many clients cannot meet? Is it reasonable for the bar at once to seek to enjoin individuals like Rosemary Furman and at the same time to fail to develop a comprehensive solution for the legal problems of the people she was trying to

28. State Bar of Arizona v. Arizona Land Title & Trust Co., 90 Ariz. 76, 366 P.2d 1 (1961), opinion on rehearing, 91 Ariz. 293, 371 P.2d 1020 (1962). The controversy is described in Merton E. Marks, The Lawyers and the Realtors: Arizona's Experience, 49 A.B.A.J. 139 (1963).

help? These questions should be considered in connection with the policy arguments relating to the general question of whether competition in legal services threatens "lawyer professionalism."

The organized bar largely acquiesces in activities carried on by powerful occupational groups, such as accountants in providing tax advice or realtors in real estate transactions. The bar's efforts to enforce unauthorized practice restrictions are strongest in situations in which unorganized individuals seek to perform activities that are of considerable economic importance to general practitioners, such as divorces, personal bankruptcies and drafting and probate of wills. Do these activities involve greater legal complexity than those carried on by accountants or realtors? Are these activities different from tax advice or real estate transactions because they involve court filings, however routine in character? Or because these activities are of considerable bread-and-butter importance to the solo practitioners who still constitute almost one-half of all lawyers in private practice?

Jerome Carlin's empirical study of solo practitioners in Chicago concludes that:

> Most matters that reach the individual practitioner—the small residential closing, the simple uncontested divorce, drawing up a will or probating a small estate, routine filings for a small business, negotiating a personal injury claim, or collecting on a debt—do not require very much technical knowledge, and what technical problems there are are generally simplified by the use of standardized forms and procedures.... [Moreover, clients in these areas are] unwilling to pay for the kind of legal advice or product that would give fullest rein to the individual practitioner's abilities. As a result, the legal work of the individual lawyer is, in most instances, reduced to a fairly routine, clerical-bookkeeping job—the very kind of job which many nonlawyers and lay organizations are as well, if not better, equipped to handle than the lawyer.... [M]uch of this work should probably be handled by lay organizations. This does not mean eliminating the lawyer, but, as in the case of the title company, transferring the job from the private lawyer to the house counsel [assisted by clerks and paralegals].[29]

On the other hand, Professors Ehrlich and Schwartz argue that such conclusions as Carlin's rest on supposition rather than solid evidence. They ask for studies that will show, for example, whether the displacement of the solo lawyer by title insurance companies is more efficient or merely the substitution of a new and more costly monopoly (e.g., that of title insurance companies) for that of lawyers. They urge studies that would "indicate the relative costs and benefits of lawyer and nonlawyer representation, and a comparison of lawyer costs for services in fields where 'lay' competition is not permitted...." [30]

---

29. Jerome E. Carlin, Lawyers on Their Own: A Study of Individual Practitioners in Chicago 206–09 (1962).

30. Ehrlich and Schwartz, supra, at 305.

Professor Rhode's comprehensive study of the enforcement of unauthorized practice regulation concludes that the burden of proof and persuasion rests on the legal profession to justify its monopoly rather than on actual or potential competitors: [31]

> Invoking standards that are conclusory, circular, or both, courts have typically inquired only whether challenged activity calls for "legal" skills, not whether lay practitioners in fact possess them. At every level of enforcement, the consumer's need for protection has been proclaimed rather than proven.... Absent evidence of significant injuries resulting from lay assistance, individuals should be entitled to determine the cost and quality of legal services that best meet their needs. Where there are demonstrable grounds for paternalism, it should emanate from institutions other than the organized bar [which has such a strong self-interest in a broad sphere of professional monopoly].[32]

Rhode's empirical study finds the following: Prosecutors rarely bring criminal charges of unauthorized practice; nearly all complaints emanate from the organized bar rather than from consumers of legal services; the bar's enforcement efforts primarily take the less visible forms of pressure, negotiation and threat, followed occasionally by injunction proceedings against recalcitrant competitors; and the bulk of the enforcement effort (three-quarters of all investigations and 68 percent of reported cases) involves lay form preparation and related advice. How much significance should be given to the fact that enforcement is at the initiative of the bar rather than either the public prosecutor or consumers of the nonlawyer's services? Is it relevant that lay people, and sometimes legislators, seem to prefer a choice between service providers of differing price and quality? Or is this one of the questions on which the legal profession, acting through the highest state court, knows what is best for consumers and the public?

A considerable body of professional and scholarly literature defends or attacks various professional restrictions on the production and distribution of legal services as either essential to the preservation of the virtues of professionalism, on the one hand, or as unjustified restrictions on free competition, on the other. An underlying issue, rarely discussed directly, is whether or not "professionalism," when properly understood, is inconsistent with, or threatened by, competition among lawyers and between lawyers and other service providers. This issue arises in connection with virtually every issue relating to regulation of what is offered to the public under the rubric of legal services: unauthorized practice, advertising and solicitation, group legal services, restrictions on form of practice, publicly subsidized legal services for the poor and other matters. Is competition a threat to professionalism?

31. Deborah L. Rhode, Policing the Professional Monopoly: A Constitutional and Empirical Analysis of Unauthorized Practice Prohibitions, 34 Stan. L. Rev. 1, 94–99 (1981).

32. Id. at 97–99.

What is the causal connection between the real virtues of "professional-ism," if they can be identified, and a competitive marketplace?

2. Who Regulates Lawyers?

Occupational licensing is endemic in the United States, but the regulation of lawyers has distinct characteristics. First, it is generally created, revised and enforced by the highest court of a state. As the Florida Supreme Court said in *Brumbaugh,* the court is not only an adjudicator but "acts in its administrative capacity as chief policy maker, regulating the administration of the court system and supervis-ing all persons who are engaged in rendering legal advice to members of the general public." The regulatory regimes governing other occupa-tions are created by statute and normally involve an administrative agency exercising delegated rulemaking and enforcement powers. Al-though "regulatory capture" of the responsible agency is a continuing problem with other licensed occupations, legislative oversight and pub-lic involvement may act as a check. In cases like *Brumbaugh,* on the other hand, the state supreme court combines the functions of legisla-tor, enforcer and adjudicator.

Second, in most states the legislature is excluded from partic-ipation in the regulation of lawyers.[33] Early American courts, follow-ing English practice, assumed that determining the qualifications of those who appeared before them was part of inherent judicial authori-ty. Decisions in many states draw negative implications from this doctrine of inherent authority: Because the regulation of lawyers is part of the "judicial power" vested in courts, any legislative act dealing with lawyers, unless it is fully consistent with the judicially imposed framework and policy, is violative of separation of powers.[34] Why should the most broadly competent policy-making body be excluded from dealing with matters that have a large effect on the availability, cost and quality of legal services, such as group legal services, lawyer advertising and the like? Would the negative-implications approach make sense if confined to the lawyer's in-court representation of clients?

Third, bar associations retain a privileged and influential role in the formulation of professional standards. Standards and model codes promulgated by the ABA are studied by state bars, which issue reports that initiate rulemaking consideration by the high court of a given state. Because the judges have heavy judicial caseloads, the rulemak-ing function may be treated in a perfunctory manner or delegated to the chief judge or a small group of judges. Although state supreme

33. For discussion of the inherent-powers doctrine, see Wolfram, Modern Legal Ethics 27–31 (1986); and Charles W. Wolfram, Lawyer Turf and Lawyer Regulation—The Role of the Inherent–Powers Doctrine, 12 U.Ark.Little Rock L.J. 1 (1989–90).

34. See, e.g., Hustedt v. Workers' Compensation Appeals Bd., 30 Cal.3d 329, 178 Cal.Rptr. 801, 636 P.2d 1139 (1981) (invalidating a statute authorizing an administrative agency to discipline lawyers in agency proceedings).

courts have exercised more independence in recent years, substantial deference typically is given to bar association views.[35]

Is self-regulation of the profession an essential element of "professionalism?" Or would it be desirable, as Professor Rhode and others contend, if public regulation of the practice of law were carried on by legislatively created bodies that included nonlawyers as well as lawyers?

3. Market Imperfections in the Delivery of Legal Services

Is the professional monopoly in the best interests of society generally, or is it merely a tactic by which the legal profession seeks to protect its own turf? Both conservative economists and Marxist analysts view much of the profession's regulation of itself (through the instrumentality of the highest court of a state) as designed to enhance the incomes and status of lawyers. Milton Friedman, for example, argues that fears that consumers are incapable of making choices for themselves are paternalistic and wrong; registration or certification are adequate to overcome market imperfections such as inadequate information.[36] He "find[s] it difficult to see any case in which licensure [e.g., exclusion of competitors] rather than certification can be justified." [37] From Friedman's point of view, restraints on competition have adverse effects on the quality, variety and cost of services. Innovation is reduced, and the flow of information impeded. And it is almost inevitable that the producer group will dominate occupational licensing at the expense of the public.

The persistence of occupational licensing and the continuing public support for some types of regulation of legal and medical services have stimulated economic arguments in defense of at least some occupational regulation. Consider the following arguments:

Information imperfections in the legal services market may lead to consumer harm or a debasement of the quality of service.

- Some consumers of legal services need to be protected against their own ignorance. They may be harmed as a result of information deficiencies that are costly or impossible to correct. Individuals who have no experience with lawyers and are involved in a personal plight, such as injury, divorce or a criminal charge, lack information as to choosing or supervising a lawyer. The gap between the client's information and that of the lawyer requires the client to make a leap of faith, trusting that the lawyer is competent and honest. Professional regulation seeks to justify the client's trust by assuring a minimal level of integrity, competence and performance.

---

35. Professor Wolfram states (too broadly?) that "lawyers, and *only* lawyers, now regulate the legal profession. Lawyers entirely control the process by which lawyer rules of conduct are written and adopted." Wolfram, Modern Legal Ethics 16 (1986).

36. Milton Friedman, Capitalism and Freedom 130–60 (1962).

37. Id. at 149.

- If consumers cannot differentiate between high quality and low quality legal services, producers will not be compensated for the higher cost of high quality service. Information asymmetry may result in a "market for lemons," in the sense that producers are forced to make price and quality reductions that in turn lead to only cheap products being sold and the market shrinking.[38] The problem may be overcome by certification, advertising or other measures that remedy the typical consumer's information deficiencies. Alternatively, a regulatory regime may define performance standards and provide adequate incentives for lawyers to invest time, education and resources in providing quality services.[39]

Neighborhood effects (externalities) of sufficient size and frequency may justify governmental intervention. Even if it is paternalistic and undesirable to deny consumers the freedom to choose the type of service they want, costs to third persons or to the public generally may justify regulation. If an unlicensed and incompetent person builds a bridge or skyscraper that collapses, huge costs are imposed on others. After-the-fact remedies, such as negligence law, may not prevent a sufficient number of such incidents. In the context of legal services, externalities come into play most obviously when the issue is representation in litigation, which involves the interests of the court, opposing parties and the public in just and expeditious resolution of disputes. Regulation of advocates may serve those goals.

Finally, *free rider* problems may support some governmental intervention. Free riders are those who benefit from collective goods without contributing for their payment. In a sense, the public trust created by the profession's scheme of entry regulation and control of conduct is a collective good of the profession or the public. "[A]bsent effective regulatory structures, individual attorneys will have inadequate economic incentives to avoid cheating; they can benefit as free riders from the bar's general reputation without adhering to the standards that maintain it."[40]

How serious are these market imperfections? Are they applicable to all sectors of law practice or only a few? Would certification of lawyers be a satisfactory alternative to exclusive licensing? Would provision of public information about the practice and qualifications of lawyers solve the information problem? Why not rely solely on moral suasion and peer pressure from within the profession? Or is the current regulatory regime, including exclusive licensing, necessary?

38. See George A. Akerlof, The Market for Lemons: Quality Uncertainty and the Market Mechanism, 84 Q. J. Econ. 488 (1970); Hayne E. Leland, Quacks, Lemons, and Licensing, 87 Pol.Econ. 1328 (1979); and Hayne E. Leland, Minimum Quality Standards and Licensing in Markets with Asymmetry of Information, in Simon Rottenberg (ed.), Occupational Licensure and Regulation 265 (1980).

39. See generally Robert Dingwall and Paul Fenn, 'A Respectable Profession'?, Sociological and Economic Perspectives on the Regulation of Professional Services, 7 Int'l Rev. of Law and Econ. 51 (1987).

40. Deborah L. Rhode and David Luban, Legal Ethics 647 (1992).

B. ADVERTISING, SOLICITATION AND PRACTICE RESTRICTIONS

1. Professional Traditions and Rules

Traditional Ban on Lawyer Advertising [41]

The world has changed so much since 1976, when the Supreme Court first accorded free speech protection to "commercial speech," [42] that today's law students need to be reminded of the way things were when lawyer advertising was prohibited. In the 19th century lawyers sometimes advertised their services in newspapers or distributed business cards. But a professional tradition that it was unseemly for a lawyer to advertise, carried over from England, dominated the profession and was included in the ABA Canons of Professional Ethics in 1908.

Canon 27 stated in part (in its original form):

The most worthy and effective advertisement possible, even for a young lawyer, is the establishment of a well-merited reputation for professional capacity and fidelity to trust. This cannot be forced, but must be the outcome of character and conduct.... [S]olicitation of business by circulars or advertisements, or by personal communications, or interviews not warranted by personal relations, is unprofessional.... Indirect advertisement for business by furnishing or inspiring newspaper comments concerning causes in which the lawyer has been or is engaged, ... the importance of the lawyer's positions, and all other like self-laudation, defy the traditions and lower the tone of our high calling, and are intolerable.

During the next six decades, ethics committees put substantial effort into defining the line between appropriate business-getting activities and impermissible ones. A lawyer could have a small, dignified sign ("shingle") to mark the office door, appear in a "reputable law list" (i.e., a directory, such as Martindale–Hubbell, primarily available to other lawyers), and make "customary use" of professional cards and business letterheads. But the sign could not be too large, any listings

---

41. For discussion of the history of lawyer advertising, see Lori B. Andrews, Birth of a Salesman: Lawyer Advertising and Solicitation (1980).

42. Virginia State Bd. of Pharmacy v. Virginia Citizens Consumer Council, Inc., 425 U.S. 748 (1976) (Virginia statute declaring it unprofessional conduct for licensed pharmacist to advertise prices of prescription drugs held invalid under First Amendment), extended to lawyer advertising in Bates v. State Bar of Arizona, 433 U.S. 350 (1977) (invalidating a total prohibition on advertising the price of routine legal services). The current standards for evaluating restrictions on commercial speech are set out in Central Hudson Gas & Elec. Corp. v. Public Serv. Comm'n, 447 U.S. 557 (1980). The *Central Hudson* test protects commercial speech (defined as "expression solely related to the economic interests of the speaker and its audience") that concerns lawful activity and is upheld only if: (1) the asserted government interest is "substantial," (2) the regulation "directly advances" that interest and (3) the regulation is no more extensive than necessary to serve that interest.

or advertisements in materials distributed to the public were prohibited and any identification of the lawyer's field of practice was improper (except for a traditional exception for three federal specialties—patent, trademark and admiralty lawyers). In an effort to deal with ingenious efforts at evasion, the professional rules became more and more elaborate. The longest and most detailed provisions of the 1969 Model Code dealt with advertising, solicitation and other efforts to provide information about legal services. See DRs 2–101 through 2–105 and ECs 2–6 through 2–15.

The reported decisions, which deal with such matters as whether distribution of a matchbook embossed with the lawyer's name is permissible,[43] often seem trivial. But the underlying issues were taken very seriously by leaders of the bar. They felt that a distinctive aspect of professionalism was a rejection of the commercial spirit, a posture that reinforced notions of the lawyer as serving larger interests than those of self. Moreover, they believed that advertising of legal services would inevitably be misleading to lay persons, resulting in deception, overreaching and incitement of litigation. "[P]ublic confidence in our legal system would be impaired by ... advertisements of legal services" because "it would inevitably produce unrealistic expectations in particular cases and bring about distrust of the law and lawyers." EC 2–9.

The scope of the ban on advertising and the profession's commitment to it are conveyed by the following cases:

• Berezniak, an immigrant from Russia, distributed a calendar to "theatrical people" describing himself as specializing in "theatrical law" and containing testimonials praising his services (e.g., "Berezniak is one of the few lawyers who look for the interest of the client first and the money second"). At the initiative of the Chicago Bar Association, Berezniak was publicly censured:

> The advertisements of respondent are very obnoxious and disgusting, not only because they are gotten up after the manner of quack doctors and itinerant vendors of patent medicines and other cure-alls, but because of the fact that they contain statements that cast reflections upon the common honesty, proficiency, and decency of the profession generally of which he insists he is a distinguished member. Any one who is knowingly guilty of such conduct as a lawyer ought to suspect that he is laying himself open to the charge of unprofessional conduct, which, if persisted in, would lead to disbarment.[44]

• Gray, a New York City lawyer, was censured for soliciting claims for collection and other legal business in letters addressed to businesses with which he had no professional relation. One letter, for example, stated: "It can do you no harm to give me a trial on some work if you have no regular attorney, and if you have an attorney, it would

---

43. In re Maltby, 68 Ariz. 153, 202 P.2d 902 (1949) (condemning matchbooks).

44. People ex rel. Chicago Bar Ass'n v. Berezniak, 292 Ill. 305, 127 N.E. 36 (1920).

undoubtedly make little or no difference to him if your smaller business was given to me." [45] The court said:

> Business men, receiving a succession of such communications, would be likely to form a very unjust estimate of the profession at large, and conclude that the law was not, as consistently maintained, a learned *profession,* but had deteriorated into a mere *business,* where the most persistent and adroit self-advertiser would be the most successful, a point of view repugnant to the conception of every honorable practitioner, condemned by the bar and bench alike.[46]

• Crocker published a classified advertisement in a daily newspaper in Nebraska offering to do "default divorces" for "$15 and costs." He was suspended for 30 days: [47]

> [T]he courts generally have condemned the practice of a lawyer advertising for professional employment and particularly for divorce cases. . . . [T]he practice of lawyers hawking their brains as wares upon the street corner [cannot] be approved. An advertisement in a newspaper by an attorney at law soliciting divorce cases is conduct requiring discipline.[48]

• In 1962 *LIFE* magazine published a feature article dealing with the practice of corporate law in New York City. The Olwine firm of New York City had agreed to be interviewed as an illustrative medium-sized firm (25 lawyers). The firm was described in generally laudatory terms in the article (e.g., a "blue chip" firm that enjoys "the cream of corporate business"). Four partners were censured for these self-promotion activities.[49] The court said:

> Canon 27, in wording and in spirit, is clearly violated by conduct of an attorney which is plainly calculated to publicize the magnitude of the interests handled by him or, in any way, his special skills, capabilities or talents in the practice of law. . . . These actions tending prominently to publicize the names of these attorneys and their special qualifications, constitute indirect advertising. They "offend the traditions and lower the tone of our profession and are reprehensible" (see Canon 27), and require disciplinary action.[50]

• Marvin Belli, the self-styled "King of Torts," was suspended in California for 30 days for sending to *Time* and *Newsweek* a news release puffing the 20th anniversary of his annual seminar for trial lawyers

45. In re Gray, 184 App.Div. 822, 172 N.Y.S. 648 (1st Dept.1918).

46. 172 N.Y.S. at 652.

47. State ex rel. Hunter v. Crocker, 132 Neb. 214, 271 N.W. 444 (1937).

48. 271 N.W. at 447.

49. Matter of Connelly, 18 A.D.2d 466, 240 N.Y.S.2d 126 (1st Dep't 1963).

50. 240 N.Y.S.2d at 139.

and for appearing in a *New York Times* advertisement endorsing Glenfiddich Scotch whiskey.[51]

Beginning in the 1960s forces within and without the profession began to challenge the total prohibition on advertising. The consumer movement, supported by the Department of Justice and the Federal Trade Commission, challenged paternalistic assumptions that consumers were incapable of intelligent use of the information provided by advertising.[52] The growth of the legal services movement, providing civil legal assistance to poor people, invoked concerns within and without the profession concerning the distribution of legal services. And some groups within a larger and more heterogeneous legal profession sought to develop new modes of delivery, such as legal clinics.[53]

First Amendment Protection of Lawyer Advertising

Lawyer efforts to gain business by various forms of advertising and solicitation are now largely protected by authoritative interpretations of the First Amendment. The major current exception is in-person solicitation of legal business.

Even before the Supreme Court extended constitutional protection to commercial speech, two Arizona lawyers, Bates and O'Steen, who had opened a legal clinic in Phoenix "to provide legal services at modest fees to persons of moderate income who did not qualify for governmental legal aid," challenged Arizona's prohibition of all lawyer advertising on antitrust [54] and First Amendment grounds. Thus began the series of landmark cases putting First Amendment protection around lawyer advertising.

> • Bates v. State Bar of Arizona [55] involved newspaper advertising of a legal clinic that offered "legal services at very reasonable rates"

---

51. Belli v. State Bar of California, 10 Cal.3d 824, 112 Cal.Rptr. 527, 519 P.2d 575 (1974).

52. E.g., Justice Department testimony on the anticompetitive effect of the ban on advertising. See 60 A.B.A.J. 791, 792 (1974).

53. Critics argued that the premise that lawyers could build a practice by gradual growth of repute in the community was inappropriate in urban settings and was perpetuated by elite lawyers as a means of suppressing competition from new entrants. See Jerold S. Auerbach, Unequal Justice 43–44 (1976) ("The Canons especially impeded those lawyers who worked in a highly competitive urban market with a transient clientele ... [and reduced] the opportunity of an accident victim to recover damages"); Philip Shuchman, Ethics and Legal Ethics: The Propriety of the Canons as a Group Moral Code, 37 Geo.Wash.L.Rev. 244, 266–77 (1968) (attacking restrictions on advertising).

54. *Bates* rejected the antitrust challenge under the state action immunity flowing from Parker v. Brown, 317 U.S. 341 (1943) (California's displacement of competition in marketing of raisins is state action not subject to federal antitrust policy). This doctrine requires that an anticompetitive policy be created and enforced by a state instrumentality. Because the ban on lawyer advertising rested on a rule adopted by the Arizona Supreme Court, it was within the state action immunity. Compare Hoover v. Ronwin, 466 U.S. 558 (1984) (a bar admission policy designed to limit the number of new entrants was a "clearly articulated state ... policy" "actively supervised" by a state agency and therefore within the state action immunity), with Goldfarb v. Virginia State Bar, 421 U.S. 773 (1975) (minimum fee guidelines of state bar as a private association violate the antitrust laws).

55. 433 U.S. 350 (1977).

and listed standard charges for certain matters (e.g., $175 plus $20 filing fee for an uncontested divorce). Such truthful advertising was held protected by the "commercial speech" component of the First Amendment.

• In Ohralik v. Ohio State Bar Ass'n,[56] the Supreme Court upheld disciplinary sanctions against a lawyer who had personally gone to the home of a person involved in an automobile accident, and also visited her in the hospital, to solicit the lawyer's employment for a personal injury case. However, in In re Primus,[57] the Court upheld "in-person" solicitation carried out by a lawyer for a civil rights organization seeking a plaintiff who would bring a civil rights "test case."

• In re R.M.J.,[58] upholding First Amendment protection of professional announcements circulated to potential clients, indicated that a state could require any such written communications to be labeled as an "advertisement."[59]

• Zauderer v. Office of Disciplinary Counsel[60] held that lawyers could use "targeted" newspaper advertisements. The newspaper advertisement in that case invited Dalkon Shield claimants to contact the attorney concerning possible personal injury claims.

Model Rules on Lawyer Advertising

In 1983, when the American Bar Association adopted the Model Rules of Professional Conduct, the ABA rejected the Kutak Commission's recommendation that "targeted" letters be permitted along with newspaper advertisements, circulars distributed by a general mailing and other forms of written communication to the general public. Model Rule 7.3 allowed lawyers to send "non-targeted" letters but not "targeted" ones. This provision was attacked in the *Shapero* case, reprinted below.

Model Rules 7.1 and 7.2 make all advertising subject to requirements of truthfulness. The Rules also require that a lawyer maintain copies of all written solicitations for a reasonable period, such as a year, following their dissemination. This was to allow enforcement authorities to verify the text of any such communications.

56.   436 U.S. 447 (1978).

57.   436 U.S. 412 (1978).

58.   455 U.S. 191 (1982).

59.   Id. at 206, note 20.

60.   471 U.S. 626 (1985).

2.   Free Speech and Lawyer Business–Getting Activities

SHAPERO v. KENTUCKY BAR ASSOCIATION
Supreme Court of the United States, 1988.
486 U.S. 466, 108 S.Ct. 1916, 100 L.Ed.2d 475.

JUSTICE BRENNAN announced the judgment of the Court and delivered the opinion of the Court as to Parts I and II and an opinion as to Part III in which JUSTICE MARSHALL, JUSTICE BLACKMUN, and JUSTICE KENNEDY join.

This case presents the issue whether a State may, consistent with the First and Fourteenth Amendments, categorically prohibit lawyers from soliciting legal business for pecuniary gain by sending truthful and nondeceptive letters to potential clients known to face particular legal problems.

I

In 1985, petitioner, a member of Kentucky's integrated Bar Association, see Ky.Sup.Ct. Rule 3.030 (1988), applied to the Kentucky Attorneys Advertising Commission [1] for approval of a letter that he proposed to send "to potential clients who have had a foreclosure suit filed against them."   The proposed letter read as follows:

"It has come to my attention that your home is being foreclosed on.   If this is true, you may be about to lose your home.   Federal law may allow you to keep your home by *ORDERING* your creditor [*sic*] to *STOP* and give you more time to pay them.

"You may call my office anytime from 8:30 a.m. to 5:00 p.m. for *FREE* information on how you can keep your home.

"Call *NOW*, don't wait.   It may surprise you what I may be able to do for you.   Just call and tell me that you got this letter.   Remember it is *FREE*, there is *NO* charge for calling."

The Commission did not find the letter false or misleading.   Nevertheless, it declined to approve petitioner's proposal on the ground that a then-existing Kentucky Supreme Court Rule prohibited the mailing or delivery of written advertisements "precipitated by a specific event or occurrence involving or relating to the addressee or addressees as distinct from the general public."   Ky.Sup.Ct. Rule 3.135(5)(b)(i).[2]   The

---

1.   The Attorneys Advertising Commission is charged with the responsibility of "regulating attorney advertising as prescribed" in the Rules of the Kentucky Supreme Court. Ky.Sup.Ct. Rule 3.135(3) (1988).   The Commission's decisions are appealable to the Board of Governors of the Kentucky Bar Association, Rule 3.135(8)(a), and are ultimately reviewable by the Kentucky Supreme Court.   Rule 3.135(8)(b).   "Any attorney who is in doubt as to the propriety of any professional act contemplated by him" also has the option of seeking an advisory opinion from a committee of the Kentucky Bar Association, which, if formally adopted by the Board of Governors, is reviewable by the Kentucky Supreme Court.   Rule 3.530.

2.   Rule 3.135(5)(b)(i) provided in full:

"A written advertisement may be sent or delivered to an individual addressee only if that addressee is one of a class of persons, other than a family, to whom it is also sent or delivered at or about the same time, and only if it is not prompted or precipitated by

Commission registered its view that Rule 3.135(5)(b)(i)'s ban on targeted, direct-mail advertising violated the First Amendment—specifically the principles enunciated in Zauderer v. Office of Disciplinary Counsel of Supreme Court of Ohio, 471 U.S. 626 (1985)—and recommended that the Kentucky Supreme Court amend its Rules. Pursuing the Commission's suggestion, petitioner petitioned the Committee on Legal Ethics (Ethics Committee) of the Kentucky Bar Association for an advisory opinion as to the Rule's validity. See Ky.Sup.Ct. Rule 3.530; n. 1, supra. Like the Commission, the Ethics Committee, in an opinion formally adopted by the Board of Governors of the Bar Association, did not find the proposed letter false or misleading, but nonetheless upheld Rule 3.135(5)(b)(i) on the ground that it was consistent with Rule 7.3 of the American Bar Association's Model Rules of Professional Conduct (1984).

On review of the Ethics Committee's advisory opinion, the Kentucky Supreme Court felt "compelled by the decision in *Zauderer* to order [Rule 3.135(5)(b)(i)] deleted," 726 S.W.2d 299, 300 (1987), and replaced it with the ABA's Rule 7.3, which provides in its entirety:

> " 'A lawyer may not solicit professional employment from a prospective client with whom the lawyer has no family or prior professional relationship, by mail, in-person or otherwise, when a significant motive for the lawyer's doing so is the lawyer's pecuniary gain. The term 'solicit' includes contact in person, by telephone or telegraph, by letter or other writing, or by other communication directed to a specific recipient, but does not include letters addressed or advertising circulars distributed generally to persons not known to need legal services of the kind provided by the lawyer in a particular matter, but who are so situated that they might in general find such services useful." ' 726 S.W.2d, at 301 (quoting ABA, Model Rule of Professional Conduct 7.3 (1984)).

The court did not specify either the precise infirmity in Rule 3.135(5)(b)(i) or how Rule 7.3 cured it. Rule 7.3 like its predecessor, prohibits targeted, direct-mail solicitation by lawyers for pecuniary gain, without a particularized finding that the solicitation is false or misleading. We granted certiorari to resolve whether such a blanket prohibition is consistent with the First Amendment, made applicable to the States through the Fourteenth Amendment, and now reverse.

II

Lawyer advertising is in the category of constitutionally protected commercial speech. See Bates v. State Bar of Arizona, 433 U.S. 350 (1977). The First Amendment principles governing state regulation of lawyer solicitations for pecuniary gain are by now familiar: "Commercial speech that is not false or deceptive and does not concern unlawful activities ... may be restricted only in the service of a substantial

a specific event or occurrence involving or relating to the addressee or addressees as distinct from the general public."

governmental interest, and only through means that directly advance that interest." *Zauderer,* supra, 471 U.S., at 638 (citing Central Hudson Gas & Electric Corp. v. Public Service Comm'n of New York, 447 U.S. 557, 566 (1980)). Since state regulation of commercial speech "may extend only as far as the interest it serves," *Central Hudson,* supra, at 565, state rules that are designed to prevent the "potential for deception and confusion ... may be no broader than reasonably necessary to prevent the" perceived evil. In re R.M.J., 455 U.S. 191, 203 (1982).

In *Zauderer,* application of these principles required that we strike an Ohio rule that categorically prohibited solicitation of legal employment for pecuniary gain through advertisements containing information or advice, even if truthful and nondeceptive, regarding a specific legal problem. We distinguished written advertisements containing such information or advice from in-person solicitation by lawyers for profit, which we held in Ohralik v. Ohio State Bar Assn., 436 U.S. 447 (1978), a State may categorically ban. The "unique features of in-person solicitation by lawyers [that] justified a prophylactic rule prohibiting lawyers from engaging in such solicitation for pecuniary gain," we observed, are "not present" in the context of written advertisements. *Zauderer,* 471 U.S., at 641–642.

Our lawyer advertising cases have never distinguished among various modes of written advertising to the general public. See, e.g., *Bates,* supra (newspaper advertising); id., 433 U.S., at 372, n. 26 (equating advertising in telephone directory with newspaper advertising); *In re R.M.J.,* supra (mailed announcement cards treated same as newspaper and telephone directory advertisements). Thus, Ohio could no more prevent Zauderer from mass-mailing to a general population his offer to represent women injured by the Dalkon Shield than it could prohibit his publication of the advertisement in local newspapers. Similarly, if petitioner's letter is neither false nor deceptive, Kentucky could not constitutionally prohibit him from sending at large an identical letter opening with the query, "Is your home being foreclosed on?," rather than his observation to the targeted individuals that "It has come to my attention that your home is being foreclosed on." The drafters of Rule 7.3 apparently appreciated as much, for the Rule exempts from the ban "letters addressed or advertising circulars distributed generally to persons ... who are so situated that they might in general find such services useful."

The court below disapproved petitioner's proposed letter solely because it targeted only persons who were "known to need [the] legal services" offered in his letter, 726 S.W.2d, at 301, rather than the broader group of persons "so situated that they might in general find such services useful." Generally, unless the advertiser is inept, the latter group would include members of the former. The only reason to disseminate an advertisement of particular legal services among those persons who are "so situated that they might in general find such services useful" is to reach individuals who *actually* "need legal services of the kind provided [and advertised] by the lawyer." But the First

Amendment does not permit a ban on certain speech merely because it is more efficient; the State may not constitutionally ban a particular letter on the theory that to mail it only to those whom it would most interest is somehow inherently objectionable.

The court below did not rely on any such theory.... Rather, it concluded that the State's blanket ban on all targeted, direct-mail solicitation was permissible because of the "serious potential for abuse inherent in direct solicitation by lawyers of potential clients known to need specific legal services." 726 S.W.2d, at 301. By analogy to *Ohralik,* the court observed:

> "Such solicitation subjects the prospective client to pressure from a trained lawyer in a direct personal way. It is entirely possible that the potential client may feel overwhelmed by the basic situation which caused the need for the specific legal services and may have seriously impaired capacity for good judgment, sound reason and a natural protective self-interest. Such a condition is full of the possibility of undue influence, overreaching and intimidation." 726 S.W.2d, at 301.

Of course, a particular potential client will feel equally "overwhelmed" by his legal troubles and will have the same "impaired capacity for good judgment" regardless of whether a lawyer mails him an untargeted letter or exposes him to a newspaper advertisement—concededly constitutionally protected activities—or instead mails a targeted letter. The relevant inquiry is not whether there exist potential clients whose "condition" makes them susceptible to undue influence, but whether the mode of communication poses a serious danger that lawyers will exploit any such susceptibility. Cf. *Ohralik,* supra, 436 U.S., at 470 (Marshall, J., concurring in part and concurring in judgment) ("What is objectionable about Ohralik's behavior here is not so much that he solicited business for himself, but rather the circumstances in which he performed that solicitation and the means by which he accomplished it").

Thus, Respondent's facile suggestion that this case is merely "*Ohralik* in writing" misses the mark. In assessing the potential for overreaching and undue influence, the mode of communication makes all the difference. Our decision in *Ohralik* that a State could categorically ban all in-person solicitation turned on two factors. First was our characterization of face-to-face solicitation as "a practice rife with possibilities for overreaching, invasion of privacy, the exercise of undue influence, and outright fraud." *Zauderer,* supra, 471 U.S., at 641. See *Ohralik,* supra, 436 U.S., at 457–458, 464–465. Second, "unique ... difficulties," *Zauderer,* supra, 471 U.S., at 641, would frustrate any attempt at state regulation of in-person solicitation short of an absolute ban because such solicitation is "not visible or otherwise open to public scrutiny." *Ohralik,* 436 U.S., at 466. See also ibid. ("[I]n-person solicitation would be virtually immune to effective oversight and regulation by the State or by the legal profession"). Targeted, direct-mail solicitation is distinguishable from the in-person solicitation in each respect.

Like print advertising, petitioner's letter—and targeted, direct-mail solicitation generally—"poses much less risk of over-reaching or undue influence" than does in-person solicitation, *Zauderer,* 471 U.S., at 642. Neither mode of written communication involves "the coercive force of the personal presence of a trained advocate" or the "pressure on the potential client for an immediate yes-or-no answer to the offer of representation." Ibid. Unlike the potential client with a badgering advocate breathing down his neck, the recipient of a letter and the "reader of an advertisement . . . can 'effectively avoid further bombardment of [his] sensibilities simply by averting [his] eyes,' " *Ohralik,* supra, 436 U.S., at 465, n. 25 (quoting Cohen v. California, 403 U.S. 15, 21 (1971)). A letter, like a printed advertisement (but unlike a lawyer), can readily be put in a drawer to be considered later, ignored, or discarded. In short, both types of written solicitation "conve[y] information about legal services [by means] that [are] more conducive to reflection and the exercise of choice on the part of the consumer than is personal solicitation by an attorney." *Zauderer,* supra, 471 U.S., at 642. Nor does a targeted letter invade the recipient's privacy any more than does a substantively identical letter mailed at large. The invasion, if any, occurs when the lawyer discovers the recipient's legal affairs, not when he confronts the recipient with the discovery.

Admittedly, a letter that is personalized (not merely targeted) to the recipient presents an increased risk of deception, intentional or inadvertent. It could, in certain circumstances, lead the recipient to overestimate the lawyer's familiarity with the case or could implicitly suggest that the recipient's legal problem is more dire than it really is. Similarly, an inaccurately targeted letter could lead the recipient to believe she has a legal problem that she does not actually have or, worse yet, could offer erroneous legal advice. See, e.g., Leoni v. State Bar of California, 39 Cal.3d 609, 619–620, 217 Cal.Rptr. 423, 429, 704 P.2d 183, 189 (1985), summarily dism'd, 475 U.S. 1001 (1986).

But merely because targeted, direct-mail solicitation presents lawyers with opportunities for isolated abuses or mistakes does not justify a total ban on that mode of protected commercial speech. See In re R.M.J., 455 U.S., at 203. The State can regulate such abuses and minimize mistakes through far less restrictive and more precise means, the most obvious of which is to require the lawyer to file any solicitation letter with a state agency, id., at 206, giving the State ample opportunity to supervise mailings and penalize actual abuses. The "regulatory difficulties" that are "unique" to in-person lawyer solicitation, *Zauderer,* supra, 471 U.S., at 641—solicitation that is "not visible or otherwise open to public scrutiny" and for which it is "difficult or impossible to obtain reliable proof of what actually took place," *Ohralik,* supra, 436 U.S., at 466—do not apply to written solicitations. The court below offered no basis for its "belie[f] [that] submission of a blank form letter to the Advertising Commission [does not] provid[e] a suitable protection to the public from overreaching, intimidation or mis-leading private targeted mail solicitation." 726 S.W.2d, at 301. Its concerns were presumably those expressed by the ABA House of Delegates in its comment to Rule 7.3:

> "State lawyer discipline agencies struggle for resources to investi-gate specific complaints, much less for those necessary to screen lawyers' mail solicitation material. Even if they could examine such materials, agency staff members are unlikely to know any-thing about the lawyer or about the prospective client's underlying problem. Without such knowledge they cannot determine whether the lawyer's representations are misleading." ABA, Model Rules of Professional Conduct, pp. 93–94 (1984).

The record before us furnishes no evidence that scrutiny of target-ed solicitation letters will be appreciably more burdensome or less reliable than scrutiny of advertisements. See *Bates,* 433 U.S., at 379 (Burger, C.J., concurring in part and dissenting in part) (objecting to "enormous new regulatory burdens called for by" *Bates*). As a general matter, evaluating a targeted advertisement does not require specific information about the recipient's identity and legal problems any more than evaluating a newspaper advertisement requires like information about all readers. If the targeted letter specifies facts that relate to particular recipients (e.g., "It has come to my attention that your home is being foreclosed on"), the reviewing agency has innumerable options to minimize mistakes. It might, for example, require the lawyer to prove the truth of the fact stated (by supplying copies of the court documents or material that lead the lawyer to the fact); it could require the lawyer to explain briefly how he or she discovered the fact and verified its accuracy; or it could require the letter to bear a label identifying it as an advertisement, see id., at 384 (dictum); In re R.M.J., supra, 455 U.S., at 206, n. 20, or directing the recipient how to report inaccurate or misleading letters. To be sure, a state agency or bar association that reviews solicitation letters might have more work than one that does not. But "[o]ur recent decisions involving commercial speech have been grounded in the faith that the free flow of commercial information is valuable enough to justify imposing on would-be regu-lators the costs of distinguishing the truthful from the false, the helpful from the misleading, and the harmless from the harmful." *Zauderer,* supra, 471 U.S., at 646.

III

The validity of Rule 7.3 does not turn on whether petitioner's letter itself exhibited any of the evils at which Rule 7.3 was directed. See *Ohralik,* 436 U.S., at 463–464, 466. Since, however, the First Amend-ment overbreadth doctrine does not apply to professional advertising, see *Bates,* 433 U.S., at 379–381, we address respondent's contentions that petitioner's letter is particularly overreaching, and therefore un-worthy of First Amendment protection. Id., at 381. In that regard, respondent identifies two features of the letter before us that, in its view, coalesce to convert the proposed letter into "high pressure solicitation, overbearing solicitation," Brief for Respondent 20, which is not protected. First, respondent asserts that the letter's liberal use of underscored, uppercase letters (e.g., "Call *NOW*, don't wait"; "it is *FREE*, there is *NO* charge for calling") "fairly shouts at the recipient . . . that he should employ Shapero." See also Brief in Opposition 11 ("Letters of solicitation which shout commands to the individual, targeted recipient in words in underscored capitals are of a different order from advertising and are subject to proscription"). Second, respondent objects that the letter contains assertions (e.g., "It may surprise you what I may be able to do for you") that "stat[e] no affirmative or objective fact," but constitute "pure salesman puffery, enticement for the unsophisticated, which commits Shapero to nothing."

The pitch or style of a letter's type and its inclusion of subjective predictions of client satisfaction might catch the recipient's attention more than would a bland statement of purely objective facts in small type. But a truthful and nondeceptive letter, no matter how big its type and how much it speculates can never "shou[t] at the recipient" or "gras[p] him by the lapels," as can a lawyer engaging in face-to-face solicitation. The letter simply presents no comparable risk of overreaching. . . .

To be sure, a letter may be misleading if it unduly emphasizes trivial or "relatively uninformative fact[s]," In re R.M.J., supra, at 205 (lawyer's statement, "in large capital letters, that he was a member of the Bar to the Supreme Court of the United States"), or offers overblown assurances of client satisfaction, cf. In re Von Wiegen, 63 N.Y.2d 163, 179, 481 N.Y.S.2d 40, 49, 470 N.E.2d 838, 847 (1984) (solicitation letter to victims of massive disaster informs them that "it is [the lawyer's] opinion that the liability of the defendants is clear") cert. denied, 472 U.S. 1007 (1985); *Bates,* supra, 433 U.S., at 383–384 ("advertising claims as to the quality of legal services . . . may be so likely to be misleading as to warrant restriction"). Respondent does not argue before us that petitioner's letter was misleading in those respects. Nor does respondent contend that the letter is false or misleading in any other respect. Of course, respondent is free to raise, and the Kentucky courts are free to consider, any such argument on remand.

The judgment of the Supreme Court of Kentucky is reversed and the case is remanded for further proceedings not inconsistent with this opinion.

JUSTICE WHITE, with whom JUSTICE STEVENS joins, concurring in part and dissenting in part.

I agree with Parts I and II of the Court's opinion, but am of the view that the matters addressed in Part III should be left to the state courts in the first instance.

JUSTICE O'CONNOR, with whom CHIEF JUSTICE REHNQUIST and JUSTICE SCALIA join, dissenting.

Relying primarily on Zauderer v. Office of Disciplinary Counsel of Supreme Court of Ohio, 471 U.S. 626 (1985), the Court holds that States may not prohibit a form of attorney advertising that is potentially more pernicious than the advertising at issue in that case. I agree with the Court that the reasoning in *Zauderer* supports the conclusion reached today. That decision, however, was itself the culmination of a line of cases built on defective premises and flawed reasoning. As today's decision illustrates, the Court has been unable or unwilling to restrain the logic of the underlying analysis within reasonable bounds. The resulting interference with important and valid public policies is so destructive that I believe the analytical framework itself should now be reexamined.

I

Zauderer held that the First Amendment was violated by a state rule that forbade attorneys to solicit or accept employment through advertisements containing information or advice regarding a specific legal problem. See id., at 639–647. I dissented from this holding because I believed that our precedents permitted, and good judgment required, that we give greater deference to the States' legitimate efforts to regulate advertising by their attorneys. Emphasizing the important differences between professional services and standardized consumer products, I concluded that unsolicited legal advice was not analogous to the free samples that are often used to promote sales in other contexts. First, the quality of legal services is typically more difficult for most laypersons to evaluate, and the consequences of a mistaken evaluation of the "free sample" may be much more serious. For that reason, the practice of offering unsolicited legal advice as a means of enticing potential clients into a professional relationship is much more likely to be misleading than superficially similar practices in the sale of ordinary consumer goods. Second, and more important, an attorney has an obligation to provide clients with complete and disinterested advice. The advice contained in unsolicited "free samples" is likely to be colored by the lawyer's own interest in drumming up business, a result that is sure to undermine the professional standards that States have a substantial interest in maintaining.

. . .

II

. . .

A standardized legal test has been devised for commercial speech cases. Under that test, such speech is entitled to constitutional protection only if it concerns lawful activities and is not misleading; if the speech is protected, government may still ban or regulate it by laws that directly advance a substantial governmental interest and are appropriately tailored to that purpose. See Central Hudson Gas & Electric Corp. v. Public Service Comm'n of New York, 447 U.S. 557, 566 (1980). Applying that test to attorney advertising, it is clear to me that the States should have considerable latitude to ban advertising that is "*potentially* or demonstrably misleading," In re R.M.J., 455 U.S. 191, 202 (1982) (emphasis added), *as well as* truthful advertising that undermines the substantial governmental interest in promoting the high ethical standards that are necessary in the legal profession.

Some forms of advertising by lawyers might be protected under this test. Announcing the price of an initial consultation might qualify, for example, especially if appropriate disclaimers about the costs of other services were included. Even here, the inherent difficulties of policing such advertising suggest that we should hesitate to interfere with state rules designed to ensure that adequate disclaimers are included and that such advertisements are suitably restrained.

As soon as one steps into the realm of prices for "routine" legal services such as uncontested divorces and personal bankruptcies, however, it is quite clear to me that the States may ban such advertising completely. The contrary decision in *Bates* was in my view inconsistent with the standard test that is now applied in commercial speech cases. Until one becomes familiar with a client's particular problems, there is simply no way to know that one is dealing with a "routine" divorce or bankruptcy. Such an advertisement is therefore inherently misleading if it fails to inform potential clients that they are not necessarily qualified to decide whether their own apparently simple problems can be handled by "routine" legal services. Furthermore, such advertising practices will undermine professional standards if the attorney accepts the economic risks of offering fixed rates for solving apparently simple problems that will sometimes prove not to be so simple after all. For a lawyer to promise the world that such matters as uncontested divorces can be handled for a flat fee will inevitably create incentives to ignore (or avoid discovering) the complexities that would lead a conscientious attorney to treat some clients' cases as anything but routine. It may be possible to devise workable rules that would allow something more than the most minimal kinds of price advertising by attorneys. That task, however, is properly left to the States, and it is certainly not a fit subject for constitutional adjudication. Under the *Central Hudson* test, government has more than ample justification for banning or strictly regulating most forms of price advertising.

. . . Soliciting business from strangers who appear to need particular legal services, when a significant motive for the offer is the lawyer's pecuniary gain, always has a tendency to corrupt the solicitor's professional judgment. This is especially true when the solicitation includes the offer of a "free sample," as petitioner's proposed letter does. I therefore conclude that American Bar Association Model Rule of Professional Conduct 7.3 (1984) sweeps no more broadly than is necessary to advance a substantial governmental interest. . . .

III

The roots of the error in our attorney advertising cases are a defective analogy between professional services and standardized consumer products and a correspondingly inappropriate skepticism about the States' justifications for their regulations.

... The best arguments in favor of rules permitting attorneys to advertise are founded in elementary economic principles. See, e.g., Hazard, Pearce, & Stempel, Why Lawyers Should Be Allowed to Advertise: A Market Analysis of Legal Services, 58 N.Y.U.L.Rev. 1084 (1983). Restrictions on truthful advertising, which artificially interfere with the ability of suppliers to transmit price information to consumers, presumably reduce the efficiency of the mechanisms of supply and demand. Other factors being equal, this should cause or enable suppliers (in this case attorneys) to maintain a price/quality ratio in some of their services that is higher than would otherwise prevail. Although one could probably not test this hypothesis empirically, it is inherently plausible. Nor is it implausible to imagine that one effect of restrictions on lawyer advertising, and perhaps sometimes an intended effect, is to enable attorneys to charge their clients more for some services (of a given quality) than they would be able to charge absent the restrictions.

Assuming *arguendo* that the removal of advertising restrictions should lead in the short run to increased efficiency in the provision of legal services, I would not agree that we can safely assume the same effect in the long run. The economic argument against these restrictions ignores the delicate role they may play in preserving the norms of the legal profession. While it may be difficult to defend this role with precise economic logic, I believe there is a powerful argument in favor of restricting lawyer advertising and that this argument is at the very least not easily refuted by economic analysis.

One distinguishing feature of any profession, unlike other occupations that may be equally respectable, is that membership entails an ethical obligation to temper one's selfish pursuit of economic success by adhering to standards of conduct that could not be enforced either by legal fiat or through the discipline of the market. There are sound reasons to continue pursuing the goal that is implicit in the traditional view of professional life. Both the special privileges incident to membership in the profession and the advantages those privileges give in the necessary task of earning a living are means to a goal that transcends the accumulation of wealth. That goal is public service, which in the legal profession can take a variety of familiar forms. This view of the legal profession need not be rooted in romanticism or self-serving sanctimony, though of course it can be. Rather, special ethical standards for lawyers are properly understood as an appropriate means of restraining lawyers in the exercise of the unique power that they inevitably wield in a political system like ours....

Imbuing the legal profession with the necessary ethical standards is a task that involves a constant struggle with the relentless natural force of economic self-interest. It cannot be accomplished directly by legal rules, and it certainly will not succeed if sermonizing is the strongest tool that may be employed. Tradition and experiment have suggested a number of formal and informal mechanisms, none of which is adequate by itself and many of which may serve to reduce competition (in the narrow economic sense) among members of the profession. A few examples include the great efforts made during this century to improve the quality and breadth of the legal education that is required for admission to the bar; the concomitant attempt to cultivate a sub-class of genuine scholars within the profession; the development of bar associations that aspire to be more than trade groups; strict disciplinary rules about conflicts of interest and client abandonment; and promotion of the expectation that an attorney's history of voluntary public service is a relevant factor in selecting judicial candidates.

Restrictions on advertising and solicitation by lawyers properly and significantly serve the same goal. Such restrictions act as a concrete, day-to-day reminder to the practicing attorney of why it is improper for any member of this profession to regard it as a trade or occupation like any other. There is no guarantee, of course, that the restrictions will always have the desired effect, and they are surely not a sufficient means to their proper goal. Given their inevitable anticompetitive effects, moreover, they should not be thoughtlessly retained or insulated from skeptical criticism. Appropriate modifications have been made in the light of reason and experience, and other changes may be suggested in the future.

In my judgment, however, fairly severe constraints on attorney advertising can continue to play an important role in preserving the legal profession as a genuine profession. Whatever may be the exactly appropriate scope of these restrictions at a given time and place, this Court's recent decisions reflect a myopic belief that "consumers," and thus our Nation, will benefit from a constitutional theory that refuses to recognize either the essence of professionalism or its fragile and necessary foundations. Compare, e.g., *Bates,* 433 U.S., at 370–372, with id., at 400–401, and n. 11 (Powell, J., concurring in part and dissenting in part). In one way or another, time will uncover the folly of this approach. I can only hope that the Court will recognize the danger before it is too late to effect a worthwhile cure.

––––––

Lawyer Advertising After *Shapero*

Targeted Mail

How did lawyer Shapero plan to expand his law practice? What result if he had included the same information in a newspaper ad in a local newspaper? Are those who have a specific legal problem (e.g., someone facing a home foreclosure) more vulnerable to advertising than those among a newspaper's general readership who have the same problem? Is Justice Brennan correct in arguing that the state's inter-

est in preventing deception or overreaching may be handled by requiring all letters to be deposited with the state disciplinary agency?

In–Person Solicitation

    Shapero interprets *Ohralik* as supporting a categorical ban on all
in-person solicitation. Thus a telephone call or home visit conveying
the same information would subject the lawyer to discipline. Yet those
soliciting charitable contributions have a constitutionally protected
right to do door-to-door solicitation.[61] So do accountants who seek to
obtain new clients by direct, in-person and uninvited solicitation.[62] Are
lawyers more dishonest than those who solicit for charities? Is abuse
more likely with lawyers than accountants? Professor Louise Hill
argues that "the categorical proscriptions on in-person solicitation ...
lack a firm historical basis and constitute a violation of the first
amendment." [63]

    If Shapero had been employed by an environmental group to bring
an action against a local polluter, could he have called on homeowners
to enlist them as representative plaintiffs in a class action? If so, why
is a home visit on someone whose home is being foreclosed not allowed?
In re Primus [64] held that solicitation for a political or associational
purpose receives a higher degree of protection than when the lawyer's
motive, as in *Ohralik*, is financial. Primus, a lawyer acting on behalf
of the ACLU, met with and later wrote several women subject to a
South Carolina policy of requiring sterilization of welfare mothers as a
condition of continued Medicaid eligibility. She invited them to participate in litigation attacking the state's policy. The Court held that
South Carolina could not discipline Primus for solicitation when she
was acting without compensation on behalf of the associational and
political interests of a nonprofit group. Justice Rehnquist, dissenting,
criticized the majority for relying on assumptions about the motives of
lawyers rather than focusing on the nature of the conduct regulated by
the state. From Rehnquist's viewpoint, a personal injury lawyer, such
as Ohralik, may act with lofty motives, and a public interest lawyer
may be moved by considerations of power, status, or, when a fee-
shifting statute is involved, money. Is Rehnquist right?

    61. Village of Schaumburg v. Citizens for a Better Environment, 444 U.S. 620 (1980)
(ordinance prohibiting most door-to-door and on-the-street solicitation of charitable contributions invalid under First Amendment). The Court in *Schaumburg* distinguished
Ohralik, stating, "charitable solicitation is not so inherently conducive to fraud and
overreaching as to justify its prohibition." Id. at 637–38, note 11.

    62. Edenfield v. Fane, 113 S.Ct. 1792 (1993) (Florida's prohibition of in-person solicita-
tion of clients violates the First Amendment; *Ohralik* distinguished on grounds that
lawyers, unlike accountants, are trained in the art of persuasion and that an accountant's
clients are not likely to be unsophisticated, injured or distressed).

    63. Louise L. Hill, Solicitation by Lawyers: Piercing the First Amendment Veil, 42
Maine L.Rev. 369, 369–70 (1990).

    64. 436 U.S. 412 (1978).

Subsequent Developments

After the decision in *Shapero* invalidated M.R. 7.3 as promulgated in 1983, the ABA amended Model Rules 7.2 and 7.3. The text of amended Model Rules 7.2 and 7.3 should be studied at this point.

The revised rule, M.R. 7.3(c), adopts the suggestion in *In re R.M.J.* that the First Amendment does not preclude a requirement that advertising material be labeled as such. Also, M.R. 7.3(a) differentiates between in-person solicitation resulting in pecuniary gain and other solicitation. This attempts to track *Ohralik* and *Primus,* supra.

Unless changes in the Court's personnel provide a majority for Justice O'Connor's position, *Shapero* has largely settled the law. All forms of written advertising are protected by the First Amendment, subject to the requirement that they not involve deception or harassment. On the other hand, in-person solicitation by lawyers seeking fee-paying cases continues to be prohibited pursuant to Ohralik, subject to the *Primus* exception for public interest cases.

Unresolved Questions

Some questions remain unresolved. The Court has declined to consider any cases involving radio and television advertisements that are cast in symbolic, evocative and emotional terms or that employ dramatizations or celebrity endorsements.[65] Several states regulate lawyer advertising on the electronic media more stringently than print advertisement.[66] Should the Court, which has been careful to limit its general pronouncements to "written" ads, give states greater leeway in regulating lawyer advertising on radio and television?

Questions also remain concerning advertising containing qualitative claims not subject to verification. Ads that compare the quality of a lawyer's services to other lawyers (a matter not susceptible to objective determination) may be viewed as inherently misleading. Ads that recite past victories (e.g., "three million-dollar verdicts last year") may be deceptive because they give rise to unreasonable expectations.

Claims of special expertise may be regulated even though they cannot be entirely prohibited. In Peel v. Attorney Registration and Disciplinary Comm'n of Illinois,[67] the Court held that Illinois could not

---

65. A California lawyer was disciplined for a radio ad in which a former client described the lawyer's handling of a personal injury case and stated: "If I had any legal problem, car accident or anything, I would definitely go back...." Oring v. State Bar of California, 4 Law.Man.Prof.Conduct (ABA/BNA) 206 (July 6, 1988), appeal dismissed for want of a properly presented federal question, 488 U.S. 590 (1989). Subsequently, California changed its rule to permit testimonials and endorsements if accompanied by a disclaimer that no "guarantee, warranty, or prediction" of outcome is involved.

66. See, e.g., Petition of Felmeister & Isaacs, 104 N.J. 515, 518 A.2d 188 (1986) (forbidding "drawings, animations, dramatizations, music or lyrics ... in connection with televised advertising"); Committee on Professional Ethics v. Humphrey, 377 N.W.2d 643 (Iowa 1985), appeal dism'd, 475 U.S. 1114 (1986) (prohibiting background sound, visual displays and more than one nondramatic voice in radio and television advertisements). Florida has special provisions dealing with ads on the electronic media. Rule 4–7.1(b).

67. 496 U.S. 91 (1990).

prohibit a lawyer's truthful statement that he had been "certified" as a "civil trial specialist" by the National Board of Trial Advocacy (NBTA). The NBTA is a private group that has "developed a set of standards and procedures for periodic certification of lawyers with experience and competence in trial work." The plurality opinion of Justice Stevens held that the letterhead was neither actually nor potentially misleading. Justice Marshall, however, who provided the fifth vote for reversal, indicated that a state could require disclaimers to protect against potentially misleading impressions that NBTA was a governmental body or that Peel's certification might "cause people to think that [Peel] is necessarily a better trial lawyer than attorneys without the certification." [68] The dilemma is that bar associations hostile to advertising may rely on disclaimers to destroy its usefulness. A Texas lawyer, for example, was disciplined because a newspaper ad offering to do uncontested divorces for $75–$175 did not include a disclaimer that he was "not certified [by the state] as a specialist in family law"—even though his ad did not claim that he was a specialist. [69]

Use of lay intermediaries to refer legal business may also be subject to state regulation. This is clearly the case when a lawyer pays someone, such as a paramedical or a nurse or a funeral home attendant, to inform potential clients of the lawyer's services. The prohibition of solicitation of professional employment by direct contact, stated in Model Rule 7.3, is extended to the use of agents by M.R. 8.4(a), which forbids a lawyer from violating a professional rule "through the acts of another." [70] But may a lawyer in person or in writing urge intermediaries to recommend her services? Discipline was upheld in Matter of Alessi,[71] involving a lawyer's letter to 1,000 realtors listing his fees for housing closings and impliedly seeking referrals of those buying or selling homes. The court thought that conflict of interest considerations were brought in play when the broker acted as an intermediary.[72]

3. Is "Professionalism" Consistent with Competition in Legal Services?

Professionalism and Advertising

Although the law may be settled that lawyer advertising and written solicitation are protected by the First Amendment, the thesis developed by Justice O'Connor in her dissent in *Shapero* has implica-

---

68. 496 U.S. at 114.

69. Daves v. State Bar of Texas, 691 S.W.2d 784 (Tex.Ct.App. 1985), appeal dism'd, 474 U.S. 1043 (1986).

70. See also DR 2–103(C), stating that a "lawyer shall not request a person or organization to recommend or promote the use of his services," with certain limited exceptions.

71. 60 N.Y.2d 229, 469 N.Y.S.2d 577, 457 N.E.2d 682 (1983).

72. Compare Grievance Committee v. Trantolo, 192 Conn. 27, 470 A.2d 235 (1984) (lawyer's letter providing information to realtors was protected by free speech provisions of state and federal constitutions).

tions that reach much further. The practice of law is a social institution performing unique functions in the administration of justice. Indeed, the unique place of legal services in our social order was one of the premises advanced by the decisions challenging lawyer advertising as well as by bar leaders supporting a continuing prohibition. The bar's fears of "incitement of litigation," however, are replaced by the Court's recognition of the role of lawyers in providing access to justice. In *Zauderer,* for example, the Court said:

> Nor does the traditional justification for restraints on solicitation—the fear that lawyers will "stir up litigation"—justify the restriction imposed in this case.... Over the course of centuries, our society has settled upon civil litigation as a means for redressing grievances, resolving disputes, and vindicating rights when other means fail.... The State is not entitled to interfere with that access by denying its citizens accurate information about their legal rights.[73]

The Report of the ABA Commission on Professionalism states that "professionalism" is an "elastic concept" that gets meaning from the historic traditions of the bar as a "learned profession." [74] The Report quotes with approval Roscoe Pound's definition:

> The term refers to a group ... pursuing a learned art as a common calling in the spirit of public service—no less a public service because it may incidentally be a means of livelihood. Pursuit of the learned art in the spirit of a public service is the primary purpose.[75]

Justice O'Connor states that professionalism "entails an ethical obligation to temper one's selfish pursuit of economic success" by giving

---

73. 471 U.S. at 642–43. See also Bates v. State Bar of Arizona, 433 U.S. 350 at 376 (1977).

74. ABA Commission on Professionalism, " ... In the Spirit of Public Service:" A Blueprint for the Rekindling of Lawyer Professionalism, 112 F.R.D. 243, 261 (1986). On the complex and subtle concept of "professionalism," and the professionalism of lawyers in particular, a classic statement is Talcott Parsons, The Professions and Social Structure (rev. ed. 1954). For a valuable collection of essays on lawyer professionalism, see Robert L. Nelson, David M. Trubek and Rayman L. Solomon (eds.), Lawyers' Ideals/Lawyers' Practices: Transformation in the American Legal Profession (1992).

75. 112 F.R.D. at 261. The Report also provides a more detailed definition of "professionalism" prepared for the Commission by Professor Eliot Freidson, an authority on the sociology of professions:

An occupation whose members have special privileges, such as exclusive licensing, that are justified by the following assumptions:

1. That its practice requires substantial intellectual training and the use of complex judgments.

2. That since clients cannot adequately evaluate the quality of the service, they must trust those they consult.

3. That the client's trust presupposes that the practitioner's self-interest is overbalanced by devotion to serving both the client's interest and the public good, and

4. That the occupation is self-regulating—that is, organized in such a way as to assure the public and the courts that its members are competent, do not violate their client's trust, and transcend their own self-interest.

112 F.R.D. at 261–62.

primacy to interests of clients and the legal order. She argues that social arrangements dealing with the recruitment, preparation and conduct of lawyers need to reinforce this altruistic and public service orientation. Practices such as lawyer advertising will cause a diminution in the profession's public-service orientation: "[F]airly severe constraints on attorney advertising" will "act as a concrete, day-to-day reminder to the practicing attorney of why it is improper for any member of this profession to regard it as a trade or occupation like any other."

Is Justice O'Connor correct in concluding that lawyer advertising gives rise to lawyer greed, which is antithetical to "professionalism?" Does her argument rest on the notion that something about the selection and socialization of lawyers makes them more altruistic than the population at large? Were lawyers less self-serving or more altruistic in the days prior to lawyer advertising? Are lawyers a special breed who, despite the materialism of American society and the economics of present-day law practice, are motivated to subordinate their interest in doing well to public interests that often conflict with that goal? [76] And how in concrete terms does lawyer advertising undermine professionalism?

As Justice O'Connor's opinion indicates, the rule against advertising and solicitation helped sustain the special character of the practice of law. Another example of a rule having that effect is the custom in most other countries that an advocate, as well as a judge, must wear a black robe in court. One could say that having to wear a black robe involves suppression of one's freedom of expression, while at the same time recognizing that the rule "says something" about the nature of the advocate's function.

Other kinds of rules could more rigorously inhibit the "commercialization" of law practice. Lawyers could be prohibited from engaging in any other vocation or business as long as they are engaged in law practice.[77] Lawyers could be prohibited from holding public office or corporate directorships if they are also engaged in practice. They could be prohibited from forming law firms of "bureaucratic" size, for example larger than 20 members. (English barristers still are required to be solo practitioners; 30 years ago the largest firm in many states was no bigger than 20 lawyers.)

The present character of American law practice is significantly shaped by the *absence* of rules against the foregoing kinds of "commercialization" and "bureaucratization." Justice O'Connor does not mention these rules in her dissent in *Shapero.* Does allowing advertising

---

76. See Nancy J. Moore, Professionalism Reconsidered, 1987 Am.B.Found.Research J. 773, 788, criticizing the Report of the ABA Commission on Professionalism: lawyers "should immediately reject both the pious exhortation to renounce wealth as a primary goal of legal practice, as well as the more dangerous (if only implied) suggestion that any incursions on the tradition of self-regulation are inevitably inimical to the public interest."

77. See the discussion of ancillary businesses and dual practice below at p. 983.

"commercialize" the legal profession in different ways than allowing lawyers to sit on corporate boards? Are different socio-economic interests involved?

Effects of Lawyer Advertising

Most lawyer advertising is addressed to individual consumers of moderate income. About one-third of lawyers purchase advertising messages, but the advertising of most of them consists of yellow-page listings and notices.[78] Newspaper advertising is used by about 16 percent of lawyers who advertise. Only 3 percent of lawyers who advertise use radio or television. In 1990 lawyers spent $82.3 million on television advertisements; about one-fourth of this amount was spent by the five largest users (two national legal clinics and three groups of personal injury lawyers).[79] Studies show that consumers support lawyer advertising, but lawyers are less willing to accept it.[80]

Lawyers who provide individualized services to wealthy or corporate clients rarely use the forms of lawyer advertising that are criticized—billboards, newspaper ads, radio spots and television commercials. Lawyers in the corporate sector of practice, however, do use a variety of techniques to bring themselves to the attention of potential clients. Social connections through business and social clubs provide opportunities for informing clients of the experience and talents of firm lawyers. Newsletters that summarize current developments in fields in which a firm has expertise are distributed to potential clients. Many large law firms have engaged marketing and public relations consultants who seek to place stories or gain interviews in newspapers of general circulation or in the lawyer press (e.g., *American Lawyer, National Law Journal*). Bolder marketing efforts are now encountered: Baker & McKenzie purchased a six-page color insert in *California Lawyer*, a trade publication, highlighting the firm's personnel, experience and international practice.[81]

Economic analysts generally conclude that advertising is an efficient means to market legal services that are capable of standardization but not those that require highly individualized treatment.[82] With

78. Paul Reidinger, Lawpoll: More Lawyers Now Advertise Their Practice, 73 A.B.A.J. 25 (Nov. 1, 1987).

79. Record TV Legal Ads, Nat'l L.J., Apr. 16, 1990, at p. 6.

80. Paul Marcotte, Who Likes Lawyer Ads?, 74 A.B.A.J. 28 (Oct. 1, 1988).

81. Large Firms Overcome Marketing Reticence, Wall Street Journal p. B1 (Sept. 17, 1990). The ad cost about $35,000.

82. See, e.g., Geoffrey C. Hazard, Jr., Russell G. Pearce and Jeffrey W. Stempel, Why Lawyers Should Be Allowed to Advertise: A Market Analysis of Legal Services, 58 N.Y.U.L.Rev. 1084 (1983); Timothy J. Muris and Fred S. McChesney, Advertising and the Price and Quality of Legal Services: The Case for Legal Clinics, 1979 Am.B.Found.Research J. 179 (comparing the price and quality of services offered by an advertising legal clinic and other law firms); Federal Trade Commission, Improving Consumer Access to Legal Services: The Case for Removing Restrictions on Truthful Advertising (1984) (study concluding that state restrictions on price advertising of five routine legal services resulted in higher prices; "the dominant effect of advertising is to enhance price competition by lowering consumer search costs"). The empirical studies are reviewed in

respect to standardized services, advertising expands awareness of a legal need, provides information about which lawyers provide the service and communicates some information of possible cost. Even on the critical decision of choosing a particular lawyer, advertising adds to information coming from prior experience or word-of-mouth. "For the consumer of standardizable services, the probable result of permitting lawyers to advertise will be lower priced services of better quality." [83] Professor Macaulay agrees that "[l]awyer advertising may play some part in enlarging access to legal services," but warns against viewing it as either a devil or a panacea:

> Advertising alone is not likely to push the bar into crass commercialism or produce a nation of rational informed clients seeking to maximize utility. Recognizing this, we must be concerned that largely symbolic debates about lawyer advertising may divert us from concern with more pressing issues of access and equality.[84]

Solicitation of Another Firm's Clients

Subject to the restrictions on in-person solicitation in provisions such as M.R. 7.3, and subject to the prohibition in M.R. 4.2 against dealing directly with an opposing party, a lawyer is legally free to suggest to a prospective client that she switch lawyers. This does not constitute tortious interference with a contract relationship because any client has a right to discharge a lawyer at any time.[85] However, additional problems are presented when a lawyer leaves a firm and seeks to take clients with her. When the departing lawyer acts secretly, soliciting firm clients before announcing a decision to leave, the lawyer may be liable for fiduciary breach.[86] Recognition of the client's interest in a choice of lawyers, and consequently the need to protect the lawyer's right to compete for clients, suggests that a degree of open communication is desirable.[87]

4. Restrictions on Form of Practice

Group Legal Services

Consider the following departures from the traditional model of a lawyer or law firm providing fee-for-service legal assistance to private clients:

> • A nonprofit advocacy group, e.g., NAACP, seeks to challenge racial discrimination in public education by seeking out blacks who

Stewart Macaulay, Lawyer Advertising: Yes But ..., U. Wis. Inst. for Legal Studies: Working Paper 7–3 (1985).

83. Hazard, Pearce, and Stempel, supra, at 1109.

84. Macaulay, supra, at 75.

85. See the *Balla* case and the notes following it in Chapter 6 above at p. 604.

86. See Adler, Barish, Daniels, Levin & Creskoff v. Epstein, 482 Pa. 416, 393 A.2d 1175 (1978); Meehan v. Shaughnessy, 404 Mass. 419, 535 N.E.2d 1255 (1989).

87. See Vincent R. Johnson, Solicitation of Law Firm Clients by Departing Partners and Associates, 50 U.Pitt.L.Rev. 1 (1988); Robert W. Hillman, Law Firms and their Partners: The Law and Ethics of Grabbing and Leaving, 67 Tex.L.Rev. 1 (1988).

would be willing to serve as plaintiffs in actions attacking racially segregated schools; the NAACP offers to provide legal services without cost to the plaintiffs.[88]

• A labor union, concerned about the quality and cost of legal services available to injured members of the union, advises its members not to settle worker's compensation or personal injury claims without consulting a lawyer and offers the services of designated attorneys who have agreed to handle claims on specified terms.[89] Alternatively, the union hires staff attorneys who are made available to handle the claims of members.[90]

• A nonprofit organization of motorists uses members' annual dues to hire a staff of lawyers and provide legal services, without charge, to members of the association in certain court proceedings arising out of the operation of members' automobiles.[91]

• A large retail chain, e.g., Sears or Montgomery Ward, hires a staff of lawyers and opens law offices in many of its stores. The offices offer a limited menu of routine legal services (e.g., real estate closings, divorces, wills, individual bankruptcies) to customers at advertised rates.

• A large insurance company advertises "a prepaid legal services plan" under which, in return for an annual premium, the insured is entitled to receive a variety of legal services during the plan year, including telephone and office consultation with lawyers who have agreed with the insurance company to provide these services.

These arrangements for the provision of legal services to groups of people (hence the term "group legal services") differ in a number of important respects. The NAACP case involves the assertion of civil or political rights that are close to the heart of freedom of expression; the union cases involve the assertion of employment-related rights; and the others involve the broad array of legal interests of ordinary Americans. Some of them (e.g., the NAACP case and the motorists' association) involve not-for-profit organizations, whereas the retail chain and the

---

88. See NAACP v. Button, 371 U.S. 415 (1963) (First Amendment protects NAACP's right to seek plaintiffs and provide them with counsel; state's interest in preventing barratry, maintenance and champerty are not a compelling state interest justifying limiting First Amendment freedoms).

89. See Brotherhood of Railroad Trainmen v. Virginia ex rel. Virginia State Bar, 377 U.S. 1, 8 (1964) ("[T]he First and Fourteenth Amendments protect the right of the members through their Brotherhood to maintain and carry out their plan for advising workers who are injured to obtain legal advice and for recommending specific lawyers.... And, of course, lawyers accepting employment under this constitutionally protected plan have a like protection which the State cannot abridge.")

90. See United Mine Workers of America, District 12 v. Illinois State Bar Assn., 389 U.S. 217 (1967) (reversing a lower court decision enjoining the union's program); United Transportation Union v. State Bar of Michigan, 401 U.S. 576 (1971) ("The common thread running through our decisions in NAACP v. Button, *Trainmen,* and *United Mine Workers* is that collective activity undertaken to obtain meaningful access to the courts is a fundamental right within the protection of the First Amendment.")

91. See People ex rel. Chicago Bar Assn. v. Motorists' Assn. of Illinois, 354 Ill. 595, 188 N.E. 827 (1933) (motorists' association enjoined from practicing law without a license).

insurance company are engaged in profit-making activity. Should that make a difference? Some employ staff lawyers to deliver legal services, and others rely on members of the private bar who are affiliated with a particular plan. The insurance plan involves two distinctive features: prepayment and insurance.

Yet the common features of group legal services plans have made them a center of controversy for more than thirty years. In general, as with lawyer advertising, the ABA and state bar associations have attempted to prohibit or restrict arrangements for group legal services while the Supreme Court has forced the bar to accommodate them.[92] Yet the profession has not been monolithic in opposition: Important elements of ABA leadership have seen group legal services as a vital part of the long-term future of the legal profession because of their potential role in expanding the demand for legal services. Despite bar opposition, group and prepaid plans have grown rapidly, reaching an estimated 15 million Americans by the mid–1980s. Much of the growth has been due to the recognition of lawyer advertising, beginning with the *Bates* decision in 1977, and changes in federal law that made group and prepaid plans attractive as an employment-related fringe benefit.

Group legal services plans present a variety of standard professional responsibility problems. First, in most the lawyer is paid for and often selected by the organizers of the plan. Will the independent judgment of the lawyer in serving a client through the plan be distorted or controlled by the interests of the operator of the plan? The same possibilities are present whenever a third person selects and pays a client's lawyer (e.g., a liability insurer providing a defense to an insured) or an organization hires staff lawyers (e.g., corporate legal staff). Second, group legal services plans often rely on advertising, raising the same issues involved in other advertising of legal services. Should an insurance company be permitted to call or solicit members of the public to enroll in a prepaid legal services plan in the same manner in which those companies merchandise life and health insurance to the public? Third, many plans employ nonlawyers to administer plans and to perform paralegal functions. These staffing arrangements raise issues of unauthorized practice of law. Underlying all of these issues is one of competition with general practitioners in the provision of legal services to ordinary Americans. Hostility to group legal services comes primarily from bar leaders who represent the interests of general practitioners who are threatened by competition from group legal services plans (e.g., the loss of work injury cases handled by a union plan).

92. For discussion of the ABA's grudging response to the constitutional decisions requiring recognition of group legal services plans, see Wolfram, Modern Legal Ethics § 16.5.5 (1986). The 1969 Model Code limited lawyer participation in group legal service plans to those operated by a nonprofit organization that used "open panels" of lawyers (under an "open panel" a plan member is entitled to choose any lawyer from the private bar; under a "closed panel," a member is restricted to a staff lawyer or a group of lawyers selected by the plan).

The Kutak Commission's draft of what became Model Rule 5.4 eliminated the form-of-practice restrictions that restricted group legal services. Under the proposal, a lawyer could be employed by any organization engaged in the delivery of legal services as long as the organization respected a lawyer's professional judgment, protected a client's confidential information, avoided impermissible advertising or solicitation and charged only reasonable fees. The Commission's proposal, however, was dropped from the Model Rules by the ABA House of Delegates at the last minute. Professor Geoffrey Hazard, the reporter for the Kutak Commission, reports: "During the debate someone asked if [the Kutak] proposal would allow Sears, Roebuck to open a law office. When they found out it would, that was the end of the debate." [93]

Model Rule 5.4(a), (b) and (d) forbid a lawyer to "form a partnership with a nonlawyer if any of the activities of the partnership consist of the practice of law," forbids a lawyer "to share legal fees with a nonlawyer," and says that a "lawyer shall not practice with or in the form of a professional corporation or association . . . if . . . a nonlawyer owns any interest therein . . .; a nonlawyer is a corporate director or officer thereof; or . . . a nonlawyer has the right to direct or control the professional judgment of a lawyer." The Comment states that these "limitations are to protect the lawyer's professional independence of judgment." They are drawn from and substantially replicate DR 3–102(A), DR 3–103(A) and DR 5–107(C) of the Model Code and may be traced back to Canon 33 of the Canons of Professional Ethics.

Are the limitations of M.R. 5.4 justifiable? Why should nonlawyers be prohibited from investing in, managing and profiting from companies that provide legal services? Why should these activities be reserved to lawyers? Critics of form-of-practice restrictions argue that the legal services market would benefit from enlarged competition and increased investment.[94] Allowing banks, insurance companies or retailers to diversify into legal services would serve that purpose. On the other hand, especially when legal services are combined with another business activity, such as provision of banking or insurance services, legal advice may be distorted by the desire to sell the other services. Would malpractice liability provide a sufficient deterrent to such distortion?

M.R. 5.4 (and its Model Code antecedents) assumes that lay management of a legal services organization will be tempted, more than are lawyer managers, to interfere with the professional relationships of employed lawyers when it is profitable to do so and that the problem is

93. David Kaplan, Want to Invest in a Law Firm?, Nat'l L.J., Jan. 19, 1987, at p. 28.

94. For criticism of M.R. 5.4, see Stephen Gillers, What We Talked About When We Talked About Ethics: A Critical View of the Model Rules, 46 Ohio St.L.J. 243, 266–69 (1985). Gillers argues that M.R. 5.4 serves the interests of established firms, with accumulated capital and clientele, rather than the interests of lawyers generally, especially younger lawyers who would benefit from increased opportunities in salaried employment. Gillers also says that M.R. 5.4 harms consumers by suppressing competition in the supply of services.

so serious that a prophylactic rule prohibiting lay management is necessary. Are these assumptions correct? Why aren't after-the-fact remedies for violation of professional rules sufficient?

Dual Practice and Affiliated Business Activities

Dual practice refers to two related problems: (1) a lawyer, who is also qualified in accounting, engineering or some other field, holds herself out as practicing in a dual capacity, and (2) a lawyer forms a partnership with a nonlawyer such as an accountant. DR 2–102(E) of the 1969 Model Code prohibited "a lawyer who is engaged both in the practice of law and another profession" from indicating the dual qualifications on a letterhead or sign. This prohibition was repealed in 1980, four years after the Supreme Court had held that the First Amendment protected truthful advertising.

Dual practice in the form of a partnership of a lawyer and a nonlawyer presents additional problems: Is the lawyer aiding unauthorized practice by a nonlawyer (M.R. 5.5)? Is the lawyer sharing fees or management of a law firm with a nonlawyer (M.R. 5.4)? The combination of the two rules generally means that the nonlawyer must be supervised by the lawyer and may not act in a legal capacity, such as making a court appearance. Does this position reflect an assumption that lawyers are superior to other professionals? That lawyers must be in charge?

In recent years the topic has become a controversial one within the organized bar under the rubric of "ancillary business." [95] A number of major law firms, especially in Washington, D.C., have created affiliated organizations that employ nonlawyers in various consulting activities, such as providing financial and regulatory assistance to real estate developers.

Some segments of the bar, centered in the ABA Section of Litigation, charge that these activities raise serious professionalism concerns, including the following: compromising lawyer's independent judgment, endangering confidentiality and creating conflicting interests. Opponents of ancillary business activity fear that this "business" activity will impair lawyer professionalism by paving the way for nonlawyer ownership of or participation in law firms, distract lawyers from their professional responsibilities as lawyers and ultimately lead to a displacement of self-regulation. Lawrence Fox, a leading advocate of a professional rule prohibiting ancillary business activities, states:

> [T]he ancillary business movement introduces non-lawyers into positions of influence and control of the profession. All the safeguards one can imagine do not overcome the reality that those who come to prominence and success in the operations of the ancillary

95. See, e.g., Stephanie B. Goldberg, More than the Law: Ancillary Business Growth Continues, A.B.A.J. 54 (Mar. 1992); Alexander Stille, When Law Firms Start Their Own Businesses, Nat'l L.J. 1, Oct. 21 1985, at p. 1; Thomas F. Gibbons, Branching Out, A.B.A.J. 70 (Nov. 1989) ("at least 45 law firms have opened non-law businesses").

business will end up with real power in the governance of the overall enterprise. Quite simply, money talks, and dependence on money changes perspectives in a way that people of the utmost good will cannot overcome....

Also disquieting is the possibility that, if lawyers enter other fields of endeavor, non-lawyer enterprises such as Household Finance, Coldwell Banker, American Express and WalMart are likely to wish to add legal services to their array of consumer products. As lawyers cloak their drive for financial hegemony in arguments such as "it's a public service to offer the public one-stop shopping," it becomes a very small leap, if a leap at all, to argue that these other non-law-firm, non-lawyer-controlled entities are entitled to an equal opportunity to provide this "public service," particularly when law firms seek to offer the services to non-clients of the firm and/or without any relation to the provision of legal services.[96]

Defenders of ancillary business operations counter that the activities are no different from others in which lawyers traditionally have been involved, that clients benefit from the broad array of services that are provided, that professional rules protecting confidentiality and prohibiting conflicting interests provide adequate protection against these very real dangers, and that efforts to define "the practice of law" for these purposes are unwise and counter-productive.

James Jones, managing partner of Arnold & Porter, a firm that offers non-law services in several areas—lobbying, public relations, real estate development and financial services—argues that the future of the legal profession lies in these arrangements and that existing form-of-practice restrictions such as M.R. 5.4 should be revised to permit non-lawyers to become partners.[97] Jones states:

The practice of law—however it may be defined and whatever its scope—has become far more complex and diverse in recent years than could have been imagined even 20 years ago.

The growing complexity of both the law and the economic and social activities that the law attempts to regulate increasingly requires lawyers, in the course of representation, to understand and apply the precepts of other disciplines.

. . . .

96. Lawrence Fox, Restraint Is Good in Trade, Nat'l L.J., Apr. 19, 1991, at p. 17. See also L. Harold Levinson, Independent Law Firms that Practice Law Only: Society's Need, the Legal Profession's Responsibility, 51 Ohio St. L.J. 229 (1990).

97. The version of M.R. 5.4 adopted in the District of Columbia provides that a lawyer "may practice law in a partnership or other form of organization in which a financial interest is held or managerial authority is exercised by an individual nonlawyer who performs professional services which assist the organization in providing legal services to clients" under several conditions, including that these persons "undertake to abide by these rules" and lawyer-partners or owners "undertake to be responsible for the nonlawyer participants to the same extent as if nonlawyer participants were lawyers under Rule 5.1." A number of law firms in the District of Columbia have named nonlawyer partners.

These demands have led to the use of non-lawyer professionals, working in tandem with (and often at the direction of) lawyers in analyzing client problems, structuring transactions and managing litigation. . . .

In the past 10 years or so, law firms of all sizes with practice areas requiring interdisciplinary collaboration have begun to bring these services in-house by hiring non-lawyer professionals in areas ranging from economics and international trade to engineering and health care, from accounting and social work to lobbying and family counseling.

Sometimes, these lawyers have been hired as employees of the law firms; in other cases, the firms have established separate companies to make these services available. But in all cases the motivation has been to improve the quality of service to clients by assuring that complex matters requiring interdisciplinary skills can be handled efficiently and economically.[98]

In 1992 the ABA Standing Committee on Ethics and Professional Responsibility proposed an amendment to the Model Rules that would have allowed ancillary services to be provided by law firm subsidiaries to nonclients, subject to a regulatory regime designed to ensure that lawyers' professional obligations toward clients were not impaired.[99] A customer of an ancillary business entity would be informed in writing of the entity's relationship to the law firm and that the relationship was not that of lawyer and client. The ABA Section of Litigation proposed a substitute prohibiting all ancillary services unless such services were provided by employees of the firms to clients of the firm in connection with the provision of legal services. In August 1991 the ABA adopted the prohibitory version by a narrow margin (197–186).[100]

M.R. 5.7 proved to be short-lived. General practitioners in smaller cities, who have always combined law practice with other activities, such as title search companies, service on corporate boards and real estate development, awoke to the fact that M.R. 5.7 might prohibit these long-standing activities. A renewed debate in August 1992 resulted in another narrowly divided vote, repealing M.R. 5.7. No state had adopted M.R. 5.7 during its short life.

Why do powerful groups within the ABA seek to prohibit ancillary businesses when these groups do not oppose practices that involve an equal or greater interference with "independent professional judgment," such as lawyers serving on the board of directors of a corporation represented by the lawyer's firm or business transactions between lawyer and client?

98. James R. Jones, Law Firm Diversification, A.B.A.J. 52 (Sept. 1989).

99. See 7 L.Man.Prof.Conduct (ABA/BNA) 256 (Aug. 28, 1991).

100. The text of former M.R. 5.7, which should be read at this point, raises many questions of application and interpretation. Did the Rule prohibit a law firm from monitoring legislation or engaging in lobbying activities? Did it prohibit a lawyer from selling title insurance?

C. LOCAL CONTROL IN AN ERA
OF MULTISTATE PRACTICE

Introduction

Admission to the bar and lawyer discipline are functions that from the earliest days have been carried on by state courts. Admission to the bar in a state carries authority to represent others in any state tribunal and in any transactions within the state coming within the state's definition of the "practice of law." Admission to the bar of a state is ordinarily a prerequisite to admission to the bar of a federal court within that state or which entertains appeals from that state. Admission in one state, however, does not authorize practice in another. Professional rules are violated when a lawyer "practice[s] law in a jurisdiction where doing so violates the regulation of the legal profession in that jurisdiction." M.R. 5.5(a); see also DR 3–101(B). For a New York lawyer to give advice on California law concerning a transaction with California contacts may be unauthorized practice.

Yet we are one nation with a national economy, bound together by a common language and a common legal culture. Federal law, increasingly important in the practice of law, is uniform throughout the nation. The legal systems of all states except Louisiana are based on the common law; uniform laws and the unifying effect of Restatements and legislative imitation provide sufficient commonality that legal education is relatively homogeneous everywhere. A substantial portion of the population moves each year, often across state lines, and business transactions involve people and events almost without regard to state lines. In this setting, clients want and expect their lawyers to handle all aspects of a transaction, even litigation, that crosses state lines.

In today's world the state-based control of admission and discipline is in tension with the reality of multistate legal problems and practice. This tension has produced fracture lines involving three questions: (1) When may a lawyer admitted to practice in one state be eligible for permanent admission in another (geographic restrictions based on local residence, a local office or association of local counsel)? (2) When may a lawyer admitted in one state be specially authorized to handle litigation in another state's courts (admission pro hac vice)? And (3) to what extent may an office lawyer provide advice to clients that crosses state lines (multistate practice)?

1. Exclusion of Nonresidents

SUPREME COURT OF NEW HAMPSHIRE v. PIPER

Supreme Court of the United States, 1985.
470 U.S. 274, 105 S.Ct. 1272, 84 L.Ed.2d 205.

JUSTICE POWELL delivered the opinion of the Court.

The Rules of the Supreme Court of New Hampshire limit bar admission to state residents. We here consider whether this restriction violates the Privileges and Immunities Clause of the United States Constitution, Art. IV, § 2.

I

Kathryn Piper lives in Lower Waterford, Vermont, about 400 yards from the New Hampshire border. In 1979, she applied to take the February 1980 New Hampshire bar examination. Piper submitted with her application a statement of intent to become a New Hampshire resident. Following an investigation, the Board of Bar Examiners found that Piper was of good moral character and met the other requirements for admission. She was allowed to take, and passed, the examination. Piper was informed by the Board that she would have to establish a home address in New Hampshire prior to being sworn in.

On May 7, 1980, Piper requested from the Clerk of the New Hampshire Supreme Court a dispensation from the residency requirement. Although she had a "possible job" with a lawyer in Littleton, New Hampshire, Piper stated that becoming a resident of New Hampshire would be inconvenient. Her house in Vermont was secured by a mortgage with a favorable interest rate, and she and her husband recently had become parents. According to Piper, these "problems peculiar to [her] situation ... warrant[ed] that an exception be made." Letter from Appellee to Ralph H. Wood, Esq., Clerk of N.H. Supreme Court, App. 13.

On May 13, 1980, the Clerk informed Piper that her request had been denied. She then formally petitioned the New Hampshire Supreme Court for permission to become a member of the bar. She asserted that she was well qualified and that her "situation [was] sufficiently unique that the granting of an exception ... [would] not result in the setting of any undesired precedent." Letter of Nov. 8, 1980, from Appellee to Hon. William A. Grimes, then Chief Justice of the N.H. Supreme Court, App. 15. The Supreme Court denied Piper's formal request on December 31, 1980.... [2]

2. Piper was not excluded totally from the practice of law in New Hampshire. Out-of-state lawyers may appear pro hac vice in state court. This alternative, however, does not allow the nonresident to practice in New Hampshire on the same terms as a resident member of the bar. The lawyer appearing pro hac vice must be associated with a local lawyer who is present for trial or argument. See N.H. Sup.Ct. Rule 33(1); N.H. Super.Ct. Rule 19. Furthermore, the decision on whether to grant pro hac vice status to an out-of-state lawyer is purely discretionary. See Leis v. Flynt, 439 U.S. 438, 442 (1979) (per curiam).

II

Article IV, § 2, of the Constitution provides that the "Citizens of each State shall be entitled to all Privileges and Immunities of Citizens in the several States." [6] This Clause was intended to "fuse into one Nation a collection of independent, sovereign States." Toomer v. Witsell, 334 U.S. 385, 395 (1948). Recognizing this purpose, we have held that it is "[o]nly with respect to those 'privileges' and 'immunities' bearing on the vitality of the Nation as a single entity" that a State must accord residents and nonresidents equal treatment. Baldwin v. Montana Fish & Game Comm'n, [436 U.S. 371, 383]. In *Baldwin*, for example, we concluded that a State may charge a nonresident more than it charges a resident for the same elk-hunting license. Because elk hunting is "recreation" rather than a "means of a livelihood," we found that the right to a hunting license was not "fundamental" to the promotion of interstate harmony. 436 U.S., at 388.

Derived, like the Commerce Clause, from the fourth of the Articles of Confederation, the Privileges and Immunities Clause was intended to create a national economic union. It is therefore not surprising that this Court repeatedly has found that "one of the privileges which the Clause guarantees to citizens of State A is that of doing business in State B on terms of substantial equality with the citizens of that State." *Toomer v. Witsell*, supra, 334 U.S., at 396. . . . [I]n *Toomer*, supra, the Court held that nonresident fishermen could not be required to pay a license fee of $2,500 for each shrimp boat owned when residents were charged only $25 per boat. Finally, in Hicklin v. Orbeck, 437 U.S. 518 (1978), we found violative of the Privileges and Immunities Clause a statute containing a resident hiring preference for all employment related to the development of the State's oil and gas resources.

There is nothing in [these cases] suggesting that the practice of law should not be viewed as a "privilege" under Art. IV, § 2.[10] Like the occupations considered in our earlier cases, the practice of law is important to the national economy. As the Court noted in Goldfarb v.

---

6. Under this Clause, the terms "citizen" and "resident" are used interchangeably. See Austin v. New Hampshire, 420 U.S. 656, 662, n. 8 (1975). Under the Fourteenth Amendment, of course, "[a]ll persons born or naturalized in the United States ... are citizens ... of the State wherein they reside."

10. In Corfield v. Coryell, 6 F.Cas. 546 (No. 3,230) (CCED Pa.1825), Justice Bushrod Washington, sitting as Circuit Justice, stated that the "fundamental rights" protected by the Clause included:

"The right of a citizen of one state to pass through, or to reside in any other state, for purposes of trade, agriculture, professional pursuits, or otherwise; to claim the benefit of the writ of habeas corpus; to institute and maintain actions of any kind in the courts of the state; to take, hold and dispose of property, either real or personal. . . ." *Id.*, at 552.

Thus in this initial interpretation of the Clause, "professional pursuits," such as the practice of law, were said to be protected.

The "natural rights" theory that underlay *Corfield* was discarded long ago. Hague v. CIO, 307 U.S. 496, 511 (1939) (opinion of Roberts, J.); see Paul v. Virginia, 8 Wall. 168 (1869). Nevertheless, we have noted that those privileges on Justice Washington's list would still be protected by the Clause. Baldwin v. Montana Fish & Game Comm'n, 436 U.S. 371, 387 (1978).

Virginia State Bar, 421 U.S. 773, 788, the "activities of lawyers play an important part in commercial intercourse."

The lawyer's role in the national economy is not the only reason that the opportunity to practice law should be considered a "fundamental right." We believe that the legal profession has a noncommercial role and duty that reinforce the view that the practice of law falls within the ambit of the Privileges and Immunities Clause. Out-of-state lawyers may—and often do—represent persons who raise unpopular federal claims. In some cases, representation by nonresident counsel may be the only means available for the vindication of federal rights. See *Leis v. Flynt*, 439 U.S., at 450 (Stevens, J., dissenting). The lawyer who champions unpopular causes surely is as important to the "maintenance or well-being of the Union," *Baldwin*, 436 U.S., at 388, as was the shrimp fisherman in *Toomer*, or the pipeline worker in *Hicklin*.

Appellant asserts that the Privileges and Immunities Clause should be held inapplicable to the practice of law because a lawyer's activities are "bound up with the exercise of judicial power and the administration of justice." [12] Its contention is based on the premise that the lawyer is an "officer of the court," who "exercises state power on a daily basis." Appellant concludes that if the State cannot exclude nonresidents from the bar, its ability to function as a sovereign political body will be threatened.

Lawyers do enjoy a "broad monopoly . . . to do things other citizens may not lawfully do." In re Griffiths, 413 U.S. 717, 731 (1973). We do not believe, however, that the practice of law involves an "exercise of state power" justifying New Hampshire's residency requirement. In *In re Griffiths*, supra, we held that the State could not exclude an alien from the bar on the ground that a lawyer is an " 'officer of the Court who' . . . is entrusted with the 'exercise of actual governmental power.' " We concluded that a lawyer is not an "officer" within the ordinary meaning of that word. 413 U.S., at 728. He " 'makes his own decisions, follows his own best judgment, collects his own fees and runs his own business.' " Moreover, we held that the state powers entrusted to lawyers do not "involve matters of state policy or acts of such unique responsibility as to entrust them only to citizens."

Because, under *Griffiths*, a lawyer is not an "officer" of the State in any political sense,[15] there is no reason for New Hampshire to exclude

---

12. Justice Rehnquist makes a similar argument in his dissent. He asserts that lawyers, through their adversary representation of clients' interests, "play an important role in the formulation of state policy." He therefore concludes that the residency requirement is necessary to ensure that lawyers are "intimately conversant with the local concerns that should inform such policies." We believe that this argument, like the one raised by the State, is foreclosed by our reasoning in In re Griffiths, 413 U.S. 717 (1973). There, we held that the status of being licensed to practice law does not place a person so close to the core of the political process as to make him a "formulator of government policy." Id., at 729.

15. It is true that lawyers traditionally have been leaders in state and local affairs—political as well as cultural, religious, and civic. Their training qualifies them for this

from its bar nonresidents. We therefore conclude that the right to practice law is protected by the Privileges and Immunities Clause.[16]

III

The conclusion that Rule 42 deprives nonresidents of a protected privilege does not end our inquiry. The Court has stated that "[l]ike many other constitutional provisions, the privileges and immunities clause is not an absolute." *Toomer v. Witsell*, 334 U.S., at 396.... The Clause does not preclude discrimination against nonresidents where (i) there is a substantial reason for the difference in treatment; and (ii) the discrimination practiced against nonresidents bears a substantial relationship to the State's objective. In deciding whether the discrimination bears a close or substantial relationship to the State's objective, the Court has considered the availability of less restrictive means.

The Supreme Court of New Hampshire offers several justifications for its refusal to admit nonresidents to the bar. It asserts that nonresident members would be less likely (i) to become, and remain, familiar with local rules and procedures; (ii) to behave ethically; (iii) to be available for court proceedings; and (iv) to do pro bono and other volunteer work in the State.[18] We find that none of these reasons meets the test of "substantiality," and that the means chosen do not bear the necessary relationship to the State's objectives.

There is no evidence to support appellant's claim that nonresidents might be less likely to keep abreast of local rules and procedures. Nor may we assume that a nonresident lawyer—any more than a resident— would deserve his clients by failing to familiarize himself with the rules. As a practical matter, we think that unless a lawyer has, or anticipates, a considerable practice in the New Hampshire courts, he would be unlikely to take the bar examination and pay the annual dues of $125.[19]

type of participation. Nevertheless, lawyers are not in any sense officials in the government simply by virtue of being lawyers.

16. Our conclusion that Rule 42 violates the Privileges and Immunities Clause is consistent with Leis v. Flynt, 439 U.S. 438 (1979). In *Leis*, we held that a lawyer could be denied, without the benefit of a hearing, permission to appear pro hac vice. We concluded that the States should be left free to "prescribe the qualifications for admission to practice and the standards of professional conduct" for those lawyers who appear in its courts. Id., at 442.

Our holding in this case does not interfere with the ability of the States to regulate their bars. The nonresident who seeks to join a bar, unlike the pro hac vice applicant, must have the same professional and personal qualifications required of resident lawyers. Furthermore, the nonresident member of the bar is subject to the full force of New Hampshire's disciplinary rules....

18. A former president of the American Bar Association has suggested another possible reason for the rule: "Many of the states that have erected fences against out-of-state lawyers have done so primarily to protect their own lawyers from professional competition." Smith, Time for a National Practice of Law Act, 64 A.B.A.J. 557 (1978). This reason is not "substantial." The Privileges and Immunities Clause was designed primarily to prevent such economic protectionism.

19. Because it is markedly overinclusive, the residency requirement does not bear a substantial relationship to the State's objective. A less restrictive alternative would be to

We also find the appellant's second justification to be without merit, for there is no reason to believe that a nonresident lawyer will conduct his practice in a dishonest manner. The nonresident lawyer's professional duty and interest in his reputation should provide the same incentive to maintain high ethical standards as they do for resident lawyers. A lawyer will be concerned with his reputation in any community where he practices, regardless of where he may live. Furthermore, a nonresident lawyer may be disciplined for unethical conduct. The Supreme Court of New Hampshire has the authority to discipline all members of the bar, regardless of where they reside....

There is more merit to the appellant's assertion that a nonresident member of the bar at times would be unavailable for court proceedings. In the course of litigation, pretrial hearings on various matters often are held on short notice. At times a court will need to confer immediately with counsel. Even the most conscientious lawyer residing in a distant State may find himself unable to appear in court for an unscheduled hearing or proceeding. Nevertheless, we do not believe that this type of problem justifies the exclusion of nonresidents from the state bar. One may assume that a high percentage of nonresident lawyers willing to take the state bar examination and pay the annual dues will reside in places reasonably convenient to New Hampshire. Furthermore, in those cases where the nonresident counsel will be unavailable on short notice, the State can protect its interests through less restrictive means. The trial court, by rule or as an exercise of discretion, may require any lawyer who resides at a great distance to retain a local attorney who will be available for unscheduled meetings and hearings.

The final reason advanced by appellant is that nonresident members of the state bar would be disinclined to do their share of pro bono and volunteer work. Perhaps this is true to a limited extent, particularly where the member resides in a distant location. We think it is reasonable to believe, however, that most lawyers who become members of a state bar will endeavor to perform their share of these services. This sort of participation, of course, would serve the professional interest of a lawyer who practices in the State. Furthermore, a nonresident bar member, like the resident member, could be required to represent indigents and perhaps to participate in formal legal-aid work.

In summary, appellant neither advances a "substantial reason" for its discrimination against nonresident applicants to the bar, nor demon-

require mandatory attendance at periodic seminars on state practice. There already is a rule requiring all new admittees to complete a "practical skills course" within one year of their admission. N.H. Sup. Ct. Rule 42(7).

New Hampshire's "simple residency" requirement is underinclusive as well, because it permits lawyers who move away from the State to retain their membership in the bar. There is no reason to believe that a former resident would maintain a more active practice in the New Hampshire courts than would a nonresident lawyer who had never lived in the State.

strates that the discrimination practiced bears a close relationship to its proffered objectives.

. . .

[Justice White, concurring, thought the New Hampshire residency requirement was invalid as applied to Ms. Piper, given the facts of this case, but that it was unnecessary to reach the broader issue of the constitutionality of residency requirements generally.]

JUSTICE REHNQUIST, dissenting.

Today the Court holds that New Hampshire cannot decide that a New Hampshire lawyer should live in New Hampshire. This may not be surprising to those who view law as just another form of business frequently practiced across state lines by interchangeable actors; the Privileges and Immunities Clause of Art. IV, § 2, has long been held to apply to States' attempts to discriminate against nonresidents who seek to ply their trade interstate. The decision will be surprising to many, however, because it so clearly disregards the fact that the practice of law is—almost by definition—fundamentally different from those other occupations that are practiced across state lines without significant deviation from State to State. . . .

. . . My belief that the practice of law differs from other trades and businesses for Art. IV, § 2, purposes is not based on some notion that law is for some reason a superior profession. The reason that the practice of law should be treated differently is that law is one occupation that does not readily translate across state lines. Certain aspects of legal practice are distinctly and intentionally *nonnational*; in this regard one might view this country's legal system as the antithesis of the norms embodied in the Art. IV Privileges and Immunities Clause. Put simply, the State has a substantial interest in creating its own set of laws responsive to its own local interests, and it is reasonable for a State to decide that those people who have been trained to analyze law and policy are better equipped to write those state laws and adjudicate cases arising under them. The State therefore may decide that it has an interest in maximizing the number of resident lawyers, so as to increase the quality of the pool from which its lawmakers can be drawn. A residency law such as the one at issue is the obvious way to accomplish these goals. Since at any given time within a State there is only enough legal work to support a certain number of lawyers, each out-of-state lawyer who is allowed to practice necessarily takes legal work that could support an in-state lawyer, who would otherwise be available to perform various functions that a State has an interest in promoting.[3]

Nor does the State's interest end with enlarging the pool of qualified lawmakers. A State similarly might determine that because

___

3. In New Hampshire's case, lawyers living 40 miles from the state border in Boston could easily devote part of their practice to New Hampshire clients. If this occurred a significant amount of New Hampshire legal work might wind up in Boston, along with lawyers who might otherwise reside in New Hampshire.

lawyers play an important role in the formulation of state policy through their adversary representation, they should be intimately conversant with the local concerns that should inform such policies. And the State likewise might conclude that those citizens trained in the law are likely to bring their useful expertise to other important functions that benefit from such expertise and are of interest to state governments—such as trusteeships, or directorships of corporations or charitable organizations, or school board positions, or merely the role of the interested citizen at a town meeting. Thus, although the Court suggests that state bars can require out-of-state members to "represent indigents and perhaps to participate in formal legal-aid work," the Court ignores a host of other important functions that a State could find would likely be performed only by in-state bar members. States may find a substantial interest in members of their bar being residents, and this insular interest—as with the opposing interest in interstate harmony represented by Art. IV, § 2—itself has its genesis in the language and structure of the Constitution.

. . .

There is yet another interest asserted by the State that I believe would justify a decision to limit membership in the state bar to state residents. The State argues that out-of-state bar members pose a problem in situations where counsel must be available on short notice to represent clients on unscheduled matters. The Court brushes this argument aside, speculating that "a high percentage of nonresident lawyers willing to take the state bar examination and pay the annual dues will reside in places reasonably convenient to New Hampshire," and suggesting that in any event the trial court could alleviate this problem by requiring the lawyer to retain local counsel. Assuming that the latter suggestion does not itself constitute unlawful discrimination under the Court's test, there nevertheless may be good reasons why a State or a trial court would rather not get into structuring attorney-client relationships by requiring the retention of local counsel for emergency matters. The situation would have to be explained to the client, and the allocation of responsibility between resident and nonresident counsel could cause as many problems as the Court's suggestion might cure.

Nor do I believe that the problem can be confined to emergency matters. The Court admits that even in the ordinary course of litigation a trial judge will want trial lawyers to be available on short notice; the uncertainties of managing a trial docket are such that lawyers rarely are given a single date on which a trial will begin; they may be required to "stand by"—or whatever the local terminology is—for days at a time, and then be expected to be ready in a matter of hours, with witnesses, when the case in front of them suddenly settles. A State reasonably can decide that a trial court should not have added to its present scheduling difficulties the uncertainties and added delays fostered by counsel who might reside 1,000 miles from New Hampshire. If there is any single problem with state legal systems that this Court might consider "substantial," it is the problem of delay in litigation—a subject that has been profusely explored in the literature over the past several years.... Surely the State has a substantial interest in taking steps to minimize this problem....

Geographic Restrictions and Exclusions

Until the 1970s, most states restricted eligibility to the bar to persons who were residents of the state or who affirmed an intention to become a resident upon admission or both. These restrictions were particularly rigorous in states adjacent to large metropolitan centers, e.g., New Jersey, and in "sunshine" states such as Florida and Arizona. The former feared competition from big city lawyers; the latter feared that senior lawyers from other states would come there to retire and engage in incidental practice. In the 1980s these restrictions were challenged on grounds of Equal Protection and the Privileges and Immunities Clause. The line of cases beginning with *Piper* has drastically curtailed these restrictions.[1]

Doesn't Justice (now Chief Justice) Rehnquist advance a strong argument in his *Piper* dissent that substantial state interests support the residency requirement? How is a small state, nestled among large urban states, to preserve the special character of its law and bar unless it can impose a residency requirement?

Three other Supreme Court decisions have dealt with geographic restrictions and exclusions on bar admission. In Supreme Court of Virginia v. Friedman,[2] the Court struck down a Virginia provision permitting lawyers who were Virginia residents, but not those who maintained a nonresident status, to be admitted on motion without taking the bar examination. If Friedman, who lived in Maryland and worked on a corporation's legal staff, had moved to Virginia and affirmed an intention to practice full-time in Virginia, she could be admitted on motion, but not if she retained her Maryland residency. This differential treatment was held to violate the Privileges and Immunities Clause.

In Barnard v. Thorstenn,[3] the Court invalidated on statutory grounds a rule of the Virgin Islands requiring for admission to the bar that an applicant reside for a year in the Islands and affirm an intention to reside there. A durational residency requirement of this type is virtually a ban on outsiders, who must spend a year in the Virgin Islands before becoming eligible for admission. The Court rejected as insubstantial five interests claimed to justify the residency

---

1. In re Griffiths, 413 U.S. 717 (1973), held citizenship requirements invalid; a state could not meet the heavy burden of sustaining the "suspect classification" of alienage under the strict scrutiny standard.

2. 487 U.S. 59 (1988).

3. 489 U.S. 546 (1989).

requirement: the geographical isolation of the Virgin Islands, court delays flowing from any effort to accommodate the schedules of nonresident attorneys, difficulties of nonresidents in maintaining competence in local law given publication delays of Virgin Islands' legal materials, inadequacy of disciplinary resources to supervise nonresident lawyers, and difficulties in getting nonresidents to participate on a fair basis in assigned defense of indigent criminal defendants.[4]

In a third case, the Court invalidated a local rule of a United States district court that imposed a residency requirement for admission to that federal court.[5] The ground for the ruling was not the Privileges and Immunities Clause but the Court's inherent supervisory power over the lower federal courts.

Although the *Piper* line of cases eliminates residency requirements, other barriers still impede multistate practice. A lawyer can be required to maintain an office where papers can be served on her.[6] And states need not permit nonresident lawyers to be admitted on motion, but may require all applicants to take the bar examination (about one-half of the states have reciprocity statutes that allow nonresidents to be admitted on motion if the applicant's state also does so).

2. Admission Pro Hac Vice

By long-established practice, a lawyer admitted in one jurisdiction may be permitted by a court of another jurisdiction to participate in a specific case. Normally, permission is sought through a motion by a lawyer already admitted to the court. This is called admission pro hac vice. A typical situation is bringing in a trial specialist from out of state to present a particularly difficult or important matter. Most courts have specific rules concerning such admissions, and the rules often impose the requirement that a locally admitted lawyer also be associated in the case.[7]

In Leis v. Flynt,[8] an out-of-state lawyer claimed a right to appear on behalf of a criminal defendant (Larry Flynt of *Hustler* fame) without being admitted pro hac vice, on the ground that the right to practice constituted a constitutionally protected interest that other states had to recognize. This contention was rejected:

> ... We do not question that the practice of courts in most States is to allow an out-of-state lawyer the privilege of appearing upon motion, especially when he is associated with a member of the local bar. In view of the high mobility of the bar, and also the trend toward specialization, perhaps this is a practice to be encouraged.

---

4. 489 U.S. at 553.

5. Frazier v. Heebe, 482 U.S. 641 (1987).

6. Generally see Note, Invalidation of Residency Requirements for Admission to the Bar: Opportunities for General Reform, 23 U.Rich.L.Rev. 231 (1989).

7. See generally Samuel J. Brakel and Wallace D. Loh, Regulating the Multistate Practice of Law, 50 Wash.L.Rev. 699 (1975); Annot., 20 A.L.R. 4th 855 (1983).

8. 439 U.S. 438 (1979).

But it is not a right granted either by statute or the Constitution....

A claim of entitlement under state law, to be enforceable, must be derived from statute or legal rule or through a mutually explicit understanding. The record here is devoid of any indication that an out-of-state lawyer may claim such an entitlement in Ohio, where the rules of the Ohio Supreme Court expressly consign the authority to approve a pro hac vice appearance to the discretion of the trial court....

Nor is there a basis for the argument that the interest in appearing pro hac vice has its source in federal law. There is no right of federal origin that permits such lawyers to appear in state courts without meeting that State's bar admission requirements.... [9]

Leis v. Flynt involved the lawyer's interest in pro hac vice admission. What about the client's right to be represented by counsel of choice? [10] In Ford v. Israel,[11] a Wisconsin criminal defendant was represented by a public defender because a Wisconsin rule required him to retain and pay local counsel if he was defended by the Chicago lawyer retained by his parents. He was unable to do so and, after being convicted, challenged the "local counsel" rule in a habeas proceeding. Judge Posner conceded that the rule "has about it the air of a guild restriction and may for all we know be motivated by a desire to increase the fees of Wisconsin lawyers." [12] But the attack on the conviction failed because the rule was not arbitrary, especially in a criminal case where a convicted defendant might well attack a conviction on ground that the out-of-state lawyer did not provide effective assistance. Thus the state had a legitimate reason to require local counsel.

The upshot is that pro hac vice admission is required for a lawyer to appear in a court to which she has not been regularly admitted. However, a court's refusal to admit pro hac vice a lawyer who meets the standard requirements, depriving the defendant of counsel of

---

9. 439 U.S. at 441–43. The dissenting opinion of Justice Stevens, joined by Justices Brennan and Marshall, argues that a lawyer's right to "pursu[e] his calling is protected by the Due Process Clause ... when he crosses the border" of the State that licensed him. Justice Stevens identifies two "protected" interests that "reinforce" each other: the lawyer's interest in "discharging [his] responsibility for the fair administration of justice in our adversary system" and "the implicit promise' inhering in Ohio custom" of permitting out-of-state lawyers to handle particular cases. The dissent relies on the historic role of pro hac vice admissions in vindicating rights and in defending unpopular persons or causes.

10. The abstention rule of Younger v. Harris, 401 U.S. 37 (1971), prevented defendant Flynt from seeking a federal court order enjoining Ohio's criminal prosecution of Flynt and *Hustler* magazine.

11. 701 F.2d 689 (7th Cir.1983).

12. 701 F.2d at 692.

choice, may be reversible error under state law or ground for a collateral attack on the conviction.[13]

The absence of any constitutional protection for pro hac vice admission places a premium on the willingness of states to be receptive to out-of-state trial lawyers. Some states, such as New York, permit pro hac vice representation "in the discretion of the court" without requiring local counsel. Others, such as New Jersey, permit out-of-state lawyers to appear pro hac vice, but require that all papers filed in a court proceeding be signed by a lawyer authorized to practice in the state. Statutes and court decisions in a number of states set standards for pro hac vice admission and provide for hearings before denial.

In Hahn v. Boeing Co.,[14] two California lawyers brought suit in Washington on behalf of representatives of persons killed when a plane manufactured by Boeing crashed in Kenya. Boeing challenged the California lawyers' applications for pro hac vice admission on ground that they had solicited the plaintiffs in violation of Washington's professional rules. The trial court's order prohibiting the lawyers' pro hac vice admission until the court ruled on the solicitation charge was reversed on appeal. The appellate court stated that the required association of local counsel served one legitimate judicial interest: reasonable assurance that local rules of practice will be followed. The other interest—that "the attorney is competent and will conduct himself in an ethical and respectful manner in the trial of the case"—was met by the lawyers' out-of-state admission. Because Washington trial courts lack jurisdiction to try disciplinary matters and "[s]olicitation has no relevance per se to the conduct of the trial, nor is it prejudicial to the defendant," the trial court was required to grant pro hac vice admission unless it was shown that the out-of-state lawyer would not conduct a competent, ethical trial. This and other decisions support the view that pro hac vice admission may not be denied without substantial cause.[15]

13. See, e.g., Fuller v. Diesslin, 868 F.2d 604 (3d Cir.1989) (trial court's arbitrary denial of pro hac vice admission of two nonresident lawyers resulted in grant of habeas); Herrmann v. Summer Plaza Corp., 201 Conn. 263, 513 A.2d 1211, 1214 (1986) ("The right to have counsel of one's own choice, although not absolute, is important enough to require a legitimate state interest before a person can be deprived of that right.... In this period of greater mobility among members of the bar and the public, and the corresponding growth in interstate business, a court should reluctantly deny an application to appear pro hac vice"). Compare Panzardi–Alvarez v. United States, 879 F.2d 975 (1st Cir.1989) (standard for reviewing district court's denial of attorney's application for pro hac vice admission to bar is abuse of discretion).

14. 95 Wn.2d 28, 621 P.2d 1263 (1980).

15. See Note, Due Process and Pro Hac Vice Appearances by Attorneys: Does Any Protection Remain?, 29 Buffalo L.Rev. 133 (1980) (suggested standards and procedures for handling pro hac vice applications); Comment, Leis v. Flynt: Retaining a Nonresident Attorney for Litigation, 79 Colum.L.Rev. 572 (1979).

3. Handling Multistate Transactions

RANTA v. McCARNEY

Supreme Court of North Dakota, 1986.
391 N.W.2d 161.

VANDE WALLE, JUSTICE

Robert P. McCarney appealed from a judgment of the Burleigh County Court in favor of Esko E. Ranta for recovery of fees for legal services. We reverse and remand.

Ranta is an attorney licensed to practice in Minnesota. Since 1966 he has travelled to North Dakota to provide various legal advice to McCarney, primarily in the area of taxation. He never has been licensed to practice law in the State of North Dakota. Details of the fees to be charged were traditionally left open, with Ranta billing McCarney the amount Ranta believed was fair and reasonable for the services rendered. Ranta states that they never had any problems so far as fees were concerned, and that McCarney "referred to me at least twenty clients in this area, ..." At one point, Ranta opened what he called a "branch office" in Bismarck, apparently to serve those additional clients.[1]

McCarney hired Ranta in 1977 in connection with the sale of McCarney's Ford, Inc. On November 7, 1977, the final documents selling the business were negotiated and signed in an all-day closing in Bismarck. On or about June 1, 1978, McCarney paid Ranta $5,000. At the end of that month Ranta sent McCarney his bill of $22,500, showing the $5,000 paid as a credit and a $17,500 balance due. The bill contained no statement of hours or costs incurred. At trial office records that showed approximately sixty-one hours of work on behalf of McCarney were submitted. According to Ranta, the only other time records were kept in his mind.

At the end of the trial McCarney moved to amend his answer to include the defense that Ranta never was licensed to practice law in the State of North Dakota and therefore could not recover compensation. The trial court granted the motion, but in a later memorandum opinion stated that McCarney

---

1. Ranta freely admitted at trial to rendering services to "at least twenty clients in this area" and opening a branch office in Bismarck. Ranta gave the following justification for providing McCarney with legal advice in this State:

"I know it's a criminal act as far as the courts are concerned, but to take matters like tax planning or representing clients before the Internal Revenue Service, I have had clients in at least half of the fifty states that I have represented on tax matters, and the question has never been raised. This was basically a tax matter that I was counselling Mr. McCarney on."

Although in-State practice before a Federal court pursuant to that court's rules commonly has been construed as an authorized practice of law, this Court has no knowledge of any special exception given to persons practicing in the area of tax law. The unlicensed practice of law in this State by non-resident attorneys is allowed only when court permission, pursuant to the applicable Federal or State court rules, is granted for the limited purposes of appearing in relation to a particular matter before the court. See Rule 2, North Dakota Admission to Practice Rules. Any other unauthorized practice of law is prohibited by § 27–11–01, N.D.C.C.

"has received the total benefits of the contract and should not now be allowed to claim that Mr. Ranta is not entitled to his fee. There is nothing in the law of the State of North Dakota which prohibits Mr. Ranta from collecting his fee, and in addition, the doctrine of equitable estoppel should preclude Mr. McCarney from advancing such an argument."

Section 27–11–01, N.D.C.C., prohibits the practice of law in this State without proper authorization. . . .

Although our statutory law does not specifically prohibit compensation of out-of-State attorneys who practice law in the State in violation of § 27–11–01, the statute is clearly intended to provide protection to our citizens from unlicensed and unauthorized practice of law. . . . Although Ranta may be competent (a factor which is irrelevant), he is not authorized to practice law in this State. The purpose of the statute is to determine *before* an individual practices in this State whether that person is competent and qualified to do so.

Prior to this case we have not had occasion to determine whether an out-of-state attorney not authorized to practice law in this State may recover compensation for his or her services. There are, however, two North Dakota cases which are analogous. Application of Christianson, 215 N.W.2d 920 (N.D.1974), involved legal work performed by a suspended lawyer which, the lawyer alleged, could be lawfully performed by a layperson. The Court held that the suspended attorney "is subject to the same restrictions as are laymen, such as the limitation that [the acts performed] involve his own business and *that he charge no fee.*" 215 N.W.2d at 925. (Emphasis added.)

We believe a fair reading of Section 27–11–01 and *Christianson* indicate a preference by both the Legislature and our Court of furthering the strong policy considerations underlying the prohibition against the unauthorized practice of law that occurs in this State by barring compensation for any such activities. The statute is intended to protect the public from unlicensed attorneys and is to be liberally construed "with a view to effecting its objects and to promoting justice." Section 1–02–01, N.D.C.C. An out-of-State lawyer who is not authorized to practice law in this State (such as Ranta) sits in the same position as a suspended attorney previously admitted to practice law in this State (as in *Christianson*); such a person cannot lawfully practice law in this State, nor can that person charge a fee for such services. We therefore hold that an out-of-State attorney who is not licensed to practice law in this State cannot recover compensation for services rendered in the State of North Dakota. This position is in accord with the majority view on the issue. . . . We further hold that a violation of § 27–11–01 precludes the application of equitable principles, such as equitable estoppel, because such a violation constitutes unclean hands. . . .

A problem develops, however, in relation to exceptions to the rule that many jurisdictions have developed. The exception of Federal court practice (as opposed to State court practice) does not apply because Ranta's conduct did not involve an appearance in a federal court. See, e.g., Spanos v. Skouras Theatres Corporation, 235 F.Supp. 1 (S.D.N.Y.1964), affirmed in relevant part, 364 F.2d 161 (2d Cir.), cert. denied, 385 U.S. 987 (1966); Cowen v. Calabrese, 230 Cal.App.2d 870, 41 Cal.Rptr. 441 (1964). Nor do we perceive a justification for Ranta's conduct under the interstate practice exception. Although some States allow an out-of-State attorney to recover fees where the attorney made proper disclosure to the client and associated with local counsel, such as Massachusetts [Brooks v. Volunteer Harbor No.4, 233 Mass. 168, 123 N.E. 511 (1919)], we need not reach the issue because such is not the situation here. Another State has adopted a "sister-State" exception, allowing recovery when the attorney is licensed to practice law in a sister State and has not offended the spirit of intention of the statutes regulating the practice of law. See Freeling v. Tucker, 49 Idaho 475, 289 P. 85 (1930). But even if we were to adopt an interstate or sister-State exception (a point which we do not reach), such an exception would not apply here in light of Ranta's long-term unauthorized practice in this State, his involvement with many other area clients, and his opening a branch office in Bismarck. Such conduct is a clear violation of § 27–11–01.

The dissent attempts to frame the question as whether the protection of the economic interests of the attorneys of the State and the estate of McCarney is more justifiable than the forfeiture to Ranta and windfall to McCarney occasioned by this opinion. It apparently urges that because Ranta is licensed in another State Section 27–11–01, N.D.C.C., should not apply or, alternatively, that the Federal-court-practice exception should apply. Justice Levine makes an eloquent plea that our statute is not meant to govern this situation in which the attorney is licensed in another State. It may be that such an exception is warranted, but such a plea is more properly made to a legislative committee considering a bill enacting such an exception or to this court in its rule-making function than it is in a judicial decision....

. . .

The dissent further argues that because the advice given was "tax advice," it must involve the Federal court and thus the Federal-court-practice exception should apply. The Federal-court-practice exception was not relied upon by the trial court nor by Ranta in his brief to this court and there is little in the record to sustain the conclusion reached by the dissent as to the precise nature of the legal advice. More important, however, the dissent does not provide even one citation for its sweeping application of the Federal-court-practice exception to this case and, as we have heretofore concluded, the application of such an exception in this case is not warranted.

According to our holding, an out-of-State lawyer not authorized to practice law in this State is prohibited from recovering any fees relating to the practice of law actually conducted in this State (unless that attorney falls within a recognized exception to the rule). Because

Ranta does not fall within any of the recognized exceptions to the rule, the only issue remaining is the determination of which fees relate to the practice of law conducted outside of North Dakota....

LEVINE, JUSTICE, dissenting.

I agree that the purpose of 27–11–01 is to protect the public from unqualified legal advisors. But I disagree that Mr. Ranta is the unqualified legal advisor intended to be protected against....

The only protection effected by the holding in this case is the protection of the economic interests of the attorneys of this state and the estate of Mr. McCarney. While there may be some justification for the former, the question is whether that justification outweighs the forfeiture to Ranta and windfall to McCarney occasioned by our holding. I do not believe it does and, therefore, I dissent.

.   .   .

MESCHKE, JUSTICE, respectfully dissenting.

... For my part, I prefer the approach of In Re Estate of Waning, 47 N.J. 367, 221 A.2d 193 (1966), approving an award of fees to out-of-state counsel for a New Jersey estate for "federal tax matters, largely involving federal law and out-of-state activities." I believe the reasoning of that opinion is more realistic:

> "Multistate relationships are a common part of today's society and are to be dealt with in common sense fashion. While the members of the general public are entitled to full protection against unlawful practitioners, their freedom of choice in the selection of their own counsel is to be highly regarded and not burdened by "technical restrictions which have no reasonable justification." Id. 221 A.2d at 197.

Local Control or National Bar ?

Local control is enforced against trial lawyers by rules that limit court appearances to licensed local practitioners or those admitted pro hac vice for a specific litigation. The presence of an adversary in the courtroom setting provides an enforcement mechanism. A practical restraint on pro hac vice admission is also operative: The client must be willing to pay the additional cost of the local counsel required by most states' rules. Application and enforcement of local control is more difficult, however, with respect to counselors engaged in providing advice or facilitating transactions. Most of what they do occurs in the privacy of the law office. The *Ranta* case illustrates one enforcement device: denial of the opportunity to collect a fee for work performed. Lawyer Ranta might also be disciplined by North Dakota, the sanction being an order forbidding him from further practice in the state. Finally, it is possible, although highly unlikely, that Ranta's conduct will be viewed as a disciplinary violation by his home state, Minnesota.

Are such restrictive rules justified by substantial local interests, or are they a form of economic protectionism for the local bar? The interests generally relied on in defense of local control are those discussed throughout the domain of unauthorized practice: the harmful effects on local consumers of the provision of allegedly incompetent or unethical services by out-of-state practitioners; the relative ignorance of local substantive law and procedure on the part of out-of-state practitioners; and the difficulty of applying local disciplinary machinery to out-of-state lawyers. The restrictions pose the most difficulties for certain categories of lawyers: lawyers who move from one state to another for personal reasons, who are transferred by their corporate employers, who seek to develop a national practice in a specialty field, and who are sought by unpopular clients who encounter difficulty in obtaining local representation.

Two important New York decisions deal with the activities of out-of-state lawyers in New York. In Spivak v. Sachs,[16] a California lawyer spent 14 days in New York assisting a client who was involved in acrimonious matrimonial litigation with her spouse. The client was a New York resident, the divorce proceeding was pending in Connecticut, and the advice involved negotiation tactics, choice of local counsel and some issues of New York law. When the lawyer sought to collect a fee of $10,575 plus expenses of $1,600, the client claimed that the fee was uncollectible because the lawyer had violated New York's unauthorized practice law. The court refused to enforce the fee contract because the out-of-state lawyer had engaged in illegal practice. But it also stated that the statute should not be construed to prohibit "customary and innocuous practices:" "[R]ecognizing the numerous multi-State transactions and relationships of modern times, we cannot penalize every instance in which an attorney from another State comes into our State for conferences or negotiations relating to a New York client and a transaction somehow tied to New York." [17]

The second decision, El Gemayel v. Seaman,[18] allowed a Lebanese lawyer to collect a fee of $22,350 plus $6,000 of expenses for work primarily performed in Lebanon in a successful effort to regain custody for defendant's daughter of a child who had been taken to Lebanon by the father in violation of a Massachusetts' custody decree. The lawyer, a Lebanese national who resided in Washington, made frequent phone calls to defendant-client and her daughter, then residing in New York, and met with them in New York on one occasion. The court, affirming the fee award, stated:

> Here, unlike *Spivack*, plaintiff's contacts with New York were ... incidental and innocuous. Although plaintiff engaged in substantial litigation in Lebanon, where he was licensed, and even

16. 16 N.Y.2d 163, 263 N.Y.S.2d 953, 211 N.E.2d 329 (1965).

17. 211 N.E.2d at 331. See also Lozoff v. Shore Heights, Ltd., 66 Ill.2d 398, 6 Ill.Dec. 225, 362 N.E.2d 1047 (1977) (nonresident lawyer denied compensation for work on an Illinois real estate transaction).

18. 72 N.Y.2d 701, 536 N.Y.S.2d 406, 533 N.E.2d 245 (1988).

arguably provided legal services while in Washington, D.C., and Massachusetts, ... phone calls to New York by plaintiff ... did not, without more, constitute the "practice" of law in this State in violation of Judiciary Law § 478.... To adopt a per se rule such as advanced by defendant would impair the ability of New York residents to obtain legal advice in foreign jurisdictions on matters relating to those jurisdictions since the foreign attorneys would be unable to recover for their services unless they were licensed both in New York as well as in the foreign jurisdiction.[19]

May a lawyer who is handling a matter involving federal law engage in nationwide practice? In Spanos v. Skouras Theatres Corp.,[20] Judge Friendly encouraged an affirmative response by stating: "[U]nder the privileges and immunities clause of the Constitution, no state can prohibit a citizen with a federal claim or defense from engaging an out-of-state lawyer to collaborate with an in-state lawyer and give legal advice concerning it within the state."[21] Spanos, a California lawyer, assisted a theater chain in planning a major antitrust action in New York. Spanos did not seek admission pro hac vice but performed extensive work over several years, mostly in New York. After the case was settled, the client refused to pay. The court, in addition to its broad statement of constitutional principle, quoted above, held that the failure of the client's New York lawyer to move for Spanos' pro hac admission, which would have been granted as a matter of course by the federal court under its rules, could not be used to defeat the out-of-state lawyer from collecting his fee.

Commentators have suggested a variety of solutions to the realities of multijurisdictional practice. A national bar examination qualifying those who pass for practice in any state is one possibility. A less dramatic proposal would be a separate national admissions process for practice involving federal courts and federal law. Another possibility is to separate trial court representation from other aspects of the practice of law, with state admission (either permanent or pro hac vice) required for in-court representation, but legal advice and other practice of law opened to nationwide competition. Would one of these proposals be desirable? How likely is it that a change of this type will come about? Is this a fit subject for federal legislation?

In August 1993 the ABA amended Model Rule 8.5 to clarify which jurisdiction's professional code applies to lawyers who are admitted and practice in more than one jurisdiction. The amended rule provides that in litigation, a lawyer, including one admitted pro hac vice to

19. 533 N.E.2d at 248–49.

20. 364 F.2d 161 (2d Cir.1966) (en banc).

21. 364 F.2d at 170. The per curiam opinion in *Leis v. Flynt,* discussed above at p. 995, pointedly stated that this portion of the *Spanos* decision "must be considered to have been limited, if not rejected entirely, by [subsequent Supreme Court decisions]." 439 U.S. at 438, 442 n. 4. But *Leis* itself is impaired as a precedent by language of the Court in *Piper,* reprinted above at p. 987. So the current status of Judge Friendly's view is in doubt.

handle a particular case, is subject to the professional rules of the forum state. In all other situations, lawyers are subject to the rules of the jurisdiction in which they "principally" practice, with one exception—where the particular conduct in question "clearly has its predominant effect" in another jurisdiction. For example, the Comment states that a lawyer, principally practicing in State A but also admitted in State B, who handles an acquisition for a company whose headquarters and operations are in State B, would be subject to the professional rules of State B.

Chapter 11

LAW, LAWYERS AND JUSTICE

Introductory Note

One tradition in Judaism explains the Jews' place as the chosen people with the following story. God's presence in the world, the Shekinah, was once whole in the form of a giant crystal globe. This globe was shattered into millions of tiny pieces of glass. The Jews were chosen as the people whose responsibility it is to collect the pieces of glass to try and restore God's presence in the world. In Hebrew this responsibility is captured by the words "*tikun olum*," which means to repair the world. The story explains that the Jews were given the Torah, the law, at Mount Sinai as the means to fulfill their responsibility. The moral of the tale is that by living a life dedicated to studying and living the law one helps to repair the world.

We begin our examination of law, lawyers and justice with this story because most law students and many lawyers believe that law is an important and necessary means of repairing the world and at its best a life in the law is devoted to this task of repair, to bringing justice into the world. In this chapter we investigate the connection between law and justice, between being a lawyer and repairing the world. We begin with the grand gesture, repairing the world, if you will, by shaking it. We move next to lawyers for the poor and public interest lawyers, repairing the world by trying to even out the odds. We conclude with the day-to-day work of ordinary lawyers—lawyers who draft contracts, litigate tort suits, negotiate messy divorces, advise corporations and the like. Are these lawyers, one of whom you will most likely be, helping to repair the world? Is the disappointment that many lawyers feel a function of the contradiction between their ideal of practice, that lawyers should help repair the world, and the reality of practice as they experience it? Do we need to abandon the ideal of repairing the world because the ideal does not correspond to reality or can we reformulate what it means to repair the world? Does picking up one tiny piece of glass at a time count? [1]

---

1. A Christian story provides an affirmative answer: Jesus is describing God inviting the righteous at the last judgment to "inherit the kingdom prepared for you," and saying to them: " 'for I was hungry and you gave me food, I was thirsty and you gave me something to drink, ... I was naked and you gave me clothing, I was sick and you took care of me, I was in prison and you visited me.' Then the righteous will answer him, 'Lord, when was it that [we did these things]?' And the Lord will answer them, 'Truly, I tell you, just as you did it to one of the least of us, you did it to me.' " Matt. 25: 31–40.

1005

In Gideon v. Wainwright,[2] the Warren Court held that due process "cannot be realized if the poor man charged with a crime has to face his accusers without a lawyer to assist him."[3] In *Gideon*, the Court offered two explanations for the essential connection between lawyers and justice. First, quoting "the moving words of Justice Sutherland in Powell v. Alabama,"[4] the Court explained:

> The right to be heard would be, in many cases, of little avail if it did not comprehend the right to be heard by counsel. Even the intelligent and educated layman has small and sometimes no skill in the science of law. If charged with crime, he is incapable, generally, of determining for himself whether the indictment is good or bad. He is unfamiliar with the rules of evidence. Left without the aid of counsel he may be put on trial without a proper charge, and convicted upon incompetent evidence, or evidence irrelevant to the issue or otherwise inadmissible. He lacks both the skill and knowledge adequately to prepare his defense, even though he have a perfect one. He requires the guiding hand of counsel at every step in the proceedings against him. Without it, though he be not guilty, he faces the danger of conviction because he does not know how to establish his innocence.[5]

Justice Sutherland's explanation of the connection between lawyers and justice emphasizes commutative justice—justice envisioned as fairness through neutrality in adjudicating guilt and innocence, rights and duties. Lawyers, here, are part of justice itself. Adjudication that is fair and just normally requires the participation of a lawyer to be realized.[6] Is this less true in civil proceedings than in criminal proceedings?

A second quotation, from the *Gideon* case, emphasizes a different aspect of justice and thus a different connection between lawyers and justice.

> Governments, both state and federal, quite properly spend vast sums of money to establish machinery to try defendants accused of crime. Lawyers to prosecute are everywhere deemed essential to protect the public's interest in an orderly society. Similarly, there are few defendants charged with crime, few indeed, who fail to hire the best lawyers they can get to prepare and present their defenses. That government hires lawyers to prosecute and defendants who have the money hire lawyers to defend are the strongest indica-

2. 372 U.S. 335 (1963).

3. 372 U.S. at 344 (1963). The evolution of an indigent criminal defendant's right to counsel at state expense is discussed in Chapter 3 above at p. 193.

4. 372 U.S. at 344, referring to Sutherland's majority opinion in Powell v. Alabama, 287 U.S. 45 (1932) (involving the Scottsboro Boys), discussed above at p. 193.

5. 372 U.S. at 344–45, quoting Powell v. Alabama, 287 U.S. 45, 68–69 (1932).

6. But cf. Faretta v. California, 422 U.S. 806 (1975) (establishing the right to proceed without counsel).

tions of the widespread belief that lawyers in criminal courts are necessities, not luxuries.[7]

Justice here is distributive—justice as providing for the poor and unfortunate in society. Justice here is giving the poor what those with means have and consider essential, lawyers. Why those with means consider lawyers essential is explained by the connection between lawyers and commutative justice.

Few, if any, well-to-do civil litigants would proceed to trial without a lawyer, and governments use lawyers in civil proceedings with the same regularity as in criminal proceedings. Thus the same widespread belief—that lawyers are necessities not luxuries in contested proceedings involving substantial stakes—extends to civil as well as criminal cases. Should a poor person have a right to a lawyer in a civil proceeding? This issue is discussed below at p. 1035.

Both aspects of justice, commutative and distributive, are included in the American concept of justice, meaning that the ideal of justice is that society will be even-handed in dealing with all litigants and decently open-handed in dealing with the poor. But there is yet a third aspect of the ideal of justice as it is conceived in this country that is important to this discussion and which complicates the picture drawn thus far. Substantively the ideal of justice in America affirms individual equality, notwithstanding that in practice a denial of equality to women, blacks and other minorities was and is an acknowledged fact. On the positive side, justice as the political equality of individuals signifies that everyone has an equal right to participate in various political and legal processes. On the negative side, however, the principle of individual political equality signifies that no class or group has a recognized and accepted special responsibility to carry the burden of social justice. It follows that no chosen people have a special duty to repair the world through pursuit of justice.

Fulfilling either the commutative or distributive aspects of justice entails great intellectual and practical difficulties. Enhancing these difficulties, however, is the very real tension between the special responsibility for justice that both the commutative and distributive aspects of justice assign to lawyers and the American ideal that rejects, if it does not abhor, assigning such special responsibility to one group. Moreover, it is not just non-lawyers who have serious doubts about the justice of assigning lawyers a special responsibility for justice, lawyers too have such doubts. Who appointed *us* as the special guardians of justice? This question resurfaces in different forms in the materials discussed below: Why should lawyers have to volunteer to represent the poor without adequate compensation? Who anointed us to represent the public interest? What gives a lawyer the right to try to stop an individual client from doing something because the lawyer thinks it is of questionable legality or unjust or unwise? We return to these questions at the end of this chapter, but we raise them now so that you

7. 372 U.S. at 344.

may consider them in thinking about the issues raised in the materials that follow.

A. SHAKING THE WORLD: LAWYERS FOR AND AS REVOLUTIONARIES

1. Politics and the Courtroom

Professor Cover penetrates to the heart of the use of force that lies behind legal authority: [8]

> The act of sentencing a convicted defendant is among [the] most routine of acts performed by judges. Yet it is immensely revealing of the way in which [legal] interpretation is shaped by violence. First, examine the event from the perspective of the defendant. The defendant's world is threatened. But he sits, usually quietly, as if engaged in a civil discourse. If convicted, the defendant customarily walks—escorted—to prolonged confinement, usually without significant disturbance to the civil appearance of the event. It is, of course, grotesque to assume that the civil facade is "voluntary" except in the sense that it represents the defendant's autonomous recognition of the overwhelming array of violence ranged against him, and of the hopelessness of resistance or outcry.... [17]

> There are societies in which contrition or shame control defendants' behavior to a greater extent than does violence.... But I think it is unquestionably the case in the United States that most prisoners walk into prison because they know they will be dragged or beaten into prison if they do not walk. They do not organize force against being dragged because they know that if they wage this kind of battle they will lose—very possibly their lives.

> If I have exhibited some sense of sympathy for the victims of this violence it is misleading. Very often the balance of terror in this regard is just as I would want it. But I do not wish us to pretend that we talk our prisoners into jail. The "interpretations" or "conversations" that are the preconditions for violent incarceration are themselves implements of violence.

What then is the criminal defense lawyer's role—or for that matter, the role of a lawyer in a civil proceeding that threatens to divest a client of her child, her property or something else held dear—when the client decides to respond by breaking the rules of the proceeding as a

---

8. Robert M. Cover, Violence and the Word, 95 Yale L.J. 1601, 1608–09 (1986).

17. ... Bobby Seale taught those of us who lived through the 1960's that the court's physical control over the defendant's body lies at the heart of the criminal process. The defendant's "civil conduct," therefore can never signify a shared understanding of the event; it may signify his fear that any public display of his interpretation of the event as "bullshit" will end in violence perpetrated against him, pain inflicted upon him. Our constitutional law, quite naturally enough, provides for the calibrated use of ascending degrees of overt violence to maintain the "order" of the criminal trial. See, e.g., Illinois v. Allen, 397 U.S. 337 (1970)....

protest, as a challenge, as a statement that what is going on will not be calmly accepted?

NORMAN DORSEN AND LEON FRIEDMAN
DISORDER IN THE COURT

Pp. 56–64, 272, 276–277 (1973).[9]

The Chicago Conspiracy Trial

The most notorious disorderly trial in recent years was the Chicago conspiracy trial of 1969–70. In that case, eight leading members of the Vietnam antiwar movement were indicted under the federal anti-riot statute of 1968 for conspiring, organizing, and inciting riots during the 1968 Democratic National Convention in Chicago. It appears from the evidence introduced at the trial that seven of the eight defendants—David Dellinger, Abbie Hoffman, Jerry Rubin, Rennie Davis, Tom Hayden, Lee Weiner, and John Froines—had planned to hold massive demonstrations in the streets and parks of Chicago at the time of the 1968 convention to protest the continuation of the Vietnam war. After extensive negotiations with city officials, permits for large-scale demonstrations were refused. Nevertheless, rallies were held, which led to violent confrontations between the demonstrators and the Chicago police.

Subsequent investigations by a special committee of the National Violence Commission concluded that the disturbances that ensued were the result of a "police riot"....

The trial drew considerable public notice because of the notoriety of the defendants and because this was the first use of a statute which was of doubtful constitutionality. From its inception numerous incidents occurred which attracted even more attention. In the week before the trial began, four of the attorneys who had appeared earlier in the case for specific pretrial motions telegrammed that they were withdrawing from further participation. On the motion of the United States attorney, Judge Julius Hoffman took the unusual step of issuing bench warrants to have all four arrested and brought before him. Five days later, after a storm of protest from lawyers and law professors, he vacated the order.

Additional contention arose because of the judge's refusal to postpone the trial until Charles Garry of California, who was engaged to act as Bobby Seale's lawyer, had recovered from a gall bladder operation. Seale insisted from the first days of the trial that he was unrepresented until Garry appeared. On September 26, he said to the court:

> If I am consistently denied this right of legal defense counsel of my choice who is effective by the judge of this Court, then I can only see the judge as a blatant racist of the United States Court.

---

9. Copyright © 1973 by the Association of the Bar of the City of New York. Reprinted with permission.

On the same day the court reprimanded Tom Hayden for giving a clenched fist salute to the jury and Abbie Hoffman for blowing them kisses. On September 30, the court discharged one juror after reading to her the contents of a threatening letter signed "The Black Panther," which had been sent to her home. On October 15, the defendants asked to celebrate Vietnam Moratorium Day and tried to drape the counsel table with American and N.L.F. flags. On October 22 the defendants tried to bring a birthday cake into the courtroom for Bobby Seale.

The ... particular incidents that gave rise to the greatest number of contempt citations were as follows:

Gagging and Binding of Bobby Seale

The most serious disorders occurred over the problem of representation for Bobby Seale. After Charles Garry became unavailable, William Kunstler filed an appearance for Seale ostensibly in order to see him at the county jail. On the first day of the trial, he also filed a general appearance for four of the defendants, including Seale. On September 26 Seale rejected Kunstler as his lawyer and thereafter insisted on his right to defend himself. The court and Seale argued about this issue at almost every opportunity. On October 14, the following colloquy occurred:

Mr. Seale:	I don't have counsel, Judge, I don't stand up because—
The Court:	Mr. Kunstler filed his appearance for Mr. Seale. The record shows it orally and in writing, sir....
Mr. Seale:	Hey, you don't speak for me. I would like to speak on behalf of my own self and have my counsel handle my case in behalf of myself.
	How come I can't speak in behalf of myself? I am my own legal counsel. I don't want these lawyers to represent me.
The Court:	You have a lawyer of record and he has been of record here since the 24th.
Mr. Seale:	I have been arguing that before the jury heard one shred of evidence. I don't want these lawyers because I can take my own legal defense and my lawyer is Charles Garry.
The Court:	I direct you, sir, to remain quiet.
Mr. Seale:	And just be railroaded?
The Court:	Will you remain quiet?
Mr. Seale:	I want to defend myself, do you mind, please?

On October 20 Bobby Seale made a motion to act as his own lawyer. The U.S. attorney opposed the motion and Judge Hoffman ruled that Seale was represented by Kunstler and could not discharge him. The court of appeals later ruled that Judge Hoffman acted improperly in not inquiring whether Seale wanted Kunstler to represent him.

The conflict escalated on October 28, when Seale again insisted on his right to represent himself.

Mr. Seale :	... You are in contempt of people's constitutional rights. You are in contempt of the constitutional rights of the mass of the people of the United States. You are the one in contempt of people's constitutional rights. I am not in contempt of nothing. You are the one who is in contempt. The people of America need to admonish you and the whole Nixon administration.
Mr. Hayden :	Let the record show the judge was laughing.
Mr. Seale :	Yes, he is laughing.
The Court :	Who made that remark?
Mr. Foran [prosecutor] :	The defendant Hayden, your Honor, made the remark....
The Court :	You are not doing very well for yourself.
Mr. Seale :	Yes, that's because you violated my constitutional rights, Judge Hoffman. That's because you violated them overtly, deliberately, in a very racist manner. Somebody ought to point out the law to you....

On the next day, October 29, Seale addressed a group of his followers in the courtroom before the judge appeared. As soon as the court was called into session, Richard Schultz, the assistant United States attorney, spoke:

Mr. Schultz :	If the Court please, before you came into this courtroom, if the Court please, Bobby Seale stood up and addressed this group.
Mr. Seale :	That's right, brother. I spoke on behalf of my constitutional rights. I have a right to speak on behalf of my constitutional rights. That's right.
Mr. Schultz :	And he told those—people in the audience, if the Court please—and I want this—on the record. It happened this morning—that if he's attacked, they know what to do. He was talking to these people about an attack by them.
Mr. Seale :	You're lying. Dirty liar. I told them to defend themselves. You are a rotten racist pig, fascist liar, that's what you are. You're a rotten liar. You are a fascist pig liar.
	I said they had a right to defend themselves if they are attacked, and I hope that the record carries that, and I hope the record shows that tricky Dick Schultz, working for Richard Nixon and [his] administration all understand that tricky Dick Schultz is a liar, and we have a right to defend

ourselves, and if you attack me I will defend myself.

Seale was forcibly put into his chair by the marshals. After he again
insisted on his right to represent himself, the court took a brief recess.
Seale was then taken out of the courtroom by the marshals and
returned bound and gagged in his chair. The gag was not secure, and
he could still speak through it. Kunstler described the scene for the
record:

> *Mr. Kunstler*: I wanted to say the record should indicate that Mr.
> Seale is seated on a metal chair, each hand hand-
> cuffed to the leg of the chair on both the right and
> left sides so he cannot raise his hands, and a gag is
> tightly pressed into his mouth and tied at the rear,
> and that when he attempts to speak, a muffled
> sound comes out.
>
> *Mr. Seale (gagged)*: You don't represent me. Sit down, Kunstler.
>
> *The Court*: Mr. Marshal, I don't think you have accomplished
> your purpose by that kind of a contrivance. We
> will have to take another recess.

On the next day, October 30, 1969, Seale was again bound and
gagged.

> *Mr. Weinglass*: If your Honor please, the buckles on the leather
> strap holding Mr. Seale's hand is digging into his
> hand and he appears to be trying to free his hand
> from that pressure. Could he be assisted?
>
> *The Court*: If the marshal has concluded that he needs assis-
> tance, of course.
>
> *Mr. Kunstler*: Your Honor, are we going to stop this medieval
> torture that is going on in this courtroom? I think
> this is a disgrace.
>
> *Mr. Rubin*: This guy is putting his elbow in Bobby's mouth and
> it wasn't necessary at all.
>
> *Mr. Kunstler*: This is no longer a court of order, your Honor; this
> is a medieval torture chamber. It is a disgrace.
> They are assaulting the other defendants also.

The three days from October 28 through October 30 produced the
most serious crisis in the trial. Of the 137 citations for contempt
against the defendants, 47 occurred then. Seale was cited six times for
his actions and the remaining defendants for their support of Seale and
their protest against what was happening to him. One week later, on
November 5, 1969, Seale was held in contempt by Judge Hoffman and
severed—from the trial. He was sentenced to forty-eight months in
jail—three months for each of sixteen acts of misconduct. The court of
appeals later held that four of the sixteen specifications dealing with

Seale's attempt to defend himself were insufficient to justify contempt charges. After the case was reversed and sent back by the court of appeals for retrial before a different judge, the government decided not to reprosecute the contempt charges because it did not wish to disclose information concerning wiretaps of Seale.

Ralph Abernathy Incident

Two other triggering events that led to numerous contempt citations were the refusal to allow Reverend Ralph Abernathy to testify and the revocation of the bail of David Dellinger. On Friday, January 31, the defense indicated it was prepared to rest its case on Monday, February 2, after submitting some television film. Over the weekend, another witness, Ralph Abernathy, became available. On Monday morning, Kunstler asked to reopen the case to allow Abernathy to testify. Judge Hoffman refused the request.

New Evidence wanted to re-open [handwritten marginalia]

> *The Court*: There have been several witnesses called here during this trial ... whose testimony the Court ruled could not even be presented to the jury—singers, performers, and former office holders. I think in the light of the representations made by you unequivocally, sir, with no reference to Dr. Abernathy, I will deny your motion that we hold—
>
> *Mr. Kunstler*: ... Your Honor.... I think what you have just said is about the most outrageous statement I have ever heard from a bench, and I am going to say my piece right now, and you can hold me in contempt right now if you wish to. You have violated every principle of fair play when you excluded Ramsey Clark from that witness stand. The New York Times, among others, has called it the ultimate outrage in American justice.
>
> *Voices*: Right on.
>
> *Mr. Kunstler*: I am outraged to be in this court before you. Now because I made a statement on Friday that I had only a cameraman, and I discovered on Saturday that Ralph Abernathy, who is the chairman of the Mobilization, is in town, and he can be here.... I am trembling because I am so outraged, I haven't been able to get this out before, and I am saying it now, and then I want you to put me in jail if you want to. You can do anything you want with me... because I feel disgraced to be here.

Kunstler was then ordered to make no reference to Abernathy before the jury.

> *Mr. Schultz*: Your Honor, may the defendants and their counsel then not make any reference in front of this jury that they wanted Dr. Abernathy to testify?
>
> *Mr. Kunstler*: No, no.

> *The Court*:   I order you not to make such a statement.
>
> *Mr. Kunstler*: We are not going to abide by any such comment as that. Dr. Ralph Abernathy is going to come into this courtroom, and I am going to repeat my motion before that jury.
>
> *The Court*:   I order you not to.
>
> *Mr. Kunstler*: Then you will have to send me to jail, I am sorry. We have a right to state our objection to resting before the jury.
>
> *The Court*:   Don't do it.

After the jury was brought into the court, Abernathy arrived and Kunstler immediately asked that he be allowed to testify. The request was refused.

. . .

Lawyer Contempts

The contempt citations against the two lawyers in the case did not involve abusive language or obscene remarks. The government said in its appellate brief, "The attorneys present a far different case; they did not heap vituperation upon the judge as did their clients, but rather repeatedly contested rulings by the judge to the point of obstructing the trial." Thus Weinglass was cited for refusing to sit down immediately after being ordered to do so, for asking questions on cross-examination beyond the scope of the direct examination, for repeating citations of legal authorities, for continuing an argument after the judge had ruled on it, and for making disrespectful remarks about the prosecution. He also was cited for making "invidious comparisons" between the court's treatment of the government's case and of the defense's.

Kunstler was cited for similar transgressions, such as refusing to sit down or continuing to argue. The court also cited him for going into the substance of a document not introduced in evidence and for arguing about the time of recess. In addition he defied specific orders of the court not to mention before the jury certain matters which the court had ruled on. Kunstler was given the maximum sentence of six months for these transgressions and an additional six months for his intemperate remarks on the morning of the Abernathy affair. He also received four months for telling the court, "You brought this on [referring to fistfights between the marshals and spectators.] This is your fault," and four months for accusing the government of using violence in the courtroom and of liking to strike women. He was also cited for referring to the gagging of Bobby Seale as "medieval torture" and for expressing his approval of disapproving groans from the spectators.

Total Contempt Citations

Aside from the cluster of disruptions described above, the trial proceeded without significant interruption for four and a half months.

There were individual incidents from time to time, produced in part by the unconventional life style and political activism of the defendants: Rubin was cited twice for wearing judicial robes in court; Hoffman, for blowing kisses to the jury and asking the court, "How is your war stock doing"; Dellinger, for requesting a moment of silence on Moratorium Day; and all of the defendants were cited for interrupting the court or making comments on political subjects or the proceedings. At the very end of the trial, immediately after the jury was charged, Judge Hoffman handed down a total of 159 citations for contempt, 121 against the defendants other than Seale and 38 against the two lawyers. The largest single category (36 citations) consisted of defendants refusing to rise at the beginning or close of a court session. In 27 cases they called the judge a name or accused him of prejudice or injustice or made sarcastic comments to him, mostly arising from the incidents described above. In 10 cases they interrupted or insulted the prosecution, and in 11 cases they applauded or laughed in the courtroom.

On May 11, 1972, all the contempt convictions of the defendants and the lawyers were reversed by the Seventh Circuit Court of Appeals. The appellate court held that the judge cannot wait until the end of the trial to punish the defendants and the lawyers.

> ... the trial judge must disqualify himself if he waits to act until the conclusion of the trial. When the trial proceedings have terminated, the need for proceeding summarily is not present.

The court also determined that Bobby Seale could not be punished summarily by the judge.

The court of appeals sent the case back to the district court level for retrial of the contempt before a judge other than Judge Hoffman....

GEOFFREY C. HAZARD, JR.
"SECURING COURTROOM DECORUM"
80 Yale L.J. 433 (1970).[10]

The spectacle of United States v. Dellinger, has impelled two distinguished organizations of the legal profession to promulgate rules designed to secure courtroom decorum. In July, 1970, the American College of Trial Lawyers, through a special Committee on Disruption of the Judicial Process, published its Report and Recommendations. In January, 1971, the American Bar Association received a report on Standards Relating to the Function of a Trial Judge from its Advisory Committee on the Judge's Function, a constituent of the ABA's Project on Standards for Criminal Justice.

. . .

---

10. Copyright © 1970 by the Yale Law Journal Company, Inc. Reprinted by permission.

... [The intertwined problems of judicial intemperance and lawyer misconduct] are difficult to solve simply because the possible remedies and sanctions by which to control them are so limited as compared to those which may be invoked against a litigant or spectator. A disruptive spectator may simply be excluded from the trial. Members of the news media can be excluded if their presence intrudes on calm and orderly procedure.... As to litigants, Illinois v. Allen [32] has now made clear that a defendant's presence at trial is a right that can be denied if he refuses to conform to elemental requirements of courtroom decorum. Accordingly, where a litigant's disturbances obstruct fulfillment of his opportunity to participate, he may be excluded and his trial conducted in absentia. But while in special circumstances bystanders and even litigants can be dispensed with and a trial still be held, the same is not true of the judge nor, in an adversary system, of counsel. In the extraordinary case that would test our definition of a trial, they are the primary participants.[33]

A. Who Adjudicates?

The central question at the stage of adjudicating a contempt is who shall preside. The ABA Report's proposal is equivocal. It says that the trial judge may ordinarily hear the contempt, but provides for referral where "his conduct was so integrated with the alleged contempt that he contributed to it or was otherwise involved, or his objectivity can for any reason plausibly be questioned." [34] As applied to misconduct by lawyers, the exception nearly swallows the rule.... [For example,] where a lawyer's trial conduct has been grossly disruptive, it may have been that the judge's efforts to control the trial were simply ineffectual, which is itself an involvement of a very disturbing kind, or were even provocative, which is also a form of involvement. Putting the matter differently, under the ABA proposal arguments suggest themselves that would render legally infirm any attempt by the trial judge to hear a contempt except in the most clear-cut instances. Those are not the cases that test a code.

32. 397 U.S. 337 (1970).

33. The defendant who represents himself would still be subject to the *Allen* requirements of maintaining elementary decorum, and could be excluded if he, after proper warning, continued to disrupt the trial. In that case the court would presumably endeavor to appoint counsel, even over defendant's objection. *Cf.* Mayberry v. Pennsylvania, 400 U.S. 455, 468 (1971) (concurring opinion); ABA Report, Standards C.2, C.3, and C.4.

34. ABA Report, Standard F.5. The Supreme Court has recently given substantial support to this approach to hearing courtroom contempts. In Mayberry v. Pennsylvania, 400 U.S. 455 (1971), the Court reversed the contempt sentence of a defendant who represented himself, noting that "[w]here ... [a judge] does not act the instant the contempt is committed, but waits until the end of the trial, on balance, it is generally wise where the marks of the unseemly conduct have left personal stings to ask a fellow judge to take his place." Id. at 504. At the end of its opinion, the Court also stated an apparently broader rule: "Our conclusion is that by reason of the Due Process Clause of the Fourteenth Amendment a defendant in criminal contempt proceedings should be given a public trial before a judge other than the one reviled by the contemnor." Id. at 466.

The Trial Lawyers Report does not attempt considered analysis of the question of who should preside at the contempt hearing. The position taken is the traditional one that the trial judge should conduct the hearing. The Report recognizes that the trial judge may refer the matter to another judge but its commentary disaffirms and even disparages such a possibility.

The Trial Lawyers Report concedes that "some persons are troubled by the thought of a judge acting not only in that capacity [as judge] but also as accuser and prosecutor" and responds by saying that the trial judge has the responsibility to "keep a case moving" and to "keep it under control at all times." The response is true but irrelevant: the police have the duty to keep a crowd moving and to keep it under control, but we do not for that reason give them exclusive authority to punish misconduct at a police line. Perhaps recognizing the weakness of this response, the Trial Lawyers Report goes on to suggest that impartiality in adjudicating the contempt can be secured through appeal....

This must be one of the few occasions where an association of barristers has argued that a fair appeal procedure is a sufficient corrective for an apparently biased trial procedure. There are other paradoxes in the argument. The assumption that an appeal will be taken contradicts the assumption that summary determination is essential. Treating the trial court contempt conviction as in effect only an indictment returnable in the appellate court denigrates the tribunal whose stature is sought to be enhanced....

Contemplation of these consequences leads one to reconsider the premises. Why shouldn't the traditional view be abandoned and instead the rule adopted that lawyer contempts shall be heard by another judge, if possible one from another locality? Administering such a rule would not entail much additional cost, unless it is supposed that a summary contempt conviction can rest solely on the trial judge's memory of the events at issue—a procedure which would be the ultimate form of trial *in camera*.[37] Requiring a contempt hearing to be held by another judge expresses the same principle as the rule which bars a judge from hearing a case in which he has a financial or familial interest, and recognizes that professional probity is at least as precious to a judge as money or kinship.

What would be lost? If the trial judge was fair and the lawyer intemperate, what clearer vindication of the judge? If the judge was not fair or the lawyer not intemperate, what surer vindication of the

---

37. Both federal and state law require the presiding judge to support a summary contempt conviction with some record of the incidents in question. In federal courts, Rule 42(a) of the Federal Rules of Criminal Procedure provides that: "A criminal contempt may be punished summarily if the judge certifies that he saw or heard the conduct constituting the contempt and that it was committed in the actual presence of the court. The order of contempt shall recite the facts and shall be signed by the judge and entered of record." The general rule applicable in most states is that "the record must set out the proceedings of the lower court and the facts which support its jurisdiction and constitute the contempt." 17 C.J.S. *Contempt* § 122 (1963).

lawyer? The adversary method of eliciting facts can be employed before another trial judge but is unavailable in an appellate court—is the adversary method less useful when the complaining witness is a judge? Is the ugly spectacle of judging the judges more repugnant than refusing to subject them to searching judgment? One can almost hear the anxious rejoinder welling up only to be suppressed by awareness of its implication: what if most, or all, of these lawyer contempt citations were found to be unwarranted? What, indeed?

C. Trial Procedures

. . .

The ... Trial Lawyers Report [proposes] that the lawyer has the obligation

> to advise any client appearing in a courtroom of the kind of behavior expected and required of him there, and to prevent him, so far as lies within the lawyer's power, from creating disorder or disruption in the courtroom.

The reach of the duty is not elaborated. It is not stated, for example, what a lawyer is supposed to do if the client persistently misbehaves despite his advice to the contrary. The Manson case in Los Angeles Superior Court presents that problem and suggests that it is no real answer to say the lawyer should resign from the case, for what will his successor do? But if the outer limits of the duty are imprecise the same is not true of its initial form: the lawyer should tell his client to behave himself, and do so with sincerity or at least its verisimilitude.

Of late it has been argued otherwise—that his client's courtroom conduct is none of the lawyer's business. The contention is that the lawyer is but an agent, that the client as principal can have his case presented any way he wants to, and that the agent's responsibility ends with giving the principal advice. More fundamentally, it is suggested that there are cases where the defendant's style is itself on trial and in such cases the defendant has, as it were, a right of affirmative defense.

There is something to this. The client does have certain procedural initiatives which the advocate can neither waive nor exercise on the client's behalf: the right to speak before pronouncement of sentence, the right to advice on consequences before tendering a guilty plea, the right to be present and to confront witnesses, and perhaps the right to testify against his counsel's advice. Furthermore, the hippy or yippy defendant has a right to insist that the impartiality by which he is adjudged not depend on changing his life-style *pendente lite*, just as the poor man should not have to change his clothes nor the black man his skin. It is also no doubt true that judges and prosecutors often confuse *dishabille* with disorder and perceive loud mannerisms as literally making noise.

When due allowance is made for all these considerations, however, the fact is that we have witnessed some trials in which the defendants have talked when they should have been silent, moved about when they should have been seated, gesticulated when they should have been in repose. The lawyer's duty to admonish his clients against such misbehavior is sometimes supported by the argument that he has special leverage on them and should use it to help his professional colleague on the bench in keeping order. There is truth in this but also odium, particularly to the members of a generation that is highly and understandably sensitive to manipulation. The lawyer's duty to admonish his clients surely rests on more substantial ground than that as an officer of the court he is also one of its bailiffs.

The duty, it may be suggested, is a component of the lawyer's own role as advocate. The role of advocate is that of speaking to questions of law and fact in a particular kind of forum in accordance with specified opportunities and sequences. It would be quite clear that the lawyer could not play his role if whenever he tried to speak he was ignored, or interrupted or drowned out by a bullhorn. The lawyer's part, however, is not soliloquy but—the pun is irresistible—a trialogue, a series of ordered exchanges with the judge and opposing counsel. If the judge and opposing counsel cannot speak without disruption or hindrance, then the lawyer's appearances and cues are lost or disordered and at some point his role and reason for being there simply collapse. If the advocate does not contribute to sustaining these forensic requirements, he has to that extent abdicated his role and literally has no place in the performance. And if he does not believe in his role and cannot live it, he should seek another calling, just as an atheist should leave the priesthood.

The same, of course, goes for the judge and the prosecutor. To some who observed the "Chicago Eight" trial, one of the appalling things was the noisome patter of witticism and jokes by Judge Hoffman. It is conceivable that if he had consistently avoided playing it like a minstrel show, the defendants might not have played it like a circus.

Courtroom Order in the Political Trial

The immediate inspiration of the recommendations by the Trial Lawyers and the ABA was a "political" trial. Their appositeness to that kind of dispute requires brief further analysis.

A political trial is one in which the defendants—they are usually plural—are tried for conduct that is interpreted by them and by the community at large as a challenge to the legitimacy of the political order. The conduct may be pure challenge, such as advocating overthrow of the government, or a challenge manifested in conduct that is independently unlawful, such as a riot or sit-in. When uttered, the challenge constitutes an appeal to some public or other for support. The subsequent trial is of itself conclusive evidence that the challenge failed, for if it succeeded the defendants would have been vindicated and not face prosecution.

From the viewpoint of the challenged authority, the issues in a political trial are defined by its positive law: whether the challenge enjoys the immunity afforded to free speech; whether all defendants were accomplices to the illegal elements of the enterprise; whether, regarding challenges expressed as action, there were excuses or justifications such as antecedent illegal action by officials; and so on. From the viewpoint of the defendants, however, these are only some of the issues. If the defendants desire exoneration, their surest recourse is not legal defense but public contrition, for in that event there would usually be no trial. A political case that goes to trial is one in which the defendants have counterclaims.

The counterclaims in a political trial are based on a maddening combination of transcendental political or ethical issues and procedural technicality. One counterclaim is that the regime—all of it or the part directly involved in the altercation—is illegitimate according to some theory of political justice so that the actions of its officials are not clothed with legal authority and therefore amount to naked coercion. A subsidiary count is that the court trying the case is part of the illegal system and that its proceeding is a juridical pretension and a farce, as indeed it is if the premise is accepted.

The second counterclaim is that the court will not try the case with proper observance of its own legal procedure. This claim depends on technical and sometimes hypertechnical interpretation of procedural law and may involve tactics which seek to make it a self-fulfilling prophecy. Like the first counterclaim, it asserts that the court is not really a court. But the second counterclaim is supported by an argument which is diametrically opposite to that supporting the first counterclaim. The argument is that according to the tribunal's own law, the tribunal is not functioning as one.

A political trial thus involves two and perhaps three concurrent proceedings. In the "straight" one, the prosecutor is the accuser, the defendants are the accused and the judge and jury are arbiters. In the trial of defendants' first counterclaim, the defendants are the accusers, the prosecutor and the judge (and sometimes the jury) are the accused, and the arbiter is indefinitely the jury (hence the struggles at voir dire), the defendants' circle of sympathizers, the world at large, or history. The alignment of the parties is the same in the defendants' second counterclaim except that the arbiter is the appellate courts.

The confusion over the participants' position is confounded by evidentiary problems. The evidence for the government in a political trial consists largely of the defendants' utterances—writings, speeches, discussions. These are what actuated the prosecution in the first place and what constitute the legal basis for regarding the defendants' conduct as peculiarly wrongful. Hence, in putting on its case the prosecution inevitably rebroadcasts the defendants' challenge of the regime and thus introduces evidence which defendants regard as relevant to their first counterclaim, that the tribunal is illegitimate. Defining the proper scope of these proofs involves continual rulings that are subject to the claim of prejudicial error. Sometimes the defendants seek to introduce even fuller accounts of their utterances. If this effort is successful, it buttresses their first counterclaim; if it is unsuccessful, it buttresses the contention that the court is not trying the case fairly.

The proceeding as a whole is thus suffused with ambiguity: proofs consisting of speeches, which bear simultaneously on issues that have been pleaded and others that have not been, which are punctuated by evidentiary and procedural issues laden with double or triple meaning, which are advanced by participants who are intermittently forgetful that the conflict encompasses the agenda and their respective roles. Rules that clarify the official roles and responsibilities in the hearing of such a case can help define the issues in the underlying struggle over whether the official version of the proceedings shall prevail. Reaffirmation of the contempt power confirms the consequences if the established order does prevail. The established order, however, by its own terms cannot win the struggle by the threatening mechanisms of legal prescription and penal sanction. It can win only through steadfast and unpretentious fulfillment of official roles, especially that of the judge. In the emphasis it tries to give this aspect of the problem, the ABA Report may have made a particularly important contribution. At the same time, it is well to recognize that the struggles represented in political trials will not disappear until fundamental political dissension also disappears. That day may be less welcome than many might think.

———————

On the obligation to provide representation to "unpopular" clients, see Model Rule 1.2(b) and its comment; see also EC 7–9 and EC 7–17.[11]

Lawyer as Revolutionary

During the 1960s Professor Richard Wasserstrom addressed the relationship of the lawyer to radical or revolutionary programs.[12]

> [L]awyers and revolution don't mix especially well.... [T]he legal system—any legal system—is an essentially conservative institution [in a fundamental sense].... First, the law is conservative in the same way in which language is conservative. It seeks to assimilate everything that happens to that which has happened.... Thus the lawyer's virtually instinctive intellectual response when he is confronted with a situation is to look for the

11. See also Mark Green, The Other Government 270–88 (1975); Abe Krash, Professional Responsibility to Clients and the Public Interest: Is There a Conflict?, 55 Chicago Bar Record 31 (1974); Andrew L. Kaufman, Introduction: A Professional Agenda, 6 Hofstra L.Rev. 619 (1978) (describing how the ethics rules embody and have always embodied a tension between the obligation owed one's client and the obligation owed to the public at large).

12. Richard Wasserstrom, Lawyers and Revolution, 30 U.Pitt.L.Rev. 125 (1968).

respects in which that situation is like something that is familiar and that has a place within the realm of understood legal doctrine. . . . [P]ersons who are genuinely concerned with far-reaching and radical . . . solutions to social ills ought to be on guard against and ought to mistrust this powerful tendency on the part of the lawyer to transmogrify what is new into what has gone before or to reject as unworkable or unintelligible what cannot be so modified.

The second way in which the law is conservative comes about through the very basic character of the lawyer qua lawyer. . . . First, there is the obvious, but important, fact that when an individual is a lawyer he is playing an institutional role. As such, there are all sorts of explicit and implicit constraints upon his thought and action. As a *lawyer*, there are some things he simply cannot do—without ceasing to play the role of a lawyer. . . . Second, the lawyer qua advocate plays an essentially non-critical role. The very essence of the lawyer's institutional role is to submerge himself in his clients' position and to represent that interest in the legal arena as forcefully as possible. . . . [B]eing an advocate in our legal system—where one does not or need not choose one's causes—encourages a non-critical, non-evaluative, uncommitted state of mind. . . .

. . . The attorney's role is intimately connected with securing for his client the greatest possible advantage that can be wrung for him from the institutional system. Paradoxically enough, this leads not to the single-mindedness of purpose that so typically characterizes the revolutionary and the radical, but leads rather to a penchant for compromise, accord and accommodation. The attorney is in many respects the system's broker. . . . [T]he processes of litigation and adjudication derive from and are infected by the model of the market place in which a good bargain consists in each of the parties making concessions and compromises.

[The lawyer's cast of mind] is at best neutral and more typically uncongenial to that of the revolutionary's. . . . The revolutionary may, for instance, simply not be interested in winning in any conventional sense. Or, he may be interested in winning if and only if certain very special conditions obtain. In either case, the tension that is latent in the lawyer's whole approach to problems becomes manifest and intense.

. . . [T]he lawyer's ambitions to try to get the best he can for client *within the legal order* can be not so much inconsistent with his client's interest as genuinely corruptive of them. For there are innumerable situations in which the lawyer's inclination to take what he can get leads to the compromise of interests and rights about which no accommodation ought ever be tolerated.

. . .

[T]he third major issue that falls within the heading of the lawyer and revolution . . . [is] whether we ought to be radical in respect to the law, and if so, of what such radicalism would consist.... [I]t is not very easy or very sensible to be radical in respect to the *idea* of a legal system.... The trouble begins when we move beyond ... [ameliorative] proposals to genuinely radical suggestions for social innovation and change.... [We can't get along without law or lawyers and intermediate steps, such as getting rid of the adversary system, are] an extraordinarily difficult undertaking, particularly for lawyers.[13]

In 1981 Professor Duncan Kennedy urged Harvard law students to subvert the "demonic" and "antisocial" practice of corporate law from within.[14] A leftist student might take actions within the corporate law firm, such as refusing to work on cases that are offensive to one's beliefs.

... I'm not advocating self-immolation—more like sly, collective tactics within the institution where you work, to confront, outflank, sabotage or manipulate the bad guys and build the possibility of something better.

... What I am suggesting is the politicization of corporate law practice, which means doing things and not doing things in order to serve left purposes, not because they fit or don't fit the Canons. The point is to turn down clients because they want you ... to delay implementation of environmental controls, even though it's all totally within the law. But the point also is to reconceive the internal issues of firm hierarchy as an important part of one's political life, fighting the oligarchy of senior partners, opposing the oppression of secretaries by arrogant young men who turn around and grovel before their mentors....

... If you fight now, if you come to stand for something now, you'll be able to make things different when you own the place.

... If you think before you act, if you are subtle, collusive, skillful and tricky, if you use confrontation when confrontation will work, you should able to do left office politics without being fired, and make partner.[15]

Among the many responses provoked by Kennedy's article was one from a Harvard colleague, Detlev Vagts: [16]

... In brief, the radical lawyer of 1982 has three choices: to go to a corporate law firm and resist through "sly" tactics, to go there and resist openly or to go somewhere else. I take Professor Kennedy to advise the first, though the layers of irony are so thick as to obscure the message. I would disagree. The disadvantages of the "sly" alternative start with the short-range problem that it is

13. Id. at 128–33.

14. Duncan Kennedy, Rebels from Principle: Changing the Corporate Law Firm from Within, Harvard L.S.Bull. 36 (Fall 1981).

15. Id. at 36, 37, 39.

16. Harv.L.S.Bull. (Winter 1991).

unlikely to work, given the perceptiveness of the opposition. It certainly won't work a second time. Meanwhile, the practice of using subtle and tricky messages corrupts one's ability to communicate with anybody....

One can combine mild reformism with work in a high pressure law practice but one simply cannot survive in it if one is involved in a constant series of battles of conscience over what one is asked to do.

... One is left, then, with going elsewhere and taking up the very difficult task of building or creating a left organization.... [T]here are organizations—law firms, law communes, some government offices, some parts of law school faculties—that offer beginnings.... [T]his is where the talented young radical lawyer belongs. To hold out the alternative that one can keep one's leftist conscience and "still make partner" is to disguise an inescapable dilemma. Those who think that they can have both through a few sly schemes are likely to end up as weary court jesters in motley shaking their bells at the passing parade.[17]

2. Free Speech Rights of Lawyers

The degree of protection accorded to lawyer speech depends upon the context in which the speech occurs. Statements made by a lawyer in the course of representation of a client are protected by common law privilege. An absolute privilege protects statements made in or reasonably related to a judicial proceeding.[18] A qualified privilege protects statements in the course of representation outside of judicial proceedings.[19] See the discussion of these privileges in Chapter 5 above at p. 412.

In other contexts, however, lawyers are accorded less protection for their speech than nonlawyers. Lawyers' free speech issues arise in several recurring contexts. Disruptive and improper speech in the courtroom itself, discussed in the materials above, may be punished by civil or criminal contempt or by professional discipline. The materials below deal with, first, public comment about pending cases; second, extrajudicial comments of lawyers about judges generally or the administration of justice; and third, public criticism of particular judges.

---

17. Id. at 30.

18. See Restatement (Second) of Torts § 586; W. Prosser and P. Keeton on Torts § 114 (5th ed. 1984); e.g., DeVivo v. Ascher, 228 N.J.Super. 453, 550 A.2d 163 (1988) ("We ... favor a broad interpretation of the phrase 'in the course of a judicial proceeding.' ").

19. See Restatement (Second) of Torts § 595, Comment d; W. Prosser and P. Keeton, supra, § 115.

Public Comment About Pending Cases

GENTILE v. STATE BAR OF NEVADA

Supreme Court of the United States, 1991.
___ U.S. ___, 111 S.Ct. 2720, 115 L.Ed.2d 888.

CHIEF JUSTICE REHNQUIST delivered the opinion of the court with respect to parts I and II, and delivered a dissenting opinion with respect to part III in which Justice White, Justice Scalia, and Justice Souter have joined.

Petitioner was disciplined for making statements to the press about a pending case in which he represented a criminal defendant. The State Bar, and the Supreme Court of Nevada on review, found that petitioner knew or should have known that there was a substantial likelihood that his statements would materially prejudice the trial of his client. Nonetheless, petitioner contends that the First Amendment to the United States Constitution requires a stricter standard to be met before such speech by an attorney may be disciplined: there must be a finding of "actual prejudice or a substantial and imminent threat to fair trial." ... We conclude that the "substantial likelihood of material prejudice" standard applied by Nevada and most other states satisfies the First Amendment.

I

Petitioner's client was the subject of a highly publicized case, and in response to adverse publicity about his client, Gentile held a press conference on the day after Sanders was indicted. At the press conference, petitioner made, among others, the following statements:

> "When this case goes to trial, and as it develops, you're going to see that the evidence will prove not only that Grady Sanders is an innocent person and had nothing to do with any of the charges that are being leveled against him, but that the person that was in the most direct position to have stolen the drugs and the money, the American Express Travelers' checks, is Detective Steve Scholl.

> "There is far more evidence that will establish that Detective Scholl took these drugs and took these American Express Travelers' checks than any other living human being."

[Petitioner also stated at the press conference that a number of the witnesses against his client were "known drug dealers and convicted money launderers;" that his client was "an innocent man;" and he implied that Detective Scholl was a drug user.]

Articles appeared in the local newspapers describing the press conference and petitioner's statements. The trial took place approximately six months later, and although the trial court succeeded in empaneling a jury that had not been affected by the media coverage and Sanders was acquitted on all charges, the state bar disciplined petitioner for his statements.

The Southern Nevada Disciplinary Board found that petitioner knew the detective he accused of perpetrating the crime and abusing drugs would be a witness for the prosecution. It also found that petitioner believed others whom he characterized as money launderers and drug dealers would be called as prosecution witnesses. Petitioner's admitted purpose for calling the press conference was to counter public opinion which he perceived as adverse to his client, to fight back against the perceived efforts of the prosecution to poison the prospective juror pool, and to publicly present his client's side of the case. The Board found that in light of the statements, their timing, and petitioner's purpose, petitioner knew or should have known that there was a substantial likelihood that the statements would materially prejudice the Sanders trial.

The Nevada Supreme Court affirmed the Board's decision, finding by clear and convincing evidence that petitioner "knew or reasonably should have known that his comments had a substantial likelihood of materially prejudicing the adjudication of his client's case." Gentile v. State Bar of Nevada, 106 Nev. 60, ___, 787 P.2d 386, 387 (1990). The court noted that the case was "highly publicized"; that the press conference, held the day after the indictment and the same day as the arraignment, was "timed to have maximum impact"; and that petitioner's comments "related to the character, credibility, reputation or criminal record of the police detective and other potential witnesses." The court concluded that the "absence of actual prejudice does not establish that there was no substantial likelihood of material prejudice."

II

[The Court first summarized the history of the efforts of bar and public groups to balance fair trial concerns against free speech interests.]

When the Model Rules of Professional Conduct were drafted in the early 1980's, the drafters ... adopted the "substantial likelihood of material prejudice" test. Currently, 31 States in addition to Nevada have adopted—either verbatim or with insignificant variations—Rule 3.6 of the ABA's Model Rules. Eleven States have adopted Disciplinary Rule 7–107 of the ABA's Code of Professional Responsibility, which is less protective of lawyer speech than Model Rule 3.6, in that it applies a "reasonable likelihood of prejudice" standard. Only one State, Virginia has explicitly adopted a clear and present danger standard, while four States and the District of Columbia have adopted standards that arguably approximate "clear and present danger."

Petitioner maintains, however, that the First Amendment to the United States Constitution requires a State, such as Nevada in this case, to demonstrate a "clear and present danger" of "actual prejudice or an imminent threat" before any discipline may be imposed on a lawyer who initiates a press conference such as occurred here.[4] He relies on decisions such as Nebraska Press Assn. v. Stuart, 427 U.S. 539 (1976), Bridges v. California, 314 U.S. 252 (1941), Pennekamp v. Florida, 323 U.S. 331 (1946), and Craig v. Harney, 331 U.S. 367 (1947), to support his position. In those cases we held that trial courts might not constitutionally punish, through use of the contempt power, newspapers and others for publishing editorials, cartoons, and other items critical of judges in particular cases. We held that such punishments could be imposed only if there were a clear and present danger of "some serious substantive evil which they are designed to avert." Bridges v. California, supra, 314 U.S., at 270. Petitioner also relies on Wood v. Georgia, 370 U.S. 375 (1962), which held that a court might not punish a sheriff for publicly criticizing a judge's charges to a grand jury.

.... [N]one of these cases involved lawyers who represented parties to a pending proceeding in court....

.... [T]he theory upon which our criminal justice system is founded [is that] the outcome of a criminal trial is to be decided by impartial jurors, who know as little as possible of the case, based on material admitted into evidence before them in a court proceeding. Extrajudicial comments on, or discussion of, evidence which might never be admitted at trial and *ex parte* statements by counsel giving their version of the facts obviously threaten to undermine this basic tenet.

At the same time, however, the criminal justice system exists in a larger context of a government ultimately of the people, who wish to be informed about happenings in the criminal justice system, and, if sufficiently informed about those happenings might wish to make changes in the system. The way most of them acquire information is from the media. The First Amendment protections of speech and press have been held, in the cases cited above, to require a showing of "clear and present danger" that a malfunction in the criminal justice system will be caused before a State may prohibit media speech or publication about a particular pending trial. The question we must answer in this case is whether a lawyer who represents a defendant involved with the criminal justice system may insist on the same standard before he is disciplined for public pronouncements about the case, or whether the State instead may penalize that sort of speech upon a lesser showing.

It is unquestionable that in the courtroom itself, during a judicial proceeding, whatever right to "free speech" an attorney has is extremely circumscribed. An attorney may not, by speech or other conduct, resist a ruling of the trial court beyond the point necessary to preserve a claim for appeal. Sacher v. United States, 343 U.S. 1, 8 (1952) (criminal trial); Fisher v. Pace, 336 U.S. 155 (1949) (civil trial). Even outside the courtroom, a majority of the Court in two separate opinions in the case of In re Sawyer, 360 U.S. 622 (1959), observed that lawyers

4. ... Petitioner challenged Rule 177 as being unconstitutional on its face in addition to as applied.... The validity of the rules in the many states applying the "substantial likelihood of material prejudice" test has, therefore, been called into question in this case.

in pending cases were subject to ethical restrictions on speech to which an ordinary citizen would not be....

Likewise, in Sheppard v. Maxwell, where the defendant's conviction was overturned because extensive prejudicial pretrial publicity had denied the defendant a fair trial, we held that a new trial was a remedy for such publicity, but

> "we must remember that reversals are but palliatives; the cure lies in those remedial measures that will prevent the prejudice at its inception. The courts must take such steps by rule and regulation that will protect their processes from prejudicial outside interferences. Neither prosecutors, counsel for defense, the accused, witnesses, court staff nor enforcement officers coming under the jurisdiction of the court should be permitted to frustrate its function. *Collaboration between counsel and the press as to information affecting the fairness of a criminal trial is not only subject to regulation, but is highly censurable and worthy of disciplinary measures.*" 384 U.S., at 363 (emphasis added).

We expressly contemplated that the speech of *those participating before the courts* could be limited. This distinction between participants in the litigation and strangers to it is brought into sharp relief by our holding in Seattle Times Co. v. Rhinehart, 467 U.S. 20 (1984). There, we unanimously held that a newspaper, which was itself a defendant in a libel action, could be restrained from publishing material about the plaintiffs and their supporters to which it had gained access through court-ordered discovery. In that case we said that "[a]lthough litigants do not 'surrender their First Amendment rights at the courthouse door,' those rights may be subordinated to other interests that arise in this setting," id., at 32–33, n. 18, (citation omitted), and noted that "on several occasions [we have] approved restriction on the communications of trial participants where necessary to ensure a fair trial for a criminal defendant." Ibid.

. . .

We think that the quoted statements from our opinions in In re Sawyer, 360 U.S. 622 (1959), and Sheppard v. Maxwell, supra, rather plainly indicate that the speech of lawyers representing clients in pending cases may be regulated under a less demanding standard than that established for regulation of the press in Nebraska Press Assn. v. Stuart, 427 U.S. 539 (1976), and the cases which preceded it. Lawyers representing clients in pending cases are key participants in the criminal justice system, and the State may demand some adherence to the precepts of that system in regulating their speech as well as their conduct. As noted by Justice Brennan in his concurring opinion in *Nebraska Press*, which was joined by Justices Stewart and Marshall, "[a]s officers of the court, court personnel and attorneys have a fiduciary responsibility not to engage in public debate that will redound to the detriment of the accused or that will obstruct the fair administration of justice." 427 U.S., at 601, n. 27. Because lawyers have special access to information through discovery and client communications, their extrajudicial statements pose a threat to the fairness of appending proceeding since lawyers' statements are likely to be received as especially authoritative. See, e.g., In re Hinds, 90 N.J. 604, 627, 449 A.2d 483, 496 (1982) (statements by attorneys of record relating to the case "are likely to be considered knowledgeable, reliable and true" because of attorneys' unique access to information); In re Rachmiel, 90 N.J. 646, 656, 449 A.2d 505, 511 (N.J.1982) (attorneys' role as advocates gives them "extraordinary power to undermine or destroy the efficacy of the criminal justice system"). We agree with the majority of the States that the "substantial likelihood of material prejudice" standard constitutes a constitutionally permissible balance between the First Amendment rights of attorneys in pending cases and the state's interest in fair trials.

Balancing Rights
-limiting test to substantial likelihood of material prejudice is appropriate when balancing states interest in fair trials.

When a state regulation implicates First Amendment rights, the Court must balance those interests against the State's legitimate interest in regulating the activity in question. See, *e.g., Seattle Times,* supra, 467 U.S. at 32. The "substantial likelihood" test embodied in Rule 177 is constitutional under this analysis, for it is designed to protect the integrity and fairness of a state's judicial system, and it imposes only narrow and necessary limitations on lawyers' speech. The limitations are aimed at two principal evils: (1) comments that are likely to influence the actual outcome of the trial, and (2) comments that are likely to prejudice the jury venire, even if an untainted panel can ultimately be found. Few, if any, interests under the Constitution are more fundamental than the right to a fair trial by "impartial" jurors, and an outcome affected by extrajudicial statements would violate that fundamental right. See, e.g., *Sheppard,* 384 U.S., at 350–351; Turner v. Louisiana, 379 U.S. 466, 473 (1965) (evidence in criminal trial must come solely from witness stand in public courtroom with full evidentiary protections). Even if a fair trial can ultimately be ensured through voir dire, change of venue, or some other device, these measures entail serious costs to the system. Extensive voir dire may not be able to filter out all of the effects of pretrial publicity, and with increasingly widespread media coverage of criminal trials, a change of venue may not suffice to undo the effects of statements such as those made by petitioner. The State has a substantial interest in preventing officers of the court, such as lawyers, from imposing such costs on the judicial system and on the litigants.

The restraint on speech is narrowly tailored to achieve those objectives. The regulation of attorneys' speech is limited—it applies only to speech that is substantially likely to have a materially prejudicial effect; it is neutral as to points of view, applying equally to all attorneys participating in a pending case; and it merely postpones the attorney's comments until after the trial. While supported by the substantial state interest in preventing prejudice to an adjudicative proceeding by those who have a duty to protect its integrity, the rule is limited on its face to preventing only speech having a substantial likelihood of materially prejudicing that proceeding.

[Part III of Chief Justice Rehnquist's opinion, which was joined by three other justices, argued that Model Rule 3.6 was not overbroad or void for vagueness. "The Rule provides sufficient notice of the nature of the prohibited conduct." M.R. 3.6(c), allowing an attorney to state "the general nature of the claim or defense," uses terms of degree ("general" and "elaboration"), but "convey[s] the very definite proposition that the authorized statements must not contain the sort of detailed allegations that petitioner made at his press conference" (referring to the specific charges against Detective Scholl and the other witnesses).]

JUSTICE KENNEDY announced the judgment of the Court and delivered the opinion of the court with respect to Parts III and VI, and an opinion with respect to Parts I, II, IV, and V in which JUSTICE MARSHALL, JUSTICE BLACKMUN and JUSTICE STEVENS join.

[In Parts I and II of his opinion, joined by three other justices, Justice Kennedy argued that the standard stated in M.R. 3.6 might be interpreted to be consistent with the "clear and present danger" test, but Nevada's interpretation and application of it violated the First Amendment. Petitioner's actions were preceded by pre-indictment publicity by law enforcement officials that were damaging to his client; in holding the press conference, petitioner acted deliberately and after investigating the ethics rule; at the conference he refused to elaborate on his description of his client's defense; most of the information in his "abbreviated, general comments six months before trial" had been published in one form or another. "There is no support for the conclusion that petitioner's statement created a likelihood of material prejudice, or indeed of any harm of sufficient magnitude or imminence to support a punishment of speech."]

III

As interpreted by the Nevada Supreme Court, the Rule is void for vagueness, in any event, for its safe harbor provision, Rule 177(3), misled petitioner into thinking that he could give his press conference without fear of discipline. Rule 177(3)(a) provides that a lawyer "may state without elaboration . . . the general nature of the . . . defense." Statements under this provision are protected "[n]otwithstanding subsection 1 and 2(a-f)." By necessary operation of the word "notwithstanding," the Rule contemplates that a lawyer describing the "general nature of the . . . defense" "without elaboration" need fear no discipline, even if he comments on "[t]he character, credibility, reputation or criminal record of a . . . witness," and even if he "knows or reasonably should know that [the statement] will have a substantial likelihood of materially prejudicing an adjudicative proceeding."

Given this grammatical structure, and absent any clarifying interpretation by the state court, the Rule fails to provide " 'fair notice to those to whom [it] is directed.' " Grayned v. City of Rockford, 408 U.S. 104, 112 (1972).   A lawyer seeking to avail himself of Rule 177(3)'s protection must guess at its contours.   The right to explain the "general" nature of the defense without "elaboration" provides insufficient guidance because "general" and "elaboration" are both classic terms of degree.   In the context before us, these terms have no settled usage or tradition of interpretation in law.   The lawyer has no principle for determining when his remarks pass from the safe harbor of the general to the forbidden sea of the elaborated.

. . .

. . . The fact Gentile was found in violation of the Rules after studying them and making a conscious effort at compliance demonstrates that Rule 177 creates a trap for the wary as well as the unwary.

The prohibition against vague regulations of speech is based in part on the need to eliminate the impermissible risk of discriminatory enforcement, Kolender v. Lawson, 461 U.S. 352, 357–358, 361 (1983); Smith v. Goguen, 415 U.S. 566, 572–573 (1974), for history shows that speech is suppressed when either the speaker or the message is critical of those who enforce the law.   The question is not whether discriminatory enforcement occurred here, and we assume it did not, but whether the Rule is so imprecise that discriminatory enforcement is a real possibility.   The inquiry is of particular relevance when one of the classes most affected by the regulation is the criminal defense bar, which has the professional mission to challenge actions of the State. Petitioner, for instance, succeeded in preventing the conviction of his client, and the speech in issue involved criticism of the government.

. . .

Notes on *Gentile*

Was there a "substantial likelihood" that lawyer Gentile's televised charges would "materially prejudice" the impending trial?   Note that Gentile charged that a police detective was responsible for the crime with which his client had been indicted and that specific prosecution witnesses were "money launderers and drug dealers."   Should a "clear and present danger" test be applied rather than the looser test of "substantial likelihood of material prejudice" to an adjudication?   Are the "safe-harbor" provisions of Model Rule 3.6(c) unconstitutionally vague, as Justice Kennedy and four of his colleagues held?

The ABA is in the process of amending Model Rule 3.6 to conform to the *Gentile* case.   In February 1994 the ABA House of Delegates will consider a proposed amendment to M.R. 3.6 submitted by the ABA Standing Committee on Ethics and Professional Responsibility.   The proposed amendment eliminates the "safe harbor" language of M.R. 3.6(c) which was found to be unconstitutionally vague in *Gentile,* and deletes from the black-letter rule the itemized lists of permissible and impermissible extrajudicial statements now contained in M.R. 3.6(b) and (c). The resulting black-letter rule thus would consist only of what is now M.R. 3.6(a). The lists of permissible and impermissible statements would be transferred to the amended rule's comment as guidelines.

Extrajudicial Criticism of Administration of Justice

Legal systems invariably require or expect lawyers to treat judges with courtesy and respect. Deference to judges is part of the ritual aspect of public judicial proceedings and contributes to their public acceptance and legitimacy. Lawyers who participate in these public ceremonies conform themselves to the tribunal's customs of dress, demeanor and deference either out of conviction or self-interest or both. For similar reasons, lawyers are hesitant to make public criticisms of judges. The judicial tradition of not being drawn into public controversies leaves judges unable to defend themselves against groundless public charges. Yet the official conduct of an occasional judge is subject to just censure of a kind that a lawyer may be in the best position to make. The lawyer codes express a special obligation of lawyers not to criticize judges through false accusations,[20] as well as the hope that lawyers might come to the defense of judges unfairly accused.[21]

The permissible limits on extrajudicial criticism of judges by lawyers have expanded in recent decades. Formerly, a number of decisions took the position that vigorous public criticism of judges was sanctionable, regardless of the truth or falsity of the criticism, because it created public disrespect for the law or the judiciary. In those cases it was the tone of criticism rather than its factual content that was considered objectionable. For example, in In re Snyder,[22] a lawyer was suspended from practice in all federal courts in the circuit for six months for a private letter sent to a district judge's secretary criticizing the court's system of compensating court-appointed lawyers. The lawyer's letter referred to the "extreme gymnastics" required to receive "puny amounts" and expressed "extreme disgust" at his treatment by the court of appeals, which twice rejected his undocumented requests for additional compensation. Without reaching First Amendment issues, the Supreme Court reversed.[23] Speaking for a unanimous court, Chief Justice Burger stated:

> We do not consider a lawyer's criticism of the administration of the [Criminal Justice] Act or criticism of inequities in assignments under the Act as cause for discipline or suspension.... Officers of the court may appropriately express criticism on such matters.

20. M.R. 8.2(a); DR 8–102(B).

21. M.R. 8.2 comment [3]; EC 8–6.

22. 734 F.2d 334 (8th Cir.1984).

23. In re Snyder, 472 U.S. 634 (1985).

The record indicates the Court of Appeals was concerned about the tone of the letter; petitioner concedes that the tone of his letter was "harsh," and, indeed it can be read as ill-mannered. All persons involved in the judicial process—judges, litigants, witnesses, and court officers—owe a duty of courtesy to all other participants. The necessity for civility in the inherently contentious setting of the adversary process suggests that members of the bar cast criticisms of the system in a professional and civil tone. However, even assuming that the letter exhibited unlawyer-like rudeness, a single incident of rudeness or lack of professional courtesy—in this context—does not support a finding of contemptuous or contumacious conduct, or a finding that a lawyers is "not presently fit to practice law in the federal courts." Nor does it rise to the level of "conduct unbecoming a member of the bar" warranting suspension from practice.[24]

Criticism of Particular Judges

Although general criticism of the judiciary or of the administration of justice will receive a great deal of constitutional protection, lawyers who make false charges against a particular judge are subject to professional discipline.[25] The special requirements applicable when public figures sue speakers for defamation—proof of both falsity and "actual malice"—[26] have not been applied to a lawyer's accusations against a judge that turn out to be false.

Elizabeth Holtzman, a prominent political figure in New York, was reprimanded for a press release made while she was serving as a prosecutor.[27] Holtzman charged a named judge with judicial misconduct by staging a replay of a pending sexual assault incident. The judge, she stated,

> asked the victim to get down on the floor and show the position she was in when she was being sexually assaulted.... The victim reluctantly got down on her hands and knees as everyone stood and watched. In making the victim assume the position she was forced

24. 472 U.S. at 646–47. See also Justices of Appellate Division, First Dep't v. Erdmann, 39 A.D.2d 223, 333 N.Y.S.3d 863 (1972), rev'd, 33 N.Y.2d 559, 347 N.Y.S.2d 441, 301 N.E.2d 426 (1973) (reversing censure of a lawyer whose critical quotes about New York trial and appellate judges—the latter as "the whores who became madams"—were published in a magazine article; the court held that "isolated instances of disrespect for ... Judges and courts expressed by vulgar and insulting words ... uttered ... outside the precincts of the court are not subject to professional discipline").

25. See, e.g., Ramirez v. State Bar, 28 Cal.3d 402, 169 Cal.Rptr. 206, 619 P.2d 399 (1980) (accusations against state court of appeals judges in federal court pleadings); In re Crumpacker, 269 Ind. 630, 383 N.E.2d 36 (1978) (disbarment for intemperate and unfounded attacks upon character and integrity of judge who had ruled against lawyer in emotion-laden litigation).

26. Harte–Hanks Communications, Inc. v. Connaughton, 491 U.S. 657 (1989) (actual malice defined as knowledge of a statement's falsity or reckless (i.e., conscious) disregard for its truth); New York Times v. Sullivan, 376 U.S. 254 (1964).

27. Matter of Holtzman, 78 N.Y.2d 184, 573 N.Y.S.2d 39, 577 N.E.2d 30 (1991).

to take when she was sexually assaulted, Judge Levine profoundly degraded, humiliated and demeaned her.[28]

Holtzman had relied on the memorandum of a trial assistant reporting the incident, but she did not obtain the minutes of the criminal trial, discuss the incident with the trial assistant or speak with persons present during the alleged misconduct. Members of her staff counseled her to delay publication until the trial minutes were received. The court accepted the lower court's finding that the accusation was false.

Petitioner's act was not generalized criticism but rather release to the media of a false allegation of specific wrongdoing, made without any support other than the interoffice memoranda of a newly admitted trial assistant, aimed at a named judge who had presided over a number of cases prosecuted by her office. Petitioner knew or should have known that such attacks were unwarranted and unprofessional, serve to bring the bench and bar into disrepute, and tend to undermine public confidence in the judicial system.

Therefore, petitioner's conduct was properly the subject of disciplinary action under DR 1–102(A)(6) [prohibiting "conduct that adversely reflects on his fitness to practice law"]. . . .

Petitioner contends that her conduct would not be actionable under the "constitutional malice" standard enunciated by the Supreme Court in New York Times v. Sullivan (376 U.S. 254). Neither this Court nor the Supreme Court has ever extended the *Sullivan* standard to lawyer discipline and we decline to do so here.

Accepting petitioner's argument would immunize all accusations, however reckless or irresponsible, from censure as long as the attorney uttering them did not actually entertain serious doubts as to their truth. . . .

. . .

In order to adequately protect the public interest and maintain the integrity of the judicial system, there must be an objective standard, of what a reasonable attorney would do in similar circumstances. It is the reasonableness of the belief, not the state of mind of the attorney, that is determinative.[29]

------

28. 577 N.E.2d at 31.

29. 577 N.E.2d at 33–34. For another case involving reprimand of a prosecutor for public criticism of a particular judge, see Matter of Westfall, 808 S.W.2d 829 (Mo.1991) (lawyer stated that a judge's opinion was "somewhat illogical" and "a little bit less than honest," the judge "distorted the statute," and represented a conclusion the judge had reached before he wrote the decision). The Supreme Court denied review in both the *Holtzman* and *Westfall* cases.

B. LAWYERS SERVING POOR PEOPLE AND "THE PUBLIC INTEREST"

1. A Constitutional Right to Civil Legal Assistance?

After Gideon v. Wainwright, it seemed possible that a similar right to counsel might be recognized for civil matters. The high water mark of this development was Boddie v. Connecticut,[30] in which the Court on due process grounds struck down a state statute requiring prepayment of a $45 filing fee by divorce plaintiffs. *Boddie* was subsequently narrowed to situations where judicial process provided the only means for vindicating a fundamental interest[31] and was then displaced by a balancing-of-factors approach in Lassiter v. Department of Social Services.[32]

In *Lassiter* the Court held that a state's failure to appoint counsel for an indigent, imprisoned mother, before terminating her parental rights to custody of her minor child as an unfit parent, did not violate due process. The Court's three-part balancing process, carried over from other due process cases, considers (1) the private interests at stake, (2) the government's interests and (3) the extent of the risk that the claimed procedural right, here the absence of publicly provided counsel, will lead to erroneous results in the litigation. In *Lassiter*, however, the Court added something to the balancing process. The Court identified a presumption that there is a right to appointed counsel only when the indigent person faces a loss of personal liberty in the form of confinement by the state. After balancing the three elements identified above, the Court "set[s] their net weight in the scales against the presumption"[33] that there is a right to appointed counsel only when confinement is a possibility. This thumb-on-the-scales form of balancing sounded the death knell for a right to counsel in most civil cases.

Four dissenting justices asserted that termination of parental rights involves a more important interest than is involved in many misdemeanor cases. They also argued that appointment of counsel is particularly important for a fair adjudication of cases of this type, which involve the application of an imprecise standard in formal adversarial proceedings in which the opposing party, the state, is represented. As the dissenters predicted, few situations under *Lassiter's* balancing-of-interests approach turn out to require the appointment of counsel in civil cases.[34] States are free to provide counsel to

---

30. 401 U.S. 371 (1971).

31. United States v. Kras, 409 U.S. 434 (1973) (bankruptcy not a fundamental interest); Ortwein v. Schwab, 410 U.S. 656 (1973) (upholding a $25 filing fee to obtain state court appellate review of a state agency's reduction of welfare benefits).

32. 452 U.S. 18 (1981).

33. Id. at 27.

34. See, e.g., United States v. Bobart Travel Agency, 699 F.2d 618 (2d Cir.1983) (civil contempt charges that may lead to imprisonment require the appointment of counsel).

indigents in civil cases either generally or in specific categories of cases, but with limited exceptions have not done so.[35]

David Luban argues that the premises of the American political system require the provision of counsel to indigents in important civil matters, and especially in civil enforcement proceedings against a poor person.[36] Equality before the law is a fundamental principle embodied in constitutional text. Its effective implementation requires access to the legal system, which in turn is dependent upon the assistance of lawyers. In Luban's view, the failure to provide counsel impairs the legitimacy of government.

Geoffrey Hazard states some of the reasons why "[t]he notion that due process meant lawyer-assisted process never took hold in civil matters:" [37]

> For one thing, there was a long tradition, exemplified in worker's compensation proceedings, juvenile court, and small claims, that legal dispute resolution could be more just, more expeditious and less expensive if lawyers were kept out. For another thing, in civil cases there was no apparatus of legal assistance provided by the state to assist one side, as was provided for the prosecution in criminal cases.
>
> There was a more fundamental difficulty in fixing the provision of civil legal aid. The measure of necessary legal aid in criminal cases was the quantum provided the prosecution. There was no similar measure for civil legal aid. To provide a lawyer to an indigent civil grievant was in effect to confer a subsidy in the amount of nuisance settlement value to beneficiaries arbitrarily selected in terms of income or wealth and self-selecting in terms of disposition to litigate. Implicitly recognizing this, the courts were willing to say that due process required legal aid only in narrowly limited civil categories.

In the absence of any constitutional entitlement, provision of counsel to indigents in civil matters depends upon the volunteered services of lawyers, judicial actions appointing lawyers for indigents and legislative provision of subsidized legal services.

---

35. In Payne v. Superior Court,17 Cal.3d 908, 132 Cal.Rptr. 405, 553 P.2d 565 (1976), a prisoner seeking to defend a civil action was held entitled to appointed counsel. *Payne* was reaffirmed in Yarbrough v. Superior Court, 39 Cal.3d 197, 216 Cal.Rptr. 425, 702 P.2d 583 (1985) (expressing a hope that the legislature would provide funding for representation that otherwise depended on appointed counsel serving without compensation).

36. David Luban, Lawyers and Justice: An Ethical Study c. 11 (1988) (equality-of-rights-not-fortunes is a basic legitimation right of society; its denial undermines the legitimacy of the system and may generate a right of resistance).

37. Geoffrey C. Hazard, Jr., After Professional Virtue, 1989 Sup.Ct.Rev. 213, 219–20.

STEVEN BRILL
"THE STENCH OF ROOM 202"

The American Lawyer, Pp. 1, 15–18, 20 (April 1987). [38]

Tracy Miller, NYU Law class of '85, Order of the Coif and Root–Tilden scholar, steps through the cigarette butts and heads up the dark, graffiti-lined stairway. At the top of the landing, she pushes open the door just lightly enough not to hit any of the several dozen blacks and Puerto Ricans lingering in the corridor, then whirls around through another door.

This room, with the paint peeling, with the fluorescent lights half out, with the yellow newspapers stacked in the soot against the window sill under the "In God We Trust" sign, with the white people with briefcases in front of the bench and the nonwhites, clutching pieces of official-looking paper, milling around in the back, is the seat of justice every day for hundreds of Americans: Brooklyn housing court, room 202.

It is also a place, as I'll explain below, that I would like the American Bar Association's president . . . to think about every day he is in office.

As Miller waits for her case to be called, a short, wiry white man in a dark, double knit suit, his tie already loosened at 9:30 in the morning, stands in front of the bench calling out names. The first ten bring no answer. The eleventh yields an eager black man with a mock-fur hat. He rushes up to the white man and identifies himself.

"Yes, that's me, sir," he whispers.

There is some discussion, apparently about money, which I cannot hear completely, then: "Sign this stip, and you can go," the white man explains, not looking at him.

The black man signs quickly, says, "Thank you, Your Honor," and rushes out.

His Honor is not a judge. He is Kenneth Mintz, counsel to the landlord in this case. Mintz has just gotten his tenant-opponent to sign some sort of stipulation in an eviction proceeding that the tenant had— by virtue of his having shown up in this courtroom—been fighting.

Mintz's firm, Gutman & Mintz of Queens, counts among its clients J. Leonard Spodek, known in New York as the "Dracula Landlord" for the way he has rendered heatless, threatened with goon squads, and otherwise abused tenants so brazenly that he has been jailed twice recently.

Mintz later said that the stipulation involved a client other than Spodek and was "probably just an adjournment." The man who signed

---

38. Steven Brill is the Editor in Chief of The American Lawyer. This article is reprinted with permission from the April 1987 issue of The American Lawyer. Copyright © 1993 The American Lawyer.

it could not be found by the time I realized what had happened and went looking for him in the corridor.

(Asked why he had allowed the man to think he was the judge, Mintz said, "I always introduce myself.... You must not have ... heard me. It's impossible that he thought I was the judge.... Sometimes people in court call lawyers 'Your Honor,'" Mintz added.)

"It could have been an adjournment, or a stip waiving all defenses and promising to be out," Tracy Miller explains, "or it could be a stip saying he'll pay on time from now on...." It could also, Miller notes, have been a stipulation saying that although the rent was withheld because the landlord didn't make repairs, those repairs have now been made and the rent will be paid.

"It could have been anything," Miller concludes.

But, adds Miller, because this particular courtroom is, in part, for tenants who have gotten notices of dispossession and have then filed papers asserting some kind of defense, it's likely the stipulation was a substantive waiver of something.

Mintz, now joined by a red-nailed, white-bloused associate who hands him file after file, calls out a half dozen more case names, then lets another member of the landlords bar have his turn.

"The only lawyers other than us," says Miller, are landlord lawyers. "Except for us, it's a landlords bar versus pro se tenants."

Miller is a staff attorney with Brooklyn Legal Services Corporation B. She is one of ten attorneys in the housing unit. (Brooklyn Legal Services Corporation A, the citywide Legal Aid Society, and other legal services organizations together have about two dozen more lawyers working on housing cases in Brooklyn, which has a larger population than Houston.)

Last year there were 111,000 cases in Brooklyn housing court, making estimates by Miller and her colleagues that 95 percent of all tenants in housing court go without lawyers seem conservative. As a result, Legal Services lawyers are reduced to providing what they call "triage service"—taking only one in ten housing cases that come through the door, and trying to make sure those cases have unusually strong fact situations, such as a landlord harassing a tenant in a gentrifying neighborhood in order to get him to move out so that the building can be turned into a co-op or a luxury rental.

At about 10 a.m. civil court judge Richard Goldberg and a clerk enter the room. Goldberg, a small white-haired man who seems almost frightened by the proceedings, sits quietly while the clerk, Norman Botwin, takes over. Botwin orders everyone to "listen carefully, because if you miss your name when it is called you will be in default," and then calls out a series of 30 case names. In only one instance does he get an answer from both parties, whereupon Judge Goldberg sends them up to a sixth-floor courtroom.

"This [courtroom] is just so the judge can assign motions to the other judges," explains Miller, who apparently has been doing this work long enough—15 months—for that explanation to make sense.

In the 29 cases where one or both parties don't answer, the clerk dismisses the tenants' motions if they don't answer but holds over the motions if the landlords don't answer.

"He figures the landlord's lawyer is somewhere in the building," says Miller, who like her colleagues I will meet later, seems so coolly professional about how unhallowed these hallowed halls of justice are that you suspect she's been emotionally numbed by it all. "I know, it's not fair," she adds matter-of-factly, "but it's the way it works."

After Miller's case has been sent up to the sixth floor, she hurries down to a first-floor auditorium-like courtroom where tenants first come when they've received eviction notices.

Miller says that she's "trying to round up" the landlord's lawyer who has the case with her on the sixth floor so that she can get out before lunch. "These guys are handling maybe a hundred cases at a time, and the judge will never dismiss if they don't show. He'll just hold it over," she explains.

I count 121 blacks and Hispanics, mostly women, among the 124 people sitting on bridge chairs. (Brooklyn is about 50 percent black and Hispanic.) All but one of the lawyers—including Mintz, who has found his way to the bench here, too—are white.

It is almost impossible to hear the names called above the wailing of two infants, one bundled on a bridge chair, another sleeping fitfully on the linoleum floor under his mother's feet.

Down a hallway outside this first-floor "courtroom" is the waiting area where tenants will be sent if they are lucky enough to hear their names in the auditorium and answer correctly "tenant by the court" (which means the tenant is here and wants the case adjudicated by the court rather than by arbitration) and to have the landlord's lawyer answer as well.

Here, these people who believed enough in our system to show up when sent that piece of paper saying, in the name of our justice system, that they were about to become homeless will wait for their cases to be assigned to another judge, after which time they will wait, again, for one of the landlord's lawyers to decide to show up.

The room's light bulbs are all out except one. The place looks like the arcade of an abandoned subway station. It is dark. Filthy. Virtually chairless. An affront to justice.

It is not simply a matter of people holding out on rent that they owe. New York, especially many areas of Brooklyn, is in the midst of a real estate upheaval that has seen values skyrocket in many neighborhoods where the renters are the working poor or lower middle class. So many landlords are doing anything they can—claiming rent hasn't been paid, raising rents illegally, claiming leases don't exist, and not offering to renew leases when they are obligated to—in order to bring dispossession actions.

Other tenants face dispossession even though they are only withholding rent because repairs to which they are entitled have not been made. Still others may, indeed, be far behind on their rents for no reason other than inability or unwillingness to pay. But even they could—if they had lawyers—raise defenses ranging from the landlord's not having kept up his end of the bargain because of some significant fault in the building (such as no heat or no locks on the doors), to invalid or just plain nonexistent service by the process server. A lease, after all, is supposed to be a contract, and due process is supposed to be due process.

Russell Engler, who works with Miller at the Brooklyn Legal Services housing unit, may be exaggerating when he says, "We could successfully fight ninety percent of all evictions if we could take the cases." But he may not be far off.

But because Miller, Engler, and their cohorts can't take all the cases, they pick their fights carefully. Engler—who graduated from Harvard Law School in 1983 and clerked for Fourth Circuit Court of Appeals Judge Francis Murnaghan, Jr., before coming to Brooklyn in 1984—splits his time between individual cases having what he says are particularly compelling facts and what he calls "impact litigation," which are suits designed to improve things generally for his clients.

Thus, last December Engler began attacking the kangaroo-court aspects of Brooklyn housing court by suing the chief judge of civil court, as well as the administrator of the overall state court system, among others, for not acting on complaints he had made that one judge— Ferdinand Pellegrino—was particularly biased.

Engler charged that Pellegrino, who declined comment on the case, "enters orders granting judgments of possession to landlords against unrepresented tenants without conducting a trial or making a record of the proceeding; approves stipulations prepared by landlords' attorneys without reading the stipulations ... to unrepresented tenants; ... [and] rules against tenants after having heard an ex parte communication from the landlord's attorney...."

This kind of impact litigation can yield broad results, and its logic as a client service is compelling. (For example, in 1985 Engler's colleagues won a suit requiring the city's Housing Authority to overhaul its procedures for accepting and acting upon applications for its scarce apartments.) It's also exactly the kind of litigation that the Reagan administration has attacked when brought by Legal Services lawyers, claiming it represents political activism rather than the lawyering that a taxpayer-paid program is meant to support.

Miller and another lawyer, Sheryl Karp, also do work that is strategically well-targeted, but controversial: "They're a two-lawyer illegal eviction unit established with a grant from the city last year to help tenants who are threatened with illegal evictions or who have already been evicted illegally. Thus, the two young women often end up representing and even helping to organize tenants' associations that are fighting landlord harassment.

As Miller and I leave a courtroom up on the fourth floor, we run into Karp. They stop and talk just long enough in the crowded hall under the "Pay All Fees To Court Cashiers Only" signs to attract two women who need help. Legal Services lawyers are not supposed to pick up cases in the courthouse. But Miller takes ten minutes to advise the first woman informally; and Karp, realizing that the second woman's case may fall within the scope of their special unit's work—the woman claims she is being harassed in a building where Karp knows the landlord is trying to force everyone out—darts into a courtroom to tell a judge that she's just taken the case and needs a postponement.

"Wall Street lawyers work nights, and I work nights," says Karp as we walk back to her office two blocks from the courthouse. "Only we work different places. I'm usually at a tenants' association meeting or in a client's apartment."

. . .

"I figure we're saving the city money by keeping people from becoming homeless," explains Miller, having come back from court and settled into her small office. "It costs the city thousands to take care of people who become homeless. But, of course, what we do is much more important than the money it saves."

Does she ever feel so frustrated or worn down that she'd like to move on, say, to a more conventional Wall Street job? "No, I love what I do," Miller answers quickly. "I can see the law I practice have an effect on people. I can work in a subject area that I love"—Miller got a master's in urban planning at Columbia before going to law school and wrote her thesis on rent control—"and I get more freedom and responsibility than just about any lawyer I know from my law school days."

"I know that what I'm doing is what I want to do for the rest of my life," says Karp, who is 31 and came to Brooklyn Legal Services in 1986. "And I have to tell you that I used to be embarrassed to admit that, because I don't know too many people my age who feel that way."

"This is the only type of legal work I think I could ever enjoy," echoes Engler, who spent part of the summer between his second and third years at Harvard at San Francisco's McCutchen, Doyle, Brown & Enerson. "I would guess that fifty percent of the people we represent would become the homeless people everyone's reading about if we didn't represent them," he adds. "Or they'd be one more stop—maybe a relative's home or one more rental—away from being homeless. I spend my time preserving what is probably a man's most basic property right, his home."

. . .

One could argue that a rough measure of our commitment to justice is the difference between what we, in the way we organize our legal and economic systems, pay Engler or Miller and what we pay a starting associate on Wall Street. In 1971, the year the Legal Services Corporation started, the going rate on Wall Street was roughly $16,000. That year, staff lawyers at Brooklyn Legal Services were paid $12,000. That's about 4:3; starting salaries on Wall Street [in 1987] are about $75,000 including bonuses, or about three times what Engler and Miller make. And on Wall Street Miller and Engler, it should be remembered, would be getting second- and fourth-year salaries, not starting salaries.

[Brill then argues that the American Bar Association should propose "practical, relatively radical measures" to achieve equal justice: First, encourage law graduates to work for the non-rich by requiring ABA-approved law schools to provide full student loans to any student who wants one combined with a substantial loan forgiveness program for graduates who work for "a nonprofit organization providing legal services to the poor." The program would be paid for out of tuition charges, thus shifting the cost to students who take higher paying jobs after graduation. Second, a "justice tax" of 0.5-1.0 percent of law firms' gross revenues be imposed to finance legal services for the poor. Third, companies that make money by selling things to lawyers, such as *The American Lawyer* (Brill's publication) and LEXIS, should be asked to contribute the same percentage.]

No one is ever going to even things up so that the mirror in Tracy Miller's tiny office can become a window with a harbor view, her linoleum a carpet, her subway token a Dialcab voucher. She doesn't expect that.

But she and every other lawyer and every other American has a right to expect that the rest of her profession will do more. That her profession won't allow Americans to go homeless because they didn't have a lawyer to nag a judge into doing his job. That her colleagues at the bar will remember that more people see room 202 in a week than see a deposition room in a month, and that for these people the "litigation crisis" isn't about docket delay, interrogatories, and hourly rates but about simple justice.

Miller and every other lawyer and every American have a right to expect that places like room 202—scenes that seem taken from Soviet propaganda texts—won't continue to be the true images of justice in our country.

And we all have a right to expect that the justice profession in the country that is supposed to stand for equal justice will push itself, reexamine itself, even tax itself, to produce more [lawyers] like Miller and Engler.

2. Professional Obligation to Represent Poor People

The legal profession in the United States has regarded itself, uniquely among legal professions in the world, as charged with a responsibility to provide legal assistance to the poor. Various rationales are offered. One is that a lawyer, as an officer of the court, has a concern that justice be done, and that representing an indigent person who requires legal assistance is an obvious way to act upon this concern. Another rationale is that the bar has a monopoly of law practice, and as a monopolist it should reallocate its monopoly profits to a manifest public need that is related to the monopoly. A third rationale is that representation of the poor is a special kind of continuing legal education that exposes the lawyer to the realities of justice as administered to the poor.[39]

The bar's commitment to representing the poor has always been and remains more rhetorical than actual. The scope and depth of the legal needs of the poor began to be taken more seriously by the public and the bar after the upheavals of the 1960s and the development of the federal legal services program. Even before that, however, "legal aid" organizations in many communities provided poor people with some free legal help. This aid was provided by private lawyers who would volunteer their time and effort. Although lawyers in other countries recognized some similar obligation, the obligation was not treated as seriously, in legal or moral terms, as in this country. Is this different response rooted in an aspect of the American concept of justice?

Mandatory Pro Bono

Volunteered services may have worked reasonably well in small-town America at an earlier time. Lawyers were general practitioners who had contacts with a wide range of people in their communities. A poor person who came to a lawyer's office with a substantial and meritorious legal problem may have had a decent chance of getting necessary help. A competent general practitioner could tell a meritorious case when he saw it, especially if he was free to decline it. Toward the end of the 19th century, the face-to-face character of American society gave way in urban centers. During the 20th century legal practice increasingly became specialized in character. Absent institutional arrangements channeling willing lawyers to needy clients, volunteered efforts proved ineffective.

Lawyers have embodied their aspirations concerning access to justice in their codes of professional ethics, but have not stated them in

---

39. For discussions of the "pro bono" obligation see Barlow F. Christensen, The Lawyer's Pro Bono Public Responsibility, 1981 Am.Bar Found.Research J. 1; Geoffrey C. Hazard, Jr., The Lawyer's Pro Bono Obligation, in ABA Proceedings of the Second National Conference on Legal Services and the Public (1981); David L. Shapiro, The Enigma of the Lawyer's Duty to Serve, 55 N.Y.U.L.Rev. 735 (1980).

mandatory terms.[40] The wording of Model Rule 6.1, as adopted in 1983, reflects an explicit rejection of earlier drafts which mandated 40 hours per year of pro bono service from each lawyer. A 1993 amendment to M.R. 6.1 edges back toward the original Kutak Commission proposal: "A lawyer *should aspire* to render at least [50] hours of pro bono publico legal services per year [primarily to persons of limited means or organizations that address the needs of such persons]."[41] Note that M.R. 6.1 departs from the general pattern of the Model Rules in stating an aspirational rather than a disciplinary standard.

Mandatory pro bono proposals have arisen in states and localities with increasing frequency since the 1980s, partly stimulated by cutbacks in federal funding of the Legal Services Corporation. Thus far state-wide proposals have been defeated or tabled after extensive discussion.[42]

A New York proposal provides a specific focus for discussion. In 1990 a committee appointed by the chief judge of the New York Court of Appeals proposed that the courts adopt rules compelling New York lawyers to donate 40 hours every two years to advance the legal needs of the poor.[43] The mandatory pro bono proposal contained the following details: Law firms could credit the excess hours of some firm lawyers to meet the obligations of others. Lawyers in small firms of less than ten lawyers could satisfy their obligation by paying $1,000 each, in lieu of time, to support legal services for the poor. A third alternative permits law firms or unaffiliated lawyers to hire an attor-

---

40. See Model Rule 6.1 and its comment; and Model Code ECs 2–25, 8–3 and 8–9.

41. The full text of M.R. 6.1 is now as follows:

A lawyer should aspire to render at least [50] hours of pro bono publico legal services per year. In fulfilling this responsibility, the lawyer should:

(a) provide a substantial majority of the [50] hours of legal services without fee or expectation of fee to (1) persons of limited means or (2) charitable, religious, civic, community, governmental and education organizations in matters which are designed primarily to address the needs of persons of limited means; and

(b) provide any additional services through: (1) delivery of legal services at no fee or substantially reduced fee to individuals, groups or organizations seeking to secure or protect civil rights, civil liberties or public rights, or charitable, religious, civic, community, governmental and educational organizations in matters in furtherance of their organizational purposes, where the payment of standard legal fees would significantly deplete the organization's economic resources or would be otherwise inappropriate; (2) delivery of legal services at a substantially reduced fee to persons of limited means; or (3) participation in activities for improving the law, the legal system or the legal profession.

In addition a lawyer should voluntarily contribute financial support to organizations that provide legal services to persons of limited means.

42. For discussion of mandatory pro bono proposals, see Symposium, 19 Hofstra L. Rev. 739 et seq. (1991); David Luban, Lawyers and Justice: An Ethical Study 240–89 (1988); Steven B. Rosenfeld, Mandatory Pro Bono: Historical and Constitutional Perspectives, 2 Cardozo L. Rev. 255 (1981); Michael A. Millemann, Mandatory Pro Bono in Civil Cases: A Partial Answer to the Right Question, 49 Md.L.Rev. 18 (1990).

43. Committee To Improve the Availability of Legal Services, Final Report to the Chief Judge of the State of New York (April 1990), reprinted in 19 Hofstra L. Rev. 755 (1991) (generally referred to as the Marrero Report after its chairman).

ney to discharge their collective obligation to devote time.   Is this proposal desirable and fair?

The proposal, like mandatory pro bono plans elsewhere, divided the New York bar.   Most bar associations opposed it, but individual lawyers and a few bar associations supported it.   The Association of the Bar of the City of New York, which is representative of New York City's largest firms, " 'reluctantly' but forcefully endorsed the proposal as essential to meet a 'desperate' need."   In light of this mixed reaction, Chief Judge Wachtler postponed action on the report for a period of time in the hope that the stimulus it provided to voluntary pro bono would suffice to meet the problem.

What is the scope of the problem?   No one knows the proportion of the legal needs of the poor that are now going unmet, an issue discussed further below.[44]   In the modern administrative/welfare state, however, corporations and poor people may be two groups in society most in need of competent legal assistance.   The corporate need is obvious to most law students, undoubtedly because law school courses that explicate the corporation's legal and regulatory problems abound.   On the other hand, few law students take courses that study the complex law and practice of Aid for Dependent Children, Social Security disability, federal and state housing laws or any of the multitude of other legal areas that directly impinge on the lives of poor people.   Corporations, however, able to pay for needed legal services, receive the legal assistance they want.

The federally-funded national legal services program meets a portion of the legal needs of the poor, although funding cuts since 1981 have reduced it from more than 6,000 total lawyers to about 4,000 nationwide.   Efforts to encourage and support private bar involvement in local legal services programs have met with some success.   Various studies show that most lawyers do participate in some pro bono work, but much of that time is directed toward activities that build relations with other lawyers, such as bar association work, or work that is designed to attract clients, such as free or reduced-fee work for local charities.[45]

The argument for mandatory pro bono usually proceeds along the following lines: (1) Many individuals, and especially the poor, have an unmet need for vital legal services.   (2) A lawyer is necessary for meaningful access to the justice system.   (3) The American ideal of equal justice under law is undermined by lack of access to justice.   (4)

---

44.   See the Curran excerpt below at 1066.

45.   Although most lawyers donate some free services, little of it involves the representation of indigents.   Miskiewicz, Mandatory Pro Bono Won't Disappear, Nat'l L.J. 1 (Mar. 23, 1987).   Some reports indicate that as many as 16 percent of lawyers participate in pro bono services for the poor, but other studies report that only about 6 percent of lawyer time is pro bono, much of it devoted to charities rather than poor people.   See the materials cited in Roger C. Cramton, Mandatory Pro Bono, 19 Hofstra L.Rev. 1113, 1121, 1124 (1991).

Although voluntary pro bono is commendable, it has proven insufficient even when supplemented by modest public funds in the form of the national legal services program. Therefore (5) lawyers must satisfy the unmet need with mandated services at least until other alternatives, such as adequate provision of publicly-funded services, are put in place.[46]

Even if one accepts the premises of this argument, serious legal, moral and practical questions are raised when a general moral obligation of lawyers to represent the poor is converted into a detailed legal requirement. The legal objections rest on various constitutional provisions, including freedom of speech and association, the takings clause, equal protection and involuntary servitude. The legal arguments have generally been rejected in the context in which they have the greatest force: court-appointment programs which require an appointed lawyer to devote a substantial amount of time to handling a particular matter.[47] Such appointments commit a lawyer to a specific client and cause, bear heavily on trial lawyers and may require a large amount of uncompensated time. On the other hand, the imposition of a modest annual pro bono obligation on lawyers who are extensively regulated and have an exclusive license to practice is hard to perceive as involuntary servitude.[48] If the lawyer is given a great deal of choice concerning how the required service is performed, as is the case in most mandatory proposals, a claim that free speech and associational rights are impaired is also difficult to maintain. Whether mandatory pro bono is wise or desirable is perhaps a more important inquiry than whether it would pass constitutional muster.

The moral objections to mandatory pro bono are that mandated service intrudes on personal autonomy; that it converts a gift of volunteered services into the duty of a compelled exaction, thus depriv-

---

46. For a more extended argument, see David Luban, Lawyers and Justice 267–89 (1988).

47. See, e.g., Unites States v. Shackney, 333 F.2d 475, 485–87 (2d Cir.1964) (only physical restraint or legal confinement constitutes involuntary servitude); United States v. Dillon, 346 F.2d 633 (9th Cir.1965) (compulsory appointment of a lawyer not a taking); Family Div. Trial Lawyers v. Moultrie, 725 F.2d 695 (D.C.Cir.1984) (compulsory appointment of lawyers for uncompensated representation of parents in child neglect and parental termination cases was not a taking; but case remanded for a further hearing on an equal protection claim arising out of limitation of that obligation to juvenile defenders). But see State ex rel. Scott v. Roper, 688 S.W.2d 757 (Mo.1985) (suggesting that uncompensated service presents a constitutional question); and DeLisio v. Alaska Superior Court, 740 P.2d 437 (Alaska 1987) (court appointment was a temporary taking requiring just compensation). See David L. Shapiro, The Enigma of the Lawyer's Duty to Serve, 55 N.Y.U.L.Rev. 735, 765 (1980) (arguing that compelling a lawyer to represent a particular client or to assert certain positions is "more troublesome than a tax in dollars"). See Note, Court Appointment of Uncompensated Legal Assistance in Civil Cases, 81 Colum.L.Rev. 366 (1981).

48. Although the practice of law is a property interest protected by the takings clause of the Fourteenth Amendment, Konigsberg v. State Bar, 353 U.S. 252 (1957), a requirement that a relatively small number of hours be devoted to public service each year is supported by the bar's historic tradition of response to court appointment and falls short of a "taking."

ing the actor of the moral significance of the gift of service; [49] and that in application it tends to be regressive and inequitable, falling with a heavier hand on less affluent and less successful lawyers. Consider these arguments in the context of the New York mandatory pro bono proposal summarized above.

The legal and moral objections to mandatory pro bono reflect an underlying theme discussed earlier: the emphasis on the political equality of individuals in the American concept of equality, which entails a rejection of elitism and of assigning of special responsibilities for justice to one group. [50]

The principal practical objections to mandatory pro bono rest on concerns about the quality and efficiency of mandated services, the burdensome problems of administration and enforcement, the discouragement of charitable and bar association work if these activities are excluded from the required pro bono category, as in the New York proposal, and, finally, a concern that, if adopted in only one jurisdiction, lawyers in that state will be adversely affected vis-a-vis their competitors in other states. A pro bono obligation imposed on New York lawyers will operate essentially as a tax on legal services, putting New York lawyers in a less favorable position with respect to clients who can go elsewhere for legal services.

Doubts about the quality and efficiency of mandatory services rest on the specialized character of the legal needs of poor people. Is an office lawyer engaged in bond debenture work likely to be an effective advocate for poor people? [51] The most common legal problems faced by poor people involve highly technical subjects with which most lawyers are unfamiliar. Law schools generally do not teach these subjects, at least in any depth. Representation of indigent criminal defendants requires familiarity with criminal law and its practice. Representation of poor people in disputes with a welfare department requires familiarity with a complicated body of federal and state law and with local administrative practice in administering that law. The law of landlord and tenant, which affects many poor people, is similarly complicated. From a political-economic viewpoint, most poor people exist in a semi-

---

49. Moral philosophers and economists have debated whether the provision of blood for transfusions may best be met exclusively by voluntary donation (as in the United Kingdom) or by purchase as well as gift. Richard Titmuss's comparative study concludes that the British approach, forbidding the development of a market for blood, fosters "the gift relationship" and is more effective in providing blood, while the more commercial approach in the United States results in chronic shortages. See Richard Titmuss, The Gift Relationship: From Human Blood to Social Policy (1971); Kenneth Arrow, Gifts and Exchanges, 1 Phil. & Pub. Affairs 343 (1972); and Peter Singer, Altruism and Commerce: A Defense of Titmuss Against Arrow, 2 Phil. & Pub. Affairs 312 (1973). The altruistic impulse was the target of President Bush's frequent references to "a thousand points of light."

50. See discussion above at p. 1007.

51. Some believe that the costs of arranging and supervising pro bono opportunities (training, administering referrals and monitoring performance) exceed the benefits. Esther Lardent, Pro Bono in the 1990s, in American Bar Association, Civil Justice: An Agenda for the 1990s (1990) (mandatory pro bono programs will make a "very small dent in a very large problem").

socialist regime in which their lives are continuously dependent on government regulation and discretion. Hence, in most localities, certainly in all major cities, a very sophisticated system would be required to provide that every lawyer shall be on call for whatever may be the legal needs of the poor.

A related problem is equalizing the burden of service on all members of the bar. Although the bar as a whole may have a monopoly of law practice, no single lawyer or law firm does. If the burden of discharging the collective responsibility were not equitably apportioned, widely disparate burdens would be involved. Lawyers who had undertaken to learn a specialty in the "law of the poor" would be particularly vulnerable, and that would create perverse incentives to remain unskilled in poverty law.[52] The difficulties could be ameliorated if lawyers were exposed in law school or through continuing legal education and practice to some field of "poverty law."[53] But the acceptance of such a duty would require the bar to take seriously its rhetorical claim that it has a special responsibility for justice in this country, a notion that many lawyers and much of the public resist.

Should law students be required during law school to assist in providing legal assistance to the poor?

The *Mallard* Case [54]

John Mallard, an Iowa lawyer with a securities and bankruptcy practice, was appointed by a federal magistrate in Iowa to represent inmates of a state prison in their civil suit against prison officials seeking redress for brutalities and other wrongs. The appointment was pursuant to a program, begun as a voluntary pro bono effort by the Iowa bar and the state legal services organization, subjecting every lawyer who had been admitted to the federal district court's bar to compulsory appointment, which worked out to one appointment about every three years. Mallard refused the appointment, stating that "he had no familiarity with the legal issues presented in the case, that he lacked experience in deposing and cross-examining witnesses, and that he would be willing to volunteer his services in an area in which he possessed some expertise, such as bankruptcy and securities law."[55] After being ordered by the magistrate, the district judge and the court

52. See, e.g., Family Division Trial Lawyers v. Moultrie, 725 F.2d 695 (D.C.Cir.1984), in which lawyers who had signed up to receive compensated court assignments as juvenile defenders were required, as a condition of receiving compensated assignments, to accept court appointments for uncompensated representation of indigent parents in child neglect and parental termination proceedings.

53. As of 1992 a handful of law schools imposes such a requirement. See John R. Kramer, Law Schools and the Delivery of Legal Services—First, Do No Harm, in American Bar Association, Civil Justice: An Agenda for the 1990s (1991) ("the best way to alter attorneys' attitudes is from the ground up by instilling in law students a sense of the responsibilities they must shoulder when they become members of the bar").

54. Mallard v. United States District Court for the Southern District of Iowa, 490 U.S. 296 (1989). The case is discussed in Geoffrey C. Hazard, Jr., After Professional Virtue, 1989 Sup.Ct.Rev. 213.

55. 490 U.S. at 299.

of appeals to provide service, Mallard sought certiorari from the Supreme Court, which heard the case and reversed.

In *Mallard* the Court held, 5–4, that the federal statute empowering a federal judge to "request" an attorney to represent an indigent in a civil case [56] did not create a legally binding obligation on the part of the attorney. Justice Brennan's opinion for the majority relied on the fact that other provisions of the same statute imposed mandatory duties; the opinion did not reach the question whether a district court had inherent authority apart from the statute to require a lawyer to serve. Justice Brennan acknowledged the tradition that members of the bar have an obligation to represent indigents,[57] but interpreted the history as establishing an ethical rather than legal obligation: " 'To justify coerced, uncompensated legal services on the basis of a firm tradition in England and the United States is to read into that tradition a story that is not there.' " [58]

Justice Stevens' dissenting opinion argued that the statute was using polite language to describe an order an attorney was legally obligated to accept. Citing the history of court appointments in England and the United States, as well as that of the statute, Stevens quoted Justice Field's statement in 1860: "Counsel are not considered at liberty to reject ... the cause of the defenseless, because no provision for their compensation is made by law." [59] Brennan's opinion reflects the American ideal of individual political equality, whereas Stevens' opinion reflects an acceptance of the bar's special obligation to see justice done.

3. Publicly Financed Civil Legal Assistance

Background [60]

Legal aid in various forms began around 1900, sometimes as self-help associations of worker and immigrant groups, sometimes as charities. Through the 1950s legal aid programs were funded almost entirely by charity and subscription of members of the bar. The programs usually had a small staff, often one person, assisted by volunteers and law students. The agencies were few in number, located almost exclusively in major cities, thinly funded and relatively passive, concentrat-

---

56. 28 U.S.C. § 1915(d), which provides: "The court may request an attorney [to represent the indigent in certain proceedings]."

57. "In a time when the need for legal services among the poor is growing and public funding for such services has not kept pace, lawyers' ethical obligation to volunteer their time *pro bono publico* is manifest." 490 U.S. at 310.

58. 490 U.S. at 304 (quoting from David L. Shapiro, The Enigma of the Lawyer's Duty to Serve, 55 N.Y.U.L.Rev. 735, 753 (1980).

59. 490 U.S. at 313–14, quoting from Rowe v. Yuba County, 17 Cal. 61, 63 (1860).

60. For general and historical background, see Earl Johnson, Jr., Justice and Reform: The Formative Years of the OEO Legal Services Program (1974); Reginald Heber Smith, Justice and the Poor (1919); Emery A. Brownell, Legal Aid in the United States (1951); Elliot Cheatham, A Lawyer When Needed (1963); Jerome E. Carlin, Jan Howard & Sheldon L. Messinger, Civil Justice and the Poor (1966); Barlow F. Christensen, Lawyers for People of Moderate Means (1970).

ing on individual cases and having the aura of a charity. In the 1960s the Ford Foundation made legal aid a major undertaking and infused it with new money, new stature and new assertiveness. In 1964, the Economic Opportunity Office of President Lyndon Johnson's "war on poverty" program provided funding for a quantum leap in civil legal assistance. The federal legal services program, discussed more fully below, originated in the OEO initiative.

Public defender programs originated in the western states, notably California, in the early part of the 20th century. They are publicly funded law offices providing representation to indigent criminal accused and to juveniles.[61]

Development of Federal Legal Services Program

The visionaries and activists who started the legal services movement in the turbulent 1960s had three missions in mind: (1) the individual client-service mission of traditional legal aid, (2) law reform and institutional change and (3) empowering poor people by creating organized groups that might engage in direct action such as boycotts, demonstrations and political activity. The activists in the legal services movement ridiculed individual-client assistance as "band-aid" work that failed to get at fundamental problems.[62] They sought to direct the program's resources into social advocacy and organizational activity. The provision of lawyers for otherwise represented persons in dealing with public or private institutions resulted in numerous decisions requiring fuller procedure or establishing new substantive law. The ultimate objective—a substantial redistribution of societal wealth and power—proved to be too large and too politically controversial to be accomplished by lawyers through the mechanism of the courts.

The social reform potential visualized in the 1960s for the federal legal assistance program excited hopes of reformers and fears of conservatives, both greatly exaggerated. The result was a political struggle for control of the program, involving the organized bar at various levels, political action groups, factions in Congress and a variety of governmental agencies. Broadly speaking, the reformers sought to make legal aid programs a vehicle for structural legal reform, through test cases, class actions and legislative activity, in such areas as housing, civil rights, education, welfare benefits and employment. The conservatives sought to maintain legal aid as a service program for needy individuals in such traditional matters as child support and

---

61. For discussion of public defenders, see Lisa J. McIntyre, The Public Defender: The Practice of Law in the Shadows of Repute (1987) (empirical study of Cook County, Illinois, public defender office); Michael McConville and Chester L. Mirsky, Criminal Defense of the Poor in New York City, 15 N.Y.U.Rev. of Law & Soc. Change 581–964 (1986–87); and Lee Silverstein, Defense of the Poor in Criminal Cases in American State Courts (1965).

62. See Stephen Wexler, Practicing Law for Poor People, 79 Yale L. J. 1049, 1053 (1970) ("If all the lawyers in the country worked full time, they could not deal with even the articulated problems of the poor.... In this setting, the object of practicing poverty law must be to organize poor people, rather than to solve their legal problems.").

custody, landlord-tenant disputes, debtor-creditor disputes and securing governmental benefits.[63]

In 1974, a detente of sorts was reached. The federal legal services program was established on a permanent basis through the Legal Services Corporation Act.[64] The statutory objectives are stated in politically neutral terms of "equal access to justice" and "high-quality legal assistance" for the poor. Political and organizational activities on the part of legal services lawyers are largely excluded by specific restrictions: a ban on political activity by lawyers in the field, a prohibition on participation in organizational activity (as distinct from legal advice concerning it) and procedural constraints on the use of class actions. These restrictions suggest that individual-client service and test-case litigation arising out of it constitute the central statutory mission.

The structure of the national program involves the Legal Services Corporation (LSC) as a funding agency for local non-profit organizations that actually represent clients and deliver legal services. LSC is forbidden to provide legal services to poor people directly, but it has an uncertain extent of regulatory authority over the operation of local programs. Restrictions on the matters that could be undertaken by local programs were included in the original Act (e.g., abortion and school desegregation cases). These restrictions have since been modified, elaborated and fought over, each time in highly political battles. Parallel struggles over the level of funding regular recur.[65]

President Reagan was strongly against any reformist tendency in legal aid and favored abolishing the Legal Services Corporation. Major bar associations, led by the American Bar Association, in company with various civil rights and other activist groups, held out for continuing the program. In the 1980s, the program survived but with funding diminished by budget cuts and inflation. The federal legal aid program has achieved permanence with modest funding, a distinctive structure and a legacy of bitter political controversy.

Legislative Controls

Lobbying

The 1974 Act prohibited use of LSC funds to "directly or indirectly" influence the passage or defeat of federal, state or local legislation or regulation except where "necessary to the provision of legal advice and representation with respect to such clients' legal rights and responsibilities" or where a government agency or legislative body or committee

---

63. For one view at the time, see Carlin, Howard & Messinger, supra; for another, see Geoffrey C. Hazard, Jr., Social Justice Through Civil Justice, 36 U.Chi.L.Rev. 242 (1970); Hazard, Law Reforming in the Anti–Poverty Effort, 37 U.Chi.L.Rev. 242 (1970).

64. Pub.L. 93–355, 88 Stat. 378, codified as 42 U.S.C. § 2996 et seq.

65. See generally Roger C. Cramton, Crisis in Legal Services for the Poor, 26 Vill.L.Rev. 521 (1981); Carrie Menkel–Meadow, Legal Aid in the United States: The Professionalization and Politicization of Legal Services in the 1980s, 22 Osgoode Hall L. J. 28 (1984).

or member thereof requested assistance.[66] A recipient legal aid agency was also prohibited from using private funds for lobbying. The restriction on lobbying was relaxed somewhat in 1977, but tightened in appropriation statutes beginning in 1983. In 1984, LSC issued highly controversial regulations interpreting the lobbying restrictions. Congress responded by requiring, first, that these and all new regulations be submitted to the appropriations committee for review, and second, by prohibiting LSC from implementing or enforcing either the 1984 or 1986 lobbying regulations.[67]

Class Actions

The Legal Services Corporation Act requires that class actions be approved by the project director of a recipient agency in accordance with policies established by the agency's governing body.[68] Beginning with the 1983 appropriation statute, new restrictions were added, notably that prior to filing a class action against a government entity, the project director must determine that the government entity is unlikely to change the policy or practice in question, that the policy or practice will continue to adversely affect eligible clients and that responsible efforts to resolve the matter without litigation have been unsuccessful or would be adverse to client interests.

Specific Causes

LSC funds may not be used to provide legal assistance with respect to abortions, desegregation of school systems, violations of military selective service acts or military desertion or criminal proceedings. Some of these restrictions rest on rationing grounds (e.g., since states are required to provide defense lawyers to criminal indigents, federal funds should be restricted to civil legal assistance); others are frankly political. How can the denial of legal services to those seeking school desegregation be justified? Is the suspicion that desegregation is the mission of lawyers and not poor people generally enough to justify the ban? Why should it matter whose mission it is, if desegregation is a goal of American justice? What justifies the abortion ban?

Legal services programs are also prohibited from engaging in direct political activity. "Political activity" is defined by the Act to include any activity involving transportation of voters to the polls, voter registration activity other than legal advice or representation and various partisan and election activities. The 1977 amendments prohibit a staff attorney from being a candidate in a partisan political election.

Fee–Generating Cases

LSC recipients may not provide legal assistance in any fee-generating case except in accordance with guidelines promulgated by LSC.

66. Public Law 93–335, § 1007(a)(5).

67. See Pub.L. 99–591.

68. See § 1006(d)(5).

Thus LSC grantees may not undertake personal injury claims that can be handled by private lawyers under contingent-fee arrangements.[69]

Organizing

The LSC Act forbids use of LSC funds "to organize, assist to organize or encourage to organize or to plan for the creation or formation of, or the structuring of, any organization, association, coalition, alliance, federation, confederation or any similar entity."[70] Changes in 1977 made it clear that local programs may give legal advice to those seeking to organize a group of poor people or to such an organization once it is formed. But legal services lawyers may not themselves organize the group.

STEPHEN WEXLER
"PRACTICING LAW FOR POOR PEOPLE"
79 Yale Law Journal 1049, 1049–1059 (1970).[71]

Poor people are not just like rich people without money. Poor people do not have legal problems like those of the private plaintiffs and defendants in law school casebooks. People who are not poor are like casebook people. In so far as the law is concerned, they lead harmonious and settled private lives; except for their business involvements, their lives usually do not demand the skills of a lawyer. Occasionally, one of them gets hit by a car, or decides to buy a house, or lets his dog bite someone. The settled and harmonious pattern of life is then either broken or there is a threat that without care it may be broken. This is the law school model of a personal legal problem; law schools train lawyers to take care of such problems and to understand the role of a lawyer in those terms.

Poor people get hit by cars too; they get evicted; they have their furniture repossessed; they can't pay their utility bills. But they do not have personal legal problems in the law school way. Nothing that happens to them breaks up or threatens to break up a settled and harmonious life. Poor people do not lead settled lives into which the law seldom intrudes; they are constantly involved with the law in its most intrusive forms. For instance, poor people must go to government officials for many of the things which not-poor people get privately. Life would be very difficult for the not-poor person if he had to fill out an income tax return once or twice a week. Poverty creates an abrasive interface with society; poor people are always bumping into sharp legal things. The law school model of personal legal problems, of solving them and returning the client to the smooth and orderly world in television advertisements, doesn't apply to poor people.

. . .

69. See § 1007(b)(1); 45 C.F.R. § 1609.

70. Pub.L. 93–355, § 1007(b)(6).

71. Copyright © Yale Law Journal, 1970. Reprinted with permission.

Poverty will not be stopped by people who are not poor. If poverty is stopped, it will be stopped by poor people. And poor people can stop poverty only if they work at it together. The lawyer who wants to serve poor people must put his skills to the task of helping poor people organize themselves. This is not the traditional use of a lawyer's skills; in many ways it violates some of the basic tenets of the profession. Nevertheless, a realistic analysis of the structure of poverty, and a fair assessment of the legal needs of the poor and the legal talent available to meet them, lead a lawyer to this role.

If all the lawyers in the country worked full time, they could not deal with even the articulated legal problems of the poor. And even if somehow lawyers could deal with those articulated problems, they would not change very much the tangle of unarticulated legal troubles in which poor people live. In fact, only a very few lawyers will concern themselves with poor people, and those who do so will probably be at it for only a while. In this setting the object of practicing poverty law must be to organize poor people, rather than to solve their legal problems. The proper job for a poor people's lawyer is helping poor people to organize themselves to change things so that either no one is poor or (less radically) so that poverty does not entail misery.

Two major touchstones of traditional legal practice—the solving of legal problems and the one-to-one relationship between attorney and client—are either not relevant to poor people or harmful to them. Traditional practice hurts poor people by isolating them from each other, and fails to meet their need for a lawyer by completely misunderstanding that need. Poor people have few individual legal problems in the traditional sense; their problems are the product of poverty, and are common to all poor people. The lawyer for poor individuals is likely, whether he wins cases or not, to leave his clients precisely where he found them, except that they will have developed a dependency on his skills to smooth out the roughest spots in their lives.

The lawyer will eventually go or be taken away; he does not have to stay, and the government which gave him can take him back just as it does welfare. He can be another hook on which poor people depend, or he can help the poor build something which rests upon themselves— something which cannot be taken away and which will not leave until all of them can leave. Specifically, the lawyer must seek to strengthen existing organizations of poor people, and to help poor people start organizations where none exist. There are several techniques for doing this, but all of them run counter to very deeply rooted notions in law school training, professionalism and middle-class humanism. I shall say something about the techniques which have already been used by lawyers to help organize poor people; but the techniques are not nearly so important as the mentality of the lawyer who uses them. The techniques will prove unsuccessful if applied by a lawyer who misunderstands his role; and the lawyer who knows what he is about will find the techniques to do his job.

The starkest picture of the "proper" mentality for a poor people's lawyer is painted in a story told by a very successful welfare rights organizer:

> I once found a recipient who worked hard at organizing, and was particularly good in the initial stages of getting to talk to new people. I picked her up at her apartment one morning to go out knocking on doors. While I was there, I saw her child, and I noticed that he seemed to be retarded. Because the boy was too young for school and the family never saw a doctor, the mother had never found out that something was seriously wrong with her son. I didn't tell her. If I had, she would have stopped working at welfare organizing to rush around looking for help for her son. I had some personal problems about doing that, but I'm an organizer, not a social worker.

I have heard this story related several times; each time, the people who have not heard it before gasp, fidget in their seats, and shrink away from the organizer. It is natural for them to be repelled, for this story embodies the very hardest line about organizing. Not everyone can handle the "personal problems" which arise from a primary commitment to organizing. The very things which make a lawyer want to work for poor people make it difficult to help them in the most effective way. Few can accept the organizer's model fully; but the more one is able to accept it, the more he can give poor people the wherewithal to change a world that hurts them.

If organizing is the object of a poverty practice, what are the methods for achieving that object? One method by which an existing organization can be strengthened is for a lawyer to refuse to handle matters for individuals not in the organization. A lawyer is a valuable piece of property in a poor community; an organization that can command his skills for its members, and deny them to non-members, has a powerful means of building its membership.

Turning people away is difficult: The values which made a lawyer want to help poor people will make it hard to turn away a person with a problem; the professional ethic is full of talk about representing all who need representation; moreover, the government, which often pays the lawyer, has guidelines designed to ensure that all who come get served. The latter points are weakened when one realizes that there are too many poor people seeking or in need of aid to help them all. A seemingly neutral policy of "first-come, first-served" cuts against the least informed, the least mobile, and the most oppressed. Some sieve is inevitably applied to the work a poverty lawyer does; that sieve can be one he chooses consciously in order to serve a particular end, or it can be one he chooses without thinking, and with no aim at all....

Selection of clients is only the first step; the cornerstone of a practice is the kind of service a lawyer provides for his clients. The hallmark of an effective poor people's practice is that the lawyer does not do anything for his clients that they can do or be taught to do for themselves. The standards of success for a poor people's lawyer are how well he can recognize all the things his clients can do with a little of his help, and how well he can teach them to do more.

There are several reasons for building a practice with these goals. First, there aren't enough lawyers to serve poor people, so poor people must be helped and taught to serve themselves. Second, it is better for poor people to acquire new skills than new dependencies. Third, poor people can often do what lawyers cannot or will not do. Finally, the law ought to be demystified for all laymen, but especially for the poor. More important than the specific techniques is the lawyer's belief that his clients are able to do a great many "legal" things for themselves. Most people who are not poor believe that poor people are unable to take care of themselves, let alone do work traditionally reserved for professionals. In addition to this general belief in the incompetence of poor people, lawyers are taught to believe, and have a three-year investment in believing, that what they have learned in law school was hard to learn, and that they are somehow special for having learned it. It is difficult for a lawyer to commit himself to believing that poor people can learn the law and be effective advocates; but until he believes that, a lawyer will create dependency instead of strength for his clients, and add to rather than reduce their plight.

Four ways in which a lawyer can help his clients use his knowledge are (1) informing individuals and groups of their rights, (2) writing manuals and other materials, (3) training lay advocates, and (4) educating groups for confrontation. None is particularly glamorous, but all are extremely important.

These techniques are some of the possible ways in which a lawyer can help poor people to use his knowledge and skills. While these techniques are important, the most important thing for a poor people's lawyer is to avoid playing the "lawyer's game." From all that one hears in law school, one comes to believe that a lawyer is doing his job and being a good person if he is honest and works as hard as he can for the interests of his client. This technical "morality" is a fraud; it is a way to avoid, rather than to address, the real moral questions which a lawyer ought to face. It is morality within a game.

The chief theoretical justification for the game is the adversary notion of law: each side has an advocate, each advocate is competent and fully devoted to the interests of his client, and from this structure justice will emerge. Among the not-poor, the adversary system might lead to justice; the most usual criticism of lawyers from not-poor people concerns their dishonesty and failure to be fully committed and fully competent advocates. But if justice can be obtained for the not-poor through an adversary system of law, it is because they are involved with the law on a case-by-case basis. But a case-by-case injustice is not what poor people face; they confront a host of unjust institutions, acting for and within an unjust society. The whole notion of an adversary proceeding is unsuited to dealing with social problems.

4. Recurring Policy Issues

Staff–Attorney System or Judicare System?

The United States is distinctive in that civil legal assistance to the poor is provided primarily by organizations that employ "poverty lawyers"—lawyers who are employed full time by local non-profit organizations engaged in delivering legal services to eligible poor persons (generally defined as persons whose household incomes are below 125 percent of the federal "poverty line"). In other countries eligible poor persons are referred to members of the private bar, who are then paid by the state at rates fixed by statute or regulation. The latter system, by analogy to Medicare, is referred to as "judicare" in the United States.

The staff-attorney system, which is favored by most participants in the U.S. legal services movement, provides a cadre of lawyers who are intellectually and personally committed to serving the poor; the delivery of service may be organized so that clients are served by experienced specialists in various areas of poverty law, such as welfare, housing or education; and it permits more aggressive pursuit of institutional reform that benefits groups of poor people rather than merely an individual client.

Proponents of judicare as a replacement of or alternative to the staff-attorney system argue that use of private lawyers permits a more normal lawyer-client relationship (the client chooses the lawyer and controls the objectives of the representation) and leads to greater client satisfaction.[72] Some proponents favor judicare for precisely the reasons that those enamored of law reform litigation prefer the staff-attorney system: Judicare is more likely to stick to individual-client service. Studies performed by the Legal Service Corporation indicate that both systems are feasible, the existence of some staff component is essential in controlling costs and the staff system offers a potential of having a larger impact on the legal rights and living conditions of eligible clients.[73]

Who Should Be Served?

The demand for free goods, even if their use involves time and inconvenience, is likely to exceed the available supply. The result is an inevitable rationing problem. Because lawyers cannot and will not be provided to all poor people who feel aggrieved and who lack the

72. Samuel J. Brakel, Judicare: Public Funds, Private Lawyers, and Poor People (1974); Brakel, Styles of Delivery of Legal Services to the Poor, 1977 Amer.Bar Found. Research J. 219.

73. Legal Services Corporation, The Delivery Systems Study: A Policy Report to the Congress and President of the United States (1980).

resources or capacity to seek relief on their own, someone must decide who will be served. Local legal services programs are required to establish priorities after consultation with representatives of client groups, but it is recognized that staff lawyers play a large role in shaping and then administering priorities. The establishment of a priority in one area, such as public housing issues, may lead to refusing service in categories of other cases. A number of legal services programs, for example, refuse to accept matrimonial cases. Critics of the current program advocate adoption of more neutral principles, such as queuing or some effort to replicate the private market, as with a voucher system or client copayments.[74]

Current arrangements rely on utilitarian arguments of *triage*: Because funding is so limited, scarce resources must be devoted to handling the most serious problems that will do the most good for poor people as a whole. This argument places group interests above the right of individuals to obtain access to justice to defend or enforce their legal rights.[75] Inevitably, it places authority in staff lawyers who decide what cases to take and, in doing so and in handling the subsequent representation, to make decisions as to what is in the best interests of poor people.[76] Finally, critics argue, it departs from the traditional lawyer-client relationship by putting lawyers too much in control. A poor client, unlike a rich one, is unable to choose her lawyer, define the objectives of representation and the resources devoted to it and to select a new lawyer if the initial one is unsatisfactory.

What Should Be the Standard of Service?

Ordinary people who desire a lawyer to prepare a will, get a divorce or facilitate a transaction must pay the customary charge of lawyers for that service. Numerous studies indicate that many of them forego the use of legal services because of cost, inconvenience or fear of

74. See Douglas J. Besharov, Legal Services for the Poor: Time for Reform xiv, xvi (1990) (staff lawyers, who dominate priority setting, devote little effort to the problems associated with family breakdown, which are the most critical problem of poor people today; client copayments would force clients to choose among their needs); and Marshall J. Breger, Legal Aid for the Poor: A Conceptual Analysis, 60 No.Car.L.Rev. 282 (1982) (utilitarian justifications of a lawyer-centered rationing of service should be replaced by an individual-rights approach).

75. Breger, supra, argues that the claims of poor people of access to justice are best protected through allocation and litigation procedures that give equal weight to each person's complaint, not by procedures that turn on the group impact of a given poor person's case. Marie A. Failinger and Larry May, Litigating Against Poverty: Legal Services and Group Representation, 45 Ohio State L. J. 1 (1984), responding to Breger's argument, dispute his claim that access rights are more important than welfare rights.

76. See Paul R. Tremblay, Toward a Community–Based Ethic for Legal Services Practice, 37 U.C.L.A. L.Rev. 1103, 1111 (1990), arguing that the legal services lawyer faces the dilemma of choosing between "allegiance to the individual client" and making choices and imposing limits that serve interests of groups of poor people. Tremblay states:

Legal services offices must engage in a form of triage, or "screening of [clients] to determine their priority for treatment [i.e., representation]. They cannot allocate their services according to the usual method of price, so they must choose other means to decide between potentially eligible clients.

becoming involved in the legal machinery. Those with little choice, who are cast as defendants in a proceeding brought by someone else, reluctantly hire lawyers, but generally push them to handle the matter as cheaply as possible. The result is a world in which most people "lump it" on many legal matters and get low-cost or minimal representation on many others. That is the reality of the legal market place in which most private persons make their decisions.

The most ambitious vision of legal services for the poor, however, looks to the representation provided to wealthy individuals and large corporations in high-stakes matters as the appropriate analogy. Earl Johnson, who headed the OEO legal program in the 1960s, states that he learned what full-servicing lawyering for a client really meant from a partner at Covington & Burling who represented American Airlines in major controversies. Poor people, Johnson concluded, are entitled to the same quality and extent of legal service that is provided to a wealthy client in a high-stakes matter: aggressive advocacy at every stage, including appeals; representation in administrative and legislative matters, including lobbying; and use of representative or class actions when in the interest of clients as a group. The implication is that eligible clients of publicly-funded legal services offices are entitled to what only a few wealthy persons and large corporations actually receive in high-stakes matters: unrestricted full-service lawyering that leaves no stone unturned and is largely unrestrained by considerations of cost.

The stakes involved in some test cases or class actions clearly justify full-service lawyering. The aggregation of small, related claims may collectively constitute a major claim that justifies a substantial commitment of legal resources whether the case is pursued by a legal services lawyer, without fee, or a class action lawyer who anticipates a fee award from a successful action. See the discussion of class action lawyers in Chapter 8 above at p. 836.

Other matters, however, present issues of proportionality and fairness. A private litigant ordinarily will not pursue a $1,000 matter by expending more than some fraction of that amount on legal services. But a publicly-funded lawyer is not similarly constrained in litigation on behalf of a poor client. As Gary Bellow and others have recognized, this fact confers enormous leverage on legal services lawyers in dealing with private persons and some leverage in dealing with government agencies. Because the costs of litigation from the point of view of a private person may be larger than the amount at stake, the possibility of extortionate settlements exist. The constraints on this behavior on the part of legal services lawyers are the practical ones of heavy caseloads and limited staffs, constraints that advocates of full-service lawyering on behalf of the poor vigorously lament and want removed.

Social Advocacy v. Individual Client Service [77]

The activist vision is one in which lawyers improve the lives of poor people by redistributing power to them to influence decisions that will affect them. Gary Bellow, for example, criticized the tendency of most legal service organizations to devote most of their effort to individual client service.[78] Poorly trained and inexperienced lawyers were thrown into frustrating and tension-laden situations that resulted in minimal service and did little to ease the larger problems of the poor. The legal services program's potential for social change, he argued, could not be achieved unless its priorities were reversed, so that political organization of the poor would come first, followed by aggressive pursuit of strategic priorities in a way that would apply maximum pressure in favor of institutional and legal changes that affect large numbers of poor people.

> A massive expansion of minimal, routinized legal assistance throughout the low-income areas of the country, mediated by selective efforts at "law reform", is potentially a powerful system of social control, capable of defining and legitimating particular grievances and resolutions and ignoring others. Legal aid lawyers, unwilling or unable to respond to client concerns in ways which link them to a larger vision of social justice, can readily become purveyors of acquiescence and resignation among the people that they are seeking to help. Clients can be literally "taught" that their situations are natural, inevitable, or their own fault, and that dependence on professional advice and guidance is their only appropriate course of action; that is, legal assistance for the poor can become a bulwark of existing social arrangements. To echo a now familiar phrase, a profession that is not part of the solution can soon become part of the problem. The legal aid experience may soon be a troubling illustration of the modern homily.[79]

One of the ironies of modern political debate is that members of the political right, most notably Jack Kemp, HHS Secretary under President Bush, have recently appropriated the term "empowerment" to describe their approach to the problems of the poor. Those on the right who speak of empowerment view the liberal programs of the 1960s, including the legal services movement, as disempowering the poor and empowering instead liberal do-good program employees, such as legal

---

77. See generally Marshall J. Breger, Legal Aid for the Poor: A Conceptual Analysis, 60 No.Car. L. Rev. 282 (1982); Failinger and May, supra.

78. Gary Bellow, Turning Solutions Into Problems: The Legal Aid Experience, 34 N.L.A.D.A. Briefcase 106, 122 (1977). See also Gary Bellow, Legal Aid in the United States, 14 Clearinghouse Rev. 337 (1980).

79. Bellow, Turning Solutions Into Problems, at 122. See also Jack Katz, Poor People's Lawyers in Transition (1982). Katz's study of the legal services program in Chicago finds that during the 1970s "law reform" activities replaced an earlier emphasis on organizing and community education. The result was what Katz calls the "legalization of poverty." Legal services lawyers helped create government programs for the poor that were professionally administered, confined by formal procedures and limited by rules and standards. Poverty lawyers became poverty managers and "helped rationalize the state's organization of the poor as a homogeneous segregated social class."

services lawyers. This critique reflects the American suspicion of groups who see themselves as having a special obligation to serve social justice. This suspicion is grounded in the belief that, like all other individuals, members of such groups are really serving their individual needs and not the needs of others. The irony is that this same charge can be and is leveled against the "new right" advocates of empowerment.

David Luban provides an elaborate philosophical defense of a vision of politicized legal services.[80] As a foundation for doing so, he constructs a worst-case scenario of public housing representation in order to then argue that, even in the occasional instances of worst-case social activism, the activity is needed and desirable. In considering the issues raised here, the student should recall two cases previously considered that involved social advocacy by legal services lawyers: *Fiandaca,* printed above in Chapter 7 at p. 644, dealing with conflicts of interest in concurrent representation, and *Jeff D.,* printed in Chapter 6 above at p. 548, dealing with attorney-fee waivers.

Luban's scenario involves a legal services program (the Center) in a metropolitan area that decides to focus its attention on reforming the city's public housing program. The agency responsible for public housing has allowed the housing to deteriorate, has not maintained basic services and has violated state and federal law in perpetuating racial patterns. The staff attorneys in the program decide to mount an attack against the agency's tenant-selection practices, its failure to correct project conditions and its construction policies for new units. The Center cuts back on provision of other legal aid to handle the tenants who are well-situated to raise these issues. To build the morale and loyalty of housing clients who agree to accept representation on the Center's terms, a broad range of legal services other than housing is provided to them. A series of lawsuits over a period of years results in a federal judge appointing a receiver to administer the housing agency, ousting the elected officials who have been unresponsive to prior court orders. The existing units are fully integrated and new construction is targeted for transitional areas mixed in racial composition. The Center's activities produce a great deal of hostility in the city, including some from poor groups who are declined service or who disagree with the Center's housing location policies.

Luban's example graphically raises all the important objections to politicized public interest law practice:

> ... The Center's lawyers manipulated clients, took sides in a dispute within the client community (over whether the development should be built in an integrated neighborhood), spent public money to take a partisan stand on several divisive and politically controversial issues, switched from a general legal services practice to a politicized legal campaign, and used the courts to take control

---

80. See David Luban, Lawyers and Justice (1990).

of a political institution.   All of these are highly debatable tactics.... [81]

Luban's conclusion, however, is that, choice of tactics aside,

There is absolutely nothing illegitimate about impact work being done by legal services lawyers, even highly politicized legal services lawyers. On the contrary, law reform of this sort is at once an admirable attempt to further social justice and a professional responsibility to help more clients rather than fewer. It is precisely what lawyers ought to be doing.[82]

Luban argues that successful law reform solves the problems of many poor people at once and is therefore the most efficient use of scarce legal resources. Although Luban concedes that client control and manipulation are sometimes involved, "one cannot succeed in political action without dirtying one's hands." [83] Moreover, the people and groups served by the lawyer's political use of the legal machinery are aware of what is going on. Their free and mutual commitment to the lawyer's cause justifies the unusual degree of lawyer control. Winning the battle in the courts rather than in the legislatures does not violate democratic principles because the courts are intervening on behalf of groups that are under-represented in the legislatures. Luban concludes that public interest lawyers, by helping "fragmented constituencies to organize themselves, ... serve the highest goal of democracy: to engage citizens in responsible deliberation about the ends of action." [84]

Is the lawyering described by Luban consistent with the role of the lawyer envisioned by professional ideology and ethics rules? With the role for which legal education prepares law students?

Is Luban's justification for public interest lawyers, that they work to correct democratic failures, persuasive? [85] Public interest lawyers might be seen instead in republican versus democratic terms: an elite group working toward some vision of the public good. Is this description more accurate, if less appealing? If it is less appealing, how so?

---

81. Id. at 297–98. The authors do not believe that Luban's scenario reflects the attitudes and conduct of the legal services lawyers in the one housing receivership case of which we are aware.

82. Id. at 302.

83. Id. at xiv.

84. Id. at xv.

85. Contrast the following quote from deTocqueville.

The influence that [the bar] exerts in America is the most powerful existing security against the excesses of democracy. Without this admixture of lawyer-like sobriety, with democratic principles, I question whether democratic institutions could long be maintained, and I cannot believe that a republic could exist at the present time, if the influence of lawyers in public business does not increase in proportion to the power of the people.

Alexis deTocqueville, Democracy in America, quoted in Randall, Our Professional Responsibility: Lawyers Make Freedom a Living Thing, 43 A.B.A. J. 315, 318, n.13 (1957).

Compare Brill's description of the work of legal services' lawyers in his article on Room 202, p. 1037, Wexler's description of what the ideal poor person's lawyer would do, p. 1053, and Luban's description of the tactics necessary in the name of social justice. Would Wexler approve of the lawyers Brill praises or those Luban critiques and defends? Would Luban approve of Brill's lawyers? What responsibility do you think the bar has to stop the Stench of Room 202? To remedy conditions in public housing projects? To organize the poor so that they get a bigger piece of the American promise?

Or are housing conditions in a city such as New York the result of political, legal and financial structures that are unlikely to be amenable to lawyering activity (e.g., unrealistic and unenforced building codes, inequities and shortages resulting from a rent-controlled housing market and absence of social provision for homeless people)?

C. JUSTICE AND ORDINARY LAWYERING

1. Access to Justice for the Non–Poor

Is there too much or too little access to justice in the United States? Are lawyers the problem of or the solution to the contemporary problems of access and litigiousness? In 1983 Derek Bok, former dean of the Harvard Law School and then president of Harvard University, expressed widely-held views in a broad critique of the American legal system, the legal profession and legal education.[1] "The legal system," Bok said, is "grossly inequitable and inefficient; ... there is far too much law for those who can afford it and far too little for those who cannot."[2] Legal rules and procedures, he argued, are unclear and unnecessarily complex; lawyers are too numerous and too litigious;[3] legal uncertainty and conflict, combined with overelaborate procedures, fuel more (and more complex) regulation and litigation, resulting in social expenditures on legal services that have grown to about $80 billion annually.[4] The excessive cost and delay have harmful effects on

1. Derek C. Bok, A Flawed System of Practice and Training, 33 J.Legal Educ. 570 (1983), reprinted from Harvard Magazine 38–45, 70–71 (May–June 1983).

2. Id. at 571.

3. Bok lamented that the wastefulness of our legal system "attracts an unusually large proportion of the exceptionally gifted" college graduates:

The net result ... is a massive diversion of exceptional talent into pursuits that often add little to the growth of the economy, the pursuit of culture, or the enhancement of the human spirit.... [F]ar too many of these rare individuals are becoming lawyers at a time when the country cries out for more talented business executives, more enlightened public servants, more inventive engineers, more able high school principals and teachers.

... A nation's values and problems are mirrored in the ways in which it uses its ablest people.... As the Japanese [who have fewer lawyers] put it, "Engineers make the pie grow larger; lawyers only decide how to carve it up."

Id. at 573–74.

4. In 1982, when Bok wrote, annual expenditures on legal services in the United States were estimated at $30–40 billion; ten years later they are probably closer to $80

everyone; they tax the well-to-do and deprive the poor and the middle class of effective access to justice. Bok urged a combined program of simplification of law (delegalization) and enlarged access, cautioning that either by itself will only make things worse. Society, he asserted, needs simpler procedures and fewer rules which are "more fundamental, better understood, and more widely enforced throughout society."[5] Simultaneously, new forms of delivery of legal services could provide access to justice to the poor and the middle class at reasonable cost and quality.

Others echo some of Bok's critique without necessarily sharing his proposed cures. Aleksandr Solzhenitsyn, criticizing the West's reliance on legal forms and requirements, stated that overemphasis on "the letter of the law" erodes moral values, creating "an atmosphere of spiritual mediocrity that paralyzes man's noblest impulses."[6] Vice President Quayle, speaking to the American Bar Association in support of a battery of proposals designed to improve civil justice, asked:

> Does America really need 70 percent of the world's lawyers? ... Is it healthy for our economy to have 18 million new lawsuits coursing through the system annually? Is it right that people with disputes come up against staggering expense and delay?[7]

Allegations that lawyers bring frivolous suits, increase health care costs, stifle innovation in pharmaceuticals and other products, and hamper the U.S. economy in world economic competition became issues in the 1992 presidential election.

The underlying issues are important, complex and highly controverted.[8] The argument that American society is excessively litigious and over-lawyered is attacked by leaders of the bar and by a substantial group of legal scholars. Marc Galanter's studies of available historical and comparative data on the volume and frequency of litigation demonstrate that patterns of litigation vary over time and place, but that current figures in the United States are not markedly different from

billion. In 1987 the services of lawyers in private practice (not all lawyers) added $62.3 billion to the economy. Richard H. Sander and E. Douglass Williams, Why Are There So Many Lawyers? Perspectives on a Turbulent Market, 14 J. Law & Soc. Inquiry 431 (1989).

5. Id. at 580.

6. Aleksandr I. Solzhenitsyn, A World Split Apart, in R. Berman (ed.), Solzhenitsyn at Harvard 7–8 (1980). Compare Grant Gilmore: "The better the society, the less law there will be. In heaven, there will be no law, and the lion will lie down with the lamb.... In Hell there will be nothing but law, and due process will be meticulously observed." Grant Gilmore, The Age of American Law 111 (1977).

7. Dan Quayle, "Isn't Our Legal System in Need of Reform," Legal Times 9–10 (Aug. 19, 1991). Quayle's facts and proposals were immediately attacked by leaders of the bar. See David Margolick, A Speech by Quayle on the Legal System Unsettles Lawyers, N.Y.Times (Aug. 14, 1991), at pp. A1, A14. Quayle's data were challenged by Marc Galanter, American Lawyer 82–86 (April 1992).

8. For a good survey of this subject, see Thomas D. Rowe, Study on Paths to a "Better Way": Litigation, Alternatives, and Accommodation, 1989 Duke L. J. 824.

those of the American past or of other countries with a similar legal system.[9] Recent decades have shown, however, an increase in the volume, complexity, length and cost of high-stakes litigation, especially in the federal courts.

Do the benefits of litigation outweigh its costs? Americans resort to court because other mechanisms of social control—the family, the church, the neighborhood—have lost some of their effectiveness. Some matters that other countries handle without adjudication, such as compensation for accidental injuries, are left to the courts in the United States. The unwillingness or inability of other branches of government to deal decisively with social problems—witness abortion, deficit spending, or conditions in schools or prisons—relegates problems to the courts or encourages efforts to do so. The diffusion of authority among federal, state and local governments adds complexity, uncertainty and opportunities for manipulation.

But are these aspects of American society vices or virtues? An alternative vision converts what critics view as vices into virtues.[10] Governmental authority is diffused in order that liberty may flourish. The complex blend of reliance on private economic activity and public regulation is designed to provide opportunity and material well-being. The quest for equality in a society characterized by racial, ethnic and religious pluralism centers on the pursuit of individual legal rights. The quest for accountability presses for fairer procedures and better outcomes in private and public institutions. From this point of view, justice through law is a distinctive American virtue rather than a vice. Those who share this vision point to problems of access and conclude that America is underlawyered rather than overlawyered, or at least that the distribution of legal services is badly skewed. In any event, the intangible and immeasurable benefits of litigation should also be considered: expanded opportunities for women and minorities, expansion of civil liberties, fair procedures within institutions, limits on government. "Who would deny that these are significant gains?

9. See Marc Galanter, Reading the Landscape of Disputes: What We Know and Don't Know (and Think We Know) About Our Allegedly Contentious and Litigious Society, 31 U.C.L.A. L. Rev. 4 (1983); Marc Galanter, The Day After the Litigation Explosion, 46 Md. L. Rev. 3 (1986) ("civil court filings are [not] dramatically higher than in the recent past" and are comparable to those of countries with similar legal systems; settlement rates remain high; and the greatest single sources of increased filings are divorce cases in state courts and social security cases in federal courts, which are not brought because people are "enamored of litigation or beguiled by lawyers").

10. Deborah Rhode argues that determining whether a particular claim is frivolous turns on normative judgments. In 1976 a prominent legal educator, then president of the Legal Services Corporation, stated that sex discrimination suits against Little Leagues were an example of "legal pollution" that endangered the legal system. Thomas Ehrlich, Legal Pollution, New York Times 17 (Feb. 8, 1976). But gender stereotyping in the provision of athletic opportunities in a society that takes sports so seriously raises important social and legal issues. See Deborah L. Rhode, Justice and Gender 299–301 (1989).

Whether they are worth the cost is a question that models and equations cannot answer." [11]

The purpose here is not to resolve the unanswerable questions posed by differing attitudes concerning the American reliance on law, lawyers and litigation, but to put more specific and perhaps answerable questions against the backdrop of the larger normative controversy. Who uses the services of lawyers? Are some important "legal needs" left unserved by current patterns of availability and distribution? How, why and at what cost can these needs be met? [12]

Public's Use of Legal Services

BARBARA CURRAN
REPORT ON THE 1989 SURVEY OF THE
PUBLIC'S USE OF LEGAL SERVICES
(American Bar Foundation, 1989). [13]

Summary of Survey Results

In 1974, a national survey of a representative sample of the U.S. adult population examined the incidence of personal, non-business legal problems and the use of legal services in their resolution. In February, 1989, a second national survey was conducted for the purpose of determining whether changes had occurred in the public's need for or use of legal services. This paper reports on the results of the 1989 survey. The following are the principal findings discussed in this paper.

A. Overall Use of Legal Services

1. The use of legal services for personal and family legal matters has increased since 1974. A larger proportion of the 1989 adult population had consulted lawyers at least once in their lives than was the case for the 1974 population. Moreover, wider use of legal services in the 1989 population was also reflected in recent use patterns, i.e., the

---

11. Lawrence Friedman, Litigation in Society, 15 Am.Rev.Sociol. 17, 27 (1989). Marc Galanter states that the "consternation about litigation" is partly due to the accountability to public standards fostered by litigation:

> The sense of being held to account has multiplied far more than cases or trials, for it depends ... not on the direct imposition of court orders, but on the communication of messages about what courts might do. Law as a system of symbols has expanded; information about law and its workings is more widely circulated to more educated and receptive audiences.... The [former] predominance of cases enforcing market relations has given way to tort, civil rights, and public law cases "correcting" the market.... [The increase in this type of litigation] by outsiders and clients and dependents against authorities and managers of established institutions ... excites most of the reproach....

Galanter, supra, 46 Md. L. Rev. at 38.

12. For an excellent collection of materials on topics treated more summarily here, see Deborah L. Rhode and David Luban, Legal Ethics 784–894 (1992).

13. Copyright © American Bar Foundation, 1989. Reprinted with permission.

proportion of the population using legal services in the three year period preceding the 1989 survey was greater than that for the comparable period preceding the 1974 survey.

Percent of adults ever having used legal services:	Percent of adults having used legal services within 3 years of survey:
1974: 64%	1974: 27%
1989: 72%	1989: 39%

2.   The rise in lawyer use occurred primarily among persons over the age of 40.

3.   The disparity in lawyer use rates is substantial between highest and lowest income groups.   While 49% of adults in the top 25% of the income scale had consulted lawyers in 1986–89, only 27% of adults in the lowest 10% used legal services during the same period.

4.   Use of legal services increased for all income groups, but at the slowest rate among persons of limited means and at the highest rate among persons of moderate means. . . .

C.   Considerations Surrounding Use of Lawyers' Services

1.   Cost remains a significant element in the decision to seek legal assistance.   Those considering consulting lawyers are most likely to refrain from doing so in the case of consumer and marital problems.

2.   The overwhelming majority of persons considering using legal services turn to friends and relatives for advice and help in choosing a lawyer.   Almost 10% rely on advertisements and yellow pages.

3.   Current income remains the principal way in which lawyers' services are financed by all income groups.   Forty-two percent of those of limited means pay for lawyers' service out of current income or by borrowing. . . .

Reasons for Not Consulting Lawyers

In both the 1974 and 1989 surveys, respondents were asked whether they had considered consulting a lawyer on a personal, family matter but had not done so.   Of those responding to the question, 9% of the 1989 survey group indicated they had considered consulting a lawyer at some time during the three years preceding the survey while 14% of the 1974 survey group had done so in the three year period preceding the 1974 survey.

Table 24.   Distribution of reasons given for not consulting lawyers (1986–89) N=91

Solved other way	29%
Cost	22%
Decided not to pursue further	15%
Procrastination	12%
Finding the right lawyer	6%

Problems ought to be solved without lawyer	3%
Didn't think attorney would be of any help	3%
Didn't know why lawyers not consulted	4%
Other reasons	6%
TOTAL	100%

The reasons given are not mutually exclusive. Concern about cost or selecting the "right" lawyer may well have influenced decisions not to pursue the matter further or solving the problem in some other way.

———

Other efforts to measure the public's legal needs show that many people think they have been legally wronged by another; [14] that some grievances (e.g., a tort matter) are much more likely to be pursued than others (e.g., a discrimination claim); [15] and that low income households eligible for publicly-funded civil legal assistance report many grievances for which lawyers were not available but would have been helpful.[16]

The time and energy of lawyers is primarily devoted to relatively well-to-do individuals, small businesses and large organizations. Lawyers in private practice spend only a small portion of their time in the representation of low income clients.[17] Only about 4,000 lawyers work for the legal services organizations that provide free civil legal assistance to eligible poor people. The Council for Public Interest Law reports that in 1989 there were 200 tax-exempt non-profit groups that devoted a substantial portion of their resources to the representation of previously unrepresented interests on matters of public policy, but these groups employed only about 1,000 lawyers.[18] Thus less than 1 percent of U.S. lawyers are engaged full time in representing poor people or otherwise unrepresented interests in civil matters. Social advocacy litigation—efforts to vindicate the collective interests of groups such as prisoners, welfare recipients and victims of institutional

14. Richard E. Miller and Austin Sarat, Grievances, Claims, and Disputes: Assessing the Adversary Culture, 15 Law & Soc'y Rev. 525 (1980–81) (reporting that 40 percent of randomly selected households experienced a grievance involving $1,000 or more during a three-year period; 79 percent of those experiencing a grievance made a claim and 68 percent obtained some recovery, but only 11 percent filed a lawsuit).

15. William Felstiner, Richard Abel, and Austin Sarat, The Emergence and Transformation of Disputes: Naming, Claiming, and Blaming, 15 Law & Soc'y Rev. 631 (1980).

16. The Spangenberg Group, American Bar Association National Civil Legal Study (1989) (no legal assistance was available in about 80 percent of the civil legal problems encountered during the prior year by 43 percent of those surveyed). Principal reasons for not consulting a lawyer were cost (28 percent) and lack of knowledge about how to obtain assistance (17.5 percent).

17. See Joel Handler, Ellen Hollingsworth, and Howard Erlanger, Lawyers and the Pursuit of Legal Rights (1978) (estimating that only about 10 percent of the effort of those lawyers who represent individual clients is devoted to those with incomes in the bottom one-third of the population).

18. Nan Aron, Liberty and Justice for All: Public Interest Law in the 1980's and Beyond 55–56 (1989).

discrimination—is largely dependent on the efforts of this small band of public interest lawyers.

Alternative Prescriptions

How important are the unserved needs described above in social and individual terms? Poor people have many needs and the pursuit of legal claims with the help of lawyers may be much less important than other needs, such as housing, education and employment. Social resources are finite and other programs and benefits for poor people compete with the provision of lawyers. Moreover, legal services are different from other professional services in two respects: First, because equality in their provision is important (the adversary system operates best when both parties have advocates of equal skill and resources), it is argued that poor or limited services carry some negatives and limited benefits.[19] Second, the availability to one party of subsidized legal services imposes costs on other persons, who are forced to hire lawyers to defend their interests, and on the public.

If all needs cannot be met because of cost or normative objections, who should decide what needs will be met? In Europe, where a right to civil legal assistance is generally recognized, its actual provision is restricted by screening mechanisms and by severe restrictions on the fees lawyers earn in handling matters that survive the screening process.[20]

If some specific needs should be met, perhaps because they enable poor people to take control over their own lives, does it follow that law, lawyers and litigation are the best or most desirable approach? Alternatives include the simplification or modification of legal rules or processes so that individuals could handle their own problems. This approach, often referred to as "delegalization," is favored by Bok and other commentators because it reduces the need for legal intervention by substituting an alternative regime. Drastic simplification of transactions or events that now require the use of lawyers, such as probate of wills, sale of houses and divorces, might reduce the need for lawyers for millions of routine matters. Simpler statutes and regulations written in "plain English" might be followed without resort to professional advice. Changes in substantive law would also eliminate the need for lawyers and lawsuits, for example, the substitution of national health care for most personal injury and accident losses. All of these proposals are highly controversial. In each case the legal profession tends to resist substantive or procedural change, whether out of concern for the substantive or procedural rights that would be sacrificed or out of economic self-interest. In each area lawyers opposing change

19. Richard L. Abel, Legal Services (1981), reprinted in G. Hazard and D. Rhode, The Legal Profession: Responsibility and Regulation 417 (2d ed. 1988) (unlike health care and other services, "the services of a lawyer are valuable only if they are roughly equal, in quality and quantity, to the services possessed by adversaries").

20. See Earl Johnson, Jr., The Right to Counsel in Civil Cases, 19 Loy.-L.A. L.Rev. 341 (1985) (comparative study).

(e.g., probate lawyers opposing simplified probate or personal injury lawyers opposing compensation plans) are joined by powerful economic and social interests (e.g., insurance companies and health care providers who oppose compensation and health care proposals that would affect their interests).

A second set of reform proposals seeks to reduce the cost of legal services and court proceedings by handing them more efficiently. Alternative dispute resolution (ADR) is a favorite proposal. Frank Sander, for example, proposes extensive use of ADR techniques in a multi-door courtroom, with some official deciding which technique, or series of techniques, are appropriate for a particular dispute.[21] Repetitive and routinized adjudicatory functions would be handled by procedures less cumbersome than normal adjudication. Most cases, even the complex ones, would be disposed of in arbitration or mediation stages that would precede the trial stage. Skeptics respond that the efficiency gains will occur only if the parties waive constitutional rights or the procedures deal effectively with intractable procedural dilemmas. Others attack the fundamental premises of ADR. Owen Fiss, for example, argues that social values inherent in judicial declaration of public norms are sacrificed by substitution of more informal processes of private settlement.[22] Richard Abel and others worry that compulsory ADR will be confined in practice primarily to poor people, resulting in second-class justice for those who are already deprived.[23]

Another way to reduce the cost of legal services, favored by a number of commentators, involves deregulation of the practice of law.[24] Increased competition within the legal profession and with nonlawyer service providers, it is argued, would lower the cost of routine legal services and make them more available to the public at acceptable levels of quality. This approach would eliminate the professional monopoly and the remaining restrictions on form of practice. Nonlawyers would be able to compete with lawyers in the provision of legal services by delivering services directly to clients (with a possible exception for representation of criminal defendants) or by employing various

21. See Frank Sander, Varieties of Dispute Processing, 70 F.R.D. 111 (1976); Stephen Goldberg, Eric D. Green and Frank Sander, Dispute Resolution (1985).

22. Owen Fiss, Against Settlement, 93 Yale L.J. 1073 (1984).

23. Richard Abel, Delegalization, reprinted in G. Hazard and D. Rhode, The Legal Profession: Responsibility and Regulation 388 (2d ed. 1988). See also Jerold Auerbach, Justice Without Law? Resolving Disputes Without Lawyers 115–37 (1983).

24. See, e.g., W. Clark Durant, Maximizing Access to Justice: A Challenge to the Legal Profession (speech of Feb. 12, 1987), reprinted in D. Rhode and D. Luban, Legal Ethics 832–40 (1992). Durant, then chairman of the board of the Legal Services Corporation, called for replacement of the Corporation by deregulation of the legal profession:

> The overall effect of this system created and operated by lawyers is to limit entry into the profession, to discourage competition, to increase prices, delays and costs and ultimately to deny access to justice for the poor, for all of us. The legal cartel's heaviest burden falls on the poor. They are denied choices and access. They are denied advocates and opportunities.

Rhode and Luban, supra, at 838.

combinations of lawyers and paralegals to perform legal tasks on a high-volume, low-cost basis. Judge Richard Posner also favors the deregulation of legal education: individuals should be able to sit for bar examinations without attending accredited law schools, a change that would require law schools to justify their costs in a free market—costs that now are built into the cost of legal services.[25]

2. Justice in the Law Office

Introductory Note

Do private lawyers have an obligation to see that justice is done? It is fairly well accepted that trial lawyers may and should leave justice to the judge and jury. In the stylized world of a trial, lawyers are expected to play the role of partisan advocate; judges and juries are to worry about just results. Because partisanship must be kept "within the bounds of law," law constrains the trial lawyer's partisanship. For example, the law on suborning perjury, Rule 11 on honesty in papers filed in civil proceedings, the prosecutor's obligations to provide the defense with exculpatory information and not to seek the conviction of the innocent, all set limits on the partisanship of trial lawyers.

Nonetheless, the theory of adversary proceedings is that each side's lawyers will be partisan—through adversary representation under the supervision of an impartial referee (the judge), the fact finder, be it judge or jury, will arrive at a just result. The advocate should not supplant the fact finder's role in the name of justice. Justice in American society is in large part defined by the assumption that lawyers will play the role of partisan at trial, and citizens in the form of a jury, not professionals, will decide the litigants' fate.

Most lawyering, however, is other than trial lawyering. The vast majority of lawyering occurs in the offices of lawyers and consists of lawyers helping clients arrange their affairs or transact business with other people. No referee charged with keeping partisanship within the limits of the law is present in the lawyer's office; no entity charged with determining facts or applying law to concrete situations passes on assertions. Those present are limited to the lawyer, her client, sometimes the opposite party and sometimes a lawyer for that party. Whose job is it in this situation to see that justice is done? That the law is followed? That the parties operate in good faith? Should it be anyone's job?

---

25. Richard Posner, The Uncertain Future of Legal Education (talk to AALS annual meeting, Washington, D.C., Jan. 5, 1991), reported in Nat'l L. J. 4 (Jan. 21, 1991). Posner stated that legal education "has been distorted and quite possibly distended by state regulation." Law schools "have a captive audience, insulating [them] from a true market test of the value of the services they provide. . . . The students recognize that they are paying for a credential, rather than an education."

Drafting Contracts

The American concept of justice, emphasizing as it does individualism and autonomy, reserves much room for the private ordering of relations among citizens, including citizens acting through business organizations. This private law is created for the most part by lawyers acting for individual fee-paying clients. Are these lawyers, who create law for the parties, responsible for the justice and injustice of the law they create? When both parties to a contract are represented by competent counsel, lawyers may relinquish some responsibility for the justice of what they create by relying on the adversary excuse: "It's my job to further my client's interest and it's the other side's job to further her client's interest." Of course, the private contracting model lacks some features of an adversary proceeding that are important to the excuse, such as an effective referee and discovery procedures to ensure the availability of material information. The adversary excuse is thus only partially available in reciprocally lawyered contract formation. It fails completely, however, when only one party to a contract is represented by a lawyer.

In most other Western democracies the terms of contracts, particularly adhesion (take-it-or-leave-it) contracts, are closely regulated, and often specified in detail, by legal codes. In this country, such regulation is exceptional. As a result, the fairness and justice of the private law created by contracts are far more dependent on the lawyers who draft such agreements.

In 1973, the Massachusetts Supreme Judicial Court held in litigation between a landlord and tenants that an implied warranty that the premises are fit for human occupation was part of all rental agreements for dwellings and that this implied warranty of habitability could not be waived by any contract provision.[26] Landlords eager to escape the implications of this ruling set their lawyers to work. One landlord included in his lease the following provision, presumably drafted by his lawyers:

> There is no implied warranty the premises are fit for human occupation [are habitable] *except so far as governmental regulation, legislation or judicial enactment otherwise requires.* (Emphasis in original).

The landlord's lawyer argued that this provision was not deceptive because it included "in small print, [the words] 'except so far as governmental regulation, legislation or judicial enactment otherwise requires.' "[27] Was it unethical for the lawyers to have included this provision? In thinking about this question, consider the following proposed Model Rule, which was rejected by the ABA House of Delegates when adopting the Model Rules:

26. Boston Hous. Auth. v. Hemingway, 363 Mass. 184, 199, 293 N.E.2d 831, 843 (1973). Similar rules are in effect in many other jurisdictions.

27. Leardi v. Brown, 394 Mass. 151, 155, 474 N.E.2d 1094, 1099 (1985).

Proposed Rule 4.3: Illegal, Fraudulent, or Unconscionable Transactions

A lawyer shall not conclude an agreement, or assist a client in concluding an agreement, that the lawyer knows or reasonably should know is illegal, contains legally prohibited terms, would work a fraud, or would be held to be unconscionable as a matter of law.

Presumably one of the reasons the ABA rejected Proposed Rule 4.3 was the uncertainty about which terms "would be held to be unconscionable as a matter of law." [28]   Prior to a court ruling on a specific term, how is a lawyer to assess which terms would be held unconscionable? Should a lawyer assess contract terms favorable to her client as if the lawyer were a judge called upon to rule on the conscionability of the term in question?   Does it matter whether the other side is represented?   Is represented competently?

What of the justification for the habitability clause offered by the lawyers for the Massachusetts landlord?   In Leardi v. Brown,[29] the Massachusetts court held that the habitability clause quoted above violated the state's consumer protection law.[30]   The Massachusetts consumer protection law expressly incorporates judicial interpretations of the Federal Trade Commission Act.[31]   Under the federal statute (and many state consumer laws like the one in Massachusetts), a practice is deceptive if it possesses "a tendency to deceive." [32]   Moreover, in judging whether an act is deceptive "regard must be had, *not to fine spun distinctions and arguments that may be made in excuse*, but to the effect which it might reasonably be expected to have upon the general public." [33]   The Massachusetts Supreme Judicial Court thus held the clause deceptive, rejecting the fine spun distinctions offered by the landlord's lawyers.   The court said that the clause suggested that the implied warranty of habitability was

> "the exception and not the rule, if it exists at all."   Indeed, the average tenant, presumably not well acquainted with [the court's precedent on the implied warranty] is likely to interpret the provision as an absolute disclaimer of the implied warranty of habitability.[34]

28.   See Geoffrey C. Hazard, Jr., The Obligation to Be Trustworthy, 33 S.Car.L.Rev. 181 (1981) (discussing the rejection of the Kutak proposal); Gary T. Lowenthal, The Bar's Failure to Require Truthful Bargaining by Lawyers, 2 Geo.J.Legal Ethics 411 (1988); Rex R. Perschbacher, Regulating Lawyers' Negotiations, 27 Ariz.L.Rev. 75 (1985); and James J. White, Machiavelli and the Bar: Ethical Limitations on Lying in Negotiation, 1980 Am.Bar Found. Research J. 926. A classic discussion of truthfulness in negotiation is Alvin Rubin, A Causerie on Lawyers' Ethics in Negotiation, 35 La.L.Rev. 577 (1975).

29.   *Leardi*, supra.

30.   Mass. General Laws c. 93A.

31.   15 U.S.C. § 45 (1982).

32.   Trans World Accounts, Inc. v. FTC, 594 F.2d 212, 214 (9th Cir.1979).

33.   P. Lorillard Co. v. FTC, 186 F.2d 52, 58 (4th Cir.1950) (emphasis added).

34.   *Leardi*, 474 N.E.2d at 1099 (quoting the trial judge in the case).

If it is unlawful for landlords to include such provisions in leases, may lawyers include them in rental agreements drafted for landlords? DR 7–102(A)(7) of the Model Code prohibits assistance "that the lawyer knows to be illegal or fraudulent." Model Rule 1.2(d) narrows the prohibition to "conduct that the lawyer knows is criminal or fraudulent." Inclusion of an unlawful and deceptive contract provision may be unfair and unconscionable, but it is "illegal" or "criminal?" Even if it is, how does a lawyer "know," before a court rules, that a particular clause is unconscionable?

On the other hand, if landlords and other providers of consumer goods can be fined for violating consumer protection laws by including unconscionable provisions that are declared unconscionable ex post, then surely it is not unfair to expect lawyers to exercise reasonable foresight in deciding which clauses are likely to be ruled unconscionable. Of course, the exercise of such foresight assumes that a lawyer is able to exercise nonpartisan judgment. An ingenious advocate can articulate "fine spun distinctions" in defense of virtually any provision. But it is another matter for an office counselor to write such clauses into contracts. Was the ABA thus unwise to reject Rule 4.3?

CARNIVAL CRUISE LINES v. SHUTE
Supreme Court of the United States, 1991.
499 U.S. 585, 111 S.Ct. 1522, 113 L.Ed.2d 622.

JUSTICE BLACKMUN delivered the opinion of the Court.

In this admiralty case we primarily consider whether the United States Court of Appeals for the Ninth Circuit correctly refused to enforce a forum-selection clause contained in tickets issued by petitioner Carnival Cruise Lines, Inc., to respondents Eulala and Russel Shute.

I

The Shutes, through an Arlington, Wash., travel agent, purchased passage for a 7–day cruise on petitioner's ship, the *Tropicale*. Respondents paid the fare to the agent who forwarded the payment to petitioner's headquarters in Miami, Fla. Petitioner then prepared the tickets and sent them to respondents in the State of Washington. The face of each ticket, at its left-hand lower corner, contained this admonition:

"Subject to Conditions of Contract on Last Pages Important!

PLEASE READ CONTRACT—ON LAST PAGES 1, 2, 3"

The following appeared on "contract page 1" of each ticket:

Terms and Conditions of Passage Contract Ticket

. . .

3. (a) The acceptance of this ticket by the person or persons named hereon as passengers shall be deemed to be an acceptance and agreement by each of them of all of the terms and conditions of this Passage Contract Ticket.

. . .

8. It is agreed by and between the passenger and the Carrier that all disputes and matters whatsoever arising under, in connection with or incident to this Contract shall be litigated, if at all, in and before a Court located in the State of Florida, U.S.A., to the exclusion of the Courts of any other state or country."

The last quoted paragraph is the forum-selection clause at issue.

II

Respondents boarded the *Tropicale* in Los Angeles, Cal. The ship sailed to Puerto Vallarta, Mexico, and then returned to Los Angeles. While the ship was in international waters off the Mexican coast, respondent Eulala Shute was injured when she slipped on a deck mat during a guided tour of the ship's galley. Respondents filed suit against petitioner in the United States District Court for the Western District of Washington, claiming that Mrs. Shute's injuries had been caused by the negligence of Carnival Cruise Lines and its employees.

[The court of appeals reversed the district court's grant of defendant's motion for summary judgment. It held that defendant's contacts with Washington were sufficient for personal jurisdiction and that the forum-selection clause was unenforceable because it "was not freely bargained for."   897 F.2d 377 (9th Cir.1990).]

III

We begin by noting the boundaries of our inquiry. First, this is a case in admiralty, and federal law governs the enforceability of the forum-selection clause we scrutinize. . . .   Second, we do not address the question whether respondents had sufficient notice of the forum clause before entering the contract for passage. Respondents essentially have conceded that they had notice of the forum-selection provision. . . .

Within this context, respondents urge that the forum clause should not be enforced because, contrary to this Court's teachings in The Bremen [v. Zapata Off–Shore Co., 407 U.S. 1 (1972)], the clause was not the product of negotiation, and enforcement effectively would deprive respondents of their day in court. Additionally, respondents contend that the clause violates the Limitation of Vessel Owner's Liability Act, 46 U.S.C.App. § 183c. We consider these arguments in turn.

IV–A

. . .

In *The Bremen*, this Court addressed the enforceability of a forum-selection clause in a contract between two business corporations. An American corporation, Zapata, made a contract with Unterweser, a

German corporation, for the towage of Zapata's ocean-going drilling rig from Louisiana to a point in the Adriatic Sea off the coast of Italy. The agreement provided that any dispute arising under the contract was to be resolved in the London Court of Justice. After a storm in the Gulf of Mexico seriously damaged the rig, Zapata ordered Unterweser's ship to tow the rig to Tampa, Fla., the nearest point of refuge. Thereafter, Zapata sued Unterweser in admiralty in federal court at Tampa. Citing the forum clause, Unterweser moved to dismiss. The District Court denied Unterweser's motion, and the Court of Appeals for the Fifth Circuit, sitting en banc on rehearing, and by a sharply divided vote, affirmed. 446 F.2d 907 (1971).

This Court vacated and remanded, stating that, in general, "a freely negotiated private international agreement, unaffected by fraud, undue influence, or overweening bargaining power, such as that involved here, should be given full effect." 407 U.S., at 12–13. The Court further generalized that "in the light of present-day commercial realities and expanding international trade we conclude that the forum clause should control absent a strong showing that it should be set aside." Id., at 15. The Court did not define precisely the circumstances that would make it unreasonable for a court to enforce a forum clause. Instead, the Court discussed a number of factors that made it reasonable to enforce the clause at issue in *The Bremen* and that, presumably, would be pertinent in any determination whether to enforce a similar clause.

In this respect, the Court noted that there was "strong evidence that the forum clause was a vital part of the agreement, and [that] it would be unrealistic to think that the parties did not conduct their negotiations, including fixing the monetary terms, with the consequences of the forum clause figuring prominently in their calculations." Id., at 14 (footnote omitted). Further, the Court observed that it was not "dealing with an agreement between two Americans to resolve their essentially local disputes in a remote alien forum," and that in such a case, "the serious inconvenience of the contractual forum to one or both of the parties might carry greater weight in determining the reasonableness of the forum clause." Id., at 17. The Court stated that even where the forum clause establishes a remote forum for resolution of conflicts, "the party claiming [unfairness] should bear a heavy burden of proof." Ibid.

In applying *The Bremen*, the Court of Appeals in the present litigation took note of the foregoing "reasonableness" factors and rather automatically decided that the forum-selection clause was unenforceable because, unlike the parties in *The Bremen*, respondents are not business persons and did not negotiate the terms of the clause with petitioner. Alternatively, the Court of Appeals ruled that the clause should not be enforced because enforcement effectively would deprive respondents of an opportunity to litigate their claim against petitioner.

. . .

In evaluating the reasonableness of the forum clause at issue in this case, we must refine the analysis of *The Bremen* to account for the realities of form passage contracts. As an initial matter, we do not adopt the Court of Appeals' determination that a nonnegotiated forum-selection clause in a form ticket contract is never enforceable simply because it is not the subject of bargaining. Including a reasonable forum clause in a form contract of this kind well may be permissible for several reasons: First, a cruise line has a special interest in limiting the fora in which it potentially could be subject to suit. Because a cruise ship typically carries passengers from many locales, it is not unlikely that a mishap on a cruise could subject the cruise line to litigation in several different fora. See *The Bremen*, 407 U.S., at 13 and n. 15; *Hodes*, 858 F.2d, at 913. Additionally, a clause establishing ex ante the forum for dispute resolution has the salutary effect of dispelling any confusion about where suits arising from the contract must be brought and defended, sparing litigants the time and expense of pretrial motions to determine the correct forum, and conserving judicial resources that otherwise would be devoted to deciding those motions. See *Stewart Organization*, 487 U.S., at 33 (concurring opinion). Finally, it stands to reason that passengers who purchase tickets containing a forum clause like that at issue in this case benefit in the form of reduced fares reflecting the savings that the cruise line enjoys by limiting the fora in which it may be sued. Cf. Northwestern Nat. Ins. Co. v. Donovan, 916 F.2d 372, 378 (CA7 1990).

We also do not accept the Court of Appeals' "independent justification" for its conclusion that *The Bremen* dictates that the clause should not be enforced because "[t]here is evidence in the record to indicate that the Shutes are physically and financially incapable of pursuing this litigation in Florida." 897 F.2d, at 389. We do not defer to the Court of Appeals' findings of fact. In dismissing the case for lack of personal jurisdiction over petitioner, the District Court made no finding regarding the physical and financial impediments to the Shutes' pursuing their case in Florida.... Furthermore, the Court of Appeals did not place in proper context this Court's statement in *The Bremen* that "the serious inconvenience of the contractual forum to one or both of the parties might carry greater weight in determining the reasonableness of the forum clause." 407 U.S., at 17. The Court made this statement in evaluating a hypothetical "agreement between two Americans to resolve their essentially local disputes in a remote alien forum." Ibid. In the present case, Florida is not a "remote alien forum," nor—given the fact that Mrs. Shute's accident occurred off the coast of Mexico—is this dispute an essentially local one inherently more suited to resolution in the State of Washington than in Florida. In light of these distinctions, and because respondents do not claim lack of notice of the forum clause, we conclude that they have not satisfied the "heavy burden of proof," ibid., required to set aside the clause on grounds of inconvenience.

It bears emphasis that forum-selection clauses contained in form passage contracts are subject to judicial scrutiny for fundamental fairness. In this case, there is no indication that petitioner set Florida as the forum in which disputes were to be resolved as a means of discouraging cruise passengers from pursuing legitimate claims. Any suggestion of such a bad-faith motive is belied by two facts: petitioner has its principal place of business in Florida, and many of its cruises depart from and return to Florida ports. Similarly, there is no evidence that petitioner obtained respondents' accession to the forum clause by fraud or overreaching. Finally, respondents have conceded that they were given notice of the forum provision and, therefore, presumably retained the option of rejecting the contract with impunity. In the case before us, therefore, we conclude that the Court of Appeals erred in refusing to enforce the forum-selection clause.

IV–B

Respondents also contend that the forum-selection clause at issue violates 46 U.S.C.App. § 183c, [which makes unlawful any contract provision for maritime passenger transportation "purporting ... to lessen, weaken, or avoid the right of any claimant to a trial by court of competent jurisdiction on the question of liability for [personal] injury, or the measure of damages therefor."]

By its plain language, the forum-selection clause before us does not take away respondents' right to "a trial by [a] court of competent jurisdiction" and thereby contravene the explicit proscription of § 183c. Instead, the clause states specifically that actions arising out of the passage contract shall be brought "if at all," in a court "located in the State of Florida," which, plainly, is a "court of competent jurisdiction" within the meaning of the statute.

... [R]espondents cite no authority for their contention that Congress' intent in enacting § 183c was to avoid having a plaintiff travel to a distant forum in order to litigate. The legislative history of § 183c suggests instead that this provision was enacted in response to passenger-ticket conditions purporting to limit the shipowner's liability for negligence or to remove the issue of liability from the scrutiny of any court by means of a clause providing that "the question of liability and the measure of damages shall be determined by arbitration." [Citing legislative history.] Because the clause before us allows for judicial resolution of claims against petitioner and does not purport to limit petitioner's liability for negligence, it does not violate § 183c.

The judgment of the Court of Appeals is reversed....

JUSTICE STEVENS, with whom JUSTICE MARSHALL joins, dissenting.

The Court ... implies that a purchaser of a Carnival Cruise Lines passenger ticket is fully and fairly notified about the existence of the choice of forum clause in the fine print on the back of the ticket.... I begin my dissent by noting that only the most meticulous passenger is likely to become aware of the forum selection provision. I have therefore appended to this opinion a facsimile of the relevant text, using the type size that actually appears in the ticket itself. A careful reader will find the forum-selection clause in the eighth of the twenty-five numbered paragraphs.

Of course, many passengers, like the respondents in this case, will not have an opportunity to read paragraph 8 until they have actually purchased their tickets. By this point, the passengers will already have accepted the condition set forth in paragraph 16(a), which provides that "[t]he Carrier shall not be liable to make any refund to passengers in respect of ... tickets wholly or partly not used by a passenger." Not knowing whether or not that provision is legally enforceable, I assume that the average passenger would accept the risk of having to file suit in Florida in the event of an injury, rather than canceling—without a refund—a planned vacation at the last minute. The fact that the cruise line can reduce its litigation costs, and therefore its liability insurance premiums, by forcing this choice on its passengers does not, in my opinion, suffice to render the provision reasonable. . . .

Even if passengers received prominent notice of the forum-selection clause before they committed the cost of the cruise, I would remain persuaded that the clause was unenforceable under traditional principles of federal admiralty law and is "null and void" under the terms of Limited Liability Act, 49 Stat. 1480, as amended, 46 U.S.C.App. § 183c, which was enacted in 1936 to invalidate expressly stipulations limiting shipowners' liability for negligence.

Exculpatory clauses in passenger tickets have been around for a long time. These clauses are typically the product of disparate bargaining power between the carrier and the passenger, and they undermine the strong public interest in deterring negligent conduct. For these reasons, courts long before the turn of the century consistently held such clauses unenforceable under federal admiralty law. . . .

Clauses limiting a carrier's liability or weakening the passenger's right to recover for the negligence of the carrier's employees come in a variety of forms. Complete exemptions from liability for negligence or limitations on the amount of the potential damage recovery, requirements that notice of claims be filed within an unreasonably short period of time, provisions mandating a choice of law that is favorable to the defendant in negligence cases, and forum-selection clauses[4] are all similarly designed to put a thumb on the carrier's side of the scale of justice.

Forum selection clauses in passenger tickets involve the intersection of two strands of traditional contract law that qualify the general rule that courts will enforce the terms of a contract as written.

---

4. All these clauses will provide passengers who purchase tickets containing them with a "benefit in the form of reduced fares reflecting the savings that the cruise line enjoys by limiting [its exposure to liability]." See ante, at 8. Under the Court's reasoning, all these clauses, including a complete waiver of liability, would be enforceable, a result at odds with longstanding jurisprudence.

Pursuant to the first strand, courts traditionally have reviewed with heightened scrutiny the terms of contracts of adhesion, form contracts offered on a take-or-leave basis by a party with stronger bargaining power to a party with weaker power. Some commentators have questioned whether contracts of adhesion can justifiably be enforced at all under traditional contract theory because the adhering party generally enters into them without manifesting knowing and voluntary consent to all their terms. See, e.g., Rakoff, Contracts of Adhesion: An Essay in Reconstruction, 96 Harv.L.Rev. 1173, 1179–1180 (1983); Slawson, Mass Contracts: Lawful Fraud in California, 48 S.Cal.L.Rev. 1, 12–13 (1974); K. Llewellyn, The Common Law Tradition 370–371 (1960).

The common law, recognizing that standardized form contracts account for a significant portion of all commercial agreements, has taken a less extreme position and instead subjects terms in contracts of adhesion to scrutiny for reasonableness. Judge J. Skelly Wright set out the state of the law succinctly in Williams v. Walker–Thomas Furniture Co., 350 F.2d 445, 449–450 (D.C.Cir.1965):

> Ordinarily, one who signs an agreement without full knowledge of its terms might be held to assume the risk that he has entered a one-sided bargain. But when a party of little bargaining power, and hence little real choice, signs a commercially unreasonable contract with little or no knowledge of its terms, it is hardly likely that his consent, or even an objective manifestation of his consent, was ever given to all of the terms. In such a case the usual rule that the terms of the agreement are not to be questioned should be abandoned and the court should consider whether the terms of the contract are so unfair that enforcement should be withheld.

See also ... Henningsen v. Bloomfield Motors, Inc., 32 N.J. 358, 161 A.2d 69 (1960).

The second doctrinal principle implicated by forum-selection clauses is the traditional rule that "contractual provisions, which seek to limit the place or court in which an action may ... be brought, are invalid as contrary to public policy." See Dougherty, Validity of Contractual Provision Limiting Place or Court in Which Action May Be Brought, 31 A.L.R.4th 404, 409, § 3 (1984). See also Home Insurance Co. v. Morse, 20 Wall. 445, 451 (1874). Although adherence to this general rule has declined in recent years, particularly following our decision in The Bremen v. Zapata Off–Shore Co., 407 U.S. 1, the prevailing rule is still that forum-selection clauses are not enforceable if they were not freely bargained for, create additional expense for one party, or deny one party a remedy. See 31 A.L.R.4th, at 409–438 (citing cases). A forum-selection clause in a standardized passenger ticket would clearly have been unenforceable under the common law before our decision in *The Bremen*, see 407 U.S., at 9, and n. 10, and, in my opinion, remains unenforceable under the prevailing rule today.

The Bremen, which the Court effectively treats as controlling this case, had nothing to say about stipulations printed on the back of passenger tickets. That case involved the enforceability of a forum-selection clause in a freely negotiated international agreement between two large corporations providing for the towage of a vessel from the Gulf of Mexico to the Adriatic Sea. The Court recognized that such towage agreements had generally been held unenforceable in American courts, but held that the doctrine of those cases did not extend to commercial arrangements between parties with equal bargaining power.

The federal statute that should control the disposition of the case before us today was enacted in 1936 when the general rule denying enforcement of forum-selection clauses was indisputably widely accepted. The principal subject of the statute concerned the limitation of shipowner liability, but as the following excerpt from the House Report explains, the section that is relevant to this case was added as a direct response to shipowners' ticketing practices. "During the course of the hearings on the bill (H.R. 9969) there was also brought to the attention of the committee a practice of providing on the reverse side of steamship tickets that in the event of damage or injury caused by the negligence or fault of the owner or his servants, the liability of the owner shall be limited to a stipulated amount, in some cases $5,000, and in others substantially lower amounts, or that in such event the question of liability and the measure of damages shall be determined by arbitration. The amendment ... is intended to, and in the opinion of the committee will, put a stop to all such practices and practices of a like character." H.R.Rep. No. 2517, 74th Cong., 2d Sess., 6–7 (1936); see also S.Rep. No. 2061, 74th Cong., 2d Sess., 6–7 (1936).

. . .

The stipulation in the ticket that Carnival Cruise sold to respondents certainly lessens or weakens their ability to recover for the slip and fall incident that occurred off the west coast of Mexico during the cruise that originated and terminated in Los Angeles, California. It is safe to assume that the witnesses—whether other passengers or members of the crew—can be assembled with less expense and inconvenience at a west coast forum than in a Florida court several thousand miles from the scene of the accident.

... The forum-selection clause here does not mandate suit in a foreign jurisdiction, and therefore arguably might have less of an impact on a plaintiff's ability to recover. See Fireman's Fund American Ins. Cos. v. Puerto Rican Forwarding Co., 492 F.2d 1294 (CA1 1974). However, the plaintiffs in this case are not large corporations but individuals, and the added burden on them of conducting a trial at the opposite end of the country is likely proportional to the additional cost to a large corporation of conducting a trial overseas.[6]

6. The Court does not make clear whether the result in this case would also apply if the clause required Carnival passengers to sue in Panama, the country in which Carnival is incorporated.

Under these circumstances, the general prohibition against stipulations purporting "to lessen, weaken, or avoid" the passenger's right to a trial certainly should be construed to apply to the manifestly unreasonable stipulation in these passengers' tickets. Even without the benefit of the statute, I would continue to apply the general rule that prevailed prior to our decision in *The Bremen* to forum-selection clauses in passenger tickets.

I respectfully dissent.

Unconscionability

After the *Carnival* decision, Congress outlawed forum-selection clauses in passenger tickets, effectively overruling the precise holding of the case. This change was accomplished in late 1992 by a "technical clarification" of 46 U.S.C. § 183c "buried in a 68–page act which was passed under a motion to suspend the normal rules." [35] Is that poetic justice? Does the swift congressional reversal of *Carnival* cast some doubt on the soundness of the decision?

On what grounds did the Court find the forum-selection clause "fundamentally fair?" Contracts of pre-specified form, whose terms are not actually negotiated, are not in and of themselves unconscionable. Generally, courts will invalidate a contract on the ground that it is an adhesion contract only if unfairness is found both in the procedure by which the contract was formed and in the contract terms being challenged.[36] Should the Court in *Carnival* have paid more attention to the fairness of the contract process? Recall that before the Shutes ever saw the ticket, they were bound because the money they paid for the ticket was unrefundable. Under these circumstances, was the Shutes' lawyer negligent to have "conceded" notice?

Courts rarely, if ever, will find a contract void as an adhesion contract when both parties are business entities. When two business entities have entered into a contract, the first requirement, procedural unfairness, is rarely found. Notice that *The Bremen* case, on which *Carnival* is based, involved two business entities (sophisticated contractors, presumably, each represented by counsel). Business entities whose counsel fail to read and alert their clients to harsh provisions in "fine print" may sue their lawyers for malpractice if those provisions later come back and bite them.

35. Michael F. Sturley, Forum Selection Clauses in Cruise Line Tickets: An Update on Congressional Action "Overruling" the Supreme Court, 24 J. Maritime L. & Commerce 399, n. 5 (1993). The amendment invalidates any provision in a passenger contract that purports "to lessen, weaken, or avoid the right of any claimant to a trial by *any* court of competent jurisdiction." (Emphasis added.)

36. See, e.g., Williams v. Walker–Thomas Furniture Co., 350 F.2d 445, 449 (D.C.Cir. 1965) (setting forth the standard of unconscionability as "includ[ing] an absence of meaningful choice on the part of one of the parties together with contract terms which are unreasonably favorable to the other party").

Consider Justice Stevens' description of the ticket. Assuming the Shutes' money was refundable or that they had seen the ticket before purchasing it, should a lay person be expected to read, understand and comprehend the implications of the ticket terms? Do you read the fine-print contract terms on your airline tickets? The ticket you get when you park your car in a commercial lot?

Do you agree with the majority that no evidence of fraud or overreaching by Carnival was presented? Judge Posner, no big fan of unconscionability doctrine, had this to say about the Ninth Circuit's decision in this case, while the case was pending review before the Supreme Court:

> The [Ninth Circuit's] opinion bristles with hostility to nonnegotiated form contracts, but the facts were special. A passenger was injured on a cruise ship and brought suit. The cruise line sought to dismiss the suit on the basis of a forum selection clause printed on the passenger's ticket. The ticket had not even been mailed to the passenger until after she bought the ticket and as a result she had had no knowledge of the clause until the transaction was complete. If ever there was a case for stretching the concept of fraud in the name of unconscionability, it was [*Carnival*]; and perhaps no stretch was necessary.... If a clause really is buried in illegible "fine print"—or if as in [*Carnival*] it plainly is neither intended nor likely to be read by the other party—this circumstance may support an inference of fraud, and fraud is a defense to a contract.[37]

Carnival's Lawyers

Assuming that Carnival's lawyers wrote the forum-selection clause relying on *The Bremen*, was it reasonable at that time to believe that *The Bremen* justified the inclusion of such a clause in a consumer contract? If the law on what is conscionable is unclear, may the lawyer simply include the term and hope for the best, i.e., a decision like *Carnival* approving the clause after the fact? Is that "the best?" Or is "the best" outcome one that results in waiving the clause for those parties who threaten to challenge its enforceability and assuming that most people will adhere to the term on the (perhaps mistaken) belief that it is enforceable? Is the later strategy ethical?

A form contract prepared by lawyers has an air of legality about it. Why shouldn't unrepresented parties who sign such a document be entitled to believe—what most ordinary people do believe—that the terms included are lawful? Doesn't a lawyer who drafts a form contract implicitly represent as much, knowing that unrepresented persons will rely on that representation? Recall that in many jurisdictions, third parties who reasonably rely on a lawyer's negligent misrepresentations can now sue the lawyer.[38] Moreover, those who are

---

37. Northwestern Nat'l Ins. Co. v. Donovan, 916 F.2d 372, 376, 377 (7th Cir.1990).

38. See, e.g., *Greycas v. Proud*, p. 75.

intentionally deceived by someone else's lawyer have always been allowed to maintain an action for fraud against that lawyer.[39] Do these tort principles suggest that it is unlawful or unethical for a lawyer to intentionally or negligently include unconscionable terms in a form contract? Should lawyers who draft form contracts be expected to flag provisions of doubtful enforceability for consumers?

Consider now the lawyers' responsibility for the procedure employed by Carnival to sell its tickets. Assuming Carnival's lawyers believed the forum-selection clause was valid under *The Bremen* as long as ticket buyers had notice of the clause, should the lawyers have refused to include the clause so long as Carnival sold its tickets on a sight-unseen nonrefundable basis? Should the lawyers have insisted that some other notice of the provision be given, perhaps in the Carnival brochure?

What changes, if any, should Carnival's lawyers have recommended to their client after the Court's decision? After the legislative overruling of *Carnival*? Consider that in a later class action brought against Carnival by passengers injured on a cruise, a California intermediate appellate court held that the forum-selection clause was not enforceable against any plaintiff who did not have sufficient notice.[40] Of course, Carnival might not want to draw attention to such clauses because notice might frighten passengers or passengers might not agree to such terms for other reasons. If, on the other hand, that is Carnival's reason for selling tickets without notice or hiding the clause, doesn't that suggest "overreaching or fraud?" Should a lawyer be a party to that?

Rescission and Mistake

Professor Murray L. Schwartz argues that lawyers in nonadversarial settings should refrain from the use of "unconscionable" means and from assisting clients toward "unconscionable" ends:

> [T]he client has no "legal right" to a noncriminal or nonfraudulent result which would nonetheless be unenforceable or which could be avoided were a court to review the transaction, and ..., therefore, the client has no right to receive professional assistance for this purpose. A lawyer has a professional responsibility to decline to accomplish on behalf of a client that which the formal processes of the law themselves would not tolerate.[41]

Schwartz relies on an ethics opinion stating that it is unethical for a landlord's lawyer to insert in a lease a provision previously held void

---

39. See the discussion of a lawyer's liability for intentional fraud above at p. 86.

40. Carnival Cruise Lines v. Superior Court of Los Angeles County, 234 Cal.App.3d 1019, 286 Cal.Rptr. 323 (1991).

41. Murray L. Schwartz, The Professionalism and Accountability of Lawyers, 66 Calif.L.Rev. 669, 687 (1978).

as against public policy.[42]   Schwartz also relies on cases and ethics opinions involving inadvertent mistakes by one party's lawyer that are known to the other's party's lawyer.   In Stare v. Tate,[43] for example, the wife's lawyer in negotiating a property settlement in connection with a divorce proceeding made an arithmetic error of about $50,000 in a settlement offer.   The husband's lawyer, recognizing the error, which resulted in a figure very close to that desired by his client, prepared a counteroffer that was prepared in a way designed to minimize the possibility that the wife or her lawyer would discover the mistake. When the parties met, the counteroffer was accepted after some minor give and take.   The upshot was that the wife received about $50,000 less than she would have received if her valuation of the disputed property had been accepted.

Immediately after the divorce became final, the brash former husband mailed his former spouse a copy of the offer containing the erroneous computations, with an exultant note pointing out the "$100,-000 mistake in your figures. . . ."   She brought an action to reform the property settlement agreement to reflect the parties' acceptance of her valuation of the disputed property.   Established law, the court said, vitiated an agreement based on fraud, mutual mistake of the parties or a mistake of one party, which the other party knew of when the agreement was made.   Since the husband's lawyer was aware of the mistake, the settlement agreement was set aside.   The court stated:

> . . . [It does not matter] what Joan would have done had Tim been more frank.   By permitting her to enter into the contract in the belief that he had accepted her $550,000 value, he simply took the risk that if she discovered the mistake and sought judicial redress, the contract would be enforced on the terms which she mistakenly thought she had already received.

If substantive law will invalidate an agreement reached under circumstances of mistake or fraud, what implications does this have for lawyer behavior in negotiating the agreement? [44]

---

42. Comm. on Prof. Ethics of Ass'n of Bar of City of New York, Op. 722 (1948) (including unlawful provision purporting to waive tenant's right to a sixty-day period in which to cancel an agreed-upon rent increase is unethical conduct).

43. 21 Cal.App.3d 432, 98 Cal.Rptr. 264 (1971).

44. See also Comm. on Prof. Ethics, Ass'n of Bar of City of New York, Op. No. 477 (1939) (when a lawyer negotiating a settlement makes an arithmetical error that hurts her client, the opposing lawyer, recognizing the inadvertent error, should urge her client to reveal the mistake and, if the client refuses, do so herself).

D. DO LAWYERS HAVE A SPECIAL RESPONSIBILITY FOR JUSTICE?

Introductory Note

American society has always been radically heterogeneous in terms of ethnic and religious identity. Locally, ethnic and religious groups provided social leadership in defining and working toward the public good and aiding the poor well until the 19th century. These groups still had considerable strength until World War II, when the accumulating effects of urbanization, the automobile and mobility through education broke down this pattern. While these groups were strong sources for justice on a local basis in the past and still retain some force today, they were not generally active agents at the state level, let alone the national level.

Instead, at various times and in various places in the United States there was a more or less recognized political aristocracy that professed responsibility for social justice at the state and national level—notably the New England church oligarchy in the late 18th and early to mid–19th centuries, and the planter aristocracy in the pre-Civil War South. deTocqueville saw lawyers as such an aristocracy [45] and to some extent the bar still sees itself that way.

LOUIS D. BRANDEIS
"THE OPPORTUNITY IN THE LAW" (1905)
In Brandeis, Business—A Profession (1914).

... Standing not far from the threshold of active life, feeling the generous impulse for service which the University fosters, you wish to know whether the legal profession would afford you special opportunities for usefulness to your fellow-men, and, if so, what the obligations and limitations are which it imposes....

For centuries before the American Revolution the lawyer had played an important part in England. His importance in the State became much greater in America. One reason for this, as deTocqueville indicated, was the fact that we possessed no class like the nobles, which took part in government through privilege. A more potent reason was that with the introduction of a written constitution the law became with us a far more important factor in the ordinary conduct of political life than it did in England. Legal questions were constantly arising and the lawyer was necessary to settle them. But I take it the paramount reason why the lawyer has played so large a part in our political life is that his training fits him especially to grapple with the questions which are presented in a democracy.

The whole training of the lawyer leads to the development of judgment. His early training—his work with books in the study of legal rules—teaches him patient research and develops both the memo-

---

45. See the quote from deTocqueville printed below at 1091.

ry and the reasoning faculties. He becomes practiced in logic; and yet the use of the reasoning faculties in the study of law is very different from their use, say, in metaphysics. The lawyer's processes of reasoning, his logical conclusions, are being constantly tested by experience. He is running up against facts at every point. Indeed it is a maxim of the law: Out of the facts grows the law; that is, propositions are not considered abstractly, but always with reference to facts....

If the lawyer's practice is a general one, his field of observation extends, in course of time, into almost every sphere of business and of life. The facts so gathered ripen his judgment. His memory is trained to retentiveness. His mind becomes practiced in discrimination as well as in generalization. He is an observer of men even more than of things. He not only sees men of all kinds, but knows their deepest secrets; sees them in situations which "try men's souls." He is apt to become a good judge of men....

His experience teaches him that nearly every question has two sides; and very often he finds—after decision of judge or jury—that both he and his opponent were in the wrong. The practice of law creates thus a habit of mind, and leads to attainments which are distinctly different from those developed in most professions or outside of the professions. These are the reasons why the lawyer has acquired a position materially different from that of other men. It is the position of the adviser....

[B]y far the greater part of the work done by lawyers is done not in court, but in advising men on important matters, and mainly in business affairs. In guiding these affairs industrial and financial, lawyers are needed, not only because of the legal questions involved, but because the particular mental attributes and attainments which the legal profession develops are demanded in the proper handling of these large financial or industrial affairs. The magnitude and scope of these operations remove them almost wholly from the realm of "petty trafficking" which people formerly used to associate with trade. The questions which arise are more nearly questions of statesmanship. The relations created call in many instances for the exercise of the highest diplomacy. The magnitude, difficulty and importance of the problems involved are often as great as in the matters of state with which lawyers were formerly frequently associated. The questions appear in a different guise; but they are similar. The relations between rival railroad systems are like the relations between neighboring kingdoms. The relations of the great trusts to the consumers or to their employees is like that of feudal lords to commoners or dependents....

It is true that at the present time the lawyer does not hold as high a position with the people as he held seventy-five or indeed fifty years ago; but the reason is not lack of opportunity. It is this: Instead of holding a position of independence, between the wealthy and the people, prepared to curb the excesses of either, able lawyers have, to a large extent, allowed themselves to become adjuncts of great corporations and have neglected the obligation to use their powers for the protection of the people. We hear much of the "corporation lawyer," and far too little of the "people's lawyer." The great opportunity of the American Bar is and will be to stand again as it did in the past, ready to protect also the interests of the people....

For nearly a generation the leaders of the Bar have, with few exceptions, not only failed to take part in constructive legislation designed to solve in the public interest our great social, economic and industrial problems; but they have failed likewise to oppose legislation prompted by selfish interests. They have gone further in disregard of common weal. They have often advocated, as lawyers, legislative measures which as citizens they could not approve, and have endeavored to justify themselves by a false analogy. They have erroneously assumed that the role of ethics to be applied to a lawyer's advocacy is the same where he acts for private interests against the public, as it is in litigation between private individuals.

The ethical question which laymen most frequently ask about the legal profession is this: How can a lawyer take a case which he does not believe in? The profession is regarded as necessarily somewhat immoral, because its members are supposed to be habitually taking cases of that character. As a practical matter, the lawyer is not often harassed by this problem; partly because he is apt to believe, at the time, in most of the cases that he actually tries; and partly because he either abandons or settles a large number of those he does not believe in. But the lawyer recognizes that in trying a case his prime duty is to present his side to the tribunal fairly and as well as he can, relying upon his adversary to present the other side fairly and as well as he can. Since the lawyers on the two sides are usually reasonably well matched, the judge or jury may ordinarily be trusted to make a decision as justice demands.

But when lawyers act upon the same principle in supporting the attempts of their private clients to secure or to oppose legislation, a very different condition is presented....

Here, consequently, is the great opportunity in the law. The next generation must witness a continuing and ever-increasing contest between those who have and those who have not. The industrial world is in a state of ferment ... The labor movement must necessarily progress. The people's thought will take shape in action; and it lies with us, with you to whom in part the future belongs, to say on what lines the action is to be expressed; whether it is to be expressed wisely and temperately, or wildly and intemperately; whether it is to be expressed on lines of evolution or on lines of revolution. Nothing can better fit you for taking part in the solution of these problems, than the study and preeminently the practice of law. Those of you who feel drawn to that profession may rest assured that you will find in it an opportunity for usefulness which is probably unequalled. There is a call upon the legal profession to do a great work for this country.

Is Brandeis' justification for the special responsibility of lawyers for justice persuasive? Has law school trained you as Brandeis suggests?

ROBERT W. GORDON
"THE IDEAL AND THE ACTUAL IN THE LAW"

In Gerald W. Gawalt, Ed., The New High Priests:
Lawyers in Post–Civil War America (1984).[46]

. . .

[We can think of lawyers] as having "ideal interests" as well as material ones, and as struggling to work out a relationship between their beliefs and their practices—between the ideal and the actual—with which they could live in comfort. Lawyers are perhaps ... double agents. They have obligations to a universal scheme of order, "the law," understood as some fairly coherent system of rules and procedures that are supposed to regulate social life in accordance with prevailing political conceptions of the good.

The law, to put this another way, is an artificial utopia of social harmony, a kind of collectively maintained fantasy of what society would look like if everyone played by the rules. But lawyers are also supposed to be loyal toward and advance the interests of clients pursuing particular ends. The lawyer's job, thus, is to mediate between the universal vision of legal order and the concrete desires of his clients, to show how what the client wants can be accommodated to the utopian scheme. The lawyer, thus, has to find ways of squeezing the client's plan of action into the legally recognized categories of approved conduct. Of course, the law's view of the client's reality is often a highly distorted one, since its categorizing forms are administratively manageable only if they drastically abstract and simplify from that reality, and legitimate only if they seem to be part of the system of universal normative order. Even so, the lawyer's job is selling legitimacy: reassurance to the client and its potential regulators, investors, or business partners that what it wants to do is basically all right; and the lawyer cannot deliver unless she can make plausible arguments rationalizing her client's conduct within the prevailing terms of legal discourse. She must, in short, be able to understand the day-to-day world of the client's transactions and deals as somehow approximating, in however decayed or imperfect a form, the ideal or fantasy world of legal order.

Reform-minded lawyers of 1870 had no trouble perceiving that their world was, from this point of view, in lots of trouble. The

---

46. Copyright © 1984 by Gerald W. Gawalt.

articulate ones are most easily described as modified or pragmatic classical liberals, that is, their ideal society was one in which (adult male) individuals were left free to pursue self-interest within a framework of property rights, exchange rules, and public order guaranteed by law—rules of general application, treating individuals as formally equal, and impartially and predictably applied.... Within their ideal scheme of order, all participants had definitely bounded rights and powers—the individual vis-á-vis other individuals and the state, the states vis-á-vis one another and the federal government, the separate branches of government vis-á-vis one another—which it was the role of the judiciary, the natural arbiter of the system as well as a player in it, to enforce.

Yet this scheme had for some years—since the '50s or '60s, depending on whether one blamed the railroads or Reconstruction—been in a process of total breakdown. Liberal lawyers analyzed the breakdown much as other reformers did, except that they were more prone to see it as the result of *legal* failure that was remediable by legal reform. The present evils could be summed up as lack of generality in framing laws, and lack of predictability and impartiality in applying them. Southern black codes, debtor's stay laws, legislation relieving municipalities from contracted bond obligations, handouts of subsidies, exemptions, and privileges to railroad corporations—all had in common the vice of *particularly* favoring or disfavoring special classes of citizens. Impartiality of application had been subverted by patronage appointments or machine-controlled election of corrupt judges or officials. Predictability was undermined by the same factors, as well as by sloppiness in statutory draftsmanship, judicial decision making, and administration of procedural rules, and by the wild variety of law-making jurisdictions.

The lawyers proposed to restore all this unruly mess to the dominion of the rule of law....

[H]igh-minded lawyers were embarked on a practical program of reform. As leaders of the bar, they belonged to a tradition, communicated through endless reiteration in formal speeches, of patrician Whig aspirations to play a distinctive role in American society as a Third Force in politics (in fact the role of "the few" in classical republican theory), mediating between capital and labor, between private acquisitiveness and democratic redistributive follies; thus, they kept looking for social stages on which to enact the role of Tocqueville's lawyer-aristocrats....

Lawyers as Aristocracy

Gordon suggests that the leaders of the New York bar of the 1870s faced a conflict between their idealized conception of the law and their role in its administration, on the one hand, and the seamy actuality they confronted in everyday life on the other hand. It seems clear that the same contradictions are confronted by all lawyers, not just those in New York City or a century ago.

Gordon refers to the underlying wish to "enact the role of de-Tocqueville's lawyer-aristocrats." In this he is referring to deTocqueville's famous observation:

> Men who have made a special study of the laws and have derived therefrom habits of order, something of a taste for formalities, and an instinctive love for a regular concatenation of ideas are naturally strongly opposed to the revolutionary spirit and to the ill-considered passions of democracy.

> Study and specialized knowledge of the law give a man a rank apart in society and makes of lawyers a somewhat privileged intellectual class. The exercise of their profession daily reminds them of this superiority; they are the masters of a necessary and not widely understood science; they serve as arbiters between the citizens.... Add that they naturally form *a body* ....

> So, hidden at the bottom of a lawyer's soul one finds the tastes and habits of an aristocracy.[45]

The problem with viewing lawyers or the ideal of the legal profession as aristocratic is that the concept of an especially responsible republican class implies a legitimate social inequality. But social inequality is presumed unjust in America, particularly since such cases as Brown v. Board of Education[46] and Baker v. Carr[47] elevated the concepts of social and political equality to positions of primacy in our constitutional order as that order exists in ideal form.

But the elevation of social and political equality to positions of constitutional primacy delegitimates claims of other groups to special positions of social and moral leadership and the First Amendment renders religious claims to social leadership suspect at the very time it protects the existence of religious groups. By default then, the norms that constitute our common reference points in the debate on social justice are norms supplied by positive law not the ethic of elite groups. The American judiciary's special role in the political order, expressed by the judiciary's expansive power to invalidate legislation as unconstitutional, enhances the role of positive law in the debate on social justice. And our federalist system, which celebrates diversity and decentralized power at the same time that it subordinates local decisions to federal ones within the federal government's legitimate sphere, also acts to transform questions of social justice and legitimate social action into complicated questions of law.

45. Alexis deTocqueville, Democracy in America, P. 11, Ch. 8.

46. 347 U.S. 483 (1954).

47. 369 U.S. 186 (1962).

In this diffuse, complex and pluralistic system, lawyers are the caretakers of the law. Although the notion of a group charged with special responsibilities to see justice done inherently contradicts other premises of American society, the very structure of American justice elevates the bar to such a position. The question is whether we are worthy of the task given us and what happens to justice if we are not.

Chapter 12

BECOMING AND BEING A LAWYER

On the one hand ...

But the lawyer is always in a hurry.... The consequence has been, that he has become keen and shrewd; he has learned how to flatter his master in word and indulge him in deed; but his soul is small and unrighteous.... [F]rom the first he has practiced deception and retaliation, and has become stunted and warped [although he thinks of himself as] a master of wisdom.

—Plato, Theatetus

There was a society of men among us, bred up from their youth in the art of proving by words multiplied for the purpose, that white is black and black is white, according as they are paid.

—Jonathan Swift, Gulliver's Travels

On the other hand ...

When I think then of the law, I see a princess mightier than she who once wrought at Bayeux, eternally weaving into her web dim figures of the ever-lengthening past—figures too dim to be noticed by the idle, too symbolic to be interpreted except by her pupils, but to the discerning eye disclosing every painful step and every world-shaking contest by which mankind has worked and fought its way from savage isolation to organic social life.

—Oliver Wendell Holmes, Jr. (in steel letters on marble at the University of California School of Law, Berkeley)

[O]ur profession in its highest walks afforded the best employment in which any man could engage.... To be a priest, and possibly a high priest in the Temple of Justice; to serve at her alter and aid in her administration; to maintain and defend the inalienable rights of life, liberty and property upon which the safety of society depends; to succor the oppressed and defend the innocent; to maintain constitutional rights against all violations, whether executive, by the legislature, by the restless power of the press, or worst of all by the ruthless rapacity of an unbridled majority; to rescue the scapegoat and restore him to his proper place in the world—all this seemed to me to furnish a field worthy of any man's ambition.

—Joseph H. Choate, in an address delivered to the Bench and Bar of England, 1905

I have a high opinion of lawyers. With all their faults, they stack up well against those in every other occupation or profession. They are better to work with or play with or fight with or drink with, than most other varieties of mankind.

—Harrison Tweed, accepting the Presidency of the Association of the Bar of the City of New York, 1945

Introductory Note

This coursebook is about the law and morals of a profession, the practice of law. The law consists of the regulations and common law directly addressing the lawyer's conduct, and the substantive and procedural law that is the material with which the lawyer works and in which her practice is embedded. The moral issues are the questions of right and wrong that are unresolved by the law or which arise because the law, as written or as administered, does not correspond to a sense of justice.

In the course of addressing these problems, the materials herein convey a great deal of information about the practice of law. It is not a systematic presentation, for this is not a coursebook in the demographics, sociology or economics of the legal profession. Nevertheless, the cases report real-life vignettes in the practice of law and yield a composite picture that is fairly accurate. There are cameos of big firm practitioners, small firm and sole practitioners, corporate law department lawyers, lawyers in government practice and prosecutors and defenders. There are men and women, and individuals of various ethnic, religious and geographical backgrounds. Along with the other sources of information that a law student has, informal as well as formal, the whole is a reasonable description of the profession at work.

In very general terms, the professional activity of lawyers is directed primarily at protecting property and claims to property and wielding or seeking to deflect the coercive power of government. That is, law practice is concerned with the use of money and power. Yet the lawyer's relationship to money and power is secondary and mediatory. A lawyer is not an investment banker or a business entrepreneur, although many people trained as lawyers migrate into those lines of work. Nor is a lawyer a public official even though a lawyer is appropriately called, as in the Preamble to the Model Rules of Professional Conduct, "an officer of the legal system." A lawyer provides assistance to those who directly own or manage property and who directly exercise or are subject to political authority. In doing so, a lawyer acts with loyalty to the client, but a loyalty qualified by responsibilities to the legal system.

As Canon 7 of the Code of Professional Responsibility states, "A lawyer should represent a client zealously within the bounds of the law." This seemingly simple axiom reveals the conflicting commitments involved in the practice of law. The practice of law is a continual encounter with such personal conflict.

What are the rewards of practice? Why go through the labor, and bear the opportunity costs, of preparing to practice law? Why pursue it afterwards? There are some obvious answers. Entry into the practice of law is fairly open to people of a wide range of backgrounds and talents, so long as they have relatively high levels of verbal facility, stamina and diligence. Becoming a lawyer does not require a political constituency or extensive capital (other than the willingness to borrow against future earnings). The legal profession can be entered even without social or political connections, although those certainly can help. Work in law practice generally has considerable variety and novelty, and often involves an inside view of fascinating and sometimes bizarre human affairs. It usually requires active use of a person's intelligence. Most kinds of practice involve a relatively high degree of autonomy—freedom from bureaucratic or direct regulatory control— although employment in large organizations is becoming more common. Most practitioners make a decent living, certainly compared to the general population, and many achieve substantial influence in the councils of business, government or politics. Most find repeated satisfactions in using their abilities to help people plan their affairs or extricate themselves from messy situations.

So what are the discontentments in the practice of law, and how do they arise? The following materials seek to frame that problem and to suggest responses.

A. MORALITY OF RHETORIC

The first excerpt, from Gorgias, provides Socrates' moral critique of the lawyers of his day—rhetoricians—and more particularly, his moral challenge to those who practice or teach law. Gorgias was the most famous rhetorician of his age; he practiced and taught. The word "gorgeous" is derived from his name, bearing witness to the beauty and power of his speech.

PLATO'S GORGIAS

Reprinted From the Dialogues of Plato, Translated Into English by B. Jowett.
(D. Appleton and Co.: New York 1898).

. . .

Gorgias: Rhetoric, Socrates, is my art.

Socrates: Then I am to call you a rhetorician?

Gor. Yes, Socrates, and a good one too, if you would call me that which, in Homeric language, "I boast to be."

Soc. I should wish to do that.

Gor. Then pray do.

Soc. And are we to say that you make other men rhetoricians?

Gor. Yes, that is exactly what I profess to make them, not only at Athens, but in all places.

Soc. And will you continue to ask and answer questions, Gorgias, as we are at present doing, and reserve for another occasion the longer mode of speech which Polus was attempting? and will you keep your promise, and answer shortly the questions which are asked of you?

Gor. Some answers, Socrates, are of necessity longer; but I will do my best to make them as short as I can; for a part of my profession is that I can be as short as any one.

Soc. That is what is wanted, Gorgias; exhibit the shorter method now, and the longer one at some other time.

Gor. Well, I will; and I am sure that you will commend my brevity of speech as unrivaled.

Soc. Well, then, as you say that you are a rhetorician, and a maker of rhetoricians, what is the business of rhetoric in the sense in which I might say that the business of weaving is making garments—might I not?

Gor. Yes.

Soc. Might I not say, again, that the business of music is the composition of melodies?

Gor. Yes.

Soc. By [the god] Here, Gorgias, I admire the surpassing brevity of your answers.

Gor. Yes, Socrates, and I do think that I am good at that.

Soc. I am glad to hear it; answer me in like manner about rhetoric: what is the business of rhetoric?

Gor. Discourse.

Soc. What sort of discourse, Gorgias?—such discourse as would teach the sick under what treatment they might get well?

Gor. No.

Soc. Then rhetoric does not treat of all kinds of discourse?

Gor. Certainly not.

Soc. And yet rhetoric makes men able to speak?

Gor. Yes.

Soc. And to understand that of which they speak?

Gor. To be sure.

Soc. But does not the art of medicine, which we were just now mentioning, also make men able to understand and speak about the sick?

Gor. Certainly.

Soc. Then medicine also treats of discourse?

Gor. Yes.

Soc. Of discourse concerning diseases?

Gor. Certainly.

Soc. And does not gymnastic also treat of discourse concerning the good or evil condition of the body?

Gor. Very true.

Soc. And the same, Gorgias, is true of the other arts: all of them treat of discourse concerning the subject of which they are the arts.

Gor. That is evident.

Soc. Then why, if you call rhetoric the art which treats of discourse, and all the other arts treat of discourse, do you not call them arts of rhetoric?

Gor. Because, Socrates, the knowledge of the other arts has only to do with some sort of external action, as of the hand; but there is no such action of the hand in rhetoric which operates and in which the effect is produced through the medium of discourse. And therefore I am justified, as I maintain, in saying that rhetoric treats of discourse.

Soc. I do not know whether I perfectly understand you, but I dare say that I shall find out: please to answer me a question; you would allow that there are arts?

Gor. Yes.

Soc. And in some of the arts a great deal is done and nothing or very little said; in painting, or statuary, or many other arts, the work may proceed in silence; and these are the arts with which, as I suppose you would say, rhetoric has no concern?

Gor. You perfectly conceive my meaning, Socrates.

Soc. And there are other arts which work wholly by words, and require either no action or very little, as, for example, the arts of arithmetic, of calculation, of geometry, and of playing draughts; in some of which words are nearly coextensive with things: and in most of them predominate over things, and their whole efficacy and power is given by words: and I take your meaning to be that rhetoric is one of this sort?

Gor. Exactly.

Soc. And yet I do not believe that you really mean to call any of these arts rhetoric; although the precise expression which you used was, that rhetoric is an art of which the effect is produced through the medium of discourse; and an adversary who wished to be captious might take a fancy to say, "And so, Gorgias, you call arithmetic rhetoric." But I do not think that you would call arithmetic rhetoric, any more than you would call geometry rhetoric.

Gor. You are quite right, Socrates, in your apprehension of my meaning.

Soc. Well, then, let me have now the rest of my answer: seeing that rhetoric is one of those arts which works mainly by the use of words, and there are other arts which also use words, tell me what is that quality of words by which the effect of rhetoric is given: I will suppose some one to ask me about any of the arts which I was mentioning just now; he might say, "Socrates, what is arithmetic?" and I should reply to him as you replied to me just now, that arithmetic is one of those arts in which the effect is produced by words. And then he would proceed: "Words about what?" and I should say, Words about odd and even numbers, and how many there are of each. . . . And suppose, again, I were to say that astronomy works altogether by words—he would ask, "Words about what, Socrates?" and I should answer, that the words of astronomy are about the motions of the stars and sun and moon, and their relative swiftness.

Gor. Very true, Socrates; I admit that.

Soc. And now let us have from you, Gorgias, the truth about rhetoric: which you would admit (would you not?) to be one of those arts which operate and produce all their effects through the medium of words?

Gor. True.

Soc. Tell me, I say, what are the words about? To what class of things do the words which rhetoric uses relate?

Gor. To the greatest, Socrates, and the best of human things.

Soc. That again, Gorgias, is ambiguous; I am still in the dark: for which are the greatest and best of human things?   . . .

Gor. That, Socrates, which is truly the greatest good, being that which gives men freedom in their own persons, and to rulers the power of ruling over others in their several States.

Soc. And what would you consider this to be?

Gor. I should say the word which persuades the judges in the courts, or the senators in the council, or the citizens in the assembly, or at any other public meeting: if you have the power of uttering this word, you will have the physician your slave, and the trainer your slave, and the money-maker of whom you talk will be found to gather treasures, not for himself, but for you who are able to speak and persuade the multitude.

Soc. Now I think, Gorgias, that you have very accurately explained what you conceive to be the art of rhetoric; and you mean to say, if I am not mistaken, that rhetoric is the artificer of persuasion, having this and no other business, and that this is her crown and end. Do you know any other effect of rhetoric over and above that of producing persuasion?

Gor. No; the definition seems to me very fair, Socrates; for persuasion is the crown of rhetoric.

Soc. Then hear me, Gorgias, for I am quite sure that if there ever was a man who entered on the discussion of a matter from a pure love of knowing the truth, I am one, and I believe that you are another.

Gor. What is coming, Socrates?

Soc. I will tell you: I am very well aware that I do not know what, according to you, is the exact nature, or what are the topics of that persuasion of which you speak, and which is given by rhetoric; although I have a suspicion both about the one and about the other. And I am going to ask—what is this power of persuasion which is given by rhetoric, and about what? But why, if I have a suspicion, do I ask instead of telling you? Not for your sake, but in order that the argument may proceed in such a manner as is most likely to elicit the truth. And I would have you observe, that I am right in asking this further question. If I asked, "What sort of a painter is Zeuxis?" and you said, "the painter of figures," should I not be right in asking, "What sort of figures, and where do you find them?"

Gor. Certainly.

Soc. And the reason for asking this second question would be, that there are other painters as well, who paint many other figures?

Gor. True.

Soc. But if there had been no one but Zeuxis who painted them, then you would have answered very well?

Gor. Certainly.

Soc. Now I want to know about rhetoric in the same way;—is rhetoric the only art which brings persuasion, or do other arts have the same effect? I mean to say this—Does he who teaches anything persuade of what he teaches or not?

Gor. He persuades, Socrates,—there can be no mistake about that.

Soc. Again if we take the arts of which we were just now speaking,—do not arithmetic and the arithmetician teach us the properties of number?

Gor. Certainly.

Soc. And therefore persuade us of them?

Gor. Yes.

Soc. Then arithmetic as well as rhetoric is an artificer of persuasion?

Gor. That is evident.

Soc. And if any one asks us what sort of persuasion, and about what,—we shall answer, of that which teaches the quantity of odd and even; and we shall be in a position to show that all the other arts of which we were just now speaking are artificers of persuasion, and of what kind of persuasion, and about what.

Gor. Very true.

Soc. Then rhetoric is not the only artificer of persuasion?

Gor. True.

Soc. Seeing, then, that not only rhetoric works by persuasion, but that other arts do the same, as in the case of the painter, a question has arisen which is a very fair one: Of what persuasion is rhetoric the artificer, and about what? is not that a fair way of putting the question?

Gor. I think that is.

Soc. Then, if you approve the question, Gorgias, what is the answer?

Gor. I answer, Socrates, that rhetoric is the art of persuasion in the courts and other assemblies, as I was just now saying, and about the just and unjust.

Soc. And that, Gorgias, was what I was suspecting to be your notion; yet I would not have you wonder if by and by I am found repeating a seemingly plain question; for as I was saying, I ask not for your sake, but in order that the argument may proceed consecutively, and that we may not get the habit of anticipating and suspecting the meaning of one another's words, and that you may proceed in your own way.

Gor. I think that you are quite right, Socrates.

Soc. Then let me raise this question; you would say that there is such a thing as "having learned"?

Gor. Yes.

Soc. And there is also "having believed"?

Gor. Yes.

Soc. And are the "having learned" and the "having believed," and are learning and belief the same things?

Gor. In my judgment, Socrates, they are not the same.

Soc. And your judgment is right, as you may ascertain in this way: If a person were to say to you, "Is there, Gorgias, a false belief as well as a true?" you would reply, if I am not mistaken, that there is.

Gor. Yes.

Soc. Well, but is there a false knowledge as well as a true?

Gor. No.

Soc. No, indeed; and this again proves that knowledge and belief differ.

Gor. That is true.

Soc. And yet those who have learned as well as those who have believed are persuaded?

Gor. That is as you say.

Soc. Shall we then assume two sorts of persuasion,—one which is the source of belief without knowledge, as the other is of knowledge?

Gor. By all means.

Soc. And which sort of persuasion does rhetoric create in courts of law and other assemblies about the just and unjust, the sort of persuasion which gives belief without knowledge, or that which gives knowledge?

Gor. Clearly, Socrates, that which only gives belief.

Soc. Then rhetoric, as would appear, is the artificer of a persuasion which creates belief about the just and unjust, but gives no instruction about them?

Gor. True.

Soc. And the rhetorician does not instruct the courts of law or other assemblies about just and unjust, but he only creates belief about them; for no one can be supposed to instruct such a vast multitude about such high matters in a short time?

Gor. Certainly not.

Soc. Come, then, and let us see what we really mean about rhetoric; for I do not know what my own meaning is as yet. When the assembly meets to elect a physician or a shipwright or any other craftsman, will the rhetorician be taken into counsel? Surely not. For at every election he ought to be chosen who has the greatest skill; and, again, when walls have to be built or harbors or docks to be constructed, not the rhetorician but the master workman will advise; or when generals have to be chosen and an order of battle arranged, or a position taken, then the military will advise and not the rhetoricians: would you admit that, Gorgias? As you profess to be a rhetorician and a maker of rhetoricians, I shall do well to learn the nature of your art from you. And here let me assure you that I have your interest in view as well as my own. For I dare say that some one or other of the young men present might like to become your pupil, and in fact I see some, and a good many too, who have this wish, but they would be too modest to question you. And therefore when you are interrogated by me, I would have you imagine that you are interrogated by them. "What is the use of coming to you, Gorgias?" they will say; "about what will you teach us to advise the State? about the just and unjust only, or about those other things also which Socrates has just mentioned?" How will you answer them?

Gor. I like your way of leading us on, Socrates, and I will endeavor to reveal to you the whole nature of rhetoric. You must have heard, I think, that the docks and the walls of the Athenians and the plan of the harbor were devised in accordance with the counsels, partly of Themistocles, and partly of Pericles, and not at the suggestion of the builders.

Soc. Certainly, Gorgias, that is what is told of Themistocles, and I myself heard the speech of Pericles when he advised us about the middle wall.

Gor. And you will observe, Socrates, that when a decision has to be given in such matters the rhetoricians are the advisers; they are the men who win their point.

Soc. I had that in my admiring mind, Gorgias, when I asked what is the nature of rhetoric, which always appears to me, when I look at the matter in this way, to be a marvel of greatness.

Gor. A marvel indeed, Socrates, if you only knew how rhetoric comprehends and holds under her sway all the inferior arts. And I will give you a striking example of this. On several occasions I have been with my brother Herodicus or some other physician to see one of his patients, who would not allow the physician to give him medicine, or apply the knife or hot iron to him; and I have persuaded him to do for me what he would not do for the physician just by the use of rhetoric. And I say that if a rhetorician and a physician were to go to any city, and there had to argue in the Ecclesia or any other assembly as to which should be elected, the physician would have no chance; but he who could speak would be chosen if he wished, and in a contest with a man of any other profession the rhetorician more than any one would have the power of getting himself chosen, for he can speak more persuasively to the multitude than any of them, and on any subject. Such is the power and quality of rhetoric, Socrates. And yet rhetoric ought to be used like any other competitive art, not against every-body,—the rhetorician ought not to abuse his strength any more than a pugilist or pancratiast or other master of fence; because he has powers which are more than a match either for enemy or friend, he ought not therefore to strike, stab, or slay his friends. And suppose a man who has been the pupil of a palestra and is a skillful boxer, and in the fulness of his strength he goes and strikes his father or mother or one of his familiars or friends, that is no reason why the trainer or master of fence should be held in detestation or banished,—surely not. For they taught this art for a good purpose, as an art to be used against enemies and evil-doers, in self-defense, not in aggression, and others have perverted their instructions, making a bad use of their strength and their skill. But not on this account are the teachers bad, neither is the art in fault or bad in itself; I should rather say that those who make a bad use of the art are to blame. And the same holds good of rhetoric; for the rhetorician can speak against all men and on any subject, and in general he can persuade the multitude of anything better than any other man, but he ought not on that account to defraud the physician or any other artist of his reputation merely because he has the power; he ought to use rhetoric fairly, as he would also use his combative powers. And if after having become a rhetorician he makes a bad use of his strength and skill, his instructor surely ought not on that account to be held in detestation or banished. For he was intended by his teacher to make a good use of his instructions, and he abuses them. And therefore he is the person who ought to be held in detestation, banished, and put to death, and not his instructor.

Soc. You, Gorgias, like myself, have had great experience of arguments, and you must have observed, I think, that they do not always terminate to the satisfaction or mutual improvement of the disputants; but disagreements are apt to arise, and one party will often deny that the other has spoken truly or clearly; and then they leave off arguing and begin to quarrel, both parties fancying that their opponents are only speaking from personal feeling. And sometimes they will go on abusing one another until the company at last are quite annoyed at their own condescension in listening to such fellows. Why do I say this? Why, because I cannot help feeling that you are now saying what is not quite consistent or accordant with what you were saying at first about rhetoric. And I am afraid to point this out to you, lest you should think that I have some animosity against you, and that I speak, not for the sake of discovering the truth, but from personal feeling. Now if you are one of my sort, I should like to cross-examine you, but if not I will let you alone. And what is my sort? you will ask. I am one of those who are very willing to be refuted if I say anything which is not true, and very willing to refute any one else who says what is not true, and just as ready to be refuted as to refute; for I hold that this is the greater gain of the two, just as the gain is greater of being cured of a very great evil than of curing the evil in another. For I imagine that there is no evil which a man can endure so great as an erroneous opinion about the matters of which we are speaking; and if you claim to be one of my sort, let us have the discussion out, but if you would rather have done, no matter; let us make an end.

Gor. I should say, Socrates, that I am quite the man whom you indicate; but, perhaps, we ought to consider the audience, for, before you came, I had already given a long exhibition, and if we proceed the argument may run on to a great length. And therefore I think that we should consider whether we may not be detaining some part of the company when they are wanting to do something else.

Chaerephon: You hear the audience cheering, Gorgias and Socrates, which shows their desire to listen to you, and for myself, Heaven forbid that I should have any business which would take me away from so important and interesting a discussion.

· · ·

Soc. I may truly say ... that I am willing, if Gorgias is.

Gor. After this, Socrates, I should be disgraced if I refused, especially as I have professed to answer all comers; in accordance with the wishes of the company, then, do you begin, and ask of me any question which you like.

Soc. Let me tell you then, Gorgias, what makes me wonder at your words; though I dare say that you may be right, and I may have mistaken your meaning. You say that you can make any man, who will learn of you, a rhetorician?

Gor. Yes.

Soc. Do you mean that you will teach him to gain the ears of the multitude on any subject, and this not by instruction but by persuasion?

Gor. Certainly.

Soc. You were saying, in fact, that the rhetorician will have greater powers of persuasion than the physician, even in a matter of health?

Gor. Yes, with the multitude,—that is.

Soc. That is to say, greater with the ignorant; for with those who know, he cannot be supposed to have greater powers of persuasion than the physician has.

Gor. Very true.

Soc. And if he is to have more power of persuasion than the physician, he will have greater power than he who knows?

Gor. Certainly.

Soc. Though he is not a physician,—is he?

Gor. No.

Soc. And he who is not a physician is obviously ignorant of what the physician knows?

Gor. That is evident.

Soc. Then, when the rhetorician is more persuasive than the physician, the ignorant is more persuasive with the ignorant than he who has knowledge? is not that the inference?

Gor. In the case which is supposed, yes.

Soc. And the same holds of the relation of rhetoric to all the other arts; the rhetorician need not know the whole truth about them; he has only to discover some way of persuading the ignorant that he has more knowledge than those who know?

Gor. Yes, Socrates, and is not this a great blessing?—not to have learned the other arts, but the art of rhetoric only, and yet to be in no way inferior to the professors of them?

Soc. Whether the rhetorician is or is not inferior on this account is a question which we will hereafter examine if the inquiry is likely to be of any service to us; but I would rather begin by asking, whether he is as ignorant of the just and unjust, base and honorable, good and evil, as he is of medicine and the other arts; I mean to say, does he know anything actually of what is good and evil, base or honorable, just or unjust in them; or has he only a way with the ignorant of persuading them that he not knowing is to be esteemed to know more than another who knows? Or must the pupil know and come to you knowing these things before he can acquire the art of rhetoric? And if he is ignorant, you who are the teacher of rhetoric will not teach him, for that is not your business, but you will make him seem to know them to the multitude, when he does not know them; and seem to be a good man, when he is not. Or will you be wholly unable to teach him rhetoric unless he knows the truth of these things first? What is to be said, Gorgias, about all this? I swear that I wish you would, as you were saying, reveal to me the power of rhetoric.

Gor. Well, Socrates, I suppose that if the pupil does chance not to know them, he will have to learn of me these things as well.

Soc. Say no more, for there you are right; and so he whom you make a rhetorician must know the nature of the just and unjust, either of his own previous knowledge, or he must be taught by you.

Gor. Certainly.

Soc. Well, and is not he who has learned carpentering a carpenter?

Gor. Yes.

Soc. And he who has learned music a musician?

Gor. Yes.

Soc. And he who has learned medicine is a physician, in like manner. He who has learned anything whatever is that which his knowledge makes him.

Gor. Certainly.

Soc. And in the same way, he who has learned what is just is just?

Gor. To be sure.

Soc. And he who is just may be supposed to do what is just?

Gor. Yes.

Soc. And must not the rhetorician be just, and is not the just man desirous to do what is just?

Gor. That is clearly the inference.

Soc. Then the just man will surely never be willing to do injustice?

Gor. That is certain.

Soc. And according to the argument the rhetorician ought to be a just man?

Gor. Yes.

Soc. And will therefore never be willing to do injustice?

Gor. Clearly not.

Soc. But do you remember saying just now that the trainer is not to be accused or banished if the pugilist makes a wrong use of his pugilistic art; and in like manner, if the rhetorician makes a bad and unjust use of his rhetoric, that is not to be laid to the charge of his instructor, neither is he to be banished, but the wrong-doer himself who made a bad use of his rhetoric is to be banished—was not that said?

Gor. Yes, that was said.

Soc. And now it turns out that this same rhetorician can never have done any injustice.

Gor. True.

Soc. And at the very outset, Gorgias, there was an assertion made, that rhetoric treated of discourse, not about odd and even, but about just and unjust. Is not that true?

Gor. Yes.

Soc. And I thought at the time, when I heard you saying this, that rhetoric, which is always discoursing about justice, could not possibly be an unjust thing. But when you said, shortly afterwards, that the rhetorician might make a bad use of rhetoric, I noted with surprise the inconsistency into which you had fallen; and I said, that if you thought, as I did, that there was a gain in being refuted, there would be an advantage in discussing the question, but if not, I would leave off. And in the course of our examination, as you will see yourself, the rhetorician has been acknowledged to be incapable of making an unjust use of rhetoric, or of unwillingness to do injustice. By the dog, Gorgias, there will be a great deal of discussion, before we get at the truth of all this.

Polus : And do you, Socrates, seriously incline to believe what you are now saying about rhetoric? What! because Gorgias was ashamed to deny that the rhetorician knew the just and the honorable and the good, and that he could teach them to any one who came to him ignorant of them, and then out of the admission there may have arisen a contradiction; you, as you always do, having recourse to your favorite mode of interrogation. For do you suppose that any one will ever say that he does not know, or cannot teach, the nature of justice? The truth is, that there is great want of manners in bringing the argument to such a pass.

Soc. Illustrious Polus, the great reason why we provide ourselves with friends and children is that when we get old and stumble a younger generation may be at hand, and set us on our legs again in our words and in our actions; and now, if I and Gorgias are stumbling, there are you a present help to us, as you ought to be; and I for my part engage to retract any error into which you may think that I have fallen—upon one condition.

Pol. What is that?

Soc. That you contract, Polus, the prolixity of speech in which you indulged at first.

Pol. What! Do you mean that I am not to use as many words as I please?

Soc. Only to think, my friend, that having come on a visit to Athens, which is the most free-spoken State in Hellas, you of all men should be deprived of the power of speech—that is hard indeed. But then look at my case: should not I be very hardly used if, when you are making a long oration and refusing to answer what you are asked, I may not go away, but am compelled to stay and listen to you? I say rather, that if you have a real interest in the argument, or, to repeat my former expression, have any desire to set me on my legs, take back again anything which you please; and in your turn ask and answer, like myself and Gorgias—refute and be refuted: for I suppose that you would claim to know what Gorgias knows?

Pol. Yes.

Soc. And you, like him, invite any one to ask you about anything which he likes, and you will know how to answer him?

Pol. To be sure.

Soc. And now, which will you do, ask or answer?

Pol. I will ask; and do you answer me, Socrates, the same question which Gorgias, as you suppose, is unable to answer: What is rhetoric?

Soc. Do you mean what sort of an art?

Pol. Yes.

Soc. Not an art at all, in my opinion, if I am to tell you the truth, Polus.

Pol. Then what, in your opinion, is rhetoric?

. . .

Soc. I should say a sort of routine or experience.

Pol. Then does rhetoric seem to you to be a sort of experience?

Soc. That is my view, if that is yours.

Pol. An experience of what?

Soc. An experience of making a sort of delight and gratification.

Pol. And if able to gratify others, must not rhetoric be a fine thing?

Soc. What are you saying, Polus? Why do you ask me whether rhetoric is a fine thing or not, when I have not as yet told you what rhetoric is?

Pol. Why, did you not tell me that rhetoric was a sort of experience?

Soc. As you are so fond of gratifying others, will you gratify me in a small particular?

Pol. I will.

Soc. Will you ask me what sort of an art is cookery?

Pol. What sort of an art is cookery?

Soc. Not an art at all, Polus.

Pol. What then?

Soc. I should say a sort of experience.

Pol. Of what? I wish that you would tell me.

Soc. An experience of making a sort of delight and gratification, Polus.

Pol. Then are cookery and rhetoric the same?

Soc. No, they are only different parts of the same profession.

Pol. And what is that?

Soc. I am afraid that the truth may seem discourteous; I should not like Gorgias to imagine that I am ridiculing his profession, and therefore I hesitate to answer. For whether or no this is that art of rhetoric which Gorgias practises I really do not know: from what he was just now saying, nothing appeared of what he thought of his art, but the rhetoric which I mean is a part of a not very creditable whole.

Gor. A part of what, Socrates? Say what you mean, and never mind me.

Soc. To me then, Gorgias, the whole of which rhetoric is a part appears to be a process, not of art, but the habit of a bold and ready wit, which knows how to behave to the world: this I sum up under the word "flattery"; and this habit or process appears to me to have many other parts, one of which is cookery, which may seem to be an art, and, as I maintain, is not an art, but only experience and routine: another part is rhetoric, ... And Polus may ask, if he likes, for he has not as yet been informed, what part of flattery is rhetoric: he did not see that I had not yet answered him when he proceeded to ask a further question,—Whether I do not think rhetoric a fine thing? But I shall not tell him whether rhetoric is a fine thing or not, until I have first answered, "What is rhetoric?" For that would not be right, Polus; but I shall be happy to answer, if you will ask me, What part of flattery is rhetoric?

Pol. I will ask, and do you answer: What part of flattery is rhetoric?

Soc. Will you understand my answer? Rhetoric, according to my view, is the shadow of a part of politics.

Pol. And noble or ignoble?

Soc. Ignoble, as I should say, if I am compelled to answer, for I call what is bad ignoble,—though I doubt whether you understand what I was saying before.

Gor. Indeed, Socrates, I cannot say that I understand myself.

Soc. I do not wonder at that; for I have not as yet explained myself, and our friend Polus, like a young colt as he is, is apt to run away.

Gor. Never mind him, but explain to me what you mean by saying that rhetoric is the shadow of a part of politics.

Soc. I will try, then, to explain my notion of rhetoric, and if I am mistaken, my friend Polus shall refute me. Are there not bodies and souls?

Gor. There are.

Soc. And you would further admit that there is a good condition of either of them?

Gor. Yes.

Soc. Which condition may not be really good, but good only in appearance? I mean to say, that there are many persons who appear to be in good health, and whom only a physician or trainer will discern at first sight not to be in good health.

Gor. True.

Soc. And this applies not only to the body, but also to the soul: in either there may be that which gives the appearance of health and not the reality?

Gor. Yes, certainly.

Soc. And now I will endeavor to explain to you more clearly what I mean: the soul and body being two, have two arts corresponding to them: there is the art of politics attending on the soul; and another art attending on the body, of which I know no specific name, but which may be described as having two divisions, one of which is gymnastic, and the other medicine. And in politics there is a legislative part, which answers to gymnastic, as justice does to medicine; and they run into one another, justice having to do with the same subject as legislation, and medicine with the same subject as gymnastic, yet there is a difference between them. Now, seeing that there are these four arts which are ever ministering to the body and the soul for their highest good, flattery, knowing or rather guessing their natures, has distributed herself into four shams or simulations of them; she puts on the likeness of one or other of them, and pretends to be that which she simulates, and has no regard for men's highest interests, but is ever making pleasure the bait of the unwary, and deceiving them into the belief that she is of the highest value to them. Cookery simulates the disguise of medicine, and pretends to know what food is the best for the body; and if the physician and the cook had to enter into a competition in which children were the judges, or men who had no more sense than children, as to which of them best understands the goodness or badness of food, the physician would be starved to death. A flattery I deem this and an ignoble sort of thing, Polus, for to you I am now addressing myself, because it aims at pleasure instead of good. And I do not call this an art at all, but only an experience or routine, because it is unable to explain or to give a reason of the nature of its own applications. And I do not call any irrational thing an art; if you dispute my words, I am prepared to argue in defense of them.

Cookery, then, as I maintain, is the flattery which takes the form of medicine, and the art of tiring [cosmetics], in like manner, takes the form of gymnastic, and is a knavish, false, ignoble, and illiberal art, working deceitfully by the help of lines, and colors, and enamels, and garments, and making men affect a spurious beauty to the neglect of the true beauty which is given by gymnastic.

I would rather not be tedious, and therefore I will only say, after the manner of the geometricians (for I think that by this time you will be able to follow),

As the art of tiring : gymnastic :: cookery : medicine; or rather—

As tiring : gymnastic :: sophistry : legislation; and—

As cookery : medicine :: rhetoric : justice.

And this, I say, is the natural difference between them, but by reason of their near connection, the sphere and subject of the rhetorician is apt to be confounded with that of the sophist; neither do they know what to make of themselves, nor do other men know what to make of them. For if the body presided over itself, and were not under the guidance of the soul, and the soul did not discern and discriminate between cookery and medicine, but the body was made the judge of them and the rule of judgment was the bodily delight which was given by them, then the word of Anaxagoras, that word with which you, friend Polus, are so well acquainted, would come true: chaos would return, and cookery, health, and medicine would mingle in an indiscernible mass. And now I have told you my notion of rhetoric, which is in relation to the soul what cookery is to the body. I may have been inconsistent in making a long speech, when I would not allow you to discourse at length. But I think that I may be excused, as you did not understand me, and could make no use of my shorter answer, and I had to enter into an explanation. And if I show an equal inability to make use of yours, I hope that you will speak at equal length; but if I am able to understand you, let me have the benefit of your brevity, for this is only fair; and now this answer of mine is much at your service.

Pol. What do you mean? Do you think that rhetoric is flattery?

Soc. Nay, I said a part of flattery; if at your age, Polus, you cannot remember, what will you do by and by, when you get older?

Pol. And are the good rhetoricians meanly regarded in States, under the idea that they are flatterers?

Soc. Is that a question or the beginning of a speech?

Pol. I am asking a question.

Soc. Then my answer is, that they are not regarded at all.

Pol. How not regarded? Have they not very great power in States?

Soc. Not if you mean to say that power is a good to the possessor.

Pol. And I do mean to say that.

Soc. Then, in that case, I think that they have the least power of all the citizens. . . .

.   .   .

Soc. Well then, I say to you that here are two questions in one, and I will answer both of them. And I tell you, Polus, that rhetoricians and tyrants have the least possible power in States, as I was just now saying; for they do nothing, as I may say, of what they will, but only what they think best.

Pol. And is not that a great power?

Soc. Polus has already denied that.

Pol. Denied? Nay, that is what I affirm.

Soc. By the—what do you call him?—not you, for you say that great power is a good to him who has the power.

Pol. I do.

Soc. And would you maintain that if a fool does what appears best to him he does what is good, and would you call this great power.

Pol. I do not say that.

Soc. Then you must prove that the rhetorician is not a fool, and that rhetoric is an art and not a flattery,—that is the way to refute me; but if you leave me unrefuted, then the rhetoricians who do what they think best in States, and the tyrants, will be deprived of this power: for you assume that power is a good thing, and yet admit that the power which is exercised without understanding is an evil.

————

Questions

How do the tone and "rules" of the dialogue as conducted by Socrates differ from the "Socratic method" used in law school? What values are implicit in Socrates' style? In the "Socratic method"?

Gorgias concedes that if a student does not know the right and wrong of those things upon which he will argue, it is the law professor's responsibility to teach the student this. Do you agree? [1]

Is the practice of law a "routine" or "experience" as Socrates called "rhetoric"? Does Socrates' critique apply only to lawyers acting as advocates and not to counseling or other lawyer roles?

What arguments in defense of a lawyer's role would a modern lawyer make that Gorgias did not? Professor James Boyd White has attempted to answer this question. White's dialogue features two

1. For contemporary discussion of the propriety or obligation of a law teacher addressing issues of "right and wrong," see Symposium, Beyond the Ordinary Religion, 37 J.Legal Educ. 509 (1987) (articles by Roger C. Cramton, Katherine T. Bartlett, James R. Elkins, Peter M. Shane and James Boyd White).

American lawyers, Euerges and Euphemes, "successful attorneys in a firm with a diverse general practice," who seek to defend their lives and endeavors in a conversation with Socrates.[2]

White's Euerges argues that the lawyer's function is to advise people about their legal rights and duties, and to represent clients' interests or desires, by increasing their power, range of choices, liberty and wealth. A course of action is chosen only after a detailed consultation with clients, viewed as responsible and intelligent actors, concerning their needs and wants. In response to the charges equating lawyers with prostitutes, Euerges claims that a lawyer's work is part of an overarching system whose overall aim is justice. A lawyer serves justice by playing his part in such a system which, despite its imperfections, experience has shown to be the best. This is shown by the progress that our law has made over time, and by the ethical constraints and circumscribing rules of law that have evolved to control attorneys' misrepresentations. In appealing to a judge, the lawyer may use only the techniques of persuasion permitted by the system. This excludes, for example, appeals to bigotry. Finally, traditional legal procedures originate in a democratic form of government, founded with the people's consent, and thus are the most just. In sum, White's Euerges justifies the lawyer's role and function in a manner similar to that of the organized profession.[3]

White's Euphemes, on the other hand, justifies the modern lawyer's activity on a different basis. Euphemes, after rejecting the "idealistic" justifications of Euerges, claims instead that the practice of law specifically and uniquely enables one to attain the difficult-to-reach goal of becoming "trustworthy".[4] The most important factor in attaining such a character is the "ethical community that one establishes both with one's clients and with other lawyers and judges."[5] The function of lawyers in the community is to preserve and improve a language of description, value and reason—a culture of argument—without which it would be impossible even to ask the important questions, such as those about the nature of justice.[6]

In its practical application, a concept like that of justice is not ideal or universal, but rather culturally conditioned. Concepts concerning justice are the tools or materials lawyers use to "maintain the materials essential to these cultural activities and the conventions and under-

2. James Boyd White, The Ethics of Argument: Plato's *Gorgias* and the Modern Lawyer, in White, Heracles' Bow, c. 10 (1985), reprinting in modified form the article of the same title in 50 U.Chi.L.Rev. 849 (1983).

3. See the discussion of the views of Charles Fried and Richard Wasserstrom on role morality in Chapter 2, and those of David Luban in Chapter 5 concerning the "adversary system excuse."

4. Brandeis in his essay, The Opportunity in the Law, excerpted in Chapter 11 at p. 1086, also argues that everyday law practice cultivates judgment and virtue. For another contemporary argument to this effect, see Anthony T. Kronman, Living in the Law, 54 U.Chi.L.Rev. 835 (1987).

5. Id. at 232.

6. Id. at 223.

standings that make them possible." Cultural continuity requires a stable language, procedures to regulate it and a vocabulary of shared cultural norms, values and expectations. New facts and circumstances constantly test and reshape this language. Lawyers are essential participants in the cultural discourse and framework by which law is made and remade. Lawyers preserve and refurbish the law itself as "a way in which the community defines itself, not once and for all, but over and over, and in the process educates itself about its own character and the nature of the world."[7]

Euphemes then discusses the ethical dimensions of this approach to lawyering. The alleged "insincerity" of an advocate's assertions in the dynamic process described above is irrelevant because it is transparent; it deceives no one. It is but a small, recognized aspect of a formalized procedure that plays only a part in reaching the overall goal—well-known to the decision-maker—of achieving a lawful result. A given attorney's "best" argument does not reflect justice in the abstract, but rather the means that the culture allows one to use in attempting to reach a just result. In so doing, the lawyers also instruct the judge concerning the nature of the case and the scope of disagreement. The "trustworthy" lawyer is one who does this honestly and intelligently, and whose standards of argument are heightened by being addressed to an "ideal" judge. Such an approach justifies the activity of being a lawyer in any community, just or unjust, since it entails making the best case the materials of the culture will allow. Of course, no one can know whether the lawyer's arguments or her conception of the "ideal" judge are "best", but the important thing is to know how to approach these questions, and how to strive for the best possible use of cultural materials.

If, however, a culture appears so repugnant as to warrant its destruction, one must first evaluate "the materials for argument that the culture makes available."[8] Would it be possible to appeal to its "better" side? Is any improvement possible? Here Euphemes affirms the role of ideals, the values of equality and reason that make up the rule of law. How should one evaluate ideals? Certain basic standards exist, but in the case of more complicated issues the question is rather how best to engage in dialogue on such unresolved questions. To preserve this dialogue's useful character for others, one must encourage an interplay between a realistic and an idealistic language: the latter alone may be impractical and useless, whereas the former alone may devolve into a cynical instrumentalism.

Thus, one of the lawyer's functions is to preserve the tension between the two poles of realism and idealism. The language of the law must reflect both "factual congruence with reality" and the "element of aspiration"; and the lawyer must use these tools to "convert and translate" the facts of human experience into arguments about

7. Id. at 235.
8. Id. at 232.

justice. A lawyer always remains an advocate during this process, but the "trustworthy" lawyer spells out to his client, implicitly or explicitly, the limits of his advocacy. The lawyer's credibility, and thus his effectiveness before the judge, actually depends upon such self-restraint. In sum, her duty is to present, and thus become, a "trustworthy" character, the very opposite of Socrates' amoral rhetorician. The uniquely equivocal situations that an attorney encounters offer her a unique opportunity to develop her character; such a career then becomes "not a life worthy of no one', but a life worthy of anyone." [9]

Are White's arguments more persuasive than those offered in Plato's dialogue?

B. FORMATIVE INFLUENCE OF LEGAL INSTITUTIONS

Introduction

Erving Goffman's project in Asylums was the examination of "total institutions," e.g., prisons, monasteries and mental hospitals. The institutions in which lawyers train and work are not "total." Law schools, which come closest to his model, allow "inmates" to interact more or less freely with the outside world. Law firms, corporations and government bureaucracies are all further along the spectrum, controlling the lives of "inmates" and "staff" by less obvious, although not necessarily less effective, means. Finally, the court system is obviously not a "total" institution. Although some of its participants, judges and court personnel, are more or less "fixed" participants, parties and jurors are transitory actors; many lawyers and some parties are repeat players. There are, however, two factors that make the connection between courts and total institutions closer than it might appear at first. One, the power of courts, in civil and criminal matters, is dependent on their ability to transform people into inmates of total institutions. The power of law in the end *is* the power of total institutions. The court system may therefore be seen as the portal to society's involuntary total institutions. Second, courts, while ostensibly "open" to the public, are not open in the sense that Grand Central Station is open. The court wields enormous power on all within its domain: lawyers, litigants, jurors and even spectators to a lesser degree are expected to play by special rules and act in accordance with roles not appropriate in other settings. [10]

Despite the sometimes striking parallels between legal institutions and total institutions, it is important to remember two important distinctions. First, "inmates" in legal institutions retain active mem-

---

9. Id. at 237.

10. See the materials in Chapter 11 discussing the contempt charges against lawyers and defendants in the Chicago conspiracy trial and the Hazard excerpt on courtroom decorum, pp. 1009, 1015.

bership in other "institutions" or communities—families, ethnic and religious groups, community-organizations, political parties and the like—which serve as continuing sources of traditions, norms and commitments that provide grounds by which the individual may critique, resist and revise the institutions of law. Second, an "inmate" in a law school or law firm, unlike one in a prison or asylum, can always choose to leave.

ERVING GOFFMAN
ASYLUMS

Pp. 3–18, 44–45, 60–65, 99 (1961).[11]

INTRODUCTION

I

Social establishments—institutions in the everyday sense of that term—are places such as rooms, suites of rooms, buildings, or plants in which activity of a particular kind regularly goes on. In sociology we do not have a very apt way of classifying them. Some establishments, like Grand Central Station, are open to anyone who is decently behaved; others, like the Union League Club of New York or the laboratories at Los Alamos, are felt to be somewhat snippy about who is let in. Some, like shops and post offices, have a few fixed members who provide a service and a continuous flow of members who receive it. Others, like homes and factories, involve a less changing set of participants.... In this book another category of institutions is singled out and claimed as a natural and fruitful one because its members appear to have so much in common—so much, in fact, that to learn about one of these institutions we would be well advised to look at the others.

II

Every institution captures something of the time and interest of its members and provides something of a world for them; in brief, every institution has encompassing tendencies. When we review the different institutions in our Western society, we find some that are encompassing to a degree discontinuously greater than the ones next in line. Their encompassing or total character is symbolized by the barrier to social intercourse with the outside and to departure that is often built right into the physical plant, such as locked doors, high walls, barbed wire, cliffs, water, forests, or moors. These establishments I am calling *total institutions*, and it is their general characteristics I want to explore.

The total institutions of our society can be listed in five rough groupings. First, there are institutions established to care for persons

11. Copyright © 1961 by Erving Goffman.

felt to be both incapable and harmless; these are the homes for the blind, the aged, the orphaned, and the indigent. Second, there are places established to care for persons felt to be both incapable of looking after themselves and a threat to the community, albeit an unintended one: TB sanitaria, mental hospitals, and leprosaria. A third type of total institution is organized to protect the community against what are felt to be intentional dangers to it, with the welfare of the persons thus sequestered not the immediate issue: jails, penitentiaries, P.O.W. camps, and concentration camps. Fourth, there are institutions purportedly established the better to pursue some work-like task and justifying themselves only on these instrumental grounds: army barracks, ships, boarding schools, work camps, colonial compounds, and large mansions from the point of view of those who live in the servants' quarters. Finally, there are those establishments designed as retreats from the world even while often serving also as training stations for the religious; examples are abbeys, monasteries, convents, and other cloisters. . . .

Before I attempt to extract a general profile from this list of establishments, I would like to mention one conceptual problem: none of the elements I will describe seems peculiar to total institutions, and none seems to be shared by every one of them; what is distinctive about total institutions is that each exhibits to an intense degree many items in this family of attributes. In speaking of "common characteristics," I will be using this phrase in a way that is restricted but I think logically defensible. At the same time this permits using the method of ideal types, establishing common features with the hope of highlighting significant differences later.

III

A basic social arrangement in modern society is that the individual tends to sleep, play, and work in different places, with different co-participants, under different authorities, and without an over-all rational plan. The central feature of total institutions can be described as a breakdown of the barriers ordinarily separating these three spheres of life. First, all aspects of life are conducted in the same place and under the same single authority. Second, each phase of the member's daily activity is carried on in the immediate company of a large batch of others, all of whom are treated alike and required to do the same thing together. Third, all phases of the day's activities are tightly scheduled, with one activity leading at a prearranged time into the next, the whole sequence of activities being imposed from above by a system of explicit formal rulings and a body of officials. Finally, the various enforced activities are brought together into a single rational plan purportedly designed to fulfill the official aims of the institution.

Individually, these features are found in places other than total institutions. For example, our large commercial, industrial, and educational establishments are increasingly providing cafeterias and free-time recreation for their members; use of these extended facilities remains voluntary in many particulars, however, and special care is taken to see that the ordinary line of authority does not extend to them. Similarly, housewives or farm families may have all their major spheres of life within the same fenced-in area, but these persons are not collectively regimented and do not march through the day's activities in the immediate company of a batch of similar others.

The handling of many human needs by the bureaucratic organization of whole blocks of people—whether or not this is a necessary or effective means of social organization in the circumstances—is the key fact of total institutions. From this follow certain important implications.

When persons are moved in blocks, they can be supervised by personnel whose chief activity is not guidance or periodic inspection (as in many employer-employee relations) but rather surveillance—a seeing to it that everyone does what he has been clearly told is required of him, under conditions where one person's infraction is likely to stand out in relief against the visible, constantly examined compliance of the others. Which comes first, the large blocks of managed people, or the small supervisory staff, is not here at issue; the point is that each is made for the other.

In total institutions there is a basic split between a large managed group, conveniently called inmates, and a small supervisory staff. Inmates typically live in the institution and have restricted contact with the world outside the walls; staff often operate on an eight-hour day and are socially integrated into the outside world. Each grouping tends to conceive of the other in terms of narrow hostile stereotypes, staff often seeing inmates as bitter, secretive, and untrustworthy, while inmates often see staff as condescending, highhanded, and mean. Staff tends to feel superior and righteous; inmates tend, in some ways at least, to feel inferior, weak, blameworthy, and guilty.

Social mobility between the two strata is grossly restricted; social distance is typically great and often formally prescribed. Even talk across the boundaries may be conducted in a special tone of voice ... Although some communication between inmates and the staff guarding them is necessary, one of the guard's functions is the control of communication from inmates to higher staff levels ... Just as talk across the boundary is restricted, so, too, is the passage of information, especially information about the staff's plans for inmates. Characteristically, the inmate is excluded from knowledge of the decisions taken regarding his fate. Whether the official grounds are military, as in concealing travel destination from enlisted men, or medical, as in concealing diagnosis, plan of treatment, and approximate length of stay from tuberculosis patients, such exclusion gives staff a special basis of distance from and control over inmates.

All these restrictions of contact presumably help to maintain the antagonistic stereotypes. Two different social and cultural worlds develop, jogging alongside each other with points of official contact but little mutual penetration. Significantly, the institutional plant and name come to be identified by both staff and inmates as somehow belonging to staff, so that when either grouping refers to the views or interests of "the institution," by implication they are referring (as I shall also) to the views and concerns of the staff.

The staff-inmate split is one major implication of the bureaucratic management of large blocks of persons; a second pertains to work.

In the ordinary arrangements of living in our society, the authority of the work place stops with the worker's receipt of a money payment; the spending of this in a domestic and recreational setting is the worker's private affair and constitutes a mechanism through which the authority of the work place is kept within strict bounds. But to say that inmates of total institutions have their full day scheduled for them is to say that all their essential needs will have to be planned for. Whatever the incentive given for work, then, this incentive will not have the structural significance it has on the outside. There will have to be different motives for work and different attitudes toward it. This is a basic adjustment required of the inmates and of those who must induce them to work.

. . .

There is an incompatibility, then, between total institutions and the basic work-payment structure of our society. Total institutions are also incompatible with another crucial element of our society, the family. Family life is sometimes contrasted with solitary living, but in fact the more pertinent contrast is with batch living, for those who eat and sleep at work, with a group of fellow workers, can hardly sustain a meaningful domestic existence. Conversely, maintaining families off the grounds often permits staff members to remain integrated with the outside community and to escape the encompassing tendency of the total institution.

. . .

THE INMATE WORLD

I

It is characteristic of inmates that they come to the institution with a "presenting culture" (to modify a psychiatric phrase) derived from a "home world"—a way of life and a round of activities taken for granted until the point of admission to the institution. . . . Whatever the stability of the recruit's personal organization, it was part of a wider framework lodged in his civil environment—a round of experience that confirmed a tolerable conception of self and allowed for a set of defensive maneuvers, exercised at his own discretion, for coping with conflicts, discreditings, and failures.

. . .

The full meaning for the inmate of being "in" or "on the inside" does not exist apart from the special meaning to him of "getting out" or "getting on the outside." In this sense, total institutions do not really look for cultural victory. They create and sustain a particular kind of tension between the home world and the institutional world and use this persistent tension as strategic leverage in the management of men.

II

The recruit comes into the establishment with a conception of himself made possible by certain stable social arrangements in his home world. Upon entrance, he is immediately stripped of the support provided by these arrangements. In the accurate language of some of our oldest total institutions, he begins a series of abasements, degradations, humiliations, and profanations of self. His self is systematically, if often unintentionally, mortified. He begins some radical shifts in his *moral career,* a career composed of the progressive changes that occur in the beliefs that he has concerning himself and significant others.

The processes by which a person's self is mortified are fairly standard in total institutions; analysis of these processes can help us to see the arrangements that ordinary establishments must guarantee if members are to preserve their civilian selves.

The barrier that total institutions place between the inmate and the wider world marks the first curtailment of self. In civil life, the sequential scheduling of the individual's roles, both in the life cycle and in the repeated daily round, ensures that no one role he plays will block his performance and ties in another. In total institutions, in contrast, membership automatically disrupts role scheduling, since the inmate's separation from the wider world lasts around the clock and may continue for years. Role dispossession therefore occurs. In many total institutions the privilege of having visitors or of visiting away from the establishment is completely withheld at first, ensuring a deep initial break with past roles and an appreciation of role dispossession.... I might add that when entrance is voluntary, the recruit has already partially withdrawn from his home world; what is cleanly severed by the institution is something that had already started to decay.

Although some roles can be re-established by the inmate if and when he returns to the world, it is plain that other losses are irrevocable and may be painfully experienced as such. It may not be possible to make up, at a later phase of the life cycle, the time not now spent in educational or job advancement, in courting, or in rearing one's children. A legal aspect of this permanent dispossession is found in the concept of "civil death": prison inmates may face not only a temporary loss of the rights to will money and write checks, to contest divorce or adoption proceedings, and to vote but may have some of these rights permanently abrogated.

The inmate, then, finds certain roles are lost to him by virtue of the barrier that separates him from the outside world. The process of entrance typically brings other kinds of loss and mortification as well. We very generally find staff employing what are called admission procedures, such as taking a life history, photographing, weighing, fingerprinting, assigning numbers, searching, listing personal possessions for storage, undressing, bathing, disinfecting, haircutting, issuing institutional clothing, instructing as to rules, and assigning to quarters. Admission procedures might better be called "trimming" or "programming" because in thus being squared away the new arrival allows himself to be shaped and coded into an object that can be fed into the administrative machinery of the establishment, to be worked on smoothly by routine operations....

Because a total institution deals with so many aspects of its inmates' lives, with the consequent complex squaring away at admission, there is a special need to obtain initial co-operativeness from the recruit. Staff often feel that a recruit's readiness to be appropriately deferential in his initial face-to-face encounters with them is a sign that he will take the role of the routinely pliant inmate. The occasion on which staff members first tell the inmate of his deference obligations may be structured to challenge the inmate to balk or to hold his peace forever. Thus these initial moments of socialization may involve an "obedience test" and even a will-breaking contest; an inmate who shows defiance receives immediate visible punishment, which increases until he openly "cries uncle" and humbles himself.

An engaging illustration is provided by Brendan Behan in reviewing his contest with two warders upon his admission to Walton prison:

"And 'old up your 'ead, when I speak to you."

" 'Old up your 'ead, when Mr. Whitbread speaks to you," said Mr. Holmes.

I looked round at Charlie. His eyes met mine and he quickly lowered them to the ground.

"What are you looking round at, Behan? Look at me."

. . .

I looked at Mr. Whitbread. "I am looking at you," I said.

"You are looking at Mr. Whitbread—what?" said Mr. Holmes.

"I am looking at Mr. Whitbread."

Mr. Holmes looked gravely at Mr. Whitbread, drew back his open hand, and struck me on the face, held me with his other hand and struck me again.

My head spun and burned and pained and I wondered would it happen again. I forgot and felt another smack, and forgot, and another, and moved, and was held by a steadying, almost kindly hand, and another, and my sight was a vision of red and white and pity-coloured flashes.

"You are looking at Mr. Whitbread—what, Behan?"

I gulped and got together my voice and tried again till I got it out.   "I, sir, please, sir, I am looking at you, I mean, I am looking at Mr. Whitbread, sir."

Admission procedures and obedience tests may be elaborated into a form of initiation that has been called "the welcome," where staff or inmates, or both, go out of their way to give the recruit a clear notion of his plight.   As part of this rite of passage he may be called by a term such as "fish" or "swab," which tells him that he is merely an inmate, and, what is more, that he has a special low status even in this low group.

The admission procedure can be characterized as a leaving off and a taking on, with the midpoint marked by physical nakedness.   Leaving off of course entails a dispossession of property, important because persons invest self feelings in their possessions.   Perhaps the most significant of these possessions is not physical at all, one's full name; whatever one is thereafter called, loss of one's name can be a great curtailment of the self.

Another clear-cut expression of personal inefficacy in total institutions is found in inmates' use of speech.   One implication of using words to convey decisions about action is that the recipient of an order is seen as capable of receiving a message and acting under his own power to complete the suggestion or command.   Executing the act himself, he can sustain some vestige of the notion that he is self-determining.   Responding to the question in his own words, he can sustain the notion that he is somebody to be considered, however slightly.   And since it is only words that pass between himself and the others, he succeeds in retaining at least physical distance from them, however unpalatable the command or statement.

The inmate in a total institution can find himself denied even this kind of protective distance and self-action.   Especially in mental hospitals and political training prisons, the statements he makes may be discounted as mere symptoms, with staff giving attention to non-verbal aspects of his reply.   Often he is considered to be of insufficient ritual status to be given even minor greetings, let alone listened to.   Or the inmate may find that a kind of rhetorical use of language occurs: questions such as, "Have you washed yet?"   or, "Have you got both socks on?"   may be accompanied by simultaneous searching by the staff which physically discloses the facts, making these verbal questions superfluous.   And instead of being told to move in a particular direction at a particular rate, he may find himself pushed along by the guard, or pulled (in the case of ... mental patients), or frog-marched....

· · ·

VI

Although there are solidarizing tendencies such as fraternalization and clique formation, they are limited.   Constraints which place inmates in a position to sympathize and communicate with each other do not necessarily lead to high group morale and solidarity. In some concentration camps and prisoner-of-war installations the inmate cannot rely on his fellows, who may steal from him, assault him, and squeal on him, leading to what some students have referred to as anomie. In mental hospitals, dyads and triads may keep secrets from the authorities, but anything known to a whole ward of patients is likely to get to the ear of the attendant. (In prisons, of course, inmate organization has sometimes been strong enough to run strikes and short-lived insurrections; in prisoner-of-war camps, it has sometimes been possible to organize sections of the prisoners to operate escape channels; in concentration camps there have been periods of thoroughgoing underground organization; and on ships there have been mutinies; but these concerted actions seem to be the exception, not the rule.) But though there is usually little group loyalty in total institutions, the expectation that group loyalty should prevail forms part of the inmate culture and underlies the hostility accorded those who break inmate solidarity.... The same inmate will employ different personal lines of adaptation at different phases in his moral career and may even alternate among different tacks at the same time.

First, there is the tack of "situational withdrawal." The inmate withdraws apparent attention from everything except events immediately around his body and sees these in a perspective not employed by others present. This drastic curtailment of involvement in interactional events is best known, of course, in mental hospitals, under the title of "regression." ...

Secondly, there is the "intransigent line": the inmate intentionally challenges the institution by flagrantly refusing to co-operate with staff. The result is a constantly communicated intransigency and sometimes high individual morale. Many large mental hospitals, for example, have wards where this spirit prevails. Sustained rejection of a total institution often requires sustained orientation to its formal organization, and hence, paradoxically, a deep kind of involvement in the establishment. Similarly, when staff take the line that the intransigent inmate must be broken (as they sometimes do in the case of hospital psychiatrists prescribing electroshock or military tribunals prescribing the stockade), then the institution shows as much special devotion to the rebel as he has shown to it. Finally, although some prisoners of war have been known to take a staunchly intransigent stance throughout their incarceration, intransigence is typically a temporary and initial phase of reaction, with the inmate shifting to situational withdrawal or some other line of adaptation.

A third standard alignment in the institutional world is "colonization": the sampling of the outside world provided by the establishment is taken by the inmate as the whole, and a stable, relatively contented existence is built up out of the maximum satisfactions procurable within the institution. Experience of the outside world is used as a point of reference to demonstrate the desirability of life on the inside, and the usual tension between the two worlds is markedly reduced, thwarting the motivational scheme based upon this felt discrepancy which I described as peculiar to total institutions. Characteristically, the individual who too obviously takes this line may be accused by his fellow inmates of "having found a home" or of "never having had it so good." The staff itself may become vaguely embarrassed by this use that is being made of the institution, sensing that the benign possibilities in the situation are somehow being misused. Colonizers may feel obliged to deny their satisfaction with the institution, if only to sustain the counter-mores supporting inmate solidarity. They may find it necessary to mess up just prior to their slated discharge to provide themselves with an apparently involuntary basis for continued incarceration. Significantly, the staff who try to make life in total institutions more bearable must face the possibility that doing so may increase the attractiveness and likelihood of colonization.

A fourth mode of adaptation to the setting of a total institution is that of "conversion": the inmate appears to take over the official or staff view of himself and tries to act out the role of the perfect inmate. While the colonized inmate builds as much of a free community for himself as possible by using the limited facilities available, the convert takes a more disciplined, moralistic, monochromatic line, presenting himself as someone whose institutional enthusiasm is always at the disposal of the staff. In Chinese P.O.W. camps, we find Americans who became "Pros" and fully espoused the Communist view of the world. In army barracks there are enlisted men who give the impression that they are always "sucking around" and always "bucking for promotion." In prisons there are "square johns." In German concentration camps, a long-time prisoner sometimes came to adapt the vocabulary, recreation, posture, expressions of aggression, and clothing style of the Gestapo, executing the role of straw boss with military strictness....

The alignments that have been mentioned represent coherent courses to pursue, but few inmates seem to pursue any one of them very far. In most total institutions, most inmates take the tack of what some of them call "playing it cool." This involves a somewhat opportunistic combination of secondary adjustments, conversion, colonization, and loyalty to the inmate group, so that the inmate will have a maximum chance, in the particular circumstances, of eventually getting out physically and psychologically undamaged. Typically, the inmate when with fellow inmates will support the counter-mores and conceal from them how tractably he acts when alone with the staff.[124] Inmates who play it cool subordinate contacts with their fellows to the

124. This two-facedness is very commonly found in total institutions. In the state mental hospital studied by the writer, even the few elite patients selected for individual psychotherapy, and hence in the best position to espouse the psychiatric approach to self, tended to present their favorable view of psychotherapy only to the members of their intimate cliques. For a report on the way in which army prisoners concealed from fellow offenders their interest in "restoration" to the Army, see the comments by Richard Cloward in Session Four of New Perspectives for Research on Juvenile Delinquency, eds. Helen L. Witmer and Ruth Kotinsky, U.S. Dept. of Health, Education, and Welfare, Children's Bureau Publication No. 356 (1956), especially p. 90.

higher claim of "keeping out of trouble"; they tend to volunteer for nothing; and they may learn to cut their ties to the outside world just enough to give cultural reality to the world inside but not enough to lead to colonization.

.   .   .

An interesting institutional ceremony, often connected with the annual party and the Christmas celebration, is the institutional theatrical. Typically the players are inmates and the directors of the production are staff, but sometimes "mixed" casts are found. The writers are usually members of the institution, whether staff or inmate, and hence the production can be full of local references, imparting through the private use of this public form a special sense of the reality of events internal to the institution. Very frequently the offering will consist of satirical skits that lampoon well-known members of the institution, especially high-placed staff members. If, as is frequent, the inmate community is one-sexed, then some of the players are likely to perform in the costume and burlesqued role of members of the other sex. Limits of license are often tested, the humor being a little more broad than some members of the staff would like to see tolerated....

———

Questions

How do law schools use admission procedures and obedience tests to initiate recruits? Why are these techniques necessary? What lines of adaptation have you used in your career as a law student? Why? Have you perceived among your fellow students variations on the lines of adaptation described by Goffman? What values does the structure of law school inculcate? Are these necessary for "good" lawyering? What changes in law school would you suggest?

What are the admission procedures and obedience tests used by law firms and other institutions in which lawyers work? Are there similar lines of adaptation present? In what ways are clients like inmates in the lawyer's office? Since neither the model of inmate or staff works well to describe the client in a law firm, how would you go about describing the client's relationship to the institution?

How are lawyers like inmates in the courts? How are they like staff? What role do the litigants play in the court system? The jurors?

C. PROFESSIONAL RHETORIC

Professional Detachment and Superiority

A number of readings in this book, from deTocqueville in the early 19th century, p. 1091, to Wasserstrom in contemporary times, p. 474, have emphasized qualities that give lawyers a shared identity and make them special: the hard years of mastering a difficult subject matter; the collegial relationship with other lawyers in law office and courtroom; the acquisition of skill and language not possessed by ordinary citizens; the perquisites of the professional license; the relatively high income and social status that flow from professional accomplishments and privileges; the shared stories of the lawyer as zealous champion and courageous vindicator of rights; etc. Do the professed ideals of the legal profession concerning its own role reflect these characteristics of the profession?

Rhetorical expressions of professional ideals are constantly reshaped by contemporary social conditions and moral values. David Hoffman's lectures to those about to enter the profession, first presented in 1836, are a classic of the times. Note both the similarity of some of his propositions to modern-day ethical formulations, and also the loftily high-minded position he professed. It is difficult to imagine that he actually acted out the role he describes, but it is easy to imagine that he *believed* he did. At any rate, the same tone persisted in the Canons of Professional Ethics adopted by the American Bar Association in 1908, which remained the ABA's official position until 1969. Thus, compare Hoffman's *Resolution III,* regarding the lawyer's proper attitude toward the courts, with Canon 1 of the 1908 Canon:

> It is the duty of the lawyer to maintain towards the Courts a respectful attitude, not for the sake of the temporary incumbent of the judicial office, but for the maintenance of its supreme importance....

So also, compare Hoffman's *Resolution XIV* with the recitals in Canon 15 of the 1908 Canons:

> Nothing operates more certainly to create or to foster popular opinion against lawyers as a class, and to deprive the profession of that full measure of public esteem and confidence which belongs to the proper discharge of its duties than does the false claim, often set up by the unscrupulous in defense of questionable transactions, that it is the duty of the lawyer to do whatever may enable him to succeed in winning his client's cause.

DAVID HOFFMAN
A COURSE OF LEGAL STUDY (1836)

Resolutions in Regard to Professional Deportment

. . .

III. To all judges, when in court, I will ever be respectful: they are the Law's viceregents; and whatever may be their character and deportment, the individual should be lost in the majesty of the office.

V. In all intercourse with my professional brethren, I will be always courteous. No man's passions shall intimidate me from asserting fully my own, or my client's rights; and no man's ignorance or folly shall induce me to take any advantage of him; I shall deal with them all as honourable men, ministering at our common altar.

. . .

X. Should my client be disposed to insist on captious requisitions, or frivolous and vexatious defences, they shall be neither enforced nor countenanced by me. And if still adhered to by him from a hope of pressing the other party into an unjust compromise, or with any other motive, he shall have the option to select other counsel.

XI. If, after duly examining a case, I am persuaded that my client's claim or defence (as the case may be,) cannot, or rather ought not, to be sustained, I will promptly advise him to abandon it. To press it further in such a case, with the hope of gleaning some advantage by an extorted compromise, would be lending myself to a dishonourable use of legal means, in order to gain a *portion* of that, the *whole* of which I have reason to believe would be denied to him both by law and justice.

XII. I will never plead the Statute of Limitations, when based on the *mere efflux of time;* for if my client is conscious he owes the debt; and has no other defence than the *legal bar,* he shall never make me a partner in his knavery.

. . .

XIV. My client's conscience, and my own, are distinct entities; and though my vocation may sometimes justify my maintaining as facts, or principles, in doubtful cases, what may be neither one nor the other, I shall ever claim the privilege of solely judging to what extent to go. In *civil* cases, if I am satisfied from the evidence that the *fact* is against my client, he must excuse me if I do not see as he does, and do not press it; and should the *principle* also be wholly at variance with sound law, it would be dishonourable folly in me to endeavor to incorporate it into the jurisprudence of the country, when, if successful, it would be a gangrene that might bring death to my cause of the succeeding day.

XV. When employed to defend those charged with crimes of the deepest dye, and the evidence against them, whether legal, or moral, be such as to leave no just doubt of their guilt, I shall not hold myself privileged, much less obliged, to use my endeavors to arrest, or to impede the course of justice ... & c. Persons of atrocious character, who have violated the laws of God and man, are entitled to no such special exertions from any member of our pure and honourable profession; and indeed, to no intervention beyond securing to them a fair and dispassionate investigation of the *facts* of their cause, and the due application of the law; all that goes beyond this, either in manner or substance, is unprofessional, and proceeds, either from a mistaken view of the relation of client and counsel, or from some unworthy and selfish motive, which sets a higher value on professional display and success, than on truth and justice, and the substantial interests of the community.

The second excerpt is an address by Justice, later Chief Justice, Harlan Fisk Stone. The address created a stir when made because it was a lamentation on the fallen state of the bar from one who stood at the pinnacle of the legal establishment. Observe how Stone derives a unique position for the legal profession from the Constitution, and, on this basis, attributes to lawyers a special competence and responsibility in matters of public policy. Was this claim subsequently vindicated by the Warren Court's activism in constitutional interpretation? Did that activism have roots arising from sectors of the legal profession that had little connection to the sector of the bar that Stone was talking about? Is there some kind of relationship between the idea of protecting corporate property through legal devices and protecting equality of citizenship through legal devices? Is the concept of such a relationship one that would readily occur to lawyers as a body, but be unlikely to occur either to businessmen or to oppressed minorities or the average citizen? Could some such idea be the basis of the ideology of the legal profession? Or is it a self-delusion—the profession's lie?

HARLAN FISKE STONE
"THE PUBLIC INFLUENCE OF THE BAR"
48 Harv.L.Rev. 1 (1934).[12]

. . .

We meet at a time when, as never before in the history of the country, our most cherished ideals and traditions are being subjected to searching criticism. The towering edifice of business and industry, which had become the dominating feature of the American social structure, has been shaken to its foundations by forces, the full significance of which we still can see but dimly....

[If] tradition and history are guides ... we may rightly look to the Bar for leadership in the preservation and development of American institutions. Specially trained in the field of law and government, invested with the unique privileges of his office, experienced in the world of affairs, and versed in the problems of business organization and administration, to whom, if not to the lawyer, may we look for guidance in solving the problems of a sorely stricken social order?

No tradition of our profession is more cherished by lawyers than that of its leadership in public affairs. We dwell upon the part of lawyers in the creation of the Federal Constitution and in the organiza-

---

12. Copyright © 1934 by the Harvard Law Review Association.

tion of the national government and of our federal and state judicial systems. The role they played in politics and government in the first half of the last century is a familiar part of our history.... In a very real sense they were guardians of the law, cherishing the legitimate influence of their guild as that of a profession charged with public duties and responsibilities.... Yet candor would compel even those of us who have the most abiding faith in our profession, and the firmest belief in its capacity for future usefulness, to admit that in our own time the Bar has not maintained its traditional position of public influence and leadership. Although it tends to prove the point, it is not of the first importance that there are fewer lawyers of standing serving in the halls of legislatures or in executive or administrative posts than in earlier days. Public office is not the only avenue to public influence. Representatives of other professions in public position have always been comparatively few, but wherever questions of professional concern to them touch the public interest, they are nevertheless profoundly influential. In matters of sanitation and public health, in great public undertakings involving engineering knowledge and skill, we place ourselves unreservedly in their hands.... [M]ost laymen, at least, would deny that there is today a comparable leadership on the part of lawyers, or a disposition of the public to place reliance upon their leadership where the problems of government touch the law.

... While it has not inherited the completely independent status of the English bar, to no other group in this country has the state granted comparable privileges or permitted so much autonomy. No other is so closely related to the state, and no other has traditionally exerted so powerful an influence on public opinion and on public policy. That influence in the past has been wielded chiefly in the courts, in the forum of local communities, in legislative halls, in the councils of government. In all its varying aspects, it has been most potent when public questions have been closely associated with legal questions in whose discussion the lawyer was peculiarly at home, and when, with a developed consciousness of its social responsibility, it was inevitable that the Bar should draw upon all its special knowledge and skill and resourcefulness for their solution.

In appraising the present-day relationship of the lawyer to his community, we cannot leave out of account either the altered character of public questions or the change in the function which the lawyers, as a class, are called upon to perform. It was in 1809 when Jefferson wrote: "We are a rural farming people; we have little business and few manufactures among us, and I pray God it will be a long time before we have much of either." Profound changes have come into American life since that sentence was penned....

· · ·

The changed character of the lawyer's work has made it difficult for him to contemplate his function in its new setting, to see himself and his occupation in proper perspective. No longer does his list of clients represent a cross section of society; no longer do his contacts make him the typical representative and interpreter of his community. The demands of practice are more continuous and exacting. He has less time for reflection upon other than immediate professional undertakings. He is more the man of action, less the philosopher and less the student of history, economics, and government.

The rise of big business has produced an inevitable specialization of the Bar. The successful lawyer of our day more often than not is the proprietor or general manager of a new type of factory, whose legal product is increasingly the result of mass production methods. More and more the amount of his income is the measure of professional success. More and more he must look for his rewards to the material satisfactions derived from profits as from a successfully conducted business, rather than to the intangible and indubitably more durable satisfactions which are to be found in a professional service more consciously directed toward the advancement of the public interest. Steadily the best skill and capacity of the profession has been drawn into the exacting and highly specialized service of business and finance. At its best the changed system has brought to the command of the business world loyalty and a superb proficiency and technical skill. At its worst it has made the learned profession of an earlier day the obsequious servant of business, and tainted it with the morals and manners of the market place in its most anti-social manifestations. In any case we must concede that it has given us a Bar whose leaders, like its rank and file, are on the whole less likely to be well rounded professional men than their predecessors, whose energy and talent for public service and for bringing the law into harmony with changed conditions have been largely absorbed in the advancement of the interests of clients.

. . .

... The loss and suffering inflicted on individuals, the harm done to a social order founded upon business and dependent upon its integrity, are incalculable. There is little to suggest that the Bar has yet recognized that it must bear some burden of responsibility for these evils....

We must remember, nevertheless, that the very conditions which have caused specialization, which have drawn so heavily upon the technical proficiency of the Bar, have likewise placed it in a position where the possibilities of its influence are almost beyond calculation. The intricacies of business organization are built upon a legal framework which the current growth of administrative law is still further elaborating. Without the constant advice and guidance of lawyers business would come to an abrupt halt. And whatever standards of conduct in the performance of its function the Bar consciously adopts must at once be reflected in the character of the world of business and finance. Given a measure of self-conscious and cohesive professional unity, the Bar may exert a power more beneficent and far reaching than it or any other non-governmental group has wielded in the past.

... Before it can function at all as the guardian of public interests committed to its care, there must be appraisal and comprehension of the new conditions and the changed relationships of the lawyer to his clients, to his professional brethren and to the public. That appraisal must pass beyond the petty details of form and manners which have been so largely the subject of our codes of ethics, to more fundamental consideration of the way in which our professional activities affect the welfare of society as a whole. . . .

. . .

[T]he Bar must assume the responsibility of consciously bringing its conduct to conform to new standards fitting the times in which we live. And unless history reverses itself the cooperation and support of leaders of the Bar will not be wanting. . . .

D. SATISFACTIONS AND DISSATISFACTIONS OF PRACTICE

How satisfied are lawyers today with their work? A 1984 study by Ronald Hirsch for the ABA Young Lawyers Division provides some contemporary data. Following the Hirsch article, and a 1990 update, is a table that relates overall satisfaction in practice to position in practice, years in practice and gender. Observe that law practice is not regarded by lawyers as being all wine and roses, but on the other hand that the level of satisfaction seems pretty high in this age of discontent. Observe also how intellectual challenge is salient in the sources of satisfaction. That ties back to deTocqueville's observation, quoted earlier, that "study and specialized knowledge of the law give a man a rank apart in society and makes of lawyers a somewhat privileged intellectual class."

RONALD L. HIRSCH
"ARE YOU ON TARGET?"

The Barrister Magazine, Vol. 12, No. 1, p. 17 (1985).[13]

. . .

In an effort to accurately study the state of the profession, the Young Lawyers Division, with the generous support of the ABA Board of Governors, undertook the first comprehensive survey of the legal profession: the National Survey of Career Satisfaction/Dissatisfaction.

A random probability sample of 3,018 lawyers of all ages was drawn from both ABA member and nonmember lists totalling 569,706

---

13. Copyright © 1985 by the American Bar Association.

lawyers. The sampled individuals were sent a lengthy survey covering many aspects of their work environment, job history, educational background, health and psychological profile and basic demographics....

. . .

... The good news is that the overall level of dissatisfaction is less than was expected, albeit still substantial: 16 percent of all lawyers (25 percent of junior associates and staff attorneys) are dissatisfied.

However, despite the high level of overall satisfaction, the survey confirms that there are serious problems in the workplace, even for those who are satisfied overall. Problems concerning training, feedback from superiors, time for one's nonwork life, among others, are widespread throughout the profession. Also, serious problems concerning control of work, office intrigue, and even financial reward exist in many firms and other job settings.

Another way of looking at problems within the profession is to look at the 25 percent of all lawyers planning to change jobs within the next two years. When we look at those in private practice who plan to change, the data is astonishing: Only 26 percent plan to look for a job in private practice and 31 percent plan to look at non-legal positions. Further, almost no one currently in a large firm wants to stay in one, and few lawyers want to move to one.

. . .

In looking at this data, we see that junior associates in most firms and lawyers in general in 2–3 man firms are far more dissatisfied than those in other positions and settings. And women are far more dissatisfied generally, regardless of position.

However, although being a junior associate and being a woman account for a small amount of the variation in satisfaction levels, it is the particular mix of positive and negative work environment factors that primarily accounts for satisfaction or dissatisfaction.

. . .

Intellectual Challenge Conquers All

Just what are these positive and negative factors? The most important positive factor is the existence of intellectual challenge in the job.

The results of this analysis are also supported by other data from the survey. In looking at the data on why people choose law as a career, as well as the factors important to their overall feeling about their jobs, intellectual challenge was by far the single most important factor—for both men and women. If one then looks at the job descriptor for intellectual challenge, we find that the overwhelming majority find the amount of challenge to be either great or somewhat so.

As a result, 60 percent are satisfied with the extent of challenge present in their jobs, 27 percent feel neutral, and only 14 percent are dissatisfied. Clearly, the overwhelmingly satisfactory presence of intellectual challenge in their jobs is enough to overcome the various negative aspects of their jobs. The result: an overall feeling of satisfaction in most cases.

After intellectual challenge, the next most important positive factor contributing to job satisfaction is the presence of a warm and personal work atmosphere. Other important factors are opportunity to advance, treatment by superiors as a professional colleague and control over one's work.

Two other positive factors, although not significant statistically, are both the substantive and activity mix—client contact, memo writing, court appearances—in a lawyer's job.

There is a popular belief that many lawyers, especially junior associates, are very dissatisfied with the mix of their work, that many are stuck in library stacks, and that others work on one big case for years. Although such cases obviously do exist, the survey found that such cases are relatively rare. The survey also found, not surprisingly, that those lawyers who have a good mix of activities were significantly more satisfied overall than either those lawyers who were acting as "drones," doing mostly research and memo writing and other nonclient-contact work, as well as those lawyers who had a very heavy concentration in activities such as trials, court appearances and depositions. In total, only 5 percent of all attorneys find the substantive mix of their work unattractive, and only 9 percent find the mix of activities to be unattractive.

Why Are Women More Dissatisfied?

Why, then, are so many more women lawyers dissatisfied? The answer is that women experience far more negative work environments in a number of critical areas. Significantly more women report that their job atmosphere is not warm and personal, that advancement is not determined by the quality of work, that they have no control over the cases they handle, that tension is high, and that they have virtually no time for themselves. Finally, the income of women lawyers is far below that of their male counterparts in most situations. Thus, even though their intellectual challenge is almost as high as reported by men, the other positive factors are not present to the same extent—and various negative factors are more pronounced.

Negative Factors: Politics and Personal Time

On the negative side, the most important factor for lawyers is the existence of political intrigue and backbiting, followed by an extreme lack of time for themselves. A high score on these factors results in an attorney being dissatisfied, regardless of position or setting.

One frequent complaint about the practice of law is that it is all-consuming to the exclusion of one's personal life. A severe problem is identified by the survey in the area of vacation time. Although most lawyers have relatively generous vacation allowances, the comparison between time allowed and time taken shows that far less time is taken.

Thus, we find that 40 percent of all lawyers are dissatisfied with the amount of vacation they are able to take. This should not be surprising. Given the number of hours that lawyers regularly work, 1 or 2 weeks vacation a year is not enough to recover and replenish one's physical and mental reservoirs.

The survey shows that many lawyers work long hours: 11 percent work in excess of 240 hours a month, while 44 percent of all lawyers work in excess of 200 hours a month. Twenty percent felt that their hours were unattractive, while 34 percent felt neutral. "Hours worked" includes all activities that were considered by the respondent or his employer to be part of the job, regardless of whether defined as "billable" or not.

One surprising fact is the comparison of the hours worked by junior associates with those of senior associates and partners. Conventional wisdom is that junior associates work longer hours than others. However, ... junior associates in fact work slightly less hours, with senior associates shouldering the heaviest burden. It is also interesting to note that solo practitioners work less than lawyers in firms, which is probably a function of the amount of work they have.

. . .

Training and Feedback: Too Infrequent

The survey also supports the often-heard statement that supervision within firms is very poor. Forty-seven percent of junior associates reported negatively on the extent of supervision—whether defined as feedback on work, or provision of instruction and training. Only 14–17 percent of junior associates report receiving frequent training and feedback from superiors. However, although many attorneys complain about this problem, ... only 21 percent report dissatisfaction with this individual factor and it is rather unimportant in its effect on overall satisfaction.

Is Money the Name of the Game?

Lawyers have a reputation in American folklore for being an avaricious group who will do anything for money. However, the survey shows that the majority of lawyers earn far less than many would expect. Further, in spite of the fact that 41 percent are dissatisfied with their earnings, most of these attorneys are still satisfied overall with their jobs. Money, then, is not the name of the game. The amount of financial reward, although a factor of some importance in its effect on overall satisfaction, did not account for a large degree of variation in satisfaction.

Thus, 45 percent of all lawyers report job incomes under $45,000. . . .

Although the general public might not find these salaries bad, the expectations of most people who go to law school and work very hard in their practices are not being met.

. . .

Dissatisfaction Affects Law Firm Profits

Many lawyers feel that law firms could care less if their attorneys are dissatisfied or not; as long as the work gets out, that's all that matters. However, the findings of the survey show clearly that it is in a firm's enlightened self-interest to do what it can to increase lawyer satisfaction, the reason being that dissatisfaction increases lawyer turnover and decreases lawyer productivity.

Twenty-five percent of all attorneys plan to change jobs within the next two years; as a lawyer's satisfaction decreases or dissatisfaction increases, the likelihood of his changing jobs increases dramatically. However, . . . it is not only malcontents that change jobs. Even those who score neutral on the satisfaction scale have an uncomfortably large propensity to change jobs. This is again the result of the complex interaction of work environment factors, with many attorneys having considerable dissatisfaction with various aspects of the workplace— even though they overall feel satisfied or neutral.

. . .

Of those in private practice, 11 percent of partners, 26 percent of senior associates and 35 percent of junior associates plan to change within the next two years. The economic impact of the loss of a partner or a senior associate cannot help but be substantial. However, there is also economic impact in the loss of associates after they get to the point where they can truly start to "earn their keep," especially when, as in most reported cases, they leave their firms because they are dissatisfied with the firm rather than that the firm is dissatisfied with them. All the time, effort and money that firms have invested in individuals is lost.

RONALD L. HIRSCH
THE STATE OF THE LEGAL PROFESSION
P. 81 (1990).

In the past six years [between the initial survey in 1984 and its replication in 1990], the extent of lawyer dissatisfaction has increased throughout the profession. It is now reported in significant numbers by lawyers in all positions—partners as well as junior associates. It is now present in significant numbers in firms of all sizes, not just the largest and the smallest firms. This increased dissatisfaction is directly caused by a deterioration of the lawyer workplace, by the increasing number of lawyers who have experienced negative work environments. In particular, the amount of time lawyers have for themselves and their families has become an issue of major concern for many lawyers.

Further, the survey documents that while the exposure of men to negative environments has increased, it has gotten even worse for women. In 1984, far more women experienced a negative environment than men, and that is still true in 1990; they have both gotten worse. Across the board, women are worse off than men and the survey documents that this difference in experience is due to men having better opportunities than women—which is to say that it is due to general bias. Further, the survey documents that sexual harassment on the job is something that most women have to deal with in one way or another and that the younger generation of male lawyers is in general no better than older lawyers on this issue.

. . .

The problems that have been identified are not new. They are the same that were identified in the 1984 survey. Only the extent of the problems has grown. . . .

ANALYSIS OF 1984 HIRSCH DATA BY ROBERT L. NELSON

Project Director, American Bar Foundation

Mean Satisfaction Level by Law Position,
Years in Practice, and Sex

(1 to 5 scale: 1 = very sat.; 5 = very dissat.)

Years in Practice

Law Position	1–4 yrs Male	Female	5–9 yrs Male	Female	10 + yrs Male	Female	Total Male	Female	(n)
Solos, 2–3	2.04	2.43	2.18	2.23	2.18	3.00	2.14	2.41	(368)
4–30 lawyers	1.95	2.46	1.93	2.62	1.69	2.33	1.89	2.48	(447)
31 + lawyers	2.32	2.74	2.21	2.64	1.67	2.00	2.10	2.68	(244)
Government	2.34	2.75	2.05	2.29	1.88	1.67	2.08	2.54	(196)
Corp./Other	2.00	1.78	2.23	2.06	1.73	3.00	1.97	1.95	(171)
(n)	(383)	(153)	(361)	(78)	(436)	(15)	(1180)	(246)	(1426)

significant effects: law position, years in practice, sex, interaction of law position and years in practice

Range: Males 10 years or more in practice,
            large firm: 1.67
            to
            Females 10 years or more in practice,
            solo practice or corp./other: 3.00

E. SOME FUNDAMENTAL QUESTIONS [14]

Whose Morality? (Finding a Moral Compass)

This ancient question has lots of answers but no single answer. The content of the answer varies greatly depending upon whether the inquirer is thinking in philosophic, religious or anthropologic terms. The major strands in Western philosophy are familiar to most law students. One prominent stream of thought, undergoing a renaissance in recent years, stems from Aristotle and his concept of human flourishing. The basic idea is that reflection and discourse about the conditions and circumstances that lead to human flourishing will lead to a broad range of agreement concerning such matters as virtue and vice, good character, presumptive moral principles and practical judgment.[15] A second prominent strand, stemming from Kant, attempts to build an elaborate superstructure of rights, duties and moral rules from simple foundations, such as Kant's principle that human beings are not to be used solely as means. A third strand, originating in Hobbes and Locke, is often lumped together under the rubric "social contract theory." Johns Rawls' egalitarian principle of justice as fairness, derived from the point of view of a detached observer standing behind the "veil of ignorance," is an influential modern version of social contract thought.[16] A fourth major school of moral philosophers emphasizes the consequences of action or inaction—"the greatest good for the greatest number." A prominent modern version of utilitarian consequentialism, stemming from Bentham and Adam Smith, is committed to an economic approach to issues of law and justice.[17]

At a high level of abstraction any of these philosophic traditions can be consistent and satisfying, but each is elusive and frustrating to a person with a particular history, background and role who confronts a messy situation in which two or more moral principles appear relevant.

14. These preliminary and tentative thoughts are the joint product of the authors. Some portions draw on papers prepared by one of us, Geoffrey C. Hazard, Jr.: My Station as Lawyer, 6 Ga.St.U.L.Rev. 1 (1989); Doing the Right Thing, 70 Wash.U.L.Q. 691 (1992); Personal Values and Professional Ethics, 40 Cleve.St.L.Rev. 133 (1992); and Dimensions of Ethical Responsibility: Relevant Others (unpublished lecture, University of Pittsburgh, Feb. 1993).

15. See Alasdair MacIntyre, After Virtue (1982), and MacIntyre, Whose Justice? Which Rationality? (1988); Martha Nussbaum, The Fragility of Goodness: Luck and Ethics in Greek Tragedy and Philosophy (1986); John Finnis, Natural Law and Natural Rights (1980).

16. John Rawls, A Theory of Justice (1971). See also Ronald Dworkin, Taking Rights Seriously (1978) (a theory of rights applied to judicial decision-making), and Dworkin, Law's Empire (1986) (the objective of law is not to report consensus or provide efficient means to social goals, but to answer the requirement that a political community act in a coherent and principled manner toward its members); David Gauthier, Morals by Agreement (1986) (deriving an ethical system from a principle of rational cooperation that should be accepted by self-interested individuals).

17. See Richard A. Posner, Problems in Jurisprudence (1992) and The Economics of Justice (1981). See also Robert H. Frank, Passions Within Reasons (1988) (the role of moral sentiments in rational choice). Other modern consequentualists, following John Stuart Mill, do not emphasize economic consequences.

Philosophy then becomes both too abstract and too conflicted—a Babel of contradictory approaches and assertions all couched in esoteric jargon.[18] Most of us at that point retreat for guidance to the commitments we have made and the community from which we draw our image of ourselves.

Robert Fulghum expresses this approach in a popular, secular form: [19]

> Most of what I really need to know about how to live and what to do and how to be I learned in kindergarten. Wisdom was not at the top of the graduate school mountain, but there in the sandpile at Sunday school. These are the things I learned:
>
> Share everything.
>
> Play fair.
>
> Don't hit people.
>
> Put things back where you found them.
>
> Clean up your own mess.
>
> Don't take things that aren't yours.
>
> Say you're sorry when you hurt somebody.
>
> Wash your hands before you eat.
>
> Flush.
>
> Warm cookies and cold milk are good for you.
>
> Live a balanced life—learn some and think some and draw and paint and sing and dance and play and work every day some.
>
> Take a nap every afternoon.
>
> When you go out into the world, watch out for traffic, hold hands and stick together....

For most Americans, this sort of popular morality derives from the religious and cultural values explicitly or implicitly conveyed in home, church, school, college and, for budding lawyers, law school. Religion is the neglected stepchild of the academic world even though for most Americans it is one of the most powerful influences on moral development. Moreover, social scientists tell us that most Americans are believers and take their religion seriously enough to participate on a regular basis.[20] For many of us a religious tradition, fostered in the home and in church or synagogue, provides a moral compass that is directional to a greater or lesser degree.

18. See Alasdair MacIntyre, After Virtue (1982) (the Enlightenment project of providing a shared, rationally justifiable, secular basis for morality has failed).

19. Robert Fulghum, All I Really Need to Know I learned in Kindergarten: Uncommon Thoughts on Common Things 4–5 (1988).

20. See Andrew M. Greeley, Religious Change in America (1989); Phillip L. Berman, The Search for Meaning (1990); Christopher Lasch, The True and Only Heaven: Progress and Its Critics (1991).

Although it is trendy in moral philosophy to talk about dialectic rationality—mature, responsible, intelligent adults sitting around a table calmly and endlessly discussing the aims of life—in practice agreement on many specific matters of morality seems impossible to achieve (e.g., abortion, assisted suicide).[21]   And the concept of dialogic exercise signifies a detached rationality that lacks the warmth, fervor and commitment that can be supplied either by religious experience and belief or by absorption in a secular cause that builds strong ties among its adherents.   People who do important things usually are fired by the kind of enthusiasm that flows from being committed to narratives of human aspiration, suffering and redemption that have implications in terms of moral behavior.

Man is a rational animal, but the image of man as only a rational decision-maker does not describe most people's experience.   Human beings are seldom as rational and free as most modern philosophical ethics assume, an important point discussed below.   Stanley Hauerwas, drawing on the work of Iris Murdoch, argues that how we view the world is more fundamental than deciding particular moral questions.[22] Moral virtue, according to Hauerwas and Murdoch, is not so much the result of making ethically correct decisions as it is a matter of orienting ourselves according to what is good, beautiful and true.   We create our world as well as live in it.   It is thus a world in which "reality" is elusive and our imagination of reality is central.   Murdoch refers to "unselfings," moments in which through an act of will the self is denied—forgotten, if you will—in order to allow us to discover an essential component of reality, the reality of the other.   Freedom is living in accordance with reality, but that means we must take responsibility for imagining the reality of others, which requires the humility to "unself."   The truly moral life is located in these moments of "unselfing."

Social scientists tell us that Americans find it difficult to express ideas concerning moral values.[23]   Religious terms such as sin, grace and repentance have been banned from the secular public forum, crippling our moral language.   By default, this leads to heavy reliance on the language and symbols of either managers or therapists, such as in the profusion of "self-help" books that crowd the bookstores (e.g., "How to win friends and influence people" and "I'm OK, you're OK").

21. The existence of moral disagreement is sometimes taken, erroneously, as establishing the truth of relativism or subjectivism. But the fact that rational people can disagree on some matters does not prove that the world is governed solely by subjectivism, force or irrationality. See Isaiah Berlin, The Crooked Timber of Humanity (1991). Human beings, located within history, exchange reasons and arguments about things that are good and bad, sound or unsound. This effort to persuade (a search for truth) is not equivalent to manipulation and unreason. See Martha Nussbaum, Human Functioning and Social Justice, 20 Political Theory 202 (May 1992).

22. Stanley Hauerwas, Vision and Virtue (1974), drawing on Iris Murdoch, The Sovereignty of Good (1970).

23. See Robert N. Bellah et al., Habits of the Heart: Individualism and Commitment in American Life (1985).

Anthropologists tell us that most human beings get a sense of self, community and hope from membership in a community. Carol Greenhouse's study of how Baptists in a Georgia community think and act in dealing with disputes concludes that "people tend to explain their morals by claiming membership in a community—a family, an ethnic group, a region of the country, or in the case of her Baptists, a congregation." [24] As Thomas L. Shaffer puts it, "We account for our morals, unintentionally, by naming what we belong to." [25] Shaffer argues that most people at the moment of moral choice do not engage in the sort of "ethical dilemma" thinking that pervades teaching of moral and legal ethics—discussion of a moral quandary based on highly abstracted and limited facts.[26] Instead, people remember or discover who they are, a psychological homecoming, and then, having remembered or discovered that they belong to a community or are living out a story, act as if they were members of that community or engaged in that story. Moral action is founded not on "principles" or on "choice" as much as it is on the commitments of participation in community. As deTocqueville said, America is "a society built not on obedience [to principles] but on participation." [27]

Moral life is simpler if one is brought up in a single community in which one moral language expresses a relatively coherent set of ideals, commitments, roles and expectations. Today we must cope with multiple moral traditions: with a Western tradition that is highly eclectic, diverse and pluralistic, and also with a multicultural world in which the cacophony of religions and philosophies is compounded by voices expressing the old divisions of class, race, ethnicity and sex and newer ones of sexual preference and "life style."

Is Role Relevant?

A basic criticism of legal ethics by some moral philosophers is the argument that the nature of law practice itself, when conducted in faithful adherence to official standards, is inherently amoral or immoral. That is, a good person, observing the ordinary morality of people generally, cannot also be a good lawyer who observes professional requirements. When an abstract vision of ordinary morality is compared with the stereotypical description of legal ethics, lawyers look bad. Lawyers appear to be partisan rather than disinterested, as ordinary morality would prescribe, guileful rather than open, grasping rather than generous and duplicitous rather than truthful. Things that lawyers do as a matter of course, such as asserting the statute of limitations to bar a "just" claim or assisting an immoral cause, become morally questionable.

---

24. Thomas L. Shaffer and Mary M. Shaffer, American Lawyers and Their Communities: Ethics in the Legal Profession 25 (1991), discussing Carol J. Greenhouse, Praying for Justice: Faith, Order, and Community in an American Town (1986).

25. Id.

26. Robert M. Cover makes a similar point. See Cover, Nomos and Narrative, 97 Harv.L.Rev. 4.10 (1983) (normative behavior is communal in character).

27. Quoted in Shaffer and Shaffer, supra, at 26.

One response to this criticism is that the moral philosophers have built their edifice on a shaky foundation: The law and ethics of lawyering is much less single-minded than the straw figure that the moral philosophers have sought to destroy. First, ethics rules provide lawyers with a great deal of moral choice in selection of clients, control of procedure and tactics, opportunities for moral suasion of clients, withdrawal from representation of a client who will not take a lawyer's advice and, in the versions adopted by most states, disclosure of a client's confidences to prevent serious harm to courts and third persons. But this argument does not respond to the basic point that the lawyer's traditional role permits and generally commits lawyers to a partisan presentation on behalf of clients that puts client interests first.

A more fundamental response to the philosophers' critique of the lawyer's partisan role rests on a skepticism about whether the abstract universalism of the moral philosophers fairly reflects the contextuality and complexity of moral action. The universalism generated by Kantian and Benthamite premises—that all human beings are of equal value—may lead to silly conclusions such as that a mother's preference for her own child, as against the claims of a distant child in Somalia, is morally unworthy. Ordinary morality, however, involves conceptions of doing the right thing in the family, the neighborhood, the workplace and as a citizen in a range of communities (local, state, national and international). Moral actors are also located in time, space and circumstance. Any meta-ethics that ignores these brute facts is simplistic, unrealistic and predicated upon misconceptions about moral action.

The idealized ordinary person of some moral philosophers has no personal history and thus acts in problematic situations without constraining commitments to others. She confronts stipulated facts that are perfectly comprehensible at the point of fateful decision. Her ethical repertoire is clearly apparent to her, and she is readily able to determine the relative priority of her values in whatever circumstances may be presented. Her ethical choices are never subject to being second-guessed. This idealized ordinary person does not exist in this world.

In the real world actors have personal histories which determine their position in life at any moment of ethical choice. Having a position in life limits one's options in taking action and therefore limits one's ethical options. People in the real world operate in a web of commitments to others. Having commitments to others—children, family members, fellow believers, friends, co-workers, co-adherents to a cause, etc.—makes one a partisan, whether willingly or unwillingly. Information relevant to a decision arrives disjointed and is often contradictory. Having fragmentary information means that ethical choices are often based on factual assumptions that turn out to be wrong. Among other consequences, this uncertainty often requires decisions modulated by concern that one should, as Oliver Cromwell said, "think it possible that you may be mistaken." So far as competing values are concerned, most people discover that their repertoire of values is not fully apparent to them until the moment of decision, and even then remains disorganized and often internally discordant. Perhaps most important, in the real world people have to answer to others for the consequences of what they have done. Accusation and recrimination are agonizing possibilities that must be considered at the time of action.

Circumstances such as these have the result that, as a practical matter, values that we affirm as fundamental in the abstract often turn out to be incompatible in concrete application. Isaiah Berlin tellingly expounds the incommensurability of values:

> [S]cientifically minded rationalists declared that conflict and trage-
> dy arose only from ignorance of fact [and] inadequacies of method
> ... so that, in principle, at least, ... a harmonious, rationally
> organized society [can be] established.... But if it is the case that
> not all ultimate human ends are necessarily compatible, there may
> be no escape from choices governed by no overriding principle,
> some of them painful, both to the agent and to others.[28]

Thus the real world of ordinary people, as Berlin argues, may offer "no escape from choices governed by no overriding principle." [29] Lawyers' ethics should be compared with those of real world people rather than idealized cardboard figures.

Some of the classic "hard cases" of legal ethics—defending a person that the lawyer knows is guilty, pleading the statute of limitations against a person who has a good claim and interjecting the lawyer's own moral and prudential values into advice given the client [30]—have analogs in ordinary life: The parent who is confronted with a police officer who believes the parent's child has stolen merchandise from a store; the situation in which one person says to another, concerning an old grievance, "Can't we just forget about it?"; and the many situations where business or family advice is offered, often unsolicited, to colleagues, friends and family members. In all these situations, for good reasons, ordinary people have difficulty doing what some moral universals say is the right thing.

Doing the right thing in law practice is no easier. Defending the guilty, pleading the statutes of limitations and giving hard advice are often the right things to do, even if they involve a conflict in values. Trying to do the right thing, when it is impossible to do so without

---

28. Isaiah Berlin, The Crooked Timber of Humanity 234–35 (1991).

29. The contextuality and complexity of moral decision-making makes it difficult to state or agree upon a set of rationally ordered principles. But the existence of rational disagreement should not be viewed as establishing the dominance or inevitability of unreason. Power alone does not govern the affairs of human beings; persuasion by rational argument remains central.

30. The governing rule of legal ethics is clear in all three cases. A lawyer retained or appointed to defend a guilty person has an ethical obligation to provide effective assistance in defending the case; if a client wishes to assert the defense of statute of limitations, the lawyer has an ethical duty to interpose the statute; and, with regard to interjection of personal moral and prudential values, professional rules give the lawyer the authority and at times the duty to be assertive.

conflict of values, is one of society's necessary but messy jobs. However, no one is compelled to become a lawyer or, generally, to represent a particular client. If doing so is repugnant in a particular case, one should withdraw; if doing so is repugnant as a more general matter, one should leave the profession. But can the ethical problems arising from circumstance, background and commitment be escaped in any station in life other than as an inmate in an insane asylum?

Does the Legal Profession Provide Sure Moral Guidance?

The professional rhetoric of lawyers and bar associations carries the implication that a lawyer can find sure guidance in facing problems encountered in law practice in the traditions and ethics of the legal profession. At the individual level, the moral example of professional mentors—teachers, practitioners and judges—is an energizing source of guidance and aspiration. At the collective level the resonance of images and stories, such as those suggested by the Holmes and Choate quotations at the beginning of this chapter, helps form a lawyer's professional persona. But the guidance from rules of formal ethics is less sure and more troubling.

First, an unthinking obedience to professional rules that state a clear duty involves a moral simplification that may lead to wrongdoing. Consider, for example, the blanket obligation to report of Model Rule 8.3 or the limited disclosure options of Model Rule 1.6. Would a truly moral lawyer conform woodenly to those prescriptions? Reliance on a handbook of rules is tempting but results in a simplified moral framework that fails to include some moral aspects of a particular situation.[31] A good lawyer who is also a good person may be faced with some situations in which civil disobedience of the profession's edicts may be the truly moral choice.

Second, the profession's rules fail to give guidance in many problematic situations. Sometimes the rules are self-contradictory, with one rule pointing in one direction and another in a different direction. Sometimes the ethics rules are contradicted by other law, especially agency law, criminal law, procedural law or regulatory law, containing provisions that permit or require a lawyer to take action that the profession's rules appear to prohibit or vice versa.[32] More frequently, the ethics rules fail to tell a lawyer what to do but leave it to the individual lawyer's discretion. Whether to accept a client, whether to conform to a client's direction on a matter of procedure or tactics, whether to try to persuade the client to take a particular course of action, whether to withdraw when the client rejects advice or wants assistance that the lawyer finds repugnant and whether to disclose a client's future crime or fraud—the ethics rules leave these decisions to lawyer discretion. Such guidance as exists in these situations comes

---

31. See John Ladd, The Quest for a Code of Professional Ethics: An Intellectual and Moral Confusion, reprinted in Geoffrey C. Hazard, Jr. and Deborah L. Rhode (eds.), The Legal Profession: Responsibility and Regulation 105 (2d ed. 1988).

32. See the discussion of client fraud at p. 294 above.

from the ideology and practice of professional subcultures of which the lawyer is part: the criminal defense bar, legal services lawyers, plaintiff's personal injury lawyers, outside or inside counsel to large corporations, etc. But even within a legal subculture, ideology and practice are highly variable and often rest on unexamined assumptions.

Third, the profession's messages may be influenced by the self-interest of the profession itself. In the 19th century the moral framework of American lawyers was heavily influenced by the "lawyer as gentleman" in a largely white, Protestant, capitalist culture.[33] In the 20th century efforts to make the profession more open, more accountable to consumers and to the public and more competitive were generally resisted by the organized bar.[34] Every group that has a strong collective identity tends to view the world from a special vantage point. The tendency of individuals and groups to believe that what is in their own interest is also in the general interest is a constant danger. Thus a skeptical evaluation of the profession's rules, rather than an uncritical obedience, is called for.

Finally, the profession's preference for clients is itself limited by the responsibilities of lawyers to courts, other legal institutions and third persons. Whose interests must be considered?

Who Are the Relevant Others?

Each of us exists in a world in which individual uniqueness is shaped by social and cultural forces. The structure of our world is determined by such objective or external factors as our sex, age, race, religion, nationality, circumstances of birth and upbringing, education and family status at any given time. It is also determined by our occupation in life. Thus, it is one thing to be male, another to be female; to be a child, a young aspiring professional, or a retired person; to be a Caucasian in the Orient or an Asian in the United States; to have had supportive nurturing as a child or to have suffered privation or abuse; and to be married with responsibilities for children or not. Similarly, it is one thing to be a lawyer and another to be a teacher, a business manager or a blue-collar worker. These and other aspects of circumstance may have moral significance in a specific situation.

The world of the self is determined by internal factors as well. In aggregate these constitute a person's subjective viewpoint—the world as it appears from inside one's station in life. People having substantially the same background and education, and engaged in essentially the same vocation, respond very differently to different kinds of ethical problems, as anyone knows who has participated with other committee members in deliberating upon such a problem. These differences in "personality" can be crudely correlated with various personal background factors. For example, some feminists and many commentators

33. See Thomas L. Shaffer and Mary M. Shaffer, supra, cc. 2–4 (discussing and critiquing the American tradition of the "lawyer as gentleman").

34. See Richard Abel, American Lawyers (describing and critiquing the professional project to increase the status, authority and income of lawyers).

assert that many men respond to ethically charged situations in ways different from most women.[35]   People who are verbally articulate usually respond in different terms than people who express themselves dramatically or in body language.[36]   Different nurture also seems to reveal different nature, as attested by Sigmund Freud and embodied in the lay desire to try to explain "where someone is coming from" in order to predict and interpret his or her response to ethically problematic situations.

A person, however, is not simply a summation of his or her life experience.   Stated one way or another, this is the problem of free will—the realization that, whoever and whatever one of us may be, an element of subjective freedom is involved in every ethically significant decision.[37]   The response to an ethically problematic encounter on the part of one specific person thus is a product of the unique mind and spirit which that person brings to that unique encounter.

These aspects of one's station in life—objective circumstance, personal history and unique occasion for action—apply both to lawyers and to nonlawyers.[38]   Every lawyer has such a station in every moment of practice.   Being a lawyer entails having clients and having clients in turn entails special ethical responsibilities.   In addition to professional identity as a lawyer, every lawyer practices in a context that has its own legal subculture.   Within each legal subculture, substantial variation is found: Although corporate lawyers tend to have some characteristic attitudes different from those of criminal lawyers, lawyers in each subgroup are not all cut to the same pattern.   Everyone who practices law gives the vocation a personal definition.

To recognize station in life and personal subjective viewpoint, and their relevance to ethical choice, is not to reject the notion that there are general ethical principles that speak to situations in life.   We believe that foundational ethical principles, or at least a universal ethical perspective, can be identified.[39]   A society cannot exist at all, let alone flourish, without some generally accepted rules against harming other people, stealing, lying, breaking of promises and the like.   Language itself is dependent upon some degree of truth-telling.   Moreover, if ethical perspectives were not shared, we could not make ethical comparisons, whether in terms of station in life or personal experience or otherwise.

35. See, e.g., Carol G. Gilligan, In a Different Voice 25 (1982).

36. See Herman Melville, Billy Budd (published posthumously in 1924) (portraying and contrasting an inarticulate person's response to evil with the response of a "rational," educated actor).

37. See Primo Levi, The Drowned and Saved (1988).

38. Nonlawyers also have stations in life, as accountants or mechanics, homemakers or breadwinners, parents or children, neighbors or strangers.   They combine various personal attributes in infinite variation, each one in his or her own way of life.   They encounter ethical problems similar to those encountered by lawyers.

39. See James Q. Wilson, The Moral Sense (1993) (arguing that empirical studies suggest a core of near universal moral attitudes).

Another aspect of a universal ethical perspective is that, in the absence of other considerations, all people should be treated equally. Of course, other considerations are always present, so that the ethical universal never has unqualified application. But that does not diminish the ideal of universal equality.

Ethical responsibility requires consideration of who are the "relevant others" for whom an actor should have ethical concern. A second dimension consists of the established and recognized rules governing the situation—the rules of the game. A third dimension consists of time, including time past and the future. Another factor, that of uncertainty, modifies these other dimensions. All real-world ethical problems have these dimensions: pre-existing rules, a placement in time and actors functioning under conditions of uncertainty. Thus, ethical analysis is more complicated than generally conceived.

Virtually every serious ethical problem involves at least two or three potentially significant "relevant others" and often as many as five. The first player is the actor who is called on to make the ethical choice (e.g., a lawyer); the second is the person who may immediately gain or lose according to whether or not the actor acts beneficently toward that player (e.g., the lawyer's client); a third player sometimes involved is another person who will lose if the actor acts beneficently toward the second player (e.g., the opposing party in negotiation or litigation). The ethical problem could be whether the lawyer should disclose to the other party a fact known to the lawyer that would adversely affect the client's position vis-a-vis the third party. Although a lawyer is generally required to give preference to the interests of the client, legal rules and norms of common decency sometimes require disclosure.[40] It is often a judgment call whether these "other regarding" norms apply.[41]

Defining an ethical problem in terms of only three participants, however, results in misleading oversimplification.[42] In Kolhberg's problem involving the protagonist, the sick spouse and the recalcitrant druggist, discussed by Carol Gilligan at p. 31 above, and in the situation confronted by a lawyer representing a probably-guilty client, at least two other participants can be identified. The fourth participant is a person (or set of persons) for whose benefit the protagonist could have committed her moral concern and practical efforts. The fifth participant consists of another person (or set of persons) to whom the protagonist is answerable, apart from the other participants immediately involved. Let us refer to that broader audience as political or legal

---

40. See, e.g., Greycas, Inc. v. Proud, 826 F.2d 1560 (7th Cir.1987), p. 75.

41. Scenarios involving three participants are involved in standard ethical analysis of ethical dilemmas of people who are not lawyers, such as Kohlberg's case of the impoverished husband whose wife needs an expensive drug that apparently can be procured only by stealing it from a druggist. The protagonist is the first participant, the wife is the second and the druggist is the third.

42. Limiting an ethical problem to three participants radically and artificially reduces the complexity involved in real-world ethical problems. The number of possible relationships multiplies rapidly as the number of participants increases.

authority. Real-world ethical dilemmas include these additional participants.

Consider the parable of the Good Samaritan (Luke 10:29–37). A
traveler had been waylaid by robbers and left wounded and unattended.
Two persons passed by during the day without heeding or stopping.
Finally, a Samaritan—a member of a despised alien ethnic group—
stopped, provided help to the victim and found him shelter and assistance. The story of the Good Samaritan is a model of beneficence.
According to Christian tradition, the story teaches us who is the
neighbor whom we should love as we love ourselves.

Yet those who passed by may have believed they had good reasons
for doing so. In the Bible story, they had religious reasons for not
stopping. But one can imagine other reasons. Perhaps one of them
was bent on important community business, such as warning his tribe
of an impending attack by enemies. Perhaps another was hurrying to
minister to another victim to whom a greater duty was owed, such as a
parent or a child. Perhaps a third was acting out Kohlberg's quandary
of the vital drug, carrying a stolen drug to another victim whose life
depended on it.[43] In short, those who passed by may have been
responding to another need or political authority or both.

Thus the Samaritan, if he was morally responsible, made a calculation that caring for the victim before him would not unduly interfere
with responsibilities he owed to other persons. Sometimes such a
fourth "relevant other" can be immediately present. For example,
suppose in the druggist hypothetical only one dose of the drug is
available, but the protagonist has two sick friends. This is the familiar
"triage" problem, in which a benefaction must be rationed among
potential recipients who are equally deserving from a moral viewpoint.[44]

Suppose, in the case of a lawyer, the choice is between preparing
oneself adequately in the case now on trial, including cross examination
of a frail witness, and preparing adequately to examine a difficult
witness in a second case in which trial will commence next week. The
rules of ethics say that a lawyer should not have undertaken the second
case if doing so would interfere with adequate preparation in the cases
she already has, thus preferring an existing client to a prospective
client, regardless of their relative need.[45] In the absence of such a "tie-

---

43. Perhaps another of the passersby previously had the experience of being conned
by a robber feigning injury and did not want to risk repeating that experience. This
introduces another dimension in the problem.

44. Triage refers to the procedure used by military doctors to allocate their time and
energy. All wounded from the battlefield are classified into those who could probably
survive without treatment, those who probably would not survive regardless of treatment
and those who apparently could be helped. Treatment is provided to the last group. On
triage, See Gerald R. Winslow, Triage and Justice (1982). See also the analysis of many
similar examples in Jon Elster, Local Justice (1992).

45. See, e.g., IBM v. Levin, 579 F.2d 271 (3d Cir.1978).

breaker" rule emanating from outside the problem, a Good Samaritan lawyer lacks a principle for deciding which client to prefer.

In principle, the mandate to be a Good Samaritan covers everyone who could be better off as a result of a protagonist's beneficence. Rigorous adherence to the principle of moral equality would require the Good Samaritan to have considered all possible victims in all degrees of need before deciding whether to minister to the needy person immediately before him. If the Samaritan had reason to think that a worse-off victim lay around the bend of the road, should he stop to minister to the victim before him?

Ethically conscious actors are aware that the world is full of such relevant others. Many of them are much in need of our benefactions, including legal services from those who practice law.[46] The principle of moral equity provides no basis for choosing which is most deserving. The triage problem thus plays out in infinite variation. Explaining the triage problem is the basic insight of economic analysis: Human needs, or at least human wants, forever outrun available resources to meet them. The principles of economics, of course, do not exhaust ethical analysis. But ethical analysis that is unmindful of economics fails to take account of relevant others.

And yet, we should pause before relying on the calculating rationality that suggests the moral superiority of weighing a response to a neighbor in need against the claims of real and hypothetical others who are not present. The parable of the Good Samaritan was a response to a lawyer's question: "Who is my neighbor?" The answer in narrative form was that everyone in the community, regardless of class, race or religion, is a neighbor whom we should treat with the care and respect that we give to ourselves. Jesus was not engaged in a philosophic analysis of problems of triage but was vividly portraying the ideal of reaching out to those in the community whose need confronts us face-to-face. We are present, we see the need, we have the capacity to help, and we should respond.[47]

The person who stops first to ponder the conflicting and more distant claims of the engagement for which he is heading or the alternate uses of his time and money may end preferring the convenience and profit of not becoming involved. A terrible truth about human rationality is its tendency to find rationalizations for what is convenient and profitable. Rejecting the passionate response to the immediate needs of the injured and helpless victim in order to serve

46. Is it immoral to choose to become a corporate lawyer rather than a public defender or a legal services lawyer? Charles Fried, The Lawyer as Friend: The Moral Foundations of the Lawyer–Client Relation, 85 Yale L.J. 1060, 1076–80 (1976), argues that individual autonomy provides a moral justification for choosing a type of practice one prefers rather than one that satisfies utilitarian considerations of "the greatest good to the greatest number." Is he right?

47. Recall the Jewish story of "repairing the world" by picking up bits of glass and the Christian statement to the effect that he who does good to "the least among us" also does it to God. See p. 1005 above.

some more abstract good may involve a terrible paradox. At what point does the calculated rationality of such a person so diminish her humanity that she is no longer able to recognize or serve the larger good?

Everyone Is Accountable

The simple binary choices of moral quandaries such as that involving the husband, the druggist and the sick spouse postulate complete autonomy in the protagonist's decision whether or not to steal the drug. That kind of freedom rarely if ever exists in the real world. Rather, every protagonist is in some way accountable to someone beyond those whose interests are immediately involved, whether it be family members, a co-worker, an employer, a governmental authority or the court of public opinion.

Accountability means having to answer to someone else for what one has done—explaining and justifying the course of action that has been chosen. When contemplating action, the actor must calculate whether the justification will be convincing to the relevant audience. Such a calculation must include an estimate of how the facts will look to that other person. Accountability often turns not on questions about the governing norms, but on questions of fact. Questions of fact can arise whether accountability takes the form of legal responsibility or discussion within a family or organization as to how a relative, neighbor or co-worker should have been treated. The calculation about accountability must also include an estimate of how the balance that was struck by the actor between the competing interests—stealing versus helping a sick spouse—will be regarded by those to whom the actor is accountable. The actor knows that some people regard stealing as an inadmissible course under any conditions, whereas others think that property interests should always yield to personal interests. Similar problems are involved when a lawyer must exercise professional judgment within the limits imposed by law and the rules of ethics.

One statement can be made with certainty: The problem of choice will not look precisely the same in retrospect as reviewed by the protagonist's reference group as it did to the protagonist at the moment of choice. All forms of review involve an element of second-guessing.

Accountability is the essence of political and managerial responsibility in our modern bureaucratized world. Even political leaders who are momentarily beyond the reach of retribution are accountable to history, which means the collective memory of the community. In the case of professionals, such as doctors and lawyers, the lines of accountability are designedly loose but always present. The professional ideal of independent judgment involves a sphere of autonomous authority.[48] Nevertheless, a lawyer who is a member of a firm is directly accountable to her partners or associates for ethically debatable decisions. More than one law firm has fallen apart when such a decision did not sit well

---

48. See M.R. 5.4(c); Model Code, Canon 5.

with colleagues. Accountability for a solo practitioner is less direct but nevertheless real. A solo practitioner depends on "reputation" for a continued flow of referrals, and reputation is the community's informal system of accountability. Also, all lawyers in principle must answer to the state's disciplinary agency. When a breach of ethics also involves violation of criminal or tort law, for example, in misappropriation of client funds or a departure from ordinary care, lawyers are also accountable to the criminal and civil law.

Accountability to legal authority is especially significant in legal ethics. In most forms of law practice a lawyer is an agent for the client.[49] As an agent for a client, a lawyer owes legal and ethical duties to the client. Not all lawyers equally understand that an agent also owes legal and ethical duties to the third person with whom the lawyer deals on behalf of the client.[50] The principle of agency accountability is not merely a legal concept; it is an ethical concept as well.

Two things are clear about an agent's accountability. First, an agent may not be fully chargeable with the principal's purposes. If an agent is directed or encouraged by a principal who has political authority to perform an act that is otherwise illegal, a more complicated problem of responsibility is presented than if the agent were acting on his own. This is essentially the position taken by Oliver North in his well-known foreign exchange dealings. Even if we do not accept this "Nuremberg defense" in a specific case, it would be a relevant consideration under some circumstances, and perhaps decisive in a few.[51]

For lawyers the matter of political authority is essential to the legitimacy of many aspects of our calling. After all, how else could one justify defending a person who, one has every reason to believe, is guilty of a serious crime? In this case, political authority is the community's collective judgment that defending those accused of crime, even ones who appear certainly to be guilty, is warranted by moral and constitutional considerations that redound to everyone's benefit. That is, the constitutional concept of due process entails the right to counsel, and the right to counsel entails the right to a lawyer who will give her best lawful effort for the accused, whatever she may think about whether the accused is guilty. The same principle applies in other social relationships. For example, a similar kind of authority undergirds a parent's protective efforts in favor of a guilty child.[52]

49. An exception, or perhaps only an apparent exception, is a lawyer who also holds authority as a principal. The most common instance is a government attorney who is a legally constituted public official, such as a prosecutor or an attorney general. The merger of the function of lawyer and public official presents a problem often referred to in terms of "who is the client?" See Chapter 8 above.

50. See generally Restatement (Second) of Agency § 343 et seq. (tort liability); Lucas v. Hamm, 56 Cal.2d 588, 15 Cal.Rptr. 821, 364 P.2d 685 (1961) (malpractice liability of will drafter to intended beneficiaries); United States v. Benjamin, 328 F.2d 854 (2d Cir.1964) (criminal liability).

51. See M.R. 5.2 (accepting a severely circumscribed "Nuremberg defense" for junior lawyers acting under the direction and supervision of a senior lawyer).

52. See Geoffrey C. Hazard, Jr., Doing the Right Thing, 70 Wash.U.L.Q. 691 (1992).

The other aspect of agency accountability, however, is that at some point and degree of involvement, an agent is equally chargeable with the principal for an ethically problematic choice. In legal terms, this is the liability that is described as "aiding and abetting." [53] In the practice of law, a similar limitation is expressed in the canon that a lawyer's zeal on behalf of a client must be "within the bounds of the law." [54] In the language of ordinary ethics, the same idea is expressed in the proposition that it is not a defense simply to say "they made me do it" or "I was only doing my job." Ethically conscious actors are aware that while political authority is a source of ethical justification or excuse, and often an impetus to doing good, it is also an impetus to complicity in doing evil.

The fact of accountability in all real world relationships thus implicates problems of politics. Politics *is* the allocation of power and authority. Politics in this classical sense is not everything there is to ethics, but ethical analysis unmindful of politics is incomplete. These complications come into view, however, only if we include political authority among the "relevant others" who are involved in real world ethical dilemmas.

In summary, real-world ethical problems have unavoidable complications arising from the number of relevant others whose interests are involved in resolving such problems. Analytically, there are at least five such players, even in relatively simple situations. In actual life, the number of others whose interests are at stake usually is larger. The resulting complexity would be unmanageable without rules and conventions that impose priorities and give preferred position to various "relevant others." For lawyers, the qualified preference is given to a client, but not in disregard of the interests of "relevant others" who are not clients. For those in other stations in life, such as parent or business manager, there are counterpart rules of qualified preference. One of the functions of legal rules and institutions is to establish, maintain and circumscribe such rules of preference.

Some Final Thoughts

When lawyers or future lawyers gather for ceremonial occasions, such as a Law Day banquet or a law school graduation ceremony, speakers call forth the kind of rhetoric found in talks at other ceremonies marking beginnings and endings: some aspiration, some nostalgia, perhaps even some pretense. Pretense can be a bad thing, of course, but there are many worse things than having ideals we know we do not fully live up to—active participation in evil, for example, or acquiescence in evil committed by others.

Karl Llewellyn, a teacher and mentor of one of the authors, used to tell his students: "Technique without compassion is a menace; compas-

---

53. See Sanford H. Kadish, Complicity, Cause and Blame: A Study in the Interpretation of Doctrine, 73 Calif.L.Rev. 323 (1985).

54. See M.R. 1.2(d), Model Code, Canon 7.

sion without technique is a mess." Both are necessary to a successful and happy professional life.

Some years ago the National Institutes of Health did a study of the quality of medical care delivered to patients by a large group of general practice physicians. The study was designed to shed some light on what characteristics were highly correlated to high quality medical care. Thousands of bits of information about the physicians and the circumstances of their practice were fed into the computers along with an objective evaluation of the patients' files. On almost every item the study came up with negative results: Most differences between physicians—age, ethnicity, experience, medical school, size of practice, etc.— did not seem to matter. But significant findings emerged on a tantalizing series of items that tell something about what it takes to be a good physician. The physicians who always delivered good medical care subscribed to and read medical journals; they attended out-of-town medical education meetings (attending local ones was not significant); they responded to their patients' emergency needs and requests; and they worked long hours.

What does this study tell us? The good physician cares about medicine, possessing an intellectual interest in and continuing curiosity about this area of human knowledge. He cares about his patients. And he cares about his own self-integrity and performance as a physician. The result is an internalized value system that finds doing good work rewarding and doing sloppy work a source of shame and guilt.

The same things are true of the good lawyer: She cares about the law, maintaining throughout her career an intellectual interest in it and a desire to improve it. She cares about her clients and suffers with them if they suffer. She cares about herself as a professional—a skilled, principled and compassionate technician who delivers honest work for honest pay.

Law graduates sometimes delude themselves into believing that work can be separated from the rest of life, that "doing time" in hateful professional work for big bucks will be made up by the enjoyments of leisure and personal life, now or in some future stage of life. The problem is that being a good professional takes too much time and attention; it cannot be separated from the rest of life. Work turns out to be too important a part of one's self and one's life.

An African–American spiritual has it right:

> O you gotta get a glory in the work you do,
>
> A Hallelujah chorus in the heart of you.
>
> Paint or tell a story, Sing or shovel coal,
>
> But you gotta get a glory Or the job lacks soul.[55]

55. Quoted in Caroline Royds, Prayers for Children 36 (1988).

*

INDEX

References are to Pages

†